Nineteenth-Century Literature Criticism

Topics Volume

Guide to Thomson Gale Literary Criticism Series

For criticism on	Consult these Thomson Gale series
Authors now living or who died after December 31, 1999	*CONTEMPORARY LITERARY CRITICISM (CLC)*
Authors who died between 1900 and 1999	*TWENTIETH-CENTURY LITERARY CRITICISM (TCLC)*
Authors who died between 1800 and 1899	*NINETEENTH-CENTURY LITERATURE CRITICISM (NCLC)*
Authors who died between 1400 and 1799	*LITERATURE CRITICISM FROM 1400 TO 1800 (LC)* *SHAKESPEAREAN CRITICISM (SC)*
Authors who died before 1400	*CLASSICAL AND MEDIEVAL LITERATURE CRITICISM (CMLC)*
Authors of books for children and young adults	*CHILDREN'S LITERATURE REVIEW (CLR)*
Dramatists	*DRAMA CRITICISM (DC)*
Poets	*POETRY CRITICISM (PC)*
Short story writers	*SHORT STORY CRITICISM (SSC)*
Literary topics and movements	*HARLEM RENAISSANCE: A GALE CRITICAL COMPANION (HR)* *THE BEAT GENERATION: A GALE CRITICAL COMPANION (BG)* *FEMINISM IN LITERATURE: A GALE CRITICAL COMPANION (FL)* *GOTHIC LITERATURE: A GALE CRITICAL COMPANION (GL)*
Asian American writers of the last two hundred years	*ASIAN AMERICAN LITERATURE (AAL)*
Black writers of the past two hundred years	*BLACK LITERATURE CRITICISM (BLC)* *BLACK LITERATURE CRITICISM SUPPLEMENT (BLCS)*
Hispanic writers of the late nineteenth and twentieth centuries	*HISPANIC LITERATURE CRITICISM (HLC)* *HISPANIC LITERATURE CRITICISM SUPPLEMENT (HLCS)*
Native North American writers and orators of the eighteenth, nineteenth, and twentieth centuries	*NATIVE NORTH AMERICAN LITERATURE (NNAL)*
Major authors from the Renaissance to the present	*WORLD LITERATURE CRITICISM, 1500 TO THE PRESENT (WLC)* *WORLD LITERATURE CRITICISM SUPPLEMENT (WLCS)*

ISSN 0732-1864

Volume 168

Nineteenth-Century Literature Criticism

Topics Volume

Criticism of Various
Topics in Nineteenth-Century Literature,
including Literary and Critical Movements,
Prominent Themes and Genres, Anniversary
Celebrations, and Surveys of National Literatures

Jessica Bomarito
Russel Whitaker
Project Editors

THOMSON
★
GALE
™

Detroit • New York • San Francisco • New Haven, Conn. • Waterville, Maine • London • Munich

THOMSON
GALE

Nineteenth-Century Literature Criticism, Vol. 168

Project Editors
Jessica Bomarito and Russel Whitaker

Editorial
Kathy D. Darrow, Jeffrey W. Hunter, Jelena O. Krstović, Michelle Lee, Rachelle Mucha, Thomas J. Schoenberg, Noah Schusterbauer, Lawrence J. Trudeau

Data Capture
Frances Monroe, Gwen Tucker

Rights and Acquisitions
Emma Hull, Jacqueline Key, Ron Montgomery

Imaging and Multimedia
Dean Dauphinais, Robert Duncan, Leitha Etheridge-Sims, Lezlie Light, Michael Logusz, Dan Newell, Kelly A. Quin, Denay Wilding

Composition and Electronic Capture
Carolyn A. Roney

Manufacturing
Rhonda Dover

Associate Product Manager
Marc Cormier

LIBRARY OF CONGRESS CATALOG CARD NUMBER 84-643008

ISBN 0-7876-8652-2
ISSN 0732-1864

Printed in the United States of America
10 9 8 7 6 5 4 3 2 1

Contents

Preface vii

Acknowledgments xi

Literary Criticism Series Advisory Board xiii

Preface

Since its inception in 1981, *Nineteeth-Century Literature Criticism* (*NCLC*) has been a valuable resource for students and librarians seeking critical commentary on writers of this transitional period in world history. Designated an "Outstanding Reference Source" by the American Library Association with the publication of is first volume, *NCLC* has since been purchased by over 6,000 school, public, and university libraries. The series has covered more than 450 authors representing 33 nationalities and over 17,000 titles. No other reference source has surveyed the critical reaction to nineteenth-century authors and literature as thoroughly as *NCLC*.

Scope of the Series

NCLC is designed to introduce students and advanced readers to the authors of the nineteenth century and to the most significant interpretations of these authors' works. The great poets, novelists, short story writers, playwrights, and philosophers of this period are frequently studied in high school and college literature courses. By organizing and reprinting commentary written on these authors, *NCLC* helps students develop valuable insight into literary history, promotes a better understanding of the texts, and sparks ideas for papers and assignments. Each entry in *NCLC* presents a comprehensive survey of an author's career or an individual work of literature and provides the user with a multiplicity of interpretations and assessments. Such variety allows students to pursue their own interests; furthermore, it fosters an awareness that literature is dynamic and responsive to many different opinions.

Every fourth volume of *NCLC* is devoted to literary topics that cannot be covered under the author approach used in the rest of the series. Such topics include literary movements, prominent themes in nineteenth-century literature, literary reaction to political and historical events, significant eras in literary history, prominent literary anniversaries, and the literatures of cultures that are often overlooked by English-speaking readers.

NCLC continues the survey of criticism of world literature begun by Thomson Gale's *Contemporary Literary Criticism* (*CLC*) and *Twentieth-Century Literary Criticism* (*TCLC*).

Organization of the Book

An *NCLC* entry consists of the following elements:

- The **Author Heading** cites the name under which the author most commonly wrote, followed by birth and death dates. Also located here are any name variations under which an author wrote, including transliterated forms for authors whose native languages use nonroman alphabets. If the author wrote consistently under a pseudonym, the pseudonym will be listed in the author heading and the author's actual name given in parenthesis on the first line of the biographical and critical information. Uncertain birth or death dates are indicated by question marks. Single-work entries are preceded by a heading that consists of the most common form of the title in English translation (if applicable) and the original date of composition.

- The **Introduction** contains background information that introduces the reader to the author, work, or topic that is the subject of the entry.

- A **Portrait of the Author** is included when available.

- The list of **Principal Works** is ordered chronologically by date of first publication and lists the most important works by the author. The genre and publication date of each work is given. In the case of foreign authors whose works have been translated into English, the list will focus primarily on twentieth-century translations, selecting those works most commonly considered the best by critics. Unless otherwise indicated, dramas are dated by first performance, not first publication. Lists of **Representative Works** by different authors appear with topic entries.

- Reprinted **Criticism** is arranged chronologically in each entry to provide a useful perspective on changes in critical evaluation over time. The critic's name and the date of composition or publication of the critical work are given at the beginning of each piece of criticism. Unsigned criticism is preceded by the title of the source in which it appeared. All titles by the author featured in the text are printed in boldface type. Footnotes are reprinted at the end of each essay or excerpt. In the case of excerpted criticism, only those footnotes that pertain to the excerpted texts are included. Criticism in topic entries is arranged chronologically under a variety of subheadings to facilitate the study of different aspects of the topic.

- A complete **Bibliographical Citation** of the original essay or book precedes each piece of criticism.

- Critical essays are prefaced by brief **Annotations** explicating each piece.

- An annotated bibliography of **Further Reading** appears at the end of each entry and suggests resources for additional study. In some cases, significant essays for which the editors could not obtain reprint rights are included here. Boxed material following the further reading list provides references to other biographical and critical sources on the author in series published by Thomson Gale.

Indexes

Each volume of *NCLC* contains a **Cumulative Author Index** listing all authors who have appeared in a wide variety of reference sources published by Thomson Gale, including *NCLC*. A complete list of these sources is found facing the first page of the Author Index. The index also includes birth and death dates and cross references between pseudonyms and actual names.

A **Cumulative Nationality Index** lists all authors featured in *NCLC* by nationality, followed by the number of the *NCLC* volume in which their entry appears.

A **Cumulative Topic Index** lists the literary themes and topics treated in the series as well as in *Classical and Medieval Literature Criticism, Literature Criticism from 1400 to 1800, Twentieth-Century Literary Criticism,* and the *Contemporary Literary Criticism* Yearbook, which was discontinued in 1998.

An alphabetical **Title Index** accompanies each volume of *NCLC*, with the exception of the Topics volumes. Listings of titles by authors covered in the given volume are followed by the author's name and the corresponding page numbers where the titles are discussed. English translations of foreign titles and variations of titles are cross-referenced to the title under which a work was originally published. Titles of novels, dramas, nonfiction books, and poetry, short story, or essay collections are printed in italics, while individual poems, short stories, and essays are printed in roman type within quotation marks.

In response to numerous suggestions from librarians, Thomson Gale also produces an annual paperbound edition of the *NCLC* cumulative title index. This annual cumulation, which alphabetically lists all titles reviewed in the series, is available to all customers. Additional copies of this index are available upon request. Librarians and patrons will welcome this separate index; it saves shelf space, is easy to use, and is recyclable upon receipt of the next edition.

Citing *Nineteenth-Century Literature Criticism*

When citing criticism reprinted in the Literary Criticism Series, students should provide complete bibliographic information so that the cited essay can be located in the original print or electronic source. Students who quote directly from reprinted criticism may use any accepted bibliographic format, such as University of Chicago Press style or Modern Language Association style.

The examples below follow recommendations for preparing a bibliography set forth in *The Chicago Manual of Style,* 15th ed. (Chicago: The University of Chicago Press, 2003); the first example pertains to material drawn from periodicals, the second to material reprinted from books:

Franklin, J. Jeffrey. "The Victorian Discourse of Gambling: Speculations on *Middlemarch* and *The Duke's Children.*" *ELH* 61, no. 4 (winter 1994): 899-921. Reprinted in *Nineteenth-Century Literature Criticism.* Vol. 168, edited by Jessica Bomarito and Russel Whitaker, 39-51. Detroit: Thomson Gale, 2006.

Frank, Joseph. "*The Gambler*: A Study in Ethnopsychology." In *Freedom and Responsibility in Russian Literature: Essays in Honor of Robert Louis Jackson,* edited by Elizabeth Cheresh Allen and Gary Saul Morson, 69-85. Evanston, Ill.: Northwestern University Press, 1995. Reprinted in *Nineteeth-Century Literature Criticism.* Vol. 168, edited by Jessica Bomarito and Russel Whitaker, 75-84. Detroit: Thomson Gale, 2006.

The examples below follow recommendations for preparing a works cited list set forth in the *MLA Handbook for Writers of Research Papers,* 6th ed. (New York: The Modern Language Association of America, 2003); the first example pertains to material drawn from periodicals, the second to material reprinted from books:

Franklin, J. Jeffrey. "The Victorian Discourse of Gambling: Speculations on *Middlemarch* and *The Duke's Children.*" *ELH* 61.4 (Winter 1994): 899-921. Reprinted in *Nineteenth-Century Literature Criticism.* Eds. Jessica Bomarito and Russel Whitaker. Vol. 168. Detroit: Thomson Gale, 2006. 39-51.

Frank, Joseph. "*The Gambler*: A Study in Ethnopsychology." *Freedom and Responsibility in Russian Literature: Essays in Honor of Robert Louis Jackson.* Eds. Elizabeth Cheresh Allen and Gary Saul Morson. Evanston, Ill.: Northwestern University Press, 1995. 69-85. Reprinted in *Nineteenth-Century Literature Criticism.* Eds. Jessica Bomarito and Russel Whitaker. Vol. 168. Detroit: Thomson Gale, 2006. 75-84.

Suggestions are Welcome

Readers who wish to suggest new features, topics, or authors to appear in future volumes, or who have other suggestions or comments are cordially invited to call, write, or fax the Associate Product Manager:

Associate Product Manager, Literary Criticism Series
Thomson Gale
27500 Drake Road
Farmington Hills, MI 48331-3535
1-800-347-4253 (GALE)
Fax: 248-699-8054

Acknowledgments

The editors wish to thank the copyright holders of the criticism included in this volume and the permissions managers of many book and magazine publishing companies for assisting us in securing reproduction rights. We are also grateful to the staffs of the Detroit Public Library, the Library of Congress, the University of Detroit Mercy Library, Wayne State University Purdy/Kresge Library Complex, and the University of Michigan Libraries for making their resources available to us. Following is a list of the copyright holders who have granted us permission to reproduce material in this volume of *NCLC*. Every effort has been made to trace copyright, but if omissions have been made, please let us know.

COPYRIGHTED MATERIAL IN *NCLC*, VOLUME 168, WAS REPRODUCED FROM THE FOLLOWING PERIODICALS:

Cahiers Victoriens et Édouardiens, v. 44, October, 1996. Reproduced by permission.—*CLCWeb: Comparative Literature and Culture: A WWWeb Journal,* v. 3.2, June, 2001, for "British Travel Writing about the United States and Spanish America, 1820-1840: Different and Differentiating Views" by Frank Lauterbach. Copyright © 2001 Purdue University Press. Reproduced by permission.—*Cultural Critique,* fall, 1986 for "The Return of William James" by Frank Lentricchia. Copyright c 1986 by University of Minnesota. Reproduced by permission.—*Early American Literature,* v. 31, 1996. Copyright © 1996 by the University of North Carolina Press. Used by permission.—*ELH,* v. 61, winter, 1994. Copyright © 1994 The Johns Hopkins University Press. Reproduced by permission.—*Feminist Studies,* v. 21, fall, 1995 for "Alternatives to the Missionary Position: Anna Leonowens as Victorian Travel Writer" by Susan Brown. Copyright © 1995 by Feminist Studies, Inc. All rights reserved. Reproduced by permission of the publisher, Feminist Studies, Inc.—*Henry James Review,* v. 18, fall, 1997. Copyright © 1997 The Johns Hopkins University Press. Reproduced by permission.—*Leviathan,* v. 6, March, 2004. Reproduced by permission.—*Partisan Review,* v. 64, winter, 1997 for "'We Pragmatists …': Peirce and Rorty in Conversation" by Susan Haack. Copyright © 1997 by Susan Haack. Reproduced by permission of the author.—*Philological Papers,* v. 44, 1998-1999. Reproduced by permission.—*PTL: Journal for Descriptive Poetics and Theory of Literature,* v. 3, October, 1978. Reproduced with permission from Elsevier.—*Raritan,* v. 8, winter, 1989. Copyright © 1989 by *Raritan: A Quarterly Review*. Reproduced by permission.—*Southwest Review,* v. 85, autumn, 2000. Copyright © 2000 Southern Methodist University. All rights reserved. Reproduced by permission.—*Victorian Literature and Culture,* v. 24, 1996 for "'That Ain't no Lady Traveler … It's a Discursive Subject': Mapping and Re-mapping Victorian Women's Travel Writing" by Catherine Barnes Stevenson. Reprinted by permission of Cambridge University Press and author.—*The Victorian Newsletter,* v. 79, spring, 1991 for "Images of Middle-Eastern Women in Victorian Travel Books" by Charisse Gendron; spring, 2001 for "The Travels of RLS as a Young Man" by Gordon Hirsch. Both reproduced by permission of the publishers and the respective authors.

COPYRIGHTED MATERIAL IN *NCLC*, VOLUME 168, WAS REPRODUCED FROM THE FOLLOWING BOOKS:

Brennan, Bernard P. From *William James*. Twayne Publishers, 1968. Copyright © 1968 by Twayne Publishers, Inc. All rights reserved. Reproduced by permission of The Gale Group.—de Waal, Cornelis. From *On Peirce*. Wadsworth, 2001. © 2001. Reprinted with permission of Wadsworth, a division of Thomson Learning: www.thomsonrights.com.—Fitzpatrick, Kristin. From "American National Identity Abroad: The Travels of Nancy Prince," in *Gender, Genre, and Identity in Women's Travel Writing*. Edited by Kristi Siegel. Peter Lang, 2004. Copyright © 2004 Peter Lang Publishing, Inc., New York. All rights reserved. Reproduced by permission.—Frank, Joseph. From "The Gambler: A Study in Ethnopsychology," in *Freedom and Responsibility in Russian Literature: Essays in Honor of Robert Louis Jackson*. Edited by Elizabeth Cheresh Allen and Gary Saul Morson. Evanston: Northwestern University Press, 1995. Copyright © 1995 by Northwestern University Press. All rights reserved. Reproduced by permission.—Frawley, Maria H. From *A Wider Range: Travel Writing by Women in Victorian England*. Fairleigh Dickinson University Press, 1994. Copyright © 1994 by Associated University Presses, Inc. All rights reserved. Reproduced by permission.—Hollinger, David A. From "The Problem of Pragmatism in American History: A Look Back and a Look Ahead," in *Pragmatism: From Progressivism to Postmodernism*. Edited by Robert Hollinger and David Depew. Praeger, 1995. Copyright © 1995 by Robert Hollinger and David Depew. Reproduced by permission of Greenwood Publishing Group, Inc., Westport, CT.—Lawrence, Karen R. From *Penelope Voyages: Women and Travel in the British Literary Tradition*. Cornell University Press, 1994. Copyright © 1994 by Cornell

Thomson Gale Literature Product Advisory Board

The members of the Thomson Gale Literature Product Advisory Board—reference librarians from public and academic library systems—represent a cross-section of our customer base and offer a variety of informed perspectives on both the presentation and content of our literature products. Advisory board members assess and define such quality issues as the relevance, currency, and usefulness of the author coverage, critical content, and literary topics included in our series; evaluate the layout, presentation, and general quality of our printed volumes; provide feedback on the criteria used for selecting authors and topics covered in our series; provide suggestions for potential enhancements to our series; identify any gaps in our coverage of authors or literary topics, recommending authors or topics for inclusion; analyze the appropriateness of our content and presentation for various user audiences, such as high school students, undergraduates, graduate students, librarians, and educators; and offer feedback on any proposed changes/enhancements to our series. We wish to thank the following advisors for their advice throughout the year.

Gambling in Nineteenth-Century Literature

The following entry provides commentary on the treatment of gambling in nineteenth-century literature.

INTRODUCTION

The rise in democracy, industrialism, and capitalism in European and American societies during the nineteenth century brought about a rise in opportunities for attaining wealth, access to gambling, and commercial enterprises. Prior to the nineteenth century, gambling, or "gaming," in Europe was a purely recreational activity. Men of the privileged class gathered in exclusive, private clubs to affirm their wealth by demonstrating that they could afford to lose large sums of money. Depictions of gambling in the literature of this period reflect this reality. The size of the middle class greatly increased in America during the nineteenth century, and as more and more Americans and Europeans gained access to sources of wealth previously unavailable to them, the nature of gambling and the prevailing social opinion of it changed from one of a seemingly harmless pastime of the wealthy to a threat to social responsibility and morality. American literature presented an ideal man who was both financially successful and socially responsible, characterizing those who amassed fortunes through success in trade or commerce as respectable and those who achieved financial success through speculation and gambling as disreputable. Literature warned that luxury could lead to the valuing of personal gain over the public good. Critics have noted that the members of the landed aristocratic classes feared the upsetting of the traditional social hierarchy, and believed that the members of the middle and lower classes—perceived by the elite as less educated and less inclined toward social responsibility—who gained wealth would spend their money irresponsibly on luxury items, or recklessly engage in gambling, ultimately leading to the corruption of society as a whole. Anti-gambling tracts offered fictionalized versions of supposedly true stories of good people's lives being ruined by gambling.

Commentators have also discussed gambling in Russian literature of the nineteenth century, assessing Russian authors' treatment of the theme of "chance" as a means of grappling with the political and social realities faced by individuals seeking to assert themselves in imperialist Russia. In the works of many Russian authors, cards and card games serve as a metaphor for the idea of fate and destiny being controlled by external forces.

REPRESENTATIVE WORKS

Anonymous
The Gambler; or, Memoirs of a British Officer Distinguished in the War of the American Revolution (novel) 1802
Crockford's; or, Life in the West (novel) 1828

Benjamin Disraeli
The Young Duke (novel) 1831
Henrietta Temple (novel) 1836
Sybil; or, The Two Nations (novel) 1845

Fyodor Dostoevsky
Igrok [*The Gambler*] (novella) 1867

George Eliot
Middlemarch: A Study of Provincial Life (novel) 1871-72
Daniel Deronda (novel) 1876

Percy Fitzgerald
Fatal Zero (novel) 1868; published serially in the journal *All the Year Round*

James Grant
The Great Metropolis (essays) 1837

Vasilii Ivanovich Maikov
Igrok lombera (epic poem) 1763

Herman Melville
Redburn: His First Voyage (novel) 1849

George Meredith
The Amazing Marriage (novel) 1895

Alexander Pushkin
Pikovaia dama [*The Queen of Spades*] (short stories) 1834

Charles Reade
A Woman-Hater (novel) 1877

Rebecca Rush
Kelroy (novel) 1812

Andrew Steinmetz
The Gaming Table: Its Votaries and Victims, in All Times and Countries, Especially in England and France (history) 1870

Aleksandr Vasil'evich Sukhovo-Kobylin

Kartiny proshedshego [*The Trilogy of Alexander Sukhovo-Kobylin*] (plays) 1869

William Makepeace Thackeray

The Kickleburys on the Rhine, by Mr. M. A. Titmarsh (sketches) 1850

Anthony Trollope

The Duke's Children (novel) 1880

Caroline Matilda Warren

The Gamesters; or, Ruins of Innocence (novel) 1805

Mason Locke Weems

God's Revenge against Gambling (sketches) 1810

Sarah Wood

Dorval; or, The Speculator (novel) 1801

OVERVIEW

Gerda Reith (essay date 1999)

SOURCE: Reith, Gerda. "The Nineteenth Century: Playing with Numbers." In *The Age of Chance: Gambling in Western Culture*, pp. 74-87. London and New York: Routledge, 1999.

[*In the following excerpt, Reith surveys the various forms of gambling popular during the nineteenth century and discusses how certain scientific, political, and economic shifts "dramatically changed the face of gambling."*]

In the nineteenth century, various changes occurred which dramatically changed the face of gambling. The commercialisation of games of chance during the Industrial Revolution converged with the commercialisation of economic life and with the denouement of probability theory—the science that had 'tamed' chance. As the calculation of odds became more fully understood, the nature of the games played changed so that they became more amenable to commercial organisation, more homogeneous and, ultimately, more 'sellable'. It is in this period that the recognisably modern forms of the casino, the public racetrack and the mechanised slot-machine first appeared. In place of the huge sums wagered by the individuals of the seventeenth-century aristocracy came more democratic games for many

players organised around modest stakes which allowed for prolonged rather than excessive play. These conventions are still visible in the gambling behaviour of today. . . .

THE CASINO

In the industrial discipline of the nineteenth century, the separation of the spheres of leisure and work, which had been ongoing for the previous two hundred years, was finally consolidated. Such a development was particularly evident in the gambling arena which at this time was disengaged from its surrounding social life and organised into distinct, highly commercial spheres. The casino was perhaps most representative of the trend; it emerged in the second half of the century as a collection of public rooms devoted exclusively to gambling, away from its earlier formulation as a dancing saloon and summer-house (McMillen 1996).

In this period, the fashionable watering places of the aristocracy continued to be popular gaming centres and were supplemented by the development of a series of resorts throughout Europe, in which gaming houses—now casinos—were the central attraction. This development of what Turner and Ash (1975) describe as a decadent and extravagant 'Pleasure Periphery' in the French Riviera included Nice, Cannes and Monte Carlo, or, as the French called them, 'the World, the Flesh and the Devil'. Baden Baden, Bad Homberg and Wiesbaden were small localities whose deliberate expansion turned them from health spas into gambling resorts (a process which would be perfected in the twentieth century in the creation of Las Vegas).[1] Although generally exclusive, the commercialism of at least some of these resorts bore witness to some degree of democratisation. In Bad Homberg and Wiesbaden the great mass of visitors were of the middle and lower-middle classes, causing Steinmetz to note with disapproval that 'the general run of guests is by no means remarkable for birth, wealth or respectability' (Steinmetz 1870, p. 213).

By the end of the nineteenth century then, dramatic changes had transformed the nature of commercial games of chance, overseeing the formulation and codification of what we now recognise as modern casino games. Just as the economic imperatives of emergent capitalism were reflected in the growth of commercial gaming houses, so the games themselves came to reflect the social logic of a capitalist system. It is these changes we shall turn to next.

CARDS

In cards, traditional games that revolved around various kinds of patterns and sequences, such as the gaining of suits, trumps and tricks or the making of combinations like flushes and marriages in melds, were being sup-

Photo of men seated at a gambling table in a Monte Carlo casino, c. 1897.

planted by a new form of game. This new style of play was based on the arithmetical values of the cards in their properties as individual numerals, and forms the basis of all modern casino card games.

Such a shift was made possible by an experiment of the Woolley Card Company. In 1884, in keeping with the statistical spirit of the times, they printed a numerical value at diagonally opposite corners of each card in what was known as an *indice* (Hargrave 1966, p. 189). As numbers 'poured into' the nineteenth century, so they poured on to packs of cards. With this seemingly trivial development, the face of cards was literally changed forever. The value of these new cards was depicted by a bold unequivocal number, no longer represented by an image, which was necessarily more ambiguous. The authority of the number was not open to interpretation; it was a fact. Not only was it instantly more striking, in the new style of games, but the number on these cards was also more *important* than all the other information they contained. In games based on the speedy calculation of number, it was vital that each card be immediately recognisable to the player. A simple digit in each corner met this requirement in a way that a more vague pictorial depiction never could. Given the commercial environment of the new games, it was not only important that players should quickly recognise their cards, but equally, that other players should *not*. Until now, the backs of cards had been either plain or decorated with a single one-way design. This meant that they could easily be marked, or, in the case of

decorated cards, arranged with some backs upside-down, for example, to distinguish high cards from low ones, face cards or suits (Sifakis 1990, p. 57). The possibilities for cheating with such packs were unlimited; even a player with a poor memory could not fail to recognise specific cards from their backs after a while. In the nineteenth century this golden age of cheating was ended when companies began experimenting with uniform back designs so that, by the end of the century, simple two-way designs had rendered cards indistinguishable. These twin developments made cards at once both unique *and* standardised. As instances of 'the same kind of thing' they were indistinguishable, yet within this general category each one was recognisably the bearer of a specific value. Similarly, in the wider society, *l'homme moyen* was characterised by his representativeness of all others of his kind. At the same time, these characteristics came out in individual properties which displayed as much statistical variation in their particular sample as, say, the individual cards in their particular pack. In the nineteenth century then, both *l'homme moyen* and the new-style cards came to be represented as individual variations on a single, standard theme. By streamlining them, the numbering and standardisation of cards was integral to the development of new styles of play, loosely termed banking games, which evolved into casino games.

In the game of *vingt-et-un* (which later grew into pontoon, and then the casino game of blackjack), and *chemin de fer* (baccarat), suits and court cards were irrelevant, numerical values paramount. From their regal status as the most important cards in the pack (many bearing the image of their owner), in baccarat, picture cards were dethroned and given no value at all. A similar fate befell court cards in blackjack which were also democratised and given a single numerical value—ten. Consonant with the statistical spirit of the times, cards in these games, like all the others in the pack, were only important through their representation of number. Both games were basically arithmetical exercises whose principle was to assemble cards whose value did not exceed a specified number: twenty-one in blackjack, nine in baccarat.

With their emphasis on calculation and the irrelevance of any distinctions other than numerical ones, we can see in these games the mirror of the commercial, statistical interests of an increasingly capitalist society.

It was not only in card games that the dynamic relation between games and society was apparent. The early probabilists used games of chance to develop their theorems, and their discoveries in turn affected the games they experimented with. As probability became more fully understood, the games it was applied to became more complex, so that games and theory developed by feeding off each other in an ever more complex dialectic of theoretical and practical application.

ROULETTE

The game of E-O (even-odd) was popular during the eighteenth century in fashionable resorts like Bath and consisted of a wheel with forty cups alternately marked E for even and O for odd. A ball was released as the wheel rotated and players wagered whether it would fall into an E or O pocket. Pascal experimented with a similar ball and wheel device, but did not, as is sometimes claimed, 'invent' roulette. The game as we know it today was actually developed in the nineteenth century when the French addition of thirty-six numbers and colours to the wheel revolutionised the simplicity of the original game (Sifakis 1990, p. 256). The impact of the addition was enormous, greatly increasing the variety of betting available from one to ten, with different odds on each. Players could still bet odd or even, but now any single number or combination of numbers as well. The addition of numbers made roulette a far more exciting and complex game than its rather staid predecessor, and, with the inclusion of a zero (two in America), also made it a very commercial one, for when the ball landed in this pocket all bets were won by the house.

DICE

Advances in the study of probability, aided by commercial developments, also transformed the ancient game of hazard into a faster, more streamlined version known as craps. Hazard had been played in the same way for centuries, with players betting that they would eventually throw a certain number with two dice, throwing until they did and then continuing to throw until the original number or 'point' came up again. However, since the odds of certain numbers coming up before others varies, a competent player would require a basic understanding of probability to play well. Such an understanding of averages and odds in relation to dice simply did not exist until the seventeenth century, with the result that most bettors did not comprehend all the ways various combinations could be achieved with two dice. For hundreds of years 'A hustler could indeed have made a fortune' (Sifakis 1990, p. 147)!

In France, hazard was known as krabs (after the English word for a throw of two or three), later corrupted to creps or craps. When introduced into America by French colonists, a modified version grew in popularity among black slaves in New Orleans and took its name from French craps (Scarne 1974, p. 39). In the nineteenth century, the incorporation of ever-increasing knowledge about odds and percentages reformulated the rules of hazard into what we now know as the modern game of craps. Dozens of types of bets now became available to the player, with many more variations of each type.

With its multitude of betting strategies and combinations of odds, the appeal of craps as a lucrative commercial game was obvious. To entice it into the casino, further modifications were made, which changed its structure yet again. A small charge was made by the house whenever the thrower made two or more passes. This was known as a take-off game. Next, the house took the opposition against the thrower, so that *all* players now had to bet the dice to win against the house. A simple table layout bearing the six and eight, the field, win and come bets, was drawn up to play on, exactly half of the table layout today. The house now took its cut 'not as a direct charge, but indirectly and less noticeably by offering short odds so that it gained a percentage' (Scarne 1974, p. 41). A further development offered players the opportunity to bet the dice to *lose,* as well as to win. In effect, every bet could now be either for or against the dice or the house. Betting opportunities were doubled, and the craps table reflected the change, changing its shape from a semi-circle to a full oval, with one half a mirror image of the other. The game of craps at times appeared as the archetypal game of probability theory, with its complex permutations of odds, pay-offs and house percentages, a working (or rather *playing*) example of a theoretical construction.

GAMING MACHINES

One of the most significant developments of the nineteenth century was the introduction of gaming machines. The Industrial Revolution had laid the foundations for automatic gambling when a London bookseller created a vending machine in order to sell proscribed literature, although the introduction and proliferation of coin-operated machines did not appear on a mass scale until the last quarter of the nineteenth century. During this period of technological innovation, the automation of the leisure sphere was complemented by that of the workplace, so that the development of what Costa (1988) called 'automatic pleasures' was symptomatic of the automation of the wider world of the late nineteenth century.

Being born into a secular, industrial age, the ancient image of divinatory drama which ran as a leitmotif through most older, established types of gambling would not be expected to feature in this young form. However, slot-machines did manage to maintain the link of all gambling with the sacred, for the automated machines from which the early gaming machines drew their inspiration were originally used for fortune-telling. In the white heat of the technological revolution, the art of divination was not made redundant, it was simply mechanised.

The earliest gaming machines invited individuals to discover their future by means of a spinning pointer, a card dispenser or some kind of animated figure (Costa 1988, p. 21). Their patents stated that they could be used either as divinatory devices or as games of chance, although in an attempt to limit their appeal, both forms of amusement were only allowed to return tokens such as cigarettes and chewing-gum and not cash, as prizes. The design of many of these first machines was simply an automatic adaptation of already existing games—hence the popularity of images of cards and horses, as well as of pieces of fruit, from which the term 'fruit machine' is derived.

The first automatic three-reel machine, or 'one-arm bandit'—the prototype of our modern gambling machines—appeared in San Francisco in 1905 when Charles Fey developed a device in which a handle was pulled to spin three wheels and, if a winning combination was made, a stream of nickels poured out into a tray below (Sifakis 1990). The one-armed bandit (which Fey patriotically named the Liberty Bell) was developed in a rush of pioneering individualism typical of the Gold Rush state of that time. Throughout the nineteenth century risk-hungry Californians, whom Findlay (1986) called 'people of chance', were possessed of a dynamic, innovative spirit which culminated in their westward advance across Nevada and the subsequent creation of Las Vegas. It is no wonder then that in an era of technological advance, it was these 'people of chance' who gave slot-machines their final configuration and so created the most modern form of gambling device.

HORSES

The numerical preoccupation of the nineteenth century, along with technological innovation, was to dramatically change the face of horse-race betting. The role of newspapers became steadily more important in this process, along with newly established journals such as *Sporting Life* (1863) and *Sporting Chronicle* (1871), disseminating tips, news and forecasts to a hungry audience. For the second time in history,[2] print encouraged—and was encouraged by—gambling. This plethora of sporting journals fed the voracious public appetite for information, and was crammed full of facts and statistics about horses, races, jockeys and odds. Aided by the electronic telegraph system, which meant the press could quickly publish results and starting odds, and the establishment of a credit network, the 1880s saw the development of large-scale organised betting (McKibbon 1979; Chinn 1991; Clapson 1992; Munting 1996). In a move which the aristocracy would have fought bitterly against, railways helped to make horse-racing a national spectator sport by sponsoring races and linking towns (and therefore fee-paying punters) to courses.

These nineteenth-century developments revolutionised racing. Now thoroughly democratised, its status was reversed from being the prerogative of a rich elite to being a massive working-class entertainment. Under the sway of commercial developments, spectacular, individual upper-class bets disappeared and popular betting between a mass of punters—both on and off the track—took over. Such bets were subject to strict odds: the chances of a horse winning a race were calculated by taking many variables into account, and expressed in a numerical equation. Pay-offs were equally subject to strict calculation, based on the amount of the original stake and the odds on the particular horse. No longer a simple 'gentlemen's agreement' for a set amount, betting became a complex contract between bettors and central race organisers, relayed through a number of betting shops. The physiognomy of betting also changed: from being private and limited it became public and widespread. Its role in providing a source of excitement as well as hope of financial gain at a time when poverty made alternative forms of economic advance, such as saving, unrealistic, meant the popularity of betting was assured (Chinn 1991; Clapson 1992). This broad place in working-class culture was reflected in an increasing dissemination of bookmakers, runners and their agents on street corners, in the backs of shops and throughout private homes. The first betting house opened in Britain in 1847: three years later over 400 existed, and almost immediately, an 'epidemic of gambling was declared to have attacked even the poorest class' (Neville 1909, p. 99). Needless to say, a wave of legislation—the Street Betting Acts of 1853, 1874 and 1892—swiftly appeared, designed to eradicate all forms of popular, working-class betting.[3] Again, it was too late. The popular tide of betting simply went underground, largely unaffected by the 'suppression', until betting shops were reinstated in 1961.

THE NEW STYLE OF PLAY

The highly numerical nature of all these forms of gambling was consonant with the statistical milieu of the nineteenth century, and was particularly suited to the imperatives of commercial organisation. These developments were to change the experience of play forever. In gaming halls and public houses, people played all day and all night at games like craps and roulette, which had been refined and organised in such a way as to include a 'space' for a 'player' who always won—the house, or dealer. Commercialisation encouraged dealers to rely increasingly 'upon the more predictable and more secure profits provided by odds fixed inflexibly in their favour' (Findlay 1986, p. 91). Realising the impossibility of winning the games they operated, these commercial interests—'the house'—made a brilliant move whereupon winning was assured. Rather than participate in a game, they removed themselves from it altogether and allied themselves with the very law that told them they had to lose. By placing themselves actually *within* the probability equation, they could simply sit back and await the profits which would inevitably result from favourable odds once the law of large numbers was given enough time to come into effect. Backed by the indomitable authority of probability, the house could not possibly lose. On the other hand, the alliance of both odds *and* house edge meant that individual gamblers could not possibly win. They found themselves competing against an invisible opponent with a permanent place at every table and unlimited resources. What is more, they were forced to play against the house, for this element of competition had been built into the commercial games and was now inherent in their structure. Gamblers no longer played against each other but against the house, whose invisible impersonal force mirrored the imperatives of economic behaviour, the 'invisible hand' of market forces.

Commercialisation also changed the social composition of play by encouraging less wealthy players. As wagers became smaller, participation dramatically increased. Hiding behind the iron laws of probability, gambling entrepreneurs made profits, not by increasing the stakes of games, but by increasing the volume of players. They might not make 'leviathan' wagers, but these more modest players could be relied on to place a regular flow of smaller bets, so guaranteeing the profits of the house.

As its nature was transformed through commercialisation, the experience of gambling itself underwent a change. Participation, not winning *per se,* became paramount and, as Findlay points out, this changed the meaning of gambling itself: 'Players still hoped to win . . . but they looked upon betting more as a commodity for sale . . . as an experience worth purchasing with losing wagers' (Findlay 1986, p. 92). In a capitalist economy, gambling had finally succumbed to commodification. But this was no ordinary commodity, for it had a unique experiential component. Players continued to gamble, but as much for the thrills and excitement of the game itself as for financial rewards. Fast games and moderate stakes became valued for prolonging participation and therefore maximising excitement. Now that their main motivation was participation, gamblers played simply to *play,* for: 'Next to the pleasure of winning is the pleasure of losing, only stagnation is unendurable' (Bankcroft, in Findlay 1986, p. 94).

Out of this process of commercialisation emerged a distinctive type of gambling which, despite distinct differences, also shared common elements with the gambling of the seventeenth-century aristocrat. Crucially, for both, money served only as a measure of play, unimportant in itself. The high stakes of the aristocracy showed their indifference to money and as such, the aristocrat played to *participate,* never to win. The low stakes of the nineteenth-century gambler at first seem far removed from the leviathan bets of the aristocrat, but they served a similar purpose: to lengthen participation. Again, money was only a *means* of play, and the indifference of these latter gamblers to it stemmed from their participation in play itself. These orientations are also to be found in modern gamblers. . . .

The commercialisation of gambling was to gather speed over the following hundred years, overseeing its gradual development into a widespread, popular and—just as importantly—legal form of consumption. In this process centuries of condemnation which had persistently attempted to eliminate games of chance from social life—and especially the social life of the poor—were finally overturned.

Notes

1. See Russell T. Barnhart's history of these gambling centres, as well as the illustrious figures who frequented them (Barnhart 1983).

2. The first being the dissemination of cards from the printing presses of the fifteenth century.

3. Both of these Acts were hugely unpopular, and largely unworkable. In particular, the 1906 legislation represented an attempt by anti-gambling lobbies (mainly the National Anti-Gambling League) to outlaw all forms of working-class gambling. In this, it has been described as 'a monstrous sample of class legislation' (Clapson 1992, p. 31), which ensured that gambling was to remain a political issue.

References

Barnhart, R. T. (1983) *Gamblers of Yesteryear,* Las Vegas: Gamblers Book Club Press.

Chinn, C. (1991) *Better Betting with a Decent Feller: Bookmakers, Betting and the British Working Class 1750-1990,* Hemel Hempstead, Herts: Harvester Wheatsheaf.

Clapson, M. (1992) *A Bit of a Flutter: Popular Gambling and English Society 1823-1961,* Manchester: Manchester University Press.

Costa, N. (1988) *Automatic Pleasures: The History of the Coin Machine,* London: The Bath Press.

Findlay, J. (1986) *People of Chance: Gambling in American Society from Jamestown to Las Vegas,* Oxford: Oxford University Press.

Hargrave, C. (1966) *A History of Playing Cards,* New York: Dover Publications, Inc.

McKibbon, N. (1979) 'Working class gambling in Britain 1880-1937', *Past and Present,* 82, 147-178.

McMillen, J. (ed.) (1996) *Gambling Cultures: Studies in History and Interpretation,* London: Routledge.

Munting, R. (1996) *An Economic and Social History of Gambling in Britain and the USA,* Manchester and New York: Manchester University Press.

Neville, M. (1909) *Light Come, Light Go,* London: Macmillan.

Scarne, J. (1974) *Scarne on Dice,* Harrisburg, PA: Stackpole Books.

Sifakis, C. (1990) *The Encyclopedia of Gambling,* New York: Facts on File.

Steinmetz, A. (1870) *The Gaming Table,* vol. 2, London: Tinsley Brothers.

Turner, L. and Ash, J. (1975) *The Golden Hordes: International Tourism and the Pleasure Periphery,* London: Constable.

GAMBLING IN AMERICAN LITERATURE

Karen A. Weyler (essay date 1996)

SOURCE: Weyler, Karen A. "'A Speculating Spirit': Trade, Speculation, and Gambling in Early American Fiction." *Early American Literature* 31, no. 3 (1996): 207-42.

[In the following essay, Weyler examines American novelists' treatment of such subjects as the desire for and accumulation of wealth within the context of social morality during the late eighteenth and early nineteenth centuries.]

"We thought when once our liberty was gain'd,
And Peace had spread its influence thro' the land,
That Learning soon would raise its chearful head,
And arts on arts would joyfully succeed;
'Till all Columbia's genius 'gan to blaze,
And in true science more than rival'd Greece:
But *Speculation,* like a baleful pest,
Has pour'd his dire contagion in the breast:
That monster that would ev'ry thing devour. . . ."

From *The Glass or Speculation: A Poem: Containing an
Account of the Ancient, and Genius of the Modern,
Speculators*

The excerpt quoted above, from a poem printed in pamphlet form in 1791, captures both the hope and the disappointment wrought by changing economic conditions in the newly formed United States after the Revolution. "Speculation" and its companion vices avarice and greed dismayed republicans throughout the United States as the self-sacrificing civic virtue of the war years gave way to more profit-oriented forms of individualism.[1] Novels written in America arose at precisely the time when this postcolonial economy was in great flux, and they point to the possibilities and dangers inherent in a capitalist economy that placed grave demands upon trust between widely separated and differing individuals. Novelists, poets, political writers, and belletrists, regardless of their political orientation, expressed considerable anxiety about how this changing economy would affect the moral virtue of American citizens. The luxuries resulting from this changing economy became a locus for these fears, and luxury came to refer not only to specific items procured in international trade, but also to an urbanized, sophisticated lifestyle.[2] Although novelists were concerned about abuses of luxury, they were perhaps more concerned about the problematic issue of accumulating capital. While most early American novels exalt industry and the potential for economic advancement that the American economy offered, these novels simultaneously point to contemporary economic anxieties, primarily the fear that people would attempt to make money without industry through such means as gambling, speculating, and counterfeiting. I argue in this essay that reading novels alongside political pamphlets, economic tracts, and belles lettres reveals that American fiction was an active and significant link in the nexus of public discourse during the 1790s and the first two decades of the nineteenth century. Deeply engaged with economic issues facing Americans of the rising middle-class, fiction contributed to public economic discourse by exploring ways to reconcile desire for personal economic advancement with larger civic interests; at the same time, fiction contributed to the gendering of the American economic system by presenting trade as a virtuous means of making money and by simultaneously constructing economic desire as a specifically masculine prerogative.

Novels written between 1789 and 1815 provide a window into post-Revolutionary America that allows us to understand both American cultural values and cultural anxieties. Increased social choices and sexual freedom for young women caused considerable anxiety among writers of early American fiction, for private female virtue—meaning chastity, among other things—was integral to republican conceptions of female virtue.[3] Although these novels place many of the same demands upon male and female characters—among these demands are patriotism, fidelity, and chastity—they differ in one key respect. While the primary challenge women face is to be sexually and emotionally chaste, the challenge male characters face is to be economically virtuous—meaning that they must balance self-interest and public interest. The difficulty of this balancing act obviously evoked tremendous anxiety on the part of writers of early fiction, for virtually every novel written during this time betrays considerable apprehension about the issue of accumulating capital. Novels portray money being made or amassed in a variety of ways—sometimes legally, through trade, and other times illicitly, through some other means such as counterfeiting, forgery, gambling, or speculation. Yet contemporary political disputes meant that even a legal means of making money such as trade carried with it certain overtones of political and class conflict. The provocative question these novels pose is this: How does one balance the competing desire of making money and the goal of being economically virtuous? Or in other words, How does one balance individual and public or community economic interests? The agenda of much early American fiction is precisely this regulation and control of economic desire in a republic anxious about the dangerous effects of luxury. Fiction mediates between such desires, and a fictional battle emerges, pitting money earned through virtuous trade against that acquired through gambling, speculation, or inheritance.

The problem of making money is a natural one for writers of early American fiction to explore, for the task of the American protagonist is literally to become Crèvecoeur's "new man"; many protagonists of early American fiction are disinherited, both literally and metaphorically, perhaps as a parable for the severing of the colonial relationship with England. The response of these protagonists to this disinheritance serves as a driving force within the plot of many novels.[4] Charles Brockden Brown, the best known of America's early fiction writers, frequently relies upon this trope. In Brown's *Edgar Huntly* and *Arthur Mervyn,* for example, both protagonists initially express their economic anxiety by searching for a surrogate father, a wealthy man who might adopt them and eliminate their economic anxieties and their need to make money. Ultimately, the events of the novels snatch these father figures away from both Huntly and Mervyn, although Mervyn does find a surrogate mother in his fiancée, Achsa Fielding. Brown's interest in economic issues has been ably explored by a number of critics.[5] What I am concerned with instead in this essay is how a number of other early American novels, particularly Rebecca Rush's *Kelroy* (1812) and Sarah Wood's *Dorval; or, The Speculator* (1801), explore alternatives to inherited wealth and the possibilities present in a changing economy.

While many early American novels exhibit a definite Republican bias, exalting a healthy, virtuous lifestyle on a landed estate, inherited wealth and land-ownership are precisely what most disinherited protagonists lack; instead, land ownership is extended as a tantalizing reward for a life of virtue and industry.[6] The anonymous work *Moreland Vale* (1801) provides an excellent example of this trope. After serving for years as a clerk in a counting-house in Canton, China, Henry Walgrove, the male protagonist of the novel, inherits a substantial fortune; he and his wife then retire to country life. He explains why he does so: "In the peaceful bosom of calm retirement, you do not give up the world; but you have the pleasure of enjoying the company of your friends unaccompanied by the ceremony and bustle of a town life. You have leisure to attend to the calls of humanity and to relieve the wants of your fellow creatures" (144). It is the very orderliness of rural life that provides such a happy resolution to so many early American novels, for rural life generally symbolizes a life ordered by class and hierarchy, where systems of philanthropy enable each individual to neatly categorize others.[7] The corollary to this praise of rural life is the relative absence in early American fiction of novels portraying details of life in urban industrial centers—not surprising since widespread industrialization did not take place until the second decade of the nineteenth century. With the exception of Sarah Savage's 1814 novel *The Factory Girl,* early American fiction thus paints a landscape largely free of manufacturing, populated instead by farmers, artisans, professionals such as doctors, lawyers, ministers, and soldiers, and, most interestingly, merchants.[8] Merchants and trade are the key to economic opportunity, since trade offered a proactive approach to the problem of earning an income, as well as a virtuous means of halting post-Revolution downward mobility.

Yet merchants and trade held an unsettled status among writers of the day. Numerous historians of the early national era, including Drew R. McCoy and Carroll Smith-Rosenberg, among others, have commented on the ambivalence of the citizens of the new Republic toward trade.[9] Much of this ambivalence seems to stem from two different problems, the first directly involving merchants and the "ethics" of trade. The second problem centers around the results of international trade, chiefly the increased importation of luxury goods into the United States. Certainly these concerns about luxury were already present; indeed, as T. H. Breen has persuasively argued, colonial theories that the appearance of luxury led to increased taxes fostered pre-

Revolutionary antagonism to British commercial policies and precipitated the subsequent nonimportation agreements.[10] Dramatically increased opportunities for international trade and commerce after the Revolution, and especially with Asia after 1793, when Britain was involved in the war with France, undoubtedly fomented anxieties about the consequences of trade. Despite unsettled views about the social status of merchants, trade represented a quick and yet relatively virtuous means of acquiring wealth. In his study *The Social Structure of Revolutionary America,* Jackson Turner Main indicates that the merchant class in the post-Revolutionary period offered significantly increased opportunities for social mobility, particularly in large cities like Boston, New York, and Philadelphia (190-92). He concludes that trade, along with law, offered the most fruitful way to wealth. Novels of the time such as *Dorval; or The Speculator, Moreland Vale,* and *Fidelity Rewarded; or, The History of Polly Granville,* to name just a few, use the motif of virtuous trade to illustrate the mobility inherent in the American economy, whereas the conclusions of these novels, which inevitably feature settlement on a landed estate, emphasize the return of order, social stability, and hierarchy.

In order to constitute trade as a virtuous means of earning one's wealth, however, novelists had to establish a difference between those who dealt in honest trade and those who dealt in unsavory or potentially dishonest economic practices like gambling and land, currency, or commodity speculation. In other words, they had to find a means of separating trade from its sometimes attendant or at least associated economic practices, because many Americans still associated success in trade with some degree of chance. Novelists differentiated between these practices by linking economic speculation with gambling, which is universally damned in early American fiction and belles lettres; trade thus came to be viewed by some as a practice distinct from speculation. Furthermore, by encasing trade in a rhetoric and logic of sentimentality, novels associated trade not only with individual benefits, but also with the economic health and security of families, communities, and the nation at large. Characters engage in foreign trade not out of greed or desire for luxuries, but rather for reasons of sentiment or honor, such as the need to support aged parents or to redeem a father's debts. In an era in which land owning was valorized and trade still slightly suspect, fiction portrayed the East India and China trade as a daring, even romantic, venture, yet one that offered the possibility of tremendous legitimate profit gained not at the expense of other Americans—an important distinction, and one that novelists carefully portray.

THE CULTURAL SIGNIFICANCE OF THE EAST INDIA AND CHINA TRADE

The East India and China trade had a tremendous cultural resonance during the early national period, for it symbolized American entrepreneurship, as well as America's new freedom from the trading restraints of the British mercantile system. Partisans of free trade like minister-turned-merchant Pelatiah Webster also claimed that a vigorous international trade would actually serve to unite the new country, thereby giving additional impetus and significance to the sea trade (*A Dissertation* 219). Although British mercantilist policy prohibited direct American trade with the British West Indies, the former colonies' closest trading partner, and blocked American trade with the French West Indies colonies during the Napoleonic war, Great Britain tolerated American participation in the East India and China trade until the commencement of the hostilities that later led to the War of 1812. Furthermore, the Jay Treaty guaranteed reception of American ships in important British ports throughout the trade routes to East India and China.[11]

Post-Revolutionary direct trade with Asian countries allowed Americans to trade for their own luxuries—precisely the kind of luxuries that conspicuously appear in a number of novels. Americans would ship goods such as ginseng (used for medicinal and aphrodisiac purposes), tobacco, pitch, tar, turpentine, furs, and silver to China and East India. Export of commodities such as ginseng and tobacco was acceptable, even necessary, according to Jeffersonian political doctrine, in order to expand the agricultural basis of the new nation. In return, traders would receive tea, cotton nankeen cloth, silk, porcelain (which was so inexpensive in China that it was often shipped as ballast), pepper, and Chinese cinnamon. Americans might also ship home more exotic luxury goods, including such items as hand-painted wallpaper, lacquered trays and boxes, silk slippers, and decorative fans made from a variety of materials, such as paper, mother-of-pearl, silk, and lacquer.[12] Formerly a symbol of British mercantilist policy, tea procured in free trade had obvious cultural significance for Americans, as did these other conspicuous luxury items—not of British manufacture, but luxury items procured through free trade with the exotic Orient. The tremendous popularity of special-order China export porcelain decorated with patriotic motifs lends special significance to mention of China plate in shipping lists, newspapers, and novels, and further suggests how American patriots valued American participation in the East India trade. The conspicuous presence of these items, and tea in particular, in virtually every early American novel would have signaled to readers not only patriotic pride in American entrepreneurship, but also approval of American participation in international trade. Henry Walgrove, the honorable merchant protagonist of *Moreland Vale,* for instance, presents to his new wife a trunk filled with Chinese porcelain, elegant fans, and silks—gifts that she generously shares with her friends. In such a situation, proper display and use of these cultural signifiers not only celebrated American trade, but also denoted consumer sophistication that in itself came to symbolize a shared culture.[13]

The luxury goods procured during voyages to China and East India offered both owners and investors opportunities for remarkable profits. For example, in 1784-85, the first American voyage to China, that of Robert Morris's *Empress of China,* netted the owners a twenty percent return on their original investment. Other voyages generated even more profit, such as the 1785 voyage of the *Experiment,* which netted investors returns of seventy-two percent on their investment (Goldstein 30; Dulles 43).[14] The Asian trade was a very fluid business, and ship owners were not the only ones to profit from such voyages. Merchants other than the owners or original investors might invest in a voyage by shipping cargo on the same ship. The captain and other members of the crew, such as the supercargo, might also be allowed to engage in small private commercial ventures. Supercargoes might also carry out commissions for private individuals for a flat fee or a percentage of the profits (Dulles 44-7). Thus, there was considerable opportunity for individual participation in the trade with the Far East. Once in the East, individuals might also choose to remain in India or China in a managerial capacity as a commercial agent for a number of years beyond the usual fifteen to eighteen month round trip for such a voyage, a situation that frequently occurs in fiction of the time: Henry Walgrove of *Moreland Vale* becomes a clerk in a counting-house in Canton, while one of the sons of the Dunbar family in *Dorval* remains in India as an agent for seven years, amassing an enormous fortune.

The impact of the first direct voyage to China was of great importance and was widely documented and discussed in east coast newspapers of the time such as Boston's *Massachusetts Centinel,* the *New-York Packet,* and Philadelphia's *Pennsylvania Packet,* undoubtedly providing information and inspiration to American writers of fiction. In *Philadelphia and the China Trade,* Jonathan Goldstein claims that "In private correspondence, newspaper articles, and books, two themes emerged that would be echoed down to the end of Philadelphia's old China trade: the China trade was of unprecedented economic importance for the new nation; and because of that great commercial value, the Chinese people as a whole were to be held in esteem" (31). The China and East India trade immediately burgeoned after this initial venture. Goldstein claims that "Between 1784 and 1804, as many as seven ships a year went from Philadelphia to China, and as many as thirty-one per year from the entire United States. After 1804, until the end of the old China trade in 1846, the number of American voyages leveled off at about thirty or forty per annum, with Philadelphia ships comprising about one-third of these passages" (34). The entrepreneurial possibilities inherent in international trade seem to have

enthralled the imagination of writers of fiction, and merchants and the separations demanded by trade become favored characters and situations in diverse novels such as Mrs. Patterson's *The Unfortunate Lovers, and Cruel Parents* (1799), Wood's *Dorval; or The Speculator,* and Rebecca Rush's *Kelroy.*

Patriotic pride in such trading ventures pervades newspapers and other writings of the 1780s and 1790s. Philip Freneau's *envoi,* entitled "On the First American Ship That Explored the Route to China, and The East-India, After the Revolution," aptly captures this celebratory patriotism in the new freedom for American shipping.

> With clearance from BELLONA won
> She spreads her wings to meet the Sun,
> Those golden regions to explore
> Where George forbade to sail before.
>
> Thus, grown to strength, the bird of Jove,
> Impatient, quits his native grove,
> With eyes of fire, and lightning's force
> Through the blue aether holds his course.
>
> No foreign tars are here allow'd
> To mingle with her chosen crowd,
> Who, when return'd, might, boasting, say
> They show'd our native oak the way.
>
> To that old track no more confin'd,
> By Britain's jealous court assign'd,
> She round the STORMY CAPE shall sail
> And, eastward, catch the odorous gale.
>
> To countries plac'd in burning climes
> And islands of remotist times
> She now her eager course explores,
> And soon shall greet Chinesian shores,
>
> From thence their fragrant TEAS to bring
> Without the leave of Britain's king;
> And PORCELAIN WARE, enchas'd in gold,
> The product of that finer mould.
>
> Thus commerce to our world conveys
> All that the varying taste can please:
> For us the Indian looms are free,
> And JAVA strips her spicy TREE.
>
> Great pile proceed!—and o'er the brine
> May every prosperous gale be thine,
> 'Till, freighted deep with eastern gems,
> You reach again your native streams.[15]

Despite his patriotic pride in being free of "Britain's jealous court," Freneau himself embodies the ambivalence that many American writers felt toward trade, ambivalence that also permeates political and economic pamphlets and tracts of the 1790s. Although he could thrill patriotically at the freedom of American shipping, at the same time Freneau feared that the luxuries procured by this trade would foster greed and avarice among his countrymen. Just a few years later, in 1797,

Freneau printed in *The Time Piece* an excerpt from the anonymous work *Of Commerce and Luxury,* which questions the wisdom and benefits of a developed international trade in luxury goods. While granting the necessity of economical trade, the author of this piece clearly feared that an advanced trade in luxury goods would create an ever greater disparity in wealth among the population.[16] This fear of altering the status quo of wealth in the new Republic was only one of the problems associated with the sea trade.

The other problems associated with the rise of American participation in international trade represent significant conflicts with republican political ideology, as merchants and trade became a locus for generalized anxieties about the American economy and culture. These anxieties range along a spectrum that extends from dislike of unproductive labor to the negative effects of a luxurious, speculative lifestyle. The first of these anxieties centers around the concern that all labor be productive labor. Although Scottish political economist Adam Smith considered trade to be productive labor, many American writers followed the general tenets of the French physiocrats in arguing that trade was, in fact, unproductive.[17] Thomas Cooper, who would later teach one of the first American courses on political economy at the University of South Carolina, argues in *Political Arithmetic* (1798) that the military costs of protecting international trade far outweigh its profits. But equally a matter of concern for Cooper was that "*merchants, and all the people directly employed by him, rank among the unproductive classes of society*" (14; emphasis in original); Cooper includes in this group agents, factors, clerks, sea captains, and sailors, all of whom merely arrange and transport the labor of others, while producing nothing new themselves. Other Jeffersonians, like the Virginian John Taylor, agreed that the sea trade, when compared with the practice of agriculture, was unproductive (78). Hence, the nature of the wealth procured through trade was itself problematic.

Attendant to this fear about the unproductive nature of foreign trade was the belief that involvement with trade would bring about wealth too quickly when compared to the slow and steady prosperity of agriculture. In *An Enquiry Into the Principle and Tendencies of Certain Public Measures* (1794), Taylor describes merchants as "brokers, honourable and useful, whilst adhering to a steady line of commerce, and supplying the wants of a nation; but pernicious and dangerous, whilst speculating indiscriminately on foes and friends for the acquisition of wealth, and aspiring to exclusive privileges and prerogatives" (78). Thomas Cooper makes a similar argument, claiming

> Nor is it a slight objection, that while by the peaceful products of agriculture, gains can be made but slowly, gradually, and by the regular exertions of habitual,

> wholesome industry, the commercial speculator often gets rich by accident, by unfair venturing, by sudden exertions. Wealth thus suddenly obtained is in many respects detrimental to the community. It operates as a lottery: it tempts capital into trade beyond prudent bounds: it entices to unjustifiable boldness: it introduces ostentation, luxury and pride, and manners out of harmony with republican principles.

(14-15)

This emphasis on agriculture as noncompetitive, "habitual," and "wholesome" points to anxiety that trade itself might not be wholesome and, further, that the vagaries of trade themselves are a danger. Trade is dangerous not so much from the possibility of losses but rather from the possibility of too-sudden gains, a possibility that explicitly links the merchant with the speculator, just as the mention of the lottery links trade to gambling. This association demonstrates the uncertain status that merchants and trade continued to hold for some people during the early national era, for both Taylor and Cooper associate merchants with a dangerous tendency toward avarice and greed and a subsequent appetite for a luxurious lifestyle. At the same time, Taylor, Cooper, and others feared that this desire for luxuries would spread throughout the population at large. These fears are precisely those that novelists of the early Republic era address and counter, as I will argue later in my essay.

The Link between Luxury, Gambling, and Speculation

Other Americans were also critical of the newly formed United States' access to these new sources of luxuries, for concomitant with this changing economy were anxieties about how people would behave in an economy filled with luxuries. The vituperative 1785 debate between Samuel Adams and the supporters of the Boston Tea Assembly (the "San Souci Club") exemplifies this anxiety about the kind of society a changing economy might produce. Even the author signing himself "One of a Number," who was himself a supporter of the Tea Assembly, links an increase in commerce with luxury; he views amusements such as dancing and card playing at the Tea Assembly as the natural outcomes of an increasingly luxurious lifestyle (rptd. in Wood, *Rising Glory* 144).[18] Adams, advocate for a very Spartan version of republicanism, had numerous concerns about the Tea Assembly, particularly about the promiscuous mixing of social classes he believed such a public entertainment might entail. But more dangerous, he believed, was the possibility that card playing at the Assembly would lead to it becoming a decadent gambling den, where such speculative acts would be publicly performed and might lead "to the destruction of everything good or virtuous" (rptd. in Wood 138). Adams sees card playing as the slippery slope to ruin: "Those who play frequently get an itch for it, and although they may begin small, will play more largely as they are more attached to it. The gamester by being fortunate this night, is desirous to risk again:—Or by being unfortunate the last night, has imbibed such a desire for gaming, as never to be easy but when at play" (rptd. in Gordon 147). Benjamin Austin concurs with Adams about the potential dangers of card playing, for such gambling might lead to "the *ruin of their [the gamblers'] fortunes,* and *misery of their families* . . . for though [the] independent gentleman may claim this right, within his *private sphere,* yet a *public amusement* may prove fatal to a community, and may with propriety be *supprest as such*" (rptd. in Wood 151; emphasis in original). Indeed, Austin seems to fear that private vices like gambling would no longer remain so, but would permeate society, an end brought about by the luxurious lifestyle that international trade enabled and fostered. Austin's position here is typical of American republicanism in its rejection of Bernard Mandeville's equation of private vices with public virtues, for most Americans feared the effects of private vice.

Although there had always been a streak of antigambling sentiment running through the religious and literary culture of colonial America, this rhetoric reaches a new pitch in the late eighteenth century, as gambling becomes understood as a result of luxury, and at the same time as part and parcel of the practice of economic speculation. A prime example of this confusion of economic practices is Mason Locke Weems's 1810 anti-gambling tract *God's Revenge Against Gambling.* Weems provides numerous lurid examples, some of which are obviously fictionalized sketches, while others are based in fact, of the violence and tragedy that result from gambling; one anecdote in particular strikingly illustrates the cultural association between gambling, speculation, and trade. After enumerating the tragic loss of fortune and subsequent suicide or murder of several gamblers, Weems concludes that "this just judgment of poverty inflicted on Gamblers, is a universal truth none can deny" (34). He challenges readers to show him "one single Gambler, who *has liv'd and died rich*" (34; emphasis in original). Weems himself promises he could "name . . . hundreds, and here in the town of Augusta too, to go no farther, hundreds of industrious, honest men, who started poor and now are rich" (34). Among the doctors and lawyers he mentions, Weems includes "honorable Merchants, who, thirty years past, open'd shop with hardly more than pedlars packs, and yet now drink as good wine as the *great Emperor*; and parry, with a shrug only, the loss of 50,000 dollars on a cotton speculation" (35; emphasis in original). Clearly, honest trade was not completely free of all ties with speculation in 1810, but by this time, the kind of speculation involved in basically honest trade has taken on a more positive connotation—at least in Weems's view—as a legitimate risk of the marketplace.

Novel-length fictions of the 1790s and the first decade of the nineteenth century, however, are careful to isolate gambling as a seductive obsession, as a practice separate from virtuous trade, and as an economic practice with no possibility of redemption.[19] One typical such novel is *The Gambler, or The Memoirs of a British Officer* (1802), which combines a number of themes popular in fiction of the time. The main character is, of course, a British officer who gambles away his family's fortune, is imprisoned along with his family for debt, and eventually dies from disappointment and grief. The British officer is the natural choice to represent the gambler in this text, for in his character, American readers see embodied Britain's lack of virtue, as well as their own fears about the outcome of a luxurious, riotous lifestyle. Telling his tale while imprisoned, the officer describes himself as a man in the grip of an obsession, unable to overcome it even though he regrets his actions. Through its use of first person narration, the tale borrows from the genre of the conversion narrative. Despite this first person narration, the tale remains flat, and it never gains the power of a true conversion narrative, perhaps because there is no possibility of redemption for this gambler.

Another, more complicated, antigambling novel that also bills itself as a conversion narrative of sorts is *St. Hubert* (1800). *St. Hubert* begins the conversion process by including on its title page the motto "Exemplo aliorum discite," or "Profit by example." Interestingly enough, in spite of, or perhaps because of, its status as a quasi-conversion narrative, the preface takes a very different tack from that of most prefaces in early American fiction. The frame narrator, no apologist, explains in the preface that he is telling his tale in the form of a novel in order to aid the "rising generation" in the face of "the many difficulties" and the "numerous temptations" they face (iii). He prefers the novel form because he fears that "the austere manners and jesuitical denunciations which priestcraft has too often invented to answer the purposes of fraud and deception" will not appeal to the youth of his time (iv); he goes on to condemn sermonic literature, claiming that "the awful and silent exhortations of the pulpit . . . [have] not had the salutary effect which they merited, inasmuch as they [are] too serious and . . . gloomy" (iv). Instead, the frame narrator finds the novel to be the most "captivating mode of recommending virtue in her simple and comely garb, and of exhibiting vice in her native hideous colors" (iii-iv).

The tale itself illustrates a fascinating intertwining of the seduction of moral and economic virtue. St. Hubert, who narrates the inside narrative, is a Frenchman led into debauchery by his friend Delaferre, who introduces him to card playing and to the seductive widow, Madam de Trenville. The widow and cards are twin seducers, each furthering St. Hubert's descent into debauchery, as

St. Hubert gambles in order to be near Madam de Trenville, and she in turn encourages him to gamble. After St. Hubert has lost his entire fortune, he learns that Madame de Trenville, who is the picture of "hardened vice, of experienced seduction" (30), has merely feigned love in order to seduce his fortune away from him. Learning of St. Hubert's debauchery, his wife dies of shock and grief. St. Hubert then enters a religious order and practices acts of "charity and beneficence, to make [his] being not hateful in [Heaven's] sight" (36). *St. Hubert* is a relative rarity among early American fiction, because few novels show male chastity under such a tempting attack. But Madame de Trenville represents a double threat, for she not only challenges St. Hubert's chastity, but also represents a means of corrupting his economic virtue. Indeed, it is the failure of St. Hubert's economic virtue and the subsequent loss of his fortune that seem to trigger the death of his wife.

Economic virtue is similarly under attack in Caroline Matilda Warren's 1805 novel *The Gamesters,* as Leander Anderson is seduced into vice by Edward Somerton, his corrupt and dissipated friend. Somerton is the proverbial snake in the garden of Leander's rural married bliss, using specious logic to sway Leander from virtue. Knowing that gaming is Leander's weakness, Somerton argues that there is no reason for Leander not to pursue his passion. He asks Leander, "Were [the passions] not implanted into the soul when it first animated a mortal form? You will undoubtedly answer, they were; if so, they must proceed from Deity, and is it not the height of presumption and impiety to pretend that any *evil* can flow from the *Fountain of all Good*?" (190; emphasis in original). What Somerton here proposes—that passions are indeed a normal part of human existence—was widely accepted in eighteenth-century pedagogical and religious writings. However, this same pedagogical literature also argued that it was the duty of rational humans to regulate and control the passions.[20] Nonetheless, Somerton easily convinces Leander that he should thus "acquiesce in the will of Heaven, and not attempt to stifle the growth of that which God himself implanted in [his] soul" (190-91). Untested and unskilled in regulating his own behavior, Leander succumbs to this seductive rhetoric, games away his inheritance, commits suicide, and leaves his wife and son destitute.

The common link among *The Gamesters, St. Hubert, The Gambler,* and Weems's *God's Revenge Against Gambling,* aside from their obvious antigambling rhetoric, is the light they shed on the relationship between gambling and speculation. Gambling is a small-scale, private form of speculation, one that wreaks havoc on the domestic life of the gambler by decimating family finances and destroying the family itself. But if gambling is speculation on the domestic scale, then speculation is gambling on a large, public scale—gambling that affects the entire community and its web of economic relationships with far-reaching public implications, for it is private vice made public. No good emerges from *this* private vice, for greed and self-interest triumph over public interest.

Indeed, medical and political discourse of the time demonstrate a culture-wide apprehension about how greed and avarice were fueling speculative economic practices, and vice versa. Such anxiety is understandable considering events in the transatlantic community during the preceding seventy-five years. The John Law currency fiasco in France, the failure of the Mississippi Company, the South Sea bubble in England, and numerous land scandals in America all rocked the financial security of the transatlantic community. In the early national era, the Yazoo land speculation fraud vividly exemplified the fortunes to be made by some speculators and the tremendous costs to be borne by others.[21] When American writers of the late eighteenth and early nineteenth centuries use the term "speculation," clearly they are viewing American speculation as part of an unfortunate transatlantic history of greed and economic fraud. In *Travels in New England and New York,* for instance, Timothy Dwight refers specifically to the "Mississippi and South Sea schemes" in the context of a discussion of American land and currency speculation (1:158). And in what amounts to a mini-jeremiad on the evils of speculation, Dwight extravagantly praises the New England states for their success in commerce while condemning his greedy countrymen for their desire to profit through speculation. He finds the post-Revolutionary currency speculation particularly repugnant, claiming that

> At the first effusion of this evil upon the community, every sordid passion of man was stimulated to the most vigorous exertion. Wealth, for such it seemed to the fancy, was acquired with an ease and rapidity which astonished the possessor. The price of labor, and of every vendible commodity, rose in a moment to a height unexampled. Avarice, ambition, and luxury saw their wishes anticipated, and began to grasp at objects of which they had not before even dreamed.
>
> (4: 261)

Although at a different point on the political spectrum from many of his Jeffersonian contemporaries, Dwight, too, worries about the dangers of wealth too rapidly acquired, claiming "Sudden wealth rarely fails of becoming sudden ruin; and most of those who acquire it are soon beggared in morals, if not in property" (4: 261). In addition, Dwight felt that speculation was undermining the work ethic of his country, arguing that "Fortunes, they [enterprising men] will easily believe, may be amassed at a stroke, without industry or economy, by mere luck, or the energy of superior talents for business" (1: 158). Even Pelatiah Webster, a partisan for trade, similarly warned of the dangers of speculation decades before Dwight, claiming in 1779 that "fortunes acquired suddenly without the *industry* of the possessor, rarely ever increase his happiness and welfare, help his virtuous habits, or continue long with him; they must commonly ruin him" ("A Second Essay on Free Trade and Finance" 37). But what most incensed Dwight was the fact that those who bear the costs of speculation, whether in currency or land, are too often those who can least afford to lose their money: "widows and orphans" and "great multitudes of sober, industrious people [launching] the earnings of their whole lives," and "the honest purchaser, stripped of his possessions . . . left to meet old age without property, consolation, or hope" (1: 159-60).

Dwight was only one of many public figures who excoriated speculation. Solomon Aiken, a frequently published anti-Federalist minister, condemned the currency and scrip speculation by Federalists during the 1790s in his 1811 fast day sermon, *The Rise and Progress of the Political Dissension,* and concluded that "These gross and bare-faced instances of speculation, have a tendency to break down all barriers to common honesty. Hence the increase of dishonesty, defrauding and overreaching, in private and individual dealings; and consequently an augmentation of vexations and expensive law suits" (13). Speculation was not merely a private vice, as gambling was supposed to be, for speculation had wide-ranging public implications. Benjamin Rush took an even more dramatic point of view in his multifaceted work *Medical Inquiries and Observations Upon the Diseases of the Mind.* He suggests that the tremendous opportunities for various kinds of financial speculation in the decades following the revolution caused a corresponding increase in cases of insanity. Rush asserts that

> In the United States, madness has encreased since the year 1790. This must be ascribed chiefly to an increase in the number and magnitude of the objects of ambition and avarice, and to the greater joy or distress, which is produced by gratification or disappointments in the pursuit of each of them. The funding system, and speculations in bank scrip, and new lands, have been fruitful sources of madness in our country.
>
> (66)

Unlike many of his contemporaries, who tended to see the flow of influence in one direction and thus believed that the central issue was the danger of private vice contaminating the public sphere, Rush saw these public events as deeply influencing private life and the individual.

Even works in popular circulation expressed dismay about the greed, avarice, and ambition that seemed rampant in American culture. In his "Chronology of Facts," a satiric piece published in the *National Gazette,* Freneau labels the year 1791 "The Reign of Speculators,"

due to the "Banks, bubbles, tontines, lotteries, monopolies, usury, forgery, lying, gambling, swindling, & c. & c." that he saw as plaguing the nation during that year. In another savage but amusing satire, Freneau constructs a plan for an American nobility based upon practitioners of speculation, ranging from the lowest rank, the "order of the Leech," to a middling order, "Their Hucksterships," to the highest order, "The Order of Scrip."[22] But perhaps most interesting is how antipathy for speculation entered into the realm of popular culture in the form of song. A. W.'s *A Dandy Song,* a broadside ballad dating back at least to 1806, cleverly expresses some of the disillusionment of the age, as it heaps scorn upon the greediness of speculators who hold government offices and professionals such as doctors and lawyers. The final lines of the song aptly sum up its message: "But I'm sure you'll not be beat if I call the world a cheat, / And he that reaps the harvest is the dandy O."

Greed and avarice alone did not cause the public problem of rampant speculation: it was overweening ambition fueled by greed and avarice, and vice versa, that led to public speculations. Thus ambition, too, comes under attack in countless pamphlets, poems, and sermons of the early national period. Hezekiah Woodruff, for example, in his 1804 sermon *The Danger of Ambition Considered,* militates against ambition, arguing that ambition "is a selfish exercise" that "aims primarily at its own advancement" (7). What emerges in the literature of the time—both fictional and nonfictional—is the notion that ambition had to be tempered by a sense of justice and fair play for one's fellow Americans. Above all, ambition had to be regulated by industry, which writings of the day praise in its stead.[23]

Benjamin's Franklin's *Autobiography,* a tale of the transformation of a private individual into a public servant and statesman, is perhaps the best-known written example from the early Republic era of this tempering of ambition with industry. Although Franklin's own life serves for us today as convincing evidence of his ambition, "ambition" is a word he uses only twice in all four parts of his memoirs, on one occasion of which, when discussing how contemporary writers categorize the moral virtues, he explicitly links ambition with avarice (149). Instead, the touchstones for Franklin's autobiography are those character traits that I discuss throughout this essay: industry, virtue, honesty, truth, and justice. As the life story he recounts illustrates, self-interest is best advanced not through ambition, but through private virtue and industry, which in turn benefit the larger community. This harmony or balance between self and society is precisely what Franklin seeks to uncover or recover in his autobiography. Furthermore, Franklin spends a great deal of time explaining how he himself countered the appearance of ambition through his deliberate displays of modesty, the most famous of which is the iconic image he paints of the industrious younger

Franklin, aproned and trundling a wheelbarrow through the streets of Philadelphia.

Throughout his autobiography, Franklin emphasizes the importance of civic virtue, of acting in what he calls a "publick-spirited" manner. His illustrations of how to act, such as his refusal to accept a patent on the improvements he made to the wood-burning stove, arguing that part of our public duty is to contribute to the betterment of our community and to serve others, have appeared to many critics as monuments to his ego. Nonetheless, Franklin also emphasizes that in pursuing these civic achievements it is important to de-emphasize the self—not only to ensure the cooperation of others, but also to mitigate charges of self-serving personal ambition. When Franklin began raising money for the academy that later would become the University of Pennsylvania, he explains, "In the Introduction to these Proposals, I stated their Publication not as an Act of mine, but of some *publick-spirited Gentlemen*; avoiding as much as I could, according to my usual Rule, the presenting myself to the Publick as the Author of any Scheme for their Benefit" (193; emphasis in original). For Franklin, it was not enough merely to be virtuous—one had to perform virtue, over and over again.

TRADE AND THE FICTIONAL GENDERING OF ECONOMIC DESIRE

In order to present trade as a virtuous economic practice, novelists focused on many of the same issues that Franklin identifies as crucial in conveying the appearance of virtue. Novelists had to distinguish between honest trade and vices such as gambling or lottery playing, as well as between honest trade and potentially dishonest practices like speculation. Novelists also had to demonstrate that one needed industry to succeed in trade—not merely superior business sense or good fortune. Finally, novelists had to show the productive fruits of trade, fruits that serve a triple purpose of patriotically celebrating America's trading freedom while benefiting individual and public interests.

Although many novels include one or more of these tropes, two novels in particular emphasize and draw them together in a coherent fashion, framing trade as a viable, virtuous means of accumulating capital, while at the same time gendering economic desire. Significantly, both of these novels are by women; juxtaposing them against one another emphasizes the diversity of fiction written by women during the early national period, for while Rebecca Rush's *Kelroy* emphasizes private life and the effect of individual vice on domestic life, Sarah Wood's *Dorval; or The Speculator* attempts to show the impact of national economic events and trends upon the individual and upon domestic life. Yet both novels show the relative permeability of public and domestic spheres.

Kelroy is the more consciously gendered of the two novels in its exposé of the snares of ambition. Mrs. Hammond, one of the central characters of the novel, is the mother of Emily and Lucy and the widow of a well-connected Philadelphia merchant. The narrator describes her as "a woman of fascinating manners, strong prejudices, and boundless ambition, which extended itself to every circumstance of her life" (3-4). Despite her limited funds, Mrs. Hammond's appetite for luxurious living, as well as her confidence in her ability to broker economically advantageous marriages for her daughters, encourage her to "[launch] fearlessly into the wide sea of dissipation, and in the incense, and adulation of the giddy multitude" of Philadelphia (11). Indeed, Mrs. Hammond's lifestyle nearly caricatures contemporary notions of luxury. She has every accoutrement of contemporary concepts of luxury: a city house in Philadelphia and a country estate bordering the Schuylkill River, numerous servants, expensive furniture, plate and crystal, diamonds, her own carriage, and silk and satin gowns—all of which are financed by credit, her expectations, and loans finagled from her future son-in-law. Mrs. Hammond also engages in what someone like Samuel Adams could only have viewed as an extremely dissipated lifestyle: once her daughters are of marriageable age, their lives become an endless round of balls, social calls, tea parties, and card parties. Although Mrs. Hammond has no active role in Philadelphia's foreign trade, she is a voracious consumer of luxury trade goods, and foreign trade both enables and encourages her participation in social rituals.[24] The conspicuous presence of trade goods points to the permeability of the domestic sphere, yet women like Mrs. Hammond are themselves not able to participate in the profit-making aspects of this trade.

Eventually Mrs. Hammond's financial extravagance squanders her remaining money, but perversely, her very poverty drives her to "feverish extravagance," both from the self-denial she has practiced in the past and the struggle she has to maintain appearances (164). Unlike the hapless Gurnet family, Mrs. Hammond knows how to use and display trade goods as status symbols, enabling her to maintain her place in a social hierarchy that has material wealth as its basis. Eventually, however, her creditors force her to settle some of her bills in order to avoid exposure. The final calamity which befalls her is a fire which burns down her townhouse, the insurance policy for which she had let lapse only the week before. Nearly destitute and "half wild with perturbation," Mrs. Hammond plays the lottery with money borrowed from a friend (129). She has the true gambler's mentality, always convinced that "it was possible the scale might still turn in her favour" (129). In her final venture in the lottery, the first ticket drawn is a blank, but the second ticket amazingly wins Mrs. Hammond $50,000.

To the characters of *Kelroy,* this lottery win appears to be the stroke of fortune that saves Mrs. Hammond from financial ruin; subsequent events, however, reveal to the reader that this fortunate gamble ultimately sets in motion the tragic events of the novel's denouement. Although Mrs. Hammond's youngest daughter, Emily, is at this time happily engaged to a young man named Kelroy, Mrs. Hammond has long conspired to marry Emily to a wealthier man. Kelroy was raised and educated as a gentleman, but his father lost the family fortune in "a wild speculating scheme, which he fancied would at least double his property, but on the contrary it failed, and ruined him" (36). After Mrs. Hammond wins the lottery, Kelroy believes that Emily will be financially secure under her mother's care, so he travels to India to recoup the family fortune. However, Kelroy's absence leaves his relationship with Emily vulnerable to the manipulation of Mrs. Hammond, who now has no other worries to distract her and thus can direct her full attention to controlling her youngest daughter. Consequently, Mrs. Hammond and her confederate Marney intercept letters between Kelroy and Emily and forge still others, severing their engagement. Mrs. Hammond then manipulates Emily into accepting the proposal of Dunlevy, a young man whose considerable fortune ensures Mrs. Hammond status and financial security for the rest of her life. Her luck runs out, however, when she has a crippling stroke during the post-wedding festivities. Unable to walk or speak, she dies, leaving in her desk incriminating evidence of the forgeries, which Emily later discovers. Disillusioned and crushed by grief over her mother's treacherous betrayal, Emily soon follows her to the grave. Thus, the payoff from the ambitious Mrs. Hammond's last great gamble destroys her, Emily, and Kelroy; and in a bizarre twist of fate, a misfiring pistol later blinds Marney and blows up his forging hand.

As I earlier claimed, *Kelroy* is far more gendered in its critique of economic desire than is Wood's *Dorval.* Indeed, *Kelroy* provides a potent argument that, among early American novels, economic desire is a legitimate desire only for men. Although the novel ends with Kelroy's death during a shipwreck, the narrative condones his economic desire, for his voyage to India is a financial success. Mrs. Hammond's economic desire is a vastly different matter, however. Mrs. Hammond's economic desire could easily have been sentimentalized as the story of a widowed mother who merely desires for her daughters financially secure marriages with respectable young men—an outcome which she does effect; instead, *Kelroy* indicts Mrs. Hammond as an ambitious, greedy, grasping woman who views her daughters as commodities or, as Cathy N. Davidson has suggested, as another investment on which she can wager (233). Indeed, the most positive view of this situation is that Mrs. Hammond is unable to guarantee herself an income through any method other than bartering her daughters, for as Dana D. Nelson argues in her introduction to a recent reprint of *Kelroy,* "If Mrs. Hammond is vicious, so too is the situation to which she responds" (xvi). That *Kelroy* does indeed accurately represent the financial difficulties women faced during the early nineteenth century is in some ways less important than the cultural value it propagates: that economic desire is neither becoming nor appropriate for women. In *Kelroy,* as throughout early American fiction, economic desire is consistently configured as part of a masculine plot, and women who seek unsentimentalized economic advancement through marriage, virtually the only means open to them, are literally struck down, by a stroke as is Mrs. Hammond, or by death in childbirth as is Eliza Wharton in *The Coquette* (although Eliza's situation is admittedly complicated). Trade is implicated as part of this project of gendering economic desire, for while it is a virtuous means of accumulating capital, it is strictly a masculine occupation.

Gendering of economic desire is a far less important issue in Sarah Wood's *Dorval; or The Speculator,* which focuses more broadly and generally on the problem of economic ambition and speculation in America during the 1790s. By bringing together and merging the character of the merchant and speculator, Wood plays upon her audience's apprehensions that no type of virtue is sacrosanct, and that even model republicans can be corrupted, given the right set of temptations. Equally important, Wood explicitly parallels challenges to male and female virtue, for the character of Dorval unites the seducer of female chastity with the seducer of male economic virtue. Rather than concentrating on the personal and the domestic, Wood's sentimental novel instead portrays how national economic trends influence the individual and impact domestic life. Just as fictional seducers were counterfeiting love to despoil the virtue of young women, so were speculators and their ilk seducing the economic virtue of the nation with their promises of quick and easy wealth without industry.

Wood pairs Colonel Morely, a virtuous, patriotic merchant, with Dorval, a walking compendium of cultural evils of the early Republic, characters who, respectively, epitomize the best and the worst that America has to offer. Colonel Morely, a New York delegate to the Constitutional Convention, is honorable, philanthropic, public-spirited, and faithful—in short, he is a catalog of republican virtues. Dorval, on the other hand, is a murderer, a bigamist, a seducer, a forger, a gambler, and a speculator. Hiding these evils behind a mask of sincerity, Dorval tempts Colonel Morely with the seductive allure of unearned wealth. By exploiting the greed lying dormant in apparently virtuous men, the figure of the speculator thus served to question that seeming virtue, as well as to exploit the greed and naiveté of the American character.

In order to provide her readers with a context for understanding Colonel Morely's patriotic virtue, the narrator of *Dorval* describes how Morely personally acted to stave off economic catastrophe for the individual and the nation in the years after the Revolution. When the war veterans were paid in devalued scrip, the Colonel bought their securities for their full face value, at great financial risk to himself, in order to ensure fairness for those who had fought for American freedom. "Determined to do every thing in his power to support the sinking reputation of his country," the narrator explains, Colonel Morely "bought up, at their original value, as many certificates and securities, as his own finances would allow. For these he paid in silver and gold, and in the produce of his lands" (13). Morely dangerously overextends himself, but his patriotic venture is vindicated when these securities are later redeemed at face value, and the country becomes more economically stable.[25] Contemporary readers of *Dorval* would have instantly recognized and acknowledged Morely's self-sacrificing civic virtue, since he paid many times the going rate for those securities.

Even though the Colonel is once again a wealthy man, happily ensconced on a rural estate, his economic ambition eventually prevails over his interest in the public good. Dorval, as agent for a Georgia land company, tempts the Colonel with visions of wealth to be gained through land speculation from the Yazoo purchase. Morely enthusiastically pursues this speculation, even though his adopted daughter, Aurelia, anxiously cautions him to avoid land speculation. Aurelia emerges as the true republican when she questions Morely's motives and means: "I don't know anything about the value of land; but it appears to me, there must be some deception when it is sold for a cent an acre. . . . Perhaps it is the observations, I have heard my aunt make upon the evils of speculation, and the impositions, that are often practiced, that give me this disgust to the most distant appearance of speculation" (35-36). Aurelia understands that good intentions are not enough—one must avoid even the hint of impropriety. Indeed, Aurelia is the voice of sensible virtue, as she explains to her friend Elizabeth Dunbar that

> I am sorry to remark, that my father seems to have an ambition, to which I thought he was superior, that of possessing great wealth. He talks as if millions of acres were not large enough for a farm, and thousands too contracted for a garden. My mother is quite delighted with the idea that every dollar, my father now pays away, will produce a hundred, twelve months hence. But every passion must have its reign; and I am inclined to say with the Preacher: 'Surely man, in his best state, is altogether vanity.'
>
> (36-37)[26]

The Colonel does not deliberately choose to rob or bilk others to gain his wealth, but his greed and ambition overcome his natural virtue and reason. The narrator

explains that "The time was, when [Morely] became a poor man to secure his country; but the time had now arrived, when, as he supposed, he was amassing great wealth, and this at the expense of the ruin of thousands.—He was not aware, however, though Dorval was, that such ruin would be the consequence" (51).[27]

Despite Aurelia's continued misgivings, the Colonel and Dunbar, his partner, pursue their land speculation deals with the unscrupulous Dorval, with repercussions that Morely never anticipates. Morely and Dunbar sign a contract typical of the land deals of the time, which the narrator describes in dramatic detail:

> The fatal deeds were drawn, which conveyed to these gentlemen millions of acres of land. The boundaries were specified, the lines mentioned, as marked upon the maps, and every appearance of honest and just dealings exhibited to sanctify the fraud and conceal deceit. In exchange for these deeds, which were signed by Dorval, as agent for the Georgia proprietors, bonds and notes of hand were given. One fourth of the money was to be paid in three months, one fourth in six, and the remainder in one year.
>
> (68-69)

Morely and Dunbar are true speculators, for they do not pay the money up front, but instead confidently gamble on future sales: "They had no doubt but the land would sell so well, that they should dispose of enough within three months to pay the whole" (89). Despite strenuous efforts, they are unable to sell the land either in America or Europe. The financial burden of these debts forces Morely to undermine his own policy of economic virtue and benevolence, driving him to call in a number of small loans made to assist young tradesmen in starting businesses (84). These recalled debts are merely the first of the repercussions that emanate outward in a republic when an individual or group of citizens lack economic virtue. Indeed, selfish focus on private interests inevitably produces such public repercussions, as the epigraph to chapter 10 makes clear: "'Tis avarice that suggests a thousand schemes, / A thousand plans, and fills our waking dreams, With hopes of gain, bids speculation come, / And forces ruin to a happy home, / And love of country turns to love of self, / And centers all our pleasures in ourself" (49). This self-focus becomes selfishness, and excessive self-interest demands the sacrifice of the public good.

After Morely fails to sell any of the land, his creditors have him imprisoned for debt in Philadelphia, where he dies repentant and cognizant of the temptations that overcame him. He explains to Aurelia:

> I now view the motives that induced me to become concerned in the Georgia purchase in a light very different from that in which I have been used to see them. Divested of that glare, which variety, avarice, and self love threw upon them, I behold myself as nothing more

nor less than a speculator, who was willing to risk his paternal inheritance and the produce of honest industry for the vain, the foolish hope of acquiring immense sums. I had a fortune sufficiently large to gratify every reasonable wish of my heart; and had I never attempted to increase it by this species of fraud, I should now have been happy; but I have followed the phantom, that enchanted me, until it has stripped me of my property, of my happiness, of the peace of my mind, and left me an inhabitant of a prison.

(151)

Morely's self-condemnatory speech focuses on the key issues of post-Revolutionary anxiety that I have discussed: the dangers of greed, avarice, and fraud, culminating in the cultural problem of speculation, juxtaposed against the need for honest industry. Moreover, the dying Morely himself describes speculation as merely another form of gambling—risky, vain, and foolish. Aurelia's biological father, Major Seymour (with whom she is reunited at the end of the novel), emphasizes this connection between speculation and gambling when he visits Morely's grave. Although Major Seymour recognizes Dorval's "iniquity," he concludes that "An ambition to be wealthy was the cause of [Morely's] ruin" (284). He advises Aurelia's half-brother: "For, whatever arguments we may use to deceive ourselves or others, we may be certain of this, that the *man who aims at immoderate riches, without intending to give an equivalent, is building his own glory upon the ruin of his fellow creatures, and must be considered as a speculator.* Do all you can, my son, by precept and example, to discourage every species of gaming . . ." (284).

Not one for subtlety, Wood continues to drive home her message that speculation is merely a large-scale version of gambling through the character of Dorval. Dorval is the most interesting character of the book, uniting in one person multiple evils, for he is a seducer of both economic and moral virtue; yet Wood insists in a footnote to her novel that "The character and history of Dorval are not a fiction. What is related in the subsequent sheets, however romantic and melancholy it may appear, is well known by many to be strictly agreeable to the truth" (62). Dorval's identity is fluid, and with each incarnation he becomes increasingly depraved. He is the consummate speculator; even his romantic intrigues are a form of speculation, for he is driven not by love or even by lust, but by the profit that he speculates he can gain from each marriage or seduction. Before the time of the novel, Dorval's avarice has already driven him to marry in secret a Jamaican heiress and to commit multiple murders. To avoid imprisonment, Dorval escapes to America, where he becomes the agent for a land company which typically employs "wretches . . . more cruel and more criminal than the convict who makes his exit on a gallows" (52). Dorval cleverly hides his greed and depravity behind a mask of "frankness and bluntness" that conceals "deception and deep laid plans of villainy" (40). After ruining the reputation of Elizabeth Dunbar through an elopement and causing the bankruptcy of Colonel Morely, Dorval flees to Philadelphia, where he then gambles away the money of his victims. Greed and the seductive lure of chance drive him to risk this money. In order for readers to understand the relationship between his activities as a land speculator and as a gambler—that these guises are two sides of the same coin—the narrator explains that "From one species of gaming he had descended to another far more injurious to him than was speculation: in the latter he dealt with honest men, whose unsuspecting probity laid them open to imposition; but his other associates were rascals like himself, and equally artful and knavish" (130). These "gamesters" and "sharpers" entice Dorval into games of billiards, cards, and dice, with the result that "from the possession of a large sum of money, he found himself reduced to a single dollar" (130).

With Colonel Morely disposed of, only Aurelia's discerning nature and republican virtue protect her from Dorval. Attempting to recoup his fortune, Dorval once more assumes a guise of forthrightness and proposes to Aurelia, who wisely rejects him. Dorval next turns his attentions to the widowed Mrs. Morely, who demonstrates her lack of perspicacity as well as her love of luxurious, dissipated living by accepting his proposal. Dorval marries her in a bigamous ceremony, quickly defrauds her of her money and estate, and later murders her. After his arrest, Dorval spuriously blames Aurelia for his troubles, claiming that it was her rejection of him that drove him to such lengths. Foiled in his attempt to murder Aurelia, Dorval shoots himself, but lingers for five agonizing and self-deluded days. Although Dorval wreaks havoc upon a community, he directly harms only those who are themselves culpable—those whose ambition, greed, or gullibility make them susceptible to his enticements. However, Aurelia's republican virtue and all that it entails—her chastity, fidelity, patriotism, self-sacrifice, industry, and philanthropy—ultimately triumph over Dorval's seductive powers, as she escapes him and aids several of his victims, among them Elizabeth Dunbar and Dorval's Jamaican-born wife.

The virtue and industry of one of the younger Dunbar sons and Burlington, whom Aurelia ultimately marries, serve to balance the greed of Dorval and Morely. Burlington and the younger Dunbar represent the hope of the rising generation of families in the novel, as they seek to earn their fortunes through industry in the East Indies. Their actions signal self-sacrifice, industry, and a sentimental justification of trade. Although they profit from their voyages, this accumulation of capital results from personal effort, and they use this money not for vain luxuries, but to fulfill social and familial obliga-

Illustration of a poker game at a tavern in Atlanta, Georgia.

tions. The cumulative effect of these actions is more powerful than any individual example; a brief listing of some of the events enabled by their participation in the Asian trade will illustrate my point. The return voyage from the East Indies allows Burlington to exhibit his compassion and disinterested benevolence as he endangers himself to rescue a dying, shipwrecked man, who returns the favor by bequeathing him $30,000. One of the Dunbar sons, unnamed in the novel, because it is not who he is but what he does that is important, returns fantastically wealthy after seven years of labor in the East Indies. He has amassed a fortune large enough to settle all of his impoverished father's debts, as well as to bestow a $2,000 dowry on his sister, Elizabeth. And Major Seymour, Aurelia's biological father, returns from the East Indies with enough money to settle the debts of individuals who befriended Aurelia and to buy her a large country estate.

The repetition of these sentimental rewards provides more than an easy way to resolve plot difficulties. Rather, the continued presence of the East Indies and China points to this area as a free economic space, as a space for trade justified by sentimental rhetoric, and as a space where Americans can vent economic aggressions without harming their fellow citizens. This displacement of economic aggression is not a replication of the colonial process. Nor do these references to non-Western countries enable the concept of empire, as Edward W. Said has suggested of the British novel in *Culture and Imperialism*.[28] To American novelists, China and East India represented not colonies to be subjugated—since East India was already under British control—but rather resources that could be exploited for the mutual benefit of both parties. China, East India, and their inhabitants—themselves virtually unmentioned, which in the case of China is not surprising given the strictly limited contact between the Chinese and foreigners—nonetheless represent a cultural lacuna on which economic aggression could be profitably displaced or inscribed. The juxtaposition in early American fiction of this foreign trade against gambling and speculation emphasizes the need for individuals to balance self-interest with concern for the public good of America and its communities. The difficult and virtuous labor of these merchant characters highlights Dorval's depravity and the foolishness of men like Colonel Morely and Dunbar, who seek wealth without industry.[29]

Within the context of individual novels, participation in international trade was for the most part figured as a temporary expedient, yet as a whole, use of this theme had widespread ramifications for the development of American fiction. First, the participation of women such as Rebecca Rush and Sarah Wood in actually writing this bourgeois agenda into being demonstrates American women's vested interest in issues that extend outside the home and the domestic sphere. Writing itself allowed women to enter into the bourgeois public world of commerce—both literally and metaphorically—when other means of access were denied to them. At the same time, the procommerce advocacy of American fiction pointed to the increasingly egalitarian nature of American society and the potential mobility inherent in such a society. As a form of vernacular print culture, American fiction also patriotically affirmed the success and benefits of the newly formed United States' trading freedom and encouraged increased American commerce with the rest of the world, thereby contributing to the creation of a national identity.[30] In the rogues' gallery that was early American fiction, the virtuous merchant and businessman begin to stand out against a backdrop that warns against the speculator, the con man, the cheat, the counterfeiter, and the gambler.

The figure of the speculator himself represents both the unbounded economic potential of the American economy as well as the dangers inherent in such freedom. Equally interesting, the speculator also symbolizes the dangers of too much self-creation—the dark side of the myth of self-creation that Benjamin Franklin's autobiography promulgates. As William E. Lenz has explained of the emergence of the confidence man in America, "he relies not on supernatural powers or charms or courts but on the fluid nature of society in the New World with its unique opportunities for self-government, self-promotion, self-posturing, and self-creation. He appears to trace his ancestry most directly from the ambiguities of the New World, which had earlier given rise to the regional images of the peddler, the Yankee, and the rustic Jonathan" (1). The same ambiguities and possibilities that could give rise to a benevolent Franklin could also give rise to a Dorval, a Marney, or a Stephen Burroughs, because it is but an easy step from Franklin's "projector" to Sarah Wood's "speculator."[31] This issue of economic virtue was a crucial one for people of the early Republic, since the economic seduction practiced by speculators was a matter for grave public concern; once freed from the restraints imposed by the colonial government, speculators bankrupted countless families and communities. The emer-

gence in the nineteenth century of the confidence man, that peculiarly American version of the picaro, undoubtedly owes much to the seducer of economic and moral virtue so prevalent in the fiction of the early national period.

Notes

Research for this essay was supported in part by a Stephen Botein Fellowship from the American Antiquarian Society and by a research fellowship from the Graduate School at the University of North Carolina at Chapel Hill.

1. See Gordon S. Wood, *The Creation of the American Republic, 1776-1787,* especially chapter 10: "The Vices of the System."

2. The anonymous author of *Of Commerce and Luxury* defines luxury as "the abuse of riches: it consists in an extravagance for fantastical superfluities, disproportioned to the situation and abilities of him that spends" (23).

3. For more information about republican conceptions of female virtue, see Ruth H. Bloch, "The Gendered Meanings of Virtue in Revolutionary America," especially 52. Also useful is Jan Lewis's essay, "The Republican Wife: Virtue and Seduction in the Early Republic."

   For information about increased social and sexual choices available to young women, see Ellen K. Rothman, "Sex and Self-Control: Middle-Class Courtship in America, 1770-1870." See also Rothman, *Hands and Hearts: A History of Courtship in America,* especially chapter 1. Particularly valuable for explaining changing patterns of sexual behavior during the post-Revolutionary years are Daniel Scott Smith, "Parental Power and Marriage Patterns: An Analysis of Historical Trends in Hingham, Massachusetts," and Daniel Scott Smith and Michael S. Hindus, "Premarital Pregnancy in America 1640-1971." William E. Nelson's "Emerging Notions of Modern Criminal Law in the Revolutionary Era: An Historical Perspective" provides a useful overview of changing legal perspectives toward extramarital sex.

4. In her essay "Original Vice: The Political Implications of Incest in the Early American Novel," Anne Dalke notes in passing the frequency with which wealth is inherited in early American fiction. Discussing *Margaretta,* Dalke argues that "opportunity is open in this novel only to those already well-to-do. No man rises here by his own efforts: De Burling's failure in trade is marked, and he and his father-in-law both succeed finally by means of inherited wealth. Upward mobility is possible in this book only through inheritance"

(199). Ultimately, the same might be said of several other novels, including *Moreland Vale; or, The Fair Fugitive* and *The Fortunate Discovery*. In these novels, the male characters struggle to earn a virtuous living either through trade or a professional occupation. Yet the conclusions of both novels hinge upon a denouement of newly discovered British patrimonies with inherited wealth. A number of other novels, however, explore possibilities for earning wealth through virtuous economic practices.

For further discussion of economic desire as a driving force of narrative, see chapter 2 of Peter Brooks's *Reading for the Plot: Design and Intention in Narrative.*

5. Although numerous studies discuss economic issues in Brown's novels, I have found several to be particularly valuable. For useful discussions of *Arthur Mervyn,* see Bill Christophersen, *The Apparition in the Glass: Charles Brockden Brown's American Gothic,* especially 111-15, and Alan Axelrod, *Charles Brockden Brown: An American Tale,* 134-59.

Elizabeth Jane Wall Hinds explicitly discusses the issue of Edgar Huntly's disinheritance in "Charles Brockden Brown's Revenge Tragedy: *Edgar Huntly* and the Uses of Property." Hinds argues that "The novel's revenge elements both establish the basis for Edgar's actions and enter the current dialogue about economic policy and practice, a discussion registering the shift in power, during the American 1790s, from a landed to an entrepreneurial class" (52). Hinds notes that Edgar perceives his economic potential to be "family- and land-based rather than entrepreneurial. Edgar never considers making money; he merely bemoans his lack of inheritance"; Hinds concludes that Edgar's resentment at his disinheritance "precipitates Edgar into a new round of revenge" (60).

Also helpful is the first chapter of Steven Watt's *The Romance of Real Life: Charles Brockden Brown and the Origins of American Culture.* Watts explores interactions between the novel and "the shaping of capitalist culture in America," arguing that the novel "promoted the consolidation of liberal hegemony not only in class and cultural terms, but in psychological terms as well. By constructing and disseminating what Raymond Williams has aptly called "structures of feeling," American fictional texts helped establish the growing dominance of bourgeois values by the late 1700s and early 1800s. They did so in part, of course, by promoting values of individualism, material ambition, self-control, and privatization" (24-25).

6. The America of the 1780s and 1790s that Drew R. McCoy portrays in *The Elusive Republic: Political Economy in Jeffersonian America* is one of constant tension between those generally aligned with the Jeffersonian Republican camp, who favored agricultural pursuits combined with limited domestic manufactures of necessary items such as clothing and household furnishings, opposed to Alexander Hamilton and the Federalists, who favored increased foreign commerce and more sophisticated domestic manufactures like those in England. There was, however, considerable division within these general groupings. Further, there was fluidity even between groups, as some who held a general orientation towards Jeffersonian Republicanism favored trade as a means of disposing of excess agricultural produce and also as a way of staving off further development of domestic manufacturing; this position gained adherents throughout the 1790s (188). See also chapter 3: "Commerce and the Independent Republic." Steven Watts makes a similar argument in *The Republic Reborn: War and the Making of Liberal America, 1790-1820,* although he seems to see even more fluidity across party lines than does McCoy (12-14; 329-30).

However, in *Capitalism and a New Social Order: The Republican Vision of the 1790s,* Joyce Appleby argues that the Jeffersonian Republicans were far more interested in commerce than most scholars credit. She points to the anticapitalist bias of most historians and suggests that this bias and a tendency to view capitalism as a monolithic system "have obscured the role that the expectation of commercial growth played in the social thought of the Jeffersonian Republicans" (46). She concludes that "Where Republicans differed from Federalists was in the moral character they gave to economic development. . . . Capitalism thus disclosed itself in a benign and visionary way to Republicans who drew from its dynamic operation the promise of a new age for ordinary men" (49-50). Appleby extends this thesis in chapters 2 and 12 of *Liberalism and Republicanism in the Historical Imagination,* where she examines what she sees as the agrarian, yet decidedly progressive and commercial, vision Jefferson had for America, in which grains sold in the transatlantic market would provide funds for European manufactured goods.

7. Despite this exaltation of agricultural life, few novels actually portray the life of the gentleman farmer. Enos Hitchcock's 1793 bildungsroman *The Farmer's Friend, or The History of Mr. Charles Worthy* is a notable exception.

8. Sarah Savage's *The Factory Girl,* which depicts the female protagonist reeling cotton in a mill, is the only early American novel to portray any type

of advanced manufacturing. Although Hamilton and some of the Federalists advocated sophisticated manufactures in the United States, most writers of fiction regarded such development unfavorably, since it would require a dense urban population working for low wages, as in England.

In "Separate Spheres and Extensive Circles: Sarah Savage's *The Factory Girl* and the Celebration of Industry in Early Nineteenth-Century America," Thomas B. Lovell discusses at length the topics of virtuous and productive labor—crucial issues in justifying female labor in factories—and uses *The Factory Girl* to call into question current historiography about the development of the separate spheres ideology. Despite the narrative's defense of factory work, I would argue that it still demonstrates considerable anxiety about the issue of female work outside the home, as well as the danger of "mixing" with workers of unknown virtue within the factory. Nevertheless, *The Factory Girl* also features a significant subplot involving the dangerous seductions entailed by playing the lottery; clearly virtuous work—even if carried out in a factory—is preferable to insidious lottery-playing.

9. J. G. A. Pocock considers the attitudes of the British gentry toward trade during the early part of the eighteenth century in *The Machiavellian Moment: Florentine Political Thought and the Atlantic Republican Tradition* (440-61).

In her essay entitled "Domesticating 'Virtue': Coquettes and Revolutionaries in Young America," Carroll Smith-Rosenberg discusses the contested nature and definitions of republicanism in the eighteenth century. She claims that "The man of trade occupied a more ambivalent position within classical-republican discourse. The value of the gentry's land, the source of the gentry's political dependence, depended on trade, and hence on the actions of the traders and on events occurring in London and in ports around the world. Their independence thus circumscribed by men and processes beyond their control or ken, the gentry responded with nervous suspicion. Trade, they wrote each other, was productive, linked to England's and their own prosperity. But trade also 'introduces luxury . . . and extinguishes virtue.' It depended on credit which hung upon opinion and the passions of hope and fear. It was cathected with desire. It might seduce independent men away from the simple ways of their fathers. It could entrap them in an endless web of debt and ruin" (164).

10. See T. H. Breen, "Narrative of Commercial Life." Breen discusses these issues in several other essays as well, including "'Baubles of Britain': The

American and Consumer Revolutions of the Eighteenth Century" and "An Empire of Goods: The Anglicization of Colonial America, 1690-1776." In "Baubles of Britain," Breen also notes the importance of consumer goods in creating a shared cultural identity (79-87).

11. This tolerance arose from self-interest: American shipping provided an essential backup service for British merchants, especially during the Napoleonic war (Goldstein 24-25; Furber 240-45). British policy, however, expressly prohibited American ships from participating in the opium trade, although some did so anyway. For more on American participation in the opium trade, see Goldstein, chapter 4: "Philadelphians and the China Opium Trade: Commercial, Diplomatic, and Attitudinal Consequences" (46-70).

12. Numerous studies examine the import-export trade with East India and China. For a sampling, see Dulles, *The Old China Trade,* especially 40-49; Furber, "The Beginnings of American Trade with India, 1784-1812"; Goldstein, *Philadelphia and the China Trade,* 30; Doerflinger, *A Vigorous Spirit of Enterprise, Merchants and Economic Development in Revolutionary Philadelphia,* 291-97; and Smith, *The Empress of China.* Also useful is appendix I of volume 7 of *The Papers of Robert Morris,* which contains correspondence with detailed annotations about Morris's trading ventures. I would like to thank Mary Gallagher for allowing me to see this appendix in galley form.

Also, the Peabody-Essex Museum in Salem, Massachusetts has a remarkable collection of goods imported from China and East India, as well as an extensive library of materials on the East India and China trade.

13. The nouveau riche Gurnet family in *Kelroy* demonstrates the ludicrous *misuse* of luxury items, as they unintentionally caricature the polite ritual of taking tea by wearing gaudy and inappropriately lavish satin gowns. Their discourse itself also makes them look ridiculous; Mrs. Gurnet, for example, repeatedly calls their porcelain dishes "chany" (156). That the visit to the Gurnet's house was obviously intended for comic relief highlights the sophisticated cultural values and assumptions about luxury goods that Rush assumes her readers will share.

14. Profits for voyages varied widely, depending on the kind of goods exported to China, the amount of competition for goods in Canton, and the timing of the return to American ports with Chinese goods. By the mid-1820s, increased competition caused the China trade to flatten out, and there were fewer opportunities for individual profit, as

the trade became dominated by large firms who established permanent American agents in Canton and eliminated the need for supercargoes (Dulles 113-14).

15. See *Poems Written Between the Years 1768 & 1794* (291).

16. See "On Commerce and Luxury" in *The Time Piece* (November 17, 1797, and November 20, 1797), which Freneau abstracted from *Of Commerce and Luxury. Of Commerce and Luxury* is frequently attributed to John Mills (d. 1784?). Although the American edition claims to be reprinted from the British edition, I have been unable to locate an edition prior to the 1791 American edition.

17. For Smith's critique of the French physiocrat system, see vol. 3, book 4, chapter 9 of *An Inquiry into the Nature and Causes of the Wealth of Nations.* Appleby notes that Smith's work did not become influential in America until the early nineteenth century (*Liberalism and Republicanism* 4).

18. See chapter 9, "The Problem of Luxury," in Gordon Wood, *The Rising Glory of America,* for excerpts from this debate.

19. In *Card Sharps, Dream Books, & Bucket Shops: Gambling in Nineteenth-Century America,* Ann Vincent Fabian argues that in the mid- to late nineteenth century, "Gambling . . . became a 'negative analogue,' the one form of gain that made all other efforts to get rich appear normal, natural, and socially salubrious" (5). Thus, she argues, because gambling in a narrowly defined sense was damned, speculative economic practices became rehabilitated and normalized. In the 1790s, however, this rehabilitation had not yet begun. Instead, gambling and land speculation are described in unmitigatedly negative terms; indeed, the link between gambling and speculation serves to make activities such as the East India trade appear virtuous by comparison, since it potentially benefited both Americans and their Asian trading partners.

20. For a representative sampling of pedagogical texts on this subject that were popular in America, see Locke, *Some Thoughts Concerning Education*; Watts, *Logic: Or, the Right Use of Reason* and *Improvement of the Mind*; Burder, *The Closet Companion*; and Hitchcock, *A Discourse on Education.*

Medical discourse also explored the importance of controlling the passions. See, for example, Parrish, *An Inaugural Dissertation on the Influence of the Passions Upon the Body in the Production and Cure of Diseases,* and Haslam, *Observations on Madness and Melancholy.*

21. Speculation itself was at the center of political controversy between the Jeffersonian Republicans and the Federalists. As McCoy explains, "While supporters of a bankruptcy law generally viewed speculation as the necessary basis for economic growth, Republicans tended to consider it a dangerous activity to be discouraged, not promoted. Perhaps this fear of the social and moral repercussions of uncontrolled speculation was the strongest fear the Jeffersonians had, especially in the wake of a speculative fever in the early months of 1798 that resulted in a wave of defaults and insolvencies" (183).

Jefferson frequently discussed the issue of speculation in his correspondence. In an August 17, 1785, letter to Nathaniel Tracy, Jefferson writes, "It is much to be wished that every discouragement should be thrown in the way of men who undertake to trade without capital. . . . The consumers pay for it in the end, and the debts contracted, and bankruptcies occasioned by such commercial adventurers, bring burthen and disgrace on our country. No man can have a natural right to enter on a calling by which it is at least ten to one he will ruin many better men than himself" (399).

22. "Plan for a Nobility," in *National Gazette,* May 7, 1792. Also in the *National Gazette* (November 3, 1793), in "Detached Reflections from a Correspondent," Freneau claims that "A speculating spirit, if prevalent, is always dangerous in any country." Freneau also wrote satiric poetry about greedy land speculators. See "The Projectors" (224-25).

23. Juvenile works, in particular, praise industry, rather than ambition. The distinction they make seems to have its origins in class, since these works generally feature the working class or the worthy poor as inspirational models. Clearly honest industry was seen as a more suitable goal for the poor than ambition, which could be construed as overweening pride. A sampling of such juvenile works published in America in multiple editions includes: *The Instructive Story of Industry and Sloth,* an allegorical tale comparing two households; Maria Edgeworth's *Idleness and Industry Exemplified in the History of James Preston and Lazy Lawrence,* a story comparing the behavior of two children; and *Dame Partlet's Farm: Containing an Account of the Great Riches She Obtained by Industry . . . ,* a tale of a poor widow who through industry gains a farm. The anonymous work *The Little Islanders: or, Blessings of Industry,* a brief novel in which the children of titled parents imitate Crusoe and thereby learn habits of industry, crosses class lines in an interesting way and provides a notable exception to the advocacy of industry for the poor.

Not until the mid- to late nineteenth century does ambition supplement or supplant industry as a central tenet of male conduct and advice literature, as Sarah E. Newton notes in *Learning to Behave: A Guide to American Conduct Books Before 1900* (53-54).

24. Kathryn Zabelle Derounian convincingly argues that *Kelroy* is a hybrid of the romance and the novel of manners, since Rush pits two essentially romantic characters, Emily and Kelroy, against the social reality of the novel of manners as represented by Mrs. Hammond, who is, above all, the shallow product of materialistic cultural expectations.

25. For a contemporary, nonfiction discussion of the scrip problem, see Pelatiah Webster's *A Plea for the Poor Soldiers,* reprinted in Webster's *Political Essays on the Nature and Operation of Money, Public Finances, and Other Subjects Published During the American War, and Continued Up to the Present Year, 1791* (306-43).

26. Indeed, through her opposition to gambling and excessive luxury, Aurelia emerges as an advocate of near-Spartan Republicanism. As part of a discussion about the dangers of fashion, Aurelia argues that "I have often thought . . . we should be better and happier for sumptuary laws. If we were obliged by the legislature not to alter the make of our dress but once in ten years, it would save a great deal of trouble, needless expense, and waste of time" (80).

27. At this time, the Yazoo purchase was the linchpin in frontier land speculation, because those lands, which compose the present-day states of Alabama and Mississippi, bordered the Mississippi River, which would open that part of the county up to profitable trade. The land in question was under dispute, however, since it was claimed by Spain, various Indian tribes, and the states of Georgia and South Carolina. Induced by bribes, the Georgia legislature sold 30,000,000 acres to four separate companies for $500,000—about 1½ cents per acre. As Sakolski explains, "Georgia did not guarantee title against other claimants, and disclaimed responsibility for the acts or claims of the Indians" (133). Following these sales, there was tremendous speculation of shares; many purchasers bought these shares on credit and such amassed speculative fortunes, which they lost just as quickly when land values stabilized. Outraged Georgians soon protested the sale of what they viewed as their land and demanded that the legislature repudiate the act authorizing the sale of the land. Although Georgia offered to refund payments, most purchasers did not take advantage of this offer and instead continued to speculate in shares of this land. The claims on this property were not settled until 1815, at which time the settlement benefited wealthy speculators who could afford to buy up shares and gamble on a future profit at the time of settlement.

28. See Said, *Culture and Imperialism,* especially chapter 2.

29. While novels like *Dorval, or The Speculator* were successful in rehabilitating trade by vilifying gambling and by distinguishing the speculator from the honest trader, what early American fiction generally could not envision was a life-long engagement with trade. As I suggested earlier, most novels conclude with the return of the male protagonist from the east, bearing gifts of porcelain, fans, and silks, while an important part of the resolution of these novels is settlement on a landed estate— which is exactly the situation in *Dorval.*

30. In *Imagined Communities: Reflections on the Origin and Spread of Nationalism,* Benedict Anderson addresses the importance of vernacular print culture in the formation of "imaginary communities," which he claims contributed to the rise of modern nationalism.

31. Several recent works on confidence men discuss Franklin and Stephen Burroughs as such. In particular, see Gary Lindberg's *The Confidence Man in American Literature,* chapter 3, "Benjamin Franklin and the Model Self." Also useful is Daniel E. Williams's essay, "In Defense of Self: Author and Authority in *The Memoirs of Stephen Burroughs.*" The fact that Burroughs's work moves easily between fact and what appears to be fiction helps it bridge the differences among the genres of autobiography, polemical political tracts, and fiction; while Burroughs is certainly concerned with the creation of self, it is not the ideal, public self modeled by Franklin, but rather a fluid self more closely akin to that of the confidence man.

Works Cited

Aiken, Solomon. *The Rise and Progress of the Political Dissension.* Haverhill, Mass.: Allen, 1811.

Anderson, Benedict. *Imagined Communities: Reflections on the Origin and Spread of Nationalism.* London: Verso, 1983.

Appleby, Joyce. *Capitalism and a New Social Order: The Republican Vision of the 1790s.* New York: New York Univ. Press, 1984.

———. *Liberalism and Republicanism in the Historical Imagination.* Cambridge, Mass.: Harvard Univ. Press, 1992.

Axelrod, Alan. *Charles Brockden Brown: An American Tale.* Austin: Univ. of Texas Press, 1983.

Bloch, Ruth. "The Gendered Meanings of Virtue in Revolutionary America." *Signs* 13.1 (1987): 37-58.

Breen, T. H. "'Baubles of Britain': The American and Consumer Revolutions of the Eighteenth Century." *Past and Present* 119 (1988): 73-104.

——. "An Empire of Goods: The Anglicization of Colonial America, 1690-1776." *Journal of British Studies* 25 (1986): 467-99.

——. "Narrative of Commercial Life: Consumption, Ideology, and Community on the Eve of the American Revolution." *William and Mary Quarterly* 50.3 (1993): 471-501.

Brooks, Peter. *Reading for the Plot.* Cambridge, Mass.: Harvard Univ. Press, 1992.

Brown, Charles Brockden. *Arthur Mervyn; or, Memoirs of the Year 1793.* Philadelphia, 1799; second part, New York, 1800.

——. *Edgar Huntly; or, Memoirs of a Sleep-Walker.* 3 vols. Philadelphia, 1799.

Burder, George. *The Closet Companion: or, An Help to Serious Persons, in the Important Duty of Self-Examination. Intended to be Kept in the Christian's Usual Place of Retirement, In Order to Remind Him of, as Well as to Assist Him in, This Work.* Hartford: Hosmer, 1810.

Burroughs, Stephen. *Memoirs of Stephen Burroughs.* Ed. Philip F. Gura. Boston: Northeastern Univ. Press, 1988.

Christophersen, Bill. *The Apparition in the Glass: Charles Brockden Brown's American Gothic.* Athens: Univ. of Georgia Press, 1993.

Cooper, Thomas. *Political Arithmetic.* Philadelphia: 1798.

Dalke, Anne. "Original Vice: The Political Implications of Incest in the Early American Novel." *Early American Literature* 23 (1988): 188-201.

Dame Partlet's Farm: Containing an Account of the Great Riches She Obtained by Industry. . . . Philadelphia: J. Johnson, 1806.

Davidson, Cathy N. *Revolution and the Word: The Rise of the Novel in America.* New York: Oxford Univ. Press, 1986.

Derounian, Kathryn Smith. "Lost in the Crowd: Rebecca Rush's *Kelroy.*" *American Transcendental Quarterly* 47-48 (1980): 117-26.

Doerflinger, Thomas. *A Vigorous Spirit of Enterprise: Merchants and Economic Development in Revolutionary Philadelphia.* Chapel Hill: Univ. of North Carolina Press, 1986.

Dulles, Foster Rhea. *The Old China Trade.* Boston: Houghton Mifflin, 1930.

Dwight, Timothy. *Travels in New England and New York.* Vols. 1 and 4. 1822. Ed. Barbara Miller Solomon with Patricia M. King. Cambridge: Belknap Press of Harvard Univ. Press, 1969.

Edgeworth, Maria. *Idleness and Industry Exemplified in the History of James Preston and Lazy Lawrence.* Philadelphia: J. Johnson, 1803.

Fabian, Ann Vincent. *Card Sharps, Dream Books, & Bucket Shops: Gambling in Nineteenth-Century America.* Ithaca: Cornell Univ. Press, 1990.

Fidelity Rewarded: or, The History of Polly Granville. Boston: Young and Minns, 1796.

Franklin, Benjamin. *The Autobiography of Benjamin Franklin.* Ed. Leonard W. Labaree et al. New Haven: Yale Univ. Press, 1964.

The Fortunate Discovery. Or, The History of Henry Villars [by the author of *Moreland Vale*]. New York, 1798.

Freneau, Philip. *Poems Written Between the Years 1768 & 1794.* Mount Pleasant and Monmouth, 1795.

——. "Chronology of Facts." *National Gazette.* May 31, 1792.

——. "Detached Reflections from a Correspondent." *National Gazette.* November 3, 1793.

——. "On Commerce and Luxury." Abstract printed in *The Time Piece.* November 17, 1797, and November 20, 1797.

——. "Plan for a Nobility." *National Gazette.* May 7, 1792.

Furber, Holden. "The Beginnings of American Trade with India, 1784-1812." *The New England Quarterly* 11.2 (June 1938): 235-65.

The Gambler, or The Memoirs of a British Officer. 2nd ed. Washington City, 1802.

The Glass; or Speculation: A Poem: Containing an Account of the Ancient, and Genius of the Modern, Speculators. New York: printed for the author, 1791.

Goldstein, Jonathan. *Philadelphia and the China Trade 1682-1846.* University Park and London: Pennsylvania State Univ. Press, 1977.

Haslam, John. *Observations on Madness and Melancholy.* London: J. Callow, 1809. Reprint. New York: Arno Press, 1976.

Hitchcock, Enos. *A Discourse on Education, Delivered at the Meeting-House on the West Side of the River, in Providence, November 16, 1785.* Providence: Bennett Wheeler, 1785.

Hinds, Elizabeth Jane Wall. "Charles Brockden Brown's Revenge Tragedy: *Edgar Huntly* and the Uses of Property." *Early American Literature* 30 (1995): 51-70.

Hitchcock, Enos. *The Farmer's Friend, or the History of Mr. Charles Worthy.* Boston, 1793.

The Instructive Story of Industry and Sloth. Hartford: John Babcock, 1798.

Jefferson, Thomas. *The Papers of Thomas Jefferson.* Ed. Julian P. Boyd. Princeton: Princeton Univ. Press, 1950-.

Lenz, William E. *Fast Talk & Flush Times: The Confidence Man as a Literary Convention.* Columbia: Univ. of Missouri Press, 1985.

Lewis, Jan. "The Republican Wife: Virtue and Seduction in the Early Republic." *William and Mary Quarterly* 44 (October 1987): 689-721.

The Little Islanders: or, Blessings of Industry. Philadelphia: Johnson & Warner, 1809.

Lindberg, Gary. *The Confidence Man in American Literature.* New York: Oxford Univ. Press, 1982.

Lovell, Thomas B. "Separate Spheres and Extensive Circles: Sarah Savage's *The Factory Girl* and the Celebration of Industry in Early Nineteenth-Century America." *Early American Literature* 31 (1996): 1-24.

Main, Jackson Turner. *The Social Structure of Revolutionary America.* Princeton: Princeton Univ. Press, 1965.

Mandeville, Bernard. *The Fable of the Bees.* 2 vols. Ed. F. B. Kaye. Oxford: Clarendon, 1924.

McCoy, Drew. *The Elusive Republic. Political Economy in Jeffersonian America.* Chapel Hill: Univ. of North Carolina Press, 1980.

Moreland Vale; or the Fair Fugitive [by the author of *The Fortunate Discovery*]. New York, 1801.

Morris, Robert. *The Papers of Robert Morris.* Volume 7. Edited by Elizabeth M. Nuxoll and Mary A. Y. Gallagher. Pittsburgh: Univ. of Pittsburgh Press, 1995.

Nelson, Dana A. Introduction. *Kelroy, a Novel.* By Rebecca Rush. New York: Oxford Univ. Press, 1992. xi-xxiv.

Nelson, William E. "Emerging Notions of Modern Criminal Law in the Revolutionary Era: An Historical Perspective." *New York University Law Review* 42 (May 1967): 450-82.

Newton, Sarah E. *Learning to Behave: A Guide to American Conduct Books Before 1900.* Westport, Conn.: Greenwood Press, 1994.

Of Commerce and Luxury. Rptd. from the British edition. Philadelphia: T. Lang, 1791.

Parrish, Joseph. *An Inaugural Dissertation on the Influence of the Passions Upon the Body in the Production and Cure of Diseases.* Philadelphia: Kimber, Conrad & Co., 1805.

Patterson, Mrs. *The Unfortunate Lovers, and Cruel Parents: A Very Interesting Tale Founded on Fact.* 17th ed. n.p., 1797.

Pocock, J. G. A. *The Machiavellian Moment: Florentine Political Thought and the Atlantic Republican Tradition.* Princeton: Princeton Univ. Press, 1975.

Rothman, Ellen K. *Hands and Hearts. A History of Courtship in America.* New York: Basic Books, 1984.

―――. "Sex and Self-Control: Middle-Class Courtship in America, 1770-1870." *The American Family in Social-Historical Perspective.* 3rd. ed. Ed. Michael Gordon. New York: St. Martin's Press, 1983. 393-410.

Rush, Benjamin. *Medical Inquiries and Observations Upon the Diseases of the Mind.* 1812. New York: Hafner, 1962.

[Rush, Rebecca]. *Kelroy, a Novel.* 1812. Reprint. Ed. Dana D. Nelson. New York: Oxford Univ. Press, 1992.

Said, Edward W. *Culture and Imperialism.* New York: Knopf, 1993.

Sakolski, A. M. *The Great American Land Bubble.* New York: Harper & Brothers, 1932.

[Savage, Sarah.] *The Factory Girl.* Boston, 1814.

Smith, Adam. *An Inquiry into the Nature and Causes of the Wealth of Nations.* Revised ed. 3 vols. Philadelphia: Dobson, 1789.

Smith, Daniel Scott. "Parental Power and Marriage Patterns: An Analysis of Historical Trends in Hingham, Massachusetts." *Journal of Marriage and the Family* 35 (August 1973): 419-28.

Smith, Daniel Scott, and Michael S. Hindus. "Premarital Pregnancy in America 1640-1971: An Overview and Interpretation." *Journal of Interdisciplinary History* 5.4 (Spring 1975): 537-70.

Smith, Philip Chadwick Foster. *The Empress of China.* Philadelphia: Philadelphia Maritime Museum, 1984.

Smith-Rosenburg, Carroll. "Domesticating 'Virtue': Coquettes and Revolutionaries in Young America." *Literature and the Body: Essays on Populations and Persons.* Ed. Elaine Scarry. Baltimore: Johns Hopkins Univ. Press, 1986: 160-84.

St. Hubert; or, Mistaken Friendship. District of Columbia: W. W. Wood, 1800.

Sullivan, James. *The Path to Riches: An Inquiry into the Origin and Use of Money. . . .* Boston: By P. Edes, for I. Thomas and E. T. Andrews, 1792.

Taylor, John. *An Enquiry Into the Principles and Tendency of Certain Public Measures.* Philadelphia: Thomas Dobson, 1794.

W., A. *A Dandy Song.* [Boston?: s.n. between 1806 and 1826].

Warren, Caroline Mailda. *The Gamesters; or Ruins of Innocence. An Original Novel, Founded in Truth.* Boston: Carlisle for Thomas & Andrews et al., 1805.

Watts, Isaac, D. D. *The Improvement of the Mind: or a Supplement to the Art of Logic. In Two Parts. To Which is Added, a Discourse on the Education of Children and Youth.* Exeter, N.H.: J. Lamson and T. Odiorne, for David West, Boston, 1793.

———. *Logic: Or, the Right Use of Reason, in the Inquiry After Truth. With a Variety of Rules to Guard Against Error in the Affairs of Religion and Human Life, As Well as in the Sciences.* 2nd American ed. Newburyport: printed by W. Barrett for Thomas and Andrews, Boston, 1796.

Watts, Steven. *The Republic Reborn: War and the Making of Liberal America, 1790-1820.* Baltimore: Johns Hopkins Univ. Press, 1987.

———. *The Romance of Real Life: Charles Brockden Brown and the Origins of American Culture.* Baltimore: Johns Hopkins Univ. Press, 1994.

Webster, Pelatiah. *Political Essays on the Nature and Operation of Money, Public Finances, and Other Subjects Published During the American War, and Continued up to the Present Year, 1791.* Philadelphia: Joseph Crukshank, 1791.

———. "A Plea for the Poor Soldiers: Or, An Essay to Demonstrate that the Soldiers and Other Public Creditors, who really and actually supported the Burden of the late War, Have Not Been Paid, Ought to Be Paid, Can Be Paid and Must Be Paid." 1790. *Political Essays.* . . . Philadelphia: Joseph Crukshank, 1791. 306-43.

———. "A Second Essay on Free Trade." 1779. *Political Essays.* . . . Philadelphia: Crukshank, 1791. 27-49.

Weems, Mason Locke. *God's Revenge Against Gambling: Exemplified in the Miserable Lives and Untimely Deaths of a Number of Persons of Both Sexes, Who Had Sacrificed Their Health, Wealth, and Honor at Gaming Tables.* Augusta, Ga.: Hobby & Bunce, 1810.

Williams, Raymond. "Base and Superstructure in Marxist Cultural Theory." *New Left Review* 82 (1973): 3-16.

Wood, Gordon S. *The Creation of the American Republic, 1776-1787.* New York: W. W. Norton, 1969.

———, ed. *The Rising Glory of America 1760-1820.* Revised ed. Boston: Northeastern Univ. Press, 1990.

Wood, Sarah. *Dorval: or The Speculator. A Novel, Founded on Recent Facts.* Portsmouth, N.H., 1801.

Woodruff, Hezekiah N. *The Danger of Ambition Considered, in a Sermon Preached at Scipio, N.Y., The Lord's Day, August 12, 1804: Occasioned by the Death of General Alexander Hamilton, Who Fell in a Duel with Aaron Burr, Vice-President of the United States of America, on the 11th Day of July, 1804.* Albany: Charles R. and George Webster, 1804.

Jonathan A. Cook (essay date March 2004)

SOURCE: Cook, Jonathan A. "The Historical and Literary Sources of *Redburn*'s 'Mysterious Night in London.'" *Leviathan* 6, no. 1 (March 2004): 9-33.

[*In the following essay, Cook explains that Herman Melville had not yet visited London at the time he wrote* Redburn, *and offers details about establishments and literary sources that may have influenced the novel's well-known gambling scene set in that city.*]

Chapter 46 of *Redburn*, "A Mysterious Night in London," has long remained a sticking point in a number of critical evaluations of the novel. The story of young Redburn's traumatic overnight experience with his new friend Harry Bolton at Aladdin's Palace, a fashionable London gambling "hell," is, in the opinion of some commentators, a melodramatic excrescence in an otherwise compelling account of a teenage boy's initiation into the evils and injustices of the world. Hershel Parker, for example, argues that the scene is "lurid" and "unconvincing," an exercise in literary padding. Robert K. Martin similarly suggests the inadequacy of the same episode, adducing the author's attempt to depict an upper-class London gambling club and ostensible "male brothel" without actually having patronized these establishments.[1] Although the scene has defenders who point to its garish intensity and its revelation of the character of Harry Bolton, others agree with Parker and Martin that the events at Aladdin's Palace are too factitious and overdrawn to serve as an authentic picture of fashionable vice in what was intended as an upper-class counterpart to the depiction of lower-class misery in the port of Liverpool.[2] Moreover, despite its alleged artificiality, several critics assume, like Martin, that Aladdin's Palace hints at a male brothel as well as a gambling hell; but no one so far has attempted to substantiate this claim with relevant literary or historical evidence.[3]

In his informative study of *Redburn*, William H. Gilman first demonstrated that the experience described in "A Mysterious Night in London" could not have been based on the author's firsthand experience since during his stay in Liverpool in August 1839 Melville apparently had no time for a trip to London. As a result,

Melville presumably relied on literary and historical sources for the conception and details of this chapter. Gilman notes the similarities in imagery between the luxurious furnishings in Aladdin's Palace and the lush setting of the second of Melville's 1839 "Fragments from a Writing Desk," both of them bearing the stamp of the popular Romantic Orientalism of the day, as found in Byron ("The Bride of Abydos," *Don Juan*), Moore (*Lalla Rookh*), and *The Arabian Nights' Entertainments*. In addition to these influences, Parker has also identified a melodramatic story, "The Gambler's Fate," published in the July 1837 *Albany Microscope*, as a revealing analogue. The unsigned story, which Melville may have read, tells of a young man named "Melvil" who accompanies a friend, Russell, to a London gambling hell, with disastrous consequences. Parker makes no claim for "The Gambler's Fate" as a source for the scene at Aladdin's Palace (or for Melville as the unacknowledged author of the story), but he effectively demonstrates that Melville's chapter might have a more varied literary ancestry than Gilman suggests.[4]

Given that Melville had no firsthand experience of a fashionable London gambling club at the time he wrote *Redburn,* the question remains, what other literary or historical sources could he have used for the creation of Chapter 46? In fact, the description of Redburn's and Harry Bolton's visit to Aladdin's Palace was almost certainly inspired by the most famous London gambling club of the era, Crockford's on St. James's Street, opened in 1828 and closed in 1845, membership to which was *de rigueur* for the contemporary man of fashion. By combining an examination of the visit to Aladdin's Palace in *Redburn* with the many evocations of the famous club in both fact and fiction, we can identify Melville's likely sources for Chapter 46 of *Redburn* and also make better sense of what actually happens at the luridly elegant "hell" depicted therein. We will also discover that the scene enacted at Aladdin's Palace bears a generic resemblance to scenes found in some of the fashionable "silver fork" novels of the era, while the character of Harry Bolton conforms to the type of elegantly dressed "dandy" who flourished in the early decades of the nineteenth century and often played a conspicuous role in silver fork fiction. This historical and literary evidence should allow us to appreciate the dramatic function of Redburn's mysterious night in London and to gain added insight into the role of Harry Bolton.

Crockford and His Gambling "Hell"

Various forms of gambling had long been a regular feature of eighteenth-century London life, often hand-in-glove with prostitution; but though widely perceived as a moral blight at the time, as in Hogarth's *Rake's Progress* (1735), only a relatively limited number of clubs, or "hells," were devoted to the pastime. ("Hell"

for gambling club dates to the late eighteenth century.) Gambling gained a wider popularity during the last two decades of the century, however, especially with the arrival of French emigrés fleeing the Revolution; and it was given additional impetus with the cessation of hostilities in Europe in 1815. By 1820 there were about fifty gambling clubs in London, many of which featured games brought over from the Continent such as the card games of écarté, faro, loo, macao, piquet, rouge-et-noir, and vingt-et-un; or the roulette wheel; or the dice-based game of hazard. The center of London gambling in the early nineteenth century was in the fashionable West End, where clubs such as Roubel's, Fielder's, Taylor's, Holdsworth's, and Davis's clustered in the vicinity of Piccadilly and Pall Mall. As a writer for *Bentley's Miscellany* in 1845 wryly noted in a retrospective survey of London gambling, "The regal, episcopal, and aristocratic parish of St. James's has ever been, as it still is, the favoured locality of the speculative and enterprising gaming-house keeper." At the heart of this district was St. James's Street, running the short distance between Piccadilly to the north and Pall Mall to the south. By the late 1820s the street was the site of the city's four leading gentlemen's clubs—White's, Brooks's, Boodle's, and Crockford's—where gambling was pursued in varying degrees. Yet it was only Crockford's that offered a combination of luxurious accommodations, aristocratic clientele, and extraordinary opportunities for deep—and often ruinous—play.[5]

The undisputed king of London gambling from the late 1820s to the early 1840s was William Crockford (1775-1844), the founder and proprietor of the establishment bearing his name situated at 50 St. James's Street, across from White's. The son of a fishmonger doing business at Temple Bar in the working-class East End of London, Crockford was an avid and astute gambler who saw an opportunity to reap great rewards from the pockets of Regency dandies, bucks, aristocrats, and men-about-town. Crockford's club was the consummation of its proprietor's career as a gambling club operator and bookmaker originally connected to the Newmarket Heath racecourse. In the early 1820s, Crockford and a partner ran Watier's, a club founded in 1807 by the Prince of Wales and named after its chef, where superior cuisine and highstakes gambling were combined; a decade before Crockford assumed control, Watier's, located on Piccadilly at Bolton Street, had been patronized by the likes of Byron and Beau Brummell. In the mid-1820s, Crockford obtained the lease to a building on the west side of St. James's Street, where he set up a gambling hell; but after obtaining the leases to three adjacent buildings, he razed all four and set about building a palatial and opulently furnished gentlemen's club devoted to gambling that contemporary wits were quick to dub "Pandemonium." Another interested observer called it "the leviathan hell." After over a year's construction, "Crockford's" opened in January 1828.[6]

Society architect Benjamin Wyatt modeled the club's neoclassical design and décor on Louis XIV's Versaille. Construction costs amounted to £60,000 and furnishings another £35,000. With its privileged clientele paying £25 annually for membership and a roster of over a thousand members, Crockford's fulfilled all contemporary notions of ease and elegance. Among its members, many of whom served in Parliament, was the acknowledged leader of English society, the Duke of Wellington, as well as a host of other aristocrats such as the Lords Alvanley, Bentinck, Chesterfield, Lennox, Raglan, Rivers, and Sefton; men-about-town such as Colonel Armstrong, Edward Hughes Ball ("Ball" Hughes), Sir Joseph Copley, John Wilson Crocker, Thomas Slingsby Duncombe, Captain Gronow, and George Payne; distinguished foreigners like the Count d'Orsay, Prince Paul Esterhazy, Prince Lieven, Louis Napoleon, and Tallyrand; and a few fashionable authors such as Bulwer, Disraeli, Theodore Hook, and Henry Luttrell.[7] Crockford's was famous for the quality of its cuisine, prepared by the French chef, Eustache Ude. Food and wine were served to players "on the house" and to others at a reasonable rate in the club dining room. While low-stakes gambling at Crockford's might involve a variety of card games, the dice-based game of French hazard was the center of the proprietor's high-stakes gambling operations. The hazard room opened at 11 p.m. for an all-night session, with the bank set at £5,000. Neither servants nor smoking was allowed in the room, while three new pairs of dice, each pair costing a guinea, were provided every night for play. During the time that Parliament was in session, from February to August, a special hazard room upstairs was available; otherwise, hazard was played downstairs adjacent to the public rooms.

The law of the day formally forbade gambling hells, but Crockford's escaped closing, despite the enormous amounts of money that changed hands there, because of laxity of legal enforcement and the prestige of the club's members. Crockford's was ostensibly operated by an aristocratic management committee, but Crockford himself was its principal manager, assisted by an underling named Gye. With his cockney accent and undistinguished appearance, the corpulent Crockford always presented himself as a humble servant of the club's privileged clientele. After a dozen years of personal enrichment estimated at over a million pounds (partially depleted by his continuing career as a racecourse "leg," horse owner, and speculator in mining and real estate), Crockford announced his retirement in 1840. By 1844 there were at least twenty other gambling hells in the vicinity of Pall Mall and Picadilly seeking to emulate Crockford's success. Despite Crockford's official dissociation from the club bearing his name, it was widely believed that he still had a hand in its operations until

his death in May 1844, at which time a parliamentary committee was beginning to crack down on gambling after a notoriously fixed Derby race.[8]

Crockford's finally closed its doors at the end of 1845. During its years of operation, the club was known to cater to the most select London society and was never implicated in any cheating or scandal. For all Crockford's elegant food and furnishings, however, the club's ultimate purpose was to lure the contemporary man of fashion into squandering his money. Among the biggest losers, Lords Sefton and Chesterfield each lost about £200,000 there, while Lord Rivers (dubbed in France "*le Wellington des joueurs*") lost £23,000 at hazard in a single sitting. To keep such a lucrative system operating efficiently, Crockford's allegedly had a regular system for luring in prospective candidates for "plucking," as the journalist James Grant noted in *The Great Metropolis,* a two-volume account of London in the mid-1830s:

> In Crockford's, very large sums are played for with the cards; but it is at the hazard table, when the game is French hazard, that the work of plunder is carried on on the most extensive scale. There, to use gambling phraseology, the "pigeon is plucked." And to get the flat [dupe] prevailed on to throw down the cards, and repair to the hazard room, is the great, though concealed object of those in the interest of the house. A few hours, most probably, will do the work in the latter place. The stakes are usually high: he loses, perhaps, a fourth part of his fortune in less than an hour: he "tables" another fourth—he loses again. He becomes desperate: in the delirium, or madness (for that is the proper word) of the moment, he determines on risking his all at one throw. The dice turn up—his all is lost: he who a few hours before was a rich man, is now a beggar. The sums which young thoughtless noblemen lose at Crockford's in one night, are sometimes incredibly large. Seven years ago one pigeon was plucked, in a few hours, to the tune of 60,000*l.*—the stakes were 10,000*l.* . . . . Losses of 5,000*l.*, 7,000*l.*, and 10,000*l.*, in one night, are by no means uncommon when a rich flat is caught.

> (Grant 1:170-71)

Crockford already had a European reputation as England's premier gambling proprietor even before he opened his newly constructed club on St. James's Street. Symptomatic of the influential reputation that the club had quickly obtained even in America was the fact that the anonymously authored *Crockford's, or Life in the West,* a monitory fictionalized report on the new London gambling sensation, was immediately reprinted in New York by Harper Brothers in 1828. Near the end of this didactic narrative, the author notes of a young "flat" named Rosefield who is lured into deep play at hazard: "There was nothing wanting to give this magnificent palace of knavery and ruin, (it was Crockford's club where this mere youth was allured,) every charm that splendour can convey, beneath which lurks unseen, but not unfelt, robbery and wretchedness."[9]

The republication of James Grant's *Great Metropolis* in New York in 1837 enhanced Crockford's notoriety in America. The author opens his chapter on "The Gambling Houses" in London by noting: "Who has not heard of Crockford's? Everybody has heard of it, and everyone knows that it is a great gambling establishment; but that is the extent of the public's knowledge on the subject" (Grant 1:159). In the following decade, an extensive account of William Crockford's career, as well as the cultural significance of his club, appeared in 1845 in *Bentley's Miscellany,* followed by a wide-ranging survey of London gambling in several installments over the next year. Finally, Crockford's was later mentioned in the memoirs of some of its former frequenters such as Captain Gronow, who summarized the economic impact of the fashionable club: "One may safely say, without exaggeration, that Crockford won the whole of the ready money of the then existing generation."[10]

CROCKFORD'S CLUB AND ALADDIN'S PALACE

To what extent might Melville have relied on Crockford's as a model for "Aladdin's Palace" in *Redburn*? Traveling by train from Liverpool, Redburn and Harry Bolton arrive in London at Euston Station near Regents Park, on the edge of the West End. From there they would have traveled a relatively short distance south to St. James's Street, the center of fashionable gentlemen's clubs. Disguised to prevent recognition by his former associates in the fashionable world, Bolton stops the cab in which he and Redburn are riding at "no. 40" of an unnamed street, a building having "high steps" and illuminated by a "purple light."[11] Crockford's club at 50 St. James's Street had a short flight of stone steps leading to the main entrance, and a well-lit classical facade. While the exterior of the club at which Bolton and Redburn stop is not as conspicuous as the historical Crockford's, the general appearance and décor inside the famous club clearly suggest a source for much of the brilliant appearance and questionable activities taking place at "Aladdin's Palace."

Thus, when the parliamentarian John Wilson Crocker visited the lavish new club on St. James's Street shortly after its opening in 1828, he noted in his diary: "I went to Crockford's to look at his fairy palace, which certainly beats the drop-scene of a pantomime. The lamp in the staircase cost £1200, and so in proportion. The whole house is as splendid as marble, scagliola, gilding, and glasses [mirrors] can make it."[12] James Grant also noted the stunning effect of walking into Crockford's club for the first time: "No one, I believe, not even those accustomed to visit the mansions of the aristocracy, ever entered the saloon for the first time, without being dazzled with the splendour which surrounded him. A friend and myself lately went throughout the whole of it; and for some moments, on entering the saloon, we stood confounded by the scene" (Grant 1:160).

The article on "Crockford and Crockford's" in *Bentley's Miscellany* in 1845 described the details of the same scene:

> On entering from the street, a magnificent vestibule and staircase break upon the view; to the right and left of the hall are reading and dining-rooms. The staircase is of a sinuous form, sustained in its landing by four columns of the Doric order, above which are a series of examples of the Ionic order, forming a quadrangle with apertures to the chief apartments. Above the pillars is a covered ceiling perforated with luminous panels of stained glass, from which springs a dome of surpassing beauty; from the dome depends a lantern containing a magnificent chandelier.
>
> *The State Drawing Room* next attracts attention,—a most noble apartment, baffling perfect description of its beauty, but decorated in the most florid style of the school of Louis Quatorze. The room presents a series of panels containing subjects, in the style of *Watteau,* from the pencil of Mr. Martin, a relative of the celebrated historical painter of that name: these panels are alternated with splendid mirrors. A chandelier of exquisite workmanship hangs from the centre of the ceiling, and three large tables, beautifully carved and gilded, and covered with rich blue and crimson velvet, are placed in different parts of the room. The upholstery and decorative adjuncts are imitative of the gorgeous taste of George the Fourth. Royalty can scarcely be conceived to vie with the style and consummate splendour of this magnificent chamber.

("Crockford and Crockford's," 253)

According to a mid-Victorian historian of London clubs, the entrance hall at Crockford's featured "a screen of Roman-Ionic scagliola columns with gilt capitals, and a cupola of gilding and stained glass. The library has Sienna columns and antae of the Ionic order, from the Temple of Minerva Polias; the staircase is panelled with scagliola, and enriched with Corinthian columns."[13] William Crockford's twentieth-century biographer has described the interior of the club in similar terms, noting its "capacious cellars suitable for later development as a cockpit, and providing also a secret exit from the Club in case of a police raid"; conspicuous, too, was "the latest form of gas lighting" used in the club's central chandelier.[14]

Upon entering Aladdin's Palace with Harry Bolton, Redburn describes the scene that first meets his eye:

> It was some semi-public place of opulent entertainment; and far surpassed any thing of the kind I had ever seen before.
>
> The floor was tesselated with snow-white, and russet-hued marbles; and echoed to the tread, as if all the Paris catacombs were underneath. I started with misgivings at that hollow, boding sound, which seemed sighing with a subterranean despair, through all the magnificent spectacle around me; mocking it, where most it glared.

The walls were painted so as to deceive the eye with interminable colonnades; and groups of columns of the finest Scagliola work of variegated marbles—emerald-green and gold, St. Pons veined with silver, Sienna with porphyry—supported a resplendent fresco ceiling, arched like a bower, and thickly clustering with mimic grapes. Through all the East of this foliage, you spied in a crimson dawn, Guido's ever youthful Apollo, driving forth the horses of the sun. From the sculptured stalactites of vine-boughs, here and there pendent hung galaxies of gas lights, whose vivid glare was softened by pale, cream-colored, porcelain spheres, shedding over the place a serene, silver flood; as if every porcelain sphere were a moon; and this superb apartment was the moon-lit garden of Portia at Belmont; and the gentle lovers, Lorenzo and Jessica, lurked somewhere among the vines.

(NN *Redburn* 228)

In Redburn's description of the club, we find many of the same architectural and decorative elements found at Crockford's. First, Redburn's observation of how hollow their steps sounded on entering hints at the extensive underground cellars beneath Crockford's club. Second, the classical columns in both clubs exhibit "scagliola" marble surfaces. (The term denotes a stone-like plaster veneer consisting of a matrix of gypsum and glue, to which marble or granite chips were added and then polished to a high gloss.) Third, both Crockford's and Aladdin's Palace feature Baroque neoclassical paintings: those at Crockford's, in keeping with the Louis XIV décor, were in the style of the French Rococo painter Antoine Watteau (1684-1721), who specialized in pleasure excursions, or *fêtes galantes,* set off by mythological backgrounds; at Aladdin's Palace the ceiling fresco is a copy of the Italian Baroque painter Guido Reni's *Aurora* (1613), which featured the sun god driving his chariot while being led forward by the goddess of the dawn. Finally, the elaborate gas lighting fixtures at both Crockford's and Aladdin's Palace lend an air of enchantment to the opulent scene, and help create an ineffable, dazzling effect on the individual seeing such luminous and gilded splendor for the first time.

Redburn and Harry enter the brilliantly lit room, in which sit "knots of gentlemanly men," and seating themselves, Harry calls for wine. After drinking, Harry talks to an elderly man who appears to be the steward of the premises, "a very handsome florid old man, with snow-white hair and whiskers, and in a snow-white jacket—he looked like an almond tree in blossom" (NN *Redburn* 228). Characterized by an ambiguous whiteness, the old man is associated with the almond tree, which in the form of a "rod" (i.e., branch) of almond was a sign of God's blessing in the Old Testament (Num. 17:8; Jer. 1:11), an ironic association, needless to say, for a gambling club employee. Harry Bolton confers with the old man, we may assume, about the accommodations to be made for Redburn overnight while

Harry is busy gambling. Harry then disappears with the steward while Redburn is left alone to fantasize a moment about the aristocratic personages he might meet through Harry, in the meantime self-consciously assuming a "careless and lordly air . . . like a young Prince Esterhazy" (NN *Redburn* 229). Reference to this wealthy scion of the Austrian Empire, who served as its ambassador to Britain in the 1830s, is relevant in this context since he was a well-known member of Crockford's.[15] Redburn's attempt to assume a pose of studied nonchalance is, of course, unsuccessful; as he continues waiting, he sees groups of gentlemen retiring together "as if going to a private apartment" and then overhears "one of them drop the word *Rouge*; but he could not have used rouge, for his face was exceedingly pale. Another said something about *Loo*" (NN *Redburn* 229-30). The exact nature of the establishment, and its various forms of play at cards and dice, are still unknown to the inexperienced young American, thrust into a foreign social world.

Redburn and Harry subsequently ascend "the long winding slope of those aristocratic stairs" and enter a luxuriously furnished room on the second floor:

As we entered the room, methought I was slowly sinking in some reluctant, sedgy sea; so thick and elastic the Persian carpeting, mimicking parterres of tulips, and roses, and jonquils, like a bower in Babylon.

Long lounges lay carelessly disposed, whose fine damask was interwoven, like the Gobelin tapestry, with pictorial tales of tilt and tourney. And oriental ottomans, whose cunning warp and woof were wrought into plaited serpents, undulating beneath beds of leaves, from which, here and there, they flashed out sudden splendors of green scales and gold.

In the broad bay windows, as the hollows of King Charles' oaks, were Laocoon-like chairs, in the antique taste, draped with heavy fringes of bullion and silk.

The walls, covered with a sort of tartan-French paper, variegated with bars of velvet, were hung round with mythological oil-paintings, suspended by tasseled cords of twisted silver and blue.

(NN *Redburn* 230)

The luxurious room is a kind of modern Spenserian Bower of Bliss or House of Busirane, with seductive flowers on the floor into which Redburn sinks; moreover, a dominant image pattern here is of *twisted* décor, casting doubt on the moral tenor of the club's activities. The imagery of the room in which Redburn finds himself thus suggests an inextricable union of sensuality and sin, as in the arabesque-style "plaited serpents" visible in the "oriental ottomans" or the serpent-like "Laocoon-like chairs," both of which are symbolically appropriate for the furnishings of a high-class "hell." All of the décor, moreover, suggests a morally dangerous confusion between the natural and the artificial.[16]

While no contemporary description of a room at Crockford's exactly matches the furnishings of this upstairs lounge, *Bentley's Miscellany* describes the principal drawing room as "decorated in the most florid style of the school of Louis Quatorze," with its tables "beautifully carved and gilded, and covered with rich blue and crimson velvet." Another description in a nineteenth-century history of gambling represents the rooms at Crockford's as "panelled in the most gorgeous manner; spaces are left to be filled up with mirrors and silk, or gold enrichments; while the ceilings are as superb as the walls." In addition, "A billiard-room on the upper floor completes the number of apartments professedly dedicated to the use of the members. Whenever any secret manoeuvre is to be carried on, there are smaller and more retired places, both under this roof and the next, whose walls will tell no tales."[17]

Redburn's subsequent description of the "mythological" (i.e., erotic) paintings in the upstairs room at Aladdin's Palace is not directly evocative of any known décor at Crockford's (although the Watteau-like paintings there may have been mildly lubricious); but the paintings do suggest the visual presentation of sexuality as yet another aspect of the club's luxurious furnishings, and an appetitive stimulus to "deep play":

> They were such pictures as the high-priests, for a bribe, showed to Alexander in the innermost shrine of the white temple in the Libyan oasis: such pictures as the pontiff of the sun strove to hide from Cortez, when, sword in hand, he burst open the sanctorum of the pyramid-fane at Cholula: such pictures as you may still see, perhaps, in the central alcove of the excavated mansion of Pansa, in Pompeii—in that part of it called by Varro *the hollow of the house*: such pictures as Martial and Suetonius mention as being found in the private cabinet of the Emperor Tiberius: such pictures as are delineated on the bronze metals, to this day dug up on the ancient island of Capreae: such pictures as you might have beheld in an arched recess, leading from the left hand of the secret side-gallery of the temple of Aphrodite in Corinth.

(NN *Redburn* 230-31)

The décor of the room in which Redburn spends the evening hints at a world of sexual as well as financial profligacy among the upper classes. But we see no explicit signs of prostitution in this chapter and can only assume that the lewd pictures at Aladdin's Palace are simply there as pornographic entertainment. The contemporary literature on gambling says almost nothing about sex being available at clubs in the second quarter of the nineteenth century, and it is clear that this was not a regular feature of current gambling culture (unlike the previous century). The normally outspoken James Grant, for example, only briefly mentions that the proprietors of some clubs "have always on hand a sufficient quantity of flash apparel in which to deck out any unfortunate girl who engages to pamper to their avarice, by her own prostitution" (Grant 1:212).

The "mythological" paintings on the wall at Aladdin's Palace are nevertheless appropriate for the taste and educational level of the patrons of an upper-class gambling club with a neoclassical design scheme. In this regard we may look to the equally suggestive classical décor at another well-known contemporary hell for the better class of players, as described by the writer on "Gaming, Gaming-Houses, and Gamesters" in *Bentley's Miscellany*:

> The rouge et noir department at Taylor's was somewhat remarkable from the walls of the room being adorned with a handsome paper of French manufacture and design, illustrative of the story of the descent of Aeneas with the sybil [*sic*] into the infernal regions, as related by Virgil—and what was most singularly appropriate in the arrangement of the panels descriptive of the subject was, that at the immediate opening or doorway to the play-room, was the very apposite representation of Cerberus guarding the entrance to hell, and the sybil in the act of throwing the sop, which was to be effective in lulling the monster to a comfortable nap, so that the "facilis descensus Avernii" [easy descent to hell] might be safely accomplished. Whether this arrangement was attributable to the classic taste of the gaming-house proprietor, or to the wit and waggery of some intelligent paper-hanger, is not known; but it was a frequent subject of jocose observation amongst the visitors.[18]

Unlike this amusing visual pun on the nature of the establishment it is decorating, the images in the upstairs lounge at Aladdin's Palace convey a disquieting message to Redburn of a debased mixture of the sacred and the profane, thereby repeating a motif found elsewhere in the décor of the club and in its most conspicuous employee, the white-haired steward. Significantly, *Bentley's Miscellany* attributed a mock-sacramental aura to the gambling operation at Crockford's, describing its modest-sized hazard room as the "Sanctum Sanctorum" and its supervisor (Crockford himself) the presiding "Pluto."

Redburn's description of the quasi-pornographic art at Aladdin's Palace seems to be a mixture of fact and fantasy.[19] His allusion to ancient temples evokes a traditional association between pagan religions and ritualized sexual representation, here attributed to the temple of the Egyptian supreme god Amen-Ra (also known as Zeus or Jupiter Ammon) in the Libyan desert, the temple of the Aztec Quetzalcoatl at Cholula, and the temple of Aphrodite at Corinth. But contrary to Redburn's overheated imagination, none of the aforementioned temples would seem to have actually featured erotic imagery. On the other hand, the references to the "excavated mansion" ascribed to the aedile Gaius Cuspius Pansa at Pompeii and the "private cabinet" of the Emperor Tiberius on the island of Capri are more authentically evocative of the decadent, sexually candid culture of the first-century Roman empire. (The word "pornography" and its linguistic variants first came into the English language in the mid-nineteenth century, shortly after *Redburn* was published, in connection with the recently recovered erotic art at first-century Pompeii and Herculaneum.) But if the house of Pansa, unlike a number of other Pompeian villas, was not known for any erotic art, the allusion to the Roman historian Suetonius on Tiberius (emperor 14-37 A.D.) is a more reliable clue to the lascivious images that Redburn evokes. The pictures and medals that Redburn mentions are probably derived from the pornographic paintings and displays that formed part of Tiberius's extensive repertoire of sexual entertainment and artwork at Capri, according to Suetonius.[20]

After Harry and Redburn have entered the risqué second-floor lounge at Aladdin's Palace, Harry speaks into the ear of a sculpted bust representing "a bald-headed old man, with a mysteriously-wicked expression, and imposing silence by one thin finger over his lips" (NN *Redburn* 231). Harry is simply ordering a servant for cigars. Significantly, in their subsequent conversation Redburn unknowingly pronounces the name of the gambling club, imaginatively identifying it as "this Palace of Aladdin" where Harry seems almost at home. The reference to Aladdin and the world of *The Arabian Nights* is particularly appropriate at this point in terms of the seemingly magical means of ordering in the servant, and the instantaneousness of his appearance, like a genie out of a lamp. As the astonished Redburn observes, "In obedience to a summons so singularly conveyed, to my amazement a servant almost instantly appeared, standing transfixed in the attitude of a bow." In the well-known story of Aladdin and his magic lamp (often performed as a theatrical pantomime in the nineteenth century), Aladdin used his genie to create a resplendent palace for his new bride, the sultan's daughter. The instantaneous, obsequious service that Harry obtains is also suggestive of the plethora of "amazingly polite" round-the-clock servants who waited on the clientele at Crockford's (Grant 1:167).

Yet if "Aladdin's Palace" is evocative of the Romantic Orientalism of the day, and also suggests the factitious splendor of the gambling establishment it describes, Melville might have actually conceived the name of his gambling club from a contemporary journalistic source relating to Crockford's. In a July 1844 article in the *Edinburgh Review* devoted to a recent biography of George Selwyn (1719-1791), a celebrated eighteenth-century wit, politician, rake, and gambler, the appearance of William Crockford's sumptuous club is described as rising "like a creation of Aladdin's lamp; and the genii themselves could hardly have surpassed the beauty of the internal decorations."[21] Given the fact that Melville used two *Edinburgh Review* articles from the 1820s as sources for several passages in *White-Jacket*, written immediately after he completed *Redburn*, Melville may

have also seen this 1844 article and gotten the idea for the name of the London gambling establishment depicted in the earlier-written novel.[22] If not, the coincidence is still revealing.

After telling Redburn that he has to disappear for some time (in order to begin gambling), Harry makes reference to the "old duke here" in connection with Redburn's overnight accommodation. Redburn mistakes this as an allusion to the Duke of Wellington, whereas Harry is only referring to the elderly steward of the premises. Such a confusion of identities suggests the reduction of Redburn's hopes for his London visit, but it also may operate as an inadvertent reminder of the Duke of Wellington's membership at Crockford's, and the aristocratic cachet he gave the club. Harry thereupon makes Redburn swear to deliver a letter to Bury St. Edmunds if he hasn't reappeared by morning. The implication is that Harry is going to do away with himself if he doesn't succeed at his gambling. The mood of the scene intensifies as Harry leaves Redburn alone for the night, for it is clear that Harry is about to wager his remaining worldly resources at the hazard table. As Redburn notes while trying to understand what is happening around him, he "only heard the hum from the roomful below, scattered voices, and a hushed ivory rattling from the closed apartments adjoining" (NN *Redburn* 233). He thereupon feels a "terrible revulsion":

> I shuddered at every footfall, and almost thought it must be some assassin pursuing me. The whole place seemed infected; and a strange thought came over me, that in the very damasks around, some eastern plague had been imported. And was that pale yellow wine, that I drank below, drugged? thought I. This must be some house whose foundations take hold on the pit. But these fearful reveries only enchanted me fast to my chair; so that, though I then wished to rush forth from the house, my limbs seemed manacled.
>
> While thus chained to my seat, something seemed suddenly flung open; a confused sound of imprecations, mixed with the ivory rattling, louder than before, burst upon my ear, and through the partly open door of the room where I was, I caught sight of a tall, frantic man, with clenched hands, wildly darting through the passage, towards the stairs.
>
> (NN *Redburn* 233)

The scene has a nightmarish Dostoevskian quality, as the moral corruption of the establishment is imaginatively projected as both a physically tainted atmosphere and a paralyzing bondage. Underlying the boyish Redburn's growing horror is a vague awareness of the ruinous gambling at hazard at the center of the club's operations, just as it was at Crockford's. At the same time, Redburn begins to question Harry's identity and ultimate purpose in coming to the club, and thinks of looking for him; but after reconsidering the situation Redburn remains faithful to his original promise to dispose of the letter and purse that Harry has left, should his friend not return. Redburn's doubts eventuate in a climactic realization for an American youth who has habitually idealized the aristocracy of England: "But spite of these thoughts, and spite of the metropolitan magnificence around me, I was mysteriously alive to a dreadful feeling, which I had never before felt, except when penetrating into the lowest and most squalid haunts of sailor iniquity in Liverpool. All the mirrors and marbles around me seemed crawling over with lizards; and I thought to myself, that though gilded and golden, the serpent of vice is a serpent still" (NN *Redburn* 234). The low haunts in Liverpool already described in Chapter 39, "Booble-Alleys of the Town," are "putrid with vice and crime," while the "sooty and begrimed bricks of the very houses have a reeking, Sodom-like and murderous look" (NN *Redburn* 191). Though framed in evangelical terms, Redburn's insights have a legitimate sociological bearing on the condition of England at the onset of the "hungry forties," in particular, the existence of "two nations" of rich and poor that troubled leading writers and social critics such as Carlyle, Disraeli, Dickens, Gaskell, Marx, and Engels.

After a fitful sleep, Redburn awakens when Harry Bolton mysteriously returns, having lost his money and so declaring, "I am off for America. The game is up" (NN *Redburn* 234). Harry's behavior now fits the contemporary model of the desperate and suicidal gambler who has succumbed to deep play and lost. Significantly, Harry gives his "dirk" to Redburn as a protective measure, and then alludes to a nearby bell-rope as an instrument for hanging. Such behavior may seem melodramatic, but in the context of the London gambling mania of the early nineteenth century, it suggests the social costs of gambling that many critics were decrying, and that eventually led to more strictly enforced laws against the practice. Thus, after describing the inner "Sanctum" at Crockford's where hazard was played and "the Pluto of the place was wont to preside," William Crockford's biographer in *Bentley's Miscellany* went on to note:

> It is a lamentable truth, and pregnant with most serious and melancholy feeling and reflection, that, within the narrow limit of the Sanctum, or play-room, described, the ruin has been wholly or partially effected, and the doom sealed, of many noble, high-minded, and opulent men, once proud in position of rank, station, and circumstance, and happy in all the social blessings and relations of life. Many such, fallen from their elevated and envied estate, by the direful infatuation of, and indulgence in, play, unable to bear up against the ruin that has overtaken them, have died by their own hands. To such distressing cause, and the fatal influence of the hazard-table, may be ascribed the lamentable and suicidal acts of the late highly-respected nobleman, Lord R—, and the no less esteemed gentleman, the late

Henry B—. Others of like grade and character have, owing to the same afflicting cause, become beggars in means, and outcasts alike from society and their country.

> ("Crockford and Crockford's," 254)

In *The Great Metropolis*, James Grant was similarly outspoken in his attack on contemporary gambling, and accordingly highlighted the addictive behavior and self-destructive end of many players:

> Of all the passions of which human nature is susceptible, a passion for gambling is inconceivably the most pernicious. Once indulge it, and you are inevitably hurried forward to irretrievable ruin. There is scarcely an instance on record of a person having yielded to the temptation to a certain extent, and then breaking off from it. There is a sort of fatality in it; its victim has no free-will of his own. He sees the folly of the course he is pursuing: he sees the issues too, and yet he cannot, or will not, help himself. He acts like a man who knows his destiny, and seems resolved, frightful though it be, on fulfilling it with the least possible delay. . . . Gambling is, I believe, the source of more evils to society in the metropolis, as well as to the individuals themselves, than any other vice which exists. My own impression is, that neither our moralists nor our legislators have any conception of the share it contributes to the crimes and immoralities with which this great city abounds. I have not a doubt that the cause of half the suicides which occur in the higher and middle walks of life, is gambling,—though the fact be carefully concealed by the friends of the parties.

> (Grant 1:97-200)

Here, too, we find a textbook analysis of what is happening behind the scenes at Aladdin's Palace, and the suicidal behavior of Harry Bolton when he returns from the hazard table. Nevertheless, after stabbing his empty purse with the "dirk" he has snatched back from Redburn, Harry calms himself with brandy, and for the rest of the night sits up with his decanter while Redburn tries to sleep.

HARRY BOLTON AND SILVER FORK FICTION

While the depiction of Aladdin's Palace strongly evokes London's most famous gentleman's club and gambling hell of the 1820s and 1830s, Melville also draws on a recognizable contemporary literary tradition. For the scene in which the dandy-like Harry Bolton gambles away his last resources is reminiscent of similar episodes in numerous novels of fashion of the "silver fork" school, most of them published by Henry Colburn. Such novels focused on manners, morals, and matrimony in the realm of genteel and aristocratic society, and were widely read among the rising middle class eager for glimpses into the privileged world of the "exclusives" or the "*haut ton*." "The principal ingredients in Colburn's formula," writes Ellen Moers, "were balls, gambling scenes, social climbers, political gossip, Almack's, the clubs, younger sons looking for heiresses, dowagers protecting their daughters from younger sons. Most of the novels produced on this pattern were mere handbooks of exclusive manners, pseudo-literary gossip journalism concerned with neither characterization nor plot, but with the illusion of authenticity."[23] In an 1827 review in the *Examiner*, William Hazlitt dismissively identified the new type of society novel as the "dandy school" of fiction, which drew attention to the details of fashionable life such as the use of silver forks to eat fish; as a result, the term "silver fork" has become associated with this genre.

The school began to develop in the mid-1820s in such works as Theodore Hook's *Sayings and Doings* (1824), Plumer Ward's *Tremaine, or the Man of Refinement* (1825), and Thomas H. Lister's *Granby* (1826), and continued with Disraeli's *Vivian Grey* (1826-27) and Bulwer's *Pelham* (1828), the latter two reaching wide audiences in England and America. Both Disraeli and Bulwer continued in this profitable vein—Disraeli's *The Young Duke* (1831) and *Henrietta Temple* (1837), and Bulwer's *Godolphin* (1833) being the chief examples—before the authors turned their talents elsewhere, Disraeli to the political, Bulwer to the "metaphysical" and historical novel. In the meantime, silver fork fiction continued in the 1830s and 1840s in the hands of such socially informed female observers as Lady Charlotte Bury, the Countess of Blessington, and Catherine Gore. (Out of all these writers, Melville was most familiar with the works of Bulwer and Disraeli.)[24] In her study of the social milieu of the writers of silver fork fiction, Alison Adburgham observes that gambling scenes in these novels mirrored the extravagant habits of the contemporary upper classes: "Just as in some silver fork novels a turning point in the young hero's life is a twenty-four hour sitting at Crockford's or some less recherché gambling 'hell,' so in very fact it was with many young men of rank and fortune who faced the moment of truth after their carefree years in 'the world'."[25] We may conclude, then, that Harry Bolton's desperate attempt in *Redburn* to win money at gambling in order to stave off financial ruin is reminiscent of a number of comparable scenes in silver fork fiction that reflected the epidemic spread of gambling in Regency and Reform-era Britain.

Two of Disraeli's novels in particular illustrate the contemporary vice of gambling. *The Young Duke* was the author's most extravagant foray into silver fork fiction. Its scene of ruinous gambling provides a somber contrast to the otherwise high-spirited social comedy found elsewhere in the novel. The young Duke of St. James engages in fashionable love affairs and expensive dissipations while avoiding the altruistic guidance of his Roman Catholic guardian, Mr. Dacre, and discrediting

himself with Dacre's beguiling daughter May. While Crockford's is mentioned several times in the narrative, the climactic gambling scene takes place in Brighton at the residence of the Baron de Berghem (Book IV, Chapters VII-VIII) where the combined forces of the Baron, Lord Castlefort, Lord Dice, and Temple Grace manage, in a prolonged session at cards, to win £100,000 off our dismayed hero. The young duke redeems himself and partially recoups his fortunes by giving a speech in favor of Catholic Emancipation in Parliament, thereby earning the hand of the now-willing May Dacre.

In *Henrietta Temple*, young Captain Ferdinand Armine is secretly in love with the heroine of the title, but is deeply in debt. In order to procure needed funds, Armine appeals to a Mr. Bond Sharpe, a money lender and gambling proprietor based on both Ephraim Bond (a Jewish operator of the Athenaeum club from whom Disraeli himself had borrowed money) and William Crockford. After Sharpe lends him £1,500, Armine meets Count Alcibiades de Mirabel, a character modeled on Disraeli's dandified friend and fellow Crockford's habitué, the Count d'Orsay. Following the dinner where the two meet, the party adjourns to an elegant gentleman's club on St. James's Street highly suggestive of Crockford's. Inviting Armine into the unnamed club, the Count makes a Dantean allusion to its identity as a gambling hell: "Come, we will make you an honorary member, mon cher Captain Armine . . . and do not say, '*Oh! lasciate ogni speranza,*' when you enter here."[26] After further developments in the love plot, Armine is arrested and taken to a "spunging house" (forced confinement preceding legal process for debt); but his new friend Count Mirabel comes to his rescue by winning £15,000 at Crockford's, thereby allowing him to finally marry Henrietta. In Disraeli's silver fork novel, then, we find both a visit to an unnamed gambling hell resembling Crockford's, and a hero who has his near-disastrous fortunes retrieved by the help of a friend at an establishment explicitly identified as the famous London club.

As a young man of means who "in the company of gambling sportsmen and dandies" had "lost his last sovereign" (NN *Redburn* 217), Melville's Harry Bolton is well-suited to the world of silver fork fiction. Redburn's first acquaintance with him in Liverpool demonstrates that Harry is naturally formed according to contemporary standards of genteel physical refinement: "He was one of those small, but perfectly formed beings, with curling hair, and silken muscles, who seem to have been born in cocoons. His complexion was a mantling brunette, feminine as a girl's; his feet were small; his hands were white; and his eyes were large, black, and womanly; and, poetry aside, his voice was as the sound of a harp" (NN *Redburn* 216). While the modern reader may be tempted to think that the androgynous-looking Bolton must be gay, this identification fails to take into consideration the contemporary cultural stereotype of the dandy.[27] Like Harry Bolton, the heroes of Bulwer's and Disraeli's early autobiographical fiction possess great personal beauty along with foppish tastes in dress, but they are nevertheless heterosexual in their behavior. That Harry Bolton is a contemporary type of England's young man of fashion is made evident from Harry's familiarity with the world of London high society: "Harry enlarged upon the fascinations of a London life; described the curricle he used to drive in Hyde Park; gave me the measurement of Madame Vestris' ankle; alluded to his first introduction at a club to the madcap Marquis of Waterford; told over the sums he had lost upon the turf on a Derby day; and made various but enigmatical allusions to a certain Lady Georgiana Theresa, the noble daughter of an anonymous earl" (NN *Redburn* 221).[28] In this résumé of a leisured existence, the realms of genteel public display, theater, club, turf, and aristocratic amours are all represented, although Redburn subsequently hints that Harry may have been "squandering his aristocratic narrations with a careless hand; and, perhaps, sometimes spending funds of reminiscences not his own" (NN *Redburn* 221).

Harry is an orphaned prodigal son from Bury St. Edmunds who has squandered his £5,000 inheritance by gambling and fast living. And as Redburn later realizes when he sees Harry's "incredible ignorance" (NN *Redburn* 253) of nautical matters as a sailor on the *Highlander,* Harry's claim of having been a midshipman or "guinea pig" in the East India service is just another fiction. What is certain is that Harry is a charming fraud and dandified spendthrift whose downfall has been gambling and extravagance. Harry's one last fling at the gambling table before shipping out to America is in keeping with the capricious temperament and irresponsible habits that have undermined his position in society, and forced him to seek a future in the New World. Unlike most silver fork spendthrifts, however, Harry's fate is radical dispossession from English society; and his distressed situation is later made worse by ridicule from the crew of the *Highlander,* who "put [him] down for a very equivocal character" (NN *Redburn* 254). As Redburn remarks, "I do not know exactly what they thought Harry had been; but they seemed unanimous in believing that, by abandoning his country, Harry had left more room for the gamblers. Jackson even asked him to lift up the lower hem of his trowsers, to test the color of his calves" (NN *Redburn* 254). In other words, Jackson is mockingly checking to see if Harry is a *blackleg* or sharper. Redburn had earlier revealed his familiarity with such jargon when he meditated on whether he could trust Harry Bolton before their visit to London: "What little money he has, he spends freely; he can not be a polite blackleg, for I am no pigeon to pluck; so *that* is out of the question;—perish such a

thought, concerning my own bosom friend!" (NN *Redburn* 223). Just as Redburn has good reason to doubt his friend's honesty with regard to his past, the sailors on the *Highlander* are aware that such a *déclassé* young dandy may be a cheat and a con artist.

Some of the same critics who have argued that the scene at Aladdin's Palace is unconvincing have asserted that the character of Harry Bolton is an imperfectly integrated addendum to the ending of *Redburn.* However, when viewed within the literary and historical contexts of the era, Harry emerges as a forceful characterization of a fallen young Englishman of taste and refinement— a dandy, in short—infected with a moral malady that Redburn is helpless to remedy, and that is inextricably mixed with Harry's considerable charm and personal gifts. Appearing two-thirds of the way through the novel, Harry is an English alter ego to the keenly sensitive, lonely, and downwardly mobile Redburn, and acts as an embodiment of Old World glamour and refinement tainted with moral corruption. As such Harry plays an important role in filling out the image of England presented in the novel and providing a dramatic foil to the more experienced and self-reliant Redburn on the return voyage to New York.[29]

CONCLUSIONS

Based on the available historical and literary evidence, we may conclude that the gentleman's club depicted in Chapter 46 of *Redburn* was largely modeled on Crockford's of London, while Harry Bolton's squandering of his last resources at Aladdin's Palace repeats a scene that was played out many times in the lives of upper-class Englishmen, and reflected in a specific class of contemporary novels of fashion that mirrored this milieu. Moreover, once we establish the links between *Redburn,* Crockford's, the contemporary dandy, and the world of silver fork fiction, it becomes evident that the character of Harry Bolton—who has struck some critics as an insufficiently developed or sexually ambiguous figure—is recognizable as a literary and cultural type, while Harry's ruination at Aladdin's Palace and subsequent self-imposed exile suggest the fate of some well-known dissolute dandies of the period—even though most bankrupt Regency and Early Victorian dandies, from Beau Brummell in 1816 to the Count d'Orsay in 1849, fled to nearby France, not America.

Yet there remains one more question to be answered. Given the fact that Aladdin's Palace is, with the relevant historical data in hand, a recognizable fictional adaptation of the most famous gambling hell of the era, why didn't any contemporary—and especially English—reviewers of *Redburn* point this out? In England, for example, the writer for the *Spectator* praised the novel for its "quiet naturalness," but took exception to the "episodical trip to London" because of its "melodramatic exaggeration." The writer for the London *Morning Herald* remarked of Redburn and Harry Bolton that "among the places [*sic*] of entertainment they frequent is one of those splendid gambling houses which are to be met with in London"; but the writer didn't provide any further details. On the other hand, the longest English review of the novel, appearing in *Blackwood's Edinburgh Magazine,* categorically asserted that an establishment like Aladdin's Palace "certainly exists nowhere (at least in London) but in our sailor-author's lively imagination." The writer went on to note: "We unhesitatingly qualify the whole of the London expedition as utter rubbish, intended evidently to be very fine and effective, but which totally misses the mark." In America, the reviewer for the New York *Albion* was also dismissive: "A flying visit to a London gambling-house, made by the sailor-boy under absurdly improbable circumstances, does but show the author's inability to paint scenes of this sort." The reviewer for the *Southern Literary Messenger* mentioned in passing "the melodramatic midnight trip to London," but claimed "no room" for further remark. Finally, the writer for *Holden's Dollar Magazine,* comparing the amount of fact and fiction evident in the narrative, noted that "there are a few palpable inventions—the story of the London Hell for instance—that do not give us a very exalted idea of Mr. Melville's imaginative capacities." Such is the failure of contemporary reviewers to acknowledge the validity of Melville's depiction of the London gambling milieu in *Redburn.*[30]

But, of course, *Redburn* was published in England and America in the fall of 1849, more than a decade after Crockford's heyday and five years following its final demise, after which time much London gambling had been curtailed in reaction to the parliamentary crackdown in 1844. Then, too, it is reasonable to assume that none of the reviewers quoted above had ever been to Crockford's or witnessed the epidemic of upper-class London gambling that peaked in the 1820s and 1830s, and dropped significantly by the later 1840s. (The American reviewers would obviously have been at a special disadvantage here.) Consequently, the failure of contemporary reviewers to identify the background of Redburn's mysterious night in London need not be a stumbling block for a historical understanding of the episode today.

Redburn's "Mysterious Night in London" has been frequently misunderstood, but when we are apprised of the particular upper-class world of fashionable vice and opulent excess it faithfully mirrors, we gain a deeper appreciation of its artistic merits. That Melville had no direct personal experience of Crockford's or its imitators did not keep him from creating a historically accurate fictional likeness, or from dramatizing an upper-class young man's terminal losses at the hazard table. Harry Bolton's disastrous experience at Aladdin's Palace represents the young dandy's final act of dispossession from his homeland, and informs us of the tainted world of privilege he is leaving in order to seek his fortunes in democratic America. The fact that we see Harry's fall from grace through the naive and puritanical eyes of Redburn adds a special note of poignancy to this event as another of the many bitter lessons that Melville's narrator must absorb, completing the destruction of his illusions about the storied romance of the Old World.

Notes

1. Hershel Parker, *Herman Melville: A Biography: Volume I, 1819-1850* (Baltimore: Johns Hopkins University Press, 1996), 642; Robert K. Martin, *Hero, Captain, and Stranger: Male Friendship, Social Critique, and Literary Form in the Sea Novels of Herman Melville* (Chapel Hill: University of North Carolina Press, 1986), 50-51.

2. Among earlier critics, Newton Arvin noted that the scene at Aladdin's Palace was "the one chapter of *Redburn* in which Melville seems to be indulging in deliberate mystification. . . . For the rest, though the chapter is not without a genuine vein of dreamlike intensity, it is vitiated as a whole by the kind of unnaturalness into which Melville so easily fell with such themes"; see *Herman Melville* (William Sloane Associates, 1950), 105, 106. So, too, for Ronald Mason, "The fanciful and unconvincing London episode belongs to the early stages of Redburn's acquaintanceship with Harry—a melodramatic and rather confused picture of what Melville presumably thought was a typical scene of night-life among the well-to-do"; see *The Spirit Above the Dust: A Study of Herman Melville* (London: John Lehmann, 1951), 76. In a more positive evaluation of the scene, William B. Dillingham observes: "The description of Aladdin's Palace constitutes a highly imaginative and elaborate metaphor for Harry Bolton. . . . He does not know what it is, but Redburn is sure that there is something badly wrong with Harry much as there seems to be some secret evil lying below the surface of Aladdin's Palace"; see *An Artist in the Rigging: The Early Work of Herman Melville* (Athens: University of Georgia Press, 1972), 43, 44.

3. James H. Justice gives a favorable judgment of the episode of *Redburn* while asserting that Aladdin's Palace is a male brothel: "Nominally a gentlemen's gambling club, the quarters are described in terms that make gambling one of the lesser iniquities. The club's exteriors glow with a purple light, and its interiors, a triumph of stylistic indirection, suggest that 'No. 40' is a male bordello as well as a gambling den"; see "*Redburn*

and *White-Jacket*: Society and Sexuality in the Narratives of 1849," in *Herman Melville: Reassessments*, ed. A. Robert Lee (Totowa, NJ: Barnes & Noble, 1984), 51. Other critics who allude, in passing, to Aladdin's Palace as a male brothel include Michael Paul Rogin, *Subversive Genealogy: The Politics and Art of Herman Melville* (Berkeley: University of California Press, 1985), 70; Nicholas K. Bromell, *By the Sweat of the Brow: Literature and Labor in Antebellum America* (Chicago: University of Chicago Press, 1993), 76; Christopher Sten, *The Weaver God, He Weaves: Melville and the Poetics of the Novel* (Kent, OH: Kent State University Press, 1996), 108; and Elizabeth Hardwick, *Herman Melville* (New York: Viking, 2000), 29.

4. On the impossibility of Melville traveling to London in August 1839, see William H. Gilman, *Melville's Early Life and* Redburn (New York: New York University Press, 1951), 196-97; on the resemblances between Aladdin's Palace and the second of the two "Fragments," see 194-96; on the influence of Romantic Orientalism evident in the latter, see 112-20. On "The Gambler's Fate," see Parker, 643.

5. For an informative contemporary overview of London gambling, see the three-part article, "Gaming, Gaming-Houses, and Gamesters," in *Bentley's Miscellany* XVIII (1845): 333-40, 489-97, 593-600 (quote on p. 491); see also the continuation of the series in XIX (1846): 44-51, 127-33, 276-81, 399-403. For a wide-ranging anecdotal survey of the history of gambling through the mid-nineteenth century, see Andrew Steinmetz, *The Gaming Table: Its Votaries and Victims, in all Times and Countries, Especially in England and France*, 2 vols. (1870; rpt., Montclair, NJ: Patterson Smith, 1969), http://www.etext.lib.virginia.edu/toc/modeng; see especially Vol. 1, Ch. 6, "The Rise and Progress of Modern Gambling in England," and Vol. 2, Ch. 6, "The Gaming Clubs." For background information on contemporary London clubs, see John Timbs, *Club Life of London*, 2 vols. (London: Richard Bentley, 1866). A useful recent survey of upper-class English social life in the late eighteenth and early nineteenth centuries is Venetia Murray, *High Society: A Social History of the Regency Period, 1788-1830* (New York: Viking, 1998). (Murray [66] notes that the British pound has appreciated about fifty times since the early nineteenth century.)

6. "Crockford and Crockford's," in *Bentley's Miscellany* XVII (1845): 142-55, 251-64; hereafter cited as "Crockford and Crockford's." See also [James Grant], *The Great Metropolis*, 2 vols. (New York: Sanders and Otley, 1837), 1:159-91 (hereafter

cited as Grant); John Raymond, ed., *The Reminiscences and Recollections of Captain Gronow* (New York: Viking, 1964), 255-59; and John L. Bradley, ed., *Rogue's Progress: The Autobiography of "Lord Chief Baron" Nicholson* (Boston: Houghton Mifflin, 1965), Ch. 7. (The reference to Crockford's as "leviathan hell" is on p. 45.) For twentieth-century studies of Crockford and his club, see Arthur Lee Humphreys, *Crockford's; or the Goddess of Chance in St. James's Street, 1828-1844* (London: Hutchinson, 1953); and Henry Blyth, *Hell and Hazard; or William Crockford versus the Gentlemen of England* (Chicago: Henry Regnery, 1970).

7. For more on Crockford's clientele, see Humphreys, Chs. 4-14, and Blyth, Ch. 5.

8. On the latter stages of Crockford's career, see Blyth, Chs. 6 and 7.

9. [Anonymous], *Crockford's, or Life in the West,* 2 vols. (New York: J. & J. Harper, 1828), 2:181.

10. Raymond, 256. For the articles on London gambling in *Bentley's Miscellany,* see the references in notes 5 and 6 above. For mention of Crockford's in Victorian diarists, see Humphreys, *passim.*

11. *Redburn: His First Voyage,* ed. Harrison Hayford, Hershel Parker and G. Thomas Tanselle (Evanston and Chicago: Northwestern University Press and The Newberry Library, 1969), 227; hereafter cited as NN *Redburn.*

12. Louis J. Jennings, ed., *The Crocker Papers: The Correspondence and Diaries of the Late Right Honourable John Wilson Crocker, L.L.D., F.R.S.,* 3 vols. (2nd ed., rev., London: John Murray, 1885), 1:404.

13. Timbs, 1:283.

14. Blyth, 106-7.

15. Prince Paul Anton Esterhazy von Galantha (1786-1866) first arrived in England as Austrian ambassador in 1815, and finally departed in 1842. On Prince Esterhazy's membership at Crockford's, see Raymond, 258. Redburn's attempt to appear "like a young Prince Esterhazy" does not imply that the prince was young at this time but that Redburn wants to look like a younger version of the elegant prince.

16. See Harold Beaver's remarks in his "Introduction" to *Redburn,* ed. Harold Beaver (New York: Penguin, 1976), 25. On the scene's twisted décor, see also Justus, 51. On the parallels with Spenser's Bower of Bliss, see Mina Herman Maltz, "Aladdin's Palace and the Bower of Bliss: Melville and

Spenser," *Theoria* (University of Natal, South Africa) 63 (1984): 55-66.

17. Steinmetz, 2:187.

18. "Gaming, Gaming-Houses, and Gamesters," *Bentley's Miscellany,* XVIII, 593.

19. For an informed distinction of fact from fantasy in these erotic images, see Gilman, 355 n.31. Gilman claims that the images "are further evidence that Melville could not confine himself to strict realism indefinitely" (224). For Beaver, on the other hand, they are a "hoax" (*Redburn,* ed. Beaver, 437).

20. On the development of the term and concept of "pornography" in the mid-nineteenth century, see Walter Kendrick, *The Secret Museum: Pornography in Modern Culture* (1987; Berkeley: University of California Press, 1996), Chs. 1-4. A useful survey of erotic art at Pompeii is Antonio Varone, *Eroticism in Pompeii,* trans. Maureen Fant (Los Angeles: J. Paul Getty Museum, 2001); on p. 12, Varone notes that a bakery adjoining the House of Pansa featured an phallic bas relief. Willard Thorp traced the reference to the house of Pansa in *Redburn* to the *Penny Cyclopaedia* entries on "Atrium" and "House" (NN *Redburn* 329). On Tiberius's sexual practices on the island of Capri, see Suetonius, *The Twelve Caesars,* trans. Robert Graves (New York: Penguin, 1979), 135-36.

21. Rev. of John Heneage Jesse, *George Selwyn and his Contemporaries; with Memoirs and Notes,* in *Edinburgh Review* LXXX (July 1844): 1-42. The relevant passage is on p. 36.

22. Thomas Philbrick, "Melville's 'Best Authorities'," *Nineteenth-Century Fiction* 15 (1960): 171-79. See also Parker, 652-53.

23. Ellen Moers, *The Dandy: Brummell to Beerbohm* (New York: Viking, 1960), 52-53. See also Matthew Whiting Rosa, *The Silver Fork School: Novels of Fashion Preceding "Vanity Fair"* (New York: Columbia University Press, 1936).

24. Melville knew Bulwer's silver fork fiction well enough to allude to *Pelham* in *White-Jacket* (Chs. 4 and 6). The privileged milieu of Pierre Glendinning in *Pierre* also resembles that of several of Disraeli's heroes. See *Pierre; or, The Ambiguities,* ed. Henry A. Murray (New York: Hendricks House, 1949), xxiv, xli, and lxvii-lxviii.

25. Alison Adburgham, *Silver Fork Society: Fashionable Life and Literature from 1814 to 1840* (London: Constable, 1983), 110.

26. *Henrietta Temple: A Love Story* (New York: Knopf, 1934), 370.

27. For the theory that Harry Bolton is homosexual, see Martin, 51-54. See also Bromell, 69-79.

28. On the famously shapely legs of the Italian actress and dancer Madame Vestris (born Lucy Bartolozzi), see Murray, 223. The "madcap" Marquis of Waterford was a member of Crockford's; see Humphreys, Ch. 5.

29. Noting that Melville enlarged his allegedly completed manuscript at the end of June 1849, Parker writes dismissively: "The best guess as to how he enlarged the manuscript is that he added the character of the specious dandy Harry Bolton, after having first gotten Redburn safely back to New York City without his dubious companionship" (642). Asserting Melville's inability to deal candidly with homosexual themes, Martin claims that Harry Bolton's alleged weakness as a character "seems to coincide with the author's artistic (and perhaps personal) difficulty" (52). In an early article that clarified Melville's double point of view in the novel (older narrator and younger subject), Merlin Bowen remarked: "Bolton remains to the end an unconvincing and static figure, while Redburn's further progress is to be measured only in a wider, and essentially undramatic, extension of his sympathies" ("*Redburn* and the Angle of Vision," *Modern Philology* 52 [1954], 108). For a more favorable discussion of Harry Bolton's role in the novel as a corrupt European counterpart to Redburn's democratic man, see Nicholas Canaday, Jr., "Harry Bolton and Redburn: The Old World and the New," in *Essays in Honor of Esmond Linsworth Marilla,* ed. Thomas Austin Kirby and William John Olive (Baton Rouge: Louisiana State University Press, 1970), 291-98. See also Sten, 107-11.

30. Brian Higgins and Hershel Parker, eds., *Herman Melville: The Contemporary Reviews* (New York: Cambridge University Press, 1995), 258, 261, 269, 270, 282, 287, 289. See NN *Redburn* 333, for attributions of some of these reviews.

GAMBLING IN BRITISH LITERATURE

J. Jeffrey Franklin (essay date winter 1994)

SOURCE: Franklin, J. Jeffrey. "The Victorian Discourse of Gambling: Speculations on *Middlemarch* and *The Duke's Children.*" *ELH* 61, no. 4 (winter 1994): 899-921.

[*In the following essay, Franklin asserts that an analysis of the treatment of gambling in such nineteenth-century novels as George Eliot's* Middlemarch *and An-*

thony Trollope's The Duke's Children *reveals a central concern about changing values that underlies Victorian debates over money, marriage, and work.*]

> When I was young, people called me a gambler. As the scale of my operations increased I became known as a speculator. Now I am called a banker. But I have been doing the same thing all the time.
>
> —Sir Earnest Cassel, Banker to Edward VII[1]

> At a time when the poor were existing on wages that could be counted in shillings per week rather than pounds, and women could be employed at a penny an hour in the Welsh coal-mines, Harry Hastings lost more than one hundred thousand pounds in the two-and-a-half minutes in which it took to run the Derby.
>
> —Henry Blyth, *Hell and Hazard*[2]

I

The discourse of money is so ubiquitous in the British Victorian novel that any analysis of it runs the risk, on the one hand, of becoming trivial and, on the other hand, of becoming embroiled in the broadest and most pressing issues of the nineteenth century. One such issue that cannot be avoided is the bourgeois revolution, the widely noted social paradigm shift from the predominantly aristocratic, status-based ideologies of the eighteenth century to the Whig ideologies of commerce and work that came to dominate the nineteenth century.[3] Thus it may not be surprising that the readings of George Eliot's *Middlemarch* and Anthony Trollope's *The Duke's Children* offered here find the discourse of money to be a primary vehicle for the progressive or liberal ideologies of the ascending middle class. However, I move beyond this general, speculative level toward more specific inquiries: exactly how is money represented in these novels, and how might those representations be read in relation to the ways in which subjects and social institutions were constructed and served? The analysis concentrates on the figure of gambling as a component of the discourse of money, and gambling is shown to link together all other components within that discourse. The figure of gambling is used to trace connections at a broader level between the discourse of money and two other Victorian discourses: marriage and work. Gambling is analyzed as that which binds together and problematizes this central trinity of Victorian concerns.

Almost every character in novels such as *Middlemarch* and *The Duke's Children* is connected to other characters by specified and publicly observed monetary relations. In *Middlemarch,* for example, Fred Vincy is connected to his miserly uncle Featherstone by inheritance; Rosamond Vincy's marriage to Dr. Lydgate comes to be dominated by the issue of debt; Dorothea Brooke's relation to Lydgate, as to Reverend Farebrother, is one of charity; the banker Bulstrode is bound to the dispu-

table character Raffles (and to his own past deeds) by ill-gotten money and blackmail. While money is by no means the only, and often not the primary, determinant of relationships in Victorian fiction, it is the primary form that social evaluations of relationships assume. So while Dorothea's scandalous second marriage to Will Ladislaw is *not* about money, it is evaluated by Middlemarch society in terms of money. The same may be said of Frank Tregear's marriage to Lady Mary Palliser in *The Duke's Children* (although his motives are arguably more mixed). While Lydgate's motive for twice standing by Bulstrode when the rest of Middlemarch has turned against him is not primarily pecuniary, it is socially evaluated in terms of money, specifically bribery.

Money, then, is the public yardstick of private relationship; part of the ideological work of the discourse of money was to make the private public.[4] The danger of gambling, whether with money or relationships, is that it can transpose private loss or gain into the public domain of scandal: on being told by his son Silverbridge that his gambling is "nothing to speak of," the Duke of Omnium replies, "Nothing to speak of is so apt to grow into that which has to be spoken of."[5] The very same sort of risks are shown in Victorian fiction to exist in relation to marriage, which never is considered entirely apart from issues of money. Indeed, the discourse of money and the discourse of marriage are alike in that they each operate to regulate romantic desires that were perceived as dangerous. Consider for example the way that the issue of money moderates the matrimonial intentions of Frank Tregear and Lady Mabel Grex in *The Duke's Children* or Fred Vincy and Mary Garth in *Middlemarch*. In particular, I will argue that the figure of gambling comes to function in Victorian fiction as a medium of expression for human desire, such that many relationships in novels like *Middlemarch* and *The Duke's Children* are shown to teeter between the gamble of romance and the romance of gambling.

The pervasiveness of the discourse of money in Victorian fiction and in Victorian society may in part be a result of the heterogeneity of money. Money comes and goes in many forms, and the forms of monetary relationship "diversified" significantly during the first half of the nineteenth century, paralleling the following well-known trends: 1) the maturation of the banking profession, as indicated by the rise in the number of incorporations and the increased sophistication of financing; 2) the institutionalization of the stock exchange in its current form and the popularization of financial speculation, as exemplified by the "Railway Mania" of the 1840s; 3) the professionalization of gambling, as represented by the rise to prominence of gentlemen's "gambling hells," the commercialization of horse racing, the marked increase in both on-track (upper-class) and off-track (lower-class) betting, and, in general, the replacement of the gentlemanly wager by the professional bookmaker; and, 4) the general increase in the rate of financial circulation, particularly through speculation and gambling, due to advances in transportation and communication technology.[6] Victorian fiction thoroughly records and responds to such developments as these, just as it shapes the discourses that constituted them. As a result, wealth is circulated in Victorian novels— gained, earned, lost or given—through at least nine different social forms: inheritance and dispossession; marriage; individual labor; charity; financial speculation; debt; bankruptcy (generally as an outcome of speculation, debt or gambling); foul play, particularly bribery and blackmail; and, not the least among these, gambling.

Different forms of money come with different valuations in Victorian novels. It can be argued that one of the primary social functions of the discourse of money is to mediate between various forms of wealth, between, in effect, "good" money and "bad" money. The "bad" forms—among which gambling is exemplary—are designated as such in relation to identifiable ideological interests. One trademark of the ascending nineteenth-century middle-class ideology was (as it still is) the universalization of a definition of culture as that which transcends social difference, politics and class.[7] The advantage of erasing class in particular as a meaningful distinction was twofold: it eased upward social mobility for the middle classes by replacing aristocratic status boundaries with financial, educational or meritocratic standards of gentlemanliness (as exemplified by Frank Tregear and Mr. Boncassen in *The Duke's Children* and, parodically, the Veneerings and the Podsnaps in Dickens's *Our Mutual Friend*); and, 2) it applied the socially controlling—not to mention profitable— middle-class values of hard work and self-denial to the lower classes, while at the same time obscuring historical inequalities by offering the ideal of "equality" as compensation for disruptive social changes. Two observations follow from this. First, in order to be effective, *embourgeiosement* had to operate bi-directionally on both the upper and the lower classes. It is for this reason that the aristocratic figure of the gentleman and its counterpart, the figure of the idle poor, are both so problematic in Victorian fiction. Victorian novels strive to mediate these two figures, and the distinction between good money and bad money is used for this purpose. Secondly, the discourse of work was pivotal in distinguishing good from bad, in character as in money. Gambling, which is one of the terms most frequently opposed to work, served particularly as a marker of this distinction. I will argue that it is within the discourse of gambling that the issues of monetary value and personal worth become enmeshed. More generally, the image of financial speculation comes to be associated disturbingly with moral and metaphysical speculations. As a result, value—as both the foundation of economic ex-

change and the estimation of individual character— threatens to be revealed as depending precariously on nothing but human desire.

II

> Very good indeed, my Lord Duke; very good indeed! Ha, ha, ha!—all horses have heads and all have tails! Heads and Tails.
>
> —Major Tifto, *The Duke's Children*

It was commonplace to observe, prior to the Victorian era, that gambling brought different classes together at race tracks, gambling establishments, and other venues of popular entertainment. By the time of *The Duke's Children,* one of the chief dangers of gambling was considered to be its proximity to the lower classes. For example, while Silverbridge believes that he can avoid "the fouls and rascals" who bet along side of the lords at the Derby, he does mix with them and does bet on the horse in which he owns a "share" with Major Tifto, eventually "plunging" for a loss of 70,000 pounds (*DC*, 147). (This is not a ruinous amount to the Duke, but it is an amount that "has to be spoken of," and widely.) Trollope did not invent this sort of tale, since not a few lords and knights ended up in the tabloids after losing their fortunes either at "gambling hells," such as that run by William Crockford, or at the track, whether fairly or as a result of Tifto's style of "fixing."[8] (Trollope himself was known to be a gambler and to suffer debts for it.) Silverbridge's fraternization with Tifto, and Tifto's with a yet lower class of rascal, Captain Green, is portrayed by Trollope as a primary cause for Silverbridge's fall. The critical question is whether Tifto is a gentleman, and the negative answer the question receives is fundamental to the plot of money in this novel.

Furthermore, Trollope uses the story of Lord Grex's gambling to illustrate the threat that gambling poses by bringing together the high and the low. The threat is realized in the character of Lady Mabel Grex, who tragically is compromised by her father's gambling. Lady Mabel expresses the question of gambling again in terms of the figure of the gentleman:

> "Of all things men do this is the worst. A man who would think himself disgraced for ever if he accepted a present of money will not scruple to use all his wits to rob his friend of everything that he has by studying the run of cards or by watching the paces of some brutes of horses! And they consider themselves to be fine gentlemen! A real gentleman should never want the money out of another man's pocket;—should never think of money at all."
>
> (*DC*, 159)

Lady Mabel might have been a spokesperson for the middle-class movements that had been attempting to "reform" the track against unyielding aristocratic opposition since the end of the eighteenth century: their argument was that one who gambles for money is not only not a gentleman, but is equal to a pick-pocket.[9]

Perhaps even more threatening than the risk of the high being made low, however, was the risk of the low rising to unnatural heights. Gambling, like all forms of speculation, was seen as threatening "natural" social boundaries by facilitating rapid social mobility. One commentator noted as early as 1700 that the "greatest scoundrel of the town, with his money in his pockets, shall take his turn before the best duke or peer in the land, if the cards are on his side."[10] So Trollope notes that Major Tifto, through horse-trading and track-betting canniness, can join the Beargarden, the preeminent private gentlemen's club.

Throughout nineteenth-century fiction, gambling is linked not only with undesirable social mobility but also more generally with dangerous social and financial upheaval. Indeed, one reason for the pervasiveness of the discourse of gambling, and for the scapegoating of gambling, is that the Victorian era was a time of economic panics and of revolution (however tightly controlled) in social institutions. Serious financial crises occurred in 1825 and 1836, spanning the period in which *Middlemarch* is set and in which the second Reform Act of 1832 was signed.[11] Sixty country banks, such as Bulstrode's in Middlemarch, failed in 1825-26. 1845 saw the "Railway Mania" speculation schemes—"the most wonderful era of gambling in modern times"—and the subsequent crisis when the shares collapsed in 1847.[12] There was another financial crisis in 1857, a money-market crash in 1866 and a massive panic in 1873 (the year after *Middlemarch* was published) followed by a sustained depression. Lord and Lady Grex in *The Duke's Children* and the Lydgates in *Middlemarch* both face a bankruptcy, which also is linked with gambling.[13] In short, "financial speculation became the major spectre of economic disorder."[14] The obvious similarities between stockbroking and gambling increased general anxiety about market stability, and those in the commercial world concerned with respectability strove to maintain a precarious distinction between the two.[15] Significant in this regard was the passage of the Limited Liability act of 1855, which broke one of the last barriers limiting corporate expansion. Stock speculation, which previously had been reserved for those wealthy enough to afford the generally high price of entry and the risks of unlimited liability, was suddenly opened to a new class of speculators. Dramatic economic growth followed; hundreds of new companies were "floated," some of which sailed into prosperity, but many of which sank, taking investors down with them. As one critical member of Parliament noted, the new law "enable[d] persons to embark in trade with a limited chance of loss, but with an unlimited chance for gain. That was a direct encourage-

ment to a system of vicious and improvident speculation. . . ."[16] Barbara Weiss summarizes: "With the advent of corporate capitalism, economic life turned once and for all from a simple endeavor for a livelihood to quest for the highest possible return for investment."[17] Although one may be skeptical that a time of "simple endeavor for livelihood" ever existed, there is no doubt that limited liability brought wealth to certain creditors and brokers (represented with searing irony by Fledgeby in *Our Mutual Friend*), infused the discourse of money with a new sense of limitless opportunity, and accelerated market fluctuation and social mobility.

In general, then, it is clear that at least by the mid nineteenth century the discourses of gambling and of finance capitalism had fully penetrated each other. As the speculative dangers of finance were demonstrated by events, the need increased to rhetorically distance finance capitalism from gambling. Further, gambling posed a paradoxical dilemma for the middle classes: it was associated with the market economy by which middle-class upward mobility was effected, while at the same time it represented a fearful spectre of an economy out of control and of a lower class threatening revolt.

III

The people of Middlemarch variously are suspicious, resentful and appreciative of Mr. Bulstrode's mixture of finance capitalism and puritanical piety, and the issue of gambling consistently plays a crucial role in these judgments. For example, the old miser Featherstone, representing the "landed" interests of aristocratic ideology, is disdainful and jealous of Bulstrode's "spekilations."[18] This issue also arises in a discussion of Dr. Lydgate's ambitions for helping humanity through research, medical reform, and the opening of a new infectious disease hospital, sponsored by Bulstrode. The reader is told that he

> did not mean to imitate those philanthropic models who make a profit out of poisonous pickles to support themselves while they are exposing adulterations, or hold shares in a gambling-hell that they may have leisure to represent the cause of public morality.
>
> (*M*, 145)

It is part of George Eliot's irony that neither Lydgate nor the reader will know for five hundred pages that this is a chillingly accurate description of Bulstrode, who, we discover, "won his fortune" through a speculative marriage and foul play and is attempting to absolve himself through a combination of hospital charity and self-righteous condemnations of others' lack of religious zeal (*M*, 705).[19] It is doubly ironic, then, that the hand of fate brings Bulstrode's past back to haunt him in the form of a man who appropriately is named Raffles and who is characterized by Caleb Garth as looking like "one of those men one sees about after the races" (*M*,

507). As the narrator confides to the reader, "Destiny stands by sarcastic with our dramatis personae folded in her hand" (*M*, 95)—folded like manuscript pages, principally, but also, perhaps, like a hand of cards.

Bulstrode's downfall begins with Raffles's appearance at the very moment in the novel when he is poised to breach the barrier between landed gentry and monied townie by inhabiting Stone Court, the estate of the deceased Featherstone. Similarly, Fred Vincy, the son of a manufacturer, is initially thwarted from crossing the same barrier into the same estate for the same reason: Fred gambles. What is worse, he does so with the air of a gentleman; when he accepts money from Featherstone with feigned diffidence, he is told: "You take money like a lord; I suppose you lose it like one" (*M*, 133). Indeed he does, and he needs Featherstone's money to pay debts incurred from having done so. He is understood by Middlemarch society to be one of those young men who is "addicted to pleasure" (*M*, 223). He plays billiards for money, he makes a very "unlucky" horse trade (*M*, 106), and he publicly speculates on his expected inheritance from Featherstone, perhaps in order to secure loans. His speculations are contagious; out of trust and goodness, Caleb Garth "takes a chance" on Fred by co-signing a loan note on which Fred defaults. Fred is unable to repay after he is dispossessed, "purely by the favour of Providence in the shape of an old gentleman's caprice" (*M*, 333). It is thus that the discourse of gambling thoroughly infects the discourses of inheritance and money-lending.

The same is true for the discourse of marriage. While the endings of Victorian novels typically suggest that marriage is a natural fruition, matrimony is represented at the same time as an extremely risky gamble. At least since Marianne Dashwood's insistence to her sister that marriage not be a "commercial exchange" (her sister Elinor responds, "But wealth has much to do with it"), the economics of marriage had been central to Victorian fiction.[20] Seventy years after *Sense and Sensibility, The Duke's Children* shows marriage as an honor-regulated, gossip- and money-based economy in which some, such as Frank Tregear, are long-shot winners and some, such as Lady Mabel Grex, are ruined. References to gambling, speculation and fate suffuse the discourse of marriage in both *The Duke's Children* and *Middlemarch*. Marriage repeatedly is discussed in terms of an "unfortunate lot" or of "winning" a "fortunate match" ("fortune" being used alternately to mean wealth and fate). For instance, Lady Mabel's pursuit of Lord Silverbridge frequently is cast in terms of a "sport" or "game," paralleling the novel's horse racing and fox hunting themes. She describes Silverbridge as her "prey," but, in the course of the novel, she instead is figured as his horse. She is described as a "horse of another colour" in relation to Lady Mary Palliser, and we are told that in almost snaring Silverbridge the "cup had come within the reach of her fingers," but that, like Silverbridge's thoroughbred "Prime Minister," she failed to place because "she had dallied with her fortune" (*DC*, 376, 432). She later explains her failure to Tregear by saying: "I craned at the first fence . . ." (*DC*, 611). Similar imagery appears in *Middlemarch* when Fred Vincy's "unlucky" horse "Diamond" lames itself and, in the process, "just miss[es] killing the groom" (*M*, 235). The reader is told that there "was no more redress for this than for the discovery of bad temper after marriage" (*M*, 235).

Indeed it is the potential for the discovery of "bad temper after marriage" that makes marriage truly chancy. The role of chance in making marriages is evidenced from the outset by the fate-like role that chance meetings play (for example, Tregear's and Lady Mary Palliser's meeting in Rome, or the repeated accidental meetings of Dorothea and Will Ladislaw in *Middlemarch*, the second of which is also in Rome). But Dorothea is determined to depend neither on fate nor custom. Concerning her prospects, the reader is told (with no small amount of bitter irony), "Certainly such [unfeminine and over-arduous] elements of a marriageable girl tended to interfere with her lot and hinder it from being decided according to custom, by good looks, vanity, and merely canine affection" (*M*, 10).

While a bad marriage, such as Lydgate's to Rosamond Vincy, may lead to gambling, drugs, and a generally "narrowed lot" (*M*, 648, 775), a good marriage operates within Victorian discourse as that which can save one from such evils. The Duke of Omnium's pressure on Silverbridge to marry clearly is an attempt to redirect the son's passions from gambling, hunting and club-going to a more domestic outlet. Indeed, that is the very effect that even the contemplation of marriage to Isabel Boncassen seems to have on Silverbridge:

> When she had told him what she would do for him to make his home happy [in addition to what he clearly has imagined], it had seemed to him that all other delights must fade away from him for ever. How odious were Tifto and his racehorses, how unmeaning the noise of his club.
>
> (*DC*, 543)

The prospect of marriage to a good woman, Mary Garth, has a similar effect on Fred Vincy. It is this prospect that leads him—albeit with periodic backsliding—away not only from billiards but also from gentlemanly pretensions.

What is it, then, that makes a marriage good? What permits certain Victorian romances to be "true" while others are shown to be false? One answer seems to be that marriage requires a disillusionment about romance itself, a surrendering of the belief that romance, like the

Fate or Destiny of the gambler, magically will provide one with an ideal mate. This sort of debunking, which often is represented with humor, seems in turn to require an understanding between partners of each other's individuality and, most importantly, of one's own limitations and desires. The good (generally middle-class or working-class) couplings in Victorian fiction—such as Mary Garth and Fred Vincy, or perhaps even Silverbridge and Isabel Boncassen—typically are brought to fruition through a trial, a passage of time, or as in the case of Fred and Silverbridge, a brush with gambling. As a result, these couples are represented as being able to present themselves, and to take each other, at "face value," or, as Isabel Boncassen says several times, "as good as gold" (*DC*, 568).[21]

Within the Victorian discourse of marriage, then, the falsity of romance, as in the case of Dorothea or Lydgate or Mabel Grex, arises from a dual mis-valuation. It involves an over-valuing of the other, which is tantamount to a negation of the intended partner through self-projection, and an under-valuing or negation of one's self. Consider the way in which Lydgate's fall into gambling is described:

> But just as he had tried opium, so his thoughts now began to turn upon gambling—not with appetite for its excitement, but with a sort of *wistful inward gaze* after that *easy way* of getting money which implied no asking and brought no responsibility.
>
> (*M*, 648; emphases added)

Lydgate is not the stereotypical figure of the rabidly addicted gambler; his "wistful inward gaze" is toward the self. He hungers to recapture the selfhood he has surrendered in marrying Rosamond, but he cannot do so within the discourse of the novel through gambling's "easy" abnegation of responsibility. Dorothea must go through the self-denial of Casaubon before she is finally able to discover "her passion to herself" in her desire for Will Ladislaw and thus reunite her severed subjectivity (*M*, 762-63). According to this discourse, as represented in the second half of the nineteenth century, the risk of marriage is of not knowing one's own desires until it is too late. One cannot take the gamble out of marriage through either the romance of gambling or the gamble of romance, but only by being equal to one's self and, as a result, to one's partner.

What is required, then, in the discourse of marriage, as in the discourse of money, is an equality of value. The question noted earlier—"Is Frank Tregear a gentleman?"—and the figure of the gentleman itself raise this very question about value. Is Tregear "worthy" of Lady Mary? Is Isabel Boncassen, a now wealthy American of working class stock, worthy of Silverbridge?[22] Tregear has the status (if somewhat equivocally) but not the money; Isabel has the money but not the status. Is money equal to status? Certainly not, according to Lady Mary's father, the Duke of Omnium, for whom "maintenance of the aristocracy of the country was second only in importance to maintenance of the Crown" (*DC*, 174). However, status without money will not suffice either. When Mr. Boncassen points out that "men generally like to marry their equals," Silverbridge responds: "People don't always know who are their equals" (*DC*, 424). This is the dilemma of value.

The brilliance of *The Duke's Children*—and the way in which the novel may subvert its dominant discourses—is that the ongoing debate about worthiness for marriage is counterpointed by the debate, primarily in the Duke's mind, about social equality:

> As by the spread of education and increase of general well-being every proletaire was brought nearer to a Duke, so by such action would the Duke be brought nearer to a proletaire. Such drawing-nearer of the classes was the object to which all this man's political action tended. And yet it was a dreadful thing to him that his own daughter should desire to marry a man so much beneath her own rank and fortune as Frank Tregear.
>
> (*DC*, 175)

The irony is that it is not the Duke but Tregear, the conservative, who fears equality most. Tregear fears that the Duke's liberal party will be swayed too far by its radical wing toward the dangers of equality represented in the British mind of the time by the French Revolution. Speaking of that subject to Silverbridge, Tregear says:

> "There were a lot of honest men who thought they could do a deal of good by making everybody equal. A good many were made equal by having their heads cut off. . . . [A]s he [Tregear's Liberal opponent running for Parliament] hasn't thought much about anything, he is quite willing to lend a hand to communism, radicalism, socialism, chopping people's heads off, or anything else."
>
> (*DC*, 439)

Two points are clear. First, social equality—like the too easy social mobility that gambling threatens, and like the illusion of an easy marriage that romance promises—is dangerous and must be regulated. Second, a great deal of ambivalence and mystification about the origins of value is taking place here. The contradiction between the Duke's public practice and private policy on the worth of equality is mirrored, and therefore reversed, by the contradiction between Tregear's private practice (in thinking himself worthy of Lady Mary) and public policy on the same issue.

IV

Money is bad, then, when it has too easy an origin, whether that origin be market speculation, a speculative marriage, debt, bribery, blackmail or gambling itself.

The discourse of money shared by *Middlemarch* and *The Duke's Children* strives to keep money pure, honorable, good. In *Middlemarch,* for example, Dorothea's and Lydgate's crusade to save Farebrother from his one moral shortcoming, playing whist for money, is expressed as "a strong desire to rescue him from his chance-gotten money" (*M,* 481). In *The Duke's Children,* the Duke impresses on Gerald that money "is a commodity of which you are bound to see that the source is not only clean but noble" (*DC,* 517). One gets the sense here, and elsewhere in Victorian fiction, that money has been internalized as though it were something that circulates *through* human beings. Indeed, it nearly is described as such in Lydgate's remembrance (in free-indirect discourse) of the moment in childhood when he "chanced" to open a "cyclopaedia" to a description of the heart's valves (which one is tempted to read as "heart values") and recognized his desire to become a doctor:

> He had no more thought of representing to himself how his blood circulated than how paper served instead of gold. But the moment of vocation had come, and before he got down from his chair the world was made new to him by a presentiment of endless processes filling the vast spaces planked out of his sight by the wordy ignorance which he had supposed to be knowledge.
>
> (*M,* 142)

Historically, the world of Victorian England had indeed been "made new" by a spreading "presentiment of endless processes filling the vast spaces." The change to which I refer is the widely noted replacement, within and through the discourse of money, of use value by exchange value. This transformation was described at the time in great length, although in very different terms, by commentators ranging from Adam Smith to Karl Marx, Thomas Carlyle and Andrew Ure.[23] In short, with the full institutionalization of *laissez-faire* capitalism, the perceived stability of traditional sources of value was replaced by the unpredictability of speculation within a "fictitious" value system of paper money. The financial panics of the 1830s, 1840s and 1850s were characterized by flights away from paper value back to the "real" value of gold and land.[24] Yet at the same time, new vistas of opportunity and progress were opened by the magicality of paper fictions. The issuing of money from banks appeared no less magical than a stock-market killing or a run of luck at cards.[25] For the fortunate, money translated magically into status and possessions, while its effect on the less fortunate working class was to make the social origins of value in labor disappear, as if by magic. Most advantageous for the ascending middle class, then, was the fact that *embourgeoisement* of both the upper and lower classes was effected simultaneously by the replacement of both landed value *and* labor value with money value.

Is it not contradictory, or at least paradoxical, then, that both *Middlemarch* and *The Duke's Children* repeatedly argue for the virtue of just these good sources of value: the inheritance of land and work? (The other two good sources are appropriate marriage, on which I have touched, and charity, to which I will return.) For example, during a telling lecture to his son Gerald about the evils of gambling, the Duke asks, "Do you ever think what money is?" and Gerald timorously answers: "Cheques, and sovereigns, and bank notes" (*DC,* 517). The Duke's reply merits lengthy quotation:

> "Money is the reward of labour . . . or rather, in the shape it reaches you, it is your representation of that reward. You may earn it yourself, or, as is, I am afraid, more likely to be the case with you, you may possess it honestly as prepared for you by the labour of others who have stored it up for you. . . . There is nothing so comfortable as money,—but nothing so defiling if it be come by unworthily. . . . If a man have enough, let him spend it freely. If he wants it, let him earn it honestly. Let him do something for it, so that the man who pays it to him may get its value. But to think that it may be got by gambling . . .—that I say is to have left far, far behind you, all nobility, all gentleness, all manhood!"
>
> (*DC,* 517-18)

Note that in this passage the Duke has already changed labor into a "representation" and value into that which the employer, not the laborer, receives. Also, labor is defined very broadly to include the most likely means by which the Duke's forebears came to be one of the wealthiest aristocratic families in England. Elsewhere, the Duke, who is known for his abstinence from the pleasures of eating, associates himself with what he calls the "power" of "the rural labourer who sits on the ditch-side with his bread and cheese and onion" (*DC,* 194). Certainly he appears in contrast here to Gerald, who can only mildly remark that "not to have money for your wants;—that must be troublesome," and Silverbridge, who observes, "I cannot bear to think that I should like to have a thing and that I cannot afford it" (*DC,* 195). Like Lady Mabel Grex ("A real gentleman . . . should never think of money at all" [*DC,* 159]) and like Dorothea in *Middlemarch* ("I hate my wealth" [*M,* 787]), the Duke can afford the luxury of viewing wealth as "a burden which [one] must carry to the end" (*DC,* 197).[26] It is not with a little irony, then, that the reader must view the Duke's sincere comparison between himself and a field hand, or recognize that lack of money is more than "troublesome" to some people for whom "lik[ing] to have a thing" is overshadowed by genuine need.[27] Nevertheless, the Duke is associated throughout the novel with the "gospel of work," "the only pleasure in life which [he] has . . . enjoyed without alloy" (*DC,* 123). It is similarly ironic that the Duke is coupled in this litany of work-for-work's-sake with Caleb Garth, the lower middle-class estate manager in *Middlemarch* who values work even to the extent of working without concern for remuneration.[28] It thus appears that the upper classes and the lower classes are to be lumped together within a discourse that posits work as the real source of value, thereby serving dominant middle-class interests.

V

A telling feature of the Victorian discourse of work is its commentary on pleasure and on business, for which the issue of gambling once again serves as a key. In *Middlemarch,* Reverend Farebrother's sin is less that he plays whist than that he plays for money. It is this feature of Farebrother's character—this "blot" of "money-winning business," as Lydgate describes it to Dorothea (*M,* 481)—that must be overcome in Dorothea's mind before she can offer him the vicar's position at the Lowick Manor chapel.[29] She finally decides to do so specifically as a means of saving him from the financial need that she assumes drives him to gambling; in other words, she helps him with a form of charity. After his "conversion" from gambling, Farebrother may still play for pleasure ("a rubber to satisfy his mother") but not for money (*M,* 624). Like Mr. Farebrother, Silverbridge in *The Duke's Children* makes the mistake of confusing pleasure with business. The Duke comments on Silverbridge's reasons for associating with Major Tifto: "If you associate with him, not for pleasure, then it surely must be for profit. That you should do the former would be to me . . . surprising. . . . That you should do the latter—is, I think, a reproach" (*DC,* 213-14). Similarly, Silverbridge's more experienced colleague Mr. Lupton tells him: "A man in your position can hardly make money by it, but he may lose so much! If a man really likes the amusement,—as I do,—and risks no more than what he has in his pocket, that may be very well" (*DC,* 356). But it is Lady Mabel Grex who sums up the novel's discourse of gambling from an aristocratic viewpoint:

> "I like a man to like pleasure. But I despise a man who makes a business of his pleasures. When I hear that this man is the best whist-player in London, and that man the best billiard-player, I always know that they can do nothing else, and then I despise them."
>
> (*DC,* 78)[30]

Caleb Garth—the discourse of work's leading proponent in *Middlemarch,* and one who is noted for his lack of interest and ability in finance—represents the prescribed attitude in these matters: "It must be remembered that by 'business' Caleb never meant money transactions, but the skillful application of labour" (*DC,* 533).

Clearly, then, work, pleasure, and business must be kept separate; or, preferably, pleasure and business should be subsumed under work, erased *into* work. Work is the only completely positive term, though it should not be considered so much a value-producing activity (which might stimulate a more demanding labor force) as much as an end in itself.[31] In particular, business must be kept separate from work and pleasure and optimally should not be thought of at all. Pleasure, on the other hand, is dangerous to the extent that it distracts from work and threatens to lead the weak to mix it with business. Therefore, while business disappears, pleasure must be regulated.

This is the very conclusion on which a middle-class consensus seems to have been reached sometime around 1834, the date of the New Poor Law. The establishment of workhouses and severe vagrancy laws came with a change in social attitude toward the poor. A shift took place from the traditional aristocratic view that it was the duty of the rich to look after the poor through personal husbandry and charity to the *laissez-faire* liberal view that "poverty was the fault of the poor and that the middle and upper classes had no responsibility to relieve it."[32] This shift in particular served the need of a burgeoning manufacturing sector for a disciplined work force. At the same time, and for the same reasons according to some historians, working-class recreation, which was perceived as a threat to order, came under increased scrutiny. The police force was enlarged; betting shops were prohibited and gambling codes were strengthened; ordinances restricting mass meetings, demonstrations and street bazaars were enacted; liquor licensing was instituted after zealous campaigning by the Temperance League; "blood sports" like bear baiting were prohibited on humanitarian grounds (excluding, of course, upper-class equivalents such as fox hunting); fairs and race courses were required to buy licenses.[33] These and other factors operated to regulate working-class (and sometimes upper-class) recreation. On the other hand, certain recreations were prescribed, specifically those that centered on the family unit rather than the ale house, those that encouraged solitary self reflection (fishing, for example), those such as organized team athletics that aimed at wholesome fraternizing and physical improvement, and those that "instruct[ed] workingmen in the elementary accomplishments of social economy—time-budgeting and money management—and introduced them to the satisfactions of mental recreation."[34] In short, a propaganda of rational recreation, in conjunction with a broad and diverse range of "re-socialisation" mechanisms in other spheres of daily life, constructed an industrial discipline through "the house-training of the English proletariat."[35]

A recognition of these changes in recreation casts a new light on that characteristic activity for which Dorothea Brooke comes to be known: charity. Through financial charity, in combination with a prescription to work, Dorothea saves Lydgate from gambling, debt, and the tainted charity offered by Bulstrode; by the same means, she reforms Farebrother from gambling, redirecting his energies toward a more industrious religious practice. Using "sympathy without check," she puts aside all considerations of self and attempts to rescue Rosamond Vincy Lydgate from the selfishness that threatens to destroy the Lydgates' marriage (*M*, 774). Indeed throughout *Middlemarch*, Dorothea is described in terms of an almost Christ-like martyrdom; but no matter how much Dorothea resembles Christ (or Saint Theresa) in her charity, she also resembles Fortune, the patron saint of gamblers and religious predestinationists. After Dorothea grants the estate vicarage to Farebrother, his mother says to Dorothea, "They say Fortune is a woman and capricious. But sometimes she is a good woman and gives to those who merit, which has been the case with you, Mrs. Casaubon, who have given a living to my son" (*M*, 522). The terms in which Dorothea justifies her charity to Lydgate are also interesting in this regard: "It is so difficult to make shares at all even. This is one way" (*M*, 744).

Charity is a domesticated form of fortune or fate, one that takes care of the needy not on the basis of caprice but on the basis of merit.[36] This is consistent with the traditional system of *noblesse oblige,* and Dorothea's charity initally appears to be an example of the operation of that system, which survived roughly up until the time in which the novel is set, the 1830s.[37] By the 1860s and 1870s when Eliot was writing *Middlemarch, noblesse oblige* had been replaced by *laissez-faire* doctrines according to which poverty was a sign of degradation that needed to be dealt with not through personalized charity but by state correction on the one hand, and the "invisible hand" of the market on the other.

This context recommends a reconsideration of Dorothea's most ambitious experiment in charity, her workers' cottages. From the first chapters, Dorothea proposes that her uncle, who is known for the poor maintenance of his tenant farms, build a set of such cottages. The proposal is received sympathetically only by Sir James Chettam, and then because it coincides with his interest in "scientific farming," by which he hopes to set "a good pattern of farming among [his] tenants," and because he is romantically interested in Dorothea (*M*, 19, 33). In the early part of the novel, Dorothea conceives of her plan in an aristocratic combination of humanitarian and aesthetic terms: "Life in cottages might be happier than ours if they were real houses fit for human beings from whom we expect duties and affections" (*M*, 33). She reacts to her uncle's resistance to her plan and to the idyllic representation of rustic life portrayed in paintings that hang on his wall as follows:

> "And those poor Dagleys, in their tumble-down farmhouse, where they live in the back kitchen and leave the other rooms to the rats! That is one reason why I did not like the pictures here, dear Uncle—which you

> think me stupid about. I used to come from the village with all that dirt and coarse ugliness like a pain within me."
>
> (*M*, 378)

Here Dorothea's reaction is personal to the point of being internalized. But later, after her self-negating marriage to Casaubon, his death (the good fortune of which cannot be admitted), and her resulting financial independence, the "plan" begins to take on a new purpose: "I have a delightful plan. I should like to take a great deal of land, and drain it, and make a little colony where everybody should work, and all the work should be done well" (*M*, 532). Finally, near the end of the novel when it seems Dorothea may have abandoned the plan, she reconfirms her desire for a "village which should be a school of industry" (*M*, 742).

The progression in Dorothea's conception of her plan charts the *embourgeiosement* of aristocratic ideology. The end of the trajectory is what Peter Bailey describes as "the coercive power implicit in the semi-custodial institutions of factory villages or board schools."[38] While we must read Dorothea's charity and sympathy as sincere, we must also recognize the way in which it is infiltrated by the discourse of gambling and, more significantly, the way in which it is reexpressed through the discourse of money and the discourse of work to meet ideological ends that Dorothea Brooke, and perhaps George Eliot, confused with more traditionally aristocratic humanitarian measures.

Finally, then, the ideological work of the discourse of gambling now can be read through *The Duke's Children* and *Middlemarch,* and can be seen to circumscribe dangerous desires and recreations and to prescribe, and inscribe, work and industry.

VI

> To deal with property on the principle of chance, which is non-moral, must be immoral because it involves the false proposition that property itself is non-moral.
>
> —N. D. Mackenzie, *The Ethics of Gambling*, 1895[39]

The pervasiveness of the discourse of gambling in Victorian fiction—its infection of all forms of money, "good" as well as "bad"—perhaps is unexpected until one considers the historical context: the rise to dominance of finance capitalism and of a teleology of progress coupled with declining beliefs in a benevolent, controlling deity. Certainly the randomness of chance and the belief in individual fate (as opposed to society-wide "manifest destiny") appear antithetical to progressive, bourgeois ideology. What is most threatening—or perhaps promising—about gambling in this regard is the implication that, as a billboard for the Florida state lottery puts it, "Anything can happen!" This is an invitation to recognize the desiring subject as the only knowable source of value. Nothing would seem to be more threatening to Victorian sensibility (as evidenced by the reactions from prominent Victorians like Thomas Carlyle and Charles Dickens to Utilitarianism, for example). Some amelioration of the threat is offered by another aspect of progressive ideology, which this essay has attempted to delineate: a belief in the necessary equality of value, whether between marriage partners, mediums of exchange, or social classes. However, this precept also threatens to slip into a form of radical democratic individuality, a leveling of all distinctions, of which the even odds of gambling may be particularly representative. While the prospect of a society thus composed of autonomous self-satisfying individuals was perceived by many Victorians as threatening to moral foundations and social order, it at the same time directly served the interests of finance capitalism. Desire may not be moral, but it certainly is consuming.

In the light of these agonistic social and cultural currents, it is not surprising that this essay has found the discourse of money to be highly conflicted, particularly around the key figure of gambling. The conflicts generate questions: Why is it that at this time in history—when labor was being systematically devalued relative to exchange value and when inherited land, like precious metals, was being replaced as the basis of value by the magic of money—labor and land were seen to be the true sources of value? At the same time, why is it that a rhetoric of equality was launched at a point when the non-equivalency of face value and fictional value was seen as threatening financial panic or class revolt? In this respect, the previously noted separation of work from business and the implicit directive to concentrate on the former and ignore the latter is telling. We must first note that "work"—the venerated term in *Middlemarch* and, to a lesser extent, in *The Duke's Children*—denotes an individualized endeavor in response to a moral imperative and therefore already has been separated from "labor," which denotes a collective activity *within* society. Once labor has been erased and business has been mystified, all that is left is work— "you can succeed on your own if you try hard enough"—and equality—"we are all in this together" or "your opportunity is as good as anybody's." Work becomes a value in itself—"work for work's sake"—while business, meaning finance capitalism, which increasingly *was* the site of the construction of economic value, is removed from attention. Thus social values are separated from economic value. "Equality" functions then to mystify the relation between values and value so that the former appears as the source of the latter when it is not, or when financial value in fact may have become the primary source of moral values. Between the level of individual responsibility, on the one hand, and the culture-wide "fable of consensus" on the other, the middle—which is society itself, the site of local practice and struggle—has been removed.[40]

Here a less familiar (and perhaps ulterior) function of the discourse of gambling can be glimpsed. The similarities between market speculation and gambling required that a distinction be drawn between them. At the same time that the stock exchange solidified as a social institution, gambling became both more professionalized and more circumscribed by law. For example, in America the Chicago Board of Trade mounted a campaign against gambling shops in the 1840s "because of the fear that they would bring into general disrepute the legitimate exchange, since trade in futures would be viewed as mere gambling."[41] On both sides of the Atlantic, gambling legislation and a concerted effort to distinguish between gambling and investment facilitated the stock exchange's establishment as a pillar of society and an unquestioned source of real value. Gambling was the necessary evil other toward which critical attention now needs to be directed.

Finally, the Victorian novel participates in the nineteenth-century struggle over the issue of value formally as well as thematically. "Paper fictions" can refer equally to pound notes and to novels, to scrip and to script.[42] The realist novel approaches a dialogue about its own form in broaching the question of what constitutes real value. Foregrounding this issue is risky to the extent that it threatens to reveal the performativeness of the text, thereby admitting that the reality the text purports to *be* is of no more substance than paper and ink. Perhaps a novel like *Middlemarch,* one that relies on its realism to convey what it takes to be a vitally important morality, cannot but scapegoat gambling and related forms of value as fictitious. On the other hand, *Middlemarch, The Duke's Children,* and other Victorian novels demonstrate a willingness to take the gamble of exposing the artifice of the text in order to confront the issues that emerge through the figure of gambling.

Notes

1. Quoted in Reuven Brenner and Gabrielle A. Brenner, *Gambling and Speculation: A Theory, a History, and a Future of Some Human Decisions* (Cambridge: Cambridge Univ. Press, 1990), 90.

2. Henry Blyth, *Hell and Hazard, or William Crockford Versus the Gentlemen of England* (London: Weidenfeld and Nicolson, 1969), xiii.

3. One discussion of the pre-Victorian origins of these broad social and ideological trends in relation to the development of the novel form is Michael McKeon, *The Origins of the English Novel 1600-1740* (Baltimore: Johns Hopkins Univ. Press, 1987). McKeon summarizes: "Class criteria [of what he calls "progressive ideology"] gradually 'replace' status criteria [of "aristocratic ideology"]: which is to say not that the regard for status is obliterated but that it is subsumed under and

accommodated to the more dominant and insistent regard for financial income and occupational identity" (163).

4. At the same time, money as a medium of exchange makes the public private and secretive, both because of its physical compressibility and because of its abstractness. See Laurence Lerner, *The Literary Imagination: Essays on Literature and Society* (Sussex, England: Harvester, 1982), 46.

5. Anthony Trollope, *The Duke's Children* (Oxford: Oxford Univ. Press, 1990), 56; hereafter cited parenthetically in text as *DC*.

6. Though a few gambling clubs existed in London in the mid-eighteenth century and though the health resort at Baden-Baden, Germany had a casino by the 1760s, it was not until William Crockford's club at St. James was opened in 1827 that the gambling club became fashionable, and not until the early 1860s, which is when Monte Carlo opened, that the casino became the recognized institution that it is today. See Alan Wykes, *Gambling* (London: Aldus Books, 1964), 282-98. I am indebted for historical details to Brenner (note 1), 14; John Ashton, *The History of Gambling in England* (Montclair, N.J.: Patterson Smith, 1969), 297; Wykes (note 6), 297; and Peter Bailey, *Leisure and Class in Victorian England: Rational Recreation and the Contest of Control, 1830-1885* (London: Routledge & Kegan Paul, 1978), 23, 87, 134.

7. The exemplar of this is of course Matthew Arnold's *Culture and Anarchy*. Also see Daniel Cottom, *Social Figures: George Eliot, Social History, and Literary Representation* (Minneapolis: Univ. of Minnesota Press, 1987), particularly 9, 21-22. Two contemporary corollaries to (or perhaps outcomes of) the Victorian "ideal of a classless discourse" are the American myth of the classless society and, in criticism, the substitution of "cultural poetics" for social context by some new historicists.

8. According to Wykes (note 6), 298, in one evening at Crockford's club—of which the Duke of Wellington and Disraeli were members—Lord Rivers, Lord Sefton and Lord Grenville each lost the equivalent of over $500,000. The British sporting set of the 1830s and 1840s witnessed a number of scandalous derbys due to false registration or tampering similar to that described in *The Duke's Children*.

9. Bailey (note 6), 22-23.

10. Quoted without full attribution in Brenner (note 1), 60.

11. The dates for economic crises and panics are taken primarily from John Reed, "A Friend to Mammon: Speculation in Victorian Literature," *Victorian Studies* 27.2 (1984): 179-202. I also am indebted for historical particulars to Gillian Beer, "Circulatory Systems: Money and Gossip in *Middlemarch*," *Cahiers Victoriens & Edouardiens* 26 (October 1987): 46-62; and Barbara Weiss, *The Hell of the English: Bankruptcy and the Victorian Novel* (Lewisburg, PA: Bucknell Univ. Press, 1986).

12. Ashton (note 6), 259.

13. Weiss (note 11), argues that in "the world of Victorian capitalism the individual suddenly became vulnerable as never before to the vicissitudes of the economy" (17). Bankruptcy, she argues, became "the perfect structural metaphor for the vulnerability of the individual" and was perceived as a "moral problem" challenging the "Victorians' most cherished ideas about economic virtue" (20, 29, 71).

14. Reed (note 11), 180.

15. See David Miers and David Dixon, "National Bet: The Reemergence of Public Lottery," *Public Law* (1979): 372-403: "It was not only that stockbrokers sold lottery tickets along with shares; their whole business was regarded as a type of gambling" (379). For examples of nineteenth-century views on financial speculation and its perceived similarity to gambling, see Ashton (note 6), 274 and David Moirer Evans, *Speculative Notes and Notes on Speculation, Ideal and Real* (1864; rpt., New York: Burt Franklin, 1968), 52.

16. *Hansard's Parliamentary Debates,* 3d ser., vol. 139 (1855): col. 1378, quoted in Weiss (note 11), 138.

17. Weiss, 138.

18. George Eliot, *Middlemarch: A Study of Provincial Life* (New York: New American Library, 1981), 134; hereafter cited parenthetically in text as *M*.

19. Concerning the reader's speculations on the pasts and futures of characters, Gillian Beer, "The Reader's Wager: Lots, Sorts, and Futures," *Essays in Criticism* 40.2 (1990): 99-123, develops the notion of the reader's wager in reading fictions, particularly Victorian fictions, which Beer also argues are especially concerned with gambling. Beer writes: "Gambling and reading are both acts of desire whose longing is to possess and settle the future, but whose pleasure is in active uncertainty" (111).

20. Jane Austen, *Sense and Sensibility* (Oxford: Oxford Univ. Press, 1980), 32, 78.

21. In *The Gold Standard and the Logic of Naturalism: American Literature at the Turn of the Cen-*

tury (Berkeley: Univ. of California Press, 1987), Walter Benn Michaels develops the idea of "face value" in relation to the definition of the human subject.

22. The debate about equality and "worthiness" is also played out in the Major Tifto plot of *The Duke's Children.* Tifto's motivating concern is that he be "able to assume that appearance of equality" to Silverbridge (*DC,* 211).

23. See McKeon (note 3), for a summary of the eighteenth-century origins of this transition between competing models of value. He writes, for example: "The crystallization of conflict between progressive and conservative ideology owed a great deal to the ferment generated by the gradual recognition that human appetite was in some real sense value-creating: by the discovery, that is, of exchange value" (204). See also: Igor Webb, *From Custom to Capital: The English Novel and the Industrial Revolution* (Ithaca: Cornell Univ. Press, 1981); and Robert J. Werlin, *The English Novel and the Industrial Revolution: A Study in the Sociology of Literature* (New York: Garland, 1990), particularly 27-64.

24. See Ann Fabian, "Speculation on Distress: The Popular Discourse of the Panics of 1837 and 1857," *Yale Journal of Criticism* 3.1 (1989): 127-42.

25. Webb (note 23), 35.

26. In *The Civilized Imagination: A Study of Ann Radcliffe, Jane Austen, and Sir Walter Scott* (Cambridge: Cambridge Univ. Press, 1985), Daniel Cottom develops the idea of the aristocratic "criterion of disinterest" by which all but those who can financially afford to appear above self interest are excluded from any test of objectivity.

27. Trollope, often considered the most bourgeois of authors, should receive credit for the subtle irony with which he treats the Duke's attitude about the burden of wealth. This irony becomes clear with Gerald's final observation on the matter: "He says that a property is no better than a burden. But I'll try and bear it" (*DC,* 198).

28. For an example of Caleb Garth's Carlylean doctrine of work, see his lecture to Fred Vincy on that subject (*M,* 543).

29. It is ironic that Lydgate, who was the first to criticize Farebrother's gambling and who, the reader is told, "had an ideal of life which made this subservience of conduct to the gaining of small sums thoroughly hateful to him" (*M,* 176), is forced into just such "subservience" and into gambling through marriage and debt. Only after those experiences, when Farebrother comments, "I have no need to hang on the smiles of chance now," does Lydgate respond: "I don't see that there's any money-getting without chance, . . . if a man gets it in a profession, it's pretty sure to come by chance" (*M,* 625).

30. The biting irony of *The Duke's Children* concerning Lady Mabel Grex is that she in fact does make a "business of her pleasure" in speculatively pursuing Silverbridge when she does not love him. This falsity of motive and lack of self knowledge—as well as the social conditions that defined the options for a woman in her position—condemn her within the discourse of the novel.

31. Webb (note 23), 34.

32. Werlin (note 23), 46, 48.

33. I draw here on Bailey (note 6).

34. Bailey, 170.

35. Bailey, 174.

36. The question of free will versus fate that permeates Victorian fiction—often in relation to the issue of grace-by-works versus grace-by-faith—has obvious relevance to any consideration of gambling. I have excluded it from the scope of this essay. I would note simply that gambling has its roots in ancient religious ceremonies where "lots" were cast and that the casting of lots outside of such ceremonies was considered a sin against God; see Brenner (note 1), 1-7. For some discussion of the will/fate question, see, Felicia Bonaparte, *Will and Destiny: Morality and Tragedy in George Eliot's Novels* (New York: New York Univ. Press, 1975). For a consideration of similar issues in relation to *Daniel Deronda,* see E. A. McCobb, "*Daniel Deronda* as Will and Representation: George Eliot and Shopenhauer," *Modern Language Review,*" 80.3 (1983): 533-49.

37. For a consideration of *noblesse oblige,* see Werlin (note 23), 47.

38. Bailey (note 6), 172.

39. William Douglas MacKenzie, *The Ethics of Gambling* (London: Sunday School Union/Morrison and Gibb Printers, 1895), quoted in Brenner (note 1), 73.

40. Cottom, *Social Figures* (note 7), 175.

41. Brenner (note 1), 92. The language and practices of the stock exchange are interesting in themselves and deserve more attention than given here. One buys "futures" on commodities that one generally never intends to possess. This is truly a bet on an

imaginary future. "Options" on futures are one more step removed from any tangible basis: they are a bet on a bet.

42. Within the context of this essay, I am able only to break the surface of the issues raised about representation in relation to money and realist fiction. The topic deserves, and has received, its analysis. See Marc Shell's *The Economy of Literature* (Baltimore: Johns Hopkins Univ. Press, 1978) and *Money, Language, and Thought: Literature and Philosophical Economics from the Medieval to the Modern Era* (Berkeley: Univ. of California Press, 1982) as well as John Vernon, *Money and Fiction: Literary Realism in the Nineteenth and Early Twentieth Centuries* (Ithaca: Cornell Univ. Press, 1984), and Michaels (note 21). For a somewhat more thorough consideration of representation in relation to *Middlemarch,* see Beer (note 11).

Robert Dingley (essay date October 1996)

SOURCE: Dingley, Robert. "Playing the Game: The Continental Casinos and the Victorian Imagination." *Cahiers Victoriens et Édouardiens,* no. 44 (October 1996): 17-31.

[*In the following essay, Dingley outlines the depiction of gambling casinos in Victorian literature as exclusive establishments in which aristocrats could affirm their power in highly seductive, theatrical fantasy worlds, and relates these depictions to tensions within upper-class Victorian society regarding religion and morality.*]

Benjamin Disraeli opens the first chapter of *Sybil; or the Two Nations* with a description of Crockford's gaming club on the eve of the 1837 Derby:

> In a vast and golden saloon, that in its decorations would have become, and in its splendour would not have disgraced, Versailles in the days of the grand monarch, were assembled many whose hearts beat at the thought of the morrow. . . . The gleaming lustres poured a flood of soft yet brilliant light over a plateau glittering with gold plate, and fragrant with exotics embedded in vases of rare porcelain.
>
> (1-2)

Crockford's, as that wide-eyed account by a non-member suggests, was consciously designed as the aristocracy's exclusive preserve. It was, according to *Baily's Magazine of Sports and Pastimes,* "more difficult to get elected to it than to White's, Brooks's, or Boodle's" (qtd. in Humphreys 210) and the management committee included three earls. Bound together by social, and often by political, affiliations, the membership of Crockford's and similar clubs formed a relatively homogeneous elite in which the redistribution of wealth that

followed success or failure at the tables was safely confined within a single class. Gaming itself, moreover, could function, in this jealously defended milieu, as an implicit confirmation of the economic, and even of the moral, exclusiveness of the participants. The careless prodigality of titled punters like Lord Chesterfield and Lord Alvanley in the 1830s seems almost to have been calculated as an affront to bourgeois financial proprieties, and the nonchalance with which catastrophic reversals were met could appear to guarantee the superior quality of noble blood. Disraeli's young Duke of St. James, in his first novel, after a marathon card game lasting twenty-four hours, rises from the table poorer by about £100,000 and observes (not altogether ingenuously) to Lord Castlefort: "I wished to know what gaming was. I had heard a great deal about it. It is not so very disgusting; but I am a young man, and cannot afford to play tricks with my complexion" (246-47).

But Disraeli's fiction itself, as it moves hesitantly from emulous wonderment at princely extravagance to the advocacy of a politically responsible peerage, reflects, however idiosyncratically, a more general shift in social attitudes. The successive years in which *Coningsby* and *Sybil* appeared were also those in which evangelical pressure and a series of public scandals on the Turf finally compelled Peel's government to address itself to betting in all of its various guises. In 1844, a Select Commons Committee chaired by Palmerston hauled the reluctant Crockford before it as the centrepiece of a rigorous and widely publicised enquiry; in the following year, a new Gaming Act resulted in the closure of several hundred clubs and houses. (Crockford's was not among them, but it too had ceased to operate by the end of 1845.) Thereafter, English gambling could no longer be conducted as a glamorous public spectacle, but was driven underground, to flourish only in seedy "hells" or at furtive private parties. And because the great Parisian *maisons de jeu* had been outlawed even earlier, in January 1838, gamblers who required their activities to be sanctioned and dignified by opulent surroundings now had no option but to travel to the spa towns of Germany: to Ems and Wiesbaden, Kissingen and Aix, Baden and Homburg. Of these, the two last quickly established an ascendancy over their rivals and preferences seem to have been fairly evenly divided between them. By common consent, Baden was the more attractive town of the two ("older and more rococo" according to Dickens's protégé Percy Fitzgerald (*"Le Sport at Baden"* 25) but Homburg was felt to generate a more excitingly frenetic atmosphere. At Homburg, according to a writer in the *Dublin University Magazine,* "liveried or impudent-looking footmen . . . accost every newcomer", while at Baden, by contrast, "black-coated attendants . . . move about quietly and decently" ("Gambling-Houses in Germany" 472-73). Despite such superficial differences, however, the new and distinctive strategies developed by mid-Victorian commentators to represent the various German resorts remain relatively uniform, and this consistency extends even to their Mediterranean successor at Monte Carlo (which first achieved prominence when Louis Blanc transferred his interests there on the closure of the Homburg Kursaal in 1873).

However, rather more had occurred to change the characterisation of gambling between the early and the mid-nineteenth century than its mere geographical relocation. A writer on Crockford's in the *Westminster Review* in October 1829 could state with absolute confidence and a fair degree of accuracy that gambling was "an aristocratic occupation—a pursuit truly gentlemanly", from which the "honest and industrious middle class" was happily excluded ("English Gaming-Houses" 315-6). But the continental casinos—even Frascati's in its palmiest days—had never aspired to the upper class cliquishness of the London clubs, and this, coupled with enormously expanded opportunities for cheap European travel, meant that increasingly, after about 1850, accounts of gambling in Germany and elsewhere became preoccupied with its subversive effect on precisely those bourgeois decencies which had been felt to be securely immune only twenty years before. In his semi-autobiographical novel *Make Your Own Game* for example, G. A. Sala notices with surprise "the grave English families . . . that come sailing into the Kursaal, marshalled by pater and mater familias as demurely as though they were coming to church" (204). Another observer, the novelist Langford Cecil, describes, in his book *Fenacre Grange,* a character who "would rather have died than taken his daughter to a gambling-house in London, but thought nothing of doing it abroad" (III 13). Confronted with such extraordinary reversals of social convention, the author of an article which appeared in *All the Year Round* in 1859 could only conclude that the Kursaal at Homburg somehow exercised a "mesmeric influence" ("Moloch's Chapel of Ease" 35), and other writers felt able to locate the source of that influence more exactly. Each of the major spas, it was noticed, subsidised a permanent orchestra and the omnipresence of music was held by the *Dublin University Magazine* contributor to form one of the "snares" set by the Blanc brothers to "attract customers" to the tables at Homburg ("Gambling-Houses in Germany" 469). An article in *Chambers's Journal* called "Broken on the Wheel" observed sardonically that at Baden the casino's victims were at any rate "soothed by the most dulcet strains of Mendelssohn and Rossini" (34) and Matilda Edwards in her novel *John and I* describes how the "sound of Mozart's or Rossini's most thrilling melodies . . . engulph your senses with a drowsy overwhelming of sensuous enjoyment" (III 155).

But the ubiquitous music, in addition to its soothingly hypnotic effect, served also to enhance what was widely perceived as a theatrical quality in the casino resorts. The article in *Chambers's Journal* draws attention to the artificiality of Baden scenery:

> The forest is a show-forest. The mountains even, have been pressed into service, and are show-mountains. There is something theatrical in their sharp volcanic cones, and bold peaks, and exuberantly timbered sides.
>
> ("Broken on the Wheel" 34)

To Percy Fitzgerald, too, the houses in Baden look like "flats, and as it were, on loan from the theatre" (*"Le Sport"* 16), and the novelists C. N. and A. M. Williamson, describing Monte Carlo in *Pearson's Magazine* in 1904 call it "a vast theatre—perhaps the best . . . stage-managed theatre in the world—which differs conspicuously from other theatres because the public are its actors" (57).

That last quotation, I think, encapsulates a broad consensus among nineteenth-century writers about the primary source of the casino's dangerous fascination. The pervasive music, the theatrical appearance of the buildings, the powdered footmen, the palatial rococo rooms—all of these things combine to enforce a sense of distance from prosaic realities, and the visitor is subliminally coerced into enacting roles which will conform to the exotic stage-sets. Any rigid demarcation of illusion from actuality becomes problematic in locations which assign paramount value to playing. One P. Fendall, writing about Monaco in the magazine *Belgravia* in 1874, recalls how

> at Homburg a few years ago . . . when Patti was holding her audience spell-bound in the madscene of *Lucia,* a man suddenly rushed in and exclaimed, "There is a run of twelve red"; and in one moment the theatre was empty.
>
> (125)

"Spell-bound": the word used of Patti's impact on her audience suggests also that mesmeric effect regularly imputed to the casinos, and the staged insanity of Lucia di Lammermoor becomes interchangeable with the madness of compulsive gamblers. Passage from the theatre to the tables marks—or appears to mark—not the substitution of real life for fantasy, but the exchange of one intense dramatic experience for another. The setting of Homburg, observes the neurotic protagonist of Percy Fitzgerald's novel *Fatal Zero,* is "ever so pastoral"; but, he adds, it is "the pastoral . . . of the theatre or the opera" (44).

Fitzgerald's association there of pastoral innocence with imaginative role-playing hints at the possibility that casinos might induce a regression to childhood, a relaxation of properly adult restraints, and indeed, a rather nostalgic article published in *All the Year Round* in 1880 (nearly a decade after the closure of the Kursaal) reminisces about the "old fairy-like Homburg" where even "elderly professional men . . . became positively juvenile in manner and gaiety of apparel" in the "beautiful gardens" and "tree-fringed avenues" ("A Day at Homburg" 353).

The various related conventions with which, I have been suggesting, Victorian writers sought to evoke the distinctive ambience of the gambling towns might all be contained within the multiple significations of the word "play", which can refer equally to the harmlessly ludic activity of children, to the performance of theatrical roles, and, of course, to dedicated self-destruction at the roulette-tables. When Percy Fitzgerald, for example, refers to Baden as "a Town of Play" (*"Le Sport"* 119), it is unclear from the context which of the possible range of meanings he intends, and Meredith brilliantly sustains a similar indeterminacy when he describes Baden in *The Amazing Marriage*:

> The simple fools, performing in character, were a neutral people, grotesques and arabesques wreathed about the margins of the scene . . . Here, however, as elsewhere, the core of interest was with the serious population, the lovers and the players in earnest, who stood round the furnace and pitched themselves into it, not always under a miscalculation of their chances of emerging transfigured instead of serving for fuel. These, the tragical children of folly, were astute; they played with lightning, and they knew the conditions of the game; victories were to be had.
>
> (96)

"Players", there, seems unequivocally to refer to participation at the tables—until we notice the thread of theatrical imagery running through the passage: "performing in character"; "margins of the scene"; "tragical"; the resultant ambiguity is further complicated by the image of children playing with lightning, an analogy which appears to undermine the simultaneous assertion that these sophisticated adult gamblers "knew the game". Meredith's serpentine sentences contrive not only to expose but also to enact that semantic elision by which innocent playing can imperceptibly shade into experienced gaming.

It is, however, the conscious project of most Victorian accounts precisely to fracture that facile transition, to foreground the discrepancies rather than the continuities between the casino's festive appearance and the deadening reality at its centre. The flamboyant surfaces of Baden or of Homburg seem designed to naturalise a liberating suspension of adult responsibility; but the very act of gambling, instead of conferring the freedom it has appeared to promise, only imposes a new set of constraints and repressions. At Noirbourg, Thackeray reports in "The Kickleburys on the Rhine",

You don't see any frantic gamblers gnashing their teeth or dashing down their last stakes. . . . What you call the good company is very quiet and easy. A man loses his mass of gold, and gets up and walks off, without any particular mark of despair.

> (193-4)

"I regret," wrote Charles Clarke of Baden in 1867, "that I have nothing more to record than the bare fact that a more well-regulated society of ladies and gentlemen I never saw" (385), and when Zoe visits Homburg in Charles Reade's *A Woman-Hater,* she experiences a similar sense of anticlimax:

> Instead of the wild excitement she had heard of, there was a subdued air, a forced quiet, especially among the seated players. A stern etiquette presided, and the gamblers shrouded themselves in well-bred stoicism—losing without open distress or ire, winning without open exultation.
>
> (95)

The concept of "play", by implication, can hardly seem appropriate for such concentrated effort, and the repeated insistence on the tedious decorum of gambling is used by commentators to dissociate it from that air of sportive liberation with which the casinos seek to glamourise it. But this strategy of demystification in fact raises as many problems as it solves; for if, at the tables, play becomes earnest, then the distinction between gambling and other, socially legitimated, forms of work is itself rendered problematic. In the first chapter of *Daniel Deronda,* for example, George Eliot notes the presence at the tables of a "respectable London tradesman" who, as a holiday from "winning money in business and spending it showily", can find no better resource than "winning money in play and spending it yet more showily" (36-7). Again, an article by Percy Fitzgerald in *Household Words* for 1857 begins, typically enough, by stressing the contrast between the pastoral appearance of the spas and the sober and sobering reality it conceals: "It is certainly hard", we are told, "to associate the bright country aspect of such places . . . with the heat and glare of the rooms of play, and the worn, sallow countenances of players" (571). "Heat and glare"; "worn, sallow countenances": the phrases seem more appropriate to a factory and its workforce than to a roomfull of gamblers, and this possibility actually appears to strike Fitzgerald: "They are more in harmony," he goes on, "with the crush and awful mysteries of great cities" (571).

In his essay "Some Motifs in Baudelaire", Walter Benjamin makes very much the same point. Gambling, he argues, possesses the "futility, the emptiness, the inability to complete something" of "industrial work processes".

> The manipulation of the worker at the machine has no connection with the preceding operation for the very reason that it is its exact repetition. Since each opera-

tion at the machine is just as screened off from the preceding operation as a coup in a game of chance is from the one that preceded it, the drudgery of the labourer is, in its own way, a counterpart to the drudgery of the gambler. The work of both is equally devoid of substance.

(134-135)

It is, of course, possible to contest the detail of Benjamin's analysis, but his broad analogies between the production-line and the gaming-table serve at the very least to highlight the dully regimented pointlessness of the latter. However, this mechanically repetitive activity (and Mrs. Trollope was reminded at Baden of "the monotonous progress of the tread-mill" (II 69)) is being performed not by alienated wage-slaves but by what Charles Clarke calls "a well-regulated society of ladies and gentlemen", and its futility derives not only from the perpetual incompletion of the process, but also from the fact that nothing more is happening than the endless, arbitrary, and uncontrollable circulation of wealth among the players. Gambling in this form therefore threatens to transgress at least three central positions within the ideology of nineteenth-century capitalism. In the first place, the discernible similarity between industrial labour and casino betting tends to erode any clear qualitative distinction between proletarian (unskilled) and bourgeois (skilled) versions of "work". Secondly, gambling, in its ceaseless redistribution of wealth and its failure to generate anything more than an essentially meaningless exchange of capital, provides a disconcertingly appropriate model for a significant portion of commercial enterprise. As a writer in the *Westminster Review* shrewdly remarked in 1863: "Men who were formally attracted to the gaming-table in the hope of growing rich . . . now crowd to the Stock Exchange, and speculate there" ("Gamesters and Gaming-Houses" 86). Finally, and perhaps most importantly, the powerlessness of the player, his or her reduction to the status of an interchangeable component in an impersonal process, exposes the impotence of the individual will in the determination of its own financial destiny. What might be called Victorian popular ethics notoriously insisted on a direct correlation between personal merit and material reward. "There are," wrote Henry Mayhew, after a disconsolate inspection of the play-tables at Ems, "but two ways of making money in the world, the slow and the quick,—the former is the process of patient industry, the latter that of hasty speculation; and it is the rule, that whereas the one *almost invariably succeeds* in compassing its end, the other *almost as invariably fails*" (145-6). What is, of course, overlooked by such comforting formulae is the extent to which, in the era of high capitalism, even the most hard-working and meritorious of individuals are at the mercy of anonymous economic forces which they have no means of regulating. Mrs Gaskell's John Thornton, for example, in *North and South,* is carefully established as a Carlylean hero

of industry, but a slump in cotton prices summarily reduces him to the role of passive spectator at his own bankruptcy. It is, we might argue, precisely this disempowerment of the individual subject by the intractable fluctuations of the market that the game of chance threatens to uncover. Describing the Spielbank at Baden in 1853, a writer in *Sharpe's London Magazine* notes that "Rank, nationality, even individuality, is dropped, and all mankind become 'merely players' . . . from the moment they touch the level of this table" ("Baden-Baden in 1853" 102). A not dissimilar observation has been made by the cultural historian Franco Moretti, who argues that, during the course of the nineteenth century, games like faro and baccarat in which the "players are . . . explicitly direct adversaries" get displaced by roulette, in which "binary opposition . . . undergoes a process of multiplication and overdetermination" so that "it is never clear who the enemy is, to what extent, or why" (121-2). Although Moretti relates this development specifically to the expansion of cities, it seems equally pertinent as a model for the economic structures of which urban growth was partly an outcome, and in which the qualities and endeavours of the individual are rendered largely irrelevant by the arbitrary dispensations of the "free" market.

But if gambling threatens to demythologise some of the cherished certainties of bourgeois economic thought it also challenges a still more hallowed (though not entirely unrelated) system of rewards and penalties. The hushed, decorous and repetitive activity of the players reminds many nineteenth-century observers not only of mechanical process but of ritual devotion. "Surely," proclaims an article of 1859, significantly entitled "Moloch's Chapel of Ease",

> never was such piety as this; never do pilgrims in church struggle so painfully for front places, strain their necks so cruelly to hear and to see, not to lose a word or a form of the great ceremonial.

(35)

Two years later, in 1861, the contributor to *Chambers's Journal* wrote of "Juggernaut . . . leering in his flower-adorned car", of gamblers throwing themselves under "the gigantic gilt wheels", and of "Brahmins" whisking away the marks of sacrifice "with their cambric handkerchiefs" (33). As midnight approaches at the Baden Spielbank, notes Percy Fitzgerald, the players become increasingly excited—"a sort of 'revival' sets in, and worshippers grow fiercer and more importunate in their prayers, singing 'Hear us, Baal!' frantically" (*"Le Sport"* 105).

Baal, Moloch, Juggernaut—these deities have been fixed on less because of any distinctive attributes they may possess (though each has a taste for human blood) than for the negative quality they share: all of them are false idols and so attempts to propitiate them must inevitably fail; their exotic names merely confer specious identity on what is, in fact, absence. Their worship, moreover, is not only deluded but is positively inimical to Christianity, and several commentators foreground this feature of gambling ritual with heavy insistence. Meredith, for example, presents roulette as a form of Black Mass, presided over by "our medieval Enemy", "an ancient hoary Goat-Satan" (105), while the composition of Gustave Doré's painting *Le Tapis vert,* exhibited at the Salon in 1867 (and then at the Egyptian Hall in London), is clearly suggested by conventional groupings for the Last Supper: an elderly croupier stares out from the centre of a roulette table while the gamblers seated about him peer devotedly at the wheel he has set spinning.

Such images, of course, are intended, whether openly or implicitly, to set up a binary opposition between the certainties of Christian faith and an irresponsible surrender to the random dispensations of Chance, an opposition graphically prefigured at the moment of Christianity's inception, when Roman troopers played with dice at the foot of the Cross. God and gambling are perceived as mutually exclusive, and Guy Lawrence encapsulates what might almost be described as the official consensus when he writes of a character in his novel *Maurice Dering* that he "believed in Luck, just as implicitly as he disbelieved in Revealed Religion" (II 120). The very form of such a proposition, however, and the repeated construction of gambling as an antitype, a mirror reversal, of Christian observance, will almost inevitably tend to suggest precisely what it seeks to deny—a covert relationship between the two terms whose irreconcilable hostility is being asserted. The more Percy Fitzgerald, for example, ponders the functional similarities between discarded calculations on the floor of the Kursaal and prayer-books left lying about in a church (*"Le Sport"* 62), the more difficult it becomes to locate the precise grounds on which they might be absolutely differentiated. Such analogies, indeed, appear to rely for their impact largely upon the reader's prior conviction of the "truth" they affirm. But any such confidence in a universal assent to the self-evident dichotomy between Christian belief and other forms of superstition will almost inevitably seem misplaced by the second half of the nineteenth century. At a time when T. H. Huxley, for instance, could describe "religion nowadays" (i.e. 1885) as "for the most part, Hellenized Judaism", infused with a "mighty remnant of old-world paganism" and burdened with "fragments of Persian and Babylonian, or rather Accadian, mythology" (Goodwin 116), any claims for an essential contrast between the worship of Baal or Moloch, say, and the worship of Christ would automatically run the risk of being read or of being readable against their grain. In the first place, as that passage from Huxley suggests, the study of comparative religion tended towards the

erosion of Christianity's claims to uniqueness. Indeed, *The Golden Bough,* which appeared in its original form in 1890, should, I think, be regarded less as an innovatory text than as the culminating synthesis of a half-century of anthropological research, and its implicit reduction of Christianity to one among a whole family of Eastern religious systems is effected with a great deal more caution than had been displayed by some of Frazer's predecessors. But of more central importance than research into comparative mythology in problematising a binary opposition between the rituals of gambling and those of Christian religion was the degree to which increasingly dominant scientific models rendered the traditional bases of prediction intellectually suspect. Gillian Beer, in her 1990 F. W. Bateson Lecture, has argued that the effect both of evolutionary and of thermodynamic theory is to replace a future constituted by the "constant rediscovery of stable norms" with something "irregular, chancy" (102). And in such a climate "God" is liable to seem little more than an outmoded explanation for a universe whose structure has been determined largely by accident and whose future is hardly more certain than the sequence of winning numbers in roulette. Belief in a Christian first cause, so far from being in diametrical opposition to gambling, must now itself become a form of desperate wager, a "gamble", as Elinor Shaffer has put it, "on an impossibility" (282). And indeed, it was on precisely those terms that T. H. Huxley selected among the various available ontological hypotheses in a letter to Charles Kingsley of 1863. Deciding, after some hesitation, that a form of Pantheism "chimes in better with the rules of the game of nature" than any of the other options, Huxley is nevertheless far from sanguine:

> But who knows when the great Banker may sweep away table and cards and all, and set us learning a new game? What will become of all my poor counters, then?
>
> (qtd. in Irvine 104)

Huxley tentatively places his stake, but he does so uncertain even that the rules he plays by are still in force, and fearful that he may forfeit his investment. Huxley's agnostic gamble is, I suspect consciously, a nineteenth-century reversal of Pascal's more famous one, which had been based upon an implicitly Christian confidence that all of the available outcomes were knowable in advance and that nothing was to be lost by a mistaken wager on God's immanence. But it is, I have been arguing, precisely the idea of faith as a form of gambling (and of gambling as a form of faith) that so many Victorian writers so recurrently struggled to conceal in their insistent and finally self-defeating efforts to polarise the two concepts.

* * *

So far, I have been looking at the Victorian presentation of gambling in terms of a series of binary oppositions—between the innocent surface and the corrupt reality of the casino; between gambling and work; between Christianity and Chance—whose oppositional form is intended to pre-empt, but in fact exposes, a possibility of resemblance between the contrasted terms. I would like to conclude by trying to relate these various constructs through a very cursory examination of a single, very brief passage from Percy Fitzgerald's *Fatal Zero*, which first appeared as a serial in *All the Year Round* in 1868 and was reprinted in two volumes in the following year. The unbalanced narrator of this remarkable novel, Austen, has been sent to Homburg to recover from a nervous collapse. Priding himself on his evangelical piety, he feels complacently immune to the temptations of the Kursaal, and goes there only in order to witness the colourful spectacle and to feel smugly superior to the abandoned wretches who cluster about the roulette-wheel. Over a number of days, however, he starts to notice a pattern emerging in the sequence of winning numbers and he begins, merely as a mathematical exercise, to work out probabilities. Finally, and in order to assert his confidence in the accuracy of his calculations, he places a small bet—and wins. He becomes "hooked" and for a few days his luck holds. "God Almighty in his infinite goodness be praised," he gloats in his journal after one frenetic session: "There they are—fifteen golden napoleons torn from the clutches of the villains" (255). Austen has been able to persuade himself of two things. In the first place, the success of his wagers can be attributed to the labour he has invested in his preliminary research; indeed, unlike the other players, he has hardly been gambling at all, merely reaping the rewards of prudence and hard work. Secondly, he is able to regard his wins as a sign of God's special favour, a favour conferred, moreover, precisely because of his meritorious industry. For Austen, that is, gambling has become merely an extension of the familiar alliance between capitalist enterprise and Protestant faith, another sphere in which the Puritan work-ethic will guarantee success.

Predictably, Percy Fitzgerald goes to extreme lengths to ensure that the novel's readers will not endorse its protagonist's heresy. From his fictional diary, Austen emerges not only as half-cracked from the start, but also as weak, selfish, and arrogant. Furthermore, after his initial triumph, he begins to lose regularly; finally, having lost everything, he kills himself. Now Austen's steady decline can be read in two very different ways, and because his story is mediated to us only through his journal, there is no omniscient narrator to decide between the alternatives and direct our choice. On the one hand, his losses at the table can be regarded as a confirmation that the system he has so elaborately devised is illusory—that roulette is after all an unconnected series of random moments rather than a sequence dictated by stable laws of probability. On the other hand, however, the very consistency with which Austen loses suggests

precisely that a providential system *is* in place and that it is dispensing condign punishment for blasphemy. In other words, the novel can only seek to distance itself from its protagonist's confusion of God with Chance, Chaos with Order, by creating that same confusion in its narrative structure. Austen's catastrophe may be the result either of accident or of design; the evidence would support either conclusion and the question therefore becomes undecidable. In this sense, consequently, it would seem legitimate to describe *Fatal Zero* as an essentially agnostic text; but it is also, as I hope I have been able to suggest, a representative one for the way in which it tries to mask radical uncertainties with a confident binary demarcation of truth from falsehood, right from wrong; representative, too, in its repelled fascination with gambling as a disquietingly informative mirror-reflection of so much that was fundamental to the values and the beliefs of Victorian Britain.

Works Cited

"A Day at Homburg." *All the Year Round* ns 24 (1880): 352-55.

"Baden-Baden in 1853." *Sharpe's London Magazine* ns 37 (1870): 97-103; 137-42; 199-204.

Beer, Gillian. "The Reader's Wager: Lots, Sorts, and Futures." *Essays in Criticism* 40 (1990): 99-123.

Benjamin, Walter. *Charles Baudelaire: A Lyric Poet in the Era of High Capitalism.* Trans. Harry Zohn. London: Verso, 1983.

"Broken on the Wheel." *Chambers's Journal* 15 (1861): 33-6

Cecil, Langford. *Fenacre Grange.* 3 vols. London: Tinsley Brothers, 1870.

Clarke, Charles. "Baden Baden in 1867." *Temple Bar* 21 (1867): 383-92.

Disraeli, Benjamin. *The Young Duke.* 1831. London: Longman, n.d.

———. *Sybil; or, The Two Nations.* 1845. London: Oxford University Press, 1956.

Edwards, Matilda B. *John and I.* 3 vols. London: Hurst and Blackett, 1862.

Eliot, George. *Daniel Deronda.* 1876. Harmondsworth: Penguin, 1967.

Fendall, P. "Money-Making at Monaco." *Belgravia* 3rd. ser. 4 (1874): 125-27.

Fitzgerald, Percy. "Make Your Game, Gentlemen!" *Household Words* 15 (1856-7): 570-73.

————. *"Le Sport" at Baden. A Picture of Watering-Place Life and Manners.* London: Chapman and Hall, 1864.

————. *Fatal Zero. A Homburg Diary.* 1869; new ed. London: Chatto and Windus, 1886.

"Gambling-Houses in Germany." *Dublin University Magazine* 77 (1871): 466-76.

"Gamesters and Gaming-Houses." *Westminster Review* ns 24 (1863): 63-87.

Goodwin, Michael, ed. *Nineteenth-Century Opinion.* Harmondsworth: Penguin, 1951.

Humphreys, A. L. *Crockford's; or, The Goddess of Chance in St. James's Street 1828-1844.* London: Hutchinson, 1953.

Irvine, William. *Apes, Angels and Victorians. A Joint Biography of Darwin and Huxley.* London: Weidenfeld and Nicolson, 1956.

Lawrence, Guy. *Maurice Dering; or, The Quadrilateral.* 2 vols. London: Tinsely Brothers, 1864.

Mayhew, Henry. *The Upper Rhine: The Scenery of its Banks and the Manners of its People.* London: Routledge, 1858.

Meredith, George. *The Amazing Marriage.* 1895. London: Constable, 1911.

"Moloch's Chapel of Ease." *All the Year Round* 2 (1859): 35-7.

Moretti, Franco. *Signs Taken for Wonders: Essays in the Sociology of Literary Forms* Trans. Susan Fischer, David Forgacs and David Miller, Rev. ed. London: Verso, 1988.

Reade, Charles. *A Woman-Hater.* 1877. London: Chatto and Windus, 1896.

Sala, G. A. *Make Your Own Game* London: Ward Lock, 1860.

Shaffer, E. S. *'Kubla Khan' and the Fall of Jerusalem. The Mythological School in Biblical Criticism and Secular Literature 1770-1880.* Cambridge: Cambridge University Press, 1975.

Thackeray, W. M. "The Kickleburys on the Rhine." 1850. In *The Christmas Books.* London: Smith Elder, 1898. Vol. 9 of *The Biographical Edition of the works of W. M. Thackeray.* 13 vols. 1898-99.

Trollope, Frances. *Belgium and Germany in 1833.* 2 vols. London: John Murray, 1834.

Williamson, C. N. and A. M. "Behind the Scenes at Monte Carlo." *Pearson's Magazine* 17 (1904): 57-68.

GAMBLING IN RUSSIAN LITERATURE

Jurij M. Lotman (essay date 1975)

SOURCE: Lotman, Jurij M. "Theme and Plot: The Theme of Cards and the Card Game in Russian Literature of the Nineteenth Century." *PTL: Journal for Descriptive Poetics and Theory of Literature* 3, no. 3 (October 1978): 455-92.

[*In the following essay, first published in Russian in 1975, Lotman surveys the use of the card game as a motif in nineteenth-century Russian literature.*]

We must begin by defining the meaning given to the concept of "theme" in the following discussion.[1] It is not difficult to conclude from an examination of the different types of narrative text that they can be reduced to a surprisingly limited number of invariant plots. Not only do these plots occur in widely differing national cultures, they can be found in remarkably similar form throughout the history of literary texts, from the most ancient myths that can be reconstructed to the narratives of the twentieth century. The reasons for this recurrence have often been studied, and they are extraneous to the problems with which we are concerned here. It cannot be said, however, that all the scholar has to do is to go up through successive levels of abstraction in an attempt to reconstruct the invariant basis of diverse texts; for there is another aspect of the problem which is no less important,—the examination of the mechanism by which an original single plot schema develops into fundamentally different texts.

The mechanisms which guarantee the individuality of the plot design in any given text are complex and varied. The intention of the present work is to draw attention to one of these mechanisms. On the level at which plot is embodied in text, words which refer to specific objects are to be found in the narrative; because of their particular importance and frequent repetition in the culture of that type, these words have also accumulated certain fixed meanings and situational links. Indeed, they have undergone a process of "mythologization": they thus become sign-signals of other texts and are associated with specific plots external to the given text. Such words may condense in themselves whole complexes of texts. When inserted into the narrative in order to name an object, they gradually unfold into plot constructions which not only have no connection with that of the text, but form with it complex conflict-situations. The confrontation between these factors may produce a far-reaching deformation of the original plot. We shall call such words "themes" of the narrative. This concept of theme is similar in several of its features to the "motif," as understood by A. N. Veselovskij (1940: 500; cf. Tomashevskij, 1925), who emphasized the difference in level between plot and motif when he wrote that plot is that "into which several different motif-situations are thrust." Our interpretation of the correlation of "theme" and "motif" will be discussed below.

The capacity of plot-realia to become themes is dependent on many factors. The first of these to be noted is the importance of the given object in the given system of culture. Such realia as "house," "road" or "fire" permeate the whole density of human culture, thereby acquiring whole complexes of associations in every age. They thus become saturated with complicated connotations, which are so rich in associations that the introduction of them into a text immediately makes possible a multitude of twists and turns in the narrative, which are unforeseen in terms of the basic plot.

Themes of this type penetrate through all levels of culture and become supratemporal in nature, although they are naturally concretized in the forms of any one culture. However, there are other themes, which are characterized by markedly historical concretization and which relate to less fundamental structures of the text. Examples of such themes are, for instance, "the duel," "the parade" and "the automobile"—themes with a markedly historical concretization—or "the bull-fight" and "the harem," which for the literature of European Romanticism have become references to certain "exotic" cultures.

It is also important that the transformation of realia into a textual theme may stimulate the particular ways in which they function artistically, this being dependent on the nature, structure, function and external appearance of the realia. Some themes become means of modelling space ("the house," "the road"), others model the internal structure of a collective ("the social order," "the parade," "Ward No. 6" or "prison") or the nature of conflicts ("duel," "fight" and "game").

In this article we shall be discussing a very concrete aspect of theme, one which is clearly specific to a well-defined historical period. This will allow us to identify and discuss some theoretical problems.

Cards are an example of specific cultural realia. However, their immanent internal organization and their function in the society of a given period, together with the historical and cultural associations which have been accepted as meaningful analogues of the card game, have combined to transform them into a semiotic fact. During the Baroque age, the world was seen as a huge book composed by God and the image of the Book became the model for numerous complex concepts (and consequently, when it occurred in a text, became a plot

theme). In the same way, in the late eighteenth and early nineteenth centuries cards and the card game came to be seen as a universal model, the Card Game, which becomes the center of a unique mythopoeia of the time.

> Whatever Voltaire or Descartes may say—
> The world for me is a pack of cards,
> Life is the bank; fate deals, I play
> And the rules of the game I apply to people.
>
> (Lermontov, 1956:339)

Through their social function and their immanent mechanism, cards, as a specific theme, imposed such severe limitations on the behavior both of real people and of literary characters that the very introduction of them into the action made the further development of a story to some extent predictable. The following is evidence of this fact. In 1820 Hoffmann published his story *Spielerglück*. Russian translations of it were not long in coming: in 1822 V. Poljakov published his in No. 13-14 of *The European Herald* [*Vestnik Evropy*] and in 1836 that of I. Bezsomykin appeared in the book *E. T. A. Hoffman, The Serapion Brothers, Part 6* (see Zhitomirskaja, 1964:48-49). The plot unfolded in the story, that of the loss of one's beloved at cards, did not pass unnoticed. It is quite possible that it was known to Lermontov, who apparently began work on *The Wife of the Tambovsk Treasurer* [*Tambovskaja kaznachejsha*] (Shtein, 1947:275) in the second half of 1837. However, it is safe to assume that Hoffmann, when working on his story, knew nothing of the affair which had caused such a sensation in Moscow in 1802, when Prince Aleksandr Nikolaevich Golitcyn, the famous Cosa-rara, a spendthrift, gambler and society wastrel, staked and lost his wife, the Princess Marija Grigorevna (née Vjazemskaja) to one of the most colorful Moscow grandees, Count Lev Kirillovich Razumovskij, known in society as "le comte Léon." He was the son of a hetman, a freemason and patron of the arts, and the festivities that took place in his house on the Tverskaja and in Petrovskoe-Razumovskoe were the talk of all Moscow. The subsequent divorce of the Princess from her husband and her remarriage lent notoriety to the scandal. When the same plots emerge independently in literature and in life, one can only conclude that some mechanism has been introduced which greatly restricts the variety of possible actions and, by filtering a situation, so to speak, reduces the practically limitless number of impulses and motivations to an extremely limited group of actions. In this case, such a "filter" will function as a peculiar code: this code determines the encoding of the numerous situations which exist "at input" and correlates them with the limited number of plots "at output." The entire sum of possible plot developments is already potentially concealed within such a code. Any "theme" constitutes just such a code, which is introduced as an addition into the text, creating plot moves which, in Veselovskij's phrase, are "thrust" into the basic outline of the plot. Thus, for example, in V. J. Propp's invariant plot schema of the fairy tale, the actual nature of the magical agent is immaterial, be it a horse, a sword, a psaltery or a steel (Propp, 1969). However, it is obvious that as soon as some choice is made from this selection in an actual text, a whole series of events in the further development of the text is thereby predetermined. In the case with which we are concerned here, it is the theme of cards which constitutes this filtering agent, the introduction of which ensures a marked limitation of plot variety.

The semiotic specificity of the card game in its immanent essence is connected with its dual nature. On the one hand, the card game is a *game,* i.e., it acts as a model of a conflict situation. In this sense, it functions in its totality as an analogue of several real conflict situations. It also contains within itself the rules which control the hierarchical system of the relative values of the individual cards and the rules which govern the various possible combinations of them, the two factors which together form the situations of "winning" and "losing." But individual cards within the limits of the card game do not have any semantic relationship to denotations which lie outside the sphere of cards. When in Hermann's distraught imagination the cards acquire a semantic value outside the game ("the three blossomed in front of him like a lush flower, the seven took on the appearance of a Gothic gateway and the ace was like an enormous spider" (Pushkin, 1948: VIII, 1, 249)), they are having meanings ascribed to them which they do not possess in their own system. However, on the other hand, cards are used not only in card games, but also in fortune-telling (see Lekomceva & Uspenskij, 1965; Egorov, 1965). In this hypostasis other functions are activated, those of forecasting and programming. At the same time, another type of modeling emerges into the foreground, one in which the semantic values of the individual cards are activated.

In the functioning of cards as a unified semiotic mechanism, these two aspects have a tendency to blend into each other. When we encounter the epigraph to Pushkin's *The Queen of Spades* [*Pikovaja dama*],—"The queen of spades denotes hidden malice. *The Newest Fortune-Telling Book*" (Pushkin, 1834:187)—and then in the text of the work the queen of spades appears as a playing card, we are dealing with a typical instance of the mutual influence exerted between these two planes. This is one of the reasons why the card game occupied such a special place in the imagination of Pushkin's contemporaries and in the literature of the time, a place with which the other games fashionable then, for example, chess, which was popular at the end of the eighteenth century, could not compare. A vital factor in this position was, apparently, the fact that the single concept of "card game" covers the modeling of two completely different types of conflict situation,—the so-called

games of "bidding" and the games of "chance."There is a great deal of evidence to show that the former are regarded as "decent," while the latter are definitely subject to adverse moral judgment. Similarly, the former are attributed to "respectable people" and a propensity for them does not have the connotation of excessive modishness which is attributed to the latter. In her *Critical and Systematic Dictionary of Court Etiquette,* Madame de Genlis (1818:304-305) writes:

> It is to be hoped that drawing-room hostesses will be sufficiently discriminating not to tolerate games of chance in their homes: it is more than enough to permit billiards or whist, which over the last ten to twelve years have incorporated a great many innovations which have spoiled them. In particular, they have begun to involve much more money, thus increasingly resembling games of chance. The venerable piquet alone has retained its original purity—not for nothing is it now held in little repute.

In N. Straxov (1791:31-32), Card Game presents to Fashion the service records of his subjects:

I

Money games which deserve promotion:

1. Banque

2. Reste

3. Quintiche

4. Vingt-Un

5. *Kuchki*

6. Jourdon

7. *Gora* [mountain]

8. Macao, which is somehow extremely offended by the neglect shown to it.

II

Games which have recently been imported and deserve to be taken into service and introduced into general use:

1. Stoss

2. Three and three

3. Rocambole

III

Games which have submitted requests to be placed in service with respectable people:

1. Ombre

2. Whist

3. Piquet

4. Tenteret

5. A la mouche

IV

Games which have submitted a request to be dismissed to the provinces and villages:

1. Panfil

2. Tressette

3. Bassette

4. Shnip-shnap-shnur

5. Mariage

6. *Durachki s par* [from pairs]

7. *Durachki v navalku* [loose]

8. *Durachki vo vse karty* [with all cards]

9. *Eroshki or khrjushki* [ruffles or grunts]

10. Three leaves

11. Seven leaves

12. *Nikitishny*

And

13. *V noski* [into the socks]—straight into retirement.

Both the above quotations draw a firm line between the "respectable" and "moral" bidding games and the "fashionable" and dangerous games of chance; it is worth noting that first place among the latter in Straxov's list is occupied by banque and stoss, varieties of faro. It is known that between the late eighteenth and early nineteenth centuries, games of chance were formally suppressed in Russia as being immoral, although in practice they flourished.

The difference between these forms of games, which also determined the differences in their social function, consists firstly in the degree of information which the players possess and, secondly and consequently, in the factor which determines the win: calculation or chance. In bidding games the player's task is to guess the strategy of his opponent, each player possessing enough information to sift through the variants and make the calculations necessary in order to do so. In the first place, bidding games have relatively complicated rules (compared with games of chance) and the number of possible strategies in them is thus limited by the very nature of the game. Secondly, the player's own psy-

chology imposes limitations on the selection of strategies available to him. Thirdly, this selection is also dependent on an element of chance, namely the cards which happen to be dealt to the player. This latter aspect is the most obscure, but it is still quite possible to make probable propositions about it on the basis of the way the game develops. But at the same time the player in the bidding game is able to determine his own strategy, while trying to conceal it from his opponent.

In this way, the bidding game, which is an intellectual duel, may act as the model of conflicts of a specific kind.

These include, firstly, conflicts between equal opponents, i.e., between people, and secondly, conflicts which entail the availability of complete (or rather, sufficiently complete) information to the participants, regarding the aspects of the conflict which interest them and, consequently, the rationally regulated possibility of winning. Bidding games model conflicts in which the intellectual superiority and the greater amount of information possessed by one of the players guarantees his success. It comes as no surprise that the eighteenth century produced, in V. Majkov's *The Ombre Player* [*Igrok lombera*], an acclamation not only of the bidding game, but also of the principles of *strict adherence to rules,* calculation and moderation:

> [. . .] a dwelling-place for those is defined,
> Who can play with restraint at ombre;
> And if anyone can restrain himself thus,
> So that without four games he doesn't buy more cards,
> And without five he does not play *sans prendre* [*sanprander*] in his time [. . .]
> [. . .] That if he comes in future to play with more restraint,
> Then he may be even more fortunate than before at the game.

(Tomashevskij, 1933:109)

B. V. Tomashevskij maintained (1933:704) with good reason that "in his poem Majkov supports the moderate card game and recommends the use of calculation rather than chance in games." The appearance of poems about the *rules* of games, for example chess (Ejxenbaum, 1929:15-16), is in this sense a quite natural development.

Games of chance are constructed in such a way that the punter is required to take decisions when he actually has little or no information to help him[2]. There are various forms of possible strategy, which are denoted in the game of banque by such terms as "playing mirandole," "double stake corner" [*paroli*], "quadruple stake corner" [*paroli pe*], "run of luck" [*rute*], and "quinze-elle-va" [*kenselva*] (see Chernyshev, 1935:402-404; Ashukin, 1913; Chixadze, 1960). However, each deal of the pack is an independent event in relation to all other deals and the same can also be said of the sequence of cards in the deal: therefore, the effectiveness of choosing one strategy or another depends on chance. In an attempt to define what this concept entails, W. J. Reichmann (1969:168) writes:

> Measurement depends on the observance of specific rules. The French philosopher J. Bertrand once put the following question: "How can we talk about the laws of chance? Surely chance is the antithesis of any law?" To say that the result of an event is determined by chance is the same as admitting that we have no notion of how it is determined.

It follows, therefore, that the punter is playing not with another person, but with Chance. And if we recall that the same author goes on to say that "chance is a synonym [. . .] for unknown factors and, to a significant extent, it is precisely this which the ordinary man understands by luck" (Reichmann, 1969: 168-169) then it becomes obvious that the game of chance is a model of man's struggle with Unknown Factors. It is at this point that we approach the heart of the question as to *what* conflict was modeled in Russian life of the time by games of chance, and why these games became the passion of entire generations (cf. Pushkin's admission to Wulf: "The passion for gaming is the strongest of all") and a persistently recurrent motif in literature.

World literature has often dealt with the problems of chance, luck and their connection with individual destiny and human activity. Different aspects and stages of the interest in this question are reflected in the classical novel, the Renaissance novella, the picaresque novel of the seventeenth to eighteenth centuries, and the psychological prose of Stendhal and Balzac. It is easy to discover in each of these phenomena features of the historical process. However, there had to be national as well as historical reasons for the increasing prominence of this problem. One cannot help noticing that the whole of the so-called "Petersburg" imperial period of Russian history is marked by thoughts about chance (and its eighteenth-century manifestation as "good fortune" [cf. Novikov, 1951:105; Krylov, 1945:I, 43]—the specific form given to the structure of individual destiny by the circumstances of "woman's rule"). These thoughts also concerned the role of fate and the contradiction between the unbending laws of the external world and the individual's thirst for personal success and self-assurance, the play of the individual with circumstances, history, and the Whole, the laws of which are Unknown Factors so far as the individual is concerned. And throughout this period the more general plot collisions—together with certain other key theme-images—are concretized through the theme of banque, faro, stoss and roulette—the games of chance.

On the one hand, this question involves both the complex problem of chance in the non-religious Europeanized consciousness of the Enlightenment and Romanticism, and the unrestricted play of individual wills in the bourgeois post-revolutionary European world. Balzac's prose demonstrates very clearly the way in which the individual is ruled by egoism: in each case, the strategy of this egoism may well be guessed, but the attendant social integration turns out to be for every individual a partner who represents Unknown Factors; the strategy employed by the partner acquires an irrational character. However, on the other hand, a specifically Russian situation also begins to emerge. Beginning with the Petrine reforms, the life of educated Russian society developed on two different levels: its intellectual, literary and philosophical development corresponded in tempo and direction to the European movement, while the socio-political basis of society changed more slowly, following other laws. This led to a marked increase in the role of chance in the historical process. Each factor of one category appeared from the point of view of the other to be anarchic and accidental, while the continuous inter-penetration of phenomena from these different categories led to the unevenness and apparent causelessness of events, of State measures and the destinies of individuals, all of which made men of the time declare entire aspects of Russian life to be "inorganic," illusory and non-existent. Pushkin, for example, stated that there was no genuine aristocracy in Russia; Andrej Turgenev, the Decembrist critics, Polevoj, Nadezhdin, Venevitinov, the young Belinskij and Pushkin again declared, each in their own time, that there was no literature in Russia; Chaadaev said the same of Russian history; the Slavophils directed the charge at the post-Petrine State and society. One could continue the list indefinitely. In each case, the fact which was being denied did, of course, exist and this was perfectly well understood by the very people who were denying it. But it was felt to be inorganic, phantom and illusory. All this influenced the literary perception of the two basic spheres in which plot collisions were realized in Russia between the late eighteenth and early nineteenth centuries: that of service, rank and career on the one hand and of money on the other.

By the second half of the eighteenth century there had come into being a literary canon in which "chance" and "career" (the latter being used mainly in the masculine gender) were perceived as the results of the unpredictable play of circumstances, the caprices of Fortune. The "good fortune" of the Russian nobleman of the eighteenth century came about from the conflict of the diverse and often mutually exclusive laws of social life. "Service," as constituted by the system of the table of ranks, the hierarchy of titles, the power of the authorities and the order of production, came to form a relatively controlled and extremely active mechanism. By the reign of Nicholas I [1825-1855], this mechanism was in process of becoming the dominant State mainspring—the bureaucracy. However, even when questions of service promotion were at issue, the laws of the bureaucratic machine were not the only ones which came into effect. We need only recall the following well-known passage from *War and Peace*:

> It was at that moment that Boris clearly understood what he had earlier foreseen,—namely, that in the army, besides the principles of seniority and discipline embodied in the regulations which were known to him and everyone else in the regiment, there existed another, more vital system of seniority, which compelled this tightly-buttoned, purple-faced general to wait respectfully while captain Prince Andrej pleased himself by chatting to corporal Drubetskoj.
>
> (Tolstoj, 1951: IV, 306)

Family and kinship connections constituted a very real form of social organization in the life of the Russian nobility of the eighteenth to early nineteenth centuries and provided opportunities and means of advancement quite separate from the table of ranks. The fact that it was possible for any superior officer to behave sometimes according to one norm of conduct (for example, in treating a junior officer as befitted his rank) and on other occasions according to different rules (treating him as a relative or, for example, as a member of a certain influential family) turned service life from what should have been the controlled development of a predictable text into a series of anomalies. Such notions as "good fortune," "good luck,"—and the action which conferred them on people,—"favor," were thought of not as the realization of immutable laws, but as an anomaly, an unpredictable violation of such laws. The play of various quite separate factors made unexpectedness into a constantly active mechanism. People waited for the unexpected and then were either glad of it or indignant about it, but they were never surprised by its appearance; for them, it came within the confines of the possible, just as a man who takes part in a lottery is pleased if he wins, but is not astounded at having done so.

The possibility of receiving exceptional favors, which existed in every section of the service hierarchy, found its most extreme form in the favoritism which was so characteristic of the Russian state system in the eighteenth century. From the point of view of the state norm, which was fixed by laws, this phenomenon appeared as a violation of the prescribed order. It was precisely on these grounds that favoritism was criticized by the Russian constitutionalists of the eighteenth century. However, when viewed "from within," it displays a distinct and intelligible system. Pushkin was, therefore, quite justified in noting that "the very voluptuousness of this cunning woman [Catherine II] established her sovereignty" (Pushkin, 1948: XI, 15). But the intrusion of the laws of favoritism into the sphere of State activity was regarded there as a violation of all laws and a triumph for unpredictability and "chance." Pushkin went on to say in the same comment that "one didn't need

intelligence, merit or talent to reach the second place in the State." In his short but very perceptive introduction to the publication of Catherine II's letters to Count P. V. Zavadovskij, Ja. L. Barskov claimed that favoritism in Russia was quite different from the analogous phenomenon in other European states. It was a "kind of institution, with a wide but constantly changing sphere of affairs and a vast but unspecified budget." According to Barskov, "debauchery was a secondary feature of favoritism, and the latter was, in moral terms, a particular manifestation of a general decline in morals, a product rather than a root cause," and he goes on to demonstrate the essence of favoritism as an institution of autocratic monarchy.

The intersection of these laws in an individual's destiny appeared to contemporaries, the living participants of the age, as the rule of Chance. It is this fact which gives rise to the image of political life as a succession of chance elements, inevitably reminiscent of the card game, which in this context functions as a natural model of this aspect of being. We find a similar picture of the universal "faro" in Derzhavin's ode *To Fortune* [*Na shchast'e*]:

> In these days when all are given over to merry-
>   making:
> Politics and justice,
> Intelligence, conscience and holy law,
> And logic hold banquets,
> They stake the golden age on cards,
> And punt with the destinies of mortals
> They bend the universe into a *trente-elle-va*[3]
> Like the poles and the meridians,
> The sciences, muses, gods are drunk,
> All skip and dance and sing [. . .]
>
> (Derzhavin, 1957:126)

The acquisition of wealth also appeared to men of the age to be just as random and internally unmotivated. Depending on the caprices of fortune, vast amounts of money could be made overnight, in spheres of activity which were very far removed from the normal course of economic affairs. Castéra maintains that the Orlovs received from the Empress 17,000,000 roubles, Vasil'chikov 1,100,000, Potemkin 50,000,000, Zavadovskij 1,380,000, Zorich 1,420,000, Lanskoj 7,260,000 and the Zubov brothers 3,500,000. According to his information, the various favorites during Catherine II's reign were paid in total 92,500,000 roubles, quite apart from the payments which were made to their relatives, the gifts of the favorites themselves, the leases they controlled and all the other opportunities for easy riches which were at their disposal. Pushkin recorded the following conversation which he had with N. K. Zagrjazhskaja:

> Potemkin once remarked, while visiting me: "Natal'ja Kirillovna, would you like some land?"—"What land?"—"I have some in the Crimea."—"Why should I

take land from you, to what purpose?"—"Well, naturally, the Empress will give it to you, I shall just ask her to grant me a favor"—"Be so kind." [. . .] A year goes by and some people bring me 80 roubles.—"What is this from, gentlemen?"—"From your new lands, there are herds there and this is money for them" [. . .] At that time Kochubej was courting Masha. So I said to him: "Kochubej, please take my Crimean lands, they're nothing but trouble to me." What do you think? Those lands later brought Kochubej an income of 50,000 roubles. I was very pleased for him.

(Pushkin, 1948: XII, 176)

The huge fortunes which were accumulated by some individuals were rarely retained by their direct descendants for more than two generations. This extraordinary transference of wealth was very reminiscent of the way in which gold and bank notes changed hands over the green cloth during a card game. The action of economic laws, planning and productive efforts in the acquisition of wealth was associated with the bidding game, in which calculation and skill were conducive to winning. But it is banque or stoss which were the accepted analogies for instances of sudden and irregular acquisition of wealth, such enrichments being characteristic of the nobility's interpretation of the very concept of wealth: as an example, the "acquisitor" Chichikov (in Gogol's *Dead Souls,* tr.), who since his childhood had been determined to amass money for himself, became not a factory owner but a swindler who tried to achieve instantaneous and irregular riches.

But it was not only these areas of life, to do with service and financial affairs, which were subject to the law of non-motivation and the unexpected, factors which changed the succession of events from the unfolding of a structure with increasing redundancy into a sequence of mutually independent anomalies. Chaadaev saw in this a more general situation:

It is natural for a man to feel lost when he has no means of establishing contact with what has preceded him and with what follows him. He is then deprived of any security, any assurance. Not being guided by a *feeling of continuity,* he sees himself as a lost wanderer in the world. Such bewildered people can be found in every country; but in Russia it is a general feature [. . .] We have absolutely nothing in common in our minds; everything in them is individual and everything is unstable and incomplete.

(1941: II, 114-115)

Following this line of interpretation, contemporaries often explained the culture of the nobility of the "Petersburg period" by reference to the decisive break with the tradition of Russian culture, which came about as a result of the reforms made in the early eighteenth century. It is possible, however, that the reason for this lay in a quite contrary phenomenon, namely the fact that a whole series of social structures—primarily sociopoliti-

cal—turned out to be unusually persistent. Cultural polyglotism was intensified as a result of the reforms and this led, on the one hand, to the heightened semiotic value of eighteenth-century Russian culture and, on the other hand, to the discordant (not polyglot) nature of the culture. People of the age saw their culture as a contradictory whole, modeled on the high points of life by distinct and intelligible models, but in real life giving the appearance of chaos and the triumph of chance, whose image is the world of the card game of chance. Rationalistic theory ("Voltaire or Descartes") and a pack of cards in the hands of the dealer constitute a two-part form which, in the very extent of its inter-correlation, covers, in Lermontov's formula, the entire density of Russian life of the time, from the elegant theories of the mind to the play with the Unknown Factors of real life.

In this way, the game of chance was accepted as a model both of the social world and of universum. As we have seen, this position was determined, from one point of view, by the fact that some features of these worlds were regarded as being analogous to the card game. But a contrary analogy also emerged: the card game became a language into which various phenomena of the external world were translated and it exerted an active modeling influence on the conception of the object itself. V. V. Vinogradov has written persuasively about the modeling effect of the lexis of this language, which divides the picture of the world thus created into units:

Every cant is characterized by the fact that its system of understanding the world has two dimensions of meaning. Cant speech embodies in itself the reality and structure of its own professional world, in the form of an ironic correlation and juxtaposition of its world with the culture and daily life of the surrounding social milieu. But, on the other hand, it also interprets the general principles of life, even the bases of the world order, in the internal symbolic forms of those productive processes, their instruments and their accessories, which fill the cant-consciousness. In essence, these are two sides of the one process of the symbolic interpretation of the world through the prism of a professional ideology; and this ideology is sometimes polemically opposed to the norms of the Weltanschauung of that "society" or of those classes which occupy the dominant position in the state.

(1936:99-100)

The situation of faro is, above all, that of a duel: it models the conflict of two opponents. However, the inequality between them is built into the very essence of this model: the punter is the man who wants to win everything, although at the same time he risks losing everything; he behaves as a man who is compelled to take important decisions without having the necessary information; he can only act by guesswork and can construct propositions only by attempting to deduce some statistical regularities. (It is well known that Pushkin's library contained books on the theory of probability, evidently connected with his attempts to devise the optimal strategy for himself as a punter.) The banker, however, does not have to select any strategy. Moreover, the banker when he deals does not himself know how the cards will fall. He becomes a kind of figurehead under the control of the Unknown Factors which stand behind him. In itself such a model could give rise to particular interpretations of real-life conflicts. The game became a clash with a powerful and irrational force, frequently treated as demonic:

> [. . .] this is a demon [who]
> Twists [. . .] there is no plan in the game.

> (Cvetaeva, 1965:446)

The feeling of the senselessness of the "banker's" behavior was an important feature of the free-thinking consciousness of the eighteenth to early nineteenth centuries. Pushkin, on hearing of the death of Vjazemskij's child, wrote to Prince Petr Andreevich in the following terms:

> Fate will not stop playing tricks with you. Do not be angry with her, for she doesn't know what she's doing. Think of her as an enormous ape which has been given complete freedom. Who will put her on a chain? Not you, nor I,—no one.

> (1948: XII, 278)

But it was just this senselessness and unpredictability of the opponent's strategy which made his behavior seem a mockery, and thus made the Unknown Factors appear infernal in nature.

It is in this way that the opponent is modeled. The model of the "faro" type is oriented: any person operating with it may put himself in only one place, that of the punter, the place of the banker being given most often in the third person. One example of the few exceptions to this rule is Silvio in Pushkin's story, *The Shot* [*Vystrel*]: this is easily explained by the fact that Silvio plays the role of the "man of fate," the representative of destiny, and not its plaything. It is significant that in the scene of the card game he acts like the master of the house,—the banker, who both in life and in literature is always master of the place where the game is taking place, while as a rule, the plot hero is a guest. Similarly, Doloxov thinks of himself as the romantic "man of fate" in his game with Nikolaj Rostov (in *War and Peace*).

However, faro also models its own universum. This is marked, above all, by extreme discreteness (like any modelling of the phenomena of life by means of language): the unit is each "round," enclosed between the "beginning" and the "end" of the action, the former being marked by a transition from an undisturbed and non-signifying state (non-being, from the point of view of the Game) to actions directed towards a radical improvement in status (a win). The psychological condition of the hero at this point in the plot is one of hope. The concluding moment is marked by final ruin (losing, which is never partial or not very significant, but entails the ruin or madness of the character), or by victory, which is also eschatological in nature.

Neither is the text continuous between these two boundaries: it fragments into the separate indivisible sign-states—the cards—and the intervals between them. In addition, each card possesses a certain significance in another system, that of fortune-telling, and the succession of cards consequently forms some kind of narrative. Both in terms of the meanings involved (the "long road," the "official building," etc.) and the unconnectedness of the episodes, this narrative is reminiscent of the picaresque novel. It would, indeed, be quite possible to demonstrate the obvious parallelism of composition between the picaresque novel and a model composed of the elements of cartomancy and the rounds of faro.

The essence of the thing in a text is two-fold: it may appear in its everyday reality, thus constituting one object among others, and it may become a sign of specific cultural meanings. If, in addition, the given meaning is motivated by the nature of the thing itself, its organization or its function, then an analogous organization or function is attributed to the phenomena which it denotes. In other words, it acts as their model. The essence of these phenomena is interpreted by analogy with the object which is mentioned in the text. It is this kind of object-sign-model which becomes a plot theme and may exert an influence, in terms of plot, either on adjacent or neighboring episodes in its capacity as a localized theme, or on the plot as such.

The ability of faro to become a theme of localized and even of general plot significance determined the specific aspects of its use in the text. Interpretation of the composition of the picaresque novel or the novel in general, as rich in its succession of varied episodes as the rounds of faro, led to the card game's being viewed as a compositional unity and emphasized its real discreteness, its division into separate, scarcely connected episodes,—a "collection of motley chapters":

> And gradually into oblivion
> Of feelings and thoughts he falls,
> While before him Imagination
> Deals its varied faro.
> Now he sees: on the thawing snow
> As if sleeping at a night lodging,
> Motionless lies a youth,
> And he hears a voice: what's this? dead.
> Now he sees forgotten enemies,
> Scandalmongers, and spiteful cowards,

And a swarm of young unfaithfuls,
And the circle of despised comrades [. . .]

(Pushkin, 1948: VI, 183-184)

Compare this with the following imitative verse:

[. . .] of prison, of post-road journeys
The varied and fickle faro [. . .]

(Vs. Rozhdestvenskij, *Manon Lesko*)

The contrasts in bourgeois society, the conflict of poverty with wealth, and the power of money, became one of the leading plot fields of European literature as a whole in the 1830s and 1840s. In Russian literature, this complex of problems is linked sometimes with Western European material—Pushkin's works, *The Covetous Knight* [*Skupoj rycar'*], *Maria Schoning* [*Marija Shoning*], *Scenes from Knightly Times* [*Sceny iz rycarskix vremen*],—and sometimes with Russian reality. Each of these two plot varieties has its own specific features: the Western European material usually stimulates the writer to adopt historical subjects, while the Russian material will move him to take up contemporary subjects, even going as far as the complete confluence of narrative and reader time. However, another aspect is even more crucial: plots of the first type are concerned with what is regular, those of the second with what is chance; the former reveal the immanent essence of "the age of money," while the latter deal with the anomalies to which it gives rise. The clash of father and son, the death on the scaffold of the innocent Maria Schoning and Anna Garlin inevitably derive from the mechanism of the tyranny of money over man. In the plots taken from Russian reality, yet another link is introduced between social causes and the plot consequences: the link is chance, "events which may or may not take place as a result of an experiment" (Jaglom & Jaglom, 1973:21-22). It is not surprising, therefore, that Pushkin and Gogol stand at the head of a tradition which specifically links the idea of self-enrichment in Russian plots with cards (from *The Queen of Spades* to Dostoevskij's *The Gambler*) or with speculation (from Gogol's Chichikov to Suxovo-Kobylin's Krechinskij). It is worth noting that the "knight of money"—the baron in Pushkin's *The Covetous Knight* [*Skupoj rycar'*]—emphasizes the importance in his self-enrichment of long-term planning, a gradual approach and purposeful economic efforts:

Thus I, bringing by the poor handful
My wonted gift here into the cellar,
Built up my hill [. . .]
Here is an ancient doubloon [. . .] here it is. Today
A widow gave it to me [. . .]
[. . .] And this one? it was brought to me by Tibo.

(Pushkin, 1948: VII, 110-111)

On the other hand the behavior of Hermann when he becomes a gambler is dominated by the attempt to acquire instant wealth, which is not determined by economic factors:

When sleep overtook him, he dreamed of cards, the green board, stacks of banknotes and piles of gold coins. He played card after card, turning down the corners without hesitation, winning continually. He raked in the gold for himself and laid flat his banknotes.

(Pushkin, 1948: VIII, 1, 236)

The momentary appearance and disappearance of "fantastic wealth" also characterizes Chichikov. Whereas in Hermann it is calculation and chance which conflict and whereas in Chichikov calculation triumphs, it is hazard which takes the upper hand with Krechinskij. Fedor's words demonstrate this quite clearly:

But when we lived in Petersburg—Heavens above!—what money there was! What gaming! [. . .] And he was always like that: money was nothing but straw or firewood to him. At university he did his share of high living, but when he left the university it just went on and on, like some kind of whirlpool. Acquaintances, counts, princes, friendships, drinking and cards.

(Suxovo-Kobylin, 1886:63)

This may well be compared with Raspljuev's parodically dismissive attitude, as expressed in his words—"Money . . . cards . . . destiny . . . fortune . . . an evil, awful madness" (Suxovo-Kobylin, 1886:65). The observe of this tradition is the eventual transformation of the "Russian German" Hermann into another "Russian German," Andrej Shtolcs (in Goncharov's *Oblomov*).

It would be inappropriate in the present work to examine the plot of *The Queen of Spades* in all its complexity, particularly as this question has already been the subject of several analyses.[4] We can, however, record our agreement with the group of scholars who see in the conflict between Hermann and the old countess a clash between the age of the 1770s and the age of the 1830s, between the age of the "porcelain shepherdesses, table clocks by the famous Leroy, all kinds of little boxes, roulettes, fans and various lady's toys," invented in the eighteenth century, "together with the Montgolfiers' balloon and Mesmer's magnetism," and the age of money. The clash of the two generations was selected as the plot language for the construction of this historical conflict, just as was done in Pushkin's *The Covetous Knight* [*Skupoj rycar'*] or *To a Grandee* [*K vel'mozhe*]; through this confrontation we are able to distinguish the ancient archetype plot of the struggle between parents and son.[5]

However, our interest at the moment is not in this question, but in one which is much more restricted, namely, what influence is exerted on this given type of plot by the historically inevitable, but typologically accidental, circumstance that cards became a plot-propelling mechanism.

The theme of the card game introduces chance—an unpredictable course of events—into the mechanism of the plot and into the link between the motives of the hero and the results of his actions. Chance becomes both the mechanism of the plot and the subject of the hero's and author's deliberations. The plot begins to be constructed as the hero's approach to his aim, closely followed by an unexpected catastrophe (the "suddenly—madness" of Gogol and the "It's all over!!!" of Krechinskij in the work of Suxovo-Kobylin).

One of the consequences of this mechanism of the plot is the characterization of the hero as a man of will, who strives amid the turbulent movement of surrounding life to achieve an aim which he has set himself. The "probability" picture of the world, the conception of life as being ruled by Chance, opens before the individual opportunities of unlimited success, and sharply divides people into the passive slaves of circumstance and the "men of Fate," whose appearance in European culture in the first half of the nineteenth century is invariably associated with the figure of Napoleon. A hero characterized in this way needs for there to be with him in the text a suffering character, in relationship with whom the hero reveals his Bonaparte-like qualities. In another aspect of the plot construction, the hero will be correlated with Game and with the power which conducts this game. This power,—an irrational one, because of the very nature of the relationships between the banker and the punter,—may easily be seen as an infernal force which mocks the Napoleonic hero and plays with him. Hence the narrative necessity for the chain of heroes *Liza-Hermann-the old countess,* a chain which gives rise to a particular tradition in Russian prose and is later reflected in the series of characters *Sonia-Raskolnikov-the old money-lender* (in *Crime and Punishment*).[6]

However, this question is complicated by the fact that the old countess fulfils two different functions in Pushkin's story: that of Hermann's victim and that of the representative of the forces with whom Hermann is playing his game ("I came to you against my own will . . . ," "I am ordered to . . .").

The influence of the theme of cards on the plot of *The Queen of Spades* emerges in the clash of chance and regularity and in the actual treatment of the concept of chance. Hermann is an engineer, with a cold, precise mind. Calculation and hazard confront each other in Hermann's consciousness. However, Hermann sees himself as acting with dispassionate, automatic reason. Indeed, he would like to expel chance from the world and from his own destiny. He can only bring himself to take a seat at the green board when he is certain of the outcome of the game and he is not disturbed by the ethical aspect of his actions. In fact, he reveals his credo on the very first page of the story in a phrase which is remarkable for its strict logicality, its exactitude of expression and complete neutrality of style, thus standing out clearly against the background of the other players' emotional utterances: "Card playing interests me greatly,—said Hermann,—but I am not in a position to sacrifice the necessary in the hope of acquiring the superfluous." "Calculation, moderation and hard work; these are my three true cards"—he muses later. Calculation stands in first place and not only can Hermann not rely on chance, he rejects its very existence: "'Chance'—said one of the guests. 'A fairy-tale!'—remarked Hermann."

Pushkin emphasizes that Hermann's head remains cool even at the height of passion and fantasy. Thus, after the ghost's visit, he "returned to his room, lit a candle and wrote down what he had seen." Hermann's first win was not only a realization of his dream of wealth, but was also evidence of the reality of the supernatural phenomena; it signified that the secret of the three cards really existed and that the appearance of the old woman was not the hallucination of an inflamed imagination. Nevertheless, Hermann merely "drank a glass of lemonade and set off home." Hermann is born for such a duel with destiny, where his cold mind and his iron principles of planning are of use in his intellectual rivalry with the world. It also follows from what we said earlier that another motif runs through the story, together with that of calculation, namely that of the bidding game. The whole of the duel between Hermann and Chekalinskij is accompanied by a parallel description of a game of another type, which is going on in a neighboring room: "Several generals and privy counsellors were playing whist" (the first day of Hermann's game); "The generals and privy counsellors left their game of whist in order to see this extraordinary game" (the third day). It is therefore obvious that whist, which in Straxov's listing is still reckoned to be a game "in use among steady and respectable people," is not an instrument for the rapid and unmotivated acquisition of wealth. But Hermann is a man of dual nature, a Russian German with a cold mind and a fiery imagination, who longs for sudden riches and this forces him to enter the sphere of Chance, which is alien to him.

In 1869 A. Suxovo-Kobylin derided belief in the rationality of the world in the epigraph which he selected for his trilogy: "Wer die Natur mit Vernunft ansieht, den sieht sie auch vernünftig an. Hegel, *Logik.* 'Do as you would be done by'—*Russian translation.*" Hermann, who has tried to look at the world "mit Vernunft," is nevertheless obliged to act in the conditions of a world based on chance and probability, which looks chaotic to the individual being, who observes only insignificant fragments of the separate processes. The need to select effective tactics in a world which does not provide enough information of value about itself (and is therefore modeled by faro) compels Hermann to resort to signs ("not having any real faith, he was extremely superstitious"). V. V. Vinogradov (1936:87,88) also perceived the equivalence, in this respect, of plots constructed on the mathematical or the mystical solution to the secret of "the true card." Both mathematics and cabbalism have here a single function—as the means of expelling Chance from its own domain. The atttempt "to discover the firm mathematical formulas and laws of winning and thus release the game from the power of chance and the accidental" played the same role in the general system as "a mystical attitude to the cards which bring a win."

However, if faro is taken to be the ideal model of the conflict situation "man versus the external world," it becomes obvious that the probability of winning is different for each side. The external world, which possesses an inexhaustible supply of time and unlimited possibilities of resuming the game, inevitably outplays every individual. At the very moment when it seems to Hermann that *he* is playing (and not risking anything), it turns out that fate is playing *with him*. This is emphasized by the complex structure of the plot. In the first chapters, Hermann conducts a game with partners who are in his power (Liza, and the old countess in the scene in the bedroom). Liza thinks that she is taking part in one game, that of love. (The word "game" here, incidentally, does not signify in any way the degree of sincerity of feeling, but identifies the type of behavior and the choice of a corresponding system of actions.) Hermann actually does imitate this type of behavior: he carefully reproduces the established literary ritual of "the siege of the heart"—standing under the window, writing love letters and so on. The key to Hermann's success lies in the fact that he was actually playing a quite different game, the essence and the rules of which remain unknown to Liza until the last minute. In this way he transforms her from a partner into an instrument. The situation in the countess's bedroom is more complicated: here as well, Hermann attempts to offer his interlocutor a false move—a partnership in a whole collection of games. He has previously prepared himself to become the old woman's lover, he appeals to her "feelings as a wife, lover, mother," knowing in advance that he will in fact be playing a quite different game—the struggle to acquire wealth, in which the countess must function as an instrument and not a partner.[7] However, the old countess, who, a minute before Hermann's appearance, "was sitting, her skin quite yellow, her flabby lips trembling, *rocking to right and to left*" (my italics—Ju. L.), has already become not only a person but also a card, an instrument, not of Hermann's game, but of someone else's, in which Hermann will be the plaything.

Hermann attempts to transfer the situation of the type of his relationship with Liza onto the green board: he imitates the risk involved in a game of faro, but in reality he is playing a certainty. However, he in fact ends up in the same position as Liza, that of someone who does not know what game the world is playing with him. The fantastic element here is not a "thing" (which is evidence of an author's naive belief in the direct intervention of supernatural forces in reality), but a sign, whose meaning may be any force. Such a force may be historical, economic, psychological or mystical, but always seems irrational from the point of view of "planning, moderation and hard work" as a program for the behavior of an individual personality. This is not contradicted even by the derision shown by those forces which Hermann thinks he can outplay (e.g., the winking of the old woman). Similarly, from the point of view of Evgenij in Pushkin's *The Bronze Horseman* [*Mednyj Vsadnik*], the Petersburg flood may be viewed as "the sky's gibe at the earth."

By the time Pushkin came to work on *The Queen of Spades* his interest in the role of chance was already of long standing. He had rejected the romantic conceptions of the determining role played by individual arbitrary action and of chance in the flow of historical events,[8] as well as the extreme historical determinism which was at first contrasted with them and which led to various forms and degrees of "reconciliation with reality." In Pushkin's complex and philosophically comprehensive thinking in the 1830s, "chance" had already ceased to be only a synonym for chaos, and "law"—for regulation and order. Pushkin repeatedly contrasted dead and inflexible law with chance, as death with life. Entropy appeared to him not only as complete disorganization, but also as rigid super-regularity. This led to the concentration on the antithesis of dead-alive and motionless-moving, like that of predictable-unpredictable, which has been studied in depth by Roman Jakobson in his discussion of the thematic element of the statue and the motif of its coming to life (1973).

In this connection, the meaning of another—apologetic—attitude to chance becomes clear: this attitude sees chance as a means of increasing the internal flexibility of the social mechanism by introducing into it unpredictability. Reflecting on the paths of human thought, Pushkin allotted to chance a place among the three most important factors of its progress:

> O how many wonderful discoveries for us
> The spirit of enlightenment prepares
> And Experience, (son) of difficult mistakes,
> And Genius, (of paradoxes) the friend,
> (And Chance, the inventor-god)[9]
>
> (Pushkin, 1948: III, 1, 461)

Earlier variants of the last line contained:

> And Chance, the friend
> And Chance, the leader
>
> (Pushkin, 1948: III, 2, 1059)

It is possible to guess the general nature of the unfinished section, in that its rhythmical line was obviously intended to appear as ⌣–⌣–⌣–⌣–⌣ , while grammatically the continuation was to include a definition group (of the type, "the friend of new discoveries") or an adjunct (of the type, "leader-guide"). The content, however, could be only a formula that defined the positive place of chance in the progress of knowledge. However, in the interval between the first draft and the surface layer of the work (which was also crossed out and was consequently not a final version), Pushkin found the most expressive formula:

> And Chance   the father
> The inventive blind one
>
> (Pushkin, 1948: III, 2, 1060)

A variant of this line is: "And you blind inventor." The gap in the first line may easily be filled, following the sense, by words of the type "of knowledge" or "of truth." However, the very fact that the poet did not use these words which suggested themselves so readily is evidence that they did not contain the nuance of meaning which he needed—that of the moment of invention, the finding of the new, unexpected even by the seeker himself. We may compare this with the situation in *Scenes From Knightly Times* [*Sceny iz rytsarskix vremen*], where brother Bethold was to find gunpowder during his quest for the philosopher's stone.

In connection with this, Pushkin's attitude to chance in history became much more complex. In several lines of an excerpt devoted to N. Polevoj's *History* [*Istorija*], he saw in chance, on the one hand, a superficial layer which obscured the core of the historical process and, on the other hand, a mechanism which revealed the laws of this process. He wrote:

> Guizot has explained one of the events of Christian history: the *European enlightenment*. He locates its embryo, describes its gradual development and, leaving aside all extraneous, marginal and *accidental* factors, presents it to us.

And further on:

> The h(uman) mind, in the vernacular expression, is not a prophet but a diviner. It sees the general course of things and can deduce from it profound propositions, often justified by time, but it is impossible for the mind to foresee *chance*,—the powerful, instantaneous instrument of Providence.
>
> (Pushkin, 1948: XI, 122; Pushkin's italics)

The second aspect of the philosophical interpretation of chance could not but be reflected in the treatment of its plot model—the game of chance. It would be an oversimplification to see in this only a negative factor—the irruption of chaotic forces into the cultural macrocosm and the egoistic drive towards instant self-enrichment in the human microcosm. The same mechanism of the game also serves other purposes: in the world external to man, it serves as the manifestation of higher laws, irrational only when seen from the standpoint of human ignorance; in man's internal world, this mechanism is determined not only by the lust for money, but also by the need for risk, the necessity to de-automatize life and to give space to the play of forces which are suppressed by the weight of everyday reality.

From this point of view, the characters and events of *The Queen of Spades* appear in another light. Whereas in the antithesis "rational (regular)   chaotic (accidental)," the first member of the opposition represented information and the second entropy, in the opposition "dead (immobile or moving automatically)   alive (mobile or changeable)," the places of these categories will change over. Consequently, the accidental (the unpredictable) stands out in the first case as a factor of entropy, in the second as a factor of information. In antithesis to the mechanical flow of the predictable, dead life of Petersburg "high society," faro acts as a mechanism by which the element of alternativity, unpredictability and de-automatization is introduced into everyday reality.

From this point of view, the episodes, events and characters of the story may be divided into the living (mobile, changeable) and the dead (immobile, automatized), although in certain situations they may also move from one category into the other. The whole plot of the story represents an intervention of chance circumstances, which could at the same time be understood as the "powerful, instantaneous instrument of Providence." Although "the anecdote of the three cards made a strong impression" on Hermann's imagination, he opposed calculation to temptation and decided to reject any hope of unexpected wealth,—"No! calculation, moderation and hard work: these are my three true cards." However, at this very moment, Hermann finds himself in the power of chance:

> Reasoning in this way, he found himself in one of Petersburg's main streets, in front of a house of old-fashioned architecture [. . .]—Whose house is this?—he asked the constable on duty.—It belongs to Countess _____,—replied the constable. Hermann started. The extraordinary anecdote once again came into his imagination.

The next day he again *chanced* to find himself in front of the house: "An unknown force, it seemed, drew him to it." Lizaveta Ivanovna at that instant *chanced* to be sitting at the window,—"she happened to look down at the street." "That moment decided his fate."

The heroes move in turn from the sphere of the predictable into the domain of the unpredictable and back again, now coming to life and now turning into dead (literally and metaphorically) automata. Even in the initial situation, Hermann—the man of calculation and a gambler in his heart—is characterized by words with a semantic content of immobility ("sitting [. . .] and looking at the game," "firmness saved him,") and of suppressed movement ("he followed the various turns of the game with feverish excitement").

The heroes of *The Queen of Spades* at one moment turn to stone, at another tremble.

—Something like remorse tugged at his heart and then lay quiet again. He had turned to stone

—trembling inexplicably she got into the carriage

—he followed, trembling feverishly

—Hermann started trembling

—The dead old woman sat there, as if petrified

—Hermann quivered like a tiger

—her hands and feet turned to ice
—Hermann clasped her cold, unresponsive hand

—He stopped and, trembling, waiting for her to reply

—Herman [. . .] crashed backwards on the ground
—Lizaveta Ivanovna was carried out in a faint.

—She began to tremble

The old countess in particular is characterized more than once by her passage from life to death. Roman Jakobson (1973) has pointed out that the titles of three works by Pushkin—*The Bronze Horseman* [*Mednyj vsadnik*], *The Stone Guest* [*Kamennyj gost'*] and *The Golden Cockerel* [*Zolotoj petushok*]—all contain a contradiction between inanimate materials (bronze, stone and gold) and animate characters, thus anticipating the motif of the inanimate's coming to life. The same contradiction is contained in a somewhat different form in the title of *The Queen of Spades,* which refers both to the old countess and to the playing card. The alternating transformation of the countess into the card and the card into the countess activates the semantic marker living / lifeless, animate / inanimate. But even within the limits of her "human incarnation," the countess changes states, according to these markers:

> Suddenly this dead face changed inexplicably [. . .] the eyes came to life.

> The old woman was looking at him in silence apparently without hearing him—

> The countess was obviously embarrassed. Her features expressed a state of inner turmoil, but she soon relapsed into her former insensibility.

> The countess was silent.

> At the sight of the pistol, the countess for the second time showed strong emotion. She shook her head and

raised her arm, as if to protect herself from a shot. Then she fell back [. . .] and remained motionless.

> The countess did not reply. Hermann saw that she was dead.

The transition from insensibility, immobility, mechanicalness and death to excitement, inner movement and life, and the reverse, is encountered several times during this scene. Later, the countess, although already dead, moves, shuffling in her slippers; while lying in her coffin, she winks at Hermann. Her ability to feel emotion, which is directly opposed to the petrification of egoism, emerges in the fact that only beyond the grave does she show any concern for the victim of her whims, Lizaveta Ivanovna. After obeying the command ("I am ordered") to give Hermann the names of the three cards, she "for her own part" forgives him, on condition that he marry Lizaveta Ivanovna. Chekalinskij also is characterized by similar transitions from the deathlike mask of society politeness and ostentatious cordiality to live feeling and emotion:

> His full, fresh face bore a good-natured expression; His eyes shone, enlivened by his *constant smile.* Chekalinskij smiled and bowed in silence, as a token of his humble agreement.

> "Allow me to point out to you," said Chekalinskij with *his unchanging smile,* "that your stake is very high."

> Chekalinskij *frowned,* but the *smile* immediately returned to his face.

> Chekalinskij bowed *affectionately* to him.

> Chekalinskij was obviously *embarrassed.* He counted out 94,000 and handed the sum to Hermann.

> Hermann stood by the table, getting ready to bet alone against the *pale,* but still *smiling,* Chekalinskij.

> Cheksalinskij began to deal, *his hands trembled.*

> Your queen is beaten—said Chekalinskij *affectionately.*

> (My italics: Ju. Lotman)

At first, the smile seems to "enliven" Chekalinskij's face but it later becomes obvious (cf. the epithet "unchanging") that it is in fact a mask, constant and immobile. In other words, it is a dead smile, which conceals from view the true and vital movements of his heart.

The "strong passions and ardent imagination" of Hermann introduce unpredictability, i.e., life, into the measured and mechanically moving, but internally immobile and dead automaton of everyday society life. The game of faro is the mechanism for making this entry.

A thing that comes to life, a corpse which moves and a monument which gallops—these are not living beings, but machines, in that understanding of the word "machine" which the age of mechanics produced. Their unnatural movement only emphasizes their essential deadness. In this sense, the situation of *The Queen of Spades* is different in principle from that of *The Bronze Horseman.* In *The Bronze Horseman,* the inhuman is opposed to the human, the "bronze horseman" to the "poor riches" (Gogol') of the simple human soul. All the heroes in *The Queen of Spades* are automata, who come to life only temporarily, under the disturbing influence of their passions, of chance and the unpredictability which lies hidden both in the depths of their souls and beyond the boundaries of the artificial, mechanical world of Petersburg. Hermann having decided that he must get into the countess's house sets in motion the mechanism of seducing a young girl. He writes "a confession of love: it was tender, respectful and had been taken word-for-word from a German novel." In her confrontation with this machine, Liza behaves like a human being—she falls in love. Her letter is dictated by feeling and emotion. However, it turns out that in fact her reaction is automatic—Hermann is able to foresee it and count on it: "he had expected just that." However, the cards get mixed up, because forces hidden in Hermann's own heart enter the affair, and he ceases to be an automaton. His letters "were no longer translated from the German. Hermann, inspired by passion, wrote them in his own words; the letters expressed both the inflexibility of his desires and the disorder of his uncontrolled imagination."

But the game disrupts the mechanical order of life, violates the automatic politeness of Chekalinskij, brings a rush of life to the dying countess and kills her. It allows Hermann to burst into the world around him "like a wayward comet," but turns him into an automaton, because faro is also a machine: it possesses the illusory life of mechanical movement (to right and to left) and the ability to freeze and kill the soul. In the countess's bedroom, Hermann turned to stone, in Liza's room he "reminded her amazingly of a portrait" and, during the game, the more Chekalinskij's mask comes alive, the more Hermann freezes and turns into a moving statue. Human feelings lose their meaning for him:

> Neither the tears of the poor girl, nor the rare charm of her grief could move his stern soul. He felt no pangs of conscience at the thought of the old woman's death.

And whereas in *The Bronze Horseman* "the sky's gibe at the earth" is the mockery of the inhuman at the living, the taunting of the queen of spades, who "winked her eye and grinned mockingly," is the laughter of an automaton coming to life at one becoming paralyzed.

The story concludes with the complete victory of the automatic world—"the game took its course." All the heroes find their place in the immobility of life's cyclical repetitions: Hermann is a patient in a lunatic asylum

and *repeats* the same words, Lizaveta Ivanovna *repeats* the path taken by the old countess ("Lizaveta Ivanovna is bringing up a poor relative") and Tomskij *repeats* the usual course for a young man—he is promoted to captain and gets married.

Pushkin gives us two models superimposed upon each other:

1. The everyday world (the "inner space" of culture) is ordered and intelligible; it is contrasted to the chaotic world of the irrational, chance, the game. This second world represents victorious entropy, which sweeps away the calculations made by people: the countess died, Hermann breaks with the world of calculation and moderation, and finds himself in a madhouse—the plot ends in catastrophe.

2. The everyday world, which constitutes the "inner space" of culture, is *over-ordered,* inflexible and dead. This is where entropy reigns. Opposed to it is Chance—"the powerful, instantaneous instrument of Providence." It is chance which breaks into the mechanical state of existence and brings it to life. However, automatic order prevails in the end, "the game takes its course." The entropy of inert automatism is victorious. The world where everything is chaotically accidental, and the world where everything has gone dead, to such an extent that there is no place left for an "event," show clearly through each other.

The mutual imposition of these models is still further complicated by the fact that the "outer" and the "inner" space of culture are presented both outside each hero, as the world surrounding him, and within him, as an immanent contradiction.

Both possible exegeses are realized in Pushkin's story in the same "plot machine," namely the theme of cards and the game of chance. This gives the image of faro in *The Queen of Spades* exceptional meaning-capacity and force for modeling action on the text. It is this, indeed, which gives rise to the possibility of opposing interpretations of this theme in the different literary traditions which to an equal extent derive from Pushkin.

Pushkin says of Hermann's last hand that "it was like a duel." It is true that all texts which contain the theme of the game of chance bear a certain similarity to the plot theme of the duel: the outcome of the confrontation in both cases is fatal for one of the parties (as distinct from the theme of the bidding game, in which there is only a problem of insignificant changes (see Andreev, 1913). However, the quite different role played by chance makes a comparison of the duel and faro somewhat remote—in fact one could say, accidental. There is an organic relationship between the theme of cards and the basic plot of Lermontov's *The Fatalist* [*Fatalist*].

In this story (the concluding section of Lermontov's novel, *A Hero of our Time,* trs.) the antithesis between chance and law is interpreted philosophically as the opposition between, on the one hand, the unpredetermined freedom of the human will and, on the other, the complete subjugation of man to a fated chain of cause and effect, the predetermined course of events. K. A. Kumpan has demonstrated convincingly in his thesis on this subject that the former conception was connected with the idea of man prevalent in Western civilization, that of the over-developed personality, individualism, the longing for happiness and the absence of extra-personal stimuli. The latter conception, however, is linked to the Oriental idea of man, inseparable from tradition, alien both to duality and to personal responsibility for his doings, steeped in fatalism (see Kumpan, 1973; 1972).

The "plot machine" of this story is the theme of the game of chance. The very beginning of the story introduces the antithesis between the bidding game ("we were once sitting round at the house of Major S_____; we had got bored with boston and had thrown the cards under the table"), which is associated with the commonplace majority, and the game of chance, the destiny of passionate natures. In the case of Pechorin, one can guess at this (during the course of the story he twice tempts fate: in concluding the fatal bet with Vulich and then in attacking the Cossack murderer). This element is emphasized, however, in the character of his "Eastern" antipode, the Serb Vulich: "There was only one passion which he made no attempt to conceal: his passion for the game" (Lermontov, 1956: VI, 339).

Long before, Sumarokov had written about the fact that banque may in essence be reduced to the making of a random choice in a system with a binary code:

> I soon understood this stupidly devised game, and I thought,—why do they need cards, why do they go to so much trouble in this game? One could play it just as well without cards, thus: draw some signs—*bell, clapper, clapper, bell,* shuffle them and ask people to choose,—*bell or clapper*: if the player guesses what the banker has, he can make a stake on a corner, play sept-elle-va, etc.
>
> (Sumarokov, 1787: X)

If, in addition to the conditions which govern the chance factors in the choice between the two equally probable outcomes, we introduce the belief, which is normal for the literary theme of the game of chance, that life and death are in the bank, we arrive at the schema of Pechorin's and Vulich's bet. Indeed, the comparison is made by the heroes themselves: Vulich, having won his bet when the pistol he placed to his head failed to fire, added, "smiling in a self-satisfied manner:—this is better than banque or stoss" (Lermontov, 1957: VI, 342).

The identification of the game with murder, suicide and death (*The Queen of Spades,* Lermontov's play *Masquerade* [*Maskarad*] and *The Fatalist*) and of the opponent with the infernal forces (*The Queen of Spades,*

Lermontov's fragment *Stoss* [*Shtoss*] etc.) is connected with the interpretation of chance as chaotic and destructive, and of the sphere of entropy as evil. However, it is possible to have a model of the world in which chance will not be negative, but ambivalent in character: being the source of evil, it is also the means of overcoming it.

The eschatological consciousness, for which the triumph of evil is also a sign of its approaching final extinction, and this very transformation is interpreted as an instantaneous and final act, cannot do without miracle. But miracle, by its very nature, must appear in relation to the series of events preceding it as completely unmotivated and in the perspective of natural connections as accidental.

It has long been noted that in Dostoevskij's novels the everyday layer of the plot is unfolded as a sequence of accidental events and scandals, which seem to follow chaotically one after the other (see Slonimskij, 1922b). The abundance of unexpected meetings, "accidental" plot coincidences and the "clumsy" combinations of circumstances organize this level of Dostoevskij's narration. However, it is not only the negative world of Dostoevskij which is characterized by the logic of such sequences of episodes, in which the probability of everyday and unique events is equalized. Such is also the logic of miracle. Take, for example, Xomjakov's lines:

> O, unworthy of selection,
> You are chosen! [. . .]
>
> (1969:137)

Therefore, the same mechanism—the mechanism of the game of chance—is capable of describing both the nightmare world of everyday absurdity and the eschatological destruction of this world, which is followed by the miraculous creation of "a new earth and a new heaven." Dostoevskij's *The Gambler* is very interesting in this respect.

On the one hand, Ruletenburg is the quintessence of that world of absurdities and scandals which is so characteristic of Dostoevskij, while roulette is the center and model of this world. The phrase with which Chapter Four of the novel begins—"today was a funny, chaotic and ridiculous day" (1956: IV, 303)—could have been the epigraph of the entire everyday line of the plot. Throughout the novel run descriptions of situations of the following type:

> What shouting, noise, gabbling and banging there was! And what disorder, upheaval, stupidity and complacency this all is.
>
> (1956: IV, 318)

On the other hand, roulette is characterized as a means of salvation, with the help of which a miracle can be accomplished:

> You are definitely still convinced that roulette is your only way out and your sole salvation?

(1956: IV, 298)

> I rely on roulette alone

(1956: IV, 298)

> Something miraculous happened [. . .] to me that evening. It may well be completely validated by arithmetic, but nevertheless, it is still miraculous, so far as I am concerned.

(1956: IV, 396-397)

This is the familiar theme of the game played to the death ("my whole life was standing on that stake!" (1956: IV, 398). At the same time, this is also an event which is described eschatologically—not only as a miracle, but as death and resurrection in a new and better form:

> I can rise from the dead and begin to live again! I can find the man in myself before he is lost!

(1956: IV, 423)

> To rise again, to be resurrected.

(1956: IV, 432)

There is no genuine miracle in *The Gambler*: the hero, like Raskolnikov in *Crime and Punishment,* considers that money is the source of evil, but, at the same time, he expects salvation from it ("money is everything!" [1956: IV, 312]). The regeneration of the world lies either in replacing a lack of money by an abundance of it,—the idea which gave birth to Masonic Utopian alchemy at the end of the eighteenth century and which was parodied by Goethe in the second part of *Faust,*—or in redistributing money fairly. This means is rejected in Dostoevskij's work. However, the principle of the saving quality of miracle remains—the sudden and unmotivated regeneration of the world. Moreover, it is precisely this belief in the non-motivation and suddenness of salvation that Dostoevskij considers to be a typically Russian feature. It is in this sense that one must understand his claims that the "terrible longing for risk" (1956: IV, 401) is a typical trait of the Russian psyche, and that "roulette is a supremely Russian game" (1956: IV, 431), which is based on the longing "in one hour" "to change one's entire destiny" (1956: IV, 432).

The position of bidding games in *The Gambler* is dominated by a persistent antithesis between the bourgeois practice of accumulative economy in Europe and the Russian striving to change one's destiny in "one hour": "why is the game a worse means of getting money than any other, for example, trade?" (1956: IV, 293). "To the catechism of the virtues and merits of civilized Western man has been added [. . .] the ability to acquire capital" (1956: IV, 306), as opposed to the belief in sudden happiness, "where it is possible to get rich suddenly, in

two hours, without trying." Later, the hero adds: "I don't know which is more vile—ugly Russian disorder or the German way of accumulation by honest toil" (1956: IV, 306).

It is not one of the aims of the present work to examine the socio-historical causes for the heightened role played by the card game in the period between the late eighteenth and early nineteenth centuries. It is only possible to indicate that this problem is an integral part of a more general one: the investigation of the cybernetic mechanisms which are used by a culture as a whole to heighten the internal non-determinateness of the system and to introduce probability links into several of its couplings. This is a complicated question, which is significant in its own right, but we have been principally concerned with the role played by the theme in constructing plot and in thus creating its historically more concretized variants.[10] Our understanding of "theme" is close to the idea of the plot "machine" in A. K. Zholkovskij's article (1967), although there are several differences: we interpret the theme as one of the possible variants, by means of which the invariant typological plot coupling is realized. In more abstract description it may be "removed." However, each theme has *its own* set of "natural" object functions and its own "mythology" (within the limits of the given culture), which endows it with an independent set of predicates.[11] In other words, each theme possesses its own plot-principles, which are quite independent of the general plot, in the realization of which it is used. The way from plot archetype to text is, therefore, that of plot deformation. On taking the opposite direction, the scholar will find, when he is faced with the problem of reconstructing the archetypal plot, that knowledge of the "private mythology" of individual plot themes may help him to calculate the initial archetype, even when he stands at an enormous temporal and cultural distance from it.

Notes

1. [This essay was first] published in *Trudy po znakovym sistemam,* VII, Tartu, 1975: 120-142. Translated into English by C. R. Pike, Russian Studies, University of Keele. Throughout, all quotations have been translated by the translator.

2. In the game of faro, or banque, the banker held one pack of cards and the punter(s) a second pack. Each punter selected a card from the punters' pack and laid it face down on the table. The banker then began to deal, placing his cards alternatively to the right and to the left of the punter's card. If the righthand card was of the same value as the punter's card the banker won, and if the left hand card was of the same value then the punter won. Vladimir Nabokov in his commentary to Pushkin's *Eugene Onegin* suggests that the phrase "quinze-elle-va" should properly be "quinze-et-le-

va," similarly "sept-et-le-va" instead of "sept-elle-va," etc. (trans.).

3. The footnote in the original explains that a "trente-elle-va" is a stake which has been raised by 30 times (trans.).

4. See, for example, Gukovskij (1957: 337-365); Vinogradov (1936: 99-100; 1941: 171-180); Slonimskij (1922a: 171-180). The general problems of *The Queen of Spades* are examined also in the following works: Jakubovich (1935); Lerner (1929); Sidjakov (1973). This latter contains a perceptive analysis of the artistic structure of the story (see, in particular, the analysis of the problems connected with shifts in the point of view and the complex structure of the image of the author [115-121]), and a short bibliography (214). I take this opportunity to express my sincere gratitude to L. S. Sidjakov, who kindly took the trouble to read the present work in manuscript and made a number of valuable suggestions.

5. The presence of such an unrealized possibility is hinted at in the text of *The Queen of Spades,* when, as Hermann falls unconscious beside the coffin of the countess, "a thin man dressed as a court chamberlain, a close relative of the deceased, whispered in the ear of an Englishman standing beside him that the young officer was the natural son of the countess" (VIII, 1, 247). V. V. Vinogradov (1941:587) made the perceptive comment that the reader of the 1830s would sense the unrealized possibility of the construction of the plot as a conflict which disrupts family ties: "The image of an involuntary matricide, the scene of a card duel between brothers, the natural sons of the old crone, together with the striking finale in the eventual madness of one of them,—this is what the French 'nightmare novel' would have manufactured from the material of *The Queen of Spades.*" The possibility of treating the plot in conjunction with its translation into the language of an earlier tradition may be reduced to the mythological archetype (cf. "This hero is the one who boldly opposes his father and eventually overcomes him") (Freud, 1966:13). In this case, the preceding tradition will appear each time as a kind of language, and the analyzed work as a text which belongs partly to this language and can to a certain extent be decoded by means of it, but which is also a text *in another language,* for the understanding of which a special system of decoding must be constructed. Before the emergence on this basis of a tradition, the work in question will appear to be the *only* text in this language, one which has still to be reconstructed on its basis. It is another matter that this new language, as a rule, is already present in the old one,—in the form of extrasystematic or peripheral substructures of it, which pass unnoticed in synchronic description and emerge only in the light of historical perspective.

6. The relationship between Hermann and the old countess has another, semiparodic, parallel, which was noted by Andrej Belyj: that between Chichikov (in Gogol's *Dead Souls*) and Korobochka (see Belyj, 1934: 99-100); it is not without interest that Dostoevskij, when he was creating the confrontation of "Raskolnikov and the old woman," was conscious not only of Hermann, but also of Chichikov, who is after all called a "Napoleon in disguise" (Gogol, 1951: VI, 205). Compare the fact that Hermann has a "Napoleon's profile" with the fact that Chichikov, "if he turns round and stands with his side towards one, very much resembles a portrait of Napoleon" (1951: VI, 206). A possibly unconscious retention of images from *Dead Souls* may be detected in the nickname "German hatter," which is given to Raskolnikov by a drunk at the beginning of *Crime and Punishment* and which rephrases the "German trouser-maker" (and the "Bonaparte") which the coachman Selifan calls his horse in *Dead Souls.*

7. Incidentally, it was precisely this feature that Pushkin identified as the essence of "Bonapartism":

> We all look like Napoleons;
> Millions of two-legged creatures
> Are for us one instrument [. . .]
>
> (1948: VI, 37)

8. From the numerous examples of the romantic treatment of this problem we have selected the words of A. A. Bestuzhev, as preserved by the evidence of G. S. Baten'kov. After the murder of Nastas'ja Minkina, the company, assembled at one of the literary suppers, "were all talking about the changes which might follow as a result of the resignation of Count Arakcheev. A. Bestuzhev said on this occasion that the determined action of one young girl would produce an important change in the destiny of fifty million people. After supper, people began to talk about the fact that there were virtually no great characters or enterprising people left among us." (Quoted from Elagina, 1936:215.) The idea behind Pushkin's *Count Nulin [Graf Nulin]* was in fact a polemic with such conceptions; see Ejxenbaum (1937).

9. Cf. S. I. Vavilov that the quoted excerpt "is evidence of Pushkin's perceptive understanding of the methods of scientific creation" (Pushkin, 1951: 33); for a discussion of this fragment in connection with the problem of science and in relation to *The Queen of Spades,* see Alekseev, (1972:80, 95-109).

10. Cf. yet another thematic aspect of the story. The paralysis—coming to life of characters, which is characteristic of *The Queen of Spades* and which is an integral part of the opposition "live-dead" (one of the basic oppositions for the later Pushkin), has another, more particular sense: in the game of chance, one of the partners inevitably becomes the object of the game, the *plaything*. In *The Queen of Spades* there is a sharp division of function between the *player* and the *plaything*. On assuming the first position, characters come to life, whereas on moving into the second position they freeze: "The queen of spades winked and grinned mockingly"—"Hermann stood motionless" (VIII, 1, 251-252). At that moment, the card is the player and Hermann is the plaything. Hermann thought he was playing cards but in fact the cards are playing with him. Things, in playing with people, come to life, whereas people, when they become the playthings of things, are paralyzed.

11. The predicates which are related to a given theme either in the system of culture as a whole or in some specific category of texts may be defined as *motifs*.

References

Alekseev, M. P., 1972. *Pushkin. Sravnitel'no-istoricheskie issledovanija [Pushkin. Comparative Historical Studies]* (Leningrad).

Andreev, Leonid, 1913. *Bol'shoj shlem [The Grand Slam]*, in: *Polnoe sobranie sochinenij* (St. Petersburg).

Ashukin, N. S., 1913. *Kartochnaja igra [The Card Game]*, in: *Putevoditel' po Pushkinu* (Moskva-Leningrad).

Belyj, Andrej, 1934. *Masterstvo Gogolja [The Mastery of Gogol]* (Moskva-Leningrad).

Chaadaev, P. Ja., 1941. *Sochinenija i pis'ma [Works and Letters]* (Moskva).

Chernyshev, V. I., 1935. "Temnye slova v russkom jazyke" ["Obscure Words in the Russian Language"], in: *AN SSSR akademiku N. Ja. Marru* (Moskva-Leningrad).

1960 "Θ real'nom znachenii motiva trex kart v 'Pikovoj dame'" ["On the Real Meaning of the Motif of the Three Cards in 'The Queen of Spades'"], in: *Pushkin. Issledovanija i materialy, III* (Moskva-Leningrad).

Cvetaeva, Marina, 1965. *Izbrannye proizvedenija [Selected Works]* (Moskva-Leningrad).

Derzhavin, G. R., 1957. *Stixotvorenija [Poems]* (Leningrad).

Dostoevskij, F. M., 1956. *Sobranie sochinenij v 10 tt. [Works I-X]* (Moskva).

Egorov, B. F., 1965. "Prostejshie semioticheskie sistemy i tipologija sjuzhetov" ["Elementary Semiotic Systems and the Typology of Plots"], in: *Trudy po znakovym sistemam, II* (Tartu).

Ejxenbaum, B. M., 1929. *Moj vremennik [My Chronicle]* (Leningrad).

1937 "O zamysle 'Grafa Nulina'" ["On the Conception of 'Count Nulin'"], in: *Vremennik Pushkinskoj kommissii, 3* (Moskva).

Elagina, 1936. *Iz arxiva Elaginyx. Pis'ma G. S. Baten'kova, I. I. Pushchina i E. G. Tollja [From the Archive of the Elagins. Letters of G. S. Batenkov, I. I. Pushchin and E. G. Tolle]* (Moskva).

Freud, Sigmund, 1966. *Moïse et monothéisme* (Paris).

Genlis, Mme de, 1818. *Dictionnaire critique et raisonné des etiquettes de la cour, des usages du monde, des amusements, des modes, de moeurs etc., des françois, depuit le mort de Louis XIII jusqu'á nos jours [. . .] ou l'esprit des etiquettes et des usages anciens, comparés aux moderns* (Paris).

Gogol, N. V., 1961. *Polnoe sobranie sochinenij [Complete Works]* (Moskva).

Gukovskij, G. A., 1957. *Pushkin i problemy realisticheskogo stilja [Pushkin and the Problems of Realistic Style]* (Moskva).

Jaglom, A. M. & I. M. Jaglom, 1973. *Verojatnost' i informacija [Probability and Information]* (Moskva).

Jakobson, Roman, 1973. "La statue dans la symbolique de Pouchkine", in: *Questions de poétique* (Paris)

Jakubovich, D., 1935. "Literaturnyj fon 'Pikovoj damy'" ["The Literary Background of 'The Queen of Spades'"], in: *Literaturnyj sovremennik*.

Krylov, I. A., 1945. *Polnoe sobranie sochinenij [Complete Works]* (Moskva).

Kumpan, K., 1972. "Problema russkogo nacional'nogo xaraktera v tvorchestve M. Ju. Lermontova" ["The Problem of Russian National Character in the Work of M. Ju. Lermontov"], in: *TPI 17 uliopilaste teaduslik konverents* (Tallinn).

1973 "Dva aspekta 'Lermontovskoj lichnosti'" ["Two Aspects of the 'Lermontov Personality'"], in: *Sbornik studensheskix rabot (kratkie soobshchenija)* (Tartu).

Lekomceva, M. I. & B. A. Uspenskij, 1965. "Opisanie odnoj sistemy s prostym sintaksisom" ["Description of a System with Simple SKSEE !! E,"] in: *Trudy po znakovym sistemam, II* (Tartu).

Lermontov, M. Ju., 1956. *Sochinenija [Works]* (Moskva).

Lerner, N. O., 1929. "Istorija 'Pikovoj damy'" ["The History of 'The Queen of Spades'"] (Leningrad).

Lotman, Ju. & V. V. Fursenko, 1963. *"Sochuvstvennik" A. N. Radishcheva. A. M. Kutuzov i ego pis'ma k I. P. Turgenevu [A. N. Radishchev's "Sympathiser." A. M. Kutuzov and His Letters to I. P. Turgenev]*, in: *Trudy po russkoj i slavjanskoj filologii.*

1973 "Proisxohozhdenie sjuzheta v tipologicheskom osveshchenii" ["The Origin of the Plot in Its Typological Illumination"], in: *Stat'i po tipologii kul'tury (Tartu).*

Novikov, N. I., 1951. *Satiricheskie zhurnaly N. I. Novikova [The Satirical Journals of N. I. Novikov]* (Moskva-Leningrad).

Propp, V. Ja., 1969. *Morfologija skazki [The Morphology of the Fairy Tale]* (Moskva).

Pushkin, A. S., 1834. *Povesti, izdannye Aleksandrom Pushkinym [Stories published by Alexander Pushkin]* (St. Petersburg).

1948 *Polnoe sobranie sochinenij [Complete Works]* (Moskva).

1951 *A. S. Pushkin. 1799-1949. Materialy jubilejnyx torzhestv [A. S. Pushkin. 1799-1949. Materials of the Jubilee Celebrations]* (Moskva-Leningrad).

Reichman, W. J., 1918. *Russkij istoricheskij zhurnal [Russian Historical Journal]*, (Moskva).

1969 *Primenenie statistiki [The Use of Statistics]* (Moskva).

Shtein, S., 1947. *Pushkin i Gofman. Stravnitel'noe istoriko-literaturnoe issledovanie [Pushkin and Hoffmann. A Comparative Historical-Literary Study]* (Derpt).

Sidjakov, L. S., 1973. *Xudozhestvennaja proza A. S. Pushkina [The Artistic Prose of A. S. Pushkin]* (Riga).

Slonimskij, A. L., 1922a. "O kompozicii 'Pikovoj damy'" ["On the Composition of 'The Queen of Spades'"], in: *Pushkinskij sbornik pamjati prof. S. A. Vengerova, Pushkinist* (Moskva-Prague).

1922b "'Vdrug' u Dostoevskogo" ["'Suddenly' in Dostoevskij"], in: *Kniga i revoljucija* (Peterburg).

Straxov, N., 1791. *Perepiska Mody, soderzhashchaja pis'ma bezrukix Mod, razmyshlenija neodushevlennyx narjadov, razgovory besslovestnyx chepcov, chuvstvovanija mebelej, karet, zapisnyx knizhek, pugovic i starozavetnyx manek, kuntashej, shlaforov, telogrej i pr. Nravstvennoe i kriticheskoe sochetanie, v koem s istinnoj storony otkryty nravy, obraz zhizni i raznye smeshnye ic vazhnye sceny modnogo veka [The Correspondence of Fashion, Containing the Letters of Armless Fashions, the Thoughts of Inanimate Costumes, the Conversations of Dumb Bonnets, the Feelings of Furniture, Carriages, Note Books, Buttons and Old-fashioned Sleeves, Kaftans, Housecoats, Padded Jackets, etc. A Moral and Critical Compendium, in which the Morals, the Way of Life and Various Humorous and Important Scenes of the Age of Fashion Are Truthfully Revealed]* (Moskva).

Suxovo-Kobylin, A., 1869. *Kartiny proshedshego. Pisal s natury A. Suxovo-Kobylin [Pictures of the Past. Drawn from Nature by A. Suxovo-Kobylin]* (Moskva).

Sumarokov, A. P., 1787. "O pochtenii avtora k prikaznomu rodu" ["On the Respect of the Author for the Official Order"], in: *Polnoe sobranie sochinenij v stixax i proze* (Moskva).

Tolstoj, L. N., 1951. *Sobranie sochinenij v 14 tt. [Collected Works in 14 Volumes]*, (Moskva).

Tomashevskij, B. V., 1925. *Teorija literatury [Theory of Literature]* (Leningrad).

1933 *Ironi-komicheskaja poema [The Mock-Heroic Poem]* (Leningrad).

Veselovskij, A. N., 1940. *Istoricheskaja poetika [Historical Poetics]* (Leningrad).

Vinogradov, V. V., 1936. "Stil' 'Pikovoj damy'" ["The Style of 'The Queen of Spades'"], in: *Pushkin. Vremennik Pushkinskoj kommissii, 2* (Moskva-Leningrad).

1941 *Stil' Pushkina [Pushkin's Style]* (Moskva).

Xomjakov, A. S., 1969. *Stikhotvorenija i dramy [Poems and Dramas]* (Leningrad).

Zhitomirskaja, Z. V. & L. Z. Kopilev, 1964. *E. T. A. Gofman. Bibliografija russkix perevodov i kriticheskoj literatury [E. T. A. Hoffmann. Bibliography of Russian Translations and Critical Literature]* (Moskva).

Zholkovskij, A. K., 1967. *Deus ex machina*, in: *Trudy po znakovym sistemam, III* (Tartu).

Joseph Frank (essay date 1995)

SOURCE: Frank, Joseph. *"The Gambler*: A Study in Ethnopsychology." In *Freedom and Responsibility in Russian Literature: Essays in Honor of Robert Louis Jackson,* edited by Elizabeth Cheresh Allen and Gary Saul Morson, pp. 69-85. Evanston, Ill.: Northwestern University Press, 1995.

[*In the following essay, Frank interprets Fyodor Dostoevsky's novella* Igrok *(*The Gambler*) as an exploration of both the author's personal psychology and of a Russian national psychology.*]

The Gambler, as Robert Louis Jackson has pointed out, is "among the works of Dostoevsky . . . that [has] received the least attention," even though it is among the "most brilliant and rewarding" of his shorter creations.[1]

This does not mean, of course, that *no* criticism has been devoted to it, only that most discussion has tended to focus on its obvious biographical correlations. Dostoevsky himself was subject to accesses of gambling fever, and the novella was thus considered a thinly disguised transcription of his own experiences. Well known, too, was that *The Gambler* was written in great haste—actually, in the course of one month—when Dostoevsky was under pressure to fulfill a contract that he had imprudently signed several years earlier. It was thus assumed that, under such conditions, he simply set down a slice of his own life as best he could to meet a deadline, without being able to endow his story with any particular thematic significance, except, perhaps, that of illustrating the ravages of gambling, with which he was all too familiar.

In fact, however, the idea of writing a story about a gambler had occurred to Dostoevsky three years earlier, and he mentioned it at that time in a letter to N. N. Strakhov. "I have in mind," he wrote, "a man who is straightforward, highly cultivated, and yet in every respect unfinished, a man who has lost his faith but *who does not dare not to believe,* and who rebels against the established order and yet fears it." The letter continues:

> The main thing, though, is that all his vital sap, his energies, rebellion, daring, have been channeled into *roulette.* He is a gambler, and not merely an ordinary gambler, just as Pushkin's Covetous Knight is not an ordinary miser. . . . He is a poet in his own way, but the fact is that he himself is ashamed of the poetic element in him, because he feels it is despicable, although the need to take *risks* ennobles him in his own eyes. The whole story is the tale of his playing roulette in various gambling houses for over two years.[2]

In the next paragraph, Dostoevsky compares his projected story with *Notes from the House of the Dead,* which had portrayed convicts for the first time, and explains that he will now do the same thing for gamblers. He then remarks that, aside from the "fact that materials of this type are read with considerable curiosity in our country, gambling at spas, especially where Russian expatriates are concerned, has some (perhaps not unimportant) significance."[3] This last remark, which has been completely neglected, is really of extreme importance; indeed, it provides the chief clue to the interpretation of *The Gambler* that will be offered here.

The circumstances in which this letter was written nonetheless appeared to confirm the strongly biographical character of the work. Dostoevsky was then traveling in Europe with his erstwhile mistress Apollinaria Suslova, who was refusing him her sexual favors; while she was tormenting Dostoevsky with this cat-and-mouse game of advance and withdrawal, she herself was consumed with bitterness and resentment at having just been abandoned by her Spanish lover, a medical student named Salvador. Dostoevsky was gambling uninterruptedly during this trip, and it is not difficult to see *The Gambler* as a version of these events. The two main characters are a young Russian who becomes a confirmed gambler, Aleksei Ivanovich, and his capricious ladylove, Polina, who confides in him one moment and repulses him the next; the resemblance of these two figures to what we know of Dostoevsky and Suslova could not seem more self-evident. That Polina has recently been seduced and abandoned by the suavely treacherous Frenchman de Grieux (Dostoevsky ironically gives him the name of the passionate lover in Prévost's *Manon Lescaut*) only makes the parallel with Suslova more close-fitting.

No one would wish to deny that Dostoevsky used such events from his own life (particularly in the gambling episodes) to provide the ingredients for his narrative. But the question still remains whether he was really as unambitious as this approach to *The Gambler* assumes. D. S. Savage, in an essay that has become classic, argues quite convincingly that Dostoevsky remained true to himself as a writer in his novella, and that the work "is no mere scandalous revelation of a personal history." On the contrary, it is organized, "as is usual in Dostoevsky's works," by a "dominating and shaping imaginative *idea* to which everything in the action is related."[4] Savage's article is valuable because it shifts attention away from a narrowly biographical reading of the work and raises the question of its larger artistic import. Moreover, Savage rightfully insists that the gambler himself, a highly intelligent young university graduate, is an unreliable first-person narrator, and that the picture he offers of Polina—a view that has led to her identification with the supposedly "demonic" Suslova— cannot withstand a careful reading of the text.

Aleksei's image of Polina is a woefully distorted one, and Dostoevsky indicates this in numerous (if unobtrusive) ways. The two characters who serve as moral yardsticks (the allegedly moribund old Auntie, a wealthy Russian matriarch who erupts on the scene in Roulettenberg large as life, and the English lord and wealthy manufacturer Mr. Astley, who shyly courts Polina from a respectful distance) both speak of her in the highest terms. Their view of her character is totally different from that of the presumably love-struck Aleksei, who vehemently maintains he would throw himself down from the Schlangenberg mountaintop, a local tourist attraction, if she should give the command. Up to this point, no objection can be made to Savage's views; but a number of questions arise when we come to his explanation of the cause of Aleksei's gambling mania and of his behavior toward Polina.

"Implicit in Dostoevsky's treatment from the beginning," Savage writes, "is the idea that to the man who, having lost God, is in the process of losing himself, free and responsible choice has been eliminated, so that he is left facing a universe which is subject down to the minutest details to an irreversible deterministic law." Gambling is a revolt against such determinism, similar to the revolt of the underground man, and the soul of the gambler is thus drawn toward "an ultimate irrational and groundless freedom, which, containing equally within itself every possibility, is devoid of the power to actualize any of these possibilities and can give birth only to an ineluctable necessity."[5]

Aleksei's love-hate relationship with Polina, in which he feels she is treating him as a lackey or a "slave," is analyzed in similar terms. "When a limitless egotism, acknowledging no authority and therefore deprived of meaning and value, is brought into an erotic relationship, there results the convulsive lacerations described by Dostoevsky—the writhings of the disintegrating self in the throes of the knowledge of its own nothingness." Aleksei's "limitless egotism" thus determines the conditions of his infatuation with Polina, and "they meet, not as persons, but as unbounded egos capable of nothing between total domination and absorption of the other, or total and suicidal submission." Polina, by contrast, strives "toward a relationship of love which is conceivable only when each party ceases to be an ego and becomes a personality in an inward relation to the authority of truth (through faith in God)."[6] Savage thus relies quite literally on Dostoevsky's statement that his gambler-character would be someone who had "lost his faith in God" and attempts to force the novella into the framework of such an "imaginative idea."

My own difficulty with this reading of *The Gambler,* which would place it on the same thematic level as Dostoevsky's major works dealing with questions of religious faith (or lack of such faith), stems from a variety of sources. One is simply based on the *tonality* of the novella, which is jaunty, bouncy, and full of a certain youthful high spirits: Aleksei is a lively and irreverent character, and Mr. Astley comments on his "independence of spirit, and even cheerfulness," while also calling him "clever, enthusiastic, yet, at the same time, cynical."[7] These are the impressions his character conveys, and they are not those of someone plunged into the "convulsive lacerations" of Savage's portrayal. Nor does Polina herself take very seriously Aleksei's overheated and frenzied declarations of love, cast in the pseudo-Romantic rhetoric of a Marlinskii novel (exactly the type of novel whose falsity Dostoevsky had parodied as far back as *Poor Folk*). The perception of unreliable narration might well be extended beyond what Aleksei tells us of Polina and applied as well to the latter's professions of love; the course of the action shows how little reliable love there was, except on the part of Polina herself. If so, then perhaps Aleksei's supposed

desperation should be taken with a great deal of salt, and not attributed to so elevated a cause as loss of faith in God.

To be sure, this may be considered only a private, personal reaction; but it can be buttressed with more objective data in the text. What are we to make of the adventures of Auntie, for example, who arrives unpredictably and promptly begins to gamble uncontrollably until she is entirely wiped out? If Dostoevsky had really meant to attribute a passion for gambling to a loss of faith in God, why should this sturdy pillar of authentic Russian virtues (including a devotion to religion—she goes back home determined to rebuild the local parish church in penance for her gambling sins) behave exactly like Aleksei at the roulette wheel? The appearance of Auntie is usually considered only a comic diversion, if any attention is paid to her at all (Savage does not even mention this episode). But if we accept Savage's view (as I do) that all the important incidents of a Dostoevsky work are controlled by an "imaginative idea," then his definition of an "idea" for *The Gambler* allowing for such an important lacuna can hardly be considered satisfactory.

Nor is this the only aspect of the text that remains obscure. Why, for instance, is there not a single word to suggest that Aleksei's loss of faith in God presumably motivates his behavior? Indeed, if we look carefully, we find something quite different and a little more complex. When Aleksei steps into the gambling casino for the first time in his life, he writes: "As for my innermost moral convictions, there is no place for them, of course, in my present reasoning [about gambling]. I'll leave it at that. I am saying this to relieve my conscience" (19). Aleksei thus affirms quite clearly that he retains both his "innermost moral convictions" and his "conscience," whose validity he does not question for a moment; he simply sets them aside for the purposes of gambling. There is not a trace of any questioning of the accepted moral code, to which Aleksei continues to adhere; and this is why he feels the atmosphere of the casino to be "very sordid, somehow, morally rotten and sordid" (16). It can scarcely be a loss of faith in God, from whom this moral code derives, that turns him into an addicted gambler.

If there is not a shred of textual evidence to support Savage's interpretation, a good deal of space is taken up with discussions of various types of national character, and the Russian type is continually contrasted with that of others (French, German, English). Even more, Dostoevsky offers, through the utterances of both Aleksei and Mr. Astley, a perfectly forthright explanation for Aleksei's gambling (as well as Auntie's). "Roulette," Aleksei says, "is simply made for Russians" (33). In the last chapter Mr. Astley, who speaks here as an authorial surrogate, confirms Aleksei's opinion. By this time Aleksei has become a confirmed gambler, and Mr. Astley sees him as typical: "It seems to me that all Russians are like that, or are disposed to be like that" (196). Oddly enough, Savage does not comment on such passages at all, nor has anyone else, so far as my knowledge goes, given them much attention; yet we must assume that Dostoevsky meant them to be taken seriously. And if it seems dubious, for all the reasons already given, that Aleksei's regrettable fate can be attributed to a loss of faith in God, then perhaps we should look more carefully at what *is* mentioned, and what Dostoevsky tells us so positively and frequently.

If we do so, we shall find that Dostoevsky had, as it were, altered the thematic register of his initial idea for *The Gambler* by the time he got around to the actual writing, and that he substituted an ethnic-psychological "imaginative idea" for his initial conception of a character who has "lost his faith." His letter, as we have seen, also mentions as an afterthought that the gambling of Russian expatriates "has some (perhaps not unimportant) significance"; this significance becomes the focus of Dostoevsky's novella. Of great importance too is the comment about the gambler's being "a poet in his own way," who "is ashamed of the poetic element in him . . . although the need to take *risks* ennobles him in his own eyes." Dostoevsky explains this idiosyncratic notion of "poetry" by a reference to Pushkin's Covetous Knight, who amasses a fortune not for the sake of the money itself but solely for the psychological sense of power it enables him to acquire over others. "Poetry" in this Dostoevskian sense means acting, not for immediate material self-interest or for the gratification of any fleshly physical desire, but rather solely to satisfy a powerful craving of the human personality in some way (whether for good or evil). The underground man in part 1 of *Notes from Underground* would thus be a "poet," because he acts *contrary* to any rational idea of self-interest and only for the sake of preserving the right to exercise his free will—which means to keep alive his power of psychic self-affirmation.

The characters of *The Gambler,* which may be considered Dostoevsky's one and only contribution to the line of "international" works in Russian literature (which includes Turgenev's *A Nest of Gentry,* Goncharov's *Oblomov,* and of course Tolstoy's *War and Peace,* among others), divide into two groups: there are the Russians, and there are the Europeans. These groups are contrasted along lines that may be described, to use Dostoevsky's own categories, as "poetic" and "nonpoetic." Among the Europeans are the fake (or exceedingly dubious) count or marquis de Grieux and his supposed cousin, Mademoiselle Blanche de Cominges; *her* presumably noble origins are quite clearly sham, and she is in fact a high-priced cocotte. Both of these French figures are linked with the lives of a Russian family, that of the widowed General Z—(his family name is given only in a garbled form), who lives in a grand patriarchal style, squandering money with both hands, though he has given promissory notes to de Grieux on all his Russian estates in return for loans and is in fact completely in the latter's power. The sensual and provocative Mademoiselle Blanche would also dearly love to improve her social position by becoming *madame la générale,* and as long as the smitten General is in funds, she allows him to pay his court. All the hopes of the General depend on Auntie, whose momentarily expected demise will pour a considerable fortune into the General's lap. Even after paying off his debts, he would still remain an extremely wealthy Russian nobleman (*barin*), and what de Grieux has not taken will be left to Mademoiselle Blanche.

Both de Grieux and Mademoiselle Blanche are thus moved by exclusively mercenary motives (though the latter has a few upsurges of sentimental generosity), and Mademoiselle Blanche's relation to the General is paralleled by that of de Grieux to Polina, the General's stepdaughter. De Grieux had seduced Polina earlier in the belief that she was a wealthy heiress, but he becomes increasingly cool as the General's financial prospects grow dimmer. Unlike the aging General, who is deeply and genuinely smitten (this is *his* way of being a "poet"), Polina no longer has any illusions about de Grieux. "The moment he finds out that I, too, have inherited something from [Auntie]," she tells Aleksei, "he will immediately propose to me. Is that what you wanted to know?" (11). The only other important foreign character is Mr. Astley, an exemplar, it is true, of all the gentlemanly virtues but also the partner in a sugar-refining firm who is thus limited by his English world of prosaic practicality and common sense.

The Russian characters, by contrast, are all moved by feelings whose consequences may be practically disastrous but that in every case are sympathetically human even in their excess. Both the General and Polina have been stirred by love, and Polina has now transferred her affections to Aleksei, though he is too self-absorbed and self-preoccupied to understand that her presumed coldness would dissolve in an instant if he did not continually insist on his slavish subservience to her supposed tyranny. What obsesses Aleksei is the sense of his own social inferiority as a humble tutor in the General's household; despite his culture, education, and status as a Russian nobleman, he is treated little better than a servant. He *is* treated outright as a servant by the de Grieux-Mademoiselle Blanche tandem as well as by the hotel staff, and he totally misunderstands Polina because he believes that she looks down on him for that reason. He cannot possibly imagine that she might favor him over her two other much more imposing suitors, de Grieux and Mr. Astley, and he exhibits a rankling resentment, to which she responds in kind. "To be sure," Aleksei admits, "our relationship has had a strange beginning. Some time ago, in fact, quite some time ago, maybe two months back, I had noticed that she was trying to make me her friend, her confidant, and that she was actually sounding me out. For some reason [?] it did not work out at the time, and instead, there remained this present, strange relationship of ours" (142). The "reason" was simply Aleksei's ineradicable conviction that Polina could not but regard him with contempt because of his menial social position.

Even before arriving, Aleksei had been convinced that "something would happen to me in Roulettenberg, that there would be something, quite without fail, that would affect my destiny radically and definitively" (16). Roulette would thus change his life, and he explains how to Polina when she inquires what the "object" of such a change could be. "Nothing more," he replies, "than that with money I'll be a different man, even for you, and not a slave" (41). Aleksei thus counts on roulette to enhance his social status and, in lifting him from his inferior social position, to allow him to compete for Polina. When she accuses him, quite justly, of counting on "buying me with money," he rejects such an idea with indignation. But her reply hits the nail on the head: "If you aren't thinking of buying me, you certainly think you can buy my respect with money" (43). The climax of their relation will turn exactly on this issue, when Aleksei's behavior toward Polina parallels that of de Grieux, though for different reasons.

Aleksei begins to gamble with Polina's money and on her behalf, since it would be unseemly for her to set foot in the casino. He wins but feels constrained by his obligation to her. He leaves when, he reports, "I felt overcome by a strange and unusual feeling which I found unbearable" (20). It is only the second time, when he plays for himself, that he is really bitten by the gambling bug. After winning a considerable amount "in five minutes or so," instead of quitting—which he would have done if obtaining money had been his genuine goal—"some kind of strange sensation built up in me, a kind of challenge to fate, a kind of desire to give it a flick on the nose, or stick out my tongue at it" (31). He bets all his winnings, loses, bets again with the remainder of his funds, and is wiped out entirely. The psychic desire to challenge fate, his sudden act of defiance in total disregard of self-interest so far as money is concerned, gives rise to the "strange sensation" that he cannot (and does not wish to) control.

Aleksei's losses soon become common knowledge and lead de Grieux to remark to his face, "caustically and spitefully," that "Russians were . . . lacking in talent even in gambling" (33). It should be mentioned that Aleksei has previously been shown to be an ardent Russian patriot, who vigorously defends his country's very

unpopular policies against European (French and Polish) critics. (The time of *The Gambler* is set just after the suppression of the Polish rebellion of 1863-65.) At first, nonetheless, he seems to agree with de Grieux's insulting observation, but then he turns this denigration around into an encomium of the refusal of Russians to dedicate their lives entirely to the accumulation of wealth. "Roulette is simply made for Russians," Aleksei declares, because "the faculty of amassing capital has become, through a historical process, virtually the main point in the catechism of the virtues and qualities of civilized Western man" (33). Russians have never learned to revere such amassing of capital as an end in itself, but since they need money too, they "are very fond of, and susceptible to, methods such as, for example, roulette, allowing one to get rich suddenly in two hours, and without work. And since we gamble to no purpose, and also without real effort, we tend to be losers!" (33-34). But then Aleksei immediately transforms these seemingly uncomplimentary admissions into a tribute. "Really, who can tell which of the two is more repulsive," he replies to a rebuke from the General, "Russian shapelessness and lack of discipline or the German method of saving money by honest work" (34).

From the tirade that follows, in Dostoevsky's best vein of satiric grotesquerie, it is quite clear which of the two Aleksei finds more repulsive. For he declares roundly, "I would much rather spend my whole life in a Kirghiz nomad's tent . . . than worship the German idol." This "German idol" is caricatured in imagery taken from the pastoral-idyllic strain of German literature (e.g., Goethe's *Hermann und Dorothea*). "They have here, in every house, a *Vater,* who is extremely virtuous and extraordinarily honest. . . . Every such *Vater* has a family, and in the evening they read instructive books aloud to each other. Elms and chestnut trees rustle over the little house. Sunset, storks on the roof, and all of it is so extraordinarily poetic and touching" (34). But the honest *Vater* keeps his family "in a condition of complete servitude and submission," and "they all work like mules and they all save money like Jews." The daughter is denied a dowry and dies as an old maid; the younger son is "sold for a soldier"; the older docilely waits to marry until he has acquired enough gulden and leads his Amalchen to the altar with "her chest dried up and her nose red" (35). This appalling display of rectitude and virtue goes on for several generations, the family grows as rich as "Baron Rothschild, or Hoppe & Co.," but for Aleksei, "I'd much rather indulge in debauchery Russian style, or make my fortune at roulette." The reason is simply that "I [am not] willing to consider my person as a necessary accessory to capital" (36).

Aleksei thus links the Russian passion for roulette to an essential aspect of the Russian character, with its refusal to trim down all the needs and desires of the personality simply to a piling up of wealth. One might be inclined to interpret Aleksei's peroration merely as a clever riposte to de Grieux's withering disdain, but Dostoevsky meant it to be taken as more than just another instance of Aleksei's nationalistic rambunctiousness. This is evident from the quite diverting episode involving Auntie, who, instead of expiring on schedule in Moscow, explodes unexpectedly on the Roulettenberg scene and sends all the hopes pinned on acquiring her fortune flying out the window. The blunt old matriarch, despotic and high-handed but fundamentally humane and kindhearted, represents the traditional down-to-earth virtues of the Russian gentry when unspoiled by any truckling to foreign tastes and fashions. She instantly sees through de Grieux and Mademoiselle Blanche, calling the first a "mountebank" (83) and the second an "actress" (84), takes an instant liking to Mr. Astley, and is kind to both Polina and Aleksei. Her commanding presence inspires immediate respect and deference, and even the imposing *Oberkellner* of the fashionable hotel, used to receiving the best European society, is overawed.

Auntie's behavior, so far as gambling is concerned, provides a textbook illustration of Aleksei's ethnic-psychological theory concerning the Russian attraction to roulette. Curious to investigate this European pastime, she visits the casino and cannot believe her ears when Aleksei explains how much it is possible to win on certain stakes. Instantly tempted by the prospect of such a miraculous and seemingly effortless enrichment, she hardly listens to Aleksei's warning that the odds are "thirty-six to one" against winning and promptly begins to play. What takes over in Auntie (also called Grandmother in some translations) is the imperious pride of someone used to giving commands and to being obeyed, the pride of a Russian landowner all-powerful on her estates. "'There, look at it,' Grandmother said angrily, 'how long will I have to wait until that miserable little zero comes up? For the life of me, I'm not going until that miserable little zero comes up!'" (102). It finally does, and Auntie is hooked. She wins a large sum and returns to the hotel in triumph; but when she comes back to the tables, the disaster that everyone foresees inevitably occurs. Possessed entirely by the need to impose her will on the velleities of the wheel, she loses heavily, stubbornly cashes all her securities at a ruinous rate to continue to play, and only stops when she has lost everything. A loan from Mr. Astley is necessary to enable her to limp contritely home to Russia.

Two other aspects of this Auntie episode are thematically important. Even before beginning to gamble herself, she notices a young man in the midst of a winning streak, whose "eyes were flashing and his hand trembling. He was already making his bets quite aimlessly, just putting down what he could grab with his hand, yet he kept winning and winning, raking in more and more money" (99). Auntie wishes to tell him to stop but is warned not to raise her voice: "What a shame! The man is lost!" (100). (She also sees another gambler, well known to Aleksei, who comes every day between one and two o'clock, places her bets "quietly, coolly and calculatingly," and wins considerable sums before leaving after one hour. On learning that this methodical gambler is a Frenchwoman, Auntie comments: "Ah, one can tell a bird by its flight. This one has sharp claws. You can see that" [100].) The nationality of the young man is not given, but he is, so to speak, a "poetic" gambler in the Russian style, whose will is not controlled solely by a desire for money. Auntie, of course, will go the same way as the young man, winning for a time but doomed to lose everything.

This young man here foreshadows the fate both of Auntie and Aleksei, and the change that occurs in Auntie when *she* temporarily becomes a gambler foreshadows the denouement of the Aleksei-Polina romance. On her first visit to the casino, Auntie embarrasses everyone by insisting on entering its august precincts accompanied by her majordomo Potapych and her peasant maid Marfa. "So she is a servant, so I have to leave her behind!" she retorts to the General's warnings about propriety. "She is a human being too, isn't she? . . . How could she go anywhere, except with me?" (94). Later, when her gambling fury has taken over, she loses all concern for Marfa and snappishly dismisses her when the maid devotedly begins to escort her mistress again. "Why must you drag along! I can't take you with me every time. Go back home!" (118). Once the passion for gambling gains the upper hand, which means the passion of her will to dominate, all of Auntie's kindlier instincts and genuine fellow feeling simply vanish.

On a much higher level of emotive complication, exactly the same situation occurs as a result of the crisis created by Auntie's appearance and departure. It is clear that she will not give any money whatsoever to the General and that she is very much alive; de Grieux thus announces his intention to leave for Russia and claim the General's property. At the same time, he sends a letter to Polina explaining ceremoniously that he must renounce all further hopes for their future together but that, as a man of honor, he is willing to turn over fifty thousand francs to the General on her behalf. Aleksei finds her sitting in his room that night and realizes that this could only mean one thing. "Why, that meant that she loved me! She came to see *me* and not Mr. Astley. She, a young girl, had come alone to my hotel room, meaning that she had compromised herself before everybody, and I, I was just standing there, refusing to understand it!" (152). How he might have behaved is indicated the next day by Mr. Astley, who remarks acidly that Polina "was on her way here yesterday, and I should have taken her to a lady relative of mine. But as she was ill, she made a mistake and went to you" (167). Instead of thinking first of how to protect his presumed beloved, Aleksei rushes off to play roulette and win the fifty thousand francs necessary for Polina to wipe out de Grieux's insult. Nothing has changed in their relations, and he still behaves as though it were necessary to "buy her respect."

At the casino, Aleksei hits a sensational winning streak, playing frantically and frenziedly in the "Russian" style, "haphazard, at random, quite without thought" (154). As his luck continues to hold, he observes, "Now I felt like a winner *and was afraid of nothing, of nothing in the world,* as I plunked down four thousand on black" (155; emphasis added). The pall of social inferiority that had been the bane of his life so far is thus lifted, and he experiences "an overwhelmingly pleasurable feeling" from "scooping up and raking in the banknotes" (157). Losing all recollection of why he had come, he concedes, "I don't remember whether I thought of Polina even once in all this time," but notes, "I remember distinctly how all of a sudden a terrible craving for *risk* took possession of me, quite apart from any promptings of vanity" (158). He stakes on what seemed to be impossible odds solely to satisfy this craving. His hitherto crushed personality is freed from its crippling limits, and he loses consciousness of everything except the intoxication of this release. He breaks off play only when the voices of onlookers suddenly awaken him to the extent of his winnings; otherwise he would have continued to play until his luck turned and he had lost everything.

Just as he had forgotten Polina while playing, so now, on the way back to her, she scarcely looms any larger on his emotive horizon. What dominates is "a tremendous feeling of exhilaration—success, triumph, power—I don't know how to express it. Polina's image flitted through my mind also. . . . Yet I could hardly remember what she had told me earlier, and why I had gone to the casino" (159). As he enters the room, Aleksei notices "Polina's terribly intent gaze" as she looks at him "without moving from her seat or even changing her position." When his first words concern the problem of how best to safeguard the pile "of banknotes and rolls of gold," she looks at him "with a strange expression on her face. . . . I would not be wrong if I said there was hatred in it" (160). A bit later, after Aleksei offers to take the fifty thousand francs and return them to de Grieux "first thing in the morning," she suddenly bursts into laughter. "This laughter of hers was a lot like the sarcastic laughter I had heard so often, even recently, every time I made one of my passionate declarations to her" (161). Polina had not believed such declarations in the past, and Aleksei's behavior now only confirms her suspicions: his so-called love has more to do with the frustrations of his ego than with her.

It is at this moment, when Polina realizes that Aleksei's attitude is not really different from that of de Grieux—both men assume, one naively and unreflectingly, the other cynically, that her innermost feelings can be compensated for by money—that her ulcerated pride and dignity bring on a crisis of hysteria. Only then does Aleksei report becoming aware that "something had happened to her in my absence, she seemed quite out of her mind." Turning on him with the detestation of despair, she says bitterly, "I won't take your money," and then reveals the full truth of her affair with de Grieux: "'You are giving too much,' she said with a laugh, 'de Grieux's mistress is not worth fifty thousand francs'" (161). Polina then breaks down completely, alternating between embracing and caressing Aleksei and holding him at arm's length to scrutinize him with mistrust. The pathos of her condition is amply indicated, in the midst of her delirium, by her recurring question to Aleksei when, he says, she "put her hands on my shoulders, again giving me that intent look and saying over and over again: 'You love me . . . love me . . . will you love me?'" (162).

Unable to master himself sufficiently to come to the aid of a suffering Polina no longer responsible for her own actions, Aleksei yields to the combined temptation of her crazed caresses and his newly acquired sense of strength and mastery: he spends the night with her in his room. On waking, she looks at him "with infinite loathing" (164) and asks for the fifty thousand francs. On being assured they are hers, she flings them in his face, as she had wished to do with de Grieux, and runs out of the room to take refuge with Mr. Astley. Aleksei is still puzzling over this even in his manuscript, written a month after the event occurred, and his pretended lack of comprehension (really a guilty self-deception) is reminiscent of the underground man's self-excuses for his mistreatment of the prostitute Liza who had come to him for help. "To be sure," writes Aleksei, "it all happened in a delirious state, and I knew it too well, and . . . yet I refused to take that fact into consideration." But then he reconsiders: "Why, she wasn't all that delirious and all that ill as to be totally oblivious of what she was doing when she came to me with de Grieux's letter, or was she? So it must be she knew what she was doing" (165). What Polina certainly did know was that Aleksei's love had not been strong enough, nonegoistic enough, for him to resist taking sexual advantage of her deranged and helpless condition.

What occurs at this point, when Aleksei goes off with his winnings to Paris in the company of Mademoiselle Blanche, has been found by some commentators to be quite unconvincing. "The act confounds us," the usually helpful Edward Wasiolek has written, "and seems unprepared for in any way."[8] Well, in the first place, Aleksei's initial description of Mademoiselle Blanche strongly suggests that he is far from being impervious to her well-displayed attractions. Moreover, the prescient Mr. Astley, "in a tone as if he were quoting information from a book," has no doubt about Aleksei's destination: "All Russians, when they have some money, go to Paris!" (168). Aleksei will follow the usual Russian path and kick up his heels in Paris, but Dostoevsky motivates him a little more individually all the same. Mademoiselle Blanche is not lacking in either psychological acumen or a smattering of education, and she propositions the newly affluent Aleksei with a quotation from Corneille's *Le Cid,* asking him if he has the courage to dare. Since his personality is still under the spell of the psychic afflatus provided by his gambling exploit, he goes off with her on the spot. "I can't say I felt very cheerful," he confesses, "but, since the previous day, I had been conditioned to risking everything on one card" (171).

The Paris pages of *The Gambler* are more or less a blur of impressions similar to the scenes in *A Nest of Gentry* during which the frivolous and unfaithful wife of an idealistic aristocratic landowner plunges him into the Parisian social maelstrom as a sickened spectator. Mademoiselle Blanche is honest enough in her own way and, while spending Aleksei's money hand over fist, does not neglect to pay attention to him occasionally. To take up the slack, she introduces him to a friend, Hortense, whose nickname is Thérèse-philosophe, the title of a well-known eighteenth-century pornographic novel. Presumably Hortense keeps Aleksei amused and occupied, and he admits to having no complaints. He does, though, become terribly bored at Mademoiselle Blanche's parties, where he is forced to play host to the dullest businessmen with newly minted fortunes, insolent and ignorant military types, and "a bunch of wretched minor authors and journalistic insects" with "a vanity and conceit of such proportions as would be unthinkable even back home in Petersburg—and that is saying a great deal!" (174). How Aleksei might have known this is not clear, but Dostoevsky was certainly in a position to make such a comparison. The escapade is over, and Aleksei is sent on his way, once all his money—to which he displays a total indifference ("Un vrai Russe, un calmouk!" Mademoiselle Blanche says admiringly [181])—has been dissipated, much to the benefit of Mademoiselle Blanche's social prestige.

The main story of *The Gambler* ends with this episode, and a final chapter, set down a year and eight months later, provides a sort of commentary. Aleksei has now become an addicted gambler, traveling around Europe and picking up odd jobs as a flunky until he can scrape together enough money to return to the tables. He has become completely dependent on the "strange sensation" afforded by gambling, the thrill that enables him to affirm his identity and triumph momentarily over his gnawing sense of inferiority. Remembering one of his winning moments, he writes: "I now had seventeen

hundred gulden, and this in less than five minutes! Yes, it is at moments like this that one forgets all one's earlier failures. Why, I had got this at the risk of more than life itself. But I had dared to risk it, and there I was once again, a man among men!" Nevertheless, he also feels that "I have grown numb, somehow, as though I were buried in some sort of mire" (189). This feeling is particularly aroused in him by a supposedly accidental meeting with Mr. Astley; in fact, it is one carefully arranged for the sake of Polina.

Auntie has died meanwhile and left Polina a comfortable inheritance; she has been keeping a protective eye on Aleksei all this time and once secretly arranges to pay his bail for a bad debt. Mr. Astley, sent to see if Aleksei has changed in any way, discovers that he is much the same—if not worse. Aleksei is still convinced that Polina is really in love with de Grieux because, like all Frenchmen, "he's got elegance of form, Mr. Astley, and the young lady [especially a Russian one] takes that form for his own soul, for the natural form of his heart and soul, and not for what it is: an external garment, which has come to him by inheritance" (195). As for himself, "I am simply a small-time gambler at roulette" (196). How could he (or for that matter Mr. Astley) compete with de Grieux cast as Apollo Belvedere?

At this Mr. Astley explodes with anger and reveals to Aleksei not only that he has come to see him expressly on Polina's behalf but also that it is Aleksei she has loved all along. Even more, "what's worse, even if I were to tell you that she still loves you, why, you would stay here just the same! Yes, you have destroyed yourself. You had some abilities, a lively disposition, and you are not a bad man. *In fact, you might have been of service to your country, which needs men so badly. . . .* I am not blaming you. It seems to me that all Russians are like that, or are disposed to be like that. If it isn't roulette, it's something else but similar to it. . . . You are not the first who does not understand what work is (I'm not talking of your plain people). Roulette is preeminently a Russian game" (196-97; emphasis added).

Aleksei himself said much the same thing earlier, in his rejection of the "German idol," but now Mr. Astley shows the obverse of this refusal to discipline the personality in some way and to harness it for the achievement of a desired result. The "poetic" character of the Russian personality can lead both to personal disaster and to the obliteration of all sense of civic or moral obligation, if left to operate unchecked. Aleksei apparently wants to take this lesson to heart, and with the ten louis d'or left him at parting by Mr. Astley, who embraces him with warmth before leaving, he thinks about gambling in a new way for the first time: "Yes, all it takes is to be calculating and patient just once in a lifetime—that is all! All it takes is to keep control of yourself just once, and your whole life will be changed in an hour!" (198). This last phrase, however, betrays the old, incorrigibly Russian Aleksei, and what he remembers in the last paragraph is the exhilaration he had felt once when he bet the small sum he had been saving for dinner and won 170 gulden. "And what if I had lost heart that time, if I had not dared to take that chance . . ." (198). He will, it appears, continue to gamble in the "Russian" style.

If one reads *The Gambler* from this ethnic-psychological point of view, for which there is ample warrant in the text, then it may be seen to have a unique place in Dostoevsky's work. It is the only creation in which his view of the Russian national character, which appears sporadically (most notably, but not exclusively, in his journalism), provides him with an artistic and thematic focus.[9] Disorderly and "unseemly" though the Russian character may be, it still has human potentialities closed to the narrow, inhuman, Philistine parsimony of the Germans, the worldly, elegant, and totally perfidious patina of the French, and even the solidly helpful but unattractively stodgy virtues of the English. "For the most part," as Aleksei remarks to Polina, "we Russians are so richly endowed that, to know how to behave, we need genius. Well, and much more often than not there simply isn't any genius available, since it's a very rare commodity. It is only among the French and perhaps some other Europeans that certain forms of behavior have been developed to such perfection that a man may very well have an air of the utmost dignity and yet be a quite worthless character" (42).

Even if Russians have not yet worked out their own code of manners, however—and the dangers of such a lack have become quite obvious—they can only demean themselves by attempting to imitate any of the European models. For all his weaknesses, Aleksei arouses sympathy both because of his honesty about himself (except in the case of his night with Polina, which she has obviously forgiven) and because of his unerring eye and refreshing disrespect for the hypocrisies, pretensions, and falsities by which the Europeans cover up their own shortcomings. One of the most amusing episodes, which can be mentioned only in passing, involves Aleksei's "insult" to the insufferably pompous German baron and baroness; he refuses to apologize and ties everybody into knots by pretending to insist on the punctilio of the European gentlemanly code of *politesse* and *point d'honneur*. There is an engaging brashness and sincerity about him that wins the friendship of all the "positive" characters (Polina, Auntie, Mr. Astley), and Dostoevsky certainly hoped the reader would share some of their sentiment. Nor was Aleksei perhaps meant to be seen as *entirely* a lost man. On learning that Mr. Astley had been sent by Polina, "'Really, really!' I exclaimed, as tears came gushing from my eyes. I just could not hold them back. I be-

lieve that it was the first time in my life this had happened" (196). Such tears may presage something for the future, and they surely indicate a depth of feeling of which the earlier Aleksei had been incapable; but whether this is to be taken as a hint of possible recovery may be left undecided.

Having rejected a simplistic biographical view of *The Gambler* at the beginning of this essay, I should now, all the same, like briefly to return to the question of the relation of the novella to Dostoevsky's life. Works of art are never mere transcriptions of personal experience, but this does not mean that they have no relation to a writer's biography; they enter into symbiosis with it in manifold and intricate ways, and if literary biography has any justification at all except curiosity, it is because it may better help us to understand some of these mysterious interconnections. Certainly Dostoevsky utilized his own sensations as a gambler in this work, and it may be considered as a self-condemnation and an apologia at the same time. Clearly, it must have been some consolation to believe, as he probably did, that his own losses, which almost always resulted from a failure to stop playing in time, were the consequence of a national Russian trait carried to excess and not only a personal defect of character. He was, after all, a "poet" both in the literal and symbolic senses of that word. If his "poetry" led to unhappy outcomes when he gambled, it was nonetheless proof that he found it impossible to subordinate his personality to the flesh-god of money, before whom, as he had written in *Winter Notes on Summer Impressions,* all of Western civilization was then lying prostrate. He lost materially, but in some sense he gained a psychological reassurance from his very losses.

Dostoevsky never gambled except when he went abroad, and there is more than a suggestion that the fate of Aleksei is tied up with his expatriation. Auntie can return to a solidly rooted Russian life, sadder but wiser after her fling, but Aleksei's uprootedness throws him back on gambling as the only means of expressing his identity in the face of a world he despises. Mr. Astley says he would gladly give Aleksei a thousand pounds on the spot if he were sure he would quit gambling and return to Russia; the implication seems to be that one is tied up with the other. In life, Dostoevsky resembled Auntie much more than Aleksei, and it is worth remarking that, although *The Gambler* had already been written and published, Dostoevsky's most prolonged and disastrous periods of gambling occurred when he was *forced* to live abroad in 1867-70. If he had gone back to Russia, he would have been thrown into debtor's prison; the hope of winning enough to return home was his (at least ostensible) major motive. He gambled most desperately, we might say, to be able to escape from the exile that invariably led him into gambling.

Most interesting of all, perhaps, is the dialectical relation that can be observed between Dostoevsky's gambling and his creativity. His second wife, Anna, records in her memoirs that, after a while, she made no objection to his gambling trips because, "having convinced himself of the futility of his hope of winning, he would settle down to his novel with new energy and make up for all the lost time in two or three weeks."[10] Each time he lost, he returned to his work with renewed vigor and determination; it was as if, having proved to himself that he was too Russian to win at roulette, he decided to put into practice his belief that Russians must learn to discipline themselves through work. Dostoevsky may thus be seen as combining both Aleksei and Mr. Astley in his own personality; it was his hope for the future that the Russian character might one day embody these two extremes in a more harmonious fusion than it had as yet been able to achieve, as he knew only all too well.

Notes

1. See Robert Louis Jackson, Introduction to *Dostoevsky: New Perspectives,* ed. Robert Louis Jackson (Englewood Cliffs, N.J.: Prentice-Hall, 1984), 15.

2. Joseph Frank and David I. Goldstein, eds., *Selected Letters of Fyodor Dostoevsky,* trans. Andrew R. MacAndrew (New Brunswick, N.J.: Rutgers University Press, 1987), 184-88.

3. Ibid., 185-86.

4. D. S. Savage, "Dostoevsky: The Idea of *The Gambler,*" in Jackson, *Dostoevsky: New Perspectives,* 113. Savage's essay first appeared in 1950 in the *Sewanee Review.*

5. Ibid., 120.

6. Ibid., 122-23.

7. Fyodor Dostoevsky, *The Gambler,* trans. Victor Terras, ed. Edward Wasiolek (Chicago: University of Chicago Press, 1972), 191. Subsequent page references are included in parentheses in the essay.

8. See Wasiolek's introduction to Dostoevsky, *The Gambler,* xxxv.

9. See, for example, Razumikhin's remarks in *Crime and Punishment* (pt. 2, chap. 5) about the recent growth of crime among the Russian educated class: "Well, what did that Reader of yours in Moscow answer when he was asked why he had counterfeited the tickets?: 'Everybody else gets rich by various means, and we wanted to get rich too as quickly as we could.' . . . The idea was to do it at other people's expense, as quickly as possible, *and without labour.* They were used to having everything found for them, to being in leading-strings, to being spoon-fed" (emphasis added). The translation is that of Jessie Coulson in Fyodor Dostoevsky, *Crime and Punishment,* ed. George Gibian (New York: Norton, 1975).

10. Anna Dostoevsky, *Dostoevsky, Reminiscences,* trans. and ed. Beatrice Stillman (New York: Liveright, 1975), 165.

FURTHER READING

Criticism

Beer, Gillian. "The Reader's Wager: Lots, Sorts, and Futures." *Essays in Criticism* 40, no. 2 (April 1990): 99-123.
　　Examines gambling in late nineteenth-century society and fiction, and in Peter Carey's 1988 novel *Oscar and Lucinda.*

Flavin, Michael. *Gambling in the Nineteenth-Century English Novel: 'A Leprosy Is O'er the Land.'* Brighton, England: Sussex Academic Press, 2003, 254 p.
　　Full-length study of gambling in nineteenth-century English novels, focusing on works by Benjamin Disraeli, Charles Dickens, William Makepeace Thackeray, George Eliot, Thomas Hardy, Anthony Trollope, and George Moore.

Helfant, Ian M. *The High Stakes of Identity: Gambling in the Life and Literature of Nineteenth-Century Russia.* Evanston, Ill.: Northwestern University Press, 2002, 211 p.
　　Full-length study of gambling in nineteenth-century Russia; examines the writings of Fyodor Ivanovich Tolstoy, Aleksandr Pushkin, I. E. Velikopol'sky, Mikhail Lermontov, Dmitry Begichev, and Fyodor Dostoevsky.

Sournia, Jean-Charles. "Alcoholism, Gambling and Creativity." In *Beyond the Pleasure Dome: Writing and Addiction from the Romantics,* edited by Sue Vice, Matthew Campbell, and Tim Armstrong, pp. 58-61. Sheffield, England: Sheffield Academic Press, 1994.
　　Examines the correlation between creativity and risk.

Pragmatism in the Nineteenth Century

The following entry provides criticism on Pragmatism, a school of philosophy that began during the late nineteenth century in the United States.

INTRODUCTION

Pragmatism, a philosophical tradition that originated in the United States near the end of the nineteenth century, is characterized by a focus on outcomes and usefulness as evidence of truth. Pragmatism, unlike such philosophical traditions as Formalism and Rationalism, rejects the idea that reality can be discerned solely by the application of human intellect and conceptualization. Pragmatists assert that theories and concepts must be tested—to determine their ultimate utility to the human race—through active, concrete experimentation in the world. Using a process of experimentation and inquiry directed by the best interests of humankind, Pragmatists argue, will reveal the theories and concepts that are truly and lastingly useful.

During the nineteenth century, the most prominent figure associated with Pragmatism was noted psychologist and thinker William James. Following the nineteenth century, Charles Sanders Peirce, who coined the term "Pragmatism" but was extremely unpopular among his contemporaries, was acknowledged as a major contributor to the development of Pragmatism. Peirce referred to his own school of thought as "Pragmaticism" to distinguish it from James's views, and in 1897 James himself acknowledged Peirce as the originator of Pragmatism. In the early twentieth century, several American thinkers, including Arthur O. Lovejoy, who outlined thirteen different "Pragmatisms," and John Dewey, who developed a pragmatist theory called Instrumentalism, contributed to a wide-ranging discussion of Pragmatism and various approaches to pragmatic theories of truth. Critics suggest that Pragmatism grew out of a response to a combination of scientific advances and political events that took place during the nineteenth century, such as Charles Darwin's theory of evolution, the discovery and application of certain statistical patterns to historical events and social phenomena, and the American Civil War. Critics have also maintained that Pragmatists were influenced by the Humanist ideals of Ralph Waldo Emerson, the theological writings of Horace Bushnell, and the poetry of Walt Whitman. Commentators have traced a relationship between the Realism of author Henry James and the Pragmatism of his brother, William James, and have noted the influence of Pragmatic thought on such Modernist poets as Ezra Pound, Wallace Stevens, and T. E. Hulme.

REPRESENTATIVE WORKS

Horace Bushnell
God in Christ (lectures) 1849
Sermons for the New Life (sermons) 1858

John Dewey
"The Postulate of Immediate Empiricism" (essay) 1905; published in the journal *The Journal of Philosophy*
"The Experimental Theory of Knowledge" (essay) 1906; published in the journal *Mind*
"The Control of Ideas by Facts" (essay) 1907; published in the journal *The Journal of Philosophy*
"What Does Pragmatism Mean by Practical?" (essay) 1908; published in the journal *The Journal of Philosophy*
"The Development of American Pragmatism" (essay) 1925; published in volume two of *Studies in the History of Ideas*

Ralph Waldo Emerson
Nature (essay) 1836
An Oration, Delivered before the Phi Beta Kappa Society, at Cambridge, August 13, 1837 (lecture) 1837; also published as *The American Scholar,* 1901
Essays (essays) 1838; also published as *Essays: First Series,* 1854
An Address Delivered before the Senior Class in Divinity College, Cambridge . . . 15 July, 1838 (lecture) 1841
Essays: Second Series (essays) 1844
The Conduct of Life (essays) 1860

T. E. Hulme
"A Lecture on Modern Poetry" (lecture) c. 1908
Notes on Language and Style [edited by Herbert Read] (essay) 1929

William James
The Principles of Psychology. 2 vols. (psychology) 1890
The Will to Believe, and Other Essays in Popular Philosophy (essays) 1897
The Varieties of Religious Experience (lectures) 1902

*This essay appeared in the collection *Creative Intelligence: Essays in the Pragmatic Attitude,* 1917, which contains essays by Mead, Dewey, Addison W. Moore, Harold Chapman Brown, Boyd H. Bode, Henry W. Stuart, James H. Tufts, and Horace M. Kallen.

OVERVIEWS

Charles Sanders Peirce (essay date April 1905)

SOURCE: Peirce, Charles Sanders. "What Pragmatism Is." In *Peirce's Pragmatism: The Design for Thinking,* by Phyllis Chiasson, pp. 219-34. Atlanta, Ga. and Amsterdam, Netherlands: Rodopi, 2001.

[*In the following essay, first published in* The Monist *in April, 1905, Peirce argues that Pragmatism is a "recognition of an inseparable connection between rational cognition and rational purpose."*]

The writer of this article has been led by much experience to believe that every physicist, and every chemist, and, in short, every master in any department of experimental science, has had his mind molded by his life in the laboratory to a degree that is little suspected. The experimentalist himself can hardly be fully aware of it, for the reason that the men whose intellects he really knows about are much like himself in this respect. With intellects of widely different training from his own, whose education has largely been a thing learned out of books, he will never become inwardly intimate, be he on ever so familiar terms with them; for he and they are as oil and water, and though they be shaken up together, it is remarkable how quickly they will go their several mental ways, without having gained more than a faint flavor from the association. Were those other men only to take skillful soundings of the experimentalist's mind—which is just what they are unqualified to do, for the most part—they would soon discover that, excepting perhaps upon topics where his mind is trammeled by personal feeling or by his bringing up, his disposition is to think of everything just as everything is thought of in the laboratory, that is, as a question of experimentation. Of course, no living man possesses in their fullness all the attributes characteristic of his type: it is not the typical doctor whom you will see every day driven in buggy or coupé, nor is it the typical pedagogue that will be met with in the first school-room you enter. But when you have found, or ideally constructed upon a basis of observation, the typical experimentalist, you will find that whatever assertion you may make to him, he will either understand as meaning that if a given prescription for an experiment ever can be and ever is carried out in act, an experience of a given description will result, or else he will see no sense at all in what you say. If you talk to him as Mr. Balfour talked not long ago to the British Association saying that "the physicist seeks for something deeper than the laws connecting plausible objects of experience," that "his object is physical reality" unrevealed in experiments, and that the existence of such non-experiential reality "is the unalterable faith of science," to all such ontological meaning you will find the experimentalist mind to be color-blind. What adds to that confidence in this which the writer owes to his conversations with experimentalists is that he himself may almost be said to have inhabited a laboratory from the age of six until long past maturity; and having all his life associated mostly with experimentalists, it has always been with a confident sense of understanding them and of being understood by them.

That laboratory life did not prevent the writer (who here and in what follows simply exemplifies the experimentalist type) from becoming interested in methods of thinking; and when he came to read metaphysics, although much of it seemed to him loosely reasoned and determined by accidental prepossessions, yet in the writings of some philosophers, especially Kant, Berkeley, and Spinoza, he sometimes came upon strains of thought that recalled the ways of thinking of the laboratory, so that he felt he might trust to them; all of which has been true of other laboratory-men.

Endeavoring, as a man of that type naturally would, to formulate what he so approved, he framed the theory that a *conception,* that is, the rational purport of a word or other expression, lies exclusively in its conceivable bearing upon the conduct of life; so that, since obviously nothing that might not result from experiment can have any direct bearing upon conduct, if one can define accurately all the conceivable experimental phenomena which the affirmation or denial of a concept could imply, one will have therein a complete definition of the concept, and *there is absolutely nothing more in it.* For this doctrine he invented the name *pragmatism.* Some of his friends wished him to call it *practicism* or *practicalism* (perhaps on the ground that πρακτικός is better Greek than πραγματικός). But for one who had learned philosophy out of Kant, as the writer, along with nineteen out of every twenty experimentalists who have turned to philosophy, had done, and who still thought in Kantian terms most readily, *praktisch* and *pragmatisch* were as far apart as the two poles, the former belonging in a region of thought where no mind of the experimentalist type can ever make sure of solid ground under his feet, the latter expressing relation to some definite human purpose. Now quite the most striking feature of the new theory was its recognition of an inseparable connection between rational cognition and rational purpose; and that consideration it was which determined the preference for the name *pragmatism.*

Concerning the matter of philosophical nomenclature, there are a few plain considerations, which the writer has for many years longed to submit to the deliberate judgment of those few fellow-students of philosophy, who deplore the present state of that study, and who are intent upon rescuing it therefrom and bringing it to a condition like that of the natural sciences, where investigators, instead of condemning each the work of most of the others as misdirected from beginning to end, cooperate, stand upon one another's shoulders, and multiply incontestable results; where every observation is repeated, and isolated observations go for little; where every hypothesis that merits attention is subjected to severe but fair examination, and only after the predictions to which it leads have been remarkably borne out by experience is trusted at all, and even then only provisionally; where a radically false step is rarely taken, even the most faulty of those theories which gain wide credence being true in their main experiential predictions. To those students, it is submitted that no study can become scientific in the sense described, until it provides itself with a suitable technical nomenclature, whose every term has a single definite meaning universally accepted among students of the subject, and whose vocables have no such sweetness or charms as might tempt loose writers to abuse them,—which is a virtue of scientific nomenclature too little appreciated. It is submitted that the experience of those sciences which have conquered the greatest difficulties of terminology, which are unquestionably the taxonomic sciences, chemistry, mineralogy, botany, zoölogy, has conclusively shown that the one only way in which the requisite unanimity and requisite ruptures with individual habits and preferences can be brought about is so to shape the canons of terminology that they shall gain the support of *moral principle* and of every man's sense of decency; and that, in particular (under defined restrictions), the general feeling shall be that he who introduces a new conception into philosophy is under an obligation to invent acceptable terms to express it, and that when he has done so, the duty of his fellow-students is to accept those terms, and to resent any wresting of them from their original meanings, as not only a gross discourtesy to him to whom philosophy was indebted for each conception, but also as an injury to philosophy itself; and furthermore, that once a conception has been supplied with suitable and sufficient words for its expression, no other *technical* terms denoting the same things, considered in the same relations, should be countenanced. Should this suggestion find favor, it might be deemed needful that the philosophians in congress assembled should adopt, after due deliberation, convenient canons to limit the application of the principle. Thus, just as is done in chemistry, it might be wise to assign fixed meanings to certain prefixes and suffixes. For example, it might be agreed, perhaps, that the prefix *prope-* should mark a broad and rather indefinite extension of the meaning of the term to which it was prefixed; the name of a doctrine would naturally end in *-ism,* while *-icism* might mark a more strictly defined acception of that doctrine, etc. Then again, just as in biology no account is taken of terms antedating Linnaeus, so in philosophy it might be found best not to go back of the scholastic terminology. To illustrate another sort of limitation, it has probably never happened that any philosopher has attempted to give a general name to his own doctrine without that name's soon acquiring in common philosophical usage, a signification much broader than was originally intended. Thus, special systems go by the names Kantianism, Benthamism, Comteanism, Spencerianism, etc., while transcendentalism, utilitarianism, positivism, evolutionism, synthetic philosophy, etc. have irrevocably and very conveniently been elevated to broader governments.

After awaiting in vain, for a good many years, some particularly opportune conjuncture of circumstances that might serve to recommend his notions of the ethics of terminology, the writer has now, at last, dragged them in over head and shoulders, on an occasion when he has no specific proposal to offer nor any feeling but satisfaction at the course usage has run without any canons or resolutions of a congress. His word "pragmatism" has gained general recognition in a generalized sense that seems to argue power of growth and vitality. The famed psychologist, James, first took it up, seeing that his "radical empiricism" substantially answered to the writer's definition of pragmatism, albeit with a certain difference in the point of view. Next, the admirably clear and brilliant thinker, Mr. Ferdinand C. S. Schiller, casting about for a more attractive name for the "anthropomorphism" of his *Riddle of the Sphinx,* lit, in that most remarkable paper of his on *Axioms as Postulates,* upon the same designation "pragmatism," which in its original sense was in generic agreement with his own doctrine, for which he has since found the more appropriate specification "humanism," while he still retains "pragmatism" in a somewhat wider sense. So far all went happily, But at present, the word begins to be met with occasionally in the literary journals, where it gets abused in the merciless way that words have to expect when they fall into literary clutches. Sometimes the manners of the British have effloresced in scolding at the word as ill-chosen—ill-chosen, that is, to express some meaning that it was rather designed to exclude. So then, the writer, finding his bantling "pragmatism" so promoted, feels that it is time to kiss his child good-by and relinquish it to its higher destiny; while to serve the precise purpose of expressing the original definition, he begs to announce the birth of the word "pragmaticism," which is ugly enough to be safe from kidnappers.[1]

Much as the writer has gained from the perusal of what other pragmatists have written, he still thinks there is a decisive advantage in his original conception of the doctrine. From this original form every truth that follows from any of the other forms can be deduced, while some errors can be avoided into which other pragmatists have fallen. The original view appears, too, to be a more compact and unitary conception than the others.

But its capital merit, in the writer's eyes, is that it more readily connects itself with a critical proof of its truth. Quite in accord with the logical order of investigation, it usually happens that one first forms an hypothesis that seems more and more reasonable the further one examines into it, but that only a good deal later gets crowned with an adequate proof. The present writer having had the pragmatist theory under consideration for many years longer than most of its adherents, would naturally have given more attention to the proof of it. At any rate, in endeavoring to explain pragmatism, he may be excused for confining himself to that form of it that he knows best. In the present article there will be space only to explain just what this doctrine, (which, in such hands as it has now fallen into, may probably play a pretty prominent part in the philosophical discussions of the next coming years), really consists in. Should the exposition be found to interest readers of *The Monist,* they would certainly be much more interested in a second article which would give some samples of the manifold applications of pragmaticism (assuming it to be true) to the solution of problems of different kinds. After that, readers might be prepared to take an interest in a proof that the doctrine is true,—a proof which seems to the writer to leave no reasonable doubt on the subject, and to be the one contribution of value that he has to make to philosophy. For it would essentially involve the establishment of the truth of synechism.

The bare definition of pragmaticism could convey no satisfactory comprehension of it to the most apprehensive of minds, but requires the commentary to be given below. Moreover, this definition takes no notice of one or two other doctrines without the previous acceptance (or virtual acceptance) of which pragmaticism itself would be a nullity. They are included as a part of the pragmatism of Schiller, but the present writer prefers not to mingle different propositions. The preliminary propositions had better be stated forthwith.

The difficulty in doing this is that no formal list of them has ever been made. They might all be included under the vague maxim, "Dismiss make-believes." Philosophers of very diverse stripes propose that philosophy shall take its start from one or another state of mind in which no man, least of all a beginner in philosophy, actually is. One proposes that you shall begin by doubting everything, and says that there is only one thing that you cannot doubt, as if doubting were "as easy as lying." Another proposes that we should begin by observing "the first impressions of sense," forgetting that our very percepts are the results of cognitive elaboration. But in truth, there is but one state of mind from which you can "set out," namely, the very state of mind in which you actually find yourself at the time you do "set out"—a state in which you are laden with an immense mass of cognition already formed, of which you cannot divest yourself if you would; and who knows whether, if you could, you would not have made all knowledge impossible to yourself? Do you call it *doubting* to write down on a piece of paper that you doubt? If so, doubt has nothing to do with any serious business. But do not make believe; if pedantry has not eaten all the reality out of you, recognize, as you must, that there is much that you do not doubt, in the least. Now that which you do not at all doubt, you must and do regard as infallible, absolute truth. Here breaks in Mr. Make Believe: "What! Do you mean to say that one is to believe what is not true, or that what a man does not doubt is *ipso facto* true?" No, but unless he can make a thing white and black at once, he has to regard what he does not doubt as absolutely true. Now you, *per hypothesiu,* are that man, "But you tell me there are scores of things I do not doubt. I really cannot persuade myself that there is not some one of them about which I am mistaken." You are adducing one of your make-believe facts, which, even if it were established, would only go to show that doubt has a *limen,* that is, is only called into being by a certain finite stimulus. You only puzzle yourself by talking of this metaphysical "truth" and metaphysical "falsity," that you know nothing about. All you have any dealings with are your doubts and beliefs,[2] with the course of life that forces new beliefs upon you and gives you power to doubt old beliefs. If your terms "truth" and "falsity" are taken in such senses as to be definable in terms of doubt and belief and the course of experience (as for example they would be, if you were to define the "truth" as that to a belief in which belief would tend if it were to tend indefinitely toward absolute fixity), well and good: in that case, you are only talking about doubt and belief. But if by truth and falsity you mean something not definable in terms of doubt and belief in any way, then you are talking of entities of whose existence you can know nothing, and which Ockham's razor would clean shave off. Your problems would he greatly simplified, if, instead of saying that you want to know the "Truth," you were simply to say that you want to attain a state of belief unassailable by doubt.

Belief is not a momentary mode of consciousness; it is a habit of mind essentially enduring for some time, and mostly (at least) unconscious; and like other habits, it is, (until it meets with some surprise that begins its dissolution), perfectly self-satisfied. Doubt is of an altogether contrary genus. It is not a habit, but the privation of a habit. Now a privation of a habit, in order to be anything at all, must be a condition of erratic activity that in some way must get superseded by a habit.

Among the things which the reader, as a rational person, does not doubt, is that he not merely has habits, but also can exert a measure of self-control over his future actions; which means, however, *not* that he can impart to them any arbitrarily assignable character, but, on the contrary, that a process of self-preparation will tend

to impart to action, (when the occasion for it shall arise), one fixed character, which is indicated and perhaps roughly measured by the absence (or slightness) of the feeling of self-reproach, which subsequent reflection will induce. Now, this subsequent reflection is part of the self-preparation for action on the next occasion. Consequently, there is a tendency, as action is repeated again and again, for the action to approximate indefinitely toward the perfection of that fixed character, which would be marked by entire absence of self-reproach. The more closely this is approached, the less room for self-control there will be; and where no self-control is possible there will be no self-reproach.

These phenomena seem to be the fundamental characteristics which distinguish a rational being. Blame, in every case, appears to be a modification, often accomplished by a transference, or "projection," of the primary feeling of self-reproach. Accordingly, we never blame anybody for what had been beyond his power of previous self-control. Now, thinking is a species of conduct which is largely subject to self-control. In all their features (which there is no room to describe here), logical self-control is a perfect mirror of ethical self-control,—unless it be rather a species under that genus. In accordance with this, what you cannot in the least help believing is not, justly speaking, wrong belief. In other words, for you it is the absolute truth. True, it is conceivable that what you cannot help believing to-day, you might find you thoroughly disbelieve tomorrow. But then there is a certain distinction between things you "cannot" do, merely in the sense that nothing stimulates you to the great effort and endeavors that would be required, and things you cannot do because in their own nature they are insusceptible of being put into practice. In every stage of your excogitations, there is something of which you can only say, "I cannot think otherwise," and your experientially based hypothesis is that the impossibility is of the second kind.

There is no reason why "thought," in what has just been said, should be taken in that narrow sense in which silence and darkness are favorable to thought. It should rather be understood as covering all rational life, so that an experiment shall be an operation of thought. Of course, that ultimate state of habit to which the action of self-control ultimately tends, where no room is left for further self-control, is, in the case of thought, the state of fixed belief, or perfect knowledge.

Two things here are all-important to assure oneself of and to remember. The first is that a person is not absolutely an individual. His thoughts are what he is "saying to himself," that is, is saying to that other self that is just coming into life in the flow of time. When one reasons, it is that critical self that one is trying to persuade; and all thought whatsoever is a sign, and is mostly of the nature of language. The second thing to remember is that the man's circle of society, (however widely or narrowly this phrase may be understood), is a sort of loosely compacted person, in some respects of higher rank than the person of an individual organism. It is these two things alone that render it possible for you—but only in the abstract, and in a Pickwickian-sense,—to distinguish between absolute truth and what you do not doubt.

Let us now hasten to the exposition of pragmaticism itself. Here it will be convenient to imagine that somebody to whom the doctrine is new, but of rather preternatural perspicacity, asks questions of a pragmaticist. Everything that might give a dramatic illusion must be stripped off, so that the result will be a sort of cross between a dialogue and a catechism, but a good deal more like the latter,—something rather painfully reminiscent of *Mangnall's Historical Questions.*

Questioner: I am astounded at your definition of your pragmatism, because only last year I was assured by a person above all suspicion of warping the truth—himself a pragmatist—that your doctrine precisely was "that a conception is to be tested by its practical effects." You must surely, then, have entirely changed your definition very recently.

Pragmatist: If you will turn to Vols. VI and VII of the *Revue Philosophique,* or to the *Popular Science Monthly* for November 1877 and January 1878, you will be able to judge for yourself whether the interpretation you mention was not then clearly excluded. The exact wording of the English enunciation, (changing only the first person into the second), was: "Consider what effects that might conceivably have practical bearings you conceive the object of your conception to have. Then your conception of those effects is the WHOLE of your conception of the object."

Questioner: Well, what reason have you for asserting this is so?

Pragmatist: That is what I specially desire to tell you. But the question had better be postponed until you clearly understand what those reasons profess to prove.

Questioner: What, then, is the *raison d'être* of the doctrine? What advantage is expected from it?

Pragmatist: It will serve to show that almost every proposition of ontological metaphysics is either meaningless gibberish—one word being defined by other words, and they by still others, without any real conception ever being reached—or else is downright absurd; so that all such rubbish being swept away, what will remain of philosophy will be a series of problems capable of investigation by the observational methods of the true sciences—the truth about which can be

reached without those interminable misunderstandings and disputes which have made the highest of the positive sciences a mere amusement for idle intellects, a sort of chess—idle pleasure its purpose, and reading out of a book its method. In this regard, pragmaticism is a species of prope-positivism. But what distinguishes it from other species is, first, its retention of a purified philosophy; secondly, its full acceptance of the main body of our instinctive beliefs; and thirdly, its strenuous insistence upon the truth of scholastic realism, (or a close approximation to that, well stated by the late Dr. Francis Ellingwood Abbot in the Introduction to his *Scientific Theism*). So, instead of merely jeering at metaphysics, like other prope-positivists, whether by long-drawn-out parodies or otherwise, the pragmaticist extracts from it a precious essence, which will serve to give life and light to cosmology and physics. At the same time, the moral applications of the doctrine are positive and potent; and there are many other uses of it not easily classed. On another occasion, instances may be given to show that it really has these effects.

Questioner: I hardly need to be convinced that your doctrine would wipe out metaphysics. Is it not as obvious that it must wipe out every proposition of science and everything that bears on the conduct of life? For you say that the only meaning that, for you, any assertion bears is that a certain experiment has resulted in a certain way: Nothing else but an experiment enters into the meaning. Tell me, then, how can an experiment, in itself, reveal anything more than that something once happened to an individual object and that subsequently some other individual event occurred?

Pragmatist: That question is, indeed, to the purpose—the purpose being to correct any misapprehensions of pragmaticism. You speak of an experiment in itself, emphasizing "*in itself.*" You evidently think of each experiment as isolated from every other. It has not, for example, occurred to you, one might venture to surmise, that every connected series of experiments constitutes a single collective experiment. What are the essential ingredients of an experiment? First, of course, an experimenter of flesh and blood. Secondly, a verifiable hypothesis. This is a proposition[3] relating to the universe environing the experimenter, or to some well-known part of it and affirming or denying of this only some experimental possibility or impossibility. The third indispensable ingredient is a sincere doubt in the experimenter's mind as to the truth of that hypothesis. Passing over several ingredients on which we need not dwell, the purpose, the plan, and the resolve, we come to the act of choice by which the experimenter singles out certain identifiable objects to be operated upon. The next is the external (or quasi-external) ACT by which he modifies those objects. Next, comes the subsequent *reaction* of the world upon the experimenter in a perception; and finally, his recognition of the teaching of the experiment. While the two chief parts of the event itself are the action and the reaction, yet the unity of essence of the experiment lies in its purpose and plan, the ingredients passed over in the enumeration.

Another thing: in representing the pragmaticist as making rational meaning to consist in an experiment (which you speak of as an event in the past) you strikingly fail to catch his attitude of mind. Indeed, it is not in an experiment, but in *experimental phenomena,* that rational meaning is said to consist. When an experimentalist speaks of a *phenomenon,* such as "Hall's phenomenon," "Zeemaun's phenomenon" and its modification, "Michelson's phenomenon," or "the chessboard phenomenon," he does not mean any particular event that did happen to somebody in the dead past, but what *surely will* happen to everybody in the living future who shall fulfill certain conditions. The phenomenon consists in the fact that when an experimentalist shall come to *act* according to a certain scheme that he has in mind, then will something else happen, and shatter the doubts of skeptics, like the celestial fire upon the altar of Elijah.

And do not overlook the fact that the pragmaticist maxim says nothing of single experiments or of single experimental phenomena, (for what is conditionally true *in futuro* can hardly be singular), but only speaks of *general kinds* of experimental phenomena. Its adherent does not shrink from speaking of general objects as real, since whatever is true represents a real. Now the laws of nature are true.

The rational meaning of every proposition lies in the future. How so? The meaning of a proposition is itself a proposition. Indeed, it is no other than the very proposition of which it is the meaning: it is a translation of it. But of the myriads of forms into which a proposition may be translated, what is that one which is to be called its very meaning? It is, according to the pragmaticist, that form in which the proposition becomes applicable to human conduct, not in these or those special circumstances, nor when one entertains this or that special design, but that form which is most directly applicable to self-control under every situation, and to every purpose. This is why he locates the meaning in future time; for future conduct is the only conduct that is subject to self-control. But in order that that form of the proposition which is to be taken as its meaning should be applicable to every situation and to every purpose upon which the proposition has any bearing, it must be simply the general description of all the experimental phenomena which the assertion of the proposition virtually predicts. For an experimental phenomenon is the fact asserted by the proposition that action of a certain description will have a certain kind of experimental result; and experimental results are the only results that can affect human conduct. No doubt, some unchanging idea may come to influence a man more than it had done;

but only because some experience equivalent to an experiment has brought its truth home to him more intimately than before. Whenever a man acts purposively, he acts under a belief in some experimental phenomenon. Consequently, the sum of the experimental phenomena that a proposition implies makes up its entire bearing upon human conduct. Your question, then, of how a pragmaticist can attribute any meaning to any assertion other than that of a single occurrence is substantially answered.

Questioner: I see that pragmaticism is a thorough-going phenomenalism. Only why should you limit yourself to the phenomena of experimental science rather than embrace all observational science? Experiment, after all, is an uncommunicative informant. It never expiates: it only answers "yes" or "no"; or rather it usually snaps out 'No!" or, at best, only utters an inarticulate grunt for the negation of its "no." The typical experimentalist is not much of an observer. It is the student of natural history to whom nature opens the treasury of her confidence, while she treats the cross-examining experimentalist with the reserve he merits. Why should your phenomenalism sound the meagre jews-harp of experiment rather than the glorious organ of observation?

Pragmaticist: Because pragmaticism is not definable as "thorough-going phenomenalism," although the latter doctrine may be a kind of pragmatism. The *richness* of phenomena lies in their sensuous quality. Pragmaticism does not intend to define the phenomenal equivalents of words and general ideas, but, on the contrary, eliminates their sential element, and endeavors to define the rational purport, and this it finds in the purposive bearing of the word or proposition in question.

Questioner: Well, if you choose so to make Doing the Be-all and the End-all of human life, why do you not make meaning to consist simply in doing? Doing has to be done at a certain time upon a certain object. Individual objects and single events cover all reality, as everybody knows, and as a practicalist ought to be the first to insist. Yet, your meaning, as you have described it, is *general.* Thus, it is of the nature of a mere word and not a reality. You say yourself that your meaning of a proposition is only the same proposition in another dress. But a practical man's meaning is the very thing he means. What do you make to be the meaning of "George Washington"?

Pragmaticist: Forcibly put! A good half dozen of your points must certainly be admitted. It must be admitted, in the first place, that if pragmatism really made Doing to be the Be-all and the End-all of life, that would be its death, For to say that we live for the mere sake of action, as action, regardless of the thought it carries out, would be to say that there is no such thing as rational purport. Secondly, it must be admitted that every proposition professes to be true of a certain real individual object, often the environing universe. Thirdly, it must be admitted that pragmaticism fails to furnish any translation or meaning of a proper name, or other designation of an individual object. Fourthly, the pragmaticistic meaning is undoubtedly general; and it is equally indisputable that the general is of the nature of a word or sign. Fifthly, it must be admitted that individuals alone exist; and sixthly, it may be admitted that the very meaning of a word or significant object ought to be the very essence of reality of what it signifies. But when, those admissions have been unreservedly made, you find the pragmaticist still constrained most earnestly to deny the force of your objection, you ought to infer that there is some consideration that has escaped you. Putting the admissions together, you will perceive that the pragmaticist grants that a proper name, (although it is not customary to say that it has a *meaning*), has a certain denotative function peculiar, in each case, to that name and its equivalents; and that he grants that every assertion contains such a denotative or pointing-out function. In its peculiar individuality, the pragmaticist excludes this from the rational purport of the assertion, although *the like* of it, being common to all assertions, and so, being general and not individual, may enter into the pragmaticistic purport. Whatever exists, ex-sists, that is, really acts upon other existents, so obtains a self-identity, and is definitely individual. As to the general, it will be a help to thought to notice that there are two ways of being general. A statue of a soldier on some village monument, in his overcoat and with his musket, is for each of a hundred families the image of its uncle, its sacrifice to the Union. That statue, then, though it is itself single, represents any one man of whom a certain predicate may be true. It is *objectively* general. The word "soldier," whether spoken or written, is general in the same way; while the name "George Washington" is not so. But each of these two terms remains one and the same noun, whether it be spoken or written, and whenever and wherever it be spoken or written. This noun is not an existent thing: it is a *type,* or *form,* to which objects, both those that are externally existent and those which are imagined, may *conform,* but which none of them can exactly be. This is subjective generality. The pragmaticistic purport is general in both ways.

As to reality, one finds it defined in various ways; but if that principle of terminological ethics that was proposed be accepted, the equivocal language will soon disappear. For *realis* and *realitas* are not ancient words. They were invented to be terms of philosophy in the thirteenth century, and the meaning they were intended to express is perfectly clear. That is *real* which has such and such characters, whether anybody thinks it to have those characters or not. At any rate, that is the sense in which the pragmaticist uses the word. Now, just as conduct controlled by ethical reason tends towards fixing

certain habits of conduct, the nature of which, (as to illustrate the meaning, peaceable habits and not quarrelsome habits), does not depend upon any accidental circumstances, and *in that sense,* may be said to be *destined*; so, thought, controlled by a rational experimental logic, tends to the fixation of certain opinions, equally destined, the nature of which will be the same in the end, however the perversity of thought of whole generations may cause the postponement of the ultimate fixation. If this be so, as every man of us virtually assumes that it is, in regard to each matter the truth of which he seriously discusses, then, according to the adopted definition of "real," the state of things which will be believed in that ultimate opinion is real. But, for the most part, such opinions will be general. Consequently, *some* general objects are real. (Of course, nobody ever thought that all generals were real; but the scholastics used to assume that generals were real when they had hardly any, or quite no, experiential evidence to support their assumption; and their fault lay just there, and not in holding that generals could be real.) One is struck with the inexactitude of thought even of analysts of power, when they touch upon modes of being. One will meet, for example, the virtual assumption that what is relative to thought cannot be real. But why not, exactly? *Red* is relative to sight, but the fact that this or that is in that relation to vision that we call being red is not *itself* relative to sight; it is a real fact.

Not only may generals be real, but they may also be *physically efficient,* not in every metaphysical sense, but in the common-sense acception in which human purposes are physically efficient. Aside from metaphysical nonsense, no sane man doubts that if I feel the air in my study to be stuffy, that thought may cause the window to be opened. My thought, be it granted, was an individual event. But what determined it to take the particular determination it did, was in part the general fact that stuffy air is unwholesome, and in part other *Forms,* concerning which Dr. Carus has caused so many men to reflect to advantage—or rather, *by* which, and the general truth concerning which Dr. Carus's mind was determined to the forcible enunciation of so much truth. For truths, on the average, have a greater tendency to get believed than falsities have. Were it otherwise, considering that there are myriads of false hypotheses to account for any given phenomenon, against one sole true one (or if you will have it so, against every true one), the first step toward genuine knowledge must have been next door to a miracle. So, then, when my window was opened, because of the truth that stuffy air is malsain, a physical effort was brought into existence by the efficiency of a general and non-existent truth. This has a droll sound because it is unfamiliar; but exact analysis is with it and not against it; and it has besides, the immense advantage of not blinding us to great facts—such as that the ideas "justice" and "truth" are, notwithstanding the iniquity of the world, the mightiest of the forces that move it. Generality is, indeed, an indispensable ingredient of reality; for mere individual existence or actuality without any regularity whatever is a nullity. Chaos is pure nothing.

That which any true proposition asserts is *real,* in the sense of being as it is regardless of what you or I may think about it. Let this proposition be a general conditional proposition as to the future, and it is a real general such as is calculated really to influence human conduct; and such the pragmaticist holds to be the rational purport of every concept.

Accordingly, the pragmaticist does not make the *summum bonum* to consist in action, but makes it to consist in that process of evolution whereby the existent comes more and more to embody those generals which were just now said to be *destined,* which is what we strive to express in calling them *reasonable.* In its higher stages, evolution takes place more and more largely through self-control, and this gives the pragmaticist a sort of justification for making the rational purport to be general.

There is much more in elucidation of pragmaticism that might be said to advantage, were it not for the dread of fatiguing the reader. It might, for example, have been well to show clearly that the pragmaticist does not attribute any different essential mode of being to an event in the future from that which he would attribute to a similar event in the past, but only that the practical attitude of the thinker toward the two is different. It would also have been well to show that the pragmaticist does not make Forms to be the only realities in the world, any more than he makes the reasonable purport of a word to be the only kind of meaning there is. These things are, however, implicitly involved in what has been said. There is only one remark concerning the pragmaticist's conception of the relation of his formula to the first principles of logic which need detain the reader.

Aristotle's definition of universal predication, which is usually designated, (like a papal bull or writ of court, from its opening words), as the *Dictum de omni,* may be translated as follows: "We call a predication, (be it affirmative or negative), *universal,* when, and only when, there is nothing among the existent individuals to which the subject affirmatively belongs, but to which the predicate will not likewise be referred (affirmatively or negatively, according as the universal predication is affirmative or negative)." The Greek is: λέγομεν τὸ κατὰ παντὸς κατηγ ορεῖσθαι ὅταν μηδέν ᾖ λαβεῖν τῶν τοῦ ὑποκειμένου καθ' οὗ θάτερον οὐ λεχθήσεται· καὶ τὸ κατὰ μηδενὸς ὡσαύτως. The important words "existent individuals" have been introduced into the translation (which English idiom would not permit here to be literal): but it is plain that existent individuals were what Aristotle meant. The other departures from literalness only serve to give modern English forms of expression. Now, it is well known that propositions in formal logic go in pairs, the two of one pair being convertible into another by the interchange of the ideas of antecedent and consequent, subject and predicate, etc. The parallelism extends so far that it is often assumed to be perfect; but it is not quite so. The proper mate of this sort to the *Dictum de omni* is the following definition of affirmative predication: We call a predication *affirmative,* (be it universal or particular), when, and only when, there is nothing among the sensation affects that belong universally to the predicate which will not be, (universally or particularly, according as the affirmative predicate is universal or particular), said to belong to the subject. Now, this is substantially the essential proposition of pragmaticism. Of course, its parallelism to the *dictum de omni* will only be admitted by a person who admit the truth of pragmaticism.

Suffer me to add one word more on this point—for, if one cares at all to know what the pragmaticist theory consists in, one must understand that there is no other part of it to which the pragmaticist attaches quite as much importance as he does to the recognition in his doctrine of the utter inadequacy of action or volition or even of resolve or actual purpose, as materials out of which to construct a conditional purpose or the concept of conditional purpose. Had a purposed article concerning the principle of continuity and synthesizing the ideas of the other articles of a series in the early volumes of *The Monist* ever been written, it would have appeared how, with thorough consistency, that theory involved the recognition that continuity is an indispensable element of reality, and that continuity is simply what generality becomes in the logic of relatives, and thus, like generality, and more than generality, is an affair of thought, and is the essence of thought. Yet even in its truncated condition, an extra-intelligent reader might discern that the theory of those cosmological articles made reality to consist in something more than feeling and action could supply, inasmuch as the primeval chaos, where those two elements were present, was explicitly shown to be pure nothing. Now, the motive for alluding to that theory just here is, that in this way one can put in a strong light a position which the pragmaticist holds and must hold, whether that cosmological theory be ultimately sustained or exploded, namely, that the third category—the category of thought, representation, triadic relation, mediation, genuine thirdness, thirdness as such—is an essential ingredient of reality, yet does not by itself constitute reality, since this category, (which in that cosmology appears as the element of habit), can have no concrete being without action, as a separate object on which to work its government, just as action cannot exist without the immediate being of feeling on which to act. The truth is that pragmaticism is closely allied to the Hegelian absolute idealism, from which, however, it is sundered by its vigorous denial that the third category, (which Hegel degrades to a mere stage of thinking), suffices to make the world, or is even so much as self-sufficient. Had Hegel, instead of regarding the first two stages with his smile of contempt, held on to them as independent or distinct elements of the triune Reality, pragmaticists might have looked up to him as the great vindicator of their truth. (Of course, the external trappings of his doctrine are only here and there of much significance.) For pragmaticism belongs essentially to the triadic class of philosophical doctrines, and is much more essentially so than Hegelianism is. (Indeed, in one passage, at least, Hegel alludes to the triadic form of his exposition as to a mere fashion of dress.)

Notes

1. To show how recent the general use of the word "pragmatism" is, the writer may mention that, to the best of his belief, he never used it in copy for the press before today, except by particular request, in *Baldwin's Dictionary*. Toward the end of 1890, when this part of the *Century Dictionary* appeared, he did not deem that the word had sufficient status to appear in that work. But he has used it continually in philosophical conversation since, perhaps, the mid-seventies.

2. It is necessary to say that "belief" is throughout used merely as the name of the contrary to doubt, without regard to grades of certainty nor to the nature of the proposition held for true, i.e., "believed."

3. The writer, like most English logicians, invariably uses the word *proposition,* not as the Germans define their equivalent, *Satz,* as the language-expression of a judgment (*Urtheil*), but as that which is related to any assertion, whether mental and self-addressed or outwardly expressed, just as any possibility is related to its actualization. The difficulty of the, at best, difficult problem of the essential nature of a Proposition has been increased, for the Germans, by their *Urtheil,* confounding, under one designation, the mental *assertion* with the *assertible.*

Arthur O. Lovejoy (essay date 1908)

SOURCE: Lovejoy, Arthur O. "The Thirteen Pragmatisms." In *The Thirteen Pragmatisms and Other Essays,* pp. 1-29. Baltimore, Md.: The Johns Hopkins Press, 1963.

[*In the following essay, first published in* The Journal of Philosophy *in 1908, Lovejoy differentiates between various, and often divergent, Pragmatic theories of truth.*]

Part I

In the present year of grace 1908 the term "pragmatism"—if not the doctrine—celebrates its tenth birthday. Before the controversy over the mode of philosophy designated by it enters upon a second decade, it is perhaps not too much to ask that contemporary philosophers should agree to attach some single and stable meaning to the term. There appears to be as yet no sufficiently clear and general recognition, among contributors to that controversy, of the fact that the pragmatist is not merely three but many gentlemen at once. Some recent papers by Perry set, as it seems to me, the right example in discriminating a number of separate pragmatistic propositions and discussing each of them by itself. But perhaps even these papers do not insist so emphatically, as it is worth-while to do, upon the utter disconnection and even incongruity that subsists between a number of these propositions; and there are one or two important ambiguities of meaning in certain of the pragmatists' formulas which do not seem to find a place in Perry's careful enumeration. A complete enumeration of the metamorphoses of so protean an entity is, indeed, perhaps too much to expect; but even after we leave out of the count certain casual expressions of pragmatist writers which they probably would not wish taken too seriously, and also certain mere commonplaces from which scarcely any contemporary philosopher would dissent, there remain at least thirteen pragmatisms: a baker's dozen of contentions which are separate not merely in the sense of being discriminable, but in the sense of being logically independent, so that you may without inconsistency accept any one and reject all the others, or refute one and leave the philosophical standing of the others unimpugned. All of these have generally or frequently been labeled with the one name and defended or attacked as if they constituted a single system of thought—sometimes even as if they were severally interchangeable.

I shall try to put down all the logical doctrines of importance that seem to have been improperly reduced to unity in current discussions; and I shall try to exhibit the fact of their reciprocal independence in as clear a light as possible. To contribute to the determination of the truth or falsity of any one of these doctrines is no part of the business of the present discussion; for I venture to think that the question of truth has sometimes been not very profitably dealt with during the past ten years, in the absence of a sufficiently considerate prior clearing up of the question of meaning. The pragmatist school itself seems, thus far, more distinguished for originality, inventiveness, and a keen vision for the motes in the eye of the intellectualist, than for patience in making distinctions or the habit of self-analysis. And its critics, on the other hand, have occasionally made haste to take the utmost advantage of this unassorted commingling of doctrinal sheep and doctrinal goats in the ample fold of pragmatic theory and have made the apparently caprine character of some members of the flock a warrant for the wholesale condemnation of the entire multitude. In view of this situation, nothing seems more indicated than an attempt at clear differentiation of the separate pragmatist assertions and tendencies.

Certainly it is probable that the following list could be extended. I hope that it will be found to include all the genuinely independent contentions that are most frequently illicitly identified, and all the ambiguities of meaning that are so central and important as to call for serious consideration from both the defenders and the critics of the several opinions to which the one name has been applied.

1.

Primarily, it is obvious, pragmatism—the pragmatism of Peirce, and of James's Berkeley address—was merely a doctrine concerning the meaning of propositions, concerning the way in which the really significant issue in any controversy could be determined. It maintained that one meaning of any proposition whatever is reducible to the future consequences in experience to which that proposition points, consequences which those who accept the proposition *ipso facto* anticipate as experiences that somebody is subsequently to have. Now, a theory about the meaning of propositions is not the same thing as a theory about the criterion of truth in propositions; a formula which professes to tell you how to ascertain precisely what a given assertion really signifies does not thereby profess to tell you whether or not that assertion is true. James, at least, in his recent book and elsewhere, has clearly noted this distinction between pragmatism as a theory of meaning and pragmatism as a theory of truth; Schiller does not appear to do so, since he identifies the "principle of Peirce" with a view concerning the mark that "establishes the *real* truth and validity" of a proposition.[1] But I do not think that even James has sufficiently insisted upon the logical disconnectedness of the two theories. Indeed, the whole topic of the relation of meaning and truth might advantageously receive more extended discussion than it has yet had. It may at first sight seem that a close logical relation can be made out between the two, in at least one direction. To know what a proposition exactly means may appear to involve a knowledge of just where to look for the evidence of its truth and for the test by which its claim to truth can be brought to proof. If a judgment *means* merely certain future experiences, it might appear that its truth could be known only through—and, therefore, only at the time of—the occurrence of the predicted experiences. But I can not see that this really follows. The assertion "God exists and mere materialism is false" may possibly mean only the anticipation of a cosmic future different in specific ways from that which the acceptance of the contrary proposi-

tion would lead one to expect; but the criterion of the truth of the assertion need not be correspondingly future. Its truth may conceivably be known *now,* through a mystical intuition or by a "necessity of thought"; or (and this is apparently good pragmatist doctrine about knowledge) it may be a proposition that we are obliged and entitled proleptically to accept as a true acceptance of the postulate, because it satisfies a present (not a future) need. The experiences whose occurrence constitute the meaning of the judgment may have one date; the apprehension of the judgment's validity, or legitimacy as a belief, may have quite another. According to one of the pragmatist theories of truth, a proposition is known as true (in the only sense of "true" which that theory regards as intelligible) at the moment at which it effectually operates to put an end to a felt inner discord or to open a way through a practical *impasse*; but the matter to which the proposition refers not only may be, but normally will be, subsequent to that moment of acceptance and mental relief. A "plan of action" presumably relates to the future; but the determination of its "truth," or whatever kind of acceptability is pragmatically to pass for such, can not be postponed until the future to which it relates has been "verified" by becoming past; else all our "true" plans of action would, paradoxically, be retrospective, and we should have to say that the pragmatic man never is, but always is about to have been, blest with knowledge. If, then, the legitimacy of a belief is, upon pragmatist principles, to be known at one moment, while the experiences which it "means" may run on into later moments, it appears to follow that the fullest knowledge of the belief's meaning may throw no light whatever upon the question of its legitimacy. That—until the belief has (presumably) *lost* all meaning by coming to refer purely to past experiences—still remains, from the standpoint of pragmatism as a theory of meaning, a separate and unsettled question; it is impossible to infer that the pragmatist theory of validity is any more correct than another. The acceptance of either one of these theories, equally known as "pragmatism," leaves you an entirely open option with respect to the acceptance of the other.

2.

This pragmatic theory of meaning, as used by James, who has been its principal expounder and defender, seems designed to function chiefly as a quieter of controversy, a means for banishing from the philosophic lists those contestants between whose theories there appears, when this criterion is applied, to be no meaningful opposition, in whose differences there lies no issue that "makes a difference." In this application, however, the criterion clearly exhibits a radical ambiguity. The "effects of a practical kind" which our conception of an object must (we are told) involve, the "future consequences in concrete experience, whether active or passive," to which all significant propositions must point, may consist in either: (a) future experiences which the proposition (expressly or implicitly) predicts as about to occur, *no matter whether it be believed true or not*; or (b) future experiences which will occur *only upon condition that the proposition be believed*. The consequences of the *truth* of a proposition (in the sense of its correct prerepresentation of a subsequent experience to which its terms logically refer) and the consequences of *belief* in a proposition have been habitually confused in the discussion of the pragmatic theory of meaning. Taken in the one sense, the theory is equivalent to the assertion that only definitely predictive propositions—those which by their proper import foretell the appearance of specific sensations or situations in the "concrete" experience of some temporal consciousness—have real meaning. Taken in the other sense, the theory does not require that propositions *refer* to the future at all; it is enough that, by being carried along into the future as beliefs in somebody's mind, they be capable of giving to that mind emotional or other experiences in some degree different from those which it would have in the absence of the beliefs. No two doctrines could be "pragmatically" more dissimilar than the pragmatic theory of meaning when construed in the first sense, and the same theory when construed in the second sense. If the formula includes only "future experiences" of the class (a), it has the effect of very narrowly limiting the range of meaningful judgments, and of excluding from the field of legitimate consideration a large number of issues in which a great part of mankind seems to have taken a lively interest; and it must assuredly be regarded as a highly paradoxical contention. But if it includes also future consequences of class (b), it is no paradox at all, but the mildest of truisms; for it then is so blandly catholic, tolerant, and inclusive a doctrine that it can deny real meaning to no proposition whatever which any human being has ever cared enough about to believe. In James's *Pragmatism* his criterion is applied to specific questions sometimes in one sense and sometimes in the other; and the results are correspondingly divergent. Using his formula in the first sense, he argues, for example, that the only "real" difference between a theistic and a materialistic view of the universe is that the former entitles us to predict a future in human experience that contains certain desirable elements for the expectation of which materialism gives no warrant. In other words, the whole "meaning" of theism is declared to be reducible to the anticipation of a specific cosmic or personal future; and the only genuine issue between it and the opposing doctrine lies in the question of the legitimacy of this anticipation. "If no future detail of experience or conduct is to be deduced from our hypothesis, the debate between materialism and theism becomes quite idle and insignificant." Supposing matter capable of giving us just the same world of experience as a God would give us, "wherein should we suffer loss if we dropped God as an hypothesis and made the matter alone responsible? Where would any special deadness, or crassness, come in? And how, experience being what is once for all, would God's presence in it make it any more living or richer?"[2] "Treated as it often is" (i.e., treated nonpragmatically), "this question becomes little more than a conflict between esthetic preferences," between different ways of talking about, imagining, or explaining the ancestry of precisely the one, identical, actual world of past, present, and future experiences; and such differences in esthetic preferences are treated by James as "abstract" things that really make no difference. In the spirit of this chapter of James's book—which is the spirit of the Enlightenment at its narrowest, most utilitarian, least imaginative—one might go on to eliminate from consideration, as pragmatically meaningless, a large part of the issues over which metaphysicians and theologians have divided; one might show that (apart from the having of the beliefs themselves, which from the present point of view does not count) it makes no difference whether you believe or reject most of the dogmas of theology or the hypotheses of speculative philosophy. For these largely refer to alleged permanent, unvarying factors of reality from which no specific contents of experience (beyond, once more, the experiences directly arising from the presence of those factors) can be clearly deduced. The trinitarian presumably does not necessarily anticipate "concrete future experiences" different from those anticipated by the unitarian; nor need the pantheist expect the cosmos to behave in a manner other than that expected by the pluralistic theist. Later in James's book, however, we find his criterion taken in the opposite sense; for example, while the author observes of the monistic doctrine of the absolute that "you can not redescend into the world of particulars by the Absolute's aid or deduce any necessary consequences of detail important for your life from your idea of his nature," just this nonpredictive doctrine is credited with genuine pragmatic meaning, because "emotional and spiritual" consequences flow from the belief in it (*Pragmatism,* pp. 273-74). And in *this* spirit, all beliefs with which human emotions have in any degree become entangled would have to be regarded by the pragmatist as *ipso facto* meaningful and serious. It would not even be necessary that the beliefs should, in the ordinary logical sense, have any intelligible import at all. There are some who feel pretty sure that those who adhere, for instance, to the nihilistic monism of the Vedanta, or to the Athanasian doctrine of the Trinity, never really *conceive together* the elements of the propositions that they affirm; but no one can deny that, out of the maintenance of the posture of belief toward these propositions, believers derive highly distinctive and vivid experiences which they could scarcely have in any other way. And for all such beliefs our pragmatist—who, but a moment ago, seemed so narrow and fe-rocious an Aufklärer—would now be compelled to find a place among the significant issues.

This pragmatic theory of meaning thus breaks up into two possible doctrines that are not merely different, but incongruous. We seem to be justified in calling upon the pragmatist to make an election between them. If I may, for a moment, go beyond the province chosen for this paper, I venture to predict that neither choice will be found welcome; for I suspect that all the charm and impressiveness of the theory arises out of the confusion of its alternative interpretations. It gets its appearance of novelty and of practical serviceableness in the settle-ment of controversies from its one meaning; and it gets its plausibility entirely from the other. But (when the distinction is made) in the sense in which the theory might be logically functional, it seems hardly likely to appear plausible; and in the sense in which it is plau-sible, it appears destitute of any applicability or func-tion in the distinguishing of "real" from meaningless is-sues.

3.

But the pragmatic theory of meaning in its first sense—with its characteristic emphasis upon the ultimately pre-dictive import of all judgments—leads to a theory con-cerning the way in which judgments are verified; in other words, to a theory about the meaning of truth. If all judgments must refer to specific future experiences, their verification consists in the getting of the experi-ences which they foretold. They are true, in short, if their prediction is realized; and they can, strictly speak-ing, be known to be true only through that realization, and concurrently with the occurrence of the series of experiences predicted. James presents this doctrine with an apparent exception in favor of "necessary truths"; which, since they coerce the mind as soon as they are clearly presented to it, are (he seems to admit) verified "on the spot," without waiting for the presentation in experience of all empirical phenomena that may be re-ferred to by them. But even this exception is not recog-nized entirely unequivocally; and in any case, for the great mass of our judgments, their truth consists in the correspondence of the anticipations properly evoked by them with subsequent items of experience; and the veri-fication of their truth comes only when the whole series of such items which they foreshadowed has been com-pletely experienced. "All true processes must lead to the face of directly verifying experiences *somewhere,* which somebody's ideas have copied." "Truth *happens* to an idea. It becomes true, is made true by events. Its verity *is,* in fact, an event, a process: the process, namely, of its verifying itself, its veri-*fication.*"[3]

Now, I have already tried to show that such a theory of truth is neither identical with, nor properly deducible from, the original pragmatic theory of meaning—in ei-

ther of its senses. I wish now to make more fully clear the precise import of this theory of truth, and to show its contrast with another type of theory of truth which also and, I think, more properly figures as pragmatism. Observe that the words quoted give us a theory of truth which is obviously not at the same time functionally serviceable as a theory of knowledge—which seems a strange trait in a pragmatist theory. According to this phase of pragmatism, judgments are not known to be true until they become true, and until they become true they have no use or importance (and, as I have sug-gested, they even ought to be said, on some "pragmatist principles," to have no meaning), for their reference is to the dead past. Our intellect is condemned, according to this doctrine, to subsist wholly by a system of de-ferred payments; it gets no cash down; and it is also a rule of this kind of finance that when the payments are finally made, they are always made in outlawed cur-rency. Now, of course, what we practically want and, indeed, must have from a theory of knowledge is some means of telling what predictions are to be accepted as sound *while they are still predictions.* Hindsight is doubtless a good deal more accurate than foresight, but it is less useful. No one is likely to deny that a valid proposition (in so far, at least, as it is predictive at all) must "lead us finally to the face of some directly veri-fying experience"; but I can conceive no observation which it can be more unprofitable to dwell upon than this one. If this were all that a pragmatic epistemology had to tell us, it would assuredly be giving us a stone where we had asked for bread.

But, of course, there is a form—or more than one form—of pragmatic epistemology that offers to meet the real needs of the situation in which the problem of knowledge arises, that seeks to tell us what predictive judgments ought, and what ought not, to be believed, before the "veri-*fication*" of those judgments in actually possessed experience makes the question concerning their truth as irrelevant and redundant a thing as a coro-ner's inquest on a corpse is—to the corpse. And these pragmatist theories about the criterion of truth—i.e., about the marks of the relative validity of proposi-tions—which attempt to be really functional ought to be completely distinguished from this sterile doctrine which insists that the only true proposition is a dead proposition.

PART II

The purpose of this paper, as indicated at the beginning of the former installment, is to discriminate all the more important doctrines going under the name of pragma-tism which can be shown to be not only distinct, but also logically independent *inter se.* Three such diver-gent pragmatist contentions have thus far been noted. "Pragmatism" was primarily a theory concerning the "meaning" of propositions; but this theory, because of a latent ambiguity in its terms, breaks up into two: (1) The meaning of a proposition consists in the future consequences in experience which it (directly or indirectly) predicts as about to occur no matter whether it be believed or not; (2) The meaning of a proposition consists in the future consequences of believing it. The first of these was seen to suggest (though it by no means necessarily implies) the third variant of pragmatism, namely, a doctrine concerning the nature of truth; viz., that the truth of a proposition is identical with the occurrence of the series of experiences which it predicts and can be said to be known only after such series is completed. "Its truth *is* its verification." This contention, that judgments acquire truth only in the degree in which they lose predictive character and practical bearings, has been shown to be wholly barren and useless, since its affords no answer to the real epistemological question concerning the criterion of the truth of propositions whose specific predictive implications have not yet been experienced.

4.

It is, however, not difficult to see through what associations of ideas some pragmatists have been led to emphasize this notion of the *ex post facto* character of all truth. Largely, it would appear, it derives its plausibility from its resemblance to the ordinary empirical doctrine that those general propositions are to be regarded as true which, so far as they have been applied, have been found to be realized in past experience. This latter doctrine, from which the former is often not clearly distinguished, may be set down as another of the things that pragmatism is frequently supposed to be. It is the doctrine sometimes sententiously expressed by the observation that those propositions are true which "will work" or "which you can live by." What the evolutionary empiricists who are fond of this observation almost always really mean by it is that those judgments are true which hitherto *have* worked; in other and more precise words, that I am, in advance of the actual realization or verification of the future experiences which may be predicted by a given judgment, entitled to regard it as true if it is *similar* to, or is a special application of, a general *class* of judgments which historical records or my own memory tell me have thus far had their implied predictions realized. But this is by no means identical with the principle previously mentioned and vigorously insisted upon by some pragmatists, that each *individual* judgment can *become* true only through, and contemporaneously with, the presentation in consciousness of those specific subsequent experiences which it points to and prognosticates.

5.

If, now, we are to set down this evolutionary empiricist criterion of truth as one expression of pragmatism—at least as that is popularly understood—it is necessary to add that this formula, too, suffers from ambiguity, and therefore breaks up into two quite distinct criteria. The ambiguity is analogous to that already pointed out in the pragmatist's theory of meaning. A belief may "work" in two very different senses, either by having its actual predictions fulfilled, or by contributing to increase the energies or efficiency or chance of survival of those who believe it. The Jews, for example, believed persistently for many centuries that a national Messiah would come in the next generation to restore the independence and establish the supremacy of Israel. In one sense, this belief did not work; for the events which it predicted did not occur. But biologically considered it worked wonderfully well; for it assuredly did much to produce the extraordinary persistency of the Jewish racial character, and the exceptional energy, self-confidence, and tenacity of purpose of the individual Jew. Many beliefs involving false predictions are biologically unfavorable, namely, if they lead to physical conduct ill-adapted to the conditions of the believer's physical environment. You can not "live by" the belief that fire will not burn. But, also, some false or never-realized predictions, and many beliefs having apparently no predictive character—and no capacity for empirical verification—have shown themselves to be excellent things to live by. And if we are to take the doctrine that the true is the "livable" in its second and more unquestionably pragmatistic sense—if we are to identify the validity of beliefs with their biological serviceableness—we should apparently have to classify as "true" many judgments which predict nothing, and many which confessedly predict what is not going to occur.

6.

Partly, however, what I have called the theory of the *ex post facto* nature of truth is a somewhat blurred reflection of a certain metaphysical doctrine which, although not always very explicitly put forward, appears to me to have a rather fundamental place in the characteristic mode of thought of most representatives of pragmatism. This is the doctrine of the "open-ness" of the future, and of the determinative or "creative" efficacy of each "present" moment in the ever-transient process of conscious judgment, choice, and action. The two parts of the doctrine obviously enough go together: if the process truly brings into being at each new moment a genuinely new and unique increment of reality, then, so long as any moment's increment has not yet been brought forth, it can not yet be called in any intelligible sense real; and if, similarly, the thing that is to be is a sheer nonentity until it enters into actual, temporal experience, the moment in which it becomes an experience must be credited with the creation *ex nihilo* of a new item of being. This doctrine of what M. Bergson calls a *devenir réel,* and of the creative function of consciousness, which is the pregnant ontological preconception from which a great variety of confused pragmatistic ideas have proceeded, unquestionably has certain epistemological implications. Such a metaphysics appears to imply the partial contingency and (from the standpoint of any "present" knowledge) indeterminateness of the future content of reality. But these implications are not synonymous with the *ex post facto* theory of truth in the generality with which that has usually been expressed. The future may be—and by the same pragmatists, when they adumbrate this sort of metaphysics, apparently is—regarded as presenting to our understanding only a narrow margin of the unpredictable; its general character and the greater mass of its content may be supposed, without departing from the conception in question, to be predetermined by the accumulated and crystallized results of reality up to date, of which any possible future and novel increment of being must be the child, and to which it must be capable of accommodation. And at all events, there is nothing in this sort of thoroughgoing metaphysical temporalism which justifies the denial of the possibility of the making of "true" judgments about contemporaneous or past (but not yet consciously verified) realities.

7.

It is a frequently repeated observation of pragmatists, in moments when they are more mindful of the psychological than of the metaphysical antecedents of their diversely descended conceptions, that the true, in its more generalized character, is "the satisfactory"; it is, says James, that which "gives the maximal combination of satisfactions." Or, in Perry's careful formulation—with an amendment which we have recently been told, upon good authority, would make it entirely acceptable to a pragmatist—"the criterion of the truth of knowledge is the satisfying character of the practical transition from cognitive expectation to fulfillment, or the resolution of doubt into practical immediacy."[4] Now this doctrine which identifies the truth with the satisfactoriness of a given judgment may mean any one of three things. It may, in the first place, be a simple psychological observation—from which, I fancy, few would dissent—indicating the genus of feelings of which the "emotion of conviction" is a species. To doubt, to inquire, or to have before the mind certain potential material of judgment that is not yet accepted as true is, of course, to experience dissatisfaction; a specific sense of discomfort and of nonfulfillment is the emotional concomitant of the doubting or the deliberative moment, and is doubtless the principal spring which prompts men's search for truth. And to believe, to hold true, whatever more it may be, is always at least to be satisfied in some degree with one's mental content of the moment, to find it good, or at all events not so bad as some contrary judgment which, for its sin of insufficient satisfyingness, has been shut away into the outer darkness of nonacceptance.

8.

But this psychological truism, that to pass from doubt to belief is to pass from dissatisfaction to a relative satisfaction, is quite a different thing from the first of the pragmatist epistemological contentions that appear to be based upon it. This asserts that the way to determine whether a proposition is true is to apply the test of "satisfyingness"; and to apply it directly and *simpliciter.* There is, according to this version of the nature of truth, to be no attempt to determine the differentia which distinguishes the species "conviction" from the genus "satisfaction," or the subspecies "highest discoverable type of certitude" from "conviction" in general; and there is to be no arranging of satisfactions in a hierarchy and no pretension to define the conditions under which a maker of rational judgments *ought* to be satisfied. From many expressions of pragmatist writers it would appear that while the term "satisfaction" is "many dimensional" one dimension is as good as another; and that the final and decisive warrant for belief—the mark of the valid judgment—is the capacity of the judgment to yield the maximum bulk of satisfaction, measured indifferently in any of its dimensions. But since the dimensions *are* many, it may manifestly turn out that the greatest total volume may not give the potential maximum of any given dimension taken singly. The liking for luminosity of meaning, or for conceptual consistency, or for completeness of empirical verification may fail to get full satisfaction in a judgment; but the judgment may, it would seem, still be "true," if it compensates for these limitations by a preponderant satisfactoriness with reference to other desires or interests: by its congruency with our habitual ways of belief, or its charm for the imagination, or its tendency to beget a cheerful frame of mind in those who accept it.

I think it possible that some pragmatists may at this point protest that they know of no one who seriously holds this view; certainly, it appears to me to be a curious view to hold. But I think one is justified in calling upon all of the name who reject this doctrine to take (and faithfully observe) an oath to abstain from a fashion of language which they have much affected; to refrain from identifying the true with the satisfactory *simpliciter,* to cease speaking of satisfaction as a "*criterion*" of validity, and to confine their assimilation of the two concepts to the much more qualified and common-place thesis which follows.

9.

This is pragmatism number seven *plus* a more or less explicit admission that our "theoretic" satisfactions have a special character and special epistemological pretensions; that our "intellectual" demands—for clear meanings, for consistency, for evidence—are *not,* and can not be, satisfied, unless their peculiar claim to precedence in the determination of belief is recognized; and that this claim is a legitimate one to which men should (though they often do not) subordinate their impulse to accept any conclusions that have any other kind of satisfactoriness. According to this view, "satisfaction" is still insisted upon as an essential mark of the apprehension of "truth"; but it is precisely a satisfaction which is not to be had except upon condition that other possible satisfactions be ignored or, in many cases, flatly rejected. Between this and the preceding (eighth) doctrine some pragmatist writers seem to waver. James, for example, often uses expressions (some of which have been quoted in the two foregoing paragraphs) implying the doctrine of the commensurability and equivalence of all satisfactions. But he elsewhere (e.g., in a controversy with Joseph in *Mind,* 1905) expressly distinguishes the "theoretic" from the "collateral" satisfactions connected with the processes of judging thought; and he does not appear to deny that the former may conflict with the latter, or that, in the event of such conflict, they ought to be preferred. To the objection offered by his critic, that if such admissions be made the pragmatist's criterion of validity is not practically distinguishable from the intellectualist's, James opposes nothing more relevant than a sketch of the genesis and evolution of the demand of the human mind for consistency.[5] This sketch purports to show—if I understand it—that the desire (more characteristic of some minds than of others) to avoid self-contradiction is historically engendered through the crystallization of repeated experiences of uniformity in "things" into fixed subjective habits of expecting specific uniformities—habits so fixed that when such an expectation is disappointed "our mental machinery refuses to run smoothly." How the transition from the idea of uniformity to that of consistency is accomplished here remains obscure to me; but even supposing the evolution of the one into the other to be completely and convincingly traced, these interesting historical speculations do not show, they do not even tend to suggest, that the demand for consistency in our judgments as we now find it—playing its captious and domineering role among our mental cravings—is not quite distinct from all its fellows and their rightful, though their often flouted, overlord. In the present sense, then, the pragmatist's criterion of truth, whether right or wrong, seems entirely destitute of any distinctive character; it is simply the old, intellectualist criterion supplemented by the psychologically undisputable, but the logically functionless, remark that, after all, a "theoretic" satisfaction is a kind of satisfaction.

10.

Another pragmatism, and one that undoubtedly has real epistemological bearings, is the doctrine of radical empiricism conjoined with the doctrine of the necessity and legitimacy of postulation; the doctrine, in other words, that "axioms are postulates" and that postulates are as valid as any human judgment ever can be, provided they be the expression of a genuine "practical" need. This may look like our eighth kind of pragmatism over again, expressed in other terms; but in certain important particulars it is really a distinct theory. It contains, in the first place, a special negative contention: namely, that there are no strictly compulsive or "necessary" general truths, no universal propositions that can force themselves upon the mind's acceptance apart from an uncoerced act of voluntary choice. And on its positive side, it identifies the true, not with those judgments which slip so easily into the mind that they afford a present emotional state of satisfaction, but with those that man's active nature requires as working presuppositions to be followed in its reaction upon present experience and its instinctive endeavor to shape future experience. This doctrine seems to me to be quite unequivocally expressed by Schiller in a well-known essay in *Personal Idealism.* "The 'necessity' of a postulate," we are told, "is simply an indication of our need. We want it, and so must have it, as a means to our ends. Thus its necessity is that of intelligent, purposive volition, not of psychical, and still less of physical, mechanism." "Behind the 'can't' there always lurks a 'won't'; the mind can not stultify itself, because it will not renounce conceptions it needs to order its experiences. The feeling of necessity, therefore, is at bottom an emotional accompaniment of the purposive search for means to realize our ends."[6]

11.

A kindred but a much less thoroughgoing doctrine seems to constitute one of the pragmatisms of James. The author of *The Will to Believe* would, I suppose, still vigorously deny the possibility of reaching "necessary" conclusions with respect to many issues, including some of the greatest importance in relation both to the purely utilitarian requirements of our living and to our higher interests; and he would, clearly, still maintain the propriety and the practical inevitableness of voluntary postulation in such cases. But that there are *some* truly coercive and indubitable truths, some items of a priori knowledge inhering in the native constitution of a rational mind, James pretty fully and frankly declares in his recently published volume of lectures. "Our ready-made ideal framework for all sorts of possible objects follows from the very structure of our thinking. We can no more play fast and loose with these abstract relations than we can with our sense experiences. They coerce us; we must treat them consistently, whether or not we like the results."[7] This, obviously, is no doctrine that axioms are postulates or that behind every "can't" there lies a "won't"; it is the doctrine that axioms are necessities and that the action of voluntary choice in belief is always limited by a permanent system of a priori principles of possibility and impossibility inhering in the nature of intellect, at least as intellect is now evolved. It is compatible, at most, with the opinion that there are not so numerous, nor so useful, axioms as some dogmatic philosophers have supposed, and that, when axioms fail us, postulates must in many cases be resorted to.

12.

A point of pragmatist doctrine separable from (though not inconsistent with) either of the two last mentioned is the assertion of the *equal* legitimacy of those postulates (such as the uniformity of causal connection, the general "reliability" of nature, and the like) which appear indispensable as presuppositions for effective dealing with the world of our physical experience, and of those which, though lacking this sort of "physical" necessity as completely as they do the logical sort, yet seem demanded in order to give meaning to, or encouragement in, men's moral strivings, or to satisfy the emotional or esthetic cravings of our complex nature. It is conceivable enough that some pragmatists should refuse to recognize the equal standing of these two classes of postulates and should accept the first while rejecting the second; and it is a fact that not all who find a place for both agree as to the number and range of the second sort. The more extremely liberal forms of the doctrine of the right to postulate freely and to treat postulates as truths tend to lapse into identity with the eighth variety of pragmatism which identifies the true with the "maximally satisfying"; but in its more cautious and critical forms, the argument from the practical inevitableness of certain scientific to the legitimacy of certain ethicoreligious postulates must be regarded as a distinct type of pragmatist epistemology, and perhaps the one which—if pragmatism ought to have practical bearings—best deserves the name.

13.

Lastly, there remains a second pragmatist theory of the *meaning* of concepts or judgments—which brings us back to the topic, though by no means to precisely the doctrine, with which our enumeration began. It may be expressed thus: an essential part of our idea of any object or fact consists in an apprehension of its relation to some purpose or subjective interest on our part; so that no object of *thought* whatever could be just what, for our thought, it *is*, except through the mediation of some idea of purpose or some plan of action. The language of some pragmatist writers might lead one to suppose that they consider the *whole* meaning to be reducible to this teleological reference; but such a view does not seem to me intelligible, and it does not appear certain that any one really intends to maintain it. But it is evident that there are several logicians who think it both true and

important to declare that a relation to a purpose constitutes an intrinsic and a determinative element in the connotation of any notion. It is, I suppose, such a principle that Moore intended to illustrate in recently pointing out that, however objective the virtues of a given candidate for office may be, he could neither be "clean" nor a candidate were there not present in the mind of every one so representing him the idea of possible voting to be done. And I suppose the same view is, in part at least, what Schiller has sought to enforce in insisting that nobody can be "lost" except with the aid of the existence in the universe of some purpose in some mind, requiring the presence of the "lost" person (or of the persons from whom he is lost) in some place or relation from which he is (or they are) excluded by virtue of his "lostness."[8] Schiller appears to me to have entangled this theory of meaning in a confusing and illegitimate manner with questions about "truth" and "reality"; but to pursue this distinction would involve a somewhat long and complicated analysis which may not here be undertaken.

These thirteen pragmatisms have been set down, not in a topical order, but according to the leading of those associations of ideas through which the ambiguities of the several doctrines, and the transitions from one to another, become relatively intelligible. But it may be useful to arrange them here in a more logical manner, while still retaining the original numbering. Those forms of theory, the separate enumeration of which results from distinctions made by this paper, but overlooked by pragmatist writers themselves—in other words, the doctrines formulated by pragmatists in more or less equivocal terms—are indicated by the sign (a); each group of doctrines hitherto improperly treated as single and univocal has a common superior number:

I. *Pragmatist Theories of Meaning.*
　　1. The "meaning" of any judgment consists wholly in the future experiences, active or passive, predicted by it.
　　2. The meaning of any judgment consists in the future consequences of believing it (a^1).
　　13. The meaning of any idea or judgment always consists in part in the apprehension of the relation of some object to a conscious purpose (a^1).

II. *Pragmatism as an Epistemologically Functionless Theory concerning the "Nature" of Truth.*
　　3. The truth of a judgment "consists in" the complete realization of the experience (or series of experiences) to which the judgment had antecedently pointed; propositions *are* not, but only *become*, true (a^2).

III. *Pragmatist Theories of Knowledge, i.e., of the Criterion of the Validity of a Judgment.*
　　4. Those general propositions are true which so far, in past experience, have had their implied predictions realized; and there is no other criterion of the truth of a judgment (a^2).
　　5. Those general propositions are true which have in past experience proved biologically serviceable to those who have lived by them; and this "livableness" is the ultimate criterion of the truth of a judgment (a^2).

7. All apprehension of truth is a species of "satisfaction"; the true judgment meets some need, and all transition from doubt to conviction is a passage from a state of at least partial dissatisfaction to a state of relative satisfaction and harmony (a^3). This is strictly only a psychological observation, not an epistemological one; it becomes the latter by illicit interpretation into one of the two following.

8. The criterion of the truth of a judgment is its satisfactoriness, as such; satisfaction is "many dimensional," but all the dimensions are of commensurable epistemological value, and the maximum bulk of satisfaction in a judgment is the mark of its validity (a^3).

9. The criterion of the truth of a judgment is the degree in which it meets the "theoretic" demands of our nature; these demands are special and distinctive, but their realization is none the less a kind of "satisfaction" (a^3).

10. The sole criterion of the truth of a judgment is its practical serviceableness as a postulate; there is no general truth except postulated truth, resulting from some motivated determination of the will; "necessary" truths do not exist.

11. There are some necessary truths, but these are neither many nor practically adequate; and beyond them the resort to postulates is needful and legitimate.

12. Among the postulates which it is legitimate to take as the equivalent of truth, those which subserve the activities and enrich the content of the moral, esthetic, and religious life have a co-ordinate place with those which are presupposed by common sense and physical science as the basis of the activities of the physical life.

IV. *Pragmatism as an Ontological Theory.*

6. Temporal becoming is a fundamental character of reality; in this becoming the processes of consciousness have their essential and creative part. The future is strictly nonreal and its character is partly indeterminate, dependent upon movements of consciousness the nature and direction of which can be wholly known only at the moments in which they become real in experience. (Sometimes more or less confused with 3.)[9]

Each pragmatism of the thirteen should manifestly be given a name of its own if confusion in future discussions is to be avoided. The present writer has neither the necessary ingenuity nor the ambition to devise a nomenclature so extensive. But however the several theories be designated, the fact of their difference, and of the incompatibility of some of them with some others, can hardly, just now, be too much insisted upon—in the interest of pragmatism itself. What the movement commonly so named most needs is a clarification of its formulas and a discrimination of certain sound and important ideas lying behind it from certain other ideas that are sound but not important, and certain that would be important if only they were not unsound. The present attempt to list the chief varieties and to clear up the hidden ambiguities of a doctrine nominally one and indivisible is accordingly offered as a species of *Prolegomena zu einem jeden künftigen Pragmatismus.*

Notes

1. "The Definition of Pragmatism and Humanism" in F. C. S. Schiller, *Studies in Humanism* (1907), p. 5.

2. William James, *Pragmatism* (1907), Lecture III, *passim.*

3. James, *op. cit.,* pp. 215, 201.

4. A. W. Moore, in *Journal of Philosophy,* V (1908), p. 576.

5. *Mind,* N.S., XIV., p. 196.

6. F. C. S. Schiller, "Axioms as Postulates," para. 11, in *Personal Idealism.*

7. James, *op. cit.,* p. 211.

8. *Journal of Philosophy,* IV (1907), p. 42, and pp. 483, 488.

9. It is impossible to bring out the nature, motives, and reciprocal relations of dependence or incompatibility of these theories in any such condensed formulas. I hope no reader will attempt to take the above recapitulation as a substitute for the analytical discussion contained in the preceding paragraphs.

Philip P. Wiener (essay date 1973)

SOURCE: Wiener, Philip P. "Pragmatism." In *Dictionary of the History of Ideas: Studies of Selected Pivotal Ideas,* Vol. III, edited by Philip P. Wiener, pp. 551-70. New York: Charles Scribner's Sons, 1973.

[*In the following essay, Wiener surveys the history and development of Pragmatism within literary, historical, cultural, and philosophical contexts.*]

I. DIFFICULTIES IN DEFINING PRAGMATISM

When Arthur O. Lovejoy (in 1908) discriminated thirteen meanings of pragmatism and showed that some of them were in contradiction with one another, he raised the problem of whether there was any coherent core of ideas that could define the doctrine or movement that was so widely discussed by American and European thinkers in various disciplines. Certainly Charles S. Peirce and William James (who credited Peirce in 1897 with inventing the doctrine) had divergent ideas in their "pragmatic" theories of truth. There were also divergences among those writers in the United States and abroad who defended their own particular versions of pragmatism, e.g., John Dewey, George H. Mead, F. C. S. Schiller, G. Vailati, G. Papini, Mario Calderoni, Hans Vaihinger, and others on the fringes of philosophy. The latter group, ranging from scientists like Henri Poincaré and Percy Bridgman to legal, political, and even literary minds such as O. W. Holmes, Jr., Georges Sorel, and Luigi Pirandello respectively, make it especially difficult to include their varieties of pragmatism within the same set of ideas that are common to Peirce, James, and Dewey. At one extremity one can find self-styled pragmatists with a Jamesian tendency to regard their personal experience as a sufficient source and test of truth; the extreme group in the undefined fringe can only charitably be included in Peirce's ideal community of minds whose opinions in the long run are destined to converge on the one unalterable Platonic truth.

From the standpoint of the history of ideas a well tried and useful method of arriving at a common core of component ideas of any group's doctrines is to consider historically the ideas which that group of thinkers was opposing or trying to combat intellectually with regard to some problem viewed in its cultural and historical context. It will become evident that we can discern historically a substantial though complex core of such component ideas that came to the fore in the nineteenth and twentieth centuries in opposition to certain long established traditional modes of belief. Common to this substantial core of pragmatism is an opposition to the absolute separation of thought from action, of pure from applied science, of intuition or revelation from experience or experimental verification, of private interests from public concern—concrete applications of older philosophical problems concerning the relation of universals to particulars. It will also be evident that each alleged historical example of pragmatism shows a wide variety of individual ways of resolving these problems, especially when we include the outer fringe of those calling their very personal effusions "pragmatic."

It is not the intellectual historian's task to decide which of the many variants of pragmatism is the "correct" one. Usage in all its culturally varied ramifications is the primary concern here, and the historical effects of such usages on subsequent intellectual developments in various fields are difficult enough to trace. The usage or core of ideas central to pragmatism that has been most influential historically in many fields is found in contributions to methodology and the theory of value judgments. Against supernaturalism, authoritarianism, and eternally fixed norms of belief and values stand the more flexible method and dynamic values of naturalistic empiricism, temporalism, and pluralistic individualism as the chief component ideas at the center of what is most coherent and enduring in the many varieties of pragmatism. However, we cannot overlook the historical deviations from this central core, especially as they provide evidence of the pluralism, individualism, and relativism defended by our "core" pragmatists. Since some of these ideas are also found in other philosophical schools, we must acknowledge the difficulty of defining the borders of pragmatism.

Hence it is not surprising that here is no one general definition of pragmatism that covers all the historical doctrines that have been given that name. In the comprehensive account of the subject by H. S. Thayer an attempt at a general definition makes pragmatism stand for (1) a procedural rule for explicating meanings of certain philosophical and scientific concepts; (2) "a theory of knowledge, experience, and reality maintaining that (a) thought and knowledge are biologically and socially evolved modes by means of adaptation" and control; (b) reality is transitional and thought is a guide to satisfying interests or realizing purposes; (c) "all knowledge is a behavioral process evaluative of future experience" and thinking is experimentally aimed at organizing, planning, or controlling future experience; and (3) "a broad philosophic attitude toward our conceptualization of experience" (H. S. Thayer [1968], p. 431). However, Thayer's summary outline of a definition of "the aim and formative doctrines of pragmatism," despite its comprehensiveness does not dwell sufficiently on the very varied character and conflicting theories of method, knowledge, and reality maintained by pragmatists of different schools in diverse fields of thought and of diverse cultural and historical backgrounds.

The opening paragraph of G. Papini's work on *Pragmatismo* (*1905-1911*), a collection of his articles introducing that doctrine to Italian philosophers, reads: "Pragmatism cannot be defined. Whoever gives a definition of Pragmatism in a few words would be doing the most antipragmatic thing imaginable" (*Il Pragmatismo non si può definire. Chi desse in poche parole una definizione del Pragmatismo farebbe la cosa più antipragmatista chi si possa immaginare,* p. 75). Papini was (in 1906) echoing William James's romantic aversion to fixed definitions, and even mistakenly placed Peirce in the same boat with James, thus overlooking the important difference between James's nominalism (emphasis on particular perceived consequences of ideas) and Peirce's Scotistic realism (positing the reality of universals in logic and value judgments: truth and justice being two of the most powerful ideas in the world, according to Peirce).

The historical and cultural facets of various pragmatisms do not all fit under any general definition for two reasons. First, the philosophical writings of a leading pragmatist like C. S. Peirce are concerned with and defend theories of truth and reality that are not merely procedural, behavioristic, transitional, or conceptual. Peirce's metaphysical writings contain a speculative, idealistic version of pragmatism which he called "pragmaticism" in order to disassociate his philosophy from the pragmatisms of William James and James's disciple F. C. S. Schiller. Secondly, whole areas of knowledge, other than those mentioned in the general definition above, have been discussed by diverse pragmatists in their interpretations of the nature of history, of law and politics, of language, and of mathematical logic. It is true that some pragmatists have pursued some parts of these subjects, but some have not; some have professed a profound concern for religion and others have not. Hence, instead of trying to find a general definition to cover the conflicting beliefs and widely divergent interests of all pragmatistic philosophies, the historian of ideas will find it more instructive to trace various components of the various doctrines historically held by pragmatists.

Arthur O. Lovejoy was a student of William James at Harvard, and outlined more than sixty years ago the most discriminating criticism of pragmatism in two short articles, "The Thirteen Pragmatisms" (1908, pp. 1-12, 29-39). Lovejoy's analysis of pragmatism into its component ideas yields four groups of internal conflicts and ambiguities: (1) those claims to truth which rest, on the one hand, on the psychological properties of belief as a disposition to act from those, on the other hand, which are based on the changing characters of the *objects* of belief; (2) the identification of knowledge with a form of action based on some form of immediate perception (e.g., James's "radical empiricism") versus knowledge as the result of the mediation of ideas which interpret experience; (3) ethical and aesthetic judgments validated, on the one hand, by subjective emotional criteria, e.g., in the "will to believe" doctrine of William James and the personalism of F. C. S. Schiller; and on the other hand, by objective, verifiable social consequences along utilitarian lines, e.g., in John Dewey's "instrumentalism" and George Herbert Mead's social criteria of meaning; (4) Bergson's and James's appeal to immediate experience versus Peirce's "long run" theory of truth as the opinion that an indefinite community of scientific investigators will ultimately agree upon after continued experimental inquiry.

Lovejoy thus insisted that there are incompatible theories of knowledge, of truth, and of values present in these diverse ideas maintained by different pragmatists. F. C. S. Schiller's dramatic response to Lovejoy's discriminations was to welcome the fact that there are as many pragmatisms as there are pragmatists, but Schiller's response does not eliminate the internal discrepancies among the ideas of pragmatists. Schiller's "humanistic personalism" is diametrically opposed to Peirce's claims for logic, and reduces the definition of pragmatism to the problem of ascertaining whether there are any common ideas shared by all pragmatists in the light of the incompatible components of their philosophies.

One historical investigation of the American founders and evolutionary background of pragmatism (Wiener [1949], Ch. 9), by minimizing the differences and stressing optimistically "the common features," attempted to establish the following general components: (1) a *pluralistic empiricism* or method of investigating piecemeal the physical, biological, psychological, linguistic, and social problems which are not resolvable by a single metaphysical formula or *a priori* system; e.g., Chauncey

Wright, William James, John Dewey, C. I. Lewis, John H. Randall, Jr., Sidney Hook, Ernest Nagel, Y. Bar-Hillel, Charles W. Morris; (2) a *temporalistic* view of reality and knowledge as the upshot of an evolving stream of consciousness (W. James) or of *objects* of consciousness (C. S. Peirce), including ideas and claims to truth, processes of observation, measurement, and experimental testing; (3) a *relativistic* or contextualistic conception of reality and values in which traditional eternal ideas of space, time, causation, axiomatic truth, intrinsic and eternal values are all viewed as relative to varying psychological, social, historical, or logical contexts (Chauncey Wright, William James, George Herbert Mead, John Dewey, Stephen C. Pepper, F. P. Ramsey, and C. I. Lewis); (4) a *probabilistic* view of physical and social hypotheses and laws in opposition to both mechanistic or dialectical determinism and historical necessity or inevitability, yielding a fallibilistic theory of knowledge and values opposed to dogmatic certainty and infallibility (W. James, C. S. Peirce, O. W. Holmes, Jr., J. Dewey, Ernest Nagel, Sidney Hook, H. Reichenbach); (5) a secular *democratic* individualism asserting the right of individuals to live in a free society without the sanctions of supernatural theological revelation or totalitarian authority. This pragmatic individualism of the American pragmatists is linked to a political tradition that goes back to John Locke and the European Enlightenment, and is represented historically in the United States by thinkers from all walks of life: John Woolman, Benjamin Franklin, Thomas Paine, Thomas Jefferson, Ralph Waldo Emerson, Henry David Thoreau, Abraham Lincoln, and Walt Whitman.

It is typical of pragmatic ideas that they are not restricted to the ideas of professional philosophers, but often find influential expression among lawyers and judges like Nicholas St. John Green (the "grandfather of pragmatism," according to C. S. Peirce), Oliver Wendell Holmes, Jr., Jerome Frank, Carl Llewellyn; among logicians and scientists like Chauncey Wright, C. S. Peirce, G. Vailati, Pierre Duhem, Henri Poincaré, Edward Le Roy, C. I. Lewis, W. V. O. Quine, Percy Bridgman; among historians like Carl Becker and Charles Beard; among literary figures such as Irwin Edman and Luigi Pirandello; and even the syndicalist Georges Sorel.

We cannot simply equate the "pragmatic" with the "practical" as is so commonly done by popular writers. For technically in philosophy, "practical" may refer to Kant's idea of the categorical imperative in his *Critique of Practical Reason,* which placed the *pragmatische* on a much lower level than the *praktische.* Furthermore, "practical" in ordinary discourse is often synonymous with the "convenient," the "useful," and the "profitable" and thus contributes to enormous misunderstandings of the serious aims of pragmatism. Among the empirical varieties of pragmatism "practical" refers to what is experimental or capable of being tested in action, not quite the same as Marx's use of "praxis" or alleged "identity of theory and practice." The American pragmatists preferred the experimental meaning without the dialectics. At Harvard, in the first decades of the twentieth century, George Santayana criticized William James and John Dewey for failing to subordinate "practical thought" to eternal Platonic values.

Santayana's chapter on "How Thought is Practical" in the first volume of his *Life of Reason* (5 vols., 1905-06) is far from making him a pragmatist. Writing at Harvard as a younger colleague of William James, Santayana did not consider his own peculiar blend of Platonism and naturalism in accord with the pragmatic movement at Harvard; he regarded James as a romantic subjectivist. Santayana, in this first major work, *The Life of Reason,* maintained against the instrumentalist theory of consciousness that "In so far as thought is instrumental it is not worth having, any more than matter, except for its promise; it must terminate in something truly profitable and ultimate which being good in itself, may lend value to all that led up to it. . . . In a word the value of thought is ideal" (I, 218-19). From Santayana's aristocratic standpoint, "thought is in no way instrumental or servile; it is an experience realized, not a force to be used" (ibid., 214). It is no wonder then that neither James nor Dewey could accept Santayana's Platonic naturalism. Santayana was certainly not as democratic as James or Dewey in political theory, but followed the classical tradition of Plato and Aristotle in associating democracy with demagoguery and in favoring a form of intellectual timocracy. Thus the component features of pragmatism discussed above appear in the American variety, deeply hued by its British ancestry, and also in some of the continental European forms of pragmatism to be discussed below. However, each of the component aspects of even the American and British forms of pragmatism has had its antecedents in the more distant cultural and intellectual history of Europe, and may be traced back to some of the ideas of ancient classical and the Enlightenment's versions of both "practical" and speculative thought, yielding among its important fruits a pragmatic transformation of the basis of law in civilization and an empirical theory of value judgments in general. The next section explores some of the "old ways of thinking" for which "pragmatism is only a new name," as James put it.

II. Historical Roots

The very term "pragmatic" with its Greek root *pragma* ("affair, practical matter") was borrowed by the Romans to mean "skilled in business, and especially, experienced in matters of law"; hence, a *pragmaticus* was "one skilled in the law, who furnished orators and advocates with the principles on which they based their speeches" (Cicero, *Orationes* 1, 59; cf. also Quintilian

12, 3, 4; Juvenal 7, 123; Ulpian, *Digest* 48, 17, 9). In late Latin juridical writings a pragmatic sanction (*pragmatica sanctio*) was an imperial decree that permitted an activity in the community's affairs (*Justinian Code* 1, 2, 10).

When James and Peirce generously refer to Socrates as a forerunner of pragmatism, they perhaps had in mind Plato's dramatized Socratic activity of inquiring into the meanings of ideas about friendship, courage, justice, piety, and so forth in dialogues with the young citizens of the Athenian community. However, the logic of Plato was more of a semantic exercise than "pragmatic" in either James's psychological sense or Peirce's experimental methodology. Without going into the philological question raised by W. Lutoslawski's thesis that Aristotle's logic was a continuation of Plato's, it is safe to say that the problems of the syntax and semantics of language were more systematically treated in Aristotle's logical treatises. Plato's inquiry in the *Parmenides* whether "Being is One or Many" and whether "Non-Being is or is not" proceeds semantically to avoid verbal contradictions, but to imagine that such exercises of language suffice to understand the problems of existence, such as the struggle for existence, would be unfair to Plato's purpose. The semantic analysis is only part of Plato's thinking, but it predominates over any pragmatic intent. For example, viewing the State as "the individual writ large" (*Republic,* Book II) leads metaphorically to an ideal utopia. When Plato seems to be practical in the *Laws,* the pragmatic aspects of his political proposals (e.g., censorship and religious intolerance with possible death penalty) are shocking to modern liberals; the result is that scholars differ in deploring or explaining away the totalitarian aspects of the *Laws.*

Aristotle's use of the "practical syllogism" in ethics and his notion of each subject having its own method belong to the ancient sources of the functional and pluralistic methodology of those pragmatists who link their ideas to an Aristotelianism stripped of medieval supernaturalism (e.g., G. H. Mead; J. H. Randall, Jr.). Aristotle's "practical syllogism" consists in stating in the major premise the object desired or goal to be achieved, and in the minor premise the means which experience has shown necessary to attain the desired end, so that one can conclude that a good result may be attained by acting with the means indicated. For example, one who wishes to be a good musician must learn how to play a certain instrument; a practical syllogism would demonstrate that practice in mastering that instrument is necessary in order to achieve the desired goal. The *pluralism* of methods, categories, and goals of human endeavor also characterizes certain "pragmatic" aspects of Aristotle's applied logic. For example, Aristotle states it would be practically foolish for a mathematician to prove theorems in his science by the same methods of argumentation that an orator uses in a political speech, and conversely.

According to G. H. Mead and John Dewey, what is *not* pragmatic in Plato and Aristotle is their belief that nature, especially human nature, was essentially fixed in its eternal features. A Sophist like Protagoras and Sextus Empiricus was closer to the relativistic and empirical view of modern pragmatists, a view that can be found even in "God-intoxicated" Spinoza, namely, that the good is not what eternally determines our nature or desires; it is the variety of natures and desires that determines what is good. "Music is good for the melancholy, bad for the mourner, and neither good nor bad to the deaf" (*Ethics*, Part IV, preface). Again we cannot simply bring under the rubric "pragmatism" the philosophies of Aristotle, Spinoza, or Santayana or of any other thinker who espouses this relativistic view of values, when in fact there are so many nonempirical aspects present in their philosophies, such as Aristotle's "unmoved mover," Spinoza's "intellectual love of God," or Santayana's eternal "realms of being."

Medieval and modern forms of casuistry are considered by some writers as "pragmatic" insofar as general rules are adapted to practical situations; but we should not therefore regard the Tartuffes as pragmatists. Critics of pragmatism often wish to condemn the doctrine as sheer opportunism, or as "guilt by association" with such self-styled "pragmatic" theories as Georges Sorel's doctrine of violence.

In his "Lessons from the History of Science," Peirce viewed science as an outgrowth of the thinking of ancient and medieval philosophers; Peirce was more appreciative of medieval logic in the history of the sciences than nearly all his contemporaries. (Pierre Duhem, of course, is an outstanding exception among partly pragmatic philosophical historians of medieval science.) Peirce adopted Duns Scotus' theory of true universals as inherent in particulars, and called it "Scotistic realism." Peirce had translated Petrus Peregrinus' difficult manuscript on the magnetic properties of the lodestone. In these medieval thinkers Peirce saw some continuity with the modern scientific method of treating hypotheses (based on analogical comparisons of present with past observations), drawing inferences (preferably mathematically) from these conjectured hypotheses, and testing the deduced consequences by experiment. However, he rejected the scholastics' recourse to the authority of the Church Fathers and to their version of Aristotle, and favored the "self-corrective method" of experimental inductive science. His logic of relations went far beyond the classical logic, Peirce developing logic as a continuation and generalization of the subject-predicate logic of statements, after De Morgan and Boole.

Among the Renaissance precursors of the pragmatic union of experimental action and theoretical contemplation we may surely place the experimentalism in art and science represented by the works of such masters as Leonardo da Vinci and Galileo. Rudolfo Mondolfo, in his essay on the idea of manual and intellectual work, following a Hippocratic text which declared that man knows best what he makes (an idea developed in the *Scienza nuova* [1725] by G. B. Vico), has suggested a plausible Renaissance source of this interrelationship in Galileo's development of an intuition expressed in Ficino's *Theologia platonica*: "What is human art? A kind of nature that treats matter from the outside." This external treatment of nature takes the place of the scholastic idea of nature as "being within matter itself; but human art can produce any reality produced by nature, so long as man can struggle successfully with matter and with the necessary instruments. . . . Leonardo had already expressed his view of mechanics as the noblest and most useful of the sciences as well as the paradise of mathematical sciences because it yields the harvested fruit of these sciences in practical application" (R. Mondolfo [1950], p. 22, notes 9 and 10).

Of course, the Renaissance sources pertinent to the roots of pragmatism go back to the revival of classical ideas of natural processes and ways of living with them such as were explored by the pre-Socratics, Plato, Aristotle, Archimedes, the Epicureans, and the Stoics, and include those medieval thinkers who (like Roger Bacon and the Padovan Averroists) saw the advantages of combining experimental activity with theoretical speculation. Philosophy in the seventeenth and eighteenth centuries developed rival schools, later labelled "empiricism" and "rationalism" depending on the emphasis given to sense-experience or "pure" reasoning, but that these two aspects of knowledge are inseparable in scientific knowledge was the great achievement of Immanuel Kant before the pragmatists developed their philosophical versions of the interplay of thought and experience in all scientific and value judgments.

A sharp separation of theory and practice, however, is reflected in Kant's distinction between ethical and "pragmatic" rules. Kant's ethical rule is a "categorical imperative" based on the individual's inner "pure practical" reason, free will, and universal consciousness of one's *a priori* duty to respect all persons as ends in themselves; Kant's pragmatic (*pragmatische*) rule is practical in the very different sense of having to do only with rules of prudence which belong to the technical imperatives or means required to achieve desired ends: "For what is prudence but the skill to use free men and even natural dispositions and inclinations for one's own purposes?" (Kant, *Critique of Judgment*, Introduction). This Kantian distinction so sharply separates subjective from objective considerations, ends from means, and pure reason from social experience that post-Kantian thinkers, including the romantic Schelling, as well as Schopenhauer and Hegel and some of the American pragmatists (especially C. S. Peirce and John Dewey) were led to seeking a closer and more organic relationship between morality and mankind's other intellectual and cultural concerns.

Knowing that Chauncey Wright and C. S. Peirce daily discussed Kant's philosophy for two years at Harvard in the third quarter of the nineteenth century, the historian of pragmatism is not surprised to find that Kant's limitation of our knowledge of nature to what is observable became a cardinal empiricistic principle of some of the Harvard pragmatists, along with controversies about the role of *a priori* categories in interpreting the sensory manifold. There was also critical discussion of Kant's absolute separation of means and ends in ethics. Peirce, for example, could accept the *a priori* elements in Kant's theory of knowledge but not his categorical imperative in ethics; for Peirce, as for James and Dewey, all value judgments are hypothetical, of the form: if men desire to attain certain ends in any harmonious way, they will probably achieve these ends by acting in accord with certain specifiable empirical conditions. Only by conducting themselves according to such hypothetical rules, will men discover after "trial and error" (often painful) experience, whether they really find the attained ends desirable.

Hegel made an impressive attempt to establish the unity of means and ends, of the subjective and objective aspects of experience and thought, of the individual and the state, and of universal reason and particular events in his monistic metaphysics and philosophy of history. In this respect Hegelianism is part of the intellectual background of early forms of pragmatism and of Marxism.

"Pragmatic history," is a subspecies of "reflective history" in Hegel's classification of three kinds of history: (1) "original history" written by those historians observing events in their own lifetime; (2) "reflective history," not limited to the time of the historian "whose spirit transcends the present"; and (3) "philosophical history," which allegedly shows that "Reason is the Sovereign of the World." *Pragmatic history* consists of didactic reflections on the past for the purpose of drawing lessons from it that can be applied to moral and political problems of the present. Examples of pragmatic history appear in patriotic histories and the biographies of heroes and spiritual leaders that are supposed to teach rulers, statesmen, and moralists how to be guided by the experience of the past. However, Hegel clearly shows his contempt for this pragmatic kind of history when he states emphatically:

> But what experience and history teach is this—that peoples and governments never have learned anything from history, or acted on principles deduced from it.
>
> (*Philosophy of History,* Introduction, trans. W. Sibree)

This sentence is often quoted by antihistorical writers; they fail, however, to note that Hegel obviously draws this meta-historical statement from his rather extensive study of history. They fail also to note that Hegel concludes his remarks on pragmatic history by observing that the more objective reflective historian will insist on the distinctiveness of his own age as well as of the age whose history he depicts. Pragmatic historians still insist that our knowledge of the past is or should be determined by the interest and problems of the present, thus ignoring Hegel.

Peirce, in his later years, and Dewey, in his early career, show the influence of the Hegelian ideas of organic unity and historical continuity in the cultural life of mankind. However, their pragmatic attitudes toward experience and history diverge radically from Hegel's absolutism and dialectical method: Peirce was sharply critical of Hegel's logic and deficiency in mathematics, although he shared with Josiah Royce sympathy for Hegel's spiritual monism:

> My whole method [of using triadic categories] will be found to be in profound contrast with that of Hegel; I reject his philosophy *in toto,* nevertheless, I have a certain sympathy with it, and fancy that if its author had only noticed a very few circumstances he would himself have been led to revolutionize his system. . . . He has usually overlooked external Secondness, altogether. In other words, he has committed the trifling oversight of forgetting that this is a real world with real actions and reactions. Rather a serious oversight that. Then Hegel had the misfortune to be unusually deficient in mathematics.
>
> (*Collected Papers,* 1.368, "A Guess at the Riddle," ca. 1890)

While Peirce criticized Hegel's logic and neglect of physics and mathematics, Dewey abandoned Hegel's *a priori* dialectical method because it was not experimental and had too fixed a conception of human nature, society, and history. In the United States from the 1860's to the 1880's we can trace the growth of the impact of Hegelianism. John Dewey's *Psychology* (1885) reflected the impact of the St. Louis School of W. T. Harris and Denton J. Snyder. Hegelian ideas mark the first writings of the positivist Benjamin Stallo, and the Spencerian Hegelian, Francis Ellingwood Abbot. Also, among the origins of the American pragmatists was an antimetaphysical "back to Kant" movement in a reaction to Hegel, stimulated by the rapid growth of the physical sciences and Darwin's evolutionary theory (Wiener [1949], pp. 2f.).

Kant's separation of phenomena from the metaphysical unknowable "thing-in-itself" (*Ding an sich*) led to the positivistic element in empiricistic pragmatism. It appears in Chauncey Wright's antimetaphysical attack on both the Hegelian absolutists and the Spencerian "social

Darwinists" (as they were later called; Wright, after reading Haeckel, labelled their ideas "German Darwinism"). There is also a positivistic strain in the early work of William James, as he admits in the Preface to his first book, *Principles of Psychology* (1890).

III. PRAGMATISM AS OPERATIONAL LOGIC

Early twentieth-century developments in logic and philosophy of science led away from Comte's positivism and Mill's psychologism to the Viennese school of logical positivists with whom many pragmatists share an operational and antimetaphysical viewpoint. Later, on removal to England and the United States, as well as in Poland and other countries in Europe, logical positivists preferred the name "logical empiricists." Rudolf Carnap offered a definition of "pragmatics" following "syntactics" and "semantics" in order to show the relationship of formal logic to empirical and psychological aspects of meaning, as well as to distinguish all three. "Syntactics" is the formal study of the logical rules of formation and transformation of statements. In any formal language, e.g., of logic or mathematics, the "rules of formation" determine what statements are "well formed" combinations of the elements of the language used. The syntactical "rules of transformation" determine the equivalences, inferences, and forms of proof which are logically acceptable within a system whose elements and elementary or basic statements conform to the principles of formation. "Semantics" (in logic) is concerned with the relationship of well formed statements or of ordinary language to what they designate. The interpretation or application of a set of axioms in pure mathematics, for example, would be a semantic question. Finally we come to "pragmatics" which deals with the behavioral or experimental conditions for verifying the inferences or testing the truth claims of hypotheses, laws, and theories. "Pragmatics" will ask for specification of the *operations* that need to be performed and the empirical conditions that should be met by all experimenters if their findings are to be acceptable to others. This "operational" requirement is what is meant by the criterion of "intersubjectivity" or public verifiability.

Pragmatism then, in this twentieth-century version, is another name for the operational theory of scientific method, and is closely linked to logical empiricism. This operational variety of pragmatism is the historical outcome of the many attempts of philosophers, mathematicians, and experimental scientists to avoid sterile speculation, subjective intuitions, and unverifiable hypotheses (of the sort Newton rejected when he said *hypotheses non fingo,* although he accepted absolute space and time as the ultimate framework of the physical universe). Bar-Hillel has criticized the separation of syntax and semantics from the pragmatic elements of language; he and Roman Jakobson refer to Peirce's

theory of signs (*Linguaggi nella società e nella tecnica,* Milan [1970], pp. 3-16, 269-84), and find useful Peirce's classification of signs as icons, indices, and symbols.

Among the mathematical philosophers, especially in France, Italy, England, and Germany for the last hundred years, the study of formal axiomatic systems and their relation to experience led to a rejection of Descartes' view of intuitively self-evident truth based on his criterion of clear and distinct ideas. This criterion of intuitive self-evidence had been employed to justify the indubitable metaphysical truth of Euclid's axioms epitomized in Galileo's view that the book of nature was written in the language of Euclid's geometry. The advent of non-Euclidean geometries in the first part of the nineteenth century put an end to the exclusive ontological claims of Euclid's axioms, and reopened fundamental questions in the philosophy of science about the grounds for determining the meaning and truth of axiomatic sets. The proofs of the consistency and isomorphism of non-Euclidean and Euclidean systems made it clear that self-evidence was not an adequate test of meaning or truth, since the non-Euclidean axioms were not obvious or self-evident, e.g., that through a point outside a line no lines or (in an alternative system) an infinite number of lines can be drawn parallel to a given line. The meaning of such abstract axioms can only be ascertained by working out the deducible theorems or logical consequences of the axioms, and their interpretation or application. This orientation of the mind to developing the consequences of logically primitive statements instead of attempting to grasp their meaning in an immediate mental act of intuition provides the basis for the views of those German, French, and Italian mathematical philosophers (e.g., Leibniz, Dedekind, Frege, Hilbert, Cantor; Poincaré, Herbrand, Couturat; Peano, Vacca, Vailati) who explored the logical foundations of axiomatic systems of the theory of numbers. By establishing alternative sets of axioms and tests of internal consistency, mutual independence, and completeness of axiom-sets, these scientists showed little or no concern for any "indubitable" self-evidence of their axioms. Felix Klein and Henri Poincaré also made it clear that in pure mathematics no axioms are privileged; the upshot of these developments is to support a sort of democratic equality among axioms with respect to claims of truth (Vailati, *Scritti*). Thus, in pure mathematics, historically the "queen of the sciences," meaning was reducible to the "pencil and paper operations," as Percy Bridgman called them in his operational theory of meaning, for the purely mathematical and logical aspects of scientific research. The experimental aspects that yield more concrete empirically applicable meanings for hypotheses about "matters of fact" depend on specifying what must be done experimentally to test the logical consequences of the hypotheses in question.

C. S. Peirce was the best equipped of the American founders of pragmatism to develop the operational logic of mathematical and physical science, and to extend it to the analysis of philosophical concepts and problems of meaning. As a first-rate mathematician, astronomer, physicist, and chemist, he kept in touch with the new views of Dedekind, Cantor, Mach, Ostwald, and others who were digging deep into the foundations of mathematics and physical science. Peirce translated the chapter on weights and measures of Mach's important history of the science of mechanics (1883; trans. 1893), and even claimed prior discovery of the principle of the "economy of thought" before Mach.

IV. CHARLES S. PEIRCE'S "PRAGMATICISM"

Alexander Bain, whom Peirce regarded as the Scottish ancestor of pragmatism, had in his psychological writings defined an idea or belief as a disposition to act in a certain way under certain conditions. Applying this definition to the problem of meaning, Peirce formulated his famous prescription for fixing the meaning of a concept: "Consider what effects that might conceivably have practical bearings you conceive the object of your conception to have. Then your conception of those effects is the WHOLE of your conception of the object." This rule for attaining a higher grade of clarity than Cartesian intuition or Leibnizian calculus of reasoning is the *locus classicus* of Peirce's form of pragmatism. He stated it first in the early 1870's before the informal "Metaphysical Club" in Cambridge, Massachusetts, where a group consisting of the mathematical empiricist Chauncey Wright, the psychologist William James, three lawyers (Oliver Wendell Holmes, Jr., Nicholas St. John Green, Joseph B. Warner), the historian John Fiske, and the "scientific theist" Francis E. Abbott met from time to time to discuss the philosophical questions of the day. Among those questions the Darwinian controversy loomed large and led to disputes about science and religion, positivism and metaphysics, scientific method and the introspective investigation of the mind, ethics and legal institutions, the roles of the individual and the environment in history. The writings of Hume, Bentham, Bain, Mill, Kant, Comte, Hegel, Spencer, and Darwin furnished these Harvard Square thinkers with the fuel for illuminating problems and issues in their various fields of interest. After much crossfire and heated discussion, they found themselves more concerned with problems of method than with agreeing on a single system. The experimental method for matters of fact and logical analysis for relations of ideas were accepted as the best instruments of investigation for the natural and social sciences.

Peirce began philosophizing by discussing problems of method. His two now classic papers "The Fixation of Belief" and "How to Make Our Ideas Clear," (*Popular Science Monthly,* 1877-78) were the first two of a series of "Illustrations of the Logic of Science." He claimed, about twenty years later, that these two articles were the first formulations of his variety of pragmatism (although that term does not appear in either paper). Peirce challenged traditional "seminary" types of bookish learning and contrasted them with the "laboratory" type of thinking which he advocated (in 1905) as "pragmaticism," his own brand of pragmatism. Peirce said (about thirty years after his Metaphysical Club papers) of his variety of pragmatism:

> It will serve to show that almost every proposition of ontological metaphysics is either meaningless gibberish—one word being defined by other words, and they by still others, without any real conception ever being reached—or else is downright absurd; so that all such rubbish being swept away, what will remain of philosophy will be a series of problems capable of investigation by the observational methods of the true sciences—the truth about which can be reached without those interminable misunderstandings and disputes which have made the highest of the positive sciences a mere amusement for idle intellects, a sort of chess—idle pleasure its purpose, and reading out of a book its method.

("What Pragmatism Is," *Monist* 15 [1905], 171)

Peirce went on to deny that he was "merely jeering at metaphysics, like other prope-positivists" because "the pragmaticist extracts from it [metaphysics] a precious essence, which will serve to give life and light to cosmology and physics. At the same time, the moral applications of the doctrine are positive and potent and there are many other uses of it not easily classed" (ibid.).

Peirce's "Classification of the Sciences" was composed for his Lowell Institute Lectures in 1903. The adult education movement in the United States had taken to talks on the growth of sciences with their Baconian "promise of providing the relief of man's estate" as seriously as the older generation had taken their Bible lessons. These lectures reveal the progressive or futuristic outlook of Peirce's philosophy of science. There were for Peirce three classes of science in a descending order of importance: (a) Sciences of Discovery, (b) Sciences of Review, (c) Practical Sciences. It is well known that classifications of sciences vary with each new period in the history of science, but such classifications are a clue to the cultural role and value of various sciences and the philosophy of each period. To Peirce, the "Sciences of Discovery" were first and foremost because Peirce conceived of science primarily as a method of inquiry, as the most promising way of exploring the nature of Kant's "starry heavens above and the moral world within." The method of science was not a Baconian new instrument, because science for Peirce had always been an organon of the mind, although Peirce would agree with Bacon's idea that we moderns are the true ancients since we in our evolution have accumulated the knowledge and fruits of the experience of our predecessors.

In his experimentalism, Peirce placed great importance on the neglected role of Hypothesis as a mode of reasoning. He called the discovery of hypotheses "Abduction" to supplement what logic books previously had been mainly concerned with, viz., "Deduction" and "Induction." The reason for this novel importance which Peirce attached to the role of hypothesis is based on the logical ground that all generalizations from particular facts of observation have to be continuous extensions of what is typical or representative in these facts as gathered from previous experience. For example, although the life span of man has increased, the historical fact of man's mortality is the basis of the major premiss of the argument that proves that even Socrates was a mortal. No historical record of all human lives is complete, so that our general judgment that all men are mortal is a well grounded hypothesis on the rather large sample of what our limited historical records and observation have shown. To the extent that the randomly sampled cases are alike, some ground for their similarity may be "abducted" as a probable hypothesis. "Abduction" and "retroduction" were Peirce's synonyms for the form of reasoning leading to conjectural hypotheses. All historical statements about individual events are hypotheses drawn ("abducted" or "retroducted," in Peirce's terminology) from documents, monuments, remains which serve as our only links to the past if interpreted carefully. Every medical diagnosis consists of a hypothesis about the observed "symptoms" of a disease. Deciphering a secret code or strange language starts with hypotheses interpreting certain recurrent signs with the aid of frequency tables. Predictions or prognoses are hypotheses which when verified become scientific generalizations.

Peirce defined laws of nature as predictive generalizations with varying degrees of probability according to experimental tests. Peirce's contribution to the logic of hypothesis was regarded by him as the keystone of his variety of pragmatism; his "pragmaticism," armored with symbolic logic, attacked the more psychological and nominalistic views of William James and F. C. S. Schiller. Facts or the truth about reported events are always subject to and inseparable from the interpretations or hypotheses assumed by the interpreter in his reports, which are signs. To Peirce, James's "radical empiricism" as a form of direct immersion in facts lacked logical awareness of the role of hypotheses or interpretation of signs in such allegedly immediate forms of perception. The theory of signs is central to Peirce's pragmaticist logic. Peirce's pragmaticism is a theory of meaning based on the logical analysis of the conceivable consequences of adopting an hypothesis in so far as its signs and their implications affect the conduct of the inquirer in relation to what is designated by the signs. For example, if a student is puzzled over the meaning of an abstract set of axioms, and asks a mathematician to explain or justify his adoption of such a queer set of "postulates," the pragmatist's answer generally will take several forms. From the standpoint of technique, the axioms enable one to prove with the aid of acceptable rules of inference a body of theorems or consequences deducible from the axioms, thus reducing a large number of theorems to what is contained in a small number of axioms. This reduction is a practical aid to the memory. Another explanation or justification would consist in seeking out and showing by concrete interpretations (in which the axioms are all true) that the axioms are consistent; hence, the whole system of axioms and theorems must be consistent (this assumes a metalogical rule that only consistent results can be deduced from consistent axioms). Again, we may be told pragmatically that this axiomatic set permits certain "interpretations" or applications to empirical domains. Euclid's geometry is still useful to surveyors and engineers, whereas non-Euclidean geometry is applicable in modern applications of relativity theory to atomic physics and cosmology. Proof of the consistency of non-Euclidean geometry establishes the consistency of Euclid. Peirce's formulation of his pragmaticism repeatedly applied to formal sciences the above mentioned test of meaning: *Consider what conceivable consequences the object of your conception has in its bearing on human conduct. Then the sum total of all these conceivable consequences constitute the total meaning of your conception.*

The notion of *conceivability* rather than of actual perception plays a central role in Peirce's analysis of meaning in which he tried to generalize criteria of meaning to cover both formal systems and empirical statements (in physical sciences and everyday expressions). For example, "diamonds are hard" is explicated by considering what conceivable experimental consequences the hypothesis of the constant hardness of diamonds has on the bearing of that hypothesis in human conduct. To an experimenter the conduct involved would consist chiefly in testing the hypothesis by trying to penetrate or scratch a diamond with other materials or with another diamond. There is a Moh's scale of hardness, based on the results of such laboratory testing of different substances, from which it becomes predictable which substance can penetrate or scratch others. The need to specify the *operations* required to test such properties led scientific thinkers from Charles Babbage (1792-1871) to Percy Bridgman to defend a generalized operational methodology. It is therefore historically justifiable to claim that the hard core of the American, British, French, German, and Italian varieties of pragmatism was largely a generalization of the reflections of mathematical logicians and philosophical experimenters in the nineteenth and twentieth centuries.

G. Vailati in 1906 was the first European to recognize Peirce's importance as greater than James's in the formulation of pragmatism. In his article in the journal *Leonardo* (1906): "Pragmatismo e Logica Matematica,"

Vailati saw three intimate relations between pragmatism and symbolic or mathematical logic; symptomatic of this close connection, he said, "is the fact that the very inaugurator of the term and conception of pragmatism, Charles S. Peirce, is also at the same time the initiator and promoter of an original direction of logico-mathematical studies" (Vailati [1957], p. 197). He indicated three points of contact between modern operational logic and pragmatism: (1) "Their common tendency is to regard the validity and even meaning of any assertion as something intimately related to the use that one could or wished to make of it through the deduction or construction of definite consequences or sets of consequences" (p. 198); postulates and axioms would then no longer be privileged in any autocratic or aristocratic fashion but be "simple employees in great 'associations' that constitute the various branches of mathematics" (p. 199). (2) "The common concern of Pragmatism and modern logic is to avoid vague and imprecise generalities by reducing or analyzing every assertion into its simplest terms: those referring directly to facts or to relations among facts." The laws of science can thus be seen as expressions of hypothetical relations, contingent on such facts as "boundary conditions." The classical opposition of "facts" and "laws" begins to disappear. (3) "A third point of contact between pragmatists and mathematical logicians is their interest in historical inquiry into the development of scientific theory and in the importance that many of them attribute to such inquiry as a means of recognizing the equivalence or identity of theories which have appeared in diverse forms at various times or in different fields, though expressing substantially the same facts and serving the same purposes" (p. 200).

A further common feature is the interest in economy of expressions in order to enhance their instrumental value. Vailati's friend, a mathematical logician, G. Vacca, reported (ibid., p. 206) that when concepts or terms introduced in a theory grow arithmetically, the number of corresponding propositions to be verified grows much more rapidly in a geometrical progression according to an exponential law, stated by W. K. Clifford, and cited by G. Peano (*Calcolo geometrico*, 1888).

What distinguishes Peirce's "pragmaticism" is his elaboration of metaphysical categories going far beyond his proclaimed adherence to the logic of the "laboratory mind" of the experimenter, and even beyond his attempt to revive the medieval doctrine of objective universals (Scotistic realism). His unpublished "Hume on the Laws of Nature" was rejected by the scientific director of the Smithsonian Institution, Samuel P. Langley, as too abstruse. Instead of defending the "laws of Nature" as absolute, Peirce insisted on the absolute reality of one of his favorite metaphysical triads: (1) Immediately felt Qualities, (2) Brute Existence, and (3) Ordered Reasonableness, so that the laws of nature dis-

covered by scientists were approximations, probable guesses (hypotheses) whose logical consequences had been tested by controlled experiments. Peirce, at various times in his metaphysical thought-experiments, stated his categories in various triads: Feeling, Habit, Purpose; Sensation, Resistance, Order; Spontaneity, Contingency, Law; and in evolutionary terms, Sporting Mutation, Habit, and Adaptation. The generalization of these triadic categories was simply Firstness, Secondness, and Thirdness. Peirce offered applications of these very broad categories in many fields, e.g., in logic: terms, propositions, inferences; in his theory of signs: icons, indices, symbols; in his metaphysical doctrines: tychism, synechism, agapism—Greek-derived words for Chance, Continuity, and Love.

Critics of Peirce have no difficulty showing the confusing ambiguities of his categories. "Chance" shifts meaning as Peirce applies it to spontaneity, feeling, contingency, approximation, random distribution of energy, unpredictability, individuation, uniqueness, inexplicability; "Continuity" is ambiguously applied to the laws of natural phenomena, to human habits, to all evolution including the history of scientific discoveries, and to the history of civilization. "Evolutionary Love" is a very speculative use of the Platonic idea of the attraction of all things for order emerging in millenarian fashion out of a primordial chaos of sporting feelings. No wonder then that Peirce's "Guess at the Riddle of the Universe" was not taken seriously by the more hardheaded utilitarian followers of John Stuart Mill, Herbert Spencer, and the "Social Darwinists" of his day.

It remains nevertheless true that Peirce made pioneer contributions to the logic of relations, to the foundations of mathematics, to the theory of probability and induction, and to the theory of signs—contributions which have paved the way for rapid progress in mathematical logic and the logic of the sciences. Only in 1967, for example, was it discovered (by the mathematical logician A. R. Turquette) that Peirce had, in his unpublished papers, worked out a truth-table for a three valued logic, together with a proof of its completeness (*Transactions of the Charles S. Peirce Society*, III, 66-73). Whitehead and Russell have acknowledged their debt to Peirce's calculus of relations; Frank P. Ramsey paid tribute to Peirce's theory of probable inference as truth-frequency and instrumentalist view of theories in science as "leading principles." Whether or not Peirce would have made his discoveries (e.g., in his physical and psychological experiments, in his symbolic logic, etc.) without his restless metaphysical speculations is a difficult historical and psychological question, even though one can easily prove that *logically* there is no necessary connection between his truth-frequency analysis of probability and his tychistic cosmology.

Josiah Royce, in his *The Problem of Christianity* (2 vols., 1913, Preface), paid tribute to Peirce: "I owe much more to our great and unduly neglected American logician, Mr. Charles Peirce, than I do to the common tradition of recent idealism, and certainly very much more than I have ever owed, at any point of my own philosophical development to the doctrines which . . . can be justly attributed to Hegel" (ibid., p. xi). In fact, Royce by defining an idea as a "plan of action" developed a theory of knowledge and reality with the outcome "a sort of absolute pragmatism, which has never been pleasing either to rationalists or to empiricists, either to pragmatists or to the ruling type of absolutists" (ibid., II, 122f.). Royce's theory of knowledge was, like Peirce's, based on a social theory of inquiry, meaning, and truth. Both he and Peirce were very critical of the subjective individualism of William James. Royce's "absolute pragmatism" required an ideal community of minds as a logically necessary condition for knowledge and reality.

V. WILLIAM JAMES'S PRAGMATISM AND "WILL TO BELIEVE"

It was William James who, in 1897, credited Charles S. Peirce, his friend and admirer, with having originated pragmatism. James made this announcement in a public lecture (at the Philosophical Union of the University of California in Berkeley) entitled "Philosophical Conceptions and Practical Results." In subsequent correspondence between Peirce and James, both acknowledged their debt to Chauncey Wright. Wright's stimulating analytical mind and empiricist methodology had been inspired by John Stuart Mill's critical examination of the Scottish intuitionism of Sir William Hamilton, and by Charles Darwin's theory of natural selection. Wright was a mathematician for the *Nautical Almanac,* and had applied his knowledge to a theory about the optimal arrangement of leaves around the stems of plants (phyllotaxis) to obtain maximum exposure to air and sunlight. The paper interested Charles Darwin, who thanked Chauncey Wright for this evidence of evolutionary adaptation.

Wright also argued for a neutral view of science with regard to moral and religious values, and for John Stuart Mill's utilitarian, relativistic theory of objective morality. William James, under the influence of his Swedenborgian father's religious philosophy, argued against Wright's skepticism. The "right" and later "duty" and "will to believe," which James defended, was the counterpoise to Wright's positivistic and "nihilistic" agnosticism. However, James admitted Wright's influence on his own scientific approach in the preface to the *Principles of Psychology* (1890), the forerunner of nearly all of James's ideas as developed in his later formulations

of his doctrines of the will to believe, of "radical empiricism," and of pluralism—the three major components of his variety of pragmatism and of his general philosophy.

James's article "The Function of Cognition," written for a psychological journal in 1885, shows the influence of Peirce's realism as well as elements of the operational theory of knowledge developed later by John Dewey and Percy Bridgman. James's realism and "radical empiricism" went beyond Berkeley's idealistic view that external objects are merely passive groups of sensations or ideas. That nothing exists "without the mind" was for James a totally inadequate expression of the creative dynamism and transformative powers of the mind. The same critique was levelled at the classical rationalists (Descartes, Spinoza, Leibniz) who maintained that the order and connections of things were simply reflected by the order and connection of ideas. The mind, for James, Peirce, Dewey, and Mead—and their followers—is active in knowledge, operating on and transforming its experience in order to grasp the changing relations of things and events, utilizing ideas tested experimentally as tools needed to understand and to adapt the mind to nature. We know the earth's physical properties only when we can take some of its materials into our laboratories, break down compounds into elements, discover and create new ones by experimental activities that control some of the conditions governing nature's secret powers. So long as philosophers refer knowledge to antecedent untouched sensations and eternal ideas, which do nothing and give the mind nothing to do, they will discover nothing new and continue to produce static, unproductive models of mythical ontologies. *Homo faber* can best understand what he can create, but in order to understand nature man must learn to create and control the processes at work in nature. While Peirce, astronomer, mathematical physicist, and chemist, was concerned with cosmic evolution, James, physiological psychologist and humanist, was drawn to the trials and tribulations of the individual mind, perplexed by the complexity of environing forces and seeking the freedom to create a life worth living.

After much pondering over metaphysical and theological arguments—especially influenced by R. H. Lotze, Charles Renouvier, and Jules Lequier—James offered his "will to believe" as a solution to the age-old problem of the freedom of the will. Wright's early influence on James's thought here had been twofold. First, Wright followed Kant's and Mill's antimetaphysical views that absolute freedom of a disembodied will was beyond logical or empirical proof, but held that a practical justification for the belief in free will was to be sought in the moral benefits of holding the self responsible for the knowable empirical consequences of one's deliberate actions. James agreed with Wright's empirical approach, and explored the psychological and physiological experimental facts that might throw light on the force of instincts, habits, and association of ideas resulting from previous sensations, and on the Will, in various chapters of the *Principles of Psychology* but emerged with a negative result. The last chapter ("Necessary Truths and the Effects of Experience") concluded that the scientific study of the human mind yielded no decisive idea about the precise relation of bodily behavior to states and acts of consciousness, and thus left James with the "dilemma of determinism."

In his paper bearing this title, James distinguished "soft" from "hard" determinism. The "hard" determinist (James preferred to deal with persons rather than with doctrines) was one who denied absolutely that any act was "free" from complete determination by strict causation, so that freedom of the will was simply an illusion due to ignorance of the causes behind one's actions and decisions. The "soft" determinist was less of a pessimist by admitting the impossibility of knowing *all* the determining causes of one's actions, and by affirming a positive knowledge only of the probable empirical consequences of choosing between equally determined alternatives. Soft determinism appealed to James as more in harmony with the common-sense belief in the freedom to make some practical, moral, and religious decisions. The will to believe might then help release untapped energies.

Furthermore, there are occasions when one is confronted empirically by what James called "genuine, live, momentous, and forced options" with vital consequences foreseeable with some degree of probability as one chooses on the basis of previous experience and present feeling among two or more apparent alternatives. And there are many human situations when all the scientifically foreseeable consequences are so equally balanced between two alternatives that there is no decisive preponderance of evidence in favor of one over the other. Wright would have argued that *scientific* evidence is neutral with regard to moral decisions about ultimate valuations, and—as the mathematician W. K. Clifford later advocated—would suspend judgment if there were no further evidence to favor one alternative as more useful, socially or individually, than another. At this point William James departed from Wright's negative neutrality and Clifford's paralyzing suspension of judgment, because for James action is demanded in genuine, live, momentous, and forced options, and because it is absurd to expect human beings to suspend their natural inclinations indefinitely.

The criticisms made by both Chauncey Wright and C. S. Peirce did affect James's doctrine of "the will to believe" to the extent that James was led to laying down a condition for the application of his doctrine, namely, that no belief was to be accepted as true if it went contrary to available evidence. In other words, the appeal

to the emotional willingness to believe was, in James's critical judgment, applicable and relevant only when all the available evidence for and against a possible decision or action was equally balanced or indecisive. James's position is saved from the charge of "mere" subjectivism by his adherence to this condition, although at times it seems as though he ignored it, especially when he insists that the very desire to act in the direction of one's natural inclinations is part of the objective situation. Such insistence on the objective status of emotional factors is not surprising for a philosopher who had devoted so many years to the scientific study of psychology. The famous "James-Lange theory of the emotions" is a forerunner of the objective approach of behaviorists. We tremble not because we are afraid, but we are afraid because we tremble. James was not an extreme behaviorist; he would not dismiss or reduce to physical symptoms the immediate experience of conscious states or the effects of subconscious forces. He was willing to adopt the dual language of physiological and introspective methods of psychologizing. With G. Stanley Hall, he early recognized the importance of Freud's ideas.

Later criticisms of the James-Lange theory of emotions by W. B. Cannon and other psychologists show that James oversimplified the physiological conditions by referring only to visceral and muscular states. While James would have welcomed further knowledge and physiological research on glandular, neurological, and psychoanalytical conditions of emotional responses, he would still have left open the question whether conscious voluntary effort (such as the "will to believe" entails) is not also a possible cause for producing emotions that can be beneficial to the human organism. Like Freud, who accepted analysis of a patient's history, while awaiting physiological details, William James accepted introspective reports as equally important as behavioral data. His sympathy for Freud's approach was similar to the way in which he opened his mind to philosophical arguments for free will by the neo-Kantians Renouvier and Lotze, and even by the more mystical views of Lequier and Henri Bergson.

Although James died (1910) before the appearance of Bergson's *Two Sources of Morals and Religion* (Paris, 1932; London, 1935), he would have approved Bergson's defense of the "open" as against the mechanistically "closed" world as well as his sympathetic account of the Christian mystics. Bergson's "creative evolution" and dynamic spiritualism were not alien to James's own pluralistic and open-ended world view and interest in the varieties of religious experience. For James could argue passionately for pluralistic, democratic individualism and at the same time feel deeply the self's need for spiritual unity. The many kinds of "self" (material, social, moral, and spiritual) which he analyzed in his *Principles of Psychology* were not simply Hume's "bundles of habits" and atomistic sensations; they were the varied organic forms and directions of the stream of consciousness of an organism striving not only to survive but to create meaning and value in its finite existence. James's pragmatism was as unfinished as his open universe. He died knowing that he had not solved the eternal enigmas of the relationship of the Many to the One, of the Material to the Spiritual. In his own romantic way he had found spiritual excitement in the quest for truths which are practically unattainable with either certainty or final satisfaction, but worth pursuing if only for the glimpses of their transcendent, elusive values.

VI. EUROPEAN VERSIONS OF PRAGMATISM

James's democratic temper and tender-minded sensitivity to human suffering and political injustice were clearly evidenced in his attack on the curse of bigness in the rapid growth of America's giant monopolistic industries, on the military expansion in the Philippines and Latin America, and the growing agnosticism and cynicism. It is, therefore, surprising to note that some European thinkers referred to James's emphasis on feeling and action in their own violently antidemocratic programs of political action. For example, Mussolini, in his socialistic days, said that he admired James's philosophy though there is no evidence that he had ever read or understood it. Giovanni Papini, an enthusiastic supporter of a "magical pragmatism," had been hailed earlier by James as a leader of the pragmatic writers of articles in *Leonardo,* the philosophical journal founded by Papini in 1903.

Although Papini had said that it was impossible to give a unique and precise definition of pragmatism, he offered to indicate ". . . the dominant feature which forms the internal unity of all the various elements that go together under the mantle of its name" (. . . *il carattere dominante che forma l'unità interna di tutti i vari elementi che vanno riuniti sotto il mantello del suo nome*) namely, "*the plasticity or flexibility of theories and beliefs,* that is, the recognition of their purely *instrumental value*; . . . their value being only *relative* to an end or group of ends which are susceptible to being changed, varied, and transformed when needed" (Papini's emphases, *Pragmatismo,* p. 91).

The elements united thus by Papini turn out to be more Jamesian than Peircean, more romantic and "magical" than classical and realistic. He enumerates six such component ideas: (1) *nominalism,* (2) *utilitarianism,* (3) *positivism* (antimetaphysical scientific method), (4) *kantianism* (emphasis on the "practical reason" of the free will), (5) *voluntarism* of a Schopenhauerian sort (ontological priority of the will over science), (6) *fideism* or Pascalian apologetics aimed at restoring religious faiths. Papini adds that different emphases and combinations of these elements go to make up the "va-

riety of pragmatism" (ibid., p. 92), but he lumps Peirce and James together as emphasizing in the theory of meaning the *particular* consequences of ideas in future *practical* experiences, thus ignoring the criticism of nominalism by Peirce (ibid., p. 93).

Papini's "magical" pragmatism owes the adjective to his own emphasis on the personal power of ideas to transform what we experience by a romantic activity of the "imitative" imagination. He leans heavily on James's notion that "*faith in a fact can help create the fact*" (quoted with emphases by Papini, ibid., p. 145). He agrees also with James's statement in "The Sentiment of Rationality" (*Will to Believe,* pp. 63-110), that truths cannot become true till our faith has made them so" (ibid., p. 96). The confusion between meaning and truth remains a common feature of James's and Papini's versions of pragmatism. Papini found James' *Will to Believe* "among the most exciting and fruitful theories of contemporary thought" (Papini, p. 153), but regretted that in James "there is no trace of the belief in *magical* powers, that is to say, in the possibility that certain men have the power to change by their will external things and natural phenomena; for James restricted this power to internal psychological reality" (Papini's emphasis, ibid., p. 151).

An interesting brief chapter of Papini's book is entitled "Il Pragmatismo e i parti politici" ("Pragmatism and Political Parties," written in 1905), in which the eight Italian political parties of his day (Catholic, Conservative, Liberal, Radical, Republican, Socialist, Democratic, and Anarchist) are taken to task for using common locutions but acting differently. They all talk of aiming at Italy's *unity, freedom, prosperity* but pragmatically these terms must have as many different meanings as the various means or actions that are specifically proposed and pursued by each party's leaders. On this point, Dewey, Mead, and Hook would surely agree with Papini in applying the instrumentalist interpretation of social and political programs as no better than possible hypotheses. But the American pragmatists would also reject Papini's resort to an antimodernistic and mystical Catholicism, a far cry from his initial subjective pragmatism.

Although Luigi Pirandello (1867-1936) was not a professional philosopher, his many plays, translated in many languages and successfully performed in many countries in the 1920's and 1930's, almost always contain a Protagorean relativism with respect to truth and values. The conversations of Pirandello's characters reflect the version of the subjective relativism in the pragmatism made current in Italy by Papini's personalism and Mario Calderoni's "corridor theory" of truth. Pirandello himself disavowed any philosophical content in his plays:

> In Italy people seem to be intent on following the misleading line (*la falsariga*) of some critic who believed

he discovered a philosophical content in my things that isn't there (*un contenuto filosofico che non c'è*), I guarantee its non-existence.

(quoted in L. Pirandello, ed. C. Simioni, p. xxvii; trans. P. P. Wiener)

Yet there was a stormy, philosophical controversy over so-called Pirandellism; Pirandello's relativism was criticized by followers of Benedetto Croce, Italy's dominating metaphysician of the absolutistic Hegelian type against which the *Leonardo* group led by Papini, had led a rebellion in the first decade of the century. Croce had himself accepted Adriano Tilgher's (one of Croce's epigoni's) dialectical analysis of "the central problem" of Pirandello's art, viz., the antithesis of Life and Form (A. Tilgher, *Teoria della critica d'arte*, 1913). A. Gramsci, on the other hand, suggested that Pirandello was merely displaying his satirical sense of humor, by creating "philosophical" and nasty doubts about truth and goodness in order to flaunt subjectivism and philosophical solipsism (ibid., p. xxviii).

The most extreme form of this abuse of James's notion of the usefulness of ideas as adaptive means of action is the theory of the syndicalist Georges Sorel in his *Réflexions sur la violence* (Paris, 1908); in what he took to be a pragmatic justification of using the weapon of a general strike to bring about the revolutionary overthrow of the existing capitalistic system, Sorel argued as follows: "The myth must be judged as a means of acting on the present; any attempt to discuss how far it can be taken literally as future history is devoid of sense. . . . The question whether the general strike is a partial reality, or only a product of popular imagination, is of little importance." Thanks to revolutionary leaders, "we know that the general strike is indeed what I have said: the *myth* in which Socialism is wholly comprised, i.e., a body of images capable of evoking instinctively all the sentiments which correspond to the different manifestations of the war undertaken by Socialism against modern society. Strikes have engendered in the proletariat the noblest, deepest, and most moving sentiments that they possess . . ." (pp. 360-61).

Sorel's pragmatic conclusion to his peculiar "scientific ethics" and revolutionary myth of the general strike, reveals the missionary zeal of the syndicalist's hopes: "It is to violence that Socialism owes those high ethical values by means of which it brings *salvation* to the modern world" (ibid., p. 365). This variety of revolutionary pragmatism—surely on the extreme fringe of the solid core of pragmatism—makes a dangerous appeal to men's instincts and to irrational disregard of the consequences of the means employed. Sorel's appeal to violence, so common to extreme militants of both fascistic and communistic camps, is certainly confuted by our core pragmatists who are concerned as reformers about the human effects or social consequences of re-

sort to violence which so often breeds greater violence. Sorel owes some of his ideas, especially the appeal to instinctive drives, to Bergson's *élan vital* and emphasis on action, although Bergson never advocated violence, and preferred the mystical road to salvation.

Further illustration of the rich variety to which pragmatism lends itself, within the French group of pragmatic thinkers as well as among other nationalities, is provided by the dispute between Abel Rey and Pierre Duhem on the philosophical foundations of physical theory. Professor Rey defended an anti-metaphysical, positivistic principle of verifiability against Duhem's attempt to weld experimental physics to a neo-Thomistic theory of knowledge and reality. Duhem was perfectly willing and even anxious to have physical science aim at convenient theories that "save the appearances," provided however, that the structure of physical theories reflected the overarching ultimate nature of the supernatural invisible reality of God. Abel Rey, of course, dismissed such theological overtones as irrelevant to the aims and structure of physical theory.

A French fascist, Drieu La Rochelle, in 1927, took pride in his epistemological "pragmatism" which to him meant that "knowledge is the product only of experience," that is, of *personal* experience, as Robert Soucy explains in his article on "Romanticism and Realism in the Fascism of Drieu La Rochelle," in the *Journal of the History of Ideas* (31 [Jan. 1970], 78 and notes 30, 31). Truth had to be "lived," thus La Rochelle espoused "a kind of fascist existentialism" without knowing anything of existentialist philosophy (ibid.).

Bergson's form of pragmatism only tenuously merits that label (which he did not adopt for his philosophy); his metaphysical and spiritualistic theory of action bears all the marks of the *fin-de-siècle anti-scientisme* which appears in his criticism of the analytical, conceptual, abstract, and static modes of scientific understanding. The flux of immediate experience (*les données immédiates de la conscience,* the subject of his dissertation) could not be grasped by the abstract intellect but required an immersion in the real moving duration (*durée*) of the vital impulse (*élan vital*) which surges through the dynamic universe. William James was greatly impressed and awed by the imaginative sweep and psychological insights of Bergson's ardent defense of concrete intuitive data of consciousness so similar to James's "stream of consciousness." Bergson's *Creative Evolution* (1907) was Lamarckian, however, and was not compatible with James's defense of August Weismann's refutation of the Lamarckian theory of the inheritance of acquired characters. Despite their many differences, the kinship of Bergson's and James's pragmatic philosophies is based on their common concern to transcend static, impersonal conceptual analysis and to make of man's active, dynamic, emotional nature the source of a creative moral and spiritual order. This aim was a far cry from Sorel's appeal to the myth of a violent class war on the Marxist ground of historical materialism, but the dynamism is there, and the existentialists claim Bergson as one of their own.

Sorel, in his work on the *Utility of Pragmatism* (*De l'utilité du pragmatisme,* 1917), during World War I and nine years after his *Réflexions sur la violence,* hoped "to convince readers of this book that the pragmatic manner of considering the pursuit of truth is bound to become one of the essential elements of modern thought" (Sorel [1908], p. 4). He noted that Peirce in his 1878 essay, "How to Make Our Ideas Clear," had said that Catholics and Protestants ought not be concerned about the idea of transubstantiation so long as they agree on the effects on moral conduct of the real Presence. He noted also that Édouard Le Roy (1870-1954), the Bergsonian physicist, interpreted Catholic dogmas in Peircean fashion when Le Roy maintained that these "dogmas would impose strict rules of conduct on the faithful, but would leave a great deal of freedom for the intellectual representation of things" (ibid., pp. 5-6, with reference to Le Roy's *Dogme et critique,* pp. 19-23, 32). To Peirce, of course, "conduct" referred to "conduct of the mind," whereas James broadened the scope of the term to include, and indeed to emphasize, moral and religious behavior.

Sorel defended James's idea of the "will to believe" against the critics who misinterpreted it to mean "the will to make-believe" or to indulge in wishful thinking. Sorel also took to task those critics who had picked on James's phrase "cash value of an idea" as a reflection of Yankee commercialism. Against this gross and yet common European misinterpretation of James's lively rhetorical way of discussing epistemological theories of truth, Sorel as a political thinker and Marxist, looked with favor upon James's condemnation of undemocratic State authority and of an infallible Church that imposed its dogmas upon its members.

Sorel's brand of pragmatism was critical of Bergson's spiritualism, although Bergson shared with him an admiration for William James's break away from traditional, eternalistic metaphysics. What further distinguishes Sorel's from Bergson's pragmatic ideas is Sorel's unwavering confidence in the certainty of scientific knowledge and of historical materialism. He could find no value in Bergson's vitalism, antiscientific intuition, and religious mysticism. He did, however, praise Bergson's theory of intelligence as "the faculty of manufacturing artificial objects, especially tools for making tools, and for varying their manufacture indefinitely" (quoted by Sorel from Bergson's *L'évolution créatrice,* p. 151).

Sorel's revolutionary, syndicalist brand of pragmatism appealed strongly to Mussolini and the fascists. Of course, the very different varieties of pragmatism of James, Peirce, Mead, and Dewey can hardly be held responsible for either the Marxist or fascist interpretations of James. The very opposite defence of liberal democracy is at the cultural base of the American, British, Italian (pre-Mussolini), German (H. Vaihinger), and French varieties of pragmatism.

Communistic ideologists have criticized pragmatism as a bourgeois capitalistic doctrine of American imperialism despite James's attacks on big business and American policies in the Philippines, Cuba, and Venezuela. At the same time communist philosophers urge the union of theory and practice in very narrowly practical terms. "Praxis" occurs often in their theory of truth; it is the title of a philosophical periodical in Yugoslavia, edited by more liberal Marxists than in the USSR or Red China. So long as philosophy is chiefly an ideological tool among communist theoreticians, it is subject to modification by the leaders of the party or state. Thus Soviet philosophy becomes instrumental in the worst opportunistic sense, the polar opposite of Dewey's instrumentalism and Peirce's pragmaticism or of any of the other liberal varieties of pragmatism, so crudely regarded by its critics as advocating crass opportunism with respect to truth and human values.

For the social and political forms of pragmatism, more moderate or liberal than Sorel's or other Marxist versions of praxis, we must turn to the legal writings of philosophers like Vaihinger, and the American pragmatic realists.

In the years 1876 to 1878, while Oliver Wendell Holmes, Jr. was preparing the chapters of his work *The Common Law,* the Kantian commentator Hans Vaihinger was writing a pragmatic masterpiece, *Die Philosophie des Als Ob.* It was not published until 1911, and not translated into English until 1924. The legal philosopher, Lon L. Fuller, has devoted the last third of his work on *Legal Fictions* to explaining the contribution to legal thinking made by Vaihinger's "as if" philosophy. Though conceived independently, Vaihinger's pragmatic philosophy is similar to James's and Holmes's views in showing how the mind tends to project or reify its own conceptual constructions, which are primarily evolutionary means of adaptation to a changing world. Whatever and whenever such adaptive ideas serve to help us confront reality, they are regarded *as if* they were real properties. Perhaps Vaihinger may be considered "more pragmatic than the American school because . . . he has obtained his generalizations about human thinking, not by deduction from some premise concerning the nature of thought in general, but from an examination of the ways and byways of thought in particular sciences" (Fuller [1967], p. 96). These sciences range from the mathematical to the legal. "Imaginary numbers" (roots of negative numbers) can be treated as if they were quantitative properties of electromagnetic fields. The fictive "personality" of a corporation is regarded by the courts as if it were a person subject to specific laws of liability, bankruptcy, and so forth. In short, "Vaihinger taught German legal science how to use its own intellectual tools" (ibid.).

VII. PRAGMATISM IN THE LAW

Three of the members of the Metaphysical Club at Harvard in the 1870's, where Peirce claimed "pragmatism saw the light of day," were concerned, as students, practitioners, or teachers of law, with the cultural evolution and philosophical foundations of the law. They were Nicholas St. John Green (the "grandfather of pragmatism" who followed A. Bain's idea of belief as a disposition to act), Oliver Wendell Holmes, Jr. (busily editing the twelfth edition of Kent's *Commentaries on the American Law,* 4 vols.), and Joseph B. Warner (future lecturer in the Harvard Law School, 1886-87, and who in 1896 before the American Bar Association gave an address on "The Responsibilities of the Lawyer"). A fourth law student, John Fiske, who occasionally came to the Metaphysical Club, turned from law to history. He was a disciple of Comte and Spencer and wrote a four-volume survey, *Outlines of Cosmic Philosophy* (1874), developing an evolutionary philosophy of civilization along Spencerian lines.

The law schools were steeped in classical syllogistic methods of applying the law to individual cases as previously decided and in the Hobbesian-Austinian view that the law was "the command of the sovereign." The Lockean view of the social contract was mingled with the Puritan idea of the Covenant with God. Sir Henry Maine's *Ancient Law* (1861) and *History of Early Institutions* (1875) were reviewed by Chauncey Wright in the *Nation* (July 1, 1875) after he had previously remarked: "In the Law School there is a vigor of thought and a stimulus to study which can't be found elsewhere" (Wiener, p. 272). Maine's work emphasized the evolution of the law as paralleling the evolution of society from slavery and feudalism to modern free enterprise: "from status to contract." A similar emphasis on historical development as an essential key to understanding the cultural role and evolution of the law was the prominent feature of Holmes's great work *The Common Law* (1881):

> The felt necessities of the time, the prevalent moral and political theories, intuitions of public policy, avowed or unconscious; even the prejudices which judges share with their fellow-men have had a good deal more to do than the syllogism in determining the rules by which men should be governed. The law embodies the story of a nation's development through many centuries, and it cannot be dealt with as if it contained only the axi-

oms and corollaries of a book of mathematics. In order to know what it is, we must know what it has been, and what it tends to become. We must alternately consult history and existing theories of legislation. But the most difficult labor will be to understand the combination of the two into new products at every stage. The substance of the law at any given time pretty nearly corresponds, so far as it goes, with what is then understood to be convenient; but its form and machinery and the degree to which it is able to work out desired results, depend very much upon its past.

> (Holmes, p. 1)

Holmes illustrated his evolutionary and pragmatic approach by tracing the change from the primitive basis of revenge in the punishment of criminals to the more pragmatic justification of deterring future crimes. In civil cases, Holmes explained, the evolution of the laws of liability is shaped mainly by "considerations of what is expedient for the community concerned" (ibid., pp. 15, 35).

A progressive combination, and at times radical application, of British empiricism and utilitarian ethics was deployed by the American legal pragmatists against the metaphysical idealism of the German romantic variety that had come to the United States in the Hegelian school (mentioned above) of W. T. Harris in St. Louis, where the *Journal of Speculative Philosophy* was launched in 1868. The upshot of pragmatic jurisprudence was the dissociation of the law from its scholastic accretions of eternal theological standards and imputations of original sin and hell-fire for the nonconformist and iconoclast. The criminal law with its medieval system of punishment and torture "for the good of one's soul" was subjected to unsparing criticism by Nicholas St. John Green (1830-76) in his *Essays and Notes on the Law of Tort and Crime* (published in 1933). He insisted on an historical approach in his projected annual publication of criminal law reports and cases in both the United States and the British Empire. Before Green's death he had completed the editing and annotation of the first two volumes (1874-75) of this bold venture in historical jurisprudence. Peirce showed the influence of Green's analytical use of legal history when he pointed out, as Green had in the *American Law Review* (4 [Jan., 1870], 201), that key terms like "proximate cause" could not simply be transferred from Aristotelian physics to the laws of liability. "The idea of making the payment of considerable damages dependent on a term of Aristotelian logic or metaphysics is most shocking to any student of these subjects, and well illustrates the value of Pragmatism" (C. S. Peirce, "Proximate Cause and Effect," *Baldwin's Dictionary of Philosophy*). "Proximate cause" in civil law has to do with the negligence of a party with respect to the legal rights of others and nothing to do with spatio-temporal contiguity or a mechanical chain of causes. Rights and liabilities are determined by the civil law in the case of property damages which can even be inflicted at a distance, e.g., by hiring others to commit arson.

Green's influence on the shaping of legal pragmatism is not as well known as that of Oliver Wendell Holmes, Jr. (Wiener, pp. 164ff.). Common to their legal philosophies were: (1) a behavioristic method of determining intention by regarding an act "as a voluntary muscular contraction and nothing else" (Holmes, *American Law Review,* 14, 9) or consisting "as such of inward feelings and outward motions, the motions forming the evidence of the feelings" (Green, *Essays and Notes,* p. 192); (2) the irrelevance of the internal phenomena of conscience (Holmes, *Common Law,* pp. 62, 110; Green, *Essays and Notes,* p. 67); (3) the primacy of public policy over individual idiosyncrasies. Holmes applied a tough-minded principle of interpreting the law by the external standard of the consequences for public policy as set by the legislature, regardless of the private feelings or moral ideals that might be affected. The rule of eminent domain might seem harsh to a property owner not compensated with as much as he thinks "just," but the public interest must prevail, if the community or state budget is too limited to award more compensation. The right of free speech must be limited in time of war, or denied to a mischievous person crying "Fire" in a crowded theater. But the same right must be rigorously protected against self-appointed censors of public morality, because (as John Stuart Mill had shown in his *Essay on Liberty*) in the long run the harm to the public will be greater if ideas are suppressed than if some allegedly harmful or "immoral" ones are tolerated. The test of how good or bad a new law is becomes a matter of predicting the social consequences or public effects of enacting and enforcing the proposed law. Since every judicial decision as to how the acts of the legislature should be interpreted or applied may modify the meaning of the law, Holmes argued that judges make the law as much as the legislature. The constitution of 1789 is not the same as that of 1865 or of 1965, not simply because amendments have been added, but because both the original articles and amendments have been interpreted differently by judges at various times in new cases having aspects unforeseen by the original makers of the law. Holmes's predictive theory of the law was offered as advice to lawyers in doubt about the meaning or applicability of a law. Holmes's counsel amounted to the rule that the law in any particular case would mean what one could predict the judges would decide in that case. Such predictions would vary with the temperament, education, prejudices, or mood of the judges. Obviously, however, this predictive theory will not help a judge who is pondering over what he should decide, for it is tautologous to state that the law will be or mean what he will decide. Holmes's realistic dictum that the law is what the courts will predictably decide also runs

afoul of legislation that aims at curbing the latitude of judicial freedom. Hence, the pragmatist is faced with the practical questions of social and political values, and criteria for judging them, in a rapidly changing society.

VIII. PRAGMATIC THEORIES OF VALUE

One common feature of all the varieties of pragmatism is the idea or "the premise that valuation is a form of empirical knowledge" (C. I. Lewis, Preface, p. vii). However, the diversified range of empirical theories of knowledge, due largely to the blurred and indefinite boundaries of "experience," leaves the idea rather vague and the premiss hardly unequivocal. For example, James's *Varieties of Religious Experience* does not exclude revelations of the supernatural, and Peirce includes purely logical and mathematical reasoning as forms of "diagramatic experimentation." In ethical theory, pragmatists will be either "emotivists" (following Wright, James, F. C. S. Schiller), or "cognitivists" (following Dewey, Mead, or C. I. Lewis). Outside this variety of pragmatic theories of value—and we must specify the type or theories of value that are excluded from the "pragmatic" if this term is to have any identifiable meaning—we can point to *a priori* or transcendental ideas of the *summum bonum* which can only be known by pure reason, by political or theological authority, or by a transcendental inner conscience or Ego untouched by common experience, and in any case, claiming moral jurisdiction not subject to any appeal to public verification.

William James, F. C. S. Schiller, and Luigi Pirandello (the latter not as a systematic philosopher, of course, but as illustrated in his play, *Six Characters in Search of an Author*) based their pragmatic humanism on the relativism of knowledge and values. On the other hand, C. I. Lewis aimed to avoid "the errors of Protagorean relativism or the moral skepticism which would destroy the normative by reducing it to merely emotive significance" (ibid., p. viii). Pragmatic ethics, for C. I. Lewis, is concerned with the nature of justice, and we have seen that legal pragmatists like Holmes always insisted on applying the "external standard" of social expediency in determining what the law considers "just."

Whether there is a "higher law" above what the law courts decide is "right" depends on whether we can appeal to a more general idea of the good or *summum bonum* that subsumes or overrides the legal idea. While it is not difficult to understand the social nature of justice in the sense of what is considered legally right or correct, it requires much more argument to accept a pragmatic criterion of public verification for the more general theory of values. But that is the kind of criterion that Peirce, Dewey, G. H. Mead, and C. I. Lewis have defended against the emotivists and the apriorists.

The verifiability theory of knowledge is shared by the core pragmatists (Peirce, James, Dewey, C. I. Lewis, and their followers) and logical empiricists (M. Schlick, R. Carnap, A. J. Ayer, and their followers) but the two schools of thought differ basically on whether value judgments are verifiable. The pragmatists affirm the idea that value judgments are verifiable to the extent that such judgments are implicit hypotheses about what is valued as desirable or enjoyable. Hypotheses, as possible truths about what objects or activities will satisfy desires or yield the enjoyments anticipated, have logical consequences that will either be falsified or verified by future experiences of such objects or activities. This view of value judgments as verifiable hypotheses is known as the "cognitivist" view. It is opposed to the "emotivist" view of those logical empiricists and others who regard value judgments as expressions of personal taste, feeling, or preference without any reference to knowledge claims. John Dewey and C. I. Lewis and their pragmatistic followers have criticized the "emotivist" view by showing how ideas, reflection, and knowledge of the consequences of actions modify emotional responses and behavior. For example, knowing that some mushrooms are poisonous will lead even a hungry person to desist from eating them until he learns to distinguish them from a nonpoisonous variety. In aesthetics, the art critic and connoisseur of music, by informed comments on the art object or musical score, the artist's or composer's, conductor's, or performer's techniques, can call attention to aspects of the works contemplated which would be overlooked or ignored by the uninformed spectator or listener, and thus enhance his enjoyment. "By their fruits, ye shall know them" was Peirce's epitome of the pragmatic logic of ethical judgments. Dewey's pragmatic analysis of aesthetic judgment in his *Art as Experience* (1934) applied a similar maxim to criticisms of works of art. William James in his *Varieties of Religious Experience* (Gifford Lectures, 1902) applied the same pragmatic justification of religious beliefs of all creeds whenever he saw evidence of their effects on transforming the lives of believers.

The general theory of values comprehends not only the legal and ethical ideas of "right" and "good" but also the logical grounds of aesthetic judgment, thus pursuing in greater detail the analysis of the ancient ideals of the true, the good, and the beautiful. Peirce had gone so far in his addiction to the romantic idealism of Friedrich Schiller and Schelling as to argue that logical theory rested ultimately on ethics because logic aims to determine what sort of reasoning we ought to adopt in conducting our inquiries into truth, and ethics is the science of what we *ought* to do. Moreover, what we ought to do ultimately depends on what goals we desire to achieve, and what is desirable in the end is a question of aesthetic judgment. Peirce, however, cannot offer any criterion of what would constitute a reasonable basis for

aesthetic judgment, although he defends reasonableness as the ultimate end of all existence. If logic determines what is "reasonable," we are back to where we started in Peirce's hierarchical triad of logic, ethics, and aesthetics.

There is a more fruitful development of the pragmatic logic of valuation in Dewey, C. I. Lewis, and their followers by assuming that our value judgments are essentially *hypotheses* or tentative claims to knowing what is good or bad, either for an individual or for a society.

By assuming that value judgments are hypotheses, we make them subject to verification by individual or public experience. There seems to be for Dewey and for Mead no absolute demarcation between "private" and "public" experience, but all verification is or should be "intersubjective," i.e., common to and communicable by all persons capable of testing an idea of what is proposed as "good" by their past, present, and anticipated future experiences and feelings of satisfaction or dissatisfaction. By regarding all value judgments as tentative, while being tested or verified, we make it possible to modify the claims on our approbation or disapprobation implicit in the value judgment. The modification after verification may range from complete rejection to some compromise or adjustment, but always with the reservation that further experience may make it necessary to reappraise the situation.

Dewey continually emphasizes the need for facing the peculiar complexities of each specific situation, the problematic and indeterminate nature of each initial stage of valuation, and the tentative character of any solution or resolution resulting from publicly testing our value judgments. Dewey had the temerity to attempt to apply his pragmatic instrumentalism to the complex psychological and social problems of education (in the experimental schools of Chicago in 1902, with George Herbert Mead), to the analysis of the turbulent scene of political revolutions in Russia, China, and Mexico, and in trying to form a third party in the United States during the depression in the 1930's, in combatting fascism and communism in the 1940's, and finally in grappling with the momentous issues of war and peace. Like James, Dewey argued for channeling the aggressive impulses of men towards combatting the common enemies of mankind: ignorance, poverty, disease, and injustice. A liberal democracy for Dewey is a social order that can be achieved in a common faith by uniting thought and action against political, economic, and social injustice.

Peirce's tychism and fallibilism, James's soft determinism, O. W. Holmes's "bet-abilitarianism," and Dewey's instrumentalism are sharply opposed to the economic determinism associated with Marxian dialectical necessity and historical materialism. Only a simplistic fallacy would link the social liberalism of these pragmatists to the totalitarianism of Marxian determinists. The fallacy consists in linking these very different views by finding a common feature in the fact that the pragmatists and Marxian determinists were both opposed to "formalism." To state that individualists like Justice O. W. Holmes, Thorstein Veblen, Charles Beard, James Harvey Robinson, and John Dewey were "all products of the historical and cultural emphases of the nineteenth century" (Morton G. White, quoted by Thayer, p. 444) is to minimize their role as shapers of nineteenth- and twentieth-century thought in the United States.

In the field of aesthetics, Peirce regarded Friedrich Schiller's *Letters on the Aesthetic Education of Mankind* (1794-95) as one of the first philosophical influences on his own intellectual development, and regarded the play element, to which Schiller attributed so much educational value, as a major factor in art and even in religious contemplation. (See Peirce's essay on "A Neglected Argument for the Existence of God" [*Hibbert Journal*, 7 (1908), 90-112] in which "musement" over the order and beauty in nature leads by a play of ideas to the idea of a divine being.)

The more detailed problems of artistic and literary criticism are treated pragmatically by Dewey in *Art as Experience* (1934), and by Stephen C. Pepper in *Aesthetic Quality: A Contextualistic Theory of Beauty* (1937). The common basis again of pragmatic criticism in aesthetics is that aesthetic judgments should not be based on fixed *a priori* ideas of classical or avant-garde models but on experimenting with every possible means or media for communicating the subtle nuances of feeling and meanings that elude the ordinary means of expression.

Knowledge and feeling, meaning and action, are organically fused in aesthetic experience and artistic creation, which finally exemplify in the most immediately enjoyable sense the pragmatic notion that knowledge can and should be instrumental to the enhancement of human values. In both the appreciation and creation of art, Dewey's pragmatism appeals to the possibilities of greater public participation than the elitist conception of art displayed in art galleries with a "holier-than-thou" aloofness. Against such an esoteric sanctuary for the arts, but without denying the artist's need for complete freedom to experiment, Dewey's pragmatic view aims to extend the field of artistic experimentation to every human from early childhood to adult life at home, in the schools, in the community and world. Knowledge of the history and problems of artistic creation can help improve our understanding of artistic values, and such understanding can also help refine our taste and make us more sensitive to the values that creative intelligence can elicit from the untapped potential capabilities of human nature. The realization of all values for Dewey is inseparable from his faith in the unlimited possibilities of a liberal civilization based on social and economic justice as well as on political democracy. Both intelligence and action—neither subordinated to the other—become creative instruments for the realization of these values in Dewey's experimentalist version of pragmatism.

Bibliography

A very full historical account of pragmatism with a comprehensive bibliography is H. S. Thayer's *Meaning and Action: A Critical History of Pragmatism* (Indianapolis and New York, 1968). A. J. Ayer, *The Origins of Pragmatism* (San Francisco, 1968) is less historical and mostly critical of James and Peirce. Alexander Bain, *The Emotions and the Will* (Edinburgh, 1859). P. W. Bridgman, *The Logic of Modern Physics* (New York, 1927). Mario Calderoni, *I postulati della scienza positiva ed il diritto penale* (Florence, 1901); idem, *Scritti*, ed. O. Campa, 2 vols. (Florence, 1924). P. Duhem, *La théorie physique—son objet et sa structure*, 2nd ed. (Paris, 1914), trans. P. P. Wiener as *The Aim and Structure of Physical Theory* (Princeton, 1954). John Dewey, "The Development of American Pragmatism," *Studies in the History of Ideas,* 3 vols. (New York, 1925), II, 353-77, repr. in *Philosophy and Civilization* (New York, 1931); idem, "The Pragmatism of Peirce," Supplementary Essay to *Chance, Love and Logic, Philosophical Essays by the Late Charles S. Peirce,* edited with Introduction by Morris R. Cohen (New York, 1923). *The Philosophy of John Dewey,* ed. P. A. Schilpp (Evanston, 1939). Southern Illinois University Press has been publishing a definitive edition of Dewey's works. Lon L. Fuller, *Legal Fictions* (Stanford, 1967). Nicholas St. John Green, *Essays and Notes on the Law of Tort and Crime* (Menasha, Wisc., 1933). G. Gullace, "The Pragmatist Movement in Italy," *Journal of the History of Ideas,* 23 (1962), 91-105. O. W. Holmes, Jr., *The Common Law* (Boston, 1881). Sidney Hook, *The Metaphysics of Pragmatism* (Chicago, 1927). Roman Jakobson, "Language in Relation to Other Communication Systems," *Linguaggi nella società e nella tecnica* (Milan, 1970), pp. 3-16; see also Y. Bar-Hillel, "Communication and Argumentation in Pragmatic Languages," ibid., pp. 269-84. William James, *The Principles of Psychology,* 2 vols. (New York, 1890); idem, *The Will to Believe and Other Essays in Popular Philosophy* (New York, 1897); idem, *The Varieties of Religious Experience* (New York and London, 1902); idem, *Pragmatism, A New Name for Some Old Ways of Thinking* (New York, 1907). C. I. Lewis, *An Analysis of Knowledge and Valuation* (La Salle, Ill., 1946). Karl N. Llewellyn, *Jurisprudence: Realism in Theory and Practice* (Chicago, 1962). Arthur O. Lovejoy, *The Thirteen Pragmatisms* (Baltimore, 1965; reprint of his articles in the *Journal of Philosophy* of 1908). George H. Mead,

Mind, Self, and Society: From the Standpoint of a Social Behaviorist, ed. with introduction by Charles W. Morris (Chicago, 1934), bibliography in pp. 390-92; see also Maurice Natanson, *The Social Dynamics of George H. Mead* (Washington, D.C., 1956); Charles Morris, *The Pragmatic Movement in American Philosophy* (New York, 1970); John W. Petras, ed., *George Herbert Mead: Essays on His Social Philosophy* (New York, 1968). R. Mondolfo, "Trabajo manual y trabajo intelectual desde la antigüedad hasta el renacimiento," *Revista de la Historia de las Ideas,* 1 (1950), 5-26. Ernest Nagel, *Principles of the Theory of Probability* (Chicago, 1939); idem, *Logic Without Metaphysics* (Glencoe, Ill., 1956); idem, *The Structure of Science* (New York, 1961). G. Papini, *Pragmatismo 1903-1911* (Milan, 1913; 3rd ed., Florence, 1927); idem, *Crepùscolo dei Filosofi* (Florence, 1925). Charles S. Peirce, *Collected Papers,* Vols. 1-6, ed. C. Hartshorne and P. Weiss; Vols. 7-8, ed. A. W. Burks (Cambridge, Mass., 1931-58). *Transactions of the Peirce Society* is a quarterly edited and published by University of Massachusetts Press and contains a supplementary list of Peirce's unpublished papers as well as articles on his philosophy. Max H. Fisch is preparing a biography of Peirce, a book to supplement Paul Weiss's valuable article in the *Dictionary of American Biography.* L. Pirandello, *La vita che ti diedi, Ciascuno a suo modo,* ed. C. Simioni, with the chronology of Pirandello's life and times, an introduction and bibliography (Verona, 1970). Frank P. Ramsey, *The Foundations of Mathematics* (London, 1931). Francis E. Reilly, *Charles Peirce's Theory of Scientific Method* (New York, 1970). George Santayana, *The Life of Reason,* 5 vols. (New York, 1905-06). A. Santucci, *Il pragmatismo italiano* (Bologna, 1963). F. C. S. Schiller, "William James and the Making of Pragmatism," *Personalist,* 8 (1927), 81-93. H. W. Schneider, *A History of American Philosophy* (New York, 1946). Georges Sorel, *Réflexions sur la violence* (Paris, 1908), trans. T. E. Hulme, *Reflections on Violence* (New York, 1920); idem, *Les illusions du progrès* (1908), trans. J. and C. Stanley as *The Illusions of Progress* (Berkeley, 1969); idem, *De l'utilité du Pragmatisme* (Paris, 1917; 2nd ed. 1928). Hans Vaihinger, *Die Philosophie des Als Ob* (Berlin, 1911), trans. C. K. Ogden as *The Philosophy of As If* (New York, 1924). Giovanni Vailati, *Il metodo della filosofia,* ed. F. Rossi-Landi (Bari, 1957), with bibliography, pp. 29-36; see also F. Rossi-Landi, article on Vailati in *Encyclopedia of Philosophy,* ed. Paul Edwards, 8 vols. (New York, 1967), Vol. 8. G. Vailati, *Scritti,* ed. M. Calderoni, U. Ricci, and G. Vacca (Florence, 1911). Philip P. Wiener, *Evolution and the Founders of Pragmatism,* with Introduction by John Dewey (Cambridge, Mass., 1949; repr. Gloucester, Mass., 1969). Ludwig Wittgenstein, *Philosophical Investigations,* 3rd ed. trans. G. E. M. Anscombe (Oxford, 1953; New York, 1968). Chauncey Wright, *Philosophical Discussions,* ed. Charles E. Norton (New York, 1877); idem, *Letters of Chauncey Wright, with an Account of His Life,* ed. James B. Thayer (New York, 1878).

David A. Hollinger (essay date 1995)

SOURCE: Hollinger, David A. "The Problem of Pragmatism in American History: A Look Back and a Look Ahead." In *Pragmatism: From Progressivism to Postmodernism,* edited by Robert Hollinger and David Depew, pp. 19-37. Westport, Conn. and London: Praeger, 1995.

[*In the following essay, Hollinger regards Pragmatism's role in and contributions to American culture and history.*]

We will not understand pragmatism as an episode in American history so long as pragmatism is either stretched to cover all of America or confined to those of its formulations sufficiently fruitful philosophically to have found places in the history of Western philosophy. In the first instance, the tradition of Peirce, James, and Dewey is flattened into a style of thought characterized by voluntarism, practicality, moralism, relativism, an eye toward the future, a preference for action over contemplation, and other traits of the same degree of generality. Each of the traits commonly attributed to pragmatism can indeed be found at some level in the writings of one or more of the leading pragmatists. And, even if we now gasp ritualistically at the thought of attributing these traits to Americans "in general," there is no reason to doubt that these traits were among the intellectual ideals of a good many of the rank-and-file Yankees with whom scholars once tried to link James and his cerebral colleagues. Yet the obligation to characterize the pragmatists as representatives of America inhibits exploration of the relationship between the pragmatist philosophers and the more specific segments—chronological and social—of America in which the writings of the pragmatists appeared and demonstrably functioned. In the second instance—the confining of pragmatism to its philosophic contributions—the tradition is sharpened into a highly distinctive theory of meaning and truth to which the writings of other modern philosophers can be contrasted. Often this theory is projected as an ideal type toward which the pragmatists strived, but which they failed to fully articulate. In this view, the task of the scholar is to fill in the holes in the formulations of the pragmatists in order to complete and clarify their arguments. Even when the pragmatic theory of meaning and truth is made the subject of more authentically historical studies, in which the actual development of the ideas of one or more of the pragmatists is reconstructed, the mission of the scholar can be achieved with little attention to the constituency won among Americans by the work of the pragmatists.

The recognition that the intellectuals who rallied to pragmatism were preoccupied with the place of science in modern life is the point at which to begin an assessment of pragmatism's role in the lives of Americans who cared about it. The writings on meaning, truth, goodness, and other basic philosophical issues on account of which Peirce, James, and Dewey became known as pragmatists were the apex of a larger intellectual edifice constructed by these three men and their followers in response not only to the great epistemological and metaphysical questions of post-Kantian thought, but also to the desire for a way of life consistent with what they and their contemporaries variously perceived as the implications of modern science. Peirce, James, and Dewey were conspicuous leaders, among Americans, in the efforts of Western intellectuals to find and articulate such a way of life. That these efforts were so widespread as to constitute the framework for much of European and American intellectual history in the late nineteenth and early twentieth centuries is well known, as are the facts that ways of life as well as epistemologies were felt to be at issue and that the pragmatists were among America's most listened-to participants in this enterprise. Yet these aspects of the scene deserve more attention in the interpretation of pragmatism than historians have accorded them, for they largely define the specific setting in which Peirce, James, and Dewey gained constituencies beyond philosophy, were perceived as part of a single tradition, and thus functioned as related presences in the history of the United States.

Viewed in this setting, the pragmatists emerge as reflectors of, and powerful agents for, a distinctive cluster of assertions and hopes about how modern culture could be integrated and energized. The particular elements in this cluster were often articulated singly and in relation to other ideas by other moralists of the period, including some critical of pragmatism, but the combination of elements found in the writings of the pragmatists and their popularizers was nowhere else advanced more persistently and with more notice from educated Americans. Since the basic texts of Peirce, James, and Dewey were the raw materials out of which the pragmatic tradition was forged, I will use these texts as the basis of my account of the combination of elements peculiar to the pragmatists.

One element in this combination was a sense of the role of scientific method in a universe of change and uncertainty. The pragmatists were more concerned than were many of their contemporaries with the integrity and durability of *inquiry*, on the one hand, and the tentativeness, fallibility, and incompleteness of *knowledge* on the other. While they sometimes compared the body of existing knowledge favorably to the smaller amount available in the past, and while they often noted the superior reliability of empirically supported propositions over other propositions, the pragmatists were never among the leading celebrants of knowledge's solidity, vastness, and stability. It was rather to what they called the "spirit" of science, or its "method" and "attitude" that they looked for a foundation stable enough to support a modern culture. Knowledge was transient, and as such was another aspect of the universe of change through the experience of which the attitude of inquiry was, in itself, the most reliable single guide. Some of the pragmatists were more eager than others to see the knowledge available at a given historical moment applied vigorously to social, religious, and political life, but the priority of method as a cultural commitment was projected vividly in the works of Peirce, James, Dewey, and a host of followers.

This projection is easiest to illustrate in the case of Dewey, who was forever insisting that if only people could become scientific in the way they went about things, the potential for human fulfillment would be liberated from the bondage of a sterile, repressive, outrageously long-lived antiquity. "The future of our civilization depends upon the widening spread and deepening hold of the scientific habit of mind."[1] This assertion of Dewey's became a favorite epigram among his admirers[2] and expressed accurately, if blandly, the methodological emphasis of his thought. This emphasis was so tightly bound up with skepticism about the adequacy of existing and yet-to-be-discovered knowledge that Dewey's prescribed "scientific attitude" was defined *in terms of* a principled openness toward, and an enthusiastic search for, new and temporarily valid knowledge in a universe of constant change.[3] Willingness to accept and act upon the facts at hand would not satisfy Dewey as it had satisfied the many Victorian moralists eager to make people obey facts; Dewey's devotion was to the process of investigation itself.

So, too, was James's. The claim of some scientists to have virtually completed their task inspired James's proudest scorn; "our ignorance," he said, is "a sea."[4] His legendary assaults on the pretensions of science turned the supposed ideals of the scientific endeavor against the arrogance of contemporary scientists: James piously and passionately reminded them of the "scientific" imperative to inquire further, to remain critical of past findings, to remain free from dogmatism.[5] If T. H. Huxley, as has often been observed, turned the tables on established Christianity by claiming for Darwinian science a Protestant morality more strict than that of the church, so, too, did James turn the tables on the established science of Huxley's generation by claiming for psychical research an ideal of free inquiry more unflinching and open-minded than that of Huxley and W. K. Clifford. Scholars have made much of James's defense of religiously conventional and scientifically unorthodox beliefs, such as the conceivable reality of spirits; what needs more emphasis is what James did and did not do with such beliefs. He supported no movement to protect such beliefs from science; instead, he instituted what he regarded as a scientific investigation of the evidence on which these beliefs were supposedly founded.[6] While James developed a reputation as a hostile critic of the worldviews of many contemporary apologists for science, he also gained a reputation as a striking exemplar of the ideals of scientific inquiry.[7]

Peirce was more inclined than either James or Dewey to suspect that the object of knowledge was, technically speaking, finite,[8] but he too depicted inquiry as virtually endless and its results as unavoidably fallible. He could be as eloquent as James on "the paucity of scientific knowledge"[9] and on the sentiment expressed in his own, often quoted injunction, "Do not block the way of inquiry."[10] Peirce was unusual—even in an age of extravagant "scientism"—in the extremity and singularity with which he identified goodness and progress with science, and he was among the first admirers of science to focus this adulation explicitly on the community of investigators and on the common methodological commitments that enabled members of this community to correct both each other and the stock of propositions they took to be true.[11] It was in direct response to Peirce's vision of an eternally self-correcting community of inquiry that Royce "solved" *The Problem of Christianity* by urging the church to model itself on the scientific community.[12]

Yet it would be misleading to imply that Peirce's vision of the scientific community and its moral functions was widely noted beyond a few departments of philosophy; he was, by virtue of his great creativity and prolonged neglect, the Melville of American philosophy. The aspects of his work that did function decisively in the discourse of his generation and of the one immediately following his death in 1914 were those singled out by James and Dewey, particularly the aspect James in 1898 dubbed the "principle" of pragmatism.[13] This principle—to the much disputed substance of which we must now attend—connoted in all its formulations a willingness to treat knowledge as temporal and to treat method as both primary and enduring.

To take account of the practical consequences an object might have is the way to form a clear idea of it, Peirce had said in 1878 in "How to Make Our Ideas Clear." In what was to become the classic illustration of the pragmatic theory of meaning, Peirce analyzed in terms of this maxim the calling of a thing "hard." To be hard, a thing must be able to resist scratching by other substances; such "effects" constitute the "whole conception" of hardness. "There is absolutely no difference between a hard thing and a soft thing so long as they are not brought to the test," said Peirce, insisting, in effect, that the "qualities" often said to inhere in objects be translated into the behavior the objects manifest in rela-

tion to other objects.[14] The uncertainty of Peirce specialists even today about just what Peirce was trying to say[15]—what consequences were "practical," for example, and was the maxim a general one or designed only for science?—need not deflect us from identifying the essential freight that this proposal of Peirce's was made to carry in the development of the pragmatist movement once James launched it in 1898.[16]

To that movement no paper was more central than James's "What Pragmatism Means," in which he presented "Peirce's principle" as the basis for an entire philosophy. That philosophy was to be more scientific in outlook, James alleged, than philosophies, as a class of intellectual constructions, tended to be. Pragmatism's predecessors and rivals were too committed to one particular set or another of "results" of inquiry, such as the conclusion that the world is made up of "Energy" or that it is all contained within "the Absolute." Such philosophies employed merely "verbal solutions," reasoned from "fixed principles," built "closed systems," and fell victim to "dogma, artificiality, and the pretence of finality in truth." Pragmatism stood for less and was capable of doing more; it carried less baggage, was more autonomous, and was open to more possibilities. The pragmatic method of tracing the consequences of ideas operated in the manner of a hotel corridor—a metaphor James adopted from his Italian follower, Giovanni Papini—through which one might pass in order to get in and out of rooms representing a virtual infinity of intellectual activities.[17]

When James moved to the explicit statement of a theory of truth, he began with the observation that to modern science "laws" were at best "approximations," too numerous and too subject to "rival formulations" to enable us to view any of them as "absolutely a transcript of reality." Theories "may from some point of view be useful" by summarizing old facts and leading us to new ones. It was to this analysis of scientific knowledge that James connected the theory of truth he attributed to himself, to the British pragmatist F. C. S. Schiller, and to Dewey and his Chicago disciples. Truth in any realm was an "idea that will carry us prosperously from any one part of our experience to any other part, linking things satisfactorily, working securely, simplifying, saving labor; [it] is true for just so much, true in so far forth, true *instrumentally.*" Such sentences put James on the defensive with other philosophers, so he spent much time during his last years trying to elaborate and defend "this pragmatist talk about truths in the plural, about their utility and satisfactoriness, about the success with which they 'work,' etc."[18] Yet in all these disputes, including those involving Dewey and other pragmatists after James's death in 1910, one thing was never in doubt: whatever else the pragmatist theory of truth entailed, it carried with it the sense that truth was a condition that happened to an idea through the course of events as experienced and analyzed by human beings. This temporality of truth was basic even to the less publicized depiction by Peirce of truth as a "fated" opinion, as something that a community of investigators would eventually agree upon.[19] What was rejected everywhere in the movement was the notion of truth as "a stagnant property inherent in" an idea, apart from the process of its emergence in history and from its possession by human beings interacting contingently with each other and with the larger natural world.[20]

That this social and physical world was responsive to human purpose was a second conviction advanced by the pragmatist tradition. If one basic element in this tradition was a belief that inquiry itself could stabilize and sustain a culture for which truths could be only tentative and plural, another was the sense that inquiry could change the world. Not that the world altogether lacked resistance to human imagination and will; but neither was the world's structure so hard-and-fast as to force human purpose into headlong retreat with each new discovery of science. In contrast to the moralists who hailed or lamented the scientific enterprise as the exploration of a one-way street, down which orders for belief and conduct came from "nature," the pragmatic tradition carried a faith in inquiry's reconstructive capabilities in the most rigorous of the sciences and in everyday life.

This faith is consistent with the pragmatic approach to truth as a form of utility, but is not entailed by it. Ideas, in this view, are instruments that not only can become true by doing their job in inquiry, but can also transform the environment to which they are applied. This effect takes place most obviously in the improvement of medical and industrial techniques, but the effect was held by Dewey and his followers to operate throughout experience even at the cognitive level, in the knowing relation itself. For Dewey, the entire knowing process is a manipulative one in which inquirers seek to rearrange to their satisfaction whatever components of a given situation stimulated inquiry.[21] Peirce's account of inquiry as a response to doubt has sometimes been taken to imply a transformative role for inquiry, but Peirce drew back from such implications, and he was in any event no agent of their popularization. Dewey did the most to identify this reconstructive vision with pragmatism, while trying over a period of several decades to clarify what he meant by it.

In precisely what sense does inquiry "change" the various "situations" it is led to confront? How do we evaluate the claims to utility that may be advanced on behalf of various reconstructive solutions? It is a striking feature of the history of pragmatism that Dewey's most detailed answer to these questions appeared only in 1938, long after his more vague and question-begging pronouncements had helped win for his reconstruction-

ist vision a following greater than it has enjoyed during the more than forty years since he did his best to justify it philosophically.[22] Persons attracted to the vision were all along held in tow by a few prominent, easily apprehended assertions of Dewey's; the world, Dewey reassured his public, has been proven by the growth of science and invention to be sufficiently amenable to human ends to warrant yet more experimentation with it, particularly its previously neglected social and moral dimensions. Here the connection between pragmatism and early-twentieth-century reform[23] was at its closest, but Dewey's social engineering was only one example of pragmatism's confidence in the responsiveness of nature to human purpose. This confidence was equally hard to miss in James's "voluntarism."

James focused on the vitality of will versus outside forces in determining the life of the individual, but he also addressed the effect of human purpose on the universe outside the self. Not only did his formidable work in psychology assist vitally in the demolition of the passive mind of the British empirical tradition;[24] James's most popular essays continually asserted that "will" was an authentic force in the world. James was particularly reassuring about the role of purpose in the inquiries carried out by scientists; the phenomena of nature would ultimately decide an issue, but all the more decisively if scientists brought to their investigation—critically, to be sure—their own most intense hopes for a given outcome.[25]

The advancement of human purpose in the world through inquiry was not to be limited to professional scientists or even to philosophers. It was a mission and a fulfillment open to virtually anyone. The pragmatist tradition consisted also in this third basic element: the sense that inquiry was accessible on meaningful levels by the rank-and-file membership of an educated, democratic society. The pragmatists did not insist that all forms of inquiry were accessible to everyone, nor did they deny that inquiry was subject to a division of labor according to which people were sometimes dependent upon the expertise of others. Inquiry was a continuum of investigatory, reconstructive endeavors exemplified above all by the work of Galileo and his scientific successors, but available for practice in appropriate contexts by any citizen capable of assimilating its spirit.

Dewey translated so many of life's activities—humble and exalted—into the terms of inquiry that Bertrand Russell once accused him of being unable to distinguish between the work of a scientist and that of a bricklayer.[26] Dewey did seek to distinguish between the controlled, reflective, experimental inquiry characteristic of specialists and the common-sense thinking of everyman, but even then he insisted on their similarity and urged a program of public education to render common sense more effective by closing the gap between it and experimental science. James, too, emphasized the continuity between the intellectual life of the average soul, on the one hand, and James's own vocation as a scientist and philosopher on the other. Always an acerbic critic of the elitist pretensions of academic professionals, James urged the laity to take on the most demanding intellectual problems it could, and to adopt in their pursuit the pragmatic method long practiced without hoopla in the laboratory and now characteristic of the best philosophers.[27]

No index of the accessibility of inquiry was more dramatic than its availability to people wanting answers to ethical questions. Not only were social scientists encouraged to extend to the social realm the search for facts pioneered by practitioners of the physical sciences; persons of any station confronting issues in politics and morals were encouraged to face them "scientifically." The continuum of inquiry as depicted by Dewey, and less explicitly by James, included ethical choices as well as the explanation of physical and social phenomena;[28] the pragmatic tradition was proverbially reluctant to make what were, to other philosophic traditions, all-too-clear distinctions between the good and the true, between value and fact. This reluctance stimulated a vast polemical literature, in which critics generally insisted that the formulations of pragmatists begged the standard philosophical questions while the pragmatists, especially Dewey, argued that these questions, as traditionally conceived, were simply outdated. Although Dewey made a determined, and increasingly technical, effort to perform his own philosophical analysis of ethical judgment in terms of "inquiry," his work also served to reinforce a feeling James had first inspired in admirers of pragmatism that many of philosophy's standard questions were irrelevant. These admirers might cheer Dewey along as he fought his learned opposition, but they knew that a *little* philosophy—provided it was, like their own, the right philosophy—was enough. The active life of inquiry, it was clear, needed to wait upon no guidelines from the cloistered men who sat and talked about "is" and "ought."

The pragmatists' combination of senses of what the possibilities were for a modern, scientific culture seems at first glance very general indeed. Yet it was specific enough to distinguish pragmatism from a number of other, highly visible signposts even within the intellectual neighborhood populated by enthusiasts about science and its cultural contributions. Pragmatism's anti-elitist bias distinguished it, for example, from the program for behaviorist research and social reorganization popularized by John B. Watson,[29] whose understanding of how the human mind worked was both similar to Dewey's and loudly applauded by many followers of both James and Dewey. Socialism, too, was offered frequently in the name of science, and it attracted some pragmatists when the latter were led to think of social-

ism as appropriately experimental and democratic,[30] but the pragmatist tradition's emphasis on the continuity of inquiry cut against the grain of class-based, revolutionary socialism. Russell's "A Free Man's Worship"—one of the most widely cited testaments of the 1910s and 1920s—celebrated an ascetic's renunciation of human hope in the face of a hard, hostile, science-discovered world.[31] Sinclair Lewis's *Arrowsmith* was built around the precious unattainability, by any but the most superhuman of heroes, of the scientific idea.[32] Nobel physicist Robert A. Millikan's *Science and the New Civilization* assured the nation's Babbitts that their conservative social values were in no way threatened by scientific knowledge or inquiry.[33] Innumerable industrialists, engineers, and medical professionals filled popular and learned magazines with adulation of past and future technological progress, without hinting that the imperatives of inquiry itself might come to occupy the spiritual landscape once supervised by the Christian church.[34] The imposing bulk and permanence of existing knowledge was incandescently hailed, and mastery of its detailed contents earnestly prescribed, by a multitude of publicists and spokesmen for scientific societies.[35] Oliver Wendell Holmes, Jr., linked adulation of scientific method with serene acquiescence in the often cruel operations of an unresponsive world.[36]

The pragmatist tradition that distinguished itself in this context, and that was yet more distinctive when contrasted to outlooks skeptical of science, was constituted by more than the careers of Peirce, James, and Dewey. Until now I have made attributions to this tradition exclusively on the basis of the most extensively absorbed texts of these three men because these texts provided the adhesive to make pragmatism a tradition: from these texts the less original pragmatists drew inspiration, and to these texts educated Americans went when they wanted to confront "pragmatism." But the tradition is manifest not exclusively in these classical texts; it is found also in the writings of those who sought to summarize, elaborate upon, defend, and sympathetically analyze the contributions of the three masters. Such writings, indeed, were instrumental in establishing the canon of pragmatist classics and in sustaining a particular sense of what was common to thinkers as diverse as Peirce, James, and Dewey.[37] Attention to such writings can confirm or correct an impression of where pragmatism's center of gravity was located as pragmatism went beyond its great texts and as it transcended departments of philosophy.

If, for example, Joseph Ratner's introduction to the Modern Library Giant of 1939, *Intelligence in the Modern World: John Dewey's Philosophy,* were difficult to assimilate into what is here characterized as the pragmatist tradition, one would want to quickly revise that characterization. Ratner's 241-page introduction serves as both an attempted summary of Dewey's thought and a polemical assertion of that thought's correctness. The essay has never been taken seriously as a contribution to the philosophical refinement of pragmatism, as have the works of C. I. Lewis and George Herbert Mead, for example.[38] Nor should it so be taken. Yet it is a crucial historical document as a representative reading of Dewey and as, in turn, an agent of this reading's dissemination. So widely circulated was this book that yellowing, pencil-annotated copies can be found today in used bookstores far from Chicago and Columbia in some of the remotest areas of the United States.

Galileo's discovery of a "*general* method, available and adaptable for use by all . . . no matter what the area," is for Ratner, as for Dewey, the central moment in history. For three centuries this discovery was taken advantage of only by a handful of people, mostly those practicing the physical sciences. Resistance by philosophers to the Galilean general method of experimental inquiry is "as bad a case of cultural lag as one could ever hope to come across." At last, Dewey has come along to lay out the implications of Galileo's breakthrough for "philosophy" in the most comprehensive sense of the term, including our understanding of and prescriptions for everyday life. In so doing, Dewey has performed for the modern world the tasks performed for the ancient world by the great Athenian philosophers, explains Ratner. Much of Ratner's time, therefore, goes into demonstrating how "the two greatest of Dewey's contemporaries," Russell and Alfred North Whitehead, despite their eagerness to take account of scientific knowledge and method, remain mired in prescientific ways of thinking: they have not fully substituted the Galilean experimental attitude for the ancient "quest for certainty." They have even failed to see how fleeting a presence our current knowledge is: Russell, for example, took Newtonian physics as given in 1914 and in 1927 took Einsteinian physics as given.[39]

Ratner's Dewey is fully consistent with the outlook of the two most prolific and popularly read interpreters of pragmatism, Horace M. Kallen and Sidney Hook.[40] Kallen and Hook have long been recognized as elaborators, respectively, of James's more individualistic, unsystematic approach to the vocation of inquiry and of Dewey's more social and organized approach. Yet the careers of Kallen and Hook illustrate how difficult the problem of pragmatism looks when it is addressed in American history rather than in Western philosophy. Both of these writers were trained as philosophers by their respective masters, and both addressed some of the same technical questions involving "truth" and "meaning" that their mentors did. Yet what Kallen and Hook wrote about these questions did not make a lasting mark on the course of philosophical argument; hence, their writings are not, as are C. I. Lewis's and Mead's, given detailed and sober treatment in philoso-

phers' histories of pragmatism. One need find no fault whatever with these histories to observe that Kallen and Hook, in their exceptionally long careers as self-defined "pragmatists," are fundamentally constitutive of pragmatism as a presence in America. The ideas attributed above to the founders of pragmatism are easily found in the writings of Kallen and Hook, often offered from forums of culturally strategic importance. Kallen wrote the article on pragmatism for the *Encyclopedia of the Social Sciences*—a monument in so many ways to the ideals of pragmatists—where he performed the standard equation of pragmatism with science and democracy.[41]

No one has ever mistaken Herbert Croly for a philosopher, nor the *New Republic* for a journal of philosophy. Yet Croly and his magazine have been routinely denoted as "pragmatist" for years, as have been Croly's *New Republic* associates, Walter Weyl and Walter Lippmann. The sense in which these three men were pragmatists is left implicit in Charles Forcey's meticulous and extremely helpful monograph on the trio, *The Crossroads of Liberalism*, in which the appellation is regularly applied.[42] Yet the intellectual portraits that Forcey constructs do, indeed, make Croly, Lippmann, and Weyl unambiguous participants in the pragmatist tradition as I have characterized it. The writings of the three confirm the impression left by Forcey. Lippmann's influential *Drift and Mastery*, for example, was a vehicle for precisely the combination of hopes and aspirations found in the classic texts of the pragmatist philosophers.[43]

Lippmann later soured on all three themes in this combination, but the tradition was carried on by other publicists and academics of various affiliations, including historians Frederick Barry and James Harvey Robinson, Senator Paul H. Douglas, and the popular radio personality and lecturer Lyman Bryson.[44] Bryson, who wrote a number of *Drift-and-Mastery*-like books of cultural criticism, taught at Columbia Teachers College, where colleagues of his had institutionalized the pragmatist tradition in the early 1920s. There some 35,000 teachers were trained by William Heard Kilpatrick, a devoted if vulgarizing disciple of Dewey who relentlessly emphasized "method over content."[45]

The pragmatist tradition, then, was considerably more concentrated in structure and constituency than have been the general tendencies—practicality, voluntarism, moralism, flexibility, openness—one or more of which have often been used to characterize James Madison, Benjamin Franklin, or John Winthrop as pragmatists. If the tradition was amorphous compared to the clearly defined philosophical work that forms the tradition's most easily identified core, this larger tradition was nevertheless more specific and concrete than the stereotypical American traits that informed some of the work of the pragmatists and motivated some Americans to identify themselves with pragmatism. Pragmatism became a tradition in the discourse of American intellectuals as the work of James, initially, then of Dewey and to some extent of Peirce, was perceived to constitute a rudimentary "philosophy of life" providing a coherent orientation toward the ill-defined but undoubtedly massive and consequential entity these intellectuals called "science."

So considered, pragmatism had a lot to offer, including the supremely important fact that it did not try to offer too much. It was so spare that one could believe in it while entertaining a whole range of other beliefs, ancient and modern, idiosyncratic and conventional. Hadn't Papini said pragmatism was not so much a philosophy as a way of doing without one?[46] There was something to this, even if only because people sympathetic to pragmatism so much enjoyed quoting it. Critics also quoted it, voicing thereby what was eventually to become the standard critique of pragmatism: that pragmatism was too shallow to accomplish anything and that its adherents had mistaken vacancy for liberation. But liberating it undoubtedly did feel to many American intellectuals. Pragmatism demanded very few commitments at a time when the need to have "a philosophy" was still felt by people who were sensitive to the risk of being burned by too large and too long a hold on beliefs of greater scope. Hadn't the Darwinian revolution shown how rapidly our assumptions about the world could change? And hadn't the increasingly discredited efforts of some thinkers to build out of "evolution" a comprehensive system now confirmed the danger of taking a philosophy too far? Wasn't the urban, industrial order of 1910 more different from American life in 1860 than the latter had been from life in 1810? Pragmatism promised a small but versatile supply of insights with which to prepare oneself for an existence in which more changes were no doubt on the way.

If the inevitability of change was to be successfully faced by society as a whole, a philosophy of limited scope was surely needed by the class of managers and bureaucrats assigned the task of supervising American public affairs. It can scarcely be a coincidence that the age in which pragmatism became popular was also the age in which American intellectuals were unprecedentedly engaged by the managerial ideal.[47] Fully consistent with this ideal was the elevation of "bold, persistent experimentation" to the level of a principle in the rhetoric of the New Deal.[48] Spare as pragmatism was, it was fleshy enough to support this much admired principle, to sustain an optimistic perspective on science, and to reinforce certain of the least contested, most familiar, and most security-providing ideals in American culture.

One such ideal concerned "action." By closing the gap between thinking and doing, pragmatism preferred ac-

tion to passivity wherever the choice presented itself. Method was emphasized over bodies of knowledge, and whatever potential for stasis knowledge might have was undercut by repeated reminders of its temporality. Humanity's relation to the universe was depicted in terms of the purposive action people might employ to affect their fate. The activity of inquiry was something confined not to a few—with the rest of the world passively looking on—but opened to as many persons as could meet the challenge of performing it.

Pragmatism was also "democratic." Not only was its method announced as widely accessible and as an engine of improvement; the very practice of that method was supposed to be open, undogmatic, tolerant, self-corrective, and thus an easily recognized extension of the standard liberal ideology articulated by Mill and cherished by so many late-nineteenth-century Americans. Pragmatism was also "moralistic," "voluntaristic," and "practical." It is no great trick to go on down the list, finding these dispositions in the writings of the pragmatists and their popularizers *as these writings specifically advance* the cluster of ideas by means of which pragmatism became a presence in American intellectual life. What needs to be emphasized is that these dispositions had a function in pragmatism other than to provide the terms for supererogatory rhetoric and to be crudely mirrored in a theory of meaning and truth: these dispositions were focused and put to use by pragmatism's capabilities as an orientation toward science at the level of "philosophy of life."

This emphasis need not prevent the recognition that theories of meaning and of truth can be important to large numbers of people and that the pragmatic theory was indeed a source of pragmatism's appeal. When James said that truth was no "stagnant property," but something that happened to ideas in the course of a particular sequence of events, one did not have to be a philosopher to take an interest in the issue. That meanings, truths, and goods were somehow functions of relationships, and not absolutes written into the structure of being, was of course an arresting concept. But the power of such concepts to obtain and keep widespread attention derived in part from the context in which they were advanced. This is to say that pragmatism's answers to philosophical questions, in the narrow sense of the term, gained interest and plausibility among nonphilosophers because these answers were, like "democracy" and "action," built into a "philosophy" in the broad, Emersonian sense, and one that was equipped with an apparently viable orientation toward science.

Pragmatism as a presence in the discourse of American intellectuals consisted essentially of three interpenetrating layers: a theory of meaning and truth that served to flag the movement, a cluster of assertions and hopes about the basis for culture in an age of science, and a range of general images stereotypical of American life. Pragmatism no doubt meant many things to different people, and enabled people to cope with a variety of concerns; yet it is of this three-layered structure that we are justified in thinking when we refer to the pragmatist tradition as manifest in the first half of the twentieth century.

To so regard pragmatism is not to insist that the historical significance of Peirce, James, or Dewey is exhausted by each one's participation in pragmatism. Much of what Peirce wrote about "signs" and what James wrote about the psychology of religion, for example, has flourished well outside of this tradition and can claim attention philosophically as well as historically. Nor does this view of pragmatism insist that, with its decline in popularity during the 1940s and after, the pragmatic themes in the writings of "the three" were rendered so anachronistic as to mock the efforts of more recent thinkers to learn something from them. Few American philosophers can claim to be more vividly contemporary than Richard Rorty, for example, who addresses and appreciates Dewey from a perspective that Croly would find hard to recognize.[49] If pragmatism has a future, it will probably look very different from its past, and the two may not even share a name.

To bring the problem of pragmatism in American history down to a question of what pragmatism did for two generations of intellectuals may seem a narrow construction of the problem. Yet this modesty enables a more authentic pragmatism to come more clearly into view. The relations between this pragmatism and both the history of philosophy and the history of the United States are then more easily identified. If "pragmatic" ideas about meaning, truth, and goodness were latent in those parts of American culture discovered by Alexis de Tocqueville and explored by Louis Hartz and Daniel J. Boorstin,[50] these ideas remained mute and inglorious until explicitly developed by certain members of a particular, science-preoccupied generation of intellectuals. These ideas, moreover, did not become part of the public culture of the United States until spread by these same intellectuals and their immediate successors. The pragmatic theory of meaning and truth could not come into being until it was rendered in specific language, and it could not become a cultural possession until that language was taught to people with a will to use it. Since this language was worked out and popularized by late-nineteenth and early-twentieth-century American intellectuals, it is in the discourse of these intellectuals that the problem of pragmatism primarily resides. The pragmatism found in that discourse performed a number of political, philosophic, and religious acts that historians have only begun to assess. Not the least of these acts was the persuading of a great many people that pragmatism was an emblem for America.

POSTSCRIPT 1995: A LOOK AHEAD

Historians should know better than to look ahead. The article of 1980, reprinted above, offered one sentence about the future of pragmatism, and it soon proved to be more wrong than right. "If pragmatism has a future, it will probably look very different from its past, and the two may not even share a name." Fourteen years later pragmatism's name is invoked in a host of contexts, mostly by people who claim to be inspired by the classical pragmatists, and who see themselves as reaffirming doctrines inherited from them. Today's pragmatists, found as often in our faculties of law,[51] English,[52] history,[53] sociology,[54] and religion[55] as in our departments of philosophy, are less inclined than were their predecessors to identify science as a basis for culture, but these pragmatists of our own time are too directly engaged with the texts of Peirce, James, and Dewey to vindicate my prediction that pragmatism's future would look "very different" from its past. One could debate in detail, to be sure, the degree of difference between the old pragmatism and the new, but I prefer to concede that my conjecture about the future was mistaken.

This concession helps to clear a space in which I can respond with more confidence to the editors' request that I look ahead. I will do so historiographically. I want to suggest that an interesting question for some future historian will be this: How and why did so many American intellectuals of the 1980s and 1990s come to believe that "pragmatism" was a desirable label for their ideas, and why were these intellectuals eager to establish connections between themselves and Peirce, James, and Dewey? I will not try to answer this question here, but I want to point out that this inquiry is very close to the one I attempted for the first half of the twentieth century in my article of 1980. Behind this question in regard to both epochs is my presumption that pragmatism is a construction, rather than a natural affinity between the ideas, texts, and careers said to be involved in it. Its character is not to be taken for granted, but to be explained historically.

The "old" pragmatism was built in the context of intense concern about the cultural promise of science. This pragmatism, as I have tried to show, was propelled by three basic assertions: that inquiry itself is a discipline that could stabilize and sustain a modern, "scientific" culture for which truths could be only tentative and plural; that the social and physical world is responsive to human purpose; and that inquiry is an activity open to the rank-and-file members of an educated, democratic society. These assertions bonded very easily with the two phenomena most often flagged by the term, "pragmatism": a) the theories of meaning, truth, and goodness contributed to philosophy by Peirce, James, and Dewey; and b) the impatience with principles, privilege, stasis, and tradition stereotypically attributed to

Americans in general. Hence, if we want to assess the character of pragmatism as a broad movement among American intellectuals from the 1910s through the 1940s, we would do well to see this movement as more than a response in peculiarly American terms to some of the classical issues in philosophy; this movement was also a specific response to contemporary uncertainties and yearnings about science's cultural capabilities. One could easily break down this movement into a "philosophy" and the "cultural motives" people had for appreciating it. I have intentionally blurred this conventional distinction in order to emphasize what made pragmatism into so powerful a movement: the sense that the philosophy of pragmatism itself directly embodied, rather than merely served, a culture geared to science.

Selected utterances of Peirce, James, and Dewey were the raw materials out of which pragmatism was constructed and maintained during the era stretching from the 1910s through the 1940s. So it is today, but the favored passages are not always the same, the work they are made to do is sometimes different, and the rival persuasions against which they are invoked vary considerably. The self-consciousness with which some of today's pragmatists construct a "pragmatic tradition" suitable to present purposes is perhaps the most striking point of contrast between the contemporary discourse about pragmatism and that of only forty years ago. Discussions of American pragmatism as late as midcentury still conveyed a belief that there existed in history a genuine pragmatic tradition that could be discovered, assessed, and critically renewed. Today, some of pragmatism's most prominent champions are quick to admit that they are all but making it up: they are designating as pragmatists those past thinkers with whom they feel the most affinity. An example of this approach to the study of pragmatism is Cornel West's *The American Evasion of Philosophy,* which includes Lionel Trilling, C. Wright Mills, W. E. B. Dubois, and Reinhold Niebuhr—along with many of the usual suspects—within a "genealogy" of pragmatism offered candidly, if somewhat immodestly, as a series of antecedents to West himself.[56] One need not find fault with West in order to identify his work as a salient source for some future historical study of how pragmatism was constructed in the 1980s and 1990s.

Such a study is likely to concentrate on two concerns felt by many American intellectuals in the wake of post-1968 French thought popular in the United States. One concern has to do with democracy as a political ideal, and the other with knowledge as a goal of inquiry. Although it was easy to discern antiauthoritarian elements in the work of Foucault, Lyotard, and Derrida, just where democracy came in was not always apparent. But pragmatism, especially as associated with Dewey and his followers, was at least forthright in trying to vindicate and promote democracy.[57] Pragmatism was also understood to combine a strong sensitivity to the contingent, constructed character of knowledge with a gut sense that the objects of knowledge were capable of putting up at least some resistance to human constructions.[58] Although the newly popular French thinkers could, again, be read as sharing this suspicion that knowledge was more than the will-to-power, their emphasis was surely on the latter. Pragmatism, whatever else it might be construed to be, was at the very least a charter to critically update these old Englightenment ideals in relation to the experiences and sensitivities that had, by the end of the twentieth century, given credibility to postmodernist critiques.

Notes

1. John Dewey, "Science as Subject-Matter and as Method," *Science* 36 (January 28, 1910): 127.

2. It is quoted without specific citation, for example, as the epigram to Leo E. Saidla and Warren E. Gibbs, eds., *Science and the Scientific Mind* (New York: Mcgraw Hill, 1930).

3. John Dewey, *The Influence of Darwin on Philosophy and Other Essays in Contemporary Thought* (New York: Henry Holt, 1910), 8-9, 19, 55-57, 70-72; John Dewey, *Reconstruction in Philosophy* (New York: Holt, 1920), 40, 54, 60-61, 67, 175-77; John Dewey, *The Quest for Certainty: A Study of the Relation of Knowledge and Action* (New York: Putnam, 1929), 99-101, 192-94, 228, 251, 296; John Dewey, *A Common Faith* (New Haven, Conn.: Yale University Press, 1934), 26, 32-33, 39.

4. William James, *The Will to Believe and Other Essays in Popular Philosophy* (New York: Holt, 1897), 54.

5. Ibid., x, xii-xiii, 7-10, 14, 18-19, 53-54, 323-27.

6. Ibid., 299-327.

7. Walter Lippmann, "An Open Mind: William James," *Everybody's Magazine,* 23 (December 1910): 800-801; Robert H. Lowie, "Science," in *Civilization in the United States: An Inquiry by Thirty Americans,* ed. Harold E. Stearns (New York: Henry Holt, 1922), 152-53; T. V. Smith, "The Scientific Way of Life with William James as Guide," in T. V. Smith, *The Philosophic Way of Life* (New York, 1934), 69-110.

8. For an interesting discussion of this problem in Peirce, see Nicholas Rescher, *Peirce's Philosophy of Science: Critical Studies in His Philosophy of Induction and Scientific Method* (South Bend, Ind.: University of Notre Dame Press, 1978), 19-39.

9. Charles Sanders Peirce, *Collected Papers of Charles Sanders Peirce,* ed. Charles Hartshorne,

Paul Weiss, and Arthur W. Burks (8 vols., Cambridge, Mass.: Harvard University Press, 1931-1958), 1.116-20.

10. This is emphatically stated in ibid., 1.135.

11. Ibid., 5.311. This aspect of Peirce has been helpfully called to the attention of historians by R. Jackson Wilson's essay, "Charles Sanders Peirce: The Community of Inquiry," in R. Jackson Wilson, *In Quest of Community: Social Philosophy in the United States, 1860-1920* (New York: Oxford University Press, 1968), 32-59. See also Jakob Liszka, "Community in C. S. Peirce: Science as a Means and as an End," *Transactions of the Charles S. Peirce Society,* 14 (Fall 1978): 305-21.

12. Josiah Royce, *The Problem of Christianity,* ed. John E. Smith (New York, 1968), 404-05. Peirce's direct influence on this crucial work of Royce's is clarified by Bruce Kuklick, *Josiah Royce: An Intellectual Biography* (Indianapolis: Hackett, 1972), esp. 214-15, 235.

13. William James, "Philosophical Conceptions and Practical Results," in William James, *Collected Essays and Reviews* (New York: Holt, 1920), 406-37, esp. 410.

14. Peirce, *Collected Papers,* 5.403.

15. According to H. S. Thayer, Peirce's maxim "is probably the unclearest recommendation for how to make our ideas clear in the history of philosophy." Thayer, *Meaning and Action: A Critical History of Pragmatism* (Indianapolis: Bobbs-Merrill, 1968), 87. See also Charles Morris, *Pragmatic Movement in American Philosophy* (New York: Braziller, 1970), 20-23; John E. Smith, *Purpose and Thought: The Meaning of Pragmatism* (New Haven, Conn.: Yale University Press, 1978), 18-32, 35; Elizabeth Flower and Murray G. Murphey, *A History of Philosophy in America* (2 vols., New York: G. P. Putnam, 1977), vol. 2, 590.

16. For a useful chronology of the development of pragmatism as a movement and a sketch of steps antecedent to this development, see Max H. Fisch, "American Pragmatism Before and After 1898," *American Philosophy from Edwards to Quine,* ed. Robert W. Shahan and Kenneth R. Merrill (Norman: University of Oklahoma Press, 1977), 78-110.

17. William James, *Pragmatism: A New Name for Some Old Ways of Thinking* (New York: Longmans 1907), 48, 51-54.

18. Ibid., 55-58, 67, 197-236.

19. Less publicized among nonphilosophers, this depiction is very much the stuff of debate among philosophers assessing the pragmatists. Peirce's relevant texts include *Collected Papers,* 5.407, 565.

20. James, *Pragmatism,* 201. See also William James, *The Meaning of Truth: A Sequel to "Pragmatism"* (New York: Longmans, 1909), v-vi. For help in sorting out the various versions of the pragmatic theory of truth, see Gertrude Ezorsky, "Pragmatic Theory of Truth," in *Encyclopedia of Philosophy,* ed. Paul Edwards (8 vols., New York: Macmillan, 1967), vol. 6, 427-30; H. Standish Thayer, "Introduction" in James, *The Meaning of Truth* (Cambridge, 1975), xi-xlvi; Smith, *Purpose and Thought,* 32-33, 50-77.

21. John Dewey, "The Need for a Recovery of Philosophy," in John Dewey et al., *Creative Intelligence: Essays in the Pragmatic Attitude* (New York: Holt, 1917), 48-50; Dewey, *Reconstruction in Philosophy,* 112-13, 121-22, 177; Dewey, *Quest for Certainty,* 3, 24-25, 85-86, 103-5, 204-5.

22. John Dewey, *Logic: The Theory of Inquiry* (New York: Macmillan, 1938). How differently the history of pragmatism looks to a historian from the way it looks to a philosopher is shown by the eagerness of philosophers to overlook the forty years of mushy work Dewey did in this area in order to focus on his most rigorous, climactic work. See Thayer, *Meaning and Action,* 190-99, and Smith, *Purpose and Thought,* 96-112. This approach is understandable if one's aim is to recover the completed structure of Dewey's philosophy; the approach makes less sense if one wants to understand the living tradition that Dewey had built before his *Logic* appeared.

23. The connection is emphasized by Morton White, *Social Thought in America: The Revolt Against Formalism* (New York: Columbia University Press, 1949); Eric F. Goldman, *Rendezvous with Destiny: A History of Modern American Reform* (New York: Vintage, 1952), 119-24; and most of the references to pragmatism that still appear in survey textbooks of American history.

24. William James, *The Principles of Psychology* (2 vols., New York: Holt, Rinehart, and Winston, 1890). See also the discussion of this work in John Wild, *The Radical Empiricism of William James* (Garden City, N.Y.: Doubleday, 1969), 1-262.

25. James, *Will to Believe,* 21, 92-93, 130.

26. Bertrand Russell, "Dewey's New Logic," in *The Philosophy of John Dewey,* ed. Paul Arthur Schilpp (Evanston, Ill.: Open Court, 1939), 143-56.

27. James, *Pragmatism,* 43-81.

28. Dewey, *Reconstruction in Philosophy,* 161-86; Dewey, *Quest for Certainty,* 254-86; James, *Pragmatism,* 75-76.

29. John B. Watson, *Behaviorism* (New York: People's Institute, 1925).

30. This was particularly true in the 1930s, when Dewey himself sometimes supported socialist candidates for public office.

31. Bertrand Russell, *Mysticism and Logic and Other Essays* (New York: Doubleday, 1917), 46-57.

32. Sinclair Lewis, *Arrowsmith* (New York: Signet, 1925).

33. Robert A. Millikan, *Science and the New Civilization* (New York: Charles Scribner's Sons, 1930).

34. See, for example, Henry S. Pritchett, "Science (1857-1907)," *Atlantic Monthly,* (November 1907): 613-25.

35. See, for example, the numerous publications during the 1920s of Edwin E. Slosson, including Edwin E. Slosson, *Chats on Science* (New York: The Century Company, 1924).

36. Oliver Wendell Holmes, Jr., *Collected Legal Papers* (New York: Little, Brown, 1920). Holmes was often claimed as a prophet of the pragmatist tradition, and it is a mark of the strength of this tradition that such claims went unchallenged for so long. Of the many warm accounts of Holmes as a "liberal" and as a "pragmatist," the most eloquent is Henry Steele Commager, *The American Mind: An Interpretation of American Thought and Character Since the 1880's* (New Haven, Conn.: Yale University Press, 1950), 385-90. For a reading of Holmes more representative of the scholarship of the last twenty years, see Yosal Rogat, "The Judge as Spectator," *University of Chicago Law Review* 31 (Winter 1964): 213-56. See also G. Edward White, "The Rise and Fall of Justice Holmes," *University of Chicago Law Review.* (Fall 1971), 51-77.

37. The recognition that Peirce, James, and Dewey shared something important philosophically was first promoted by James himself, and it was acknowledged almost as readily by Dewey as it was resisted by Peirce. This much is often said in histories of pragmatism; what deserves more attention is the process by which the idea of single "American Pragmatism" was kept alive after James's death, especially during the 1920s and 1930s. Dewey and Dewey's followers played a very large role in this process and helped to persuade most Americans who took an interest in the matter that Dewey's work was the logical culmination of the pragmatism of Peirce and of James. So it is that one can responsibly analyze "pragmatism" as a presence in American intellectual life without taking up the texts of C. I. Lewis or of the later Royce; elements in their work that a discerning historian *of philosophy* might call "pragmatic" simply were not assimilated into the tradition constructed by American intellectuals under the dominating influence of Dewey. For a document of Dewey's that is representative of the process, see "The Development of American Pragmatism," in John Dewey, *Philosophy and Civilization* (New York: G. P. Putnam's Sons, 1931), 13-35.

38. Lucid, brief analyses of C. I. Lewis and George Herbert Mead in the context of the work of Peirce, James, and Dewey can be found in Thayer, *Meaning and Action.* Although Mead has recently enjoyed a considerable vogue in several of the human sciences, he was not widely known beyond philosophy prior to his death in 1931, except in the circles of "Chicago social science." For Mead in that setting, see Egbert Parnell Rucker, *Chicago Pragmatists* (Minneapolis: University of Minnesota Press, 1959). Lewis was very much a philosopher's philosopher from the onset of his career in the 1910s through his death in 1964; his role as an examplar of professionalism in philosophy is discussed ably in Kuklick, *The Rise of American Philosophy: Cambridge, Massachusetts, 1860-1930* (New Haven, Conn.: Yale University Press, 1977). For a cogent and illuminating account of Lewis's philosophic work, see ibid., 533-62. Cf. Flower and Murphey, *History of Philosophy in America,* Holt, vol. 2, 891-958.

39. Joseph Ratner, "Introduction to John Dewey's Philosophy," in *Intelligence in the Modern World: John Dewey's Philosophy,* ed. Joseph Ratner (New York: Random House, 1939), 5, 57, 61, 115, 187, 227, 241.

40. Horace M. Kallen began writing articles about James and about pragmatism in 1910, contributed in 1917 to Dewey's pivotal anthology, *Creative Intelligence,* edited in 1925 the Modern Library edition of James's writings, and was involved in numerous symposia, *Festschriften,* and commemorative volumes honoring James and Dewey in later years. See Dewey et al., *Creative Intelligence,* 409-67; *The Philosophy of William James: Drawn from His Work,* ed. Horace M. Kallen (New York: Holt, 1925), 1-55; Horace M. Kallen, "John Dewey and the Spirit of Pragmatism," in *John Dewey: Philosopher of Science and Freedom,* ed. Sidney Hook (New York: Holt, 1950), 3-46. *Festschriften* for Kallen himself were meeting grounds for keepers of the pragmatist flame. See, for example, Sidney Ratner, ed., *Vision and Action: Essays in Honor of Horace M. Kallen on*

His 70th Birthday (New Brunswick, N.J.: Rutgers University Press, 1953). Sidney Hook's operations began with Sidney Hook, *The Metaphysics of Pragmatism* (Chicago: Open Court, 1927). His other writings included *John Dewey: An Intellectual Portrait* (New York: John Day and Co., 1939). Hook also had a tour of duty similar to Kallen's on the symposia-*Festschrift* circuit of the 1940s and 1950s. For a good example of Hook's writings as they consolidate and interpret the pragmatist tradition, see "The Centrality of Method," in *The American Pragmatists: Selected Writings,* ed. Milton R. Konvitz and Gail Kennedy (Cleveland, 1960), 360-79. The essay begins with an epigram from Kallen. Kallen, who was widely known also for his exposition of "cultural pluralism," died in 1974; Hook was one of the pragmatist tradition's most forceful, capable, and visible defenders until his death in 1989.

41. Horace M. Kallen, "Pragmatism," *Encyclopedia of the Social Sciences,* ed. Edwin R. A. Seligman and Alvin Johnson (15 vols., New York: Macmillan, 1930-1935), vol. 12, 307-11.

42. Charles Forcey, *The Crossroads of Liberalism: Croly, Weyl, Lippmann and the Progressive Era, 1900-1925* (New York: Oxford University Press, 1961).

43. Walter Lippmann, *Drift and Mastery: An Attempt to Diagnose the Current Unrest* (New York: Macmillan, 1914). For an effort to determine this text's historical significance, see David A. Hollinger, "Science and Anarchy: Walter Lippmann's *Drift and Mastery,*" *American Quarterly* 29 (Winter 1977), 463-75.

44. Frederick Barry, *The Scientific Habit of Thought: An Informal Discussion of the Source and Character of Dependable Knowledge* (New York, 1927); James Harvey Robinson, *The Mind in the Making: The Relation of Intelligence to Social Reform* (New York, 1921); Paul H. Douglas, "The Absolute, the Experimental Method, and Horace Kallen," in Ratner, ed., *Vision and Action,* 39-55; Lyman Bryson, *The New Prometheus* (New York: Macmillan, 1941); Lyman Bryson, *Science and Freedom* (New York, 1947).

45. For William Heard Kilpatrick's career at Teachers College, see Lawrence A. Cremin, *The Transformation of the School: Progressivism in American Education, 1876-1957* (New York: Macmillan, 1961), 215-24. Another work, although presented as in part a history, is richly revealing as a statement of the "progressive" educational philosophy inspired by Dewey. See John L. Childs, *American Pragmatism and Education: An Interpretation and Criticism* (New York: Macmillan, 1956).

46. Papini's aphorisms about pragmatism, published in Italian, became known to Americans primarily through James's own rendering of them. See William James, "G. Papini and the Pragmatist Movement in Italy," *Journal of Philosophy, Psychology, and Scientific Methods* 3 (June 21, 1906): 337-41.

47. Of the many accounts of the rise of this idea, the most discussed is Robert H. Wiebe, *The Search for Order, 1877-1920* (New York: Hill and Wang, 1967), 133-63. See also William E. Nelson, "Officeholding and Powerwielding: An Analysis of the Relationship Between Structure and Style in American Administrative History," *Law and Society Review* 10 (Winter 1976): 188-233.

48. R. G. Tugwell, *The Brains Trust* (New York: Macmillan, 1968), 93-105. The New Deal is perhaps the most noticed of many instances in the history of pragmatic rhetoric in which the use of that rhetoric seems to have concealed from its users the unarticulated assumptions that guided their own experimentation. See especially Thurman W. Arnold, *The Symbols of Government* (New Haven, Conn.: Yale University Press, 1935), and Thurman W. Arnold, *The Folklore of Capitalism* (New Haven, Conn.: Yale University Press, 1937). See also the critique of Arnold by Sidney Hook, "The Folklore of Capitalism: The Politician's Handbook—A Review," *University of Chicago Law Review* 5 (April 1938): 341-49.

49. Richard Rorty, "Dewey's Metaphysics," in *New Studies in the Philosophy of John Dewey,* ed. Steven M. Cahn (Hanover, N.H.: University Press of New England, 1977), 45-74. Cf. the different interest in Dewey manifest in the work of Willard van Orman Quine, *Ontological Relativity and Other Essays* (New York: Columbia University Press, 1969), 26-29.

50. Louis Hartz, *The Liberal Tradition in America: An Interpretation of American Political Thought Since the Revolution* (New York: Harcourt, 1955); Daniel J. Boorstin, *The Genius of American Politics* (Chicago: University of Chicago Press, 1953). Of the many works purporting to find "pragmatic continuities throughout American history, these two still repay the effort to come to grips with them critically.

51. Michael Brint and William Weaver, eds., *Pragmatism in Law and Society* (Boulder, Co.: Westview Press, 1991).

52. Richard Poirier, *Poetry and Pragmatism* (Cambridge, Mass.: Harvard University Press, 1992).

53. James T. Kloppenberg, "Objectivity and Historicism: A Century of American Historical Writing," *American Historical Review* 94 (1989): 1011-30.

54. Philip Selznick, *The Moral Commonwealth: Social Theory and the Promise of Community* (Berkeley: University of California Press, 1992).

55. Cornel West, *The American Evasion of Philosophy: A Genealogy of Pragmatism* (Madison: University of Wisconsin Press, 1989).

56. See West, *Evasion,* 7: "My own conception of prophetic pragmatism . . . serves as the culmination of the American pragmatist tradition." This book is most successful as a vindication of the calling of philosophically informed cultural criticism, bolstered by a series of sympathetic case studies in the performance of this calling. The book's title can easily mislead readers into expecting more of a history of an intellectual movement than West actually provides. It is interesting that West does not include Oliver Wendell Holmes, Jr., C. I. Lewis, George Herbert Mead, Alain Locke, or Horace Kallen.

57. The democratic center of Dewey's project has been emphasized, once again, in Robert B. Westbrook, *John Dewey and American Democracy* (Ithaca, N.Y.: Cornell University Press, 1991).

58. The pragmatic tradition's *via media* between narrower Enlightenment models for knowledge and radically anti-Enlightenment ideas has been emphasized in James T. Kloppenberg, *Uncertain Victory: Social Democracy and Progressivism in European and American Thought, 1870-1920* (New York: Oxford University Press, 1986).

PRAGMATISM AND LITERATURE

Harvey Cormier (essay date fall 1997)

SOURCE: Cormier, Harvey. "Jamesian Pragmatism and Jamesian Realism." *The Henry James Review* 18, no. 3 (fall 1997): 288-96.

[*In the following essay, Cormier examines the works of brothers William and Henry James and attempts "to show that the relation between Jamesian pragmatism and Jamesian realism is the relation of identity."*]

Critics both philosophical and literary have puzzled over the idea that there might be a connection between the philosophy of William James and the fiction of his brother Henry James. In a well-known 1907 letter to William, Henry himself affirmed a connection when he compared himself to Molière's character M. Jourdain in *Le Bourgeois Gentilhomme,* who was so pleased to learn from the "Philosophy Master" that he had been writing "prose" all his life. Henry described himself as having discovered, on reading William's work, that he had "pragmatized" throughout his career (Hocks 23).[1]

What was the nature of this connection? Was there a sense in which Henry James was a pragmatist? In what follows, I try to explain William James's pragmatism in such a way that we can see a clear connection to Henry James's kind of literary realism. In fact, I'll try to show that the relation between Jamesian pragmatism and Jamesian realism is the relation of identity.

The vague word "realism" has, since the Middle Ages, labeled philosophical views according to which ideas or words can and in some way ought to reflect "the real things," the things that are "external" to the mind and to language. The term "real" comes from the Latin *re* or "thing"; the *re*-al things are thus the thing-al, thinglike things, as opposed to the unthinglike things that occupy the worlds of conception, imagination, and illusion. The real things may be particular items—rocks, persons, muons—or they may be abstractions—numbers, goodness, or even "real necessity." What is constant among different philosophical realisms is not *what* the real things are, but *where* they are and originate: "outside" us thinking beings and our thoughts and words.

Since the eighteenth century, philosophical "realism" has typically been contrasted with "idealism," another ill-defined notion. Idealisms basically deny that thought or language can or should reflect an external reality: they say that instead words or thoughts should reflect something un-*re*-al and internal to language or thought itself. Rationalistic Hegelian "absolute" idealism seemed to identify the world and its things with a single concept contained in the transcendent and four-dimensional mind of God; this view competed with Berkeley's empiricist idealism, according to which the things of the world were a manifold of God's perceptions. More recently, there have also been "phenomenalisms" that have treated real objects as a product of the relationship between languages, especially scientific terminologies, and the pre-linguistic or pre-conceptual perceptions that those languages "organized" in various ways. These views are all very different, but they share the principle that the world and the objects that get thought about and discussed are "in" or are somehow dependent on the minds or the languages of thinkers and talkers.

I think that William James's pragmatism was a kind of realism, but not the kind usually opposed to philosophical idealism. Instead, James operated in what Cora Diamond calls "the realistic spirit" (*Realistic* 39-72). That is, James displays the kind of realism that people often display outside of philosophy, in more "ordinary" pursuits like politics (where it is sometimes known as "pragmatism") or writing fiction like that of James's brother Henry. This idea of ordinary, extra-philosophical realism was first invoked in philosophy by the empiricist F. P. Ramsey when he criticized theories of causality and logical necessity that were realistic—or, we might say, Realistic—in the traditional philosophical sense (252; Diamond, *Realistic* 42). I think that this idea can explain the peculiar but commonplace claim that pragmatism is an attempt to go somehow "beyond realism and idealism." Pragmatism goes beyond philosophical Realism to something like literary realism.

The realistic spirit is characterized by Diamond in terms of three interconnected features: first, an attention to phenomenological detail or the way things actually show themselves to us; second, the renunciation of myth and magic; and third, attention to coherence and causal consequences, to what we all know really would happen if such-and-such circumstances came to pass. Diamond discusses the importance of these features to George Orwell's naturalistic theories of fiction, and indicates the absence of these features in the typical work of Dickens, at the end of whose stories rich men improbably appear and solve all problems by "scattering guineas." Fictions without these realistic features are *fantasies,* and, Diamond argues, so are the traditional philosophical Realisms. They too involve a refusal to examine closely the factual details of our dealings with objects; they invoke mythical "transcendent" entities that *have to be there,* whether or not the evidence calls for them; and they fail to notice that these mythical entities are "idle wheels" that cannot play the causal or explanatory roles they are assigned by the Realists.

Though we usually think of it as a kind of idealism, and thus as opposed to Realism, empiricism is the first philosophical attempt to display the realistic spirit and thus to avoid "Realist" philosophical fantasy. Someone like the empiricist philosopher George Berkeley expresses the realistic spirit when he points out that "matter," or extra-mental stuff, unlike mental perceptions, never shows itself to us in any way, and is thus a thing in whose existence we have no reason to believe. Berkeley says that even if matter did exist, it would be an idle wheel in the machinery because it couldn't possibly play the role it is typically assigned, that of explaining our distinction between actual things and illusions. If we pay close attention to the way we really draw that distinction, we see that in doing so we check our perceptions against *other perceptions,* looking among them for the stability and persisting sameness associated with non-illusory things. We never in fact appeal to any matter beyond our perceptions.

However, says Diamond, though it reflects closer attention to the facts than do philosophical Realisms, Berkeley's immaterialistic empiricism itself fails to be fully realistic because it features fantasies of its own, especially a fantasy regarding what we are "given" in perceptual experience and therefore know unmistakably. The given, undeniable perceptions appealed to by Berkeley, and the immediately discernible similarities and differences among those perceptions that we can supposedly use in a methodical way to tell the actual from the hallucinatory, are themselves myths that have nothing to do with how we in fact know objects. Diamond holds that the perceived need for anything like these things reflects a kind of self-delusion or self-confusion: we convince ourselves that we cannot have satisfactory knowledge unless there is something absolutely certain, like these self-identifying mental entities, at the bottom of that knowledge. This conviction conceals from us our real philosophical needs and our real intellectual relationship to the world. It starts us down the wrong paths of philosophical inquiry, in search of *what we really know for sure,* or the ultimate *basis* of our language and thought (Diamond, *Realistic* 59ff.).

This criticism originates in the later work of Wittgenstein, who first describes empiricism generally as insufficiently "realistic" by the empiricists' own standards. Wittgenstein says, in criticism of Ramsey's empiricist account of deductive reasoning, "Not empiricism and yet realism in philosophy, that is the hardest thing" (*Remarks* 325; see Diamond, *Realistic* 39). That is, how can we express the realistic spirit of empiricism without embracing empiricism's own fantasies? Wittgenstein goes on immediately after this remark to say that "You do not understand any more of the rule than you can explain," (325) and Diamond reads this as the repudiation of "given" empirical facts and patterns, and assignment of their spot at the head of the chain of justifications to the ordinary public procedures we actually use in explaining things (Diamond 64).

Again, empiricist philosophers are drawn to the idea of the given because they think that there must be some "inner" unmistakable knowledge underlying those ordinary explanatory procedures. This knowledge *has to be there*: otherwise, when a person describes or explains some pattern, sameness, generality, or rule, perhaps by using a set of examples, the describer isn't in any better position to know what pattern she means to describe than is the auditor who has just received the examples. We know—or at least we think, especially when we are thinking philosophically—that such an auditor, unlike the giver of the examples, may always be under one of infinitely many conceivable misapprehensions about how to generalize what he has just seen or heard. It doesn't matter how much comprehension he *displays*: until and unless he somehow latches onto *what the example-giver knew,* he still doesn't know how to generalize or "go on in the same way" from the example.[2] Empiricists ask: "What can this inner, given knowledge be?" and they come up with answers like "knowledge of a particular way to sort similar, regular sense-data into groups," or, in Ramsey's case, "knowledge of a regular [i.e., rule-governed] way to use general terms in connection with certain of the sense-experiences, decisions, habits, etc., that constitute the rest of our mental life." But Wittgenstein focuses philosophical attention on the ordinary public procedures that the empiricists disdain, such as ordinary ways of giving examples. Wittgenstein thinks that close attention to these procedures can do the only work of philosophical explanation that really needs to be done. He *renounces the question* of inner knowledge that leads empiricists to go beyond these ordinary justifications in search of their grounds. By doing this, Diamond says, Wittgenstein finally achieves the small-*r* realism that empiricist idealism and phenomenalism had tried and failed to achieve.

There are two paths to this kind of realism, however. One, Wittgenstein's, involves explicitly renouncing certain philosophical questions; the other, William James's, involves reinterpreting the terms of those questions to such an extent before answering them that the effect is something like changing the subject. Both of these approaches can refocus our attention on the ways we actually do things and justify claims; both can help us give up the quest for a mythical foundational *something*. Wittgenstein himself actually offers both kinds of responses: he sometimes, in the *Investigations,* deals with the issue of what is "given" not with an explicit rejection of the question, but with remarks like "What has to be accepted, the given, is—so one could say—forms of life" (226; see Diamond, *Realistic* 65).

Diamond points out that this isn't Wittgenstein's attempt to solve the empiricists' problem, as some readers have taken it to be:[3] the point is not that here, in public, communal ways of reaching agreement, we find what philosophers have been looking for all along, the thing that really underwrites our ordinary procedures of speech, explanation, and justification. When he directs us to what we *could* call "the given," Wittgenstein is *not* saying the following: You were "pointing inwardly" in search of the things we know better than anything else, when you should instead have been "pointing outwardly" at the procedures, abstractly considered, of producing agreement within your community concerning what is meant. *That* is where our meanings are fixed; those procedures are the "known" things—known even better than our "inner" states, if we have any—that determine what we really mean by, e.g., "go on in this way."

Rather, Wittgenstein is telling us to quit looking for fundamental things and conditions to point at. Communal agreement can't *ground* understanding or following of rules: attribution of "agreement" *presupposes* the idea of different people "going on in the same way," in that it presupposes the notion that people are giving response-tokens of the same type (Goldfarb 484; Hoff-

man 23-28). Rather than looking to communal agreement or anything else as the thing that grounds meaning and genuine understanding, we should notice that the particular examples speakers give in particular circumstances are usually perfectly adequate to the task of determining what those speakers really mean. Wittgenstein thinks that we have no real need of a way of specifying, in the way the empiricists thought their inner "given" did, the right or wrong "same way to go on" that will "reach through the logical space of all possibilities" and resolve in advance every conceivable doubt about which rule or similarity a person is trying to communicate (see esp. Diamond, *Realistic* 71-72; Goldfarb 486-88). We are constantly tempted by philosophy to throw aside our ordinary criteria for discovering meaning and understanding: we are driven to look for other criteria that are more stable and permanent, and less a matter of what we are in fact ordinarily *inclined* to say and do.[4] Wittgenstein tries to show that the search for this kind of foundation for meaning is an artifact of our being "held captive" by a "picture" (see *Investigations* 111-15 and 208ff.)—a picture that is, in Diamond's term, a fantasy.

But despite this anti-empiricist stance, Wittgenstein sometimes makes his points using the philosophical language of the empiricists, and I think that William James proceeds in a similar way. In particular, James proceeds by means of pragmatism, a "theory" or definition of truth according to which: "*'The true,' to put it very briefly, is only the expedient in the way of our thinking, just as 'the right' is only the expedient in the way of our behaving*" (*PM* 106). This sounds as if the empiricist question concerning what the speaker knows or what stably fixes meaning is being answered in terms of "inner" desires or satisfactions: to know what will make my claims true, and thus what I mean by what I say, you must know what will satisfy me, or perhaps what will satisfy some larger group that includes me. But in fact James is not trying to define truth or meaning as an empiricist might have: he is instead moving away from the search for grounds for meaning and truth. William James offers a non-theoretical theory of truth and knowledge, a "genetic" account of those things, an un-definition.

To adopt an example of Richard Rorty's (162) and put it to a use slightly different from the one he intended, William James's account of truth is analogous to a "definition" of aspirin as the stuff that was discovered in the late nineteenth century to be good for headaches, and that is today marketed in the form of little white pills by the same company that originally sold heroin as a cough remedy. This is a funny "definition" of aspirin: it seems not quite to deserve the title "a theory of what aspirin is." It would seem to be instead something like a history of aspirin, or maybe directions regarding how to get hold of some aspirin, or directions regarding how to get rid of a headache. It is "merely" a description of aspirin, a selection of useful accidental features—features that might, as a matter of fact, have turned out not to be true of aspirin. But they are features such that they do in fact pick out aspirin among other sets of white pills, and such that if they hadn't turned out to be true of aspirin, we would have been indifferent to whatever non-accidental features aspirin may have. Whatever may be the correct "theory of what aspirin is," or whatever may give the essence or the necessary and sufficient conditions for being aspirin—"acetylsalicylic acid" may do it—if aspirin were not also the stuff that's good for headaches, we wouldn't care about aspirin, and such aspirin as did exist would do so by accident rather than through strenuous human efforts. "The stuff that's good for headaches" is, we might say, what aspirin *means to us*: it's a way of explaining the *importance* of aspirin, not its essence. Analogously, we should understand William James's definition of truth as describing the importance of truth and not the essence thereof.

William James's book on truth is not called *The Meaning of the Word "Truth,"* or *The Essence of Truth,* or *The Theory of Truth.* It is *The Meaning of Truth,* and that tells us something important—not, as one might surmise, that James wrote before anybody noticed the logical distinction between use and mention, but instead that he is offering to us the meaning of *the thing called truth*: its importance to us, how it works, what it means to us, what we use it for, what it's good for. And truth, according to James, is, as it were, the stuff that's good for intellectual, spiritual, and emotional headaches. It solves problems. The feature of "true" beliefs that makes us want them—a "merely accidental" feature—is their "goodness," or their potential to help us avoid pains, right wrongs, and clear up the confusions that stop us from acting effectively.

It's actually more complicated than this, of course: obviously, not every "expedient" belief is simply "true," if only because a belief that works today might be superseded by a still more expedient one tomorrow. But William James wants to explain all such phenomena with attention to how we actually decide what to call "true"—thus displaying, we might say, the realistic spirit. Here is how he accounts for growth and change in the body of beliefs we recognize as true:

> Messrs. Dewey, Schiller, and their allies, in reaching this general conception of all truth ["the 'instrumental' view of truth," which is "the view that truth in our ideas means their power to 'work'"], have only followed the example of geologists, biologists and philologists. In the establishment of these other sciences, the successful stroke was always to take some simple process actually observable in operation—as denudation by weather, say, or change of dialect by incorporation of new words and pronunciations—and then to generalize it, making it apply to all times, and produce great results by summating its effects through the ages.

The observable process which Schiller and Dewey particularly singled out for generalization is the familiar one by which any individual settles into *new opinions*. The process here is always the same. The individual has a stock of opinions already, but he meets a new experience that puts them to a strain. Somebody contradicts them; or in a reflective moment he discovers that they contradict each other; or he hears of facts with which they are incompatible; or desires arise in him which they cease to satisfy. The result is an inward trouble to which his mind till then had been a stranger, and from which he seeks to escape by modifying his previous mass of opinions. He saves as much of it as he can, for in this matter of belief we are all extreme conservatives. So he tries to change first this opinion, and then that . . . until at last some new idea comes up which he can graft upon the ancient stock with a minimum of disturbance of the latter, some idea that mediates between the stock and the new experience and runs them into one another most felicitously and expediently.

> This new idea is then adopted as the true one.

> (34-35)

James thus takes the same stance toward "geologists, biologists and philologists" that they take toward the phenomena they observe. He notes that the actual, observable process of discovering truth works thus: if beliefs display this kind of goodness and fit with our other beliefs, we call them true; if they don't we call them false. Inquirers make no evident use of any inner, stable, meaning-fixing essence hidden beneath observable verification processes. Thus the description of those processes is the end of the story of truth—except for the coming struggle with the philosophers who won't see how the ancient philosophical questions of truth and meaning are answered by this account of how we actually happen to tell what's true.

But William James is not, in fact, trying to answer the old questions. Perhaps there really is, out there beyond all our actual procedures of discovery and explanation, an essence of truth of the kind that empiricists and other traditional philosophers seek: perhaps all and only truths correspond, in some way irrelevant to the public, observable procedures of "geologists, biologists and philologists," either to inner perceptual phenomena or to outer ("*re*-al") material things. But despite his use of "definition" terminology, James never really joins a debate like this. He often sounds like an epistemologist, but he has no arguments concerning what truth logically or metaphysically *must be*. Instead he tells us what truth really and contingently *does*: and he thus tries, by means of his pragmatic account of the role truth actually plays in our lives, to focus our attention on the real meaning truth has for us. He hopes we will see that any such transcendent "correspondence" is irrelevant to our real interest in truth, and that, in the end, both Realistic and idealistic stories of necessary but unverifiable truth-relations are no more than fantasies.

William James's brother Henry joins him in rejecting fantasy and embracing our real experiences and interests. Henry James expresses this realistic outlook whenever he condemns "romance," and here, in his well-known critical preface to *The American,* Henry finds and critiques a bit of romance in his own work:

> The only *general* attribute of projected romance that I can see, the only one that fits all its cases, is the fact of the kind of experience with which it deals—experience liberated, so to speak; experience disengaged, disembroiled, disencumbered, exempt from the conditions that we usually know to attach to it and, if we wish so to put the matter, drag upon it, and operating in a medium which relieves it, in a particular interest, of the inconvenience of a *related,* a measurable state, a state subject to all our vulgar communities. The greatest intensity may so be arrived at evidently—when the sacrifice of community, of the "related" sides of situations, has not been too rash. It must to this end not flagrantly betray itself; we must even be kept if possible, for our illusion, from suspecting any sacrifice at all. The balloon of experience is in fact of course tied to the earth, and under that necessity we swing, thanks to a rope of remarkable length, in the more or less commodious car of the imagination; but it is by the rope we know where we are, and from the moment that cable is cut we are at large and unrelated: we only swing apart from the globe—though remaining as exhilarated, naturally, as we like, especially when all goes well. The art of the romancer is, "for the fun of it," insidiously to cut the cable, to cut it without our detecting him. What I have recognised then in "The American," much to my surprise and after long years, is that the experience here represented is the disconnected and uncontrolled experience—uncontrolled by our general sense of "the way things happen"—which romance alone more or less successfully palms off on us.

> (*AN* 33-34)

The idea of presenting experience in such a way that it is "tied" by a "cable" to the "earth," nicely sums up the way literary realists, and all others who operate in the realistic spirit, try to see and describe things. A realistic description is "related" to "the conditions that we usually know to attach to it," controlled by "our general sense of 'the way things happen,'" and "subject to all our vulgar communities."

James is here faulting one of his own works for a failure to be realistic, but in general his fictions scrupulously reflect "the way things happen." He is almost always realistic about his principal subject matter, which is the perceiving mind or self and its subtle workings in social interaction. In both traditional philosophy and fantastic, un-James-like fiction, the self, if it is taken to be real at all, is a mystical entity that exists apart from particular surrounding circumstances and events. The world of happenings and doings may affect or reveal the self, but they are distinct from it: the self is *there* already, lurking behind the scenes. It has its rules and regularities and the world has its, and if we ask ques-

tions about either set of rules, the answers are also *there* waiting for excavation. But Henry James challenged the idea of a buried self with a fixed fate, and he used the same procedures William James had used to challenge the idea of a buried and mysteriously unobservable relation of truth. As William had vividly shown how truth really works and develops in our intellectual lives, Henry showed vividly how our minds or selves really work and develop as we try to live in human society.

William James the psychologist says, in his *Principles of Psychology,* that the self as we find it is felt "just as the body is felt, the feeling of which is also an abstraction, because never is the body felt all alone, but always together with other things" (299). The self is known to us first and constantly as part of the evolving world of things, happenings, and circumstances, and the world of circumstances is known to us as something created at least in part by selves in action. Therefore, William James the pragmatist and small-*r* realist will understand the truth about the self in these experiential terms, rather than as a buried relationship to an invisible object. And Henry James the realistic novelist will adopt the same attitude, and try to show us the self *as we know it.*

We see this attitude in the self-criticism above: Henry thinks that he has failed to be realistic and to show the "known" self in *The American.* He sees himself as having been "more than commonly enamoured of his idea" that his "subject" in that narrative could "take care of itself," since fate and the nature of the human self decreed a certain ending for the story (*AN* 21; see Hocks 227-28). Allegiance to this kind of idea makes the novel an "arch-romance" because it means that events and characters there don't develop with the unpredictability and flexibility that we know they would show in real life.

Literature involving the ideas of pre-written fate and underlying human nature tends toward "romance" rather than "reality" because it represents "the unknown" rather than "the things we cannot possibly *not* know, sooner or later, in one way or another" (*AN* 30-32). The unknown, as represented especially by the mysterious, the far, and the strange, is the characteristic subject matter of romantic, fantastic writing. Therefore James accuses himself of spinning a fantasy in *The American.* He laments his failure to direct his attention and ours to the common, familiar ways in which events and selves really develop.

In his other works, when he succeeds in doing this, James displays a literary realism that amounts to a philosophical position—the position his brother William called "pragmatism."

Notes

1. Hocks cites this letter at length, and centers his book around an explanation of this remark.

2. There are many examples demonstrating how examples work in Wittgenstein's later writings: Diamond (66) cites one from Wittgenstein (*Remarks* 320-21).

3. Diamond suggests in particular that her reading of Wittgenstein can be taken as a response to the one found in Kripke. For Diamond's more explicit criticisms of Kripke, see "Rules." See also section 3 of Goldfarb, part of which expands on some of Diamond's ideas.

4. Cavell calls this inner conflict, as it is exemplified in debates among Wittgenstein's different imaginary interlocutors in the *Investigations,* "the argument of the ordinary." That is the title of the second chapter (64-100) of *Conditions Handsome and Unhandsome,* and there Cavell, too, criticizes Kripke for treating Wittgenstein as a foundationalist—that is, for treating Wittgenstein as if he were looking for explanations of language use that "exact consent" rather than ones that "attract it" (100).

Works Cited

Works by Henry James

AN—*The Art of the Novel: Critical Prefaces.* Ed. R. P. Blackmur. New York: Scribner's, 1934.

Works by William James

PM—*Pragmatism and the Meaning of Truth.* Cambridge: Harvard UP, 1978.

The Principles of Psychology. Vol. 1. New York: Dover, 1950.

Other Works Cited

Berkeley, George. *Three Dialogues Between Hylas and Philonous.* Buffalo: Prometheus, 1988.

Cavell, Stanley. *Conditions Handsome and Unhandsome: The Constitution of Emersonian Perfectionism.* La Salle: Open Court, 1990.

Diamond, Cora. *The Realistic Spirit.* Cambridge: MIT, 1991.

———. "Rules: Looking in the Right Place." *Wittgenstein: Attention to Particulars.* Ed. D. Z. Phillips and Peter Winch. New York: St. Martin's, 1989. 12-34.

Goldfarb, Warren. "Kripke on Wittgenstein on Rules." *Journal of Philosophy* 82.9 (1985): 471-88.

Hocks, Richard A. *Henry James and Pragmatistic Thought.* Chapel Hill: U of North Carolina P, 1974.

Hoffman, Paul. "Kripke on Private Language." *Philosophical Studies* 47.1 (1985): 23-28.

Kripke, Saul. *Wittgenstein on Rules and Private Language.* Oxford: Blackwell, 1982.

Ramsey, Frank P. *The Foundations of Mathematics.* London: Routledge, 1954.

Rorty, Richard. *Consequences of Pragmatism.* Minneapolis: U of Minnesota P, 1982.

Wittgenstein, Ludwig. *Philosophical Investigations.* Trans. G. E. M. Anscombe. Oxford: Blackwell, 1958.

———. *Remarks on the Foundations of Mathematics.* Ed. G. H. von Wright, Rush Rhees, and G. E. M. Anscombe. Oxford: Blackwell, 1978.

Patricia Rae (essay date 1997)

SOURCE: Rae, Patricia. "Introduction: Inspiration, Reflex-action, and Pragmatism." In *The Practical Muse: Pragmatist Poetics in Hulme, Pound, and Stevens,* pp. 25-42. Lewisburg, Penn. and London: Bucknell University Press and Associated University Presses, 1997.

[*In the following essay, Rae discusses the influence of Pragmatism on the literary theories of Modernist poets Ezra Pound, T. E. Hulme, and Wallace Stevens.*]

> The germinal question concerning things brought for the first time before consciousness is not the theoretic "What is that?" but the practical "Who goes there?" or rather, as Horwicz has admirably put it, "What is to be done?"
>
> —William James, "The Sentiment of Rationality," *WB*

William James's first aspiration was to be an artist. Why he gave up art for science is unclear; it may have been because of his father's promptings or his own perception that his artistic efforts were never to be anything but mediocre.[1] The decision led him first to studies in physiology and medicine, then to a distinguished career in psychology, with a special interest in the psychology of religious experience, and, finally, in the last eight years of his life, to the project of articulating and defending "pragmatism." But James's interest in art never entirely disappeared. His writings about religious inspiration reveal a lingering fascination with creative inspiration, and his pragmatism is as much a theory about how to paint, sculpt, and write as it is a program for making and testing truth.

James's aesthetic theory is worth reconstructing, because it indirectly shaped the theory and practice of several modernist poets. Reconstructing the theory and appreciating its full significance for these poets necessitates an understanding of James's positions on several major issues not overtly connected with art. It also requires an effort to see the vital connection between James's description of the religious consciousness and his pragmatism: an effort running counter to the prevailing tendency among James scholars to compartmentalize his various interests.[2]

REINTEGRATING JAMES: A CAREER AS
REFLEX-ACTION

That James's pragmatism and his work in the psychology of religion are integrally related is suggested by a model for human consciousness popular in James's time and central to his thought: the "reflex-action theory of mind."[3] This conception of mental activity informs *The Principles of Psychology* (1890) and James's two major works on the psychology of religion, *The Will to Believe* (1897) and *The Varieties of Religious Experience* (1902). It is also crucial to his account of truth-making in *Pragmatism* (1907) and *The Meaning of Truth* (1909). Reintegrating the two sides of James's work becomes easier both when we note the pervasiveness of the "reflex-action" theory within it and when we appreciate how appropriate the model is for describing James's *corpus* as a whole.

James discusses the reflex-action theory of consciousness in detail in *The Principles of Psychology* and in two important essays reprinted in *The Will to Believe*: "The Sentiment of Rationality" (1879) and "Reflex-action and Theism" (1881).[4] The theory derives, he tells us, from a physiological principle first entertained by Descartes and established in the eighteenth century by the physiologists La Mattric and Cabanis: the principle that "the acts we perform are always the results of outward discharges from the nervous centres, and that these outward discharges are themselves the result of impressions from the external world."[5] For James and his contemporaries, this insight has led to the recognition that our mental states are an inseparable part of a continuum beginning with impressions and culminating in actions. Cognition is the second stage in a *"triad, neither of whose elements has any independent existence,"* a "cross-section . . . of what in its totality is a motor phenomenon."[6] The sequence of events in every cognitive experience is as follows:

> Any mind, constructed on the triadic-reflex pattern, must first get its *impression* from the object which it confronts; then *define* what that object is, and decide what *active measures* its presence demands; and finally *react. The stage of reaction depends on the stage of definition,* and these, of course, on the nature of the impressing object.[7]

This view of the close relationship between thought and action was to be important for James's pragmatism, because it committed him to acknowledging the *interestedness* of all theories or "definitions"; it pointed to the

fact that all theorizing is contaminated by an awareness of how theories will "out" in action.[8] But it is also fascinating because it perfectly describes the sequence of James's interests, as he moved from the psychology of religion to pragmatism. It would not be inappropriate to describe James's career as a reflex-act writ large. On this view, *The Will to Believe* and *Varieties of Religious Experience* represent what we might call its "stage of definition." In these works James makes an effort to define a very common "impression" experienced by human beings, that is, the sense that an apparently transcendent and omniscient presence "knocks on our mental door and asks to be let in." He debates the wisdom of defining this impression in metaphysical terms, as a manifestation of "God" or of an eternal "Idea,"[9] and, deciding that such a definition would be unacceptable, proposes an alternative. The specifications for truth-making he sets out in *Pragmatism* and *The Meaning of Truth,* then, are the "active measures" corresponding to this act of "definition." More specifically, they are measures reflecting a decision to *withhold judgment* about the apparently divine being that intrudes on the consciousness and shares its secrets.[10]

The definition James ends up giving to seemingly mystical moments, or experiences of "inspiration,"[11] owes everything to the discourse of what was known in his time as the "new psychology." James's own *Principles of Psychology* was one of the first comprehensive introductions to the principles, techniques, and early results of this new science of mind. In her study of the importance of this "new psychology" for modernist literature, Judith Ryan has carefully distinguished two branches of the science—"empiricist" and "experimental" psychologies—and suggested that it is to the first of these alone that modernism is indebted.[12] But in view of James's vital work on "inspiration," and comparable work by other psychologist-philosophers such as Théodule Ribot and Henri Bergson, Ryan's distinction is far too restrictive. "Empiricist" and "experimental" psychologies differed in their techniques; the first relied on introspection, whereas the second collected physiological evidence of the mind's activities. But what they shared was important: a commitment to describing the mental experience of individuals without resorting to "metaphysical" speculation about its fundamental nature or first causes. "The mind all psychologists study," James insists, without discriminating between the experimentalist and the intuitionist, "is the mind of distinct individuals inhabiting definite portions of a real space and of a real time. *With any other sort of mind,* absolute Intelligence, Mind unattached to a particular body, or Mind not subject to the course of time, [he] *has nothing to do*" (*PP* 1: 183; italics mine).

In committing himself to giving a purely "empirical" (*VRE* 52) account of revelatory experiences, as he does in *The Varieties of Religious Experience,* James rejects the temptation to attribute them to the intervention of some transcendent Being—Plato's Over-Soul, Schopenhauer's Will, Hegel's *Geist,* or the Judaeo-Christian God. In *The Principles of Psychology,* he calls such a Being the *"perfect object of belief"* (*PP* 2: 944): nothing could be more satisfying than to claim contact with it. But attributing the experience of illumination to such a principle would amount to making a statement about the experience's primary cause, which would violate James's commitment to the discourse of psychology. Instead he chooses to define the impression in phenomenological terms: the source becomes a presence that is *felt* or something that one *"considers* divine," but its real nature is always "bracketed."[13] For a single, genuinely mystical God, in other words, James substitutes an indefinite number of beings that *function like* God; their identity, their origin inside or outside the consciousness, he deems irrelevant. Among his few specifications for such divinities is their *appearance* of otherness, their quality of *seeming* to come from outside the self.[14] It is this apparent independence from the beholder's desires that seems to authorize the propositions they whisper in his ear:

> [Mystical states] are states of insight into depths of truth unplumbed by the discursive intellect. They are illuminations, revelations, full of significance and importance, all inarticulate though they remain; and as a rule they carry with them a curious sense of authority for after-time.[15]

"Mystical" moments, then, are experiences of conviction, in which one feels that one's insights are absolutely true. Here it must be emphasized that James's emphasis is on the *feeling* of truthfulness rather than the *fact.* Being unable to claim definitively that the apparently autonomous divinity *is* what it *seems,* he must translate truth-claims into claims about the "sentiment" of a proposition's "rationality."[16] He is also obliged to concede that there may be as many divinities and apparently truthful propositions as there are self-proclaimed "mystics": disavowing all certain knowledge of first principles leads inexorably to pluralism (*VRE* 525).

If this new description of religious experience constitutes the significant act of "definition" in James's career, what are the "active measures" he devises in response to it? I propose that these "measures" are the specifications he develops for how people should handle the insights they enjoy in their moments of "illumination." James does not formulate this advice completely until *Pragmatism,* but he anticipates it in the writings on religion, where he addresses the problem of how people should deal with the conclusion to which their "mystical" experiences seem to point: that God exists.[17] James knows that his obligation to problematize the status of the divinity makes a final judgment about that proposition impossible. To decide definitively for or

against it would be to violate the "opaque limit" (*WB* 30, 33) he places on a psychologist's understanding. Yet he also senses that *some* courageous position on the matter has to be taken. The decision, he realizes, is a "momentous" one, tantamount to the decision we face when lost in a blinding snowstorm: we may make the wrong choice—follow the wrong path—but "If we stand still we shall be frozen to death" (*WB* 30, 33).[18] His solution, which he calls "empirical theism,"[19] is a middle course between gnosticism and agnosticism. On the one hand, combining respect for testimonies about divine "visitations" with an acute awareness of the benefits of faith, he recommends that we should allow ourselves to accept the proposition about God's existence—to venture off faithfully into the snowstorm. But we must temper that belief with a certain amount of skepticism. That is to say, we must treat the proposition about God's existence as a "hypothesis" (*VRE* 428): a provisional truth whose authority will always rest on its continued compatibility with empirical evidence. The proposition, James says, will retain its credibility only if, when "you proceed to act upon your theory," it is "reversed by nothing that later turns up as your action's fruit," that is, if it "harmonize[s] so well with the entire drift of experience that the latter will, as it were, adopt it."[20]

The program James outlined for dealing with the proposition about God's existence inspired a whole new tradition in "empirical" theology; the American writers James Leuba, W. E. Hocking, and D. C. Mackintosh, and many contributors to the English journal *The Quest,* took up the task of justifying the proposition "in the same way as science justifies its hypotheses, that is to say, by reference to experience."[21] More importantly as I have suggested, the program served as a prototype for pragmatism—the program James devised for dealing with *any* proposition that invites belief. In its narrowest sense, the "pragmatic method" is one of reconciling philosophical disputes by asking whether the points on which opposing factions disagree make any significant difference in the world. In its more general sense, however, and the one that concerns me here, pragmatism is a *theory of truth*: a definition of what makes a theory valid. Succinctly put, the pragmatist view is that *"the true is the name of whatever proves itself to be good in the way of belief."* There are many moments in life, James suggests, when we face decisions about whether or not to accept propositions that are as "momentous" as the proposition about God. Having no right to accept theories uncritically, as "revelations" from some transcendental Power (*P* 94), we must nonetheless make up our minds about them. In his estimation, the best thing to do in such circumstances is openly to indulge the interest that is bound to infect our theorizing anyway and to give our faith to the proposition that promises to be most useful to us. The "true" theory, in other words, is the one that "will carry us prosperously from any one part of our experience to any other part, linking things satisfactorily, working securely, simplifying, saving labor." (*P* 32). James illustrates his point by adapting his example from *The Will to Believe*: "If I am lost in the woods and starved, and find what looks like a cow-path," the "true" proposition must be that there is "a human habitation at the end of it," for believing in such a proposition, and heading down the path, may be the only means of salvation (*P* 42, 94, 34, 98). In short, with pragmatism *every* proposition must be regarded with the same calculated self-interest as the proposition about God. We must be constantly making Pascalian wagers.

Singling out self-interest as a criterion for truthfulness was one of the most contentious moves of James's career. His critics objected that such a position encouraged a complete lack of discipline in epistemological matters and that it was bound to lead many a dreamer to disaster; as James summarizes it, referring to the English philosopher whose work he regarded as compatible with his own, "A favorite formula for describing Mr. Schiller's doctrines and mine is that we are persons who think that by saying whatever you find it pleasant to say and calling it truth you fulfil every pragmatistic requirement." But as subsequent chapters will show, James's statement that truthfulness is coextensive with satisfactoriness does not mean his pragmatist is simply to believe everything he wants to believe. In both *Pragmatism* and *The Meaning of Truth,* James emphasizes that the "satisfaction" that makes a proposition true comes from much more than the indulgence of a longing: it is also dependent on seeing that proposition adequately corroborated by subsequent experience. "Following our mental image of a house along the cow-path," he says, "we actually come to see the house; we get the image's full verification. *Such simply and fully verified leadings are certainly the originals and prototypes of the truth-process.*" Just as empirical theism mediates between gnosticism and agnosticism, pragmatism "harmonizes" a "tender-minded" optimism about the truthfulness of propositions with a "tough-minded" concern that experience bears them out.[22]

The appropriate reaction to feelings of certainty, then, was for James an activity of fluctuating between faith and doubt, of making assertions and unmaking them, as "facts" demand. Recognizing that his ideal thinker respects "the coercions of the world of sense about him"[23] is vital if we are to appreciate how he and his poetic successors differ from other late nineteenth- and early twentieth-century philosophers whose programs for theory-making were predicated on uncertainty—particularly Friedrich Nietzsche, Jules de Gaultier, and the young George Santayana. Because I shall be emphasizing the empiricist responsibilities of Jamesian pragmatism throughout, I should clarify at the outset that James's commitment to testing theory against "fact" is not symptomatic of his falling back on a simple "correspondence" or "copy" theory of truth.[24] Two aspects of his theory, in particular, prevent such a lapse. First, James does not view the process of checking and revising with unadulterated confidence, but with what is best described as a cautious "epistemological optimism." He begins from the premise that the objectivity of the "facts" to be heeded cannot be definitively established. He maintains, however, that in the absence of such certainty we have as much reason to consider them right as we do to consider them wrong and to respect most those theories that best account for them. To do otherwise is both perverse and, as he explains in closely related writings on colonialism, ethically unacceptable.[25] Second, the reality James envisions the pragmatist testing his theories against is not immutable but in constant change, and the theories themselves play a role in its transformation. Instead of passively reflecting reality, the theory-maker helps to *bring about* a certain version of reality by imagining it. James gives a succinct summary of the process in *Pragmatism*:

> In the realm of truth-processes facts come independently and determine our beliefs provisionally. But these beliefs make us act, and as fast as they do so, they bring into sight or into existence new facts which redetermine the beliefs accordingly. So the whole coil and ball of truth, as it rolls up, is the product of a double influence. Truths emerge from facts; but they dip forward into facts again and add to them; which facts again create or reveal new truth (the word is indifferent) and so on indefinitely.
>
> (*P* 108)

James's conception of truth's "coil and ball" leads him to endorse an "ontological optimism" similar in rationale to his epistemological attitude. Where there is no compelling evidence to the contrary, his ideal thinker will always choose the happier theory over the sad one, knowing that his choice may be a self-fulfilling prophecy.

James appears to have been aware of the relevance of pragmatism for poetry. He includes verbal expressions among "reflex-actions," observing that "the current of life which *runs in* at our eyes or ears is meant to *run out* at our hands, feet, *or lips.*"[26] He also suggests that psychology's redefinition of the mystical moment has profound consequences for traditional notions of what constitutes poetic "genius," specifically for the conception of creative inspiration as something "divine, miraculous, and God-given."[27] The poet who feels inspired is for him no different from anyone who experiences moments of profound conviction: he must resist attributing his insight, unequivocally, to God. And the "active measures" the poet is to take, like those of any pragmatist, must respect this limitation without sacrificing either the epistemological or ontological benefits of faith. In "Reflex-action and Theism," James singles out the sculptor as someone who cannot "bid [his] . . . interests be passive," just because he can no longer testify confidently that he has been divinely inspired. The artist must express himself one way or another, and his choice is one "between operating to poor or to rich results."[28] James represents the poet's responsibilities in much the same way: his communications are not revelations of timeless Truth, but practical faith-acts taken in a moment of crisis. The poet's assertions will serve as "helps" to guide him and his audience through the intimidating "forest" of the here and now:

> They are, if I may use a simile, so many spots, or blazes,—blazes made by the axe of the human intellect on the trees of the otherwise trackless forest of human experience. They give you somewhere to go from. They give you a direction and a place to reach. They do not give you the integral forest with all its sunlit glories and its moonlit witcheries and wonders. Ferny dells, and mossy waterfalls, and secret magic nooks escape you, owned only by the wild things to whom the region is a home. Happy they without the need of blazes! But to us the blazes give a sort of ownership. We can now use the forest, wend across it with companions, and enjoy its quality. It is no longer a place merely to get lost in and never return.[29]

James uses his topographical metaphor to remind us of the transcendental realm with which the poet can no longer claim certain contact: the forest he will explicate will not be an "integral" or "essential" one, normally hidden behind the phenomenal veil, but only the pressing world of immediate "experience." This is not to say that the poet has no chance of reaching the "essential" forest. Later in the same passage, James likens the trail he blazes to a path that *may* one day terminate in the "final valley" of absolute truth, so long as he adapts the blazes to overcome empirical obstacle after empirical obstacle. But for the present, it is "using" and "enjoying" the forest, and not "getting lost" in it, that counts. It is significant that James depicts the trail-blazing poet traveling "with companions," because he repeatedly reminds the pragmatist that the process of making and unmaking truths should be a community effort.[30] Moreover, because the poet's own instructions can only be "inconclusive,"[31] they are never coercive: he lets his companions know that they are free to follow or ignore them as they choose. As James says elsewhere of his own efforts at communication, "the most any one [*sic*] can do is to confess as candidly as he can the grounds for the faith that is in him and leave his example to work on others as it may."[32]

Hulme, Pound, and Stevens shared James's views both about the poet's epistemological predicament and about the use of words that was its appropriate resolution. To demonstrate the parallel between their work and his, I shall organize my investigations into their theory and practice on the reflex-action model, examining first how they interpret the "impressions" that initiate the activity and then the "active measures" they devise in response

to it. The model suits their work because all three poets subscribe to an *expressive* poetics, in the widest sense of that term; they describe an activity in which the poet experiences what seems like a divine revelation, and then articulates the insights communicated. That is to say, they envision some "current" passing into the poet from what appears to be some other world, and passing out of him through his "lips." This model also enables us to appreciate the relationship between these poets' accounts of inspiration and the expressive measures they recommend and practice. It becomes clear that these are as mutually dependent as the "acts of definition" and "active measures" in all reflex activities, as interconnected as their parallel discussions in James.

"MUMBLING ABOUT THE INFINITE": THE "MYSTICAL" POETICS OF SYMBOLISM

Like many modernist poets, Hulme, Pound, and Stevens shared a desire to rewrite an account of the poetic process they found intolerable. Their target—in some respects chimerical—was an account they associated with the German Idealist philosophers and ultimately with Plato, one they saw at work in English Romanticism, French Symbolism, American Transcendentalism, as well as in the work of "late Romantic" poets like Swinburne, Yeats, E. C. Stedman, and G. E. Woodberry. What these philosophers and poets had in common, in their eyes, was an essentially "mystical" account of the creative process and its product: a view of inspiration as an experience of achieving contact with a higher power and of poetry as a vehicle for the divine wisdom thus attained. So far as Hulme, Pound, and Stevens were concerned, the German Idealist account of art was in all important respects identical to the one Plato espouses in the *Ion* and the *Phaedrus*: they equated the state of renunciation Kant calls "disinterestedness" and its variations in other German Idealist writers, with the act of self-annihilation Plato called "divine madness."[33] The German Idealists themselves would have objected to such an interpretation; a comprehensive reading of their documents on art reveals that they backed off from attributing moments of disinterested insight to the intervention of superhuman powers and from viewing poetry as a vehicle for absolute truth.[34] But if the later poets got German Idealist theory wrong, some of the responsibility must rest with the Romantic and Symbolist writers who appealed to its authority; Symbolist manifestos, in particular, regularly assimilated Kant, Fichte, Schelling, Schopenhauer, and Hegel to Plato.[35] And if intermediaries like Baudelaire and Mallarmé themselves failed to note the ways the German Idealists undermined the overt mysticism in their work, this is itself understandable, because of the difficulty of the writings and because some of their more accessible and memorable passages contain no hint of such restraint.

Although the scope of this study precludes a detailed account of the Symbolists and their German sources, it is impossible to appreciate Hulme's, Pound's, and Stevens's affinity with James without some understanding of the mystical account of inspiration they, like James, were reacting against. To this end I would like to digress briefly and sketch the main features of the Symbolist aesthetic as I believe the poets perceived it. Here it will become apparent that some of the Symbolist poets, at least, also follow the reflex-action model, correlating their recommendations for expression with their definitions of inspiration. In interpreting inspiration as revelation, these poets appear prepared to accept the absolute authority of the poet's insights. They then endorse stylistic principles that reflect that authority, and, further, that challenge the reader to a very different interpretive process from the one posed by James's "blazes." If the modernist poets rewrite Symbolism's account of inspiration, their pragmatic style is a more generous alternative to its authoritarian grammar.

The account of creative experience in Schopenhauer's *Die Welt als Wille und Vorstellung* (1819) provides a perfect illustration of the German Idealist assimilation of Plato. As A. G. Lehmann has noted, Schopenhauer's description of what the poet undergoes reads like a "renovated theory of Platonic Ideas."[36] The poet suspends his analytical intellect, penetrates the phenomenal "veil," and apprehends the essences, or "Ideas," that lie behind it: the best, most reliable manifestations of a transcendental force called the Will. "The apprehended Idea is the true and only source of every genuine work of art."[37] Schopenhauer makes a careful distinction between the kind of creative process inspired by this "Idea" and the kind that begins with a "concept":

> The *concept* is abstract, discursive . . . attainable and intelligible only to him who has the faculty of reason, communicable by words without further assistance, entirely exhausted by its definition. The *Idea* on the other hand . . . is absolutely perceptive, individual, and, although representing an infinite number of particular things, is yet thoroughly definite . . . the *concept* is like a dead receptacle in which whatever has been put actually lies side by side, but out of which no more can be taken out (by analytical judgments) than has been put in (by synthetical reflection). The *Idea,* on the other hand, develops, in him who has grasped it, representations that are new as regards the concept of the same name; it is like a living organism, developing itself and endowed with generative force, which brings forth what was not previously put into it.[38]

Here Schopenhauer renovates Plato's account of inspiration to emphasize that the wisdom embodied in the apprehended "Ideas" is ineffable. In this respect, as in others, the poet's experience fulfils the criteria James set out in *The Varieties of Religious Experience* for mystical experience ("no adequate account" of the content of such experiences, he says there, "can be given in words"); Schopenhauer's model may have been Kant, who had attributed the same quality to "aesthetical

ideas" in *The Critique of Judgment*.[39] Schopenhauer also follows Kant in specifying that the process the "Ideas" inspire is the heuristic one typical of organisms. When an Idea floats before his mind, the poet "is not conscious *in abstracto* of the intention and aim of his work"; he works "unconsciously, indeed instinctively," discovering new ideas and formal features as he goes. The result is a poem that itself resembles an organism—something whose full meaning will always elude analysis.[40]

Ironically, Schopenhauer identifies the poetry resulting from the apprehension of Ideas as allegory, dismissing "symbolism" as an inferior, concept-driven art.[41] Like the English Romantics, the French Symbolists inverted these terms, making symbolism the art that resists analysis, and allegory the art that succumbs to it. Albert Mockel provides a classic example of how Schopenhauer's account of the creative process was used to describe the genesis of verse, hence to elevate it:

> L'allégorie, comme le symbole, exprime l'abstrait par le concret. Symbole et allégorie sont également fondés sur l'analogie, et tous deux contiennent une image développée.
>
> Mais je voudrais appeler l'allégorie l'oeuvre de l'esprit humain ou l'analogie est artificielle et extrinsèque, et j'appelerai symbole celle où l'analogie apparaît naturelle et intrinsèque.
>
> L'allégorie serait la représentation explicite ou analytique, par une image, d'une idée abstraite PRÉCONÇUE.
>
> Au contraire le symbole suppose la RECHERCHE INTUITIVE des divers éléments idéaux épars dans les Formes.[42]
>
> [Allegory, like symbol, expresses the abstract by means of the concrete. Symbol and allegory are equally based on analogy and both contained a developed image.
>
> Allegory would be the explicit or analytical representation, by way of an image, of a preconceived abstract idea.
>
> Symbol on the other hand presupposes the intuitive search for the various scattered ideal elements in the Forms.]

Although it would be wrong to suggest that all the French Symbolists professed a kind of "absolute" idealism (some, like Remy de Gourmont, espoused a "subjective" idealism, in which the highest mind the poet contacted was his own), Mockel's comments situate him within a line of writers who did: a line running from Baudelaire, to Mallarmé and Rimbaud, to a later generation including not just Mockel but also Moréas and Gide. Influenced both by the discourse of German Idealism and by its permutations in Coleridge and Carlyle, these writers represent the poet as "l'homme chargé de voir divinement" and inspiration as an experience of piercing phenomenal veils, doors and windowpanes—with the glorious result of apprehending the objective, authoritative, and generative "Idées." For Baudelaire, Mallarmé, and Rimbaud, the revealed Idea also functions as the nexus of a divinely ordained network of synaesthetic relations. The best-known account of the universal "correspondences" is Baudelaire's poem of that name, which depicts the network of divine relations glimmering through "des forêts de symboles."[43] The poet's intuitive "moment," in other words, is one in which he is suddenly aware of objective analogies or equivalencies in the world, and the mysterious "symbol"—sometimes in the world's text, sometimes in the text the poet constructs—is the aperture of the revelation. When Mallarmé writes about the experience of apprehending the objective relations in things, he imagines himself as a spider at the center of a web of divinely ordained connections.[44] Rimbaud attributes the phenomenon to an eruption from a universal consciousness, a subconscious mind whose contents originate "là-bas."[45]

Not surprisingly, the mystical discourse the Symbolists employ to describe poetic inspiration also governs their descriptions of inspiration's product. Typically, they describe the poem as a vehicle for the Idea: an icon whose words would become transparent, enabling the reader to share in the poet's divine illumination.[46] Although it would be wrong to represent Symbolist techniques as monolithic, it is not unreasonable to say that many formal features in their work reflect the mystical definitions they give to inspiration. At the simplest level, that of diction, their verse contains numerous claims about the poet's apprehension of the Infinite: of "les Cieux inconnus" or "les splendeurs situées derrière le tombeau."[47] In a more sophisticated technique, perfected by Mallarmé, it calls attention to the ephemerality of phenomena by evoking material objects indirectly, through synecdoche or negation.[48] Perhaps most significantly the Symbolists attempt to communicate the ineffable insights of inspiration—those that exceed discursive description—by organizing images into suggestive, nondiscursive arrangements. The key feature of those arrangements is that they have no clear rationale: the images chosen bear no obvious resemblance to one another, and the poets refrain from explaining what their connection might be. Rimbaud's "Le Bateau ivre," in its presentation of a kaleidoscopic series of apparently random images, is a classic example of this policy, as are a number of the prose poems in *Les Illuminations.*[49] In the drafts of Mallarmé's poems, too, we see a very deliberate effort to excise logical connectives and other explanatory material. The same clusters of images occur in poem after poem, accruing significance, not by any overt attribution of meaning but simply by their repeated association.[50] Mallarmé's refusal ever to explain his point directly can be attributed to his confidence that the choice of images he has made reflects poetry's transcendental origins. For him, as for many of his fellow Symbolists, the analogies simply reflect relations that "existent déjà dans le sein de la Beauté." They are examples of what Baudelaire calls "l'universelle analogie."[51]

There is a direct correlation between the Symbolists' supernaturalist claims for verse and the relatively few concessions their poetry makes to its audience. Baudelaire voices a sentiment as old as Aquinas when he suggests that the obscurity of poetry is not an intrinsic property, but a function of its readers' inadequacy: "tout est hiéroglyphique, et nous savons que les symboles ne sont obscurs que d'une manière relative, c'est-à-dire selon la pureté, la bonne volonté ou la clairvoyance des âmes."[52] [all is hieroglyphic, and we know that symbols are only obscure in a relative way, that is according to the purity, the good will and the clairvoyance of souls.] The young Yeats, profoundly influenced by Symbolism in both theory and practice, says essentially the same thing in pronouncing that symbol, unlike allegory, requires only "right instinct," not "right knowledge," for its understanding.[53] This attitude is evident not just in the method of juxtaposing apparently unrelated images, but also in the images—or "symbols"—themselves, and the interpretive challenges they pose. It is typical of Symbolist poetry that a contextualist reading renders a literal interpretation of its images impossible. The windows in Mallarmé's "Les Fenêtres" and the roses in Yeats's series of "Rose" poems simply could not be literal windows and roses, given the functions ascribed to them by their context. Seeking their significance then becomes a matter of guesswork: What other objects, for which windows and roses stand, might be capable of performing these functions? The reader is put into the position of having to divine the submerged tenor in what Northrop Frye would have called an "anagogic" metaphor: one in which claims about resemblance have ceded to absolute identification. Because the symbol is deemed by its authors to have "intrinsic" rather than "extrinsic" significance, it is regarded as being a *certain* communicator of its signified. No evidence or justification is needed for equivalencies that are divinely ordained. Understanding requires only that the reader be as clairvoyant as the poet.[54]

These, then, are the essentials of the "mystical" poetics the poets challenged. Hulme, Pound, and Stevens reacted to Symbolist claims about poetry's connection with "God" or the "Absolute" or the "Infinite" with all the suspicion appropriate to psychology and pragmatism: for them, as for James, these metaphysical terms were merely "power-bringing word[s] or name[s]" (*P* 31) serving to aggrandize poetry and the poet. Hulme exemplifies this visceral distaste for metaphysical discourse in his 1909 "Lecture on Modern Poetry," when he dismisses the "attempt[s] to explain technique" by "mumbl[ing] of the infinite" as so much "hocus-pocus."[55] A fuller statement of the position occurs in a notebook entry from about the same period:

> The literary man deliberately perpetrates a hypocrisy, in that he fits together his own isolated moments of ecstasy . . . and presents them as a picture of a higher life, thereby giving old maids a sense of superiority to other people and giving mandarins the opportunity to talk of "ideals." Then makes attempt to justify himself by inventing the soul and saying that occasionally the lower world gets glimpses of this, and that inferentially he is the medium. As a matter of fact being certain moments of ecstasy perhaps brought on by drink.[56]

The reasons for Hulme's, Pound's, and Stevens's contempt for Symbolist "hypocrisy" are in each case too complex to be reduced to easy generalizations, but collectively their manifestos suggest that this feeling was at least partially inspired by class and gender considerations. Hulme and Stevens, in particular, reveal a discomfort with representations of poetry that emphasize its "nobility," where an "ennobled" poetry is one claiming to transcend the demands and complexities of experience.[57] They share a need to represent poetry-making as good, honest, hard work: a laborious, painstaking activity and something of genuine use in the world.[58] In this they are very similar to James, who disparages Josiah Royce's philosophy of the Absolute as a "noble" philosophy "in the bad sense": one that ignores the "real world of sweat and dirt" (*P* 40). Closely related to this anxiety about work is the threat these poets felt Idealism posed to their manhood. Hulme's association of Idealist hypocrisy with "old maids" is consistent with many diatribes in his work against its "femininity"; all the talk about the "Infinite" was to him a lot of "moaning" and "whining"—something associated with "sentimentality rather than . . . virile thought." Stevens articulates his distress at feminizing conceptions of poetry in his essay "The Figure of the Youth as Virile Poet," where he points to the kind of "metaphysical" thinking characteristic of Idealism as a time-wasting activity that hardly "befits a man" and poses an alternative.[59] Although the concern among male modernist poets with expunging "feminine" values from poetry has been widely acknowledged,[60] recognizing their association of femininity with mysticism enables us to see something new: the attitudes favorable to feminist interests behind the façade of modernist *machismo*. In renouncing what James called the "feminine-mystical mind" (*WB* 224), the three male poets also give up the claims to privileged, absolute insight that might be used to authorize a patriarchal dogmatism. In Stevens's case, in particular, the virile gestures dismissing one kind of literary "femininity" mark the surreptitious return of other "feminine" values in his poetics: tentativeness, subversiveness, and alterability.

Whatever their reasons, Hulme, Pound, and Stevens were all devoted to changing the language in which the poetic process and its product was described, and the new language provided by empirical psychology was perfectly suited to the task. It must be emphasized that the poets' hostility to Idealist accounts of creation did not mean throwing them out lock, stock, and barrel. They endorse the anti-intellectualist aspects of those accounts—their claims about poetry's beginnings in an intuitive moment, about the heuristic process by which its intuitions are realized, and about the poem's resistance to analysis. What they reject is the *significance* transcendentalist discourse attributes to these phenomena. An acceptance of the intuitive and organic aspects of Idealist poetics is what led Frank Kermode in the 1950s, and a host of literary historians after him, to dismiss as nonsense modernist claims to be breaking with romanticism.[61] But although the modernists share a great deal with the romantics, it is no longer possible to argue, as Kermode did, that their resistance to the mystical elements in romantic and Symbolist discourse was merely superficial, that "Hulme's artist," for example, is *simply* "the Romantic voyant expressed in terms more agreeable to a man who disliked some kinds of philosophical language," or that the "Hulmian Image, precise, orderly, anti-discursive, the product of intuition" is *nothing but* "the Symbol of the French poets given a new philosophical suit."[62] Recent theories of discourse have demonstrated the inseparability of meaning and politics from language. As the reflex-action model suggests, different choices at the "stage of definition" have different consequences for action—and in the modernist redescription of Idealist poetics, this was definitely the case.

A PRACTICAL MUSE AND A PRAGMATIST POETRY

The new psychology enabled Hulme, Pound, and Stevens to redescribe the moment of "illumination" or "epiphany" with which the creative activity begins. The result was what Judith Ryan, borrowing from the Austrian novelist Robert Musil, has described as "daylight mysticism": an account that rewrites "knowing" as *feeling that* one knows, Truth as a psychological datum, the otherworldly light of revelation as the light of common day.[63] The key sources for the "daylight mysticism" found in Pound and Hulme were, in addition to James, Théodule Ribot and Henri Bergson. Ribot was the closest counterpart to James in France, a psychologist in his own right and a major publicist for psychology generally. Bergson is best known to critics of modernism as a philosopher of time, evolution, and free will, but he derived his positions on all these issues from recent work in psychology, especially Ribot's.[64] In their accounts of art, both Ribot and Bergson campaigned against the "Idealist" account of creative activity found in Symbolism, seeking to preserve its anti-intellectualism and organicism while exorcising the metaphysical principles to which it appeals. Most fascinating is the alternative description each offers for that mystical catalyst for creation, the "Idea." Ribot defines a "conception idéale" that functions in exactly the same way as Schopenhauer's and the Symbolists' Idea: it grips the attention, alerts the poet to likenesses or analogies, and governs a heuristic process of articulation. But he disengages this construct from metaphysics, describing it as a cluster of associated images and ideas springing up from the unconscious mind, where the origin of that mind is left undecided.[65] Worried that his account of creative intuition will be equated with Schopenhauer's, Bergson adapts the concept of the *conception idéale*; in his account it becomes "une certaine image intermédiaire entre la simplicité de l'intuition concrète et la complexité des abstractions qui la traduisent, image fuyante et évanouissante, qui hante, inaperçue peut-être, l'esprit du philosophe. . . ." ["a certain intermediary image between the simplicity of the concrete intuition and the complexity of the abstractions that translate it, a receding and vanishing image, which haunts, unperceived perhaps, the mind of the philosopher. . . ."] In its position as an "intermediary" and in its function as an arbiter of expression (Bergson represents it as a "fantôme qui nous hante pendant que nous tournons autour de la doctrine et auquel il faut s'adresser pour obtenir le signe décisif"), ["a phantom that haunts us while we turn about the doctrine and to which we must go in order to obtain the decisive signal"] the *conception idéale* is not just a demystified version of the "Idea" but also a neutralized version of Plato's mystical Muse.[66] It has a counterpart in the "divinities" James substituted for God in *The Varieties of Religious Experience*: objects of prayerful communion who communicate what *seems* like timeless wisdom yet who occupy no *certain* place in a transcendental world.

Recognizing the genesis and constitution of the *conception idéale* is essential to noticing an important, previously unseen parallel between Hulme, Pound, and Stevens: all three displace the Symbolists' "Idea" with the same kind of psychologized catalyst for creativity. Versions of the *conception idéale* appear over and over again in their manifestos, central elements in their attempts to speak of verse "in a plain way." Hulme writes of an "inside image" or "idea" that "precedes [the poet's] writing and makes it firm"; in elaborating this concept, he alludes directly to Bergson's *L'Évolution créatrice*.[67] In Pound's manifestos, the *conception idéale* appears as the "Image": the "PRIMARY FORM" that "PRESENTS ITSELF TO THE VIVID CONSCIOUSNESS" of the creating poet. Here, as in Ribot and Bergson, it is a cluster of associated images and ideas, erupting from the unconscious mind and generating new images and ideas in the process of being articulated. In Stevens, finally, the *conception idéale* appears both as "the first idea" and as the "companion of the conscience," who whispers words of wisdom in the poet's ear; Stevens shrinks from attributing the "first idea" to any "voluminous master folded in his fire" and renounces the right to call his interior paramour a "mystic muse." In sum, all of these entities function like the Symbolists' Idea and the Platonic Muse: they convince the poet of something and guide him through a process of articulation that is also a process of discovery. But all of them are without the "metaphysical baggage" carried by their Idealist counterparts.[68]

The substitution of *conceptions idéales* for Ideas was much more than merely the cosmetic change that Kermode, for one, suggests. In bracketing the source of inspiration, Hulme, Pound, and Stevens are making an important point about the status of poetic knowledge. Contrary to what many commentators have suggested, this is not a claim that the poet's insights are purely subjective—the projections of desire and nothing more. Rather these insights occupy what phenomenologists would call an "epochal" space:[69] whether they originate wholly "below" the mind, in desire, is as impossible to determine as whether they originate "Beyond" the mind, in God. All that can be known for certain is that they are a *genuine part* of the poet's mental experience. As Pound says of the "Image," or as any phenomenologist might say of the contents of consciousness, it is "real" simply, and only, "because we know it directly."[70]

Aided, then, by the French psychologists, as well as by James himself, Hulme, Pound, and Stevens reduced inspiration to what it was in *The Varieties of Religious Experience*: a sudden insight, accompanied by a feeling of certainty, whose cognitive value could not be known for certain. This important move is the first thing that made theirs a "pragmatist" poetics; the second is in the programs they devise for responding to the redefined "impression." That the three theorists are committed to the central principle of the reflex action model—the principle that one's "active measures" should appropriately reflect the "stage of definition"—is suggested by the fact that each of them is a champion of "sincerity." However limited they suspect the poet's insights might be, none of them is going to make him into a rhetorician or have him lie to protect his vocation.[71] This being the case, they face a major dilemma: If the poet's insights can only ever be inconclusive, on what grounds should he ever make any assertions at all? What right does he have to consider his insight of any interest to others? Should he not, at the very least, follow the route taken by Impressionist poets and painters and refrain from venturing any generalization from his experience, aiming to record (as best as language enables him) only the unprocessed data of sense?[72] What prevents Hulme, Pound, and Stevens from discouraging any form of real assertion—from consigning the poet to the torpor of skepticism—is their very Jamesian recognition that the decision to throw one's weight behind a generalization is a "momentous" one. In their own ways, they all imagine the poet lost in the woods (or in what Hulme called the "cindery" expanse of the world).[73] They all know that believing in theories is a source of comfort in what otherwise seems like chaos and that avoiding such a practice altogether will be to condemn oneself to fear, confusion, and stasis forever. To use a term proposed by Kermode, each of their hypothetical poets lives in a moment of *kairos*: a "decisive moment" where what Stevens called "dithering" (*CP* 452) is indefensible.[74]

Believing that uncertainty should not stand in the way of assertion, Hulme, Pound, and Stevens all recommend provisional modes of expression comparable to the ones proposed by James. That is, they all encourage the poet to assert himself, but they also urge him to indicate that his propositions are contingent on empirical testing. As I shall show, the cornerstone of all three poetics is a particular form of metaphor: one preserving the tension between the pragmatist's obligation to generalize and his duty to attend to the "real world of sweat and dirt." This is the device that Pound called the "interpretive metaphor."[75] Recognizing how this trope fulfils James's specifications for pragmatism enables us to see clearly how it differs from the Symbol. In essence it is a method of simple juxtaposition (what Frye called a "literal" metaphor) or, at its most coercive, a simile (for Frye, a "descriptive" metaphor).[76] What distinguishes this trope from the Symbol[77] is its preservation of *both* the phenomenal images between which a likeness has been perceived (the Symbol submerges one of the terms, assuming their interchangeability). In Sanford Schwartz's terms, it is a trope that embodies a "dialectic of form and flux": "a form that unifies sensory particulars without losing sight of the differences between them."[78] Wielding this kind of metaphor, the pragmatist poet claims much less authority for the insight he communicates than do his transcendentalist counterparts. Instead of assuming a divinely ordained identity, he simply calls attention to an analogy. Instead of submerging one of the metaphor's terms and challenging the reader to intuit connections he believes are objective, he simply takes the first step in a process of *making* connections, preserving all the evidence for and against generalization. Thus, he gives the reader an opportunity *to judge for herself* whether or not the incipient theory will hold up, whether or not the similarities are sufficient to prevail over the differences. In effect he adopts the kind of generous communicative practice James recommended for the pragmatist, presenting "as candidly as he can the grounds for the faith that is in him and leaving an example to work on others as it may."

The "interpretive metaphor," in other words, like other, closely related devices we shall see in pragmatist poetry, is to play the role of a "blaze" in the forest. For Hulme the poem is a provisional "map," tracing a path through the cinders; for Pound it is an "equation" for building helpful "bridges and devices"; for Stevens it is

a "hypothesis," intended "to help people to live their lives" (*CP* 516; *NA* 30).[79] It is a proposition, moreover, whose usefulness *doesn't preclude its truthfulness,* so long as its readers subject it to their own processes of testing and revising. As I hope to show, pragmatist poetry—in respecting both the limitations and the potential of a "practical muse"—also makes pragmatists of its interpreters.

Notes

1. See Myers, *William James,* 19-20, 493-94.

2. For a discussion of this problem in James criticism, see Charlene Haddock Seigfried, *William James's Radical Reconstruction of Philosophy* (Albany: SUNY Press, 1990), 21, 399n.

3. James, "Reflex-Action and Theism," *WB,* 98.

4. See vol. 2, chapter 21 of *The Principles of Psychology,* particularly the section "Belief in Objects of Theory" in William James, *The Principles of Psychology,* 2 vols. (1890; reprint, New York: Dover, 1950), pp. 311-20). Further references to *The Principles of Psychology,* vols. 1 and 2, will appear in the text with the abbreviation *PP* 1, 2. Hans Vaihinger, another philosopher important to modernism, was also interested in this theory; see *The Philosophy of "As if",* trans. C. K. Ogden (London: Kegan Paul, Trench, Trubner, 1924), xxxi.

5. James, "Reflex Action and Theism," *WB* 91. For an account of the physiological principle and its importance for psychology, see Edwin G. Boring, *A History of Experimental Psychology* (New York: Meredith, 1957), 29ff. and 35-39.

6. James, "Reflex Action and Theism," 92 (italics mine) and "The Sentiment of Rationality," 72.

7. James, "Reflex Action and Theism," 98 (italics mine).

8. James comments that the reflex action theory of mind commits those who accept it "to regarding the mind as an essentially teleological mechanism. I mean by this that the conceiving or theorizing faculty—the mind's middle department—*functions exclusively for the sake of ends* that do not exist at all in the world of impressions we receive by way of our senses, but are set by our emotional and practical subjectivity altogether" ("Reflex Action and Theism," 94-95).

9. Ibid., 107, 97.

10. That James might have thought it appropriate to use the reflex-action model to describe his own, interrelated philosophical concerns is suggested by his comment that the endeavor to interpret or de-

fine a divine "presence" (without question his own concern in *The Varieties of Religious Experience*) belongs to "Department two" of a reflex action ("Reflex Action and Theism," 107).

11. James, *The Varieties of Religious Experience* (Harmondsworth: Penguin, 1982), 25. Further references to this volume will appear in the text with the abbreviation *VRE*.

12. Judith Ryan, *The Vanishing Subject: Early Psychology and Literary Modernism* (Chicago: University of Chicago Press, 1991), 2.

13. See also 58. For a general discussion of James's contribution to the development of phenomenology, and especially of his influence on Husserl, see James M. Edie, *William James and Phenomenology* (Bloomington: Indiana University Press, 1987). For Edie the key phenomenological texts in James's *corpus* are "The Sentiment of Rationality" and *The Varieties of Religious Experience.*

14. See *The Varieties of Religious Experience,* 510-11.

15. Ibid., 380-81.

16. James, "The Sentiment of Rationality," *WB* 19.

17. For evidence that James made a conscious effort to devise an appropriate response to this question, see *VRE* 422-29. James's concern in this section is to "inquire whether we can invoke [the mystical state] as authoritative" (*VRE* 422). The methods he recommends for dealing with the state correspond to the methods outlined in *Pragmatism.* For further evidence of the pragmatic method in *VRE,* see 455-56.

18. On p. 33, James cites Fitz James Stephen, *Liberty, Equality, Fraternity* 2d ed. (London: n.p., 1874), 353.

19. James, "Reflex-action and Theism," *WB* 112.

20. James, "The Sentiment of Rationality," *WB* 86.

21. James Leuba, *A Psychological Study of Religion, Its Origin, Function and Future* (New York: Macmillan, 1912). For an account of the development of empirical theology in America, see Nancy Frankenberry, *Religion and Radical Empiricism* (Albany: SUNY Press, 1987), 1-35. Following Bernard M. Loomer, Frankenberry defines empirical theology as "a methodology which accepts the general empirical axiom that all ideas are reflections of concrete experience, either actual or possible. All propositional or conceptual knowledge originates from and is confirmable by physical experience. The limits of knowledge are defined by the limits of the experienceable, by the limits of relationship. Reason functions in the service of

concrete fact and experience" (*Religion and Radical Empiricism* 2-3).

22. Ibid., 111, 99, 39, 13.

23. Ibid., 13, 112.

24. For a fuller account of how James insists on verification without falling back on the "correspondence" theory, see Seigfried, *William James's Radical Reconstruction of Philosophy,* 292-94.

25. For James's fullest account of the problematics of fact, see *Essays in Radical Empiricism,* eds. Frederick H. Burkhardt, Fredson Bowers, and Ignas K. Skrupselis (Cambridge: Harvard University Press, 1976), passim. Further references to this volume will appear in the text with the abbreviation *ERE.* I discuss the relationship between James's antiimperialism and the pragmatist's duty to attend to fact in chapter 5 of this study.

26. James, "Reflex Action and Theism," *WB* 33; my italics.

27. *William James on Exceptional Mental States: The 1896 Lowell Lectures,* ed. Eugene Taylor (Amherst: University of Massachusetts Press, 1984), 150. James draws from the work of psychologists who equate genius with degenerative insanity: L. F. Lelut, Jacques-Joseph Moreau, John F. Nisbet, and Césare Lombroso. For an account of these psychologists and their work, see 203.

28. "Reflex Action and Theism," *WB* 103.

29. James, "Philosophical Conceptions and Practical Results," in *Writings 1878-1899,* ed. Gerald E. Myers (New York: Library of America, 1992), 1078.

30. See for example *Pragmatism,* 44, 144.

31. James, "Philosophical Conceptions and Practical Results," 1079.

32. Compare James's remark that the writings of the philosopher "must more and more ally themselves with a literature which is confessedly tentative and suggestive rather than dogmatic." See "The Moral Philosopher and the Moral Life," *WB* 159.

33. Plato, *Phaedrus,* trans. and ed. R. Hackworth (Cambridge: Cambridge University Press, 1952), 58.

34. For a description of the German Idealists' efforts in this area, and the tendency of their contemporaries to ignore them, see David Simpson, *The Origins of Modern Critical Thought* (Cambridge: Cambridge University Press, 1988), 14-16. For more about the variety of epistemological claims made by self-described Idealists and the inherent

contradictions in the subjectivist version of Idealism's subjectivist version that makes it easily, though mistakenly, assimilated to Plato, see Ralph Barton Perry, *Present Philosophical Tendencies* (New York: George Braziller, 1955), 113-93. The modernist poets I consider appear to have read the Romantics and Symbolists as espousing what Perry calls "Absolute Idealism": a form of Idealism that incorporates the "terms of a devotional mysticism—Spirit, Perfection, Eternity, Infinity—[into the] . . . very letter of its discourse" (164).

35. For an account of the Symbolists' tendency to do this, see A. G. Lehmann, *The Symbolist Aesthetic in France 1885-1895* (Oxford: Blackwell, 1968), 38, 42.

36. Lehmann, *The Symbolist Aesthetic in France,* 57.

37. Arthur Schopenhauer, *The World as Will and Representation,* trans. E. F. J. Payne (New York: Dover, 1969), vol. 1 of 2: 144, 235. That Schopenhauer understood the "Idea" to constitute a form of universal, absolute knowledge is suggested by his remarks in the same volume, 250-53.

38. Ibid., 234-35.

39. See Immanuel Kant, *The Critique of Judgment,* trans. J. H. Bernard (New York: Hafner, 1951), 157ff.

40. Schopenhauer, *The World as Will and Representation,* 1: 235. For Kant's description of the organic process and its product, see *Critique of Judgement,* 19-24. Schopenhauer comments that "the transition from the Idea to the concept" that takes place in translation "is always a descent." *The World as Will and Representation,* 1: 238.

41. Ibid., 239.

42. Albert Mockel, *Propos de littérature* (1894), in Guy Michaud, *Message poétique du symbolisme* (Paris: Librairie Nizet, 1947), 752. The translation is mine.

43. For examples of absolute Idealism in Moréas and Gide, see Michaud, *Message poétique du symbolisme,* 725, 731. See also Stéphane Mallarmé, *Oeuvres complètes,* ed. Henri Mondor and G. Jean-Aubry (Paris: Gallimard, 1945), 378, and Charles Baudelaire, *Oeuvres complètes,* vol. 1 of 2 vols., ed. Charles Pichois (Paris: Gallimard, 1975), 11.

44. Stéphane Mallarmé, letter to Théodore Aubanel, 28 July 1866, in *Correspondance complète 1862-1871,* ed. Bertrand Marchal (Paris: Gallimard, 1959), 315-16.

45. Arthur Rimbaud, *Oeuvres complètes,* ed. Rolland de Renéville and Jules Mouquet (Paris: Gallimard,

1946), 255. Generally the Symbolists' renunciation of any control over inspiration, their habit of attributing it to the intervention of some higher power, extended to the whole process of committing that inspiration to words. Mallarmé, for example, represented the process of articulation as one in which a transcendental *Geist* worked out its intentions. See Robert Gibson, *Modern French Poets on Poetry* (Cambridge: Cambridge University Press, 1961), 85. The Symbolists' commitment to representing the poetic process as an instinctive, organic one, also manifested itself in numerous claims about the identity of form and content. The Symbolist poet claimed never to know what he was to say before he has said it and after he said it that he could never say it again in any other way.

46. See Michaud, *Message poétique du symbolisme,* 731.

47. Baudelaire, *Oeuvres complètes,* 1: 127, 2: 334.

48. Mallarmé said that the poet's aim ought to be to evoke "l'objet tu, par des mots allusifs, jamais directs" (*Oeuvres complètes,* 400). For examples of his use of synecdoche and negation, see the poems "Sainte," "Ses purs ongles . . . ," and "Prose: pour des Esseintes," in *Oeuvres complètes,* ed. Henri Mondor and G. Jean-Aubry (Paris: Gallimard, 1945), 53, 68, 55-57.

49. See Rimbaud, "Le Bateau ivre," *Oeuvres complètes,* 66-69. For prose poems that demonstrate this practice, see "Après le déluge," "Enfance," and "Ornières," *Illuminations,* in *Oeuvres complètes,* 121-22, 122-23, 135.

50. Over the course of several poems, for example, women are juxtaposed with roses, and roses with diamonds, and diamonds with ice, and ice with virgins; when we then see a woman juxtaposed with an image of a weeping diamond, we may (or may not) intuit the point that the loss of virginity is a cause for sadness. For this repeated cluster of images, see the poems "Surgi de la croupe et du bonde," "Dame," "O si chère de loin . . . ," and "Hérodiade" in *Oeuvres complètes,* 74, 61, 41-49.

51. Baudelaire, *Oeuvres complètes,* 2: 133.

52. Ibid.

53. W. B. Yeats, *Essays and Introductions* (London: Macmillan, 1961), 147.

54. Northrop Frye discusses the "anagogic" metaphor in *Anatomy of Criticism: Four Essays* (Princeton: Princeton University Press, 1957), 124. Frye says that when metaphor reaches the anagogic level, the "literary universe . . . is a universe in which everything is potentially identical with everything

else" and that "there is no metaphor, not even 'black is white,' which a reader has any right to quarrel with in advance." For examples of claims about the "intrinsic" rather than "extrinsic" significance of symbols, see Mockel, above, and Thomas Carlyle, *Sartor Resartus* (London: Chapman and Hall, 1885), 168-69. Rimbaud's and Mallarmé's faith in the intrinsic power of symbols led them to experiment with what they believed to be the intrinsic power of individual letters. See Rimbaud, "Voyelles" (*Oeuvres complètes,* 53) and Mallarmé, "Un Coup de dés" (*Oeuvres complètes,* 457).

55. T. E. Hulme, "A Lecture on Modern Poetry," in *The Collected Writings of T. E. Hulme,* ed. Karen Csengeri (Oxford: Oxford University Press, 1994), 51. Subsequent references to this volume will appear in the text with the abbreviation *CW.*

56. Hulme, "Notes on Language and Style," *CW* 44-45.

57. For Hulme's disgust with Yeats's efforts to "ennoble" the poetic vocation and other comments against the concept of poetry's "nobility," see Hulme, "Notes on Language and Style," *CW* 43 and 38. For Stevens's critique of "the fortunes of the idea of nobility as a characteristic of the imagination," see "The Noble Rider and the Sound of Words," in *The Necessary Angel* (London: Faber and Faber, 1960), 7. Subsequent references to this volume will use the abbreviation *NA.* Read only in excerpts, the "Noble Rider" essay might be mistaken for a straightforward *defense* of the nobility of poetry, but its main point is that a kind of nobility in poetry that does not acknowledge concrete realities is unacceptable. A fuller account of the essay and of how its argument can be misconstrued is found in chapter 4 of this study.

58. See Hulme's comment that "people anxious to be poets think there is no work, just as haymaking. . . . [They are c]oncerned in the field with ecstasy, but the pains of birth and parturition are sheets and sheets of paper." See also his comment that poetry's "intensity of meaning" is the product of "agony and bloody sweat." "Notes on Language and Style," *CW* 43, 36. I discuss Stevens's concern that poetry performs useful work in the world at length in chapter 4 of this study. For an account of how pragmatist poets tend to associate poetry making with physical labor, see Richard Poirier, *Poetry and Pragmatism,* 79.

59. Hulme, "Romanticism and Classicism," and "A Lecture on Modern Poetry," *CW* 66, 51; Stevens, "The Figure of the Youth as Virile Poet," *NA* 30.

60. Suzanne Clark explores this issue and surveys the criticism of it in *Sentimental Modernism* (Bloomington: Indiana University Press, 1991). She notes the irony in the modernists' conflation of romanticism and femininity, because romanticism has been regarded by some critics (and in some ways by itself) as an aesthetic that renounced feminine values (27-28).

61. See Frank Kermode, *Romantic Image* (London: Routledge and Kegan Paul, 1957). I discuss Kermode's argument at length in chapter 1 of this study. The position that Hulme's "new classicism" was muddled, because it is based largely on Romantic tenets, is also espoused by Alun R. Jones, *The Life and Opinions of T. E. Hulme* (London: Victor Gollancz, 1960), 57; Murray Krieger, *The New Apologists for Poetry* (Minneapolis: University of Minnesota Press, 1956), 35; Graham Hough, *Image and Experience* (London: Duckworth, 1960), 30.

62. Kermode, *Romantic Image,* 130.

63. Judith Ryan, *The Vanishing Subject,* 219. Ryan defines "Daylight mysticism" as a representation of mystical experience that "divest[s] mystical experience of its mystery" (223). Where Ryan's recent study is mainly concerned with the representations of epiphany in literary texts—especially in the fiction of Proust, Musil, Woolf, Joyce and others—my study focuses on the examples of "daylight mysticism" in modernist manifestos. In my argument the carefully demystified accounts of epiphany found in Hulme's, Pound's, and Stevens's poetry are measures taken to coordinate poetic style with the redescriptions of inspiration in the manifestos.

64. For the full range of Bergson's psychological sources, see Ben-Ami Scharfstein, *Roots of Bergson's Philosophy* (New York: Columbia University Press, 1943), 32ff and 59ff. Bergson had tremendous respect for the work of James and corresponded with him regularly after the turn of the century. Despite the strong resemblance between his conception of pure mental experience as *durée réelle* and James's conception of the "stream of consciousness," Bergson denied that James was in any way responsible for his own views (Scharfstein, 30-31).

65. Théodule Ribot, *Essai sur l'imagination créatrice* (Paris: Félix Alcan, 1921), 67. I discuss Ribot's and Bergson's accounts of the *conception idéale* in chapter 1 of this study. For a comparable notion in James, see *PP* 1: 269-71; 2: 1168-69.

66. Henri Bergson, *La Pensée et le mouvant* (Paris: Presses Universitaires de France, 1938), 119, 130. Translations from Bergson, *The Creative Mind,* trans. Mabelle L. Andison (Westport, Conn.: Greenwood, 1968), 128, 139.

67. Hulme, "A Lecture on Modern Poetry," and "Notes on Language and Style," *CW* 49, 34, 26, 25. Hulme alludes to *L'Evolution créatrice* in "The Philosophy of Intensive Manifolds," *CW* 189. Paraphrasing Bergson, Hulme emphasizes that the idea that governs the process of expression is not to be confused with Schopenhauer's Idea ("Bergson's Theory of Art," *CW* 194).

68. Pound, "Vortex. Pound," in *Blast,* ed. Wyndham Lewis (1914; reprint. Santa Barbara: Black Sparrow Press, 1981), 154; Stevens, *The Collected Poems of Wallace Stevens* (New York: Knopf, 1954), 381; Stevens, *Opus Posthumous,* 253; Stevens, *Collected Poems,* 381; Stevens, "The Figure of the Youth as Virile Poet," *NA* 60; Hulme, "Bergson's Theory of Art," *CW* 194. Subsequent references to Stevens's *Collected Poems* will appear in the text with the abbreviation *CP*. For evidence that Pound and Stevens agree with Hulme's desire to eliminate "metaphysical baggage," see Pound's insistence that his claims about the "Image" do not entail any presumption about the poet's apprehension of a "deathless light" or about his insights into a "permanent world" ("Vorticism," *GB* 86). Stevens stresses that he makes no claims for the mystical origins either of the "first idea" or of the "companion of the conscience." He refuses to trace the idea back to any "voluminous master folded in his fire" (*CP* 381), and, as I explain in chapter 3, he pulls his muses back from the Beyond onto the threshold of the self, a move similar to James's treatment of his deflated "divinities" in *The Varieties of Religious Experience.*

69. Throughout this study, I shall use the term *epoche* as Husserl used it: to denote the condition of being detached from all consideration of origins or of being subjected to phenomenological reduction. See Edmund Husserl, *Ideas: General Introduction to Pure Phenomenology,* trans. W. R. Boyce Gibson (New York: Collier-Macmillan, 1962), 99-100.

70. Pound, "Vorticism," *GB* 86.

71. One of the best-known expressions of this commitment is Pound's statement in "Vorticism," where he describes the "image" (in the second sense of the term) as a type of poem: "The 'image' is the furthest possible remove from rhetoric. Rhetoric is the art of dressing up some important matter so as to fool the audience for the time being. . . . Even Aristotle distinguishes between rhetoric, 'which is persuasion,' and the *analytical examination of truth*" (*GB* 83; my italics). Pound also describes serious art as "sincere self-expression" and twice cites Remy de Gourmont's statement of the principle (*GB* 85; *SP* 386; *LE* 349). Hulme's call for sincerity is implicit in his concern that the extravagant claims of Symbolists and Romantics did not reflect the truth about the creative experience and in his repeated injunctions against the use of cliché. See, for example, "Notes on Language and Style," *CW* 55-56. In "Bergson's Theory of Art," he insists that the poet should make an extraordinary effort to bend the "curves" of language, so as to represent himself truthfully; in the best poet, he says, there is "a passionate desire for accuracy" (*CW* 200). Stevens distinguishes the "poetry of experience," which he endorses, from the "poetry of rhetoric" (*OP* 187), which he does not. His values are apparent in his explanation for citing "The Emperor of Ice-Cream" as his favorite poem: the poem, he says, "represented what was in my mind at the moment, with the least possible manipulation" (*OP* 212). The poets' concern with sincerity is the hallmark of their expressive poetics and a reflection of their concession that truth in the absolute sense may not be a standard the poet can realistically be expected to meet. See I. A. Richards's distinction between "scientific" truth and the truth of "Sincerity" in poetry, *Principles of Literary Criticism* (London: Routledge and Kegan Paul, 1967), 212-14.

72. The Impressionist painters and poets like Wilde and Symons aimed above all to capture the particularity of things—to avoid what Walter Pater called the "roughness of the eye that makes any two persons, things, situations, seem alike." *Walter Pater: Essays on Literature and Art,* ed. Jennifer Uglow (London: Dent, 1973), 40-41. The impulse was to resist any device that would translate things into *types*: it included a resistance to metaphor (more successful, inevitably, in painting than in poetry). Pound excoriated the tentativeness of such art, calling it "flaccid" ("Vortex. Pound," 153) and emphasized that Imagisme was not Impressionism.

73. The picture of a cindery chaos, probably derived from Bergson, is the central image in Hulme's intriguing notebook fragments, both those collected under the title "Notes on Language and Style" and those called "Cinders" (*CW* 7-45). Pound uses a similar image to describe empirical data in one of his best-known metaphors for the organizational principle in art: the "rose in the steel dust." *The Cantos* (London: Faber and Faber, 1975), 449. Stevens also represents experience as a gritty flux awaiting and resisting theoretical organization. See *CP* 412, 529.

74. Frank Kermode, *The Sense of an Ending* (Oxford: Oxford University Press, 1966), 49.

75. See Pound, *LE* 162, and Ernest Fenollosa, *The Chinese Written Character as a Medium for Poetry,* ed. Ezra Pound (San Francisco: City Lights, 1936), 23n.

76. Frye, *Anatomy of Criticism,* 123.

77. Or from what Gelpi has called the "type": "A type [is] an inherently significant and signifying symbol, a manifestation of spiritual truth in material form, to be communicated verbally, whereas a trope [is] itself figurative language, a metaphorical invention." Albert Gelpi, *A Coherent Splendour: The American Poetic Renaissance, 1910-1950* (Cambridge: Cambridge University Press, 1987), 68.

78. Sanford Schwartz, *The Matrix of Modernism: Pound, Eliot and Early 20th-Century Thought* (Princeton: Princeton University Press, 1985), 62, 75. In describing the Image this way, I agree with Schwartz's representation of Pound's metaphor: "Pound's interpretive metaphor . . . is neither fact nor fiction but a construct that bridges the distinction between them. It transcends fiction in that it discloses reality exactly as it appears in a special state of mind . . . Pound avoids both Nietzsche's fictionalism and Fenollosa's realism: the interpretive metaphor enables us to view the world 'as if' it possesses certain forms, but it projects these forms as experiential rather than factual, as 'interpretation' rather than explanation" (95). Schwartz's use of Stevens's favorite qualifier, "as if," points to one of my major points in this study: Pound and Stevens were more alike than they were different, and what united them was a commitment to a particular kind of provisional expression, incorporating the principles of phenomenological reduction.

79. Hulme, *CW* 22; Pound, "The Wisdom of Poetry," *SP* 332.

Abbreviations

Works frequently cited are identified throughout the text and notes by the following abbreviations:

CP: Wallace Stevens. *The Collected Poems of Wallace Stevens.* New York: Knopf, 1954.

CSP: Ezra Pound. *Collected Shorter Poems.* London: Faber and Faber, 1952.

CW: T. E. Hulme. *The Collected Writings of T. E. Hulme.* Edited by Karen Csengeri. Oxford: Oxford University Press, 1994.

ERE: William James. *Essays in Radical Empiricism.* Edited by Frederick H. Burkhardt, Fredson Bowers, and Ignas K. Skrupselis. Cambridge: Harvard University Press, 1976.

GB: Ezra Pound. *Gaudier-Brzeska.* New York: New Directions, 1970.

LE: Ezra Pound. *Literary Essays of Ezra Pound.* Edited by T. S. Eliot. London: Faber and Faber, 1960.

MT: William James. *The Meaning of Truth.* Edited by Frederick H. Burkhardt, Fredson Bowers, and Ignas K. Skrupskelis. Cambridge: Harvard University Press, 1979.

NA: Wallace Stevens. *The Necessary Angel.* London: Faber and Faber, 1960.

OP: Wallace Stevens. *Opus Posthumous.* Edited by Milton J. Bates. Revised, enlarged, and corrected edition. New York: Knopf, 1989.

P: William James. *Pragmatism.* Edited by Frederick H. Burkhardt, Fredson Bowers, and Ignas K. Skrupskelis. Cambridge: Harvard University Press, 1975.

PP 1, 2: William James. *Principles of Psychology.* 2 vols. New York: Henry Holt, 1890; reprint Dover, 1950.

PU: William James. *A Pluralistic Universe.* Edited by Fredson Bowersand Ignas K. Skrupselis. Cambridge: Harvard University Press, 1977.

SP: Ezra Pound. *Selected Prose: 1909-1965.* Edited by William Cookson. London: Faber and Faber, 1960.

VRE: William James. *The Varieties of Religious Experience.* Harmondsworth: Penguin, 1982.

WB: William James. *The Will to Believe.* Edited by Frederick H. Burkhardt, Fredson Bowers, and Ignas K. Skrupskelis. Cambridge: Harvard University Press, 1979.

CHARLES SANDERS PEIRCE

Susan Haack (essay date winter 1997)

SOURCE: Haack, Susan. "'We Pragmatists . . .': Peirce and Rorty in Conversation." *Partisan Review* 64, no. 1 (winter 1997): 91-107.

[*In the following essay, Haack uses excerpts from the works of Charles Sanders Peirce and Richard Rorty to construct an imaginary interview between herself and the two thinkers for the purpose of illuminating, comparing, and contrasting Peirce's and Rorty's positions on such subjects as the nature of truth and reality, metaphysics, and scientific inquiry.*]

[*Haack*]: *Let me begin by asking Professor Rorty to explain how he feels about philosophers like you, Mr. Peirce, who take themselves to be seeking the truth.*[1]

[Rorty]: It is . . . more difficult than it used to be to locate a real live metaphysical prig. [But] you can still find [philosophers] who will solemnly tell you that they are seeking *the truth,* not just a story or a consensus but an honest-to-God, down-home, accurate representation of the way the world is . . . lovably old-fashioned prigs (*EHO,* p. 86).

[*Haack*]: Mr. Peirce?

[Peirce]: In order to reason well . . . , it is absolutely necessary to possess . . . such virtues as intellectual honesty and sincerity and a real love of truth (2.82). The cause [of the success of scientific inquirers] has been that the motive which has carried them to the laboratory and the field has been a craving to know how things really were . . . (1.34). [Genuine inquiry consists] in diligent inquiry into truth for truth's sake (1.44), . . . in actually drawing the bow upon truth with intentness in the eye, with energy in the arm (1.235).

[When] it is no longer the reasoning which determines what the conclusion shall be, but . . . the conclusion which determines what the reasoning shall be . . . this is sham reasoning. . . . The effect of this shamming is that men come to look upon reasoning as mainly decorative . . . The result of this state of things is, of course, a rapid deterioration of intellectual vigor . . . (1.57-8).

[*Rorty*]: *"Justification" [is] a social phenomenon rather than a transaction between "the knowing subject" and "reality"* (PMN, p. 9), . . . *not a matter of a . . . relation between ideas (or words) and objects, but of conversation, of social practice . . . We understand knowledge when we understand the social justification of belief, and thus have no need to view it as accuracy of representation (p. 170).*

[Peirce]: The result [as I said] is, of course, a rapid deterioration of intellectual vigor. This is just what is taking place among us before our eyes. . . . Man loses his conceptions of truth and of reason (1.58, cont. and 1.59).

[*Rorty*]: *I do not have much use for notions like . . . "objective truth" (TWO, p. 141). [The] pragmatist view [is] of rationality as civility, . . . [as] respect for the opinions of those around one, . . . of "true" as a word which applies to those beliefs upon which we are able to agree . . . (SS, pp. 44, 40, 45).*

[Peirce]: [As I was saying,] man loses his conceptions of truth and of reason. If he sees one man assert what another denies, he will, if he is concerned, choose his side and set to work by all means in his power to silence his adversaries. The truth for him is that for which he fights (1.59, cont.).

[*Rorty*]: *Truth [is] entirely a matter of solidarity (ORT, p. 32). There is nothing to be said about either truth or rationality apart from descriptions of the familiar procedures of justification which a given society—ours— uses . . . (SS, p. 42).*

[Peirce]: You certainly opine that there is such a thing as Truth. Otherwise, reasoning and thought would be without a purpose. What do you mean by there being such a thing as Truth? You mean that something is SO . . . whether you, or I, or anybody thinks it is so or not. . . . The essence of the opinion is that there is *something* that is SO, no matter if there be an overwhelming vote against it (2.135). Every man is fully satisfied that there is such a thing as truth, or he would not ask any question. *That* truth consists in a conformity to something *independent of his thinking it to be so,* or of any man's opinion on that subject (5.211).

Truth [is] overwhelmingly forced upon the mind in experience as the effect of an independent reality (5.564). The essence of truth lies in its resistance to being ignored (2.139).

[*Rorty*]: *Some philosophers . . . insist that natural science discovers truth rather than makes it. . . . Other philosophers [like myself] . . . have concluded that science is no more than the handmaiden of technology (CIS, pp. 3-4).*

[Peirce]: There are certain mummified pedants who have never waked to the truth that the act of knowing a real object alters it. They are curious specimens of humanity, and . . . I am one of them . . . (5.555).

[*Rorty*]: *My rejection of traditional notions of rationality can be summed up by saying that the only sense in which science is exemplary is that it is a model of human solidarity (SS, p. 46).*

[Peirce]: Other methods of settling opinion have [certain advantages] over scientific investigation. A man should consider well of them; and then he should consider that, after all, he wishes his opinions to coincide with the fact . . . (5.387).

[*Rorty*]: *. . . I think that the very idea of a "fact of the matter" is one we would be better off without (PDP, p. 271).*

[Peirce]: . . . he should consider that, after all, he wishes his opinions to coincide with the fact, and . . . there is no reason why the results of those . . . [other] methods should do so (5.387, cont.).

[*Rorty*]: *"True sentences work because they correspond to the way things are" . . . [is an] empty metaphysical compliment, . . . [a] rhetorical pat on the back. . . .*

*[The pragmatist] drops the notion of truth as corre-
spondence with reality altogether . . . (CP, p. xvii).*

[Peirce]: Truth is the conformity of a representamen to
its object, *its* object, ITS object, mind you (5.554).

[However], that truth is the correspondence of a representation to its object is, as Kant says, merely the nomi-
nal definition of it. Truth belongs exclusively to propositions. A proposition has a subject (or set of subjects)
and a predicate. The subject is a sign; the predicate is a
sign; and the proposition is a sign that the predicate is a
sign of that of which the subject is a sign. If it be so, it
is true. But what does this correspondence . . . of the
sign to its object consist in? The pragmaticist answers
this question as follows. . . . If we can find out the
right method of thinking and can follow it out . . . then
truth can be nothing more nor less than the last result to
which the following out of this method would ultimately
carry us (5.553).

*[Rorty]: There are . . . two senses apiece of 'true' and
'real' and 'correct representation of reality,' . . . the
homely use of 'true' to mean roughly 'what you can defend against all comers,' . . . [the] homely and shop-
worn sense [and] the specifically 'philosophical' sense
. . . which, like the Ideas of Pure Reason, [is] designed
precisely to stand for the Unconditioned . . . (PMN,
pp. 308-9.)*

[Peirce]: That to which the representation should conform, is itself . . . utterly unlike a thing-in-itself
(5.553).

*[Rorty]: [A] pragmatist theory . . . says that Truth is
not the sort of thing one should expect to have a philosophically interesting theory about . . . (CP, p. xiii).
Pragmatists think that the history of attempts to . . .
define the word "true" . . . supports their suspicion
that there is no interesting work to be done in this area
(p. xiv).*

[Peirce]: Truth is that concordance of an abstract statement with the ideal limit towards which endless investigation would tend to bring scientific belief. . . . The
truth of the proposition that Caesar crossed the Rubicon
consists in the fact that the further we push our archaeological and other studies, the more strongly will
that conclusion force itself on our minds forever—or
would do so, if study were to go on forever. . . . The
same definitions equally hold in the normative sciences
(5.565-6).

*[Rorty]: I do not think . . . that [your account] is de-
fensible . . . [It] uses a term—'ideal'—which is just as
fishy as 'corresponds' (PDT, pp. 337, 338).*

[Peirce]: [A] false proposition is a proposition of which
some interpretant represents that, on an occasion which
it indicates, a percept will have a certain character,

while the immediate perceptual judgment on that occasion is that the percept has not that character. A true
proposition is a proposition belief in which would never
lead to such disappointment so long as the proposition
is not understood otherwise than it was intended (5.569).

Prof. Royce [like you] seems to think that this doctrine
is unsatisfactory because it talks about what would
be. . . . It may be he is right in this criticism; yet to
our apprehension this "would be" is readily resolved
. . . (8.113). [The] most important reals have the mode
of being of what the nominalist calls "mere" words,
that is, general types and would-bes. [His] "mere" reveals a complete misunderstanding . . . (8.191). The
will be's, the *actually is's,* and the *have beens* are not
the sum of the reals. . . . There are besides *would be's*
and *can be's* that are real (8.216).

*[Haack]: I suspect, Professor Rorty, that your sympa-
thies lie with the nominalist . . .*

[Rorty]: Nominalists like myself—those for whom language is a tool rather than a medium, and for whom a
concept is just the regular use of a mark or noise—. . .
see language as just human beings using marks and
noises to get what they want. (EHO, pp. 126-7).

The right idea, according to us nominalists, is that "recognition of meaning" is simply ability to substitute sensible signs . . . for other signs, . . . and so on indefinitely. This . . . doctrine is found . . . in [your
writings] . . . (TMoL, p. 211).

[Peirce]: The nominalistic Weltanschauung *has become
incorporated into what I will venture to call the very
flesh and blood of the average modern mind. (5.61).
Modern nominalists are mostly superficial men . . .
(5.312).*

*[A] realist is simply one who knows no more recondite
reality than that which is represented in a true representation (5.312, cont.). I am myself a scholastic realist
of a somewhat extreme stripe (5.470). Nomenclature involves classification; and classification is true or false,
and the generals to which it refers are either reals in
the one case, or figments in the other (5.453).*

*Pragmaticism could hardly have entered a head that
was not already convinced that there are real generals
(5.503).*

[Haack]: I wonder how Professor Rorty feels about
your references to "true representations" . . .

*[Rorty]: Pragmatism [is] anti-representationalism (PPD,
p. 1).*

[Peirce]: REPRESENT: to stand for, that is, to be in
such a relation to another that for certain purposes it is
treated by some mind as if it were that other. . . .

When it is desired to distinguish between that which represents and the . . . relation of representing, the former may be termed the "representamen," the latter the "representation" (2.273).

A sign, or *representamen,* is something which stands to somebody for something in some respect or capacity. It . . . creates in the mind of that person an equivalent sign, or perhaps a more developed sign. That sign which it creates I call the *interpretant* of the first sign. The sign stands for something, its *object* . . . in reference to a sort of idea, which I have sometimes called the *ground* of the representamen (2.228).

[*Rorty*]: *The notion of "accurate representation" is simply an . . . empty compliment which we pay to those beliefs which are successful in helping us do what we want to do (PMN, p. 10).*

[Peirce]: It is as though a man should address a land surveyor as follows: "You do not make a true representation of the land; you only measure lengths from point to point . . . you have to do solely with lines. But the land is a surface . . . You, therefore, fail entirely to represent the land." The surveyor, I think, would reply, "Sir, you have proved that . . . my map *is not* the land. I never pretended that it was. But that does not prevent it from truly representing the land, as far as it goes" (5.329).

[*Haack*]: *I am beginning to think that you may disagree with each other not only about nominalism, but about the nature and status of metaphysics . . .*

[Rorty]: The pragmatist . . . does not think of himself as *any* kind of a metaphysician . . . (CP, p. xxviii).

[*Peirce*]: *[The Pragmatic Maxim] will serve to show that almost every proposition of ontological metaphysics is either meaningless gibberish—one word being defined by other words, and they by still others, without any real conception ever being reached—or else is downright absurd; so that all such rubbish being swept away, what will remain of philosophy will be a series of problems capable of investigation by the observational methods of the true sciences. . . . So, instead of merely jeering at metaphysics . . . the pragmaticist extracts from it a precious essence . . . (5.423).*

We should expect to find metaphysics . . . to be somewhat more difficult than logic, but still on the whole one of the simplest of sciences, as it is one whose main principles must be settled before very much progress can be gained either in psychics or in physics. Historically we are astonished to find that it has been a mere arena of ceaseless and trivial disputation. But we also find that it has been pursued in a spirit the very contrary of that of wishing to learn the truth, which is the

most essential requirement. . . . Metaphysics is the proper designation for the third, and completing department of coenoscopy. . . . Its business is to study the most general features of reality and real objects. But in its present condition it is . . . a puny, rickety and scrofulous science. It is only too plain that those who pretend to cultivate it carry not the hearts of true men of science within their breast (6.4-6).

Here let us set down almost at random a small specimen of the questions of metaphysics which press . . . for industrious and solid investigation: Whether or no there be any real indefiniteness, or real possibility and impossibility? Whether there be any strictly individual existence? Whether there is any distinction . . . between fact and fancy? Or between the external and the internal worlds? What general . . . account can be given of the different qualities of feeling . . . ? Do all possible qualities of sensation . . . form one continuous system . . . ? . . . Is Time a real thing . . . ? How about Space . . . ? . . . Is hylozoism an opinion, actual or conceivable, rather than a senseless vocable . . . ? . . . What is consciousness or mind like . . . ? (6.6).

[Rorty]: Metaphysicians see [books] as divided according to disciplines, corresponding to different objects of knowledge. [We] ironists see them as divided according to traditions . . . (*CIS,* pp. 75-6).

[*Peirce*]: *All science is either, A. Science of Discovery; B. Science of Review; or C. Practical Science. . . . Science of Discovery is either, I. Mathematics; II. Philosophy; or III. Idioscopy. . . . Philosophy is divided into a. Phenomenology; b. Normative Science; c. Metaphysics. . . . Phenomenology is . . . a single study. Normative Science has three widely separated divisions: i. Esthetics; ii. Ethics. iii. Logic. . . . Metaphysics may be divided into, i, General Metaphysics, or Ontology; ii, Psychical, or Religious, Metaphysics, concerned chiefly with the questions of 1, God, 2, Freedom, 3, Immortality; and iii, Physical Metaphysics, which discusses the real nature of time, space, laws of nature, matter, etc. (1.181-192).*

[Haack]: Could you please explain your reference to "ironists," Professor Rorty?

[*Rorty*]: *[Ironists] take naturally to the line of thought developed in . . . [my] book. . . . The opposite of irony is common sense. (CIS, p. 74).*

[Peirce]: Pragmaticism will be sure to carry critical common-sensism in its arms . . . (5.499).

[*Rorty*]: *Sentences like . . . "Truth is independent of the human mind" are simply platitudes used to inculcate . . . the common sense of the West (CIS, p. 76-7).*

[Peirce]: The Critical Common-sensist holds that all the veritably indubitable beliefs are *vague* . . . (5.505); [that they] refer to a somewhat primitive mode of life . . . (5.511); [he] has a high esteem for doubt (5.514); [he] criticizes the critical method (5.523).

[*Rorty*]: [*We ironists emphasize] the spirit of playfulness . . . (CIS, p. 39). [We are] never quite able to take [our]selves seriously . . . (p. 73).*

[Peirce]: [The Critical Common-sensist] is none of those overcultivated Oxford dons—I hope their day is over—whom any discovery that brought quietus to a vexed question would evidently vex because it would end the fun of arguing around it and about it and over it (5.520).

[*Rorty*]: *. . . I have spent forty years looking for a coherent . . . way of formulating my worries about what, if anything, philosophy is good for (TWO, p. 146).*

[Peirce]: It is true that philosophy is in a lamentably crude condition at present; . . . most philosophers set up a pretension of knowing all there is to know—a pretension calculated to disgust anybody who is at home in any real science. But all we have to do is to turn our backs upon all such truly vicious conduct, and we shall find ourselves enjoying the advantages of having an almost virgin soil to till, where a given amount of really scientific work will bring in an extraordinary harvest . . . of very fundamental truth of exceptional value from every point of view (1.128).

[*Haack*]: *How do you feel about Mr. Peirce's description of philosophy as "scientific work," Professor Rorty?*

[Rorty]: [One] side of pragmatism has been scientific. . . . Let me call the claim that there is [a] "reliable [scientific] method" "scientism" . . . If one takes the core of pragmatism to be its attempt to replace the notion of true beliefs as representations . . . and instead to think of them as successful rules for action, then it becomes . . . hard to isolate a "method" that will embody this attitude (PWM, pp. 260-262).

[*Peirce*]: *It is far better to let philosophy follow perfectly untrammeled a scientific method. . . . If that course be honestly and scrupulously carried out, the results reached, even if they be not altogether true, even if they be grossly mistaken, can not but be highly serviceable for the ultimate discovery of truth (1.644). Rational methods of inquiry . . . will make that result as speedy as possible . . . (7.78).*

The first problems to suggest themselves to the inquirer into nature are far too complex . . . for any early solution. . . . What ought to be done, therefore, . . . is at first to substitute for those problems others much . . .

more abstract. . . . The reasonably certain solutions of these last problems will throw a light . . . upon more concrete problems. . . . This method of procedure is that Analytic Method to which modern physics owes all its triumphs. It has been applied with great success in psychical sciences also. . . . It is reprobated by the whole Hegelian army, who think it ought to be replaced by the "Historic Method," which studies complex problems in all their complexity, but which cannot boast any distinguished successes.

There are in science three fundamentally different kinds of reasoning, Deduction, . . . Induction, . . . and Retroduction . . . Analogy combines the characters of Induction and Retroduction (1.63-6).

[Haack]: Do you share Mr. Peirce's high regard for logic, Professor Rorty?

[*Rorty*]: *Rigorous argumentation . . . is no more* generally *desirable than blocking the road of inquiry is generally desirable (CP, p. xli).*

[Peirce]: There are two qualifications which every true man of science possesses. . . . First, the dominant passion of his whole soul must be to find out the truth in some department. . . . Secondly, he must have a natural gift for reasoning, for severely critical thought (7.605). Logic is the theory of *right* reasoning, of what reasoning ought to be . . . (2.7).

[*Rorty*]: *We no longer think of ourselves as having reliable "sources" of knowledge called "reason" or "sensation" . . . (OE, p. 531).*

[Peirce]: The data from which inference sets out and upon which all reasoning depends are the *perceptual facts,* which are the intellect's fallible record of the *percepts,* or "evidence of the senses" (2.143).

[*Rorty*]: *Eventually I got over [my] worry about circular argumentation by deciding that the test of philosophical truth was overall coherence, rather than deducibility from unquestioned first principles. But this didn't help much (TWO, p. 145).*

[Peirce]: The reader will, I trust, be too well grounded in logic to mistake . . . mutual support for a vicious circle in reasoning (6.315).

Philosophy ought . . . to trust . . . to the multitude and variety of its arguments. . . . Its reasoning should not form a chain which is no stronger than the weakest link, but a cable whose fibers may be ever so slender, provided they are sufficiently numerous and intimately connected (5.265).

[*Rorty*]: *But [as I said] this didn't help much. For coherence is a matter of avoiding contradictions, and St.*

Thomas' advice, "When you meet a contradiction, make a distinction," makes that pretty easy (*TWO*, p. 145).

[Haack]: How do you feel about Professor Rorty's observation that making distinctions is "pretty easy," Mr. Peirce?

[Peirce]: . . . *Kant's conception of the nature of necessary reasoning is clearly shown by the logic of relations to be utterly mistaken, and his distinction between analytic and synthetic judgments, . . . which is based on that conception, is so utterly confused that it is difficult or impossible to do anything with it (5.176).*

[Haack]: Perhaps, while we are on the subject of logic, you could explain your attitude to the principle of bivalence . . .

[Rorty]: *The pragmatist . . . should not succumb to the temptation to . . . take sides on the issue of "bivalence"* (CP, p. xxvi).

[Peirce]: Triadic logic is universally true (*Logic Notebook* for 1909).

[Haack]: *Perhaps, Professor Rorty, it would be helpful if you would explain how you see the relation of philosophy to science . . .*

[Rorty]: The pragmatist is betting that what succeeds the "scientific," positivist culture which the Enlightenment produced will be *better* (*CP*, p. xxxviii). Science as the source of "truth" . . . is one of the Cartesian notions which vanish when the ideal of "philosophy as strict science" vanishes (p. 34). Pragmatism . . . views science as one genre of literature—or, put the other way around, literature and the arts as inquiries, on the same footing as scientific inquiries (p. xliii). Philosophy is best seen as a kind of writing. It is delimited, as is any literary genre, not by form or matter, but by tradition. . . . Philosophy as more than a kind of writing—is an illusion. . . . [One] tradition takes scientific truth as the center of philosophical concern (and scorns the notion of incommensurable scientific world-pictures). It asks how well other fields of inquiry conform to the model of science. The second [pragmatist] tradition takes science as one (not especially privileged nor interesting) sector of culture, a sector which . . . only makes sense when viewed historically (pp. 92-3). Literature has now displaced religion, science, and philosophy as the presiding discipline of our culture . . . (p. 155).

[Haack]: *Mr. Peirce?*

[Peirce]: [I] desire to rescue the good ship Philosophy for the service of Science from the hands of lawless rovers of the sea of literature . . . (5.449).

[Rorty]: *A few [lovably old-fashioned prigs] will even claim to write in a clear, precise, transparent way, priding themselves on manly straightforwardness, on abjuring "literary" devices (*EHO, p. 86*).*

[Peirce]: As for that phrase "studying in a literary spirit" it is impossible to express how nauseating it is to any scientific man . . . (1.33).

[Rorty]: *As soon as a program to put philosophy on the secure path of science succeeds, it simply converts philosophy into a boring academic specialty (*PMN, *pp. 384-5).*

[Peirce]: In order to be deep it is requisite to be dull . . . The new pragmatists . . . are *lively* . . . (5.17). The apostle of Humanism [F. C. S. Schiller, like you] says that professional philosophists "have rendered philosophy like unto themselves, abstruse, arid, abstract, and abhorrent." But I conceive that some branches of science are not in a healthy state if they are *not* abstruse, arid, and abstract, in which case, . . . it will be as Shakespeare said . . .

> Not harsh and crabbèd, as dull fools suppose,
>
> But musical as is Apollo's lute . . .
>
> (5.537)

The reader may find the matter [of my "Minute Logic"] so dry, husky and innutritious to the spirit that he cannot imagine that there is any human good in it. . . . But the fault is his. It shall not be more tedious than the multiplication table, . . . and as the multiplication table is worth the pains of learning, . . . so shall this be . . . (2.15).

[Haack]: *Professor Rorty, your view of philosophy as a genre of literature puzzles me; surely pragmatism is a form of empiricism?*

[Rorty]: Pragmatism has gradually broken the historical links that once connected it to empiricism . . . (*PPD*, p. 4).

[Peirce]: *The kind of philosophy which interests me and must, I think, interest everybody is that philosophy, which uses the most rational methods it can devise, for finding out the little that can as yet be found out about the universe of mind and matter from those observations which every person can make in every hour of his waking life . . . laboratory-philosophy . . . (1.126, 129).*

[Rorty]: From the radically anti-representationalist viewpoint I . . . commend . . . pragmatism can be seen as gradually . . . escaping from scientism (*PPD*, p. 4).

[*Peirce*]: *[Philosophical theories] have the same sort of basis as scientific results have. That is to say, they rest on experience—on the total everyday experience of many generations. . . . Such experience is worthless for distinctively scientific purposes . . . although all science . . . would have to shut up shop if she should manage to escape accepting them. No "wisdom" could ever have discovered argon; yet within its proper sphere, . . . the instinctive result of human experience ought to have so vastly more weight than any scientific result, that to make laboratory experiments to ascertain, for example, whether there be any uniformity in nature or no, would vie with adding a teaspoonful of saccharine to the ocean in order to sweeten it (5.522).*

[Rorty]: The basic motive of pragmatism was . . . a continuation of the Romantic reaction to the Enlightenment's sanctification of natural science (*EHO*, p. 18).

[*Peirce*]: *[Science] embodies the epitome of man's intellectual development (7.49). Iconoclastic inventions are always cheap and often nasty (4.71).*

[Haack]: May we go back for a minute to Professor Rorty's reference to Romanticism?

[*Rorty*]: *The Platonist and the positivist share a reductionist view of metaphor: They think metaphors are either paraphrasable or useless for the one serious purpose which language has, namely, representing reality. By contrast, the Romantic has an expansionist view . . . Romantics attribute metaphor to a mysterious faculty called the "imagination," a faculty they suppose to be at the very center of the self . . . (CIS, p. 19).*

[Peirce]: When a man desires ardently to know the truth, his first effort will be to imagine what that truth can be . . . there is, after all, nothing but imagination that can ever supply him an inkling of the truth. . . . For thousands of men a falling apple was nothing but a falling apple; and to compare it to the moon would by them be deemed "fanciful." It is not too much to say that next after the passion to learn there is no quality so indispensable to the successful prosecution of science as imagination. . . . There are, no doubt, kinds of imagination of no value in science, mere artistic imagination, mere dreaming of opportunities for gain. The scientific imagination dreams of explanation and laws (1.46-8).

Cuvier said that Metaphysics is nothing but Metaphor. . . . If metaphor be taken literally to mean an expression of a similitude when the sign of predication is employed instead of the sign of likeness—as when we say this man *is* a fox instead of this man is like a fox,—I deny entirely that metaphysicians are given to metaphor . . . but if Cuvier was only using a metaphor himself, and meant by metaphor broad comparison on the ground of characters of a formal and highly abstract kind,— then, indeed, metaphysics professes to be metaphor . . . (7.590).

[*Rorty*]: *[A] philosopher . . . like myself . . . thinks of himself as auxiliary to the poet rather than to the physicist. . . . Interesting philosophy is . . . a contest between an entrenched vocabulary which has become a nuisance and a half-formed new vocabulary which vaguely promises great things. (CIS, pp. 7-9).*

[Haack]: But I don't think Mr. Peirce would deny the importance of linguistic innovation . . .

[*Peirce*]: *Every symbol is a living thing, . . . its meaning inevitably grows, incorporates new elements and throws off old ones. . . . Science is continually gaining new conceptions; and every new* scientific *conception should receive a new word. . . . Different systems of expression are often of the greatest advantage (2.222).*

[Rorty]: It is a feature of . . . science that the vocabulary in which problems are posed is accepted by all those who count as contributing to the subject. The vocabulary may be changed, but that is only because a new theory has been discovered. . . . The vocabulary in which the *explicanda* are described has to remain constant (*CP*, pp. 141-2).

[*Peirce*]: *How much more the word* electricity *means now than it did in the days of Franklin; how much more the term* planet *means now than it did in the time of Hipparchus. These words have acquired information . . . (7.587).*

Symbols grow. . . . In use and in experience, [the] meaning [of a symbol] grows. Such words as force, law, wealth, marriage, *bear for us very different meanings from those they bore to our barbarous ancestors (2.302).*

[Haack]: I gather, Professor Rorty, from your references to "irony" and "playfulness," that you disapprove of too solemn an attitude to philosophy as a profession . . .

[*Rorty*]: *I would welcome a culture dominated by "the Rich Aesthete, the Manager and the Therapist" so long as* everybody *who wants to gets to be an aesthete . . . The ironic, playful intellectual is a desirable character-type . . . (FMR, pp. 16, 15).*

[Haack]: Mr. Peirce?

[*Peirce*]: *We remark three classes of men. The first consists of those for whom the chief thing is the qualities of feelings. These men create art. The second consists of the practical men . . . The third class consists of men to whom nothing seems great but reason. . . . Those are the natural scientific men . . . (1.43).*

It is infinitely better that men devoid of genuine scientific curiosity should not barricade the road of science with empty books and embarrassing assumptions . . . (1.645).

[Rorty]: Intellectual gifts—intelligence, judgment, curiosity, imagination, . . . kinks in the brain . . . provide these gifts . . . (*CIS*, pp. 187-8).

[*Peirce*]: *There is a kink in my damned brain that prevents me from thinking as other people think . . .*

[Rorty]: As we look about at the manly, aggressive and businesslike academics of our . . . time, . . . the well-funded professor[s], jetting home after a day spent advising men of power . . . [we see that the] American academic mind has long since discovered the joy of making its own special enterprise "greater and better organized and a mightier engine in the general life" (*CP*, p. 61).

[*Peirce*]: *Wherever there is a large class of academic professors who are provided with good incomes and looked up to as gentlemen, scientific inquiry must languish. Wherever the bureaucrats are the more learned class, the case will be still worse (1.51).*

[Haack]: And how do you see the relation of philosophy to society?

[*Rorty*]: *Pragmatism must be defined as the claim that the function of inquiry is, in Bacon's words, to "relieve and benefit the condition of man" . . . (EHO, p. 27).*

[Peirce]: [A] modern reader who is not in awe of [Bacon's] grandiloquence is chiefly struck by the inadequacy of his view of scientific procedure. . . . "He wrote on science like a Lord Chancellor," indeed, as Harvey, a genuine man of science said (5.361).

[*Rorty*]: *Philosophy [is] in the service of democratic politics . . . (CIS, p. 196). We pragmatists commend our antiessentialism and antilogocentrism on the ground of its harmony with the practices and aims of a democratic society . . . (EHO, p. 135).*

[Peirce]: I must confess that I belong to that class of scallawags who purpose, with God's help, to look the truth in the face, whether doing so be conducive to the interests of society or not. Moreover, if I should ever attack that excessively difficult problem, 'What is for the true interest of society?' I should feel that I stood in need of a great deal of help from the science of legitimate inference . . . (8.143). Against the doctrine that social stability is the sole justification of scientific research . . . I have to object, first, that it is historically false . . . second, that it is bad ethics; and, third, that its propagation would retard the progress of science (8.135).

[*Rorty*]: *[There have been in our century] three conceptions of the aim of philosophizing. They are the Husserlian (or 'scientistic') answer, the Heideggerian (or 'poetic') answer, and the pragmatist (or 'political') answer (EHO, p. 9).*

[Peirce]: In my opinion, the present infantile condition of philosophy . . . is due to the fact that . . . it has chiefly been pursued by men who have not . . . been animated by the true scientific *Eros*; but who have . . . been inflamed with a desire to amend the lives of themselves and others . . . (1.620). The two masters, *theory* and *practice,* you cannot serve (1.642).

[*Haack*]: *It seems to me that the two of you have radically different conceptions of what pragmatism is . . .*

[Rorty]: "Pragmatism" is a vague, ambiguous and overworked word (*CP*, p. 160).

[*Peirce*]: *Many writers, . . . in spite of pragmatists' declarations, unanimous, reiterated, and most explicit, still remain unable to "catch on" to what we are driving at, and persist in twisting our purpose and purport all awry. . . . [Pragmatism] is merely a method of ascertaining the meanings of hard words and of abstract concepts (5.464).*

[Rorty]: The pragmatist . . . must struggle with the positivist for the position of radical anti-Platonist. . . . At first glance he looks like just another variety of positivist. (*CP*, p. xvii).

[*Peirce*]: *Pragmaticism is a species of prope-positivism (5.423).*

[Rorty]: My first characterization of pragmatism is that it is simply anti-essentialism applied to notions like "truth," "knowledge," "language," "morality," and similar objects of philosophical theorizing. . . . There is no wholesale, epistemological way to direct, or criticize, or underwrite, the course of inquiry (*CP*, p. 162). [A] second characterization of pragmatism might go like this: there is no epistemological difference between truth about what ought to be and truth about what is, nor any metaphysical difference between facts and values, nor any methodological difference between morality and science (p. 163). . . . The pragmatists tell us, it is the vocabulary of practice rather than of theory . . . in which one can say something useful about truth (p. 162). [A] third . . . characterization of pragmatism [is]: it is the doctrine that there are no constraints on inquiry save conversational ones. . . . The only sense in which we are constrained to truth is that, as [you] suggested, we can make no sense of the notion that the view which can survive all objections might be false. But objections—conversational constraints—cannot be anticipated (p. 165).

[*Peirce*]: *To satisfy our doubts, . . . it is necessary that a method should be found by which our beliefs may be determined by nothing human, but by some external permanency—by something upon which our thinking has no effect. . . . It must be something which affects, or might affect, every man. . . . The method must be such that the ultimate conclusion of every man shall be the same. Such is the method of science (5.384).*

[Rorty]: Once human desires are admitted into the criterion of "truth," . . . we have become pragmatists. The pragmatist's claim is that to know your desires is to know the criterion of truth . . . (*EHO*, pp. 30-31).

[Peirce]: *It is necessary to note what is essentially involved in the Will to Learn. . . . I can excuse a person who has lost a dear companion and whose reason is in danger of giving way under the grief, for trying, on that account, to believe in a future life. . . . [But] I myself would not adopt a hypothesis . . . simply because the idea was pleasing to me. . . . That would be a crime against the integrity of . . . reason . . . (5.583, 598).*

[Rorty]: What I am calling "pragmatism" might also be called "left-wing Kuhnianism" (SS, p. 41).

[Peirce]: *An opinion which has of late years attained some vogue among men of science, [is] that we cannot expect any physical hypothesis to maintain its ground indefinitely even with modifications, but must expect that from time to time there will be a complete cataclysm that shall utterly sweep away old theories and replace them by new ones. As far as I know, this notion has no other basis than the history of science. Considering how very, very little science we have attained, and how infantile the history of science still is, it amazes me that anybody should propose to base a theory of knowledge upon the history of science alone. An emmet is far more competent to discourse upon the figure of the earth than we are to say what future millennia and millionennia may have in store for physical theories . . . The only really scientific theory that can be called old is the Ptolemaic system; and that has only been improved in details, not revolutionized (2.150).*

[Rorty]: [Your] contribution to pragmatism was merely to have given it a name . . . (*CP*, p. 161).

[Peirce]: *It has probably never happened that any philosopher has attempted to give a general name to his own doctrine without that name's soon acquiring in common philosophical usage, a signification much broader than was originally intended. . . . [My] word "pragmatism" . . . begins to be met with occasionally in the literary journals, where it gets abused in the merciless way that words have to expect when they fall into literary clutches. . . . So, then, the writer, finding his bantling "pragmatism" so promoted, feels that it is time to kiss his child goodbye and relinquish it to its higher destiny; while to serve the precise purpose of ex-*

pressing the original definition, he begs to announce the birth of the word "pragmaticism," which is ugly enough to be safe from kidnappers (5.143-4).

It is good economy for philosophy to provide itself with a vocabulary so outlandish that loose thinkers shall not be tempted to borrow its words. . . . Whoever deliberately uses a word . . . in any other sense than that which was conferred upon it by its sole rightful creator commits a shameful offense against the inventor of the symbol and against science, and it becomes the duty of the others to treat the act with contempt and indignation (2.223-4).

[Rorty]: Revolutionary movements within an intellectual discipline require a revisionist history of that discipline (*CP*, p. 211).

[Peirce]: *It seems to me a pity [that the pragmatists of today] should allow a philosophy so instinct with life to become infected with seeds of death in such notions as that of . . . the mutability of truth . . . (6.485).*

Note

1. Editor's Note: This piece is an imaginary confrontation between Charles Sanders Peirce and Richard Rorty.

Works Cited

EXCEPT WHERE OTHERWISE INDICATED, PEIRCE'S CONTRIBUTIONS ARE TAKEN FROM:

Collected Papers, eds Hartshorne, C., Weiss, P. and Burks, A., Harvard University Press, Cambridge, MA, 1931-58; references by volume and paragraph number.

Peirce's comment about the kink in his brain is reported by E. T. Bell in *The Development of Mathematics*, McGraw-Hill, New York and London, 1949, p. 519.

The quotation Peirce attributes to Shakespeare is actually from Milton's *Comus*.

RORTY'S CONTRIBUTIONS TO THE CONVERSATION ARE TAKEN FROM:

CIS: *Contingency, Irony and Solidarity*, Cambridge University Press, Cambridge, 1989.

CP: *Consequences of Pragmatism*, Harvester, Hassocks, Sussex, 1982.

EHO: *Essays on Heidegger and Others*, Cambridge University Press, Cambridge, 1991.

FMR: "Freud and Moral Reflection," in Smith, J. H. and Kerrigan, W., eds, *Pragmatism's Freud*, Johns Hopkins University Press, Baltimore and London, 1986, 1-27.

OE: "On Ethnocentrism: A Reply to Clifford Geertz," *Michigan Quarterly Review,* 25, 1986, 525-34.

ORT: *Objectivity, Relativism and Truth,* Cambridge University Press, Cambridge, 1991.

PDP: "The Priority of Democracy to Philosophy," in Peterson, Merrill D. and Vaughn, Robert C., eds, *The Virginia Statute for Religious Freedom,* Cambridge University Press, Cambridge, 1988, 257-82.

PDT: "Pragmatism, Davidson and Truth," in Lepore, E., ed., *Truth and Interpretation: Perspectives on the Philosophy of Donald Davidson,* Blackwell, Oxford, 1986, 333-54.

PPD: "Introduction" to Murphy, J. P., *Pragmatism from Peirce to Davidson,* Westview Press, Boulder, CO, 1990, 1-6,

PMN: *Philosophy and the Mirror of Nature,* Princeton University Press, Princeton, NJ, 1979.

PWM: "Pragmatism Without Method," in Kurtz, Paul, ed., *Sidney Hook: Philosopher of Democracy and Humanism,* Prometheus Books, Buffalo, NY, 1938, 259-74.

SS: "Science as Solidarity," in Nelson, John S., Megill, Allan, and McCloskey, Donald M., eds, *The Rhetoric of the Human Sciences,* University of Wisconsin Press, Madison, WI, 1987, 38-52.

TMoL: "Two Meanings of 'Logocentrism,'" in Dasenbrock, Reed Way, ed., *Redrawing the Lines: Analytic Philosophy, Deconstruction, and Literary Theory,* Minnesota University Press, Minneapolis, MN, 1989, 204-16.

TWO: "Trotsky and the Wild Orchids," *Common Knowledge,* 1.3, 1992, 140-53.

Cornelis de Waal (essay date 2001)

SOURCE: de Waal, Cornelis. "Pragmatism." In *On Peirce,* pp. 24-31. Belmont, Calif.: Wadsworth, 2001.

[*In the following essay, de Waal details the development of Charles Sanders Peirce's conception of Pragmatism.*]

> At present, the word begins to be met with occasionally in the literary journals, where it gets abused in the merciless way that words have to expect when they fall into literary clutches.
>
> —Charles S. Peirce[1]

William James was the first to use the term "pragmatism" in print. This was in an 1898 paper entitled "Philosophical Conceptions and Practical Results."[2] In this paper, James credited Peirce for originating both the term and the principle for which it stands. As James

explained, and Peirce later confirmed, Peirce first used the term during meetings of the Cambridge Metaphysical Club, an informal club of friends who met regularly during the early 1870s. The term "pragmatism" caught on, even though James seemed to prefer "practicalism."

Pragmatism is in a sense a new word for old ways of thinking. Peirce found traces of it in thinkers as diverse as Socrates, Aristotle, Locke, Spinoza, and Kant. Even Jesus was a pragmatist for Peirce, as he settled the question which prophets to believe by saying: "By their fruits ye shall know them" (*EP* 2:401). Peirce credited Bishop Berkeley for bringing pragmatism to the forefront. In a letter of 23 January 1903 to James, Peirce wrote: "Berkeley on the whole has more right to be considered the introducer of pragmatism into philosophy than any other man, though I was more explicit in enunciating it."

For Peirce, pragmatism was a "method of ascertaining the meanings of hard words and of abstract concepts" (*EP* 2:400). What do we mean by words like "mammal," "simultaneity," "electron," or "substance"? Ever since Descartes, philosophers had pointed out that we should ensure that such words represent clear and distinct ideas. By this they meant ideas that are fully present to the mind and sharply demarcated from other ideas. Peirce objected that this criterion of clear and distinct ideas is insufficient, and in his 1878 paper "How to Make our Ideas Clear" he added the following criterion for clarifying the meaning of words or concepts:

> Consider what effects, which might conceivably have practical bearings, we conceive the object of our conception to have. Then, our conception of these effects is the whole of our conception of the object.
>
> (*EP* 1:132)

This criterion is generally referred to as the pragmatic maxim. It states that any conception that is used in philosophy, religion, or otherwise, cannot mean anything other than the totality of the practical consequences we can conceive the object of that conception to have. Practical consequences means experiential effects that can influence future rational or deliberative conduct. In this way the maxim is related to the notion of self-control, making it clearly a maxim of normative logic.

Consider the following example. An event that is presumed to take place during the Eucharist is the transubstantiation of wine and bread into the blood and body of Christ. According to Catholic dogma, the bread and wine literally change into the body and blood of Christ, and they do so without any modification of their physical characteristics. That is to say, after the transubstantiation the bread still has the same texture as before and the wine still tastes like normal wine.

It is not difficult to obtain a clear and distinct idea of transubstantiation, especially if one admits the classical Aristotelian distinction of substance and attributes. For

Aristotle, a substance is an individual object like this man or that horse. In grammar, this substance takes the role of the subject of a sentence. Attributes, in turn, are qualities that can be predicated of a substance. For instance, we can attribute the quality of whiteness to a horse by saying "This horse is white." It will be easily granted that the substance-attribute distinction allows us to form the conception of *transformation*. In a transformation, say from caterpillar to butterfly, the substance (that is, the individual object) remains exactly the same even though most of its qualities change.

Along the very same line, we can form for ourselves the conception of *transubstantiation*. In transubstantiation, the exact opposite occurs, for it is the substance that changes while the qualities, or attributes, remain the exactly same. This means that after the transubstantiation we have a different subject even though there has not been any change in its qualities. Thus, in transubstantiation *only the substance* changes. This allows one to say that after the Eucharist one is literally eating and drinking the flesh and blood of Christ—that is, the substance of Christ—even though it tastes like ordinary bread and wine.

Even though we can in this manner obtain a clear and distinct idea of transubstantiation, Peirce dismissed the entire concept as meaningless (*EP* 1:131). Application of the pragmatic maxim makes clear why. On the pragmatic maxim, the whole meaning of any concept, including that of transubstantiation, is nothing but its conceivable practical effects. Now, by definition our conception of transubstantiation cannot have any such practical effects, since we derive all our knowledge of anything from its qualities and the very idea of transubstantiation presupposes that there is no change in qualities. Since it makes no conceivable practical difference whether transubstantiation takes place or not, Peirce argued, our conception of transubstantiation has no meaning.

It is important to note that Peirce's pragmatic maxim is *solely* a criterion of meaning. As such, it differs from Descartes's notion of clear and distinct ideas, which is at once a criterion of meaning and a criterion of truth. On the premise that God is not a deceiver, Descartes concluded that anything we clearly and distinctly perceive must be true. Peirce rejected such a view because it reduces truth to whatever we have a natural inclination to believe. Such a view is untenable, Peirce argued, because it entirely ignores the outward clash of experience. Many a time experience nullifies the cleverest of arguments:

> A man may walk down Wall Street debating within himself the existence of an external world; but if in his brown study he jostles up against somebody who angrily draws off and knocks him down, the sceptic is

unlikely to carry his scepticism so far as to doubt whether anything beside the ego was concerned in that phenomenon.

> (*CP* 1.431)

Phrased in terms of the categories, the Cartesian view ignores secondness. As we will see in the coming chapter, it is precisely the insistence on an independent reality forcing itself upon us that, on Peirce's view, separates Descartes's approach from the scientific method.

A METHOD, NOT A DOCTRINE

Peirce's pragmatism was conceived in the spirit of the laboratory, where everything is considered as a possible subject of experimentation. A complete definition of a concept, Peirce argued, entails nothing but specifying "all the conceivable experimental phenomena which the affirmation or denial of [the] concept could imply" (*EP* 2:332). Elsewhere, Peirce added that the method by which pragmatists seek to ascertain the meaning of words or concepts is precisely the experimental method of the sciences (*EP* 2:400).

Peirce did not restrict the notion of meaning to words alone, as was common with the British empiricists, or only to sentences, as was common in the Frege-Russell tradition. Anything that can act as a sign can have meaning, whether it is a word, a sentence, an entire culture, or a physical object like a weathercock. In 1905, Peirce described pragmatism as "a method for ascertaining the real meaning of any concept, doctrine, proposition, word, or other sign" (*CP* 5.6). The pragmatic maxim applies to all types of signs, from those that are most simple to the highly complex.

That pragmatism is a method of logic rather than a principle of metaphysics, Peirce considered a great advantage. As he explained it in a letter of 17 September 1892 to his friend Judge Francis C. Russell:

> Obstinate disputes in philosophy are maintained by life presenting itself under diverse aspects. . . . My great word is that the thing to go your bottom dollar on should not be a doctrine but a method. For a vital method will correct itself and doctrines too. Doctrines are crystals, methods are ferments.

PEIRCE AND POSITIVISM

During the 1920s logical positivism emerged and quickly became a dominant force in Anglo-Saxon philosophy. In the process, it almost completely wiped out pragmatism. In contrast to the other pragmatists, whose views were often antithetical to logical positivism, there is a clear affinity between the views of the logical positivists and those of Peirce. At the same time, there are important differences. Peirce does not share the positivist's blanket dismissal of metaphysics, and although both stress the importance of formal logic and the scientific method, the logical positivist's conception of both is far narrower than Peirce's. Conceding his affinity to the positivist cause, Peirce even labeled himself a positivist, a prope-positivist that is, where the prefix "prope" was added to indicate that it concerned a broader application of the term (*EP* 2:334).

There is a striking similarity between Peirce's theory of meaning and the verification principle of the later logical positivists. For Peirce, what we say or think has meaning only insofar as it has conceivable practical consequences; that is to say, the conceivable practical consequences of the object of a statement entirely exhaust the statement's meaning. The logical positivists proposed a similar stricture, which is generally referred to as the verification principle. On this principle a statement has meaning only insofar as it can be empirically verified; or as the logical positivists liked to say, the meaning of a statement is its method of verification. A statement like "this horse is white" or "God is good" has meaning only when there is some possible sense experience (which, in Peirce's terms would count as a conceivable practical consequence) relevant to the determination of its truth or falsehood.[3] Any statement that is not thus verifiable (tautologies excluded) must be thrown aside as being without meaning.

The logical positivists were adamant that this verification principle forced us to conclude that only what falls within the scope of science can be meaningful, and that because of this the traditional enterprise of metaphysics had become obsolete. Part of it can be replaced by science, the rest is better forgotten. Peirce took a somewhat different stance. Instead of discarding metaphysics and relegating all inquiry to the special sciences, as did the logical positivists, Peirce insisted that metaphysics itself should be studied in the scientific spirit. To a certain extent, this is only a difference of perspective. Whereas the logical positivists sought to eradicate everything the sciences with that method could not deal with, Peirce sought to stretch the scientific method so as to include as much as possible. Hence, much depends on how this scientific method is understood.

By viewing science in a broader vein, Peirce also avoided a key problem that the logical positivists quickly ran into. According to the logical positivists, one may use only what passes the verification principle. This implies that one may also use the verification principle only if it passes the verification principle. However, applying the verification principle to itself quickly revealed that it is not empirically verifiable, so that the verification principle itself should be discarded as metaphysical nonsense that is better forgotten. This problem does not occur with the pragmatic maxim, which is a maxim of normative logic. As such, it is based on mathematics, phenomenology, and the normative sciences, so that there is no need to subject the maxim to itself to prove its validity.

The Other Pragmatists

Shortly after James introduced "pragmatism" in print, the term caught on and Peirce was generally acknowledged as its founder. However, the term "pragmatism" suggests more of a unity among the so-called pragmatists than is justified. Not only are there important differences between the various pragmatists, but there are also significant shifts in the views of its main proponents. Consequently, the number of pragmatisms may very well outnumber the number of pragmatists.

With respect to the course pragmatism was taking, Peirce was particularly worried about what he saw as a growing tendency to use the pragmatic method too loosely. In a letter to James of November 10, 1904, he cautioned: "You and Schiller carry pragmatism too far for me. I don't want to exaggerate it but keep it within the bounds to which the evidences of it are limited" (*CP* 8.258). In a similar vein, Peirce accused Dewey of "intellectual licentiousness" (*CP* 8.241). This discomfort with what the other pragmatists were doing was by no means limited to Peirce. James, for instance, described Peirce's 1903 Pragmatism lectures as "flashes of brilliant light relieved against Cimmerian darkness," and he discouraged their publication.[4]

The two elements that most distinguish Peirce's views from the pragmatisms of James, Dewey, and Schiller, are his focus on experience as opposed to action and his insistence on conceivable effects as opposed to practical effects. The two are closely related. If one sees pragmatism as a doctrine meant to guide conduct, it makes good sense to ignore farfetched consequences that for all practical purposes do not matter. To take this route, however, has serious ramifications. Concentrating solely on practical matters means giving up the notion that philosophers should try to find out how things really are. It also means that if the meaning of our conceptions lies solely in their practical consequences, the traditional notion of truth becomes an empty notion that is better avoided. We return to this ramification in chapter six when discussing Peirce's theory of truth.

To concentrate solely on practical effects, Peirce believed, was too restrictive. Take the relation between the diagonal and the sides of a square. As the Pythagoreans had discovered already in ancient times, one cannot express the length of both the diagonal and a side in a single unit of measure. This phenomenon is generally called the incommensurability of the diagonal of a square with its sides. That the diagonal and the sides are incommensurable can be shown easily by taking a square that has a side of one (the unit of whatever measuring system you prefer). Given the theorem of Pythagoras, the length of the diagonal will be then the square root of two. But this is an irrational number. That is to say, it is a number that cannot possibly be expressed as a decimal fraction, which means that we cannot divide the unit into smaller units that can match up exactly with the diagonal. Now, as Peirce is keen to point out, for all practical purposes the diagonal can be expressed perfectly well in terms of its side. One only has to reduce the unit of measurement far enough to make the units just large enough to be discerned. If we use a measuring rod like this, and lay it beside both the diagonal and a side of the square, it would give us a fixed number of units for each. Thus, if only practical effects were to matter, the mathematical notion of incommensurability would have to be discarded as being meaningless. For Peirce, this goes too far.

Let us have a brief look at the views of the other three classical pragmatists, James, Dewey, and Schiller. James's pragmatism is markedly different from Peirce's. For James the meaning of a concept lay not so much in its conceivable effects, as with Peirce, but in whether applying the concept makes any practical difference. Meaning, as James explained in "Philosophical Conceptions and Practical Results," is the conduct it dictates or inspires.[5] James illustrated this with a discussion of the debate between the theists and the materialists. Even though no conceivable practical difference distinguishes the two (as both lead up to exactly the same universe), James argued that it does make a difference which of the two one adheres to as to how one will act and what one hopes for. By taking this route, however, James shifted away from the consequences of the belief itself, to the consequences of a person holding the belief. However, these are quite different matters.

John Dewey, who was a student of Peirce at Johns Hopkins, also preferred the concrete above the abstract and the act above the contemplation. We are not mere spectators, Dewey argued, but we are active participants who have the ability to change things. So the shift that started with James, continued with Dewey.

The British pragmatist F. C. S. Schiller took the matter even a step further by bluntly equivocating truth with what we value. Pragmatism, Schiller explained, seeks to trace out the actual "making of truth," as opposed to a so-called 'disinterested' discovery of truth.[6] The distinction between the pragmatism of Peirce and the pragmatisms of James, Dewey, and Schiller, continues until this day.[7]

To emphasize the difference between his own position and the views of the other pragmatists, Peirce finally surrendered the term to replace it with "pragmaticism," a term which, he argued, "is ugly enough to be safe from kidnappers" (*EP* 2:335). The inserted "ic" indicates that it is a more strictly defined version of the "ism" pragmatism. It should be emphasized that Peirce's change of terminology did not mean that he had changed his mind; Peirce's sole purpose was to distance

himself from the other pragmatists. Since "pragmaticism" is an ugly term indeed, and since Peirce failed to consistently stick to it himself, I will refrain from using it.

Peirce was, by the way, not the only one of the classical pragmatists to distance himself from the term "pragmatism." Dewey preferred "instrumentalism," and Schiller preferred "humanism."

Notes

1. *CP* 5.414.

2. John J. McDermott (ed.), *The Writings of William James* (Chicago: Univ. of Chicago Press, 1977), 345-62.

3. A. J. Ayer, *Language, Truth, and Logic* (London: Penguin, 1990), 16.

4. John J. McDermott, op cit., 363.

5. John J. McDermott, op cit., 348.

6. F. C. S. Schiller, *Studies in Humanism* (Westport: Greenwood Press, 1970), chapter 7.

7. For a good illustration of this divergence, see Susan Haack's rendition of a "debate" between Peirce and Richard Rorty, in *Manifesto of a Passionate Moderate* (Chicago: Univ. of Chicago Press, 1998), 31-47.

Works Cited and Suggestions for Further Reading

A fair number of editions of Peirce's texts have appeared so far. For the editions that are referred to in this volume, the abbreviations used in the text are given here as well.

A good and affordable collection is *The Essential Peirce* (2 vols), edited by the Peirce Edition Project (Bloomington: Indiana Unv. Press, 1992-98), which is referred to as *EP* [*vol.#*]:[*page#*]. For more comprehensive editions, see the *Writings of Charles S. Peirce: A Chronological Edition,* edited by the Peirce Edition Project (Bloomington: Indiana Univ. Press, 1982-), referred to as *W* [*vol.#*]:[*page#*], and the *Collected papers of Charles Sanders Peirce* (8 vols), edited by Charles Hartshorne, Paul Weiss, and Arthur Burks (Cambridge: Harvard Univ. Press, 1931-58), which is referred to as *CP* [*vol.#*].[*paragraph#*].

More topical editions are *Semiotic and Significs,* edited by Charles S. Hardwick (Bloomington: Indiana Univ. Press, 1977), referred to as *SS* [*page#*], which contains Peirce's correspondence with Victoria Lady Welby, and *Reasoning and the Logic of Things,* edited by Kenneth Ketner (Cambridge: Harvard University Press, 1992), referred to as *RLT* [*page#*], which contains Peirce's 1898 Cambridge lectures.

Harvard manuscripts that are listed in Richard Robin's *Annotated Catalogue of the Papers of Charles S. Peirce* (Amherst: Univ. of Massachusetts Press, 1967), are referred to as *R* [*manuscript#*][*ISP#*]. The ISP# is the page number given by the Institute for Studies in Pragmaticism. Both numbers combined uniquely identify each manuscript page. The numbers follow the order of the pages on a microfilm (38 reels), published by Harvard Univ. Library.

A selection of Peirce's mathematical manuscripts appeared as *New Elements of Mathematics* (4 vols.), edited by Carolyn Eisele (The Hague: Mouton, 1976). *Historical perspectives on Peirce's Logic of Science,* (Amsterdam: Mouton, 1985), which is also edited by Carolyn Eisele, contains a selection of Peirce's manuscripts related to science.

Joseph Brent's *Charles Sanders Peirce: A Life* (Bloomington: Indiana Univ. Press, 1993) is the only full biography of Peirce's life. The introductions to the volumes of the *Writings* do a better job in connecting Peirce's life with his work, but currently reach no further than 1890. Kenneth Ketner's *His Glassy Essence: An Autobiography of Charles Sanders Peirce* (Nashville: Vanderbilt Univ. Press, 1998) contains a rich collection of previously unpublished documents related to Peirce's life. But so far only the first of three volumes has appeared.

There are several monographs on Peirce's philosophy. They include Murray Murphy's *The Development of Peirce's Philosophy* (Cambridge: Harvard Univ. Press, 1961); Christopher Hookway's *Peirce* (London: Routledge, 1985); Carl Hausman's *Charles S. Peirce's Evolutionary Philosophy* (Cambridge: Cambridge Univ. Press, 1993); and Karl-Otto Apel's *Charles S. Peirce: From Pragmatism to Pragmaticism* (Amherst: Univ. of Massachusetts Press, 1981).

The number of books and papers on Peirce is too large to be listed. Apart from the *Transactions of the Charles S. Peirce Society,* which are published four times a year, to collections deserve special attention, namely Max Fisch's *Peirce, Semeiotic, and Pragmatism,* edited by Kenneth Ketner and Christian Kloesel (Bloomington: Indiana Univ. Press, 1986), and Carolyn Eisele's *Studies in the Scientific and Mathematical Philosophy of Charles S Peirce,* edited by R. M. Martin (The Hague, Mouton, 1979).

Two web sites to start with are www.iupui.edu/~peirce and www.door.net/arisbe. The former contains the companions to the *Writings* of Peirce, and the latter is host to the listserv Peirce-L. Both sites contain numerous links that are regularly updated.

Finally, both the Peirce Edition Project at Indiana University-Purdue University Indianapolis (publisher of the *Writings)* and the Institute for Pragmaticism at Texas Tech University in Lubbock have extensive research facilities that are open to the public.

WILLIAM JAMES

Ralph Barton Perry (essay date 1910)

SOURCE: Perry, Ralph Barton. "The Philosophy of William James." In *Present Philosophical Tendencies: A Critical Survey of Naturalism, Idealism, Pragmatism and Realism, Together with a Synopsis of the Philosophy of William James,* pp. 349-78. New York: Greenwood Press, 1968.

[*In the following essay, first published in* The Harvard Graduates' Magazine *in 1910, Perry offers an overview of William James's philosophy.*]

I. PHILOSOPHY OF MIND

[SECTION] 1.

The Place of the Problem of Mind in James's Philosophy

A philosophy so complete and so significant as that of William James, touching, as it does, every traditional problem, and expressing through the medium of personal genius the characteristic tendencies of an epoch, cannot be hastily estimated. There is no glory to be won by pressing the attack upon its unguarded defences; while solemn verdicts, whether of commendation or censure, would surely prove premature and injudicious. But there is perhaps one service to be rendered to James and to philosophy for which this is the most suitable time, the service, namely, of brief and proportionate exposition. Every philosophical system suffers from accidental emphasis, due to the temporal order of production and to the exigencies of controversy. Towards the close of his life, James himself felt the need of assembling his philosophy, and of giving it unity and balance. It was truly one philosophy, one system of thought, but its total structure and contour had never been made explicit. That James should not have lived to do this work himself is an absolute loss to mankind, for which no efforts of mine can in the least compensate.[1] But I should like to make a first rude sketch, which may, I hope, despite its flatness and its bad drawing, at least suggest the form of the whole and the proper emphasis of the parts.

If one could read James's writings in a day, and forget the order of their publication, one would, I think, find that they treated of three great topics—the nature of the human mind, the structure and criteria of knowledge, and the grounds of religious belief. Were one then to take into consideration the writer's development, together with his interests and his aptitudes, one would be brought to see that the first of these topics was original and fundamental. James's philosophy was a study of man, or of life. The biological and medical sciences, psychology, philosophy proper, and religion, were not for him so many independent disciplines, from which he chose now one and now another owing to versatility or caprice; but so many sources of light concerning human nature. So that while one has difficulty in classifying him within a curriculum or hierarchy of the sciences, since he ignored such distinctions and even visited the intellectual under-world when it suited his purpose, his mind was none the less steadily focussed on its object. His knowledge was on the one hand as unified, and on the other hand as rich and diversified, as its subject-matter. In the summary which follows I shall first give an account of his general views of the human mind; after which I shall discuss his view of man's great enterprises, knowledge, and religion.

[Section] 2.

Mind as Interested and Selective

In one of his earliest published articles, on "Spencer's Definition of Mind,"[2] James adopts a standpoint which he never leaves. His object is man the organism, saving himself and asserting his interests within the natural environment. These interests, the irreducible "teleological factor," must be the centre and point of reference in any account of mind. The defect in Spencer's view of mind as correspondence of "inner" and "outer" relations, lies in its failing to recognize that such correspondence is relative to the organism's interests. "So that the Spencerian formula, to mean anything definite at all, must, at least, be re-written as follows: 'Right or intelligent mental action consists in the establishment, corresponding to outward relations, of such inward relations and reactions as will favor the survival of the thinker, or, at least, his physical well-being.'"[3] The mind is not a "mirror" which passively reflects what it chances to come upon. It initiates and tries; and its correspondence with the "outer world" means that its effort successfully meets the environment in behalf of the organic interest from which it sprang. The mind, like an antenna, feels the way for the organism. It gropes about, advances and recoils, making many random efforts and many failures; but is always urged into taking the initiative by the pressure of interest, and doomed to success or failure in some hour of trial when it meets and engages the environment. Such is mind, and such, according to James, are all its operations. These characters, interest, activity, trial, success, and failure, are its generic characters when it is observed concretely; and they are the characters which should take precedence of all others in the

description of every special undertaking of mind, such as knowing, truth-getting, and believing.

The action of the mind is not, however, creative. Its ideas are not of its own making, but rather of its own *choosing*. At every stage of its development, on every level of complexity, the mind is essentially a selective agency, "a theatre of simultaneous possibilities."[4] The sense-organs select from among simultaneous stimuli; attention is selective from among sensations; morality is selective from among interests. And above all, thought is selective. The unity and discreteness of "things" first arises from interest in some special group of qualities, and from among the group the mind then selects some to represent it most truly as its "essential" characters. Reasoning is not the mere mechanism of association. Garrulousness in which the course of ideas is allowed to proceed as it will, is unreason, a symptom of mental decay. To reason is to guide the course of ideas, through discriminating and accentuating those whose associates are to the point. Human sagacity and genius, as well as the whole overwhelming superiority of man to brute, are to be attributed to a capacity for extracting the right characters from the undifferentiated chaos of primeval experience; the right characters being those which are germane to the matter in hand, or those which enable the mind to pass to similars over a bridge of identities.[5]

[Section] 3.

The Relational or Functional Theory of Consciousness

Let us now look at mind from a somewhat different angle. If its operations are selective rather than creative it follows that it derives its content from its environment, and adds nothing to that content save the circumstance of its selection. If the term 'consciousness' be used to designate the mind's content, that manifold, namely, which can be held in view and examined by introspection, then consciousness is not a distinct substance, or even a distinct quality; but a grouping, exclusive and inclusive, of characters borrowed from the environment. James first offered this account of the matter in the article entitled, "Does Consciousness Exist?" published in 1904. But he then wrote: "For twenty years past I have mistrusted 'consciousness' as an entity; for seven or eight years past I have suggested its non-existence to my students."[6] This theory is therefore both closely related to his other theories, and also of long standing.

In suggesting the non-existence of consciousness, James meant, of course, to prepare the way for an account of its true character. This turn of thought may perhaps be paraphrased as follows. If by a thing's existence you mean its separate existence, its existence as wholly other than, or outside of, other things, as one planet exists outside another, then consciousness does not exist. For consciousness differs from other things as one grouping differs from another grouping of the same terms; as, for example, the Republican party differs from the American people. But this is its true character, and in this sense it exists. One is led to this conclusion if one resolutely refuses to yield to the spell of words. What do we find when we explore that quarter to which the word 'consciousness' directs us? We find at first glance some particular character, such as blue; and at second glance another particular character, such as roundness. Which of these is consciousness? Evidently neither. For there is no discoverable difference between these characters, thus severally regarded, and certain parts of nature. Furthermore, there is no discoverable community of nature among these characters themselves. But continue the investigation as long as you please, and you simply add content to content, without finding either any class of elements that belong exclusively to consciousness, or any conscious "menstruum" in which the elements of content are suspended. The solution of the riddle lies in the fact that one term may be called by several names corresponding to the several relationships into which it enters. It is necessary only to admit that "every smallest bit of experience is a *multum in parvo* plurally related, that each relation is one aspect, character, or function, way of its being taken, or way of its taking something else; and that a bit of reality when actively engaged in one of these relations is not *by that very fact* engaged in all the other relations simultaneously. The relations are not *all* what the French call *solidaires* with one another. Without losing its identity a thing can either take up or drop another thing, like the log . . . which by taking up new carriers and dropping old ones can travel anywhere with a light escort."[7]

I have quoted this passage in full because of its far-reaching importance. But we have to do here only with the application to the question of consciousness. The elements or terms which enter into consciousness and become its content may now be regarded as the same elements which, in so far as otherwise related, compose physical nature. The elements themselves, the "materia prima" or "stuff of pure experience," are neither psychical nor physical.[8] A certain spatial and dynamic system of such elements constitutes physical nature; taken in other relations they constitute "ideal" systems, such as logic and mathematics; while in still another grouping, and in a specific functional relation, they make up that process of reflective thought which is the subject under discussion in the author's theory of ideas and of truth. The grouping or pattern which is most characteristic of the *individual* consciousness as such, is best described in connection with "the experience of activity."

But before turning to this topic it is important to call attention to a further corollary which is capable of a very

William James, 1842-1910.

wide application. The common or 'neutral' elements of pure experience serve not only to connect consciousness with the various objective orders of being, but also to connect different units of consciousness with another. Two or more minds become co-terminous and commutable through containing the same elements. We can thus understand "how two minds can know one thing."[9] In precisely the same way the same mind may know the same thing at different times. The different pulses of one consciousness may thus overlap and interpenetrate. And where these pulses are successive, the persistence of these common factors, marginal in one and focal in the next, gives to consciousness its peculiar connectedness and continuity. There is no need, therefore, of a synthesis *ab extra;* there is sameness and permanence and universality within the content itself. Finally, just as several individual minds, and the several moments of one individual mind, are "co-conscious," so there is no reason why human minds should not be "confluent in a higher consciousness."[10]

[SECTION] 4.

The Experience of Activity

A certain grouping of the elements of experience, a grouping in which activity and affectional states are the most marked characteristics, constitutes "the individualized self." "Simon pure activity," or "activity *an sich,*" is a fictitious entity. But we are not on that account to banish the word 'activity' from our philosophical vocabulary, since there is a specific experience-complex for which it may be rightly and profitably used. "If the word have any meaning it must denote what there is found. . . . The experiencer of such a situation possesses all that the idea contains. He feels the tendency, the obstacle, the will, the strain, the triumph, or the passive giving up, just as he feels the time, the space, the swiftness or intensity, the movement, the weight and color, the pain and pleasure, the complexity, or whatever remaining factors the situation may involve."[11] This specific train or pattern of experiences being taken to constitute activity, it will constitute "my" activity in so far as it is accompanied by certain affectional states; in other words, in so far as it centres in certain experiences of my own body. For affectional states are quasi-bodily. They do not belong exclusively either to the mental or to the physical order. That which is attractive or repugnant stirs the body as well as the mind. "The 'interesting' aspects of things" rule the consecution of our several conscious streams; but they are "not wholly inert physically, though they be active only in those small corners of physical nature which our bodies occupy."[12] The individualized self is thus a peculiar assemblage or field of elements, which "comes at all times with our body as its centre, centre of vision, centre of action, centre of interest. . . . The body is the storm centre, the origin of coördinates, the constant place of stress in all that experience-train. Everything circles round it, and is felt from its point of view. The word 'I,' then, is primarily a noun of position, just like 'this' and 'here.' Activities attached to 'this' position have prerogative emphasis. . . . The 'my' of them is the emphasis, the feeling of perspective-interest in which they are dyed."[13]

Precisely as there is no consciousness *an sich,* and no activity *an sich,* so there is no mental power or "effectuation" *an sich.* The causality of mind lies in the drama, train, conjunction, or series, which is peculiar to the mind-complex. "Sustaining, persevering, striving, paying with effort as we go, hanging on, and finally achieving our intention—this *is* action, this *is* effectuation in the only shape in which, by a pure experience-philosophy, the whereabouts of it anywhere can be discussed. . . . Real effectual causation . . . is just that kind of conjunction which our own activity-series reveal."[14] We meet here with a type of process that is *sui generis.* Whether human action is determined primarily by this process, or by the elementary processes of the nerve-cells, James does not attempt to decide. It is essentially a question between the activities of longer and of shorter span; "naïvely, we believe, and humanly and dramatically we like to believe," that the two are at work in life together.[15]

If we assemble these various aspects of mind, we can picture it in its concrete wholeness. The organism operates interestedly and selectively within its natural environment; and the manifold of elements thus selected compose the mind's content. But this content, when viewed by itself, exhibits certain characteristic groupings, patterns, and conjunctions. Of these the knowledge process is the most striking But as the body is the original instrument of selection and the source of individual bias, so bodily states and bodily orientation will be the nucleus of each individual field of content.

II. THEORY OF KNOWLEDGE

[SECTION] 5.

The Function of Cognition

To understand the originality and value of James's contributions to this subject, it is indispensable that one should see his problem. One must respect the difficulty before one can appreciate his solution of it. James's problem can perhaps be formulated as follows: How can idea and object be *two,* and yet one be knowledge *of* the other, and both fall within the same individual conscious field? And this problem James proposes to solve empirically, that is, by an examination of cognition in the concrete. Just what is it that takes place, just what is found, when I have an idea of an object?

Although James's discussions of knowledge relate mainly to this dual or mediated type, to knowledge about the thing *b,* which I have by virtue of the idea *a,* he does not regard this as the only type or as the standard type. "Knowledge about" is a derivative of "direct" knowledge, or "knowledge of acquaintance," and is never more than a provisional substitute for it. Representation is cognitive only in so far as it is a virtual presentation. In direct knowledge, or knowledge of acquaintance, "any one and the same *that* in experience must figure alternately as a thing known and as a knowledge of the thing, by reason of two divergent kinds of context into which, in the general course of experience, it gets woven."[16] In knowledge of this type, in other words, the thing *itself* is acted on and felt about in the manner characteristic of an individual conscious field. The most notable case of this is sense-perception. In so far as there is here any difference between the knowing and the known, the knowing is simply the context, the company into which the thing known is received. And the individual knower will be that nuclear bodily complex which has already been described. The function of such knowledge is evidently to get things thus directly acted on, or thus directly introduced into life.

But, humanly speaking, if the range of life is not to be narrowly circumscribed, it is necessary that most things should appear in it vicariously, that is, represented by what is known "about" them. "The towering importance for human life of this kind of knowing lies in the fact that an experience that knows another can figure as its *representative,* not in any quasi-miraculous 'epistemological' sense, but in the definite practical sense of being its *substitute* in various operations."[17] Thus the function of "knowledge about" is to provide substitutes for things which it is practically impossible to know directly, so that the original function of knowledge may be widely extended. It is only a special case of that which is characteristic of all organized life—namely, the broadening of its scope by delegation and indirection. And we are thus brought to the consideration of a narrow and definite problem. *When may one item be, for cognitive purposes, substituted for another?* That which may thus be substituted is "knowledge about," or "idea of," the thing for which it is so substituted; and the thing for which the substitution is made is the object. So that our question is equivalent to the traditional question, 'What is the relation between an idea and its object?' But it is important to bear in mind that James's question cannot be answered simply by saying that idea and object are identical. That in many cases they are identical, and that in all cases they are virtually identical, he does not deny. But he asks particularly about *that respect in which they are not identical;* where there is an actual otherness of content, or an actual temporal progression from the one to the other. And it must also be remembered also that James does not permit himself to deal with this question on other than empirical grounds; in other words, he assumes that all the terms referred to must be such as can be brought together within one field of consciousness.[18] The older dualism, in which the something 'inside' represents something 'outside' every possible extension of the individual's consciousness, is regarded as obsolete.[19]

The relation characteristic of an idea and its object can be analyzed into two factors, *intention* and *agreement.*[20] In the first place, the idea must somehow "mean" its object, that is, designate which thing is its object. And intention is prior to agreement. It is not sufficient that an idea should simply agree with something; it must agree with *its* object; and until its object has been identified, no test of agreement can be applied. "It is not by dint of discovering which reality a feeling 'resembles' that we find out which reality it means. We become first aware of which one it means, and then we suppose that to be the one it resembles."[21] But intention is essentially a practical matter. What one intends is like one's goal or one's destination, in being what one's actions converge on or towards. And the idea owes its existence, as such, to an intention or plan of action of which the 'intended' is the terminus. Intention is, of course, often equivocal; but the intention is revealed, and becomes less and less equivocal as the plan of action unfolds. It is this which accounts for the superiority of gesture over words. If one can hold up the object, lay one's hand on it, or even point to it, its identity becomes unmistakable.[22] So we must conclude that where the action on the object is not completed, the object is intended in so far as there is an incipient train of action which, if completed, would terminate in that thing. I may here and now have an idea of "the tigers in India," that is, mean, intend, or refer to them, inasmuch as what is in my mind is so connected circumstantially with the actual India and its tigers, that if I were to follow it up I should be brought face to face with them.[23] In other words, to have an idea of a thing is to have access to it, even when it is not present.

But an idea must not only intend its object; it must also, in some sense, "agree" with it. And here again we find that the essential thing is *practical connection;* for identity, or even similarity, is evidently not necessary. "We are universally held both to intend, to speak of, and to reach conclusions about—to know, in short—particular realities, without having in our subjective consciousness any mind-stuff that resembles them even in a remote degree. We are instructed about them by language which awakens no consciousness beyond its sound; and we know *which* realities they are by the faintest and most fragmentary glimpse of some remote context that they may have, and by no direct imagination of themselves."[24] Since it is not always necessary that the idea should resemble its object, we must conclude that the minimum agreement which is required of all ideas cannot be resemblance. And we shall understand that minimum agreement best where it is barest, where it is not complicated by the accident of agreement. The best example, then, will be the agreement of words with their objects. Now a word agrees with its intended object inasmuch as by an established convention it leads to that object, or enables one to find it. And what is true of single words will also be true of combinations of words; they will "agree," when they are so connected with a combination of things as to enable one to reverse the verbalizing operation and substitute that combination of things for them. But since it is possible that my idea should *not* prepare me for what it intends, it is evident that we are already within the domain of truth and error; agreement being the same thing as truth, and disagreement the same thing as error. And this is a matter for special and detailed examination.

Before leaving the present topic, however, it is worth while once more to point out that for James all knowledge is virtually direct or presentative. First, the safest and surest of our everyday knowledge is sense-perception. Second, while it is not necessary that the idea should resemble its object, the idea will ordinarily be some fragment of the object, abstracted and made to serve for the whole. And in so far as this is the case the idea and its object are identical. Third, even mediated knowledge is completed only when by means of it the object is brought directly into the mind. So that the best idea would be that which would "lead to an actual merging of ourselves with the object, to an utter mutual confluence and identification."[25] In other words, knowledge, generally speaking, is the entrance of things belonging otherwise to nature or some ideal order, into the context of the individual life. Mediated knowledge, in which there is a difference and an extrinsic connection between the idea and its object, is incidental to knowledge thus defined; a means, simply, of extending its scope by the method of substitution.

[SECTION] 6.

The Pragmatic Nature of Truth

The function of knowledge reveals the *locus* of the problem of truth. Truth is something which happens to ideas owing to their relation to their objects, that is, to the things which they are 'about.' Ideas are true 'of' their objects, it being assumed that the objects are both different from the beliefs and intended by them. The pragmatic theory of truth means nothing except so far as applied to this particular situation. If the specific complexity of the situation be not taken account of, then the theory becomes labored and meaningless. James convicts most of the objectors to pragmatism of overlooking, or over-simplifying, this problem. If one identifies truth with fact, one is simply ignoring James's question as to how one fact can be true *of* another, as is supposed to be the case in all mediated knowledge. If one says that true beliefs are beliefs in true propositions, truth being an indefinable property of some propositions, one is evading the troublesome question as to what is meant by belief *in;* and one is neglecting the fact that in nearly all actual knowledge the content of the believing state, or *what* is believed, differs from that which it is believed *about.* So that James's question will simply reappear as the question how a true belief about a 'true proposition' (in the opponent's sense) differs from a false belief about that same proposition. Or, finally, if one defines truth in terms of a hypothetical omniscience, one transfers the problem to a domain where its empirical examination is impossible, and meanwhile leaves untouched the question of that human truth that can be empirically examined, including the truth of the hypothesis of omniscience.[26]

Let us, then, resort to that corner of the world to which James's question invites attention. We find, on the one hand, something belonging, let us say, to the realm of physical nature. We find, on the other hand, some particular individual's particular belief, idea, or statement with reference to that thing. What, then, do we find to be characteristic of the idea in so far as true of the thing? We are not asking for a recipe for the making of truth; still less for an infallible recipe. We desire only to understand "what the *word* 'true' *means,* as applied to a statement"; "what truth actually *consists of*"; "the relation to its object that makes an idea true in any given

instance."[27] We shall be faithful to James's meaning if we articulate the situation expressly. Let *b* represent a certain individual thing, assumed to exist; and let *a* represent somebody's idea of *b,* also assumed to exist. *a* may be similar to *b,* or dissimilar; but in any case, it must 'intend' *b,* in the manner already defined. It should also be remarked that *a* and *b* belong to one manifold of experience, in the sense that the same individual mind may proceed from the one to the other. Our question, then, is this: When is *a* true of *b?* The pragmatist answer is as follows:[28] *a* owes its existence as an idea to some interest; if there were no interested minds at work in the world, then the world would consist only of *b*'s.[29] Ideas, whether they be mere conventional signs for things or selected aspects of things, arise only because of some practical motive. Furthermore, the relation of intention which connects an idea with some thing and makes that thing *its* object, is due to the same interest or motive which selected the idea.[30] Finally, then, *a* is true of *b,* when this interest which selected *a* and related it to *b,* is *satisfied.* In short, *a* is true of *b,* when it is a successful ideating of *b.*[31]

We shall gain in clearness and explicitness if we now distinguish the cases of *applied* and *theoretical* truth. We may suppose *a* to arise, first, as a mode of conceiving *b* for some use to which *b* is to be put. Then, when by virtue of the conception *a* I am enabled to handle or control *b,* and reach the desired end by so doing, I have a true idea of *a,* in the applied sense. This kind of truth is much the more common. If we include such knowledge as animals possess, and all of that human competence and skill which is not exactly formulated—all of the art which is not science—it is evident that in bulk it far exceeds the knowledge which is immediately related to the theoretical motive.

But pragmatism is not intended as a disparagement of theory. James naturally resents the description of it "as a characteristically American movement, a sort of bobtailed scheme of thought, excellently fitted for the man on the street, who naturally hates theory and wants cash returns immediately."[32] Indeed, owing to the emphasis given the matter by the turn of controversy, the pragmatist writers have devoted a somewhat disproportionate amount of space to the discussion of theoretical truth. That the theoretical process is itself interested in its own way, that it has its characteristic motive and its characteristic successes and failures, is a fact that no one has ever questioned. And 'theoretical truth,' so-called, is its success. An idea is true theoretically, when it works for the theoretical purpose. It remains only to discover what that purpose may be. What, then, is the theoretical motive for the formation of ideas? Or what is the virtue of forming ideas of things, different from the things themselves, when there is no occasion for acting on the things? In order, the pragmatist replies, to have a compact and easily stored access to these things;

in order to be able to find, should one want them, more things than there are room for within the mind at any one time. It follows, then, that the mark of a good idea, from this point of view, is its enabling one by means of it to come directly at a large number of particular facts which it means. Verification is thus the trying out, the demonstration, of an idea's capacity to lead to its objects and obtain their direct presentation to mind. Thus *a* is true of *b,* in the theoretical sense, when by virtue of having *a* in mind I can bring *b* into mind, *a* being more compact than *b.* And the adequacy of *a* will depend upon the extent to which it puts me in virtual possession of the full or complete nature of *b.* There is always a sense in which nothing can be so true of *b* as *b* itself, and were it humanly possible to know everything directly and simultaneously, as we know aspects of things in sense-perception, then there would be no occasion for the existence of ideas. But then there would be no truth, in the particular sense in which James uses the term.

It is worth while to observe that when James defines truth in terms of satisfaction, he has in mind a very specific sort of satisfaction, a determined satisfaction, of which the conditions are imposed on the one hand by the environment, and on the other hand by the interest which called the idea forth.[33] This is by no means the same thing as to say that an idea which is satisfactory is therefore true. It must be satisfactory for a particular purpose, and under particular circumstances. An idea has a certain work to do, and it must do that work in order to be commended as true. There is a situation, again a special situation, in which the general usefulness or liveableness of an idea may be allowed to count towards its acceptance. But the case is exceptional, and is not necessarily implied in the pragmatic theory. I have thought it on the whole clearer and fairer, therefore, to consider it in another connection.[34]

The pragmatic theory of truth is closely connected in the author's mind with "the pragmatic method." It emphasizes the particular and presentable consequences of ideas, and is thus opposed to verbalism, to abstractionism, to agnosticism, and to loose and irrelevant speculation. But pragmatism here merges into empiricism, where the issues are wider and more diverse.

[SECTION] 7.

Empiricism

James was an empiricist in the most general sense, in that he insisted on the testing of an idea by a resort to that particular experience which it means. An idea which does not relate to something which may be brought directly before the same mind that entertains the idea, is not properly an idea at all; and two ideas are different only in so far as the things to which they thus lead differ in some particular respect. "The meaning of any proposition can always be brought down to some particular consequence in our future practical experience, whether passive or active . . . the point lying rather in the fact that the experience must be particular than in the fact that it must be active."[35] Similarly, "the whole originality of pragmatism, the whole point in it, is its use of the concrete way of seeing."[36] Empiricism, or pragmatism, in this sense, is essentially an application of James's theory of the function of ideas. Since it is their office to pave the way for direct knowledge, or to be temporarily substituted for it, their efficiency is conditioned by their unobtrusiveness, by the readiness with which they subordinate themselves. The commonest case of an idea in James's sense is the word, and the most notable example of his pragmatic or empirical method is his own scrupulous avoidance of verbalism. It follows that since ideas are in and of themselves of no cognitive value, since they are essentially instrumental, they are always on trial, and "liable to modification in the course of future experience."[37] The method of hypothesis and experiment is thus the method universal, and the canon of verifiability applies to philosophy as well as to science.

Empiricism in a narrower sense is the postulate, "that the only things that shall be debatable among philosophers shall be things definable in terms drawn from experience."[38] We find experience itself described as "a process in time, whereby innumerable particular terms lapse and are superseded by others."[39] This cannot mean that experience is to be identified with the manifold of sense-perception, for he refers repeatedly to "nonperceptual experiences."[40] Nor can it mean that experience is to be identified with the *experienced,* that is, with consciousness. For consciousness, like matter, is a part of experience. Indeed, "there is no *general* stuff of which experience at large is made." "It is made of *that,* of just what appears, of space, of intensity, of flatness, brownness, heaviness, or what not. . . . Experience is only a collective name for all these sensible natures, and save for time and space (and, if you like, for 'being'), there appears no universal element of which all things are made."[41] Experience, then, is a colorless name for things in their spatial-temporal conjunctions. Things are *experience* when these conjunctions are immediately present in the mind; in other words, when they are directly known *here* and *now,* or when such a here-and-now knowledge is possible. In other words, we are again brought back to a fundamental insistence on direct or presentative knowledge. In respect of this insistence James is a lineal descendent of Berkeley, Hume, and Mill, and a brother of Shadworth Hodgson and Ernst Mach. In all of these writers the insistence on the immanence of the object of knowledge has tended to lead to phenomenalism; and James, like the rest, is a phenomenalist, in the sense of being opposed to dualism and transcendentalism. But in his later writings, at least, he has made it perfectly clear that while things are "what they are known as," they need not be known in order to be. Their being known is an accidental relation into which they directly enter as they are.[42] To limit knowledge to experience means only to limit it to what may be immediately apprehended as here and now, to what may be brought directly before the mind in some particular moment of its history.

James's empiricism means, then, first, that ideas are to be tested by direct knowledge, and second, that knowledge is limited to what can be presented. There is, however, a third consideration which is both an application of these, and the means of avoiding a difficulty which is supposed to be fatal to them. This is what James calls "radical empiricism," the discovery that "the relations between things, conjunctive as well as disjunctive, are just as much matters of direct particular experience, neither more so nor less so, than the things themselves."[43] "Adjacent minima of experience" are united by the "persistent identity of certain units, or emphases, or points, or objects, or members . . . of the experience-continuum."[44] Owing to the fact that the connections of things are thus found along with them, it is unnecessary to introduce any substance below experience, or any subject above, to hold things together. In spite of the atomistic sensationalists, relations are found; and in spite of Mr. Bradley, relations *relate*. And since the same term loses old relations and acquires new ones without forfeiting its identity, there is no reason why a relation should not unite things and still be adventitious and variable. Thus the idealistic theory, which, in order that there may be *some* connection, conceives of a trans-experiential and immutable connection, is short-circuited.[45] This handling of the question of relation at the same time proves the efficacy of the empirical method, and the futility of "intellectualism."

[SECTION] 8.

Percepts and Concepts: The Critique of Intellectualism

The critical application of James's theory of knowledge follows from his notion of conception and its relation to perception. "Abstract concepts . . . are salient aspects of our concrete experiences which we find it useful to single out."[46] He speaks of them elsewhere as things we have learned to "cut out," as "flowers gathered," and "moments dipped out from the stream of time."[47] Without doubt, then, they are elements of the given and independent world; not invented, but selected—and for some practical or theoretical purpose. To knowledge they owe, not their being or their natures, but their isolation or abstraction and the cognitive use to which they are put. This use or function tends to obscure the fact that they are themselves "objective." They have, as a matter of fact, their own "ideal" relations, their own "lines of order," which when traced by thought become the systems of logic and mathematics.[48]

The human importance of concepts and of ideal systems lies in their cognitive function with reference to the manifold of sense-perception. Therefore it is necessary to inquire just what kind of a knowledge of the latter they afford. Since they are extracts from the same experience-plenum, they may be, and to a large extent are, similar to their perceptual objects. But it is never the primary function of an idea to picture its object, and in this case, at least, a complete picturing is impossible. Because, in the first place, concepts are single and partial aspects of perceptual things, and never a thing's totality. Although conception exhibits these aspects clearly one by one, sense-perception, apprehending the thing all at once, or concretely, will, in spite of its inarticulateness, always convey something—it may be only the fullness of potential concepts—which conception misses. It would follow, then, that a concept is true of a percept only *so far as it goes*. But those who employ concepts are prone to use them "privatively," that is, as though they exhausted their perceptual object and prevented it from being anything more. This "treating of a name as excluding from the fact named what the name's definition fails positively to include," is what James calls "vicious intellectualism."[49]

But, in the second place, there is a more specific reason why concepts cannot adequately express the existential sense-manifold. Not only are they unequal to it because abstracted from it, but they are necessarily *unlike* it, in that the most characteristic aspects of the sense-manifold cannot be conveyed in conceptual form. This is the chief ground of James's indictment of intellectualism, and is of critical importance to the understanding of his philosophy. It is important once more to note that the cognitive use of ideas does not depend upon their similarity to their objects. They may be abstracted aspects of their objects, or they may be entirely extraneous bits of experience, like words, connected with their objects only through their functional office. Now it is James's contention that the most characteristic aspects of existence can be ideated only in this second way. They cannot be abstracted, they cannot themselves become the immediate objects of thought, although they can, of course, be led up to and functionally represented. Every bit of experience has "its quality, its duration, its extension, its intensity, its urgency, its clearness, and many aspects besides, no one of which can exist in the isolation in which our verbalized logic keeps it."[50] The error of intellectualism lies in its attempt to make up such aspects as these out of logical terms and relations. The result is either a ridiculous oversimplification of existence, or the multiplication of paradoxes. The continuity of change, the union of related things, the fulness of the existent world, has to be sensed or felt, if its genuine character is to be known, as truly as color has to be seen or music heard. So that, so far as these aspects of existence are concerned, concepts are useful for "purposes of practice," that is, to guide us to the sensible context, and not for "purposes of insight."[51]

"Direct acquaintance and conceptual knowledge are thus complementary of each other; each remedies the other's defects."[52] Knowing is always in the last analysis witnessing—having the thing itself within the mind. This is the only way in which the proper nature, the original and intrinsic character, of things, is revealed. Thought itself is the means of thus directly envisaging some aspects of things. But owing to the peculiar conditions under which the mind operates, it is practically necessary to know most things indirectly. So thought has a second use, namely, to provide substitutes for aspects of things that can be known directly only by sense. The peculiar value of thought lies, then, in its direct grasp of the more universal elements, and in the range and economy of its indirect grasp of those elements which, in their native quality, can be directly grasped only by sense.

Knowledge in all its varieties and developments arises from practical needs. It takes place within an environment to whose independent nature it must conform. If that environment be regarded as something believed, then it signifies truth already arrived at obediently to the same practical motives. But if it be conceived simply as reality, as it must also be conceived, then it is prior to all knowledge, and in no sense involved in the vicissitudes of knowledge. In short, James's theory is epistemology in the limited sense. It describes knowledge without implying any dependence of things on the knowing of them. Indeed, on the contrary, it is based explicitly on the acceptance of that non-mental world-order which is recognized by common sense, by science, and by philosophical realism.[53]

III. PHILOSOPHY OF RELIGION

[SECTION] 9.

The Right to Believe

James's contribution to the study of religion is so considerable and so important as to stand by itself, beside his psychology and his philosophy. In the present meagre summary I shall deal only with what is directly related to the fundamentals of his philosophy, namely, to his theory of mind and his epistemology. Religion, like knowledge, is a reaction of man to his environment. Its motives are practical, and its issues, tests, and successes are practical. Religion is "a man's total reaction upon life." It springs from "that curious sense of the whole residual cosmos as an everlasting presence, intimate or alien, terrible or amusing, lovable or odious."[54] The positive or hopeful religion says "that the best things are the more eternal things," and "that we are better off

even now" if we believe so.[55] There is a practical motive leading to some such belief, and there is an additional motive for taking the hopeful rather than the despairing view. Applying the theory of truth already expounded, it follows that that religious belief is true which satisfies the demands which give it birth. So far this might mean simply that it is important for life to have an idea of the ultimate nature of things, and as hopeful an idea as possible; in which case the true religion would be the idea which succeeded in meeting these requirements. It would be the verified hypothesis concerning the maximum of hopefulness which the universe justifies. But the case is not so simple as that. For no idea of the ultimate nature of things *can* be verified, that is, proved by following it into the direct presence of its object. And meanwhile it is practically necessary to adopt *some* such idea. So the question arises as to whether the general acceptability of an idea, including its service to other interests than the theoretical interest, may in this case be allowed to count. To accept an idea, or to believe under such conditions and on such grounds, is an act of faith. What, then, is the justification of faith?

Faith does not mean a defiance of proof but only a second best, a substitute where the evidence is not conclusive. "Faith means belief in something concerning which doubt is still theoretically possible; and as the test of belief is willingness to act, one may say that faith is the readiness to act in a cause the prosperous issue of which is not certified to us in advance."[56] If it can be certified in advance, so much the better; but if not, then it may be proper to act confidently none the less. Now such is the case, first when hesitation or suspension of action is equivalent to *disbelief* in a prosperous issue. Thus, "if I must not believe that the world is divine, I can only express that refusal by declining ever to act distinctively as if it were so, which can only mean acting on certain critical occasions as if it were *not* so, or in an irreligious way."[57] "Logical scrupulosity" may thus over-reach itself, and lead one to a virtual denial even in the face of probability. In the second place, there are "cases where faith creates its own verification." Belief in the success of an enterprise in which the believer is himself engaged breeds the confidence which will help to *make* success. And religion is such an enterprise. "Believe, and you shall be right, for you shall save yourself."[58]

In short, "there is really no scientific or other method by which men can steer safely between the two opposite dangers of believing too little or of believing too much."[59] We can neither limit belief to proof, for that would be to cut ourselves off from possibilities of truth that have a momentous importance for us; nor exempt our belief altogether from criticism, for that would be to forfeit our principal means to truth. There are genuine "options" for belief, options that are "live" in that there is an incentive to choose; and "forced," in that to decline to choose is still virtually to choose.[60] Where such an option exists, hope may be allowed to convert objective or theoretical probability into subjective certainty. And the one momentous case of this is religion.

[SECTION] 10.

Reflex Action and Theism

That religious belief which is at once most probable on theoretical grounds, and most rational in the broader sense of making a "direct appeal to all those powers of our nature which we hold in highest esteem,"[61] is theism. God is conceived as "the deepest power in the universe," and a power not ourselves, "which not only makes for righteousness, but means it, and which recognizes us."[62] "To coöperate with his creation by the best and rightest response seems all He wants of us."[63] Such an interpretation of the world most completely answers our needs. "At a single stroke, it changes the dead blank *it* of the world into a living *thou,* with whom the whole man may have dealings." "Our volitional nature must, then, until the end of time, exert a constant pressure upon the other departments of the mind to induce them to function to theistic conclusions."[64] Here, then, is the possible and the profoundly desirable religious truth. To neglect it is to disbelieve it, which is equally arbitrary, and involves all the practical loss besides; while to accept it is to help make it true, since human efforts may assist in establishing the supremacy of the good. But what evidence may be adduced in its support?

The answer to this question consists partly in the removal of difficulties, such as the dogmatism of science, and the problem of "the compounding of consciousness,"[65] partly in the application to the religious experience of the theory of a "subconscious self." "We have in the fact that the conscious person is continuous with a wider self through which saving experiences come, a positive content of religious experience which, it seems to me, is literally and objectively true as far as it goes."[66] When we ask "how far our transmarginal consciousness carries us if we follow it on its remoter side," our "over-beliefs begin;" but the evidence afforded by mystical experiences, thus construed by means of an established psychological theory, creates "a decidedly formidable probability" in favor of the theistic hypothesis.[67]

[SECTION] 11.

The Dilemma of Determinism

The belief in freedom, like the belief in God, cannot be proved. Here, again, belief has an option between a rigidly determined world and a world with alternative possibilities in it. Determinism "professes that those parts of the universe already laid down absolutely appoint and decree what the other parts shall be."[68] Indeterminism, on the other hand, means that several futures are really possible, in the sense of being compatible with the same past. After the fact the one sequel is as reasonable as the other, and the fact itself throws no light on the question whether "another thing might or might not have happened in its place."[69] For this reason, the facts themselves can neither establish determinism nor disprove it. And since the facts are not decisive, man is warranted in taking into account the grave practical issues that are at stake. If the hypothesis of freedom be true, it relieves man from what would otherwise be an intolerable situation; and if he fails to accept the hypothesis because his doubts are not entirely dispelled, he virtually chooses the alternative which is worse without being any more probable.

From a moral or religious point of view a determined world is a world in which evil is not only a fact, as it must be on any hypothesis, but a necessity. "Calling a thing bad means, if it mean anything at all, that the thing ought not to be, that something else ought to be in its stead. Determinism, in denying that anything else can be in its stead, virtually defines the universe as a place in which what ought to be is impossible,—in other words, as an organism whose constitution is afflicted with an incurable taint, an irremediable flaw."[70] In such a universe there are only two religious alternatives, despair or renunciation—a hopeless complaint that such a world should be, or the cultivation of a subjective willingness that *anything* should be. To adopt the latter alternative, or "gnosticism," as the only course that will bring peace of mind, is "to abandon the judgment of regret," and substitute an intellectual, sentimental, or sensual condoning of evil for the healthy moral effort to eradicate it.[71] Indeterminism, on the other hand, is a doctrine of *promise* and *relief.*[72] It offers me "a world with a *chance* in it of being altogether good;" an escape from evil "by dropping it out altogether, throwing it overboard and getting beyond it, helping to make a universe that shall forget its very place and name."[73]

Although the belief in freedom is in the end an act of faith, there is evidence for its possibility or even probability. Freedom is not incompatible with any uniformity that has been discovered, but only with the dogma that uniformity must be absolute even if it has not been found to be so. If there be any real novelty in the world, any respects in which the future is not merely an unfolding of the past, then that is enough to leaven the whole. In the case of freedom of the will all that is required is "the character of novelty in activity-situations." The "effort" or activity-process is the form of a whole "field of consciousness,"[74] and all that is necessary for freedom is that the duration and intensity of this process should not be "fixed functions of the object."[75]

That the experience of activity should contribute something wholly new when it arises, is not only consistent
with the facts ascertained by psychology, but is also in
keeping with the general principles of radical empiricism. Old terms may enter into new relations; the unity
of the world is not over-arching and static, but a continuity from next to next, permitting of unlimited change
without disconnection and disorder. Indeterminism is
thus no more than is to be looked for in a pluralistic
universe.

[SECTION] 12.

Pluralism and Moralism

Pluralism is essentially no more than the denial of absolute monism. "Absolute unity brooks no degrees";
whereas pluralism demands no more than that "you
grant *some* separation among things, some tremor of independence, some free play of parts on one another,
some real novelty or chance, however minute."[76] And
pluralism in this sense follows directly from James's
theory of knowledge. In the first place, absolute monism loses its authority the moment its a priori necessity is disproved. To account for knowledge empirically
is to render all this elaborate speculative construction
unnecessary. As a hypothesis it is not wholly out of the
question,[77] but it will not bear comparison with pluralism for intellectual economy, and it brings a number of
artificial difficulties in its train.[78] Second, there is positive evidence for the pluralistic hypothesis in the fact of
"external relations." "It is just because so many of the
conjunctions of experience seem so external that a philosophy of pure experience must tend to pluralism in its
ontology." Relations may be arranged according to their
relatively conjunctive or disjunctive character: "confluence," "conterminousness," "contiguousness," "likeness," "nearness" or "simultaneousness," "in-ness," "on-
ness," "for-ness," "with-ness," and finally mere "and-
ness." With its parts thus related the universe has still
enough unity to serve as a topic of discourse, but it is a
unity of "concatenation," rather than of "co-
implication."[79]

The importance of such a conclusion for religious purposes is apparent. On the one hand, as we have already
seen, evil is not necessarily implied by the rest of the
universe, so that the universe as a whole is not compromised or irremediably vitiated by it. But, on the other
hand, it must be admitted that the good is in a like position. The supremacy of the good is not guaranteed,
but is only made possible, and is thrown into the future
as a goal of endeavor. Pluralism "has no saving message for incurably sick souls."[80] It is no philosophy for
the "tender-minded;" it makes life worth living only for
those in whom the fighting spirit is alive.[81] In the Introduction to the *Literary Remains* of his father, James

distinguished between the religious demand for an ultimate well-*being,* and that *healthy-minded moralism* in
which "the life we then feel tingling through us vouches
sufficiently for itself, and nothing tempts us to refer it
to a higher source."[82] It is this note which dominates
James's philosophy of life. It accounts for his relatively
slight interest in immortality.[83] He did not feel the necessity of being assured in advance of his own personal
safety. With his characteristic tenderness of mind where
the interests of others were in question, he sympathized
deeply with the more importunate and helpless cravings
of the religious spirit. But for himself, he was "willing
to take the universe to be really dangerous and adventurous, without therefore backing out and crying 'no
play.'"[84] "The essence of good is simply to satisfy demand." But the tragic fact is, that demands conflict, and
exceed the supply. Though God be there as "one of the
claimants," lending perspective and hopefulness to life,
the victory is not yet won. If we have the courage to
accept this doubtful and perilous situation as it is, "there
is but one unconditional commandment, which is that
we should seek incessantly, with fear and trembling, so
to vote and to act as to bring about the very largest total
universe of good which we can see."[85]

IV. CONCLUSION

These, I believe, are the bare essentials of James's philosophy, and the thread of reasoning by which they are
connected. A summary such as this must altogether
miss the pictorial and dramatic quality of his thought.
That which is most characteristic of him cannot be re-
stated; for his own style was its inevitable and only adequate expression. But I offer this rude sketch in the
hope that it may help those who seek to apprehend this
philosophy as a whole. James's field of study, the panoramic view within which all of his special problems
fell, was the lot of mankind. On the one hand stands the
environment, an unbidden presence, tolerating only
what will conform to it, threatening and hampering every interest, and yielding only reluctantly and gradually
to moral endeavor. On the other hand stands man who,
once he gets on good terms with this environment, finds
it an inexhausible mine of possibilities. "By slowly cumulative strokes of choice," he has extricated out of
this, like a sculptor, the world he *lives* in. James never
confused *the* world with man's world, but he made
man's world, thus progressively achieved, the principal
object of his study. Man conquers his world first by
knowing it, and thus presenting it for action; second, by
acting on it, and thus remoulding it to suit his purposes.
But these operations are the inseparable parts of one activity through which a humanized and moralized world
is developed out of the aboriginal potentialities. So philosophy becomes the study of man as he works out his
salvation. What is his endowment and capacity? How
does his knowing take place, and what are the marks of

its success? What forms does reality assume as it passes through the medium of the human mind? What are the goods which man seeks? What are the grounds, and what is the justification, of his belief in ultimate success?

The characteristics of James's mind were intimately connected with his conception of the mission of philosophy. He was distinguished by his extraordinary sense for reality. He had a courageous desire to know the worst, to banish illusions, to take life at its word, and accept its challenge. He had an unparalleled capacity for apprehending things in their human aspect, as they fill the mind, and are assimilated to life. So indefatigable was his patience in observing these conjunctions and transitions in their rich detail, that few of his critics have had patience enough even to follow his lead. True to his empirical ideals, he abandoned the easier and more high-handed philosophy of abstractions for the more difficult and less conclusive philosophy of concrete particulars. And finally, he had a sure instinct for humanly interesting and humanly important problems. He sought to answer for men the questions the exigencies of life led them to ask. And where no certain answer was to be had, since men must needs live notwithstanding, he offered the prop of faith. Making no pretence of certainty where he found the evidence inconclusive, he felt the common human need of forging ahead even though the light be dim. Thus his philosophy was his way of bringing men to the wisest belief which in their half-darkness they can achieve. He was the frank partizan of mankind, undeceiving them when necessary, but giving them the benefit of every doubt.

To attribute James's power to his genius is as much as to say that it escapes analysis. He was felt in his time as an original intellectual and spiritual force, that can no more be divided and inventoried than his philosophy can be distributed among the hackneyed classifications of the schools. It is easy to say that he owed much to his style; but it is plain that his style owed everything to him. He was, it is true, a lover of form, endowed with the finest sensibilities, and stirred by the creative impulse; but his style was always his instrument. He found it above all a means of communication; for nothing was more notable about him than the social quality of his thought. He wrote for his readers, his vivid imagination of their presence guiding him infallibly to the centre of their minds. And his style was also the means of faithfully representing his experience. It was figurative and pictorial, because the world he saw was a procession of concrete happenings, abounding in novelty and uniqueness. For his originality lay, not in his invention, but in the extraordinary freshness of his perception, and in an imagination which was freed from convention only to yield itself utterly to the primeval and native quality of the world as he found it. His thought was always of the actual world spread before him, of

what he called "the particular facts of life." He relied little on dialectic, but brought his powers of observation into play where the traditional philosophy had abstracted the problem and carried it off into the closet. And to this first-hand acquaintance with particulars he added a keen zest for metaphysical speculation. He was curious, as the natural man is curious, loving the adventure of exploration, and preferring the larger riddles of existence to the purely technical problems of the schools.

His resources were by no means limited to the results of his own observation. He probably read more widely than any philosopher of his day. He did not, however, value erudition for its own sake, but only as a means of getting light. His reading was always selective and assimilative; he converted it at once into intellectual tissue, so that it gave him strength and buoyancy and never merely a burden to carry. And he learned from men as well as from books. Always governed by his likings rather than his aversions, generous and openhearted, men who shrank from others gave their unsuspected best to him. In short, his mind was instinctively discriminating. He not only knew the good from the evil, but he was guided by a remarkably independent judgment of proportion. He was never led to accept a thing as important simply because it had acquired a certain professional or academic prominence; and he was rarely imposed on by the respectable humbug, though he opened his mind to whatever was humanly significant, even though it might be socially disreputable.

It is impossible to divorce his intellectual gifts from his character. His openmindedness, which has become proverbial, was only one of many signs of his fundamental truthfulness. Having no pride of opinion, and setting little store by his personal prestige, his mind remained flexible and hospitable to the end. His very modesty and guilelessness were sources of power. For his modesty was not a form of self-consciousness, but a preoccupation with things or persons other than himself. And his guilelessness was not a childlike naïveté, but a sincerity and openness of motive. He was possessed of a certain shrewdness and directness—an ability to come to the heart of affairs at a stroke—that made him the wisest of counselors. But he had no ambitions which he attempted to conceal, and no prerogatives of which he was jealous; so that he met his students and his friends with a natural simplicity and an entirely uncalculating indifference to distinctions of social eminence. He proved the possibility of possessing taste and personal distinction without pride or aloofness. And his democracy was a matter of conviction, as well as of impulse. He believed heartily in the institutions of his country, and shared those hopes of freedom, peace, and happiness, which unite men and nerve them to take part in the work of civilization.

James did not found a school. He was incapable of that patient brooding upon the academic nest that is necessary for the hatching of disciples. The number of those who borrowed his ideas is small and insignificant beside the number of those that through him were brought to have ideas of their own. His greatness as a teacher lay in his implanting and fostering of intellectual independence. He prized his own university for its individualism and tolerance, and for the freedom which it gave him to subordinate the scholastic office and the scholastic method to a larger human service. So the circle of his influence widened to the bounds of European civilization; while his versatility, his liberal sympathies, the coincidence of his ruling passions with the deeper interests of mankind at large, and above all the profound goodness of his heart, so diversified and humanized this influence that there were few indeed too orthodox or too odd to respond to it.

Notes

1. James left an unfinished "Introduction to Philosophy," in which he had made a beginning of a systematic restatement of his thought; but owing to its incompleteness it does not, as it stands, afford the reader the total view which was in the author's mind as he composed it. It has been published since his death under the title, *Some Problems of Philosophy[: A Beginning of an Introduction to Philosophy,* edited by Horace M. Kallen (New York & London: Longmans, Green, 1911)].

2. *The Journal of Speculative Philosophy,* Vol. XII, Jan., 1878.

3. *Loc. cit.,* p. 5.

4. *Principles of Psychology,* Vol. I [(New York: Holt, 1890; London: Macmillan, 1890)], p. 288.

5. *Op. cit.,* Ch. V, IX, XIII, XIV, XXII. Cf. especially, Vol. I, pp. 284-290; Vol. II, pp. 329-366.

6. *Journal of Phil., Psych., and Sc. Methods,* Vol. I, 1904, p. 477. The article has been reprinted in *Essays in Radical Empiricism,* I [edited by Ralph Barton Perry (New York & London: Longmans, Green, 1912)].

7. *Pluralistic Universe,* [A Pluralistic Universe: Hibbert Lectures at Manchester College on the Present Situation in Philosophy (New York & London: Longmans, Green, 1909)] pp. 322-323. Cf. *Essays in Radical Empiricism,* p. 140.

8. Cf. below, pp. 364-365.

9. *Op. cit.,* pp. 123 sq.

10. *Pluralistic Universe,* p. 290, cf. Lecture VII, *passim.* For the development of James's view concerning the "compounding of consciousness," cf. *Principles of Psychology,* Vol. I, pp. 160, 161; "The Knowing of Things Together," *Psych. Rev.,* Vol. II, 1895; *Pluralistic Universe,* Lecture V.

11. "The Experience of Activity," in *Pluralistic Universe,* pp. 380, 376-377.

12. "The Place of Affectional Facts in a World of Pure Experience," *Essays on Radical Empiricism,* pp. 150-151, and *passim.*

13. *Pluralistic Universe,* p. 380, note.

14. *Ibid.,* pp. 390, 392. For the bearing of this on the question of freedom, see below, p. 373.

15. *Ibid.,* p. 387.

16. "Essence of Humanism," in *The Meaning of Truth[: A Sequel to "Pragmatism"* (New York & London: Longmans, Green, 1907)], p. 127. Cf. *passim,* and "Function of Cognition," *ibid.,* pp. 1-42.

17. *Essays in Radical Empiricism,* p. 60.

18. For the meaning of "empiricism," see below, pp. 363-366.

19. *Meaning of Truth,* pp. 126-127.

20. "Function of Cognition," *op. cit., passim,* and especially pp. 28-32.

21. *Ibid.,* p. 25.

22. Cf. *ibid.,* pp. 25, 35; also "Meaning of the Word Truth," *op. cit.,* p. 217.

23. *Op. cit.,* pp. 43-50.

24. "Function of Cognition," *op. cit.,* pp. 30-31.

25. "A Word More about Truth," *op. cit.,* p. 156.

26. The volume entitled *The Meaning of Truth* is devoted almost entirely to the removal of these misapprehensions. Cf. especially the Preface, and Nos. VI, VIII, IX, and XIV.

27. *Op. cit.,* pp. 221, 234, 235.

28. This is not a close paraphrase of any portion of the text, but is arrived at by using the polemical statement in *The Meaning of Truth* to give greater precision to the constructive statement in Lect. VI of *Pragmatism* [*Pragmatism: A New Name for Some Old Ways of Thinking. Popular Lectures on Philosophy* (New York & London: Longmans, Green, 1907)].

29. See above, pp. 350-351.

30. See above, p. 358.

31. This success may be actual or potential. What James means by "potential" is clearly stated in

Meaning of Truth, p. 93. But in any case truth cannot be defined without reference to the success.

32. *Meaning of Truth*, p. 185.

33. Cf. *op. cit.*, pp. 192 ff.

34. See below, under "The Right to Believe," pp. 369-371.

35. *Meaning of Truth*, p. 210.

36. *Op. cit.*, p. 216. For the more popular exposition of this method, and the illustrative application of it, cf. *Pragmatism*, Lectures II, III.

37. *Will to Believe* [*The Will to Believe, and Other Essays in Popular Philosophy* (New York, London & Bombay: Longmans, Green, 1897)], Preface, p. vii.

38. *Meaning of Truth*, Preface, p. xii.

39. *Ibid.*, p. 111.

40. Cf. "Does Consciousness Exist?" *Essays in Radical Empiricism*, p. 17.

41. *Ibid.*, pp. 26-27.

42. Cf. "Does Consciousness Exist?" with "The Knowing of Things Together," *Psych. Rev.*, Vol. II, 1895. Cf. also below, p. 368.

43. *Meaning of Truth*, preface, p. xii. Cf. *Pluralistic Universe*, pp. 279-280.

44. *Pluralistic Universe*, pp. 326, 356. Cf. *Principles of Psychology*, Vol. I. p. 459.

45. Cf. "The Thing and its Relations," in *Pluralistic Universe*, pp. 347-369, *passim*. Cf. also above, p. 353, and below, pp. 373-374.

46. *Meaning of Truth*, p. 246.

47. *Pluralistic Universe*, p. 235. Cf. *Principles of Psychology*, on "Conception," and "Reasoning," Chapters XII and XXII.

48. *Essays in Radical Empiricism*, pp. 15, 16. Cf. *Meaning of Truth*, pp. 42, 195, note; *Pluralistic Universe*, pp. 339-340; *Principles of Psychology*, Ch. XXVIII. Here as elsewhere of two apparently conflicting statements I have taken the later. The latest and best statement James's view of concepts is to be found in *Some Problems of Philosophy*, Ch. IV-VI.

49. *Pluralistic Universe*, p. 60. Cf. also pp. 218 ff., and *Meaning of Truth*, pp. 248, 249 ff.

50. *Pluralistic Universe*, p. 256.

51. *Op. cit.*, p. 290. Cf. Lectures V, VI, and VII, *passim*.

52. *Op. cit.*, p. 251.

53. Cf. *Meaning of Truth*, Preface, and pp. 190-197, 212-216.

54. *Varieties of Religious Experience* [*The Varieties of Religious Experience: A Study in Human Nature. Being the Gifford Lectures on Natural Religion Delivered at Edinburgh in 1901-1902* (New York & London: Longmans, Green, 1902)], p. 35. In the "Varieties" the topic is circumscribed for the sake of convenience; cf. p. 31.

55. *Will to Believe*, pp. 25, 26.

56. *Op. cit.*, p. 90; cf. p. 1; and *Meaning of Truth*, p. 256.

57. *Will to Believe*, p. 55.

58. *Op. cit.*, p. 97.

59. *Op. cit.*, p. xi. Cf. p. 128.

60. *Op. cit.*, p. 3. Cf. *Some Problems of Philosophy*, Appendix, on "Faith and the Right to Believe."

61. *Op. cit.*, p. 110. Cf. pp. 115-116.

62. *Op. cit.*, p. 122.

63. *Op. cit.*, p. 141.

64. *Op. cit.*, p. 127.

65. Cf. above, pp. 353-354.

66. *Varieties of Religious Experience*, p. 515. Cf. also "The Energies of Men," *Memories and Studies* [(New York & London: Longmans, Green, 1911)], X.

67. *Op. cit.*, p. 513; *Pluralistic Universe*, p. 309.

68. "Dilemma of Determinism," in *Will to Believe*, p. 150; cf. *passim*.

69. *Op. cit.*, p. 152. Cf. pp. 146, 156.

70. *Op. cit.*, pp. 161-162.

71. *Op. cit.*, pp. 162 ff.

72. *Pragmatism*, pp. 119 ff.

73. *Op. cit.*, p. 297; *Will to Believe*, p. 178, and pp. 173 ff.

74. *Pluralistic Universe*, p. 391, note. Cf. above, pp. 354-356.

75. *Principles of Psychology*, Vol. II, p. 571. Cf. pp. 569-579, *passim*.

76. *Pragmatism*, p. 160. Cf. Lecture IV, *passim*.

77. *Will to Believe*, p. vii; *Pluralistic Universe*, p. 292.

78. *Meaning of Truth*, pp. 125 sq.

79. *Pluralistic Universe,* pp. 321, 325; 359, 361. Cf. Lecture VIII, and Appendix A, *passim.* Cf. also above, p. 353.

80. *Meaning of Truth,* p. 228.

81. Cf. *Pragmatism,* Lecture I, and "Is Life Worth Living?" in *Will to Believe.*

82. *Literary Remains of Henry James* [*The Literary Remains of the Late Henry James,* edited by James (Boston: Houghton, Mifflin, 1884)], pp. 116-117.

83. *Varieties of Religious Experience,* p. 524; *Human Immortality* [*Human Immortality: Two Supposed Objections to the Doctrine* (Boston & New York: Houghton, Mifflin, 1898; London: Constable, 1903)], p. 3.

84. *Pragmatism,* p. 296.

85. "The Moral Philosopher and the Moral Life," in *Will to Believe,* pp. 201, 212, 209, and *passim.*

Bernard P. Brennan (essay date 1968)

SOURCE: Brennan, Bernard P. "The Philosophic Enterprise: Pragmatism and Radical Empiricism." In *William James,* pp. 44-64. New York: Twayne Publishers, 1968.

[*In the following essay, Brennan outlines the basic tenets of William James's philosophical teachings, including James's contention that Pragmatism and Radical Empiricism have "no necessary connexion with each other."*]

George Santayana insisted that William James was not *essentially* a philosopher: "His excursions into philosophy were . . . in the nature of raids. . . ."[1] "It would be incongruous . . . to expect of him that he should build a philosophy like an edifice to go and live in for good. Philosophy to him was rather like a maze in which he happened to find himself wandering, and what he was looking for was the way out."[2] Santayana saw James as a mystic with such strong anti-intellectualistic bias that it was impossible for him to be a genuine philosopher: "He was a mystic, a mystic in love with life. He was comparable to Rousseau and Walt Whitman; he expressed a generous and tender sensibility, rebelling against sophistication, and preferring daily sights and sounds, and a vague but indomitable faith in fortune, to any settled intellectual tradition calling itself science or philosophy."[3] To Santayana, James was, therefore, hostile to genuine science—despite his degree in medicine, his teaching of physiology, and his contributions to psychology!

I ANGLE OF VISION

William James became a philosopher to satisfy a profound need which penetrated every aspect of his being. His health—physical, emotional, and mental—was contingent upon his finding the answers to philosophic problems—no mere riddles for him but indispensable keys to being. These problems brought him, before he found satisfactory answers, to despair and to the brink of self-destruction. When the answers were formulated, they retained, because of the intention of the philosopher, the signature of their origins. James considered the philosophy and the philosopher inseparably linked, like the artist and his work. Even the most general of statements, having a personal origin, he saw as bearing with it a personal note. The *human* origins of philosophy James accepts and honors; the authentic *personal* elements are retained and utilized. Every genuine problem is seen as *someone's* problem; every truth is *some thinker's* truth. The individual and universal human features in philosophical thinking are not to be exorcized; they are to be purified, accepted on their merits, and given central roles in the creation of the philosopher's picture of reality.

The first philosophical problem which concerned James in a deeply personal way was that of free will, or, as he called it, "determinism versus indeterminism." Given the best scientific viewpoints of his day, the individual seemed to be compelled to believe that man is completely determined in all his actions, physical, mental, and moral. James, familiar with the science of his day, felt compelled to see himself and others as mere automata, manipulated by forces beyond their control. This belief satisfied those requirements of his being which called for scientific consistency, but it violated other beliefs and yearnings of which he was painfully conscious. These too demanded recognition and satisfaction, for example, the consciousness of moral responsibility, which required some areas of human freedom to have meaning and fulfillment.

James's early expressions on the subject of determinism revealed his mixed feelings—a reverence for science, which seemed to require determinism, and an equally strong respect for the ethical element in life, which required moral autonomy. "I feel," he wrote, "we are Nature through and through, that we are wholly conditioned, that not a wiggle of ours will happen save as the result of physical laws; and yet, notwithstanding, we are *en rapport* with reason. How to conceive it? Who knows?"[4]

The only intellectually respectable solution to the problem evident to James at the time was determinism, with its attendant sacrifice of all the moral significance in human lives. James's early acceptance of determinism involved despair and agony; and he clung to the hope that he would find an intellectually honest way to affirm freedom. When he was twenty-five, he thus recorded his feelings: "I find myself more and more drifting towards sensationalism closed in by scepticism—but the scepticism will keep bursting out in the very midst of it, too, from time to time; so that I cannot help thinking I may one day get a glimpse of things through the onto-logical window. At present it is walled up."[5]

When James took up his vocation as a philosopher, he found himself approaching the great, perennial prob-lems with the hope of vindicating man's volitional na-ture against the "intellectual" arguments which regarded free will as a mere fiction. When he examined, for ex-ample, the basic metaphysical nature of human beings, he took into account not only the demands and aspira-tions of man's intellect but also the demands and aspi-rations of his volitional and emotional nature. As he de-veloped his philosophy, it became clearly an attempt to see reality in terms of all the resources of the human person, taking into account not only his passive specu-lator role in the world but also his creator role in en-gendering new realities and introducing new relation-ships and organizations into the existing order.

In James's philosophy, man is frankly and unapologeti-cally taken as a major key to the nature of reality—not just man viewed as knowing but as doing, not just man viewed as intellect but as an emotional, volitional, cre-ative being. James insists that man is *present* in the re-ality which philosophy investigates; he argues that the objective study of reality must include, not expunge, man with his various so-called subjective elements. Man's desires are seen as being as much a part of real-ity as the tides and rainfall; they are not to be dismissed merely because of intellectualistic biases against them. Out of a patient, profound study of the *world,* in which man plays a part, and of *man,* in which the world plays a part, there could emerge a philosophy as close to truth as man can hope to come.

II The Nature of Philosophy

Emerson defined the scholar as *man thinking;* William James said, "Philosophy in the full sense is only *man thinking,* thinking about generalities rather than about particulars."[6] Both sage and philosopher agreed that there is no thinking apart from the *thinking individual;* scholarship and philosophy, no matter how removed in presentation from their personal origins, are human products. Behind the volume and in it is a writer, with all his fallibility and aspirations as man and as thinker.

One of the most dangerous pitfalls of philosophizing, James saw, is the tendency to think of philosophy as an objective, independent entity, existing apart from hu-man beings and enjoying an enviable sort of superiority. The tendency to think in such a manner is reenforced by traditions which regard the human intellect, at its best, as participating in an eternal, ideal order of being. But, actually, philosophy is, inevitably, one other hu-man production, bearing the undeniable marks of hu-man limitations. No matter how greatly various human

enterprises may differ, from the noblest achievements to the most wretched failures, they all bear the bench-marks of a very imperfect race of artisans.

This human imperfection is visible in every philosophy and cannot be entirely overcome—because man's means of philosophic understanding and expression are forever inadequate in dealing with the richnesses of reality. In-sofar as philosophy means the articulate and the scien-tifically accurate, it will not be able perfectly to formu-late reality. "Life and mysticism," as James observed, "exceed the articulate."[7] This incomplete adequation be-tween philosophy and reality is partly due to the fact that reason does not encompass all of reality, and can handle only parts of it. Other parts can be handled only by emotions or mystical intuition—and must be left to unphilosophical activities.

The limitations which reason suffers from, as it encoun-ters reality, are described in an unpublished note which James wrote in 1905: "Reason doesn't surround Being. It encounters it. Feeling only, life, penetrates being. Reason is secondary. Illustrate by water and marble, or lime which it [water] only partially dissolves. Always refractory remainder, 'surd,' brute fact. A very natural state of things, if we agree that the intellect is a super-vening faculty, added for its utility in handling what it finds, but not coeval with creation."[8]

Reason can operate most effectively and make its best contributions to life and to philosophy when its limita-tions and legitimate goals are understood. Reason must not operate in a fashion that violates the character of re-ality or denies the legitimate roles of emotions and will. Reason has indeed so operated in those philosophies which aim at establishing "schematisms with permanent and absolute distinctions": "All neat schematicisms with permanent and absolute distinctions, classifications with absolute pretensions, systems with pigeon holes, etc., have this character [of the artificial]. All 'classic,' clean, cut and dried, 'noble,' 'fixed,' 'eternal.' Weltanshauun-gen seemed to me to violate the character with which life concretely comes and the expression which it bears, of being, or at least involving, a muddle and a struggle, with an 'ever not quite' to all our formulas, and novelty and possibility forever leaking in."[9]

If permanent and absolute distinctions, absolute classifi-cations, and static systems are supposed to be avoided, can there indeed be such a thing as philosophy? Em-phatically *yes,* says James—and philosophy in all its branches, including metaphysics, ethics, and epistemol-ogy. Philosophy may well be among man's greatest achievements, and, properly constructed, one of his most practical creations in the conduct of life. Meta-physics in particular may be regarded as the "most ex-quisite work of human mind," although its progress to the present time is indeed "pathetic."[10]

Nevertheless, it must be pointed out that there are approaches to philosophic problems which lead inevitably to conclusions that are arid, pedantic, and petty. Taking such approaches is a worse course than having no articulate philosophy at all. And developing a philosophy which does no more than confirm "common sense" seems to be a process hardly worth the trouble.

> Of all forms of earthly worry, the metaphysical worry seems most gratuitous. If it lands us in permanently skeptical conclusions, it is worse than superfluous; and if (as is almost always the case with non-skeptical systems) it simply ends by "indorsing" common-sense, and reinstating us in the possession of our old feelings, motives, and duties, we may fairly ask if it was worth while to go so far round in order simply to return to our starting-point . . . Is not the primal state of philosophic innocence, since the practical difference is *nil,* as good as the state of reflective enlightenment?[11]

Philosophy, to produce good results, must be approached with freshness of outlook; while the philosophical achievements of the past should not be ignored, neither should they lead one to give up all attempts at original thinking in one's own day. Instead of being overawed by existing official answers or technical apparatus, one should remember that one's experiences are the greatest of source books. Each generation ought to attack things "as if there were no official answer preoccupying the field." But, unfortunately, as James observed, "We work with one eye on the problem, and with the other on the consequences to our enemy or to our lawgiver, as the case may be; the result in both cases is mediocrity."[12]

Technically and remoteness from the inspiration of living experiences both spell failure in philosophy: "In a subject like philosophy it is really fatal to lose connexion with the open air of human nature, and to think in terms of shop-tradition only."[13] Closeness to the concrete details of life is not an evil to be overcome but an ideal to be pursued: "In the end philosophers may get into as close contact as realistic novelists with the facts of life."[14] This closeness to the concrete facts of life is incompatible with excessive technicalities; as James's admirer Howard Knox observed, "James seems always to have felt that such philosophic truths as were intrinsically incapable of conveyance in nontechnical form must also be intrinsically of but slight importance for human guidance."[15]

The aim of the philosopher is not to construct—or discover—some changeless order of ideal beings and then formulate a description of it in rigid, technical terms. To do so would violate the nature of being, which constantly reveals itself as restless and fluid, perpetually growing and changing. The aim of the philosopher must rather be *to find paths* in this constantly expanding and pulsating universe:

> Philosophers are after all like poets. They are pathfinders. What every one can feel, what every one can know in the bone and marrow of him, they sometimes can find words for and express! The words and thoughts of the philosophers are not exactly the words and thoughts of the poets—worse luck. But both alike have the same function. They are, if I may use a simile, so many spots, or blazes,—blazes made by the axe of the human intellect on the trees of the otherwise trackless forests of human experience. They give you somewhere to go from. They give you a direction and a place to reach. They do not give you the integral forest with all its sunlit glories and its moonlit witcheries and wonders.[16]

This philosopher-pathfinder will never write a complete, definitive geography of "the woods" because they are forever expanding beyond the scope of his equipment and efforts. His descriptions and maps will never encompass all the woods, but he will explore as many areas as he can, and mark off trails where others may follow and, if they wish, open up new trails of their own.

The great achievement of philosophy down to the present time has *not* been, therefore, its answers to specific problems, which are forever being challenged, but rather the deepening of consciousness in the human race and the opening up of new areas of awareness. In this achievement the work of the philosophers has shown a genuine superiority over the works of men of narrower and more "practical" interests:

> For as yet philosophy has celebrated hardly any stable achievements. The labors of philosophers have, however, been confined to deepening enormously the philosophic *consciousness,* and revealing more and more minutely and fully the import of metaphysical problems. In this preliminary task ontologists and phenomenologists, mechanists and teleologists must join friendly hands, for each has been indispensable to the work of the other, and the only foe of either is the common foe of both—namely, the practical, conventionally thinking man, to whom . . . nothing has true seriousness but personal interests . . .[17]

Individual philosophers, constantly examining, enlarging, and clarifying the philosophic positions which appeal to them, contribute to mankind's expanding awareness of reality. For the student who undertakes to study this philosophical accumulation, there is offered the possibility of finding illuminating, though not final, answers to the classic questions of life. But there is also another equally, if not more, important reward: the reorganization of his own ways of thinking along lines of genuine philosophical wisdom. Such ways of thinking will enable him to escape from inferior modes of thought enfeebled by convention, common sense, and tradition: "philosophic study," he will find, "means the habit of always seeking an alternative, of not taking the usual for granted, of making conventionalities fluid again, of imagining foreign states of mind. In a word it means the possession of mental perspective."[18]

Thus, the student of philosophy is rewarded not only with the answers and meditations of great men—he is also repaid for his efforts by a most desirable sort of self-transformation. In this very transformation he will find the chief *educational* value of philosophic studies, a transformation which penetrates *every* area of the student's mental activities: "As for philosophy, technically so called, or the reflection of man on his relations with the universe, its educational essence lies in the quickening of the spirit to its *problems.* What doctrines students take from their teachers are of little consequence provided they catch from them the living, philosophic attitude of mind, the independent, personal look at all the data of life, and the eagerness to harmonize them."[19]

Catching the spirit of the problems of philosophy involves the student not only in alterations, for the better, in his intellectual life but also brings his intellect, will, taste, and emotions to new awarenesses and new relationships. In responding to the challenges of philosophic problems, the student responds with his entire person; and in organizing his answers to the problems, he is rewarded with an awakening and a reorganization of his own self. In this process the role of the intellect is indispensable but definitely not exclusive: "The whole man within us is at work when we form our philosophic opinions. Intellect, will, taste, and passion co-operate just as they do in practical affairs."[20]

Although philosophy has made certainly as much progress as any human discipline in history, it has not yet produced answers which satisfy the bona fide inquirer. The would-be philosopher must acknowledge this fact and try to profit by the lessons of the past:

> By what title is it that every would-be universal formula, every system of philosophy, which rears its head, receives the inevitable critical volley from one half of mankind, and falls to the rear, to become at the very best the creed of some partial sect? Either it has dropped out of its net some of our impressions of sense,—what we call the facts of nature,—or it has left the theoretic and defining department with a lot of inconsistencies and unmediated transitions on its hands; or else, finally, it has left some one or more of our fundamental active and emotional powers with no object outside of themselves to react on or to live for. Any one of these defects is fatal to its complete success.[21]

James hopes to avoid these defects by linking philosophy to the whole man and by avoiding the unrealistic procedure of erecting philosophy upon abstractions which themselves deny all those parts of reality which lie outside the abstractions. For this aim he was to be called a non-philosopher by some; by others, he was declared to be a great liberator of the human spirit.

III A REFORMED PHILOSOPHY

The philosophy of William James is not indeed a mansion among the great mansions of philosophy; it does not have the classical outlines of Aristotle's system, which explains the movements of the heavenly bodies and incorporates the Unmoved Mover in a universe explainable by universal formulas. James's philosophy is a humbler thing—a guide to the human traveler in this world.

The questions and answers of James's philosophy emerge from certain vital, central insights—much as the pattern of a bird's or animal's life develops in response to its goals and environment. These philosophic insights of James are humanistic; they are anthropocentric—the human person is placed at the center of his philosophy (subject, later, to the central position of the role of God). From man's total personality emerges a philosophy which is humanistic, pragmatic, and experiential, vindicating man's faith in his highest ideals and encouraging his noblest efforts for the well-being of himself and his fellow men.

An examination of the philosophic heritage of the West discloses a vast quantity of deadwood which each generation hauls through life. Much of this deadwood has come to occupy positions in various philosophies, and it kills much that is vital in life and thought. The anti-humanistic traditions of philosophy deserve not veneration but expulsion from the realms of philosophic activity. To free men from these hereditary idols of philosophy, William James fashioned a number of highly effective instruments; and among the most successful are Pragmatism and Radical Empiricism Pragmatism and Radical Empiricism are pivotal theories in this philosophy; they are also, unfortunately, among the most misunderstood and misrepresented teachings in modern philosophy, particularly the doctrine of Pragmatism. Radical Empiricism and Pragmatism, once properly appreciated, offer the best angles from which to view the philosophy of William James.

IV PRAGMATISM

The commonest simplification holds that Pragmatism judges a belief by its *practical* consequences: by determining whether it produces results which are *useful* or *not useful.* This description, though apparently supported by occasional inexact utterances of William James, invites misunderstanding and should be rejected in favor of another deceptively simple but more precise statement. More exactly, Pragmatism means that concepts should be reduced to their *positive experienceable operations.*[22]

In the theory of Pragmatism, James appeals to philosophers to examine their reasons for being interested in philosophy in the first place. He asks them, in effect, to put aside their philosophical biases and find for themselves the authentic reasons—apart from snobbery—for philosophical enterprise and their participation in it. In seeking such information, the philosopher will find it more fruitful to transpose the general question about philosophy into some specific counterparts. Instead of asking, "Why study philosophy?," he should inquire why he should investigate specific problems of philosophy, such as God, free will, immortality. If these problems and their answers cannot be reduced to positive experienceable operations in human life, then the philosopher must conclude that such problems are lacking in that seriousness which is essential to genuine knowledge. On the other hand, if specific concepts are found to have positive experienceable operations in life, the pragmatic insight can then be used further to explore their meanings.

Pragmatism—at once a method, a "genetic theory of what is meant by truth,"[23] "*a general theory of human action,*"[24] and a program for philosophy—is pregnant with unforeseen depths and possibilities. James confessed his own difficulties in coming to a fuller awareness of the meanings of Pragmatism. Bergson, writing to James, declared, "I ceaselessly repeat . . . that pragmatism is one of the most subtle and *nuancées* doctrines that have ever appeared in philosophy (just because this doctrine reinstates truth in the flux of experience), and one is sure to go wrong if one speaks of pragmatism before reading you *as a whole.*"[25] As late as 1906, James himself referred to the difficulties in attaining knowledge of Pragmatism: "I myself have been slow in coming into the full inwardness of pragmatism. Schiller's writings and those of Dewey and his school have taught me some of its wider reaches."[26]

The principle of Pragmatism, first of all, aids in determining which concepts are worthy of investigation and then provides the criterion for judging their value. Concepts which *cannot* be reduced to positive experienceable operations do not warrant study by the philosopher. Among such concepts are the so-called metaphysical attributes of God as distinguished from His moral attributes—such metaphysical attributes as His indivisibility, His repudiation of inclusion in a genus, and His aseity. Even though one were forced by "a coercive logic" to believe these metaphysical attributes, one would be free to ask "how do such qualities make any definite connection with our life? And if they severally call for no distinctive adaptations of our conduct, what vital difference can it possibly make to a man's religion whether they be true or false?"[27]

On the other hand, the concepts associated with God's *moral* attributes *do* make a difference in a man's life and possess, therefore, positive experienceable operations for the believer: "Pragmatically, they stand on an entirely different footing. They determine fear and hope and expectation, and are foundations for the saintly life."[28] Pragmatically, the concept of God's holiness, for example, is significant because it means, in terms of man's positive experienceable operations, that being

holy, God can will nothing but the good. Likewise, His omnipotence signifies that He can secure the triumph of the good: "Being omniscient, he can see us in the dark. Being just, he can punish us for what he sees. Being loving, he can pardon too. Being unalterable, we can count on him securely. These qualities enter into connection with our life, it is highly important that we should be informed concerning them."[29]

For first enunciating the principle of Pragmatism James acknowledged a debt to Charles Sanders Peirce and frequently called attention to Peirce's historic article "How to Make our Ideas Clear," published in 1878.[30] In 1902 James summarized the contents of Peirce's article, accepting it without criticism:

> Thought in movement has for its only conceivable motive the attainment of belief, or thought at rest. Only when our thought about a subject has found its rest in belief can our action on the subject firmly and safely begin. Beliefs, in short, are rules for action; and the whole function of thinking is but one step in the production of active habits. If there were any part of a thought that made no difference in the thought's practical consequences, then that part would be no proper element of the thought's significance. To develop a thought's meaning we need therefore only determine what conduct it is fitted to produce; that conduct is for us its sole significance; and the tangible fact at the root of all our thought-distinctions is that there is no one of them so fine as to consist in anything but a difference of practice. To attain perfect clearness in our thoughts of an object, we need then only consider what sensations, immediate or remote, we are conceivably to expect from it, and what conduct we must prepare in case the object be true. Our conception of these practical consequences is for us the whole of our conception of the object, so far as that conception has positive significance at all. This is the principle of Peirce, the principle of pragmatism.[31]

This principle of Pragmatism is a clue or compass, "by following which," said James, "I find myself more and more confirmed in believing that we may keep our feet upon the proper trail."[32] The needle of that compass points to the positive experienceable operations connected with concepts; it does so not only for relatively unimportant concepts but also for the largest and most important concepts in human knowledge: ". . . the whole function of philosophy ought to be to find out what definite difference it will make to you and to me, at definite instants of our life, if this world-formula or that world-formula be the one which is true."[33]

In 1907, three years before his death, James reported that he had grown "more and more deeply into pragmatism" and declared that it was "absolutely the only philosophy with *no* humbug." At the same time, he expressed a hope that his readers would be careful to distinguish in his own philosophy between Pragmatism and Radical Empiricism, which have "no necessary connexion with each other."[34]

V RADICAL EMPIRICISM

"I give the name of 'radical empiricism' to my *Weltanschauung*,"[35] declared James. "My philosophy is what I call a radical empiricism, a pluralism, which represents order as being gradually won and always in the making."[36] James, who admired his empirical predecessors in Britain, John Locke, George Berkeley, and David Hume, believed that the empirical British spirit in philosophy was intellectually, practically, and morally on the sane, sound, and true path.[37] But, at the same time, James was far from complete accord with the "classical" or "pure" empiricism of the British school; among other things, he criticized British empiricism for being *insufficiently* empirical, especially in Hume's failure to recognize *experienced conjunctive relations*. Therefore, he thought it necessary to give his own variety of empiricism a distinctive name, and chose to call it *Radical* Empiricism to emphasize its profoundly empiricist nature: its total marriage to experience in all its aspects.

James's education had given him an ideal preparation for being the founder of Radical Empiricism and had equipped him for the arduous task of treating experience with respect and understanding. Thanks to education and temperament, he was able to be a consistent empiricist. One observer reported: "His materials are facts. He deals with actual experience. To this he came not only by the natural disposition of his mind, but by the processes of his education. His first degree was not in arts but in medicine. He was studying bodies when his contemporaries were studying books."[38]

In equating reality with experience, James, contrary to possible expectations, does not constrict the boundaries of reality. By including *all* experiences within reality, he avoids reducing reality to certain particular types of experiences. He includes experiences of the vague and incoherent as well as the clear and distinct; so-called appearances as well as so-called realities; the subjective as well as the objective; the emotional as well as the intellectual; the unorthodox, the mystical, the non-respectable are all included from the outset. No experience, regardless of its source, is excluded *a priori;* all are admitted provisionally, subject later to the closest study on the basis of their performances and interdigitation with the rest of experience.

In his attempts to understand the general outlines of reality, the Radical Empiricist deliberately excludes the hedges and walls introduced by materialists and idealists, Platonists and Cartesians, and other earlier philosophers. In his preparation to study being, the Radical Empiricist endeavors to purify his mind of the theories of philosophy so that he can *take the fundamental aspects of consciousness at their face value,* receiving them and examining them patiently without rushing them into categories and classifications, without judging them hastily in *a priori* terms.

Bent on the study of experience, the Radical Empiricist is like a naturalist studying a living wild animal in its native habitat—as opposed to a museum specialist interested only in assigning a dead specimen to its proper place in his chart of the animal kingdom. The so-called "superiority" of the techniques of the museum specialist is "proved" by the neatness and clearness of his conclusions, which, however, are obtainable only by ignoring most of the realities of the non-museum parts of the world.

All experiences, all data of consciousness, are in some way real; and none of them should be denied to be real simply because they cannot be fitted into the museums which men have constructed. Every datum is an epiphany of reality. No matter how humble it may appear to be, a full appreciation of its meaning might reveal consequences of revolutionary dimensions. *Every fact,* said Emerson, *is an epiphany of God!*

"What is it to be 'real'?" inquired James. "The best definition I know," he replied, "is that which the pragmatist rule gives: 'anything is real of which we find ourselves obliged to take account in any way.' Concepts are thus as real as percepts, for we cannot live a moment without taking account of them."[39] And, likewise, faith is real, moral responsibility is real, and the ideals by which men live are real, no matter how poorly they may have been formulated by philosophers.

While Radical Empiricism affirms the reality of all experiences, it also denies, with equal emphasis, the unreality of all things that have been alleged to exist beyond experience. The Unknown of Herbert Spencer, the thing-in-itself of Kant, and the world of ideas of Plato, being extra-experiential, are therefore denied to exist. All such alleged beings, invented to explain and make more intelligible the objects which men experience, are rejected by the Radical Empiricist for the reason that *beings* which men experience cannot be made more intelligible by reference to "beings" which lie, by their very nature, beyond man's experience. Those who fear and distrust human experience look for security in transempirical "realities," assuming that experience is unintelligible; and, in so doing, they make *the* greatest error of philosophy.

If the data of experience are to be regarded as intelligible and if some of our beliefs about these data are to be verified, such intelligibility and verification must be sought within the context of experience itself. Philosophers must resist the very natural tendency to think in *dualistic* analogies about reality. They must not think of experience in terms of an ambassador who can be recognized only by the credentials which he bears from another, and superior, person. This analogy will not work if it is carried to the very frontiers of, metaphysics—there are no grounds for assuming a reality beyond experience and, more significantly, no practical reason for wishing to make such an assumption.

Philosophers need not assume or "prove" a being beyond experience because, as study will show, experience itself bears its own credentials and carries its own inner intelligibility. This intelligibility is to be found potentially in the data of concrete moments of consciousness and in the relationships of such data. Potential intelligibility is present in experience, and man is capable of organizing experience in a rational manner. This fact is extolled by Walt Whitman:

> Mine is no callous shell,
> I have instant conductors all over me whether I pass,
>   or stop,
> They seize every object and lead it harmless through
>   me.
>
>   . . . . .
>
> All truths wait in all things,
> They neither hasten their own delivery nor resist it,
> They do not need the obstetric forceps of the surgeon,
> The insignificant is as big to me as any,
> (What is less or more than a touch.)
>
>   . . . . .
>
> I know I am solid and sound
> To me the converging objects of the universe perpetu-
>   ally flow,
> All are written to me, and I must get what the writing
>   means.[40]

This respect for experience, this listening to the message of the present moment, is the fulcrum on which James shifts philosophy to a new orientation. This orientation brings radical changes in the understanding of change, time, unity, plurality, the subjective, the objective—all of the categories, in fact, of philosophical thinking. All of reality will be conceived no longer in the light of old analogies but now in the analogy of *moments of experience*: "If empiricism is to be radical it must indeed admit the concrete data of experience in their full completeness. The only fully complete concrete data are, however, the successive moments of our own several histories, taken with their subjective personal aspect, as well as with their 'objective' deliverance or 'content.' *After the analogy of these moments of experience must all complete reality be conceived.*"[41]

Philosophical deliverance from ignorance about being is achieved in *understanding concrete moments of experience*. The answers to the major questions of philosophy are to be organized out of these moments of experience. What God and man are shall be understood by studying the flower in the crannied wall!

Full faithfulness to the concrete moments of experience carries Radical Empiricism into a fuller knowledge of reality, one far richer than that afforded by the older, British empiricism. Hume's Empiricism, for example, was inadequate because it introduced *a priori* distinctions into judgments about experience. These distinctions led Hume to deny the concrete existence of conjunctive relations, which the Radical Empiricist declares *can be found* in concrete experience. Hume was hampered by his *incompletely* empirical approach, and his philosophy was accordingly impoverished. James wrote: "Every examiner of the sensible life *in concreto* must see that relations of every sort, of time, space, difference, likeness, change, rate, cause, or what not, are just as integral members of the sensational flux as terms are, and that conjunctive relations are just as true members of the flux as disjunctive relations are. This is what . . . I have called the 'radically empiricist' doctrine. . . ."[42]

While the Radical Empiricist emphasizes the fact that the sensible life is extremely rich, he does not mean to imply that reality is revealed only in the most naïve and unsophisticated experiences. Starting with the data of consciousness, the Radical Empiricist embarks upon a study of experience, which reveals a variety of types, all calling for the most exacting and creative thinking and observation.

This deep study of experience led James to enlarge the meaning of *experience* when he was writing *The Principles of Psychology*. In the last chapter of that book, as he discussed *necessary truths,* he found it necessary to "try to ascertain just how far the connections of things in the outward environment can account for our tendency to think of, and to react upon, certain things in certain ways and in no other, even though personally we have had of the things in question no experience, or almost no experience, at all."[43] (In the *Psychology* James provisionally assumed the common-sense dualistic distinction between knower and objects known, a distinction which is radically foreign to his philosophy.) In this chapter, written about 1885, James indicated that "the choice will then remain to us either of denying the experiential origin of certain of our judgments, or of enlarging the meaning of the word experience. . . ."[44] Since there was no intention of denying the experiential origin of any valid belief, it was necessary to enlarge the meaning of the term *experience*.

Experience in the limited, and usual, sense of that word means the experience of something foreign that is supposed to impress us. The mind's habits copy the habits of impressions, so that "our images of things assume a time- and space-arrangement which resembles the time- and space-arrangements outside."[45] (This dualistic mode of expression is not to be understood literally.) "'*The order of experience*' in this matter of the time- and space-conjunction of things is thus an indisputably *vera causa* of our forms of thought. . . . If *all* the connections among ideas in the mind could be interpreted as so many combinations of sensedata wrought into fixity in this way from without, then experience in the common sense of that word would be the sole fashioner of the mind."[46]

But much of mental life cannot be referred to such an origin. Man's "higher aesthetic, moral, and intellectual life" seems to require a different genesis, and this can be found by considering the two modes of operating which are found in "nature." In the physiological realm, for example, "nature" may make a man's ears ring

> by the sound of a bell, or by a dose of quinine; make us see yellow by spreading a field of buttercups before our eye, or by mixing a little santomine powder with our food. . . . *In the one case the natural agents produce perceptions which take cognizance of the agents themselves; in the other, they produce perceptions which take cognizance of something else.* What is taught to the mind by the "experience" in the first case, is the *order of the experience itself.* . . . But in the case of the *other* sort of natural agency, what is taught to the mind has nothing to do with the agency itself, but with some different outer relation altogether.[47]

Following out the implications of Radical Empiricism, James came to formulate them in terms of "pure experience." Despite all the profound difficulties involved in the hypothesis of pure experience, he was convinced that that hypothesis would solve the most important problems in philosophy. The "experience philosophy" offers solutions to the great problems created by the dualistic hypothesis, for example, without plunging into the unacceptable hypothesis of monism. Dualism—with its realms of matter and spirit, its distinctions between the knower and the known—makes for ease of expression and respects the individuality of beings. But it creates an unbridgeable chasm between parts of reality. Monism, on the other hand, provides unity but does so at the expense of individuality and personal freedom. Radical Empiricism, unimpeded by the abstractions of monism or dualism, seeks the truth in experience itself.

Experience has several aspects. The first, called "pure," is that aspect wherein man has not yet introduced distinctions, made selections, or established any kind of order. Associations and relationships have not yet been established as patterns for viewing experiences. No order, practical or theoretical, has yet been extracted or imposed. This "pure experience" is intrinsically neither objective nor subjective. "What we experience, what *comes before us,* is a chaos of fragmentary impressions interrupting each other . . . ."[48] "'Pure experience' is . . . the immediate flux of life which furnishes the material to our later reflection with its conceptual categories. Only new-born babes or men in a semi-coma . . . may be assumed to have an experience pure in the literal sense of a *that* which is not yet any definite *what,* tho' ready to be all sorts of whats. . . ."[49]

At the outset, the *purity* of pure experience reveals none of those distinctions which come as a result of conceptualizing. In it are to be found both the unity and the diversity needed for the solution of philosophy's most important problems. Its priority to distinctions discloses the fundamental unity of subject and object, knower and known; the discreteness revealed in data provide the basis for individuality and pluralism.

One of the tasks of philosophy is to *reconstruct* pure experience *before* it has been conceptualized and to describe reality in the terms thus gained.[50] The conceptualization of pure experience must be scrutinized to see wherein the order of nature is violated by imposing upon it patterns which are alien to its nature. Patterns are indeed necessary for men to put pure experience into forms in which it can be handled successfully; but some patterns, now firmly established, violate the nature of experience. The philosopher's task is to identify such mis-formations of reality (for example, the distortions of "vicious intellectualism"): "Make clear my own position between *pure* empiricism (tabula rasa, with impressions adding themselves . . . and no connate mental structure at all) and Kant's. There is mental structure, but the congruence of nature with it is a painfully attained compromise in which much mental structure has to be thrown away. The most *essential* features of our mental structure, viz. grammar and logic, *violate* the order of nature, as on reflexion we believe it to exist."[51]

As experience gives men new materials to digest, these materials are assimilated, rejected, or rearranged in terms of the masses of beliefs which they already possess. Most of these beliefs, or "apperceiving ideas," are common-sense traditions of the race which once were genuine discoveries of some individuals, like the comparatively modern discoveries of energy or reflex action. In their attempts "to get the chaos of their crude individual experiences into a more shareable and manageable shape," early men formulated the notions of one time and one space as single continuous receptacles, distinguished between thoughts and things, between permanent objects and changing attributes. These and other conquests, made in the distant past, are now "part of the very structure of our mind."

As a matter of fact, *some* of these ancestral discoveries are so deeply entrenched in the human mind that no experience could upset them. The concept of one time and one space and the concept of permanently existing things are so useful that men are obliged to stand by them. These beliefs "apperceive every experience and assign it to its place."[52] Their validity is attested to by their usefulness to men in organizing their lives. If these beliefs should, however, by failing to collaborate with other useful beliefs, prove to be useless, they ought to be discarded, no matter how well they may be entrenched in man's world picture.

Transformed extensively as it is, pure experience is nevertheless not an unknowable or a mysterious thing-in-itself. Like the primitive earth in the cultivated fields, it is always present and constantly transformed. It is not behind, or below, or outside man's experience; it is the very stuff of subjective experience. The dance and the dancer are one, said Emerson; pure experience is identical with the so-called natures of the "*things*" experienced. There is no *general* stuff of which experience at large is made. "If you ask what any one bit of pure experience is made of, the answer is always the same: 'It is made of *that*, of just what appears, of space, of intensity, of flatness, brownness, or what not. . . . Experience is only a collective name for these sensible natures, and save for time and space (and, if you like, for 'being') there appears no universal element of which all things are made."[53]

The dance and the dancer are one indeed. *Thought* and *thing* refer to the same reality, and differ from one another only functionally: "*Thoughts in the concrete are made of the same stuff as things are.*"[54] "There *is* no stuff anywhere but data. Within data are two parts, the objective and the subjective parts, *seen retrospectively.* . . ."[55] Moreover, James says

> The first great pitfall from which such radical standing by of experience will save us is an artificial conception of the *relations between knower and known.* Throughout the history of philosophy the subject and its object have been treated as absolutely discontinuous entities. . . . All the while, in the very bosom of the finite experience, every conjunction required to make the relation intelligible is given in full.[56]
>
> . . . . .
>
> . . . the paper seen and the seeing of it are only two names for one indivisible fact which, properly named, is *the datum, the phenomenon, or the experience.* The paper is in the mind and the mind is around the paper, because paper and mind are only two names that are given later to the one experience, when, taken in a larger world of which it forms a part, its connections are traced in different directions. *To know immediately, then, or intuitively, is for mental content and object to be identical.* This is a very different definition from that which we gave of representative knowledge; but neither definition involves those mysterious notions of self-transcendency and presence in absence which are such essential parts of the ideas of knowledge, both of philosophers and of common men.[57]

Some indication of the nature of pure experience can be distilled from the fleeting moment in which one confronts a datum before proceeding to conceptualize it. Such a moment may occur when the inattentive driver notes the traffic light flick from red to green without grasping immediately the significance of the change. He stares at the light, observes its color, but fails momentarily to classify it in the category of signals. When he finally realizes that there is a signal function in the light, he has moved from a fairly "pure experience" of the colored light to a conceptualized, social reconstruction of the datum. He has made in a fraction of a second an observation, selection, rejection, and synthesis. He has transformed a datum which had no functional value into a conceptualized experience.

This conceptualizing means selecting from the vast jungle of pure experience those data which can be made useful to men and rejecting those of no value. It means also sorting data into categories: subjective and objective, the knower and those which are known. Conceptualizing may lead to errors, for example, by postulating entities such as consciousness, the soul, or substance; and, in so doing, it violates the data of pure experience.

The differences between pure experience and the reconstructed experience by which men live are great, but they are not radically disjoined. Except in the instances in which men have substituted a fiction for fact, as when they affirm that consciousness is an entity, the parts of reconstructed experience can be referred to data of pure experience as their origin.

The conceptualizing of pure experience—the using of ideas to select and organize data—is legitimate as a general process because *concepts (as well as percepts) are given in experience*: "If we take conceptual manifolds, or memories, or fancies, they also are in their first intention mere bits of pure experience, and, as such, are single *thats* which act in one context as objects, and in another context figure as mental states."[58] These non-perceptual experiences have objectivity as well as subjectivity; they are every bit as real as percepts are. Both can determine present conduct, and both are parts of reality of which men must take account. Both come at first as a chaos of experience, in which lines of order are soon traced. This tracing of lines of order introduces the problem of human knowledge; epistemology now occupies the attention of the philosopher.

Notes

1. George Santayana, *Character and Opinion in the United States* (New York, 1955), p. 41.

2. *Ibid.*, p. 54.

3. *Ibid.*, p. 55.

4. *Letters*, I, 152-53.

5. *Ibid.*, I, 97.

6. *Some Problems*, p. 15.

7. *Letters*, II, 58-59.

8. MS (Houghton Library), "1905-6 Outline of Phil I A Course at Stanford," opp. p. 24.

9. MS (Houghton Library), "Seminar of 1903-4," pp. 74-76.

10. MS (Houghton Library), "Phil 9-1904-5."

11. "Review of *Problems of Life and Mind* by George Henry Lewes," *Collected Essays*, p. 4.

12. *Letters*, I, 190.

13. William James, *A Pluralistic Universe* (New York, 1947), p. 117.

14. *Some Problems*, p. 27.

15. Knox, *Evolution of Truth*, p. 137.

16. "Philosophical Conceptions and Practical Results," *Collected Essays*, p. 408.

17. "Chauncey Wright," *Collected Essays*, pp. 24-25.

18. *Letters*, I, 190.

19. *Ibid.*, I, 191.

20. William James, "The Sentiment of Rationality," *The Will to Believe* (New York, 1896), p. 92.

21. "Reflex Action and Theism," *The Will to Believe*, p. 125.

22. William James, *The Meaning of Truth* (New York, 1911), pp. x-xi.

23. *Pragmatism*, p. 53.

24. "Pragmatism in Italy," *Collected Essays*, p. 464.

25. Perry, II, 632.

26. "Pragmatism in Italy," *Collected Essays*, p. 465.

27. William James, *The Varieties of Religious Experience* (New York, 1903), p. 445.

28. *Ibid.*, p. 447.

29. *Ibid.*

30. *Popular Science*, January 1878.

31. *Varieties*, pp. 444-45.

32. "Philosophical Conceptions and Practical Results," *Collected Essays*, p. 410.

33. *Ibid.*, pp. 413-14.

34. *Letters*, II, 267.

35. William James, "A World of Pure Experience," *Essays in Radical Empiricism*, (New York, 1947), p. 41.

36. *Letters*, II, 203-4.

37. "Philosophical Conceptions and Practical Results," *Collected Essays*, pp. 437-38.

38. George Hodges, "William James-Leader in Philosophical Thought," *The Outlook* (February 23, 1907).

39. *Some Problems*, p. 101.

40. Walt Whitman, *Leaves of Grass, Following the Arrangement of the Edition of 1891-2* (New York, N. D.) pp. 47, 48, 39.

41. "Personal Idealism," *Collected Essays*, pp. 443-44 (italics added).

42. *Pluralistic Universe*, p. 280.

43. William James, *The Principles of Psychology* (New York, 1890), II, 617.

44. *Ibid.*, II, 624.

45. *Ibid.*, II, 619.

46. *Ibid.*, II, 620.

47. *Ibid.*, II, 625-26.

48. *Ibid.*, II, 634.

49. "The Thing and Its Relations," *Radical Empiricism*, p. 93.

50. MS (Houghton Library), "Seminar of 1903-4," p. 55.

51. MS (Houghton Library), "Article on Kant."

52. William James "Humanism and Truth," *The Meaning of Truth* (New York, 1911), pp. 61-63.

53. "Does 'Consciousness' Exist?," *Radical Empiricism*, pp. 26-27.

54. *Ibid.*, p. 37.

55. Perry, II, 366.

56. "A World of Pure Experience," *Radical Empiricism*, pp. 52-53.

57. "The Tigers in India," *The Meaning of Truth*, pp. 49-50.

58. "Does Consciousness Exist?," *Radical Empiricism*, p. 15.

Selected Bibliography

PRIMARY SOURCES

1. WRITINGS OF WILLIAM JAMES

The Principles of Psychology. 2 vols. New York: Henry Holt and Co., 1890.

Psychology, Briefer Course. New York: Henry Holt and Co., 1892.

The Will to Believe and Other Essays in Popular Philosophy. New York: Longmans, Green and Co., 1897.

Human Immortality: Two Supposed Objections to the Doctrine. Boston: Houghton, Mifflin and Company, 1899.

Talks to Teachers on Psychology, and to Students on Some of Life's Ideals. New York: Henry Holt and Co., 1899.

The Varieties of Religious Experience: A Study in Human Nature. New York: Longmans, Green, and Co., 1903.

Pragmatism, A New Name for Some Old Ways of Thinking. New York: Longmans, Green, and Co., 1907.

The Meaning of Truth; A Sequel to Pragmatism. Longmans, Green, and Co., 1909.

A Pluralistic Universe: Hibbert Lectures on the Present Situation in Philosophy. New York: Longmans, Green and Co., 1909.

Some Problems in Philosophy: A Beginning of an Introduction to Philosophy. New York: Longmans, Green and Co., 1911.

Memories and Studies. New York: Longmans, Green and Co., 1912.

Essays in Radical Empiricism. New York: Longmans, Green and Co., 1912.

Collected Essays and Reviews. Edited by R. B. Perry. New York: Longmans, Green and Co., 1920.

The Letters of William James. 2 vols. Edited by his son Henry James. Boston: The Atlantic Monthly Press, 1920.

William James on Psychical Research. Compiled and edited by Gardner Murphy and Robert O. Ballou. New York: The Viking Press, 1960.

2. MANUSCRIPT MATERIALS

The Collection of James Family Papers, in The Houghton Library at Harvard University, is the greatest center for William James materials.

3. OTHER PRIMARY SOURCES

James, Alice. *Alice James: Her Brothers, Her Journal*. Edited, with an Introduction, by Anna Robeson Burr. New York: Dodd, Mead and Company, Inc., 1934.

———. *The Diary of Alice James*. Edited, with an introduction, by Leon Edel. New York: Dodd, Mead and Company, n.d.

James, Henry (Sr.). *The Literary Remains of the Late Henry James*. Edited, with an introduction, by William James. Boston: Houghton, Mifflin and Co., 1885.

James, Henry (Jr.). *A Small Boy and Others*. New York: Charles Scribner's Sons, 1913.

———. *Letters of Henry James*. Edited by Percy Lubbock. 2 vols. New York: Charles Scribner's Son's, 1920.

Matthiessen, F. O. *The James Family: A Group Biography Together with Selections from the Writings of Henry James, Senior, William, Henry, and Alice James*. New York: Alfred A. Knopf, 1948. Contains much primary material.

McDermott, John. *The Writings of William James*. New York: Random House. A large volume of selected readings, with a good original introduction.

Perry, Ralph Barton. *The Thought and Character of William James As Revealed in Unpublished Correspondence and Notes, Together with his Published Writings*. 2 volumes. Boston: Little, Brown and Company, 1935. A treasure house of otherwise unavailable primary material.

———. *Annotated Bibliography of the Writings of William James*. New York: Longmans, Green & Co., 1920; Dubuque, Iowa: W. C. Brown Reprint Library, 1964 (?). (See also McDermott, *The Writings of William James*, for updated bibliography.)

SECONDARY SOURCES

Allen, Gay Wilson. *William James, A Biography*. New York: The Viking Press, 1967. The only true "biography" of James.

Bixler, Julius Seelye. *Religion in the Philosophy of William James*. Boston: Marshall Jones Company, 1926. A definitive study.

Bawden, H. Heath. *The Principles of Pragmatism: A Philosophical Interpretation of Experience*. Boston: Houghton Mifflin Company, 1910. Thoughtful contribution to the pragmatic-experiential philosophy.

Brennan, Bernard P. *The Ethics of William James*. New York: Bookman Associates, 1961. A systematic formulation of James's moral philosophy.

Burke, Jane Revere. *Let Us In: A Record of Communications Believed to Have Come from William James*. New York: Dutton, 1931. A postscript on Jamesian "psychical research."

Burkle, Howard R. "Toward A Christian Pragmatism," *The Christian Scholar*, XLI (December, 1958). Much still must be done to develop James's insights.

Chapman, John Jay. *Memories and Milestones*. New York: Moffat, 1915. Extravagant in contents and expression; defective in some judgments, but exciting— and valuable as a highly personal record.

Dewey, John. *Experience and Nature*. La Salle, Ill.: Open Court Publishing Co., 1958. Dewey explores the experience-philosophy.

Edel, Leon. *Henry James: The Untried Years (1843-1870)*. Philadelphia: J. B. Lippincott Company, 1953.

———. *Henry James. The Conquest of London (1870-1881)*. Philadelphia: J. B. Lippincott Company, 1962.

———. *Henry James: The Middle Years (1882-1895).* Philadelphia: J. B. Lippincott Company, 1962. This definitive series will be completed with *Henry James: The Master (1895-1916),* now in preparation.

Grattan, C. Hartley. *The Three Jameses.* New York: Longmans, Green and Co., 1932. Putting the Jameses in their family setting. Some harsh judgments on William.

Hastings, Katherine. *William James of Albany, New York (1771-1832) and His Descendants.* Reprinted from the *New York Genealogical and Biographical Record,* 1924. A splendid work of scholarship, thorough and richly documented.

Jacks, L. P. "William James and His Message," *Contemporary Review* (January, 1911). Jacks has a perfect understanding of James's "angle of vision."

Kallen, H. M. (ed.). *In Commemoration of William James, 1842-1942.* New York: Columbia University Press, 1942. Essays of varying degrees of excellence.

Knox, Howard V. *The Evolution of Truth.* London: Constable & Co. Ltd., 1930. Knox was a dedicated, intelligent exponent of James's philosophy.

———. *The Philosophy of William James.* New York: Dodge Publishing Company, 1941. Brief, excellent exposition.

Lovejoy, Arthur C. "The Thirteen Pragmatisms," *Journal of Philosophy,* vol. v. A classical essay.

Moore, Edward Carter. *William James.* New York: Washington Square Press, 1965. Perceptive, well-organized introduction to James's philosophy.

Royce, Josiah. *William James and other Essays on the Philosophy of Life.* New York: The Macmillan Company, 1911. Contains a brief essay on James.

Santayana, George. *Character and Opinion in the United States.* New York: George Braziller, 1955. Santayana misunderstands James; shows incredible lack of perception.

Warren, Austin. *The Elder Henry James.* New York: The Macmillan Company, 1934. Excellent "life and thoughts."

Young, Frederic H. *The Philosophy of Henry James, Sr.* New York: Bookman Associates, 1951. Comprehensive, scholarly account of the philosophy of the elder James.

Frank Lentricchia (essay date fall 1986)

SOURCE: Lentricchia, Frank. "The Return of William James." *Cultural Critique,* no. 4 (fall 1986): 5-31.

[*In the following essay, Lentricchia maintains that critics who purport that modern, or "new" Pragmatism is Jamesian are in error, citing James's works to support his argument and examining the social, historical, and political context surrounding the resurgence of interest in James's work.*]

William James is on his way back: under the banner of a "new pragmatism," and what they are calling "against theory," he may be on the verge of recapturing the imagination of the American literary humanist from its fascination with the French intellectual scene, even though the canons of social responsibility say that James is not responsible, that he lacks something in genuine seriousness. The return of James is all the more surprising in the light of our preoccupation with theory because what the canonical standards of seriousness declare that James lacks is nothing other than the proper sense of theory, which George Santayana, his younger colleague and competitor at Harvard, defined in its traditional Arnoldian setting when he wrote that theory is "a steady contemplation of all things in their order and worth. . . . No one can reach it who has not enlarged his mind and tamed his heart. A philosopher who attains it is, for the moment, a poet; and a poet who turns his practice and passionate imagination on the order of all things, or on anything in light of the whole, is for that moment a philosopher."[1] What Santayana says openly is what traditional theorists generally only imply when they define their activity as theorists: that to think theoretically is to concern yourself with "wholes," with "totalities," it is to think beyond the parochialisms of the schools and to achieve some ultimate humanity of inclusive broadmindedness by rising above the particular involvements of passionate commitment. Becoming nobody, no place, no time, we achieve the theorist's ideal, which Santayana's phrasing reminds us is the very ideal of reason as it has been traditionally conceived in the West since the Greeks. In this serene, epistemologically and morally secure space, beyond ideology, one has knowledge of the real order and value of all things. Early modern philosophical commentators on this view of theory—those for it and those against—called it "absolute," as in "absolute idealism" (they were thinking mainly of Hegel); recent Marxists and anti-Marxists alike (thinking of Lukács in his Hegelian mode) say "totalizing"; and more recently (after Richard Rorty, a Jamesian of sorts) the tendency is to say "foundational"—Rorty, when he uses that word, is thinking of all of philosophy with the exception of a few names: Hegel, Dewey, Wittgenstein, Heidegger, himself. James's coded synonyms for both theory and traditional philosophy are "reason" and "rational," close cousins to his pejorative of pejoratives—"abstract."

My central point will be this: independently of Marx, and as the founding gesture of his work, James makes the point of the most famous of Marx's theses on Feuerbach—that philosophy should be trying to change, not interpret the world—but James in effect out-Marxes Marx by saying that all the interpretive efforts of philosophy are always simultaneously efforts to work upon and work over things as they are. All intellectuals plays social roles, whether they like it or not, James believed, because interpretation is always a form of intervention, a factor in social change or in social conservation. The recurring double point of James's pragmatism is that all theory is practice (situated intellectual involvement with real local effects) and that all practices are not equally worthy. If all thought is a mode of action, a tool, not a representation—an instrument for doing work—then the key consequence forced upon us by this philosophy of consequences would not be the recognition (James's banal and potentially dangerous starting point) that there is nothing but practice. The key consequence of Jamesian pragmatism would be the urgent directive that we attend to the different consequences of different practices, for only in their different consequences can we know and evaluate such practices as different epistemological and political alternatives. No difference in consequences, no difference in practice. No difference in consequences, no difference in belief.

"Belief"—which is what a pragmatist prefers to "theory"—boils down to a "set of rules" for the action of changing-by-interpreting the world's various texts, verbal and otherwise.[2] Belief shapes our interpretive conduct—a redundancy: all conduct is interpretive—and conduct is the sole significance and real content of belief. It is a strong implication of what James believes about "belief" that the rules synonymous with belief are open to reflection and revision. Whether the set of rules which constitutes belief is knowable in advance of the conduct it shapes, or whether such rules are extrapolated from conduct, after the fact, the ethical and political imperative embodied in pragmatism tells us that we must evaluate the consequences of belief—action in the world—by evaluating the conduct-structuring rules of belief, and, in doing that, become responsive to and maybe responsible for the future of a belief (the conduct and consequences that belief *will* produce): Not from some transcendental standpoint in "theory" but from within a situation that is both primal and recurrent: the situation of emergency.[3] We are lost in the woods, we need to find our way home, but we have no map. Then we see a path, choose to believe (maybe because of what we take to be irrefutable olfactory evidence) that it is a cowpath which if followed will lead us to the safety of the farmhouse. Surfacing here in James's representative anecdote of cognitive emergency, which is at the same time an existential emergency, is the temporal character of belief. As tools for getting done the various works of liberation, beliefs are instruments of desire; they are born locally in crisis and have local consequences only. When they do not lead us out of the cognitive woods, we revise them—still in the woods, still in crisis, we remeasure our context—for other beliefs that might work. If it is the case that the triggering emergency (or the occasion for belief), the

actual work of belief, and the consequences (or future) of belief are always bound to local contexts, then it is also the case that all efforts to escape temporal and geographic locality are expressions of a passion that is the traditional theoretical impulse par excellence. The desire to move to theory in James is the desire to move over the arena of work to a place where all possible situations of work can be surveyed in a single glance, gathered up, and mastered. The site of theory turns out to be the totalitarian site of imposition where all local situations are coerced into conformity, and where the future itself (in the form of consequences) is known and therefore controlled and manipulated in advance. Theory is not belief because theory never sees itself restrained by its occasional status; it does not think its status occasional. With its global conception of itself, with its metaphysical confidence, theory has no need for self-revision. But if theory is in some sense like belief because it is also a form of practice, then the work of theory can only be the work of trying to convert (shape, force) experience into what theory wants to see in the world: an adequate object of its totalizing desire to rig the game of interpretation. Like belief, theory emerges from historical ground; unlike belief, theory cannot bear to live with history.

As Stanley Fish puts it in an essay whose "new pragmatist" conclusions I want eventually to challenge, theory would work as a general (rather than a "local") hermeneutics, an interpretive procedure which would always yield correct results if the proper steps were strictly followed. Fish argues convincingly that the model for "theory" (I'd say "traditional theory") is mathematics, a "rational activity" whose "constraints are not acquired through experience (education, historical conditioning, local habits) but are innate." The constraints of theory so conceived are necessarily abstract, general, and invariant. Fish's new pragmatist definition of theory is pure William James. His conclusion that theory cannot succeed because "it cannot help but borrow its terms and its content from that which it claims to transcend, the mutable world of practice, belief, assumptions, point of view," manages to be Jamesian while at the same time missing what I read as James's ironic political theme: that theory's very inability to be successful in its own terms has powerful historical consequences, that it is precisely its failure to leave history that insures that theory is a practice and that theory always marks history with its imposing ambition.[4] The fully articulated pragmatism we find in James says that there is not only nothing but practice, but that practice carries with it the obligations of revision, that practice tends to force constant scrutiny of one's work in its context. This is so because the historical pressures at the site of practice produce a reflective (and dialectical) moment, let's call it *ad hoc* theory with a lower case "t," which is in turn tested by the practice to which it is necessarily returned.

Pragmatism teaches nothing if not responsiveness to contexts of work. When not so accompanied, our practice, including theoretical practice, becomes mindless work, something like Charley Marlowe's with his rivets in *Heart of Darkness*: which is to say that such work is not really mindless, but the hopeless effort of bad faith to escape from reflection on the situation of work and a form of intellectual cowardice. For Marlowe this means the hopeless desire to escape from reflection on the imperialist site of his activity and his responsibility at, and for, that site of work. The new pragmatist demolition of theory is useful to a point: it shows us that theory, including its varieties after the new criticism, conceived and held in the traditional way, is not only defined by ahistorical hunger but is doomed to perpetual inability to satisfy such hunger. But the new pragmatist analysis, once it has uncovered that defining contradiction of theory (formalist desire, contingent setting of desire) concludes its own work too soon, not seeing that theory-desire's contingent setting in history is the ground of theory's real work, the ironic because unwanted object of its intention. The premature closure of new pragmatism's own analysis has this effect: it produces a style of dismissiveness which then comes around to haunt and seize anti-theory, turning it into precisely the sort of theory that anti-theory ought not want to be—historically and politically blind praxis, theory (if you can imagine this) as blithe-spirited Charley Marlowe.

Expressed most resonantly in key metaphoric moments, James's vision of pragmatism is irreducibly a vision of heterogeneity and contentiousness—a vision strong for criticism, self-scrutiny, and self-revision that never claims knowledge of a single human narrative because it refuses the belief and it refuses the often repressive conduct resulting from belief in a single human narrative. James's fully committed pragmatism has no way of settling, once and for all, the question it constantly asks: Does the world rise or fall in value when any particular belief is let loose in the world?[5] When we act upon others or when others act upon us? By insisting that the question be posed that way, in nonacademic form (Does the *world,* not literature, not philosophy, rise or fall in value?), James is insisting that the consequences of belief reveal themselves most fully outside the immediate domain (in his case, the discipline of philosophy) of any particular belief's application. Like the father of pragmatism, C. S. Peirce, James is no philosophical ostrich with his head in the sand. He starts with the recognition that others believe differently and just as strongly.[6] James thereby puts us in a world of different and sometimes competing choices and conducts, and of different and sometimes competing stories, a world in which resolution could be achieved only in a final solution of criticism: by the forcible silencing of the competitor.

So the world according to James is a geography of practices adjacently placed: a heterogeneous space of dispersed histories, related perhaps by counterpoint, or perhaps utterly disrelated—a cacophony of stories—but in any case never related in medley. "The world we live in exists diffused and distributed, in the form of an infinitely numerous lot of eaches."[7] Overarching metanarratives, say Marxist or Christian, which would make all the "eaches" cohere—and so eliminate heterogeneous plurality—never tempt James. He is no utopian. He believes that history conceived as teleological union is a late and nostalgic expression of classical aesthetics—the proleptic imaging forth, in the rigorous causal perfections of Aristotelean plot, of desired historical order, the harmony of time itself. Better, he believes, to think against Aristotle's preference for drama, better to prefer romance to drama, better to think that the "world is full of partial stories that run parallel to one another, beginning and ending at odd times. They mutually interlace and interfere at points, but we cannot unify them completely."[8] Together with his literary metaphor of narrative richness, James levels this backyard metaphor at the dogmas of monism: "It is easy to see the world's history pluralistically, as a rope of which each fiber tells a separate tale; but to conceive of each cross-section of the rope as an absolutely single fact, and to sum the whole longitudinal series into one being, living an individual life, is harder."[9] "It is easy," if you are James: James himself knew that the seeing of plurality, and the letting be of what you see is not a matter of just opening your eyes to the facts and having a good attitude. His philosophical project is dedicated to the cause of getting others to see it his way while showing us, at the same time, the violent effects of seeing it otherwise, the bad attitude that necessarily accompanies seeing it otherwise.

History in James, as in his master, Emerson, is no monument that demands mimetic awe. Rationalism (a key word for "theory" in James) would force a mimetic role upon the text of the world: "On the rationalist side," James writes, "we have a universe in many editions, one real one, the infinite folio, or *edition de luxe,* eternally complete; and then the various finite editions, full of false readings, distorted and mutilated each in its own way." The effort of the rational textualist must be to make all finite editions somehow "correspond" to the *edition de luxe.* But the pragmatist gives us history in a complex metaphor as both text and as the liberation of textual work—a text, James writes, "in only one edition of the universe, unfinished, growing in all sorts of places, especially in places where thinking beings are at work."[10] For the pragmatic textualist, who is the bibliographer's version of the devil, there is only one text: the forever unfinished, decentralized text of history—forever supplemented, new chapters being written in all sorts of places by all sorts of people not especially in touch with one another. There is no work of "correspondence," only of "production." James's textual metaphor is an effort to speak against the political authority which masks itself in rationalist certitude and self-righteousness, which demands mimetic fealty, and which he specifically and frequently evokes after his involvement in the New England Anti-Imperialist League in royalist, militarist, aristocratic, and papal terms.[11] James's textual metaphor speaks *for* the liberation of the small, the regional, the locally embedded, the underdog: the voice that refuses the elocutionary lessons of cosmopolitan finishing schools. His unfinished (and unfinishable) text of history, authorized by no single author, is the text of American history as it ought to be—the multi-authored book of democracy in its ideal and antinomian form.

For James, then, there may be nothing more ugly than theoretical consciousness in the rational practices it authorizes. The lectures he delivered in late 1906 and early 1907 in Boston and New York, and then shortly after published as the book *Pragmatism,* bear the mark of a decisive moment in U.S. history: our first fully-launched imperialist adventure, in the last years of the nineteenth century, in Cuba and the Philippines. Though inchoately present in his *Principles of Psychology,* he began to know his philosophy as pragmatism only after he found the political terminus of his thought in his anti-imperialist activism at the turn of the century. In the New England Anti-Imperialist League James experienced a direct and co-determinative connection between his philosophical principles and his political life. It was at that point, after his political turn, and not before, when it was abstractly possible for him to do so, that he began freely adapting from C. S. Peirce; it was at that point, and not before, that he began to understand empire as theory (as a kind of theoretical impulse), and theory or traditional philosophy as empire (as a kind of imperialist impulse). For James, the two impulses are measured and joined by the effects they produce in trying to cure the world of diversity.

James's anti-imperialism becomes the first effort in a hidden history of oddly connected American refusals of imperialism. The second was Wallace Stevens's "Anecdote of the Jar" of 1919 as read by a third, that of Michael Herr in his book on Vietnam of 1970, *Dispatches,* in which the entire focus of American military power that was concentrated in the fortification at Khe Sanh was crystallized by Herr with (of all things) Stevens's poem. Stevens, who found Dwight Eisenhower radical, is made by Herr to speak directly against the ideology of imposition and obliteration co-active in Vietnam with a strategy of defoliation. The textual expression of that strategy is the literal re-mapping of a country—"the military expediency," in Herr's ironic reflection on the sometimes mad and deadly relations of sign and referent, "to impose a new set of references over Vietnam's truer, older being, an imposition that

began most simply with the division of one country into two and continued . . . with the further division of South Vietnam into four clearly defined tactical corps." Herr concludes by glossing Khe Sanh via the imaginative imperialism that was activated and subtly evaluated in "Anecdote of the Jar." "Once it was all locked in place, Khe Sanh became like the planted jar in Wallace Stevens's poem. It took dominion everywhere."[12]

James had written his own anecdote of the jar in the opening lecture of *Pragmatism:* "The world of concrete personal experiences to which the street belongs is multitudinous beyond imagination, tangled, muddy, painful and perplexed. The world to which your philosophy professor introduces you is simple, clean and noble. The contradictions of real life are absent from it. Its architecture is classic. Principles of reason trace its outlines, logical necessities cement its parts. Purity and dignity are what it most expresses. It is a kind of marble temple shining on a hill."[13] The marble temple shining on a hill is James's metaphor for traditional philosophy in its traditional project of representation: mind as correspondence, thought as reflection of real ontological structure, thought emptied of the messes of social time, thought historically uncontingent. But philosophy so conceived, James says, is not, despite its claim, an "account of this actual world." It is an "addition built upon it": a "sanctuary," a "refuge," a "substitute," a "way of escape," a "monument of artificiality"—"cloistral and spectral." All negative qualities, of course, and quite harmless, until we add one other characteristic which gives ominous point to all the others—James's shining marble temple of philosophy, like Stevens's jar of aesthetics, like Khe Sanh, is also a "remedy."[14] In this dismantling of the classic project of reason, what James wishes to show is that the product of rationalist method is not cool, contemplative representation—"theory" above the battle: it is *purity in action.* The shining marble temple is "round upon the ground," and it does not give "of bird or bush." Like the defoliating jar in Stevens's Tennessee, or the imposed references of military need in Vietnam which attempted to recreate the referent (we had to destroy that village in order to save it), theory classically conceived is the desire for a "refined object." And theory-desire, the desire for refinement, is a "powerful . . . appetite of the mind" which gets expressed as the *will to refine*: a chilling process when considered in the political contexts within which James writes.[15] In an eerie prolepsis of both Stevens's poem and Herr's reading of Khe Sanh as the "planted jar," James evoked his sense of the perversity of the American presence in the Philippines by describing it as an effort to "plant our order."[16]

I have to this point been emphasizing what I have called, a little misleadingly, James's political period, the late phase of his career when he could with some justice refer to himself as an anarchist. Actually this late phase represents a substantial change of heart which, if ignored, would obscure by suppressing not the non-politics but the more familiar American politics of his earlier career. Two historical points may be made, the first more or less factual, the second more or less speculative. In the late 1880s James responded to the protests of exploited labor in this country by telling his brother not to be "alarmed by the labor troubles here" (Henry was not "here"). Brother William went on to explain, in all seriousness, that the turmoil of strikes was "simply a healthy phase of evolution, a little costly, but normal, and sure to do lots of good to all hands in the end." If that response to the emergence of organized labor deserves to be characterized as academic in the worst possible sense of the word—how else to understand his application of Darwin?—then his remarks on the Haymarket Riot of May 1886 need another, less kind evaluation: in his response to that violent moment in our labor history James gave voice to American xenophobic paranoia. "I don't speak," he continues in the same letter to Henry, "of the senseless 'anarchist' riot in Chicago, which has nothing to do with 'Knights of Labor,' but is the work of a lot of pathological Germans and poles [*sic*]."[17]

The missing political link, maybe the first link—in the journey from "a lot of pathological Germans and poles," to James's critique of philosophy's shining marble temple on a hill, to Stevens's critique of the jar on the hill in Tennessee, to Herr's meditation on Vietnam, Khe Sanh upon a hill—is John Winthrop's vision of Puritan community as a "city upon a hill" and Winthrop's unwittingly ugly interpretation of that city when, years after he had coined the phrase, he banished Anne Hutchinson for antinomian heresy. Hutchinson: "I desire to know wherefore I am banished." Winthrop: "Say no more, the court knows wherefore and is satisfied."[18] The city upon a hill, a metaphor of community self-consciously visible and vulnerable, is revised in Winthrop's retort to Hutchinson into a metaphor of the imperial city rigorously and violently exclusionary—a structure of male authority, purity (Puritanism) in action, poised as a "remedy" against a radically individualist principle of resistance whose most famous American representative is female. Winthrop's revision, and its impersonal authoritarian devastation of insurrectionary female conscience, just may be (more on this later) the political unconscious of Jamesian pragmatism at its radical edge.

If Anne Hutchinson is the hidden moral and political mother-figure behind James's pragmatism, then the not-so-hidden moral and political father-figure behind his pragmatist celebration of sovereignty (personal and national) is Emerson—for intellectual and biographical reasons it could not have been anyone else—the Emerson who wrote that "whenever I find my dominion over myself not sufficient for me, and I undertake the direc-

tion of my neighbor also, I overstep the truth, and come into false relations with him. . . . This is the history of government—one man does something which is to bind another."[19] Emerson found the history of the word "politics" to be the history of a pejorative, coincidental with "cunning," the indenturing of others to the imperatives of power not their own, and (as Stevens would put it) the taking of dominion everywhere.[20] In his essay "History" (1841), Emerson argued by metaphorical sleight-of-hand that in the self's true (presumably American) domain there are no medieval relations of economic and political coercion, that the privileges of the spirit are radically open to all: "He that is at once admitted to the right of reason is made a freeman of the whole estate. What Plato has thought, he may think: what a saint has felt, he may feel; what at any time has befallen any man, he can understand; who hath access to this universal mind is a party to all that is or can be done, for this is the only and sovereign agent."[21] And with the agility of the socially critical punster, Emerson trained his wit in his famous "Nature" essay of 1836 on private property in the capitalist system, writing in a famous passage that though Messrs. Miller, Locke, and Manning may claim ownership of the physical property of their farms, the very best part of those farms their warranty deeds give them no title to: the "property" of vision is "owned" by the integrating eye of the visionary capitalist, the poet who alone can "possess," because he creates, the "landscape."[22]

The point of Emerson's compressed metaphoric recollections and attacks on feudal and capitalist modes of production is that the great human values are preserved only in the world of culture, because in that world the power that accrues from economic privilege—whether lordly or bourgeois—is presumably annulled, even though apparently culture can at no point annul the actual unfreedom and oppression that obtains in material society which, in Emerson's memorable phrasing, "everywhere is in conspiracy against the manhood of every one of its members."[23] "Society" for Emerson is synonymous with the surrender of "liberty and culture," with a process of coercion that sanctions the binding of many for the benefit of a few.[24] But culture is not a way of life intervening upon and shaping social, economic, and political relations: "culture" is rather an alternative to "society," wherein governments will continue to underwrite relations of domination. So culture for Emerson is simultaneously an idealist affirmation of freedom and truth in a democratic intellectual world of equal opportunity and an implicit denial that actual collective life can be the ground of those values. At its worst, and by virtue of what Herbert Marcuse would call its affirmative inward turn, Emersonian culture becomes an implicit validation (via benign neglect) of the real injustices rooted in real economic inequalities.[25]

What now appears most dated in Emerson's American repugnance for our European social origins, where the dream of America was hatched, was perhaps for his audience the most thrilling and the most duplicitous element in his writing. His clarion call for intellectual independence, sounded on numerous occasions—"We have listened too long to the courtly muses of Europe"—was intended to urge his fellow Americans on to the cultural end of the adventure, political independence presumably having already been secured.[26] But the overt message of "The American Scholar" and other essays which touch political themes directly is subverted time after time in Emerson's American revenge against the history of economic privilege. The American poet and the American scholar are the representative men who stand in for the desire of history's dispossessed and excluded to come into possession—for possession is power and power is freedom. In taking his revenge, the Emersonian poet asserts on behalf of all the mute and all the inglorious of all times solidarity in the transhistorical community of noble spirits and brilliant minds, for it is the Emersonian poet who underwrites the proverb of American proverbs that it is not where you come from that counts but who you are; it is he, the Emersonian poet, who celebrates the natural ground of privilege. But the retreat to the interior enacted by Emerson's various metaphors against ownership in both feudal and capitalist systems of production carries the unhappy message that cultural independence will not be the grace note of American history—in the citadel of subjectivity, where we contact the "sovereign agent," it will be the only independence we know.

In spite of Emerson's obvious delight in trumping the card of capitalism, neither the poet nor any other isolable individual finally owns anything, not even himself. The primary fact of Emerson's transcendental economy is not owning but belonging, not possessing but being possessed. That to which we belong ("the only and sovereign agent") and that by which we are possessed is no individual. What Emerson liked to call the "universal soul," or "Reason," or the "oversoul" he defined strategically, with a perfection of vagueness, as an "immensity not possessed and that cannot be possessed"—"we are its property." Whatever "it" is, whatever more specifically the word "immensity" signifies in Emerson's discourse, we can say that *it* is not quantifiable, that it cannot be economized as a "commodity." "It" is precisely that which cannot be made precise, specific, an object. It neither buys nor sells; it controls no labor power. It is instead a condition of release from possessive selfhood and the commodified consciousness of liberal political vision. "*It*"—this "immensity," a cliché in the rhetoric of the sublime—is revalued on American political ground as our possession by freedom, which Emerson (at his most hopeful) calls "the background of our being."[27]

In the crucial definition of personal consciousness that he offers in the first volume of *Principles of Psychology,* James chooses to ignore Emerson's rejection of all economic conceptions of selfhood. James finds (or thinks he finds) truly inalienable private property located at (and *as*) the core of selfhood. So the price of James's anti-imperialist vision of human heterogeneity may be the most radical of all possible alienation and disconnection, which he expresses as the first commandment of his capitalized psychology—thou shalt not steal individuality: "Each of these minds keeps its own thoughts to itself. There is no giving or bartering between them. . . . Absolute insulation, irreducible pluralism, is the law. It seems as if the elementary psychic fact were not *thought* or *this thought* or *that thought* but *my thought,* every thought being *owned.* Neither contemporaneity nor proximity in space, nor similarity of quality or content are able to fuse thoughts together which are sundered by this barrier of belonging to different minds. The breaches between such thoughts are the most absolute breaches in nature. . . . The worst a psychology can do is so to interpret the nature of these selves as to rob them of their worth."[28] Or, more emphatically still: "*In its widest possible sense . . . a man's self is the sum total of all that he can call his,* not only his body and his psychic powers, but his clothes, and his house, his wife and his children, his ancestors and friends, his reputation and works, his lands and horses, and yacht and bank-account."[29] But all of the things that we think we "own," James says, are "transient external possessions" with the sole exception of the "innermost center within the circle," that "sanctuary within the citadel," the "*self of all the other selves,*" of which we can never be dispossessed: the "home," the "source," the "emanation" of "fiats of the will"—a feeling of an "original spontaneity," an active power within, without constraining ground, that becomes the ground of our personal freedom to say yes or no, to open and shut the door, and a point of departure for James's anti-imperialist pluralism.[30] That feeling of original spontaneity is James's phenomenological postulate for the inviolability of self, or of a self that should be responded to as if it were and deserved to be inviolable.

What I think James knew is that his intellectual father's transcendentalist commitment to a community of justice and dignity beyond all those historical powers of oppression that Americans like to associate with the Old World could have no material site, not even here in the so-called New World. Emerson's "active soul," an ideal instrument, working directly, if at all, from mind to mind, never works in, on, or through the mediations of actual social arrangement. In the heat of James's anti-imperialist activity, Emersonian nonconformity was simply not enough—it lacked (my anachronism is the point) James's muscular pragmatism—for the disturbing implication of Emerson's divestiture of agency and sovereignty from the individual was political passivity, not political action. What James knew is that there can be no Emersonian practice. Any act of personal will over and above the organic act of transcendental selfhood is more than neither necessary nor appropriate; it is dangerous. Any act of would-be anti-imperialist will might become (ironically) a trace of the will of the imperialist that James and Emerson abhorred. But James's pragmatism is nothing if not a philosophy of will, of personal, not transcendental, agency, of personal, not transcendental, sovereignty that would and did risk (without guarantee of moral purity) frightening appropriation of its tenets. James took that risk because, unlike Emerson, he could not be satisfied with the interiorization of cultural power and the subjectification of freedom. James would make culture instrumentally powerful; he would make intellect politically decisive to the fate of society.

What ran deep in James and what beyond argument was altogether there in Emerson (let's call it the American instinct against the imperial social gesture), but which did not surface in James until late in his career, after he had been politicized, is a sense of American history and society as severely ruptured from its European origins and from European institutions synonymous with oppression: the Roman Catholic Church, the army, the aristocracy, and the crown. James named these institutions as the true enemy of his philosophic method, which he sometimes late in his career associated with a Whitmanesque, unbuttoned, even anarchic notion of self-determination. Especially after 1900, James conceived the role of the intellectual in specific American terms as one of guarding our freedom from those European institutionalizing impulses which might and *did* insidiously rebirth themselves here from the ("theoretical") "passion of mastery" and in the form of "national destiny," a slogan which speaks for efforts to organize, first on native ground, in a "big" and "great" manner (James hated those words) against the "molecular forces that work from individual to individual," then *over there* in the form of bringing light to the uncivilized: "national destiny" as the will to impose our sense of national story—plant our order—on foreign soil.[31] It was the American intellectual's duty, James wrote in numerous letters to the *Boston Transcript* in protest against our imperialist policies, to expose the empty but murderously effective abstractions of the party of Roosevelt (like our "responsibility" for the islands, like the "unfitness" of the Filipinos to govern themselves), and James was convinced that this could be done only if intellectuals in America developed class-consciousness as intellectuals: a class with presumably no reason to align itself materially with special interests because it stood, or should stand, for ideal interests only—by which he meant the preservation of radical individual freedom. Even in the United States this cannot but be characterized as an innocent view, but it is a

view borne aloft in the morning freshness of the founding American myth—the democratic hope that with nothing resembling an aristocracy to encumber them, Americans in the new Eden had the right to think of the individual as truly prior to society. But at the same time James saw that in such presumably fluid social circumstances we could have no equivalent to a permanent presence (like an aristocratic class) responsible for overseeing the integrity of the social process as a whole. (Who, anyway, aside from Emerson, could oversee the integrity of antinomianism?) He nominated intellectuals for that role because he thought that in a society without those entrenched institutions within which European intellectuals found themselves, the American intellectual could wield "no corporate selfishness," and "no powers of corruption."[32] James underrated, though he did not ignore, the corruptive power of capital in fluid democratic contexts—he did not imagine that capital could bind intellectuals: he could not imagine American intellectuals giving voice to the impulses of imperialism.

James *did* imagine the American intellectual as defender of a self that is, or should be, inaccessibly private property; a self that is, or should be, the motor principle of American anti-imperialism. Each of us, he writes in an essay called "On a Certain Blindness in Human Beings," is bound "to feel intensely the importance of his own duties and the significance of the situations that call these forth. But this feeling is in each of us a vital secret, for sympathy with which we vainly look to others. The others are too much absorbed in their own vital secrets to take an interest in ours. Hence the stupidity and injustice of our opinions, so far as they deal with the significance of alien lives."[33] The elaborate but symptomatic difficulty in making sense of James is coming to see that his overt commitment to the inalienable private property of selfhood, the original feeling of spontaneous action, the freedom felt within, is an inscription of a contradiction at the very heart of capitalism (and theorists of capital like Adam Smith) because property under capitalism can be property only if it *is* alienable—only if it can be bought, sold, stolen, and, when necessary, appropriated. James's political turn taught him that nothing was inalienable in the coercive world of imperialism, not even the secret self that we think we possess beyond alienation. He employs the language of private property in order to describe the spiritual nature of persons and in an effort to turn the discourse of private property against itself by making that discourse literal in just this one instance: so as to preserve a human space of freedom, however interiorized, from the vicissitudes and coercions of the marketplace.

James's anti-imperialism is American anti-imperialism; his philosophical term "pluralism" is an antithetical word signifying not so much what *is,* but rather resistance to the imperialist context of his work in the modernist moment. In other words, pluralism signifies what "is *not*" and what should be. His major effort is to combat the hegemonic discourse of a capitalism rooted in a democratic political context by appropriating the cornerstone economic principle of capitalism to the advantage of his counterdiscourse and a vision of human sanctity and difference central not only to his pragmatism, but also to the originating myth of American political history. What James says in all but words is that if imperialism and capitalism on their own are capable of destroying the self, then in their unified American form they represent a global principle of structure, a world-historical menace of unparalleled proportions. In the name of pragmatism and the American dream, James wanted to turn America against the self-pollution of its foreign policy at the end of the nineteenth century; in such an act of self-criticism, he thought, we would subvert the economic and political postures which, by treating all human subjects as if they were objects, for all practical purposes convert us into objects who suffer degradations that nonhuman commodities cannot suffer. So James's quasi-Cartesian postulate of an interior spontaneity is not ontological but thoroughly instrumental. It is his great heuristic principle, the energy of his criticism, and the basis of his anti-imperialism.

After his political turn James could, in the same breath, as it were, speak against the rationalizations of theory and traditional philosophy as well as the theorizations of society, those political and economic arrangements of power that rob the self of itself by rationalizing the self in the name of capitalism and the commodification of human labor. Against the in-house economic imperialism which appropriated the self for capital in America, against his own earlier reaction to the Haymarket Riot, and against the international imperialism which denied self-determination to the Philippines and to Ireland, James brought his pragmatism as an emancipating critical force which would liberate the particular, the local, the secret self from intellectual, economic, and political structuralizations which would consume, control, deny all particularity, all locality, and all secret selfhood. James, to say it again, is no utopian: he has no vision of a future social arrangement that would insure the safety of the self, no vision of the good collective. His pragmatism is emancipatory—it would lead us out of suffocating and tyrannous theorizations; it has nothing to say about where we should be, only about where we do not want to be.

Does James's stance on the issue of traditional theory have any consequences of the sort that would bind intellectuals to the social contexts of their activity? Not an innocent question: my professional context is theory-conscious, even theory-obsessed. Passion for and against theory seems unavoidable among those who come in contact with it: in the profession of literary studies as we know it, that means most of us. For since the late 1950s and the publication of Frye's *Anatomy of Criticism,* the American scene in literary criticism has been constituted by a controversy over the role of theory carried on with theological fervor by believers and scoffers alike. And since the Summer 1982 issue of *Critical Inquiry* and the publishing of an article called "Against Theory," a new breed of scoffers, much to the delight of the old breed, has dominated the conversation. Unlike the old breed, however, this new breed comes cunningly armed with the intellectual skills associated with theorists in order to slay the dragon of theory and offer it up, lo!, on the altar of the good old American philosophy, pragmatism itself. The movement in the United States drawing most attention now, even threatening to become fashionable, is the "against theory" movement; it is being associated everywhere with the names of Peirce, Dewey, and James; it is called the "new pragmatism."[34]

I think James would have found the "against theory" position beside the point (to put it gently) because he knew that there is no sense in being for or against what you cannot escape from. There is no escape from theory because, in James's characterization of rationalism, the theory of theories, theory is "an appetite of the mind"—part of the self.[35] We are all beset by the theoretical impulse, or theory-desire, as I have called it—by the need to make the place clean and well-ordered. In its simplest and yet most far-reaching implications, theory is the need to generalize, to overcome, to forget, and to obliterate differences: a description I'd offer as an equally fair characterization of concept-formation (the obliteration of percepts) and of imperialism both as foreign policy and as a feature of the ordinary, the casual imperialism of everyday life (the obliteration of persons). Since James's temperament is shaped by nominalist, empirical, and skeptical philosophical traditions, he believes that when theory-desire expresses itself by offering itself as an explanation of the concrete world, it must necessarily fail as theory, as explanation of the way things are at all times and in all places. The world just isn't the way theory says it is. So theory cannot have the consequences that it wishes. But it does have consequences because in an effort to make over into an image of its desire the heterogeneous world of history—the romance world of many stories that do not cohere—theory acts for worse upon the world.

The jaunty little dismissal of theory by the authors of the essay called "Against Theory" is irrelevant—but it is also something more: it is self-deluded. Knapp and Michaels say that "theory is not just another name for practice. It is the name for all the ways people have tried to stand outside in order to govern practice from without." They conclude that since no one can actually achieve that transcendental perch, no one should "try" to, and "therefore" the "theoretical enterprise" should come to an end.[36] That sort of conclusion, which seems so Jamesian, is not. What James says is that though no one can actually get outside practice, the impulse to get outside is unavoidable because the practice of theory takes its point of departure not from a special venture of literary business, a "theoretical enterprise," as Knapp and Michaels suppose, but from the constitution of mind itself. One cannot "try" or "not try" to be a theorist. Theory is not simply a matter of intention or will or conscious agency. It is a matter of necessity: an impulse, an appetite. The effects of such unavoidable theoretical impulse can be the most heinous form of practice, with the most ugly sorts of political consequences. Theory—whether we call it structuralism or capitalism—is the desire which would be the "remedy" of difference. It cannot be dismissed. It can, however, be guarded against, and the method of vigilance is James's pragmatism, not "new pragmatism." Jamesian pragmatism is nothing less than the strategy for taking away rationalist theory's theoretical ambition, for encouraging us, in our impulses to theory, to recognize that we must live with differences, provisional utility, and the necessities of revision. Theory, so conceived by the old pragmatism, tentatively holding itself as *belief,* becomes a tool for getting our work done, for exploring the shifting situations we call history. But pragmatism (the vigilante within) is always on the verge of vanquishment, of giving belief over to theory (the totalitarian within).

In an effort to tame theory in the name of pragmatism, James seems to allow himself one theoretical moment, the sentimental essentialization of mind as Manichean battlefield—a struggle between traditional philosophy, or "theory," a male principle, and "pragmatism" (homage to Anne Hutchinson), which is a woman: the principle that "unstiffens" all theories and makes them useful, and a synonym for "himself" as woman in his untraditional philosophic activity. But James's essentialist portrait of mind as a conflicted androgynous unit is intended pragmatically, not theoretically, as a useful way to view, guard against, and maybe curb the aggressivity he found theoretical: aristocratic, churchly, European, and male, but not identical with the male gender. It is his way of encouraging self-critique, the braking of the ego; of saying that we have unshakeable reason to worry; of encouraging the desire for the responsible life (the life that is responsive to its contexts) while specifying the content of responsibility with American liberal vision. James's figurative language tells us that pragmatism is a woman, but not identical with the female gender: pragmatism is democratic, pragmatism is Protestant, pragmatism is inseparable from the dream of America. Pragmatism is an epistemology for isolatos who experiment at the frontier, who work without the kingly privileges of tradition and the *a priori,* who in refusing the *a priori* of rationalism would also refuse all of the encrusted pre-capitalist social contexts that James associates with the history of philosophic ratio-

nalism. Theory, on the other hand, is a social elitist, theory is a masturbatory old world gentleman who never gets his hands dirty, who cannot "unstiffen" himself. As the tool of tools, theory-erect would make unnecessary all other tools, all thinking, all revision, all worry because it is the machine for allegorizing and rationalizing and coercing all texts and all humans as instances of the same."[37]

The new pragmatists flounder on one of James's strongest insights—that theory cannot be identified with agency and the self-conscious individual, that theory is the sort of force that tends to control individuals by speaking through them. And so does James. What unifies and binds both ends of the pragmatist tradition is its political pivot, the ideology of liberalism. In the new pragmatism, the liberal commitment surfaces in the sentiment that theory can be dismissed, as if one could, as an autonomous individual, either will it away or will oneself into it. In James the liberal commitment surfaces in the belief that the central resistance to the hateful impositions of imperialism is generated autonomously in the molecular individual: molecular individualism is the great thing, and it can be saved only by efforts of molecular will. The problem is that James treats epistemological and political rationalizations as if they were the same thing. The epistemological move to generalization may well be an "appetite of the mind," well-nigh unavoidable except in moments of radical Bergsonian cherishing of perceptual particularity. And the late James is very Bergsonian. But the economic and political move to generalize—the global generalization of labor known as capitalism—is not an unhistorical appetite; it is a locatable, historical phenomenon whose role tends to be blurred and repressed by James's liberal ideology of the autonomous self. The most powerful enemy of the self is not an irrepressible impulse but the economic imperative of capital rooted in and projected from collective interests. The category missing in new and old pragmatism is the category of class which tells us, among other things, that "individuals," including intellectuals, are also representations— vessels of power not originating in themselves and directed against themselves.[38]

The typical liberal response to the destruction of selfhood that is synonymous with the commodification of labor at the economic level and the commodification of human relations in everyday life at all levels of human interaction is to ignore the historical action of capital in the American scene: the steamrolling of the individual in the name of individualism. The problem is collective, the antidote would seem to be collective, but it is precisely the decent collective that is unimaginable to the liberal mind, maybe because the underground of the liberal mind is really antinomian. When collectives are imagined by James, they tend to be represented as lifedenying "system." James's celebration of individualism, whether in its modest liberal or its wild antinomian forms, must remain at the mercy of the systematic, capitalist appropriation of the individual that he laments. Since radical individualism in America can be seen, by definition, in no cooperative venture, it would appear that James needs to keep alive a threatening principle of generalization, always at the doorstep of individualism, in order that the radical individual may feel the isolated purity of its freedom. The idea of radical individualism in America derives much of its energy from the memory of our European origins—and capitalism, in James's America, is an ironic aid to that repressed memory of the *ancien régime.* If in one way James out-Marxes Marx, in another he un-Marxes him.

The really ironic thing about the recent "against theory" position, even in its latest and most clever formulation in a recent essay by Stanley Fish called "Consequences"—in which it is argued that neither theory nor belief can have "necessary" and therefore powerful consequences that we need to be responsive to and responsible for—is that its effort to bury theory has the consequence of reinstating theory-desire in its most naked form. The "against theory" position turns out to be the "for theory" position—a powerful expression of the very theory-impulse that James so eloquently contextualized, but with none of James's feeling for its insidious and necessary impact on human behavior. The "against theory" phenomenon turns out to be a repetition, this time around in the name of *practice,* of the escape from history and political accountability so characteristic of the various formalisms that have dominated American critical thought since Frye. Whereas James counsels vigilance for the enemy within, the voices "against theory" counsel a dismissal of a nuisance from without, of recent academic origin, not realizing that they, too, like the rest of us, are the enemy, and in disturbing garb, especially when they write, as Fish now writes, without apparent awareness of the action that theory-desire takes upon their own discourse: as when Fish offers as an example of the irrelevance of theory "the case of two legislators who must vote on a fair-housing bill."

Fish offers this case hypothetically, as if such an example might conceivably have occurred to anybody—to, say, Locke or Hegel, or in any place, say in classical Athens or in feudal Europe. He argues that a legislator voting on behalf of equal access just might be a libertarian typically committed to individual freedom, that said libertarian might not side with the lobby which works for landlords and all others who like to rest their case on the rights of private property; while the utilitarian, who would ordinarily be committed to arguments on behalf of equal access just might side with advocates of property rights as the only way to insure in the long run the greatest good for the greatest number.[39] Fish's example is confusing because it is abstract; it never

touches historical earth; it is an example offered in the analytical style of Anglo-American philosophy—a philosophical style which routinely rarifies "examples" like abortion, nuclear weapons, and capital punishment. Nowhere does Fish indicate awareness of what his language indicates against his intention—what his language speaks. At the level of his example's historical unconscious we find a discourse inscribed which must be made to say, against Fish's intention, that fair housing became an issue in the United States in the heat of the Civil Rights movement in the 1950s and 1960s. Within that historical locale, the position of the libertarian was almost always the position of the covert segregationist, the position that gave comfort, energy, and ideas to the racist who clothes his arguments with the rhetoric of property rights; while the utilitarian was almost always, within that historical locale, a proponent of social change who advocated fair housing as a way of making civil rights socially concrete for blacks, a position, in other words, that gave comfort, energy, and ideas to advocates of civil rights.

Fish's abstract antagonists on the issue of fair housing *might* conceivably, as he argues, have changed sides, *might* conceivably have taken each other's typical stance, thus demonstrating Fish's point—that it *might* not matter a damn what your position is, your practice *might* be otherwise. But in historical fact these antagonists almost never did change sides because their beliefs or theories or positions were politically and historically rooted, politically and historically determinate, in a moment which militated against such possibilities, in a moment which extracted determinate consequences from the antagonists. Thus in his discourse on the problem of fair housing in which the problem is reconceived so as to have no necessary relation to any concrete historical scene, Fish's discourse becomes theoretical—it would prove some general point about the impotence of self-conscious position-taking, applicable for all times and all instances, and in so doing it would elide the differences in positions that produced the particular and potent forms of agony this country has experienced since the 50s and 60s. History exacts its revenge within Fish's discourse, and against his Anglo-American philosophical abstractness, and says not only that all ideas are rooted in specific social situations, but that expressing ideas bears specific political consequences: Fish's discourse on consequences is a prime example, especially at the moment when it denies the consequential nature of having belief and theory.

What I am saying about Fish's most recent critical incarnation amounts to this: his treatment of the issue of fair housing is a betrayal of the strong historicism that he would elaborate, and it is a particularly destructive sort of betrayal which cancels out the only sort of political responsibility that an historicist can live with. Not the Kantian sort, which makes appeals to an ahistorical world of rights and moral imperatives; not the utopian sort, which appeals to a global community-to-be grounded in no particular time or locale. The political responsiveness that Fish betrays is to the very persons and historical community within which his nexus of terms—"fair housing," "utilitarianism," "libertarianism"—takes on determinate and powerful significance. Not just *any* historical community, but the very community within which Fish writes and within which his readers must receive him.

But the commanding question about the new pragmatism's consequences cannot really be pursued with justice at this moment. It is too new. I'll conclude, then, not with any statement about its consequences, which are not especially clear at this point, but with some remarks about its stance and its omissions. 1) However misled by the allurements of formalism, what was called theory in the United States in the 60s and 70s and in the early 80s has been the site in our profession of basic and often explosive questioning about the nature and role of literature. Marxism, deconstruction, feminism, psychoanalysis—these are the current terms of opposition to the status quo of the institution of literary study: these are terms of resistance that in various ways would take literature out of the vacuums of traditional humanism and traditional formalism and into the world of economics, power, gender, and class. The rhetoric of "against theory," therefore, at this juncture, cannot help but bring comfort, energy, and ideas to the enemies of change. The rhetoric of "against theory" is reactionary. 2) The "against theory" proponents are representative of a claustrophobic form of professionalism. They speak of "theory" as if it were the invention of literary critics and philosophers, a phenomenon of the academic institution merely. But the lesson of James is that theory is a phenomenon of everyday life in history and society, a phenomenon of all of society's institutions, and the name of a disposition whose consequences are revealed in oppression. The overly narrow, single institutional focus of the "against theory" proponents trivializes the social issues of theory, as James never did, and in the process trivializes the broader social role of literary study. In the name of practice, "against theory" gives us, once more, the ivory tower. 3) The constant accompaniment to James's criticism of theory and traditional philosophy is a commitment to anti-imperialism and an extended and troubled meditation on the fate of persons in a capitalist context. Fish's example of the two legislators and the question of fair housing looks like a splendid invitation, another social document calling for the intervention of historicized Jamesian conscience, but it is not. Despite the fact that his example has everything to do with the obsessive and intertwined themes of James's critique of theory—the sanctity of selves and the rights of property—Fish's point is that

we can dance away, with impunity if we like, and keep on dancing away from the determinate responsibilities of belief that history thrusts upon us.

Since theory of the sort that James, Fish, and I are talking about works in the realm of probability, on culture and history, and not on nature, presumably the realm of rigorous causality and the classic object of scientific inquiry, it would follow that Fish's major point—that cultural theory has no "necessary" theoretical consequences—is logically correct. But his point is a trivial tautology unless pressed beyond its tautological truth that culture is not the realm of necessity. In other words, after all of contemporary theory's hermeneutical suspicions have been registered, after we have once again followed the lead of the early Roland Barthes, who encourages us to break the conspiracy of silence by refusing to let culture be naturalized by the attitude of "it goes without saying," the question of probability remains. What might be the effect of a literary theorist working to get to that transcendental perch, getting scientific? What has been the effect of imposing our will in Central America? Making them hew, in James's terms, to our story? Or, in Fish's case, where the issue is also political, what might be the (probable) effect on his readers and students of his homogenization of the terms of struggle in the Civil Rights movement, especially in the context of the 1980s when so many of our students (with the aid of Reagan's justice department) seem convinced that racism in the United States was utterly routed everywhere by the late 1960s and that its last bastion is South Africa? The question about the literary theorist who would be scientific, the question about our political relation to the Third World, and the question about Fish are not questions of the same order. But they all involve the effects of theorization: the costs of working to wipe out differences and otherness; the costs of trying to move over the realm of history, and command it from above. These costs are not the costs, or consequences, of theory as theory imagines itself and its effects; they are instead the costs, or consequences, organic to the effort of trying to succeed in the futile and inevitable adventure of theory. And they are real.

The new pragmatists maybe could learn a lesson from our godfather, Vito Corleone, who believed that one (preferably someone else) had to "answer" for one's actions. Don Corleone was a connoisseur of reason (as in "I will reason with him"; or as in "But no one can reason with him"). But the Don was no Kantian. Unlike the new pragmatists, who assign self-consciousness no historical role, he knew that the sort of worry synonymous with self-reflection takes place in a context of other wills, not in some self-contained transcendental inner sphere, but in a context of situations that make vivid, sometimes vividly red, the consequences of taking "unreasonable" positions. Critical self-consciousness, in other words, is not a pointless activity of intellectuals too enamored of philosophical idealism, but a necessity for getting on with others in the world—a necessity even for intellectuals.

If the political unconscious of the new pragmatism is liberal (in its wild phase, antinomian), its explicit political content runs all to indifference and the professionalism that would make itself a world apart. James, an integrated intellectual, a professional with an organic sense of the relation of philosophy and all other institutions, who called himself a meliorist because he thought his world needed changing and could be changed for the better, would find in the new pragmatism the thoroughgoing satisfaction that he had excoriated in Josiah Royce: the confidence that this is the best of all possible worlds. James not only thought otherwise, but he thought that the process of change must be initiated close to home, in self-worrying critique. The new pragmatism, on the other hand, would stand one of the most ancient of Western maxims on its head. It says in all but words: "The unexamined life is the only life worth living." Here at last, moving with the tides of the times, is the basis for a literary criticism of the 80s.

Notes

1. *Selected Critical Writings of George Santayana,* ed. Norman Henfrey (Cambridge: Cambridge Univ. Press, 1968), I, 149-50.

2. William James, *"Pragmatism" and "The Meaning of Truth,"* intro. by A. J. Ayer (Cambridge, Mass.: Harvard Univ. Press, 1975), 28-29.

3. Ibid., 98.

4. Stanley Fish, "Consequences," *Critical Inquiry* 11 (March 1985): 435.

5. *Pragmatism,* 122-23.

6. C. S. Peirce, *Selected Writings,* ed. Philip P. Weiner (New York: Dover Publications, 1966), 103.

7. *Pragmatism,* 126.

8. Ibid., 71.

9. Ibid.

10. Ibid., 124.

11. See, for example, *Pragmatism,* 31, 40, 125, and F. O. Matthiessen, *The James Family: A Group Biography* (New York: Alfred A. Knopf, 1961), 633.

12. Michael Herr, *Dispatches* (New York: Alfred A. Knopf, 1977), 92.

13. *Pragmatism,* 17-18.

14. Ibid., 18.

15. Ibid.

16. Matthiessen, 626.

17. Ibid., 622.

18. Quoted in *American Literature: The Makers and the Making,* I, ed. Cleanth Brooks, R. W. B. Lewis, Robert Penn Warren (New York: St. Martin's Press, 1973), 10n.

19. *The Selected Writings of Ralph Waldo Emerson,* ed. Brooks Atkinson, foreword by Tremaine MacDowell (New York: Random House, 1968), 430-31.

20. Ibid., 427.

21. Ibid., 123.

22. Ibid., 5-6.

23. Ibid., 148.

24. Ibid.

25. Herbert Marcuse, *Negations: Essays in Critical Theory,* trans. Jeremy J. Shapiro (Boston: Beacon Press, 1968); see the essay "The Affirmative Character of Culture."

26. Emerson, 62.

27. Ibid., 263.

28. William James, *The Principles of Psychology* (New York: Dover Publications, 1950), I, 226.

29. Ibid., 291.

30. Ibid., 297-98, 299-305.

31. Matthiessen, 624, 626, 633.

32. Ibid., 633, 635.

33. Ibid., 398.

34. The relevant documents are collected in *Against Theory: Literary Studies and the New Pragmatism,* ed. W. J. T. Mitchell (Chicago: Univ. of Chicago Press, 1985).

35. *Pragmatism,* 18.

36. Steven Knapp and Walter Benn Michaels, "Against Theory," *Critical Inquiry* 8 (Summer 1982): 742. The enabling and self-trivializing assumption of "Against Theory" is announced in the essay's opening words: "By 'theory' we mean a special project in literary criticism."

37. For pragmatism as a woman, see *Pragmatism,* 43-44: on rationalism as an old world gentleman, see *Pragmatism,* 38, 40. The metaphor of pragmatism as a woman is infrequent in James; rationalism as a "gentleman" is common.

38. I allude to the classic treatment of intellectuals in *The German Ideology.*

39. Fish, 444.

Hilary Putnam and Ruth Anna Putnam (essay date winter 1989)

SOURCE: Putnam, Hilary, and Ruth Anna Putnam. "William James's Ideas." *Raritan* 8, no. 3 (winter 1989): 27-44.

[*In the following essay, the Putnams assert that an understanding of James's "ethical intentions" is imperative to fully comprehend his philosophical ideas.*]

There are several ways of coping with the work of William James. In his recent *William James: His Life and Thought,* Gerald Myers seems to have understood James's *Principles of Psychology* and his pragmatism as leading ultimately to the philosophical theory that James advanced late in his career under the name "radical empiricism"; in Myers's book, the moral and religious views, though treated in detail, are not shown to be connected. Alternatively, James's conception of truth, that is to say, his pragmatism, might be taken as a key or unifying aspect of his work. (This part of James's philosophy has been most deeply misunderstood.) Or, one might recall James's own words: "You see that pragmatism can be called religious, if you allow that religion can be pluralistic or merely melioristic in type. . . . If you are neither tough nor tender in an extreme and radical sense, but mixed as most of us are, it may seem to you that the pluralistic and melioristic religion that I have offered is as good a religious synthesis as you are likely to find." If, with James, pragmatism is regarded as a religion, then he is surely its foremost preacher, one whose ultimate motivation is ethical rather than consolatory. Whether or not pragmatism is regarded as a religion, attention to James's ethical intentions is essential to an understanding of him. We shall proceed from the assumption that, early and late, James's motivation was ultimately ethical, and that his essays in, for example, *The Will to Believe and Other Essays,* and particularly "The Moral Philosopher and the Moral Life," can play a key role in understanding both his pragmatism and his radical empiricism.

James's moral philosophy has a fundamental principle that is quasi-a priori ("quasi" because, in our view, even what look like a priori elements in James's philosophy are subject to revision). At the same time, as in almost all moral philosophies, facts about what will and what will not make human beings happy are important in determining what our detailed obligations are. (Even in Kant's ethics, such facts enter through the obligation to strive to bring about a world in which "happiness is proportional to virtue.") The quasi-a priori principle, as James states it in "The Moral Philosopher and the Moral Life," is that "without a claim actually made by some concrete person there can be no obligation, but there is some obligation wherever there is a claim." What those claims are is a contingent fact. The idea that nothing is

desirable unless something is desired, comes, of course, from utilitarianism (and James did dedicate *Pragmatism* to Mill); but, as we shall see, James gives a very different twist to even such utilitarian-sounding remarks as this from "The Moral Philosopher and the Moral Life": ". . . must not the guiding principle for ethical philosophy be simply to satisfy at all times as many demands as we can?"

If there is a strong utilitarian strain in James's ethics, there are also some striking similarities to Kantianism. Like Kant, James rejects the Humean idea that free will is compatible with determinism, and like Kant he came to see a belief in free will and a belief in what he called a theistic god (or, at other times, gods) as prerequisites for ethical action. This similarity to Kant is, perhaps, most striking in *Pragmatism,* where belief in both free will and God are defended as imperatives of practice:

> Free-will thus has no meaning unless it be a doctrine of *relief.* As such, it takes its place with other religious doctrines. Between them, they build up the old wastes and repair the former desolations. Our spirit, shut within this courtyard of sense-experience, is always saying to the intellect upon the tower: "Watchman, tell us of the night, if it ought of promise bear," and the intellect gives it then these terms of promise. *Other than this practical significance, the words God, free-will, design, etc., have none.*

Like Kant (who elevated "What may we hope?" to equal significance with the philosophical questions "What can we know?" and "What should we do?"), James believed that people cannot live and function in the world on a diet of mere pessimism; a world view that can be a guide to action need not be full of rosy optimism, but it must not tell us that we are all the pawns of either blind chance or iron necessity.

This, of course, raises the question: What entitled James to believe in free will, etc.? Answering this question (and also the question, How do we know what is wrong with the world as it is, and hence what would be a better world?) will lead us deep into James's theory of truth.

Nothing is as responsible for the low esteem in which James has been held by philosophers as his so-called theory of truth, except perhaps the doctrine of "The Will to Believe." On 26 August, 1898, in the lecture at the University of California titled "Philosophical Conceptions and Practical Results" announcing his pragmatism, James gives credit to Peirce for teaching him how to think about meaning and truth. Peirce, on the other hand, often refers to the James-Dewey view on truth, and by 1907 James credits that same theory to Dewey (whose *Studies in Logical Theory* had appeared in 1903) and to Schiller. What the great pragmatists have in common—and what creates a common difficulty in understanding them—is that they do not appear to have a clear "epistemology." Unlike Mill, Reichenbach, Carnap, or Frege, they do not see it as their task to reduce rationality to a set of canons. Of course, Peirce distinguished the invention of an explanatory scientific theory (which he called "abduction") from more elementary kinds of inductive inference; of course, he set the stage for the later pragmatists by stressing the doctrine that all our beliefs are subject to revision (which he called "fallibilism"); of course, he insisted that scientific theories must be tested. But he also insisted that scientists need good intuitions: intuition suggests theories, intuition suggests the order in which to test the theories that have come to mind. Dewey and James extended Peirce's observations by making explicit the idea that methodology itself is something that evolves in the course of inquiry. In our own day, Quine has emphasized that all inquiry involves "trade-offs" between simplicity, preservation of past doctrine, and successful prediction (all constraints which James had emphasized in *Pragmatism*). Such trade-offs, he says, are "where rational, pragmatic"; yet he doubts that the making of such trade-offs can be reduced to exact rules.

For James, pragmatism as a "method for settling metaphysical disputes" and pragmatism as "a certain theory of truth" were always closely linked. Pragmatism in the former sense meant for James an appeal to the following principle, which is his own, perhaps inaccurate, paraphrase of Peirce's famous "pragmatic maxim": "To attain perfect clearness in our thought of an object, then, we need only consider what conceivable effects of a practical kind the object may involve—what sensations we are to expect from it, and what reactions we must prepare. Our conception of these effects, whether immediate or remote, is then for us the whole of our conception of the object, so far as that conception has positive significance at all." Later it can be asked whether that is indeed all there is to the Jamesian method of settling metaphysical disputes; for now it is enough to see how this method is applied to the meaning of truth.

The dictionary says that truth means agreement with reality; but what does it mean for our beliefs or thoughts or ideas to agree with reality, and what does it matter anyway? That there is no single answer to this question has been a source of perplexity for readers of James. Peirce had said, quoting his contemporary, Alexander Bain, that belief is "that upon which a man is prepared to act"; both James and Peirce hold that a true belief is one which, when acted upon, does not lead to unpleasant surprises. James emphasizes that truth serves practical interests. But, contrary to many critics, James does not mean that anything that serves practical interests is true. Rather, the nature of a true belief's "agreement with reality," and which interests it is to serve, depend on the kind of belief it is.

Perceptual beliefs have to "lead us to the object itself." (James describes this as a realist strain in his thinking and chides his interpreters for ignoring it.) James says about scientific theories, with increasing frustration at being misunderstood, that all our knowledge of the world is a product of the world and our minds. Human beings developed the conceptual framework known as common sense, and human beings develop all other conceptual frameworks. But this is not done simply by "copying" facts that somehow dictate their own description: "The trail of the human serpent is over everything." He points out, additionally, that knowledge always grows. In that sense at least the universe is not complete and finished, and it is in our power to change it. But he points out also that "knowledge never grows all over: some old knowledge always remains what it was." That old knowledge, or "previous truths" as he calls them, combines with new experience to lead to new truths. Common sense beliefs have withstood the test of experience particularly well; nevertheless, they are, in a way, merely very successful hypotheses. All our other modes of thinking, none of which succeeds in replacing all others, "are *instrumental,* are mental modes of *adaptation* to reality, . . ." not copies. Though James has no doubt that there is a world, though he himself in his radical empiricism proposes an account of the world's ultimate stuff, our common sense and scientific and philosophical beliefs are only so many versions of the world, to use Nelson Goodman's term, each good for its purposes.

Common sense beliefs are "in a way" merely successful hypotheses, even though *hypothesis* is not a term used in ordinary language to refer to the belief, say, that fire burns, or that water is wet. The term has a skeptical connotation for traditional philosophers that it does not have (or does not always have—James wobbles somewhat on this point) for pragmatists. For a traditional philosopher—for an empiricist like Hume, for instance—calling something a hypothesis suggests a certain degree of doubt. But one of the central contributions of pragmatism was to deny that doubt is always appropriate: the point of Peirce's celebrated charge that Descartes only thought he doubted the existence of the external world is that real doubt (and the pragmatists were the first to make the now widespread distinction between real doubt and "philosophic" doubt) requires a justification; it is not only beliefs that require to be justified, but also challenges to belief. Calling these common sense beliefs "hypotheses" is a way of saying that they too are subject to revision, that no belief, however secure in the present context, is in principle exempt from challenge. To call them hypotheses is not to express some general skeptical doubt of their truth.

True beliefs are of vital importance; false beliefs may prove fatal. James's insistence that "true ideas . . . would never have acquired a class-name . . . suggesting value, unless they had been useful from the outset in this way" is perhaps responsible for the charge that he simply equates truth with utility. But the usefulness of true ideas is the result of their "agreement" with reality; their usefulness alone does not constitute that agreement. They are useful by "leading" us to act in such a way that our subsequent experiences do not come as unpleasant surprises.

What we have spoken of so far are what James called "half-truths," these being the best anyone can hope to achieve, but always subject to correction by subsequent experience. James also appears to accept the Peircean idea of truth (he calls it "absolute truth") as a coherent system of beliefs which will ultimately be accepted by the widest possible community of inquirers as the result of strenuous and attentive inquiry (what Peirce called the "final opinion"). However, James accepts this notion only as a regulative ideal; in *Pragmatism* he writes that this ideal "runs on all fours with the perfectly wise man, and with the absolutely complete experience; and, if these ideals are ever realized, they will all be realized together." Like the half-truth of everyday life, "it will have to be *made,* made as a relation incidental to the growth of a mass of verification-experience, to which the half-true ideas all along are contributing their quota."

This bifurcation of the notion of truth into a notion of available truth (half truth) and unavailable but regulative "absolute truth" is obviously problematic. Dewey proposes to remove the difficulty. He jettisons the notion of "absolute truth" and settles for half truth (renamed "warranted assertibility"). But the price of this seems too high in another way; it loses a desirable distinction (and one that James recognizes) between saying of a statement that it is warrantedly assertible on the basis of all the evidence we have to date and saying that it is ("tenselessly") *true.* A majority of today's analytic philosophers would solve the problem in a way urged by Alfred Tarski and Rudolf Carnap: they would say that "half truth" (or "warranted assertibility") is not truth at all but confirmation. James was, in this majority view, confused as to his subject matter: James thought that pragmatism was a theory of truth, when what he was offering was really a theory of confirmation. The notion of "absolute truth" is also a mistake, in the Tarski-Carnap view. "True" is not the name of a property at all according to these thinkers; to say that a statement, like "Snow is white," is true, is just to affirm the statement. To say that "Snow is white" is true, is not to say that "Snow is white" has a property of correspondence to something extralinguistic. Indeed, we do not ascribe a characteristic to the statement "Snow is white" at all; rather, we just indicate our willingness to affirm "Snow is white." This has been sometimes called

a "disappearance" theory of truth—either because, on this theory, "the problem of the nature of truth" disappears, or because truth itself disappears as any kind of an attribute.

Had we agreed that the very center of pragmatism involves a confusion which has been cleared up by modern "disappearance theories of truth," we would not have written this essay. Had we held the view just described, we would have said that it is empty to say that what we are trying to do in science or anywhere else is find the truth. One wants, of course, to affirm "Snow is white" only if snow indeed is white. But an understanding of the sentence "Snow is white" does not consist, in the "disappearance" view, of grasping conditions under which it is true; it consists, rather, in grasping conditions under which "Snow is white" is confirmed. The very criticism that the modern view makes of Dewey—that he loses the distinction between warranted assertibility and truth—is, in a way, valid against the modern view itself.

Is it incumbent, then, to go back to the Peirce-James view, that "truth" (as distinct from "warranted assertibility") is to be identified with the tremendously Utopian idea of "the final opinion," the theory to be reached (and to become coercive) at the end of *indefinitely continued investigation*? Not necessarily. James and Peirce want to deny that truth outruns what humans, or other sentient beings, could verify or find out. Very often, the problem in philosophy is that a philosopher who knows what he wants to deny feels that he cannot simply do so, but must make a "positive" statement; and the positive statement is frequently a disaster. Suppose, for the moment, that what is right in pragmatism is the leading idea that truth is an *idealization*—a useful and necessary idealization—of warranted assertibility. The idealization need not involve the Utopian fantasy of a theory satisfying all the requirements that absolute idealists placed on "the ultimate coherent account" (an account which, they argued, could only be known by the Absolute, i.e. God). The idealists' ultimate coherent account had to contain the truth about every single question—it had to be what a contemporary logician would call a "complete and consistent" theory of everything. It is, perhaps, understandable that James and Peirce would accept the ideal of One Complete and Consistent Theory of Everything, as they were influenced by the very philosophy they were combating. Yet James's own pluralism eventually leads him to reject the idea that all truth must cohere in one final system. If a statement can withstand all the criticism that is appropriate given its context, perhaps that is truth enough. This general sort of idea—the idea of truth as, in some way (not in Peirce's way, but in a more humanly accessible, modest way), an idealization of the notion of warranted assertibility—has recently been revived in writings by Michael Dummett, Nelson Goodman, and Hilary Putnam.

James (as well as Dewey) takes the same approach to ethics as he does to common sense and science. Here too, he thinks, there are procedures which can be imperfectly characterized and which might be improved in the course of ethical inquiry itself. What is not available is a set of final ethical truths or a method by which they can be discovered. He tries to change our philosophical sensibility, rather than to replace one foundationalist ethical project with another, on the one hand, or to convince us that ethics is "noncognitive," on the other.

It is possible to extract from James's writings a description of how best to proceed in ethical inquiry. First, in ethics as in science, "experiment" is necessary, not in the sense of random trials (which are not done in science either), but in the sense of hypotheses to be tested in practice. In ethics the hypotheses can include our ideals, our social philosophies, our plans for a better world; and the tests in practice consist in the struggle to implement these plans in the context of a democratic polity. In James's day it was not so well understood as it is now that scientists who propose theories often do so before any real experimental evidence is available, and often defend their untested theories with a passion—without which the evidence would probably never be collected or the experiments performed. (The life of Albert Einstein affords more than one illustration of this.) James's insistence in "The Will to Believe" that "science would be far less advanced than she is if the passionate desires of individuals to get their own faiths confirmed had been kept out of the game" shocked and bewildered many, including his graduate students at Harvard. E. A. Singer, Jr. recalled that his reaction on first hearing that essay as a lecture was like a "feeling of the absurd." One of his fellow students dubbed the essay "The Will to Make Believe." That the passionate advocacy of new ideas and ideals in the face of skepticism is the prerequisite for all social change is perhaps less controversial today than it was in James's day.

Our values—our "demands" as James calls them—cannot, however, be tested one by one, nor is there an algorithm for comparing and rank ordering them. (That is why James is not a conventional utilitarian, whatever his debt to Mill.) The most important struggle is not between atomistic or isolated values, but between what James calls "ideals," visions which inform and unite large systems of demands. Individual demands may be unreconcilable, as may ideals. But with ideals there is at least the hope of incorporation in some more inclusive vision. That we should seek to work out the conflicts between our ideals in this way—by seeking more inclusive ones which bring out and preserve what was

valuable in the ideals they replace—is a central part of the methodology James recommends to us. Peirce was confident that science would go on progressing if we only remain faithful to the spirit of fallibilism and continue to engage in abduction—theory construction, as opposed to mere induction from cases—and in ethics James is no less confident that social progress will result from this same spirit of fallibilism and a continued engagement in the construction and passionate advocacy of "ideals." In ethical cases, compassion corresponds to the corrective force of experiment in science. Just as no sequence of experiments will do any good, no matter how wonderful some of the theories under test, unless we pay attention to the outcomes, so no sequence of social experiments will do any good, no matter how wonderful some of the ideals involved in the struggle, if attention is not paid to "the cries of the wounded." Our moral image of the world must include values of procedural rationality which are closely connected with the values of intellectual freedom and mutuality.

In *A Theory of Justice,* John Rawls introduced the notion of imperfect procedural justice. Trial by jury is an example of imperfect procedural justice. The ideal—that all and only the guilty be convicted—is defined without reference to the procedure, and the procedure sometimes fails to produce the ideal result. (An example of perfect procedural justice is the well-known method of dividing a cake justly, i.e. evenly, by letting one person cut and the other choose.) A conception of, say, justice which defines it by reference to a procedure is called a "pure procedural conception" by Rawls. Trial by jury does not yield a pure procedural conception of what justice is. Nevertheless trial by jury, though imperfect, is a just procedure; it is, in practice, the best method we know to minimize false guilty verdicts. The pragmatists' conception of rationality, and James's (and Dewey's) conception of morality, is an imperfect procedural conception in a different sense. (Habermas has recently employed the notion in this new sense.) It is procedural because there is no other way to find truth or goodness; it is imperfect because there is no external point of view from which one can judge whether the method has been followed correctly. This differs from the case of trial by jury; here an outsider can judge whether the procedures have been followed.

On the other hand, the pragmatist does not believe that correctness of the outcome of the procedures—rational belief or just resolution of some conflict between demands—can be defined other than in terms of the outcome of the (endlessly self-improving) procedure. For pragmatists, our conceptions of rationality and justice are almost "pure procedural conceptions" even though the procedures are imperfect. (The guilt or innocence of the accused is not a fact quite independent of the procedure by which it becomes known; truth and goodness independent of the procedures are at best "regulative ideals.")

If the Jamesian conception is procedural, it is also a vision of personal responsibility, personal feeling and commitment, bounded by respect for the moral visions and commitments of others. The question is whether we can, whether we will, arrive at better shared conceptions of the good by struggling for our own deeply held personal conceptions within a framework of a commitment to democracy, struggling in a way which combines deep commitment with hatred for dogmatism. James raised and answered this question in "The Moral Philosopher and the Moral Life." And his answer is that we will succeed on one condition, that we must not be "deaf to the cries of the wounded."

Here again there is a link with utilitarianism. In a passage in *Utilitarianism,* Mill argues that anything is desirable—in analogy with the claim that anything is visible or audible—only if people do, or under specifiable circumstances will, desire it. On the basis of that passage, philosophers never used to tire of accusing Mill of committing the fallacy of passing from the premise that each (or a large majority) desire something to its being (objectively) desirable in the normative sense. If the something desired is a system of moral desires (an ideal, in a large sense) which would be the outcome of strenuous moral inquiry—inquiry conducted through democratic debate and practical testing in the social arena, not through appeals to the method of authority or the method of what is agreeable to reason—then the missing premise in the utilitarian argument is filled in by the pragmatist theory of truth! This is how K. O. Apel reads and applies Peirce today; in this respect, Apel follows in James's footsteps. Whereas Bernard Williams and David Wiggins claim that truth in morality is one thing (truth "humanly speaking") and something else ("absolute truth") in science, pragmatism urges that truth humanly speaking is all we've got. And the best idea we have of it is the "imperfect procedural conception" of how to get to it. From this flows the insistence on avoiding authoritarianism and not being deaf to the voices of complaint (the grandfather of the "ideal dialogic situation," in which every participant has a chance both to advance and to challenge claims, that Habermas writes about today) and the simultaneous insistence on being passionate—passionate but not fanatical—about putting forward moral, religious, and political views.

Although James is, then, a modified utilitarian in this sense, he is emphatically not a utilitarian in a certain classical sense. He denies that all our desires are reducible to a desire for pleasure and/or the absence of pain;

indeed, he affirms emphatically that we have immediate moral emotions. We would recoil, James asserts in "The Moral Philosopher and the Moral Life," from the idea of securing the happiness of the whole world "on the one simple condition that a certain lost soul on the far-off edge of things should lead a life of lonely torture." Indeed, it is because we have immediate moral emotions that hearing the cry of the wounded makes a difference in our search for the good.

That search would be futile, in James's view, a sentimental self-indulgence, if the world were closed, if there were no real possibilities, if individuals could not make a difference. Thus James was driven early and late to confront what he called "The Dilemma of Determinism." He himself was pulled back—pulled himself back—from the brink of a nervous breakdown by reading Renouvier's defense of free will. There are certain questions—metaphysical questions—which are of great importance in our lives but which cannot be settled by the rational procedures discussed so far. Moreover, to suspend judgment may have the practical effect of deciding one way rather than the other. Belief in his or her own ultimate success has enabled many a person to prevail where fainter hearts have failed. It is in these situations, and these situations only, that James exhorts us to "will to believe." ("Our passional nature not only lawfully may, but must, decide an option between propositions, whenever it is a genuine option *that cannot by its nature be decided on intellectual grounds;* for to say under such circumstances, 'Do not decide, but leave the question open,' is itself a passional decision,— just like deciding yes or no—and is attended with the same risk of losing the truth.") According to James, the question of free will or determinism is one of those questions. To be sure, determinism was a regulative ideal in the Newtonian physics of James's day; but free will is also a regulative ideal for James, and when regulative ideals conflict, it is philosophy and not physics that must decide how much to give to each. James believed that moral condemnations and moral regrets are senseless "unless the right way was open to us as well." (The quote is from "The Dilemma of Determinism," but the sound is unmistakably Kantian.) Finally, and most importantly, he could not "understand the willingness to act, no matter how we feel, without the belief that acts are really good or bad."

Perhaps the most shocking claim that James makes— the claim that is the centerpiece of the very first of the *Lectures on Pragmatism*—is that the decision we make on any metaphysical question, like the question of free will or the question of the existence of objective values, is and ought to be a matter of "temperament." Almost at the very beginning of the lecture, James announces that "The history of philosophy is to a great extent that of a certain clash of human temperaments." Of course, even if this statement is true, philosophers (as James of course realized) are bound to regard it as irrelevant psychologizing. "Temperament is no conventionally recognized reason, so he urges impersonal reasons only for his conclusions. Yet his temperament really gives him a stronger bias than any of his more strictly objective premises."

Here "temperament" does not have the connotations of arbitrariness, inexplicability, or irrationality that it most often has today. Temperaments, in James's sense, can put one in better or worse touch with the universe (as James argues in the same lecture; and, indeed, in the whole series of lectures). He claims that the extreme temperaments he calls "tough minded" and "tender minded" alike make one misperceive (or worse, fail to perceive) important parts of reality. "You find empiricism with inhumanism and irreligion; or else you find a rationalistic philosophy that indeed may call itself religious, but that keeps out of all definite touch with concrete facts and joys and sorrows." (James goes on to speak of Leibniz's "feeble grasp of reality.") The pluralist temperament, James is convinced, is the best temperament for this world.

Temperament, then, is subject to criticism. Part of what philosophical conflict is about, is determining what sort of temperament is best suited to the universe we live in. At the same time, the universe we live in is not a "ready made world." It is open in many respects, and, more important, it is up to us what it shall be like. Thus, we are engaged in a struggle (a "real fight") to adapt the universe and our temperaments to each other. "I find myself willing to take the universe to be really dangerous and adventurous," James writes, "without backing out and crying 'no play.'" And a few paragraphs later in the same lecture ("Pragmatism and Religion"), a genuine pragmatist "is willing to live on a scheme of uncertified possibilities, which he trusts; willing to pay with his own person, if need be, for the realization of the ideals which he frames."

If we are careful to limit the "right to believe" to those options which "cannot by their nature be decided on intellectual grounds," then we may add this "method"—this existential leap—to our list of "acceptable" procedures. The resulting final procedural conception of truth and goodness is troublesome. One seems to be asserting that something is true (and/or warranted) and simultaneously admitting that one cannot "prove" it to be true by already accepted public standards ("intellectual grounds"). Either one must give up the notion of truth in such a case, people suppose, or give up the notion of warrant (rational acceptability), or add a relativizer like the phrase "for me" or "for my culture" to one's talk of truth or one's talk of warrant. James's pragmatism—like existentialism, to which it has a definite relation—

insists that the "publicity" of truth and warrant is something *de faciendo* and not de facto, that we are subject to both the imperative to take a stand, to be a person who stands for something, and the imperative to try to make our stand a shared one. (This was well understood by whoever selected the quotation which decorates the lobby of William James Hall at Harvard: "The community stagnates without the impulse of the individual; the impulse dies away without the sympathy of the community.") Believing that my fundamental beliefs are true (or at least on the right track) even if they cannot be proved beyond controversy by appeal to already-shared standards is part of my acceptance of the regulative ideal of absolute truth, as James describes that ideal.

At the same time, James's pragmatism is importantly different from existentialism—especially from Kierkegaard's. While defending the right of the existentialist to believe ahead of the evidence (James cites the "Danish thinker" who has taught us that "we live forwards but we understand backwards"), James equally and correlatively emphasizes fallibilism. Now, it is no part of Kierkegaard's conception of what it is to be a Christian that one is to regard one's own Christianity as subject to revision in the light of future experience: in this respect, James's existentialism, if it is an existentialism, is sui generis. Staking one's life on one's ideals while recognizing that they are, in the nature of things, not final and may (we hope, will) be improved on in the progress of the species—this is a twist on existentialism that is deeply American.

To complete this account of James's ideas, we shall end with some remarks concerning James's radical empiricism. As we mentioned at the outset, Gerald Myers makes this the focal point of his recent lengthy study of his philosophy. Myers's judgment as to the centrality of James's radical empiricism is shared by other philosophers. Bertrand Russell, for example, in spite of his hostility to pragmatism (meaning James's theory of truth as Russell misunderstood it), was deeply impressed by "radical empiricism" which he credits with inspiring his own "neutral monism" (the philosophy which is both defended and criticized in Wittgenstein's celebrated early work, the *Tractatus Logico-Philosophicus*). In a different way, Husserl, the father of phenomenology, was equally impressed, and to the present day phenomenologists are among the best students and expositors of James's thought. We cannot even attempt an account of this immense topic here. But one or two words about it are necessary to round out our account of James as the preacher to the unchurched.

Since the seventeenth century the question of the existence of the "external" world—the world inhabited in common, of stars and mountains, chairs and tables, animals and humans—has been a central issue in episte-mology. According to the traditional view, each of us is directly acquainted only with his or her own "sense data" from which he or she "infers" (Descartes) or "constructs" (Berkeley) the common sense world of sticks and stones. Neither Hume nor Kant, both of whom recognized the difficulties of the standard view, managed to overcome the source of the problem: the central assumption is that the knower and the "given" are separate from the world that is known by means of the given.

One of James's central purposes in developing the complicated metaphysics-cum-epistemology he called "radical empiricism" was to combat that central assumption. Like John Austin many years later, but in a different way, James contended that there is nothing at all wrong with the common sense idea that (apart from such special cases as illusion and hallucination) we directly perceive external things—people, trees, buildings, and the rest. James's radically non-traditional theory of perception provides a logically coherent and empirically adequate account of perception which does away with the baffling idea that one cannot really perceive external things (except in the Pickwickian sense of directly perceiving "sense data" which are caused by the external things). By putting an alternative in the field, James has shown that the sense datum theory (which continues to influence philosophers more than they are likely to admit) is at best a hypothesis; it is to be accepted, or rejected, on grounds of likelihood or plausibility or simplicity or compatibility with other beliefs. Since the sense datum theory can no longer claim to be the only possible account of what we are "given" in perception, of what we know for sure, regardless of how skeptical we may be, James, by simply putting an alternative in the field, succeeded in calling into question "foundationalist" epistemology, epistemology based upon the idea that we have indubitable knowledge of our own private sense data.

This would be fascinating to go into, but more relevant to our account of James as, first and foremost, a *moral* philosopher is his motivation for rejecting traditional sense datum epistemology. James explains his motivation in a simple but shattering remark: "I simply cannot see," he says, "how from a large number of private worlds (the private worlds constituted by my sense data, your sense data, Dick's sense data, Jane's sense data . . .) we could ever arrive at knowledge of a common world." Even in pure epistemology and metaphysics, the concern with human beings as interdependent members of a community guides James's every move.

Recognizing the centrality of this concern helps one to perceive the connections between James's many ideas. In his radical empiricism, the distinction between the il-lusory or hallucinatory and the real is not that the illusory or hallucinatory has no experiential presence—to the victim, a hallucination is terrifyingly present—but that the illusory and the hallucinatory lack, James says, "general validity." The connection James here insists upon between reality and community echoes the connection between truth and community drawn in James's earlier writings. For example, in "The Moral Philosopher and the Moral Life," James anticipated Wittgenstein's celebrated Private Language Argument. James imagined a world in which there is only one sentient being, and wrote that none of the being's beliefs could be called "true." Why not? Because "truth presupposes a standard external to the thinker." Such a world, a world with a single sentient being, James calls "a moral solitude."

In the same essay James imagines a world in which there are a number of thinkers who do *not* care about one another; he denies that the notion of truth would have application to the thought of such beings. They are, James says, in the same position as the solitary thinker in the first thought experiment; their world is a plurality of moral solitudes. Truth then, presupposes community. But community is not enough. The "truth" of a Khomeiniist sect is not worthy of the name, according to the great pragmatists, because it is not responsive to anything except the will of the leader. (For the leader, there is no distinction at all between thinking he is right and being right, for there are no checks.) A community that subjects its beliefs to test is the minimum requirement for the existence of truth. This remarkable vision of a deep connection between truth, reality, and community drives James in propounding his "melioristic religion."

FURTHER READING

Criticism

Albrecht, James M. "What's the Use of Reading Emerson Pragmatically?: The Example of William James." *Nineteenth-Century Prose* 30, nos. 1-2 (spring-fall 2003): 388-496.

> Maintains that studying the approach used by William James to the works of Ralph Waldo Emerson illuminates the assessment of Emerson's philosophical relationship to the Pragmatic tradition.

Hypatia 8, no. 2 (spring 1993): 235 p.

> Special issue devoted to Feminism and Pragmatism.

Malachuk, Daniel S. "Walt Whitman and the Culture of Pragmatism." *Walt Whitman Quarterly Review* 17, nos. 1-2 (summer-fall 1999): 60-8.

Analyzes Walt Whitman's impact upon the early development of Pragmatism.

Reid, Alfred S. "Emerson and Bushnell as Forerunners of Jamesian Pragmatism." *Furman Studies* 13, no. 1 (November 1965): 18-30.

Delineates the impact of the works of Ralph Waldo Emerson and Horace Bushnell on Pragmatism.

Rosenthal, Sandra B., Carl R. Hausman, and Douglas R. Anderson, eds. *Classical American Pragmatism: Its Contemporary Vitality,* Urbana: University of Illinois Press, 1999, 263 p.

Full-length study exploring classical American Pragmatism's relevance to modern life.

Stuhr, John J., ed. *Pragmatism and Classical American Philosophy: Essential Readings and Interpretive Essays,* New York: Oxford University Press, 2000, 707 p.

Collection of essays examining the philosophies of Pragmatism's major figures, and placing Pragmatism in historical, philosophical, scientific, and literary contexts.

Thayer, H. S. *Meaning and Action: A Critical History of Pragmatism,* Indianapolis: Bobbs-Merrill, 1968, 572 p.

Full-length critical and historical study of Pragmatism.

Travel Writing in the Nineteenth Century

The following entry presents criticism on nineteenth-century travel writing. For further discussion of travel writing, see *NCLC,* Volume 44.

INTRODUCTION

The nineteenth century is recognized as the great era of travel literature. British imperial expansion in the East, the New World in the West, and archaeological discoveries in Italy and elsewhere summoned visitors to foreign sites in unprecedented numbers. Seeking to appease the demands of curious readers hungry for adventure and escape, publishers printed hundreds of diaries and other narratives recording the journeys of both prominent and relatively unknown travelers alongside the more ambitious chronicles of scientists, explorers, and journalists. These personal accounts commonly feature an intimate, first-person narrative and an informal, nostalgic style that greatly appealed to nineteenth-century readers. Travel writing has been compared with the autobiography as a form of reflective testimonial; modern historians and literary scholars view travel narratives as valuable documents in tracing social history, particularly in terms of what they reveal about nationalism, imperialism, ethnocentrism, and gender roles during the nineteenth century.

Many nineteenth-century travel narratives describe journeys to the Far East and North America. Britain, France, and, to a lesser extent, Germany, had established firm colonial power in Africa, the Near East, India, and Southeast Asia. During the nineteenth century a great many educated upper- and middle-class Europeans visited these colonies, and frequently remained in them for years. Avant-garde artists and writers rejected European cultural values and immersed themselves in cultures outside of the Western tradition. Other European colonials took up residence in the arid climates of Egypt or the Near East for health reasons. The Europeans' accounts of their experiences in these foreign cultures reveal the simultaneous attraction and repulsion that many of these colonials felt toward non-Western people and traditions, and many commentators have noted the dynamic of dominance and submission that resulted in this confrontation of vastly different, but highly developed, cultures. Accounts of North American travel, by contrast, focus on territorial exploration and expansion in a continent that was still largely wilderness and unsettled prairie, and remark upon the magnitude and sublimity of the North American landscape. Noted nineteenth-century writers such as Mark Twain and Henry James crafted travel narratives that manipulated the traditional touring descriptions in innovative ways, using a third-person narrator, for example, or fictionalizing their accounts to create deliberate, thought-provoking ambiguity. Recent scholarship has focused on the use of the travel narrative as a vehicle for the expression of the views of disenfranchised peoples, namely women and African Americans. Such travel books—sometimes presented as a mere noting of differences between their home countries and those they visited and other times as harsh, unwavering critiques—allowed women and African Americans to openly question and even denounce the social, national, and cultural traditions and beliefs that perpetuated gender and racial discrimination and slavery.

REPRESENTATIVE WORKS

Lady Anne Blunt
Bedouin Tribes of the Euphrates. 2 vols. [edited by Wilfrid Scawen Blunt] (travel essays) 1879

John Graham Brooks
As Others See Us; A Study of Progress in the United States (essays) 1908

William Wells Brown
Narrative of William W. Brown, A Fugitive Slave, Written by Himself (autobiography) 1847
Three Years in Europe; or, Places I Have Seen and People I Have Met (travel sketches) 1852; published in the United States as *American Fugitive in Europe. Sketches of Places and People Abroad,* 1855

James Bryce
The American Commonwealth. 3 vols. (travel essays) 1888; revised edition, 1889; revised and enlarged edition, 1893-95; abridged and republished as *The American Commonwealth: Abridged Edition for the Use of Colleges and High Schools, Being an Introduction to the Study of Government and Institutions of the United States,* 1896

Sir Richard Francis Burton
Personal Narrative of a Pilgrimage to El-Medinah and Meccah. 3 vols. (travel essays) 1855-56

Madame Frances Erskine Inglis Calderón de la Barca

Life in Mexico, during a Residence of Two Years in that Country (travel journal) 1843

James Fenimore Cooper

Notions of the Americans. 2 vols. [published anonymously] (travel essays) 1828

England. 2 vols. (travel essays) 1837; also published as *Gleanings in Europe: England*

Recollections of Europe. 2 vols. (travel essays) 1837; also published as *Gleanings in Europe*

David F. Dorr

A Colored Man Round the World. By a Quadroon (travel essays) 1858

Charles M. Doughty

Travels in Arabia Deserta. 2 vols. (travel essays) 1888; abridged edition published as *Wanderings in Arabia,* 1908

Amelia Edwards

Untrodden Peaks and Unfrequented Valleys: A Midsummer Ramble in the Dolomites (travel essays) 1873

A Thousand Miles up the Nile (travel essays) 1877

Frances Minto Elliot

The Diary of an Idle Woman in Italy. 2 vols. (travel journal) 1871

The Diary of an Idle Woman in Sicily. 2 vols. (travel journal) 1881

Diary of an Idle Woman in Spain. 2 vols. (travel journal) 1884

Diary of an Idle Woman in Constantinople (travel journal) 1892

Ralph Waldo Emerson

English Traits (travel essays) 1856

Lucie Duff Gordon

Letters from Egypt, 1863-65 [edited by Sarah Austin] (letters) 1865; revised edition published as *Lady Duff Gordon's Letters from Egypt,* 1865; enlarged edition published as *Last Letters from Egypt, to Which Are Added Letters from the Cape,* edited by Janet Ross, 1875; further revised and enlarged edition published as *Letters from Egypt, 1862-1869,* edited by Gordon Waterfield, 1969

Lady Maria Callcott Graham

Journal of a Residence in India (travel journal) 1812

Three Months Passed in the Mountains East of Rome, during the Year 1819 (travel essays) 1820

Journal of a Residence in Chile during the Year 1822 (travel journal) 1824

Journal of a Voyage to Brazil, and Residence There, during Part of the Years 1821, 1822, 1823 (travel journal) 1824

Basil Hall

Account of a Voyage of Discovery to the West Coast of Corea, and the Great Loo-Choo Island (travel essays) 1818

Travels in North America in the Years 1827 and 1828 (travel essays) 1829

W. H. Hudson

Idle Days in Patagonia (travel essays) 1893

Washington Irving

The Sketch Book of Geoffrey Crayon, Gent. [as Geoffrey Crayon] (short stories) 1819-20

Henry James

A Little Tour in France (travel essays) 1885

Alexander William Kinglake

Eothen; or, Traces of Travel, Brought Home from the East [published anonymously] (travel essays) 1844; also published as *Traces of Travel Brought Home from the East,* 1845, and as *Kinglake's Eothen,* 1906

Mary Kingsley

The Ascent of Cameroons Peak and Travels in French Congo (travel essays) 1896

Travels in West Africa, Congo Français, Corisco and Cameroons (travel essays) 1897

West African Studies (travel essays and essays) 1899

Constance Larymore

A Resident's Wife in Nigeria (autobiography) 1908

Anna Harriette Leonowens

The English Governess at the Siamese Court (autobiography) 1870; also published as *Siam and the Siamese,* 1897

The Romance of the Harem (short stories) 1872; also published as *The Romance of Siamese Harem Life,* 1873; modern edition published as *Siamese Harem Life,* 1952

Life and Travel in India (travel essays) 1884

Alexander Slidell Mackenzie

A Year in Spain, by a Young American. 2 vols. [published anonymously] (travel essays) 1829

The American in England. 2 vols. [published anonymously] (travel essays) 1835

Spain Revisited. 2 vols. [published anonymously] (travel essays) 1836; also published as *Two Years in Spain, by a Young American,* 1839

Harriet Martineau

*Illustrations of Political Economy (essays) 1832-34

Society in America. 3 vols. (essays) 1837

A Retrospect of Western Travel. 3 vols. (travel essays) 1838

Eastern Life Present and Past. 3 vols. (travel essays) 1848

Nina E. Mazuchelli

The Indian Alps and How We Crossed Them: Being a Narrative of Two Years' Residence in the Eastern Himalaya and Two Months' Tour into the Interior. By a Lady Pioneer. Illustrated by Herself (travel essays) 1876

Gérard de Nerval

Scènes de la vie orientale: les femmes du Caire; Les femmes du Liban. 2 vols. (travel essays) 1848; revised edition, 1850; revised and enlarged as *Voyage en Orient*, 1851

Nancy Gardner Prince

A Narrative of the Life and Travels of Mrs. Nancy Prince (travel essays) 1850; revised edition published as *A Narrative of the Life and Travels of Mrs. Nancy Prince, Written by Herself*, 1853

Robert Louis Stevenson

An Inland Voyage (travel sketches) 1878

Travels with a Donkey in the Cévennes (travel sketches) 1879

Lady Emmeline Charlotte Elizabeth Stuart-Wortley

Travels in the United States, etc., during 1849 and 1850 (travel essays) 1851

Bayard Taylor

Views A-Foot; or, Europe Seen with Knapsack and Staff (travel sketches) 1846

Eldorado; or, Adventures in the Path of Empire (travel sketches) 1850

A Journey to Central Africa; or, Life and Landscapes from Egypt to the Negro Kingdoms of the White Nile (travel sketches) 1854

The Lands of the Saracen; or, Pictures of Palestine, Asia Minor, Sicily and Spain (travel sketches) 1855

A Visit to India, China, and Japan in the Year 1853 (travel sketches) 1855

At Home and Abroad: A Sketch-Book of Life, Scenery and Men (travel sketches) 1859

At Home and Abroad, Second Series (travel sketches) 1862

Anthony Trollope

North America. 2 vols. (travel essays) 1862

Frances Trollope

Domestic Manners of the Americans. 2 vols. (travel essays) 1832

Mark Twain

The Innocents Abroad; or, The New Pilgrim's Progress (travel sketches) 1869; also published in two volumes as *The Innocents Abroad* and *The New Pilgrims' Progress*, 1870

A Tramp Abroad (travel sketches) 1880

Sarah Lee Wallis

†*The African Wanderers* (novel) 1847

Eliot Warburton

The Crescent and the Cross (travel essays) 1844

*This work was originally published monthly in twenty-five parts.

†Sarah Lee Wallis is variously known as Mrs. T. E. Bowdich, Mrs. R. Lee, and Sarah Lee.

OVERVIEWS

Christopher Mulvey (essay date 1988)

SOURCE: Mulvey, Christopher. "Anglo-American Fictions: National Characteristics in Nineteenth-Century Travel Literature." In *American Literary Landscapes: The Fiction and the Fact,* edited by Ian F. A. Bell and D. K. Adams, pp. 61-77. London and New York: Vision Press and St. Martin's Press, 1988.

[*In the following essay, Mulvey examines the expression of stereotypes and generalizations concerning social customs and national character in works by American and English travel writers.*]

Travellers generalized no less in the nineteenth century than in any other, and there were few topics more likely to start the American traveller in England generalizing than that of the English themselves; few topics more likely to start the English in America than the Americans. Travellers were all but obliged to generalize upon the character of the nation that they were visiting. The most immediate starting-point was a simple comparative method that recorded the most immediate differences between English and American life. 'We', said Benjamin Silliman in 1806, 'eat our cheese with our apple pye and not by itself, as is the English custom.'[1] Though he was no Levi-Strauss to decode the message of these *gustemes,* Silliman was no fool and the purport of this observation was in the direction of the question of the comparative manners of the English and the Americans. The mere record of the difference in dinner custom concealed an anxiety about the status of American society and the American gentleman *vis-à-vis* European society and the European gentleman in general and English society and the English gentleman in particular. In the business of the positioning of the apple pie, there might well have been an implication of American social inferiority.

It was seldom that these travellers acknowledged that differences in social manners were a neutral matter. Following a dinner at Lord Grey's London house in 1828,

James Fenimore Cooper wrote that 'it would not have been easy to point out any very broad distinctions' between American and English manners. He judged dining-rooms to be much alike in the two countries, though he recognized that while there were butlers in the United States there were no liveried footmen.[2] The service, style and manners of a great and aristocratic London house could be matched in New England or New Yorker society, he seemed to be saying. Not until Lady Emmeline Stuart Wortley's *Travels in the United States . . . During 1849 and 1850* would there be anything from an English traveller to corroborate Cooper's claim, and then not unequivocally.

The last 200 pages of the 400 pages of Cooper's *Gleanings in Europe: England* were preoccupied with, on the one hand, his sense of the hostility towards the United States displayed by the English and, on the other, with the personal insults endlessly offered him as an American while he was in England. But mutual hostility did not deter him from his objective, which was to a large extent, like that of his one-time college instructor Benjamin Silliman,[3] to show the likeness between the English and the Americans. By doing so he would be able to establish the equality of the two nations and make a declaration of what he called 'mental emancipation'.[4] The project was boldly undertaken but was unhappily snarled by the necessity, or so it seemed to Cooper, to show that the American thing was not only as *good* as but was the very *same* as the English thing. He was driven first into making extravagant claims for the men and manners of America. He was driven next into excluding as atypical the men and manners most commonly or most easily encountered in America. He was driven finally into accepting the social standards of England, and to some extent the moral judgement of England, as the final arbiter of whether or not America had achieved mental emancipation. The task became paradoxical.

The fantastical image of American social custom that Cooper needed to construct to support him in his drawing-room battles with the English led him into innumerable contretemps. At dinner one evening at Holland House, he refused a plate of herrings served him by Lady Holland. She explained that since herring had been declared contraband in England, society considered them a delicacy, a considerable delicacy. The herrings were Dutch, she said, obtained only '*through an ambassador*'. Cooper was, obviously, fairly upset by what seemed to him an adventitious virtue in the herring that might just as easily have made the potato an object of social ambition in different political circumstances. Having wrong-footed him on the herrings, Lady Holland went on to catch him again by complimenting him on the way he spoke: 'I was asked by the mistress of this house where I had learned to speak so good English? This surprising me quite as much as the herring!'[5]

These exchanges rankled and 200 pages later he returned to them in a letter entitled 'Oblique Compliments'. In this he pointed out the bad manners and the poor taste the English showed by 'telling a man in society' that he knows how to use a fork or to speak English '"quite as well as one of us"'.[6] Cooper had a point but the English might be forgiven if they were expecting him to force his knife down his throat, 'a most universal practice here', as Mrs. Hall, wife of Captain Basil Hall, R.N., had written home to her sister from New York only the year before.[7] And to some extent the problem was rooted in the very fact that Cooper did indeed want to be so exactly like the English that his being like them would not even be the cause for comment. This posture, one that was later to be detectable in men like Henry James and T. S. Eliot, represented in Cooper a classically colonialist status. It led naturally to fierce condemnation of English men and women for failing to live up to the high standards that a man like Cooper would demand that the English should achieve. It led naturally to fierce condemnation of American men and women for failing to rebut the low standards to which a man like Cooper felt he had to deny they had fallen.

When at the end of the book Cooper came to give an overall summary of the physical differences between the peoples of England and the United States, he was only able to confirm stereotypes:

> we are taller, and less fleshy; more disposed to stoop; have more prominent features; and faces less full; are less ruddy, and more tanned; have much smaller hands and feet, anti-democratical as it maybe, and are more slouching in gait.[8]

How else than by some grand archetypal image of Englishman and American could Cooper subsume and subdue the hundreds of thousands of individual Englishmen and Americans whom he had seen and who must now be compressed into the space of some five or six lines of regular prose? If the Englishman were different from the American in all the ways that Cooper detailed, then the Englishman must be short, fleshy, upright, flat-featured, full-faced, ruddy, big of hand and of foot, striding in gait. A portrait of John Bull was inescapably suggested. The received, the conventional pattern of national characteristics dictated to Cooper exactly what he should write even as he thought he was presenting the conclusions of direct observation.

Because of this, Washington Irving's frank reproduction in 1820 in his *Sketch-book of Geoffrey Crayon, Gent.* of the newspapers' image of John Bull had about it a simple honesty. By making no attempt whatsoever to get beyond the stereotype, it seemed to say that the stereotype was as much of the truth as it was possible to present:

John Bull, to all appearance, is a plain downright matter-of-fact fellow, with much less of poetry about him than rich prose. There is little of romance in his nature, but a vast deal of strong natural feeling. He excels in humor more than wit; is jolly rather than gay; melancholy rather than morose; can easily be moved to a sudden tear, or surprised into a broad laugh; but he loathes sentiment, and has no turn for light pleasantry. He is a boon companion if you allow him to have his humor, and to talk about himself; and he will stand by a friend in a quarrel, with life and purse, however soundly he may be cudgelled.[9]

Irving could go for pages like that. In fact he went on in this instance for seventeen to make up the chapter called 'John Bull'. There was no resort at all to the pretence of empirical observation. It was as though Irving accepted the impossibility of the individual writer's being able to create any kind of real picture of the Englishman; he accepted instead that the English nation had itself been working on this task for generations. In 1712 John Arbuthnot had personified the English nation in the character of John Bull.[10] But the work had indeed begun long before Arbuthnot in the succession of figures who had presented Englishmen to themselves for centuries: John Blunt, John Cheese, John-a-dogs, John-a-nods, John Doe, John Dringle, John-hold-my-staff, John-of-all-trades, John-out-of-office, John Trot, Poor John, John Thomas. There were all manner of ancestors and relatives of John Bull.

The fabrication of the character of John Bull was a great piece of folk art in which there existed an easy relationship between the written and the spoken word. John Bull had stepped out of Arbuthnot's book into full imaginative life as a figure of semi-mythological proportions. He was a figure of fiction not of fact, but a clear demonstration that fiction transcended fact. Bull was a composite of the males of Britain in the past and in the present. They were the millions of facts; he, the supreme fiction, sprang to life as soon as language approached the millions of facts. John Bull was a work of the collective imagination of the English people, a powerful totem of the tribe, one that provided a vehicle and an excuse for the nation's appropriation of certain characteristics, by no means found only in Englishmen and certainly not found in all Englishmen. In this process Irving noted a self-reflexive quality. The English had shaped a selective image of themselves and then gone on to shape themselves towards that image. 'The common orders of English', said Washington Irving,

seem wonderfully captivated with the *beau ideal* which they have formed of John Bull, and endeavor to act up to the broad caricature that is perpetually before their eyes. Unluckily, they sometimes make their boasted Bull-ism an apology for their prejudice or grossness.[11]

For public posturing the Englishman was able then to act out the rôle that had been devised to represent the Englishman to the world at large; the Englishman could impersonate his own personification. This must have been a simple and satisfying rôle to play, a rôle that was called out inevitably by the approaching foreigner, so that the American attempting to discover real Englishmen must invoke the very phantasmagoria that he might wish to dispel. Midway through his characterization of John Bull, in fact, Irving allowed himself to drift away from the fairly standard description with which he had started of the *beau ideal* of the English common orders into a sentimental portrait of the English gentry, creating a figure exactly suited for the picturesque drawing of the English landscape that was projected elsewhere in *The Sketch-book of Geoffrey Crayon*. John Bull, the amalgam of the national oddities, metamorphosized by successive stages into the kind of figure to be represented by Squire Bracebridge of Bracebridge Hall in Irving's next book about England. Irving's John Bull became a representative of the old gentry and lost his deliberately ambiguous placing in the popular image somewhere between yeomanry and gentry. Irving's John Bull became unequivocally a representative of the old agricultural interest with little about him of the new agricultural revolutionary and nothing about him of John Bull, Ironmaster of England. Squire Bracebridge was even to resent the intrusion of the stagecoach into his eternally rural England; he was happily not faced with the railway in 1820, and the John Bull of *The Sketch-book* was already becoming the representative of a dying breed rather than the spokesman for expanding, aggressive interests.

Unlike Irving, Emerson recognized that England was a nation that lived by buying and selling. It has, he said, 'the best commercial position in the world'.[12] It was exactly in this that the English posed themselves in Emerson's view as the people in the world most to be accounted for, most to be understood:

The problem of the traveller landing at Liverpool is Why England is England? What are the elements of that power which the English hold over other nations? If there be one test of national genius universally accepted, it is success; and if there be one successful country in the universe for the last millenium, that country is England.[13]

Implicit in this was a suggestion of a nation that would in the next millenium achieve a yet greater success. England was after all only 'the best of actual nations'.[14] Emerson was an exponent of the oblique compliment even more skilled than Lady Holland. Beyond the picture of the present nation called England and the present beings called the English was the image of a transcendent nation made up of transcendent beings. This notion was not far from Emerson's portrait of idealized Americans who had appeared in essays such as 'Nature', 'Self-Reliance', and 'The American Scholar'. Emerson had too much tact and too much sense to make this point explicitly in *English Traits*. He was in 1848 at least too much of a realist not to have felt keenly how far short America and Americans fell of the ideals that this rhetoric presented as most worthy of them. But it was the unstated message of *English Traits* quite as much as it was the overt statement of the essays that America and Americans were the best of potential nations and peoples.

In this play between the actual and the potential lay an explanation of both the admiration and the contempt that the American traveller might simultaneously express for England and the English. The concealed pride of these writers, not always so concealed, was a stratagem for negotiating the mixture of reactions provoked in the cultivated nineteenth-century traveller by the encounter with English culture and society. The contrast with the meagre resources of the culture and society that the American traveller had left behind him threatened self-confidence and identity. It was said of Benjamin West that he suffered a nervous breakdown for six months when he went from Boston to Rome in 1760. To protect himself from the kind of collapse that had overwhelmed Benjamin West, the commonplace traveller had the resource of a more fully developed philistinism that would reduce to manageable proportions if not entirely subdue the rush of what Henry James called 'High Civilisation'. By the evidence of their journals and letters, it was plain that this was a liability to which Emerson, Hawthorne and James himself were prone. For these were men of unusual sensibility. But while James allowed himself to suffer, Emerson and Hawthorne co-opted the past by identifying with the achievements of the English as a race, and saw England's great men as America's great men too, and they co-opted the future as one which would exclude the English, since what was promised by the achieved past would be actualized by an American future. Having dealt with past and future satisfactorily, the traveller put up with the discomforts of the present as best he could.

American boasting about the future was a register of considerable anxiety about the meaning of the present, a need to resist potentially negative interpretations of the apparent inadequacies of American culture and society by contrast with European, especially English, culture and society. The concealed pride, then, about the superiority of the American and the American nation was, in addition to whatever else it might be, an expression of a concealed fear of the inferiority of the American and the American nation. When the traveller's sensibility or intelligence forbade the resort to the patriotic stratigems of past and future co-option, he admitted the full impact of the perceived inferiority. This entailed a psychological passage of great painfulness before the traveller, usually artist or writer, could begin to reassert himself. Only then could he make use of the cultural riches with which he had been so grievously burdened. Such a passage as that which Benjamin West travelled

in the eighteenth century, Henry James travelled in the nineteenth century, and T. S. Eliot travelled in the twentieth. It was perhaps not coincidence that they none of them ever returned permanently to America. This was an exile not easily imagined for Ralph Waldo Emerson. 'I do not wish', wrote Emerson in his journal in London in the March of 1848, 'to be mistaken for an Englishman, more than I wish Monadnock or Nahant, or Nantucket to be mistaken for Wales or the Isle of Wight.'[15] This more than love of the American scene, this merging of self and landscape, was not something to be found in Henry James. And just as loving Nantucket in the way that he did left Emerson quite able to love the Isle of Wight, so he was able to like the English along with liking his own people, the Americans. He was not driven to repudiate either, though it still remained the fact that the idealized man, the man of the future, was for Emerson to be born in Monadnock and not by the Solent.

A more coarse patriotism like that of James Fenimore Cooper was led to repudiate the England that challenged its assumptions. Such a mind frequently presumed the arrival in America of the higher type for which Emerson only called. Cooper was no transcendentalist, but a transcendent being was the hero of the travel book about his own country that Cooper published in 1828. Remarkably, he passed if off as an account of an Englishman's tour of the United States in 1824. He called it *Notions of the Americans: Picked up by a Travelling Bachelor*. It was published in Philadelphia in two volumes by Carey, Lea and Carey. The title page carried no author's name. The hero of this travel book was an American named John Cadwallader. It is appropriate to speak of the book as having a hero because Cooper's *Notions* had about it much of the novel. The narrator, supposedly an Englishman, met Cadwallader in London. He was so impressed by the character of 'this calm, reasoning American' that, he told his readers,

> I early became alive to the desire of examining a state
> of society, which I am fond of believing, must have
> had some influence in giving birth to so much indepen-
> dence and manlines of thought.[16]

Cooper created in his English character the respect for the American character that in life Cooper had not found the English willing to give to his own character. Of Cooper and *Notions of the Americans,* Van Wyck Brooks wrote:

> He had hoped in this book to correct, in the eyes of
> Europeans, the errors which their own travellers had
> spread about [America], and the American readers, as
> Matthew Carey the publisher said, appeared to prefer
> the sneers of Basil Hall.[17]

American readers were absolutely right to prefer Basil Hall's *Travels in North America, in the Years 1827 and 1828,* if only because it was racy, engrossing and immediate where Cooper's *Notions* was pious, repellent and distant. This was perhaps the final proof that *Notions . . . Picked up By a Travelling Bachelor* was not what it claimed to be: all travel books are readable but this one is not. However, despite the preference of the American readership and subsequent readerships for Hall's work, Cooper was as much entitled to his fictions about national character as was Basil Hall. Hall's portraiture of the American was exactly that designed to satisfy the rabid class fantasies that excited his imagination as much as that of his readers. The very claim to social equality with the English upper classes that Cooper was so anxious to establish for himself was exactly the claim that most angered Hall when he met with it in the general society of Boston, New York and other great cities of the Atlantic seaboard. What the upper-class English traveller found in America were the manners and values of just the group that they most disliked and in some senses feared in England—the urbanizing, industrializing middle class. In England at least, this class met with every kind of social snub, but in the United States it had occupied the high ground.

The claim made the English traveller asthmatic and it distorted his vision of American society as if the atmosphere had been poisoned. For Basil Hall proper vision was only restored in North America when he crossed the border into Canada. 'The air we breathed seemed different', he wrote,

> the sky, the land, the whole scenery, appeared to be altered; and I must say, that of all the changes I have ever made in a life of ceaseless locomotion, I have seldom been consious of any transit from one country to another more striking than this.[18]

This claim was preposterous, though attractively so. Other British travellers did not in fact go as far as Hall, but there were many who felt as he did the relief of crossing from the United States to Canada and from a society in which they must remain ever socially vigilant into one in which the priorities of aristocratic value were guaranteed in such a way that they might breathe freely.

The middle-class Fanny Trollope felt justified in being as arrogant in her condemnation of American manners as the upper-class Halls. Though they might not have met her socially, she was strong in their defence when the Halls came under attack in both America and England for their behaviour in the United States. 'Such a downright thorough-going tory and anti-reformer', wrote Fanny Trollope of Basil Hall, 'pretending to judge the workings of the American democratical system was naturally held to be a monstrous abomination.'[19] Fanny Trollope exonerated the Halls and went on herself to adopt the rôle of 'a downright thorough-going tory and anti-reformer' in order to insult the Americans just as

thoroughly in *Domestic Manners of the Americans,* published in London in 1832 and pirated in New York in the same year. The book was as popular with the Americans as Hall's *North America*; in fact it sold even more rapidly.

As if to repudiate the frivolous tone and social partiality of this body of travel literature of which Hall's and Trollope's books were only the most successful, Harriet Martineau announced herself on the title page of her three volume study *Society in America* as the author of *Illustrations of Political Economy*; in 1837 this identified her as a student of the discipline of Adam Smith, David Ricardo, Jeremy Bentham, James Mill and John Stuart Mill. She went to America well prepared to explore and present its political, social, economic and moral reality. She was in Allan Nevins's words, 'the most thorough student of American life and institutions in the decade that we think of as a period of British abuse'.[20] However, this social scientist's evaluation of the American people was one that owed a more than common debt to the rhetoric of the Romantic imagination. 'I regard', said Harriet Martineau,

> the American people as a great embryo poet: now moody, now wild, but bringing out results of absolute good sense: restless and wayward in action, but with deep peace at his heart: exulting that he has caught the true aspect of things past, and at the depth of futurity which lies before him, wherein to create something so magnificent as the world has scarcely begun to dream of.[21]

And that on page thirty-nine of the first of three volumes.

No less than was John Cadwallader a projection of Cooper's idealized self was this wild and prophetic poet an image of Martineau's idealized self, unusual only because, in that decade of British abuse, it was uncommon for a British writer to project herself or himself positively through the image of the American type. Much more common, of course, was the projection of some degraded and repellent self that could be felt to threaten the equilibrium of women and men like the Halls and Fanny Trollope. Harriet Martineau's was a beginning of serious attempts by sympathetic British commentators to provide honest, in subsequent terminology, objective descriptions of the American character. As such her work was an anticipation of the work to be done at the end of the century by James Bryce. And in the final failure of either Martineau or Bryce to identify the American national characteristics, there lay an indication of the difficulty of the task, if not an indication that it was a task improperly conceived.

In order to clear his ground and define his subject, Bryce was to begin with a narrowing definition of the American nation

And when I speak of the nation, I mean the native Americans. What follows is not applicable to the recent immigrants from Europe, and of course, even less applicable to the Southern negroes.[22]

The starting point of the exclusions was on the basis of what Bryce called 'hereditary race character'.[23] In rhetorical terms, this was to establish a special relationship between the writer and the presumed reader. The relationship was immediately recognized and reciprocated by his American readership. Woodrow Wilson acknowledged it in his review of *The American Commonwealth* written for the *Political Science Quarterly* of 1889. Mr. Byrce, 'is', said Wilson, 'an English constitutional statesman, knowing the parent stock from which . . . our institutions sprang'.[24] And the identification continued through John Graham Brooks's more popular estimate in 1910 of Bryce as America's 'Greatest Critic'.[25] As Allan Nevins put it in 1923, 'To Americans he never seemed an alien even after he received his title.'[26] His value for this line of American commentary had been expressed in Woodrow Wilson's original review, and it continued to be made whenever Bryce's evaluation of the American character was contrasted with that of Alexis de Tocqueville. '[Bryce's] conspicuous merit consists, indeed', Wilson had written,

in perceiving that democracy is not a cause but an effect, in seeing that our politics are no explanation of our character, but that our character, rather is the explanation of our politics.[27]

What Bryce had to say about the national characteristics of the inhabitants of the United States was least applicable, he said, to the Southern negroes. What Bryce had to say about these people demonstrated only too clearly the pitfalls of national or racial portrait. 'The average negro is a naturally thoughtless, light-hearted, kindly, easy-going being', he wrote in one of several similar passages in the hundred or more pages that he gave to the 'question of colour'.[28] The contemplation of such a being as the average negro drove from Bryce's estimate the sum of his own personal observations, particularly when they contradicted the received view of the subject. It was just then when he, like other writers, rose to the challenge of taking on the great subject that his sight failed him and he began to rely on the views of others to represent what he had seen with his own eyes. And indeed he had not with his own eyes ever seen 'an average negro' but only some hundreds or thousands of individual negroes.

In exactly this way, the most prepared of British observers and certainly the most diligent of British recorders failed to see with his own eyes when he came to describe that even more numerous being, the 'average American'. The myriad of acute and penetrating observations that Bryce accumulated through the length of his two volumes synthesized into something quite different when he came to write Chapter LXXX of Volume 2, a chapter that he called 'National Characteristics', the chapter in which he made the grand statement of the American type. It was not a particularly long statement, after all it was a summary of what had already been worked out in several hundred pages; now, in the space of twelve pages Bryce identified thirteen characteristics, beginning by saying 'the Americans are a good-natured people'[29] and ending by saying that 'The Americans are a conservative people.'[30] In between, he said that they were as a people humorous, hopeful, educated, moral and well-conducted, religious, unreverential, busy, commercial, impressionable, unsettled, changeful. For each characteristic he provided a couple of paragraphs of elaboration and qualification, especially where he found himself attributing to the Americans characteristics that might appear to contradict one another, as for instance by saying that the American people were both religious and unreverential, or that they were both changeful and conservative. What emerged was a description of the American people that might have been deduced from a study of the engravings of Currier and Ives, but lacking the dash and colour of the prints. Bryce worked the Americans up into an industrious, cheerful and sober form. The list of characteristics was remarkable for having no vices but it was also remarkable for having no heroic virtues either. While the image was not in a simple sense untrue, any more than the collected works of Currier and Ives could be said to be untrue, the image was not true either. It was above all disappointing that that was all that could be said after so much hard labour.

Bryce's sense of fairness had led him to explain to their causes the vices of the Americans. His method in dealing with Tammany, the Gas Ring, and other scandals across America had been to show how such corruptions were inevitable within the given social and historical conditions. That is, they would have happened to any peoples so placed. Bryce could not bring himself to explain the virtues of the Americans in the same interesting fashion because that would have been to explain those virtues away. He would have had to contradict the implicit belief in the virtues of the Anglo-Saxon peoples, a pattern reinforced by his habit of ascribing much of the vice in the country to the presence of peoples of different racial origins. The spread of virtue, like that of vice, was restrictive: 'They are also—and here again I mean the people of native American stock—. . . on the whole, a religious people.'[31] The people of native American stock were to be given the benefit of several kinds of doubt, as the subversion of the phrase 'on the whole' suggested. What this kind of portraiture was able to suggest was no more than the image with which the native American stock used to comfort itself. Just as the American traveller was driven to reproduce the portrait of John Bull, so the English traveller was driven to reproduce the portrait of a figure very close to Uncle Sam. The portraits could be repro-duced with more or less sympathy, but it was beyond the power of any of these travel writers to go outside the bold lines of cartoon.

The generalizations were verbalizations of stereotypes and preconceptions about peoples and nations. They re-peated what had been said by many travellers before and were to be said by many after. Travellers' generali-zations were as much verbalizations of verbalizations as records of personal observations. In the final pages of *England,* for instance, Cooper wrote:

> But, putting all theory out of the question neither the English nor the Americans have the air and manner of a happy people, like the French and the Italians. The first have a sullen, thoughtful look, as if distrustful of the future, which gives one the idea that their enjoy-ments are deferred to a more favourable opportunity; while the two last seem to live as time goes on.[32]

This was fairly disappointing from a man who knew three at least of these countries and three at least of these people pretty well by the time he came up with this conclusion—the ancient opposition of Catholic and Protestant, of Latin and Anglo-Saxon. But it is difficult to conceive of Cooper or Bryce, Emerson or Martineau, being able to come up with any other kinds of generali-zations.

It is also difficult to know in any final way whether these platitudes conceal or whether they reveal a truth. Was the truth so evident that generations of writers were forced to the same conclusions with every re-examination of the evidence, or had re-examination of the evidence been precluded by the frame of reference, the formulation of the questions and the descriptive lan-guage available to the traveller? To some extent, the traveller might be at a greater disadvantage because he was on foreign ground than the thinker who stayed at home and came to the very same conclusions by way of books. The empirical tradition's contempt for scholastic inquiry as against direct observation would work to the advantage of the armchair traveller here. He at least would know that his judgement was suspect and that his generalizations were at a dangerous remove from reality. The transatlantic traveller showed no awareness that speech, just like writing, came between conscious-ness and reality to deter and to defer meaning. The so-cial scene was a text and as layered and as ambiguous and as dangerous to the innocent inquirer as any pal-impsest. Henry David Thoreau, who never left North America, preferring to read travel books instead, had certainly as much to tell the reader about the English, the Americans, the French and the Italians as James Fenimore Cooper in the generalizing sections of the *Gleanings in Europe* or James Bryce in those of *The American Commonwealth*. The social scientist and the novelist alike reached for the rhetorical devices of fic-

tion when undertaking the task of describing a people. And it must be added that those portraits penned in vin-dictiveness and ignorance were no less accurate and frequently far more entertaining than those penned in generosity and knowledge.

Fiction is in many respects an alternative mode to travel literature. A disproportionately large number of those travellers, both American and British, whose books about England and America have been among the most widely read have been themselves better known as imaginative writers, especially as writers of the short story and the novel. Washington Irving and James Feni-more Cooper at the beginning of the nineteenth century were to be matched in this rôle by Mark Twain and Henry James at the end of the century. Charles Dickens and Anthony Trollope were two English commentators better known as novelists. Fanny Trollope, following the success of *Domestic Manners,* her first book, went on to become a novelist almost as prolific as her son. Even Basil Hall wrote a novel. Further, they were prone to use their journeys not only as the basis of a travel book but also as the raw material for declared fiction. Where this happened, the closest links between fiction and travelogue could be pursued. The significance of this link between novel and travel book must nonethe-less be carefully questioned, if the inference must be that the fictionalization of national character was taking place because the men and women writing the descrip-tions were novelists and short-story writers. The case of John Bull, that masterpiece of folk art in the practice of national portraiture, suggested that mythopoesis came into play as soon as the subject of national characteris-tics was taken up. The subject matter of a people was one that destabilized scientific discourse at the same time that it provoked imaginative expression, first by requiring modes designed to subvert rational apprehen-sion and then by drawing upon emotion depths that forced the ego into unacknowledged declaration. The novelists were merely more adept, it might be argued, at controlling the business of putting upon the written page the process that inevitably involved the structuring fictions.

Notes

1. Benjamin Silliman, *A Journal of Travels in En-gland* (New Haven: Converse, 1820), Vol. 2, p. 93.

2. James Fenimore Cooper, *Gleanings in Europe: England,* ed. Robert Spiller (New York: Oxford University Press, 1930), p. 120.

3. Van Wyck Brooks, *The World of Washington Irv-ing* (London: Dent, 1945), p. 256.

4. Cooper, p. xxi.

5. Cooper, pp. 70-72.

6. Cooper, p. 290.

7. Margaret Hunter Hall, *The Aristocratic Journey,* ed. Una Pope Hennessey (London, 1931), p. 21.

8. Cooper, p. 375.

9. Washington Irving, *The Sketch-Book of Geoffrey Crayon, Gent.,* Knickerbocker Press Standard Library Edition, Vol. 3 (New York: G. P. Putnam, no date), pp. 433-34.

10. See John Arbuthnot, *The History of John Bull,* ed. A. W. Bower and R. A. Erickson, (Oxford: Clarendon Press, 1976), pp. 5-20.

11. Irving, p. 432.

12. R. W. Emerson, *English Traits* (Boston: Phillips, Sampson, 1856), p. 47.

13. Emerson, *Traits,* p. 41.

14. Emerson, *Traits,* p. 298.

15. R. W. Emerson, *The Heart of Emerson's Journals,* ed. Bliss Perry, (Boston: Houghton, Mifflin, 1926), p. 229.

16. [James Fenimore Cooper], *Notions of the Americans: Picked Up by a Travelling Bachelor* (Philadelphia: Carey, Lea and Carey, 1828), p. 3.

17. Van Wyck Brooks, *Washington Irving,* p. 263.

18. Basil Hall, *Travels in North America* (Edinburgh: Cadell, 1830), Vol. 1, p. 193.

19. Frances Trollope, *Domestic Manners of the Americans* (London: Whittaker, Treacher; New York: rept. for the Booksellers, 1832), p. 290.

20. Allan Nevins (ed.), *American Social History: As Recorded by British Travellers* (New York: Holt, 1923), p. 138.

21. Harriet Martineau, *Society in America* (London: Saunders and Otley, 1837), Vol. 1, p. 39.

22. James Bryce, *The American Commonwealth* (New York: Macmillan, 1921), Vol. 2, p. 285.

23. Bryce, Vol. 2, p. 486.

24. Woodrow Wilson, 'Bryce's *American Commonwealth*', *Political Science Quarterly,* 4 (1889), 154-55.

25. J. G. Brooks, *As Others See Us* (New York: Macmillan, 1910), p. 249.

26. Nevins, p. 537.

27. Wilson, p. 165.

28. Bryce, Vol. 2, p. 554.

29. Bryce, Vol. 2, p. 285.

30. Bryce, Vol. 2, p. 295.

31. Bryce, Vol. 2, pp. 289-90.

32. Cooper, *England,* p. 359.

Charisse Gendron (essay date spring 1991)

SOURCE: Gendron, Charisse. "Images of Middle-Eastern Women in Victorian Travel Books." *The Victorian Newsletter,* no. 79 (spring 1991): 18-23.

[*In the following essay, Gendron concentrates on how the "sexual politics—what he or she considers to be the proper role of women"—of Alexander Kinglake, Eliot Warburton, Harriet Martineau, and Lucie Duff Gordon affected these authors' treatment of Middle Eastern women in their travel writings.*]

Nearly all Victorian travelers to Egypt, Turkey, and Arabia addressed the issue of the condition of Middle-Eastern women. As Eliot Warburton put it in *The Crescent and the Cross* (1844), foreign women are the first item of interest "to the moralist as well as the epicurean" abroad (1: 59). Some Western travelers—Lamartine, Flaubert, Warburton himself—were indeed epicureans, and today must face the charges of those who see the history of "Orientalism" as one in which the West attempted to recreate the East as a fantasy of the exotic Other. According to this analysis, announced in Edward Said's *Orientalism,* the male traveler's sense of boundless adventure in journeying to the Middle East, where he sheds his inhibitions and tests his will, is epitomized in his freedom to consider as sex objects women towards whom he bears no social responsibility (188-90, 207-08, 309). In any case, he encounters in the Middle-Eastern woman one whom he has already possessed, erotically and culturally, through Western appropriation of the tales of the Arabian Nights. As Algerian writer Malek Alloula suggests, however, the epicurean's gaze meets resistance in the practices of the harem and the veil, a resistance that generates in him an obsession to penetrate the obstacles to his desire (7, 14).

This analysis implies that the Victorian traveler's view of Middle-Eastern women ·will be colored by both his nation's sense of manifest destiny in the East and by his own sexuality, unleashed by the encounter with the exotic Other and by the opportunity in writing to refashion the encounter according to the requirements of his fantasy. In general terms, I accept this analysis; as I hope to show, however, from a literary point of view the analysis becomes most interesting when we look at travel books by women as well as men and see that no absolute national ideology and no single personal sexuality exist, but rather variations that produce significantly different images of women.

And what of the other category of travelers for whom women are the primary item of interest, according to Warburton? These are the moralists, whose concerns in the Middle East are with the institutions of slavery and polygamy. Florence Nightingale and Harriet Martineau are clear examples of this category, although the categories do not always remain distinct. The Victorian interest in the Woman Question at home and slavery in America lead even such epicureans as Warburton to make judgments about the harem system. Travelers with a moral agenda difficult to separate from a political agenda, particularly missionaries and colonial administrators, have of course received their share of anti-orientalist criticism. Barbara Harlow, for example, writes of colonial European efforts to discourage the practices of suttee in India, female circumcision in Kenya, and veiling in Algeria and Iran as attempts "to collaborate with the women under the pretext of liberating them from oppression by their own men" (Alloula xviii). And, since critics tend to argue that "professional Orientalism" is inseparable from "personal" or literary descriptions of the Middle east (Said 157), I am not surprised to find Leila Ahmed, in a recent article in *Feminist Studies,* categorizing people who disapprove of harems, from the seventeenth-century traveler George Sandys to American feminists of the 1980's, as Western ethnocentrists.

Although neither Alloula, Harlow, Said, nor Ahmed reproves Harriet Martineau specifically, their arguments might easily include her. Ahmed, for instance, insists that enthnocentrism prevents Westerners from seeing that the segregation of women from the world of men may oppress women less than the integration of women in a man's world (528). Martineau, who worked for women's education and against slavery and prostitution, did not see the harem as a space defined by women for women, and Ahmed herself admits that for Middle-Eastern women "it is . . . impossible, in an environment already so negatively primed against us, to be freely critical—a task no less urgent for us than for Western feminists—of our own societies" (527). Her defense of traditional Islamic social structure is implicitly refuted by turn-of-the-century Egyptian feminist and nationalist Huda Shaarawi, who, according to her memoir *Harem Years,* incorporated Western thinking into her political campaigns to abolish the veil as well as to achieve for Egypt autonomy from Western Europe (7, 99, 112, 130).

Rather than to reject Victorian moralists out of hand as culturally prejudiced or worse, I believe that the more interesting endeavor is to see how they contribute to an ongoing dialogue among Western and Eastern writers over the sometimes competing claims of feminism and nationalism. As with the epicureans', the moralists' judgments are not monolithic; they depend, not only on a writer's national ideology and personal sexuality, but upon his or her sexual politics—what he or she considers to be the proper role of women. Although sometimes these determining factors only can be inferred, let

me attempt to analyze how they shape images of women in the books of four Victorians in the Middle East: Alexander Kinglake, Eliot Warburton, Harriet Martineau, and Lucie Duff Gordon.

As a young man recently down from Cambridge in 1834, Alexander Kinglake toured the Middle East. Ten years later, he published an account of his experiences in a travel book that is, as the preface boasts, "quite superficial in its character," "thoroughly free" "from all display of 'sound learning and religious knowledge'" (*Eothen* xxi-xxii). *Eothen* made a sensation, and is still classed with Lady Mary Wortley Montagu's letters from Turkey and Sterne's *A Sentimental Journey* as a gem among travel books. Also in 1844, Kinglake published "The Rights of Women," an ironical review of Richard Monckton Milnes's poetic defense of the harem, *Palm Leaves.* Kinglake's familiar tone in this review, in which he teases the poet abut his mustachios, suggests that he knew Milnes as a member of the London literary world where Kinglake was welcomed for his conversation. Among his personal friends were Lucie Duff Gordon, the poet Bryan Procter and his wife Anne (known for her wit as "Our Lady of Bitterness"), and Caroline Norton, a writer who used her scandalous separation from her husband to publicize the injustice to women of England's marriage and property laws (Rose 182-83). Kinglake himself never married. In *Eothen,* he brings to his description of Middle-Eastern women a taste for the company of intelligent women with liberal views, as well as a bachelor's playful gallantry, quite another thing from desire.

To understand fully Kinglake's attitude towards the harem system, which puts women at an intellectual and moral disadvantage by denying them knowledge and freedom of choice, we must consider his ideal of social intercourse between men and women. This ideal is a battle of wits. In "The Rights of Women," for instance, where he proceeds from the harem to women at home, he encourages his countrywomen to abandon the pursuit of "Nothing" as a topic of conversation in favor of literary debate, which he envisions as an intellectual skirmish with erotic overtones: "how good for the taste and judgment, how stimulative of the intellect, how favourable for the love of fairness and fair play, is the gentle strife thus provoked!" (119). Kinglake, in this respect typical of the men who built the British empire, loves a challenge: in *Eothen* he tells us that he traveled to the East to strengthen his will (xxvi). The desert tests his will, but Eastern society, particularly intercourse with women, provides no challenge. "Behind me I left . . . women hushed, and swathed, and turned into waxen dolls—love flown, and in its stead mere royal, and 'Paradise' pleasures," he writes at the close of his journey, when he again faces the West. "Before me there waited glad bustle and strife—love itself, an emulous game—religion a cause and a controversy, well smitten and well defended . . . wheels going—steam buzzing—a mortal race, and a slashing pace, and the devil take the hindmost" (355-56). Kinglake prizes the "emulous game" of love, with no insistence that it lead on to paradisal pleasures. The harem system of sequestration and surveillance, by eliminating a woman's choice as to whether she will remain faithful to her spouse, puts an end to the game. "Now it is not of course by establishing a rivalry between husbands and lovers that domestic happiness is to be secured," Kinglake concedes in the review of *Palm Leaves,* "but still, when the wholesome *possibility* of rousing emulation is excluded by brutal force, the subjection and humiliation of woman are complete" ("Rights" 99). Subjected and humiliated, Kinglake opines, women are no fun.

Kinglake earns the modern reader's admiration by standing up to the demand by Mrs. Sarah Stickney Ellis, author of Victorian conduct books, that women practice self-abnegation in the service of husband and children. "We are made up of our foibles and faults," he writes in a section of "The Rights of Women" devoted to Ellis's tracts *The Women of England . . .* and *The Wives of England . . . ,* "and to destroy all these one after the other is to extinguish sweet human nature—to efface us from out of the earth" (120). Kinglake's equal disapprobation of the Victorian angel and the Oriental odalisque reminds us that the first has merely consented to internalize the suppression externalized in the harem system. He reserves his approval for women who resist being turned into wax dolls, for instance the "romping girls of Bethlehem" described in *Eothen.* In this perhaps fictionalized account, the Christian girls are free of both the modest veil that paradoxically marks the Moslem woman as a sex object and of the unnaturally confined manners of the English drawing room. "[I]f you will only look virtuous enough to prevent alarm, and vicious enough to avoid looking silly," Kinglake writes,

> the blithe maidens will draw nearer and nearer to you. . . . And if they catch a glimpse of your ungloved fingers, then . . . will they make the air ring with their sweet screams of delight and amazement, as they compare the fairness of your hand with the hues of your sunburnt face, or with their own warmer tints. . . . And when they see you, even then, still sage and gentle the joyous girls will suddenly, and screamingly, and all at once, explain to each other that you are surely quite harmless and innocent—a lion that makes no spring—a bear that never hugs. . . . But the one—the fairest and the sweetest of all, is yet the most timid: she shrinks from the daring deeds of her playmates. . . . But her laughing sisters will have none of this cowardice; . . . they seize her small wrist and drag her forward by force, and at last . . . they vanquish her utmost modesty, and marry her hand to yours. The quick pulse springs from her fingers and throbs like a whisper upon your listening palm.
>
> (207-10)

Of course, while praising the innocently bold girls of Bethlehem, Kinglake mildly satirizes them; they are *farouche,* not quite rational creatures. Even so, the passage celebrates gentle strife between near-equals, in which man, with his advantages of physique, education, and worldly experience, agrees to be "a bear that never hugs," and woman, though compelled to join hands, retains a certain wildness, a "quick pulse" indicative of independent life.

Similar to the game here described between man and woman is the game Kinglake plays with his audience, in which he again acts the part of the bear, although he never hugs. His irreverent approach to sacred Victorian topics, including womanhood and religion, raised eyebrows. John Murray refused to publish the manuscript, and Eliot Warburton, to whom the book is dedicated, warned in a review of it that the author goes rather far (56). Yet while Kinglake makes use of a rhetoric of wickedness, of seduction and betrayal, he actually insinuates nothing base. The description of the romping girls of Bethlehem, for instance, sports with the notion of sexual compromise in the tradition of *The Rape of the Lock* and *A Sentimental Journey,* a tradition appreciated by women like Lucie Duff Gordon, sophisticated and virtuous, who had nothing but praise for *Eothen* (71).

His love of the game assures that Kinglake will endorse freedom for women; it also assures that he will never be completely serious. In "The Rights of Women," sounding very much like John Stuart Mill, Kinglake asserts that "[m]en may have in their helpmate the virtues enforced by compulsion, or the virtues that spring from free will, but they cannot have both" (106). But he gives a skeptical twist to the distinction between freely willed and compulsory virtue in *Eothen,* where he plays on the cliché of the veiled woman's increased opportunities to sin:

> She turns, and turns again, and carefully glances around her on all sides, to see that she is safe from the eyes of Mussulmans, and then suddenly withdrawing the *yashmak,* she shines upon your heart and soul with all the pomp and might of her beauty. . . . She sees, and exults in your giddiness—she sees and smiles; then, presently, with a sudden movement, she lays her blushing fingers upon your arm, and cries "Yumourdjak!" (Plague! meaning, "There is a present of the plague for you!")
>
> (41-42)

This *femme fatale* seems to embody the fear of death Kinglake confesses to have suppressed while sojourning in plague-ridden Cairo (244). His more overt intention is comically to defame the image, perpetrated by Milnes's poem *Palm Leaves,* of the Middle Eastern woman as the cloistered beloved, source of solace and inspiration for her world-weary husband. The poem goes wrong from the start, as Kinglake points out in his review, by taking the "audacious poetical licence" of occupying its harem with but a single wife. By "importing into Mahometan countries a system of strict monogamy," Milnes sentimentalizes the harem and, implicitly, the subjection of women (106-07). Although the description of the hypocritical, malicious veiled woman in *Eothen* seems less flattering than that of Milnes's wife, Kinglake, in his review, assumes the Middle-Eastern woman's perspective sufficiently to see that, as one of several wives or concubines, she could hardly enjoy the crucial position in the home afforded her by Milnes. He prefers the hard-headed account of another traveler to the region, Mrs. Poole, who, "[a]t the very time that our bard was wandering on the banks of the Nile, as blind as Homer . . . was visiting many a hareem, and carefully counting the wives" (108).

The test of a traveler's attitude towards women is his or her description of those who make no attempt to charm: old or work-worn women; women who dress or act like men; savage women whose arts, if any, are alien to the traveler. While Kinglake advocates a kind of equality in social interactions between men and women, he—like most Victorians, notably Ruskin—prefers that women remain different from men, that they be traditionally feminine. In unveiled Bedouin women, for instance, who work like pack animals but carry themselves like free beings, he finds that

> [t]he awful haggardness that gave something of character to the faces of the men was sheer ugliness in the poor women. It is a great shame, but the truth is, that except when we refer to the beautiful devotion of the mother to her child, all the fine things we say and think about women apply only to those who are tolerably good-looking or graceful. These Arab women . . . may have been good women enough . . . but they had so grossly neglected the prime duty of looking pretty in this transitory life that I could not at all forgive them.
>
> (218-19)

I, for one, forgive Kinglake for attending to the prime duty in this transitory life of being amusing and self-ironic, even while confessing his gravest sins. Among male Victorian travelers to the Middle East, I can think of only one—Charles Doughty—who does not display a double standard which makes women whom the writer considers unattractive less human than men. Curiously, this reaction seems to have less to do with sex than with ideology, since writers express it when sex would not seem to be in question. The homosexual Edward Lear, for instance, in the wilds of Albania, describes a group of women who dress and work like men as "unfeminine and disagreeable," even though their eyes express "something pensive and pleasing" (104-05). And the feminist Florence Nightingale, sailing up the Nile in 1849, associates the unfeminine—nakedness, indecorum—with the demonic: "Four Ethiopian women, per-

fectly black, were washing in the river, dancing on the clothes like imps, not with movements like human creatures" (87). Kinglake does not go so far as Nightingale in expressing the fear of chaos underlying the double standard; he simply admits, in his role of "man about town" in the Middle East, that he is prejudiced against plain women. Yet this role itself seems to mask anxieties about the nature of women, glimpsed in Kinglake's comment that the confinement of women in harems was a logical outcome of "forty centuries experience of the married state" in the Middle East ("Rights" 95).

If part of my argument is that art, as represented by Kinglake's persona, can absorb a certain amount of political incorrectness, I shall attempt to prove it further by Eliot Warburton's negative example. His *The Crescent and the Cross* was published the same year as *Eothen,* imitates *Eothen* in content and style, and yet offends where *Eothen* delights. Warburton, whose cautious review of *Eothen* strikes me as hypocritical, lacks Kinglake's distancing irony, and manages in *The Crescent and the Cross* to be heavy-handed as both epicurean and moralist. Describing slaves in the market he echoes Kinglake's phrase about wax dolls to compliment English women at the expense of Georgians and Circassians: "The sunny hair and heaven-blue eyes, that in England produce such an angel-like and intellectual effect, seemed to me here mere flax and beads; and I left them to the 'turbaned Turk' without a sigh" (1: 56). Warburton's fondness for English angels, compared to Kinglake's zest for "love . . . an emulous game," blunts the point of the comparison between free women and slaves, and sounds sanctimonious. But he reveals his latent cynicism towards both Western and Middle-Eastern women—a grosser form of Kinglake's sexual skepticism—in the further comment: "As for the Georgian and Circassian beauties . . . their only ambition, like that of many fair maidens in happier lands, is to fetch a high price; and their only hope is to be first favorite in the hareem—*whose* hareem they care not" (1: 57).

Warburton seems to conflate two episodes from *Eothen* in his description of the young Christian women of Damascus who come to the Franciscan convent to confess, "which," Warburton says with a leer, "if their tongue be as candid as their eloquent eyes, must be rather a protracted business" (2: 156). His flock of "fair penitents" recalls Kinglake's romping girls of Bethlehem, while his insinuation that the women use their veils to entice men "while wandering about these cloisters, waiting till the little confessional is vacant, or, perchance, until they have more to say to its cowled occupant," suggests Kinglake's Cairene *femme fatale.* Warburton, however, imagines wickedness only in terms of sexual license, and parades his fair penitents like prostitutes. Posing as a satirist, Warburton reveals himself as a sensualist, never more so than when he broaches the topic of the unfeminine woman. He describes the typical Arab woman in the market place as "an ugly, old, sun-scorched hag, with a skin like a hippopotamus, and a veil-snout like an elephant's trunk; her scanty robe scarcely serving the purpose of a girdle; her hands, feet, and forehead tattooed of a smoke color; and there is scarcely a more hideous spectacle on earth" (1: 69). This seems an elaboration of Kinglake's description of the Bedouin woman, but, where Kinglake then disarms the reader by admitting the injustice of judging women according to sexual criteria, Warburton aggravates the offense by continuing: "But the Lady of the Hareem, on the other hand—couched gracefully on a rich Persian carpet strewn with soft pillowy cushions—is as rich a picture as admiration ever gazed on."

If Kinglake's art neutralizes much of the nationalist and sexist aggression of which Victorian travelers stand accused, and which are more clearly exposed in Warburton, we cannot defend Harriet Martineau's *Eastern Life, Present and Past,* published in 1848 when she was forty-six, on the grounds of art. Martineau wrote to inform and persuade rather than to entertain, although she sometimes used fiction to illustrate a point. The sister of Unitarian minister James Martineau, her early interest in religion survives as moral fervor in her travel books condemning slavery in America and the harem system in Cairo and Damascus. Her feminism, which derived force from her moral training but which also sprang from her own wide interests and achievements, made her question the acquiescence of other women in the assumption that their sex should be concerned exclusively with love and marriage. She questioned this assumption in the novels of Charlotte Brontë as she did in the lives of women in the harem. Her contemporary Lucie Duff Gordon suggests in *Letters from Egypt* (1865) that Martineau's opinions blinded her to the humanity of the Egyptians, so that "the difference of manners is a sort of impassable gulf, the truth being that their feelings and passions are just like our own. . . . [H]er attack upon hareems [is] outrageous; she implies that they are brothels" (120-21). Undeniably, Martineau's puritanical streak jaundiced her view of the harems so invitingly depicted by her worldly eighteenth-century predecessor, Lady Mary Wortley Montagu. At the same time, I disagree with Duff Gordon that Martineau failed to see an important reality of women's lives in the Middle East of the last century. Her analysis of the relationship between slavery, polygamy, and the harem is acute. She never implies that a harem is literally a brothel, but Duff Gordon is correct if she means that to Martineau the distinction between concubinage and prostitution would be slight.

Martineau's prudery seems to mark her as a insular traveler, as when she dismisses Egyptian female dancing as a "disagreeable and foolish wriggle" (250). Such remarks seem less arbitrary, however, if we see them as part of a larger reaction against what she saw as the over-sexualization of women's lives under the harem system. By any account, the structure of the harem defines women as sexual property and discourages them from the pursuit of learning that might allow them to redefine themselves. "[T]he only idea of their whole lives," Martineau complains, "is that which, with all our interests and engagements, we consider too prominent with us. . . . There cannot be a woman of them all who is not dwarfed and withered in mind and soul by being kept wholly engrossed with that one interest" (263-64). Not all readers will share Martineau's apparent lack of interest in sex, but some will pause thoughtfully over her assertion that the master's eunuchs, who are both his slaves and surrogates, not only bully the women of the harem but frequently establish emotional and physical intimacy with them (265). If this is true—and Huda Shaarawi attests to the bullying part at least (39-40)—harem women are rehearsed endlessly in their role as sexual possessions, and to think of the harem as separate female space becomes impossible.

Sex aside, one sees how the intrepid Martineau, who wrote books on economics, traveled in barbarous America, and ironed her clothes in the desert, would suffer under the passivity of harem life. She writes of a visit among women who assume that, like themselves, she has nothing but time: "To sit hour after hour on the deewán, without any exchange of ideas, having our clothes examined . . . and being gazed at by a half-circle of girls in brocade and shawls . . . is as wearisome an experience as one meets with in foreign lands" (263). To make matters worse, Martineau, like Florence Nightingale after her, must put up with the condescension of harem women who fail to understand that her unmarried, independent status is voluntary: "Everywhere they pitied us European women heartily, that we had to go about traveling, and appearing in the streets without being properly taken care of,—that is, watched" (263). If Martineau seems sensitive on this point, she had probably been similarly pitied at home, where even most Englishwomen were not as self-reliant as she. When she defends women's interests, however, she is thinking not only of herself; one of my favorite passages, expressing concern with Middle-Eastern women's digestions, calls for the introduction of jump ropes into the harem (269). More important, and this argues against the insularity of her views, Martineau contrasts "the cheerful, modest countenance of the Nubian girl busy about her household tasks" in primitive Upper Egypt with "the dull and gross face of the handmaid of the hareem" in civilized Cairo. What matters to Martineau, in contrast to Warburton, Kinglake, Nightingale, and Lear, is the practical freedom and social usefulness the woman enjoys, rather than her physical attractiveness or conventional femininity. That Martineau describes as modest a woman who was probably half-naked is significant.

In spite of claiming to find Milnes's *Palm Leaves* to be a beautiful poem, Martineau effectively challenges the assumptions of Western supporters of the harem. Watching the antics of eunuchs, wives, and concubines who might have been monogamous and free in Nubia, she realizes that two systems of oppression can support each other, that "slavery and polygamy . . . can clearly never be separated" (265). She follows up the implications of Montesquieu's defense of polygamy, that Middle-Eastern men must be allowed amiable companions in addition to child brides, by suggesting that society think of marriage in terms of companionship to begin with and that women be educated appropriately (266). She answers those "cosmopolitan" philosophers who view the harem system as intrinsic to Middle-Eastern culture that "[i]t is as pure a conventionalism as our representative monarchy, or German heraldry, or Hindoo caste," and so not above reform (264). Her most irrefutable argument, however, may be implicit in her description of a visit to a Damascus harem:

> But the great amusement was my ear trumpet. The eldest widow . . . put it to her ear; when I said "Bo!" When she had done laughing, she put it into her next neighbor's ear, and said "Bo!" and in this way it came round to me again. But in two minutes, it was asked for again, and went round a second time—everybody laughing as loud as ever at each "Bo!"—and then a third time!
>
> (268)

Seclusion in the harem has not liberated these women from patriarchal structures; it has infantalized them.

Martineau is a moralist rather than an epicurean, not only in her response to the condition of Middle-Eastern women, but also in her approach to writing, which is journalistic rather than artistic. Her counterpart, Lucie Duff Gordon, more subtly blends an ability to entertain not unlike Kinglake's with a desire to inform the English people about the situation in Egypt, where in the 1860's a corrupt government was starving and conscripting the peasants in order to support French projects. Duff Gordon, once described by Kinglake as "so intellectual, so keen, so autocratic, sometimes even so impassioned in speech, that nobody feeling her powers could go on feebly comparing her to a . . . mere Queen or Empress" (Ross 7), wields in *Letters from Egypt* the aristocratic tolerance of one whose London house was open to writers and parliamentarians and who, as a German translator, helped to support her noble but poor husband. She values the forms of courtesy, but overlooks infractions of puritanical religious and sexual codes. Her comment on traditional Egyptian dancing, rather unusual for a Victorian, is that the dancer "moved her breasts by some extraordinary muscular effort, first one and then the other; they were just like pomegranates and gloriously independent of stays or any support" (115).

If her worldliness helps Duff Gordon cross the gap between Western and Eastern manners, however, she is not merely one of Martineau's fashionable cosmopolitans. Tuberculosis impelled her to live in sun-baked Nubia from 1862 until her death in 1869. She makes a cross-cultural passage, in the Forsterian sense, living among her Egyptian servants in Luxor, nursing the people, and vindicating Islamic customs in the letters collected and published in 1865. Although she remains Christian and faithful to her absent husband, her identification with Egyptian culture and irritation with Western prejudices prevent her from judging the harem system according to external standards. She tells the story of a Turkish man who, when teased by an Englishman for having several wives, replies

> "Pray, how many women have you, who are quite young, seen (that is the Eastern phrase) in your whole life?" The Englishman could not count—of course not. "Well, young man, I am old, and was married at twelve, and I have seen in all my life seven women; four are dead, and three are happy and comfortable in my house. *Where are all yours?*"
>
> (101)

Candidly admitting the polygamous behavior of men in both West and East, Duff Gordon here prefers the Islamic system as more responsible and less hypocritical.

This judgment, however, does not address the consequences of the harem system, beyond physical security, for women. Duff Gordon's privileged position in rural Egyptian society may partly account for her distance from this question, especially during the earlier part of her sojourn, before she had visited a harem in Cairo. Although she lived very simply, she held a position of respect in local society. The villagers accepted that, as a foreigner, she would go unveiled and associate with the most learned men, sheiks and magistrates. She confesses her attitude towards the women's society when she writes of a French journalist's visit as "a very agreeable interlude to the Arab prosiness, or rather *enfantillage,* on the part of the women" (203). Even in England male society lauded Duff Gordon as the exception, the "manfully-minded" woman, in George Meredith's phrase (xv). Such a progressive woman, however, could not remain unmindful of the difficulties facing all women in the nineteenth century, and Duff Gordon, having made clear her advocacy of Egyptian culture, shows in later passages her concern for the victims of its sexual double standard. When the crew finds a woman's body off her houseboat on the Nile, the pilot explains, "'most likely she has blackened her father's face, and he has been forced to strangle her, poor man.' I said 'Alas!' and the Reis continued, 'ah, yes, it is a heavy thing, but a man must whiten his face'" (239). When she finally visits a Turkish harem in Cairo, she concedes that the first wife must find it "rather a bore to have to educate little girls for her husband's use" (333). "Alas" and "rather a bore" do not sound like harsh condemnations—she saves those for French-Egyptian politics—but given her urbane view of foreign marital customs, the phrases carry weight.

Duff Gordon knows how to praise when she sees another woman who has lifted herself above social expectations. She says of a Cairene widow:

> I am filled with admiration at her good sense and courage. She has determined to carry on her husband's business of letting boats herself, and to educate her children to the best of her power in habits of independence. I hope she will be successful, and receive the respect such rare conduct in a Turkish woman deserves from the English.
>
> (235-36)

Fascinating to compare with previously mentioned passages describing traditionally unfeminine Middle-Eastern women is Duff Gordon's account of an "eccentric" Arab woman traveling through a Nile village

> dressed like a young man, but small and feminine and rather pretty, except that one eye was blind. . . . I was told—indeed, I could hear—that her language was beautiful, a thing much esteemed among Arabs. She is a virgin and fond of travelling and of men's society, being very clever, so she has her dromedary and goes about quite alone. No one seemed surprised, no one stared, and when I asked if it was *proper,* our captain was surprised. "Why not? If she does not wish to marry, she can go alone; if she does, she can marry—what harm? She is a virgin and free."
>
> (110)

Duff Gordon's account of this wealthy, militant, and free virgin transcends the sexual criteria that underlie Kinglake's gallantry, Warburton's cynicism, and Nightingale's horror of the unfeminine. Most characteristic of all, she takes the opportunity to compliment the Egyptians for accepting one who has escaped the harem system.

In an article admitting how poorly the English can behave in the East, E. M. Forster salutes Duff Gordon for transcending race prejudice (244). She is not discussed by the anti-orientalist critics mentioned above. Obviously, neither Duff Gordon's cultural openness, Kinglake's irony, nor Martineau's abolitionist commitment provides a rationale for Victorian England's imperialist activities in the Middle East. Perhaps, even, by traveling to and writing critically about the region these writers contributed to that British sense of ascendancy so advantageous to imperial ventures. I feel, however, now that critics of imperialism and Orientalism have established the connections between Victorian politics and travel literature, that politics and literature may be separated somewhat again. Our political analysis continu-

ously evolves, and from where I sit Martineau's *Eastern Life* addresses the global issue of the oppression of women, whereas Said's *Orientalism* and Alloula's *The Harem* exhibit a male bias: in Said's discussion of Arab sexuality as a revolutionary force, his representative Arab is male (311-16); Alloula worries about how Western men, by gazing at forbidden Algerian women, displace Algerian male society (122). The point is that, dangerous as Victorian travel books may seem in the mass, the best of them contribute individual versions of cultural history that may be read in numerous ways. Kinglake's *Eothen* and Duff Gordon's *Letters from Egypt* even may be read, with a clear conscience, for pleasure.

Works Cited

Ahmed, Leila. "Western Ethnocentrism and Perceptions of the Harem." *Feminist Studies* 8 (1982): 521-34.

Alloula, Malek. *The Colonial Harem.* Trans. Myrna Godzich and Wlad Godzich. Intro. Barbara Harlow. Theory and History of Literature 21. Minneapolis: U of Minnesota P, 1986.

Duff Gordon, Lady [Lucie]. *Letters from Egypt.* 1865. Ed. Gordon Waterfield. New York: Praeger, 1969.

Forster, E. M. "Salute to the Orient!" *Abinger Harvest.* New York: Meridian, 1955. 243-58.

Kinglake, Alexander. *Eothen.* Intro. V. S. Pritchett. Lincoln: U of Nebraska P, 1970.

———. "The Rights of Women." Rev. of *Palm Leaves,* by R. M. Milnes; *The Englishwoman in Egypt . . . ,* by Mrs. Poole; *The Women of England . . . ,* by Mrs. Ellis; *The Wives of England . . . ,* by Mrs. Ellis; *Characteristics of Women: Moral. Poetical, and Historical . . . ,* by Mrs. Jameson; *The Romance of Biography . . .* by Mrs. Jameson. *The Quarterly Review* 75 (Dec. 1844-Mar. 1845): 94-125.

Lear, Edward. *Edward Lear in the Levant: Travels in Albania, Greece and Turkey in Europe 1848-1849.* Ed. Susan Hyman. London: Murray, 1988.

Martineau, Harriet. *Eastern Life, Present and Past.* Philadelphia: Lea and Blanchard, 1848.

Meredith, George. Intro. *Lady Duff Gordon's Letters from Egypt.* 3rd ed. London: Johnson, 1902. vi-xvi.

Murray, John. Letter to A. W. Kinglake. 18 Sept. 1843. A. W. Kinglake Papers. Add. 7633. Cambridge University Library, Cambridge.

Nightingale, Florence. *Letters from Egypt: A Journey on the Nile 1849-1850.* Sel. and intro. Anthony Sattin. New York: Weidenfeld and Nicolson, 1987.

Rose, Phyllis. *Parallel Lives: Five Victorian Marriages.* New York: Vintage-Random, 1984.

Ross, Janet. "Memoir." *Lady Duff Gordon's Letters from Egypt.* 3rd ed. London: Johnson, 1902. 1-17.

Said, Edward W. *Orientalism.* New York: Pantheon, 1978.

Shaarawi, Huda. *Harem Years: The Memoirs of an Egyptian Feminist.* Trans. and intro. Margot Badran. New York: Feminist P, 1987.

Warburton, Eliot. *The Crescent and the Cross or, Romance and Realities of Eastern Travel.* 1844. New York: Putnam, 1849.

———. Rev. of *Eothen. The Quarterly Review* 75 (Dec. 1844): 54-76.

Frank Lauterbach (essay date June 2001)

SOURCE: Lauterbach, Frank. "British Travel Writing about the United States and Spanish America, 1820-1840: Different and Differentiating Views." *CLCWeb* 3, no. 2 (June 2001): <http://clcwebjournal.lib.purdue.edu/clcweb01-2/lauterbach01.html>.

[In the following essay, Lauterbach offers a "case study of British colonial and post-colonial representations of a transatlantic Other," focusing particularly on works by Basil Hall.]

A prominent wit and Whig—Sydney Smith of the *Edinburgh Review*—made, amongst many others, the following four comments on America: 1) "Literature the Americans have none—no native literature, we mean" ("Travelers in America" 144); 2) "There does not appear to be in America at this moment one man of any considerable talents" ("To Lord Grey" 307); 3) "[The American sloth] lives not *upon* the branches, but *under* them. He moves suspended, rests suspended, sleeps suspended, and passes his life in suspense, like a young clergyman distantly related to a bishop" ("Wanderings in South America" 308); and 4) "[The American] boa constrictor swallows [the land tortoise] whole, shell and all, and consumes him slowly in the interior, as the Court of Chancery does a great estate" ("Wanderings in South America" 309). These four quotes differ in at least three ways: First, in their geographic area of reference, the first pair referring to the United States, the latter one to South America. Second, in their thematic preoccupation, dealing with the state of literature or society and with natural phenomena respectively. Third—and this seems to me the crucial difference—in the discursive relation to their object, to America: The first two statements point at the presumed lack of US-American cultural achievements and of even the possibility to change this situation soon. Smith establishes a clear difference between the cultures of Britain and the United States, which becomes a marked indicator to position

US-American society as the Other. In contrast, the second pair of comments familiarizes objectively different and remote observations through ironic similes and, therefore, subjectively minimizes the impact of difference. Smith, reviewing Charles Waterton's *Wanderings in South America* (1825), tries, in a continuous fashion, to liken Waterton's impressions of a potentially strange and hostile wilderness to fairly common experiences of the British urban middle class. Simultaneously, he relates and relates to even the remoteness of South America by superimposing an image of Britain onto that of America.

I argue that this contrast between establishing America as culturally different (in the case of the United States) and as imaginatively familiar (in the case of South America) informs, *mutatis mutandis,* a discursive duality underlying the essential assumptions of most British travelers of the post-Monroe period when they record their impressions of either part of the American continent. And I propose to describe this duality heuristically in terms of a rhetoric of colonial versus post-colonial representations of the Other. This entails two theoretical conjectures: First, by speaking of a rhetoric of representation I focus on the manner and way the Other is narrated in relation to one's own culture, that is, on the texture of power relations rather than their implied hierarchies of agency—an approach somewhat akin to the anthropological turn towards the grammatology of field work (see, for example, Brettell 128-30). Second, my approach leads me beyond the premises of most post-colonial criticism to view colonial discourse by necessity as a hegemonial expression of the imperial center and post-colonial discourse as a reaction from the (formerly colonized) margins of empire. Instead, I suggest to look at the extent to which post-colonial discourse is produced in the metropolis rather than (exclusively) at/on the periphery.

In order to enter the rhetoric of British travel writing in terms of a dichotomy of colonial and post-colonial representations of America, I am employing—as a Trojan Horse—the semantic part of Homi Bhabha's conception of colonial mimicry as expressed in his *The Location of Culture* (1994). Ironically compromising between panoptical vision and historical change, colonial mimicry emerges as an ambivalent "desire for a reformed, recognizable Other, *as a subject of a difference that is almost the same, but not quite*" (86; emphases in the original). For the purpose of analysing the texture of colonial relations, Bhabha's italics are of primary importance (rather than the hierarchically motivated impulse of reform located in the psyche of the second British empire). Colonial rhetoric, then, is intent on making the Other "recognizable" (within a mutually constitutive colonial relationship) by subjecting it to such a difference as remains penetrable and leaves sameness virtually transparent. Accordingly, I view post-colonial discourse as a conscious denial of such likening of the Other, of its almost sameness, in favor of a perspective that stresses difference, strangeness, or alterity as a (professedly factual) observation (without necessarily advocating it as a projected intention). In this sense, I argue for post-colonial discourse as a potentially neutral rhetoric—instead of describing it in terms of activities like "murderous . . . struggle" (Fanon 30), "writing back" (Ashcroft, Griffiths, and Tiffin), "massive retaliatory overcompensation" (Buell 435), "dissociation" (Frank), or "counter-discursive strategies" (Tiffin 18)—to name only a few examples of what I feel should, more appropriately, be called de-colonization (with the interest of getting rid of imperial subjection).

My case study of British colonial and post-colonial representations of a transatlantic Other are first-hand travel accounts of the years after the Monroe Doctrine and the achievement of independence on the Spanish American continent—years that were in many ways formative for American-European relations. While drawing on a variety of significant works of that time, my central examples are the two travel books by Basil Hall (1788-1844), a staunch Tory from the Scottish Lowlands and a captain of the Royal Navy, published about his trips to Chile, Perú, and México in 1824, and to the United States and Upper and Lower Canada in 1829. I argue that whereas the earlier work betrays a colonial rhetoric (in accordance with British neo-colonial interests in South America), Hall's later study adopts a remarkably post-colonial perspective towards the United States that is paralleled in most contemporary accounts of travels to North America. Furthermore, I will show that a surprisingly colonial rhetoric seeking closeness to Great Britain is apparent in a variety of US-American reactions to Hall's work of 1829.

Basil Hall's books can serve as a good starting point for various reasons: Having traveled widely (even after retiring from military service in 1825), he published his experience of places as diverse as India, Eastern Asia, South and North America, and the Mediterranean. This soon gained him both the election to the Royal Society and the friendship of Walter Scott and other important literati. Especially after the success of *A Voyage of Discovery to the Western Coast of Corea, and the Great Loo-Choo Island in the Japan Sea* (1817), he became one of the most prolific writers of his time, popular among adults and children alike (see Hall, "Biographical Preface" 5-6). Apart from his fame, Hall is significant for a comparative approach as one of the few writers who not only traveled to and published extensive accounts of *both* parts of the American continent, but who on either trip also visited more than one region (i.e., South America and Mexico on the first, and the United States and Canada on the second trip). Finally, his *Travels in North America, in the Years 1827 and 1828* (1829) was consequential within the history of

British travelogues because it aroused particularly harsh reactions, introduced the "departure from the guidebook type" to "more discursive analytical books" (see Adams 250), and set a precedent for the overtly critical tone that was to dominate subsequent books on the United States in the following decade or so. Among them number such classics as Frances Trollope's *Domestic Manners of the Americans* (1832), Thomas Hamilton's *Men and Manners in America* (1833), Isaac Fiddler's *Observations on Professions, Literature, Manners, and Emigration in the United States and Canada* (1833), Frances Kemble's *Journal* (1835), Frederick Marryat's *Diary in America* (1839), and even Charles Dickens's *American Notes* (1842). Rather unfairly, Hall's *Travels* soon became notorious on both sides of the Atlantic for his supposedly harsh indictment of US-American culture and society. While earlier travelers—such as Richard Parkinson, Thomas Moore, Charles William Janson, Thomas Ashe, Henry Bradshaw Fearon, William Faux, or Frederick Fitzgerald de Roos—had also been vehemently refuted in the US-American press, the attack on Hall's book reached a new dimension because he had been seen as a celebrity even before his arrival and, therefore, was, together with his wife, warmly welcomed into the circles of the Anglo-American elite's social life (see Mulvey, "Merchant Society" 412-14; M. Hall). Partly as a reaction to the criticism of his views, Hall's involvement with the United States did not end with the publication of his book in 1829: When Frances Trollope returned from her disastrous business (ad)venture in Cincinnati, Hall helped her publish her own interpretation of US-American "domestic manners" in March 1832 (Smalley lxi)—well timed to enter the parliamentary debate over the Reform Bill at its zenith (Parent Frazee 148-65; Neville-Sington 167-70). While some assumed (mistakenly) that Hall was actually the author of Trollope's work, he did write the laudatory critique in the Tory *Quarterly Review,* a magazine always keen on attacking the young republic. He also took the opportunity to, *en passant,* praise and defend, under the guise of anonymity, his own earlier travel account and to restate his views on the United States (see "Domestic Manners" 40-48).

These views center on the claim that British and US-American society and culture are and ought to be fundamentally different. Basil Hall (a Scotsman after all!) explicitly states in *Travels in North America, in the Years 1827 and 1828* that he "consider[s] America and England as *differing* more from one another in many essential respects, than any two European nations I have ever visited" (2, 48; my emphasis) including, as he points out, the British archrival France (2: 17). With respect to literary production, he adds that, due to both countries "writing not for each other at all, but for themselves exclusively," they are "virtually using two *different languages*" (2, 49; my emphasis). This ties in with Hall's more general observation that American and British English differ so significantly as to allow for misunderstandings as easily as if completely different languages were spoken in either country (2, 43-44; 2, 46-48). Beyond merely registering those (real or supposed) differences, Hall is even proud of the so-called "state of blissful ignorance" (2, 49; see also 2, 22-23; 2, 123-26) of the British with respect to the United States and recommends it for future relations: "It would be a very foolish sort of wisdom on our part to destroy [that ignorance], by extending our acquaintance with their literature and history beyond its present confined limits" (2, 50). Hall expresses his view of the relationship between the British Isles and the United States through what I call a post-colonial rhetoric of differentiatory representation that appears even as a prospective model for future relations. It becomes both statement and program.

This strategy far from constitutes a minority position as most British travelers, especially after the War of 1812 (see Wisneski), are eager to point out the otherness of the United States (even if they are less explicit than Hall)—in their consideration of US-American literature as inferior, for example. Henry Tudor, in a statement that is quite representative, emphasizes that he does not "esteem the enlightened citizens of the United States, taken in a body, to be as learned, as deeply versed in literature, science, and the arts, as extensively educated in the classical lore . . . as ourselves in England" (2, 394). Fanny Kemble, more pathetically acting out a pose of despair, asks: "Where are the poets of this land? . . . Have these glorious scenes [of the Hudson] poured no inspirings into hearts worthy to behold and praise their beauty? . . . [It] is strange how marvellously unpoetical these people are! . . . Even the heathen Dutch, among us the very antipodes of all poetry, have found names such as the Donder Berg for the hills, whilst the Americans christen them Butter Hill, the Crows Nest, and *such like*" (Butler 270-71). Vigorously embittered in her criticism, Frances Trollope declares in *Domestic Manners of the Americans* (1832) rather disingeniously that upon returning to some miscellaneous poetry, which she had extracted for transcription, she "thought that ill-nature and dulness, ('oh ill-matched pair!') would be more served by their insertion, than wholesome criticism" (2, 157). Finally, Lucas George, who characterizes a variety of individual US-American writers, claims that "it is not *English* that [the reviewer Johnson] writes . . . it is *American*. His periods are accompanied by a yell, that is scarcely less dismal than the warhoop of a *Mohawk*" (Davis 139).

An oft-cited reason for such perceived deficiencies of US-American literature is the swift availability of British literary productions on the American continent, which does not allow for the growth of a native literature. Basil Hall is very outspoken on this point when he states that "nearly all that [the United States] has of letters, of arts, and of science, has been, and still continues to be, imported from us, with little addition or admixture of a domestic growth or manufacture" (*Travels* 2, 19). (Sydney Smith's afterthought in the above-quoted statement that the US-Americans have no literature slyly alludes to the same fact: "no *native* literature, we mean.") While this seems like an uncharacteristic admission of similarities, it only shows, upon closer inspection, that where likenesses might exist, they are the work of US-Americans who, in this case, neither change their copyright laws nor the economic set-up of the book market. Hall clearly emphasizes this monodirectedness of creating closeness in his conclusion that US-Americans "have done scarcely any thing as yet to attach *us to them*" (2, 17; my emphasis). Thus, even this point underlines the assumption of difference in a double way: Not only are similarities not acknowledged from Hall's strictly British perspective of superiority, but the very difference of perspectives *per se,* marks the otherness of US-American culture. However, Hall's rhetoric of post-colonialism does not only pervade his overt conclusions but is, additionally, reenacted in the very structural perspective of the book. This allows him to resolve a paradoxical dialectic, which is, as Paul Fussell has noted in *Abroad: British Literary Traveling between the Wars,* potentially inherent in all travel writing: On the one hand, travel accounts generally present themselves as memoirs "in which the narrative—unlike that in a novel or romance—claims literal validity by constant reference to actuality" (Fussell 203). Hall is eager to assert this validity from the start. He emphasizes that, in all of his three volumes, he simply tells "what I conscientiously believe to be . . . assuredly nothing but the truth, and without the slightest shade of ill-will" (1, 17). On the other hand, a travel book "is addressed to those . . . who require the exotic or comic anomalies, wonders, and scandals of the literary form *romance* which their own place or time cannot entirely supply" (Fussell 203). In his insistence on the fundamental differences between the United States and Great Britain, Hall meets this demand by, from the outset, giving his observations an air of romance. Hence, his first impressions of New York seem to him "more like a dream than a sober reality" (1, 6). This aura of romance continues to pervade both the perception of the two societies, whose "views and wishes are so diametrically opposed, not merely in name but in substance" (3, 435), and of natural phenomena like the Balize which is supposedly "beyond any imagination to conceive" (3, 338), or the Mississippi in whose "wretchedness" an "artist, in search of hints for a painting of the Deluge, would . . . have found them in abundance" (3, 353).

In his attempt to resolve this dilemma between the motivation to present the object of travel in terms of a romance and the necessity to claim narrative verisimilitude in order to be effective, Hall very self-consciously reminds the reader, over and over again, that the truthfulness of whatever account he gives is derived from unbiased observation. When he maintains that his opinions and feelings were formed "by the gradual progress of a pretty extensive observation, varied and checked in a thousand ways, and under circumstances . . . perhaps better than most natives could hope to find, even if their own country were the object of research" (1, 108-09), he diminishes the impact of both his individual subjectivity and his potentially prejudiced point of view as a British foreigner. This suggestion of his narrative transparency cleverly places his own authority at the center of his report, thus attesting to the (paradoxical) truth or realism of the romance of difference underlying his rhetoric. The perpetual gestures of detached autoreflexivity, around which Hall organizes the plot of his travels, strikingly contrasts with the immediacy of perspective in his earlier account of Spanish America (see below) and constructs the United States as a field of differences within a post-colonial discourse.

The last quote, furthermore, exemplifies Hall's constant reassurance of his status as a non-participant observer, of his not being part of US-American society. Whereas Hall's Spanish American travelogue is informed by a curious attempt at immersion, his *Travels in North America* betrays an anxiety to stay disinterested and disinvolved. He negotiates (in)difference in his attempt not to be associated with US culture—as, for instance, in his uneasy reaction to the entreaty of a US-American acquaintance to "admit . . . that we are treading close on the heels of the Mother Country": "I remained silent, not knowing well how to reply to such an appeal" (3, 433-34). Even or better: Especially since Hall enjoyed the attention of US nationals, this anxiety is a reflex to the constant threat that the differences between US-American culture and his British identity might be blurred or even erased. His narrative position as an observer is, therefore, not only stylized to authorize a romance of difference, but to unmistakably position and define himself as a post-colonial subject of this difference.

Ironically though, US-Americans, keen on countering the reports of British travelers in general and of Basil Hall in particular, do so by subscribing to a colonial rhetoric of minimizing difference in order to seek sameness to an *alter ego* that is construed as recognizable. Hall himself notices the endeavour of the US-American middle class to be accepted by British standards not by their own which leads them, paradoxically, to forms of self-praise that in and of themselves become, for Hall, a mark of difference (see 1, 109-11). As Christopher Mulvey has shown, Hall's perception was, in this point, far from being wrong, considering the openly displayed desire of the urban East Coast society to match British aristocratic manners ("Anglo-American Fictions" 69). Hence, Hall's US-American acquaintance mentioned above articulates his hope that the travel report Hall is to publish upon his return will "bring the two countries

more together" (3, 434). He retains this hope, even after the Scottish captain had made his argument for irreconcilable differences, by querying if Hall is not doing both countries injustice (3, 434) and "wanting in true philanthropy" (3, 435). Yet, Hall, in the record of this discussion, which closes his three volumes of travel impressions, firmly insists on delimiting British as opposed to US-American society, whereas his counterpart is eager to bridge the remaining gap between the two countries (see also Ullreich 107-08). Later on, Hall would poignantly stress "the utter absurdity of comparing the two countries together" ("Domestic Manners" 41). Hall earnestly maintains a division that clearly defines the United States as a post-colonial Other, whereas his friend retains a colonial dependency on British opinion in his desire to negotiate stronger likenesses between both cultures in order to remove perpetual misunderstandings (*Travels* 3, 436).

This US-American gentleman's opinions closely resemble those articulated in the responses to Hall's book. Edward Everett, reviewing it for the *North American Review,* refutes Hall's (above-cited) claim that the United States and Britain fundamentally differ in many essential respects. Everett, conversely, points to the English descent of ninety percent of the people in the United States as well as to the virtual identity of the language, the law, and even the government of the two countries. He, then, concludes that he "should be glad to know what two European nations are more like each other, in these or any other respects, than England and America" (538, see also 536-37) a statement diametrically opposed to Hall's insistence on the utter lack of likeness. In a similar manner, Calvin Colton's *The Americans* (1833), which summons Frances Trollope and Basil Hall, in a rather tedious manner, before an imaginary court, sets out to refute most of their observations. Among them are those "some dozen points of radical and essential difference between Great Britain and America" (153) that Hall took up in his review of Trollope's *Domestic Manners*. Although Colton does not argue the point that neither king, nor court, nor aristocracy exist in the United States, he does take issue with Hall's implication that this makes them "destitute of the most refined state and the highest culture of society" (162). And, even though he admits that Great Britain has indeed, over the centuries, been able to develop advantages in university education, he pronounces that "the real advances of knowledge in different nations are not measured by this accident." Instead, "there are always lovers of science and devotees of learning, not a few, in every considerable community, whose ambition will keep them in equal pace with the most accomplished of their respective professions in any part of the world" (165). Thus, whatever outward differences Colton acknowledges, he does not see them as constitutive of a fundamental otherness of US-American culture. Quite on the contrary, he confidently measures the

United States by foreign standards and concludes that being "of the same blood, the same language, the same laws, and the same institutions . . . it is unnatural for [Britains and US-Americans] to differ" (364).

Rather than perceiving the pertinence of, for example, a shared language and a common (cultural) history as a burden, both Everett and Colton (among others) consciously re-cast themselves as sharing an imperial vision and opposing the differentiatory writing of British travelers. Therefore, US-American responses to British representations of the transatlantic Other remain doubly involved in British dominance through their colonial insistence on close cultural ties as well as, more intricately, through allowing British travelers to set a discursive precedent against which these ties are expressed. Even though most British writers advance post-colonial distinctions, their US-American counterparts blur such distinctions not only in what they argue but in the very act of arguing it. They ascribe to British conceptions of the United States a hegemony already significantly tuned down by some British writers. US-American identity is subjected to networks of British values and traditions rather than to differentiatory strategies. The potential of a post-colonial (cultural) independence is deferred or disseminated within a field of negotiation dominated by the aesthetic and economic power of Great Britain, strongly (if perhaps unwillingly) reinforced by US-American critics. Thus, Richard Biddle, in his book-length reply *Captain Hall in America* (1830), paradoxically defends the "reveries" of his countrymen for British poetry against Hall's indictment of them. Biddle wants to hear nothing of any "complaint . . . made of the absence of any thing peculiar distinctive in our Literature" and asks: "Why may we not be, good-naturedly, suffered to suggest that we employ a medium of thought, and of description, appropriated, irrevocably and jealously, in the reader's memory to the *chef-d'oeuvres* of the English muse?" (59). And, such rejections of the rhetorical dividing line drawn between the two countries by Hall and other travelers are not confined to essayistic treatises like Biddle's, Everett's, and Colton's. Satirical responses to Hall (and Trollope) like Frederick William Shelton's *Trollopiad* (1837), and James Kirke Paulding's 1835 revision of *The Diverting History of John Bull and Brother Jonathan,* furthermore, ridicule any attempts to narrate the Other as different as mere market strategies to sell books that would otherwise have been largely unsuccessful in Britain (see Shelton 51-53, 59; Paulding 135-39).

The books of Hall and others did, indeed, sell well. Yet, this alone is not a sign for their lack of earnesty. Rather, it reflects their participation, at home, in the public reorganization of relations to the rest of the world, in attempts to reposition the identity of the British empire on an international scale. As such, excursions to the United States are only one side of a coin whose reverse side displays, among other things, a remarkably contrary view of South America. Whereas British travelers affirm the existence of the United States through an acknowledgement of its difference—and thus provoke a paradoxical dialectic between colonial responses to a post-colonial rhetoric—they approach Spanish America in a way that ignores its very existence as a cultural (as well as a political or economic) entity in its own right. It is seen as essentially empty, as a blank sheet of paper to be written on by the British who, through *their* inscriptions, also manifest and enhance their own basic ideals and, thus, their very identity. They project an ideal(ized) perception of their homeland onto the reality of Latin America. Consequently, the travel writers appear surprisingly little troubled by the utter otherness of both South American society and nature. Instead, they focus on a prospective development designed to reflect and foster their own ideals and to further British interests. In other words, they implement a colonial (or neo-colonial) rhetoric that minimizes difference, explores it as penetrable, and relegates it to a past which, on top of it, can conveniently be associated with the arch-enemy, an Inquisition-ridden (and Inquisition-riding) "Popish" Spain not generally present as a reality but rather as the fiction of countless eighteenth and early nineteenth-century novels. While British travel writers allow very little closeness to the United States, they eagerly sustain and embrace it in South America and, thus, repress the potential persistence of strangeness in a variety of areas.

Basil Hall, for example in his *Extracts from a Journal, Written on the Coasts of Chili, Peru, and Mexico, in the Years 1820, 1821, 1822* (1824), happily welcomes the "benefits" and the "universality" of the "real and solid advantages" that the Spanish American revolutions have brought to all classes, and he remarks with satisfaction that "every successive hour of freedom will have the effect of enlarging the circle of knowledge and virtue throughout the country" (1, 28). Hall even sees freedom, republicanism, and independence as necessary prerequisites for an "encouragement [of] literature and the arts" (1, 89; see also 1, 297-98). Coming from a Tory like Hall, this is a surprising attitude towards revolution; but it does serve the essentially important end of diminishing remaining differences between South America and Europe—as Hall himself points out in reference to Chileans: "It is of essential use to their cause, that [the people] should take delight in assimilating themselves, even in trifles, with other independent nations of the world" (1, 90). Thus, revolution is not primarily laudable in itself but as an opportunity to implement standards closely resembling his own. Though not advocating a monarchy, Hall is clearly in favour of a form of government similar to that of Great Britain when he recommends the type of strong leadership he sees exemplified in San Martín (see e.g., 1, 255-62). While Hall would stress, over and over again, not only the differences between the United States and Great Britain but the desirability of such differences, he appears equally eager to point at the advantage of erasing existing divisions between Spanish America and Britain, to stake out a common ground based on his own, British standards—despite the fact that the South American republics have embarked, as it were, on a political experiment comparable to that of their Anglo-American neighbour.

In contrast to his pose of indifference, even ignorance, towards the United States five years later, Hall continually highlights the immediacy of his perspective. Despite subsequent reservations, he is instantaneously "dazzled by the brilliancy of the spectacle" of Spanish American emancipation (1, 49) and expresses his interest to participate more fully in the novel developments (see e.g., 1, 11; 2, 129). He even regrets that his position (as naval captain on a diplomatic mission) prevents him from a deeper involvement (1: 276) as well as from "examining the whole at leisure" (2, 128). Hall's difference in attitude towards the two parts of the American continent is, however, not only apparent in a comparison of his two travel books but can already be detected in this earlier work. During a stop-over in Colombia (Panamá, to be precise), he criticizes and is annoyed by the ignorance and carelessness of Panamanian merchants with respect to the South American revolutions, while he candidly admits his own indifference to affairs in New York. Whereas South America seems constantly on his mind, the United States are utterly uninteresting for him (see 2, 150-51). In his appreciation of the newly independent nations, he is even willing to downplay (perceived) breaches of etiquette in the theatre of Lima, such as the smoking of cigars so often harshly censored by British travelers to the United States. Despite his dislike, Hall explicitly writes off such occurrences as insignificant, as "little circumstances which strike the eye of a stranger, as being more decidedly characteristic, than incidents really important" (1, 132). Among these "really important" incidents is his discovery of the likeness of the houses along the Peruvian river Huaura to Grecian temples with Gothic ornamentation. This induces him to support the argument for a universal sense of natural beauty, even "amongst rude nations," thus stressing aesthetic links with Spanish America upon which a "more cultivated taste" ought to be developed (1, 264-66).

While Hall is mostly interested in the macro-political opportunities of Spanish American independence and in their cultural implications, other writers have more specific agendas. Charles Waterton—the amateur scientist reviewed by Sydney Smith—appreciates the largely unexplored rainforests of South America for both his research of the indigenous fauna and his experiments in the taxidermy of birds. Even though he points out the otherness of life in the tropical wilderness in comparison to that in the urban metropolis of London, he sees in it an experience more rewarding than alienating: "Animation will glow in thy looks, and exercise will brace thy frame in vigour" (147). Outward differences become meaningful not in themselves but only when narrowly perceived as such. Waterton considers even the dangers of distant regions "not real but imaginary," as "not half so numerous or dreadful as they are commonly thought to be." While a South American experience can enhance the traveler physically as well as mentally, the "youth, who incautiously reels into the lobby of Drury-lane . . . is exposed to more certain ruin, sickness, and decay, than he who wanders a whole year in the wilds" (148). Thus, differences, though objectively manifest, can and ought to be overcome through a proper disposition that likens the new situation to the stranger as easily as the old habits at home.

Whereas Waterton's colonial representation of topographic differences is mitigated by his adherence to an individualistic, romantic discourse of imagination, others project and advocate certain types of social action for developing sameness. George Thomas Love in his *A Five Years' Residence in Buenos Ayres* (1825), for instance, praises the Argentine government for its "most laudable anxiety to forward education, by patronizing schools upon the Lancasterian system" (97). And he concludes by positively stressing an increasing closeness between Argentines and Britains: "It is gratifying to observe that those Creolians who have been in England evince the greatest attachment to us" (99). This appreciation of seeking to adopt British manners is echoed even more emphatically by the Robertson brothers who claim that, while Spanish Americans (in Buenos Aires and elsewhere) "imitated the comfortable habits of John Bull, they avoided his dissipation" (69). Hence, the differences between British and Spanish American societies have not only been largely overcome, but Spanish Americans have actually adopted virtues that make them even better John Bulls, better Englishmen than the British themselves. Even though the Robertson brothers do not deny the differences in language, religion, habits, customs, or education, they consider these differences now a matter of almost negligible degree—as in John Parish Robertson's following panegyrical rhetoric of colonialism in *Letters on South America, Comprising Travels on the Banks of the Paraná and Río de la Plata* (1843): "There has always been some magic influence exercised over the minds of both parties, which has obliterated those strong distinctive features which often draw an almost insuperable barrier between two nations, bringing the South Americans and English into as close a contact as if they belonged to one and the same family" (277). Closeness, based on an erasure of difference, is desirable both in the present and for the future.

Despite the aspired-to and already perceived proximity of British and Spanish American societies, Frank Mac-Shane's contention in *Impressions of Latin America: Five Centuries of Travel and Adventure by English and North American Writers* (1963) that the works of Hall and others represent a "*natural* sympathy of the English toward the newly independent countries of Latin America" (70; my emphasis) is too short-sighted in its ignoring of the conflictous potential inherent in the discursive power relations established by British writers. At times, even the imagery underlying the perception of South America reveals that more specific interests are driving the desire to make similarities transparent. When James Thomson, a religious educator and major perpetuator of the *leyenda negra* (Nuñez 249), who came to Perú to establish schools and distribute vernacular Bibles, talks about "an immeasurable field," "white . . . to the harvest" and open "for the exercise of benevolence in all its parts" (*Letters* 37), his intentions to "contribute in no inconsiderable degree to the progress of this country" (73) are—at least metaphorically—tainted by the possibility of economic or agricultural gain. In fact, gold and copper mining was seen as a primary South American asset by many Britains in the second quarter of the nineteenth century. Yet to reduce the travelers, in Mary Louise Pratt's phrase, to a "capitalist vanguard" (146-55), or to state, as Noé Jitrik has done, that they "fueron impulsados a visitarnos por una poderosa curiosidad mercantil, instrumentos . . . de la inmbatible [!] expansión económica europea" (13), ignores the larger cultural work of British travelers to (re)define themselves collectively and individually in the act of establishing a relationship to a whole subcontinent beyond its momentary economic value. To be sure, British writers were very well aware of the economic opportunities of exploiting the young Spanish American republics. Nevertheless, as the social visions of Basil Hall or the Robertson brothers, the educational objectives of Love or Thomson, and even the scientific investigations of Waterton show, Spanish American societies are not "mainly incoded in this [travel] literature as logistical obstacles to the forward movement of the Europeans," as Pratt claims (148). They instead form the very stage for acting out this movement, for a positioning of ideological power and authority that helps to represent (and reassure) British identity to itself through the collective image of being a model—superior, yet a model that entails future likeness. Whatever economic power is enacted by British entrepreneurs, it is only a side-effect, not the prime and sole goal of the vision of South America as expressed (for example) by travel writers. This vision, refracted through the rhetoric of colonial discourse, is, however, an even more effective way to silence the specifics of Spanish America and to over-write it with a presumed proximity to British society—or, at least, the prospect of such proximity.

British travel writing to South America thus enhances British values not by estranging the transatlantic world (as in the case of the United States) but by projecting such values onto an appropriated similarity between Great Britain and the newly independent republics. This difference to the differentiating attitude towards the United States (observable not only in British travelers but in a large percentage of the British middle class in general) did not go unnoticed within contemporaneous Britain itself. William Jacob's "Mrs. Trollope's *Refugee*" and "Mr. Ouseley *on the United States*" (1832) observes, in ways that underscore my argument, an almost inevitable tendency among the British to be "insensible to all but the more prominent differences" in relation to Latin Americans, "while discrepancies and peculiarities of perhaps precisely the same order, among the North Americans, assume, in our eyes, the meaner and more degrading aspect of provincialism and vulgarity" (518-19). Far from recording transparent, objective relationships, British travelers (as well as authors writing from Britain itself) employ a necessarily subjective rhetoric of representation of the US- and Spanish American Other by means of post-colonial and colonial discourses respectively.

Works Cited

Adams, Ephraim Douglas. "The Point of View of the British Traveler in America." *Political Science Quarterly* 29.2 (June 1914): 244-64.

Ashcroft, Bill, Gareth Griffith, and Helen Tiffin. *The Empire Writes Back: Theory and Practice in Post-Colonial Literatures.* London: Routledge, 1989.

Bhabha, Homi K. *The Location of Culture.* London: Routledge, 1994.

Biddle, Richard. *Captain Hall in America, by an American.* Philadelphia: Carey & Lea, 1830.

Brettell, Caroline B. "Travel Literature, Ethnography, and Ethnohistory." *Ethnohistory* 33.2 (May 1986): 127-38.

Buell, Lawrence. "American Literary Emergence as a Postcolonial Phenomenon." *American Literary History* 4.3 (1992): 411-42.

Butler, Frances Anne [Fanny Kemble]. *Journal of Frances Anne Butler.* Vol. 1. London: John Murray, 1835.

Colton, Calvin. *The Americans, by an American in London.* London: Frederic Westley and A. H. Davis, 1833.

Davis, John. *Travels of Four Years and a Half in the United States of America, during 1798, 1799, 1800, 1801, and 1802.* Bristol: R. Edwards, 1803.

Everett, Edward. "Captain Hall's Travels." *North American Review* 29.65 [New Series 20.40] (October 1829): 522-74.

Fanon, Frantz. *The Wretched of the Earth.* 1961. Trans. Constance Farrington. London: MacGibbon & Kee, 1965.

Frank, Armin Paul. "Towards a Model of an International History of American Literatures." *Do the Americas Have a Common Literary History?* Ed. Barbara Buchenau, Annette Paatz, Rolf Lohse, and Marietta Messmer. Frankfurt and New York: Peter Lang, 2001. Forthcoming.

Fussell, Paul. *Abroad: British Literary Traveling between the Wars.* New York: Oxford UP, 1980.

Hall, Basil. [Anonymous], "Biographical Preface" *Voyages and Travels of Captain Basil Hall, R.N.* London: Thomas Nelson, 1895. 5-6.

Hall, Basil. "Domestic Manners of the Americans." *Quarterly Review* 47.93 (March 1832): 39-80.

Hall, Basil. *Travels in North America, in the Years 1827 and 1828.* 3 vols. Edinburgh: Cadell; London: Simpkin and Marshall, 1829.

Hall, Basil. *Extracts from a Journal, Written on the Coasts of Chili, Peru, and Mexico, in the Years 1820, 1821, 1822.* 2 vols. 3rd ed. Edinburgh: Archibald Constable; London: Hurst, Robinson, 1824.

Hall, Margaret. *The Aristocratic Journey: Being the Outspoken Letters of Mrs. Basil Hall Written during a Fourteen Months' Sojourn in America 1827-1828.* Ed. Una Pope-Hennessy. New York: Putnam; London: Knickerbocker P, 1931.

Jacob, William. "Mrs. Trollope's *Refugee*" and "Mr. Ouseley *on the United States.*" *Quarterly Review* 48.96 (December 1832): 507-23.

Jitrik, Noé, ed. *Los Viajeros.* Serie Los Argentinos 9. Buenos Aires: Jorge Álvarez, 1969.

Love, George Thomas. *A Five Years' Residence in Buenos Ayres, during the Years 1820 to 1825: Containing Remarks on the Country and Inhabitants, and a Visit to Colonia del Sacramento, with an Appendix Containing Rules and Police of the Port of Buenos Ayres, Navigation of the River Plate, & c. & c.* London: G. Hebert, 1825.

MacShane, Frank, ed. *Impressions of Latin America: Five Centuries of Travel and Adventure by English and North American Writers.* New York: William Morrow, 1963.

Mulvey, Christopher. "Anglo-American Fictions: National Characteristics in Nineteenth-Century Travel Literature." *American Literary Landscapes: The Fiction and the Fact.* Ed. Ian F. A. Bell and D. K. Adams. London: Vision P. and New York: St. Martin's P, 1988. 61-77.

Mulvey, Christopher. "Merchant Society in the Early National Period: Replication of London Patterns in Boston, New York, and Philadelphia." *The Construction and Contestation of American Cultures and Identities in the Early National Period.* Ed. Udo J. Hebel. Heidelberg: Winter, 1999. 411-25.

Neville-Sington, Pamela. *Fanny Trollope: The Life and Adventures of a Clever Woman.* New York: Viking, 1998.

Nuñez, Estuardo. *Viajes y viajeros extranjeros por el Perú: Apuntes documentales con algunos desarrollos histórico-biográficos.* Lima: P. L. Villanueva, 1989.

Parent Frazee, Monique. *Mrs Trollope and America.* Caën: Faculté des Lettres et Sciences Humaines, U of Caën, 1969.

Paulding, James Kirke. *The Diverting History of John Bull and Brother Jonathan, by Hector Bull-Us.* New ed. New York: Harper & Brothers, 1835.

Pratt, Mary Louise. *Imperial Eyes: Travel Writing and Transculturation.* London: Routledge, 1992.

Robertson, J. Parish, and W. Parish Robertson. *Letters on South America, Comprising Travels on the Banks of the Paraná and Río de la Plata.* Vol. 2. London: John Murray, 1843.

Shelton, Frederick William. *The Trollopiad; Or, Travelling Gentlemen in America, a Satire, by Nil Admirari, Esq.* New York: Shepard, Tingley & Co., 1837.

Smalley, Donald. "Introduction: Mrs. Trollope in America." *Domestic Manners of the Americans.* Ed. Donald Smalley. New York: Knopf, 1949. vii-lxxvi.

Smith, Sydney. "To Lord Grey." *30 November 1818. Letter 313 of The Letters of Sydney Smith.* Ed. Nowell C. Smith. Oxford: Clarendon, 1953. 1, 307-08.

Smith, Sydney. "Travellers in America." *Edinburgh Review* 31.61 (December 1818): 132-50.

Smith, Sydney. "Wanderings in South America." *Edinburgh Review* 43.86 (February 1826): 299-315.

Thomson, James. *Letters on the Moral and Religious State of South America, Written during a Residence of Nearly Seven Years in Buenos Aires, Chile, Peru, and Colombia.* London: James Nisbet, 1827.

Tiffin, Helen. "Post-Colonial Literatures and Counter-Discourse." *Kunapipi* 9.3 (1987): 17-38.

Trollope, Frances. *Domestic Manners of the Americans.* London: Whittaker, Treacher, & Co., 1832.

Tudor, Henry. *Narrative of a Tour in North America, Comprising Mexico, the Mines of Real del Monte, the United States, and the British Colonies, with an Excursion to the Island of Cuba, in a Series of Letters, Written in the Years 1831-2.* Vol. 2. London: James Duncan, 1834.

Ullreich, Josefine. *Urteile bedeutender englischer Schriftsteller über die Vereinigten Staaten von Nordamerika in der ersten Hälfte des XIX. Jahrhunderts.* Doctoral Diss. Wien: U of Vienna, 1950.

Waterton, Charles. *Wanderings in South America, the North-West of the United States, and the Antilles, in the Years, 1812, 1816, 1820, and 1824, with Original Instructions for the Perfect Preservation of Birds, & c. for Cabinets of Natural History.* London: J. Mawman, 1825.

Wisneski, Richard Lawrence. *Travelers in a Wilderness: Conflicting Identities in America, 1760-1812.* Diss. East Lansing: Michigan State U, 1997.

Erik S. Schmeller (essay date 2004)

SOURCE: Schmeller, Erik S. "American Travelers, 1833-1860." In *Perceptions of Race and Nation in English and American Travel Writers, 1833-1914,* pp. 42-59. New York: Peter Lang, 2004.

[*In the following essay, Schmeller considers the travel writings of American authors William Wells Brown, David F. Dorr, and Alexander Mackenzie, to "reveal the different roles race played in their perception of individual and national identity."*]

While traveling in London and speaking about his experiences as a fugitive slave, William Wells Brown was in a unique position to observe his surroundings. As a black American, he represented a rarity in the streets despite the fact that there had been over 10,000 enslaved black people in Britain prior to emancipation. What became of these black Britons after 1833 has been largely left to speculation, and Brown rarely encountered other black people.[1] Brown did meet one black Briton repeatedly. While listening to Joseph Jenkins preach, Brown recognized him as "the bill-distributor of Cheapside, the crossing-sweeper of Chelsea, the tract-seller and psalm-singer of Kensington, and the Othello of the Eagle Saloon."[2] In some ways foreshadowing Brown's own multiple careers after the Civil War, Jenkins was a former slave who had found post-emancipation life difficult and barely survivable. Through hard work and multiple professions, Jenkins had managed to eke out a living. Brown wrote, "I left Joseph Jenkins, impressed with the idea that he was the greatest genius that I had met in Europe" (p. 207).

Alexander Mackenzie, William Wells Brown, and David F. Dorr's travel writings reveal the different roles race played in their perception of individual and national identity. In many ways they revealed varying levels of uncertainty regarding identity—whether it was personal or national identity. In *Forgiving the Boundaries: Home as Abroad in American Travel Writing*, Terry Caesar ar-

gues that many American travelers felt American identity "lacked stability," and that traveling afforded Americans an opportunity to define their nationality.[3] These antebellum American travelers appeared uncertain about the qualities that made them American until they encountered English society. Mackenzie traveled with the dual purpose of discovering what it meant to be English and how much Englishness remained in the American character. Brown, and to some extent Dorr, also had a dual purpose in imagining an America free of slavery and what their future roles might be in that America. In England they experienced greater freedom as well as hints of what might be possible. In the case of Joseph Jenkins, Brown also got a hint of the difficulties that awaited black people after emancipation. While only Brown specifically went to England to speak on behalf of abolition, Dorr also discussed the issue. At the time, they represented a minority opinion in the United States.

Colonization (the returning of ex-slaves to Africa) appealed to more Americans than abolition, and in 1830 the American Colonization Society sent its first group of free black colonists to Liberia. An increasing demand for cotton, however, quickly put a damper on future colonization efforts. A year later a major slave uprising, Nat Turner's Rebellion, demonstrated a more volatile situation. Following the lead of African-American abolitionists like David Walker, white abolitionists William Lloyd Garrison, Theodore Dwight Weld and others founded the American Anti-Slavery Society in 1833. For Brown and Dorr, traveling in England where slavery had been recently abolished and where they were treated fairly, revealed a source of national difference. They largely defined America and England based on perceived differences in racial attitudes.

Despite their focus on race, Brown and Dorr also recognized other sources of national identity. Most Americans were well prepared for what to expect when they visited Great Britain. Thanks to the popularity of British writers in America, many American travelers arrived in Britain, specifically England and Scotland, well acquainted with what they saw and heard.[4] So, like his contemporaries Mackenzie built on his reading of English travel writers as well as British literature, Mackenzie devoted most of his own book to England and to an analysis of the people he encountered. During his visit to Britain in 1833 and 1834, he briefly visited Ireland, but he focused most of his energies on discovering the true character of England and the English. More than Brown and Dorr, Mackenzie—who was white—was searching for similarities between America and England. He avoided all mention of American slavery but did devote space to an analysis of English classes, voicing his thoughts on race in England and America.

Born April 6, 1803, Mackenzie joined the Navy at age twelve after briefly attending boarding school. He had a very successful career in the Navy, serving in the Pacific and West Indies between 1818 and 1824. His first book, *A Year in Spain,* received positive reviews in both America and England; and, during periods of leave from the Navy, he continued to travel and write. A trip to England from 1833 to 1834 gave him material for *The American in England.* He concluded his naval career serving as a commander during the U.S. Mexican War from 1847 to 1848.[5]

Mackenzie, in contrast to the travelers Allison Lockwood considered in *Passionate Pilgrims,* did not encounter hostile British citizens attacking the hypocrisy of an American democracy that held slaves. Lockwood's mostly white male travelers felt that slavery was constantly being thrown in their faces.[6] Instead, Mackenzie was trying to discover a sense of what it meant to be American. In the preface to his travel book, Mackenzie claimed that he discovered many similarities between America and England. Despite starting his journey "with some feeling of animosity towards England," because of British travel writers' "misrepresentation of our institutions and national character," Mackenzie did discover some common ground. Writing in the third person in his preface, Mackenzie reports:

> The author found, moreover, that there was so much identity between his own country and that which he was visiting, that it was not easy to hate the one without also hating the other. Hence, the patriotism which made America dear to him prompted him to love England: for, after all, we are ourselves but Englishmen in another hemisphere. . . . He has found, indeed, a pleasure, not easy to describe, in the observation of so many objects connected with the early history of our race, and in offering his homage at a thousand sites hallowed by the consecrating associations of genius and heroism.[7]

Exactly what characteristics America and England shared beyond the "early history of our race" was unclear, but Mackenzie left England with an impression of common "identity." After reflecting on his trip in preparing to write the preface to his travel book, Mackenzie obviously felt a sense of connection, even going so far as to refer to Americans as "Englishmen in another hemisphere." Such a comment would have appeared very out of place in the body of his journal, where he vented his frustrations with England and English ways, but this brief identification with the English helped him construct an American identity.

The closest Mackenzie came to identifying a similarity between America and England occurred in London where he noticed: "On the whole, the street population, excepting the want of elegance in the women, compared favorable [*sic*] with ours" (p. 132). Mackenzie introduces his recurring theme of women here, as well as his increasingly negative tone. What starts as a description of women shifts to race and ultimately class. Re-

garding women, he noted that "the women whom I saw were nearly all plump and comely," their faces were "almost all expressive, and many of them very beautiful." Moving down the body from "often swan-like necks, reposing on nobly-expanding bosoms," he was troubled that "in descending, the analysis became less satisfactory" as "the upper part of the bodies was too large for the lower; the foundations seemed crushed by the weight of the superstructure" (p. 129-130). He concluded that "the enthusiastic admiration of a fine female leg was a prevailing taste in England. A means of accounting for it may perhaps be found in its extreme rarity" (p. 179). In his description of women, Mackenzie introduces his concern of health. While the women had pleasing faces there were structural flaws, and as he moved on to discuss different races and economic classes, he uncovered their particular "flaws."

While Mackenzie discussed the Londoners' appearances, he began to focus more on national differences than similarities. He made no distinction between "race" and "class" and used the terms interchangeably. This was not uncommon during the nineteenth century as "people," "nation," and "race" often had the same meaning.[8] He starts his analysis of the street population by noting, "in London, the races are most distinctly marked."[9] The "races" Mackenzie specifically described were the "gentleman" and the "trader." Going into more detail on the "races," Mackenzie began to use "class." He noticed that:

> Among the humbler classes, the physical conformation seemed to announce the peculiar and separate calling of each individual. The same trade, descending perpetually from father to son through long succeeding generations, had occasioned a development of particular limbs and muscles. The absence of intellectual and moral culture, in occupations which rendered it unnecessary for those who worked only to administer food to themselves, and profit or luxury to the class of masters, could only account for the absence of forehead, of the ornamental parts of that face which was moulded after a divine model.

> (p. 129)

Just as certain physical characteristics were associated with different races in the science of the time, Mackenzie believed that, among the English working class, certain physical traits were inherited. The idea that the poor were poor because of an innate flaw was not uncommon in the nineteenth century. Historian H. L. Malchow shows that in "the late Victorian social discourse" it was commonly felt that the poorest classes of the cities were a "race apart."[10] Assuming a highly accelerated form of evolution, Mackenzie related the physical, mental, and moral capabilities of the "humbler classes" to their type of employment, essentially a worker "race."

According to Mackenzie, there were no such common physical traits among the American working class. He felt that the difference in appearance between American and English laborers resulted from the different nature of American and English societies. For Mackenzie, environment made a significant impact on the working classes:

> The contrast in the appearance and characteristics of this class of men in the two countries is the best illustration of the two very different systems of society existing in England and America. In England, owing to the peculiar character of the government, the vast accumulations of wealth, and its concentration in a few hands, in which the legislation has for centuries been placed, and naturally and necessarily exercised in their own interest, a state of things has been brought about, the inevitable consequence of which is, that one man sows and another reaps; the poor labour, and toil, and sweat; and the rich luxuriate and enjoy. Hence recklessness, indifference, servility, and the absence of pride among the inferior classes. In America, on the contrary, where the labourer is in truth worthy of his hire there is nothing to check or limit the ardour of individual exertion.[11]

The nature of English society, as Mackenzie interpreted it, maintained the status quo. In such a strictly defined, class-oriented culture, Mackenzie felt the "inferior classes" lacked the motivation to improve their lot, but the American, with the promise of social mobility, could reach any height.

Mackenzie writes that in America "there is nothing to check or limit the ardour of individual exertion." Yet, when Mackenzie introduced color into his discussion of American and English society, his argument for American social and economic freedoms lost any appearance of objectivity. For Mackenzie, in England:

> there were more good looks, and a more abounding air of health and vitality. Here one escaped entirely from the saffron hue of people from the south, and from the marshy new lands of our western rivers; as well as from all that intermediate shades between black and white, the effect of the various crossings with the race of Ham. Here were no negroes, black, green, or blue; no mulattoes, with aspect of mingled mild and molasses, brushing you away with their tattered plaid cloaks. Here the poor made way for the well-dressed, with a cringing air. They seemed to have been taught their place in succeeding ages from father to son.

> (p. 132)

Comparing Americans to English men and women, Mackenzie believed the English a healthier-looking people. He implied that skin color signified physical well-being and that the less than lily white appearance of some Americans suggested a lack of vigor. He specifically singled out black people, and his use of green and blue as other variations of "negro" color suggested an obviously unnatural and unhealthy appearance. With his criticism of "mulattoes'" ragged appearance and improper behavior, Mackenzie returned to his discussion of class, with a possible attempt at humor, noting how the poorer English classes have been taught to behave.

Even Mackenzie's praise for the "good looks" of the English was tempered by his criticism of the hierarchical and overly deferential nature of the English lower classes. His attention to the physically inherited traits of the English working class led him to a comparison with American black people. Considering that his discussion originated with an analysis of English "races," Mackenzie's introduction of the black race was interesting. The comparatively short discussion focused on one aspect of race, color. For Mackenzie, color merely represented a sign of innate flaws in American black people, just as the inherited traits of the English working class had become a sign of theirs. For Mackenzie, white Americans and the non-laboring English shared a sense of identity mostly based on the existence of people in both nations whose physical appearance designated their place in society.

Mackenzie compared English laborers to American black people to identify shared traits between America and England while pointing out the shortcomings of England. His discussion of America's black population and people of other colors gave him the chance to do both. For Mackenzie, black people's color represented the same kind of evolutionary defect that the English laborer demonstrated by such things as his "absence of forehead" (p. 129). Mackenzie argued that the shared identity between the white American and the upper-class Englishman was a shared racial superiority. England's class system was blamed for failing to allow the English laborer to work his way up, but Mackenzie did not criticize America for keeping black people in subservient positions.

Fifteen years later, William Wells Brown came to a completely different conclusion in his travel book. Brown wrote two travel narratives in his lifetime. First, in 1848, in *Narrative of William W. Brown, A Fugitive Slave,* Brown related the story of his journey from slavery to freedom. He further expanded on this theme in his second book, *The American Fugitive in Europe. Sketches of Places and People Abroad.* Before his European travel narrative begins, however, Brown quickly summarizes his life up to the point of his departure for the reader unfamiliar with his background. In his *American Fugitive in Europe,* Brown sought to discredit pro-slavery arguments, to draw attention to national differences in racial attitudes, and to demonstrate that an America free of racism was a possibility.

Foreign travel gave Brown a wider range of experiences to draw from in his role as an abolitionist speaker. As a former slave, however, his writing has been largely excluded from studies on travel writing. Mulvey has suggested that slave narratives have been overlooked as a form of travel writing because of their apparently uncritical condemnation of all things American and praise of everything English.[12] More recently, Lisa Brawley and William Stowe have argued that slave narratives allow the authors to participate in the political, social, and intellectual life of the nation that has excluded them.[13] Travel writing has always played a large role in studies dealing with American and English national identity, and while the role of race in national identity is still debated, Etienne Balibar has shown how "the discourse of race and nation are never far apart."[14] Brown's travel writing allowed him a way to fully imagine himself as an American. Brown felt American national identity was closely tied to its racial attitudes, and he hoped for a change in both in order to end slavery and racial prejudice. For Brown, race played a central role in defining American and English national identity.

Born a slave of Dr. John Young in Lexington, Kentucky, in 1814, Brown was one of seven children. In his *Narrative of William W. Brown,* Brown revealed that his mother, Elizabeth, gave birth to six other children—all of whom had different fathers. Brown's father, George Higgins, was a white man and a relative of Dr. Young.[15] While it has been generally disregarded, Brown wrote in *The Black Man, His Antecedents, His Genius, and His Achievements* that Daniel Boone was his maternal grandfather.[16] Hired out to various men after he turned twelve, Brown at one point worked for Elijah P. Lovejoy. Lovejoy, who later became the editor of an abolitionist newspaper, was murdered by pro-slavery forces in Alton, Illinois, in 1837. Not surprisingly, Lovejoy made no reference to his hiring of Brown's labor in his own writings.[17] Ultimately, Brown was sold to Captain Enoch Price from whom he successfully escaped on January 1, 1834. A Quaker family in Ohio helped him, and Brown took the Quaker father's name, Wells Brown, as his own in thanks for his help. While working on a steamer on Lake Erie for several years, Brown gradually began to work as a speaker for various anti-slavery societies.[18]

In 1844 Brown became an agent for the Western New York Anti-Slavery Society and later the Massachusetts Anti-Slavery Society. Danger of recapture and his increasingly prominent role as an abolitionist speaker ultimately led to his trip to Europe. *The American Fugitive in Europe* began with his departure as a delegate for the Peace Congress in Paris July 18, 1849. As he traveled throughout large parts of England, Scotland, Wales, and Ireland, lecturing on behalf of various anti-slavery societies, he saw many of the typical tourist sites, such as Shakespeare's home and the Tower of London.

Brown, who remained overseas until the summer of 1854, traveled to Paris and throughout the British Isles. During his travels he met many distinguished individuals, such as Victor Hugo and Harriet Martineau. While overseas, Brown completed his novel, *Clotel; or, The President's Daughter: A Narrative of Slave Life in the United States,* published first in London in 1853. *Clotel* made him the first African-American novelist. His best known work, *Clotel,* describes the life of Thomas Jefferson's illegitimate mulatto daughter and the difficulties she and her daughters faced under slavery. Unfortunately, *Clotel* was generally ignored by the English press, most likely because it was not much of a story when compared with Brown's own factual account of his escape from slavery. When Brown returned to America in 1854, he continued to speak out against slavery; when the Civil War began, he helped recruit black soldiers. Around 1865 Brown began practicing medicine while working in various organizations that fought for the rights of black people, as well as for temperance societies.[19] He wrote on various topics and in various forms, including two plays, but his best work included his own history and his histories of black people in America.

From the beginning of Brown's *American Fugitive,* it was clear how intimately connected race and nation were for him. His anger at America was obvious, but he could not deny his attachment. When departing for England on July 18, 1849, Brown considered his conflicting feelings:

> From the treatment I had received from the Americans as a victim of slavery, and the knowledge that I was at that time liable to be seized and again reduced to whips and chains, I had supposed that I would leave the country without any regret; but in this I was mistaken, for when I saw the last thread of communication cut off between me and the land, and the dim shores dying away in the distance, I almost regretted that I was not on shore.[20]

Despite the danger of remaining in America, Brown was sad to leave America and was confused by his own feelings. Part of his regret at leaving America was being separated from friends and family, but it was only partial regret as Brown was leaving behind the restrictions American society placed on a black man and runaway slave.

The thrill of arrival quickly brought about a change in Brown's tone as he noticed a significant difference between America and Britain:

> But no sooner was I on British soil, than I was recognized as a man, and an equal. The very dogs in the streets appeared conscious of my manhood. Such is the difference, and such is the change that is brought about by a trip of nine days in an Atlantic steamer

(p. 98)

The new-found feeling of respect that Brown thereby discovered in Britain changed his outlook on everything, invigorating his writing and public speaking. Brown's favorable impressions of England only increased while there. When he returned to America in 1849, Brown wrote: "I had began to fancy myself an Englishman by habit, if not by birth" (p. 221).

Not only was Brown personally transformed by his trip to England, he also hoped to inspire a larger change by encouraging an end to slavery in America. In drawing attention to the good that England had done, Brown did not completely ignore its role in the introduction and growth of slavery in North America. Instead, he argued that, "The time has come when nations are judged by the acts of the present, instead of the past. And so it must be with America" (p. 140). Brown suggested that England had cleared its name with abolition, but the jury of international opinion was still out regarding America. Ultimately, Brown was more effective when he included his own experiences with slavery when commenting on England.

For many nineteenth century travel writers, the majority of their time was spent drawing comparisons and contrasts between home and abroad. When Brown compared American and English poverty, he also drew on his experiences as a slave. In early September of 1849, Brown visited some cottages of English working people and noted:

> the more I see and learn of the condition of the working-classes of England, the more I am satisfied of the utter fallacy of the statements often made that their condition approximates to that of the slaves of America. Whatever may be the disadvantages that the British peasant labors under, he is free; and if he is not satisfied with his employer, he can make choice of another.
>
> (p. 139)

As a fugitive slave speaking in support of abolition, Brown naturally looked for evidence to challenge American slave holders' claim that slaves worked in the same or better conditions than European laborers. Unlike Mackenzie, who was hardly working class and had limited his comparison to white American laborers, Brown was able to use first-hand experiences which gave his writing greater authority.

Travel for Brown also gave him the opportunity to directly challenge slavery proponents in ways rarely seen in slave narratives. While in Paris for the Peace Conference, Brown was approached by a white American. And just as the voyage over changed Brown, he noted it also changed his fellow American. Since Brown had been introduced earlier to Victor Hugo, the white American wanted Brown to introduce him to Hugo as well. Brown tells his readers:

> I need not inform you that I declined introducing this pro-slavery American to these distinguished men. I only allude to this, to show what a change came over the dreams of my white American brother by crossing

the ocean. The man who would not have been seen walking with me in the streets of New York, and who would not have shaken hands with me with a pair of tongs while on the passage from the United States, could come with hat in hand in Paris, and say, "I was your fellow-passenger".

(p. 110)

To Brown, the brief transformation of this white American's racial attitudes does not suggest the possibility of a permanent alteration. Instead, he increasingly suggested that such negative racial attitudes were more likely national traits, traits that even the English and Irish possessed in a small degree.

Traveling in Ireland in early August of 1849, Brown wrote a great deal about social conditions, especially regarding the poverty he encountered. In Dublin near St. Patrick's Cathedral, Brown had

> a heart-sickening view of the poorest of the poor. All the recollections of poverty which I had ever beheld seemed to disappear in comparison with what was then before me. We passed a filthy and noisy market, where fruit and vegetable women were screaming and begging those passing by to purchase their commodities; while in and about the market-place were throngs of beggars fighting for rotten fruit, cabbage-stock, and even the very trimmings of vegetables. . . . Sickly and emaciated looking creatures, half naked, were at our heels at every turn.
>
> (p. 100)

Even when enslaved, Brown had not seen poverty to the extent he witnessed in Dublin. The vivid picture he drew of the market-place was one of his most detailed descriptions during his travels in Britain. This view of the market-place clearly influenced his overall view of Ireland and the Irish.

For Brown, Ireland was a highly contradictory nation; yet he chose not to compare this "land of genius and degradation, of great resources and unparalleled poverty, noble deeds and the most revolting crimes" with his home country. Though he avoided a direct national comparison, when Brown encountered some prejudice in Ireland he did refer to America. While waiting to see a royal procession in Dublin in August of 1849, he remarked that his color seemed to attract stares from the crowd. However, he was careful to note that "neither while at the window or in the streets was I once insulted. This was so unlike the American prejudice, that is seemed strange to me" (p. 102).

Brown did present some criticism of English racial attitudes as well, but it was veiled compared to his criticism of America. One example of English prejudice occurred in October of 1849, when he noticed another black man on the streets of London. Brown approached him after he concluded from his appearance that the man was an American. This man told Brown that he was an escaped Maryland slave and that upon making his way to England he had been unable to find work. After Brown gave him some money, the man told Brown, "You are the first friend I have met in London" (p. 135). The English had certainly displayed evidence of racism in their past, and they would again, but Brown avoided any direct criticism. Instead, Brown increasingly chose to emphasize how the protective environment of England could lead to something better for black people in America.

Ironically, conditions for black people in England had not radically improved with abolition in 1833. Many of the recently freed British black people were suddenly unemployed. Instead of concerning themselves with the now free British black population, British abolitionists focused their attention on American slavery, especially the escaped American slaves arriving in England after 1833.[21] Abolitionist groups financed speaking tours of escaped American slaves throughout Great Britain for the purpose of raising awareness and funds, both of which Brown did. Those favoring reform in Britain, often members of anti-slavery societies, wanted to use American democracy as their model. Before using America as a model, however, they needed to help the Americans put their house in order by abolishing slavery.[22] While British abolitionists continued their work, British black people struggling with difficulties of adjusting to freedom were mostly ignored.

Brown used his travel book to claim a place for black people in the unified America he hoped would evolve. The first evidence of this hope occurred when he renewed his acquaintance with William and Ellen Craft. Brown first met and toured with the couple in the early months of 1849 as speakers for the Massachusetts Anti-Slavery Society.[23] When the Fugitive Slave Law became law in 1850, William and Ellen Craft traveled to England where they joined Brown on his lectures in Scotland and northern England. The story of the Craft's escape from slavery was unique, as Ellen (sometimes called the "white slave") was very light skinned and easily passed as a white person. She disguised herself as a man and pretended to be the owner of William. Ellen was often the focus of attention during these talks in America and Britain because of her color. In 1860 the Crafts published the story of their escape from slavery in *Running a Thousand Miles for Freedom; or, the Escape of William and Ellen Craft from Slavery*.

When the Crafts arrived in Liverpool in December of 1850, they proceeded to Edinburgh, Scotland. While walking together in the streets, William Craft and Brown noted a gentleman with "a colored lady on each arm." Brown wrote:

> C—— remarked, in a very dry manner, "If they were in Georgia, the slaveholders would make them walk in a more hurried gait than they do." . . . When walking

through the streets, I amused myself by watching C——'s countenance; and, in doing so, imagined I saw the changes experienced by every fugitive slave in his first month's residence in this country.[24]

As with most travelers when they saw something that defied their previous experiences, they naturally contrasted it with their home country. William Craft's observation did not positively reflect on America, and Brown's pleasure in watching Craft discover such a favorable difference reminded Brown of his own discovery of freedom when he arrived. The experience of traveling throughout Britain increasingly strengthened Brown's belief that overt racism was a uniquely American trait.

On June 21, 1851, Brown, the Crafts, and some other friends went to the Crystal Palace at the World's Fair. Brown mentioned that there were Africans among the various nationalities present, but the presence of other black Americans in the microcosm of the world inspired Brown to write:

> There is a great deal of freedom in the Exhibition. I was pleased to see such a goodly sprinkling of my own countrymen in the Exhibition—I mean colored men and women—well-dressed, and moving about with their fairer brethren. This, some of our pro-slavery Americans did not seem to relish very well.
>
> (p. 164)

Noting his "own countrymen," Brown suggests a kind of exclusive nationality that he extends only to "colored men and women" and possibly to the "fairer brethren" who were not offended by their presence. Walking through the various nations on display allowed Brown to demonstrate the possibility of racial harmony to his reading audience in America.

Brown truly savored the opportunity of breaking the mores of "appropriate behavior" for a black man in front of white Americans:

> As I walked through the American part of the Crystal Palace some of our Virginia neighbors eyed me closely and with jealous looks, especially as an English lady was leaning on my arm. But their sneering looks did not disturb me in the least. I remained the longer in their department, and criticized the bad appearance of their goods the more.
>
> (p. 164-165)

Travel for Brown had given him an opportunity to experience something he never could have in the United States. When Brown returned to the United States in 1854, he noted that he returned as "a soldier in this moral warfare against the most cruel system of oppression" (p. 227). From the time of his arrival in England to his triumph at the Crystal Palace, Brown had sought to reveal the differences in national racial attitudes. The experience of travel in England gave Brown a stronger sense of the role race played in American national identity, ultimately giving him a vision of possibilities.

Like Brown, David F. Dorr would have a similar experience at the Crystal Palace at nearly the same time, but Dorr traveled in Europe not to fight for abolition but for the experience of travel. He introduced his trip through Europe and the Middle East, writing, "This day, June 15th, 1851, I commence my writings of a promiscuous voyage."[25] *Promiscuous* has several meanings, and while there was some mention of sexual adventures, Dorr's travel writing is also a mix of various impressions and adventures. Perhaps *promiscuous* was Dorr's way of referring to himself as a man composed of many identities.

Little is known of Dorr's background besides the information he provides in his book, dedicated "to my slave mother." Only in his preface, where he revealed that he had been a slave during his travels from 1851 to 1854, did Dorr mention his enslavement and that he was a quadroon. When he returned to America and asked his master and traveling companion Cornelius Fellowes for his freedom, as he had apparently been promised "in different parts of the world," he was denied. Dorr then "fled from him and his princely promises" to Cleveland, Ohio, where he had *A Colored Man Round the World* published in 1858 (p. 12).

Malini Johar Schueller, in her introduction to a new reprint of Dorr's travel book, reveals some more information regarding Dorr after his escape to Cleveland. By locating military records, she has estimated that Dorr was born in either 1827 or 1828 in New Orleans. After the Civil War began, Dorr enlisted in the Seventh Ohio Volunteer Infantry and served until August 15, 1864, when he was discharged after being seriously injured in battle. Because of those injuries, Dorr received a disability pension after the war until his death in 1872.[26] Unfortunately, Dorr left no written record of his experiences after he escaped from slavery.

Dorr's travel book is unique in that it gives no hint that Dorr was a slave except in the preface. William Stowe, one of the few scholars to study Dorr, refers to Dorr's shift in his narrative from a slave to a free voice as his "counterfactual narrative persona."[27] Stowe argues that the model for Dorr's freeman was "his master's circle of New Orleans men-about-town" and that Dorr used his book as "dry run for freedom" (p. 62). With the exception of Stowe's research, Dorr is not considered in the scholarship on American travelers, African-American autobiography, or slave narratives. Dorr does not easily fit into any classifications, since his writing at times can defy explanation. Although Stowe tries to account for some of Dorr's behavior by arguing that Dorr was modeling himself on his master's wealthy New Or-

leans bachelor acquaintances, that particular explanation does not give Dorr enough credit for the difficulties he faced as a slave traveling as a companion, promised his freedom, and then forced to return to slavery.

Despite traveling at virtually the same time as Brown, Dorr did not give England any recognition for its leadership in ending slavery. The closest Dorr came to giving England any special notice occurred when the Queen rode by and he "felt a sort of religious thrill pass over me, and I said to myself 'this is civilization.'"[28] Dorr failed to elaborate any further, but he became quite upset with some Englishmen for discussing American slavery. Shortly after he and Fellowes, his master and traveling companion, arrived in June 1851, Dorr overheard some English gentlemen discussing slavery in the newsroom of his Liverpool Hotel.

> They were quietly discussing the weak points in American policy. One held that if the negroes of the Southern States were fit for freedom, it would be an easy matter for four million slaves to raise the standard of liberty, and maintain it against 250,000 slaveholders. The other gentleman held that it was very true, but they needed some white man, well posted in the South, with courage enough to plot the entrée. He continued, at great length, to show the feasibility under a French plotter. He closed with this expression, "One intelligent Frenchman like Ledru Rollin could do the whole thing before it could be known." I came to the conclusion that they were not so careful in the expression of their views as I thought they ought to be. I was quite sure that they would not be allowed to use such treasonable language at [New] Orleans or Charleston as that they had just indulged in.
>
> (p. 16-17)

Though Dorr was essentially a free man once he touched English soil, he did not take this opportunity to join in on the men's condemnation of slavery. Stowe interprets Dorr's reaction as the effect of his "adopted persona" appropriating the views of a Southern gentleman who takes offense at foreigners suggesting a violation of American law.[29] It could be as Stowe suggests, but Dorr's reaction was similar to William Craft's reaction to seeing a white man walking with two black women. Craft also noted that things would be different if they were in the South.[30] Like Craft, this was part of Dorr becoming acclimated to the freedom of a new location. Admittedly, on this occasion Dorr gave no hint of his bondage when an hour later he referred to the conversation he overheard as "this nauseous language."[31] But despite his apparent mouthing of the Southern gentlemanly opinions, Dorr was capable of speaking out on slavery.

Dorr made his way to the Crystal Palace at the World's Fair roughly a month after Brown and the Crafts had been there. If the atmosphere was still as Brown described it with Africans and many black Americans present, then that may have been the reason Dorr was emboldened to comment on American slavery. As he walked through the various displays on July 28, 1851, the disappointing American display reminded Dorr of slavery. He wrote:

> I saw everything that was a prevailing disgrace to our country except slaves. I understood that a South Caro-linian proposed taking half a dozen haughty and sin-ewy negroes to the Fair, but was only deterred from that proposition by the want of courage to risk six fat, strong healthy negroes to the chances of escape from slavery to freedom.

> (p. 20)

Dorr opened his commentary with a critique of the American goods and did not shy away from criticizing slavery. That slaves had been a potential display clearly troubled Dorr. Despite his earlier revulsion at the dis-cussion of a slave revolt, Dorr hinted that he found sla-very a "disgrace." That Dorr voiced a Southern view at one point and condemned slavery the next reveals his conflict in attempting to define himself in a new situa-tion.

The confusion Dorr felt over his identity continued to manifest itself as he and Fellowes continued their trav-els in Europe and the Middle East. While at a nightly ball in Paris, Dorr observed Mr. Cordevoille, a "fine looking, yellow skinned man," a quadroon from Louisi-ana who occasionally resided in France. He had been the "largest talorizer in the South" but left New Orleans because of the color prejudice he encountered. Dorr de-scribed Cordevoille and his French wife in great detail, taking care to note his gentlemanly demeanor and ap-pearance. When his traveling companion and master, Fellowes, and a Mr. Holbrook of the *New Orleans Pica-yune* were invited by Cordevoille to his country home, Dorr concluded: "Lest it be a censure on these gentle-men, I refrain from going any further with a subject so delicate" (p. 39-40). Dorr, clearly impressed with the success of Cordevoille, was pleased that the white men from New Orleans showed Cordevoille due respect. At the same time, Dorr was aware that to go on at length about the friendly meeting could harm the reputation of the white men.

During his travels, Dorr was in a strange position as he switched between the role of worldly traveler and anti-slavery advocate. To all appearances he was traveling as a free man on equal standing with Fellowes. Dorr gave a glowing biographical sketch of him in his book, and if it were not for Dorr's preface, the reader would not know that Fellowes did not keep his promise and free Dorr upon their return to the United States (p. 12).

Dorr had another apparent identity slip in Istanbul where he attempted to buy a woman for "about a thousand Turkish piastres, a sum of about twenty-five dollars" (p.

123). Yet Egypt received special notice as Dorr pointed out the incredible innovations of the black man: "Egypt was a higher sphere of artistical science than any other nation on the earth. This will naturally convey an idea to the world that the black man was the first skillful animal on the earth" (p. 134). Dorr's emphasis on this example of an advanced black civilization challenged a key point in the white defense of enslaving black people. Slavery advocates argued that there had never been a black civilization, using this claim to support the superiority of the white race. Dorr did not spend much time on this topic, however, as he quickly returned to sight-seeing.

For Dorr, the confusion of his status as free or enslaved took precedence in his writings over any overt interest in American or English national identity. Unlike Mack-enzie, Dorr was not in England looking for national similarities or differences. Unlike Brown, he had yet to clearly identify himself with abolition. His own status in New Orleans as a quadroon, where he had been edu-cated or educated himself, made the kind of distinctions Brown was able to make between England and America difficult. Dorr's treatment in England and in France was likely quite similar to his reception in New Orleans as more of a companion than servant to Fellowes. It was only when the issue of slavery was put in front of him while traveling that he attacked American racial atti-tudes.

When Mackenzie, Brown, and Dorr traveled to England before 1860, they used race in different ways to define American and English national identity. Mackenzie claimed Americans were simply Englishmen on another continent. The major similarity he discovered was that the English working class and American black people were racially inferior to the white upper-class English-man and white Americans. Brown used what he per-ceived as benevolent English attitudes to criticize American slavery and the racial attitudes that allowed slavery to exist. He remained optimistic, however, that America could emulate the English and give him the same kind of freedoms he felt he had while in England. Dorr had a more difficult time coming to terms with how to represent his individual and national identity. Unless he directly encountered American slavery, he was ambiguous about the connection between national identity and race.

Notes

1. See Nigel File and Chris Power, *Black Settlers in Britain 1555-1958* (London: Heinemann Educa-tional Books, 1981); Gerzina; Norma Myers *Re-constructing the Black Past: Blacks in Britain c. 1780-1830,* Cass Series: Studies in Slave and Post-Slave Societies and Cultures. (London: Frank Cass, 1996); Panikos Panayi, *Immigration, Ethnic-*

ity, and Racism in Britain, 1815-1945 (New York: Manchester University Press, 1994); and James Walvin's *The Black Presence: A Documentary History of the Negro in England, 1555-1860* (London: Orbach & Chambers, 1971), *Black and White: The Negro and English Society 1555-1945* (London: Allen Lane and the Penguin Press, 1973), and *England, Slaves and Freedom, 1776-1838* (London: MacMillan, 1986).

2. William Wells Brown, *The American Fugitive in Europe. Sketches of Places and People Abroad,* in *The Travels of William Wells Brown,* ed. Paul Jefferson (Boston: John P. Jewett, 1855; reprint, New York: Markus Wiener Publishing, Inc., 1991), 205.

3. Caesar, 8, 36.

4. Benjamin Goluboff has also found this in, "Latent Preparedness: Allusions in American Travel Literature on Britain" *American Studies* 31, no. 1 (Spring 1990).

5. Dumas Malone, ed., *Dictionary of American Biography* (New York: Charles Scribner's Sons, 1933), vol. 6, 90-91.

6. Allison Lockwood, *Passionate Pilgrims: The American Traveler in Great Britain, 1800-1914* (New York: Cornwall Books, 1981), 16.

7. Alexander Slidell Mackenzie, *The American in England* (Paris: A & W Galignani and Co., 1836), x-xi.

8. See George L. Mosse, *Toward the Final Solution: A History of European Racism* (New York: Howard Fertig, 1978), 45.

9. Mackenzie, 128.

10. Howard L. Malchow, *Gothic Images of Race in Nineteenth-Century Britain* (Stanford: Stanford University Press, 1996), 251.

11. Mackenzie, 170.

12. Mulvey, *Anlgo-American Landscapes,* 19.

13. Lisa C. Brawley, "Fugitive Nation: Slavery, Travel and Technologies of American Identity, 1830-1860" (Ph.D. diss., University of Chicago, 1995), 10; Stowe, 62.

14. Etienne Balibar and Immanuel Wallerstein, *Race, Nation, Class: Ambiguous Identities* (London: Verso, 1991), 37.

15. William Wells Brown, *Narrative of William Wells Brown, A Fugitive Slave,* in *The Travels of William Wells Brown,* ed. Paul Jefferson (Boston: Anti-Slavery Office, 1848; reprint, New York: Markus Wiener Publishing, Inc., 1991), 28.

16. William Wells Brown, *The Black Man, His Antecedents, His Genius, and His Achievements* (New

York & Boston, 1863), 11; quoted in William Edward Farrison, *William Wells Brown: Author and Reformer* (Chicago: University of Chicago Press, 1969), 4.

17. Paul Simon, *Freedom's Champion: Elijah Lovejoy* (Carbondale and Edwardsville: Southern Illinois University Press, 1994), 16-17.

18. Brown, *Narrative of William Wells Brown,* 88-90.

19. William Edward Farrison, *William Wells Brown: Author and Reformer* (Chicago: University of Chicago Press, 1969), 401.

20. Brown, *The American Fugitive in Europe,* 95.

21. Michael P. Banton, *The Coloured Quarter: Negro Immigrants in an English City* (London: Johnathan Cape, 1955), 24.

22. David Turley, *The Culture of English Antislavery, 1780-1860* (London and New York: Routledge, 1991), 197.

23. Farrison, 134-137.

24. Brown, *The American Fugitive in Europe,* 148.

25. David F. Dorr, *A Colored Man Round the World.* (Cleveland: privately printed, 1858), 13.

26. David F. Dorr, *A Colored Man Round the* World, ed. Johar Malini Schueller (Ann Arbor: The University of Michigan Press, 1999), xi-xv.

27. Stowe, 62.

28. Dorr, 22.

29. Stowe, 65.

30. Brown, *The American Fugitive in Europe,* 148.

31. Dorr, 17.

Bibliography

Buzzard, James. *The Beaten Track: European Tourism, Literature, and the Ways to Culture, 1800-1918.* New York: Oxford University Press, 1993.

Caesar, Terry. *Forgiving the Boundaries: Home as Abroad in American Travel Writing.* Athens: University of Georgia Press, 1995.

Foster, Shirley. *Across New Worlds: Nineteenth-Century Women Travellers and Their Writings.* New York: Harvester Wheatsheaf, 1990.

Leed, Eric J. *The Mind of the Traveler: From Gilgamesh to Global Tourism.* New York: Basic Books, 1991.

Lockwood, Allison. *Passionate Pilgrims: The American Traveler in Great Britain, 1800-1914.* New York: Cornwall Books, 1981.

Mulvey, Christopher. *Anglo-American Landscapes: A Study of Nineteenth-Century Anglo-American Travel Literature.* New York: Cambridge University Press, 1983.

Mulvey, Christopher. *Transatlantic Manners: Social Patterns in Nineteenth-Century Anglo-American Travel Literature.* New York: Cambridge University Press, 1990.

Pratt, Mary Louise. *Imperial Eyes: Travel Writing and Transculturation.* New York: Routledge, 1992.

Schriber, Mary Suzanne, ed. *Telling Travels: Selected Writing by Nineteenth-Century American Woman Abroad.* DeKalb: Northern Illinois University Press, 1995.

Stowe, William. *Going Abroad: European Travel in Nineteenth-Century American Culture.* Princeton, New Jersey: Princeton University Press, 1994.

WOMEN'S TRAVEL WRITING

Karen R. Lawrence (essay date 1994)

SOURCE: Lawrence, Karen R. "'The African Wanderers': Kingsley and Lee." In *Penelope Voyages: Women and Travel in the British Literary Tradition*, pp. 103-53. Ithaca, N.Y.: Cornell University Press, 1994.

[*In the following essay, Lawrence evaluates the West African travel narratives written by British authors Mary Kingsley and Sarah Lee Wallis.*]

In the hundred years that separates Wollstonecraft's unusual "business" trip to Scandinavia and Mary Kingsley's travels to West Africa, women's travel burgeoned, much in relation to imperialist projects of church and nation. According to Dorothy Hammond and Alta Jablow in *The Myth of Africa*:

> The clearest indication that the British were now at home in Africa was the ubiquitous presence of the ladies. Previously these had been settlers' wives in South Africa, but they did not write of their lives, and it is only from the accounts of some of the early missionaries' wives that we learn something of the Englishwoman's situation. They were expected to share the work, hardship, and discomforts. . . . By the end of the century, however, administrators, traders, and even travelers were bringing their wives to Africa. The land was considered sufficiently tame for lady tourists to travel on safari.
>
> (84)

In an otherwise astute discussion of British imperialism in Africa, Hammond and Jablow find amusement in the feminization of colonial travel wrought by "the ladies."

This suggestion of the way the presence of white women on the imperial frontier not only mitigates the excitement of adventure but also impedes colonial relations among men marks even sophisticated meditations on British imperialism. For example, in O. Mannoni's and Ashis Nandy's seminal discussions of colonial psychology (in Africa and India, respectively), white women are viewed as the source of an exaggerated racism that inhibits colonial male-to-male relationships. Mannoni remarks that feminine "racialism" is often an "overcompensation" for a sense of "inferiority" (116). Nandy attributes white women's racism to their sexual anxiety. He maintains that white women in India "were generally more exclusive and racist because they unconsciously saw themselves as the sexual competitors of Indian men, with whom their men had established an unconscious homo-eroticized bonding" (9-10). The inscription of women in "plots" of sexual jealousy and powerlessness limits their roles in colonial situations to victimization in sexual relations and frustration in public action.[1]

To offset impressions of women as secondary agents of imperialism who frequently perpetuated English racism, other historians and critics have recuperated the roles of women in the colonial context in a discourse antithetical to Hammond and Jablow's generalized treatment of "the ladies." This other tradition of analysis seeks to recover the lost stories of "intrepid" women who did make it to the imperial frontier and who traveled alone rather than settling down with husbands on their missions of empire. This tradition (including some feminist analyses) makes its argument through biographies of rugged individualists, focusing on the courage and iconoclasm of women travelers to unknown parts. These very prevalent and in some senses revisionary representations of women's active roles as adventurers concentrate on the single woman rather than on woman as helpmate. Indeed, many of the women who traveled to Africa were either divorced or widowed. In the title of her book *Spinsters Abroad*, Dea Birkett emphasizes the social and sexual status of the unmarried and solitary woman traveler—a well-known Victorian type—transforming travel into the antithesis not only of domesticity but of heterosexual relationship as well. This view of travel as a flight from the oppressions of patriarchy supplies a counterpart to Paul Zweig's notion of adventure as a flight from women. In the hands of some male writers who consider women travelers, this iconoclastic image tends to become either threatening or comic. Leo Hamalian, whose book on eighteenth- and nineteenth-century women travelers applauds the "small but impressive library of first-person narratives that combined genuine learning with the spirit of individualism" (xii), nevertheless entitles his book *Ladies on the Loose,* a title that raises the specter of uncontained female sexuality. On the other hand, for Evan Connell, whose book *A Long Desire* presents various stories of travel and adventure, the solitary women travelers become comic freaks. Even Connell's admiration for their courage is tinged with condescension. In his characterization of Isabella Bird Bishop, who is "shaped like a penguin, holding court in gold-embroidered slippers and a petticoat decorated with gold and silver Japanese wheels," he transforms the traveler into a comic Miss Pickerel on her way to Mars. "They give the impression of being mildly batty," he says, "these upright, energetic, innocent, valorous, polite, intelligent, prim, and condescending British females in long skirts, carrying parasols . . . and not infrequently clinging like a huge black moth to the back of a coolie who must have thought he had been engaged by a creature from a different universe." "No, no, I'll go along with Ibn Batuta or that Chinese whose name I can't remember, but this woman is too much" (24).

But it is the feminist analysis of nineteenth-century women's travel, including, significantly, travel to British territories and colonies, with which I am most concerned. These studies provide important acts of recovery and attention, often attempting to demonstrate how women travelers to the imperial frontier managed to escape the system of exploitation that underwrites male narratives. "With very few exceptions," Katherine Frank says in "Voyages Out," "all the women rejected the virulent racism that blights most of the male accounts of Africa" (73). Frank seems to acknowledge the complex social situation of these women travelers, in whom competing claims of gender, racial, and class discourses created both a sympathy with native populations and an assumption of superiority: "The entrenched Victorian conviction of white racial supremacy, then, was responsible for nineteenth-century women's extraordinary freedom in Africa, where their identity derived from their white skins rather than their female bodies. But at the same time, the legacy of sexual oppression paradoxically fostered these women's identification with the subjugated Africans whose lower station facilitated their own liberation in Africa" (72). In this passage, Frank appears to recognize, although not analyze, the "quest for liberation" as itself complicitous in the pattern of British imperialist domination. The danger of ignoring this complicity can be seen in Birkett's description of courageous women travelers: "The Dark Continent, the Orient, the Savage Lands" provided "the stage upon which their new experiences as travellers could be realized" (47). Birkett thus ignores the way the "native" land becomes merely a backdrop for the drama of female liberation, which feminism in the 1980s seeks to recover. As Gayatri Chakravorty Spivak points out in a provocative essay on the relation between Western feminism and women in the so-called developing nations: "Historically, it is well known that we in this country take our model of militancy from the British nineteenth century. For feminist individualism in that age of imperialism, the stake was the making of human beings. That meant the constitution and interpellation of the subject, not only as individual but as 'individualist'" ("Political Economy of Women as Seen by a Literary Critic," 219). Spivak's suggestive comments attempt to unmask the universalistic rhetoric of the Western quest for self-realization, even women's self-realization, as the forging of an imperial self whose definition depends on its difference from (and domination of) others not so individuated. Spivak's essay helps us recognize the ideological assumptions in much of the individualist rhetoric in female travel writing and even its more contemporary recuperation in feminist criticism.[2]

An incident from Mary Kingsley's *Travels in West Africa* exemplifies the complexity of racial, class, and gender discourses in British women's travel writing. Kingsley relates the story of her use of what is called "trade English," a type of pidgin English the grammar of which "has no gender." Kingsley tells a purportedly humorous story of being addressed as "sir" by her African carriers because of the lack of gender markings in the language. Her point is the comical confusion of genders, the way that she as traveler becomes androgynous, but ironically, Kingsley (who is generally an extremely astute reader of cultural roles) fails to recognize not only that the *generic* gender is masculine (and not really a third, neuter gender) but also, more important, that the class and race markers of the word "sir" signify her superiority.[3]

Kingsley's *Travels in West Africa* (1897) and Sarah Lee's *The African Wanderers; or, The Adventures of Carlos and Antonio* (1847)[4] provide instructive examples of how women writers recorded and imagined British confrontation with West Africans in two very different genres—narrative-ethnography and sentimental abolitionist novel, respectively—during two different periods of the English presence in Africa. My choice to focus on travel literature concerning Africa rests on a number of considerations. Throughout the nineteenth century, Africa represented a kind of limit case for the European imagination—the unknown Dark Continent on the other side of European enlightenment and the photographic negative of its civilization. As numerous critics have observed, this evocation of Africa is particularly gender-inflected. Despite different narrative stances and rhetorical topoi in different genres, changes in the European attitude toward Africa over the course of the century, and the previously mentioned presence of women in Africa by the late 1800s, travel literature on Africa is often coded in masculinist terms. A strongly gendered semiotics marks the multiple genres recording

British encounters in Africa: fictional adventure writing ("the main form within literature" that inspired "the expansive imperialist thrust of the white race," according to Martin Green [*Robinson Crusoe Story,* 2]), nonfictional exploration narratives (using the "monarch of all I survey" rhetoric of the British explorer in Africa [see Pratt, *Imperial Eyes,* 201]), and imperial romance (with its eroticization of the African landscape as the female body waiting for male penetration [see Brantlinger]).[5]

In selecting these two examples of women's writing about Africa in the nineteenth century, my purpose is neither to praise these representations for sensitivity greater than that of "male" narratives nor to damn them for their complicity with the dominant ideologies of their time.[6] I choose these texts as examples of two very different generic and narrative strategies for handling mediation between black and white and female and male on the imperial frontier. Lee's mid-century adventure tale deploys topoi of sentimental romance in a nondomestic, fraternal mode—themes of rescue and foster-parentage give way to the more modern themes of conversion and trade; in Kingsley's more skeptical, less sentimental version of cultural confrontation (conversion, as well as conquest, is treated with great suspicion), trade serves both as chief mechanism and as metaphor for a purported reciprocity between European and African. The two writers represent different forms of "passing" in their texts: Lee's dark-skinned Latino protagonists curiously mediate between white and black, and as I said above, Kingsley represents herself as a woman traveler addressed as "sir," a comical "error" that her text records with some degree of pleasure in gender neutrality. In examining these two texts, I am also concerned with the way two women who traveled in West Africa represented Africa as a product for a home audience.

Despite the homogenizing force of Africanist discourse, the epistemological project of the "invention of Africa," as V. Y. Mudimbe calls it, encompasses many historical and geographical variations. My choice of narratives on West Africa is conditioned by the fact that, as Philip Curtin points out, West Africa supplied the earliest images of the continent because it represented the core of the slave trade (vi). It is also the source of the idea of the fetish, which the West found so powerful; I will discuss this idea in some detail in regard to Mary Kingsley's book.

By mid-nineteenth century, when Sarah Lee's novel was marketed, images of Africa were eagerly consumed by the British reading public. The commercial success of nonfictional records published earlier in the century had inspired the burgeoning of fiction about Africa, sometimes produced by explorers and travelers with firsthand experience of the continent. "By the 1850's,"

Mary Kingsley, 1862-1900.

Curtin writes, "the image [of Africa] had hardened. It was found in children's books, in Sunday school tracts, in the popular press. Its major affirmations were the 'common knowledge' of the educated classes" (vi).[7]

Indeed, the relation between the circulation of British travelers and that of their Africanist discourse at home becomes especially pressing in a colonial context. As the preface to Henry Stanley's novel *My Kalulu, Prince, King, and Slave* (1874) indicates, questions of audience and ideological function are bound up with suppositions about gender. For many books about Africa, like Stanley's novel, were conceived as "food" for future male imperialists.

> This book has been written for boys; not those little darlings who are yet bothering over the alphabet, and have to be taken to bed at sundown, and who, when they awake, put civilised and respectable families into confusion with their cries . . . but for those clever, bright-eyed, intelligent boys, of all classes, who have begun to be interested in romantic literature, with whom educated fathers may talk without fear of misapprehension, and of whom friends are already talking as boys who have a promising future before them. These boys are the guests for whom I have provided a true Africa feast. The feast provided for them is not over rich, because Africa is not far enough advanced yet to furnish

delicacies, such as puddings, cakes, confections, & c.; but what there is of it, plain rice and curry, dried meat of game, wild fruits of piquant flavour, & c., is healthy and good for such as you, and taken once in a while, between your own regular banquets, you might thrive and be better for it.

(Stanley, v-vi)

Girls and mama's boys are excluded from this manly and healthy repast. The concept of ingestion, which Conrad so powerfully transforms in his portrait of Kurtz's devouring egotism, is suitably civilized in Stanley's preface. The novel, after all, is meant as juvenile literature; the men of the growing British empire are still boys. According to F. J. Harvey Darton, however, the difference between children's books earlier in the century (including the Robinsonades, with their "mixed conceptions about savages and nature and desert islands and morality") and the boy's adventure tale of mid-century is that in the new genre, there is an absence of "appeal to a dogmatic religious belief, or any *other* theory of conduct or education. . . . The explorer was no longer a mere missionary of religion. His travels were such stuff as dreams are made on. The English boy, like Drake in Darien, could look upon the unknown seas and vow that he would sail in an English ship upon them" (252-54). The simile is telling, for what Darton only indirectly suggests is the link between Britain's imperial "prospects," suggested by the magisterial survey of Drake in Darien, and the adventure of reading these boy's tales. If Robinson Crusoe was suitable literature for girls as well as boys, these boy's adventures were strictly for future male imperialists. The cross-cultural encounters represented in such fiction fueled and reflected the changing dynamics of Britain's increasing presence in Africa during Victoria's reign; the culminating scramble for Africa was codified at the Berlin Conference of 1884-85.

In his preface, Stanley conflates his roles as host and writer, blending the feasts partaken in Africa (of "plain rice and curry, dried meat of game") and the novel as "true African feast." As packaged in the boy's adventure story, the representation of Africa is a particular kind of product, nourishing to a certain type of reader. Michel de Certeau points to the "economy of translation" that underwrites such a venture of turning the "primitive" into a useful, edible commodity. In discussing Jean de Léry's *Histoire d'un voyage faict en la terre du Brésil* (1578), de Certeau speaks of the origin of this process in de Léry's writing: de Léry as writer/interpreter of the foreign translates the tantalizing appearances of things in Brazil into intellectual food for the readers back in France. Extrapolating from the act of discriminating between those plants and animals that merely look good to the eye and those that are truly "edible," de Certeau describes an ethnological "taste" that allows the traveler/writer to distill "an intellectual edibility," an "essence that has to be distinguished from ravishments" of the ear and eye. Such edibility is a measure of "utility"; the "double diagnostic of taste corrects seductions or repulsions of the eye; is it healthy or not to eat, raw or cooked? . . . From the baroque spectacle of flora and fauna to their edibility; from primitive festivals to their utopian and moral exemplariness; and finally from exotic language to its intelligibility, the same dynamic unfolds. It is that of *utility*—or, rather, that of *production*" (*Writing of History*, 224).

Stanley prepares a similar textual feast for his readers, serving them a healthy extract of Africa, cooking the raw material of the "primitive." Cooking and feeding are figures for the civilizing process itself. (They are usually women's work as well.) This feast, however, is prepared for boys only.

Such a feast is also prepared by Sarah Lee in *The African Wanderers,* which crosses *Robinson Crusoe* with African exploration narratives. This novel appeared in a series published by Griffith and Farran, which offered "Books for the Young of All Ages, Suitable for Presents and School Prizes" under the specific heading of "The Boys' Own Favourite Library." Other titles in the series include *Chums, Tales of the White Cockade, The Three Admirals, The Fiery Cross, Travel, War, and Shipwreck, The North Pole,* and *Harty, the Wanderer.* "The Girls' Own Favourite Library," on the other hand, includes *Shiloh, Rosamond, Fane, Simplicity and Fascination, Isabel's Difficulties, Millicent and Her Cousins, Aunt Hetty's Will,* and *A Wayside Posy.*

Despite the targeting of young audiences by gender, Sarah Lee's novel was found "intellectually edible" by future woman traveler and travel writer Mary Gaunt, who begins her first-person travel narrative *Alone in West Africa* (1912), by describing the scene in which, as a young girl in Australia, she first read about Africa. The book is not named in the text, but it is identifiable as *The African Wanderers*; Gaunt refers to this reading as an inaugural experience, "the first really exciting incident in my life" (2).

> It was a January morning, the sky overcast with smoke and a furious hot wind blowing from the north. The men of the household looked out anxiously, but I sat and read a story-book. It was the tale of a boy named Carlo who was wrecked on the coast of West Africa—nice vague location; he climbed a cocoa-nut tree—I can see him now with a rope round his waist and his legs dangling in an impossible attitude—and he was taken by savages. His further adventures I do not know, because a man came riding in shouting that the calf paddock was on fire and every one must turn out. Everyone did turn out except my aunt who stayed behind to prepare cool drinks and those drinks my little sister and I, as being useless for beating out the flames, were sent to carry to the workers in jugs and "billies."
>
> "Now little girls," said my aunt who was tenderness and kindness itself, "remember you are not to get tired."

I never finished the story of Carlo. Where he went to I can't imagine, but I can't think the savages ate him else his story would never have been written; and from that moment dated my deep interest in West Africa.

We grew up and the boys of the family went a-roving to other lands. . . . When we were young we generally regarded money as a means of locomotion. We have hardly got over the habit yet. Only for us two girls was there no prospect. Our world was bounded by our father's lawns and the young men who came to see us and made up picnic parties to the wildest bush round Ballarat for our amusement. It was not bad.

(2-3)

If it is the brush fire that interrupts the scene of reading, which suggests that life might be more exciting than even art, it is the "feminine" preparation of food that definitively replaces the African feast of reading. In such a domestic economy, a boy's adventure tale is rendered useless to the little girl. Yet, the anecdote prefaces the narrative of Gaunt's own travels to West Africa twenty years later, in which she dubs her trip as a visit to "Carlo's land" (4). For Gaunt, following in Carlo's (and Lee's) footsteps, physically and textually, Africa is an alluring space of adventure rather than the actual geography found. As the destination of boys' adventures, "Carlo's land" symbolizes the girl child's never-never land of fulfilled desire. Gaunt's story suggests the appeal of boys' adventures for girls, notwithstanding Stanley's for-boys-only hospitality. As Green says: "Adventure tales were written about, and for, boys, but they were *read* by girls. For a girl to identify with boys was always, within certain limits, acknowledged as an advantage" (*Robinson Crusoe Story,* 6). But as Claudia Nelson shows, even in the hardy genre of adventure, manliness may be subtly imbricated with womanliness—the description of girls "identifying with boys" may not account for the overlap and entanglement of manliness and womanliness in mid-Victorian texts, even those of adventure. Lee created a boy's adventure tale that represents the homosocial ethos of adventure, in which kindness and courage combine in her male heroes.[8]

Gaunt never mentions the title or author of the adventure story she read, but her description of "Carlo," shipwrecked on the coast of West Africa, climbing a coconut tree with a rope around his waist, precisely captures the events and evokes a particular illustration in Lee's novel. It is possible that Gaunt forgot the author of the tale, just as she drops the *s* from the name of the hero; it is also possible, however, that she anxiously represses the gender of the author to emphasize her own originality and daring.[9]

The illustration that Gaunt must have known is reproduced here; it depicts Carlos shimmying up a coconut tree "in the manner of the natives" (*African Wanderers,*

100) while his friend Antonio watches from below. In Lee's adventure, the two protagonists have just been abandoned on an island off the coast of Africa. Later editions of *The African Wanderers* were called *The African Crusoes* (Greenstein, 134); the thematics of the castaway combine with African adventure, thus emphasizing (like Burney's redaction of Defoe in *The Wanderer*) dependency and vulnerability rather than the confident mastery of exploration. In the complex appropriation of adventure by women writers, Lee's novel exemplifies strategies of mediation—in this case, between "masculine" confidence and "feminine" dependency. Although she herself made three trips to West Africa and spent much time alone on the coast while her first husband, T. E. Bowdich, negotiated a treaty with the Ashanti,[10] Lee "cross-genders" her own African experience—not by cross-dressing her adventure heroine, as does Cavendish, but by representing the adventures of boys. Yet as the illustration from her novel makes clear, Lee replaces the stalwart blond sons of England, who serve as protagonists in the typical stories of English adventure that Darton and Green discuss, with some dusky, rather hairy Latinos. Lee's heroes supply a middle term between black and white, for Carlos is a Spanish orphan, raised by a British soldier who rescues him on the battlefield during the Carlist War of the 1830s, and Antonio, an Italian, is a former gondolier turned soldier. Both the oppositions between masculine and feminine and the Manichean oppositions between black and white are destabilized by a curiously shifting scale of European as well as African difference. The somewhat roguish and protean Spanish orphan hero (like the archetypal picaresque protagonist) is dark enough to be mistaken for an African.[11]

By introducing her plot of African wandering with the Spanish civil war of the 1830s, Lee, like Burney, crossed the topos of wandering with contemporary politics and placed African exploration within a larger European political framework. The Carlist Wars were part of a broader European ideological battle among absolutism, liberalism, and expansionism. The first Carlist War, the setting for *The African Wanderers,* was waged from 1833 to 1839 between two factions—the Carlist counterrevolutionaries, aristocrats and defenders of the Church led by Don Carlos, and the followers (called Cristinos) of Maria Cristina, queen regent of Spain, who initiated parliamentary reforms.[12] Although sympathy in Britain was somewhat divided between the two sides in the conflict, British foreign policy officially sided with the liberal Cristinos rather than the reactionary Carlists and sanctioned the British Legion (a voluntary, nonregular army) to fight on the Cristino side. As Carlos Marichal notes, "The English and French bourgeoisies supported the Spanish Liberals because they feared the possible consequences of a Carlist victory, which would not only be a victory for Metternich and the European aristocracy, but also a blow against English and French commercial expansion in the Mediterranean" (57).

In Lee's novel, the Spanish civil conflict functions as a sign of the "real," of Continental political turmoil and potential chaos, of a world the English (and adventure fiction) cannot ignore. The British fighting on the Spanish battlefields are described in the narrative as "strangers to the vengeance which men of the same country feel towards each other in civil war" (2). The novel begins with a scene of battle. Colonel Lacy, a British soldier, and his sidekick, Sergeant Brown, who are fighting on the momentarily victorious side of the Carlists, discover two crying children next to their dead parents. The aristocratic family of Carlos and Henriquez, the two orphans rescued and subsequently adopted by the British soldier, is pro-Cristino, that is, on the liberal side. The specific ideologies at war are muted in Lee's adventure tale, which foregrounds instead the chaos and cost of war: "The Carlists robbed the Christinos [sic], the Christinos plundered the Carlists, and the banditti stripped them both. . . . Numbers of British soldiers who had been serving in the Spanish armies of either party, without pay, and rendered utterly insensible to every good feeling by the lives of bloodshed, rapine, and cruelty, which they had been leading for several years; without any one to superintend them . . . crowded to the port in order to obtain shipping for their native country" (7-9). Overtly, the British are ideologically aloof from the factions in the Spanish war. Yet the generational differences between Captain Lacy, an Englishman of the old school, Carlos (named by Lacy for Don Carlos) and Henriquez represent the inevitably changing face of adventure, from an aristocratic, military genre to one that could capture the spirit of bourgeois European expansionism.[13] The more liberal, capitalistic ethos predominates in the remainder of this abolitionist novel, which finds Carlos, the more restless of the brothers—as shipwrecked sailor, pupil of African culture, and entrepreneurial trader—finally returning to England to develop an import business.[14]

The cross-cultural rescue that begins the novel establishes a recurring pattern of paternalism in the narrative—Captain Lacy rescues the Spanish orphans, just as Carlos will rescue a Negro child in Africa. When Lacy and Brown discover the two crying infants by the side of their dead parents, a gentle fatherhood is established. The confusion and brutality of war are contrasted to the Englishmen's manly tenderness. Englishmen are first represented in the novel as helpfully intervening in the internecine battles of their more "passionate" European brothers, so that English adventure is seen against the more militaristic legacy of the conquistador tradition of adventure. This scene of paternalism serves as a prototype for the English experience in Africa.

English paternalism establishes a sympathetic circle of decidedly male geometry, a gathering of fathers, sons, and, later on, brothers. After he rescues the orphans, Captain Lacy brings them to an Irish-woman, the wife of an English soldier, who agrees to be their nurse: "But her fair face and hair, and her blue eyes, in addition to the surrounding scene, so bewildered the poor little things, that they shrieked, clung to each other, and imperfectly called for their parents. Kathleen, their new nurse, could not speak a word of Spanish; but the Sergeant and Captain Lacy caressed and soothed them in their native tongue" (5-6). In this fairy-tale rescue, Kathleen is the fairest and yet the most terrifying, the most "other" to the Spanish orphans. If Kathleen's feminine kindness ultimately overcomes cross-cultural mistrust and she helps mother them for a time back in England, it is noteworthy that the English soldiers combine a masculine (and more worldly) command of languages with feminine tenderness. In the specific paternalism of this rescue, a feminizing influence is at work that is not, however, encoded as effeminate. This liberal sympathy, combining feminine virtues with a manly spirit of adventure, is played out in a male milieu that excludes pure domesticity. Kathleen is both too feminine and, somehow, too starkly fair to participate fully in this messy, yet tender scene of male bonding. Her Irish stereotype (with its overtones of lower-class status) relegates her to a subsidiary and servant-like role,[15] but her Irishness also acts as a reminder of England's colonial responsibilities elsewhere, hence, of other claims of manly duty.

All women are excluded from the charmed circle of adventure. Indeed, in fairy-tale fashion, it is the cruel behavior of the boys' stepmother, Mrs. Lacy, that impels Carlos's sea adventures in the first place. At the end of the book, Antonio (Carlos's Venetian companion in Africa), Carlos, and Henriquez live happily ever after together, with the "fairer sex" only occasionally asking Carlos for his autograph (African Wanderers, 358). Although "fairer sex" is a cliché, in a book that so insistently refers to complexion, the phrase implies how very male this ethos of cross-cultural camaraderie is. The mix of paternalism and "brotherhood," first represented as the mediation between wholly European differences, will be extended to the Africans that Carlos and Antonio encounter.

The structure of rescue that begins with the orphans' terrified encounter with the English—soon tempered by humane behavior—is repeated when Carlos and Antonio land on an island off the coast of Africa. The two men, who have formed a bond on ship because both speak Spanish, make their way along the coast after being abandoned by the rest of the crew. They first come upon the body of a dead Negro and surmise that a slave ship has passed by; they then find a deserted child who has been left behind by the "inhuman brutes," the slave dealers. Traces of the most heinous cruelty to the Africans are everywhere apparent in the novel, but here the terrifying difference involves the confrontation between well-meaning Europeans and an African child: "Frightened and bewildered, [he] screamed, and, after one look at his preservers, obstinately hid his face in his hands, not daring to glance at them again" (120). The child is momentarily comforted by the food Carlos offers, but on seeing Antonio, he again screams and clings to Carlos as if for protection. "'It's my beard and whiskers,' observed Antonio" (120). If Kathleen is too female and white to soothe the young Spanish infants, Antonio is too masculine and hairy (later we learn the Africans are unused to facial hair) to mollify the fearful Negro child. This mirroring repetition of the Spanish orphan's fear of Kathleen suggests that neither the most "feminine" nor the most "masculine" visage can bridge the difference between the races.

By repeating the topos of paternal rescue, first with the Spanish children and then the African child, Lee establishes a curiously shifting scale of difference, as the narrative plays out a series of racial substitutions. On the one hand, these shades of difference may seem merely a reflection of the "close articulation . . . between the domestic and the colonial spheres of otherness," as George Stocking puts it (234), and a strategy for mediating the foreignness of Africa for Lee's domestic readers. But in choosing to make Latinos the heroes of her novel rather than figures of a cruder form of masculinist adventure meant to contrast with English liberalism, Lee disturbs the European color "scale," which favors the whiter, more northern agent of civilization.

Indeed, Antonio's and Carlos's Latin complexions allow them to "pass" for native, a masquerade that both protects and endangers them. "It must be owned also that the Europeans were now so bronzed in complexion, that they might very easily have passed for Arabs, who occasionally approached that part of Africa, and stragglers from whom were seen even upon the coast" (239). The wanderers are thus confused with "the aristocracy of savages," as the narrator puts it (277). Therefore a curious instability exists in the racial discourse. On the one hand, the word "savages" and the idea of a racial scale among Africans bespeak a perfectly confident moral typing according to race; on the other hand, the confusion of the protagonists with their usual foils creates a potential identification with the position of the "other." Latin "blood" seems to enable Antonio, in particular, to adapt to the African heat, as if it brought him closer to the indigenous population. On board their ship, the *Hero,* before they are abandoned, Carlos admonishes Antonio for sleeping out in the open air, but "'Never fear for me, sir,' said the faithful Italian, 'my Venetian blood does better in these countries than that of the English, and so will your Spanish; but what must

be done now?'" (89). Curiously, Lee's use of rather conventional ethnic stereotypes leads to a subtle representation of difference that subverts the neat opposition of primitive and civilized, black and white. The lexicon for designating the travelers constantly shifts during the narrative, depending on the particular system of difference invoked: when Carlos and Henriquez are among the English, they are called the "young Spaniards" (24); in Africa when he is alone with Antonio, Carlos is referred to as "the Spaniard"; on the ship, when he remarks on his difference from the English, Antonio is called the "faithful Italian"; in one episode the Europeans suddenly become "the white slaves" (282). Even the title *The African Wanderers,* with the ambiguities of its adjective, creates some confusion as to whether the wanderers are African or Europeans in Africa. This complication of racial position is different from the "harmoniously unbalanced antithesis" between black sidekick and white hero in works such as Marryat's *Mr. Midshipman Easy* (Brantlinger, 58) or the fear of "going native" that marks Conrad's novels.

Although Carlos's and Antonio's abilities are never seriously questioned, their status as wanderers relegates them to a dependent position in which they are forced, like Burney's wanderer, to rely on the kindness of strangers, in this case, African strangers. "This man receives us, poor, defenceless, destitute wanderers; never asks whence we came, how we got here, or whither we are going; gives us the best of everything, and suffers us to go to rest without a single inquiry. It is sufficient for him that we are strangers, and in need," Carlos comments to Antonio (138). This emphasis is different from the use of the Crusoe story in Marryat's *Masterman Ready* (1841), in which the Seagrave family develops their desert island into a little colony, thus illustrating the resourcefulness of the English character and its natural mastery of its environment. One could compare Lee's blurring of the racial politics of her novel with what Abdul JanMohamed calls the "syncretic" desires of certain colonialist fiction, such as Kipling's *Kim,* in which an emotional identification with the "native" land occurs in the context of the ultimate security of a stable racial division that is reaffirmed by story's end (78-79). JanMohamed points out that before the novel's conclusion recovers the "paternal function," Kim's orphanhood and dusky skin color allow him considerable play with the boundaries of racial and cultural difference: "As an orphan (a fact that is inconsequential to him), [Kim] has no origins and therefore no familial, social, political, or teleological constraints either" (78). Ultimately, according to JanMohamed, the narrator restores Kim to his natural racial identity (as Irish), thus reinforcing the manichean allegory that seems to be disrupted during the course of the fiction. (It is curious, however, that JanMohamed says nothing of Kim's Irish, rather than English, origin, that is, the difference of colonial status within the European "white" realm.)

Ultimately, however, these syncretic desires and the subtle and interesting slippages of difference give way to more predictable models of mediation of European and African positions through conversion and enlightenment. In *The Invention of Africa,* Mudimbe offers a Foucauldian analysis of the episteme that characterizes mid-nineteenth-century representations of Africa. He describes a dualistic anthropology that posits homologous antitheses between primitiveness and civilization, pagan and Christian, naked (child) and civilized (adult), among others, and an "ideological model of conversion" that mediates the terms of the oppositions. Thus, conversion is the overall model of mediation, with education serving as a more secular version (50). Mudimbe speaks here specifically about missionary discourse but applies this general ideological model to the nineteenth-century European encounter with Africa.

Mudimbe's model does not seem to acknowledge the kind of surprises within Western textual representations of Africa that I have argued appear in Lee's fiction. But his model is helpful for understanding how, despite destabilizing racial difference, Lee's novel recurs to an Enlightenment faith in education and the secular religion of commerce as forms of mediating cultural conflict. In this kinder, gentler form of colonialism, European "magic," consisting of education, Christianity, and capitalism, counteracts the fetish of the African. In an episode entitled "The Power of Education," the narrator describes the force of European Enlightenment philosophy, which, in place of violence, will convert the Africans to more rational and productive beings.

> They [the Africans] began to listen to him [Carlos] as to a being of a higher nature than themselves—to believe that he was right in all things, because they found him to be right in a few. They loved both the white men—sported with both alike—shared their meals, their society, their labours with equal affection; but there was a feeling of respect and deference towards Carlos which they could not themselves define or understand. It was the power of education which thus told upon them; the *spell* which a superior and well-informed mind exerts over its inferiors, even though the influence may be unfelt by itself.
>
> (165: emphasis added)

Interestingly, the superiority here is not purely racial, that is, associated with the whiteness of the skin: it depends on the moral worth that presumably comes with a certain kind of education.

This "education" combines the teaching of capitalism and of Christianity. As Patrick Brantlinger says of *Dawn Island,* Harriet Martineau's abolitionist novel of the same decade, commodity fetishism replaces the "unprogressive fetishism" of the Africans (31) and commercial trade replaces the barbarity of slavery. Reciprocal trade becomes the model of mediation.

> The precious treasures from Africa were passed through the Custom-house . . . and as it pleased God to bless their [Carlos and Henriquez's] endeavours, they were the channel through which many blessings flowed upon their fellow-creatures. Commerce with the western coast of Africa was a principal feature in the transactions of Carlos, in the hope of benefiting a country in which he took an undying interest; and when he reflected on the immense riches of that beautiful land, and the universal spirit of traffic which pervades its inhabitants, he hoped that sooner or later its natural productions would wholly supersede the degrading and inhuman slave-trade, which stamps it with the seal of barbarity.
>
> (*African Wanderers,* 356)

The fiction here is one of equal partnership rather than coercion, projecting onto the Africans the "universal spirit of traffic." In this version of the boy's adventure story, the violence and aggression in the colonial adventure are suppressed in a vision of reciprocal trade. The vision is emblematized by the commercial city of Liverpool. Early in the story, Captain Lacy returns to the city after fighting in the Spanish civil war but finds that "the air of Liverpool, impregnated by the smoke of many chimneys and factories, did not agree with [his] health, accustomed as he had been for years to live almost entirely in the field" (11). This response exemplifies a pastoralism in the "older" generation, and indeed, Lacy moves out of the city of industrial revolution to a quieter existence in the outlying area. By the end of the novel, however, the image of Liverpool functions as a sign of the English ability to absorb and harmonize difference. The presence of Carlos and Antonio and their African servant fails to create a ripple on the surface of this industrial Mecca: "The good inhabitants of this great commercial city are too much accustomed to foreign men to spend much time in gazing at strangers; and although most of them turned their heads as the bronzed passengers, with their black servant carrying weapons, passed hastily by them, they offered no interruption" (341). The earlier suggestion that industrialism is unhealthy vanishes in this more optimistic resolution, just as the frightening cross-cultural confrontations are replaced by the blending of black, brown, and white skins in this urban landscape.

This "blending," ultimately used in the service of a Western ideal of reciprocal trade, functions in Lee's novel as a topos of mobility and freedom, despite the sometimes dangerous and harrowing adventures faced by her wandering heroes. In a nonfictional account of her own travels to West Africa, appended to her *Stories of Strange Lands,* Lee in her self-portrait offers a very different image of circulation, as everyone on the boat stares at the "lady passenger mad enough to go to Africa" (254). The ethos of free circulation, of blending, is unavailable to the "lady passenger," who constantly serves as the object of others' gazes. In the same autobiographical notes, she describes her meeting with the real-life Antonio, whom she met on the boat and whose "qualities as a *buffo*" she praises. "His powers of mimicry extended even to his voice," she says, "his gestures were perfectly irresistible; and the instant he displayed his brilliant white teeth, contrasted with his black beard and rich brown complexion, no one could avoid joining in his mirth" (256). Lee transforms Antonio into a stereotype of male charm, and in so doing, she creates an image of the traveler who can blend, mimic, and circulate freely, none of which the woman traveler can do. This figure fulfills the "syncretic" desires of the fiction. The roving, adaptable Latin orphans experience what Lee describes as "the constant excitement afforded by a life which often presents danger, and constantly requires contrivances for comfort and enjoyment" (311).[16]

In her brief discussion of Lee's *Stories of Strange Lands*, Mary Louise Pratt points to Lee's text as an example of "the gendered division of labor around travel and writing."[17] Pratt discovers biographical correlates for this division of labor: She observes that Lee dutifully edited her husband's writings but failed to produce a full account of her own years in West Africa. Pratt regards Lee's stories as a cover for her real desire to write a nonfictional account of her own journey. She notes: "As it turns out, however, Lee ingeniously makes her stories an occasion rather than a substitute for her own account of Africa. Each comes accompanied by an enormous string of footnotes, some of them pages long and complete with illustrations. It is here in the notes that we find the makings of the travel book Lee never wrote: explanatory commentary, ethnographic descriptions, observations on flora and fauna, personal anecdotes. The notes seem to be Lee's main source of pride in the book" (*Imperial Eyes*, 106). But I would argue that her fiction was more than simply compensatory; rather it gave Lee room to imagine her own adventurous circulation and to explore the complexities of racial encounter. It provided a form of displacement, a realm of possibility, that licensed a going out from experience, a textual circulation. Mary Kingsley's nonfictional *Travels in West Africa*, as we shall see, more directly represents the African wanderer as female, a traveler who is also a mobile, improvisational "trader" on the market. In her hybrid and voluminous narration—part natural history, part ethnography, part travel narrative—Kingsley, like Sarah Lee before her, found the liberal image of trading partners a fruitful figure for the woman writer of adventure. In her text, as in Lee's, Hermes, the god of travel, is also Hermes, the patron of trade.

* * *

A distinguished male scientist offered this bit of advice to his friend Mary Kingsley before her departure for West Africa in 1893: "Always take measurements, Miss Kingsley, and always take them from the adult male"

(*Travels in West Africa*, 244-45). It encapsulates some of the prevalent assumptions about gender, race, and science at the end of the nineteenth century, when Kingsley produced her enormously popular book. The admonition succinctly embodies the Western cultural assumption that the male is the generic norm. As Donna Haraway writes of museum taxidermy and collecting safaris in colonial Africa, the typical animal "in its perfect expression" had to be an adult male. The particular "tone of perfection could only be heard in the male mode. It was a compound of physical and spiritual quality judged truthfully by the [male] artist-scientist in the fullness of direct experience" (41).

As Haraway suggests, natural science is a tissue of cultural assumptions about sexuality and gender. But the avuncular advice offered to Kingsley on her departure for Africa must also be considered in the context of racial discourse (which Haraway likewise addresses in her analysis of modern science). The mania for measurement was characteristic of late Victorian anthropology. Kingsley was going out to study, as she put it, not only "fish" but also "fetish," African law and religion as well as "nature." Her study of African culture, then, must be seen in the context of late nineteenth-century anthropological discourse, a mixture of racialist and evolutionary doctrines that sought to fix "the measure of man." If, from a feminist point of view, white women were the domestic "other" for the male norm, this norm's other "other" was the dark-skinned "primitive," encountered and studied beyond the borders of the European map. The perfection of the adult white male was to be seen in marked contrast to this primitive self. The African became the object of inspection for white anthropologists and ethnologists, a specimen measured by a European yardstick and found wanting. In *The Mismeasure of Man*, Stephen Jay Gould chronicles the history of such procedures in physical anthropology (particularly craniology), showing how science in the latter half of the nineteenth century was obsessed with the idea of measurement and discovered in numbers a confirmation of racialist and racist assumptions. Cranial indexing, the ranking of races by the size of their skulls, was a respected intellectual practice in the post-Darwinian nineteenth century.

The "Miss Kingsley" addressed by the scientist is thus not only a woman in a predominantly male world of natural scientists, ethnographers, and explorers but also a white woman who is welcomed into a fraternal circle of European measurers. As I will discuss, the feminist foregrounding of gender difference should not occlude the woman traveler's own relation to an objectivist epistemology, in which knowledge and power were indissolubly linked. The difference of race cannot be divorced from the gendering of the scientific "hunt," as Haraway calls it.[18]

Indeed, as de Certeau argues, Western historiography itself is a result of travel and the colonial encounter, the voyage out and the return that provide a perspective on one's "home." In this sense, ethnography and history are the discursive equivalents of the cultural constructions of "other" and "self"; "departure" and "return" signify places on the itinerary of the voyage as well as topoi in the discourse of the self and other. As Arjun Appadurai illustrates, the binary opposition between the mobility of the traveler/ethnographer and the stasis of the "native" to be studied establishes a power differential that puts "natives . . . in one place, a place to which explorers, administrators, missionaries, and eventually anthropologists, come" (35). Appadurai is particularly interested in the way anthropological discourse links "intellectual and spatial confinement" (36), so that "natives" are "confined" to a mode of thought, which the mobile Western observer freely travels to see.

In this cautionary mode I want to interrogate the figure, which remains very popular even today, of intrepid Victorian women travelers and their appeal for feminist recuperation. For the image of these Victorian women striding in long skirts through the bush, stopping to eat manioc, constructs the female counterpart to the British male explorer and empire builder. The important Virago/Beacon Traveler Series, which republished neglected travel texts by Victorian women, displays some of the problems of this feminism in relation to colonialist discourse. The attractive cover of the 1988 Virago/Beacon reprint of Kingsley's *Travels* illustrates what I mean. One sees a black-and-white photographic insert of Mary Kingsley, a bust that shows her looking properly buttoned up and Victorian, with a firm but perceptibly humorous gaze. This photograph is superimposed on what seems to be a color painting of an African scene, replete with towering palm trees, river, five Africans perched on or standing before a big rock that looks like a large white molar, and a canoe that resembles a banana. The caption printed above this scene reads, "The witty and highly readable classic about African culture by one of the most intrepid adventurers." The back cover refers to Kingsley as "larger than life."

Here, the white woman individual is foregrounded against what Johannes Fabian has called an "ethnographic present" that effaces history from the African scene and represents instead a timeless, primitive landscape (80-87). Africa becomes a generalized setting, even a theatrical set, for the drama of female liberation that a 1980s white Anglo-American feminism seeks to recover. This iconic representation mirrors Birkett's contention that "the Dark Continent, the Orient, the Savage Lands" provided "the *stage* upon which their new experiences as travellers could be realized" (47: emphasis added). Both the cover and the critical study proffer an ideologically loaded iconography—a photo-

graphic portrait of the white Western woman and a landscape painting of the exotic stage. A celebration of aggressive individualism, albeit in "feminine" form, is repeated in the semiotics of cultural confrontation on the cover of Kingsley's book.

Kingsley's own complex relation to imperialism and the individualism of adventure is obscured by the cover. The iconography and rhetoric of feminist recuperation, for example, ignore Kingsley's own resistance to the lexicon of self-discovery. Although Kingsley constructs a narrative "I" in her text, she deliberately eschews the search for identity thematized in much nineteenth-century travel literature. Although it is tempting to see in the topos of travel a route to self-discovery, Kingsley's hybrid narrative in fact frustrates our attempts to chart the narrator or traveler as a unified psychological "self." In a stimulating discussion of types of British colonial travel narratives, Pratt argues that experiential narratives of travel on the cultural frontier produce subjects defined by the bourgeois realm of the private individual: "This sentimental, experiential subject inhabits that self-defined 'other' sector of the bourgeois world, the private sphere—home of desire, sex, spirituality, and the Individual" (*Imperial Eyes*, 78). But Kingsley's protean narrative performance resists the coherence and self-revelation that are major "products" of both domestic fiction and sentimental travel narratives of the Victorian period. One of the most telling insights into Kingsley's resistance to self-revelation is "On Not Writing a Novel" by Rosellen Brown. After spending five years researching and planning a novel with Kingsley as protagonist, Brown explains that she abandoned her attempt because she had no sense of introspection, of an "inner life" (20), in Kingsley's writings.

Furthermore, foregrounding the intrepidity of the British traveler against an exotic background obscures the crucial significance Kingsley attributed to representing African culture to a British reading public. Kingsley's travels led her to recognize the political stakes of representation. She opposed both the blatantly aggressive policies and rhetoric of imperialism practiced by the Belgians and the more ostensibly liberal but still aggressive ethos of the British, who sought to "civilize the natives." The crucial point is that the effectiveness of Kingsley's arguments against existing imperial policy depended on the power of her narrative to represent the rich and complex African cultures that were being trampled by such policy. Although she never questioned the British presence in Africa, she argued that its Crown colony ideology and practice were both stupid and insensitive. Describing this system in the preface to her other tome on West Africa, *West African Studies* (published in 1899), Kingsley wrote that the Crown colony system "brought with it suffering to the native races and disgrace to English gentlemen, who are bound to obey and carry out orders given them by the system" (xii).[19] The very terms of her rhetoric ("native race" versus "English gentlemen") confirm her implication in colonial discourse, yet one must recognize the nuances of her textual "productions" of Africa, as well as their complicities.

Kingsley's enormously popular travel books and the series of speeches she subsequently delivered back in England made her an important public and political figure. A late twentieth-century consciousness observes just how much her critique of British colonial policy still locates itself within certain imperialist assumptions; yet as a cultural figure she fascinates, as does her narrative, because her relation to the cultural and political ideologies of the 1890s is complex enough to admit diverse interpretations. Indeed, her own relation to mainstream British intellectual culture was ambivalent. The daughter and niece of eminent Victorian men of letters George and Charles Kingsley, respectively, she felt marginalized as a woman by the educational system that helped "interpellate" the young men of England into its ideological systems (including the "muscular Christianity" that her uncle Charles espoused throughout his life). In this respect she can be fruitfully compared with Virginia Woolf two decades later.

The interest of Kingsley's ambiguous status in relation to the dominant culture's imperial ethos increases when one looks at the way her writings were appropriated by political and intellectual figures of radically divergent views, such as J. A. Hobson and Michael Davitt, on the one hand, and Rudyard Kipling, on the other. In his book *Imperialism* (1903), Hobson, the British anti-imperialist economist and social philosopher, mentions Kingsley approvingly and relies on the "testimony" of her travel writing to reveal the folly of the Crown colony system in Africa (121n); Davitt, the Irish patriot and politician who fought for land reform and home rule in Ireland, argued before Parliament against a poll tax in Ireland, citing Kingsley's writing against a hut tax in Africa. Yet Kipling, who knew and admired Kingsley, could also write a tribute to her indomitable "British" spirit, representing her as belonging to the freemasonry of the male adventurer: "Being human, she must have feared some things, but one never arrived at what they were. . . . At her own wish her body was delivered to the sea from a little torpedo-boat, off Simonstown. And, as the Quartermaster of that uneasy craft used to say in after years: '*That* was how we buried Mary'" (4-5). Neither of these views of Kingsley is "mistaken." Both were available as "readings" of her cultural image and her texts. This double reading of Kingsley has been updated in the very divergent assessments of Mudimbe, who uses her to illustrate a particularly crude late Victorian misunderstanding of African fetish (10), and Sara Mills, who in her "case study" of

Kingsley argues that the clash between femininity and colonialism in Kingsley's travel narrative produces a text both inside and outside the dominant discourse (see 153-74).

Kingsley both identified with the masculine voyages of exploration and science and exposed the masculinist hubris that often attended exploration, colonization, and anthropology conducted by men. Insofar as she identifies with the ethos of masculine adventure, Kingsley appropriates conventions of adventure, as if deliberately breaking with a female domestic literary tradition. As a woman who spent the first thirty years of her life at home with her mother, while her writer/physician/adventurer father toured the world, Kingsley read voraciously, including exploration narratives and adventure. One of her favorite books was Defoe's *A General History of Robberies and Murders of the Most Notorious Pyrates* (Frank, 68). When her parents died within six months of each other and she decided to go to Africa, she seems to have embraced male adventure and a certain mischievous iconoclasm that she found in her book of pirates.[20] In *Travels* she continually praises the "old Coasters," salty traders whom she met on her voyage and generally preferred to both missionaries and colonizers.

In the self-representation with which she begins her narrative, Kingsley implicitly places herself in relation to the mercantilist tradition of adventure through the figure of speculation. Prefacing the introduction with the type of capsule summary often found in eighteenth-century picaresque novels (the introduction "relateth the various causes which impelled the author to embark upon the voyage"), Kingsley begins the text proper rather jauntily, with the following: "It was in 1893 that, for the first time in my life, I found myself in possession of five or six months which were not heavily forestalled, and feeling like a boy with a new half-crown, I lay about in my mind, as Mr. Bunyan would say, as to what to do with them" (1). Both the monetary figure and the cross-gendering in this self-representation place Kingsley's story within the tradition of travel as investment. The coin metaphor is fascinating; leisure time in her "possession" is like capital just waiting to be spent. The root meanings of "adventure" are tapped metaphorically: both "venture," as in the risking of money, and "future" (*l'avenir*) are implicitly evoked—the thirty-year-old Kingsley is like a boy about to embark on his future. The "half-crown" prophesies the importance of the marketplace in Kingsley's journey, for she subsidizes her travels in Africa by bartering from village to village. She thus deliberately aligns herself with the merchant/adventure tradition of British travelers, fictional and nonfictional, including Robinson Crusoe, whose own trip to Africa is described (unlike Kingsley's) as the most "unfortunate of all enterprises"

(*Robinson Crusoe*, 15). Although a more serious, scientific persona is fashioned in the narrative—the "Miss Kingsley" who takes measurements—this trope of speculation predominates, combining associations of fortune, risk, and investment. "If there is a great investment in travel, it is perhaps because travel models the structure of investment itself, the *transfer* of assets that institutes an economy, be it political or libidinal, 'restricted' or 'general,'" says Georges Van Den Abbeele (xvii). In various ways, Kingsley's narrative emphasizes this general economy of travel, but its images and themes also align it with a particular version of mercantile, masculine adventure.

Narratives in this venture/adventure tradition often begin with a sense of domestic dead end. Historically, this tradition of adventure often appealed to the second sons of English families or to non-English sons of Britain (Scotsmen, for example), who lacked the benefit of patrimony entailed upon their older brothers and had no reason to remain at home.[21] Even when this particular sociological scenario does not apply, the tradition of venture/adventure often acknowledges that the protagonist has nothing to lose: think of Melville's Ishmael, who explains his wandering by saying, "Some years ago—never mind how long precisely—having little or no money in my purse, and nothing particular to interest me on shore, I thought I would sail about a little and see the watery part of the world" (1). Kingsley's narrative borrows this studied casualness, which often marks the venturing/adventuring tradition, as well as the sense of England's diminished possibilities: there seems to be nothing better to do than to go exploring. Yet her adaptation of this jaunty, "masculine" tone submerges an exhausted past that has been differently shaped by gender—that of a Victorian spinster who selflessly nursed her parents and suddenly found herself alone with her life when her parents died in 1893 (a classic topos for other Victorian women travelers, such as Marianne North and Mary Taylor).[22] More like Lucy Snowe in Brontë's *Villette* than Huck Finn or Ishmael, Kingsley begins her narrative with her departure from England because England cannot support her story. In her memoirs, Kingsley figures this "bankruptcy" of the domestic situation with a vacant interior, both of "home" and the self: "The fact is I am no more a human being than a gust of wind is. . . . It never occurs to me that I have any right to do anything more than now and then sit and warm myself at the fires of real human beings" (quoted in Gwynn, 26). Domesticity and coherent identity are decentered here—Kingsley imagines herself as vaporous, empty, unfixed; the familiar motif of the Victorian hearth is displaced, located elsewhere, with "real human beings." If domestic fiction "invested common forms of social behavior with the emotional values of women" (Armstrong, 29), Kingsley, like Lucy Snowe, seems ill-suited to such "investment." Yet the pathos of blighted domesticity figured in her memoir is muted in the travel narrative, which launches itself breezily by invoking boy's adventure, a tradition that also falls short of a perfect fit.

Early on, Kingsley's narrative plays through a series of tropes borrowed from male textual traditions. In the first chapter, she adapts the heterosexual erotics so prevalent in African travel narratives written by male explorers—the romantic figure of the mysterious foreign land, both seductive and pitiless: "The West Coast of Africa is like the Arctic regions in one particular, and that is that when you have once visited it you want to go back there again; and, now I come to think of it, there is another particular in which it is like them, and that is that the chances you have of returning from it at all are small, for it is a *Belle Dame sans merci*" (11). Sandra Gilbert and Susan Gubar make much of this image in nineteenth- and twentieth-century literature, reading its pervasiveness as a sign of male anxiety about the sexuality and power of women and of the dark and mysterious others men encountered: "And She is there in continents that during the nineteenth century became increasingly accessible to European explorers, 'underdeveloped' continents where ordinary trade and comparatively ordinary geographical research inevitably became entwined with Her extraordinary existence. Rider Haggard located Her under a mountain in the heart of an African darkness" (10). Margery Perham and J. Simmons suggest that these works produce an underlying analogy between the body of the "dark slave, ravished, beautiful but untamable" and the land (*African Discovery*, 16). In Keats's poem, La Belle Dame speaks a "language strange"; she enthralls the poet, seduces him with her enigmatic otherness. The question is, How can the female traveler and travel writer make use of a topos that links racial and sexual otherness? What happens to the equation of the power of the foreign with the power of a female "language strange" that spellbinds and threatens the male traveler, like the music of the Sirens?

"I succumbed to the charm of the Coast as soon as I left Sierra Leone on my first voyage out" (11): Kingsley identifies herself with the men who choose the seductive danger of Africa rather than the boredom of "being home in England." Later on in the narrative she extends this idea, employing the image of the African forest to signify an uninterpretable mystery. Describing a night in this forest, she says:

> Unless you are interested in it and fall under its charm, it is the most awful life in death imaginable. It is like being shut up in a library whose books you cannot read, all the while tormented, terrified, and bored. And if you do fall under its spell, it takes all the colour out of other kinds of living. Still, it is good for a man to have an experience of it, whether he likes it or not, for it teaches you how very dependent you have been, during your previous life, on the familiarity of those con-

ditions you have been brought up among, and on your fellow citizens; moreover it takes the conceit out of you pretty thoroughly during the days you spend stupidly stumbling about among your new surroundings.

(102)

Kingsley represents herself as a "man" who encounters the "spells" and "charms" of a feminized land—the feminine seductions of La Belle Dame now complicated by African magic, which implicitly invokes the idea of fetish (about which I will say much more). Africa "takes the colour out of" normal living—suddenly European culture seems impossibly bleached and vacant. African travel becomes obsession, bewitchment. Yet worth noting is the way that Kingsley's rather conventional metaphor of Africa as unreadable text is offered as an *alternative* to the topos of seduction—unless a man is spellbound and seduced, he will feel as though he is imprisoned in a library, tormented by the totally opaque foreign text. It is as if Kingsley divides two normally congruent tropes of African mystery—seductiveness and illegibility—into separate images: the male traveler on the scene, seduced by the feminine power of Africa, and the daughter back in her father's library, tormented by the foreign mysteries that present themselves as maddeningly inaccessible. The latter metaphor may evoke Kingsley's frustration in her own father's library, where she read Cook, Hakluyt, and other travel literature while her father roamed the world.

But it is in the way she demystifies seduction and de-eroticizes the cultural encounter that Kingsley's canny alteration of this heterosexual cultural trope can best be seen. For example, after aligning herself with the male travelers who hear the call of La Belle Dame and sneak back to her shores, she writes: "So I warned the Coast I was coming back again and the Coast did not believe me; and on my return to it a second time displayed a genuine surprise, and formed an even higher opinion of my folly than it had formed on our first acquaintance, which is saying a good deal" (11-12). The "language strange" that haunts the romantic male traveler is transformed into a polite, if sometimes judgmental, conversation between equals. Although she speaks of her "folly," Kingsley's mode of presenting this conversation rationalizes it—converting it into a model of exchange and reciprocity that will shape both forms and themes of the succeeding narrative. Furthermore, in the transformation, the ungainly European body becomes visible. The acts of "stupidly *stumbling*" in the new surroundings of Africa and "*fall[ing]* under its charm" (emphasis added), are literalized in the text as physical comedy. The narrative is full of a slapstick that de-eroticizes the body of the traveler, making it the sort of dehumanized object Henri Bergson observes in his analysis of comedy. The traveler's body and mind caught by surprise provide a comic fall into knowledge quite different from the tragic Ancient Mariner-like fall

that, for example, Marlow experiences in Conrad's *Heart of Darkness*. By virtue of these representations, the power of the European is undermined in actual physical pratfalls equivalent to slipping on a banana peel.

This fall into knowledge "trips up" the traveler's confident intellectual schemas of understanding. Instead of purposeful male "quest" to the interior, Kingsley's travels and travel writing display an interest in having one's interest thwarted as part of the risk of travel. The white traveler's encounter with difference produces surprise that undermines his or her system of rationality and superior orientation: "The truth is, the study of natural phenomena knocks the bottom out of any man's conceit if it is done honestly and not by selecting only those facts that fit in with his pre-conceived or ingrafted notions" (*Travels,* 441). If this comment conforms in some ways to the Western representation of Africa as enigma, that kind of projection of mystery analyzed in studies such as those by Brantlinger and Christopher Miller, the writing is far removed from the imperial gothic or romantic exoticism that usually attend this topos. Kingsley's is low mimetic representation in which intellectual reconsiderations are figured physically as reversals, upheavals, bottoms knocked out—things falling apart. The traveler's awkwardness as intruder in a foreign culture metamorphoses into slapstick when she slips and falls through the roof of an unprotected hut, "dropping in" unexpectedly, as she says. She represents herself as amusing the African villagers by "diving headlong from a large rock . . . they [the observers] applauded my performance" (170). The effect of this comedy is to disspell the romantic aura; the traveler represents herself, rather than the foreign culture, as spectacle.[23]

Although Kingsley's ever present wit allows her to cope with almost every situation, the stories she tells on herself repeatedly stage a loss of mastery for the European body. As opposed to the command of a Stanley, we get at times a blow to the traveler's equilibrium that knocks stable ideas, as well as the body of the traveler, upside down. When she describes an episode in which her African guide suggests she proceed first to a very dangerous town on their path because she was "something queer" enough so the others "might not shoot [her] at sight," she remarks, "It is at such a moment as this that the Giant's robe gets, so to speak, between your legs and threatens to trip you up" (295). One could say that the image represents an emasculation of the great white male traveler, a limp phallus between the legs, like the tail of a dog that is ashamed. Again, knowledge is represented, not as confident mastery, but as a groping toward understanding.

The "Giant's robe" is a costume, and the theatrical metaphor in the two preceding examples appears repeatedly in the representation of Kingsley's encounters and reveals her canny grasp of cross-cultural theater and mastery as performance. One of the most interesting aspects of *Travels in West Africa* is the way in which Kingsley represents cross-cultural confrontation as theater on both sides, often substituting for a discourse of the essential and natural a rhetoric of masquerade and self-conscious cultural performance. In *Blank Darkness,* Christopher Miller elevates Conrad's *Heart of Darkness* (1899) to the status of an "allegory of all other Africanist texts" (170) because it is "a self-conscious meditation on misunderstanding, and its self-consciousness is what places it at a highly significant crossroads between an old and a new mode of Africanist expression, between the projection of a corrupt and ignoble Africa and the later critique of that projection and its political outgrowth, colonialism" (171). Kingsley's *Travels,* published two years before Conrad's novel, deliberately resists the impressionist mode of philosophical meditation that makes Conrad's text so haunting.[24] But Kingsley also self-consciously explores the power-knowledge complex in cross-cultural confrontation. Let me state this carefully: Kingsley, like other late Victorian ethnographers, is not free from polygeneticist, racist assumptions about the difference between Africans and Europeans. And, as Pratt points out, her "comic irreverence" itself could be seen as a form of mastery (*Imperial Eyes,* 215). Yet in her narrative she continually satirizes an imperialism of the intellect in ethnography and travel. Unlike most of her male contemporaries, she examines how the dynamics of power between African and European is gendered. She pokes fun at the project of European mastery, of Hermes the ethnographer as phallic interpreter.

The complex interaction between knowledge and power, particularly that involved in the ethnographic pursuit of Africa, is apparent in a passage in Kingsley's text that allegorizes the difficulties of what James Clifford calls "ethnographic subjectivity" ("On Ethnographic Self-Fashioning," 93-94). It occurs in a very important and even suspensefully delayed chapter on African "fetish," which is the object of Kingsley's ethnographic research.

> The difficulty of the language is, however, far less than the whole set of difficulties with your own mind. Unless you can make it pliant enough to follow the African idea step by step, however much care you may take, you will not bag your game. I heard an account the other day—I have forgotten where—of a representative of her Majesty in Africa who went out for a day's antelope shooting. There were plenty of antelope about, and he stalked them with great care; but always, just before he got within shot of the game, they saw something and bolted. Knowing he and the boy behind him had been making no sound and could not have been seen, he stalked on, but always with the same result; until happening to look round, he saw the boy behind him was supporting the dignity of the Empire at large, and this representative of it in particular, by steadfastly holding aloft the consular flag. Well, if you

go hunting the African idea with the flag of your own religion or opinions floating ostentatiously over you, you will similarly get a very poor bag.

(434-35)

In borrowing this story of the imperial white hunter (Her Majesty's representative), Kingsley creates a parable of the imperial Western intellect. Her "allegory" exposes the folly of the European's confident machismo and links it to the nationalistic ideologies that inhibit cultural encounters on the frontiers of empire. As Haraway has shown, the image of the hunt in narratives on African travel, particularly those recounting scientific enterprises, often buttresses the threatened manhood of the white traveler. African exploration of various kinds provided the white male traveler with "resources for restoring manhood in the healthy activity of sportsmanlike hunting"—"hunting" here includes capturing the African "image" in photography or gathering scientific information (53). In interrupting her description of African "fetish" with this story of the flag as trussed-up phallus, Kingsley shifts the difficulties of interpreting African culture to the mind of the adventuring ethnographer and uncannily recognizes a form of fetish worship peculiar to Western patriotism.[25]

Although in some ways her narrative participates in the typical representation of Africa as insoluble mystery, figuring the African intellect as unfathomable terrain ("I must warn you also that your own mind requires protection when you send it stalking the savage idea through the tangled forests, the dark caves, the swamps and the fogs of the Ethiopian intellect" [440]), her emphasis falls on the cultural baggage of the Western consciousness. Anticipating Marlow's warnings in *Heart of Darkness* about the "few ideas" the European must take with him to Africa, her perspective is nevertheless more ironic and skeptical; for the moly to which this Hermes-ethnographer must cling is the recognition of "the untrustworthiness of human evidence regarding the unseen, and also the seen, when it is viewed by a person who has in his mind an explanation of the phenomenon before it occurs" (440). There is a sophisticated awareness, not only of knowledge as a kind of violence done to things, but of the reflexive limitation of vision as well—in seeing the other through Western eyes, we tend to project ourselves.

Kingsley advises that "the wisest way" to study the natural and cultural phenomena of Africa, particularly the fetish, is "to get into the state of mind of an old marine engineer who oils and sees that every screw and bolt of his engines is clean and well watched, and who loves them as living things, caressing and scolding them himself, defending them, with stormy language, against the aspersions of the silly, uninformed outside world, which persists in regarding them as mere machines, a thing his superior intelligence and experience knows they are not" (441-42). Again, this advice anticipates Marlow's speech about the saving possibilities of concentrating on "rivets," a utilitarian, English antidote to the African mystery. Yet Kingsley does something quite different in her narrative by drawing an analogy between the Western form of fetishism, which attributes divinity to technological, material objects, and African fetish, which also views material objects as embodying religious and social value. The idea and discourse of the fetish, as William Pietz thoroughly demonstrates, was developed by eighteenth-century travelers to the West African coast and was produced by a specifically mercantile cross-cultural interaction ("Fetish, II," 45). Kingsley offers the idea of the fetish not as evidence of the Africans' irrationality and perversity—as it was often presented in Western discourse—but as an intelligible nexus of social, economic, and religious investments in the material object. Whereas much Western discourse on the fetish disparages what was viewed as a confusion of religious values with material objects, said to exemplify the African mentality (Pietz, "Fetish IIIa," 109), Kingsley, herself a thoroughgoing materialist, views it as a comprehensible, even valuable idea.

Yet "pursuit of the African idea," even when this phrase designates a cautious endeavor to understand the complex idea of fetish worship, entangles Kingsley in the language of mastery, even as she attempts to dissociate herself from it. As she persists in using the metaphor of "sport," she implicates herself in the discourse of mastery and capture. She calls "stalking the wild West African idea" a "pursuit" of "high sporting interest," "as beset with difficulty and danger as grizzly bear hunting" (430). Here, her analogy between the dangers of ethnography and those of hunting is meant to aggrandize intellectual pursuit.[26] The "pursuit," like the "hunt," must be approached with great caution. The long-deferred chapter entitled "Fetish" is summarized as a narrative "in which the Voyager attempts cautiously to approach the subject of Fetish, and gives a classification of spirits, and some account of the Ibet and Orundas" (429). Can the ethnographer truly be divorced from the imperialist adventurer? In implicit recognition of the difficulties of figuring ethnographic activity, Kingsley varies her metaphors. The hunt becomes a gentler zoological expedition; ideas are "netted" rather than captured as prey, and the narrative also mentions "netting" a reason for a particular practice. It's as if all the professional activities of African explorers were encompassed by these sets of metaphors, implicated in one enterprise, yet different from one another—hunters, explorers, naturalists, ethnographers.

Whatever the particular occupation of the traveler, however, Kingsley's metaphors privilege the active "pursuit" of Africa on the frontier as opposed to a second-hand, more purely speculative approach. The narrative establishes a dichotomy between on-site ethnographic activity and the musings of armchair ethnologists comfortably at home in Europe, unwilling to risk the adventure. "Bagging" the game, which stands figuratively for achieving some satisfactory understanding of African culture, fetish in particular, is contrasted with "tagging" the stories somewhere back home. The image of the sportsman is meant to suggest some wit and ingenuity in the ethnographer, qualities that are missing from the mere collector of facts. Kingsley writes:

> African stories are of great interest when you know the locality and the tribe they come from; but I am sure if you were to bring home a heap of stories like this, and empty them over any distinguished ethnologist's head, without ticketing them with the culture of the tribe they belonged to, the conditions it lives under, and so forth, you would stun him with the seeming inter-contradiction of some, and utter pointlessness of the rest, and he would give up ethnology and hurriedly devote his remaining years to the attempt to collect a million postage stamps, so as to do something definite before he died.
>
> (439)

Kingsley constantly disparages the intellectual and physical safety of the "collector" that fosters such European misconceptions of the African and his or her culture. Her armchair ethnologist is defenseless against the "trick" played by the fieldworker, who physically "stuns" him with a cascade of African "facts." In Kingsley's scenario, these "facts" become so much garbage dumped over the distinguished ethnologist's head. She chooses philately as the proper occupation for this failed and frustrated ethnologist, for collecting *stamps* serves as the emblem for the sedentary rather than for risk-taking activity. Ticketing the "heap" of stories is implicitly compared with hoarding African objects, as opposed to promoting their circulation and exchange in the field.

Thirty years before Malinowski introduced twentieth-century standards of scientific participation-observation for the ethnographer, Kingsley contrasts the traveling scientist with the armchair egghead, representing proper ethnography as movement and adventure. Although she has a high regard for "experts" such as E. B. Tylor and Dr. Nassau, she regards with suspicion various kinds of "professionals"—government administrators and ethnologists alike—who fail to combine interpretation with experience and to consider the local context of the details of culture they analyze.[27]

Kingsley in her narrative rhetorically signals skepticism about taxonomy and rigid classification (i.e., "tagging" the game), juxtaposing it with the practical, the contingent, the nonsystematic. Digressions puncture her own discourse of classification. For example, her allegory of hunting the African idea interrupts the summaries of information on African fetish. Storytelling, that is, disperses her more "scientific" descriptions and catalogues of fetish; it is the storyteller, not the scientist, who "forgets" the source of information of the story ("I heard an account the other day—I have forgotten where"). In the midst of a crucial chapter on African custom and belief, her little parable (of the flag-bearing hunter) intrudes to disrupt classification and taxonomy. The folkloristic, the serendipitous (she *happened* to hear of this story which serves as a perfect allegory) enter the picture of knowledge. The hybrid forms within Kingsley's text—the "word swamp," as she called it, of narrative, diary, ethnographic facts, and stories quoted from African and European sources—formally imitate the mixed tones and textures of the Africa she encountered, while somehow, in their entirety, attempting to give an "idea" of Africa. It is as if the African "story" cannot be told within the confines of any one tradition. Within the narrative, Kingsley often refers to her "goings on" (351), or errant behavior, and this same kind of wandering marks the narration as well as the events. Such language emphasizes the image of the wayward, risk-taking traveler who deliberately refuses the too neat summaries of African culture as well as the more aggressive, imperial "quests" of male exploration.

It is around the concept of "fetish" that Kingsley focuses her discussion of the recalcitrance of West African culture to Western systematization—there are fetishes for everything in African culture, Kingsley says, rebuking Western attempts to integrate African "religion" into a coherent whole. On the one hand, this interpretation might be read as exemplifying the European tradition of seeing Africa as the sign of the indecipherable, the unsystematic. As Gayatri Chakravorty Spivak and Christopher Miller have observed, Africa frustrated Western attempts to reify it even more thoroughly than had the Orient. Hinduism and Islam could be read as an intelligible code, but "fetish" could not. Spivak says:

> Part of my work is to notice what kinds of distinctions were made among the so-called others of the West. I have used the example of the codification of law. In this situation the Islamic code was taken as a real code, since it was a monotheistic code, but it was seen as incorrect. . . . And anything that was not either Hindu or Muslim—tribals and so on, and in a wider context, non-Islamic Africa and the Aboriginals of Australia—did not have a code, and was made the place of magic and fetishism. It is in this kind of context that one has to see the othering of the other of the West, in actual imperial practice.
>
> (*Post-Colonial Critic,* 39)

Yet, although most nineteenth- and early twentieth-century travelers and scientists considered fetish a "puerile cult of idolatry" (Christopher Miller, 44), Kingsley's treatment, as I have already noted, is quite different. She is fascinated—and captivated—by what

she considers the local and pragmatic wisdom of African "charms" and "fetish." In a section titled the "Uncertainty of Charms," she tries to convey the practical and concrete aspects of belief: "Charms are made for every occupation and desire in life—loving, hating, buying, selling, fishing, planting, travelling, hunting, & c" (448). And, "I often think it must be the commonsense element in fetish customs that enables them to survive, in the strange way they do, in the minds of Africans who have been long under European influence and education" (490). Although in this way Kingsley domesticates the uncertainties of African practice, by doing so she attempts to show that the imposition of Western moral schemas is irrational and bizarre.

Whereas the conventional Western discourse of the fetish treats the irreducible materiality and the contingent nature of African fetish as debased, unsystematic, and unspiritual, Kingsley's account gives them values. Her narrative tries to retain the sense of the foreignness of Africa not as Conradian mystique but as the stubborn resistance of the specific, the local. Kingsley records particular encounters in which the ethnographer literally bumps up against stubborn material or cultural facts and is made to recognize they have a life of their own, a fetish power. Interestingly, the twentieth-century ethnographer Steven Webster prescribes just such an immersion in the "contingencies" of everyday life: "Ethnography must hang on in good faith to the myriad contingencies and opaque personalities of reality, and deny itself the illusion of a transparent description, a luxury reserved for less reflexive sciences" (111). Webster's metaphors only inadvertently retain the physicality of Kingsley's prosaic comedy—one pictures the ethnographer literally clinging to ("hanging on" to) the "real," the quotidian detail. It is this comic, de-eroticized body of the traveler that Kingsley's narrative represents again and again which suggests one aspect of fetish that intersects with Bergsonian comedy, its "subversion of the ideal of the autonomously determined self" (Pietz, "Fetish II," 23). Thus, fetish is invoked in the narrative both as a charm, or moly, to aid the traveler and as the kind of fateful chance that leads to her sometimes humbling (and physical) confrontation with the African "fact" she has not anticipated. The narrator complains that "the worst of charms and prayers" is that the "thing you wish of them may, and frequently does, happen in a strikingly direct way, but other times it does not" (448). Again, this difficulty becomes the source of comedy: "Finding, we will say, that you have been upset and half-drowned, and your canoe-load of goods lost three times in a week, that your paddles are always breaking, and the amount of snags in the river and so on is abnormal, you judge that your canoe-charm has stopped. Then you go to the medicine man who supplied you with it and complain. He says it was a perfectly good charm when he sold it you and he never had any complaints before, but he will investigate" (449).

The iterative mode and present tense, the hypothetical exchange of European writer and European reader in the use of the second person (it is the "you" who experiences this bewilderment rather than the "I" of the writer), and the transformation of the medicine man into a local shopkeeper—all serve to domesticate the mystery and translate the foreign into terms intelligible (and ingratiating) to the English reader. The narration here suggests that African spirits are busy thwarting European travelers and that African charms produce the necessity of English "charm" and wit in the encounter between African and European. Yet here again Kingsley's narrative represents a crucial aspect of fetishism—its relation to and origin in mercantile transactions between different cultures. Fetish is a key phenomenon in her text not only for what it reveals about African custom but also for the commercial exchange it enables. The meaning of the African "fetish" becomes linked to the particular commercial transactions in face-to-face encounters.

But Kingsley shows how the element of surprise, of risk, of chance upsets the supposedly rational Western notion of economic exchange. As Pietz observes about the fetish trade between Europeans and Africans in early narratives of African travel, trading led to "a perversion of the natural processes of economic negotiation and legal contact. Desiring a clean economic interaction, seventeenth-century merchants unhappily found themselves entering into social relations and quasi-religious ceremonies that should have been irrelevant to the conduct of trade" ("Fetish II," 45). Kingsley, on the contrary, welcomed the "messiness" of commercial transaction and its two-way process, for the economic transfer was a means, not an end, leading as it did to ethnographic encounter. The transformation of cross-cultural confrontation into a series of particular "exchanges," even consumer exchanges, is linked to the important image of circulation to which I have alluded and thus leads back to the venture/adventure tradition I mentioned earlier.

I want to return to the topoi of circulation and exchange in an attempt to explain the importance of trade not only for Kingsley's overt political support of British trading concerns in Africa (at the expense of the Crown colony system of direct control) but also for what I would call the politics of representation in her text, that is, the representation of intercultural exchanges on the frontier. According to J. E. Flint, on her return to England, in her writings and speeches Kingsley became "the intellectual and philosophic spokeswoman for the British traders to West Africa" (96). As she acknowledges in the first chapters of her book, her journeys to Africa made her totally revise her impressions of traders, and she admits owing much to the trading company of Hatton and Cookson, which helped facilitate her journey. In an appendix to *Travels* called "Disease in West Africa," she lauds the "heroes of commerce, the West Coast traders" and praises England as "the greatest manufacturing country in the world." The trade carried on in West Africa "enables thousands of men, women and children to remain safely in England, in comfort and pleasure, owing to the wages and profits arising from the manufacture and export of the articles used in that trade" (691).

This tribute to men of trade is clearly an endorsement of England's expansionist policy as well as of alliance between expansion and capitalism (Kingsley contrasts capitalistic expansion, through free trade, with colonization, which is ultimately a drain on the mother country and destructive of the indigenous culture). But if Kingsley served, in part, as an apologist for the English free-trade companies; her interest in trade would be too narrowly interpreted as an idealization of capitalism. Flint reassesses Kingsley through a revisionary reading of the "real purpose" (i.e., ulterior motive) of her intense interest in African culture—to support the trader's position and to undermine that of the missionaries—yet only in a footnote does he concede that self-interest was not involved. Because he divorces the "politics" from the narrative enterprise, Flint is at a loss to explain Kingsley as a "fanatical supporter of [trade] interests" (97, n. 7).

Trade literally underwrote much of Kingsley's journey, for she partially supported herself by bartering Western goods, such as liquor and tobacco, in exchange for food, guides, conversation, and information. These exchanges are paradigmatic of mediation on the cultural frontier. Speaking of the exchange on which anthropology itself is based, Webster points out that the anthropological account usually represses this quid pro quo. Ethnography, he comments, treats as "unspoken promises" the "honorary cultural membership" for the ethnologist and the "sanguine hope of Western advantages" for the African hosts: "The impossibility of such unspoken promises is both the tragedy of cultural difference-domination and the ground of its understanding" (92). Webster is interested in demystifying and deidealizing this cultural encounter between the object of study and the Western investigator. Kingsley frankly acknowledges the role that self-interest and material exchange play in cross-cultural confrontation. What she hoped to "purchase" through African transactions was not a commodity but participation in a male intercultural social commerce facilitated and emblematized by barter—the face-to-face exchange of goods and material as well as stories, information, and access. The benefits of commodity fetishism that those at home derive from the "heroes of commerce" differ from the anthropological trade sought by Kingsley, in which the market is infused with theater, personality, and risk. If Africans and English traders are depicted as serving each other's interests, Kingsley has a strong sense of the mutual manipulations that attend the maneuvers of exchange. For her, as for Sarah Lee, this fiction of mutuality involves projecting onto the Africans a relish and pleasure in the process of trade. She calls this process "the great affair of life" for the mainlanders, who "take to it as soon as they can toddle, and don't even leave it off at death, according to their own accounts of the way the spirits of distinguished traders still dabble and interfere in market matters" (56-57). Although there is much in *Travels* to confirm the difference between Africans and Europeans, trade functions to naturalize the difference by presenting both Africans and British travelers as having needs that are satisfied in the marketplace (and this marketplace is broadly conceived as the place of exchanges of various kinds, not only of material goods).

If this sense of the Africans' willing participation licenses the presence of British traders in Africa, it also sanctions participation of the female traveler and ethnographer. The marketplace offers Kingsley a neutral ground on which to encounter Africans and Africa. She finds an emblem of this genderless mediation in "trade English," which she describes as useful not only "as a means of intercommunication between whites and blacks, but between natives using two distinct languages. . . . It is by no means an easy language to pick up—it is not a farrago of bad words and broken phrases, but is a definite structure, has a great peculiarity in its verb forms, and employs no genders. There is no grammar of it out yet; and one of the best ways of learning it is to listen to a seasoned second mate regulating the unloading or loading, of cargo, over the hatch of the hold" (432). A whole series of cultural assumptions are embedded here; Kingsley wants to see the language of trade as a model of parity rather than mastery, a terrain on which different groups meet and spar and engage in a battle of wits. The most striking emphasis in her representation of trade English is on the fact that it is ungendered. Elsewhere, when this lack of gender results in her being called "sir," one begins to realize that the idea of "genderlessness" really denotes a generic maleness and a certain class and racial status. For in stressing the idea of parity, Kingsley ignores the markers of status evident in the address "sir" as well as the fact that the lingua franca of trade has its norm in an English the "natives" speak only imperfectly. We can recognize Kingsley's investment in affirming this fraternal system, for it significantly allows her neutral participation as woman traveler, trader, and scientist.

Thus, the woman traveler circulates within a male economy centered on the marketplace. Nancy Armstrong analyzes the way nineteenth-century English novels created an ideology of the domestic that gendered the spheres of private and public, producing the private sphere as the realm of the middle-class woman. The cultural exchange that occurs in this sphere, as represented in novels, is sexual.[28] Kingsley's travel narrative provides a counterexample to this tradition—it represents the female self not as sexual commodity but as a mobile, improvisational "trader" on the market. Putting herself in circulation is not the same as discovering the self so popular in accounts of intrepid Victorian women travelers, for to equate such circulation with self-discovery is to reinvent Kingsley's story with the value of a coherent, private subjectivity from which, even at home, Kingsley withheld belief. Her awareness of the theater of the self was heightened by the sense of cross-cultural encounter and audience. Sitting and warming herself "at the fires of other human beings" (Gwynn, 26): this is how Kingsley described her selfhood in general. It is no accident that the image evokes scenes of African fires where she warmed herself on her travels. As Gwynn says, this circulation was made possible through trade (48-54).

The economy of the traveling self on the cultural frontier, if capitalistic, is protean, risky, and infused with the personality of the circulating trader. It is thus more suited to the ethos of early modern capitalism and exploration, characterized by Stephen Greenblatt as "self-fashioning," than to the anonymity of capitalist exchange at home. Face-to-face barter and improvisational encounter in the male economy of cross-cultural confrontation may seem anachronistic in the 1890s. Flint accuses Kingsley of being reactionary rather than progressive, as she is often regarded. According to him, she attempted to "re-create and fossilize the conditions of the 1880's, when government was rudimentary, and the traders untrammeled by taxation, regulations, and official control" (104). As an example of her antipathy to change, he cites her opposition to introducing coinage into the British territories. Indeed, Kingsley's positive representation of face-to-face encounter does bespeak a resistance to the anonymity of both British bureaucracy and late nineteenth-century and early twentieth-century capitalism. In speeches he delivered around the time that Kingsley wrote her book (and that were published in book form in 1900), George Simmel diagnosed this anonymity and linked it with the institution of money itself (79). Kingsley's vision of the marketplace retained the sense of personal encounter and "face."

But this "face," to return to the theatrical metaphors that abound in the narrative, is represented by Kingsley as a construction for the benefit of an audience. In this regard, Kingsley's book looks forward rather than back to an earlier time. Applying Greenblatt's idea of self-fashioning to the situation of the ethnographer in a postmodern context, Clifford describes the late twentieth-century ethnographer as a self-fashioner, conscious of the way cross-cultural exchange is always a question of dress-up and presentation ("Ethnographic Self-Fashioning," 95). Rather than the sentimental heroic dramas found in many experiential travel narratives of the century, Kingsley gives us theatrics, the performance of the ethnographer and traveler as Hermes the trickster. Kingsley's references to her "goings on," her self-representation as an errant (wandering) traveler and writer belong in this context. Indeed, Kingsley's narrative is strikingly unsentimental about cross-cultural encounters. Her advocacy of trade and exchange must be distinguished from the ethos of a work such as Harriet Martineau's mid-century travel tale, *Dawn Island,* in which the expansion of economic activity is yoked to salvation and humanitarianism. Christianity and commerce go hand in hand to liberate the "savage" from the error of his ways. Kingsley recognizes manipulations, hustling, and self-fashioning on both sides of the cross-cultural divide. The trickster in folklore, it is well to remember, is a figure of the crossroads and the marketplace (Babcock-Abrahams, 159).[29]

Kingsley went to Africa, she says, to collect fish and fetish, that is, to study specimens and species. Much of the narrative is taken up with reporting what she discovered. But her narrative self-representation acknowledges that the Western observer is the observed as well, both performer and makeup artist. The Latin root of "species," Alexander Gelley reminds us, signifies the visual—that which is seen and that which is a spectacle in the sense of theatrical illusion, but it also implies the "mirroring or reflecting back on itself of the viewing instance" (27). This reflexivity, the acute sense of the viewer viewed, characterizes Kingsley's double vision. (Hence, these implications of "species" differ dramatically from those of the related word "specie," that is, metal coinage, which would apply to the anonymity of the market.)

This double vision bespeaks Kingsley's awareness of the theatrics that characterize not only macho European exploration but also the dyad of masculinity and femininity itself. Gender in her narrative involves masquerade and in the cross-cultural encounter is imbricated in the masculinist posturing of a Stanley. Imperialistic superiority is figured as theater—the imposing European male "Giant" wears a costume ("It is at such a moment as this that the Giant's robe gets, so to speak, between your legs and threatens to trip you up" [295]). Kingsley represents her traveling and writing as participating in such masquerade. In one scene, Kingsley and her men are trapped in a swamp by the rising tide that separates them from solid land. "No need for an old coaster like me to look at that sort of thing twice to know what it

meant, and feeling it was a situation more suited to Mr. Stanley than myself, I attempted to emulate his methods and addressed my men. 'Boys,' said I, 'this beastly hole is tidal, and the tide is coming in'" (298). Here is dress-up twice over: Mary Kingsley, Victorian woman, masquerading as a salty old coaster who affects the hyper-virile swagger of a Stanley-like explorer. The "punchline" (including the representation of the "natives" as undifferentiated "boys") is vaudevillian. The travel writer as well as the African traveler must "dress up," for writing, like trading, demands a successful performance, a witty line for every occasion. Traveler and writer must be able to meet particular situations with dialogue that works.[30]

From the theatrics of gender and race in Kingsley's text, one gets a distinct sense not only that brands of masculinity are exposed as facade or performance but also that femininity, too, is shown to participate in masquerade. When she receives a note addressed to "Dear old Man" that offers her some clean men's shirts and trousers (a mistake caused by the ambiguities of gender in "trade English"), Kingsley mugs:

> Had there been any smelling salts or sal volatile in this subdivision of the Ethiopian region I should have forthwith fainted on reading this, but I well knew there was not, so I blushed until the steam from my soaking clothes (for I truly was "in a deuce of a mess") went up in a cloud and then, just as I was, I went "across" and appeared before the author of that awful note.
>
> (502)

Here Kingsley represents herself as representing the English lady. The extent to which she *feared* being taken for such a typical creature can be gauged by her anxiety about encountering a French nun at a Roman Catholic mission on the Rembwé River:

> Moreover I learnt she could not speak English, and I shrank in my condition from attempting to evolve the French language out of my inner consciousness; feeling quite certain I should get much misunderstood by the gentle, clean, tidy lady, and she might put me down as an ordinary specimen of Englishwoman, and so I should bring disgrace on my nation. If I had been able to dress up, ashore I would have gone, but as it was I wrote her a note explaining things and thanking her.
>
> (350-51)

The "audience" for her persona is European as well as African. To be an "ordinary specimen of Englishwoman" is a terrifying fate; although Kingsley is willing to spar with African traders in "trade English," she is unwilling to be disadvantaged in French with another European woman, for without her wit she might too readily be mistaken for a walking (or traveling) cliché. Indeed, some of the rare anger in the narrative vents itself against a "lady passenger" who insists on playing the role of European lady to the hilt: "Yesterday I met a lady on the shore who asked me if I would take her to Gaboon. I said, as any skipper would, 'delighted, my dear'; and here she is sitting on the top of the cargo with her head just exactly in the proper position to get it bashed in, or knocked off by the boom; and her five bundles, one tin box, a peck of limes and a husband" (412). Kingsley goes on to say:

> My lady passenger is quite the lady passenger, fright-ened of the sea, and dissatisfied with the accommoda-tion. I have stowed her with every care in the bottom of the boat . . . and she is grateful for the attention; but says "the vessel is not big enough," and goes on eating excruciatingly sour limes in a way that sets my teeth on edge. Half her sufferings arise from her disas-trous habit of falling asleep; and then her head goes flump off the seat she is leaning it against, and crack against the ribs of the boat's side; I put my leather photograph case in her usual striking place, but she dodges it in her descent seven times in ten.
>
>   (413-14)

What befalls the lady in the narrative is not the rever-sals and tumbles of the comic "I" but a more "fitting" physical punishment—a smack on the head for her brainlessness.

In Kingsley's case, the "difference" gender makes to her travel writing seems to me to lie importantly in this recognition of the theatrical dimension in cultural en-counters and the problems of ethnographic representa-tion. I do not mean to claim for Kingsley an anachro-nistic postmodern consciousness about representation; but I do want to suggest the way in which her often comic narrative functions, in particular, to acknowledge both the way European and native "dress up" to con-front each other and the way in which textual forms of-ten imply certain ideologies. Her sense of her own life as mediated and imagined through the books in her fa-ther's library gave her an especially strong sense of the need "to prepare a face to meet the faces that you meet," to quote T. S. Eliot. "When there were no more odd jobs to do at home, I, out of my life in books, found something to do that my father cared for, something for which I had been taught German, so that I could do for him odd jobs in it. It was the study of early religion and law, and for it I had to go to West Africa, and I went there, proceeding on the even tenor of my way, doing odd jobs, and trying to understand things, pursuing knowledge under difficulties with unbroken devotion" (Oliver, 78). This language comes from a narrative she fashioned in 1899, when the African exploration was all finished. An odd combination exists here: on the one hand, she seems to accept the patriarchal legacy of the name Kingsley, which included her traveler father and her two famous writer uncles, who celebrated British expansionism and adventure; on the other hand, she is aware that in this tradition she is the daughter who, run-ning out of domestic housework, must make a project

of finding some service to be done outside the home. She emerges "out of [her] life in books" in two senses—her travel is both a liberation from the confines of her father's library and a product of that same library, where her reading empowers her to cast herself in the multiple roles of adventurer, scientist, and pursuer of knowledge.

Mary Kingsley both used and transformed male models of adventure and commerce to represent her interaction with African culture and fashion herself as a participant in a male economy. But occasionally, particularly in private letters, she identified herself with a feminized Africa. To Nathan, the man to whom she was probably most attached, she wrote: "I will import to you, in strict confidence, for if it were known it would damage me badly, my opinion on the African. He is *not* 'half devil and half child', anymore than he is 'our benighted brother' and all that sort of thing. He is a woman . . . I know those nigs because I am a woman, a woman of a masculine race but a woman still." Elsewhere she calls herself an "African" and says, "We Africans are not fit for decent society" (quoted in Deborah Birkett, 16). Perhaps it is not surprising that in writing to her poten-tial lover, Kingsley figures her own neediness and (indecent) sexuality by identifying with the African. Yet this self-description also suggests the fact that it was in-creasingly difficult to figure herself without recourse to this "other" being with whom she was so intensely in-volved in her travels and writings. The feminine domes-tic tradition, the masculinist tradition of imperial adven-ture, the self-effacing topoi of scientific writing—none of these provided the conventions for representing her differences from and resemblances to the people she came to study. *Travels in West Africa* offers more than another white woman's quest for herself in the mirror of the Dark Continent. In her seven hundred-page narrative/ethnography, Kingsley attempts to record how the awkward body of a white woman traveler both col-lided and colluded with West African cultures.

Notes

1. Opposing the thesis of white women's uncon-scious racist response to colonial homoeroticism, Sara Suleri has recently analyzed the way Anglo-Indian women's writing unmasks the "disembod-ied homoeroticism" in colonial relations and in-tentionally revises the heterosexual paradigm of ravishment and possession typical of many male exploration and travel narratives (77).

2. Although I find Spivak's comments rightly suspi-cious of the rhetoric of aggressive individualism that marks the descriptions of intrepid British women travelers, her conflation of "individual-ism" and "individualist" runs the risk of too re-ductively collapsing the significances of travel for different women, for example, Gertrude Bell and Mary Kingsley, who resisted the label of "New

Woman" and rejected the claims of the women's suffrage movement. Indeed, "the making of human beings" was variously nuanced in women's travel (as demonstrated in Nupur Chaudhuri and Margaret Strobel's edited collection *Western Women and Imperialism: Complicity and Resistance)*. As Nandy says of certain women travelers to India who there discovered alternatives to the male pattern of political domination, they "found in Indian versions of religiosity, knowledge and social intervention not merely a model of dissent against their own society, but also some protection for their search for new models of transcendence, a greater tolerance of androgyny, and a richer meaning as well as legitimacy for women's participation in social and political life" (36). Nandy points to the way that Annie Besant, for example, attempted to reconcile Western and Eastern spirituality in her study of theosophy and travel to India, a reconciliation that displays a pattern different from that of the quest for the imperial self. It is fascinating that although Nandy mentions that Besant and Mira Richards (and others) were Irish, he neglects to follow up on the implications of this anomaly: that their own colonial status might have combined with their gender to produce a different sense of cultural mediation between West and East.

3. For a more recent, Foucauldian treatment of the competing discourses of femininity and colonialism in travel writing by women, see *Discourses of Difference: An Analysis of Women's Travel Writing and Colonialism* by Sara Mills. See in particular the chapter "Feminist Work on Women's Travel Writing."

4. Lee is also known as Mrs. T. E. Bowdich, Mrs. R. Lee, and Sarah Lee Wallis.

5. Dorothy Hammond and Alta Jablow identify a difference between British and French travel narratives in this regard: British adventure narratives project "a desire for freedom and withdrawal from the importunate demands of marriage, of women, and of love itself" and are therefore "less concerned with heightened sexuality" than the French narratives, which envision "some ultimate sexual experience to be found only in Africa" (154). As Zweig shows in *The Adventurer: The Fate of Adventure in the Western World,* displacement rather than absence of the feminine occurs in many British narratives, in which the woman left behind is reinvented on the other side of adventure, erotically displaced onto the foreign body of the foreign land. Recent studies of the eroticization of the discourse of African travel, such as Christopher Miller's *Blank Darkness: Africanist Discourse in French* and Dennis Porter's *Haunted*

Journeys: Desire and Transgression in European Travel Writing, tend to focus on the French tradition of travel writing, which explores as Porter puts it, "opportunities not available in the same way in Europe to push beyond the limits of the pleasure principle" (175).

6. Other narratives by European women who traveled to West Africa include those by Mary Falconbridge, Elizabeth Melville, Mary Gaunt, and May Mott-Smith. See Patricia Romero's *Women's Voices on Africa: A Century of Travel Writings* and Catherine Barnes Stevenson's *Victorian Women Travel Writers in Africa.*

7. The subject of the differences between narratives of East and West Africa, between orientalist and nonorientalist discourses, is too broad for consideration here. No few examples of travel writing concerning Africa can represent the totality of either Africa or travel writing. I have chosen to confine my examples to West Africa for the reasons stated above as well as to provide a control in my discussion.

8. That Gaunt herself was an Australian colonial, the daughter of an English prospector who went out to the colony, might have encouraged her identification with the spirit of adventure on the frontier.

9. Gaunt dates the inception of her interest in West Africa from her reading of the story of Carlo and goes on to relate how fascination with it was "put on hold" during her twenty-year marriage. Premature widowhood led to her renewed interest in traveling to Africa, but she says she first wrote books about Africa to earn the money to travel there. Her story stresses the way Africa becomes a textual product that is a blend of citation and personal record, desire and necessity. There is a certain irony in the fact that Gaunt marketed Africa as a means to travel there.

10. For a narrative of T. Edward Bowdich's "missions" in West Africa, see *Mission from Cape Coast Castle to Ashantee with a Statistical Account of That Kingdom and Geographical Notices of Other Parts of the Interior of Africa* and *Excursions in Madeira and Porto Santo, during the Autumn of 1823, While on His Third Voyage to Africa,* the latter of which contains an appendix by "Mrs. Bowdich" that offers her view of the voyage, along with details of her husband's death in Africa.

11. In an essay on Renaissance exploration to the New World, Louis Montrose says: "For the Englishmen in the New World, the Spaniards are proximate figures of Otherness: In being Catholic, Latin, and Mediterranean, they are spiritually, lin-

guistically, ethnically, and ecologically alien. . . . The sign of the Spaniard in English discovery texts simultaneously mediates and complicates any simple antinomy of European Self and American Other." This "mediation," however, occurs in the context of "manly rivalry," in which "England and Spain" vie in a "contest to deflower the new-found lands" ("Work of Gender and Sexuality in the Elizabethan Discourse of Discovery," 161). In Lee's abolitionist novel, there is no triangular relationship between manly rivals and feminized land; instead, the heroes, rather than rivals, are Latinos, adopted sons of an Englishman, who thus mediate between white traveler and African other.

12. See John Coverdale's *Basque Phase of Spain's First Carlist War* and Carlos Marichal's *Spain (1834-1844): A New Society* for an understanding of the ideological stakes of the conflict, and *The Carlist Wars in Spain* by Edgar Holt for details on British participation in the wars.

13. Historically, a Colonel Lacy served as an English commissioner with the Cristino armies in the center of Spain (Holt, 121), but in the novel, Lacy fights for the Carlists, providing an older generation more in keeping with the aristocratic-chivalric assumptions of the traditionalist Carlist cause. These assumptions retained their appeal to a writer such as Conrad, who became a gunrunner for the Carlists in a subsequent war. Conrad fictionalizes this involvement in both *The Arrow of Gold* and *The Mirror of the Sea*. Frederick Karl says of this involvement: "That Conrad should have been involved in such ventures had little to do with belief. . . . The venture itself—hopeless, adventurous, anti-establishment—would have an appeal for its very futility" (132).

14. Curtin calls the period of African exploration from the 1830s to the 1850s the "Age of Humanitarianism" (287), during which the act of 1833 was passed, emancipating the slaves in the British colonies (290). Patrick Brantlinger astutely observes the connections between the abolitionist literature of this period, which Lee's novel exemplifies, and the general project of imperialism in *Rule of Darkness: British Literature and Imperialism, 1830-1914.*

15. See George Stocking's discussion of the class dimension of Irishness in English discourse and of the way Irishness increasingly during the century provided "a mediating example for both attitude and policy in relation with 'savages' overseas" (225-35).

16. In the short stories collected with her autobiographical narrative, Lee displaces her cultural analysis of women's restricted movement in soci-

ety onto the African heroines of her fairy-tale-like stories. Adumissa, the beautiful and tragic heroine of one of her stories, plots to save herself from marriage, which she realizes will curtail her freedom. To her would-be suitor she says: "I have been an only child; I have been the principal person in my family; every one has obeyed me; and, free and happy, I have never known what it was to submit. If I were to marry, I should become as nothing; I should lose my rank and my freedom, and be mingled with the multitude" (*Stories,* 11). If the vision of a totally free woman is ultimately negated by the rebellious heroine's tragic death, it seems to have been totally unthinkable in a European fictional setting.

17. The focus on gender in Pratt's book represents something of a departure from her work on travel that had earlier appeared in *Critical Inquiry* and the collection *Writing Culture*. In those essays Pratt seemed wary of drawing a dividing line between travel writing produced by men and women. In the book, however, she discusses differences in men's and women's travel writing, finding "a division of labor" between "male travelers . . . driven by curiosity, which legitimates their every move" and certain women travelers who refuse the rhetoric of mastery (104). Yet, as Pratt goes on to say, despite their different rhetoric and stances, these texts often participate in the same agenda as texts by men which belong to the genre of "anti-conquest" narratives, a genre that paradoxically sustains rather than overturns the imperial project.

18. See Cynthia Eagle Russett's *Sexual Science: The Victorian Construction of Womanhood* as well as Haraway's *Primate Visions: Gender, Race, and Nature in the World of Modern Science* for a discussion of the intersection between categories of sexuality and race in the development of scientific discourse. Also very useful for an understanding of the development of the ethnographic imagination in the nineteenth century is Christopher Herbert's *Culture and Anomie: Ethnographic Imagination in the Nineteenth Century.*

19. In *The English Novel in the Twentieth Century,* Green takes 1897, the year when Kingsley's *Travels* was published and the year of Queen Victoria's diamond jubilee, as an exemplary time of British pride in its imperial potential (1-15).

20. This book about pirates, attributed to Defoe, contains the narratives of "the Remarkable Actions and Adventures of the Two Female Pyrates, *Mary Read* and *Ann Bonny.*" The narratives, which record "the odd Incidents of their rambling Lives" (117), might have provided Kingsley's imagination with a particularly interesting adaptation of a masculine model. Like Cavendish's Travelia, both

women cross-dress as men to gain passage aboard the pirate ships.

21. In "The Invention of Tradition in Colonial Africa," Terence Ranger discusses the way primogeniture created a whole class of insecure second sons of England, for whom the colonies provided one of the few hopes for advancement.

22. See Mary Russell, *The Blessings of a Good Thick Skirt: Women Travellers and Their World,* 150, 156.

23. See Pratt's discussion of the way Kingsley takes pleasure in play rather than aesthetic beauty. She comments on how Kingsley seeks to separate knowledge from control (*Imperial Eyes,* 215).

24. I can find no evidence that Conrad read Kingsley's book, although she mentions reading his *Nigger of the Narcissus.*

25. In *Culture and Anomie,* Christopher Herbert praises a similar recognition of the dangers of prejudice and projection on the part of the traveler in Harriet Martineau's *How to Observe Morals and Manners* (1834), a much earlier text than Kingsley's. Showing that the narrative that dates the "invention" of modern ethnography from Malinowski falsely erases early nineteenth-century precursors such as Martineau, Herbert unearths a potential "mother" of ethnography early in the century. His excellent discussion, however, does not mention that Martineau's observations concern her travels to America rather than cross-cultural and racial confrontation on the imperial frontier. Furthermore, he does not account for the differences between cultural observation in the 1830s and imperial confrontation and observation at the end of the century, after post-Darwinian evolutionary discourse had changed anthropology and European imperialism had transformed the political scene of cross-cultural confrontation.

26. This theme of the real dangers of intellectual "pursuit" is repeated throughout her narrative, echoing that of one of her favorite books from her father's library, George Craik's *Pursuit of Knowledge under Difficulties,* a Victorian, intellectual *Profiles in Courage* that classifies different types of daring mental enterprises. Craik's study testifies to a liberalism of the intellect; it ratifies the idea that the pursuit of knowledge is available to all. The stories he tells are, he reminds us, "striking proof of how independent we really are, if we choose, of those external circumstances which seem to make so vast a difference of situation between man and man" (67). Although there are few women in this compendium of courageous individuals, Craik's point is that this pursuit is open to anyone, to

"both sexes" and "young and old" (281). For Kingsley, the autodidact and female descendant of such an illustrious Victorian literary family, this book and its liberal fictions of possibility provided another plot in which to place herself: the scientist, rather than the pirate or explorer, could be the peripatetic hero.

27. Earlier in the century, in *How to Observe Morals and Manners,* Martineau had also stressed the importance of field experience and cautioned against "hasty generalisation" (19) in interpreting "the social state of a nation" (17). But Martineau's narrative account of the intellectual difficulties that attend the traveler's sociological enterprise is itself very systematic and prescriptive, as indicated by her title. Kingsley, on the other hand, made of her narrative a farraginous mix of storytelling, description, and ethnographic summary that resists master narrative and system as it purports to come to terms with the "idea" of Africa.

28. Biographies of Kingsley rarely mention her reading the types of domestic novels that Armstrong cites as central to this "homebound" tradition. Instead, they cite her as reading picaresque novels such as Smollett's or tales of pirates.

29. Although it is true that the major representational improvisations belong to the Western traveler's narrative "I" rather than to the African, Kingsley does present many scenes of verbal and material exchange where the African host and the European guest take pleasure in sparring and hustling each other. For a discussion of the trickster figure in West African myth and folklore (specifically, among the Ashanti, Fon, Yoruba, and Dogon), see Robert D. Pelton's *Trickster in West Africa: A Study of Mythic Irony and Sacred Delight.* His general description of the trickster suits the kind of comic persona Kingsley adopts in her narrative: "It is precisely the trickster's earthiness, his popular inelegance, and his delightful inconsequence that have made our intellectual equipment for dealing with him look as ponderously inept as a steam shovel grasping for a grasshopper" (19). Kingsley's tome on West Africa disarms the compulsive thoroughness of the narration with this folkloric mask of casualness.

30. At times quotation can also function as such dress-up. For example, in the footnote she supplies to her own rendition of ascending the Great Cameroons, Kingsley quotes Sir Richard Burton's account of his attempt to reach the summit in 1862. Burton describes, in dramatic, even gothic, terms the huge crater he encounters: "Not a blade of grass, not a thread of moss, breaks the gloom of this Plutonic pit, which is as black as Erebus, except where the fire has painted it red or yellow."

Kingsley comments: "This ascent was made from the west face. I got into the 'Plutonic pit' through the S.E. break in its wall, and was the first English person to reach it from the S.E., the third of my nation, all told, to ascend the peak, and the twenty-eighth ascender according to my well-informed German friends" (595n). Clearly, her double quotation of Burton's "Plutonic pit" suggests first her appropriation, then her rejection of his more dramatic terms of description. Her own authoritative claim is deliberately stated in less heated terms, the sheer "facts" of her place in the line of mountaineers ostensibly allowed to speak for themselves. This understated way of claiming authority is characteristic of the narrative and seems intended to contrast with what Brantlinger calls the "imperial gothic" (227) of much European travel writing on Africa.

Works Cited

Appadurai, Arjun. "Putting Hierarchy in Its Place." In *Rereading Cultural Anthropology,* 34-47. Edited by George E. Marcus. Durham: Duke University Press, 1992.

Armstrong, Nancy. *Desire and Domestic Fiction: A Political History of the Novel.* New York: Oxford University Press, 1987.

Babcock-Abrahams, Barbara. "'A Tolerated Margin of Mess': The Trickster and His Tales Reconsidered." *(Indiana) Journal of the Folklore Institute* 11 (March 1975): 147-86.

Birkett, Dea. *Spinsters Abroad: Victorian Lady Explorers.* New York: Basil Blackwell, 1989.

Birkett, Deborah. "West Africa's Mary Kingsley." *History Today* 37 (May 1987): 10-16.

Bowdich, T. Edward. *Mission from Cape Coast Castle to Ashantee with a Statistical Account of That Kingdom and Geographical Notices of Other Parts of the Interior of Africa.* London: John Murray, 1819.

Brantlinger, Patrick. *Rule of Darkness: British Literature and Imperialism, 1830-1914.* Ithaca: Cornell University Press, 1988.

Brown, Rosellen. "On Not Writing a Novel." *American Poetry Review* 8 (November-December, 1979): 18-20.

Burton, Sir Richard. *The Sotadic Zone.* Boston: Milford House, 1973.

Certeau, Michel de. *The Writing of History.* Translated by Tom Conley. New York: Columbia University Press, 1988.

Clifford, James. "On Ethnographic Self-Fashioning: Conrad and Malinowski." In *The Predicament of Culture: Twentieth-Century Ethnography, Literature, and Art,* 92-113. Cambridge: Harvard University Press, 1988.

Connell, Evan S. *A Long Desire.* New York: Holt, Rinehart & Winston, 1979.

Coverdale, John F. *The Basque Phase of Spain's First Carlist War.* Princeton: Princeton University Press, 1984.

Craik, George L. *The Pursuit of Knowledge under Difficulties.* London: Bell and Daldy, 1872.

Curtin, Philip. *The Image of Africa: British Ideas and Action, 1780-1850.* Madison: University of Wisconsin Press, 1964.

Darton, F. J. Harvey. *Children's Books in England: Five Centuries of Social Life.* Cambridge: Cambridge University Press, 1932.

Defoe, Daniel. *A General History of the Robberies and Murders of the Most Notorious Pyrates.* New York: Garland Publishing, 1972.

———. *Robinson Crusoe.* New York: Bantam, 1981.

Fabian, Johannes. *Time and the Other: How Anthropology Makes Its Object.* New York: Columbia University Press, 1983.

Flint, J. E. "Mary Kingsley—A Reassessment." *Journal of African History* 4, no. 1 (1963): 95-104.

Frank, Katherine. *A Voyager Out: The Life of Mary Kingsley.* Boston: Houghton Mifflin, 1986.

———. "Voyages Out: Nineteenth-Century Women Travelers in Africa." In *Gender, Ideology, and Action: Historical Perspectives on Women's Public Lives,* 67-93. Edited by Janet Sharistanian. New York: Greenwood Press, 1986.

Gaunt, Mary. *Alone in West Africa.* New York: Charles Scribner's Sons; London: T. Werner Laurie, 1912.

Gelley, Alexander. *Narrative Crossings: Theory and Pragmatics of Prose Fiction.* Baltimore: Johns Hopkins University Press, 1987.

Gilbert, Sandra M., and Susan Gubar. *The Madwoman in the Attic: The Woman Writer and the Nineteenth-Century Literary Imagination.* New Haven: Yale University Press, 1979.

Gould, Stephen Jay. *The Mismeasure of Man.* New York: W. W. Norton, 1981.

Green, Martin. *Dreams of Adventure, Deeds of Empire.* New York: Basic Books, 1979.

———. *The English Novel in the Twentieth Century (The Doom of Empire).* London: Routledge & Kegan Paul, 1984.

———. *The Robinson Crusoe Story.* University Park: Pennsylvania State University Press, 1990.

Greenblatt, Stephen. *Renaissance Self-Fashioning: From More to Shakespeare.* Chicago: University of Chicago Press, 1980.

Gwynn, Stephen. *The Life of Mary Kingsley.* London: Macmillan, 1933.

Haggard, Rider H. *She.* Oxford: Oxford University Press, 1991.

Hamalian, Leo, ed. *Ladies on the Loose: Women Travellers of the Eighteenth and Nineteenth Centuries.* New York: Dodd, Mead, 1981.

Hammond, Dorothy, and Alta Jablow. *The Myth of Africa.* New York: Library of Social Science, 1977.

Haraway, Donna. *Primate Visions: Gender, Race, and Nature in the World of Modern Science.* New York: Routledge, 1989.

Herbert, Christopher. *Culture and Anomie: Ethnographic Imagination in the Nineteenth Century.* Chicago: University of Chicago Press, 1991.

Hobson, J. A. *Imperialism: A Study.* London: George Allen & Unwin, 1963.

Holt, Edgar. *The Carlist Wars in Spain.* Chester Springs, Pa.: Dufour Editions, 1967.

JanMohamed, Abdul R. "The Economy of Manichean Allegory: The Function of Racial Difference in Colonialist Literature." *Critical Inquiry* 12 (Autumn 1985): 59-87.

Karl, Frederick Robert. *Joseph Conrad: The Three Lives.* New York: Farrar, Straus, and Giroux, 1979.

Kingsley, Mary H. *Travels in West Africa: Congo Français, Corisco, and Cameroons.* Boston: Beacon Press, 1988.

———. *West African Studies.* London: Frank Cass, 1964.

Lee, Sarah (Mrs. R. Lee). *The African Wanderers; or, The Adventures of Carlos and Antonio, Embracing Interesting Descriptions of the Manners and Customs of the Western Tribes, and the Natural Productions of the Country.* 5th ed. London: Griffith & Farran, 1877.

Mannoni, O. *Prospero and Caliban: The Psychology of Colonization.* Translated by Pamela Powesland. New York: Frederick A. Praeger, 1956.

Marichal, Carlos. *Spain (1834-1844): A New Society.* London: Tamesis Books, 1977.

Martineau, Harriet. *Dawn Island: A Tale.* Manchester: J. Gadsby, Newall's-Buildings, 1845.

———. *How to Observe Morals and Manners.* New Brunswick, N.J.: Transaction Publishers, 1989.

Miller, Christopher L. *Blank Darkness: Africanist Discourse in French.* Chicago: University of Chicago Press, 1985.

Mills, Sara. *Discourses of Difference: An Analysis of Women's Travel Writing and Colonialism.* London: Routledge, 1991.

Montrose, Louis A. "The Work of Gender and Sexuality in the Elizabethan Discourse of Discovery." In *Discourses of Sexuality: From Aristotle to AIDS,* 138-84. Edited by Domna C. Stanton. Ann Arbor: University of Michigan Press, 1992.

Mudimbe, V. Y. *The Invention of Africa: Gnosis, Philosophy, and the Order of Knowledge.* Bloomington: Indiana University Press, 1988.

Nandy, Ashis. *The Intimate Enemy: Loss and Recovery of Self under Colonialism.* Delhi: Oxford University Press, 1983.

Nelson, Claudia. *Boys Will Be Girls: The Feminine Ethic and British Children's Fiction, 1857-1917.* New Brunswick, N.J.: Rutgers University Press, 1991.

Oliver, Caroline. *Western Women in Colonial Africa.* Westport, Conn.: Greenwood Press, 1982.

Pelton, Robert D. *The Trickster in West Africa: A Study of Mythic Irony and Sacred Delight.* Berkeley: University of California Press, 1980.

Perham, Margery, and J. Simmons. *African Discovery: An Anthology of Exploration.* London: Faber and Faber, 1943.

Pietz, William. "The Problem of the Fetish, II: The Origin of the Fetish." *Res* 13 (Spring 1987): 23-45.

Porter, Dennis. *Haunted Journeys: Desire and Transgression in European Travel Writing.* Princeton: Princeton University Press, 1991.

Pratt, Mary Louise. "Fieldwork in Common Places." In *Writing Culture: The Poetics and Politics of Ethnography,* 27-50. Edited by James Clifford and George E. Marcus. Berkeley: University of California Press, 1986.

———. *Imperial Eyes: Travel Writing and Transculturation.* London: Routledge, 1992.

Ranger, Terence. "The Invention of Tradition in Colonial Africa." In *The Invention of Tradition,* 211-62. Edited by Eric Hobsbawm and Terence Ranger. Cambridge: Cambridge University Press, 1983.

Romero, Patricia W., ed. *Women's Voices on Africa: A Century of Travel Writings.* Princeton, N.J.: Markus Wiener Publishing, 1992.

Russell, Mary. *The Blessings of a Good Thick Skirt: Women Travellers and Their World.* London: Collins, 1986.

Russett, Cynthia Eagle. *Sexual Science: The Victorian Construction of Womanhood.* Cambridge: Harvard University Press, 1989.

Simmel, George. *The Philosophy of Money.* 2d ed. Edited by David Frisby. Translated by Tom Bottomore and David Frisby. London: Routledge, 1990.

Spivak, Gayatri Chakravorty. "The Political Economy of Women as Seen by a Literary Critic." In *Coming to Terms: Feminism, Theory, Politics,* 218-29. New York: Routledge, 1989.

———. *The Post-Colonial Critic: Interviews, Strategies, Dialogues.* Edited by Sarah Harasym. New York: Routledge, 1990.

Stanley, Henry M. *My Kalulu, Prince, King, and Slave: A Story of Central Africa.* New York: Negro Universities Press, 1969.

Stevenson, Catherine Barnes. *Victorian Women Travel Writers in Africa.* Boston: Twayne Publishers, 1982.

Stocking, George W., Jr. *Victorian Anthropology.* New York: Free Press; London: Collier-Macmillan Publishers, 1987.

Suleri, Sara. *The Rhetoric of English India.* Chicago: The University of Chicago Press, 1992.

Van Den Abbeele, Georges. *Travel as Metaphor from Montaigne to Rousseau.* Minneapolis: University of Minnesota Press, 1992.

Zweig, Paul. *The Adventurer: The Fate of Adventure in the Western World.* Princeton: Princeton University Press, 1974.

Maria H. Frawley (essay date 1994)

SOURCE: Frawley, Maria H. "Voyagers Out: Victorian Women Abroad." In *A Wider Range: Travel Writing by Women in Victorian England,* pp. 13-42. Rutherford, N.J., Toronto, Ontario, and London: Fairleigh Dickinson University Press and Associated University Presses, 1994.

[*In the following excerpt, Frawley evaluates travel literature written by Victorian women in England to determine how these authors used their writings as opportunities to "expand institutional and psychological borders" as well as to determine what these writings reveal about nineteenth century English culture and "relations of power and authority both between men and women and between women and the peoples of other cultures."*]

In 1902, Constance Larymore traveled with her husband to northern Nigeria. Recalling the end of her tour in *A Resident's Wife in Nigeria* (1908), Larymore wrote:

> I had ridden over 3000 miles, learnt a new language, made thousands of new friends in the animal and flower world, as well as valued human ones. I felt as if I had "enlarged my borders" mentally, and had certainly begun to know and love Africa with a deep affection that, I think, is never lost by those who once acquire it.[1]

The passage reflects much of the confidence, freedom of spirit, and sense of accomplishment felt by Victorian women who traveled abroad. This is a study of what it meant for Victorian women to cross distances, learn languages, and enlarge borders. Distance, discovery, and borders are all part of the special language with which Victorian women travelers experienced and recorded the world outside of England. For Constance Larymore, travel to Africa was taken as "a step in the darkest dark" where "no Englishwoman yet had gone."[2]

Although Larymore did traverse many hundreds of miles through the interior of Nigeria, Mary Anne Barker, Lucie Duff Gordon, Amelia Edwards, and Mary Kingsley are just a few of the Victorian women who traveled to Africa before her. Nor were they by any stretch of the imagination the only English women to travel to regions of the world remote from England. Florence Dixie and Constance Gordon Cumming visited South America; Mary Seacole and Florence Nightingale ventured to the Crimea; Isabella Bird Bishop chose as one of her many destinations Japan; Annie Taylor explored Tibet; and Annie Brassey sailed around the world. Destinations less exotic enticed Victorian women travelers as well. Frances Trollope, Harriet Martineau, Emily Faithfull, and Beatrice Webb were among the many Victorian women who went to the United States; Anna Jameson rambled in Canada. Charlotte Eaton, Mary Shelley, Frances Power Cobbe, Frances Elliot, and Vernon Lee spent extended periods of time in Italy. Victorian women traveled. Whatever their destination, though, these women shared both a determination to leave home and a sense—however misguided—that they were going where "no Englishwoman yet had gone."

Once beyond the boundaries of England, many of these Victorian women felt compelled to write about their experiences away from home. At the close of the first volume of *Diary of an Idle Woman in Italy* (1871), the Victorian travel writer Frances Elliot observes:

> I had, during the last few hours, felt, admired, and examined so much, my mind was oppressed by the weight of recollections. On returning home I caught up a pen in *furore,* determined to convey on paper, however faintly, some idea of the variety offered by one day's sight-seeing at Rome.[3]

The intensity with which Elliot takes up her pen in an attempt to record her thoughts suggests much about the complex position of a Victorian woman abroad. After a day of intense intellectual stimulation, Elliot initially appears to write simply to purge her cluttered mind of its thoughts. Yet the resolute tone with which she approaches pen and paper implies that she is desperate to preserve on paper what she has seen and learned. Like most Victorian women who traveled, Frances Elliot was anxious to record her experiences because she believed that experiences worthy of being recorded, preserved, and made public would stop once she returned to England. Other Victorian women who traveled shared her sense of urgency. Isabella Bird, for instance, kept ink warming on the stove while in the Rocky Mountains for fear that if it froze she would be unable to write. In her diary of her experiences in America, Barbara Leigh Smith (later Bodichon) admits: "I write as much as I can without blinding myself" (122). And at the end of *Diary of an Idle Woman in Italy,* Elliot laments: "I am suddenly called back to England, and 'the Idle Woman' (not so very idle after all) lays down her pen and becomes 'the woman of the period,' with *really* nothing to do!"[4]

Elliot here alludes to the kind of woman paid homage to in the popular essays of Eliza Lynn Linton—the woman whose experiences were carefully circumscribed by the boundaries and borders of a domestic sphere within which there was much for a woman to be but little for her to do.[5] For Elliot, as for many other Victorian women who chose to leave home for extended periods, travel was first and foremost a way of getting outside of those boundaries to a place where one could do more. What is noteworthy about her comment is that she implicitly equates the activity of travel with that of writing: Both occur in conjunction with one another and are necessary to one another; and both are intimately connected to the writer's sense of her self and of her relationship to others. Both give to the writer an identity with purpose and a basis for accomplishment.

The central project of this study is to ascertain how travel and writing functioned together in nineteenth-century England to enable women to cross physical and ideological distances, to expand institutional and psychological borders. What Victorian women wrote from and about their experiences abroad is by and large non-fiction, and these nonfictional letters, essays, and books are the materials of this study's cultural interpretation. Although few are today considered canonical literary texts, these works—like much Victorian fiction—index relations of power and authority both between men and women and between women and the peoples of other cultures. Many were also enormously popular. These works written by women who traveled are hence no less a part of Victorian culture or history than are the novels, poems, plays, and essays that have been accorded the status of aesthetically or historically legitimate objects of study. To examine the place of women's travel and writing in Victorian culture is necessarily to consider how certain documents come to be privileged as representative of a literary period, a social history, a class, or a gender.

Those of us who have been initiated into Victorian culture through its fiction are familiar with the use of the wider world as an imaginative realm in which to situate narratives of adventure, conquest, and liberation. The "weight of recollections" that burden the Victorian traveler Frances Elliot at the end of her day in Rome, for example, recalls the reaction of a fictitious English visitor to the eternal city. In the 1871-72 novel *Middlemarch,* Italy plays a crucial role in the emotional liberation of Dorothea Brooke.[6] In an often-quoted passage, Eliot describes the tremendous effect that the "weight of unintelligible Rome" has on Dorothea during her honeymoon (225). Before her trip to Rome, Dorothea naively anticipates a marriage filled with learning. Contemplating life with the scholar Edward Casaubon, she thinks, "It would be like marrying Pascal. I should learn to see the truth by the same light as great men have seen it by" (51). Casaubon, though, fails to lead Dorothea down the grand path of learning that she envisions. His is a mind "weighted with unpublished matter" (230), and on their honeymoon in Rome Dorothea discovers that "what was fresh to her mind was worn out to his; and such capacity of thought and feeling as had ever been stimulated in him by the general life of mankind had long shrunk to a sort of dried preparation, a lifeless embalmment of knowledge" (228-29).

In *Middlemarch,* Eliot undercuts the truth that great men have to offer by centering it initially in the effete and sickly Casaubon, whose projected *Key to All Mythologies* turns out to be a sham. It is not Casaubon but Rome that offers Dorothea the opportunity and stimulation to learn. It is not her husband but Rome that takes possession of Dorothea during the early days of her marriage; it is Rome that addresses her "great mental need" to "see the truth." Although before marriage Dorothea anticipates "a grand life here—now—in England" (51), it is significant that she must travel outside of England to begin the process of self assessment that will determine her fate once she returns home.

The paradigm of a young woman yearning to "see the truth by the same light as great men," established early on in *Middlemarch,* is found also in *The Mill on the Floss* (1860), *Romola* (1863), and *Daniel Deronda* (1876). Like these works by George Eliot, many Victorian novels condition us to associate women with the "hidden life" that Dorothea will eventually lead, one in which access to a perceived body of knowledge and culture is either restricted, prohibited, or—still worse—absent. The hidden life to which Eliot consigns Dorothea is one unaffecting and almost unaffected by the world in which the novel's ardent public men participate. *Vanity Fair* (1848), of course, opens with Becky

Sharp triumphantly pitching her copy of Johnson's dictionary out the window of her carriage, but most Victorian heroines do not derive as much pleasure rejecting the learning associated with male culture. The similar fates of Maggie Tulliver in *The Mill on the Floss* and Eustacia Vye in *The Return of the Native* (1878) are telling; their deaths suggest much about the Victorian novelist's sense of the consequences facing a young woman too eager to learn, too anxious to attach herself to a public and cultured world.

Another such woman is Rose Yorke, a marginal character in Charlotte Brontë's novel *Shirley* (1849). In an important passage in the novel one of the central heroines, Caroline Helstone, finds Rose reading from Ann Radcliffe's *The Italian* (1796), and the two women discuss their impressions of the novel. To Rose, the novel pleases because "you feel as if you were far away from England—really in Italy—under another sort of sky—that blue sky of the south which travelers describe."[7] Intrepid and outspoken Rose is prompted by her reading of Radcliffe to insist to homebound Caroline: "my life shall be a life: not a black trance like a toad's, buried in marble; nor a long, slow death like yours in Briarfield Rectory" (385). *Shirley* is about the ways women both take and lose control of their lives and, like most of Brontë's work, its ending is ambiguous. Rose, the narrator informs us, becomes no more than "a lonely emigrant in some region of the southern hemisphere" (168).

More revealing than Rose Yorke's outcome, though, is the revitalizing potential that she imagines travel to have; the light she associates with "another sort of sky" suggests energy and transformation akin to that which Dorothea Brooke discovers on her honeymoon in Rome. To Rose the mere idea of travel beyond the boundaries of England implies the acquisition of meaningful identity, the making of a life something that will be other than the "black trance" she associates with woman's life in England. In *Villette* (1853), Brontë's next and last complete novel, the heroine Lucy Snowe also travels with "nothing to lose" to a foreign country. In Labassecour, Brontë's fictional name for Belgium, immersion in a foreign culture allows Lucy the freedom both to construct an identity and to embrace anonymity, to scrutinize and to retreat from self.

Both Charlotte Brontë and George Eliot understood the capacity of travel—of distance, really—to satisfy these dual needs. In a letter written in July of 1854, just prior to leaving England in the company of a married man, George Henry Lewes, Eliot wrote to her friend Sara Hennell and enigmatically explained her intent by making subtle reference to *Villette*: "I shall soon send you a good bye, for I am preparing to go to 'Labassecour.'"[8] Both Brontë and Eliot equated travel with release, adventure, the opportunity to learn, and sexual deliverance. Eliot made her sexual liaison public by traveling to Weimar with Lewes. Brontë was intellectually stimulated by and fell in love with her teacher Constantin Heger while training for a career in teaching at the Pensionnat Heger in Brussels. Although literary histories have unduly emphasized the romantic nature of these attachments, it is significant that both Eliot and Brontë established through their relationships the satisfaction of intellectual compatibility. For both, also, that satisfaction required leaving England, at least for a time. Lewes and Eliot learned languages while abroad together; in Germany he wrote his biography of Goethe while she translated Spinoza. Working closely under Heger's supervision while in Belgium, Brontë refined her command of the French language and wrote a series of essays that grappled with issues of authority, genius, and religious faith—topics that would later permeate her fiction.[9] At the same time, however, travel abroad for both writers exacerbated a painful relationship to "home" and invited longing, separation, and the misery of displacement to compete with hopefulness, satisfaction, and companionship. In their fiction—as in their lives—travel encompassed these same narrative dynamics: it enabled energy, confidence, initiation, and inquiry to create dialogue with separation, pain, and, oddly enough, immobility.

Foreign locales nearly always function as the sites that engendered these dialogues. From the beginning of her writing career, Brontë experimented with foreign location: from her creation of an imaginary West African Kingdom in her juvenelia to her last complete novel, *Villette,* Brontë imagined foreign countries as the loci for her heroines' adventures. In *Villette* foreign culture allows Brontë to highlight the depth of Lucy Snowe's interior exile and to emphasize the extent to which a woman's retreat into anonymity signified her lack of a relation to a public, male-dominated culture. Thus in *Villette* travel becomes almost entirely interiorized; in no other Victorian novel is the heroine so often represented as motionless despite movement between rooms, houses, cities, and countries.

In Victorian literature as a whole, travel frequently functions as a means to place a narrative of female energy and control somewhere outside of England. In *Daniel Deronda,* for example, readers are first introduced to Gwendolen Harleth at the gambling tables in Germany where, before being struck down by Deronda's gaze, she plays the confident and spirited adventuress, winning in a man's world. Later she travels to Italy where her monstrous husband drowns. Her return to England signals a return to domestic conformity and emotional lethargy—and the end of her story.

Instances of female adventure and energy abroad occur in lesser-known novels as well and suggest that by taking a woman outside the boundaries of England novelists opened up the scope of possibilities from which to construct narratives of identity. These narratives of adventure and identity occur throughout the nineteenth century and may have been inaugurated by the Gothic tradition. In Radcliffe's influential *The Mysteries of Udolpho,* published in 1794, a retreat in the Apennines is the place where the sexual and moral will of Emily St. Aubert is put to test. The sensational novelists picked up where earlier Gothic novelists had left off. In Mrs. Henry Wood's 1861 best-selling novel *East Lynne,* it is Lady Isobel's flight abroad that creates the sensation and introduces themes of bigamy and adultery into a novel fundamentally about the female quest for security. A similar pattern is found in Mary Braddon's enormously popular *Lady Audley's Secret,* published just one year later. Stories that equate female adventure with foreign locale occur in more traditional domestic novels as well. In Mrs. Humphry Ward's best-seller *Robert Elsmere* of 1888, the source of female interest is less with the domestic-minded, staunchly puritan, and predictable heroine Catherine Elsmere than with her sister Rose Leyburn, a "new woman" who travels to Germany to develop fully her musical talents.

Yet the female characters of Victorian literature whose lives have tended to be taken as paradigmatic of the lives of real Victorian women are the ones who never leave England—characters like Jane Eyre, Maggie Tulliver, and Eustacia Vye. In *Jane Eyre* (1847) the possibility of life in India with St. John Rivers tempts Jane only momentarily; his sisters warn her that she would be "grilled alive in Calcutta" and soon after Jane hears the mysterious voice that summons her back to Rochester and a life in England. Intellectually ambitious Maggie Tulliver never escapes the River Floss. In *The Return of the Native,* adventure-hungry Eustacia Vye fails to convince her husband to quit Egdon Heath and live in Paris. In each of these novels the absence of travel in a woman's life is as much a determinant of her outcome as in those narratives that move her from England into the wider world.

These are but a few examples of the way travel seeps into the social fabric of Victorian fiction and colors the narratives of female identity, but they accumulate to suggest something of the hold that travel—real and metaphorical—had on the imagination of fiction writers of the period. In fact, the idea of travel and, correspondingly, of access to a world outside of England influenced almost all writers of the period, permeating English culture in ways that are only partially reflected by its literature. And with good reason. After the French Revolution, commerce with and beyond Europe increased dramatically for the British. The strength of evangelical forces at home fortified missionary activity abroad. Most important, the introduction of steam locomotion and railways in the nineteenth century—and the work of travel entrepreneur Thomas Cook—radically changed how much the English middle and upper

classes were able to explore cultures other than their own. The confidence with which the Victorians left home can be gauged by the remarks in 1845 of the art historian Elizabeth Rigby Eastlake, who ended a review essay on the travel writing of women with the following invocation:

> Let us . . . rejoice that the long continuation of peace, the gradual removal of prejudices, the strength of the British character, and the faith in British honesty, have not only made way for the foot of our countrymen through countries hardly accessible before, but also for that of the tender and delicate companion, whose participation in his foreign pleasures his home habits have made indispensable to him.[10]

The Victorian period in England was the first to see a large-scale movement of its men *and* women into the wider world on both temporary and long-term bases.

Many Victorians traveled abroad on professional or commercial ventures, making their niche in the empire as bureaucrats, traders, missionaries, and correspondents. But as John Pemble shows in *The Mediterranean Passion: Victorians and Edwardians in the South,* an increasing number of Victorians traveled at leisure, justifying their excursions away from home by turning their trips into pilgrimages that sought to improve their spiritual, cultural, or physical health.[11] Pemble observes:

> Various writers diagnosed the annual exodus from England as a symptom of restlessness, of a perpetual desire to be somewhere else that was peculiar to the British; and this they attributed to special environmental and historical circumstances.[12]

The number of Victorians traveling at leisure increased steadily, Pemble reports, as a rise in wealth and a decrease in the cost of travel made foreign vacations possible for even the lower middle classes. Victorians moved between cities and countries at relatively fast rates and consequently saw much more of the world than did their predecessors.

Many Victorians left home assured that their status as English men and women would guarantee a privileged position abroad. Indeed, some felt it their duty to elicit respect by demanding all the comforts of home. Traveling up the Nile, for instance, Amelia Edwards insisted on having a fresh bouquet of flowers brought on board to her daily. Commenting on the postures adopted by Victorians seeking to find home in abroad, Sir Charles Petrie observed:

> The impression one gets is that if the right rooms were not immediately forthcoming at an acceptable rate, or if the laundry failed to return in time, recourse would be had to the British consul without any undue delay, and that if speedy redress were not obtained Lord Palmerston would send a gunboat.[13]

Though no doubt overstated, such comments reveal an important aspect of the way many Victorians experienced the wider world; what they saw was from a privileged perspective, one that enabled them to experience and record with great confidence.

Their claim to privilege was most pronounced in those places where many traveled, where communities of English expatriates had formed, and where English "requirements" were already known. Switzerland, Germany, Belgium, and France throughout the century drew a large share of English travelers, but the "blue sky of the South" held the most allure. Italy by far attracted the majority of those travelers tempted by the Mediterranean region. Victorians disenchanted with the dense urban fog of London and its environs migrated toward the sensuous south in order to soak up its climate and ambiance—what Amelia Edwards in *Untrodden Peaks and Unfrequented Valleys* describes as "the rich Italian summer, with its wealth of fruits and flowers, its intolerable heat, and its blinding brightness."[14] Victorians flocked to Rome in hordes and often moved on to spend time in Florence, Sorrento, and Naples. Travelers dotted the coast of Greece and the French and Spanish Rivieras. Egypt enticed hundreds of travelers as well, many of whom went on to the Middle East via the Sinai peninsula or to India on the "overland" (Alexandria-Suez) route.[15] Here, as Frances Power Cobbe wrote in *Cities of the Past* (1864), travelers could "give themselves the delight of beholding the spots of earth round which imagination has hovered from childhood."[16] Accounts of African travel written by Victorians are many, and they diligently documented expeditions into South America, the United States, and Canada as well. The noticeable presence of Victorians abroad is captured by Amelia Edwards in her description in 1889 of Cairo:

> Here are invalids in search of health; artists in search of subjects; sportsmen keen upon crocodiles; statesmen out for a holiday; special correspondents alert for gossip; collectors on the scent of papyri and mummies; men of science with only scientific ends in view; and the usual surplus of idlers who travel for the mere love of travel, or the satisfaction of a purposeless curiosity.[17]

As Edwards's catalog suggests, the wider world afforded a wealth of material for the inquisitive, and travel was undertaken to satisfy a multitude of yearnings.

The effects on Victorian culture of this nineteenth-century revolution in travel are many and varied. As travel became increasingly available to the middle classes, it became correspondingly more accessible to women. English women had of course traveled outside of England before the nineteenth century, but never before had so many women traveled so extensively.[18] Several travel accounts written by women and published just prior to the nineteenth century are notable both for their contemporary popularity and for the critical attention that they have garnered in recent years. Lady Mary Wortley Montagu published her *Letters Written during her Travels in Europe, Asia, and Africa* in 1763, and in 1796 Mary Wollstonecraft published a series of letters detailing her travels, *Letters Written During a Short Residence in Sweden, Norway, and Denmark*. Eighteenth-century England also produced one of the first woman explorers to be widely celebrated: Lady Hester Stanhope traveled to Mediterranean regions and never returned to England.[19]

In the early years of the nineteenth century, women traveled even more frequently, often as family members—wives and daughters—of those bureaucrats, traders, and missionaries infiltrating the British empire. As the century progressed, however, more and more women went abroad with a defined sense of personal interest and professional purpose, going abroad, for example, as members of the World's Women's Temperance Association or as lecturing members of the International Women's Congress. Others went as governesses for families on an extended holiday or in search of permanent positions as governesses abroad. Still more Victorian women traveled on their own, however, with the loosely defined goal of "learning." In 1852, Florence Nightingale wrote *Cassandra* to announce for the benefit of all women that she needed to learn; as she had once written in a letter, "I have a mind, an active nature which requires satisfaction."[20] She left soon after to work in the Crimea. Others like her found the satisfaction of learning through travel. In 1857 Elizabeth Gaskell wrote of Charlotte and Emily Brontë's decision to go to Belgium: "They wanted learning. They came for learning. They would learn."[21] Although overstated in a way befitting the hagiographic qualities of the biography, her comment captures the spirit of many Victorian women travelers and could apply to many who left England to learn about and experience the wider world.

Travel was seen by some Victorian women as a means to keep up with world events, and this in turn was seen as necessary to intellectual survival. Consider, for instance, the remarks of Frances Power Cobbe in her chapter on Palestine from *The Cities of the Past*. After encouraging other women to undertake the journey to Palestine, Cobbe writes:

> Especially does it seem desirable that women should seek by these and all other modes of study to fit themselves for their proper part in sharing the progress of human thought in our age. Too often have their limited lives, their scope of vision . . . made women the champions of antiquated prejudices, the cruel enemies of every newly-born truth.[22]

As Cobbe's remark suggests, a Victorian woman could prove her sincere interest in learning by going abroad, by enlarging her "scope of vision." Cobbe was only one of several women eager to demonstrate the knowledge she had gained through travel. On her way to America in 1834, Harriet Martineau never came on deck to socialize with other passengers without bringing her lap board and writing utensils with her. Wanting to demonstrate the seriousness of purpose and to set herself above other women on board who "idled about in sunny places," Martineau wrote in *Retrospect of Western Travel* (1838): "I had a task to do, which is a thing that should be avoided on board ship. I had a long article to write; and nothing else would I do, on a fine morning, till it was finished."[23] Martineau's trips abroad always resulted in an abundance of such articles. In *Eastern Life, Present and Past* (1848) she prides herself on the "stores of knowledge" she would bring from the Middle East back to England. Victorian women travelers were both teachers and students. Much later in the century Mary Kingsley wrote in *Travels in West Africa* (1897) of the Gold Coast locals, "They cannot but say that I was a diligent pupil, who honestly tried to learn the lessons they taught me so kindly."[24]

Many of the Victorian women who embarked on voyages of learning traveled together, as did Vernon Lee and Clementine "Kit" Anstruther-Thompson or Amelia Edwards and the unnamed female friend of *A Thousand Miles up the Nile*. Still more accompanied a married couple, at least for the passage en route, and then embarked on their own; of this group Harriet Martineau, Mary Kingsley, and Florence Nightingale are notable examples. By far, however, the large majority of Victorian women travelers traveled alone—Mary Gaunt, Lucie Duff-Gordon, and Marianne North, for example, are just a few of the most prominent women who traveled alone in Africa. In her autobiography, Frances Power Cobbe notes that when she set out on her solitary travels in 1857 such a journey was "still accounted somewhat of an enterprise for a 'lone woman.'" John Pemble corroborates her sense of her status in *The Mediterranean Passion*:

> All females abroad without male escorts, whether traveling singly, in pairs, or in groups, were classified as "unprotected," and the term carried strong connotations of eccentricity.[25]

Travel—and especially travel alone—was at least in part a means to express one's independence. As Catherine Barnes Stevenson notes, "By the latter part of the nineteenth century, women travelers began to be singled out as exemplars of the new freedom and prowess of women."[26]

More important, travel enabled women to acquire experience unlike that available to them at home, experience that could be recorded, analyzed, and published. The Victorian women who traveled discovered more than refuge, adventure, and learning abroad; they found room to write. Like Dorothea Brooke, they found that the satisfaction of a life of learning and knowledge was not to be found in England or in marriage but abroad. But unlike Dorothea, who returns to a "hidden life" of "unhistoric acts" in England, many Victorian women used their experiences outside of England to forge identities at home with the reading public—a public that consumed writing about travel and foreign culture voraciously. They kept detailed journals about their experiences and made sketches of what they saw. They read widely about the lands and cultures that they visited, and compared their findings to those of reputable historians, geologists, anthropologists, and explorers. They wrote letters, essays, articles, and books about their experiences abroad, and they gave lectures about what they learned to audiences at home.

Travel enabled many Victorian women to create a connection to and establish authority with a part of English culture that hitherto had evaded them because they lacked the education that decreed cultural authority. One way to measure Victorian women's success in winning public recognition for their achievements is suggested by the titles of those biographical reference works so prevalent in the period. Significantly, the popular reference work titled *Men of the Time* changed its title to *Men and Women of the Time* in 1891, less in response to the burgeoning feminist movements than to the increasing number of women who could be admitted on the basis of public achievement. In addition, *Men and Women of the Time* documents how much travel was increasingly thought of throughout the century as a profession. The most common professions available to women included not just "actress," "musician," "painter," and "social reformer," but also "journalist," "archeologist," "explorer," and "travel writer."

In essence, travel conferred on many Victorian women a measure of cultural competence that derived not from education but from experience. And as a mode of experience through which they gained the authority to write about culture, travel was empowering. Travel enabled many Victorian women to gain the experience necessary to win a new kind of recognition for themselves.

Domestic Ideology and Victorian Women Travelers

To a significant extent, women writers achieved a degree of public recognition for their travel writing because it was considered to be a nondomestic genre and hence by implication an unusual and risky choice for the woman writer. Whereas many of the women who wrote fiction were thought of as popular novelists—entertainers—women who wrote nonfiction demanded a different, perhaps more serious, kind of recognition. In her work on the social history of Victorian women, Jihang Park rightly emphasizes the implications of such recognition: "The problem of women's emancipation in nineteenth-century Britain was not only how to win equal rights with men, but also how to win recognition for their achievements in a man's world."[27] One way was to move their sphere for achievement out of England, into places thought to be less circumscribed by domestic ideology—by those socially constructed boundaries of public and private, male and female, felt so powerfully at home. Travel writing was for many women quite simply a way to document achievements worthy of recognition.

That their achievements abroad were assumed to be worthy of public recognition is in part due to the powerful hold of domestic ideology on the Victorian imagination and its concomitant forms of writing. The term *separate spheres* has long been used by scholars studying women and the structure of Victorian society to denote the ostensibly rigid separation of nineteenth-century social life into a private sphere of home, family, and interpersonal relations and a public sphere of work and politics.[28] Such studies focus both on the symbolic positioning of women within the private domain and on the material conditions of this domain as well as on the symbolic positioning of men within the public domain and its corresponding material conditions. More recently historians and literary scholars have questioned the entrenchment of separate spheres ideology, showing the fluidity of public/private boundaries and basing their arguments on evidence of Victorian women's participation in public activities. Victorian women's travel writing has played a crucial role in this critical reassessment. For example, in "Victorian Women, Wisdom, and Southeast Asia," Susan Morgan argues that "many women put the notion of separate spheres to public use by defining it as incomplete and therefore as an empowering rather than a disabling paradigm."[29] Morgan rightly concludes: "The question for critics now is how many exceptions we need to gather before the weight of accumulated facts will finally deflate to its proper, and modest, size this long-favored phallic truism."[30]

Nonetheless, literary historians argue that the extent to which Victorian women were at least ideologically associated with a private domestic sphere is evidenced by the representation of their social and psychological position in such works as Ruskin's treatise "Of Queen's Gardens" and Coventry Patmore's long poem "The Angel in the House," works that ostensibly exalt women by representing their moral authority within the home. Popular advice writers like Sara Ellis and Sarah Lewis had publicly advocated this position long before Patmore or Ruskin; both women frequently admonished their fellow countrywomen to restrict their influence to the "sacred precincts of home." In the 1839 treatise *Woman's Mission,* for example, Lewis argued that a woman's influence was dependent on her maternal feeling and thus must be exercised within the boundaries of home.[31] No matter how influential one believes Ellis

and Lewis to have been, what clearly is important to appreciate is that many Victorian women felt both bounded by and bonded to the home. How much women responded to this conflictual position can be sensed in the words of the African explorer Mary Kingsley, who, in the years after her travels, recollected: "The whole of my childhood and youth was spent at home, in the house and garden. . . . The living outside world I saw little of and cared less for."[32] Kingsley felt compelled to explain her achievements in the public world as a consequence of and reaction against her early "rooting" in home and garden.

Feminist theorists more recently have emphasized how the categories of public and private basic to the concept of separate spheres point to societal divisions central to the structuring of gender in modern Western society, and they have argued that feminist criticism should seek to demonstrate the historical origins and evolution of those divisions others have assumed to be either natural or inevitable. One critic who has tried to do this is Mary Poovey, and in *Uneven Developments: The Ideological Work of Gender in Mid-Victorian England* she writes: "The model of binary opposition between the sexes, which was socially realized in separate but supposedly equal 'spheres,' underwrote an entire system of institutional practices and conventions at midcentury, ranging from a sexual division of labor to a sexual division of economic and political rights."[33] Poovey goes on in her work to demonstrate that though representations of gender often took the form of a binary organization of difference in Victorian culture, different Victorian institutions (e.g., medical, legal, and literary) interpreted this binary logic differently. Poovey's thesis has important applicability to women's travel writing, because it, too, reflects the complexities and "uneven developments" of gender difference or, to be more exact, representations of gender difference.

In fact, one of the ways that gender ideology is most prominently represented in travel writing by women is in their portrayals of "leaving home," which, while characteristic of travel literature in general, is more self-consciously addressed in the works of Victorian women. Given the depth of ideological connection between Victorian women and home, it is not surprising that their accounts of leaving home would be represented as monumental undertakings. The historian John Pemble writes that for all Victorians: "Abandoning Britain meant abandoning home. It therefore threatened all the cherished values that home implied—fidelity, obedience, connubial affection, and a stable and rooted existence."[34] These were of course the values for whose maintenance middle-class Victorian women were responsible, and travel away from the home thus required a great degree of initiative and willfulness on the part of women. This is perhaps what Gabriele Annan meant when she wrote of women travelers: "They had to be braver than men, socially as well as physically."[35]

Women did not undertake travel lightly, and their written accounts of journeys abroad are often replete with explanation and justification for finding a life beyond the boundaries of England. Mary Kingsley, for example, opens *Travels in West Africa* (1897) by cautiously explaining: "For the first time in my life, I found myself in possession of five or six months which were not heavily forestalled" (1). Like Dorothy in Oz, Victorian women who traveled abroad were expected to discover that there was no place like home. Those who chose to remain away for extended periods were subject to a level of moral censure that could only be counteracted by finding many opportunities to act out the duties associated with "home" in England: fidelity, obedience, affection, and stability. Lucie Duff Gordon was one such woman; she left a husband and child in England to recuperate from a respiratory ailment and found in Egypt hundreds of sick natives to attend to while she waited for her own health to improve. Her *Letters from Egypt* (1876) are full of defensive accounts of her activities and seemingly hollow yearnings to rejoin her family, even though she evidently believed her health to be jeopardized by the English climate and clearly enjoyed her new-found role as health facilitator abroad. Thus, part of the interest of travel literature like that written by Lucie Duff Gordon and many others is that it both challenged and accommodated those domestic ideals against which so many Victorian women were measured. How much they saw their work as accommodation and/or challenge varied greatly among individual women, but almost all viewed their travel writing as a public statement; that is, as a means through which to ratify their sense of themselves as public individuals with experience enough to write about the wider world.

TRAVEL WRITING AND CULTURAL AUTHORITY

The institution through which women writers established their credibility as cultural spokespersons was the publishing industry and, for many, the periodical presses. The Victorian period was, as many have observed, the great age of periodical literature. In the preface to their study of the Victorian periodical press, Joanne Shattock and Michael Wolff observe: "The press, in all of its manifestations, became during the Victorian period the context within which people lived and worked and thought, and from which they derived their (in most cases quite new) sense of the outside world."[36] Hence it is not surprising that many women travelers chose to place their work initially in magazines and journals.[37] As the most influential of the "opinion-making" institutions within Victorian culture and the dominant medium through which people learned about the world outside of England, the periodical press was an important avenue through which women could disseminate the results of their travel. During the century, travel literature became the bread-and-butter of both the periodical presses and book publishing industry, and often replaced religious and advice books on the best-seller lists of major publishing houses. Articles and essays about foreign experience appeared regularly in nearly all of the most widely read periodicals. This plethora of travel writing can be seen as one manifestation of a variety of Victorian desires, among them the thirst for adventure, discovery, conquest, and escape. Travel writing by women adds other clearly discernible desires to this list—among them nondomestic identity, public recognition, and cultural authority.

That so much of the travel writing of the period was written by women suggests that publishing houses and editors of periodicals were willing and eager to capitalize on the ostensibly different perspective that women were able to bring to literature about the wider world. Women travelers, in turn, were eager to capitalize on the publicity that their activities abroad could bring. Often a series of travel essays published by a reputable journal would later be published in book form, as were the series of essays on Italy written by Frances Power Cobbe for *Fraser's Magazine* and later published as *Cities of the Past* by Trubner's of London. Others like Cobbe used their experience abroad to gain access to the periodical press. And many of those who did flaunted their success. In her preface to *Diary of an Idle Woman in Italy,* for example, Frances Elliot writes, "It may be well to mention that some of these chapters (now almost entirely rewritten) have appeared from time to time in some of the leading periodicals" (preface). Elliot clearly believes her periodical press publications to signify her authority on the subject, but that she had to explicitly call them to her reader's attention suggests, at the same time, something of the frailty of her conviction.

Highly germane to the discussion of how Victorian women used travel writing to create a connection to their culture is the work of the French sociologist Pierre Bourdieu, who has studied the process whereby cultural legitimacy is conferred on literary works. In *Distinction,* Bourdieu argues that all cultural "products," from movies to newspapers and magazines to political documents, reveal a kind of publicly legitimate taste and that these products are almost always created and marketed by professionals.[38] Although Bourdieu's study is not rendered from the standpoint of gender, it logically follows from his argument that by becoming producers of a highly valued cultural product—a product that appealed to the reigning tastes of their society—Victorian women helped to advance their own status as professionals. Bourdieu writes: "Every critic declares not only his judgement of the work but also his claim to the right to talk about it and judge it. In short, he takes part in a struggle for the monopoly of legitimate discourse about the work of art, and consequently in the production of the value of the work of art."[39]

Published travel accounts can thus be read as implicit statements of the right to contribute to a discourse deemed by their society to be culturally valuable. Perhaps more important, travel can be viewed as participation, as efforts on the part of women to actively help to shape their society's beliefs—about the wider world and, in some cases, about the position of women in that world. In *Independent Women,* Martha Vicinus writes, "Women are never passive participants in the larger culture but actively transform and redefine their external constraints."[40] Ironically, travel away from England facilitated this transformation on the home front, because it gave to women experience valuable to the British public. In Bourdieu's terms, it gave them the "symbolic capital" with which to compete in the culture market of Victorian society and to appeal to institutionally recognized powers—the periodical presses and publishing houses.

As the century progressed, women travelers became increasingly comfortable with their authority, expressing opinions with less hesitation, making greater claims for their own powers of observation and analysis, and less frequently justifying their decision to publish their work. Consider for comparison's sake a relatively early woman traveler, Anne Radcliffe. In her preface to *A Journey Made in the Summer of 1794 Through Holland and The Western Frontier of Germany,* published shortly after returning home from a trip taken with her husband, the self-conscious and insecure Radcliffe writes:

> The title page would . . . have contained the joint names of her husband and herself, if this mode of appearing before the Public, besides being thought by that relative a greater acknowledgement than was due to his share of the work, had not seemed liable to the imputation of a design to attract attention by extraordinary novelty. It is, however, necessary to her own satisfaction, that some notice should be taken of this assistance.[41]

Radcliffe goes on to undercut her intellectual authority by claiming that all "economical and political" commentary was "less her own" than that of her husband. As the century progressed, such self-diminishment became increasingly less frequent, in part because more and more women had ventured into regions considered remote from England and in part because many had done so alone.

Nonetheless, even the most confident of women travelers continued to look to outside sources of authority for corroboration of their own findings. Many attempted to legitimize their own work by making frequent reference to what had already been "established" by previous

(and most typically male) historians and travelers. Frances Elliot, for example, prefaces her *Diary of an Idle Woman in Constantinople* (1893) with this exhaustive listing of outside sources:

> My principal authorities have been Gibbon, von Hammer, Lamartine, Theophile Gautier, Gallenga, and Amicis, Meyer's 'Turkei und Griechenland,' a most valuable book, an article by H. E. Sir Henry Elliott on Abdul Aziz in the 'Nineteenth Century' and various Handbooks, English and German.[42]

Elliot here finds in historical scholarship the evidence she needs to authenticate her own findings. More often, however, women were compelled to position their work in relation to other travel writing, other sources of authority. That others had traveled before them could be made to seem advantageous, as is evident in Amelia Edwards's comments on a mountain in Korosko:

> We were surprised to find no account of the geology of this district in any of our books. Murray and Wilkinson pass it in silence; and writers of travels—only two of whom notice only the pyramidal shape of the hills—are for the most part content to do likewise.[43]

As Edward's comments suggest, Victorian women travelers who wanted to establish authority had both to indicate their awareness of another (male) tradition of travel writing, and to stress their differences from that tradition.

By writing about her travels in the wider world a woman writer in the Victorian period could not help but participate in a predominantly masculine tradition. Such hesitation in voicing opinions as was expressed by Frances Elliot and others was in part a manifestation of the sense that they were encroaching on another territory, another tradition. But at the same time, in her reliance on experiences abroad to establish a basis for authority—a voice—she necessarily called attention to her displacement from that tradition. The double-voiced discourse that some feminist critics believe characterizes the fiction of Victorian women writers is evident in much of the travel literature written by women in the period, but its implications are rather different. In travel writing, the authority of the author is dependent on an ability to comfortably occupy several positions displaced from but relative to the "center," which for most women travelers was England—nation and "home." Thus, rather than pointing to a divisive identity, double-voiced discourse in travel literature more often indicates a capable traveler and author, one whose experiences abroad solidify rather than cleave identity. In travel writing, then, an ability to successfully manipulate and negotiate distance becomes a barometer of competence. Victorian women made good use of their distance from English society; indeed, the concept of distance functions variously to signal their sense of cultural gaps and boundaries and their simultaneous sense of proximity to and detachment from that culture. Travel both eliminated and exacerbated the traveler's sense of cultural difference. By going abroad to the extent that they did, women became more familiar with foreign cultures; for some this lack of distance diminished their sense of wonder at the "other." For others, it merely underscored their sense that foreign populations were foreign. In addition, the heightened awareness of a wider world complicated the context from which they assessed their own society and their position as women within that society; cultural differences demanded new modes of self-awareness.

One might argue that Victorian women travelers made too good use of distance. How much Victorian women's travel writing successfully featured the traveler's distance from the mainstream can be sensed in the degree to which this literature has been left out of history, of our accounts of and claims for Victorian literature, society, and culture. That travel literature—despite its abundance and interest—is so rarely discussed today is in part a consequence of how the Victorians themselves categorized "the woman writer" and how we continue to reify their values in our own work.

GENDER AND GENRE

The tendency to marginalize the travel writing of Victorian women is indicative of a more general devaluation or ignorance of all nonfictional writing by women. As Carol Christ summarizes in her essay on nonfiction prose and masculinity: "There were 'lady novelists,' 'feminine poets,' and 'men of letters.'"[44] The Victorian woman writer has become, by association and almost by definition, a novelist or poet, or, more rarely, a dramatist. One explanation for the tendency to equate women with fiction can be found in the fact that throughout the period the majority of novel readers and writers were believed to be women. Such a perception was not wholly unfounded because, at least initially, women dominated the field of novel writing. In *Edging Women Out: Victorian Novelists, Publishers, and Social Change,* Gaye Tuchman and Nina Fortin argue that the very success of women novelists in the early part of the century helped to ratify the judgement of "men of letters" that the novel was an important genre and to spawn the kind of criticism that "considered 'the woman writer' in order to dismiss her potential contribution to the dominant culture."[45] They write: "By 1870 men of letters were using the term 'high culture' to set off novels they admired from those they deemed run-of-the-mill. Most of these high-culture novels were written by men."[46] One important outcome of the abundance of such criticism was to make the term *woman writer* virtually synonymous with *woman novelist* and to make "woman novelist" synonymous with producer of popular, as opposed to "high culture" novels.[47] Women hop-

ing to break into a writing career did so well aware that popular novel writing offered the most promise of financial success.

The association of women writers with the genre of the novel and, to a lesser extent, poetry, is in turn indicative of a larger cultural tendency to identify women with the potential for the creative rather than with the analytical. As repositories of creative potential, women were "naturally" suited to novel writing. The critic George Henry Lewes was one of many influential Victorians whose work helped to perpetuate this claim. Lewes well represents mainstream Victorian thought when he condescendingly suggested in his midcentury essay "The Lady Novelists" that women writers restrict themselves to the "one subject which they have eternally at command—love," and it follows from his argument that the proper form with which to make manifest this procreative impulse is the novel, the Victorian literary genre most concerned with evincing domestic realism. Nonfiction, seeming to demand more analytical skill on the part of its author, was, by implication, male territory. Such a judgment seems to have been corroborated in practice as well. In *Edging Women Out,* Tuchman and Fortin find that contributors of nonfiction during the Victorian period were more likely to have a university degree than contributors of fiction.[48]

The tendency to associate women with the creative rather than with the rational and analytical was part and parcel of the widespread assumption of male intellectual superiority, a belief corroborated by the observation that the brain of a man had greater physical weight than that of a woman. In *Feminine Character: A Study of Ideology,* Viola Klein explains: "It was emphasized by brain anatomists that the frontal lobes—believed to be the seat of logical thought and of all higher intellectual process—were distinctly more developed in men than in women."[49]

George Eliot demonstrated the weightiness of her own frontal lobes when she defied Lewes's advice to stick to novel writing and proclaimed in an essay: "Women have not to prove that they can be emotional, and rhapsodic, and spiritualistic; every one believes that already. They have to prove that they are capable of accurate thought, severe study, and continuous self-command."[50] Making her statement in a published essay, Eliot by implication argues that nonfictional genres were avenues through which women could prove their analytic, critical abilities. But Eliot was an exceptional Victorian woman writer, one of the very few who managed to establish public credibility as a sage.

Many women, however, found what Michael Cotsell has called in his introduction to *Creditable Warriors* "a marginal sagedom" through travel writing,[51] an achievement recognized by Susan Morgan in "Victorian

Women, Wisdom, and Southeast Asia" and by Linda Peterson in "Harriet Martineau: Masculine Discourse, Female Sage," both published in Thais Morgan's collection of essays titled *Victorian Sages and Cultural Discourse: Renegotiating Gender and Power.* As a popular nonfictional Victorian genre, travel writing can also be understood as what Tuchman and Fortin label a "mixed specialty," a nonfictional genre through which both men and women could distinguish themselves.[52] As a mixed specialty, travel writing was a politically expedient choice for women writers interested in moving into "high-prestige" and "male specialty" genres of nonfiction. Travel writing, in other words, offered more than an opportunity to participate in a form with great popular appeal; it also offered women the opportunity to establish or solidify their credibility in a public arena shared by men. In her work on the rise of feminine authority in the Victorian period, Nancy Armstrong observes:

> Any major change in the idea of who could write literature is just one part of a much larger revision in the culture's conception of social authority. In order for female literary authority to come into being, this revision obviously must have included a redefinition of gender as well as of the powers considered appropriate for each of the sexes.[53]

Armstrong's comment provides an enticing way to see travel writing as a means of revisioning Victorian culture's distribution of social authority. Armstrong's theory is at least partially applicable to Victorian women's travel writing, but, however appealing, it does not do justice to the many diverse and complex ways that Victorian women used their work to accommodate and reaffirm, rather than revise or subvert, already existing—and largely patriarchal—forms of authority.

Deirdre David convincingly argues in *Intellectual Women and Victorian Patriarchy* that those exceptional women who did make a name for themselves as intellectuals within the male-dominated culture did so by serving an auxiliary usefulness to that culture—by fostering and implicitly ratifying its dominant political, social, and sexual ideologies and by willingly adopting for themselves an ancillary role.[54] Yet David's argument seems founded on the assumption that cultural authority belongs primarily to those overtly concerned in their works with *English* society, history, and culture. It also implicitly endorses the idea that cultural authority is a stable, even static, phenomenon that women either serve or subvert.

Recently other critics have, like David, begun to write about the relationship of Victorian women to public forms of cultural authority. Martha Vicinus's *Independent Women* and Janet Murray's *Strong-Minded Women and Other Lost Voices of the Nineteenth Century,* for instance, each pay tribute to enterprising women who implicitly sought to register complaints with their patriarchal culture and with its concomitant forms of social order.[55] Vicinus argues that single women in Victorian England organized the ideological battle for women's rights within places like church committees, sisterhoods, and women's colleges. Although valuable, these studies falsify Victorian women's history in their assumption that the so-called strong-minded Victorian women with public identities and agendas were uniformly dissatisfied with their society and with their exclusion from cultural authority.

Travel writing provides an abundance of material with which to enlarge upon, modify, and in some cases correct, the scholarship that has to date focused on the status of Victorian women writers attempting to establish cultural credibility. On one level, it counteracts the tendency to base our history of Victorian women writers so exclusively on material provided by two literary forms—the novel and the poem. On another level, it provides a way to broaden our understanding of the role of cultural authority in that history. Deirdre David claims that the cultural authority to theorize about society remained firmly in the hands of the male writer throughout the century, but travel writing provides new ways to think about how women could "theorize" about their society in nontraditional or even covert ways. Some travel writing, for example, suggests that writing about other societies enabled women to critique their own. In *Winter Studies and Summer Rambles in Canada* (1838), Anna Jameson uses the condition of American Indians to launch her attack on the position of the single English woman. Harriet Martineau studies the democratic experiment in *Society in America* to make suggestions about both American and English society. Whereas cultural criticism may have been, as David and others have contended, more explicitly a male domain, it should not be assumed that it was exclusively so. Rather, we need to expand our understanding of what cultural criticism entails to include nontraditional forms of women's writing.

Victorian women's travel writing enables us to revise our understanding of the period in yet another, equally important way. It encourages us to see that the social history of Victorian women must include activity that took place outside of England. The very title of Philippa Levine's study *Feminist Lives in Victorian England* reveals a certain one-sidedness that is almost endemic to critical studies of Victorian women; that is, that Victorian feminism evidenced itself only *in* Victorian England.[56] Work like that done by Martha Vicinus in her study of single-woman communities in Victorian England or Coral Lansbury in her work on Victorian women and the antivivisectionist movement in England contributes to this pattern as well. Although all are important to our understanding of how Victorian women empowered themselves, these studies—and many others like them—may have helped create the impression that Victorian women's only sphere for empowerment was within England. As travel writing shows so well, this process of empowerment was one that also involved leaving England and its institutions behind and finding new ways to identify one's relationship to the world.

Victorian women travelers discovered, explored, studied, and described a world beyond England. Some thought of themselves not as participants but as observers, and their works tend on the whole to be descriptive—to focus on the external. Others sought to immerse themselves in new cultures, and their works corresponding invest much in the ideal of self-development through travel. Finally, a very few Victorian women sought neither to observe nor to participate; instead, their works seek to capture the imaginative experience and appeal of travel. One extreme attempts to document abroad; the other imagines and creates it. Travel writing by Victorian women is not rigidly demarcated according to these distinctions, but the two extremes do provide competing points of perspective within the various "kinds" of travel writing that emerged during the period.

Notes

1. Constance Larymore, *A Resident's Wife in Nigeria* (London: Routledge, 1908), p. 54.

2. Ibid., p. 2.

3. Frances Elliot, *Diary of an Idle Woman in Italy*, 2 vols. (New York: Brentanos, 1871), 1: 318-19.

4. Ibid., 2: 279.

5. That Sarah Ellis and Sarah Lewis consigned their fellow English women to the domestic sphere is ironic, because both women actively pursued a public forum for their views.

6. George Eliot, *Middlemarch: A Study of Provincial Life* (1871-72; reprint, Harmondsworth, England: Penguin, 1984); references from this edition of *Middlemarch* will hereafter be cited parenthetically in the text. Curiously, Frances Elliot's *Diary of an Idle Woman in Italy* came out in the same year as *Middlemarch*.

7. Charlotte Brontë, *Shirley* (1849; reprint, Harmondsworth, England: Penguin, 1982), p. 384; subsequent citations from this work are noted parenthetically in the text.

8. *The George Eliot Letters*, ed. G. Gordon Haight, 9 vols. (New Haven: Yale University Press, 1954-78), 2: 165. For further discussion of Eliot's reasons for making reference to Labassecour see Deirdre David's "'Getting Out of the Eel Jar': George Eliot's Literary Appropriation of Abroad,"

in *Creditable Warriors*, ed. Michael Cotsell (Atlantic Highlands, N.J.: Ashfield Press, 1990) pp. 257-72.

9. For a full discussion of Brontë's intellectual relationship with Constantin Heger, see Sue Lonoff's essay, "Charlotte Brontë's Belgian Essays: The Discourse of Empowerment," in *Victorian Studies* 32 (Spring 1989), 386-409.

10. Elizabeth Eastlake, "Lady Travellers," *Quarterly Review* 76 (June 1845), 136.

11. John Pemble, *The Mediterranean Passion: Victorians and Edwardians in the South* (London: Clarendon, 1987), p. 96.

12. Ibid., p. 96.

13. Sir Charles Petrie, *The Victorians* (London: Eyre and Spottiswoode, 1960), p. 168.

14. Amelia Edwards, *Untrodden Peaks and Unfrequented Valleys* (1873; reprint, Boston: Beacon Press, 1987), p. 1.

15. John Pemble, *The Mediterranean Passion*, p. 46.

16. Frances Power Cobbe, *Cities of the Past* (London: Trubner and Co., 1864), p. 173; subsequent citations from this work are noted parenthetically in the text.

17. Amelia Edwards, *A Thousand Miles Up the Nile* (London: George Routledge, 1889), pp. 1-2; subsequent citations from this work are noted parenthetically in the text.

18. An example of an exceptionally early traveling English woman is Margery Kempe, who records her visit to Jerusalem and Rome in her autobiography, *The Book of Margery Kempe*, thought to date from 1436.

19. In addition, early women novelists made use of their experiences abroad. Aphra Behn, for example, wrote *Oroonoko* after having lived in Surinam. Charlotte Lennox incorporated some of her American experiences in *Harriot Stuart* and *Euphemia*.

20. Quoted by Cecil Woodham-Smith in *Florence Nightingale*. (New York: McGraw-Hill 1951), p. 266.

21. Elizabeth Gaskell, *The Life of Charlotte Brontë* (1857; reprint, Harmondsworth, England: Penguin, 1985), p. 225.

22. Cobbe, *Cities*, p. 176.

23. Harriet Martineau, *Retrospect of Western Travel*, 2 vols (New York: Lohman, 1838), 2: 18-19; subsequent citations from this work are noted parenthetically in the text.

24. Mary Kingsley, *Travels in West Africa: Congo Francais, Corisco, and Cameroons* (1897: reprint, Boston: Beacon Press, 1982), p. 6; subsequent citations from this work are noted parenthetically in the text.

25. Pemble, *Mediterranean Passion,* pp. 77-78.

26. Catherine Barnes Stevenson, *Victorian Women Travel Writers in Africa* (Boston: Twayne, 1982), p. 3.

27. Jihang Park, "Women of Their Time: The Growing Recognition of the Second Sex in Victorian and Edwardian England," *Journal of Social History* 21 (Fall 1987), 49.

28. For examples of work on the public/private dichotomy in Victorian life see Janet Siltanen and Michelle Stanworth's collection of essays *Women and the Public Sphere: A Critique of Sociology and Politics* (New York: St. Martin's Press, 1984) and Catherine Hall's "Private Persons Versus Public Someones: Class, Gender and Politics in England, 1780-1850" in *Language, Gender and Childhood,* ed. Carolyn Steedman, Cathy Urwin, and Valerie Walkerdine (London: Routledge and Kegan Paul, 1985), p. 10-33.

29. Susan Morgan, "Victorian Women, Wisdom, and Southeast Asia," in *Victorian Sages and Cultural Discourse: Renegotiating Gender and Power,* ed. Thais Morgan (New Brunswick, N.J.: Rutgers University Press, 1991), p. 223.

30. Ibid., p. 223.

31. Sarah Lewis, *Woman's Mission* (London: John W. Parker, 1839).

32. Quoted in Stevenson, *Women Travel Writers in Africa,* p. 87.

33. Mary Poovey, *Uneven Developments,* p. 8-9.

34. Pemble, *The Mediterranean Passion,* p. 53.

35. Gabriele Annan, "Roughing It," *The New York Review of Books* (22 December 1988), p. 3.

36. Joanne Shattock, and Michael Wolff, *The Victorian Periodical Press: Soundings and Samplings* (Leicester, England: Leicester University Press, 1982), p. xiv.

37. In her article "'The Hero as Man of Letters': Masculinity and Victorian Nonfiction Prose," Carol T. Christ notes that women account for only thirteen percent of those authors indexed in *The Wellesley Index to Victorian Periodicals* (21). Not surprisingly, many of the women she mentions were travel writers, among them Frances Power Cobbe, Lady Eastlake, and Vernon Lee.

38. Pierre Bourdieu, *Distinction: A Social Critique of the Judgement of Taste,* trans. Richard Nice (Cambridge: Harvard University Press, 1984).

39. Ibid., p. 317.

40. Martha Vicinus, *Independent Women: Work and Community for Single Women, 1850-1920* (Chicago: University of Chicago Press, 1985), p. 7.

41. Anne Radcliffe, *A Journey made in the Summer of 1794 Through Holland and the Western Frontier of Germany* (1795; reprint, Hildesheim, N.Y.: G. Olms Co., 1975), p. v.

42. Frances Elliot, *Diary of an Idle Woman in Constantinople* (Leipzig, Germany: Bernhard Tauchnitz, 1893), n.p.

43. Amelia Edwards, *Untrodden Peaks,* p. 242.

44. Carol Christ, "The Hero as Man of Letters," in *Victorian Sages and Cultural Discourse: Renegotiating Gender and Power,* ed. Thais Morgan (New Brunswick, N.J.: Rutgers University Press, 1991), p. 230.

45. Gaye Tuchman, and Nine Fortin, *Edging Women Out: Victorian Novelists, Publishers, and Social Change* (New Haven: Yale University Press, 1989), p. 215.

46. Ibid., p. 3.

47. Ironically, one of the most influential pieces of "woman writer" criticism was written by a woman: "Silly Novels by Lady Novelists" by George Eliot was published in *The Westminster Review* in October of 1856.

48. Tuchman and Fortin, *Edging Women Out,* p. 73.

49. Viola Klein, *The Feminine Character: History of an Ideology* (New York: International Universities Press, 1949), p. 42.

50. Pinney, Thomas, p. 334.

51. Michael Cotsell, ed., *Creditable Warriors, 1830-1876* (Atlantic Highlands, N.J.: Ashfield Press, 1990), p. 14.

52. Their research shows that most Victorian nonfiction can be categorized according to gender. Whereas "male specialties" included the natural sciences, physical sciences, classics, geography, and economics, "female categories" were limited to women's topics and children's books. "High-prestige" specialties, those accorded the most cultural status, included philosophy, history, politics, social theory, and public policy—many of the same areas that Deirdre David would identify as the province of the traditional intellectual.

53. Nancy Armstrong, "The Rise of Feminine Authority in the Novel," *Novel: A Forum on Fiction* 15
(Winter 1982), p. 129.

54. Deirdre David, *Intellectual Women and Victorian
Patriarchy* (Ithaca: Cornell University Press,
1987).

55. Janet Murray, *Strong-Minded Women and Other
Lost Voices from the Nineteenth Century* (New
York: Pantheon Books, 1982).

56. Phillipa Levine, *Feminist Lives in Victorian England* (Cambridge: Basil Blackwell: 1990).

Bibliography

Blaikie, W. G. "Lady Travellers." *Blackwood's Magazine* 160 (July 1896): 49-66.

Susan Brown (essay date fall 1995)

SOURCE: Brown, Susan. "Alternatives to the Missionary Position: Anna Leonowens as Victorian Travel
Writer." *Feminist Studies* 21, no. 3 (fall 1995): 587-614.

[*In the following essay, Brown assesses the works of
Anna Leonowens within the context of Victorian wom-
en's travel writing, emphasizing in particular the ways
in which Leonowens' works differ from other travel
narratives in terms of imperialist or missionary authorial viewpoint.*]

The writings of Anna Harriette Leonowens, a woman of
English extraction who lived and worked in Southeast
Asia during the period of British imperial consolidation
in the 1860s, complicate the current endeavor to understand the connections between nineteenth-century feminism and imperialism. Leonowens as the "Anna" of the
well-known musical and film *The King and I* has become for many the symbol of the earnestly civilizing
Englishwoman abroad. Yet the historical Anna's position was more ambiguous than the popularized version
of her singing and dancing her way through cultural
difference would suggest. Leonowens lived in Siam,
now Thailand,[1] from 1861 to 1867, employed by King
Mongkut as governess to his numerous wives and children and as sometime assistant in his foreign correspondence. My focus here is on her two publications about
Siam which appeared in the early 1870s, *The English
Governess at the Siamese Court* (1870) and *The Romance of the Harem* (1873).[2] These texts dramatize the
difficult position of the Victorian woman travel writer
and, in response to these difficulties and the ambiguities
of Leonowens's own position, represent a significant re-
orientation of certain conventions of the genre of travel
writing and of imperialist discourse. Obviously, the
field of travel writing by Victorian women is a vast one,

and I make no claim here to account for the entire genre.
My purpose, rather, is to situate Leonowens's writings
about Thailand within the genre by examining their articulation of an alternative to one of the more tempting
discursive positions available to the Victorian woman
writing about non-European travels, a position I will
elaborate as "the missionary position."

Nowhere are the uneven relations between gender and
imperialism clearer than in the notion of "mission" as it
circulated within various discourses in the nineteenth
century. Missionaries often preceded and prepared the
ground for direct colonial incursion into a region and
"were a powerful force in defining the imperial project
in the nineteenth century."[3] Both the evangelical missions that preceded or accompanied European expansion and the civilizing missions which were their secular version were constructed as masculine. However, a
shifting but nonetheless powerful discourse of "woman's mission," inscribed in religious texts, conduct literature, essays, fiction, poetry, and travel writing constantly challenged the boundaries between the different
spheres of influence and action established by hegemonic discourses.[4] Earlier understandings of Victorian
constructions of gender which all but eclipsed the race,
nationality, and class of the white women citizens of
the largest empire of the century have given way to
probing questions about the complicities, enablements,
and contradictions historically engendered by the intersection of differences. For despite the continuing construction of the British Empire as male space, the lives
of Victorian women were materially and ideologically
bound up with imperial and colonial projects, from the
tea they drank and the cashmere shawls they might
covet to the very notion of "Englishness."[5] In employing the phrase "the missionary position" I mean to designate not a homogeneous construction of mission but
common threads in the strategies used by many Victorian writers to position themselves as superior to the
peoples and cultures they encountered. The sexual reso-
nances of the phrase suggest at once its predominantly
masculinist orientation and the unstable positionality
missionary discourse offers to women generally and
feminists in particular when it comes to adopting a role
of superiority.

Before considering Leonowens's texts as a way into
questions about the intersecting discourses of gender
and imperialism in high Victorian writing, however, I
need to clarify the placement of both Siam and Leonowens relative to British imperialism in the 1860s. Siam
was never directly subject to Western rule. There are,
however, compelling reasons for considering the country within the context of British imperial expansion.
Siam occupied a strategic position in Southeast Asia between Burma, which was being gradually annexed by
Britain, and French-occupied Indochina.[6] Historians
such as Abbot Low Moffat argue that Siam's avoidance

of colonization was largely the result of King Mongkut's skill in international relations: "For seventeen years he steered his country through the conflicting pressures and territorial ambitions of France and England and set the course that preserved the independence of his country—the only country in Southeast Asia never to have fallen under European domination."[7] Notwithstanding Mongkut's success, however, in the 1850s and 1860s, it appeared unlikely that Siam would maintain its independence. A longtime resident of Bangkok, U.S. missionary D. B. Bradley, wrote in 1858 that "the usual thought among the Siamese rulers is that Siam is destined to pass into the hands of the English. They seem almost instinctively to think so and so to express themselves." French-Siamese tensions over Cambodia became so serious in 1866 that Mongkut wrote to Britain suggesting that he would accept a British protectorate.[8] Thus, bearing in mind Antonio Gramsci's contention that hegemonic activity must precede an accession to formal rule, there is a strong case for regarding Siam in the 1860s as a site of British imperial expansion.[9] Mongkut's pro-Western stance, as well as his emphasis on English education for himself, his wives, and children, is generally placed in this context of hegemonic activity and resistance to it.[10] As the most recent biographer of Leonowens rather naively puts it, under Mongkut "many of the benefits of colonialism were obtained, without its yoke."[11]

The popular image of Leonowens herself is inextricably bound up with the British Empire. In a lengthy posthumous tribute published in 1915, John MacNaughton called her "the type which has made the Empire."[12] Thirty years later, Margaret Landon's romanticized and highly colored version of her story, *Anna and the King of Siam* (1944), followed by the Rodgers and Hammerstein musical *The King and I* (1951, filmed 1956), firmly entrenched the popular perception of Leonowens as the proper English lady who undertook single-handedly to "civilize" the king and court of Siam. Thus, we have Northrop Frye's placement of the Leonowens story beside classic texts of the British Empire such as *Robinson Crusoe*, texts "in which the whole cultural history of the nation that produced [them] comes into focus." Leonowens epitomizes the imposition of empire in his characterization of her as

> the Victorian lady in an Oriental country which had never had any tradition of chivalry or deference to women. She expected to be treated like a Victorian lady, but she didn't so much say so as express by her whole bearing and attitude that nothing else was possible, and eventually Siam fell into line.[13]

However, despite the evident temptation to make Leonowens into a metonymic figure for British imperialism—or as Laura Donaldson has recently done, for the contradictory role played by Victorian women in the Angle-European imperial project[14]—the popular conception of her is in sharp contrast to Leonowens's more problematic and marginal relation to empire. Notwithstanding her *representation* of herself as English, she was born in India, possibly of a "Eurasian" mother and a Welsh infantryman father.[15] No evidence supports her claim to have been educated in Wales, so she may well have been raised in the squalid barracks of an East India Company infantry regiment and educated in garrison schools at Ahmednugger and Puna.[16] In short, she occupied, for an (apparently) white, English-speaking and -identified woman, a rather oblique position relative to empire.

As these factors of marginal positionality might suggest, the writings of Leonowens on Siam are much less straightforward than the popularized story implies. In their episodic structure, they bear almost no resemblance to the tightly constructed and romanticized narrative of the musical version. Her first book, *The English Governess at the Siamese Court: Being Recollections of Six Years in the Royal Palace at Bangkok,* is a roughly chronological account of her stay, but whole chapters on topics such as Siamese language and literature, religious sites and practices, and the country's political system interrupt the personal story. *The Romance of the Harem,* which Leonowens dedicated to "the noble and devoted women" of the royal harem as "a record of some of the events connected with their lives and sufferings," consists of a series of short, unconnected narratives, some told in the first- and others in the third-person, along with some expository material on various aspects of Siamese culture. Their significance thus cannot be approached in terms of a continuous, developing plot or narrative of, say, a civilizing mission but, rather, through attention to particular rhetorical devices and thematic elements which recur in the author's representation of Siam and of Mongkut's harem.

Although Leonowens resided in Thailand for six years and was thus not actually in transit in the period she describes, the anecdotal structure and subject matter of her texts present good reasons for grouping them with other women's travel texts, some of which have dealt with such periods of residence.[17] Despite the absence of some characteristics attributed to this hybrid and capacious genre, Leonowens's accounts of Siam participate in the genre of travel writing not least insofar as they were judged, by contemporary reviewers and by critics since, with the expectations that they were true accounts of true experiences. Thus, the British *Athenæum*'s negative review in February 1873 of Leonowens's second book challenges her truth claims (*Romance,* p. vi) and, alluding to the title, accuses her of writing mere "Romance" and "a sensational work," rather than adhering to the veracity associated with the genre of travel writing.[18] It is precisely the uneven, ambiguous status of such conventions in Leonowens's texts that permits interrogation of the complex relations among gender, imperialism, and travel writing by women.

Despite my emphasis here on Leonowens's unusual placement in relation to the structures of gender, race, and empire, I nevertheless reject an "experiential" theory of travel writing, particularly the sort of gendered model suggested by Catherine Barnes Stevenson in her assertion that women travel writers "tend to record, to surrender to experience; men to judge, to schematize experience."[19] The notion of "experience" is problematized by a recognition that the female travel writer is not a mobile *tabula rasa* but a social subject interpellated by institutions such as nation and discourses such as those of orientalism. As Joan Wallach Scott argues, "experience" is always already mediated[20] and differences between female and male travel narratives cannot be relegated to an opposition between a passive female "recording," and an active male "schematizing" of an "experience" assumed as given. However, the discourses that surrounded and constituted both the act of traveling and the "experience" of the Orient are gendered in ways that had a significant impact not only on the way that travel was "experienced" by a woman travel writer but also on her discursive positioning in accounts of her travels. The travel text is thus, in Sara Mill's formulation, the result of "a configuration of discursive structures with which the author negotiates."[21] Certain aspects of Leonowens's background help to clarify ways in which she negotiates discursive structures in her texts differently from other travel writers of the period.

The position of Leonowens as a Victorian travel writer was unusual. Most obviously, Victorian travel writers tended to be male, or, when they were female, were often connected to men who were either officially, as in the case of colonial administrators or diplomats, or unofficially, as in the case of missionaries, engaged in the business of empire. Leonowens, being neither, occupied an anomalous position for a Victorian woman abroad in the 1860s. Indeed, she could hardly be said to be "abroad" in the usual sense, because it seems unlikely that she set foot in England until *after* leaving Siam. Not surprisingly, Leonowens seems to have been excluded, perhaps on the basis of her background, class position, or ignorance of etiquette, from the insulating enclave of British society in Bangkok.[22] The excentricity of her position in Siam was further heightened by the fact that she had been hired by an oriental monarch to teach inside a harem. Her employment at this major site of centuries-old Orientalist constructions of a simultaneously fascinating and repellent Eastern sensuality represented a serious threat to the already dubious propriety, controversial and precarious in the 1860s, of her position as a middle-class working woman. Both *The English Governess at the Siamese Court* and *The Romance of the Harem*, in which Leono-

wens capitalizes on her experience after leaving Mongkut's employ in 1867, attest to the difficulties and differences produced in these texts by her anomalous position.

Recent attention to Leonowens has focused largely on the question of authenticity, given the revelation that many of the events she narrates in her writings and her account of her own background are historically indefensible. Both Leslie Smith Dow, her biographer, and Susan Morgan, editor of *The Romance of the Harem,* thus ask whether Leonowens was a liar and seek to defend the "real Anna," her "true character" and "true voice."[23] Laura Donaldson's more theoretical approach to the texts and their dramatic legacies, which concludes by stressing the constructedness of subjectivity and involving the notion of multiple and shifting identity, nevertheless also suggests that Leonowens's publications, referred to as "real-life diaries," might provide access to her "authentic" self.[24] Yet Leonowens's texts can no more provide us with access to the "real" woman who wrote than they can be tested against the "real" life of the imperial harem or the city and inhabitants of Bangkok in the 1860s. In this respect, they differ only in degree and not in kind from any other travel memoir, whose narrating voice and narrated material are the products of language rather than reflections of reality.

The writings of Anna Leonowens are constructed using the conventions of language and genre available to her from a specific historical and geographical location, marked by but not reducible to her own lived sense of self, and heavily influenced, although not determined, by other factors such as writing for a largely North American rather than a British readership.[25] What is most interesting in Leonowens's texts, and most amenable to analysis, is her virtual self-creation in words. This self-creation is epitomized by her invention of her unique patronymic, created at her husband's death in 1858 by joining his second and last names, so that Mrs. Thomas Leon Owens became Mrs. Anna H. Leonowens. And just as her apparent patronymic both does and does not signify a conformity to the patriarchal naming and positioning of women, her texts in different respects conform to and depart from generic and discursive conventions. *The English Governess* and *The Romance of the Harem* reveal constant negotiation with the conventional discourses and hegemonic positioning typical of Victorian travel writing.

As much recent scholarship suggests, Victorian women's relation to empire and the discourses associated with it was frequently inflected by gender.[26] Not surprisingly, Leonowens's self-construction within her texts becomes particularly difficult at points where her position in Siam conflicts with Victorian gender ideologies. One of the most autobiographical moments in the two books occurs on the opening page of *The English Gov-*

erness, when the narrator describes how her first view of the beautiful Gulf of Siam is blotted out by the pain of parting from her young daughter: "[T]he memory of two round, tender arms, and two little dimpled hands, that so lately had made themselves loving fetters around my neck, in the vain hope of holding mamma fast, blinded my outlook." This is practically *all* that the text divulges of Leonowens's having sent her daughter away to school. Sending children to England for an education was common practice and frequently figures in colonial women's writings. However, the lack of elaboration in the passage and its placement on the first page of the text mark a significant moment of discursive contradiction in terms of the passage's attempt to employ Victorian discourses of gender within a context in which the primacy of motherhood is belied by the narrator's evident need for or commitment to waged employment.[27] That is, there is a difference between the wife and mother who must stand by her husband and his imperial mission and Leonowens's situation as a young widow in the Orient. She should presumably return "home," that is, to England, rather than staying and sending her daughter away. This is a precarious position from which to employ the rhetoric of maternal suffering upon separation from a child, which assumes such separation to result from necessity. Yet Leonowens does not articulate her need to work to support herself and her children, because the traditional construction of motherhood on which her rhetoric draws was challenged by the notion of women performing public, remunerated labor.

Victorian discourse of femininity were being destabilized in the 1850s and 1860s in precisely these terms. The supposed "naturalness" of women's unwaged domestic labor was being questioned as middle-class women asserted their need for and right to waged labor. Although the profession of governess seems to twentieth-century readers a safely feminized form of waged labor for a supposedly middle-class woman to undertake, it was precisely the potential slippage between domestic, middle-class mothers and public, paid women workers that threatened midcentury constructions of gender.[28] *The English Governess* reflects this instability in Victorian discourses of gender in its attempt to reconcile the narrator's position as a working woman with a still-dominant discourse of femininity.[29] So, Leonowens's recourse to the Victorian valorization of motherhood, as for example when she represents a "wretched crone" who guards the prime minister's harem as appearing "no longer ugly" when the woman sheds tears for her dead sons, exists in tension with her self-construction as a working woman (*English Governess,* pp. 19-20); hence, her reply to the "monstrous suggestion" by the women of the prime minister's harem

that she should prefer to be his wife than Mongkut's. Leonowens's explanation begins by setting herself and European women in opposition to members of the harem:

> "The prince, your lord, and the king, your Chow-che-witt, are pagans," I said. "An English, that is a Christian, woman would rather be put to the torture, chained and dungeoned for life, or suffer a death the slowest and most painful you Siamese know, than be the wife of either."

> (p. 21)

Yet this opposition is shortly destabilized by Leonowens's articulation of her position outside the marital economy:

> "I am only here to teach the royal family. I am not like you. You have nothing to do but to play and sing and dance for your master; but I have to work for my children, and one little one is now on the great ocean, and I am very sad."

> (pp. 21-22)

This second passage sets up contradictory relations between nationality and gender roles, for in dissociating herself from marriage as a woman who must work Leonowens echoes English and American feminist critiques of marriage and arguments in favor of remunerative employment for women. In so doing, the passage destabilizes the initial opposition between Christian and pagan marriage practices by implicitly aligning married Christian women whose only role is to please their husbands with the women of the harem. The final clauses of the passage group all women under the aegis of a universal motherhood which apparently transcends differences among women, including Siamese wives and working European women such as Leonowens. My discussion will return to Leonowens's representation of motherhood as an important feature of the position she adopts in her texts.

One resolution to the tension between female vocation and independence as opposed to feminine roles and spheres was available through recourse to discourses of religious mission. It was a discursive position particularly useful to women travelers who desired to reconcile their actions with conventional gender discourse. Advocates of female missionary work abroad defended such activity as drawing on intrinsically female strengths and as subordinated to divine will rather than the result of self-determination and willfulness. Kate Marsden, for instance, positions herself in these terms in *On Sledge and Horseback to the Outcast Siberian Lepers.* Introducing her 1892 narrative of travels through Siberia to investigate the situation of lepers and track down a rumored cure for the disease, she characterizes herself as a worker "for the furtherance of

Christ's kingdom, and for the good of humanity"; she repeatedly emphasized her "mission of relief," denying that her journey was a "pleasure trip" or that she "bids high for the world's applause." Marsden's discursive position is not entirely stable, for despite her claim that she provides "the particulars of the inconveniences, dangers, and exciting incidents, which have been, as it were, the inseparable companions of my travels," as opposed to "a simple record of the conditions and wants of the lepers," merely for the sake of sales to support her mission, she advertises herself on her title page not only as a member of the Royal British Nurses' Association and Medalist of the Russian Imperial Red Cross Society but also as a Fellow of the Royal Geographic Society. Yet, notwithstanding the complex motives suggested here and elsewhere, Marsden's text consistently adheres to the missionary position as a discursive strategy. The conjunction of imperial mission with Marsden's assertion of a specifically female religious mission—she says that "this leper work is essentially women's work"—is evident in the book's dedication to the queen:

> The most Queenly Woman and the most Womanly Queen of Whom the History of the World has ever told; Whose keen Sympathy with Suffering has made Her, Personally, as Beloved as the Progress of the British Empire, under Her Rule, as made Her Throne magnificent. . . .[30]

Although Leonowens's text is hardly framed with such an assertion of mission, she at one point represents the time she spent in Siam as selfless service to the oppressed:

> But ah! if any germ of love and truth fell from my heart into the heart of even the meanest of those wives and concubines and children of a king, if by any word of mine the least of them was won to look up, out of the depths of their miserable life, to a higher, clearer, brighter light than their Buddha casts upon their path, then indeed I did not labor in vain among them.
>
> (*English Governess*, p. 282)

This assertion of mission, if less consistent than Marsden's, is more ambitious, because Marsden works through the feminized vocation of nursing while Leonowens's passage suggests unmediated missionary work for the winning of souls. Such a passage as related by a woman who is in Siam on her own account cannot address the contradictions of which it also partakes, for the desire of women to be missionaries rather than missionaries' wives was strenuously contested. In this respect, then, Leonowens's text joins those of other Victorian women travelers, including Marsden's, in undermining the opposition of private and public spheres upheld within the discourses of femininity and religious mission, and within the discourses of empire and expansion to which they contributed. The contra-

dictions are heightened in Leonowens's texts to the extent that such missionary discourse appears infrequently rather than structuring or framing them.

Leonowens's gender also shapes significantly her construction of the Orient, particularly of the harem. A substantial portion of *The English Governess*, for instance, recounts her struggle with the king to obtain a home outside the walls of his palace:

> "I beg your Majesty will remember that in your gracious letter you promised me 'a residence adjoining the royal palace,' not within it."
>
> He turned and looked at me, his face growing almost purple with rage. "I do not know I have promised. I do not know former condition. I do not know anything but you are our servant; and it is our pleasure that you must live in this palace, and—*you shall obey.*"
>
> (p. 65)

Although the prominence she gives this battle could be attributed to the paradigmatic desire of a European traveler to keep the self intact, such an interpretation ignores the possibility of Leonowens being absorbed into the harem, not to mention the risk and rebellion involved in her decision to live independently in Bangkok. As Sara Mills notes, sexual matters mark a notable silence in women's travel writing.[31] Leonowens cannot articulate fully the dangers her readers would have understood to be involved in living within a harem, even in the absence of the discussion about Leonowens becoming one of the prime minister's wives or the assertion that efforts were being made at this time to acquire an English woman for the harem. But, especially given her already ambivalent position of employment, this lengthy section of *The English Governess* indicates the necessity of managing within the text the anxieties surrounding the white woman travel writer's relation to the harem, an institution that crystallized European notions about gender and the Orient.

Leonowens's texts manage this anxiety in a number of ways. Although she relates one scene of a female dance performance in relatively standard Orientalist form near the beginning of *The English Governess*, in *The Romance of the Harem* she supplements this with an account told from the point of view of the female performer and object of the gaze. The story of Choy, told in heightened narrative style, suggests an autonomy of female desire and subjectivity even as it reproduces the stock language of heaving breasts and parted lips employed in the earlier description (*Romance*, pp. 130-31). Leonowens's texts frequently echo the horrified representations of harems by earlier women writers, such as Harriet Martineau's 1848 pronouncement: "I declare that if we are to look for a hell upon earth, it is where polygamy exists."[32] There is no question that she deplores the institution of the Siamese harem, much as she deplores the system of slavery she associates with it, for depriving its members of independence, responsibility, and useful occupation. However, Leonowens's texts also provide alternative representations of the harem in her descriptions of it as an independent city of women. She estimates the imperial harem of Nang Harm, the city of Veiled Women, populated entirely by women and children, to contain 9,000 people.

> This woman's city is as self-supporting as any other in the world: it has its own laws, its judges, policy, guards, prisons, and executioners, its markets, merchants, brokers, teachers, and mechanics of every kind and degree; and every function of every nature is exercised by women, and by them only.
>
> (*Romance*, pp. 10-11)

In this respect the harem in Leonowens's texts becomes a community of women and functions, in Nina Auerbach's words, as an emblem of female self-sufficiency.[33]

Billie Melman discusses the similar "domestication" of the harem in nineteenth-century English women's writing about the Middle East, within which the harem is seen as "an autonomous sorority, little affected by the world outside it." But in contrast to this "a-political (or, rather, un-political) interpretation of what is, undoubtedly, a patriarchal system,"[34] Leonowens insists on the coexistence of dependency and independence in Nang Harm. Although her city of women is a world unto itself made up of women in both traditional and untraditional—from an Anglo-American perspective—roles and occupations, this private, female world which contains public, masculine activities is far from apolitical. It is full of intrigue among its members and assumes continuous and varied, open and clandestine, contact with the world outside. Private and public, inside and outside, female and male spheres influence each other despite the walls, just as her representation of the harem as a city blurs the boundaries of domestic and nondomestic space. The harem's self-sufficiency is balanced by the repeated reminders of the influence of external politics on its enclosed world and indeed its very composition—because many women are placed in it to cement their high-ranking family's relationship with the king—and of the final authority of the king over the harem and its members. In Leonowens's texts, then, domestication of the space of the harem reinforces rather than counters the interpretation of the harem as a political entity.

Leonowens's attack on an institution that was integral to the political system of Siam, and that historians since have credited with cementing the political stability which allowed Mongkut to maintain the country's national independence, suggests an ideological alignment with imperial expansion and with European feminist campaigns to "liberate" "other" women.[35] Such liberation was often advocated in terms of religious mission. As an advocate of female missionaries argued, women "owe to Christianity their present free and happy state—while it is on their sex, that, in other lands, the hard bondage of heathenism presses with the heavier weight."[36] The processes by which women attempted to adopt religious or spiritual positions in their participation in colonizing activity or discourses has lately received significant scholarly attention.[37] Women's appropriation of this area of discourse was enabled by the association of women with the religious and the cultural in Victorian gender ideology: the positions particular women embraced ranged from embodiments of evangelical zeal to more dispersed senses of mission derived from the notion of "woman as a specially civilizing influence."[38] Yet Leonowens's texts, although drawing on such discursive structures, also gesture at alternative positionings.

Leonowens was hired by Mongkut on the specific condition that she not attempt to convert him or his court to Christianity, on the grounds that "the followers of Buddha are mostly aware of the powerfulness of truth and virtue, as well as the followers of Christ, and are desirous to have faculty in English language and literature, more than new religions" (letter from Mongkut in *The English Governess at the Siamese Court*, p. vi). Leonowens at times represents herself as surreptitiously attempting to inculcate Christianity in her pupils, but on the whole her texts, *The Romance of the Harem* especially, eschew a religious construction of mission. Thus, despite a footnote in *The English Governess at the Siamese Court*, which credits Siamese missionaries with "much, if not all, of [Siam's] present advancement and prosperity" (p. 242), one does not find effusive tributes to missionary activity such as, for example, that of an earlier French traveler in Siam, Henri Mouhot, who writes: "The sight of the Cross in foreign lands speaks to the heart like meeting with an old friend; one feels comforted and no longer alone. It is beautiful to see the devotion, self-denial, and courage of these poor and pious missionaries. . . ."[39] Leonowens apparently drew on Mouhot's diaries but does not emulate him in this respect.[40] Indeed, her texts stage circuitous but persuasive critiques of Christianity, through "dialogues" with Mongkut and other Buddhists. For example, she leaves unanswered Mongkut's claim that the Christian God stigmatizes marriage as "unholy in that he would not permit his Son to be born in the ordinary way; but must needs perform a miracle in order to give birth to one divinely inspired" (*English Governess*, p. 241). Both of Leonowens's books about Siam provide lengthy accounts of Buddhist principles and practices, and she argues: "We are prone to ignore or to condemn that which we do not clearly understand; and thus it is, and on no better ground, that we deny that there are influences in the religions of the East to render their followers wiser, nobler, purer" (*English Governess,* p. 184). *The Romance of the Harem* (p. 207) goes so far as to include an unflattering representation of missionary endeavors in a section describing the filth of Bangkok's Christian village and a startling account of Christian (albeit Catholic) Siamese as dishonest and sometimes murderous. She also describes experiencing an ecumenical "hope" at the peaceful death of a Siamese priest (*English Governess,* p. 202).

Refusing by and large the religious missionary position, Leonowens poses instead as a kind of cultural translator or intermediary—despite reviewers' criticism of her translation of Thai words, she was a serious student of languages and religion, preferring Persian to Latin, and acquiring at least eight non-European tongues—and her texts veer frequently between the modes of personal narrative and cultural description.[41] She criticizes those who have misunderstood Buddhism "because they preferred to observe it from the standpoint and in the attitude of an antagonist, rather than of an inquirer" (*English Governess,* p. 186).

Yet Leonowens's relation to the construction of *imperial* mission is less clear. She certainly adopts the rhetoric of imperialism at points, as when she describes Siam as "benighted" in contrast to the "light and glory" of England (*Romance,* p. 186). But such passages are unrepresentative of the tone and import of much of her texts. For instance, Leonowens's depiction of herself speaking Thai, Malay, and other Oriental languages, rather than insisting that others speak English, serves to undermine a sense of cultural power or authority. So too does the departure from the rule Mills notes in women's travel writing "that the narrator is shown in a position of power and is never portrayed as being disobeyed."[42] The Christmas Day diary entry of Annie Taylor, during a dangerous and forbidden journey into Tibet, illustrates the way that this common feature of women's travel writing can dovetail with a religious missionary stance. She writes: "I had fellowship in spirit with friends all over the world. Quite safe here with Jesus."[43] That nothing in fact *does* happen to harm the writer of course confirms that the mission is providentially ordained.

Leonowens, in contrast, frequently represents herself as powerless and as negotiating the very real dangers and threats of her situation. When she does successfully negotiate crises, it is seldom through European male protection, consular or otherwise, or through physical or political power generally, but through her use of language or moral authority, and through female community and solidarity. Thus, Mills's contention that one of the primary functions of women's travel writing was to make the empire a safe space is clearly challenged by Leonowens's texts, in which she is actually physically assaulted as a result of becoming embroiled in political

intrigue (*English Governess,* p. 126). Her texts might be read as an argument for the need to *make* Siam a safe space through colonization; this is certainly an available reading, given the hegemonic impetus of the time and her concerted attack on the political system of the country. Yet the means by which the textual figure of Leonowens negotiates her position in Siam suggest that the change these texts advocate is not so much political, to be solved by British rule, as it is moral or cultural.

The ex-centricity of Leonowens's position in terms not only of gender but also of class, racial, and national origin is evident in the degree to which her texts seem to resist the discursive positions frequently adopted by other nineteenth-century women travelers. Leonowens's attempts to inscribe herself as a proper Victorian lady abroad result in a series of gaps, silences, and fabrications in her texts. Women's travel writing frequently intersects with autobiography, yet Leonowens's texts contain almost no autobiographical material.[44] In both books, she begins very much *in media res,* on or after her arrival in Siam. So, for example, *The English Governess* opens with a chapter called "On the Threshold" relating her arrival in Bangkok but providing no information about the circumstances that brought her there. Although both books contain personal anecdotes occurring during her stay in Siam, she makes almost no reference to her previous life. Such gaps result from the suppression of her national and class origins; her later book, *Life and Travel in India: Being Recollections of a Journey before the Days of Railroads* (1884), implies a narrative, still sketchy, of a "proper" English background.[45]

These silences function in two quite different ways. First, they invite a reader to assume the author's position as the proper middle-class English woman that her discursive style and genre, some of the behavior she recounts, and occasional self-description imply her to be, although the silences remain as markers of the suppression of Leonowens's contradicted social subjectivity. On the other hand, however, despite her intermittent use of the pronoun "we" to construct an implicitly Western readership, the structural lack of a reiterated "home" in relation to which Siam is defined as foreign and other, mitigates, in conjunction with other factors, the sense of England or the West generally as a center to which all else refers. Although Leonowens recounts, for example, her difficulties in getting Mongkut to provide her with a house outside of the palace, neither text contains much domestic detail and no comparison is made, such as those found in much Victorian women's travel writing, of Siamese food, housekeeping conditions, or servants with their English counterparts. Her writings present a sharp contrast to her contemporary Emily Innes's description of Southeast Asia as a "tailorless, cobblerless, doctorless, bookless, milkless, postless and altogether comfortless jungle."[46] In this respect, at least, Leonowens's representation of Siam very rarely constructs it as the lacking other or margin of a civilized imperial center. Her decision to "return to England" is related in *The English Governess* as based on health concerns and the stresses of her job rather than on a desire to return "home"—a word significantly absent in this context, although she uses it to describe her hard-won house in Bangkok (pp. 282, 75). "Englishness" or "home," then, does not operate as an *oikos,* an established point of reference which grounds the imperialist travel narrative.[47]

The ways in which Leonowens's texts depart from dominant discursive practices and even from those of other nineteenth-century women travelers do not mean they are somehow pure of the dominant discourses of religious and imperial mission but that her texts also attest to an alternative, indeed a Victorian feminist, construction of mission. This alternative is represented in large part through the intertext of *Uncle Tom's Cabin.* Leonowens was deeply impressed by Stowe's text, which stirred up abolitionist sentiment in the years leading up to the American Civil War, and which she had read before going to Siam.[48] In both *The English Governess* and *The Romance of the Harem,* which are contemporaneous with the Civil War and written primarily for a postwar U.S. audience, she positions herself as an abolitionist in the Siamese court, one whose primary concern is the sexual slavery of the women in the harem.[49] In so doing Leonowens adopts the feminist and abolitionist impetus of Stowe's novel but largely circumvents the evangelical drive of Stowe's polemic. Significantly, the only unambiguous conversion narrative of any length in Leonowens's writings about Siam is that of a member of the harem to anti-slavery sentiment through *Uncle Tom's Cabin.*[50] This woman, Sonn Klean, or "Hidden Perfume," is depicted as a paragon of spirituality who reproaches Leonowens for suggesting that she prays to an idol rather than to "the Great One who sent me my teacher Buddha" and argues that they both pray to the same God by different names (*Romance,* p. 248). Yet Leonowens suggests that Sonn Klean's life is illuminated even more powerfully by her engagement with Stowe's novel, which is described in the manner of a biblical text: "Her favourite book, however, was 'Uncle Tom's Cabin,' and she would read it over and over again, though she knew all the characters by heart, and spoke of them as if she had known them all her life" (*Romance,* p. 248). Sonn Klean frees her many slaves, and—in a species of reverse appropriation of the name of the white woman by an Oriental other—takes to signing herself Harriet Beecher Stowe "to express her entire sympathy and affection for the author of 'Uncle Tom's Cabin,'" who she compares to Buddha (p. 249). Given Leonowens's constant stress on the evils of slavery, this conversion carried far more weight in her texts than a traditional religious one.

Leonowens draws regularly on U.S. feminist abolitionist imagery and discourse. In the most striking instance, *The Romance of the Harem* describes Leonowens unexpectedly encountering a woman imprisoned in a courtyard: "She was naked to the waist, and chained,—chained like a wild beast by one leg to a post driven into the ground, and without the least shelter under that burning sky." The terms in which Leonowens addresses the woman echo nineteenth-century abolitionist descriptions of female slaves as "women and sisters": "'My sister,' said, I, 'tell me your whole story, and I will lay it before the king'" (*Romance,* pp. 44, 47). Such language, along with the iconography of the chained and naked female slave, permeated the writings and visual representations of U.S. feminist abolitionists.[51] The passage confirms Leonowens's self-positioning in her earlier book as "set up between the oppressor and the oppressed" in Siam (p. 270).

That Leonowens draws on the rhetoric of U.S. abolitionism in general and Stowe's novel in particular to articulate her position in Siam naturally suggests a parallel between her investments and theirs. It recalls the critical debates over the terms in which an emerging white, middle-class feminism and abolitionism intersect in Stowe's text.[52] Leonowens's loosely constructed writings and Stowe's sentimental novel participate in very different textual conventions. However, it is perhaps worth noting in this context that Stowe's position as a member, albeit a female one, of the abolitionist establishment in the antebellum North of the United States differs markedly from Leonowens's position, and it is perhaps significant that Stowe does not figure herself into her texts as does Leonowens. As I have suggested, Leonowens's depiction of herself as vulnerable to the same political forces as are the Siamese women she represents—for the king and the political intrigue that surrounds him have an impact on them both—is a crucial aspect of her self-positioning.

Yet Leonowens's recourse to feminist abolitionist discourse does suggest the possibility, in the light of Karen Sánchez-Eppler's analysis of its rhetorical strategies, that asymmetry and exploitation underlie the identification between the white feminist writer and the enslaved woman: "The bound and silent figure of the slave represents the woman's oppression and so grants the white woman access to political discourse denied the slave." Although, again, one cannot conflate Leonowens's rhetorical purpose and discursive possibilities with those of feminist abolitionists several decades earlier, her adaptation of their rhetoric relies on the same dynamic of displacement. If feminist abolitionist writing repressed its authors' "fear of confronting the sexual elements of her own bodily experience,"[53] Leonowens's incorporation of their rhetoric into her articulation of mission relies not only on a degree of asymmetry and exploitation in relation to Siamese women but also a repression of her own potential subordination by the missionary position she adopts.

What can be acknowledged and spoken only intermittently in Leonowens's texts is not the similarity between the position of women and slaves: this indeed is being asserted. The comparison between the position of slaves and women was utterly commonplace in the latter half of the nineteenth century. Emily Innes, for instance, recounts an argument between herself and a Malay Resident who remarks:

> "It is too good, your making such a fuss about these slaves. You are a slave yourself, you know—all married women are slaves!"
>
> I replied, "Just so. That is precisely why I can sympathize with other slaves."[54]

What must be repressed in Leonowens's texts, however, is the origin of her rhetoric in the masculinist discourse of mission from which her feminist self-positioning derives. She elides the contradiction entailed by women's subordination in masculinist and imperialist discourse and risks replicating the same structure of asymmetry and dominance. But what if the binary terms and fixed roles within missionary discourse could be destabilized? Moments of such destabilization in Leonowens's texts suggest the possibility of not just an alternative missionary discourse which replicates the structures it seeks to avoid but of an alternative to missionary discourse.

The intertextuality of Leonowens's texts with U.S. feminist abolitionist writing does not underwrite a static characterization of herself as active liberator and Siamese women as passive victims of slavery and injustice. Martineau's outraged response to a middle-eastern "Hareem" earlier in the century inscribes the women as ignorant victims who passively accept a condition of life that horrified the writer, who describes them as "the most injured human beings I have ever seen—the most studiously depressed and corrupted women whose condition I have witnessed."[55] In contrast, Leonowens's texts represent Siamese women as active in their own and others' liberation in her narratives, of which Sonn Klean's story is one of the less dramatic. The most sensational example of such agency is perhaps the slave girl who cuts out her own tongue so as to be unable to betray the mistress whose escape from the harem prison she has engineered (*Romance,* pp. 199-201). Throughout, Leonowens's texts recall Stowe's narrative of (female or feminized) self-sacrifice for the sake of others, of which Leonowens's own actions are but one instance. The effect of this sustained intertextual engagement with feminist abolitionism generally and *Uncle Tom's Cabin* in particular is to align Leonowens's texts with what Jane Tompkins has analyzed as "a monumental effort to reorganize culture from the woman's point of view."[56]

Leonowens's texts naturalize and domesticate the exotic space of the Oriental harem to a notion of Western femininity and motherhood. Women in a harem, she asserts, are so warped by their environment that they are de-feminized—"disinterestedness vanishes"—and become "unconscious of the terrible defacement they have undergone," but they can nevertheless be redeemed by motherhood: "when a woman [in the harem] becomes a mother her life changes; she passes from the ignoble to the noble; then she becomes pure, worthy, honorable." The bound and chained slave, for instance, is "repulsive" because of her defiant expression until suffused by motherly devotion, when she becomes "glorious, clothed in the beauty and strength of a noble human love" (*Romance,* pp. 107, 45). This is a valorization of femininity and motherhood consecrated to female liberation and abolition. The ideal of femininity is clearly Western in origin but that it is represented as accessible to women regardless of race or creed—as indeed exemplified by numerous Siamese women in Leonowens's narratives—suggests that the liberating impetus here is not founded on an assertion of English superiority in the way that many English women's texts of the nineteenth century were.[57] The fluidity of roles in Leonowens's texts suggest a construction of mission which eschews the static oppositions of subject/object, active/passive, savior/victim that ground traditional missionary discourse.

Leonowens's discursive positioning departs markedly from religious or imperialist missionary stances, but she nevertheless participates in some of their structures. Leonowens constructs herself, albeit unevenly and problematically, as a white, English-educated and middle-class woman from the imperial center with a mission to "other" less privileged women, and she employs the rhetoric of feminist abolition and emancipation on which such women grounded their own claims to and inscriptions of political subjectivity and voice. In this respect, her texts anticipate, or perhaps proleptically insert into the past, a source for her later activism in the campaign for female suffrage in Canada.[58] Leonowens also profits materially from the texts produced by these means. Her texts were enthusiastically received by U.S. audiences, who, by the time she completed the lecture tour that followed the publication of *The Romance of the Harem* in 1873, were giving her credit for the abolition of slavery in Siam following Mongkut's death and the ascension of his son and Leonowens's former pupil, Chulalongkorn. Leonowens's resistance to a traditional missionary position indeed seemed to serve her well, if not in England at least with U.S. audiences accustomed to abolitionist imagery and rhetoric and swelled by their own sense of having recently abolished slavery. The material benefits and the cultural capital Leonowens gained from her texts must be acknowledged, along with the important fact that the texts were enabled by her access as a white female British subject to publication and speaking engagements, as well as to the language and discursive conventions of nineteenth-century English hegemony.

Yet, as I have attempted to demonstrate here, this complicity should not be allowed to overshadow the ways in which these texts articulate dissent and difference. Within the context of their production and reception, Leonowens's texts can be read as advocating a different mode of political interaction than one based on imperial strength and suppression. Her antislavery position is impure: it is self-serving as well as indebted to and complicit with both religious missionary discourse and the discursive circulation of British imperial power at the historical moment in which she wrote. Yet the version of mission Leonowens adapts from feminist abolitionists and rearticulates within the genre of travel writing emphasizes a model of female political efficacy based on respect for the language, culture, and agency of others, and on the power of teachers and texts. Her model is by no means unassailable, but it is an alternative.

The ambiguities of Leonowens's self-construction highlight the difficulties of assessing the extent to which feminist reorientations of Victorian notions of power are consistent with or dependent upon participation in imperialist constructions of mission toward "inferior" cultures. Her narratives participate in Victorian discourses of gender and imperialism, particularly in her construction of an English textual identity. But they also modify and depart from those discourses in ways that challenge dominant Victorian modes of representing transcultural encounters. The instability of Leonowens's self-positioning exceeds, I am arguing, even that which Mills has argued is intrinsic to women travel writers' "struggle with the discourses of imperialism and femininity, neither of which they could wholeheartedly adopt, and which pulled them in different textual directions . . . their writing exposes the unsteady foundations on which it is based."[59] Leonowens's texts destabilize dominant Victorian constructions of gender, the Orient, and the discursive positioning of the travel writer, as well as challenge the legacies of those constructions in contemporary history and scholarship that would see Victorian discourse on Southeast Asia as masculinist and monological. But, more importantly for the study of the imbrication of nineteenth-century feminism with imperial project, *The English Governess at the Siamese Court* and *The Romance of the Harem,* with their inevitable, but uneven, complicity with colonial interests and representational practices, also complicate some current notions of the function of Victorian women's travel writing and of the relation to nineteenth-century women to the British Empire.

Leonowens is an extreme instance of the tension between such differing constituents of subjectivity as race, nationality, class, and gender. Her difficulties in positioning herself through the discourses available to her are the difficulties writ large of the obliquely positioned writing subject's relation to the textual possibilities of a particular historical and cultural moment. They remind us of Teresa de Lauretis's articulation of the connection between feminism and postcolonialism in terms of an "understanding of the interrelatedness of discourses and social practices, and of the multiplicity of positionalities concurrently available in the social field seen as a field of forces: not a single system of power dominating the powerless but a tangle of distinct and variable relations of power and points of resistance."[60] Just as Leonowens's representation of the Orient manages to evade, at points, the binary models of dominant discourses, her texts exhort twentieth-century readers to eschew simplistic binary models of oppressor and oppressed, colonizer and colonized, lest we miss in the process the possibilities of an ambiguous term, another position, a complex range of alternatives. Although it is fruitless to seek an authentic voice or presence in Leonowens's texts, we can nevertheless distinguish in their discursive strategies an innovative engagement with the textual and ideological conventions of travel writing and acknowledge the extent to which such texts map out, if only partially and tentatively, alternatives to masculinist missionary positions.

Notes

1. The name of the government of the country adopted in 1939 is contested, associated as it is with a program of nationalism centered on the linguistic and ethnic Thai majority. "Siam" under King Mongkut in the mid-nineteenth century was more inclusive of minority groups, although still exclusive, for example, of Malaysians and Islamic peoples generally. See Craig J. Reynolds, "Introduction," *National Identity and Its Defenders: Thailand, 1939-1989,* ed. Craig J. Reynolds (Clayton, Australia: Centre of Southeast Asia Studies, 1991), 1-40; and Sivaraska Sulak, "The Crisis of Siamese Identity," in ibid., 41-58.

2. *The English Governess at the Siamese Court: Being Recollections of Six Years in the Royal Palace at Bangkok* (1870; rpt., Singapore: Oxford University Press, 1988), and *The Romance of the Harem,* ed. Susan Morgan (1873; rpt., Charlottesville: University Press of Virginia, 1991), hereafter referred to as *English Governess* and *Romance* in parentheses in the body of my article.

3. Catherine Hall, "Missionary Stories: Gender and Ethnicity in England in the 1830s and 1840s," in *Cultural Studies,* ed. Lawrence Grossberg, Cary Nelson, and Paula Treichler (London: Routledge, 1992), 243.

4. Hence, Gayatri Chakravorty Spivak's insight into *Jane Eyre*'s concluding tribute to the Indian mis-

sionary work of St. John Rivers has recently been extended by Jenny Sharpe's acute analysis of Jane's feminist *bildungsroman* as grounded in the extension of the force and significance of the civilizing mission to the domestic sphere. See Gayatri Chakravorty Spivak, "Three Women's Texts and a Critique of Imperialism," *Critical Inquiry* 12 (autumn 1985): 243-61; and Jenny Sharpe, *Allegories of Empire: The Figure of Woman in the Colonial Text* (Minneapolis: University of Minnesota Press, 1993), 27-55.

5. The depiction in history and scholarship of the British Empire, the Orient, and the general domain of travel literature as male spaces has recently been challenged in studies which focus on women or gender in these areas, most strenuously in Sara Mills, *Discourses of Difference: An Analysis of Women's Travel Writing and Colonialism* (London: Routledge, 1991); and Billie Melman, *Women's Orients: English Women and the Middle East, 1718-1918* (Ann Arbor: University of Michigan Press, 1992). For a general collection of essays, see Nupur Chaudhuri and Margaret Strobel, eds., *Western Women and Imperialism: Complicity and Resistance* (Bloomington: Indiana University Press, 1992), including Chaudhuri's essay, "Shawls, Jewelry, Curry, and Rice in Victorian Britain," 231-46.

6. Nicholas Tarling, *The Fall of Imperial Britain in South-East Asia* (Singapore: Oxford University Press, 1993), 47.

7. Abbot Low Moffat, *Mongkut, the King of Siam* (Ithaca: Cornell University Press, 1961), viii.

8. D. B. Bradley, quoted in B. J. Terweil, *A History of Modern Thailand, 1767-1942* (St. Lucia: University of Queensland Press, 1983), 184, 187.

9. See *Selections from the Prison Notebooks of Antonio Gramsci*, ed. and trans. Quinton Hoare and Geoffrey Nowell Smith (London: Lawrence & Wishart, 1971), 57.

10. See Sulak; Moffat; Tarling. Cf. Leonowens, *The English Governess* regarding the gradual installment of Europeans in key institutional positions such as commander of the troops and head of the police force, developments which Leonowens attributes to the activities of the British consul-general; elsewhere there are discussions of the missionary work of introducing English language and literature to Bangkok (245-46).

11. Leslie Smith Dow, *Anna Leonowens: A Life beyond "The King and I"* (Lawrencetown Beach, Nova Scotia: Pottersfield Press, 1991), 149.

12. John MacNaughton, *Mrs. Leonowens* (Montreal: Gazette Printing Co., 1915), 1.

13. Northrop Frye, "Verticals of Adam," in his *The Educated Imagination* (Toronto: Canadian Broadcasting Corporation, 1963), 52-53. Thanks to Donna Palmateer Pennee for bringing this passage to my attention.

14. Laura Donaldson, *Decolonizing Feminisms: Race, Gender, and Empire-Building* (Chapel Hill: University of North Carolina Press, 1992).

15. This revision of the life story constructed by Leonowens in *Life and Travels in India: Being Recollections of a Journey before the Days of Railroads* and expanded by her friends and family is based on the extensive research of birth and marriage registries and army records conducted by W. S. Bristowe for his biography of Leonowens's son, Louis. See his "Anna Unveiled," in *Louis and the King of Siam* (London: Chatto & Windus, 1976), 23-31.

16. Susan Morgan's suggestion, in her introduction to *The Romance of the Harem* (xvi), that the real mystery about Leonowens's background is how she became so articulate if she came from such a background seems unwarranted. Barracks schools such as the child of a sergeant would have attended were hardly luxurious, but they provided a sound education far in advance of the provision of public education in England, one which the teen-aged Leonowens seems to have furthered in her later travels and stay in the Middle East with the Reverend George Percy Badger, who superintended the school at Puna. See Denis Ryan, "Education in the British Army," in *The Education of Armies,* ed. Michael D. Stephens (London: Macmillan, 1989), 75; Dow, 3-4. Gauri Viswanathan's impressive work on the Indian school curriculum in *Masks of Conquest: Literary Study and British Rule in India* (New York: Columbia University Press, 1989) is of course not directly applicable to the regimental school system. However, the way in which the regimental schools anticipated by many years the curriculum of free public schooling suggests parallels with Viswanathan's contention that the literature curriculum in Indian schools was crucial to the introduction and maintenance of colonial hegemony in England. Although such an argument could not be made conclusively without more detailed information about the curriculum in these schools than I have been able to locate, I am suggesting that the regimental education offered to the children of noncommissioned ranks in the army of the East India Company was a primary means by which Leonowens was interpellated as an English subject, although not a highly privileged one.

17. On such writings by women in Southeast Asia, see Susan Morgan, "An Introduction to Victorian

Women's Travel Writings about Southeast Asia," *Genre* 20 (summer 1987): 189-208.

18. "The Romance of Siamese Harem Life," *Athenæum* 2364 (15 Feb. 1873): 207. Twentieth-century historians have followed this lead in denouncing her texts on these grounds. See Moffat; and A. B. Griswold, "King Mongkut in Perspective," *Journal of the Siam Society* 45 (April 1957): 1-41. Morgan's introduction to *The Romance of the Harem* defends the text against its "detractors," placing it in the tradition of Victorian fiction ("fictionalized history or historical fiction" [xvi]) rather than the travelogue but arguing that "in all its excess, [it] uncovers that consistently hidden, politically inconvenient truth" of the oppression of the women of Nang Harm (xxxvi). Leonowens's title itself suggests a destabilization of the opposition between "truth" and "romance."

19. Catherine Barnes Stevenson, *Victorian Women Travel Writers in Africa* (Boston: Twayne, 1982), 10.

20. See Joan Wallach Scott, "Experience," in *Feminists Theorize the Political,* ed. Judith Butler and Joan W. Scott (New York: Routledge, 1992), 22-40.

21. Sara Mills provides a fine account of the gendered constraints on the production and reception of women's travel writing; for discussion of the way the representation of women is bound up with the construction of the Orient, see Melman; Rana Kabbani, *Europe's Myths of Orient* (London: Pandora, 1986); and Malek Alloula, *The Colonial Harem,* trans. Myrna Godzich and Wlad Godzich (Minneapolis: University of Minnesota Press, 1986); Mills, 9.

22. Bristowe, 31.

23. Dow, xiii; Morgan, xvi, xxii.

24. Donaldson, 35, 50.

25. After leaving Siam, Leonowens settled for ten years in the United States and then moved to Canada. Her writings about Siam, later published in *The English Governess,* were first published in the *Atlantic Monthly,* a magazine well known for publication of antislavery writings by contributors like Harriet Beecher Stowe. She also supplemented her income from her writing by lecturing on Siam to North American audiences.

26. See, for an example pertinent in this context, Nancy Paxton, "Disembodied Subjects: English Women's Autobiography under the Raj," in *De/Colonizing the Subject: The Politics of Gender in Women's Autobiography,* ed. Sidonie Smith and Julia Watson (Minneapolis: University of Minnesota Press, 1992), 387-409.

27. As Shirley Foster notes, women travel writers of the nineteenth century rarely acknowledge the financial distress which was a common motivation for traveling or living abroad. Leonowens's silence on the economic difficulties which led her to work in Siam is comparable. See Foster's *Across New Worlds: Nineteenth-Century Women Travellers and Their Writings* (New York: Harvester, 1990), 9.

28. See M. Jeanne Peterson, "The Victorian Governess: Status Incongruence in Family and Society," in *Suffer and Be Still: Women in the Victorian Age,* ed. Martha Vicinus (Bloomington: Indiana University Press, 1972), 3-19; and Mary Poovey, *Uneven Developments: The Ideological Work of Gender in Mid-Victorian England* (Chicago: University of Chicago Press, 1988), 126-63.

29. Parallel moments of discursive tension in the text occur in her representation of her negotiations with her employer for a raise and her reasons for having been in and then deciding to leave Siam (*English Governess,* p. 269).

30. Kate Marsden, *On Sledge and Horseback to the Outcast Siberian Lepers* (New York: Cassell, 1892), xi, 7, 14, 7. See 2, ix, i.

31. Mills, 81.

32. Harriet Martineau, *Eastern Life Past and Present* (London: Moxon, n.d.), 236. Melman attributes Martineau's response to the Middle Eastern harem to her abolitionist sympathies, which considered polygamy and slavery concomitant evils (138, 146, 359 n. 3).

33. Nina Auerbach, *Communities of Women: An Idea in Fiction* (Cambridge: Harvard University Press, 1978), 5.

34. Melman, 144.

35. See Sharpe; and Antoinette Burton, *Burdens of History: British Feminists, Indian Women, and Imperial Culture, 1865-1915* (Chapel Hill: University of North Carolina Press, 1994).

36. Author of the anonymous essay in Jemima Thompson, *Memoirs of British Female Missionaries: With a Survey of the Condition of Women in Heathen Countries, and also a Preliminary Essay on the Importance of Female Agency in Evangelizing Pagan Nations* (London: William Smith, 1841), xv.

37. See Hall; Mills; Melman; Stevenson; and Vron Ware, *Beyond the Pale: White Women, Racism and History* (London: Verso, 1992).

38. Foster, 10.

39. *Henri Mouhot's Diary,* abrg. and ed. Christopher Pym (Kuala Lumpur: Oxford University Press, 1966), 4.

40. The concluding chapter of *The English Governess,* "The Ruins of Cambodia—An Excursion to the Naghkon Watt," appears to have been based on other sources, mainly an earlier account of Cambodian temple ruins by Henri Mouhot (Bristowe, 24). The question of the veracity of Leonowens's texts precedes the question of her identity: the review of *The English Governess* in the *Athenæum* insinuates that in addition to questionable translations and accounts of Siamese customs, the trip to Cambodia is fabricated and drawn from the French traveler's account.

41. This is not to imply the innocence or objectivity of translation, or the associated discourses of ethnography and anthropology, which developed in the mid-nineteenth century within the European imperial context but, rather, to distinguish the discursive position they construct from that of religious missionary discourse. See Patrick Brantlinger, *Rule of Darkness: British Literature and Imperialism, 1830-1914* (Ithaca: Cornell University Press, 1988), 166, on the establishment of anthropology in Britain; and Bill Ashcroft, Gareth Griffiths, and Helen Tiffin, *The Empire Writes Back: Theory and Practice in Post-Colonial Literatures* (London: Routledge, 1989) on translation and ethnography generally within transcultural writing.

42. Mills, 22.

43. William Carey, *Travel and Adventure in Tibet, Including the Diary of Miss Annie R. Taylor's Remarkable Journey from Tau-Chau to Ta-Chien-Lu through the Heart of the Forbidden Land* (London, 1902; rpt., Delhi: Mittal, 1983), 242.

44. For discussion of the overlap between travel writing and writing of the self, see *De/Colonizing the Subject.*

45. Leonowens's *Life and Travel in India: Being Recollections of a Journey before the Days of Railroads* (Philadelphia: Porter & Coates, 1884) contains more autobiographical discourse, although it is still relatively vague. The difference is possibly explained in the lapse of more than a decade since the earlier publications during which time Leonowens became successful as a writer and speaker and consolidated a middle-class social and economic position, first in the United States and then in Canada. It seems likely that these factors, in addition to the security provided by the distance in time and geography from her previous life, enabled a more specific articulation of origin and identity than was possible in the earlier, much more ambivalently positioned, texts, given that the origin and identity were in part constructed and hence subject to possible refutation.

46. Emily Innes, quoted in Jane Robinson, *Wayward Women: A Guide to Women Travelers* (Oxford: Oxford University Press, 1990), 285.

47. See Simon Gikandi, "Englishness, Travel, and Theory: Writing the West Indies in the Nineteenth Century," *Nineteenth-Century Contexts* 18, no. 1 (1994): 51-52, drawing on Georges Van Den Abbeele, *Travel as Metaphor: From Montaigne to Rousseau* (Minneapolis: University of Minnesota Press, 1992).

48. Leonowens apparently read *Uncle Tom's Cabin* in the early 1860s, long before she entered the circle of American acquaintances that eventually brought about a gratifying meeting with Stowe herself in 1872. See Margaret Landon, *Anna and the King of Siam* (New York: Harper & Row, 1943), 29, 354; Dow, 69; Morgan, xxii.

49. The slavery the texts allege should be considered in light of the doubt scholars have cast on the historical veracity of much of what Leonowens relates; Mongkut's ostensible policy was that his wives could leave if they so chose, and some did. There certainly was slavery in Thailand, of varying degrees, but, significantly, Leonowens's focus is on women.

50. A more sustained but also more ambiguous story of conversion to Catholicism in *The Romance of the Harem* suggests that the conversion is thwarted by the factionalism of priests and frames the narrative with accounts of evil Thai Christians.

51. See Jean Fagin Yellin, *Women and Sisters: The Antislavery Feminists in American Culture* (New Haven: Yale University Press, 1989).

52. See, for example, Richard Yarborough, "Strategies of Black Characterization in *Uncle Tom's Cabin* and the Early Afro-American Novel," in *New Essays on "Uncle Tom's Cabin,"* ed. Eric J. Sundquist (Cambridge: Cambridge University Press, 1986), 45-84; Hortense J. Spillers, "Changing the Letter: The Yokes, the Jokes of Discourse, or, Mrs. Stowe, Mr. Reed," in *Slavery and the Literary Imagination,* ed. Deborah E. McDowell and Arnold Rampersad (Baltimore: Johns Hopkins University Press, 1989), 25-61; and essays in the recent collection, *The Stowe Debate: Rhetorical Strategies in "Uncle Tom's Cabin,"* ed. Mason L. Lowrance Jr., Ellen E. Westbrook, and R. C. De Prospo (Amherst: University of Massachusetts Press, 1994).

53. Karen Sánchez-Eppler, *Touching Liberty: Abolition, Feminism, and the Politics of the Body* (Berkeley: University of California Press, 1993), 19, 22.

54. Emily Innes, *The Chersonese with the Gilding Off,* intro. Khoo Kay Kim (Kuala Lumpur: Oxford University Press, 1974), 2: 139.

55. Martineau, 245.

56. Jane Tompkins, *Sensational Designs: The Cultural Work of American Fiction, 1790-1860* (New York: Oxford University Press, 1985), 124.

57. My reading here tries to complicate Donaldson's claim that Leonowens "imprisons Siamese women within an ethnocentric vision of angelic motherhood" and "legitimates the agendas of a colonialist society" (35, 36). Although there is no doubt that Leonowens's texts are implicated in the discourses of colonialism and orientalism, Donaldson's conclusions are based largely on a reading of the film and script of *The King and I.* Her reading elides, in its lack of attention to Leonowens's texts, the complexity and contradictions of Leonowens's self-positioning in relation to colonial discourse, and in its conclusions conflates the author and her writings with the legacy of her texts.

58. See Dow, 109ff.

59. Mills, 3.

60. Teresa de Lauretis, "Eccentric Subjects: Feminist Theory and Historical Consciousness," *Feminist Studies* 16 (spring 1990): 131.

Catherine Barnes Stevenson (essay date 1996)

SOURCE: Stevenson, Catherine Barnes. "'That Ain't no Lady Traveler . . . It's a Discursive Subject': Mapping and Re-mapping Victorian Women's Travel Writing." *Victorian Literature and Culture* 24 (1996): 419-31.

[*In the following essay, Stevenson surveys different categories of and various critical approaches to nineteenth century women's travel writing.*]

Before the late 1970s, women's travel writing was virtually *terra incognita*—its reaches uncharted, its contours unmapped, its strategic importance unknown. With the exception of Paul Fussell's elegant study of British literary traveling, *Abroad* (1980), travel writing itself was a form of literary production still largely untheorized. Then in the 1980s literary explorers, schooled in feminist acts of recovery and in gynocriticism, opened the territory of women's travel writing to popular audiences, surveying its dimensions and charting preliminary routes. They discovered "lost" texts, unearthed the buried lives of remarkable women, tried to locate travelers within personal, cultural, and even political nexuses. In keeping with the spirit of the times, they focused on the achievements of these women worthies, documented the personal and rhetorical postures dictated by Victorian gender roles, and searched for commonalities in literary techniques or psychological dynamics.

Recently, armed with post-colonial theory, cultural studies and a heightened sense of what James Clifford calls the "predicament of culture," a second wave of explorers has ventured into a newly problematized territory. Scholars now interrogate the conventions of travel literature as they relate not only to issues of literary representation but also to imperial discourse and the construction of "the self" and "the other." They unpack the cultural baggage that women travelers carried with them. They investigate the intersecting and competing imperatives of gender, race, and imperial privilege as these played themselves out in the women's travels and writings. Although there is still much territorial mapping to be done (as evident in the work of Billie Melman on women's writing about the "Orient"), many recent scholars eschew biography and geography to focus on the traveler's "subject position" in relation to the institutions and ideologies of her home culture.

Opposing itself to earlier "celebratory" and "estheticist" traditions of studying travel writing, Mary Louise Pratt's landmark *Imperial Eyes* presents itself as a "critique of ideology" (4), specifically of the way that European travel writing about non-European parts of the world "produced" that world for its readers and engendered in a metropolitan audience imaginative investment in European "expansionist enterprises." With considerable wit, agility, and a commitment to a "dialectical" approach, *Imperial Eyes* examines the "conventions of representation" in a wide variety of travel writing over two centuries: eighteenth-century naturalists' accounts of Southern Africa, "sentimental" travel accounts from the Caribbean and West Africa (1780-1840), "discursive reinventions" of South America (1800-1840), Victorian writers in Central Africa (1860-1900), and finally post-colonial travelers of the 1960s and eighties. By elucidating the intersections of travel writing with other forms of expression, particularly natural history and sentimental literature, Pratt is able to offer a highly useful contextualization of the literature of travel within its historical, cultural, intellectual, and literary milieu.

Because of its facility with the discourses of both literary criticism and ethnography, *Imperial Eyes* has given the field of travel writing a new vocabulary for discussing cultural encounters and their representations. Pratt's contributions to the lexicon include the following. The contact zone: those "social spaces where disparate cultures meet, clash, and grapple with each other" (4); it stresses the "interactive, improvisational dimensions of colonial encounters," the way that "subjects are constituted in and by their relations to each other" (7). Transculturation: an ethnographic term that describes how subordinated or marginal groups select and use materials transmitted from the dominant culture (6); Pratt also uses this term to suggest the ways in which metropolitan European culture was constructed from the outside. Anti-conquest: those strategies of innocence adopted by the male European bourgeois subject to distinguish himself from the imperial conqueror while at the same time asserting hegemony through his imperial gaze (7). Auto-ethnography: the colonized subject's self-representations which "engage with the colonizer's own terms" (7).

Although women's travel writing is referenced in several different contexts here, I want to focus on the most extended discussion of the gender differences in travel accounts, the chapter entitled "Reinventing America II: The Capitalist Vanguard and the *Exploratrices Sociales.*" Here two traditions in early nineteenth-century travel accounts of South America are elucidated, each of them distinct from the earlier accounts of explorers or naturalists. The first—a male, heroic mode—represents travel in a "goal-oriented rhetoric of conquest and achievement" and allegorizes the journey through "the lust for progress" (148). The ideological work of this kind of writing was to invent a "backward and neglected" America, full of unclean and indolent peasants, a land very much in need of capitalist investment and "rationalized exploitation." The second tradition emerges in Flora Tristan's *Peregrinations of a Pariah* (1837) and Maria Callcott Graham's *Voyage to Brazil and Journal of a Residence in Chile* (1824). In contrast to the linear narrative pattern of the capitalist vanguard, these works are centripetally structured around the woman's place of residence in the city. Where the capitalist vanguard desires to collect and possess the surrounding world, these women travelers strive to possess themselves and a "room of their own," while at the same time registering (to a higher degree than their male counterparts) the social and political realities of colonial life. These women's narratives enact the search for "self-realization and social harmony" (168); in fact, each constructs "feminotopias," idealized worlds of autonomy, empowerment, and pleasure for women. In reinventing America in their writings, these women were, in fact, reinventing themselves.

Pratt's focus on women travelers' personal liberation through their travel writing allies her with the work of the first generation of students of women's writing, as does her identification of gender-based differences in the meaning of and representation of the travels. An earlier generation of commentators saw in the travelers' personal growth and social awakening a transformative

force that changed their understanding of their place in their own culture, their subsequent actions, even their political and social attitudes. This tradition is continued by two of the books discussed here—Frawley and Melman. However, another school of contemporary scholars represents women travel writers as enmeshed in incompatible ideologies, not so much speaking of their experiences as being spoken by contradictory discourses.

Perhaps the most extreme version of the latter approach appears in Sara Mills's *Discourses of Difference.* Writing only about women who traveled to countries that were under British economic, religious, or political control (but mysteriously omitting India), Mills positions three Victorian women's texts in both colonial and discursive frameworks. Her thesis is that women's involvement with colonialism and their representations of that involvement differ from men's because of the pull of two discursive pressures: the power of patriarchy, "which acted upon them as middle-class women" and the power of colonialism, "which acted upon them in relation to the people in the countries they describe in their books." The "convergence and conflict of these two power systems . . . determines the style and content of women's travel writing" (180). By creating a deterministic, binary system, *Discourses of Difference* oversimplifies the complex range of discursive models which women travelers employed in their writings: for example, little attention is paid to literary discourse, or the discourses of science, ethnography, religion, and women's rights. The result is a cartoon-like flattening of texts along two dimensions only.

Like other commentators on women's travel writing, Mills looks for gender-based differences; her approach, however, is general and theoretical, not specific in its analysis of the effect of destination, mode of travel, or period of travel. Women's texts, she argues, share a sense of "personal involvement and relationships with" the people among whom they traveled and possess "less authoritarian" narrative stances than those of their male counterparts. Because of their indeterminate position between discourses, women travelers produce "counter-hegemonic voices" in their writings through humor, self-deprecation, statements of affiliation, and descriptions of relationships (22). "Whereas men could describe their travel as individuals and as representatives of the colonial power, women could only travel and write as gendered individuals with clearly delineated roles" (103). That reductive "only" points to the missing element in this analysis: an understanding of the dynamic forces that operate even within those gendered roles—the way, as Susan Blake shows in "A Woman's Trek: What Difference does Gender Make?" (*Western Women and Imperialism*), that race, gender, and class intersect and modify each other in women's travel writing.

Discourses of Difference proposes to study an important, under-investigated topic: the production and reception of women's travel writing. Relying on Foucault, it analyzes the constraints on the production of women's travel writing, sometimes covering old ground in a new theoretical wagon, sometimes discovering some unexplored patches. To find a voice to accommodate gender norms even when their behaviors challenged these, women travel writers employed both the conventions of colonial writing (the male adventure hero/protagonist, the construction of the colonized "other,") and the conventions of women's writing (eschewing topics that women were not allowed to talk about, employing the discourse of femininity in their focus on the personal and domestic). Within the framework of production and reception theory, Mills asks a set of useful questions: how did these texts manage to get published? why were they read? how were they were read? Unfortunately, the answers are not sought through close analysis of the institutions of reviewing, sales practices, negotiation with publishers, or women's attempts to market their works. Instead, Mills's text focuses on the way in which cultural assumptions about women's writing—particularly the autobiographical imperative, the distrust of women's veracity, and the concern with the exceptional nature of the woman traveler—shaped the reading of these works.

The second half of the book considers three "case studies"—Alexandra David-Neel, Mary Kingsley, and Nina Mazuchelli. The aim is to produce a "symptomatic reading" of one text by each of these writers in order to exhibit the contradictions inherent in the power relations within colonialist discourse and to demonstrate how any discursive position is called into question by other elements in the text. Autobiographical readings are shunned since a "coherent self, in textual terms, is impossible" (37). By focusing on the discursive frameworks, *Discourses of Difference* claims to present new ways of understanding the texts of women travel writers; instead it offers a kind of re-categorization of some familiar concepts about women's writing. Thus, David-Neel's *My Journey to Lhasa* (1827) is seen in terms of its reception by male critics as "exaggerated." The complex, wonderful, frustrating *Travels in West Africa* (1897) by Mary Kingsley becomes simply an example of the contradictory clashes of colonialism and feminine ideology—an ultimately unstable text that is *neither* fully colonial, nor feminine, nor feminist. Finally, Nina Mazuchelli's *The Indian Alps and How We Crossed Them* (1876) is seen to inscribe the discourses of femininity and colonialism, although the narrator's behavior transgresses the norms of female conduct; the text thus exemplifies "the clashes and reinforcements of these discourses" (194). The reader is left agreeing with the author's assessment of the results of her methodology: "The reading which is produced is more unwieldy . . . and ultimately it is more difficult to make generali-

zations about the text" (195). Perhaps the readings might have been less unwieldy if, instead of employing a binary model, Mills had developed a fuller sense of the "interdiscursiveness" of these texts, as articulated by Dave Morley: "Both the text and the subject are constituted in the space of the interdiscursive; and both are traversed and intersected by contradictory discourses—contradictions which arise not only from the subject positions which these different discourses propose, but also from the conjuncture and institutional site in which they are articulated and transformed" ("Texts, Readers, Subjects" 171).

A more sophisticated application of cultural studies theory to women's travel writing, one much closer to Morley's notion of the "interdiscursive," is Alison Blunt's *Travel, Gender, and Imperialism: Mary Kingsley and West Africa*. Like Mills, Blunt eschews "any realist claim to biographical authenticity and/or authority" in her investigation of the "subject positionality" of Mary Kingsley. Specifically, she examines the construction of Kingsley's subjectivity by herself and others along the lines of gender, race, class—at home and abroad (4). With great dexterity and a real appreciation of the fluidity of these discursive categories, *Travel, Gender, and Imperialism* examines the ways in which imperialism, the sex-gender system, the discourses of race and class produced both the texts of and the public persona of "Mary Kingsley."

In an opening discussion of travel as metaphor, Blunt examines a dynamic which underlies much of her analysis: "travel . . . involves the familiarization or domestication of the unfamiliar at the same time as the defamiliarization of the familiar or domestic" (19). It both offers and contains the possibility of transgression. Travel writing itself is the construction of spatial and textual difference; imperial travel writing, the instantiation of "mythological otherness" (30). By studying Kingsley, whose many personae were spatially and temporally distinct, this book proposes to "give voice to those marginalized by such totalizations while at the same time revealing their ambivalence rather than fixity" (37). Clearly, "ambivalence" is privileged by the post-modern critic much as irony and paradox were by the new critic.

Because of its specificity, its theoretical sophistication, and its willingness to admit that a private life exists and has some importance, however, Blunt's analysis is neither reductive nor tedious. For example, by focusing on Kingsley's "gendered subjectivity" both at home and abroad, Blunt is able to frame some of the puzzling doubleness of *Travels in West Africa* and *West African Studies* (1897). Kingsley's desire to participate in the masculine tradition of trade and exploration aligned her, it is argued, with imperial authority and its construction of racial difference; this conflicts with her feminine self-consciousness, which is a source of both personal and national identity. Blunt offers a provocative formulation to help explain the ambivalences in attitude and the shifting gender identities of Kingsley the traveler: "During travel racial superiority came to supersede gender inferiority" (105). As a result, Kingsley regarded African women with a privileged male gaze, feeling no special gender bond with them while she regarded African men in terms of race. Although this blanket statement over-simplifies Kingsley's complicated attitude toward African women, Blunt goes on to acknowledge "the tensions and contradictions" in Kingsley's writing that arose from the clash of gender-based self-conceptions (105). Kingsley was liberated by travel, Blunt argues, because she was able to "identify with imperial power and authority" while at the same time maintaining her sense of "otherness" through an intact gendered subjectivity.

In a sense the book's most valuable and original contributions appear in its final chapters, "Return: Reconstituting Home" and "Institutional Responses to Women Travel Writers." Here Kingsley's marginality as a woman is shown to undergird the reception of her travels, her writings, and her political activities. Using readers' responses found in reviews and obituaries, Blunt demonstrates how the identities that Kingsley constructed on her travels were reconstructed at home. The largely favorable reviews of *Travels In West Africa* focused on the novelty of the woman traveler and on her femininity—her clothes, the dangers she encountered, her eccentricity. The mixed critical reviews of the more scientific *West African Studies,* on the other hand, highlighted the work's "chatty" feminine style and the book's intellectual content—but not her political proposals. Kingsley's relationship to the institutions that shaped policy and regulated knowledge was marginal, yet through her voluminous private correspondence, often with other women, she established a position of public political influence without violating her allegiance to the lady's proper sphere.

Also greatly concerned with the woman traveler's construction of a professional identity at home is Maria Frawley's *A Wider Range: Travel Writing by Women in Victorian England.* This work undertakes the ambitious project of describing "the major forms of Victorian women's travel writing," of correlating those forms to geographical regions, and of demonstrating "how decisions about the travel account's form and the . . . choice of region relate finally to questions of and choices about professional identity" (36). The material is organized according to the intersection of geography (Italy, the Middle East, America) and the traveler's "mode" of self-presentation (the "adventuress" versus the art historian or the sociologist). The result is a hybrid structure in which the focus shifts from the range of writing produced *about* a region to individual women

writers who sought a specific professional identity through their travel writing. Thus the opening chapter on Italy as it was written by women travelers gives way to discussion of two women who made their reputations as writers about art history. America as a destination yields to a focus on women as sociologists; the chapter on the Middle East is essentially an examination of Harriet Martineau's and Frances Power Cobbe's attempts to write a kind of history in which the traveler is an active "witness" of the past who recreates it for her readers (138). The middle chapter is not destination-specific but mode-specific, for it considers "Victorian Adventuresses"—that is, any woman who traveled to remote, exotic locales.

Following a long line of feminist critics, Frawley argues that travel enabled women to "reimagine and rework" gender differences, simultaneously to maintain distance from and proximity to their home culture, to experiment with identities. More than this, travel gave them what Bourdieu called "symbolic capital" that empowered them to speak on social, intellectual, and political issues and to compete in the Victorian marketplace of ideas. *A Wider Range* offers some valuable new insights into the way that travel writing enabled women to construct professional identities and to garner cultural authority, although it does not fully examine the institutional barriers to their complete acceptance as professionals. Drawing on Tuchman and Fortin's sociological work on Victorian authorship in *Edging Women Out,* Frawley situates travel writing as a "mixed specialty," and thus a "politically expedient" form of writing for women who wanted to break into the "high prestige" areas of non-fictional scholarly and critical writing.

The strength of Frawley's method is evident in the first two chapters on Italy: "Into the Temple of Taste" and "The Professionalization of Taste: Art Historians Abroad." Positioning women's writing within the context of the hundreds of accounts of journeys to this cultural mecca, Frawley considers those which achieved the status of "cultural commodities," that is, those that were "published, reviewed, compared in the press to male-authored accounts" (47). The writings of Mary Shelley, Frances Trollope, Frances Elliott, and Vernon Lee provide evidence that women who wrote about Italy attempted to straddle the camps of tourist and traveler, combining the tourist's acts of obeisance to prescribed spots with the traveler's more personal engagement with lesser known attractions. (In the wake of James Buzard's masterful work on the evolution and cultural valences of these terms in *The Beaten Track,* one longs for a fuller discussion of the implications of the posture of "the tourist" or "the traveler" for women.) In the attempt to rise above the status of "mere tourist" to more professional heights, these travelers "introduced into their commentaries the problematic discourse so often linked . . . with the idea of middle-class women's work" (Frawley 51). Although tourism was permissible as a lady's leisure activity, writing about one's travels, especially from a position of authority or expertise, challenged the ideology of separate spheres. So women travel writers adopted strategies that enabled them to find "authentic" authorial positions without directly challenging cultural definitions of appropriate roles. In their search for an "authentic Italy," these women "discovered an uncultivated Italy, one offering more potential for vision" (70). In striking contrast to the writers on South America that Pratt discusses, these women de-materialized the country, describing a landscape divorced from the specifics of history and politics, "one perhaps more fanciful and, in a sense, more exotic that those of their male counterparts" (70).

A subgroup of the female writers on Italy used their experiences as travelers to cultivate "professional identities" as art historians, identities that ultimately subsumed their personae as travelers. Their works strained beyond the limits of traditional travel writing by blending travel, art history, and criticism. Focusing on the lives and works of Anna Jameson and Elizabeth Rigby Eastlake, Frawley charts the evolution of each woman's sense of "authenticity and authority," the gender ideologies that shaped their definitions of themselves, and, most interestingly, the development of a professional community of women in the arts in Victorian Britain. Jameson's work gives evidence of an evolving sense of herself as an art historian and a feminist; in fact Frawley privileges a reading of *The Diary of an Ennuyée* as a "primer for beginning art historians." Because of her feminism, Jameson was able to bridge the gap between her identities at home and abroad, to be both a professional and a woman. On the other hand, the influential Lady Eastlake began as a travel writer, moved into the world of male discourse in her essays for the *Quarterly Review,* and married into a position of privilege. In Frawley's estimate she struggled with the contradictory status of the woman writer, desiring to gain legitimacy for her intellectual work yet to remain within the appropriately female sphere. Her solution was to garner authority for her work by minimizing gender issues and foregrounding class. By making class the "ultimate determinant of authority," she was able to negotiate the tensions between being a proper lady and a woman art critic.

One of the most tantalizing aspects of this chapter is its reflection on the intellectual community among women art historians and the cultural role of the museum in women's lives. Travel was the entree to the world of art but the real making of the art historian, Frawley argues, happened at home in museums and through interaction with other intellectual women. The museum, though clearly a professional site for art historians, was also a socially acceptable venue for spending leisure time; a safe place in which women could negotiate the ideological contradictions of their social position. I would like to have seen a more consistent and complete discussion of the woman writer's attempt to locate herself within various personal and institutional spaces that would allow her to develop a professional identity—something along the lines of Billie Melman's discussion of Amelia Edwards's position in the academic disciplines of Egyptology and archaeology or Alison Blunt's analysis of Kingsley's ethnographic and political contributions.

In *A Wider Range* destination is seen to determine literary and professional destiny; thus, women who journeyed to remote locales, which they mythologised as repositories of "the primitive," are treated here as "Adventuresses" whose works manifest similar attitudes and similar narrative strategies. The argument falters here, possibly because of the range of kinds of writing and of locales grouped together—Africa, Patagonia, the South Seas, Egypt. As a group, Victorian adventuresses are said to draw on two powerful male models—the military man and the intrepid explorer—in constructing identities that express the "aggressive side of their national identity" and demonstrate through their physical adventures that they could compete with men (108). Frawley ignores the ironizing of the role of the great male adventurer in the works of several adventuresses. Somehow, the book's focus on women's attempt to construct professional identities based on travel experiences seems to slip in this chapter: Mary Kingsley's struggles to be taken seriously as an ethnographer and her extensive involvement with colonial politics are dismissed in one paragraph. No mention is made of Florence Dixie's role as a war correspondent or of her later attempt to influence the political fate of the Zulu nation.

Instead, Frawley dwells on the anomalous sexual position that the adventuress occupied on returning home. She argues, not completely convincingly in the light of Alison Blunt's work, that women travelers were presented by the press as aggressively sexualized and thus demonized figures. To deflect this response, they adopted strategies of accommodation by domesticating their adventures or by adopting the pose of the ethnographer gathering data. Lumping together a wide range of women's responses to indigenous peoples, Frawley argues that "adventuresses" inspected the "natives" from a distance as scientific specimens: "Representing the peoples she [sic] encountered as either radically different—or worse, entirely absent—allowed some women travelers to preserve contrasts that made traveling new, exciting, strange, and appealing" (124). Such a generalization is painfully inadequate in accounting for the complex emotional bond forged by Dixie and Kingsley with the African peoples or Lucie Duff Gordon with the Egyptians. Frawley goes on to argue that many adventuresses, like Kingsley, construct their identities in relation to Nature, "endow[ing] the landscape with the capacity for powerful feeling and expression that they wouldn't let themselves see in the natives" (125). Again this generalization seems to flatten out the complex literary strategies that women travelers employ in describing the landscape—strategies that arise from a range of ideologies. In the end all that can be asserted about these adventurous women is that they helped to redefine the market for learned works and "could not help but have influence on opinion at home" (130). This reader, at least, was left clamoring for more specific and nuanced analyses.

If Frawley's treatment of the "Victorian adventuress" is flawed because of its attempt to lump into one category women who traveled to a range of different locales, Billie Melman's *Women's Orients* concentrates on a single loosely defined, but nonetheless circumscribed geographical location, "the Orient." She surveys two centuries of women's writing about the region with an eye to the difference that gender made in women's relations to the Orient, in their mode of travel and of writing. So as to attend to the "plurality of voices and idioms, reflecting the proliferation . . . of experiences of individuals and groups, of gender and class" (315), Melman organizes the writings into genres: Harem Literature, which focuses on the domestic; Evangelical Ethnography, a new brand of vocational literature; and autobiographical travel narratives by individuals—Harriet Martineau, Amelia Edwards—and by that "orientalist couple," the Blunts. She alternates between chapters that locate "themes, key words, and formulaic representations" (21) in groups of writers and those that focus on individuals. This "prosopography" of women's travel writing places the travelers within their cultural and literary contexts. To do so, it surveys 187 travel accounts written by women, compiles biographies of 53% of the writers, analyzes the lives along various matrices, and investigates the literary conventions found in the writings.

Although this organization sometimes produces needless repetition from chapter to chapter, it also allows the author to cover in rich detail an array of fascinating topics and to attend to the *heteroglossia* that she encounters. As part of the strategy of domesticating the Orient, Melman argues, Victorian women travel writers surfeited readers with details of Oriental women's lives, dwelling particularly on their physical features, food, hygiene, costume (including the tropes of dress and undress), and their domestic and child care arrangements. These writers also desexualized the Orient. The veil, a symbol of women's sexual liberty for Augustan writers like Mary Wortley-Montagu and Elizabeth Craven, was figured by their Victorian successors as "a trope for female virtue and respectability" (11). Similarly, the harem was represented as a bourgeois home, not as a place of sexual license.

Unlike these secular travelers, the evangelical writers featured in the second section of *Women's Orients* represented the *haremlik* as a locus of impurity, the manifestation of a patriarchal construct. Unlike Frawley, who assumes that destination determines form and attitude, Melman documents how the ideological framework of the journey structures perception. She offers a detailed portrait of female missionaries to the Middle East, documenting their numbers, the range and kind of their activities, and the leitmotifs of their writings. Throughout she points to the importance of the evangelical construction of gender; by figuring the Christian home as the woman's sphere and womankind as inherently spiritual, the agent of moral reform, evangelicalism opened the way for women to assume the role of professional missionaries. Not surprisingly, these missionary writers domesticated Palestine and "feminized" the landscape by associating it specifically with "religious experiences that are perceived as generically female as well as with women's history as it is revealed in sacred texts" (193). In fiction and travel writing, evangelical women represented themselves as "mothers" to their Jewish "daughters" (Melman observes that Muslim women and their culture were invariably excluded from Evangelical writings). When they confronted the Middle Eastern landscape, they "tamed the exotically oriental, by locating landscape and people in a conceptual and ideological framework familiar to the Christian West" (219). Of special interest is the discussion of how pictorial imagery, particularly that derived from Holman Hunt's "The Scapegoat," and Biblical typology, particularly that derived from the Naomi-Ruth story, shaped verbal landscape painting in several of these travel works.

Like Maria Frawley, Melman in her final section examines the intersection of autobiography and professional authority in travel writing and the development of stylistic techniques to represent experience. Identifying Harriet Martineau's *Eastern Life* as "the first feminine travelogue proper [about the Middle East] that is not an account of a pilgrimage" (253), Melman attests to the shaping force of the autobiographical instinct and Martineau's "notion of history" (236). Rather tartly, Melman argues for the derivative nature of Martineau's ideas (particularly the influence of Unitarian Biblical interpretation, higher criticism, and the antiquarian *récits de voyage),* the influence of her ideology of history on her representation of landscape, and the role of her inflated self-esteem in shaping the narrative. Amelia Edwards, one of the first female "Orientalists" and the author of *A Thousand Miles Up the Nile* (1889), receives a more sympathetic treatment in a chapter that discusses the evolution of archaeology and Egyptology as disciplines, Edwards's intellectual and structural position in these developing fields, and her rhetorical strategies in representing Egypt. Defeminizing her traveler/narrator and distancing herself from the peoples of contemporary Egypt (particularly the women and children), the narrator of *A Thousand Miles* presents a detailed, "scientific" account of the archaeological riches of Egypt which attempts a photographic description of objects, in a style virtually devoid of metaphor. Particularly concerned with the status of Egyptian women in history, Edwards parallels their legal and social position to that of contemporary British women, aiming to evoke a "retrospectival envy" in her Victorian female audience.

Arguing that "domestic politics shaped the rhetoric of domesticity which characterizes the co-produced accounts of travel" (277), Melman turns her attention finally to the writings of "orientalist couples," particularly Anne and Wilfrid Blunt. In this case, the complex politics of the Blunt family encompassed the traditional rhetoric of female submission on Anne's part, the affirmation of separate spheres (in *Bedouin Tribes*, 1878, Anne described life in the desert, Wilfrid added the "serious" informative chapters at the end), and a growing dissonance between the two in religious beliefs. Having investigated the "primary sources" used in the construction of the narrative of *Pilgrimage to Nejd* (1881)—Anne's travel journals, Wilfrid's travel journals, and Anne's more private pocket diaries—Melman concludes that this volume, although "edited" by Wilfrid Blunt, is decidedly Anne's allegorical account of her spiritual pilgrimage. Unlike the narratives produced by the romantic male travelers who preceded her (Burton and Palgrave), Anne's travelogue creates a self-effacing narrative persona while affirming the order and design she finds in the landscape of central Arabia that they had found so "wild."

Women travelers' relationship to the people among whom they travel seems a particularly vexed question in these works: Alison Blunt argues that a traveler like Mary Kingsley distances herself from African women; however, Melman contends, despite the example of Amelia Edwards, that in general nineteenth-century women travelers to the Orient locate "the similarities between western and exotic familial structures . . . [and] note the sameness of womankind, regardless of culture, class or ethnicity" (309). Although she argues for the emergence of an empathetic connection between women travelers and Oriental peoples, Melman does admit that "cultural smugness and ethnocentrism" were also probable outcomes of such encounters, especially among liberal feminists or reformers.

The five books under consideration here concur that no single meta-narrative can account for women travelers' representations of the other or themselves; no single model can capture the complex encoding of experiences for diverse audiences. Moreover, despite wide differences in the theoretical frameworks which inform these texts, they share a surprising number of common concerns. For instance, all of them argue for a "difference" in women's writing, even though they disagree on its determining causes: women's position as gendered subjects? or their exclusion from professional authority? or the material conditions of their journeys? or their ability to experience empathy with the people among whom they travel? or their individual values and experiences? All of these critical works find manifestations of difference in women's writing, whether in narrative paradigms, descriptive conventions, the "gazes" they employ, or the "counter-hegemonic" voices they record. Several find "ambivalence" and instability at the heart of women's travel writing. All are interested in the cultural status of travel writing itself and the extent to which the writer's gender shaped the way that the text was consumed. Finally, even in the face of profound shifts in critical consciousness over the last decade, all of the critics except Sara Mills, still circle around the central feminist insight of the criticism of the 1980s: the ways in which the experience of travel both catalyzed and symbolized Victorian women's redefinition of their private selves and their social/professional personae.

Works Considered

Blunt, Alison. *Travel, Gender, and Imperialism: Mary Kingsley and West Africa.* New York and London: Guilford, 1994.

Buzard, James. *The Beaten Track: European Tourism, Literature, and the Ways to Culture, 1800-1918.* Oxford and New York: Clarendon, 1993.

Chaudhuri, Nupur and Margaret Strobel, eds. *Western Women and Imperialism: Complicity and Resistance.* Bloomington and Indianapolis: Indiana UP, 1992.

Frawley, Maria H. *A Wider Range: Travel Writing by Women in Victorian England.* London and Toronto: Associated University Presses, 1994.

Melman, Billie. *Women's Orients: English Women and the Middle East, 1718-1918.* Ann Arbor, Michigan: U of Michigan P, 1992.

Mills, Sara. *Discourses of Difference: An Analysis of Women's Travel Writing and Colonialism.* London and New York: Routledge, 1991.

Morley, Dave. "Texts, Readers, Subjects." *Culture, Media, Language.* Ed. Stuart Hall, Dorothy Hobson, Andrew Lowe and Paul Willis. London: Unwin Hyman, 1980. 163-176.

Pratt, Mary Louise. *Imperial Eyes: Travel Writing and Transculturation.* London and New York: Routledge, 1992.

Linda Ledford-Miller (essay date 2004)

SOURCE: Ledford-Miller, Linda. "A Protestant Critique of Catholicism: Frances Calderón de la Barca in Nineteenth-Century Mexico." In *Gender, Genre, and Identity in Women's Travel Writing,* edited by Kristi Siegel, pp. 225-33. New York: Peter Lang, 2004.

[*In the following essay, Ledford-Miller interprets Frances Calderón de la Barca's criticism of Catholic traditions and practices in Mexico as an expression of the author's "desire for social justice for Mexican women."*]

Frances Calderón de la Barca's *Life in Mexico during a Residence of Two Years in That Country,* based on a series of letters home from 1839 to 1842, was published in 1843 to general acclaim in the United States and Britain. In Mexico, however, Calderón's work gave rise to concerns that her ambassador husband, who may have had access to state secrets, may have provided information or otherwise assisted his wife. The first four letters were published in Spanish over a period of four weeks in the *Siglo Diez y Nueve* [*The Nineteenth Century*] newspaper. The fourth letter, somewhat critical of Veracruz, elicited complaints that, combined with the contents of the fifth letter, which touched on General Santa Ana, then president and *de facto* dictator of Mexico, put an end to the planned serialization of her letters. Not until 1920 was a complete Spanish translation published.[1] In this century *La vida en México* (*Life in Mexico*) was considered "el mejor libro sobre México que haya escrito un extranjero" ("the best book on Mexico written by a foreigner") (Appendini 8; this and subsequent translations are mine).

Calderón's letters describe her travels to and within Mexico, giving many details of her daily life and the lives of those around her, especially women. She witnesses two small uprisings, the chaos of the copper monetary crisis, and a change of president, among other momentous events. However, it is her deep interest in women, convents, churches, and religious practice that we will investigate in this essay, focusing particularly on Calderón's outsider (Protestant) observations of insider (Catholic) religious practice, and her critique of such practices as instances of a desire for social justice for Mexican women.

Frances Calderón de la Barca was the Scottish-born American wife of Angel Calderón de la Barca, Spain's first envoy to Mexico after it had won its independence from Spain in 1821. Frances Erskine Inglis was born in Edinburgh in 1804, but she moved to Boston with her mother and sisters in 1831, where they established a school for girls. They relocated to Staten Island in 1835 and opened another girls' school. It was in New York

that she met her future husband. Fifteen years her senior, Calderón was born in 1790 in Buenos Aires, then a colony of Spain.

He was educated in England, had been a prisoner of war of the French, had served diplomatic missions in Germany and Russia, and was the Spanish minister to the United States under President Martin Van Buren when he and Fanny met. She was a confirmed Protestant; he was Catholic. They were married in the Church of the Transfiguration in New York by Father Felix Varela y Morales, a Cuban-born Catholic priest (Wood 47; Fisher and Fisher xxv). Molly Marie Wood notes that

> Upon marrying Calderón, Fanny was educated in Catholic doctrine, perhaps by Father Varela himself. She knew the terminology, memorized the prayers and attended Catholic mass in the United States. In preparation for her journey to Mexico, she read the history of the Church in Latin America and saw pictures of the splendid cathedrals. After all, she knew that she would be expected to "act Catholic" for diplomatic reasons . . . No amount of preparation, however, could transform her naive, romantic and aesthetic view of the Church into the real Church she encountered in Mexico.
>
> (48)

Indeed Calderón does "act Catholic": She attends many masses, chats with many priests, bishops, and even the Archbishop; she witnesses many processions, participates in the *posadas* and, due to her status as wife of the Spanish ambassador, and her condition as outsider, visits monasteries and convents closed to most Mexicans. Indeed, in a letter to William Hickling Prescott, Calderón comments that, because her husband is not considered a foreigner, she is "intimate" with Mexican society and has received permission from the Archbishop to visit convents, "which is never permitted" (Prescott letter from Calderón dated June 5, 1840, 128-29).

While at mass, her commentaries on churches and cathedrals tend to focus on two main topics: the beauty and wealth of the church and its images—whether the color and richness of statues of saints or the vivid purple robes of priests in procession; and the class or status of those worshipers in attendance. For example, Calderón recounts her visit to the cathedral of Our Lady of Guadalupe, contrasting the colonial church with the Temple of Tonantzin, the mild goddess of earth and corn worshipped by the Aztecs, upon which the cathedral was superimposed (85). She marvels at the quantity of silver in the rich edifice, and the quantity of beggars, unwashed lepers who beg by appealing to religious or domestic sentiment, or perhaps to superstition, calling on potential benefactors "por el amor de la Santisima Virgin!" ("for the love of the Most Sacred

Virgin"). They appeal to men "by the life of the Señorita," to women "by the life of the little child!" and to children "by the life of your mother!" (87).

At New Year's mass in the church of San Francisco, one of the cleanest in Mexico and "most frequented by the better classes," she again comments on the presence of lepers and beggars, as well as Indians (306). Though in the San Francisco you may find yourself between two well-to-do women, you might also find yourself next to "a beggar with a blanket," or an Indian woman with her baby in tow and a basket of vegetables on her head (306-7). As a result of the excessive dirtiness of the Mexican churches and the constant presence of the lepers and other (unclean) beggars who frequent them, "the principal families" frequently have their own private oratorios and contract the services of a priest for private masses at home (308).

Calderón's preoccupation with the uncleanliness of Mexican churches may elicit our sympathy when we discover that "men may sit on chairs or benches in church, but women must kneel or sit on the ground. Why? *Quien sabe* (who knows) is all the satisfaction I have ever obtained on that point" (147, original emphasis). During the very special ceremony confirming an Archbishop, Calderón complains that she "had the pleasure of kneeling beside these illustrious persons for the space of three or four hours," because no seating was provided for the wives of cabinet members or diplomats (190). Blessed by gender, the men sit comfortably; undone by gender, the women kneel at their men's feet.

During the period of *desagravios,* or public penance in which all Mexicans participate, according to Calderón, she observes the women at their morning penitence. It is 6 a.m., and no men are allowed to enter the church; in contrast, Calderón sees women doing their penance by kneeling with their arms extended in front of them in the shape of a cross, groaning with discomfort after about ten minutes of maintaining the uncomfortable pose (275).

However, the men's penitence is a much more peculiar scene, and one Calderón is able to witness due only to admission having been arranged "by certain means, *private but powerful,*" probably referring to the Archbishop (275, original emphasis). She and an anonymous female companion cloak themselves completely and go after dark to the church of San Agustin, where they look down upon about one hundred fifty men similarly cloaked and made anonymous. After the priest's homily on the torments of hell awaiting unrepentant sinners, the church suddenly goes dark and a voice calls out, "My brothers! When Christ was fastened to the pillar by the Jews, he was *scourged!*" (276, original emphasis).

To Calderón's horror, she then hears "the sound of hundreds of scourges descending upon the bare flesh . . . Before ten minutes had passed, the sound became *splashing,* from the blood that was flowing" (276, original emphasis). The scourging, sometimes done with scourges of iron designed with sharp points to pierce the flesh, continues for half an hour. Calderón finds it "sickening" and says, "had I not been able to take hold of the Señora——'s hand, and feel something human beside me, I could have fancied myself transported into a congregation of evil spirits" (276). Thus, the very act designed to drive out evil, an act of penance and repentance for one's sins, seems to her evil. We might notice as well that, although Calderón seldom names names in her text, she usually follows the convention of supplying the first and last letter of the surname. Here, however, her companion has only gender to identify her, which suggests the need for the utmost secrecy and discretion due to the improper nature of their visit.

Though laywomen did not scourge themselves, Calderón discovers that the nuns of Santa Teresa do. On a visit to that convent she sees a crown of thorns worn on certain days by one among the nuns. Similarly to the scourges she witnessed at St. Agustin, this crown is made of iron with sharp points directed toward the head, causing the wearer to suffer cuts and bleeding from the wounds made by wearing the crown (285). In the individual cells she notices instruments designed for self-inflicted torture, such as an iron band with sharpened points to wear around the waist, a cross with iron nails to enter the flesh, and a scourge like those of St. Agustin, covered with iron nails designed to wound the flesh (286). She notes that most of the nuns look happy enough, if pale, but closes with this telling comment: "[I]f any human being can ever leave this world without a feeling of regret, it must be a nun of Santa Teresa" (287).

We find a less gruesome critique of Catholic practice in Calderón's reflections after attending the *honras* of the daughter of the Marquis de S—a, or the mass for the repose of her soul, for which every possible expense was lavished.

> If this Catholic doctrine be firmly believed, and . . . the prayers of the Church are indeed availing to shorten the sufferings of those who have gone before us; to relieve those whom we love from thousands of years of torture, it is astonishing how the rich do not become poor, and the poor beggars, in furtherance of this object, and . . . if the idea be purely human, it showed a wonderful knowledge of human nature, on the part of the inventor, as what source of profit could be more sure?
>
> (110-11)

Such comments represent a typically Protestant view of purgatory and the practice of paying for prayers and masses to shorten the stay, or of "buying" God's influence, from the Protestant perspective. However, Calderón goes on to describe the elegance and richness of the ceremony, demonstrating once again her own divided reactions to the mysteries of Mexican Catholicism.

Her inner conflict is manifest to some extent even among her harshest and most direct criticisms of insider religious practice. She visits a number of convents and admires them for their fine gardens and the art they contain. (In fact, convents and monasteries were often the repositories of great works of art, particularly of paintings.) She develops a close friendship with a woman who is happily a nun. In a letter to Prescott she describes the ignorance of Mexican women as *"total,"* and suggests that sheer boredom may lead them to the convent. "They are very amiable and good natured, but I do not wonder that so many become nuns, as I think they amuse themselves quite as well in a convent as at home" (Prescott, letter from Calderón dated June 5, 1840, 128). Nevertheless, Calderón is frankly appalled by what she considers the sacrifice of young girls to the convent veil.

The convent Encarnación she says is the richest and finest in Mexico, with the possible exception of the Concepción (151). In fact, it is "a palace" where each nun has at least one servant, and some have more, for the Encarnación is not as strict as some of the other orders (153). She adds that each novice pays five thousand dollars to the convent when she enters, a fantastic sum in those years, and that pride seems to be the prevailing sin of Encarnación's wealthy nuns (153). Even here, in the gilded cage, her sympathies lie with the novices, whom she calls "poor little entrapped things!" who falsely believe that they can leave the convent at the end of the year if they should tire of the convent life. However, Calderón intimates that the novices will never be allowed to tire, never be permitted to leave (153).

Calderón witnesses the taking of the veil by three different nuns-to-be, and considers it "next to death . . . the saddest event that can occur in this nether sphere" (199). Indeed, her descriptions everywhere suggest death. One young woman embraces the nuns of her order, whom Calderón calls "dark phantoms" who "seem like the dead welcoming a new arrival to the shades" (204). At another convent entry, the young girl is "consigned . . . to a living tomb" upon entering the convent under the influence of her confessor and with her father's consent, but against her mother's will, and we recognize the powerlessness of the mother, of women, in the face of male power.

Though Calderón makes much of the strength and depth of family bonds among Mexicans, she reveals that these bonds are torn asunder when families give their daugh-

ters to convents, for they will never see them again, nor embrace them, nor will the nuns ever leave the convent, even for the death of a mother. Nevertheless, she says, "the frequency of these human sacrifices here is not so strange as might first appear" (199). Of course "here" is the foreign and Catholic Mexico, not, by implication, the "there" of sensible Protestant homes in the United States.

Why are such sacrifices so common, we wonder? Calderón believes that religion and romanticism, in combination with the status of women and girls, make the convent an attractive option. According to Calderón's observations, young Mexican girls of the upper class have little instruction beyond piano and embroidery lessons. They must remain at home, without the freedom to walk alone or even with others of their age and station, with little to occupy or interest them. The Mexican girl who "from childhood is under the dominion of her confessor, and who firmly believes that by entering a convent she becomes sure of heaven" and who, furthermore, finds the pageantry of the ceremony irresistible, with its costumes, dresses, and candles, and knows the attention of the world will focus on her, may indeed decide to take such a momentous step. Further, once taken, there is no going back. The actress cannot abandon the stage in mid-act, after all. In fact, Calderón does suggest the church-as-theater, as the guests take their seats and "the *second act* begins" (204, original emphasis). Furthermore, the girls hold it as an essential point of propriety and honor to demonstrate cheerfulness and gaiety,

> demonstrating the same feeling . . . which induces the gallant highwayman to jest in the presence of the multitude when the hangman's cord is within an inch of his neck . . . which makes the gallant general whose life is forfeited, command his men to fire on him; the same which makes the Hindoo [sic—meaning "Hindu"] widow mount the funeral pile without a tear in her eye, or a sigh on her lips. If the robber were to be strangled in a corner of his dungeon; if the general were to be put to death privately in his own apartment; if the widow were to be burnt quietly on her own hearth; if the nun were to be secretly smuggled in the convent gate like a bale of contraband goods,—we might hear another tale.
>
> (203)

Once again, metaphors of death and imprisonment abound. Calderón is clearly opposed to getting the daughters of Mexico to a nunnery. She just as clearly finds their education inadequate and their socialization insufficient, as we noted above. Although she describes the pomp and circumstance of the ceremonies with a journalist's lively eye, she sees no justice for women in the events and influences that lead them to take the veil.

In fact, Calderón's deep interest in convents and nuns may stem from the "loss" of her sister Jane, who converted to Catholicism and herself took the veil of a nun, living in a convent in France (Fisher 713, note 6). Jane was only fourteen months Fanny's senior, so Jane's "defection" from a solidly Scottish Protestant family must have marked Calderón deeply (Wood 49). Nevertheless, her ambivalence about the Church in Mexico is evident in the back-and-forth of criticism and praise throughout her letters. Although she critiques the Archbishop for the comfort in which he lives, she compliments the kindness of the parish priest. She expresses horror at the "sacrifice" of young girls to the convent veil, while maintaining a close friendship with a nun in the convent of Santa Teresa, the very convent whose masochistic practices so horrify her (Calderón 199). Though she observes Catholic religious practices as an outsider, she acts out the rituals of the Church, genuflecting and making the sign of the cross alongside her Mexican colleagues (Fisher 121). Moreover, she does comment on the beauty and mystery of the Church as a force for the subordination of the people (Wood 86), but also as a source of community. Indeed, perhaps the ambiguity of her responses, or the divided self manifest in them, is the first indication of the transformation she must have been slowly undergoing. The divided self became one, the outsider became the insider, when Calderón herself converted to Catholicism on May 10, 1847, at the Holy Trinity Church in Georgetown, Washington, D.C. There is some evidence that Calderón wished to alter, or at least temper, some of the criticisms in her letters. In a visit to her family in 1848, she apparently made marginal notes in an edition of the *Letters* at the family home, softening her earlier harsh words. Her younger sister Lydia, who also converted to Catholicism and, like her sister Fanny, later settled in Spain, wished to bring out a new, softened edition after her sister's death (Wood 90-91). That edition was never released, so we do not know how Calderón's outsider (Protestant) observations of insider (Catholic) religious practice might have been altered as a consequence of her conversion to Catholicism and, thus, to the belated, or retroactive, insider status. Nonetheless, we must agree with Prescott's comment that "none but a Spaniard or the wife of a Spaniard could have had such opportunities for observation, and no one less acquainted with the language of the country could have so well profited by them" (Prescott, Letter to Charles Dickens dated December 1842, 329).

Unlike most women's travel narratives of the period, which tend to focus on picturesque descriptions of peoples and landscapes and the details of domestic life, particularly in relation to a dominant male figure of husband or father (Helen Sanborn's *A Winter in Central America and Mexico*, 1886, for example), Calderón's *Life in Mexico* transgresses the boundaries of women's writing. Not content to receive Mexican society women in her home on calling days, or to sit quietly doing needlepoint, Calderón plays a quasi-masculine role as an adventurer. Though her husband's diplomatic status

and the Mexican view of him as not really a foreigner may have provided the needed entrée to proscribed areas, it is Fanny Calderón who enters and describes those areas. Fanny Calderón's *Life in Mexico* blends the male perspective of public life with the female perspective of domestic, or private life (Leask 187). Her convent visits fuse the private lives of nuns with the public practice of the Catholic religion, concomitantly demonstrating the private (female) price that women and girls pay to satisfy public (male) expectations.

Note

1. For a history of the book's publication and reception in the United States, Britain, and Mexico, see Ledford-Miller, "Fanny Calderón de la Barca" and "First Appearance of *Life in Mexico*; Early Comments; Subsequent History," in Fisher and Fisher 629-36. Though Fisher and Fisher's 1966 edition of *Life in Mexico* presents the letters with "new material from the author's private journals," and offers extensive endnotes and annotations, for purposes of this essay we use the 1982 Berkeley edition, which is essentially a facsimile of the original 1843 edition.

Works Cited

Calderón de la Barca, Frances. *Life in Mexico*. Berkeley, CA: U of California P, 1982.

———. *Life in Mexico during a residence of two years in that country*. London: Chapman and Hall, 1843.

Fisher, Howard T., and Marion Hall Fisher. Introduction and "First Appearance of Life in Mexico; Early Comments; Subsequent History." *Life in Mexico: The Letters of Fanny Calderón de la Barca*. Garden City, NY: Doubleday, 1966. xxi-xxix, 629-36.

Leask, Nigel. "'The Ghost in Chapultepec': Fanny Calderón de la Barca, William Prescott and Nineteenth-Century Mexican Travel Accounts." *Voyages and Visions: Towards a Cultural History of Travel*. Eds. Jás Elsner and Joan-Pau Rubiés. London: Reaktion Books, 1999. 184-209.

Ledford-Miller, Linda. "Fanny Calderón de la Barca." *Dictionary of Literary Biography. American Travel Writers, 1777-1864*. Detroit: Bruccoli Clark Layman, 1997. 43-47.

Prescott, William Hickling. *The Correspondence of William Hickling Prescott, 1833-1847*. Transcribed and edited by Roger Wolcott. Boston and New York: Houghton Mifflin Co., 1925.

Sanborn, Helen. *A Winter in Central America and Mexico*. Boston: Lee and Shepherd, 1886.

Wood, Molly Marie. *A Search for Identity: Frances Calderón de la Barca and "Life in Mexico."* Master's Thesis, U of Richmond, 1992.

Kristin Fitzpatrick (essay date 2004)

SOURCE: Fitzpatrick, Kristin. "American National Identity Abroad: The Travels of Nancy Prince." In *Gender, Genre, and Identity in Women's Travel Writing,* edited by Kristi Siegel, pp. 263-91. New York: Peter Lang, 2004.

[*In the following essay, Fitzpatrick explores how Nancy Gardner Prince utilized the travel narrative to denounce racism and raise awareness abroad of the evils of slavery in the United States.*]

> Ships at a distance have every man's wish on board. For some they come in with the tide. For others they sail forever on the horizon, never landing until the Watcher turns his eyes away in resignation, his dreams mocked to death by Time. That is the life of man.
>
> Now, women forget all those things they don't want to remember, and remember everything they don't want to forget. The dream is the truth. Then they act and do things accordingly.
>
> —Zora Neale Hurston, *Their Eyes Were Watching God*

Travel literature has traditionally been the domain of every man's wish, its texts freighted with promise moving across distant horizons. The opening lines of *Their Eyes Were Watching God* rewrite Frederick Douglass's *Narrative of the Life of Frederick Douglass, an American Slave,* where he stands on the shores of the Chesapeake Bay and longs to flee on the white-winged ships thronging the horizon (Gates 3). Zora Neale Hurston uses the horizon to reconfigure the relations between home and abroad, men and women (1). By writing in reference to an already established African American tradition of letters, Hurston complicates the whiteness of American national identity and situates at its heart what Toni Morrison calls an "unsettled and unsettling population" against which American literature and nationality define themselves (6). In speaking of her project to explore Americanness, Morrison opens with metaphors of travel and charting the New World "without the mandate for conquest" (3). Her writing, like Hurston's, has a topographical dimension that carries encoded within it movement across the middle passage and the conceptualization of identity as lost and rewoven in the movement shuttling between points, with the beyond, both a threat and a promise. She and Hurston cast the relationship between national and personal identity as one of individual to horizon, and, indeed, America has historically been formed at the crossroads of traveling cultures, many of them moving in order to escape oppression. The country is a nation of travelers, willing and unwilling, who unsettle American conceptions of self. However, most tales of travel handed down to us are the accounts predominantly of Anglo-American men. Gender and travel intersect in Hurston's rewriting of Douglass, where women and men's different relationships to the horizon throw "home" and traditional gender roles into question.

Travel literature makes a project of difference. Nations, as well as individuals, define themselves comparatively against that which they are not. If countries are, as Benedict Anderson has proposed, imagined communities, then they need to tell themselves and the international community coherent tales about themselves. Travelogues thus reaffirm or question the integrity of national identity. In nineteenth-century America, the spate of publications by women about overseas voyages allowed women to engage issues of nationalism indirectly. However, women—particularly women of color—often betrayed ambivalence toward their country, which did not grant them full access to all rights of citizenship. African American women in particular were painfully aware of these inequities at home. Considerable attention has focused on writings by Anglo-American and European women abroad, mainly because few women of color had the financial resources—or the physical liberty—to travel and publish. However, while we have access to few travel narratives by women of color, we need to explore them for the ways in which they can unsettle established conventions of travel literature and our understanding of American nationalism then and now.

Nancy Gardner Prince, one of the best traveled American women of her time, wrote the first travel narrative by an African American woman. On April 14, 1824, Prince left the United States for Russia, where she lived for nine years, married to a footman in the court of the Czar. Seven years later, inspired by the British Assembly's emancipation of former slaves in the West Indies, she traveled to Jamaica, where she witnessed the jubilation and turmoil in the aftermath of colonialism. Prince lectured on and published her travels in order to raise consciousness about racism and to support herself. On March 8, 1839, the antislavery newspaper *Liberator* carried a small notice announcing a lecture by her on Russia. She later wrote a pamphlet on Jamaica (1841) and finally combined her accounts of Russia and Jamaica in *Narrative of the Life and Travels, of Mrs. Nancy Prince,* which was first published in 1850, followed by an expanded edition in 1852, and released in a third and final edition in 1856. The edition cited here was published as *A Black Woman's Odyssey through Russia and Jamaica* (1990) with an introduction by Ronald G. Walters.

Prince's narrative raises the challenges African American women faced when writing themselves as American subjects in the predominantly white, male genre of travel. Travel literature requires the American national abroad to anchor the narrative with a clear sense of his or her own identity as an American. This proved to be doubly complicated for black women travelers writing within a genre largely dominated by white, male writers. How to claim the narrative "I," when it wasn't clear who the "I" was in terms of a nationality predicated on masculinity and whiteness? How to write within a genre that essentially demanded allegiance to these women's oppressors?

Without female literary antecedents in the field of travel, Prince drew on two particular genres, the spiritual narrative and slave narrative that allowed black, self-educated women to claim the traditionally male prerogatives of literacy and movement. Nineteenth-century women were not expected to articulate themselves publicly, much less raise voice to criticize their circumstances. They suffered a lack of authorial legitimacy, and black women doubly so. However, as critics such as Frances Smith Foster (*Written by Herself*), Hazel Carby ("Hear My Voice, Ye Careless Daughters"), and Joanne Braxton (*Black Women Writing Autobiography*) argue, slave narratives provided black women with an already established genre devoted to explicating and condemning exploitation. As William Andrews (*Sisters of the Spirit*), Joanne Braxton, and Joycelyn Moody ("On the Road with God") point out, first-person spiritual narratives, often written by itinerant women preachers, validated the mobile female voice and justified women claiming authority for themselves. Critics have generally discussed Prince's *Narrative* in the context of these genres because she draws very strongly on them to criticize slavery and colonialism. However, in doing so, critics have focused on only part of Prince's work, the sections on Jamaica and the United States, while ignoring the opening in Russia. Prince's stay in Russia indeed appears remarkably unremarkable and reads like any other nineteenth-century travelogue. Including Russia, however, and tracing the whole trajectory of the *Narrative* through Russia, Jamaica, and the United States allows us to investigate Prince as a writer at the roots of African American travel literature, one whose writing had consequences for later travelogues by black Americans.

Travel allowed black writers like Prince to create an international standpoint from which to criticize the United States. Extensive travel urged readers to see the black writer as "truly a world citizen whose knowledge extends beyond American scenes of poverty, beyond America and beyond Europe" (Martin 64). Such a writer tried "to establish credibility for the international black mind, important not for its color, but for its sensitivity and reach" (64). By portraying themselves as "world citizens," black American travelers like Prince challenged nineteenth-century America's refusal to accord them citizenship. African Americans who found respect on the other side of the Atlantic put the United States in the unsavory position of supporting an internationally condemned institution, which is the strategy Prince subtly follows by contrasting the equitable treatment she receives in Russia and the West Indies with continued slavery in the States.

Her return to the United States by way of the South is often seen by critics simply as extending her criticism of slavery to the United States; what is striking, however, is the sense in the conclusion that she is not returning home but entering another foreign country more hostile than any other she has visited. With legal actions like the Fugitive Slave Act (1850) and the Dred Scott Case (1857), the United States effectively framed all black residents as, at best, legal aliens, and we sense that in Prince's homecoming, which really highlights the absence of a home for black Americans at this time. However, this meaning only becomes apparent by recasting Prince's writing as a travel narrative and tracing the tensions that arise between home and horizon in her narrative. As Prince shuttles between the United States and abroad, she uses geography to triangulate who she is as a black American, woman, and American. By looking at the tensions among these identities in her narrative, we can develop some understanding of how gender, ethnicity, and nationality mesh to form a national identity.

Prince's narrative falls in three parts, moving through Russia, Jamaica, and back to the United States. Before beginning with Russia, however, it is worth exploring her motive for leaving the United States in the first place and how she frames her departure, because these things reveal the strategies she uses to establish authorial legitimacy vital to the narrative. Prince's foremost concern is to establish authorial legitimacy as a black American and as a woman. As a black American, she initially subordinates her skin color to nationality by detailing her family's long historical roots in the United States and expressing her deep loyalty to her country. This opening genealogy, while standard for autobiographical narratives, also documents her family's American nationality and secures her audience's trust in her as an American. Thus, her hardships cannot be brushed off as individual but rather become national difficulties. Consequently, when Prince finally does admit that she decided to leave the United States, because seven years of providing for her siblings and fighting racial prejudice had worn her out, her departure obliquely criticizes the nation and makes racial prejudice a national rather than a personal burden.

Prince's desire to leave is not only motivated by discrimination, but, she says, by a determination to do something for herself. However, it is not until her marriage to Nero Prince, one of twenty black foreigners serving in Alexander's court, that she leaves the United States. Her relationship with "Mr. Prince," as she insists on calling him throughout, seems simply to fill the narrative function of lending propriety to her movements abroad. Mr. Prince is never referred to outside his capacity as a husband, and the marriage is conflated with Nancy's desire to leave and subsequent departure. Her most intimate remarks on the subject are merely that "after seven years of anxiety and toil, I made up my mind to leave my country. September 1st, 1823, Mr. Prince arrived from Russia. February 15th, 1824, we were married. April 14th, we embarked on board the Romulus, captain Epes Sargent commander, bound for Russia" (15). We hear little more about Nero Prince, except that he was born in Marlborough, met Nancy at her mother's in-between trips in 1810 and 1812 to St. Petersburg (16), served Princess Purtossof in the Czar's court (17), and died before he could follow her back to the United States (45). Curiously, she doesn't tell us that he was also a prominent citizen in the United States, where he was elected the second grand master of the African Grand Lodge of the Masons, which he had organized and helped found in 1791 (Blakely 15). While Prince's reticence about their relationship is not unusual by nineteenth-century standards, the way in which she articulates her marriage is clearly a perfunctory nod to conventions demanding that women not travel alone. The marriage, along with her conversion to Christianity at age sixteen, and insistent propriety (she doesn't drink, dance, or gamble, even at the Russian court), set her up as a decent Christian woman whose veracity—and, by extension, that of her narrative—can be trusted.

Most importantly for narrative credibility, where the reader might expect a self-educated black woman to have limited powers of perception or stock of cultural knowledge, Prince commands a cultural mastery that rivals any other nineteenth-century traveler. While in Russia, Prince learns Sclavonian and Polish, languages of the common Russians, as well as modern Greek and French, languages of the nobility—all in the space of six months, she tells us. She writes extensive histories of the areas she visits, not only giving factual information but using the past to explain present developments. In St. Petersburg, she traces the origins of the 1825 Decembrist Revolt back to 1814, when German and Russian nobility united in the hopes of establishing a republican government, details Russia's wars with Turkey and Poland, and explains the origins of the 1831 cholera epidemic. In Jamaica and the West Indies, she shows how extant political chaos, corruption, and racial tensions were the legacy of colonialism and slavery, not proof of blacks' inherent inability to govern themselves, as many tried to argue in the United States. By working her great command of history, languages, and politics into the narrative, Prince proves her intellectual equality and demands membership in Europe and America as an equal. Due to the limited number of publications by black female contemporaries, Prince must have been aware that anything she wrote could have been seen as representative of black American women in their entirety. If, as Edward Said theorizes, cultural access also provides entrance to political communities, then literacy becomes a passport to citizenship, and Prince was literally writing herself and others into the American citizenship still denied them at that time.

The rhetorical strategies Prince uses to legitimize her narrative are set up in the section on Russia, a country seemingly free of racism. Critics have generally passed over Prince's writing on Russia because it makes little direct mention of racism, but this issue needs to be addressed precisely because the quiet acceptance Prince encounters in Russia contrasts strongly with the racially charged atmosphere in the United States and Jamaica, where such normative relations are impossible. Russia functions as an exemplar of racial tolerance in Prince's text: By the time she arrived, slavery had been outlawed in Russia since the previous century, and there were many blacks who had obtained high social and professional status, both inside the court and in Russian society at large. Along with her husband, Prince was invited to court social gatherings, accepted orders from the Empress and ladies of the court for her needlework and children's clothing, and was active in a local church. She writes that upon arrival, Emperor Alexander and Empress Elizabeth presented her with a watch and other gifts. There "was no prejudice against color; there were all casts, and the people of all nations, each in their place" (17-18). Her strategic comment on the lack of prejudice in Russia's highest institution implies that a country's racial divisiveness or tolerance flows from its highest governing seats. She insinuates that American racism is effectively condoned by its government, for if czarist Russia is enlightened enough to accept all colors, casts, and nations, surely the republican, democratic United States can do the same. As Hazel Carby notes, Prince continues to criticize the United States throughout her narrative by using indirect international parallels (60). This tactic proves particularly effective, because it avoids directly undermining the American nationalism that she draws upon to enlist her reader's empathy and trust, and yet it does shame the United States through comparison with other countries.

This international perspective also allows Prince to analyze the mechanics of oppression and theorize ways in which power operates across national, ethnic, and gender lines. Prince was one of the first black Americans to use international analysis to criticize imperialism in Jamaica and, by extension, the United States, which Prince showed as an imperial power with oppression at its foundation. While the United States tried to cast slavery as a purely internal matter, Prince's international analysis of colonialism argues otherwise. Her analysis begins, oddly enough, in Russia, where she criticizes slavery by comparing it with exploitation of the serfs: "This class of people till the land, most of them are slaves and are very degraded. The rich own the poor, but they are not suffered to separate families or sell them off the soil" (30). Her international comparison reminds readers that exploitation is not limited to a particular country. The comparison also denies biological essentialism as the grounds for American slavery: The serfs are suffering due to an imbalance of power, not to the color of their skins. Shared race does not undermine Prince's critique, as initially might seem to be the case, but becomes central to it by deessentializing American slavery. This example foreshadows Prince's much more direct attack on slavery in the next section on Jamaica, where she analyzes the wages of colonialism in the aftermath of British rule.

Prince returned home from Russia in 1833 due to failing health, unable to tolerate another Russian winter. Her husband planned to follow after a couple years but died before returning to the United States. Prince involved herself in social work and the Anti-Slavery Society, and later that year, inspired by British manumission freeing the slaves in the West Indies, she resolved to go to Jamaica. Her purpose was to aid the black community in its transition to self-government, but when she arrived in Jamaica after a harrowing voyage plagued by storms and pirates, she was appalled at the extent of colonialism's legacy. Whites still controlled the government and resources, missionaries exhorted money where they could, and sharecropping kept black Jamaicans in perpetual slavery. Racial tension was extremely high, with former slave owners destroying relinquished property and putting down celebrations with force, and blacks paying back white cruelty in turn. For example, Prince relates that the Maroons, former slaves who arrived from Sierra Leone in 1841 and now controlled Jamaica's mountainous areas, trapped whites crossing the passes. The Maroons killed their prisoners or returned in kind the cruelty they had suffered as slaves (60). Ironically, in the years following Prince's visit, the Maroons were hired by whites to hunt down black Jamaicans.

Prince traces all problems back to colonialism and concludes: "It is not surprising that this people are full of deceit and lies, this is the fruits of slavery, it makes master and slaves knaves" (65). In the process of analyzing the lasting scars of slavery and British rule, she lays out the dynamics of colonialism and extends them to the United States by connecting her stay in Jamaica with her subsequent return to the United States by way of the South. Comparison with the foreign allows for an indirect critique of home that avoids openly implicating or accusing white abolitionists in Prince's audience, yet her intention of countering American arguments for slavery is very clear.

Her principal strategy for undermining slavery is to dispel stereotypes about blacks that were used by slave owners to justify slavery's ostensible necessity. One argument slave owners regularly fronted was that African Americans were inherently lazy and therefore needed a firm hand to discipline and provide for them. Prince proves this idea as specious, noting that the farmers' markets in Jamaica are all built and run by black Jamaicans:

Thus it may be hoped they are not the stupid set of beings they have been called; here surely we see industry; they are enterprising and quick in their perceptions, determined to possess themselves, and to possess property besides, and quite able to take care of themselves. They wished to know why I was so inquisitive about them. I told them that we had heard in America that you are lazy, and that emancipation has been of no benefit to you; I wish to inform myself of the truth respecting you, and give a true account on my return.

(54)

The Jamaicans' work ethic and self-sufficiency challenge racist portrayals of American blacks and throw into question the logic of arguing inherent superiority based on skin color. Prince's insistence on the veracity of her words and theirs harkens to narratives by escaped slaves, who were in the position of convincing skeptical white audiences of the horrors they had fled. In her travels throughout Jamaica and the West Indies, Prince quotes a great number of former slaves, whose firsthand accounts lend credence to her arguments. The international context of her critique renders it even more effective because she can confront the United States with evidence of a black community's successful transition from forced dependence to freedom, and Britain's recognition of black rights across national boundaries further sanctions her critique. Manumission in countries so close to American borders added impetus to the abolition movement and left the United States with the shameful international reputation of defending slavery.

The section on Jamaica is targeted at black as well as white members of Prince's readership. Prince writes to disillusion, effectively writing an immigrant guide warning the black members of her audience who might go seeking new freedom in Jamaica. She notes that many blacks arrive in Jamaica under the impression that their passage was free: Instead, they are jailed upon landing and generally end up back on plantations, ostensibly working until they can pay back their passage (55). Even those who are free, she says, face many of the same obstacles present under slavery; given the challenges of sharecropping, opportunist merchants, and racial prejudice, whites take blacks' money as fast as they can earn it. Some have such difficulty earning a living that they return to work for their former masters, who then, one man notes bitterly, proclaim that free blacks do not know how to work. Looking at the aftermath of British rule in postcolonial Jamaica, Prince identifies violence, economic exploitation, and prejudice as strategies employed by a dominant group to maintain power. With these methods of control perpetuating white dominance even under the guise of freedom, the end of slavery does not automatically establish an egalitarian society. Through comparison, Prince warns African Americans not only against false assumptions about Jamaica but about the United States. As free blacks like

Prince already knew too well, life in the North was not free from racial prejudice, and abolishing slavery would not immediately end attempts by whites to control and subjugate black Americans. Despite this grim picture, Prince leaves her audience with some hope and little doubt about the moral imperative of abolishing slavery. During a brief visit to the liberated West Indies, she quotes an older woman who, despite her poverty, says: "'Now not bad now as in the time of slavery; then God spoke very loud to Bucker (the white people,) to let us go.'" Prince amends, "May these words be engraved on the post of every door in this land of New England. God speaks very loud . . ." (69).

Casting slavery as an abomination in terms of Christian morality was a common rhetorical practice in abolitionist texts. Many slave narratives found powerful sanction in the very religion that was also used to justify slavery. Nineteenth-century America strongly identified itself as Christian, with Christian morality forming the backbone of the nation. By arguing slavery's immorality on these religious grounds, abolitionists cast slavery as not only un-Christian but un-American. Writers like Prince used their faith to break convention conservatively, in the name of maintaining a Christian morality fundamental to American national identity. Thus, although this *Narrative* risked losing readers' sympathy by denouncing America's racism and sexism, the appeal to God as a final authority ultimately made her criticism patriotic and reinforced the status of blacks and women as American citizens.

While white women travelers could draw on male narratives and class privilege for validation, these avenues were generally closed to black women on the road, who chose to see racial and sexual differences as secondary in the eyes of God. Prince does use the form of a traditional travel narrative in describing Russia, but in writing about Jamaica and the West Indies she chooses a narrative form better designed to legitimate her authorial position vis-à-vis the highly charged topic of slavery. There is no need to invoke a higher power when describing the Frozen Market of St. Petersburg or Greek Orthodox funeral rites she observed in Russia because these hardly challenge America's self-image. Slavery, however, was the cleft in national identity at this time, and if Prince was going to argue not only against slavery, but against the myth of racial equality in the North, she needed to reach for the most powerful validation possible.

One of the institutions Prince criticizes most strongly for exploiting blacks in Jamaica and the United States is, ironically enough, the church. The extent to which white missionaries take advantage of the people tremendously discourages her in Jamaica. Prince reports being threatened by local missionaries after they discover her giving, rather than selling, Bibles to the poor.

Churches actively recruit blacks to raise membership and donations, because "colored people give more readily, and are less suspicious of imposition, if one from themselves recommends the measure; this the missionaries understand very well, and know how to take advantage of it" (49). Black Jamaicans are such a profitable source of income for the church that many of the missionaries joke about becoming "macroon" hunters (49). This exploitation is not limited to Jamaica, however. Prince also has little good to say about white Christians in the United States. As a child, she recounts, she worked for a "religious family." Her days with them often began at two in the morning and ran until late in the night. After three months, she left them, exclaiming, "They had family prayers, morning and evening. Oh! yes, they were sanctimonious!" (7).

The church, it seems, is simply yet another colonialist institution in both Jamaica and the United States that hedges white privilege and takes little interest in blacks aside from their potential as a financial resource. Prince concludes that "man has disobeyed his Maker. . . . God has in all ages of the world punished every nation and people for their sins. The sins of my beloved country are not hid from his notice" (47-48). Even men and nations are subject to divine authority, a particularly effective rhetorical strategy given that a large part of Prince's audience is Christian and will feel itself called to account. Despite her call to judgment, however, she still asserts her loyalty to the "beloved country" of her audience, thus situating the abolitionist position as truly patriotic.

However, Prince's return to the United States is not an occasion for patriotism. While her first voyage home from Jamaica is uneventful, like that from Russia, and is simply noted as "successful," her final return in 1841 was perilous in the extreme. The ship sailed through several storms, and the captain made unannounced stops in New Orleans and Key West, where Prince and the other passengers bound for New York were forced to change ships before reaching relative safety in the North. The black passengers were in great danger the moment they left the ships: As soon as their feet touched American soil, they could be taken into so-called "custody" and sold into slavery. At each stop in the South, Prince writes, "[E]very inducement was made to persuade me to go ashore, or set my feet on the wharf. A law had just been passed there that every free colored person coming there, should be put in custody on their going ashore" (77). Due to this law, Prince and the other five African Americans on board did not dare stir from the ship, at each stop spending three or four days tied up in dock, unable to go ashore for dry clothes, fresh food, or water. This second voyage meandering back through the South contrasts the freedom of black Jamaicans with the sharply proscribed freedom of ostensibly "free" African Americans like Prince. Whereas the racial egalitarianism she experienced in Europe now extends even to Jamaica and the West Indies, slavery still thrives in the United States, the single site of virulent racism and inequality in her worldly narrative. The transition in the Caribbean from colonial rule to equality is undeniably rough: The power inequities that are colonialism's legacy will, it seems, continue to distort relations between people of color and whites for years to come. However, the process has begun, whereas in the United States, colonialism continues in full force. By detailing her experiences on this final return to the United States, Prince carries over the dynamics of colonialism to home and brings the critique, subtly begun in Russia, full circle to the United States.

When the ship docks in New Orleans, it becomes clear that white Americans do not view Prince as an American citizen returning home but as a ruled subject again under their jurisdiction. The southerners demand to see her protection, saying they have heard that it is under the Russian government. She counters their demands for national identification with a biblical passage foretelling the fall of Babylon, a city grown wealthy from the slave trade: "I pointed them to the 18th chapter of Revelations and 15th verse: 'The merchants of these things which were made rich by her, shall stand afar off, for the fear of her torment, weeping and wailing. For strong is the Lord God who judgeth her.' They made no answer, but asked the Captain how soon he should get away" (81). By speaking of Babylon's fall due to slavery, Prince condemns the slave owners taunting her from the docks and the captain of her ship, who stops just short of physically putting her off board into their hands. Whether Prince's listeners realize it or not, she is prophesying the fall of at least the South, if not the entire United States, grown rich from slavery. However, Prince's listeners need not be intimately acquainted with the Bible to read the threat in this passage. As a black woman, she is without recourse to American citizenship or its attendant legal rights, but by reframing a debate about nationality, where she necessarily loses, into one of morality, she appropriates the religion of her oppressors and holds them accountable to their own beliefs. With her "citizenship" Christianity and her "protection" God, Prince has ingeniously given an answer to which there can be no objection that does not challenge the overriding authority of God. By denying the divine authority behind Prince's passage, her interlocutors, even if less than devout Christians, run the risk of proving American morality a sham, so Prince gambles on the southerners' allegiance to God and country, and she wins.

The ship becomes a contested space, which Prince defends verbally against the men cajoling and threatening her from the shore and docks. She uses "sass" to talk them down and hold them back from the ship. "I found it necessary to be stern with them," she writes; "they were very rude; if I had not been so, I know not what would have been the consequences" (80). As long as Prince and the other African Americans remain on board, they are on neutral ground outside the reach of southern law, and as long as the Southerners remain reluctant to physically assert their intentions, the fragile line of demarcation holds. Interestingly, the men outside are nearly as afraid of Prince as she is of them. They insist they do not want to harm her, but "'we do not want you here . . .' said they; 'we shall watch you like the d—until you go away; you must not say any thing to these negros whilst you are here.' 'Why, then, do you talk to me, if you do not want me to say any thing to you? If you will let me alone, I will you'" (80-81). As the Southerners' nervousness attests, Prince is dangerous. Her freedom of speech and movement defy their equation of blackness with slavery and could incite other blacks to demand the same liberties she possesses. Her very existence testifies to the possibility of black literacy, self-determination, and potential racial and gender equality.

Prince's extensive use of dialogue in this section is noteworthy as well. William Andrews explains that black nineteenth-century writers often included dialogue in their narratives to counter abolitionist and southern images of women as passive. Black women's voices were often left out of print at this time, and this silence abetted objectification and abuse. Prince writes herself as a speaking subject into the text and, by documenting her exchange with the southerners, she gives lie to their power and black women's presupposed helplessness. Prince's oratory skills essentially create a free space on board the ship: Biblical literacy and oration prove to be the currency of freedom. They hold back the Southerners and allow Prince to articulate herself as a subject demanding equal consideration in the eyes of her opponents. This is the only time Prince ever includes extensive direct dialogue in her *Narrative*: In Russia, she writes descriptively, and in Jamaica and the West Indies, she records the voices of manumitted blacks. Here, however, her status as a human being is threatened as nowhere else in her travels. By recording her exchanges with the men about her status as a sentient, self-possessed human being, Prince documents her humanity and makes a powerful argument for black Americans' rights to citizenship.

Prince seems to be aware at some level that, as a traveler crossing national and ideological boundaries, she represents a certain potential for transgression. The comparative perspectives Prince develops allowed her to survey home and herself from various angles and to question American presumptions about America's place in the world, while the need for authorial legitimacy also keeps her tethered to certain conservative ideologies of propriety and femininity. The multiplicity of cultural and national practices she encounters relativizes

American ideals and leaves readers forced to take stock of their own participation in the inequities she experiences at home. Europe afforded Prince some degree of latitude regarding her status as a black American: Repatriation therefore necessitates making a series of difficult decisions about which national ideologies to challenge upon return, with what strategy, and at what price.

Nineteenth-century women travelers usually finished their narratives by emphasizing their happy satisfaction at coming home, thus reassuring their readers that their ultimate allegiance lay with American ideologies. Freedoms enjoyed abroad can thus be recast as adventurous flirtations with foreign ways, now set aside as souvenirs—literally memories, in the French sense of the word—separate from the fabric of daily life, with no threatening implications for American ways. However, these conclusions often sound strained, suggesting that returning stateside meant giving up the freedom of movement and sometimes greater social latitude many American women reported enjoying abroad.

Prince's *Narrative* presents a startling contrast and reminds us that race has been elided in discussions of nineteenth-century travel narratives by predominantly white women. Happiness is markedly absent from Prince's return. The last words of her narrative are, rather than a move toward closure, an appeal for continued protection. She closes with a poem titled "The Hiding Place," thanking God for safe passage and continuing to provide a haven from the dangers of the world:

> . . . I'm in a wilderness below,
> Lord, guide me all my journey through,
> Plainly let me thy footsteps trace,
> Which lead to heaven, my hiding place.
> Should dangers thick impede my course,
> O let my soul sustain no loss;
> Help me to run the Christian race,
> And enter safe my hiding place.
>
> Then with enlarged powers,
> I'll triumph in redeeming love,
> Eternal ages will I praise,
> My Lord for such a hiding place.

(90-91)

While the poem's content is continuous with the faith running through her account, the way each verse concludes with the words "hiding place" coincides very uneasily with this, the end of her journey. Who or what is she hiding from if she is truly home? History gives us a clear answer, and the American nation is implicitly condemned: God, not America, is her refuge and the highest authority to which she can appeal. The freedom she experiences as an American citizen abroad melts away upon reentry, an irony not lost on Prince or her readers. Freedom at home is at best a conditional, uncertain state. As an African American, she is suspended in the hyphen in-between identities, with neither promising stability nor protection. "The Hiding Place" leaves us with the uneasy sense that the country Prince repatriates to is not, and has never been, her own. Rather than a returning citizen, she is a fugitive in her own land, where the journey out is less perilous than the journey home.

Works Cited

Andrews, William L., ed. *Sisters of the Spirit: Three Black Women's Autobiographies of the Nineteenth Century*. Bloomington: Indiana UP, 1986.

Blakely, Allison. *Russia and the Negro: Blacks in Russian History and Thought*. Washington, DC: Howard UP. 1986.

Braxton, Joanne. *Black Women Writing Autobiography: A Tradition within a Tradition*. Philadelphia: Temple UP, 1989.

Carby, Hazel. "'Hear My Voice Ye Careless Daughters': Narratives of Slave and Free Women before Emancipation." *African American Autobiography*. Ed. William Andrews. Englewood Cliffs, NJ: Prentice Hall. 1993. 59-76.

Foster, Frances Smith. *Written by Herself: Literary Production by African American Women, 1746-1892*. Bloomington: Indiana UP, 1993.

Gates, Jr., Henry Louis. "*Their Eyes Were Watching God*: Hurston and the Speakerly Text." *Zora Neale Hurston: Critical Perspectives Past and Present*. Ed. Henry Louis Gates Jr. and K. A. Appiah. New York: Amistad Press, 1993. 154-203.

Hurston, Zora Neale. *Their Eyes Were Watching God*. New York: Harper & Row, 1990.

Martin, Charles. "Coloring Books: Black Writing on Europe." *Mosaic: A Journal for the Interdisciplinary Study of Literature* 26.4 (1993): 53-67.

Moody, Joycelyn. "On the Road with God." *Religion and Literature* 27.1 (1995): 35-50.

Morrison, Toni. *Playing in the Dark: Whiteness and the Literary Imagination*. Cambridge: Harvard UP, 1992.

Prince, Nancy Gardner. *Narrative of the Life and Travels, of Mrs. Nancy Prince*. In *A Black Woman's Odyssey Through Russia and Jamaica*. Ed. Ronald G. Walters. 1850. New York: Markus Wiener Publishing, 1990.

Said, Edward. *Culture and Imperialism*. New York: Vintage Books, 1994.

Walters, Ronald G. Introduction. *A Black Woman's Odyssey Through Russia and Jamaica*. Ed. Ronald Walters. New York: Markus Wiener Publishing, 1990. 9-23.

OTHER NOTABLE TRAVEL WRITERS AND THEIR WORKS

Sylvie L. F. Richards (essay date 1998-99)

SOURCE: Richards, Sylvie L. F. "The Occidental Tourist: Nerval's *Le Voyage en Orient* as Pseudo-Documentary." *Philological Papers* 44 (1998-99): 65-72.

[*In the following essay, Richards views Gérard de Nerval's* Voyage en Orient *in relation to French Orientalist travel narratives, German Illuminism, and Nerval's own personal search for meaning and grief following his mother's death.*]

One could say that the nineteenth-century French Romantics "invented" (that is, imagined) the *voyage en Orient*. Certainly Europeans had traveled to the Near East, to those countries which bordered the Mediteranean before this time. European history had been interlaced with the history of the Near East. But the chroniclers of these expeditions always made reference to these as "voyages," as a plural noun, because their chronicles were meant to be read as documentaries of the Orient. For the writers of the *Encyclopédie*, the notion of "Orient" was more often than not a learned term associated with the Near East. The Orientalist references in Diderot's entries, for instance, are either historical (Byzantium and Constantinople), or philosophical (Zoroaster, the Gnostics, the occult tradition). The formulaic "voyages en Orient" in the plural appeared for the first time in 1772 in the French translation of the title *A Description of the East* written by R. Pococke and published in London between 1743-45. The tradition of "voyages" as documentary narrative continued until the 1835 publication of Alphonse de Lamartine's *Souvenirs, impressions, pensées et paysages pendant un voyage en Orient,* the first Romantic treatment of a personal narrative using the Orient as a backdrop. As Edward Said notes:

> When he began his trip to the Orient in 1833, Lamartine did so, he said, as something he had always dreamed about: "un voyage en Orient [était] comme un grand acte de ma vie intérieure."[1]

The change from the plural substantive "voyages" to the singular "voyage" heralded a new concept about writing about the Orient, but it was a change that went unnoticed by the vast reading public. From the time of Lamartine's "voyage," there exists in French Romantic literature a single Orient, a collectivity of ideas and impressions that subsequent literary and Occidental travelers of this space would repeat. More importantly, the singular "voyage" represents a shift from documentary writing about the Orient to a discourse using the Orient as an expression and an exploration of a personal geography. However, this paradigm shift remained unperceived by the reading public who continued to view Orientalist writings as documentaries. Hence, there arose a politics about the Orient based in large measure on a misreading of the Orient, on an unfounded substitution of personal narrative poetics for documented concrete reality. The case of Gérard de Nerval is particularly elucidating because his *Voyage en Orient* came early in his literary career and served as the framework of a new conception into which he incorporated his later writings.

From Volney [Constantin-François Chassebeuf] (*Voyage en Syrie et en Égypte,* 1787) to Chateaubriand (*Itinéraire de Paris à Jérusalem,* 1811), from Chateaubriand to Lamartine (*Voyage en Orient,* 1835), from Lamartine to Nerval (*Voyage en Orient,* 1851), from Nerval to Flaubert (his travels in the Orient are recounted in a series of letters written from 29 october 1849 and ending with his return to France in early June 1851; his travel letters were published in 1948), French Orientalist travel writers form an uninterrupted discourse about the Orient, one that is both enlightening and profitable to its writers. The "voyage en Orient" as text had an economic value, encoded with a bourgeois sign of prestige. It took a great deal of money to mount and munition an expedition. The trip required leisure time, a substantial fortune, and some diplomatic connections. Volney sacrificed his inheritance to finance his *Voyage en Syrie et en Égypte*. Chateaubriand spent over 50,000 FF. But it was Lamartine who made the Romantic "voyage en Orient" profitable. For his expedition of 1832-33, Lamartine spent twice as much as Chateaubriand. But upon his return, he sold his manuscript for 100,000 FF,[2] thereby capitalizing on the public's insatiable demand for more details about the Orient. Nerval himself made no secret of his desire to find literary fame and fortune as a result of his expedition. As Laurence Porter writes:: "(Il voulait) faire un gros livre; être bien payé par les éditeurs; relancer sa carrière en traitant un sujet bien à la mode."[3] The French appetite for travel stories, for documentaries about the Orient by Orientalists, was almost insatiable. It was a thirst for a confirmation of national manifest destiny over an area filled with mystery and sensuality that would not be quenched until after the Algerian War. Nerval's *Voyage en Orient,* therefore, would be read by this eager public as a documentary about the lives and customs of Orientals and not as an elaboration of a personal geography of an Occidental traveler in an Orientalist space.

Moreover, Nerval wanted to reestablish himself in the literary world after his nervous breakdown of 1841 and his internment in an asylum in 1842. Writing to his father, Dr. Étienne LaBrunie, from Constantinople on or about October 5, 1843, Nerval expressed his gratitude for his friends, in particular to Théophile Gautier:

L'amabilité de Théophile, en me dédiant, pour ainsi dire, son ballet, et en entretenant le public de mon voyage, m'a été d'autant plus sensible que, depuis ma maladie trop connue, il importait que mon retour à la santé fût constaté bien publiquement; et rien ne devait mieux le prouver qu'un voyage pénible dans les pays chauds; ce n'a pas été l'un des moindres motifs de me le faire entreprendre à tout prix.[4]

As he had hoped, the "voyage" would prove therapeutic not only for his mental health but also for his literary career.

What was understood by the word Orient at the time of Nerval's travels? Principally, the Orient was a series of clichés, an oasis for a *déjà vu*, a land made familiar by the stories in the *Mille et une nuits,* Antoine Galland's French translation having been published from 1704-1717. The popular conception of the Orient was thus a reconstruction beginning with a literary text or a painting. As Nerval writes in a letter to Théophile Gautier from Péra on September 7, 1843:

On sent une grande privation en Orient, c'est la musique et les intérieurs éclairés. Ensuite, on sait trop ce qu'on va voir. Partout les peintres nous ont découpé l'Asie en petits carrés pendus aux murs; hormis en Syrie, je n'ai pas trouvé un paysage imprévu.

(1: 943)

But it was always a reconstruction fabricated in the Occident, the Occidental traveler expected to find evidence of Orientalist textual fabrications in the real Orient. As Nerval noted in another letter to Théophile Gauthier at the end of August, 1843:

Oh! Que je suis curieux d'aller voir à Paris le Caire de Philastre et Cambon; je suis sûr que c'est mon Caire d'autrefois, celui que j'avais vu tant de fois en rêve, qu'il me semblait comme à toi, y avoir séjourné dans je ne sais quel temps, sous le règne du sultan Bibars ou du calife Hakem! . . . Ce Caire-là, je l'ai *reconstruit* [emphasis mine] parfois encore au milieu d'un quartier désert, ou de quelque mosquée croulante; il me semblait que j'imprimais les pieds dans la trace de mes pas anciens. . . . Je retrouverai à Paris le Caire véritable, l'Égypte immaculée, l'Orient qui m'échappe . . . c'est à cette Égypte-là que je crois et non pas à l'autre: aussi bien les six mois que j'ai passés là sont passés. . . . Le meilleur de ce qu'on y trouve, je le savais déjà par coeur.

(1: 941-42)

This reconstruction of the Orient received two important impeti in the nineteenth century: Napoleon's conquest of Egypt and his concomitant founding of the Institut d'Égypte,[5] events which seemed to confirm the powerlessness of the Orient while revealing its splendors; and the interest brought to the study of philology, initiated by Diderot's close friend Jacob Grimm, founder of the German school of philology in the eigh-

teenth century. The quest for the original language, for a primitive tongue, was at the heart of the Aryan myth promulgated by Franz Bopp in his treatise *Vergleichende Grammatik* (1832). This quest for a new Holy Grail, the original language, had to take place in the Orient.[6] To find his philological genesis, the Occidental had to excavate his linguistic roots in the Orient. Nerval's choice of Egypt as fertile Orientalist ground for his personal exploration and his insistance on incorporating Oriental words into his texts, of making them graphically Occidental, can be understood in the light of these two dimensions.

According to Orientalists, the Orient was governed by stereotypes of passivity, of impotence, of voluptuousness, of a "feminine" space ready to be conquered, to be possessed, to relinquish its secrets and mysteries. Orientals were, by implication, inferiors, who benefited from the domination of superior Occidentals. Nerval was attracted to this feminine space for psychological reasons resulting from the early loss of his mother.[7] In the Orient, he hoped to be enveloped by this "gynography" and to achieve some sort of mystical reunification with his absent mother. His subsequent literary production would be irrevocably shaped by the presence of this feminized Orientalist space, *Les Filles du Feu* being the most obvious example. The *Voyage en Orient* is a narrative dominated by the presence of women. Women form the pretext and the context of the "voyage." For instance, in the section "Les Femmes du Caire," Nerval describes private spaces for women in great detail, forbidden spaces inaccessible to Occidental travelers, even to the gaze of Oriental men. Reading Nerval's *Voyage* becomes an act of extreme voyeurism for his male and female readers.

It is no secret that, though Nerval traveled in the Orient, he plagarized most of his narrative from other writers, notably William Lane (*An Account of the Manners and Customs of the Modern Egyptians,* 1836), Silvestre de Sacy (*Principes de grammaire générale,* 1799), and Barthélémy d'Herbelot de Molainville (*Bibliothèque orientale,* 1697, with a preface by Antoine Galland).[8] His account of the Orient, therefore, conformed fully to the expectations of his readers and assuaged their need to find *their* Orient in his descriptions. But what was the Orient for Nerval? For him, it was the region long associated with the esoteric Illuminism of the secret societies which flourished after the Revolution, with their initiation rites and hermeneutic symbols.[9] "Orient" was the name given to provincial Masonic lodges, while "Grand Orient" designated the central lodge in Paris formed with representatives from all of the provincial lodges. Nerval journeyed to the Orient to discover the secrets of these mysteries. In describing his beliefs, the narrator of the *Voyage en Orient* asks this question: "Mais qui sait ce que peut représenter en Orient un Parisien nourri d'idées philosophiques, un fils de Voltaire, un impie, selon l'opinion des braves gens? (2: 263)." However, he would be deceived in his expectations of the Orient. In a letter to Jules Janin written on November 16, 1843 during his journey home on board a ship headed for Malta, he spoke of his disillusionment with the Orient:

> En somme, l'Orient n'approche pas de ce rêve éveillé que j'en avais fait il y a deux ans, ou bien c'est que cet Orient-là est encore plus loin ou plus haut, j'en ai assez de courir après la poésie; je crois qu'elle est à votre porte, et peut-être dans votre lit.
>
> (1: 950)

According to Nerval, his plans to go to the Orient were formulated during the year in which he experienced his breakdown. The Orient was to have provided solace for his broken spirit.[10] In the bosom of the Orient, he searched for connections which he hoped to find in Egypt, land of the pyramids, keeper of the mysteries about death and rebirth. There he hoped to penetrate the mysteries of the after-life which would perhaps permit him to reconnect with his mother.[11] The hermetic tradition of Nerval's Orient will become manifest in *Les Filles du feu* and *Les Chimères*. But the seeds are already found in *Voyage en Orient*. For instance, we find the following passage in "Les Femmes du Caire":

> Le soleil noir de la mélancolie, qui verse des rayons obscurs sur le front de l'ange rêveur d'Albert Dürer, se lève aussi parfois aux plaines lumineuses du Nil, comme sur les bords du Rhin, dans un froid paysage d'Allemagne. J'avouerai même qu'à défaut de brouillard, la poussière est un triste voile aux clartés d'un jour d'Orient.
>
> (2: 132)

We find the same wording in the first quatrain of "El Desdichado," the first poem in Nerval's collection of eight poems comprised of twelve sonnets which he titled *Les Chimères* when they were first published at the end of *Les Filles du feu* in 1854. Seven of the twelve sonnets had appeared in two years before in *Petits Châteaux de Bohème*[12] under the title of *Mysticisme*.

> Je suis le Ténébreux,—le Veuf,—l'Inconsolé,
> Le Prince d'Aquitaine à la Tour abolie:
> Ma seule *Étoile* est morte,—et mon luth constellé
> Porte le *Soleil noir* de la *Mélancolie*.
>
> (1: 2)

It is no strange coincidence that the esoteric image of the "soleil noir" reappears, for the image is at the heart of the dualities propounded by the Illuminists.[13] Furthermore, the association made between Germany and the Orient points to even larger issues for Nerval's *Voyage en Orient*. The first is his affinity for Germany. It is important to remember that, before the *Voyage en Orient*, Nerval was known for his translation of Goethe's *Faust*.[14] The *Voyage en Orient* begins with a necessary detour through Switzerland, Germany, and Austria because Nerval was being guided by the doctrines of German Illuminism in his journey.[15] His personal journey in the Orient sought to confirm the esoteric mysteries of the secret societies. Nerval was seeking the original initiatory rites that would allow him to penetrate into the mysteries of life and the after-life, perhaps in an effort to reconnect with his dead mother:

> Alors l'Égypte, la mère et la conservatrice de toutes les imaginations et même de toutes les extravagances religieuses, offrit une satisfaction aux besoins de l'âme et des sens. Sérapis et Isis vinrent en aide, l'un aux corps souffrants, l'autre aux âmes.
>
> (1: 1277)

He will devote a portion of *Les Filles du Feu* to Isis, this mother figure symbolized by the moon, whose zodiac was intimately tied with the Pyramids. Prior to his departure for the Orient, he had consulted Cagliostro's *Confessions du Comte de C*** avec l'histoire de ses voyages en Russie, Turquie, Italie et dans les Piramides d'Égypte* (1787), Alexandre Lenoir's *La Franche-Maçonnerie rendue à sa véritable origine* (1814), and the 1827 translation of Thomas Moore's *L'Épicurien* (2: 1321). He found in Illuminist Orientalist writings what he had been searching for: a confirmation of his own ideas on life and death, in particular metempsychosis and reincarnation. His own selection of Oriental tales, such as "Les Deux Califes," reveal as much. In this story, the Caliph Hakem believes that he has seen his *ferouer* or his double:

> Cette vision lui semblait un avertissement céleste, et son trouble augmenta encore lorsqu'il reconnut ou crut reconnaître ses propres traits dans ceux de l'homme assis près de sa soeur. Il crut que c'était son *ferouer* ou son double, et, pour les Orientaux, voir son propre spectre est un signe du plus mauvais augure.
>
> (2: 390)

This apparition occurs at the time that Hakem has decided to marry his sister Sétalmulc. This incestuous desire, a reworking of the Isis-Osiris myth, seems to be the provoking agent for the arrival of the double, as if the transference of the transgressive act to an Other who is the Same can relieve Hakem of the blameful act. The same incestuous desire reappears in *Sylvie*.[16] The narrateur est the "frère de lait" of Sylvain, Sylvie's brother. Though very attracted to Sylvie, the narrator will transfer his affections to her "double" Adrienne, a blond version of Sylvie with an angelic voice who is bathed in moonglow. Adrienne will enter the convent at her parents' behest where she will die. But at the end of *Sylvie,* she appears to have been "reborn" in the person of the actress Aurélie, a prefiguration of Aurélia. In this narrative, which begins with the phrase, "Le Rêve est une seconde vie" (1: 359), the Ideal Woman reappears and plunges the narrator into a waking dream:

Un être d'une grandeur démesurée,—homme ou femme, je ne sais,—voltigeait péniblement au-dessus de l'espace et semblait se débattre parmi des nuages épais. . . . Il était coloré de teintes vermeilles, et ses ailes brillaient de mille reflets changeants. Vêtu d'une robe longue à plis antiques, il ressemblait à l'Ange de la *Mélancolie*, d'Albrecht Dürer.—Je ne pus m'empêcher de pousser des cris d'effroi, qui me réveillèrent en sursaut.

(1: 362)

Here is the same image found in "El Desdichado" and in *Le Voyage en Orient*. In *Aurélia*, we find the genesis of the *Voyage en Orient* and the deeper meaning behind Nerval's voyage. Shortly after the apparition, the narrator is at a gathering of friends discussing art and music:

L'un d'eux, nommé Paul ***, voulut me reconduire chez moi, mais je lui dis que je ne rentrais pas. "Où vas-tu? me dit-il.—*Vers L'Orient!*" Et pendant qu'il m'accompagnait, je me mis à chercher dans le ciel une étoile, que je croyais connaître, comme si elle avait quelque influence sur ma destinée. L'ayant trouvée, je continuai ma marche en suivant les rues dans la direction desquelles elle était visible, marchant pour ainsi dire au-devant de mon destin, et voulant m'apercevoir l'étoile usqu'au moment où la mort devait me frapper. . . . ". . . Dans cette étoile sont ceux qui m'attendent. Ils sont antérieurs à la révélation que tu as annoncée. Laisse-moi les rejoindre, car celle que j'aime leur appartient, et c'est là que nous devons nous retrouver!"

(1: 362-63)

Like the Magi, Nerval chose to follow his star to the Orient, to a land which held the promise of being reunited with the Ideal Woman, with Isis, with the Mother. He renounced all affiliation with Occidental beliefs and adopted the Illuminist credence in reincarnation, the only philosophy which would, in his mind, permit union with his mother. As a new Osiris, Nerval hoped to achieve a symbolic marriage with his Isis and to rule the kingdom of the dead, in a realm that touched upon the pyramids of Egypt.[17]

What appeared to the average reader to be another documentary by an occidental traveler, Nerval's *Voyage en Orient* proved to be the genesis of his own literary work. Interspersed with the collective adaptations of the writings of others Orientalists are the seeds of Nerval's own personal narrative geography, of his own tortured search for meaning and destiny. Long neglected by scholars, who saw the *Voyage* as plagarism, as a flawed documentary, the work merits a concerted reevaluation in the light of Illuminist doctrines which inspired it. Nerval's disillusionment with the real Orient, his inability to find his promised land outside of his own Orientalist reveries, may well hold the key to his untimely death by suicide, the one means of death which forever prevented his long sought-after reunion with his dead mother. His obsession to unify with a mythic "feminine" Orientalist landscape, one in which he traveled and described, haunted him to his final moments. Eight days before his death, Nerval had drawn a portrait of several French queens in an allegorical Orientalist style (1: 1186). Quite possibly, the queens are all representations of his mother, of Isis, of the one about which he spoke in "Artemis":

Aimez qui vous aima du berceau dans la bière;
Celle que j'aimai seul m'aime encor tendrement:
C'est la Mort—ou la Morte . . . O délice! Ô tourment!
La rose qu'elle tient, c'est la *Rose trémière*.

(1: 5)

Source of knowledge about birth and death, about birth and rebirth, the image of the Mother is fixed in the Orient. Nerval's personal pilgrimage to reassemble the lost parts of himself unwittingly served a curious public with the intimate details of an Orientalist reverie which were reinterpreted as documented facts. His writings about the Orient satisfied his readers who never physically traveled there. For Nerval, who had set foot in the real Orient, the voyage had proven to be a disillusionment. He much preferred his Orientalist dreams, the ones riddled with the mysteries of Illuminist initiates. Like Claude Lantier of Zola's *L'Oeuvre*, Nerval the Occidental traveler hung himself by his painting of his feminized Orientalist Ideal, perhaps in a crazed attempt to finally enter his promised land.

Notes

1. *Orientalism* (New York: Vintage, 1978) 177.

2. Albert Marie Pierre Luppé, *Les Travaux et les jours d'Alphonse Lamartine* (Paris: Albin Michel, 1942) 174.

3. "Le Voyage initiatique de Gérard de Nerval," *Revue Internationale d'Etude de la Réception Critique des Oeuvres Littéraires* 9 (1984): 64.

4. *Oeuvres,* ed. Albert Béguin et Jean Richer (Paris: Éditions de la Pléiade, 1966) 1: 944.

5. Nerval was aware of the work of the Institut d'Égypte and makes mention of it in the *Voyage en Orient*: "Je ne pus m'empêcher de reconnaître que c'était pour les érudits prussiens une noble ambition que d'avoir voulu marcher sur les traces de notre Institut d'Égypte, dont il ne pourront, du reste, que compléter les admirables travaux" (2: 218).

6. Nerval, who began his literary career as a translator, is equally fascinated by the possibility of "translating" hieroglyphics into French for the purpose of deciphering the mysteries of Egypt. Impregnated by German mysticism, Nerval cre-

ates a German character as the one who has mastered the philological difficulies and possibilities made available by the Rosetta Stone: "Il savait le sens de ces hieroglyphes modernes inscrits d'après le système de la grammaire de Champollion" (2: 219).

7. Nerval's mother, Marie-Antoinette-Marguerite Laurent Labrunie, died on 29 November 1810 at the age of twenty-five. Nerval was only two years old. Nerval's father, the doctor Etienne Labrunie, was at the time attached to a military unit serving at the Rhine. Nerval was sent to live with his great-uncle Antone Boucher at Mortefontaine.

8. Albert Béguin and Jean Richer, in their notes for the Pléiade edition of the *Voyage en Orient,* vol. 2 (Paris: Gallimard, 1961), mention Nerval's various borrowings. For Lane, see note for p. 92 on p. 1301 and passim. For Sacy, see note for p. 358 on p. 1342 and passim. For d'Herbelot, see note for p. 104 on p. 1302 and passim. Béguin and Richer also detail Nerval's borrowings from other Orientalist writers. Their notes are invaluable for any serious study of the *Voyage.*

9. Nerval's father was a Mason as were several of his friends. He had read and was greatly influenced by the doctrines of Marinès de Pasqually, founder of a mystical-theosophical Masonic French order in Montpellier in 1754. Pasqually had written the *Traité de la Réintégration des Êtres dans leurs premières propriétés, vertus et puissances spirituelles et divines,* in which he taught that it was possible to link each individual soul with the original image of Man before the Fall.

10. After a second serious mental breakdown in 1854, Nerval once again planned to renew his strength in the Orient and planned a second voyage. He even received 600 francs from the Ministre de l'instruction publique Hippolyte Fortoul to defray the costs of a "mission en Orient ayant pour objet la continuation de vos travaux littéraires sur ces pays" (1: 1121). However, Nerval's mental state deteriorated to such a degree that he was unable to undertake this second voyage, and he subsequently returned the money.

11. In a letter to Dr. Émile Blanche dated 25 November 1853 during Nerval's internment at Dr. Blanche's clinic, Nerval alludes to the ever-present memory of his mother: "Si vous m'avez vu pleurer hier, ne croyez pas que ce fût par faiblesse; seulement je pensais que nous ne nous comprenions plus. Or c'est assez faire le fou quand on est raisonnable et ce n'est pas le jour anniversaire de la mort de ma mère que j'en aurai le courage" (1:1094).

12. Bohemia was associated in Nerval's thoughts with Jan Hus, founded of the heretical sect, the Hussites. Excommunicated in 1412, he was burned alive at the stake after being condemned by the Council of Constance. In Illuminist circles, Hus was considered an enlightened precursor. By extension, Bohemia was associated with esoteric mysteries.

13. For an analysis of *Les Chimères* in light of Illuminist thought, see my article "Alchemy as Poetic Metaphor in Gérard de Nerval's *Les Chimères,*" *WVUPP* 27 (1981): 34-41.

14. In a letter to his father dated 18 September 1838 and written from Frankfort, Gérard writes: "Il est incroyable de voirà quel point les gens de lettres français sont estimés et bien accueillis en Allemagne. Cela m'a donné l'idée d'aller l'année prochaine à Vienne, on l'on veut me recommander d'une manière suprême, et où je pourrai me fortifier dans la prononciation allemande" (*Oeuvres* 1: 815).

15. Germany had been "rediscovered" as a land of mysticism by Mme de Staël, whose publication *De l'Allemagne* inspired Romantic writers. As the daughter of Jacques and Suzanne Necker, she herself had Germanic roots which she may have wanted to validate.

16. "Sylvie, que j'avais vue grandir, était pour moi comme une soeur. Je ne pouvais tenter une séduction" (*Oeuvres* 1: 266).

17. Nerval signed a letter to Arsène Houssaye dated 20 October 1854 in this curious fashion: "Celui qui fut GERARD et qui l'est encore . . . "(1: 1175). He would hang himself on 26 January 1855.

Nicholas Howe (essay date autumn 2000)

SOURCE: Howe, Nicholas. "Deserts, Lost History, Travel Stories." *Southwest Review* 85, no. 4 (autumn 2000): 526-39.

[*In the following essay, Howe traces the desert travel narratives of several British authors, emphasizing especially Charles M. Doughty's* Travels in Arabia Deserta.]

Most travel books fall victim to the clichés of their time. In older examples, the author visits a place and then writes the desired setpiece: the harbor entrepot satisfies a taste for the seedy; the alpine vista inspires the winsomely romantic; the demimonde capital offers a glimpse of the naughty; the walled hilltown prompts effusions on the ephemeral and picturesque. Readers expected these travel books to yield predictable portraits of place, just as they expected the hotels and restaurants they patronized to match descriptions in guidebooks. Anything different meant disappointment for reader and traveler. A generation or two later, these travel books seem as dated as postcards found in junkshops. Their hasty greetings to friends back home—"Having a lovely trip, off tomorrow for Tunbridge Wells"—tell us somebody had a great time somewhere, even if it's hard now to share that excitement. So it is with most travel accounts that fill the shelves in used-book stores. They seem the sort of thing one can read only when traveling with steamer trunks and lap rugs.

Readers' expectations about travel books change as do the places themselves. Contemporary taste seems more and more to prize a self-questioningly ironic stance that worries about cultural imperialism and despoiling the environment. Having too much fun or not living dangerously enough are also grounds for concern because they might mark one as a tourist. With this ironic stance, our writers can correct the naive excesses of earlier travelers who worried about beasts of burden, restless tribes, and their dwindling supply of anti-malarial gin. But just as the over-dyed colors of their narratives now seem garish, so the muted brushwork of many of our travel books will fade to invisibility for later readers.

Time is cruel to travel books precisely and ironically because the effects of time are so often their unacknowledged subject: they mourn the golden age that slipped away years before; they memorialize places changed utterly by nature or war or simply the writer's disillusionment; they report on newly built or discovered sites. Travel books, despite grounding themselves in a feeling for place, are always vulnerable to the shiftings of time. Some old ones retain historical value by documenting their time of composition or recording the customs and people of a place. But most seem empty pages filled with inaccurate information and banal description. Curiously, this is not always true of guidebooks. Old Baedekers or E. V. Lucas' series of *A Wanderer in Paris, . . . in London, . . . in Florence,* for example, are still interesting because they were grounded in facts rather than impressions. It satisfies a genuine, if minor, curiosity to know that in 1910 the sea-lions in the Jardin des Plantes were fed daily at 3 p.m., or that in 1912 the passage between the Uffizi and Pitti was, in Lucas' phrase, "hard worked only on Sundays." These guides never make you feel like a lout for not finding a particular view or painting sublime; they merely suggest, by noting it, that others thought so.

Travel books last for many reasons but the least common, I suspect, is the choice of place, especially if the author glamorizes it as unspoiled or exotic. For a travel book to last beyond its immediate season, it may be enough if it observes a terrain with perception or per-

haps sympathy. And if its voice has some personal timbre. As I think of examples of the genre that endure even if they are not widely read—Charles M. Doughty's *Travels in Arabia Deserta* (1888) or W. H. Hudson's *Idle Days in Patagonia* (1893)—they are alike in knowingly locating their place within a sense of time. They depend on the moment of encounter between author and place, of course, but they also move within a flow of other places and other times. With a chastening sense of historical contingency, they offer neither the innocent claim of being somewhere first nor the world-weary one of being there last.

Although he did not set out to follow anyone's footsteps, Doughty is always looking in *Arabia Deserta* for the traces left by those who were there before him. Following was for him a shadowy and metaphorical act. With a writer's faith in the enduring presence of language, he devoted great efforts to tracing and recording the ancient inscriptions he found in the desert. He published a volume of these inscriptions for scholars, knowing that most readers of travel books lack the imagination to appreciate that sort of adventure. He also recorded inscriptions written in English, signs of mercantile empire, that he found in the desert. He tells of seeing flasks of gunpowder labelled with their name and place of manufacture, "Hall, Dartford," and of explaining to merchants in the souk that the wrappers for their silk thread were torn-up pages from *The Bombay Gazette.*

As Doughty's twelve-hundred pages move from place to place, they reenact the ritual more than the course of pilgrimage. He was not a believer and thus could not follow the route of the Haj, the pilgrimage into Mecca; but he refers to it continually to determine his place in the desert or the time of year. Such findings are necessary because, in its scale and detail, *Arabia Deserta* is so massive that one easily gets lost in it. As with Dickens and Tolstoy, one can skim the boring parts where nothing seems to happen and read for narrative, but that can be a mistake because Doughty, like them, is a master of gratuitous details that carry the texture and sensation of daily life. Aware that readers would get lost if his narrative lacked a clear route, Doughty opens his book with two moves: he first presents himself as a traveler in the desert, and then depicts the necessity of travel in the world he journeys through as an outsider. With each move, he makes clear he will offer something other than titillating tales from the exotic orient.

Doughty opens his travels by quoting the question that an unnamed, undescribed friend posed to him in Damascus after his return from the Arabian Peninsula: "Tell me (said he), since thou art here again in the peace and assurance of Ullah, . . . what moved thee, or how couldst thou take such journeys into the fanatic Arabia?" One might ask a similar question of any traveler, but it makes a dazzling opening for Doughty, we see in retrospect, because he answers not with a brief reply but rather with two volumes of stories about what he saw in Arabia Deserta. He never tells us explicitly that he went to the desert because . . . We can find phrases in his pages to characterize his motives or to solve the enigma of his journey. But Doughty remains intact in his faith that the best a traveler can do is to return with stories of the places he has been. Anything else risks cant.

In the second opening of *Arabia Deserta,* some two pages after he quotes his friend's question, Doughty shifts from himself to the culture in which he traveled. He writes of Damascus, the gathering point for pilgrims on the way to Mecca, in ways that reveal his complex situation. He has left England to immerse himself in the world of desert Islam with its bedouins, camels, oases, extreme physical conditions, but he has brought with him his reading in English literature, especially *The Canterbury Tales.* Doughty is too austere a traveler, too demanding a writer to cartoon the people he writes about by turning them into characters from Chaucer. Instead, he learns from Chaucer to use the telling fact— what pilgrims wear, what they speak—to shape the departure point for his narrative:

> There is every year a new stirring of this goodly Oriental city in the days before the Haj; so many strangers are passing in the bazaars, of outlandish speech and clothing from far provinces. The more part are of Asia Minor, many of them bearing over-great white turbans that might weigh more than their heads; the most are poor folk of a solemn countenance, which wander in the streets seeking the bakers' stalls, and I saw that many of the Damascenes could answer them in their own language.

Doughty enters the place and its narrative not as a religious pilgrim, for he never converted to Islam, but rather as a literary traveler. The route to Mecca is like that to Canterbury because pilgrims on both tell stories to pass the time across the landscape.

No one ever wrote an English like Doughty's—certainly not Chaucer, Malory, and Spenser, who were his favorite writers. And yet that same invented language allowed him to create a sense of place in which prescribed religious pilgrimage existed beside the rituals of warrior nomads. Some who stayed in nineteenth-century England tried to recreate this world of prayer and warfare by composing medievalesque ballads or designing tapestry wallpaper or building gothic university buildings. Doughty who called himself "a disciple of the divine Muse of Spenser and Venerable Chaucer" went further. He left home and found that world as he alone thought it might exist among the desert Arabs. For the traveler who reads, another country can become the desired past.

Today, the shock of *Arabia Deserta* is that it should be so richly populated with, as Reyner Banham puts it, "all kinds of human beings, settlements, and tribes." And each has its stories. In a characteristic passage, Doughty speaks of "the cheerful musing Beduin talk, a lesson in the traveller's school of mere humanity" and he fills his work with these stories. He tells, for instance, of his friend Abdullah who knew "endless Oriental tales" that were "the townspeople's solace." He adds, in that leisurely way of his that forces one to quote him at length, the particulars of these stories:

> The matter is most what that which was heart's joy to the good old knight in the noble English poet, *"When any man hath been in poor estate and climbeth up and wexeth fortunate."* But their long process grows in European ears (for tediousness) to a confused babble of sounds. [Abdullah] told of the climbing up of the fortunate son from the low degree to wedding with kings' daughters; mingling in his tale many delightful standings by the way,—perils and despairs, gifts of precious jewels, the power of talismans, the finding of hid treasures, and the blissful rencounters as *"the joy that lasteth evermo,"* of separated affections; the sound of the trumpet and the battle, and thereafter the secure and happy days.

In his book, Doughty sets the two quotations from Chaucer in boldface Gothic to elide the centuries and continents between *The Canterbury Tales* and Abdullah's tales.

Doughty echoed Chaucer not simply to give his text a savor of medieval chivalry and tale-telling. Chaucer's lines and the England they evoke are to Doughty another kind of monumental inscription found along a pilgrimage route, not carved in stone but incised in the mind as part of the traveler's store of memory. The "good old knight" who speaks these lines is also a traveler portrayed in Chaucer's Prologue as a veteran fighter against heathens and infidels, including those in the Holy Land. He joins the pilgrimage to Canterbury in campaigning gear stained by the rust of his armor. The lines Doughty quotes come from the Knight's response to *The Monk's Tale* and its catalogue of figures who fell from high estate and thus suffered tragedy. The knight wishes to hear instead stories of those who "abideth in prosperitee," of those who live well. Doughty uses Chaucer to acknowledge he cannot know Arabia apart from England and its medieval literature.

Doughty uses his prose to carry this long cultural memory of pilgrimage tales and quest romances. Nothing has done more to cast him as a Victorian eccentric than this prose, at once leisurely in its pacing from paragraph to paragraph and unrelenting in its local demands. He goes on for hundreds of pages but individual sentences are compressed to the point of enigma as they mix registers: they intertwine Arabic with English or, more exactly, with a variety of Englishes. Most immediately, Doughty sprinkles his sentences with Middle English. In a vivid account of the Kheyabara, he notes that "many a night they kept this morris dance," a term that is less cross-cultural metaphor for him than literal statement. He describes a prosperous and hospitable Arab, a man "gentle and liberal," with a term of office that Chaucer wrote into the language: "Hamed was a manly young franklin."

These archaisms can be annoying when read in isolation but within the flow of Doughty's prose they have a precision that gives historical density to his sense of place. T. E. Lawrence, in his introduction to *Arabia Deserta,* said this style was "so closely wrought, so tense, so just in its words and phrases, that it demands a hard reader." This hard reader also needs sufficient empathy to know that medievalism is not a lost history, a forlorn or laughable desire for the past. It can also be, as in Doughty, a means to honor a culture and place, and thus to preserve it from the rewriting of empire. Whatever sins of imperialism may have stained Doughty, thinking of the Arabs he traveled among as a barbaric people that needed to be colonized under the guise of European moral superiority was not one of them. If anything, he may have been guilty of romanticizing the desert and its people in order to distance himself from England and the English.

Doughty could within the span of a few sentences both deride and praise the Arabs he traveled among—and it is easy to quote him to either effect. More difficult but truer to his discourse and beliefs would be to read his narrative and descriptive passages, for they render the complexity of the desert culture he found and his ambivalent responses toward it. In his twelve-hundred pages readers can find single sentences to support whatever claims they wish to make, whether to defame, exalt, or even understand his book.

Once he was in the desert, the rhythms of nomadism instilled themselves in Doughty. As a non-believer in a culture that made prayer a public rite, Doughty could not hope to pass as a native; but he did not otherwise live apart from the customs of the place. This discipline required that Doughty discard all but the minimum of material goods. He buried his books ("saving *Die alte Geographie Arabiens,* and Zehme's *Arabien seit hundert Jahren"*) in a hole in the desert so that he could live true to his own maxim: "He is a free man that may carry all his worldly possessions upon one of his shoulders." The things brought from the outside and cast off as unnecessary in the desert are books, the mechanically reproduced form stories take in a modern world.

This gesture of renunciation helps us glimpse Doughty's motives as a traveler, especially when set beside this brief passage from *Arabia Deserta*:

> The Beduins asked me daily if I did not feel a home-sickness? They whispered ofttimes that I were a ban-

ished man. "Khalil [their term for him], how long wilt thou be missing from thy place and fellowship?" . . . "Tell us, art thou an outlawed man? and else, we cannot imagine what thou art!"

In his usual oblique way, Doughty does not repeat the answers, if any, he gave to these questions; he says only that the bedouins think of the outlaw as a fugitive from human justice and society. That last fact suggests Doughty thought of himself as an outlaw who'd fled an England that had grown alien to him as it became industrial and urban. Speaking of English travelers as a breed, Evelyn Waugh quipped that they alone of Europeans "have half (and wholly) killed themselves in order to get away from England." For Doughty, more complexly, Chaucer's England of the high Middle Ages was dead and in the grave, a thing never to be seen again except perhaps in fleeting glimpses by a traveler in Arabia who did not need to carry *The Canterbury Tales* on his shoulder because he had it by heart.

To read Doughty today demands a kind of double time-travel: across the desert world he traversed that is now in the past; and across an imagined sense of place he took from a medieval world that even in the 1870s was in the past. As they come together in our minds, just as they come together in his sentences of mingled Arabic and Middle English, we see how Doughty escaped the clichés of his contemporary travel writers. With his doubling vision that brought together these great pilgrimages and their stories, he made a sense of place for himself that was utterly original and largely inimitable. In his *Scenes in America Deserta,* Banham observes shrewdly that "to survive a reading of Doughty—all six hundred thousand words of his two solid volumes—is like surviving a long desert journey, and leaves the reader permanently changed."

Reading Doughty has always been an act of recovery, of returning to a different sense of time, even for those who followed closely after him in the line of British desert travelers. T. E. Lawrence, who could occasionally imitate Doughty's style to good effect, was by comparison a latecomer. His medievalism may seem much like Doughty's but it was in fact far more literal and thus could be made to serve his political activism. Drawn first to the desert while an undergraduate at Oxford, Lawrence wrote a thesis on crusaders' castles in the Holy Land. He set out to examine the surviving monuments of a medieval world rather than to use its traces as a metaphor for writing about place. As a young man, he went to study the ruins of Christian culture in the Holy Land and then journeyed into Syria; that familiarity with terrain served him well during the Arab Revolt in the desert during World War I. Yet even as he mastered the arts of dynamiting railroads and cruising the desert in Rolls-Royce armored cars, Lawrence was unable to distance himself from the medieval. Remembering in *Seven Pillars* the enforced quiet of a desert winter, living in miserable conditions of ice, vermin and boredom, Lawrence writes: "In my saddle-bags was a *Morte d'Arthur.* It relieved my disgust." Perhaps in that slow and painful threnody for a dying world, Lawrence came to understand the workings of time: that the acts of even the most heroic warriors as they roam freely across the landscape quickly fade with their noble ideals and bonds of comradeship.

After Doughty's accounts of pilgrimage routes in the desert, and Lawrence's drama of revolt, Arabia must have seemed overwritten to Wilfred Thesiger when he went there immediately after World War II. He brought with him an almost absurdly colonial pedigree: son of the British Legate in Addis Ababa, nephew of a viceroy of India, educated at Eton and Oxford, colonial officer in the Sudan, wartime service with the SAS in the North African desert, officer of the Desert Locust Research Organization. Yet beneath these signs of privilege and service there was a deep sense of the nomad in Thesiger, of the wanderer who truly hates modern civilization and its proprieties because he has known them at first hand. In a choice both physically audacious and metaphorically resonant, Thesiger twice crossed the Empty Quarter, the eastern desert of the Arabian Peninsula, between 1945 and 1950. In his typically laconic way, he explained in his account of the place, *Arabian Sands* (1958), that "it was one of the very few places left where I could satisfy an urge to go where others had not been." It was also a place where he could "win distinction as a traveler" and find comrades among the bedouin so that his journey did not become "a meaningless penance."

Thesiger shows his devotion to T. E. Lawrence by quoting him at various points in *Arabian Sands,* most notably his description of nomadism as "that most deep and biting social discipline." This phrase comes from Lawrence's statement that Doughty knew "nomadism, that most deeply biting of all social disciplines." There is a narrative line linking these writers but each moves through the desert with a different sense of time: Doughty responds to the traces of its past inhabitants, Lawrence to the political moment between Ottoman and European colonialism, and Thesiger to the enduring nomadic customs shaped by terrain and weather. As the title character of Michael Ondaatje's *The English Patient* (1992) remarks, "But in the emptiness of deserts you are always surrounded by lost history."

If *Arabian Sands* lacks the scale of *Arabia Deserta* or *Seven Pillars,* that is its point. Thesiger retreated into the last fastnesses of empty desert with a small group of bedouin because he wanted to know one final untouched territory. He was a solitary, and his ordeal was personal beyond the point of self-denial to outright masochism. He wrote *Arabian Sands* some years after

his journeys and then only at the urging of friends. That he went to the Empty Quarter to define himself rather than to gather experience for a book may well explain why his narrative keeps a dangerously stark quality. Nothing is wasted, nothing is adorned. His prose is as harshly lit as the black-and-white photographs he took in the desert. With little shadow or gradation, his writing cultivates that extremity of place where all life is reduced to a matter of water.

The name Empty Quarter had a literal truth for Thesiger when he crossed the desert in the late forties. *Arabian Sands* has fewer people in it than *Arabia Deserta* or *Seven Pillars* because Thesiger writes as a loner, but its descriptions of the shape of a day or of riding a camel are like those in Doughty and Lawrence. When Thesiger returned to Oman and Abu Dhabi in 1977, however, they had become for him an "Arabian Nightmare." Writing in his seventies of a desert world made small by motor vehicles and airplanes, Thesiger concluded the new preface to *Arabian Sands* on a familiar note of traveler's regret: "For me this book remains a memorial to a vanished past, a tribute to a once magnificent people." Amid ruin and disillusionment, all that remained was the lost history of the place.

Thesiger won the distinction he craved. Even skeptical writers who could honestly call themselves travelers thought of him as a celebrity, a throwback to the great Victorian travelers. Eric Newby ends his *A Short Walk in the Hindu Kush* (1958) with a wonderfully self-deflating scene that turns on his encounter with Thesiger in the mountains of Nuristan. Having crossed some of the most rugged mountains in Asia, Newby meets Thesiger at the end of his short walk: "a great, long striding crag of a man, with an outcrop for a nose and bushy eyebrows, forty-five years old and as hard as nails, in an old tweed jacket of the sort worn by Eton boys." They make camp that evening, eat chicken and rice together, and then prepare for sleep. With that comes Newby's final paragraph, designed to mock whatever illusions he might have nursed about the glamorous hardships of his own travels: "The ground was like iron with sharp rocks sticking up out of it. We started to blow up our air-beds. 'God, you must be a couple of pansies,' said Thesiger." So the book ends, and with it a style of travel writing.

For a writer of another generation and nationality, the American Christopher Dickey, Thesiger's Arabian nightmare could itself become a compelling subject. As a journalist covering the Islamic world of the late 1980s, Dickey signals his time and place by calling his book *Expats: Travels in Arabia from Tripoli to Teheran* (1990), that is, from Qaddafi to Khomeini. Early in his book, Dickey tells of his visit to Thesiger in his London flat, to the nomad domesticated in the city, and then closes *Expats* with a one-page "Postscript" on Thesiger's return to Abu Dhabi in 1990 for an exhibition of his desert photographs. What comes between is Dickey's account of an Arab world filled with powerful machines of the sort Thesiger loved to despise: diesel barges to service off-shore oil rigs, aircraft to connect the emirates with the world's money capitals, American warships to patrol the chokepoints of the Persian Gulf. It seems beyond even the ability of an informed reader to see this as the region Thesiger crossed a brief generation before by camel. With deft understatement, Dickey ends his book not by speculating on geopolitics or the rate of change in the Islamic world but by quoting a few sentences from an interview Thesiger gave about *Arabian Sands* to *The Gulf News* in 1990: "'I want it to be put into Arabic as a monument to a proud people,' said the old man. 'And I want it to be read by every young Arab who has never been a Bedu.'" At the end, Thesiger might have thought himself to be Doughty quoting Chaucer or Lawrence praising Malory. More sadly, he reminds me of this sentence in *Arabia Deserta*: "The Semites are wont to say of the old nations before them that they were giants."

For all that the desire to go where no one has ever gone before can seem the traveler's snobbery, it must also have been a reflex of claustrophobia for some English writers. It promised escape from a social world of hierarchies and conventions. But what happens when all the untouched regions have been seen, all the journeys without maps have been made? When Thesiger has stopped writing and the people of his other great book, *The Marsh Arabs* (1964), have become victims of Saddam Hussein's genocide? When it's all *terra cognita?*

No one who writes honestly about travel and place can evade these questions. For they shape not merely what one can say about a particular place but whether one can write about it at all. The most self-examined response I know to the impossibility of following these British Arabists comes from another island expatriate, Reyner Banham, in his *Scenes from America Deserta* (1982):

> Certainly, the reader will discover soon enough that I view the Southwest [of the United States] through a vision that has been largely formed by the powerful British tradition of writing about quite other deserts, those of the Old World; and it is in honor of that tradition that I have given this book a title that deliberately echoes that of Charles Doughty's classic *Travels in Arabia Deserta.*

As much as he admits his affection for these British writers, Banham also evades their influence or at least distances himself from it. For Banham, clearing territory does not simply mean shifting continents, it also means shaping his own style. His fluid prose has the ease of a spoken idiom far removed from Doughty's knowingly archaic diction and syntax or Thesiger's

flinty and austere notations. As Banham saw in 1982 the nomadic desert was coming to its end, at least for British writers. He may not be the last of them but his *Scenes in America Deserta* is shaped by a sense that this particular traveler's tale needs to discover a new site. Banham rewrites the desert book by going to arid openlands in the American west and accepting the traveler's fate of rental cars, motels, and fast-food restaurants. No rhapsodies from him about the old days of animal transport, sleeping in the open, and eating local dishes. He finds in America Deserta two holy places, two meccas: the entwined yet contradictory sites of Salt Lake City and Las Vegas, heaven and hell, separated by a range of mountains. But more, he distances himself from both of these pilgrimage sites—and from even the idea of following that ritual—by evoking the stillness of the desert.

Coming this late Banham survives as traveler and writer by accepting that places as well as our tales about them have changed utterly in the century between the early Doughty and the late Thesiger. We can never be that innocent again. Or so we will seem in our innocence to later generations that read our books about places and travels—unless they read us with greater sympathy than we read our predecessors. For they will know better than we that part of a place's story must be the way writers find predecessors to guide them. In an insight that reveals how hard it was for him to read through and then beyond Doughty and the other Arabists, Banham tells how, once in the Mojave, he found his best guides were science-fiction writers and illustrators: "Science fiction was one of the most relevant things I knew about America Deserta before I got there, but I didn't know that I knew it until I did get there. That flash of light in the filling station forecourt was an eleventh-hour-and-fifty-ninth minute warning of what was about to come." That this epiphany of how to see the place hit Banham as he was pumping gas marks his time and place as a desert traveler.

After twelve-hundred pages of narrative, Doughty writes the last sentence of *Arabia Deserta*: "On the morrow I was called to the open hospitality of the British Consulate." A flatter and more dazzlingly anti-climactic sentence of homecoming would be hard to imagine. It works, though, because it reminds the reader that Doughty is leaving the vast openness of the desert to return to the insularity of British life. The travel book as written by Doughty, Lawrence, and Thesiger, as well as by others such as Charles Kinglake, Mary Kingsley, Freya Stark, even our contemporaries like Bruce Chatwin, Nick Danziger, and Redmond O'Hanlon is essentially a narrative of personal testing, of setting off for a place where the soul can flourish by breaking free of all that constrains it at home. Their books are never straightforward reportage or analysis, nor merely psychological exploration but instead a mixed form that seeks to find the place where the writer-traveler can feel most fully alive, in fact, where he or she can find the home that Britain cannot provide. And part of that recovery is to locate a place that could serve as the past, often a medieval past of quest romance and knights errant.

It is partly the Britishness of these writers—their knowledge of that insular, hierarchical, claustrophobic culture—that makes them such wonderful travel writers. For islands often drive out their most talented and lively natives. And partly, it is other aspects of this Britishness that prepared them to be travel writers: a tradition of outdoor activities like riding and hunting that are useful skills in a desert; a classical education in Latin and Greek, or at least the shreds of one, that makes Jason, Odysseus, and Aeneas into compatriots; a vernacular literary tradition in Chaucer, Malory, and Spenser that prized the individual adventurer who turned the literal journey into a spiritual quest; and an essayistic prose tradition, in *The Rambler* and elsewhere, that admired a nonchalant, if careful discursiveness.

Perhaps because the desert offered a more austere setting than did, for example, the classical remains of the Mediterranean world, it set the possibilities for the travel book as a genre into sharp relief: spiritual quest-romance, as in Doughty's *Travels in Arabia Deserta*; spiritual-political adventure, as in Lawrence's *Seven Pillars of Wisdom*; elegiac celebration of nomadic austerity, as in Thesiger's *Arabian Sands*. For all that these writers may have gone to the desert to escape England, they carried with them the burden of its language and literary tradition. They portrayed the desert by working the far edge of literary decorum. A contemporary reviewer of Charles Kinglake's *Eothen* (1844), a forerunner of books by Doughty and the others, described its prose as "lively, brilliant, and rather insolent" and that set the tone for those who followed, especially if "insolent" is taken to imply a distaste for conventional good prose. The styles of the desert writers belong as much to their nomadism as do their accounts of desert life. They bend the resources of English to evoke what they brought to the place and what they found there.

Doughty, Lawrence, Thesiger and the others counter our easy use of the word "nomad": here today gone tomorrow, footloose and fancy free, pack up our troubles in the old kitbag and go. For them, the allure of desert nomadism meant thirst, extremes of heat and cold, extended marches through landscapes of lacerating rock and sand—all toward a radical simplicity that might leave behind European civilization, in its essentials as much as its excesses. Like other nomads, they learned a place by submitting to its rhythms. In turn, we learn their nomadism by submitting to their prose.

Gordon Hirsch (essay date spring 2001)

SOURCE: Hirsch, Gordon. "The Travels of RLS as a Young Man." *The Victorian Newsletter,* no. 99 (spring 2001): 1-7.

[*In the following essay, Hirsch studies the travel writings of Robert Louis Stevenson, and asserts that for Stevenson "travel served as a mode of self-discovery as well as providing material for his developing craft."*]

It is not surprising that Robert Louis Stevenson embarked on his career as an author in the genre of travel writing. In his early twenties, Stevenson traveled extensively in Scotland, England, and France, undertaking walking tours wherever he went. Stevenson's cousin and official biographer, Graham Balfour, cites a "pencil list of towns in which he had slept, compiled about 1886," including 46 in England, 50 in Scotland, 74 in France, and 40 in the rest of Europe. Balfour notes that "between 1871 and 1876 no less than nine of [Stevenson's essays] deal with travel or the external appearance of places known to him" (1:126). Stevenson's wanderlust was evident early, as was his desire to turn his journeys to use in his writing. At a time when the young Stevenson's character was still in the process of being formed, travel served as a mode of self-discovery as well as providing material for his developing craft.

In September 1876, Stevenson and a friend, Walter Simpson, set off on a canoe trip on the rivers and canals of Belgium and northern France. Intending from the first to write about these travels, Stevenson kept a journal, which he rewrote a year later and which became his first book, *An Inland Voyage*. Except for the "incessant, pitiless, beating rain" (117), Stevenson's journey itself, as described in the book, is relatively unremarkable. He encounters various individuals, towns, and difficulties along the way (including an overturned canoe), but the most unusual experience—Stevenson's brief detention by the police in France as a suspected German spy—was not fully detailed until ten years after the book was originally published (Swearingen 124). What is striking and remarkable, however, is the way Stevenson presents himself and the issues which concern his personality.[1]

At the outset Stevenson notes that he has "never been in a canoe under sail in my life" (3) His voyage is perceived as an adventure and experiment, and it is compared grandiloquently to a major life change: "I suppose it was almost as trying a venture into the regions of the unknown as to publish a first book, or marry" (4). Nonetheless, he is aware that he looks odd to the people he meets—a young, spindly-legged, long-haired bohemian wanderer, wearing "a smoking-cap of Indian work, the gold lace pitifully frayed and tarnished" (159).

A group of walkers cross the Mer de Glace at Chamonix, France.

Furthermore, Stevenson frequently turns up in towns rain-drenched and bedraggled. Mistaken by those he encounters for a rag-and-bone man, vagrant, spy, peddler, servant, or purveyor of pornographic photographs, Stevenson paints a wry portrait of his own apparent lack of defined social rank and respectability. He is shocked that the people he meets respond to his clothes and physical appearance, rather than his more complicated, subjective sense of who he is. One of the most striking passages in the book describes his expulsion from a highly praised inn at La Fere. The brisk, bustling landlady not only refuses Stevenson and his traveling companion a room, but also denies them dinner in her establishment, virtually throwing them out the door. A similar response is elicited in another town where one landlady or landlord after another wonders aloud whether the two wanderers are peddlers—"*Ces messieurs sont des marchands?*" (38)—before turning them away as wholly unsuitable guests, which leads Stevenson to muse, "I never knew a population with so narrow a range of conjecture as the innkeepers of Pont-sur-Sambre" (40). If Stevenson seems somewhat uncertain about who he is, the townspeople and innkeepers do not hesitate in locating him at the margins of society.

In fact, Stevenson has undertaken his inland voyage partly to explore deracination and marginality, and he consciously identifies with the people who share his sense of wanderlust or bohemianism whom he meets along the way. He praises, for example, the canal barge operators: "I would rather be a bargee than occupy any position under Heaven that required attendance at an office" (11). A bargeman proudly contrasts himself (and the two travelers) with "a man . . . who sticks to his own village like a bear . . . very well, he sees nothing. And then death is the end of all. And he has seen nothing" (67). Stevenson also records the envy of the travelers expressed by the omnibus driver for the Hotel *Grand Cerf* in Maubeuge: "How he longed to travel! he told me. How he longed to be somewhere else, and see the round world before he went into the grave! 'Here I am!' said he, 'I drive to the station. Well. And then I drive back to the hotel. And so on every day and all the week round. My God, is that life?' . . . It is an evil age for the gypsily inclined among men" (27). Driving a hotel's omnibus may be respectable, but why should one who finds his respectability an insufficient reward be required to cling to it? "Better a thousand times that he should be a tramp, and mend pots and pans by the wayside, and sleep under trees, and see the dawn and the sunset every day above a new horizon," Stevenson believes (28). It is worth recalling that earlier in the decade Stevenson had completed his legal studies, and was none too eager himself to settle down to become a legal drudge. No wonder, then, that he sees the omnibus driver as a "poor cage-bird! Do I not remember the time when I myself haunted the station, to watch train after train carry its complement of freemen into the night, and read the names of distant places on the time-bills with indescribable longings?" (29). Stevenson's wanderlust took hold at an early age, when every distant town in the railroad timetables seemed a putative "El Dorado."

Stevenson had turned his back on the law and in 1875 gone to stay in an artists' colony near Fontainebleau, where earlier the Barbizon school of French painting had congregated. Thus on his inland voyage he feels a special kinship with those he encounters who are "outskirters of art" (147). He spends a long time staring at one man dining in a large party at an inn, because his face stood out from the rest of the company for its "living, expressive air, and you could see that his eyes took things in." Later Stevenson finds the man "busy fiddling for the peasants to caper to" and the riddle of his identity is solved: "He was a wandering violinist" (147). Stevenson also records in loving detail his encounter with an old strolling player, who vigorously rejects the idea that he regrets his choice of a career: "Do you think I would rather be a fat burgess, like a calf? . . . I have known what pleasure was, what it was to do a thing well, what it was to be an artist. And to know what art is, is to have an interest forever, such as no burgess can find in his petty concerns" (152).

Not only does he choose to identify with the discontented and bohemian, but the young Stevenson also becomes aware of social class and some of the politics of class. He records with interest the strongly felt political convictions of a professed "Communist" (88-94). He is staggered when, because his traveling companion has a mackintosh and he himself does not, he is taken for his friend's servant. Being repeatedly shut out by innkeepers and townspeople because he doesn't look quite respectable leads Stevenson to a series of meditations on class. On the one hand, even the lower classes like to find points of superiority to somebody else, but, on the other hand, a poor individual is likely to offer charity, whereas "at a certain level of prosperity, as in a balloon ascent, the fortunate person passes through a zone of clouds, and sublunary matters [i.e. the less prosperous and less elevated individuals below] are thenceforward hidden from his view" (42).

Stevenson's responses to women in *An Inland Voyage* are also revealing. On the one hand, the category of woman he most frequently encounters seems to be the "red-handed and loud-voiced" washerwomen he frequently glimpses along the waterways (137; cf. 119, 125, 155, etc.). Yet he also occasionally notices women like the "bevy of girls in Parisian costumes playing croquet. . . . The look of these slim figures, all corseted and ribboned, produced an answerable disturbance in our hearts. We were within sniff of Paris, it seemed. And here were females of our own species playing croquet" (142). It is tempting to inquire as to what other species Stevenson thinks women might belong, and indeed the answer is not far to seek: "For, to be frank, the peasant woman is scarcely to be counted as a woman at all"—he has already "passed by such a succession of people in petticoats digging, and hoeing, and making dinner" (143). When Stevenson and his friend pass a "bevy" of bourgeois girls, it is often with a "disturbance in our hearts," as occurs again when they pass by young women in the garden of a boarding school. These girls wave handkerchiefs at the canoeists, and Stevenson responds with a wave and "a stir in my heart. . . . This is a fashion I love: to kiss the hand or wave a handkerchief to people I shall never see again, to play with possibility, and knock a pag for fancy to hang upon" (137). Even at a distance, such young women are fit subjects for fantasy, belonging as they do to the same "species" as the author. But they are also attractive precisely because they are ephemeral figures of fantasy, and thus not threatening.

The young Stevenson's identity clearly is protean and uncertain in *An Inland Voyage*. A chapter is devoted, for instance, to an encounter with the members of a Belgian boating club, and although the Belgian enthusiasts are intrigued to know all about their British counterparts, in conversation Stevenson feels somewhat distant from the "Royal Nautical Sportsmen." He can identify with their lack of interest in "dull" and "nasty" business affairs: "They were all employed over the frivolous mercantile concerns of Belgium during the day; but in the evening they found some hours for the serious concerns of life"—namely, "their spontaneous, long-suffering affection for nautical sports" (18-19). Still, Stevenson is soon left behind by their passionate enthusiasm for rowing, and he flees to avoid the arrival of a a champion canoeist. These enthusiasts evidently take their pastime entirely too seriously, cling to it with an escapism that is perhaps a bit too readily apparent.

Throughout the book, then, Stevenson's bourgeois roots are evident, yet he is most interested in people who have not fully adapted to bourgeois life, whether they be Royal Nautical Sportsmen, barge families, wandering actors and musicians, or omnibus drivers longing to travel somewhere other than back and forth between station and hotel. On the other hand, Stevenson also feels somewhat shocked by his not fitting in—at being taken for a peddler or vagabond or worse. He clearly feels envious of his traveling companion's superior respectability: "He had more aplomb altogether than I; and a dull, positive way of approaching a landlady that carried off the india-rubber bags" in which their belongings were stowed (117). Simpson's appearance and manners are somehow less likely to provoke the canoeists' immediate expulsion from an inn.

Throughout the voyage, Stevenson explicitly resists the pull of the conventional life and home. He declares that "the receipt of letters is the death of all holiday feeling" on a trip: "I have paid all this money, look you, and paddled all these strokes, for no other purpose than to be abroad; and yet you keep me at home with your perpetual communications. You tug the string, and I feel that I am a tethered bird. You pursue me all over Europe with the little vexations that I came away to avoid" (124). It is not always clear who the Stevenson-*persona* in the book is, but it is clear what he is resisting, what he wishes *not* to become.

In the course of the book, some of the most interesting moments occur when Stevenson momentarily surrenders control and loses himself entirely, hypnogogically, to canoeing. Continuing to count his individual oar strokes, he loses track of the hundreds (133). He slips into a state of Nirvana, where he cannot distinguish *me* from *not-me* and it seems that "somebody else" is managing the paddling (131). The canoe-trip as a whole is a willed, temporary separation from ordinary life: "I wish to take a dive among new conditions for a while, as into another element. I have nothing to do with my friends or my affections for the time" (124). There is a strong sense of emotional detachment and dissociation, and the Nirvana-state is clearly the journey's high-point: "Thoughts presented themselves unbidden; they were not my thoughts, they were someone else's. . . . This frame of mind was the great exploit of our voyage, take it all in all. It was the farthest piece of travel accomplished" (132). At this moment Stevenson and his fellow-voyager, Simpson, virtually become the two boats by whose names they have referred to one another, the *Arethusa* and the *Cigarette,* respectively, and the "inland" of the title becomes what in important respects it always was—the interior of Robert Louis Stevenson. The fluidity of the author's character comes to resemble the water that has borne him along, and fundamentally he is alone.

For many of Stevenson's admirers, *Travels with a Donkey in the Cevennes* contains his most perfect and picturesque travel writing. It is an elaboration of the journal he kept while roaming this mountainous region in the south of France for twelve days during September and October 1878. (The journal itself was first published one hundred years afterwards under the title *The Cevennes Journal.*) Unlike the *Inland Voyage* canoe-trip, Stevenson made this tour alone and on foot, with knapsack and pack. He purchased a mule, however,

which he named Modestine, to carry his pack. If the earlier book depicts an attempt at defining a very fluid personality, with Stevenson adopting various *personae* along his voyage and trying to reconcile his self-perceptions with others' perceptions of him, *Travels with a Donkey* is the story of a relationship, the relationship of Stevenson with his donkey.

Of course, a number of themes weave their way through *Travels with a Donkey,* and one of the more prominent of these concerns religion. Stevenson is conscious that he has been raised in a strong tradition of Scottish Presbyterianism, though he is now something of an agnostic traveling in largely Catholic France. He devotes a section of the book—reminiscent of Matthew Arnold's ambivalent response to the monastery of the Grande Chartreuse—to his stay in a Trappist monastery, where he encounters some pressure from his fellow-boarders to convert to Catholicism. Stevenson delights in resisting. His travels also take him to the region of the Camisards, French Protestants who were in armed revolt against the government in the early years of the eighteenth century, following the revocation of the Edict of Nantes, which had granted them religious toleration. Stevenson's treatment of the whole topic of religion in *Travels* amounts to an extended meditation on religious differences and a plea for mutual toleration and respect. As such, it constitutes part of the extended dialogue on religious faith that Stevenson conducted with his Calvinist father.

A second motif that one can trace through the book concerns the presence, or perhaps one should say the absence, of the married American woman who had come into Stevenson's life and was later to become his own wife, Fanny Osbourne. Stevenson met Fanny in July 1876 at Grez, where both had gone to study art. Their relationship developed over the next two years, but Fanny sailed back to the U. S. in August 1878 at the insistence of her husband, Sam. Occasionally Stevenson's "strange lack" of Fanny rises to the surface of his text, particularly in his feeling of solitude under the stars: "I wished a companion to lie near me in the starlight, silent and not moving, but ever within touch. . . . To live out of doors with a woman a man loves is of all lives the most complete and free" (297-98).[2] The importance of Fanny's presence/absence in *Travels with a Donkey* is alluded to in Stevenson's declaration to his cousin Bob Stevenson that "lots of it is mere protestations to F., most of which I think you will understand. That is to me the main thread of interest" (*Letters* 2:313); and the book's dedication to Sidney Colvin, though a more general elaboration on the theme that "we are all travelers in what John Bunyan calls the wilderness of this world" in search of "an honest friend," also hints at the *roman a clef*: "Every book is, in an intimate sense, a circular letter to the friends of him who writes it. They alone take his meaning; they find private messages, assurances of love, and expressions of gratitude dropped for them in every corner" (187).

The argument of this section of the paper will be to show, a bit more substantially and systematically, what other readers have suspected (see, for example Mackay 88, Holmes 38, and McLynn 131) that the donkey Modestine is a surrogate for Fanny, a female "other" in a relationship with Stevenson that the book is focused on developing. This thesis is an elaboration of a remark that Stevenson himself included in his *Cevennes Journal,* but chose not to publish in *Travels with a Donkey,* that "a voyage is a piece of autobiography at best" (68).

Although most modern editions of *Travels with a Donkey* follow the Tusitala edition of Stevenson's *Works* by placing the fragment "A Mountain Town in France" at the beginning of the book, as Stevenson seems to have originally intended, all versions of *Travels with a Donkey* published during his own lifetime actually begin with the section on Velay and the chapter on "The Donkey, the Pack, and the Pack-Saddle" (Swearingen 33-34). The Velay section starts with two epigraphs which immediately call attention to the donkey Modestine in some of her symbolic complexity. One is an excerpt from a well-known passage in Sophocles's *Antigone,* in which the chorus marvels at the might of man, who "masters by his devices the tenant of the fields," though the passage in *Antigone* goes on to complicate this sense of triumph by noting that such human cleverness may produce either good or evil and by denouncing the person who chooses evil. Stevenson's second epigraph— "Who hath loosed the bands of the wild ass?" (*Job* 39:5) expresses the claim of the deity, speaking as the voice from the whirlwind, to the kind of infinite power and wisdom that Job cannot hope to understand or regulate. Both epigraphs, in other words, ironically suggest the limits of humankind's power over even those creatures and things which it believes are under control or at least within its power of understanding.

The first chapter of the original book, as noted, plunges the reader immediately into the topic of "The Donkey, the Pack, and the Pack-Saddle." Stevenson determines that he will require an animal of some sort to help transport his sleeping-sack—a sort of long roll or sausage, green waterproof cart cloth without and blue sheep's fur within" (209)—along with his cooking utensils, some food, a lantern and candles, a jack-knife and a revolver, and other necessities. Stevenson's preconceptions about the animal he will purchase in order to help him are interesting. He first contemplates a horse as his preferred "beast of burden," but he concludes with a curiously volatile sense of the animal's gender:

> A horse is a fine lady among animals, flighty, timid, delicate of eating, of tender health; he is too valuable and too restive to be left alone, so you are chained to

your brute as to a fellow galley-slave; a dangerous road puts him out of his wits; in short, he's an uncertain and exacting ally, and adds thirty-fold to the troubles of the voyager. What I required was something cheap and small and hardy, and of a stolid and peaceful temper; and all these requisites pointed to a donkey.

(209-10)

From Father Adam, a peddler, he purchases Modestine, "a diminutive she-ass, not much bigger than a dog, the color of a mouse, with a kindly eye and a determined under jaw" (210), supposing her to be merely "an appurtenance of my mattress, or self-acting bedstead on four castors" (211). Modestine's clear gender-markings are striking from the very first, and she continues to be gender-marked throughout the text—as "a female" (216), "my lady" and "my lady-friend" (247, 261, 361), "my she-ass" (255, 347, etc.). Descriptively, too, Modestine is "prim" (*Cevennes Journal* 50), moves with a "sober daintiness of gait" and is "docility itself" (215). Her very name suggests female modesty, and when Modestine meets a male donkey on the road Stevenson is forced to separate the pair, noting that "the incident saddened me, as did everything that spoke of my donkey's sex" (220). Imagining her at first to be a tractable helpmate, a self-acting bedstead, Stevenson writes of his affection for Modestine, and his belief that he is rescuing her from Father Adam, who "had a name in the village for brutally misusing the ass," though Adam visibly sheds a tear upon parting from Modestine (211).

Stevenson soon encounters his own problems with Modestine, and, in fact, the editors of the *Cevennes Journal* suggest that one of the reasons for these problems is that Modestine probably had been used previously to draw the peddler's cart, not to carry a loaded pack-saddle (138). In any event, Stevenson almost immediately experiences a great deal of difficulty fitting both a pad and the pack-saddle upon Modestine, especially when he tries to add "a monstrous deck-cargo" of clothing, food, and bottles (213). A disaster is brewing.[3] The load requires constant readjustment, and at various times the pack intended for Modestine's back falls below her belly, spilling Stevenson's possessions onto the roadway. Early in their travels, particularly, Stevenson and his donkey provoke amusement in the people they encounter—so he imagines that, encouraged by these onlookers, Modestine herself "seemed to smile" (220). He is at last forced to jettison a goodly portion of his belongings, calling this "a sacrifice to the gods of shipwreck" (222).

The first great test of wills occurs as Stevenson attempts to use a cane to get Modestine to move. He is able to speed her up a bit by applying his staff, but she immediately reverts to her slowest pace when he stops. Stevenson knows himself to be a "green," and believes himself to be a "reluctant" donkey-driver (215), and he has qualms about his brutality toward his female donkey as he goes along: "I am worthy the name of an Englishman, and it goes against my conscience to lay my hand rudely on a female" (215-16); or, "The sound of my own blows sickened me. Once, when I looked at her, she had a faint resemblance to a lady of my acquaintance who formerly loaded me with kindness, and thus increased my horror of my cruelty" (220).

At the same time Stevenson is suspicious about the trustworthiness of Modestine's responses. At one point he responds sympathetically to her apparent difficulty: "The poor brute's knees were trembling and her breathing was distressed; it was plain that she could go no faster on a hill. God forbid, thought I, that I should brutalise this innocent creature; let her go at her own pace, and let me patiently follow" (216). Yet when a "peasant" passing by replaces Stevenson's cane with a switch plucked from a thicket and begins to lace Modestine "about the sternworks, uttering a cry," Stevenson notes that Modestine "broke into a good round pace, which she kept up without flagging, and without exhibiting the least symptom of distress, as long as the peasant kept beside us. Her former panting and shaking had been, I regret to say, a piece of comedy" (217). In a later chapter, as recorded in the *Cevennes Journal,* Stevenson takes a longer route "in honor of real or feigned fatigues upon the part of my loathly donkey" (53). Stevenson again humorously projects his doubts about the donkey's integrity onto her when he reports her taking and munching the black bread he offers "with a contrite, hypocritical air" (222).

Modestine's resistance to Stevenson and his beatings of her continue.[4] Stevenson keeps "one arm free to thrash Modestine, and cruelly I chastised her" (213). He complains that "my arm ached like toothache from perpetual beating" (226). At times Modestine's vagaries are represented as stereotypically female, as when she leaves the main road for a by-path, and Stevenson's responses are stereotypically male: "A little out of the village, Modestine, filled with the demon, set her heart upon a by-road and positively refused to leave it. I dropped all my bundles, and, I am ashamed to say, struck the poor sinner across the face" (222). Modestine, Stevenson complains, is always domestically inclined, preferring any open gate or doorway she encounters along the way to the open road. When bystanders laugh at him, Stevenson uncomfortably recalls "having laughed myself when I had seen good men struggling with adversity in the person of a jackass, and the recollection filled me with penitence" (222).

The landlord of an inn at which Stevenson stays makes his progress easier by preparing a goad for Stevenson to use—a wand with 1/8 inch of pin at the end to prick Modestine into progress:

Thenceforward Modestine was my slave [Stevenson adds in the *Cevennes Journal* "my chattel, my most obedient, humble servant" (39)]. . . . And what although now and then a drop of blood should appear on Modestine's mouse-colored wedge-like rump? I should have preferred it otherwise, indeed; but yesterday's exploits had purged my heart of all humanity. The perverse little devil, since she would not be taken with kindness, must even go with pricking.

(231-32)

Still, Modestine's top speed is only two and a half miles per hour, and Stevenson continues to employ his goad. Modestine suffers from the blows and goading, the rubbing of the sack and saddle, and also probably, as the *Cevennes Journal* editor has suggested, from being in heat throughout the first part of the journey (153).

Alas, there were her two forelegs no better than raw beef on the inside, and blood was running from under her tail. They told me when I left, and I was ready to believe it, that before a few days I should come to love Modestine like a dog. Three days had passed, we had shared some misadventures, and my heart was still as cold as a potato towards my beast of burden. She was pretty enough to look at; but then she had given proof of dead stupidity, redeemed indeed by patience, but aggravated by flashes of sorry and ill-judged lightheartedness. [*Cevennes Journal* adds: "I could have seen her led to the gelatine factory without a pang" (53).] And I own this new discovery seemed another point against her. What the devil was the good of a she-ass if she could not carry a sleeping bag, and a few necessaries? I saw the end of the fable rapidly approaching, when I should have to carry Modestine. Aesop was the man to know the world!

(255-56)

The "raw beef" and trickle of blood "from the poop" become a recurrent motif, especially in the unedited *Cevennes Journal* (53, 58, 95-96). Still, the struggles with Modestine continue, as, backing, rearing, and braying, she rejects a short cut up a hillside. "I plied the goad" and Modestine is forced up the steep ascent: "Half a dozen times she [the 'vile brute' in *Cevennes Journal* (77)] was nearly over backwards on top of me; half a dozen times, from sheer weariness of spirit, I was nearly giving it up, and leading her down again to follow the road. But I took the thing as a wager, and fought it through" (292). Coping with "Modestine's laggard humour," Stevenson reports that he "goaded and kicked the reluctant Modestine" to a place of rest (321). Modestine can be forced up a path, "but once on the turf or among heather . . . the brute became demented, "traveling in circles (241). Trusting Modestine's instinct to choose the correct path when the road forks is also a mistake; Modestine turns out to have "the instinct of an ass" (243).

Stevenson is not entirely uncaring and unsolicitous toward Modestine, however. He repeatedly tries to readjust and lighten the pack, even discarding some of its contents and shifting some of the rest to his own knap-sack. His sleeping-sack is at first folded in half and slung on one side of the donkey; Stevenson eventually learns to hang it full length across the saddle on both sides to ensure the donkey's stability, even though in a drizzle this is more likely to produce wet wool inside the sleeping-sack. It is clear that at certain moments he can humorously empathize with Modestine, as when she is seen as "a haggard, drenched, desponding don-key" (247) or when, before dawn, Modestine is discov-ered "tied to a beech, and standing half across the path in an attitude of inimitable patience" (250). At moments he clearly enjoys sharing his black bread with her (early on he reduces the two classes of bread, black and brown, to an egalitarian one), and there are a number of affectionate glimpses of Modestine "munching at the sward" (296), or "munching heather" (347), or recuper-ating at an inn with "stable and kitchen in a suite, so that Modestine and I could hear each other dining" (227) There are even moments of (relatively) high com-pliment: "It grew darker and darker. Modestine, sud-denly beginning to smell mischief, bettered the pace of her own accord, and from that time forward gave me no trouble. It was the first sign of intelligence I had occa-sion to remark in her" (242). As the journey progresses, Modestine herself develops "high spirits, and broke of her own accord, for the first time in my experience, into a jolting trot" (303). A while later, "even Modestine was inspired by this purified nocturnal sunshine [the moonlight on the road], and bestirred her little hoofs as to a livelier measure" (351). At times Stevenson can be quite solicitous of Modestine, making her "a pile of chestnut-leaves, of which I found her greedy" (321)

Although Stevenson's frustrations with Modestine con-tinue through the latter parts of the journey and the text, many times here his irritation is restrained or checked. For example, "I had hurried to the topmost powers of Modestine, for I dearly desired to see the view upon the other side [of the summit of St. Pierre] before the day had faded. But it was night when I reached the summit" (358). Rhetorically, the blame is deflected somewhat from Modestine: she performed at her "topmost pow-ers," but "I" failed to reach the summit in daylight. At another point, "I fed Modestine with all the haste I could" (324), and the rest of the sentence, found in the *Cevennes Journal,* is suppressed: "but it took me longer than usual, for the minx, smelling hurry, refused to eat except from my hand" (99). Stevenson's ambivalence toward Modestine comes through most clearly in sum-mary assessments like this:

> To Modestine, although I could never find it in my heart to be generous, I believe I was rigorously just. On the march, I hit upon a mean between the honest stride-legged pace of a man walking, and the pitiful,

mincing gait that seemed to suit my she-ass next best after standing still; and to this mean, I sought honestly to keep the pair of us faithful.

> (*Cevennes Journal* 58; passage not included in *Travels with a Donkey*)

Modestine and Fanny are not the only females who fig-ure in *Travels with a Donkey.* As in the *Inland Voyage,* but more prominently in this later book, there is a mi-nor motif of Stevenson's encounters with various women along the way.[5]

A number of these women are teasing, taunting, or oth-erwise unappealing. Stevenson frequently has difficulty with the young girls he encounters: there is the seven- or eight-year-old "lassie" who clearly expects respect from the wanderer, but whose mood turns to "silent dudgeon" when he laughs at her imperiousness (235); and there are two girls of whom he asks directions, "a pair of impudent sly sluts, with not a thought but mis-chief," one of whom sticks out her tongue while the other instructs him that to reach his destination he need only follow the cows (241).

There are also quite a few attractive and appealing women in the book, such as the pretty and engaging young innkeeper in a hamlet by the Tarn: "he who takes her to his heart will doubtless be a fortunate young man" (330). At another inn, there is a shrewd landlady who runs the operation while ruling her "astonishingly ignorant" husband (228). Stevenson is surprised when he is asked to share a bedroom with a married couple at this inn: "I kept my eyes to myself, and know nothing of the woman except that she had beautiful arms, and seemed no whit abashed by my appearance" (230). The blushing self-consciousness is all his, Stevenson admits, and the couple are not fazed by his presence. When Stevenson crosses into the country of the Camisards, he notes the prettier women there, exemplified by Clarisse, whose "great grey eyes were steeped in amorous lan-guor" (311). But as often appears to be the case with the women he encounters, Clarisse has serious limita-tions: she is complacent and countrified, needing "train-ing" and contact with superior society in order to achieve real elegance (312). Clearly relationships will not come easily to this writer, and in the company of women almost as much anxiety as attraction is ex-pressed.

At "Our Lady of the Snows," Stevenson muses on the practice of excluding women from male groups, whether at a Trappist monastery or at an artists' colony, such as the one he had come to know in Barbizon:

> In the neighborhood of women it is but a touch-and-go association that can be formed among defenseless men; the stronger electricity is sure to triumph; the dreams of boyhood, the schemes of youth, are abandoned after

an interview of ten minutes, and the arts and sciences, and professional male jollity, deserted at once for two sweet eyes and a caressing accent.

(274)

Yet it is also true, as Stevenson well knows, that the Trappist monks at the monastery sleep nightly in their grave-clothes and appear in more senses than one to be "the dead in life" (277). As he leaves the monastery, a French song about how *Amour* will know how to value the *belles filles* comes to mind, "And I blessed God that I was free to wander, free to hope, and free to love" (277), unlike the monks.

As the traveler approaches the end of his travels, he hears "the voice of a woman singing some sad, old, endless ballad . . . about love and a *bel amoureux*," and Stevenson wishes he "could have taken up the strain and answered her," to tell about "how the world gives and takes away, and brings sweethearts near, only to separate them again into distant and strange lands; but to love is the great amulet which makes the world a garden" (350). Once again, Fanny across the seas is doubtless the subtext of his song.

Travels with a Donkey is, indeed, a book of longing, longing for the absent, desired woman. But it is also, as we have seen, a book about the problems in the relationship with a less than idealized woman. The book is suffused with a sense that relationships involve obstinacy, struggles for mastery, suspicion, contestation, strife. However humorously Stevenson's contests with Modestine are presented—and humor is certainly his aim—there is a serious subtext of irritation and contention, defining both partners in this relationship.

In this respect *Travels with a Donkey* is a difficult book for the modern reader, and perhaps especially for a modern woman, to read. If Stevenson's contemporary, presumably male reviewers found his treatment of an animal hard to take, the book is certainly all the more difficult for a modern reader who reads directly through from donkey to woman. One is probably not justified in reading the text so transparently, however. Donkeys are, after all, notoriously willful and resistant in their own right, and Modestine was very much a real-life donkey. Still, the fact is that Stevenson himself makes much of his donkey's gender, and it is quite within the realm of biographical possibility that the other side of Stevenson's longing for the absent Fanny consisted of powerful feelings of anger and frustration at being left behind when she went off to rejoin her husband. The biographical evidence makes clear, in fact, that Fanny's return to the U. S. initiated a trying period of gloom and self-doubt for Stevenson.[6]

Whatever his exasperation with Modestine, Stevenson, after adding many pages not included in the original *Cevennes Journal* recounting the struggles of the Cam-

isards, the rebellious French Protestants, chooses to end *Travels with a Donkey* by returning to Modestine and describing their parting. "Farewell Modestine!" the book's final chapter, begins with this notation: "On examination, on the morning of October 4th, Modestine was pronounced unfit for travel. She would need at least two days' repose according to the ostler" (361). Unwilling to wait, Stevenson sells Modestine for 35 francs, about half the 65 francs he had originally paid for her, but feeling "I had bought freedom into the bargain" (361). Despite these sentiments, the last chapter is a tribute to Modestine, summarizing their relationship and their parting, with a kind of equal weighing of delight and dole, or, at any rate, a blend of affectionate melancholy and humor: "I became aware of my bereavement. I had lost Modestine. Up to that moment [of parting] I had thought I hated her; but now she was gone." Stevenson sums it all up by quoting from one of Wordsworth's "Lucy" poems: "'And, Oh, / The difference to me!' For twelve days we had been fast companions. . . . She had come to regard me as a god. She loved to eat out of my hand. She was patient, elegant in form, the color of an ideal mouse, and inimitably small. Her faults were those of her race and sex; her virtues were her own" (362-63). Stevenson claims that he wept as his coach pulled away, and this is the note on which this second book of travel ends.

The first travel book, *An Inland Voyage,* is largely about a young person's search for identity. It is concerned with how he will define himself—with what social class, vocation, and group. In it Stevenson tries out a variety of bohemian roles; he expresses disapproval of various groups he encounters, but identifies totally with none. One of the striking aspects of the book is that it describes no true relationship whatsoever, even though Stevenson has a traveling companion. The latter, however, functions in the text entirely as a yardstick for measuring the self. Stevenson presents himself as something of a free spirit, enjoying the random and circumstantial nature of his encounters with people and places. His peak experience is the inner one of Nirvana.

Travels with a Donkey, on the other hand, is primarily a book about relationship—indeed about contestation in a relationship. Fanny Osbourne is obliquely present in the book, in the few direct allusions to her, but still more in the various women represented, especially Modestine. Just as in real life Fanny was resisting Stevenson by returning to the U. S. without any firm commitment to him, Modestine was resisting too, as donkeys are wont to do. The relationship between Stevenson and Modestine occupies center stage of *Travels with a Donkey,* while the Cevennes, the district traveled in, occupies a subordinate position, even in the volume's title.

Notes

1. After this was written, I came upon the recent discussion by Alex Clunas of the two early travel

books which are also the subject of this essay. Although we both discuss the sense of estrangement and the fluid identity which permeates *An Inland Voyage,* Clunas is primarily concerned with Stevenson's grappling with aesthetic problems, his invention of himself as an author, whereas my essay looks at Stevenson's struggle with developmental issues. Clunas emphasizes aesthetic choices, whereas I am mostly concerned with matters of personality. Furthermore, although Clunas essentially sees these two travel books as identical in technique, I believe the focus on Modestine in the later text makes them significantly different.

2. In the *Cevennes Journal* the passage goes on to describe "a sort of fellowship more quiet than even solitude, and which, rightly understood, is solitude made perfect. The woman . . . whom a man has learned to love wholly . . . is no longer another person in the troublous sense" (81). This double-edged sense that the beloved might be a troubling "other" or might ideally represent perfect harmony and understanding is significant.

3. In her preface to *Travels with a Donkey* Fanny Stevenson observes that "the management of Modestine's pack must have been a source of exasperation and perplexity to her master, for my husband was, like his father before him, what the Scotch call a 'handless man.' Neither could tie a knot that would hold . . . and [Stevenson's father] would find himself helpless before the problem of cording a trunk, or even buttoning his own cuffs" (184).

4. Contemporary reviews attacked this aspect of the book. The *Fortnightly Review* noted that "most Englishmen will perhaps feel pained rather than amused by the description of Modestine's many stripes" (Maixner 66); and the *Spectator* complained about "the vivid description [Stevenson] gives of each blow, as it descended on the creature's back. . . . It is strange how he can dwell with such placid content on the sufferings that he owns to have inflicted on his companion" (Maixner 72).

5. Frank McLynn suggests that Stevenson's contemporary readers and reviewers noted "the ubiquity of sexuality" in the book (136).

6. McLynn 137-48. McLynn is in fact highly critical of Fanny's behavior before her marriage to Stevenson, describing her as a mercenary, "cold, unscrupulous and somewhat coarse coquette" (113). His biography goes on to paint the later Stevenson as "a martyr to the greedy, grasping Osbourne family" (543). It is interesting to compare another recent biographical work, Alexandra Lapierre's fictionalized study of Fanny Stevenson,

which portrays her as a modern, independent, path-breaking proto-feminist. Despite their radically different sympathies, both of these recent books have the virtue of representing the two partners as strong personalities involved in a "conflictual" rather than an "idyllic" relationship (McLynn 147; cf. Lapierre 342-43).

Works Cited

Balfour, Graham. *The Life of Robert Louis Stevenson.* 2 vols. London: Methuen, 1901.

Clunas, Alex. "'Out of my country and myself I go': Identity and Writing in Stevenson's Early Travel Books." *Nineteenth-Century Prose* 23.1 (1996): 54-73.

Holmes, Richard. *Footsteps: Adventures of a Romantic Biographer.* New York: Viking, 1985.

Lapierre, Alexandra. *Fanny Stevenson: A Romance of Destiny.* Trans. Carol Cosman. New York: Carroll & Graf, 1995.

Mackay, Margaret. *The Violent Friend: The Story of Mrs. Robert Louis Stevenson.* Garden City, NY: Doubleday, 1968.

Maixner, Paul, ed. *Robert Louis Stevenson: The Critical Heritage.* London: Routledge & Kegan Paul, 1981.

McLynn, Frank. *Robert Louis Stevenson: A Biography.* London: Hutchinson, 1993.

Stevenson, Robert Louis. *The Cevennes Journal: Notes on a Journey through the French Highlands.* Ed. Gordon Golding, Jacques Blondel, and Jacques Poujol. Edinburgh: Mainstream, 1978.

———. *An Inland Voyage, Travels with a Donkey* and *Edinburgh: Picturesque Notes.* Vol. 1 of *The Works of Robert Louis Stevenson.* Vailima Edition. 26 vols. New York: Scribner's, 1921-23.

———. *The Letters of Robert Louis Stevenson.* ed. Bradford A. Booth and Ernest Mehew. 8 vols. New Haven: Yale UP, 1994-95.

Swearingen, Roger G. *The Prose Writings of Robert Louis Stevenson: A Guide.* Hamden, CT: Archon, 1980.

Jeffrey Alan Melton (essay date 2002)

SOURCE: Melton, Jeffrey Alan. "Touring the Old World: Faith and Leisure in *The Innocents Abroad* and *A Tramp Abroad.*" In *Mark Twain, Travel Books, and Tourism: The Tide of a Great Popular Movement,* pp. 59-94. Tuscaloosa: University of Alabama Press, 2002.

[*In the following essay, Melton considers Mark Twain's travel narratives* The Innocents Abroad *and* A Tramp Abroad *as illustrative of American cultural and literary attitudes during the "Tourist Age."*]

Touring eastward in *The Innocents Abroad* and *A Tramp Abroad,* Mark Twain repeatedly snubs the grandiose pretensions of the cultures he encounters.[1] He shows readers that the Old World, especially Europe, if viewed honestly through definitively American eyes, falls far short of common, overblown expectations. Although such a reading of Twain's Old World tours helps us understand a pervasive theme—that of high anticipation meeting with deep disappointment—we should also consider that his reactions are tied more to touristic expectations than to any national braggadocio or stubborn Yankee self-reliance. Both *The Innocents Abroad* and *A Tramp Abroad,* then, are records not simply of the failure of the Old World civilizations he encounters but of the failure of touring itself, which becomes the real object of Twain's satire and cultural criticism. The Old World has a few shams, but tourism is rife with them. All the same, as his narratives indicate, Twain adapts well to the demands of tourism. His two best-selling travel books, in turn, masterfully illustrate how the new American, the tourist, should function in the new age.

Because the Old World, especially Europe, proved to be the most compelling draw for nineteenth-century American tourists, it also provided the best context for Twain's narrative examination of the "great popular movement." *The Innocents Abroad* and *A Tramp Abroad* make ideal travel-book companions,[2] both books capturing the vagaries of the Tourist Age—at its beginning with *The Innocents Abroad* and in full stride in *A Tramp Abroad.* These two literary texts are also well-crafted cultural documents that showcase, first, a new way of seeing the world, and second, a new way of participating in that world as the tide of tourism enveloped the globe.

Although in the preface to *The Innocents Abroad* Twain offers "no apologies for any departures from the usual style of travel-writing" (5), implying that his narrative does indeed take its own course, his implicit claim itself bows to convention. However, despite this innocuous wordplay, *The Innocents Abroad* does serve as a watershed in the history of American travel writing, but for different reasons. As a "record of a pleasure excursion," the first transatlantic cruise, it marks the beginning of a new Tourist Age, and neither Twain nor American tourism at large would be the same afterward. The actual tour, of course, changed Samuel Clemens forever, giving to him an opportunity that led to financial and literary status he could never have obtained as a roving journalist or newspaper editor, and the narrative tour in *The Innocents Abroad* launched Mark Twain as a consummate travel writer and tourist who would define the new Tourist Age as an elaborate "picnic on a gigantic scale."

A natural and logical theme of any travel book centers around the inevitable differences between expectations and realities, and Twain employs the subsequent disap-

pointment caused by those variances as a touchstone throughout the tour. Yet there is more to this theme than the unfulfilled wishes of an American innocent abroad for the first time; it is also the record of the too-soon failures of the Tourist Age as a whole. Twain's dilemma—balancing the needs of his skepticism and honesty in his role as a travel writer with his needs for authenticity as a tourist—becomes evident as he juxtaposes attacks on the humbugs of previous romantic travel writers (and the disingenuous reactions of other tourists) against his own willingness to imagine and then create a more favorable touristic experience.

Chapter 1 helps to clarify Twain's purpose and his early intuitive assessment of the *Quaker City* pleasure excursion and its social import. Perhaps the opening chapter, with its enthusiasm and its seeming overstatement, is not as ironic as it might appear on an initial reading. In the first paragraph, Twain explains the significance of the new undertaking and, while extolling its grand scale, implies that other expeditions will follow. The idea of the "picnic" changes considerably as a result. The first wave of participants in this gigantic outing, these *Quaker City* excursionists would be a new breed of tourists. They would not simply paddle up an "obscure creek" for a "long summer day's laborious frolicking"; they would be embarking instead on a "royal holiday beyond the broad ocean, in many a strange clime and in many a land renowned in history!" (19). The largeness of the enterprise was fit for hyperbole—even the ship's ballroom stretches "from horizon to horizon." Once he sets the stage, Twain includes the program for the tour in its entirety, saying that it will serve as a "map" and "text" for the narrative tour. In turn, *The Innocents Abroad* becomes a map and text for the touristic experience at large. As a text for this "brave conception" called "the *Quaker City* pleasure excursion," *The Innocents Abroad* records both the first great touring experiment conducted by Americans and Twain's struggle with its essential and inevitable failures.

As we have seen, all efforts of tourists to seek truly authentic experiences are by their very nature destined to fail. When we engage in any sightseeing activity, we participate in a staged production not unlike that of the theater; there are eager performers (guides, advertisers, shop owners, etc.) and attentive audience members (tourists). In recognition of the play, tourists allow for "a willing suspension of disbelief," to adapt Samuel Taylor Coleridge's well-known description of poetic faith (6).[3] For my purposes here, this obliging participation in the illusion can be called "touristic faith." As tourists move in and out of theatrical productions ("sights")—Versailles, the Colosseum in Rome, the Holy Sepulcher in Jerusalem, the Great Sphinx in Egypt—they seek varying levels of instruction, entertainment, and comfort. As audience members for a staged production, nonetheless, they demand authenticity on some level. Herein is a basic inner conflict for the tourist: how to obtain the authentic in a world of prefabricated make-believe. As both a tourist and a travel writer, Twain faced the same problem, and his narrative records the struggles that abound during the education of a novice tourist. As such, the narrative also illustrates how Twain overcomes the inherent perils of tourism within his own production called *The Innocents Abroad*.

How do Twain's palpable expectations meet with the reality of the tour itself? Twain's short side excursion to Tangier is the symbolic and definitive first contact with what he believes to be wholly "foreign" on the cruise, and it is therefore a crucial moment for establishing a point of reference and for examining touristic behavior. His reaction to the sights parallels the unbridled enthusiasm established in the opening chapter:

> Tangier is the spot we have been longing for all the time. Elsewhere we have found foreign-looking things and foreign-looking people, but always with things and people intermixed that we were familiar with before, and so the novelty of the situation lost a deal of its force. We wanted something thoroughly and uncompromisingly foreign—foreign from top to bottom—foreign from centre to circumference—foreign inside and outside and all around—nothing any where about it to dilute its foreignness—nothing to remind us of any other people or any other land under the sun. And lo! in Tangier we have found it.
>
> (76)

Rhetorically, Twain's conspicuous repetition of "foreign" highlights the readiness of the tourist abroad to see sights wholly different from those available at home; symbolically, this passage also confirms how completely tourists see the world as "other."[4] Twain and his fellow tourists are, in actuality, the foreigners in Tangier. Moreover, it is important to note that Twain witnesses people simply going about their normal daily lives (which for many meant catering to the whims and interests of tourists), yet Twain, as a tourist, defines it as a spectacle to be viewed, a production to be savored. Twain goes on to provide readers with a long list of descriptive details to clarify Tangier's "foreignness," and in one of the few direct addresses to his readers, he closes with a powerful suggestion: "Isn't it an oriental picture?"

Tourists can identify the "foreign" by its difference from home, but to define it they need a preconceived image, a picture. In the case of Tangier, it is an "oriental picture." Twain's reactions, then, must be based on what he expects to see. Although he has never been to Tangier, he has an *idea* of its appearance based on the "oriental pictures" in his mind, and it is these pictures to which Twain responds rapturously. The reality of the scene thus gains value by matching his expectations for the strange, the exotic, the "foreign." Meanwhile, the people on the street are going about their typical daily activities, unaware of the frame within which they exist in *The Innocents Abroad* and in Twain's mind, and in ours. Twain notes that he has previously "mistrusted" pictures of the Orient because of their seeming exaggeration. Presently, witnessing street life in Tangier, he acknowledges that the pictures he held previous to the tour inadequately match the strangeness of the reality. Unable to escape from the essential quality of the tourist experience despite his excitement, however, he still frames the visual experience as an "oriental picture." He carries a literary equivalent to the Claude Glass (named for French painter Claude Lorrain), a tinted or mirrored gilt frame through which a nineteenth-century tourist could view landscapes as if they were paintings. A viewer would stand on a hillside, for instance, hold the frame at arm's length toward the valley, and look at the landscape through the ornate frame. The Claude Glass orders the natural landscape into a gilded rectangle and transforms it into "art," a commodity. For the travel writer, such framing via narrative devices serves two purposes: first, like the Claude Glass, it effectively focuses the eyes on a particular part of the whole; and second, it provides a point of comparison between the actual and the preconceived tourist expectations, between the street life Twain saw in Tangier and the "oriental picture" he brought with him from home. Tourists inevitably think about, preview, and see the world initially in pictures. The same is the case for travel readers, though their pictures derive primarily from an author's language (and the illustrations that often accompany travel books). Both frames help make touristic experiences manageable, structured, and more convenient for the tourist.

For a helpful parallel, let us take a look at another "oriental picture" in *The Innocents Abroad*. Much later in the tour, Twain encounters Constantinople and witnesses a street scene strikingly similar to that in Tangier, yet the "oriental picture" he frames in this instance differs significantly from the earlier experience:

> Ashore, it was—well, it was an eternal circus. People were thicker than bees, in those narrow streets, and the men were dressed in all the outrageous, outlandish, idolatrous, extravagant, thunder-and-lightning costumes that ever a tailor with the delirium tremens and seven devils could conceive of. There was no freak in dress too crazy to be indulged in; no absurdity too absurd to be tolerated; no frenzy in ragged diabolism too fantastic to be attempted. No two men were dressed alike. It was a wild masquerade of all imaginable costumes—every struggling throng in every street was a dissolving view of stunning contrasts. Some patriarchs wore awful turbans, but the grand mass of the infidel horde wore the fiery red skull-cap they call a fez. All the remainder of the raiment they indulged in was utterly indescribable.
>
> (358-59)

The "stunning contrasts" of this subsequent "oriental picture" no longer thrill the tourist in Twain as they did in Tangier, so the picture he provides for his readers back home exudes a comic tone rife with negative overtones; a mirthful exuberance is replaced by annoyance and disdain. The variety in dress so compelling if "weird" in Tangier is now so "outrageous" and "outlandish" that there is "no freak in dress too crazy." Several factors contribute to the altered response. First, having little respect for the Ottoman Empire (see, for example, his description of Abdul Aziz in chapter 13), Twain enters Constantinople with an unprepossessing "picture" already in the forefront of his expectations. Second, he is beginning to show signs of what could be called tourist fatigue. As the days, weeks, and months pass, the tour inevitably taxes the energy (and thus enthusiasm) of any tourist, and the "foreignness" so charming and enticing at the beginning soon becomes tiresome indeed. Specifically, as the *Quaker City* moves steadily around the Mediterranean, Twain's most pleasant moments coincide with a return to the ship, especially in the Holy Land and Egypt: "It was worth a kingdom to be at sea again" (609). Third, and perhaps most important to the touristic experience, once the tourist sees the "oriental picture" and adds it to his or her basket of memories, there is little interest in seeing a similar scene again. The novelty, the "foreignness," is gone. After framing the street scene in Constantinople, Twain writes that it is "a picture which one ought to see once—not oftener" (359).

Twain does, however, see other "oriental pictures" as he continues his tour of the eastern Mediterranean. In Smyrna, in effect, he re-creates a picture similar to that of Tangier, but unlike the Constantinople version, he allows for a more positive coloring. Although the scene parallels the others, one feature is indeed new to his experience: camels. The novel sight of these beasts "laden with spices of Arabia and the rare fabrics of Persia" marching through the crowded streets recaptures Twain's imagination, and he dreams of *Arabian Nights*—the oriental pictures he remembers from childhood—as he did earlier in Tangier. He concludes contentedly, "The picture lacks nothing" (411).

Ultimately, this struggle between local reality and touristic imagining convinces Twain to make a simple judgment: reality is usually disappointing. Still traveling in Syria, he describes yet another "oriental picture" as the tourists stop at a well which was "walled three feet above ground with squared and heavy blocks of stone, after the manner of Bible pictures" (543). Significantly, the well's characteristics match pictures from the Bible, not vice versa. In assessing the crowd of people and animals surrounding the well, Twain notes:

> Here was a grand Oriental picture which I had worshiped a thousand times in soft, rich steel engravings! But in the engraving there was no desolation; no dirt; no rags; no fleas; no ugly features; no sore eyes; no feasting flies; no besotted ignorance in the countenances; no raw places on the donkeys' backs; no disagreeable jabbering in unknown tongues; no stench of camels; no suggestion that a couple of tons of powder placed under the party and touched off would heighten the effect and give to the scene a genuine interest and a charm which it would always be pleasant to recall, even though a man lived a thousand years.
>
> (543-44)

The distinction typifies Twain's struggle in the Holy Land between imagination and reality as the tangible conflict between that reality and touristic expectations presents a potentially overwhelming crisis. Twain must juxtapose the actual well scene, which includes a preponderance of unpleasant characteristics (desolation, dirt, rags, ugly features, sore eyes, feasting flies, etc.), against his more pleasing pictures derived from the Bible. Trying to define the experience, the tourist and travel writer both face a formidable challenge. Twain, confronted with the disparity, has only two options: reconcile the striking differences between the pictures, altering each, or reject one of the pictures outright. Twain ultimately chooses the latter, as do most tourists. He symbolically destroys the actual picture by wishing for its annihilation via "a couple of tons of powder." With the ugliness of the actual picture removed, Twain as tourist can return to the beloved oriental pictures he has carried with him from home. He thereby demonstrates one of the basic truths of tourism: "Oriental scenes look best in steel engravings" (544). Twain had promised in his preface to look at the Old World through his own eyes, a noble if conventional declaration. This proposition endeavors to remove from our perceptions the falsities of our imagined pictures as given to us by earlier travel writers, but Twain cannot escape such images so easily. This is especially troubling when the tourist faces the actual scenes. The "oriental pictures," in this case, are deeply interwoven with the tourist's aesthetic sensibilities, and if Twain cannot dismiss the actual pictures entirely, he can at least fantasize about their destruction.

The Old World provides more than a convenient cultural target for his Americanism; it also represents the essence of the touristic experience. Twain marvels in his first exposure to the foreign, but his enthusiasm quickly wanes and his subsequent struggles between the beauty of his expectations and the too-often dismal reality mimic the struggle of tourists at large to reconcile the contrasts between the "authentic" pictures in front of them and the delicately crafted images in their minds. Twain's method of picturing is not a rhetorical accident. His early use of the phrase "oriental picture" reflects a more general narrative strategy through which he transfers to his readers not simply a pictorial tour of the Old World, but more importantly, an overview of touristic experience itself.

In Paris, Twain delights in "recognizing certain names and places with which books had long ago made us familiar," and he continues, "we knew the genuine vast palace of the Louvre as well as we knew its picture" (112). Twain as a tourist feels "familiar" with the museum because he knows what it looks like from pictures firmly entrenched in his memory, so when the actual building matches the image, there is no need for much commentary or conflict—there are no surprises. Likewise, at Notre Dame, he writes, "We recognized the brown old Gothic pile in a moment; it was like the pictures" (130). In both instances the emphasis is on how well the actual landmark coincides with his expectations, and what seems to be important is the knowledge base of the tourists, a source of pride as they come to Paris *knowing* it. So far the tour is moving along smoothly. The actual pictures are meeting the qualities of the imagined ones except for small annoyances like the absence of soap or the dangers of a Parisian shave.

As the tour progresses, however, the frustration with failed expectations grows, and Twain faces the prototypical touristic dilemma: how to salvage a treasured picture of the Old World in the face of dissenting realities. One such threat occurs in Venice. Twain fears that his charming image of the city is teetering in the balance as he is assailed by a gondolier who sings terribly. Allowing for the humor of such a scene, the encounter also reiterates the primary goal of the tourist to reaffirm his images. In protest to the "caterwauling," Twain complains that his "cherished dreams of Venice have been blighted forever as to the romantic gondola and the gorgeous gondolier" (218). Fortunately for Twain the tourist, the gondola soon moves into the Grand Canal, and "under the mellow moonlight the Venice of poetry and romance stood revealed" (218). Twain has traveled to see the "poetry and romance," the Venice of his dreams, and only when he can match the actual scene with his expectations is he satisfied. Once this willing deception is accomplished, "Venice was complete" (219). Of course, it is his picture of Venice that is complete. When the stark realities of a city, however, conspire to challenge the image, darkness can soften the glare of the sun, and Venice, it seems, is supposed to be "dreamy." Its actual appearance, therefore, needs the softening glow of moonlight to capture the qualities of the Venice which Twain and other American tourists know, the Venice they travel to see.

Nathaniel Hawthorne's preface to *The House of Seven Gables* (1851) provides a corollary here. Hawthorne insists that a writer of romance may claim a "certain latitude" to restructure scenes regardless of probability in real life, as long as the writer does not "swerve aside from the truth of the human heart." The writer, Hawthorne continues, may "present that truth under circumstances . . . of the writer's own choosing or creation,"

and moreover, he or she may "bring out or mellow the lights, and deepen and enrich the shadows, of the picture" (1). Although Hawthorne is not referring to travel writers, his observations nonetheless apply to the genre. Because the truth of the tourist's heart is not necessarily in the actual picture but rather the imagined one, the travel writer often chooses to "mellow" the lights or "deepen" the shadows of the actual in order to preserve the aesthetic superiority of the imagined picture. Twain, in similar fashion to Hawthorne's romance author, captures the perfect touristic Venice by dimming lights and manipulating shadows: "It was a beautiful picture—very soft and dreamy and beautiful" (219). Twain affirms one of the most compelling desires of the American in Europe—to find the "shadowy grandeurs of the past," in the words of Washington Irving from *The Sketch-Book* (1819-20).[5] Twain is echoing Irving when he writes that touring Venice has seemed like "drifting back, back, back, into the solemn past, and looking upon the scenes and mingling with the peoples of a remote antiquity." Twain continues: "We have been in a half-waking sort of dream all the time. I do not know how else to describe the feeling. A part of our being has remained still in the nineteenth century, while another part of it has seemed in some unaccountable way walking among the phantoms of the tenth" (236).

Athens provides another opportunity for Twain to confront his dreamy expectations for shadowy grandeur. Unlike the jarring incompatibility of the initial visions of the actual Venice and his image, the problem in Athens is that the *Quaker City* is quarantined in the harbor and the tourists are not allowed to disembark. Although this disappointment is an unmitigated disaster for most of the excursionists, for Twain—willing and able to run the blockade, as it were—it is a fortunate break because it gives him and his comrades (and his readers) the chance to see Athens under cover of night. Walking among the fallen statues on the Acropolis at night, Twain can ignore any possible flaws in the actual picture and more easily match it to his own image. The opportunity allows him to create another touristic dream:

> The full moon was riding high in the cloudless heavens, now. We sauntered carelessly and unthinkingly to the edge of the lofty battlements of the citadel, and looked down—a vision! And such a vision! Athens by moonlight! The prophet that thought the splendors of the New Jerusalem were revealed to him, surely saw this instead! It lay in the level plain right under our feet—all spread abroad like a picture—and we looked down upon it as we might have looked from a balloon. We saw no semblance of a street, but every house, every window, every clinging vine, every projection, was as distinct and sharply marked as if the time were noonday; and yet there was no glare, no glitter, nothing

harsh or repulsive—the noiseless city was flooded with the mellowest light that ever streamed from the moon, and seemed like some living creature wrapped in peaceful slumber.

(347-48)

This romantic evocation of a "vision!" is similar to Twain's ecstatic reaction to Versailles, but it is more closely aligned with his description of Venice in the way he frames the picture. He situates himself and his readers in a comfortable perspective from which to verify a popular image of Athens, a frame that has carefully removed all evidence of modern daily life. There is no present within a frame defined solely by the past. To gain the ideal picture of Athens, Twain brushes the canvas with strokes of darkness and touristic wish fulfillment. Again, like in Venice, the picture, steeped in a romantic reverence for the past, is presented in all its shadowy grandeur. Twain celebrates not Athens but his image of Athens, a vision of "Athens by moonlight." The picture is perfect, with all its detail miraculously "distinct and sharply marked" but without a corresponding "glare." As travel writer and as tourist, Twain, by the light of the silvery moon, sees nothing "harsh" or "repulsive." He closes out the Acropolis meanderings with a carefully constructed image wherein he and his readers gain the Athens they could only have hoped to see: "Overhead the stately columns, majestic still in their ruin—under foot the dreaming city—in the distance the silver sea—not on the broad earth is there another picture half so beautiful!" (348). Twain, author of travel romance, dreams an ideal moment for the tourist. Isn't it a Grecian picture?

Touristic ways of seeing become even more pronounced as Twain enters the Holy Land. The region's most renowned body of water, the Sea of Galilee, offers Twain another opportunity to confront the issue of expectations and reality. The first picture he shares is under the harsh light of day, and it is a forthright one. According to Twain, the Sea of Galilee, no matter its marvelous associations, is a dismal, barren body of water. Again he writes in terms of pictures, noting that the sea and its environs "never, never, never do shake the glare from their harsh outlines, and fade and faint into vague perspective" (508). Twain as tourist and travel writer faces a dilemma, for his preconceived images of the Sea of Galilee contrast sharply with the actual landscape. In this reaction, Twain fulfills his promise set out in the preface—that he will see (and report) with his own eyes rather than with those of tourists who preceded him. Frustrated, he lashes out at those who have deceived him, other travel writers. Citing several lengthy passages from "Wm. C. Grimes" and "C. W. E.," Twain deconstructs their pictures and proceeds to set the record straight. Rejecting other writers' efforts to perpetuate deceptions, Twain argues that "no ingenuity

could make such a picture beautiful—to one's actual vision" (509). He ignores, for the moment, his own narrative ingenuity. Since Twain's primary concern is not the tourist's "*actual* vision" but the dream vision of expectancy, he has learned a method for reshaping a scene by simply recasting the context for his "actual vision." Using the method learned in Venice and perfected in Athens, he writes under the softening cover of night and produces a poetic and evocative picture the tourist wants to see:

> Night is the time to see Galilee. Genessaret under these lustrous stars has nothing repulsive about it. Genessaret with the glittering reflections of the constellations flecking its surface, almost makes me regret that I ever saw the rude glare of the day upon it. Its history and its associations are its chiefest charm, in any eyes, and the spells they weave are feeble in the searching light of the sun. *Then,* we scarcely feel the fetters. Our thoughts wander constantly to the practical concerns of life, and refuse to dwell upon things that seem vague and unreal. But when the day is done, even the most unimpressible must yield to the dreamy influences of this tranquil starlight. The old traditions of the place steal upon his memory and haunt his reveries, and then his fancy clothes all sights and sounds with the supernatural. In the lapping of the waves upon the beach, he hears the dip of ghostly oars; in the secret noises of the night he hears spirit voices; in the soft sweep of the breeze, the rush of invisible wings. Phantom ships are on the sea, the dead of twenty centuries come forth from the tombs, and in the dirges of the night wind the songs of old forgotten ages find utterance again.

(512-13)

This rich passage recaptures the dreamlike allure of the Sea of Galilee and the romantic image that the severe light of day had so tarnished. The imaginative picture, for Twain and thus his readers, materializes only after sunset as the moonlight and the solitude give Twain the chance to restructure his Sea of Galilee picture, invoking the powers of biblical association, the "chiefest charm" for the tourist in the Holy Land. He appears sincere in wishing he had not seen the picture during the daylight, but the unpleasant experience is not fatal to the image he wants to maintain. Twain's nighttime reverie by the sea—a touristic revision—in effect paints over the unpleasant picture created in the "rude glare of day," thereby preserving beloved images of the revered setting.

The night can offer only so much protection for the hopeful tourist, however. Another way of seeing for the tourist takes its advantage from distance. On several occasions Twain plays with the notion of distant viewing in reference to the expectation-versus-reality theme. Damascus is one such example.[6] Twain refers to the story of Mahomet's view from the mountain overlooking the city. According to legend, Mahomet claimed that "man could enter only one paradise; he preferred to go to the one above. So he sat down there and feasted his eyes upon the earthly paradise of Damascus, and then went away without entering its gates" (455). Twain sits in the same spot and views the city below, a broad, panoramic picture, and declares, "Damascus *is* beautiful from the mountain" (455). He goes on to emphasize, however, that Damascus probably seems a paradise because of the utter desolation of all that surrounds it. The city benefits by comparison with the ugliness outside its gates. Noting that the city is nestled in a "billowy expanse of green foliage," he continues: "This is the picture you see spread far below you, with distance to soften it, the sun to glorify it, strong contrasts to heighten the effects, and over it and about it a drowsing air of repose to spiritualize it and make it seem rather a beautiful estray from the mysterious worlds we visit in dreams than a substantial tenant of our coarse, dull globe" (456). Again, Twain uses dream imagery to capture an evocative picture for his readers, placing them in an ideal perspective, the mountaintop. Mahomet was wise, according to Twain, for he saved himself from facing the dreariness that is Damascus when seen from close up. Once inside the city, Twain loses the favorable and pleasant picture, and "paradise is become a very sink of pollution and uncomeliness" (456). Not even the most aggressive imagination can undo the harshness of reality and the damage it causes the preconceived image. Twain concludes that Mahomet unwittingly made the right choice aesthetically, and the tourist in Twain can only wish he had done the same and thereby avoided the unfortunate challenge to his comfortable image acquired from a distance.

The tourist to the Holy Land travels to touch the landmarks (tourist sights) authenticated by the Bible. For them, the present is largely irrelevant and, moreover, a nuisance, but it still remains as an obstacle between the tourists and what they seek. If Twain honestly points out the harshness of the actual pictures he sees, he also carefully reaffirms the imagined pictures he and his readers share. The touristic way of seeing is predisposed to the familiar, to what the tourist already *knows*. There are two essential components to that touristic knowledge: imagination and faith.

To sit at home in America and read about the Holy Land in the Bible and in works of travel requires an active, fully engaged imagination. The tourists who make pilgrimages to the places illuminated by such texts must be equally imaginative because their journey bears no connection to any realities of their present. Within his narrative tour, Twain seems to understand the two often opposing pictures of the Holy Land, and he struggles for some pleasing balance. He often shows us multiple views of the Holy Land, pictures tempered by both sharp and mellow lighting, by caustic wit as well as romantic wishfulness. As his preface indicates, Twain

does see with "his own eyes," but he fails to note that those eyes see pictures both real and imagined, both skeptical and faithful. He does, however, in the end favor the power of the imagination to render the Holy Land acceptable for the Tourist Age. In short, despite his self-image as the "sinner," he keeps the Holy Land holy. Accomplishing this task, though, requires substantive imaginative leaps and a will to see—despite the prevalence of contrary images—what he came to see. We have already examined how he revises the Sea of Galilee to maintain its poetic associations. He faces a similar conflict in Nazareth as he tours the Grotto of the Annunciation:

> The very scene of the Annunciation—an event which has been commemorated by splendid shrines and august temples all over the civilized world, and one which the princes of art have made it their loftiest ambition to picture worthily on their canvas; a spot whose history is familiar to the very children of every house, and city, and obscure hamlet of the furthest lands of Christendom; a spot which myriads of men would toil across the breadth of a world to see, would consider it a priceless privilege to look upon. It was easy to think these thoughts. But it was not easy to bring myself up to the magnitude of the situation.
>
> (527)

The grotto itself proves to be simply too small to accommodate the weighty associations that define it as a holy sight. Twain acknowledges his obligation to *feel* something remarkable, yet he confesses that he can only provide an intellectual reaction; he can only "think these thoughts." Like the "princes of art" who preceded him, Twain endeavors to place the spot on his literary canvas. He stands before it overwhelmed by its associative power but also undeniably underwhelmed by its physical smallness (dullness). He continues:

> I could sit off several thousand miles and imagine the angel appearing, with shadowy wings and lustrous countenance, and note the glory that streamed downward upon the Virgin's head while the message from the Throne of God fell upon her ears—any one can do that, beyond the ocean, but few can do it here. I saw the little recess from which the angel stepped, but could not fill its void. The angels that I know are creatures of unstable fancy—they will not fit in niches of substantial stone. Imagination labors best in distant fields.
>
> (527)

The conflict arises from the fact that the imagined "Grotto of the Annunciation" is larger, more powerful, more "shadowy" and "lustrous" than the simple stone cave in which Twain stands. The two pictures clash with one another. But once Twain removes himself metaphorically and revises the grotto by divorcing the imaginary from the actual, he recaptures the emotional context and pictures the "glory that streamed downward" so long ago. Twain closes the reverie by doubting whether anyone could stand in the actual grotto and incorporate the "phantom images of his mind" into the "too tangible walls of stone" (527). His dilemma in the grotto is that of any tourist who seeks a sight with strong historical associations. The conflict is especially sharp when that tourist is a pilgrim, who most often fills expectations with images more closely aligned with the "Throne of God" than with stone abodes in Palestine. Twain goes on to question the authenticity of the actual grotto and points out that such sights are fabrications formed by Catholic monks. Whereas he recoils at such impostures throughout his tour, he supports the deception in this case. His reasoning is simple and directly related to touristic imagination: the value of the tourist sight—especially the holy sight—lies not in its specific authenticity but in its evocative power. Whether or not the actual grotto in which he stands is the grotto wherein the Annunciation took place is irrelevant; it signifies, nonetheless, the "Grotto of the Annunciation" venerated (and thus authenticated) by thousands of tourists. The monks who originated the deception, according to Twain, have provided a service by creating "a particular spot to chain your eye, rivet your interest, and make you think" (529). Of course, seeing the actual "spot" is basically a matter of convenience for the tourist and expedience for the pilgrim. In any case, its existence helps to "drive a stake through a pleasant tradition that will hold it to its place forever" (529). The touristic imagination, then, can always infuse the "too tangible walls of stone" with "phantom images" and thus move Twain toward faith. Still, Twain needs the peace, serenity, and imaginative perspective allowed by "distant fields." His struggle, though, is not resolved. He takes his final step to touristic faith in the Church of the Holy Sepulcher.

Twain's picture of Jerusalem is the most crucial for the tourist, and it is within the walls of this ancient city that he fully reconciles the conflict between the actual and the imagined. Throughout the *Quaker City* excursion, Twain has struggled with competing impulses, one to view the Old World with skeptical eyes, the other to see with the imaginative eyes of the tourist. In Jerusalem, however, Twain fully embraces touristic faith, and in so doing he salvages his imaginative pictures of Palestine, the pictures that make the land holy. Twain's first picture of Jerusalem is typical; it offers a distant, carefully framed image so popular in travel books to the Holy Land, the same perspective used by "Grimes" (William Prime). He writes: "Perched on its eternal hills, white and domed and solid, massed together and hooped with high gray walls, the venerable city gleamed in the sun" (556). Once he establishes the image, he fills the frame with notable details: "We dismounted and looked, without speaking a dozen sentences, across the wide intervening valley for an hour or more; and noted those prominent features of the city that pictures make familiar to all men from their school days till their death. We

could recognize the Tower of Hippicus, the Mosque of Omar, the Damascus Gate, the Mount of Olives, the Valley of Jehoshaphat, the Tower of David, and the Garden of Gethsemane" (556). Twain and his fellow tourists "recognize" Jerusalem. Of course, they have never been there physically, yet due to their lifetime education from the Bible and travel writing, they react through their imaginations as if they have seen it before. They have come to verify those pictures they derived directly from Scripture. Twain writes: "I think there was no individual in the party whose brain was not teeming with thoughts and images and memories invoked by the grand history of the venerable city that lay before us" (557). Although Twain methodically differentiates himself from Prime and writers like him, he does, nonetheless, have similar touristic impulses. The difference is that Twain is a far better writer, though not necessarily a better tourist. Like Prime, Twain seeks the past, the poetical associations for which he has traveled, the pictures he can "recognize" from memory, not experience.

Still, Twain's aggravation with Prime's overt emotionalism indicates some discomfort with the imaginative picture of Jerusalem that wholly ignores the pragmatic, actual one. In the Church of the Holy Sepulcher, Twain fully integrates the two ways of seeing in a manner that, like Prime, privileges the imagination and its prefigured pictures of the Holy Land. As in the case of the Grotto of the Annunciation, Twain doubts the authenticity of the actual pictures within the Holy Sepulcher, and he struggles with his conflicting impulses: "One is grave and thoughtful when he stands in the little Tomb of the Saviour—he could not well be otherwise in such a place—but he has not the slightest possible belief that ever the Lord lay there, and so the interest he feels in the spot is very, very greatly marred by that reflection" (570). He goes on to claim that he feels the same way at each of the "spots" within the church, that "there is nothing genuine about them, and that they are imaginary holy places created by the monks." Twain is experiencing a crisis in touristic faith as he momentarily denies the importance and validity—within the tourist context—of "imaginary holy places," a validity he has already affirmed in the Grotto of the Annunciation. Describing his feelings using the third person (and thus emphasizing the plight of tourists on the whole), Twain claims that the "place of the Crucifixion affects him differently," and "he fully believes" in the authenticity of the "spot" (570). Twain justifies his belief by working through a logical, practical argument, one that could just as well apply to the other "spots." He notes that such a crucial location certainly would have been duly noted by Christ's contemporaries with a precision that matched the importance of the event, and the exact location would, then, have been passed down through the generations with accuracy and reverence. In perhaps one of the most interesting and ironic moments in *The*

Innocents Abroad, Twain credits, of all people, William Prime for the logical gamesmanship by which Twain testifies his touristic faith (he adds a footnote using Prime's actual name, not "Grimes"). Prime does more than simply provide Twain with a helpful, if flawed, logic; he also leads Twain beyond his skepticism and to touristic faith. Although the argument is presented as intellectual reasoning—as one would expect from a skeptic—it derives from the needs of the tourist to preserve the pictures of the romantic imagination. Twain effectively salvages the imaginary Church of the Holy Sepulcher for himself and his readers, despite acknowledging its "clap-trap side-shows and unseemly impostures of every kind" (573). The holy church's "tremendous associations" remain intact, its pictures safe.

Twain does not abandon his skepticism by any means, nor does he wholly dismiss the harshness of the actual Old World after his conversion in the Church of the Holy Sepulcher. However, the touristic faith embodied within the narrative encounter inside the church solidifies a desire he reveals throughout *The Innocents Abroad.* Twain, as tourist and as travel writer, wants to preserve his and his readers' pictures of the Old World, especially when such pictures are deeply rooted and spiritual. When his other motive—to identify impostures—comes in conflict with his primary goal, he holds on to his imagined pictures; he chooses faith.

If imagination is the key to maintaining preconceived pictures in the face of reality, memory is the key to redefining touristic experience in perpetuity. In this sense, as Twain observes, memory is an active process of creation and a further defense mechanism for the tourist. Following the visit to the Church of the Holy Sepulcher, the dominant theme of *The Innocents Abroad* becomes the comforting assurances of memory. Approaching the end of the Holy Land portion of the tour, Twain writes:

> We have full comfort in one reflection, however. Our experiences in Europe have taught us that in time this fatigue will be forgotten; the heat will be forgotten; the thirst, the tiresome volubility of the guide, the persecutions of the beggars—and then, all that will be left will be pleasant memories of Jerusalem, memories we shall call up with always increasing interest as the years go by, memories which some day will become all beautiful when the last annoyance that incumbers them shall have faded out of our minds never again to return.
>
> (585)

Memory is a tool on which the tourist can rely to reshape any experience, no matter how unpalatable. The ability of touristic memory in conjunction with imagination to erase the unpleasant details of a journey, to mellow the lights and soften the rough edges, allows for any experience to be salvaged and repackaged. Whatever skepticism he maintains in the moment of

viewing the actual "spots" will, according to Twain (and to his great relief), fade in the coming days, months, and years until they happily disappear altogether. In this touristic dream, Twain can always visit the Holy Land and Europe and "in fancy . . . revisit alone, the solemn monuments of the past, and summon the phantom pageants of an age that has passed away" (603). Twain reiterates this wish in the remainder of his tour, and as he leaves the Holy Land for good physically, he sums up its essential value for the tourist: "It is dream-land" (608).[7]

The imagination holds the promise of altering the actual to preserve on some level a place defined by touristic expectations, and memory completes the picture for the long term, a willful editing of experience to remove all unpleasantness. If *The Innocents Abroad* is a record of an innocent's struggle with touristic faith, then the Holy Land portions of the narrative contain absolution for Twain as he reconciles the skeptic with the dreamer. Twain recognizes the implicit failure of tourism to offer authentic experiences, but during the excursion he learns also how to temper that inherent failure and to redefine the world with the grace allowed by touristic faith and the redemption offered by touristic memory. Tourists are dreamers, and ultimately Twain's eyes are not simply those of the young American skeptic but those of the tourist.

Twain recognizes the difficulty of maintaining his pictures of the Old World, and as we have seen, he struggles with balancing his expectations with the reality he encounters throughout the *Quaker City* tour—in Tangier, Paris, Venice, Constantinople, and the Holy Land. He sees as the tourist sees, and the world is therefore a series of pictures, images he hopes to "recognize" and keep with him forever. He travels, then, to affirm them. Travel is rarely fatal to prejudice, despite his claim otherwise in the last chapter; it is, however, always potentially fatal to touristic expectations. As the imagined pictures collide with actual ones, tourists must adapt, and Twain is no exception. The conclusion is the benediction for Twain's redemption, and its rhetorical structure carefully reiterates his discovery of touristic faith in Europe and the Holy Land. The repetition in the closing paragraphs provides a hypnotic resonance of memory and imagination as the tourists define their experiences. Although the tour is over, memory remains, and it exists, like the tour itself, in the form of pictures: "Yet our holyday flight has not been in vain—for above the confusion of vague recollections, certain of its best prized pictures lift themselves and will still continue perfect in tint and outline after their surroundings shall have faded away" (650). The last three paragraphs then summarize the five-month excursion as a series of actively constructed and edited remembrances. Twain moves us again through the entire tour and (with no hint of skepticism) highlights the most special and endearing moments—"pleasant France," "majestic Gibraltar," "the delicious atmosphere of Greece," and "venerable Rome." He describes St. Peter's in Rome as standing "full of dignity and grace, strongly outlined as a mountain" (651). This passage can apply to all of the moments he recounts. Using these mellowed descriptions together with the soft repetition of "we shall remember" helps to lull Twain and his readers into the realm of dream, a somnambulant journey of pleasing images, all "perfect in tint" with their blemishes wonderfully "faded away." It is the dream of the Tourist Age.

A TRAMP ABROAD AND ADVENTURES IN LEISURE

A Tramp Abroad is a natural extension of *The Innocents Abroad* as a travel narrative, a return to the Old World. As a cultural document, it is also a natural continuation of the great popular movement of tourism, wherein the "innocent" becomes a "tramp." The energy of the first swell of the tide captured in *The Innocents Abroad* has settled into the comfortable inertia of leisure, of tourism at high tide, eleven years later in *A Tramp Abroad.* Twain, having fully accepted the possibilities of manipulating experience in his first tour, is free to push further in his second. No longer caught in the first wave of the Tourist Age, Twain enjoys in his second narrative tour of the Old World the benefits of both his social stature and the changing face of tourism. In *A Tramp Abroad* he truly drifts with the tide, or, perhaps more accurately, he floats.

A Tramp Abroad, unlike its predecessor, has no distinct itinerary, no grand program. Although for some readers the narrative suffers as a result of such floating, the rambling structure accurately captures the changing emphasis for American tourists at large, a move away from *seeing* the world as a set of pictures to *being* in the pictures themselves—more settled, more affluent, more experienced, more self-absorbed. In 1878, Twain the tourist mirrors this cultural change, and he returns to Europe with his own entourage traveling the continent at will and always in comfort, a comfort paid for from his own pockets rather than those of the *Alta California.* Not surprisingly, the theme of expectation versus reality, so prominent in *The Innocents Abroad,* is practically nonexistent in its sequel; the narrative focuses more often on Twain himself, the leisured tourist—artist, German-language student, mountain-climbing adventurer. The satire and parody within the narrative, then, depend not on what he sees but on what he does. With the security of resting comfortably on a high tide, Twain the leisure tourist does nothing at all.

If in *The Innocents Abroad* Twain struggles to hold on to his pictures of the imaginary touristic Old World, *A Tramp Abroad* shows that such struggles are the work of an innocent; the high-tide tourist has apprehended

that *all* is irrelevant. The innocent learns to manipulate pictures to suit his expectations and memory; the tramp learns to alter his sense of self to match any place, any occasion. Whereas the place for an innocent tourist becomes negotiable as he learns the vagaries of tourism, for the tramp tourist the self is fungible and the place is simply immaterial. *The Innocents Abroad* blurs the distinctions between the imaginary and the actual in touristic experience and ultimately privileges the dream of the imaginary. In *A Tramp Abroad* there are no distinctions at all—"actual" and "imaginary" are simply words that have little connection to experience. The novice tourist of the first tour confronts the basic failure of tourism to provide authentic experiences. The veteran tourist of the second tour simply does not care. By the close of *The Innocents Abroad,* the tourist comes to grips with his conflicting impulses and ultimately celebrates the impostures of tourism by embracing touristic faith and immersing himself in imagination and memory. So this conflict between expectation and reality is settled. In *A Tramp Abroad,* however, Twain takes the next logical step apropos to the swelling tide: he embraces leisure. For the leisure tourist, the primary goal is not to see the world but to be the center of it.

There is little room for disappointment in such self-indulgence. Thorstein Veblen, in his seminal study of the late-nineteenth-century gilded culture, *The Theory of the Leisure Class* (1899), provides a helpful context for touristic behavior.[8] Noting that leisure is "nonproductive consumption of time," Veblen argues that this time consumption occurs because the leisure class regards productive work as undesirable and below the dignity of the privileged and that therefore it serves as the underpinning for their desire to show a "pecuniary ability to afford a life of idleness" (46). There is a catch, however, according to Veblen. Although they endeavor to be nonproductive in the more mundane considerations, people of leisure are obligated socially to show some evidence of intellectual work, what he calls "immaterial evidences," such as "quasi-scholarly or quasi-artistic accomplishments" (46). The leisured gentleman or lady may also tackle physical challenges, as long as such challenges are conspicuous and therefore afford some distinguished notoriety. Although Veblen does not focus on tourism specifically (only as a behavior associated with the leisure class), his study is relevant to the social imperatives that helped to form Twain's own notions of touristic behavior in all of his travel narratives. This context is especially applicable to *A Tramp Abroad,* which contains in a sense Twain's own informal theory of the leisure class. Twain, of course, did not have the benefit of Veblen's study, but he had his own experience as leisured tourist to draw from, and as his premise for *A Tramp Abroad* indicates, Twain the travel writer understood well the potential that a "life of idleness" may have as a literary theme. His narrative strategy, then, offers readers a life of idleness via their beloved "innocent" who has transformed into a gentleman of leisure, a rich "tramp." The result is a record of a tourist's "non-productive consumption of time," and as such *A Tramp Abroad* is also an extended parody of life in the leisure class.

Within this self-focused tour of Europe, Twain sets up his hopeful goals right away. To show the "immaterial evidences" of his idleness, he plans to learn German and become an artist. His primary justification for the tour, however, is his proposed physical goal, to walk across Europe. Twain uses these three quasi-respectable versions of the modern tourist to provide a coherence to *A Tramp Abroad*: the artist, the student (of German), and the adventurer. Although the narrative is peppered with references and jokes based on Twain's seemingly infinite capacity for ignorance of both art and German linguistics, the primary structural tool of the narrative is his manipulation of his quasi-adventurer self. It is within this parody that Twain fully recognizes the absurdities of touristic idleness.

One of the most effective narrative personae in nineteenth-century travel books was that of the "adventurer," and the most successful purveyor of that pose was Bayard Taylor, the "Great American Traveler" (Beatty 146). Taylor, the most prolific and best-known travel writer of his era, published eleven full-length travel books, most of which earned a vast popularity and were reprinted often.[9] Although virtually unknown to twentieth-century readers, Taylor garnered widespread respect and admiration from his contemporaries. His death on 19 December 1878 prompted laudatory responses in newspapers around the world. The *New York Times* ran his obituary on the front page and called him "a great traveler, both on land and paper."[10] Much of Taylor's appeal came from his ability to create an exciting narrative persona that dominates all his travel books, an American heroic ideal—the adventurer, the essence of the rugged individualist in the American popular imagination.

Views A-Foot (1846) marks the beginning of Bayard Taylor the adventurer, establishing perhaps accidentally the identity that would serve him throughout his career. The very method of his travels showcases the narrator's adventurous spirit, recording an intimidating, often risky two-year journey on foot ("with knapsack and staff") through Europe. The novelty and scope of the idea in the mid-nineteenth century added to its charm. As indicated clearly by his voluminous sales figures, Taylor's industrious postures endeared him to readers as he persevered, aggressively overcoming all obstacles. In the narrative, Taylor is a man of action. His readers could walk alongside him, enjoying his triumphs, sharing his passion for danger and his fearlessness of the unknown. Taylor, self-reliant and strong-willed, offers readers an exciting touring partner—indestructible, inscrutable to

the last, the kind of traveler they would want to be. There is no room for leisure-minded, passive tourists.

A friend and fan of Taylor's, Twain knew well the literary and financial benefits of creating an engaging persona, but unlike Taylor, he also recognized the comic value of mocking such postures.[11] In this context, Twain's quasi-adventurer takes on an additional feature: the persona provides a vital point of parody for both tourism and travel writing. In *A Tramp Abroad*, Twain sets up a conscious, carefully crafted pattern that capitalizes on readers' familiarity with the adventurer pose. As was his preference with many travel-writing conventions, he takes well-established forms and makes them his own. His manipulations do, however, depend on reader recognition of the convention. In this case, he builds on the characteristics of the adventurer. Yet, Mark Twain is hardly a stock adventurer.

Twain first indicates the plan for *A Tramp Abroad* in a letter to Frank Bliss, his publisher, dated 20 August 1878: "I have instructed Twichell[12] to keep the title and plan of the book a secret. I will disclose them to you by letter, presently, or through Twichell—but I do not want them to get into print *until the book is nearly ready to issue from the press.*—They are in themselves a joke—and a joke which the public are already prepared for is no joke at all" (Hill, *Twain's Letters* 109). From the beginning, he intended to structure *A Tramp Abroad* around the adventurer pose, and the premise is simple: no matter how often he insists on posing as a strong, energetic, fearless traveler, he ultimately switches and becomes, more accurately, a weak, lethargic, fearful tourist—a new breed of American traveler, a lover of leisure and comfort rather than excitement and danger. The title itself would be a lie according to Twain's plan. He would promise a walking tour, much in the same spirit as Taylor's *Views A-Foot,* but would offer something quite different. A new generation requires a new type of adventurer, one more reflective of the times. Taylor constructed his persona around an image of a strong, determined, rugged narrator who sets out to face a physically demanding ordeal; over thirty years later, Twain would promise in the scope of *A Tramp Abroad* the same adventure, but he would make the pose comically absurd. Quite simply, Twain had neither the desire nor the energy to walk across Europe. He did, however, recognize the potential of implying such an intent.

Originally, Twain planned to inform his readers of the book's true nature and the irony of its title. In an unused preface, he writes:

> When I chose my book's title, I only intended it to describe the nature of my journey, which was a *walk,* through foreign lands,—that is, a tramp; but the more I think of how little I cared whither I went, or how long it took me to go, or whether I saw anything or found

out anything when I got there, so long as I had a lazy, delightful, irresponsible high-holiday time on the road, the more I perceived that in using the word Tramp I was unconsciously describing the walker as well as the walk.

(qtd. in Hill, *Twain's Letters* 109-10)[13]

Of course, there was nothing unconscious about Twain's use of the double entendre of "tramp" or his plan to undercut himself as an adventurer. In the conception Twain would promise to "tramp" across Europe, but in practice he would almost always avoid such hard work. Whenever possible, he would take any more convenient and inevitably more leisurely alternative that offered itself. Twain used laziness as a pose throughout his career, and it is a prominent character trait that he projected both within and outside his books. Yet by combining his feigned inveterate laziness with a vastly popular travel-book persona, he made his joke all the more shrewd and effective. No adventurer, Twain was a consummate leisured tourist, a man of his gilded age. In a letter to William Dean Howells, Twain shares further clues to his narrative plan: "In my book I allow it to appear,—casually & without stress,—that I am over here to make the tour of Europe *on foot*. I am in pedestrian costume, as a general thing, & *start* on pedestrian tours, but mount the first conveyance that offers, making but slight explanation or excuse, & endeavoring to seem unconscious that this is not legitimate pedestrianizing" (qtd. in Smith and Gibson 249). Twain's use of "costume" provides an interesting parallel to his manipulation of the adventurer pose in that it is itself a mocking costume of sorts throughout the narrative. He is also in leisure costume throughout, and the two poses work together to mock behavior and undermine accepted definitions of "legitimate" tramping in the Tourist Age.

Ultimately, Twain chose not to include his confessional preface, thereby allowing his joke to reveal itself within the narrative proper. He opted, instead, to open with a conventional introduction within the first chapter, in which he immediately assumes the adventurer costume: "One day it occurred to me that it had been many years since the world had been afforded the spectacle of a man adventurous enough to undertake a journey through Europe on foot. After much thought, I decided that I was a person fitted to furnish to mankind this spectacle. So I determined to do it" (17). This beginning paragraph bestows a subtle bow to Taylor's *Views A-Foot*, the original tramp across Europe, a reference that many of his readers would have recognized.[14] It is important to note that Twain's opening accomplishes two tasks: it sets up the adventure context on which the narrative's structure depends and points out that for this tour of Europe, the "spectacle" will not be the Old World but Twain himself. As a modern tourist, Twain is the subject of our gaze.

In just a few lines below the opening assertion, Twain undercuts the narrative persona and provides readers with their first clue to the full nature of his peculiar version of the adventurer: "After a brief rest at Hamburg, we made preparations for a long pedestrian trip southward in the soft spring weather, but at the last moment we changed the program, for private reasons, and took the express train" (17). Such an avoidance of actual walking establishes the joke and sets in motion the running gag that ties *A Tramp Abroad* together. He puts on the costume of the adventurer, but almost immediately he hints to readers that, like other disguises, this one is a travel-book pose, if not a standard one. In reference to tourism, Twain's premise also sets up for parody touristic practices at large, wherein American tourists spread across Europe adorning a variety of costumes seemingly oblivious to the vacuousness of their behavior. For Twain as tourist, walking across Europe requires, first, the ambition to assert the goal, and second, the willingness to dress properly for the occasion; it does not necessarily require walking. Fidelity must be applied to the details of presentation rather than actual exertion. Amusingly, Twain conducts his most extensive "walk" as he looks desperately for a sock in his room in the middle of the night (chapter 13). The pedometer he is wearing at the time indicates he travels a total of forty-seven miles during his search (114-21). After introducing his primary theme using the adventurer, Twain splices the running joke and his satire throughout the narrative using several approaches as touchstones and reminders while also fulfilling other travel-book conventional requirements.

Eventually, Twain and his agent, Harris, propose "to make a pedestrian tour" up the shores of the Neckar River to Heilbronn from Heidelberg. Twain details their extensive preparations and touts the value of the enterprise for a writer, noting that since no one has taken such a route by foot, it remains "virgin soil for the literary pioneer." He meticulously and enthusiastically prepares for the journey, mimicking the excitement usually expressed about such adventurous undertakings: "What a glorious morning it was, and how the flowers did pour out their fragrance, and how the birds did sing! It was just the time for a tramp through the woods and mountains" (102). Then Twain clarifies the picture and reasserts the primary focus of his "pedestrian tour":

> We were all dressed alike: broad slouch hats, to keep the sun off; gray knapsacks; blue army shirts; blue overalls; leathern gaiters buttoned tight from knee down to ankle; high-quarter coarse shoes snugly laced. Each man had an opera glass, a canteen, and a guide-book case slung over his shoulder, and carried an alpenstock in one hand and a sun umbrella in the other. Around our hats were wound many folds of soft white muslin, with the ends hanging and flapping down our backs,—an idea brought from the Orient and used by tourists all over Europe.
>
> (102)

The attention to detail Twain grants to his pedestrian costume as opposed to, say, the relative dearth of description of the scenery around the river emphasizes his primary focus. He and Harris are the objects of our scrutiny. In reference to Veblen's distinctions, Twain is clarifying his intention to perform a conspicuous act, which demands that he at least dress for the occasion. He does not, it seems, feel obligated to actually perform the task itself. Perfectly outfitted, having made all the correct costume choices, Twain the adventurer is ready to embark, but Twain the tourist makes an astute, practical observation: "When we got down town I found that we could go by rail to within five miles of Heilbronn. The train was just starting, so we jumped aboard and went tearing away in splendid spirits. It was agreed all around that we had done wisely, because it would be just as enjoyable to walk *down* the Neckar as up it, and it could not be needful to walk both ways" (103). Of course, Twain never walks *down* the Neckar either. He places readers on the verge of adventure only to skirt it at the first opportunity, preferring leisure over challenge and easily rationalizing away the implicit failure. Twain's theory of the tourist class is simple, as illustrated by this redefining of "pedestrian tour." The value is in the costume. In order to realize such an adventurous plan—walking up the Neckar, in this specific instance—Twain as tourist dons the proper accoutrements, and once that picture is complete the actual walking is negotiable—up and down, up or down, or neither. Twain rationalizes that *down* is sufficient, but by extension it is not "needful" to walk at all. Twain makes similar choices throughout the narrative, dressing for adventure and enjoying leisure. Twain pushes one step further by introducing several members of a German family on the train who are "greatly interested in our costumes," which, as they see it, are out of place for the terrain (104). They assume, then, that Twain and Harris are heading for "other rugged country." Of course, the family is unaware that the two adventurers are on a virtual pedestrian tour wherein plainer outfits hold little interest. There is really very little need for walking in a pedestrian tour according to Twain's understanding of touristic practices. When the family asks if the two adventurers find walking in such warm weather to be fatiguing, they answer truthfully: "We said no" (104).

In addition to avoiding walking during a pedestrian tour of Europe, Twain intersperses other methods of undermining the adventurer and updating its characteristics to the new age. He does, however, allow for stock excitement, by proxy. He employs surrogate adventurers to do the work for him, gaining the narrative excitement without placing himself under any strain. Harris becomes his primary substitute. For instance, upon noting that his itinerary does not include the Furka Pass, the Rhone Glacier, the Finsteraarhorn, and the Wetterhorn, and also upon discovering from his guidebook that they are important, he calls upon Harris to make an excursion to include each sight so Twain can insert the experience into his book. Moreover, he also wants Harris to take along a courier because, as Twain writes, "I must insist that as much style be thrown into my journeys as possible" (311-12). Twain is reasserting that, in a touristic context, actually doing something is not required to claim the experience as one's own. In his theory of the leisure class, all he needs to do is claim the experience—"my journeys." He also continues his play with the self-indulgence of such behavior, wherein the tourist becomes the focus of attention, the sight. His own *style* is a defining feature of the experience, not the act itself.[15] Later, as they travel through the Gemmi Pass in Switzerland (chapter 35), Twain refers to the "Ladders" built into the face of a precipice "two or three hundred feet high." Local peasants, according to Twain, climb these ladders in their daily routines, but he sees the potential danger of such a climb for someone unfamiliar with them. Twain the adventurer senses that danger is afoot, and he is eager for the challenge of such an exploit. Alas, Twain the tourist recognizes the same potential but prefers a more passive role:

> I ordered Harris to make the ascent, so I could put the thrill and horror of it in my book, and he accomplished the feat successfully, through a sub-agent for three francs, which I paid. It makes me shudder yet when I think of what I felt when I was clinging there between heaven and earth in the person of that proxy. At times the world swam around me, and I could hardly keep from letting go, so dizzying was the appaling [sic] danger. Many a person would have given up and descended, but I stuck to my task, and would not yield until I had accomplished it. I felt a just pride in my exploit, but I would not have repeated it for the wealth of the world. I shall break my neck yet with some such fool-hardy performance, for warnings never seem to have any lasting effect upon me.

> (397-98)

Twain directly mocks the adventurer pose—and readers' expectations, for that matter—by claiming the thrills and dangers of the experience for himself just as his readers would, vicariously. Simultaneously, he undermines both his own pretense as adventurer and his role as a travel writer. Although everybody remains safe—reader in an armchair, writer at his desk, tourist on the ground—all participants, no less, claim the adventure as their own. They do, after all, pay for it. More important to his overall structure is the continuance of his satirical assertion that proxy experience equals actual experience. For the travel writer and the tourist, there is nothing "fool-hardy" about his vicarious trip up the ladders, but there is value in the "performance" dressed in full tourist costume.

Twain also appropriates the adventures of other travel writers, and the strategy is the same as with Harris. As he travels more deeply into the Alps, the opportunities for danger inevitably increase, and Twain taps into the potential risks to continue his mock-adventure and to maintain the vitality of his structural joke. Noting that approaching the Alps offered a "chance for blood-curdling Alpine adventure," Twain claims that the Great Altels, specifically, are "daring us to an ascent" (371). Again outfitted with stock language and determination, Twain proposes to climb the mountain, placing his readers on the threshold of yet another adventure. Consistent with his pattern, however, he hesitates, claiming that he needs to study the experiences of others in order to prepare himself for his own climb. At this point, Twain introduces his next surrogate adventurer, Thomas Hinchliff, whose *Summer Months among the Alps* (1857) provides the excitement and danger typical of Alpine mountaineering.[16] Twain cites Hinchliff's descriptions of his ascent of Monte Rosa and, using extensive quotations and paraphrases, quite simply transfers Hinchliff's adventures directly into *A Tramp Abroad*. Twain uses Hinchliff in much the same way that he uses Harris (and his "sub-agent"); they both help him capture the adventurous spirit he has promised readers all along. Of course, Harris as proxy helps Twain satirize the convention and create a comic touristic approach to adventuring; Hinchliff, on the other hand, represents the convention in its pure form and thus serves as the standard pose against which Twain can counter his passive, leisure-loving tourist. As he summarizes Hinchliff's narrative, Twain carefully emphasizes its perils and thrills, and he compliments the fortitude of the climbers. It is worth noting that Twain refrains from ridiculing Hinchliff; moreover, he highlights especially daring and shocking passages by placing them in italics. This lengthy usurpation of adventure contains no hint of irony or satire. His method, however, accomplishes two crucial tasks: he gives readers the adventures they enjoy, and he sets up the convention for subsequent parody as he turns the focus back on himself as the tourist. Assuming the role of reader (of Hinchliff), Twain learns about the dangers of *actual* adventuring, and just as he finishes the narrative, Harris interrupts, announcing that preparations for their own climb are complete. Twain balks and responds as the tourist: "I said I believed I wouldn't ascend the Altels this time. I said Alp-climbing was a different thing from what I had supposed it was, and so I judged we had better study its points a little more before we went definitely to it" (379).

Twain opens the following chapter (35) with a conventional description of his newfound passion for mountain climbing:

> A great and priceless thing is a new interest! How it takes possession of a man! how it clings to him, how it rides him! I strode onward from the Schwarenbach hostelry a changed man, a reorganized personality. I walked in a new world, I saw with new eyes. I had been looking aloft at the giant snow-peaks only as things to be worshiped for their grandeur and magni-

> tude, and their unspeakable grace of form; I looked up at them now, as also things to be conquered and climbed.
>
> (381)

The adventurer reemerges, complete with courage, enthusiasm, and exclamation points, a man ready to face any peril, to earn any experience. It is important to note, however, that the passage focuses not on the Alps but on Twain's "reorganized personality." He is reformed, this time fully in the garb of Hinchliff, a true adventurer. As tourist, moreover, Twain keeps the attention where it resides normally—on the self. Twain sees "with new eyes" that satirically serve more to mirror his touristic identity than to understand the Alps. By defining their "grandeur and magnitude" as "things to be conquered and climbed," Twain firmly infuses the peaks with his self-image, a dramatic overlay that heightens his comic shallowness. The new picture of the Alps has the tourist in the foreground: "I followed the steep lines up, inch by inch, with my eye, and noted the possibility or impossibility of following them with my feet. When I saw a shining helmet of ice projecting above the clouds, I tried to imagine I saw files of black specks toiling up it roped together with a gossamer thread" (381).

His passion reestablished, Twain confronts another opportunity for adventure and again opts for a surrogate. This time he cites Edward Whymper and his *Scrambles amongst the Alps* (1871).[17] As he does with Hinchliff, Twain claims he must learn more about climbing, so he quotes and paraphrases Whymper at length. Assuming the role of reader, Twain incorporates Whymper's perilous adventures into his own narrative. His reaction to his reading is important not only for its self-parody but also because it belies the pretense of a changing self-image. A man now ready for his own adventure comments: "I was no longer myself; I was tranced, uplifted, intoxicated, by the almost incredible perils and adventures I had been following my authors through, and the triumphs I had been sharing with them" (418). A standard trope of Alpine travels, the real-life perils of mountain climbing find their way into Twain's narrative and accomplish two tasks: first, the excerpts from Hinchliff and Whymper offer readers what Twain could rightfully assume would be interesting material and thus valuable as informative and sensational content; second, together they provide an immediate springboard for the leisure tourist. Also, by overstating his "intoxication" with Whymper's (and Hinchliff's) escapades and reasserting his own adventurer pose, Twain is ready for an extended parody of the conventional demands of the adventurer and typical desires of the tourist. He begins by making a supposedly startling proposal. Riding the crest of excitement provided by his surrogates, Twain announces, "I WILL ASCEND THE RIFFELBERG" (418). Twain the adventurer has decided to embark on what he proclaims to be a highly dangerous journey, and although Harris begs him to desist, he remains constant to his intentions ("I was already wrestling with the perils of the mountains"). Thus begins Twain's mock-epic adventure—the ascent of the Riffelberg.

Putting together an expedition worthy of true adventure (and true parody), Twain gathers "198 persons, including the mules; or 205, including the cows," and among his troop are four surgeons, fifteen barkeepers, and four pastry cooks (419). In addition to the comically absurd proportions of the expedition, the massive scale of the adventure helps create a sensation, the true goal of the leisure tourist, who wants to be the spectacle. As the long procession ("3,122 feet long") gets ready to leave, Twain emphasizes the explicit value of the ascent: his performance. Isn't it an Alpine picture? With many tourists and townspeople along the roadside, Twain begins his show with the simultaneous raising of 154 umbrellas. "It was a beautiful sight, and a total surprise to the spectators. Nothing like that had ever been seen in the Alps before. The applause it brought forth was deeply gratifying to me, and I rode by with my plug hat in my hand to testify my appreciation of it" (422). This burlesque expedition (mounted on donkeys, Twain and Harris, appropriately, are the only ones not walking) quickly becomes a comedy of errors, riddled with failures and absurdities. But when the climbing party finally reaches its goal seven days later, Twain—seeming ever oblivious to the illegitimacy of his endeavors—using stock language, declares the mission a success and, for those readers unfamiliar with the Riffelberg, completes his extended joke: "At noon we conquered the last impediment—we stood at last upon the summit, and without the loss of a single man except the mule that ate the glycerine. Our great achievement was achieved—the possibility of the impossible was demonstrated, and Harris and I walked proudly into the great dining room of the Riffelberg Hotel and stood our alpenstocks up in the corner" (445). Although his cadence matches that of Whymper and Hinchliff (as well as Taylor), the conspicuous lack of substance illustrates his true intent. The meaningless double-talk—"achievement was achieved" and the "possibility of the impossible"—serves to record, again, the primary characteristic of his pedestrian tour of Europe: leisure. Moreover, he playfully reasserts that he (along with Harris) is the focus of attention as he walks "proudly into the great dining room." The mock-pride derives from the touristic assumption that the style of the performance is all and, no matter the comic failures of the climb, the success of the endeavor is marked by the quality of his entrance into the hotel. The alpenstocks placed in the corner, their badges of courage, substantiate their "achievement." Twain regrets climbing in evening dress, however, because of the wear and tear the ordeal placed on the clothing; as a result, "the general effect was unpleasant and even disreputable" (445). This mistake is the only blemish on an otherwise successful performance. He continues: "There were about seventy-five tourists at the hotel,—mainly ladies and little children,—and they gave us an admiring welcome which paid us for all our privations and sufferings. The ascent had been made, and the names and dates now stand recorded on a stone monument there to prove it to all future tourists" (446). Of course, the ascent, as Twain emphasizes, represents no true "achievement" at all. The punch line for his parody depends on simple facts: "the Riffelberg" is a hotel, not a dangerous mountain, and, moreover, it is populated by "ladies and little children" who have obviously themselves made the "climb" before Twain. Still, his tattered gentleman's clothing aside, Twain affects a grand entrance and gains from the pseudo-ordeal what he has sought all along, "an admiring welcome" and a "monument" to himself as the quintessential tourist. Maintaining the mock-solemnity of the occasion, Twain undermines his own "achievement" as he informs his readers that he can only claim to be a tourist, a man of leisure seeking out Veblen's "immaterial evidences" to justify his unremitting idleness. Twain adds factual information on the Riffelberg Hotel walk taken from the guidebook. According to *Baedeker's* guide book, the walk from Zermatt to the hotel takes three hours (Twain takes seven days), the road is unmistakable (Twain gets lost), and guides are unnecessary (Twain has seventeen). Indignant, Twain concludes that the guidebook is wrong, claiming that "the road *can* be mistaken. If I am the first that did it, I want the credit of it, too" (450).

The conspicuous self-indulgence of the Riffelberg ascent illustrates in the specific what Twain parodies in general throughout *A Tramp Abroad*: his own theory of the tourist class. Touristic behavior, as Twain shows, depends on the overriding desire to place oneself in the pictures that define the world, in this case Europe. Placing himself in many of those pictures requires of Twain a willingness for self-delusion and a belief that actual experience is irrelevant to and, moreover, undistinguishable from touristic experience. In this sense, he follows with an ascent of Mount Blanc, the highest peak in Europe, that parallels his ascent of the Riffelberg in that its primary characteristic is Twain's ability, as the tourist, to insert himself into the frame of experience. In this satire of touristic behavior, Twain uses an ideal symbol, the telescope, which becomes another proxy for him to incorporate an adventurous spirit. The telescope can perform two significant illusions: it can bring the viewer's eyes to the top of Mount Blanc without demanding any exertion (other than pulling three francs from one's pocket), and it can provide a ready-made frame into which Twain can place himself. Twain writes: "I wanted to stand with a party on the summit of Mount Blanc, merely to be able to say I had done it" (515). As he looks through the telescope and watches a climbing party reach the top of the mountain, Twain mentally places himself with them and thereby gains the experience, in a purely touristic sense: "Presently we all stood together on the summit! What a view was spread out below!" (519). He then takes the delusion one step further by describing the view not through the telescope but from the perspective of the climbers, his proxies: "The eye roved over a troubled sea of sun-kissed Alps" (520). Interestingly, Twain uses the singular "eye," but to which eye is he referring—the unified eye of the actual climbers or the eye of Twain squinting through the telescope? It is neither, of course, because Twain's understanding of the eye of the tourist renders the question moot. No matter the origin of "the eye," it sees a wonderful Alpine picture, one the tourist can "remember" always. Nearing the end of this section of his pedestrian tour of Europe, Twain asserts yet again his own vision of touristic experience and provides a tongue-in-cheek tourist's philosophy: "Nothing is gained in the Alps by over-exertion; nothing is gained by crowding two day's [*sic*] work into one for the poor sake of being able to boast of the exploit afterward. It will be found much better, in the long run, to do the thing in two days, and then subtract one of them from the narrative. This saves fatigue, and does not injure the narrative. All the more thoughtful among the Alpine tourists do this" (531). The goal of the tourist, according to Twain's astute satirical eyes, is to obtain a "narrative." Aside from its self-referential nature to Twain as the travel writer ever vigilant for content to include in his own work, this observation reasserts the self-referential obsession of tourists on the whole, for all tourists perform this deception. Reality in the Tourist Age is always negotiable.

In *A Tramp Abroad,* Twain, like most tourists, is no adventurer, but, again like most tourists, he can pretend to be one and enjoy wearing its costumes. As a thrill-seeker of a vicarious and thoroughly passive sort, Twain endeavors throughout the narrative to gather his "immaterial evidences" to justify his claims to adventure and solidify his status as a man of leisure, as a modern tourist. True to his satire and his structural plan for *A Tramp Abroad,* Twain closes out his pedestrian tour of Europe as he opens it—saving "shoe leather"—thereby concluding both his ambitious "tramp" and his extended joke upon the leisured dreams of the American tourist.

Traveling to the Old World, the mid-nineteenth-century American tourist moves back in time. Twain's versions of such time travel in his two narratives to Europe apply this nostalgia to the Tourist Age. Tourism—a process of commodifying cultures, peoples, and places—is also a process of reformatting the past into the recognizable present, a consumable present. The strengths of *The Innocents Abroad* and *A Tramp Abroad* derive from Twain's intuitive ability to illustrate this reordering of the world into a touristic context. Far more complex than youthful nationalistic exuberance or middle-age

complacency, the perspectives within these two narrative tours hold the promise as well as the failure of the Tourist Age, the new way of seeing the world based primarily on deception and self-delusion. Twain makes a provocative observation in the middle of his tour, one of the few remarks on tourism at large and its effects on European culture:

> What a change has come over Switzerland, and in fact all Europe, during this century. Seventy or eighty years ago Napoleon was the only man in Europe who could really be called a traveler; he was the only man who had devoted his attention to it and taken a powerful interest in it; he was the only man who had traveled extensively; but now everybody goes everywhere; and Switzerland, and many other regions which were unvisited and unknown remotenesses a hundred years ago, are in our days a buzzing hive of restless strangers every summer. But I digress.
>
> (345)

Twain does not digress here. More accurately, the passage illustrates his understanding of the true power of the "restless strangers" definitive of the Tourist Age. As *The Innocents Abroad* and *A Tramp Abroad* demonstrate, the great popular movement of tourists, placed astutely in context with the conquering army of Napoleon, sweeps across Europe, remaking everything in the process. Twain plays with the ridiculous notion that Napoleon traveled alone, but, of course, he traveled with armies behind him. His transformative power derived from sheer numbers as much as desire as he moved through Europe in order to call it his own. This new army of "restless strangers" ultimately carries more power, and its influences, as Twain recognizes, will long outlive those of Napoleon. There is no Waterloo for the Tourist Age.

Notes

1. *The Innocents Abroad* has garnered a wealth of critical attention, much of it highly insightful. For a few exceptional examples that address issues of tourism and travel writing, see Leon Dickinson, "Mark Twain's Revisions in Writing *The Innocents Abroad,*" *American Literature* 19.2 (1947): 139-57; Richard S. Lowry, "Framing the Authentic: The Modern Tourist and *The Innocents Abroad,*" *New Orleans Review* 18.2 (1991): 18-28, and *"Littery Man": Mark Twain and Modern Authorship* (New York: Oxford UP, 1996); Bruce Michelson, "Mark Twain the Tourist: The Form of *The Innocents Abroad,*" *American Literature* 49.3 (1977): 385-98, and "Fool's Paradise," *mark Twain on the Loose* (Amherst: U of Massachusetts P, 1995) 39-93; Hilton Obenzinger, *American Palestine: Melville, Twain, and the Holy Land Mania* (Princeton: Princeton UP, 1999); David E. E. Sloane, afterword, *The Innocents Abroad* by Mark Twain, The Oxford Mark Twain, ed. Shelley Fisher

Fishkin (New York: Oxford UP, 1996) 1-18; Henry Nash Smith, "Sinners and Pilgrims," *Mark Twain: The Development of a Writer* (Cambridge: Belknap/Harvard UP, 1962) 22-51; Jeffrey Steinbrink, "Why the Innocents Went Abroad: Mark Twain and American Tourism in the Late Nineteenth Century," *American Literary Realism* 16.2 (1983): 278-86; and Larzer Ziff, "Mark Twain," *Return Passages: Great American Travel Writing, 1780-1910* (New Haven: Yale UP, 2000) 170-221.

A Tramp Abroad, on the other hand, has been virtually ignored or dismissed. For a couple of especially valuable exceptions that address issues of tourism, see Leland Krauth, "Victorian Traveler," *Proper Mark Twain* (Athens: U of Georgia P, 1999) 51-77, especially 69-71; and James S. Leonard, afterword, *A Tramp Abroad* by Mark Twain, The Oxford Mark Twain, ed. Shelley Fisher Fishkin (New York: Oxford UP, 1996) 1-14.

2. With the exception of *Life on the Mississippi,* all of Twain's travel books were marketed so as to capitalize on the popularity of *The Innocents Abroad.* Name recognition, for example, was a benefit for subsequent narratives published in Great Britain: *The Innocents at Home* instead of *Roughing It,* and *More Tramps Abroad* for *Following the Equator.* Also, Twain used "Abroad" in his second Old World tour for its resonance.

3. Samuel Taylor Coleridge, *Biographia Literaria,* vol. 2, *The Collected Works of Samuel Taylor Coleridge,* vol. 7, pt. 2, ed. James Engell and W. Jackson Bate (Princeton: Princeton UP, 1983).

4. Discussions of applications of the term *other* in literary and cultural studies are numerous, but for an especially helpful study of tourist behavior see John Urry, *The Tourist Gaze: Leisure and Travel in Contemporary Societies* (London: Sage, 1990).

5. See "The Author's Account of Himself," *The Sketch-Book,* author's rev. ed. (New York: Putnam, 1860) 14-15.

6. He uses the same idea in his description of Naples, mocking the saying popularized by Neapolitans, "See Naples and Die," which carries the assumption that Naples represents the epitome of beauty and charm. As he does with Damascus, Twain notes that the city is beautiful from a distance, but up close the tourist encounters "disagreeable sights and smells" (316).

7. In Egypt, Twain is again frustrated by the unpleasantness of the actual in reference to his imagined pictures, and again he emphasizes that meaning for the tourist must be defined separately from the actual picture: "Why try to call up the traditions of vanished Egyptian grandeur; why try to fancy Egypt following dead Rameses to his tomb in the Pyramid, or the long multitude of Israel departing over the desert yonder? Why try to think at all? The thing was impossible. One must bring his meditations cut and dried, or else cut and dry them afterward" (623).

8. The sociological connections between leisure and tourism form the core of MacCannell's seminal work on touristic behavior, *The Tourist: A New Theory of the Leisure Class* (1976; Berkeley: U of California P, 1999), which incorporates Veblen's title.

9. Taylor's travel books include *Views A-Foot* (1846); *Eldorado* (1850); *A Journey to Central Africa* (1854); *The Lands of the Saracen* (1855); *A Visit to India, China, and Japan in the Year 1853* (1855); *Northern Travel* (1857); *Travels in Greece and Russia* (1859); *At Home and Abroad, First Series* (1859); *At Home and Abroad, Second Series* (1862); *Colorado, A Summer Trip* (1867); and *By-Ways of Europe* (1869). His sales were consistent and formidable. See S. Austin Allibone, *A Critical Dictionary of English and British and American Authors,* vol. 3 (1871; Philadelphia: Lippincott, 1908) 2340-41. *Views A-Foot* went through twenty editions in ten years; *Eldorado,* eighteen editions in twelve years; *A Journey to Central Africa,* eleven editions in eight years; *The Lands of the Saracen,* twenty editions in eight years. In addition, Putnam's issued the Caxton and Household uniform editions of his works in 1862.

10. *New York Times* 20 Dec. 1878: 1-2.

11. See Alan Gribben, *Mark Twain's Library: A Reconstruction,* vol. 2 (Boston: G. K. Hall, 1980) 687-88. Gribben provides helpful documentary evidence illuminating Twain's admiration for Taylor.

12. The Reverend Joseph Twichell was Twain's companion for much of the trip, but Twain refers to him as his agent, Harris, within the text.

13. Twain never published the preface, dated July 1879. There is no direct evidence available to explain why he chose not to include it (the narrative has no preface), but considering his letter to Bliss forbidding the release of the title and plan for the book, it seems likely that he simply did not want to give his joke away and ruin its potential effect as a structural thread for the narrative as a whole.

14. Significantly, Bayard Taylor traveled to Europe aboard the *Holsatia* during the same voyage that carried Twain and his entourage. Taylor was going to Germany to take his newly appointed post as United States minister to Germany. Also, Twain

refers to Taylor directly in chapter 18: "Bayard Taylor, who could interpret the dim reasonings of animals, and understood their moral natures better than most men, would have found some way to make this poor old chap forget his troubles for a while, but we had not his kindly arts, and so had to leave the raven to his griefs" (161-62).

15. See also chapter 33, in which Twain employs Harris to set logs adrift in a swiftly running brook because Twain "needed exercise" (363).

16. Twain refers directly to Hinchliff, giving his title and date of publication in the text.

17. Twain refers to "Mr. Whymper" but does not provide his book's title or imprint information.

Works Cited

Beatty, Richmond Croom. *Bayard Taylor: Laureate of the Gilded Age*. Norman: U of Oklahoma P, 1936.

Hawthorne, Nathaniel. Preface. *The House of the Seven Gables. The Centenary Edition of the Works of Nathaniel Hawthorne*, Vol. 2. [Columbus]: Ohio State UP, 1971. 1-3.

Hill, Hamlin, ed. *Mark Twain's Letters to His Publishers*. Berkeley: U of California P, 1967.

Irving, Washington. *The Sketch-Book of Geoffrey Crayon, Gent.* Author's rev. ed. New York: Putnam, 1860.

Smith, Henry Nash, and William M. Gibson, eds. *Mark Twain-Howells Letters: The Correspondence of Samuel L. Clemens and William Dean Howells, 1872-1910*. 2 vols. Cambridge: Belknap/Harvard UP, 1960.

Taylor, Bayard. *A Journey to Central Africa*. 1854. New York: Greenwood-Negro Press, 1970.

———. *At Home and Abroad, First Series*. 1859. New York: Putnam, 1862.

———. *At Home and Abroad, Second Series*. 1862. *Prose Writings of Bayard Taylor*. Rev. ed. New York: Putnam, 1869.

———. *Eldorado: or, Adventures in the Path of Empire*. 1850. Glorietta, NM: Rio Grande Press, 1967.

———. *The Lands of the Saracen*. New York: Putnam, 1855.

———. *Views A-Foot; or Europe Seen with Knapsack and Staff*. 1846. New York: Putnam, 1848.

Twain, Mark. *The Innocents Abroad*. 1869. The Oxford Mark Twain. Ed. Shelley Fisher Fishkin. New York: Oxford UP, 1996.

———. *A Tramp Abroad*. 1880. The Oxford Mark Twain. Ed. Shelley Fisher Fishkin. New York: Oxford UP, 1996.

Veblen, Thorstein. *The Theory of the Leisure Class*. 1899. Boston: Houghton Mifflin, 1973.

FURTHER READING

Criticism

Brantlinger, Patrick. "Victorians and Africans: The Genealogy of the Myth of the Dark Continent." In *Joseph Conrad: A Casebook,* edited by Gene M. Moore, pp. 43-88. Oxford: Oxford University Press, 2004.

> Explores Victorians' attitude toward Africa, examining the portrayal of the continent in nineteenth-century fictional travel narratives.

Fish, Cheryl J. *Black and White Women's Travel Narratives: Antebellum Explorations*. Gainesville: University Press of Florida, 2004, 183 p.

> Focuses on the travel writings of Nancy Prince, Mary Seacole, and Margaret Fuller.

Labbe, Jacqueline. "A Family Romance: Mary Wollstonecraft, Mary Godwin, and Travel." *Genre* 25, nos. 2-3 (summer-fall 1992): 211-28.

> Examines the travel narratives of mother and daughter Mary Wollstonecraft and Mary Shelley.

Ziff, Larzer. *Return Passages: Great American Travel Writing, 1780-1910*. New Haven, Conn.: Yale University Press, 2000, 304 p.

> Focuses on the travels and travel writings of John Ledyard, John Lloyd Stephens, Bayard Taylor, Mark Twain, and Henry James.

Additional coverage of Travel Writing in the Nineteenth Century is contained in the following source published by Thomson Gale: *Nineteenth-Century Literature Criticism,* **Vol. 44.**

How to Use This Index

The main references

list all author entries in the following Thomson Gale Literary Criticism series:

AAL = *Asian American Literature*
BG = *The Beat Generation: A Gale Critical Companion*
BLC = *Black Literature Criticism*
BLCS = *Black Literature Criticism Supplement*
CLC = *Contemporary Literary Criticism*
CLR = *Children's Literature Review*
CMLC = *Classical and Medieval Literature Criticism*
DC = *Drama Criticism*
FL = *Feminism in Literature: A Gale Critical Companion*
GL = *Gothic Literature: A Gale Critical Companion*
HLC = *Hispanic Literature Criticism*
HLCS = *Hispanic Literature Criticism Supplement*
HR = *Harlem Renaissance: A Gale Critical Companion*
LC = *Literature Criticism from 1400 to 1800*
NCLC = *Nineteenth-Century Literature Criticism*
NNAL = *Native North American Literature*
PC = *Poetry Criticism*
SSC = *Short Story Criticism*
TCLC = *Twentieth-Century Literary Criticism*
WLC = *World Literature Criticism, 1500 to the Present*
WLCS = *World Literature Criticism Supplement*

The cross-references

list all author entries in the following Thomson Gale biographical and literary sources:

AAYA = *Authors & Artists for Young Adults*
AFAW = *African American Writers*
AFW = *African Writers*
AITN = *Authors in the News*
AMW = *American Writers*
AMWR = *American Writers Retrospective Supplement*
AMWS = *American Writers Supplement*
ANW = *American Nature Writers*
AW = *Ancient Writers*
BEST = *Bestsellers*
BPFB = *Beacham's Encyclopedia of Popular Fiction: Biography and Resources*
BRW = *British Writers*
BRWS = *British Writers Supplement*
BW = *Black Writers*
BYA = *Beacham's Guide to Literature for Young Adults*
CA = *Contemporary Authors*
CAAS = *Contemporary Authors Autobiography Series*
CABS = *Contemporary Authors Bibliographical Series*
CAD = *Contemporary American Dramatists*
CANR = *Contemporary Authors New Revision Series*
CAP = *Contemporary Authors Permanent Series*
CBD = *Contemporary British Dramatists*
CCA = *Contemporary Canadian Authors*
CD = *Contemporary Dramatists*
CDALB = *Concise Dictionary of American Literary Biography*

CDALBS = *Concise Dictionary of American Literary Biography Supplement*
CDBLB = *Concise Dictionary of British Literary Biography*
CMW = *St. James Guide to Crime & Mystery Writers*
CN = *Contemporary Novelists*
CP = *Contemporary Poets*
CPW = *Contemporary Popular Writers*
CSW = *Contemporary Southern Writers*
CWD = *Contemporary Women Dramatists*
CWP = *Contemporary Women Poets*
CWRI = *St. James Guide to Children's Writers*
CWW = *Contemporary World Writers*
DA = *DISCovering Authors*
DA3 = *DISCovering Authors 3.0*
DAB = *DISCovering Authors: British Edition*
DAC = *DISCovering Authors: Canadian Edition*
DAM = *DISCovering Authors: Modules*
  DRAM: *Dramatists Module;* **MST:** *Most-studied Authors Module;*
  MULT: *Multicultural Authors Module;* **NOV:** *Novelists Module;*
  POET: *Poets Module;* **POP:** *Popular Fiction and Genre Authors Module*
DFS = *Drama for Students*
DLB = *Dictionary of Literary Biography*
DLBD = *Dictionary of Literary Biography Documentary Series*
DLBY = *Dictionary of Literary Biography Yearbook*
DNFS = *Literature of Developing Nations for Students*
EFS = *Epics for Students*
EXPN = *Exploring Novels*
EXPP = *Exploring Poetry*
EXPS = *Exploring Short Stories*
EW = *European Writers*
FANT = *St. James Guide to Fantasy Writers*
FW = *Feminist Writers*
GFL = *Guide to French Literature,* Beginnings to 1789, 1798 to the Present
GLL = *Gay and Lesbian Literature*
HGG = *St. James Guide to Horror, Ghost & Gothic Writers*
HW = *Hispanic Writers*
IDFW = *International Dictionary of Films and Filmmakers: Writers and Production Artists*
IDTP = *International Dictionary of Theatre: Playwrights*
LAIT = *Literature and Its Times*
LAW = *Latin American Writers*
JRDA = *Junior DISCovering Authors*
MAICYA = *Major Authors and Illustrators for Children and Young Adults*
MAICYAS = *Major Authors and Illustrators for Children and Young Adults Supplement*
MAWW = *Modern American Women Writers*
MJW = *Modern Japanese Writers*
MTCW = *Major 20th-Century Writers*
NCFS = *Nonfiction Classics for Students*
NFS = *Novels for Students*
PAB = *Poets: American and British*
PFS = *Poetry for Students*
RGAL = *Reference Guide to American Literature*
RGEL = *Reference Guide to English Literature*
RGSF = *Reference Guide to Short Fiction*
RGWL = *Reference Guide to World Literature*
RHW = *Twentieth-Century Romance and Historical Writers*
SAAS = *Something about the Author Autobiography Series*
SATA = *Something about the Author*
SFW = *St. James Guide to Science Fiction Writers*
SSFS = *Short Stories for Students*
TCWW = *Twentieth-Century Western Writers*
WLIT = *World Literature and Its Times*
WP = *World Poets*
YABC = *Yesterday's Authors of Books for Children*
YAW = *St. James Guide to Young Adult Writers*

Africa, Ben
See Bosman, Herman Charles

Afton, Effie
See Harper, Frances Ellen Watkins

Agapida, Fray Antonio
See Irving, Washington

Agee, James (Rufus) 1909-1955 ...... **TCLC 1, 19**
See also AAYA 44; AITN 1; AMW; CA 108; 148; CANR 131; CDALB 1941-1968; DAM NOV; DLB 2, 26, 152; DLBY 1989; EWL 3; LAIT 3; LATS 1:2; MAL 5; MTCW 2; MTFW 2005; NFS 22; RGAL 4; TUS

Aghill, Gordon
See Silverberg, Robert

Agnon, S(hmuel) Y(osef Halevi) 1888-1970 ..... **CLC 4, 8, 14; SSC 30; TCLC 151**
See also CA 17-18; 25-28R; CANR 60, 102; CAP 2; EWL 3; MTCW 1, 2; RGSF 2; RGWL 2, 3; WLIT 6

Agrippa von Nettesheim, Henry Cornelius 1486-1535 .... **LC 27**

Aguilera Malta, Demetrio 1909-1981 .... **HLCS 1**
See also CA 111; 124; CANR 87; DAM MULT, NOV; DLB 145; EWL 3; HW 1; RGWL 3

Agustini, Delmira 1886-1914 .... **HLCS 1**
See also CA 166; DLB 290; HW 1, 2; LAW

Aherne, Owen
See Cassill, R(onald) V(erlin)

Ai 1947- .... **CLC 4, 14, 69**
See also CA 85-88; CAAS 13; CANR 70; DLB 120; PFS 16

Aickman, Robert (Fordyce) 1914-1981 .... **CLC 57**
See also CA 5-8R; CANR 3, 72, 100; DLB 261; HGG; SUFW 1, 2

Aidoo, (Christina) Ama Ata 1942- .... **BLCS; CLC 177**
See also AFW; BW 1; CA 101; CANR 62, 144; CD 5, 6; CDWLB 3; CN 6, 7; CWD; CWP; DLB 117; DNFS 1, 2; EWL 3; FW; WLIT 2

Aiken, Conrad (Potter) 1889-1973 .... **CLC 1, 3, 5, 10, 52; PC 26; SSC 9**
See also AMW; CA 5-8R; 45-48; CANR 4, 60; CDALB 1929-1941; CN 1; CP 1; DAM NOV, POET; DLB 9, 45, 102; EWL 3; EXPS; HGG; MAL 5; MTCW 1, 2; MTFW 2005; RGAL 4; RGSF 2; SATA 3, 30; SSFS 8; TUS

Aiken, Joan (Delano) 1924-2004 ...... **CLC 35**
See also AAYA 1, 25; CA 9-12R; 182; 223; CAAE 182; CANR 4, 23, 34, 64, 121; CLR 1, 19, 90; DLB 161; FANT; HGG; JRDA; MAICYA 1, 2; MTCW 1; RHW; SAAS 1; SATA 2, 30, 73; SATA-Essay 109; SATA-Obit 152; SUFW 2; WYA; YAW

Ainsworth, William Harrison 1805-1882 .... **NCLC 13**
See also DLB 21; HGG; RGEL 2; SATA 24; SUFW 1

Aitmatov, Chingiz (Torekulovich) 1928- .... **CLC 71**
See Aytmatov, Chingiz
See also CA 103; CANR 38; CWW 2; DLB 302; MTCW 1; RGSF 2; SATA 56

Akers, Floyd
See Baum, L(yman) Frank

Akhmadulina, Bella Akhatovna 1937- .... **CLC 53; PC 43**
See also CA 65-68; CWP; CWW 2; DAM POET; EWL 3

Akhmatova, Anna 1888-1966 ..... **CLC 11, 25, 64, 126; PC 2, 55**
See also CA 19-20; 25-28R; CANR 35; CAP 1; DA3; DAM POET; DLB 295; EW 10; EWL 3; FL 1:5; MTCW 1, 2; PFS 18; RGWL 2, 3

Aksakov, Sergei Timofeyvich 1791-1859 .... **NCLC 2**
See also DLB 198

Aksenov, Vasilii (Pavlovich)
See Aksyonov, Vassily (Pavlovich)
See also CWW 2

Aksenov, Vassily
See Aksyonov, Vassily (Pavlovich)

Akst, Daniel 1956- .... **CLC 109**
See also CA 161; CANR 110

Aksyonov, Vassily (Pavlovich) 1932- .... **CLC 22, 37, 101**
See Aksenov, Vasilii (Pavlovich)
See also CA 53-56; CANR 12, 48, 77; DLB 302; EWL 3

Akutagawa Ryunosuke 1892-1927 ... **SSC 44; TCLC 16**
See also CA 117; 154; DLB 180; EWL 3; MJW; RGSF 2; RGWL 2, 3

Alabaster, William 1568-1640 .... **LC 90**
See also DLB 132; RGEL 2

Alain 1868-1951 .... **TCLC 41**
See also CA 163; EWL 3; GFL 1789 to the Present

Alain de Lille c. 1116-c. 1203 .... **CMLC 53**
See also DLB 208

Alain-Fournier .... **TCLC 6**
See Fournier, Henri-Alban
See also DLB 65; EWL 3; GFL 1789 to the Present; RGWL 2, 3

Al-Amin, Jamil Abdullah 1943- .... **BLC 1**
See also BW 1, 3; CA 112; 125; CANR 82; DAM MULT

Alanus de Insluis
See Alain de Lille

Alarcon, Pedro Antonio de 1833-1891 .... **NCLC 1; SSC 64**

Alas (y Urena), Leopoldo (Enrique Garcia) 1852-1901 .... **TCLC 29**
See also CA 113; 131; HW 1; RGSF 2

Albee, Edward (Franklin) (III) 1928- .. **CLC 1, 2, 3, 5, 9, 11, 13, 25, 53, 86, 113; DC 11; WLC**
See also AAYA 51; AITN 1; AMW; CA 5-8R; CABS 3; CAD; CANR 8, 54, 74, 124; CD 5, 6; CDALB 1941-1968; DA; DA3; DAB; DAC; DAM DRAM, MST; DFS 2, 3, 8, 10, 13, 14; DLB 7, 266; EWL 3; INT CANR-8; LAIT 4; LMFS 2; MAL 5; MTCW 1, 2; MTFW 2005; RGAL 4; TUS

Alberti (Merello), Rafael
See Alberti, Rafael
See also CWW 2

Alberti, Rafael 1902-1999 .... **CLC 7**
See Alberti (Merello), Rafael
See also CA 85-88; 185; CANR 81; DLB 108; EWL 3; HW 2; RGWL 2, 3

Albert the Great 1193(?)-1280 ...... **CMLC 16**
See also DLB 115

Alcaeus c. 620B.C.- .... **CMLC 65**
See also DLB 176

Alcala-Galiano, Juan Valera y
See Valera y Alcala-Galiano, Juan

Alcayaga, Lucila Godoy
See Godoy Alcayaga, Lucila

Alciato, Andrea 1492-1550 .... **LC 116**

Alcott, Amos Bronson 1799-1888 ... **NCLC 1, 167**
See also DLB 1, 223

Alcott, Louisa May 1832-1888 . **NCLC 6, 58, 83; SSC 27; WLC**
See also AAYA 20; AMWS 1; BPFB 1; BYA 2; CDALB 1865-1917; CLR 1, 38; DA; DA3; DAB; DAC; DAM MST, NOV; DLB 1, 42, 79, 223, 239, 242; DLBD 14; FL 1:2; FW; JRDA; LAIT 2; MAICYA 1, 2; NFS 12; RGAL 4; SATA 100; TUS; WCH; WYA; YABC 1; YAW

Alcuin c. 730-804 .... **CMLC 69**
See also DLB 148

Aldanov, M. A.
See Aldanov, Mark (Alexandrovich)

Aldanov, Mark (Alexandrovich) 1886-1957 .... **TCLC 23**
See also CA 118; 181; DLB 317

Aldington, Richard 1892-1962 .... **CLC 49**
See also CA 85-88; CANR 45; DLB 20, 36, 100, 149; LMFS 2; RGEL 2

Aldiss, Brian W(ilson) 1925- . **CLC 5, 14, 40; SSC 36**
See also AAYA 42; CA 5-8R, 190; CAAE 190; CAAS 2; CANR 5, 28, 64, 121; CN 1, 2, 3, 4, 5, 6, 7; DAM NOV; DLB 14, 261, 271; MTCW 1, 2; MTFW 2005; SATA 34; SCFW 1, 2; SFW 4

Aldrich, Bess Streeter 1881-1954 .... **TCLC 125**
See also CLR 70; TCWW 2

Alegria, Claribel
See Alegria, Claribel (Joy)
See also CWW 2; DLB 145, 283

Alegria, Claribel (Joy) 1924- .... **CLC 75; HLCS 1; PC 26**
See Alegria, Claribel
See also CA 131; CAAS 15; CANR 66, 94, 134; DAM MULT; EWL 3; HW 1; MTCW 2; MTFW 2005; PFS 21

Alegria, Fernando 1918- .... **CLC 57**
See also CA 9-12R; CANR 5, 32, 72; EWL 3; HW 1, 2

Aleichem, Sholom .... **SSC 33; TCLC 1, 35**
See Rabinovitch, Sholem
See also TWA

Aleixandre, Vicente 1898-1984 .... **HLCS 1; TCLC 113**
See also CANR 81; DLB 108; EWL 3; HW 2; MTCW 1, 2; RGWL 2, 3

Aleman, Mateo 1547-1615(?) .... **LC 81**

Alencar, Jose de 1829-1877 .... **NCLC 157**
See also DLB 307; LAW; WLIT 1

Alencon, Marguerite d'
See de Navarre, Marguerite

Alepoudelis, Odysseus
See Elytis, Odysseus
See also CWW 2

Aleshkovsky, Joseph 1929-
See Aleshkovsky, Yuz
See also CA 121; 128

Aleshkovsky, Yuz .... **CLC 44**
See Aleshkovsky, Joseph
See also DLB 317

Alexander, Lloyd (Chudley) 1924- ... **CLC 35**
See also AAYA 1, 27; BPFB 1; BYA 5, 6, 7, 9, 10, 11; CA 1-4R; CANR 1, 24, 38, 55, 113; CLR 1, 5, 48; CWRI 5; DLB 52; FANT; JRDA; MAICYA 1, 2; MAICYAS 1; MTCW 1; SAAS 19; SATA 3, 49, 81, 129, 135; SUFW; TUS; WYA; YAW

Alexander, Meena 1951- .... **CLC 121**
See also CA 115; CANR 38, 70, 146; CP 7; CWP; FW

Alexander, Samuel 1859-1938 .... **TCLC 77**

Alexeyev, Constantin (Sergeivich)
See Stanislavsky, Konstantin (Sergeivich)

Alexie, Sherman (Joseph, Jr.)
1966- .... **CLC 96, 154; NNAL; PC 53**
See also AAYA 28; BYA 15; CA 138;
CANR 65, 95, 133; CN 7; DA3; DAM
MULT; DLB 175, 206, 278; LATS 1:2;
MTCW 2; MTFW 2005; NFS 17; SSFS
18

al-Farabi 870(?)-950 .... **CMLC 58**
See also DLB 115

Alfau, Felipe 1902-1999 .... **CLC 66**
See also CA 137

Alfieri, Vittorio 1749-1803 .... **NCLC 101**
See also EW 4; RGWL 2, 3; WLIT 7

Alfonso X 1221-1284 .... **CMLC 78**

Alfred, Jean Gaston
See Ponge, Francis

Alger, Horatio, Jr. 1832-1899 .... **NCLC 8, 83**
See also CLR 87; DLB 42; LAIT 2; RGAL
4; SATA 16; TUS

Al-Ghazali, Muhammad ibn Muhammad
1058-1111 .... **CMLC 50**
See also DLB 115

Algren, Nelson 1909-1981 ..... **CLC 4, 10, 33;
SSC 33**
See also AMWS 9; BPFB 1; CA 13-16R;
103; CANR 20, 61; CDALB 1941-1968;
CN 1, 2; DLB 9; DLBY 1981, 1982,
2000; EWL 3; MAL 5; MTCW 1, 2;
MTFW 2005; RGAL 4; RGSF 2

**al-Hariri, al-Qasim ibn 'Ali Abu
Muhammad al-Basri**
1054-1122 .... **CMLC 63**
See also RGWL 3

Ali, Ahmed 1908-1998 .... **CLC 69**
See also CA 25-28R; CANR 15, 34; CN 1,
2, 3, 4, 5; EWL 3

Ali, Tariq 1943- .... **CLC 173**
See also CA 25-28R; CANR 10, 99

Alighieri, Dante
See Dante
See also WLIT 7

al-Kindi, Abu Yusuf Ya'qub ibn Ishaq c.
801-c. 873 .... **CMLC 80**

Allan, John B.
See Westlake, Donald E(dwin)

Allan, Sidney
See Hartmann, Sadakichi

Allan, Sydney
See Hartmann, Sadakichi

Allard, Janet .... **CLC 59**

Allen, Edward 1948- .... **CLC 59**

Allen, Fred 1894-1956 .... **TCLC 87**

Allen, Paula Gunn 1939- .... **CLC 84, 202;
NNAL**
See also AMWS 4; CA 112; 143; CANR
63, 130; CWP; DA3; DAM MULT; DLB
175; FW; MTCW 2; MTFW 2005; RGAL
4; TCWW 2

Allen, Roland
See Ayckbourn, Alan

Allen, Sarah A.
See Hopkins, Pauline Elizabeth

Allen, Sidney H.
See Hartmann, Sadakichi

Allen, Woody 1935- .... **CLC 16, 52, 195**
See also AAYA 10, 51; AMWS 15; CA 33-
36R; CANR 27, 38, 63, 128; DAM POP;
DLB 44; MTCW 1; SSFS 21

Allende, Isabel 1942- ... **CLC 39, 57, 97, 170;
HLC 1; SSC 65; WLCS**
See also AAYA 18; CA 125; 130; CANR
51, 74, 129; CDWLB 3; CLR 99; CWW
2; DA3; DAM MULT, NOV; DLB 145;
DNFS 1; EWL 3; FL 1:5; FW; HW 1, 2;
INT CA-130; LAIT 5; LAWS 1; LMFS 2;
MTCW 1, 2; MTFW 2005; NCFS 1; NFS
6, 18; RGSF 2; RGWL 3; SATA 163;
SSFS 11, 16; WLIT 1

Alleyn, Ellen
See Rossetti, Christina

Alleyne, Carla D. .... **CLC 65**

Allingham, Margery (Louise)
1904-1966 .... **CLC 19**
See also CA 5-8R; 25-28R; CANR 4, 58;
CMW 4; DLB 77; MSW; MTCW 1, 2

Allingham, William 1824-1889 ...... **NCLC 25**
See also DLB 35; RGEL 2

Allison, Dorothy E. 1949- .... **CLC 78, 153**
See also AAYA 53; CA 140; CANR 66, 107;
CN 7; CSW; DA3; FW; MTCW 2; MTFW
2005; NFS 11; RGAL 4

Alloula, Malek .... **CLC 65**

Allston, Washington 1779-1843 .... **NCLC 2**
See also DLB 1, 235

Almedingen, E. M. .... **CLC 12**
See Almedingen, Martha Edith von
See also SATA 3

Almedingen, Martha Edith von 1898-1971
See Almedingen, E. M.
See also CA 1-4R; CANR 1

Almodovar, Pedro 1949(?)- .... **CLC 114;
HLCS 1**
See also CA 133; CANR 72; HW 2

Almqvist, Carl Jonas Love
1793-1866 .... **NCLC 42**

**al-Mutanabbi, Ahmad ibn al-Husayn Abu
al-Tayyib al-Jufi al-Kindi**
915-965 .... **CMLC 66**
See Mutanabbi, Al-
See also RGWL 3

Alonso, Damaso 1898-1990 .... **CLC 14**
See also CA 110; 131; 130; CANR 72; DLB
108; EWL 3; HW 1, 2

Alov
See Gogol, Nikolai (Vasilyevich)

al'Sadaawi, Nawal
See El Saadawi, Nawal
See also FW

al-Shaykh, Hanan 1945- .... **CLC 218**
See also CA 135; CANR 111; WLIT 6

Al Siddik
See Rolfe, Frederick (William Serafino Aus-
tin Lewis Mary)
See also GLL 1; RGEL 2

Alta 1942- .... **CLC 19**
See also CA 57-60

Alter, Robert B(ernard) 1935- .... **CLC 34**
See also CA 49-52; CANR 1, 47, 100

Alther, Lisa 1944- .... **CLC 7, 41**
See also BPFB 1; CA 65-68; CAAS 30;
CANR 12, 30, 51; CN 4, 5, 6, 7; CSW;
GLL 2; MTCW 1

Althusser, L.
See Althusser, Louis

Althusser, Louis 1918-1990 .... **CLC 106**
See also CA 131; 132; CANR 102; DLB
242

Altman, Robert 1925- .... **CLC 16, 116**
See also CA 73-76; CANR 43

Alurista .... **HLCS 1; PC 34**
See Urista (Heredia), Alberto (Baltazar)
See also CA 45-48R; DLB 82; LLW

Alvarez, A(lfred) 1929- .... **CLC 5, 13**
See also CA 1-4R; CANR 3, 33, 63, 101,
134; CN 3, 4, 5, 6; CP 1, 2, 3, 4, 5, 6, 7;
DLB 14, 40; MTFW 2005

Alvarez, Alejandro Rodriguez 1903-1965
See Casona, Alejandro
See also CA 131; 93-96; HW 1

Alvarez, Julia 1950- .... **CLC 93; HLCS 1**
See also AAYA 25; AMWS 7; CA 147;
CANR 69, 101, 133; DA3; DLB 282;
LATS 1:2; LLW; MTCW 2; MTFW 2005;
NFS 5, 9; SATA 129; WLIT 1

Alvaro, Corrado 1896-1956 .... **TCLC 60**
See also CA 163; DLB 264; EWL 3

Amado, Jorge 1912-2001 ... **CLC 13, 40, 106;
HLC 1**
See also CA 77-80; 201; CANR 35, 74, 135;
CWW 2; DAM MULT, NOV; DLB 113,
307; EWL 3; HW 2; LAW; LAWS 1;
MTCW 1, 2; MTFW 2005; RGWL 2, 3;
TWA; WLIT 1

Ambler, Eric 1909-1998 .... **CLC 4, 6, 9**
See also BRWS 4; CA 9-12R; 171; CANR
7, 38, 74; CMW 4; CN 1, 2, 3, 4, 5, 6;
DLB 77; MSW; MTCW 1, 2; TEA

Ambrose, Stephen E(dward)
1936-2002 .... **CLC 145**
See also AAYA 44; CA 1-4R; 209; CANR
3, 43, 57, 83, 105; MTFW 2005; NCFS 2;
SATA 40, 138

Amichai, Yehuda 1924-2000 .. **CLC 9, 22, 57,
116; PC 38**
See also CA 85-88; 189; CANR 46, 60, 99,
132; CWW 2; EWL 3; MTCW 1, 2;
MTFW 2005; WLIT 6

Amichai, Yehudah
See Amichai, Yehuda

Amiel, Henri Frederic 1821-1881 .... **NCLC 4**
See also DLB 217

Amis, Kingsley (William)
1922-1995 ...... **CLC 1, 2, 3, 5, 8, 13, 40,
44, 129**
See also AITN 2; BPFB 1; BRWS 2; CA
9-12R; 150; CANR 8, 28, 54; CDBLB
1945-1960; CN 1, 2, 3, 4, 5, 6; CP 1, 2,
3, 4; DA; DA3; DAB; DAC; DAM MULT,
NOV; DLB 15, 27, 100, 139; DLBY 1996;
EWL 3; HGG; INT CANR-8; MTCW 1,
2; MTFW 2005; RGEL 2; RGSF 2; SFW
4

Amis, Martin (Louis) 1949- .... **CLC 4, 9, 38,
62, 101, 213**
See also BEST 90:3; BRWS 4; CA 65-68;
CANR 8, 27, 54, 73, 95, 132; CN 5, 6, 7;
DA3; DLB 14, 194; EWL 3; INT CANR-
27; MTCW 2; MTFW 2005

Ammianus Marcellinus c. 330-c.
395 .... **CMLC 60**
See also AW 2; DLB 211

Ammons, A(rchie) R(andolph)
1926-2001 ...... **CLC 2, 3, 5, 8, 9, 25, 57,
108; PC 16**
See also AITN 1; AMWS 7; CA 9-12R;
193; CANR 6, 36, 51, 73, 107; CP 1, 2,
3, 4, 5, 6, 7; CSW; DAM POET; DLB 5,
165; EWL 3; MAL 5; MTCW 1, 2; PFS
19; RGAL 4; TCLE 1:1

Amo, Tauraatua i
See Adams, Henry (Brooks)

Amory, Thomas 1691(?)-1788 .... **LC 48**
See also DLB 39

Anand, Mulk Raj 1905-2004 ...... **CLC 23, 93**
See also CA 65-68; 231; CANR 32, 64; CN
1, 2, 3, 4, 5, 6, 7; DAM NOV; EWL 3;
MTCW 1, 2; MTFW 2005; RGSF 2

Anatol
See Schnitzler, Arthur

Anaximander c. 611B.C.-c.
546B.C. .... **CMLC 22**

Anaya, Rudolfo A(lfonso) 1937- ...... **CLC 23,
148; HLC 1**
See also AAYA 20; BYA 13; CA 45-48;
CAAS 4; CANR 1, 32, 51, 124; CN 4, 5,
6, 7; DAM MULT, NOV; DLB 82, 206,
278; HW 1; LAIT 4; LLW; MAL 5;
MTCW 1, 2; MTFW 2005; NFS 12;
RGAL 4; RGSF 2; TCWW 2; WLIT 1

Andersen, Hans Christian
1805-1875 .... **NCLC 7, 79; SSC 6, 56;
WLC**
See also AAYA 57; CLR 6; DA; DA3;
DAB; DAC; DAM MST, POP; EW 6;
MAICYA 1, 2; RGSF 2; RGWL 2, 3;
SATA 100; TWA; WCH; YABC 1

Arden, John 1930- .... **CLC 6, 13, 15**
  See also BRWS 2; CA 13-16R; CAAS 4;
  CANR 31, 65, 67, 124; CBD; CD 5, 6;
  DAM DRAM; DFS 9; DLB 13, 245;
  EWL 3; MTCW 1

Arenas, Reinaldo 1943-1990 .. **CLC 41; HLC 1**
  See also CA 124; 128; 133; CANR 73, 106;
  DAM MULT; DLB 145; EWL 3; GLL 2;
  HW 1; LAW; LAWS 1; MTCW 2; MTFW
  2005; RGSF 2; RGWL 3; WLIT 1

Arendt, Hannah 1906-1975 .... **CLC 66, 98**
  See also CA 17-20R; 61-64; CANR 26, 60;
  DLB 242; MTCW 1, 2

Aretino, Pietro 1492-1556 .... **LC 12**
  See also RGWL 2, 3

Arghezi, Tudor .... **CLC 80**
  See Theodorescu, Ion N.
  See also CA 167; CDWLB 4; DLB 220;
  EWL 3

Arguedas, Jose Maria 1911-1969 .... **CLC 10, 18; HLCS 1; TCLC 147**
  See also CA 89-92; CANR 73; DLB 113;
  EWL 3; HW 1; LAW; RGWL 2, 3; WLIT 1

Argueta, Manlio 1936- .... **CLC 31**
  See also CA 131; CANR 73; CWW 2; DLB
  145; EWL 3; HW 1; RGWL 3

Arias, Ron(ald Francis) 1941- .... **HLC 1**
  See also CA 131; CANR 81, 136; DAM
  MULT; DLB 82; HW 1, 2; MTCW 2;
  MTFW 2005

Ariosto, Lodovico
  See Ariosto, Ludovico
  See also WLIT 7

Ariosto, Ludovico 1474-1533 ... **LC 6, 87; PC 42**
  See Ariosto, Lodovico
  See also EW 2; RGWL 2, 3

Aristides
  See Epstein, Joseph

Aristophanes 450B.C.-385B.C. .... **CMLC 4, 51; DC 2; WLCS**
  See also AW 1; CDWLB 1; DA; DA3;
  DAB; DAC; DAM DRAM, MST; DFS
  10; DLB 176; LMFS 1; RGWL 2, 3; TWA

Aristotle 384B.C.-322B.C. .... **CMLC 31; WLCS**
  See also AW 1; CDWLB 1; DA; DA3;
  DAB; DAC; DAM MST; DLB 176;
  RGWL 2, 3; TWA

Arlt, Roberto (Godofredo Christophersen)
  1900-1942 .... **HLC 1; TCLC 29**
  See also CA 123; 131; CANR 67; DAM
  MULT; DLB 305; EWL 3; HW 1, 2;
  IDTP; LAW

Armah, Ayi Kwei 1939- . **BLC 1; CLC 5, 33, 136**
  See also AFW; BRWS 10; BW 1; CA 61-
  64; CANR 21, 64; CDWLB 3; CN 1, 2,
  3, 4, 5, 6, 7; DAM MULT, POET; DLB
  117; EWL 3; MTCW 1; WLIT 2

Armatrading, Joan 1950- .... **CLC 17**
  See also CA 114; 186

Armitage, Frank
  See Carpenter, John (Howard)

Armstrong, Jeannette (C.) 1948- .... **NNAL**
  See also CA 149; CCA 1; CN 6, 7; DAC;
  SATA 102

Arnette, Robert
  See Silverberg, Robert

Arnim, Achim von (Ludwig Joachim von Arnim) 1781-1831 .. **NCLC 5, 159; SSC 29**
  See also DLB 90

Arnim, Bettina von 1785-1859 ...... **NCLC 38, 123**
  See also DLB 90; RGWL 2, 3

Arnold, Matthew 1822-1888 ..... **NCLC 6, 29, 89, 126; PC 5; WLC**
  See also BRW 5; CDBLB 1832-1890; DA;
  DAB; DAC; DAM MST, POET; DLB 32,
  57; EXPP; PAB; PFS 2; TEA; WP

Arnold, Thomas 1795-1842 .... **NCLC 18**
  See also DLB 55

Arnow, Harriette (Louisa) Simpson
  1908-1986 .... **CLC 2, 7, 18**
  See also BPFB 1; CA 9-12R; 118; CANR
  14; CN 2, 3, 4; DLB 6; FW; MTCW 1, 2;
  RHW; SATA 42; SATA-Obit 47

Arouet, Francois-Marie
  See Voltaire

Arp, Hans
  See Arp, Jean

Arp, Jean 1887-1966 .... **CLC 5; TCLC 115**
  See also CA 81-84; 25-28R; CANR 42, 77;
  EW 10

Arrabal
  See Arrabal, Fernando

Arrabal (Teran), Fernando
  See Arrabal, Fernando
  See also CWW 2

Arrabal, Fernando 1932- ... **CLC 2, 9, 18, 58**
  See Arrabal (Teran), Fernando
  See also CA 9-12R; CANR 15; DLB 321;
  EWL 3; LMFS 2

Arreola, Juan Jose 1918-2001 .... **CLC 147; HLC 1; SSC 38**
  See also CA 113; 131; 200; CANR 81;
  CWW 2; DAM MULT; DLB 113; DNFS
  2; EWL 3; HW 1, 2; LAW; RGSF 2

Arrian c. 89(?)-c. 155(?) .... **CMLC 43**
  See also DLB 176

Arrick, Fran .... **CLC 30**
  See Gaberman, Judie Angell
  See also BYA 6

Arrley, Richmond
  See Delany, Samuel R(ay), Jr.

Artaud, Antonin (Marie Joseph)
  1896-1948 .... **DC 14; TCLC 3, 36**
  See also CA 104; 149; DA3; DAM DRAM;
  DFS 22; DLB 258, 321; EW 11; EWL 3;
  GFL 1789 to the Present; MTCW 2;
  MTFW 2005; RGWL 2, 3

Arthur, Ruth M(abel) 1905-1979 ..... **CLC 12**
  See also CA 9-12R; 85-88; CANR 4; CWRI
  5; SATA 7, 26

Artsybashev, Mikhail (Petrovich)
  1878-1927 .... **TCLC 31**
  See also CA 170; DLB 295

Arundel, Honor (Morfydd)
  1919-1973 .... **CLC 17**
  See also CA 21-22; 41-44R; CAP 2; CLR
  35; CWRI 5; SATA; SATA-Obit 24

Arzner, Dorothy 1900-1979 .... **CLC 98**

Asch, Sholem 1880-1957 .... **TCLC 3**
  See also CA 105; EWL 3; GLL 2

Ascham, Roger 1516(?)-1568 .... **LC 101**
  See also DLB 236

Ash, Shalom
  See Asch, Sholem

Ashbery, John (Lawrence) 1927- .. **CLC 2, 3, 4, 6, 9, 13, 15, 25, 41, 77, 125; PC 26**
  See Berry, Jonas
  See also AMWS 3; CA 5-8R; CANR 9, 37,
  66, 102, 132; CP 1, 2, 3, 4, 5, 6, 7; DA3;
  DAM POET; DLB 5, 165; DLBY 1981;
  EWL 3; INT CANR-9; MAL 5; MTCW
  1, 2; MTFW 2005; PAB; PFS 11; RGAL
  4; TCLE 1:1; WP

Ashdown, Clifford
  See Freeman, R(ichard) Austin

Ashe, Gordon
  See Creasey, John

Ashton-Warner, Sylvia (Constance)
  1908-1984 .... **CLC 19**
  See also CA 69-72; 112; CANR 29; CN 1,
  2, 3; MTCW 1, 2

Asimov, Isaac 1920-1992 ..... **CLC 1, 3, 9, 19, 26, 76, 92**
  See also AAYA 13; BEST 90:2; BPFB 1;
  BYA 4, 6, 7, 9; CA 1-4R; 137; CANR 2,
  19, 36, 60, 125; CLR 12, 79; CMW 4;
  CN 1, 2, 3, 4, 5; CPW; DA3; DAM POP;
  DLB 8; DLBY 1992; INT CANR-19;
  JRDA; LAIT 5; LMFS 2; MAICYA 1, 2;
  MAL 5; MTCW 1, 2; MTFW 2005;
  RGAL 4; SATA 1, 26, 74; SCFW 1, 2;
  SFW 4; SSFS 17; TUS; YAW

Askew, Anne 1521(?)-1546 .... **LC 81**
  See also DLB 136

Assis, Joaquim Maria Machado de
  See Machado de Assis, Joaquim Maria

Astell, Mary 1666-1731 .... **LC 68**
  See also DLB 252; FW

Astley, Thea (Beatrice May)
  1925-2004 .... **CLC 41**
  See also CA 65-68; 229; CANR 11, 43, 78;
  CN 1, 2, 3, 4, 5, 6, 7; DLB 289; EWL 3

Astley, William 1855-1911
  See Warung, Price

Aston, James
  See White, T(erence) H(anbury)

Asturias, Miguel Angel 1899-1974 .... **CLC 3, 8, 13; HLC 1**
  See also CA 25-28; 49-52; CANR 32; CAP
  2; CDWLB 3; DA3; DAM MULT, NOV;
  DLB 113, 290; EWL 3; HW 1; LAW;
  LMFS 2; MTCW 1, 2; RGWL 2, 3; WLIT 1

Atares, Carlos Saura
  See Saura (Atares), Carlos

Athanasius c. 295-c. 373 .... **CMLC 48**

Atheling, William
  See Pound, Ezra (Weston Loomis)

Atheling, William, Jr.
  See Blish, James (Benjamin)

Atherton, Gertrude (Franklin Horn)
  1857-1948 .... **TCLC 2**
  See also CA 104; 155; DLB 9, 78, 186;
  HGG; RGAL 4; SUFW 1; TCWW 1, 2

Atherton, Lucius
  See Masters, Edgar Lee

Atkins, Jack
  See Harris, Mark

Atkinson, Kate 1951- .... **CLC 99**
  See also CA 166; CANR 101; DLB 267

Attaway, William (Alexander)
  1911-1986 .... **BLC 1; CLC 92**
  See also BW 2, 3; CA 143; CANR 82;
  DAM MULT; DLB 76; MAL 5

Atticus
  See Fleming, Ian (Lancaster); Wilson,
  (Thomas) Woodrow

Atwood, Margaret (Eleanor) 1939- ... **CLC 2, 3, 4, 8, 13, 15, 25, 44, 84, 135; PC 8; SSC 2, 46; WLC**
  See also AAYA 12, 47; AMWS 13; BEST
  89:2; BPFB 1; CA 49-52; CANR 3, 24,
  33, 59, 95, 133; CN 2, 3, 4, 5, 6, 7; CP 1,
  2, 3, 4, 5, 6, 7; CPW; CWP; DA; DA3;
  DAB; DAC; DAM MST, NOV, POET;
  DLB 53, 251; EWL 3; EXPN; FL 1:5;
  FW; GL 2; INT CANR-24; LAIT 5;
  MTCW 1, 2; MTFW 2005; NFS 4, 12,
  13, 14, 19; PFS 7; RGSF 2; SATA 50;
  SSFS 3, 13; TCLE 1:1; TWA; WWE 1;
  YAW

Aubigny, Pierre d'
  See Mencken, H(enry) L(ouis)

Aubin, Penelope 1685-1731(?) .... **LC 9**
  See also DLB 39

EXPN; EXPS; HGG; LAIT 3, 5; LATS 1:2; LMFS 2; MAL 5; MTCW 1, 2; MTFW 2005; NFS 1, 22; RGAL 4; RGSF 2; SATA 11, 64, 123; SCFW 1, 2; SFW 4; SSFS 1, 20; SUFW 1, 2; TUS; YAW

Braddon, Mary Elizabeth 1837-1915 .... **TCLC 111**
See also BRWS 8; CA 108; 179; CMW 4; DLB 18, 70, 156; HGG

Bradfield, Scott (Michael) 1955- .... **SSC 65**
See also CA 147; CANR 90; HGG; SUFW 2

Bradford, Gamaliel 1863-1932 .... **TCLC 36**
See also CA 160; DLB 17

Bradford, William 1590-1657 .... **LC 64**
See also DLB 24, 30; RGAL 4

Bradley, David (Henry), Jr. 1950- .... **BLC 1; CLC 23, 118**
See also BW 1, 3; CA 104; CANR 26, 81; CN 4, 5, 6, 7; DAM MULT; DLB 33

Bradley, John Ed(mund, Jr.) 1958- . **CLC 55**
See also CA 139; CANR 99; CN 6, 7; CSW

Bradley, Marion Zimmer
1930-1999 .... **CLC 30**
See Chapman, Lee; Dexter, John; Gardner, Miriam; Ives, Morgan; Rivers, Elfrida
See also AAYA 40; BPFB 1; CA 57-60; 185; CAAS 10; CANR 7, 31, 51, 75, 107; CPW; DA3; DAM POP; DLB 8; FANT; FW; MTCW 1, 2; MTFW 2005; SATA 90, 139; SATA-Obit 116; SFW 4; SUFW 2; YAW

Bradshaw, John 1933- .... **CLC 70**
See also CA 138; CANR 61

Bradstreet, Anne 1612(?)-1672 ...... **LC 4, 30; PC 10**
See also AMWS 1; CDALB 1640-1865; DA; DA3; DAC; DAM MST, POET; DLB 24; EXPP; FW; PFS 6; RGAL 4; TUS; WP

Brady, Joan 1939- .... **CLC 86**
See also CA 141

Bragg, Melvyn 1939- .... **CLC 10**
See also BEST 89:3; CA 57-60; CANR 10, 48, 89; CN 1, 2, 3, 4, 5, 6, 7; DLB 14, 271; RHW

Brahe, Tycho 1546-1601 .... **LC 45**
See also DLB 300

Braine, John (Gerard) 1922-1986 . **CLC 1, 3, 41**
See also CA 1-4R; 120; CANR 1, 33; CDBLB 1945-1960; CN 1, 2, 3, 4; DLB 15; DLBY 1986; EWL 3; MTCW 1

Braithwaite, William Stanley (Beaumont)
1878-1962 .... **BLC 1; HR 1:2; PC 52**
See also BW 1; CA 125; DAM MULT; DLB 50, 54; MAL 5

Bramah, Ernest 1868-1942 .... **TCLC 72**
See also CA 156; CMW 4; DLB 70; FANT

Brammer, Billy Lee
See Brammer, William

Brammer, William 1929-1978 .... **CLC 31**
See also CA 235; 77-80

Brancati, Vitaliano 1907-1954 .... **TCLC 12**
See also CA 109; DLB 264; EWL 3

Brancato, Robin F(idler) 1936- .... **CLC 35**
See also AAYA 9, 68; BYA 6; CA 69-72; CANR 11, 45; CLR 32; JRDA; MAICYA 2; MAICYAS 1; SAAS 9; SATA 97; WYA; YAW

Brand, Dionne 1953- .... **CLC 192**
See also BW 2; CA 143; CANR 143; CWP

Brand, Max
See Faust, Frederick (Schiller)
See also BPFB 1; TCWW 1, 2

Brand, Millen 1906-1980 .... **CLC 7**
See also CA 21-24R; 97-100; CANR 72

Branden, Barbara .... **CLC 44**
See also CA 148

Brandes, Georg (Morris Cohen)
1842-1927 .... **TCLC 10**
See also CA 105; 189; DLB 300

Brandys, Kazimierz 1916-2000 .... **CLC 62**
See also CA 239; EWL 3

Branley, Franklyn M(ansfield)
1915-2002 .... **CLC 21**
See also CA 33-36R; 207; CANR 14, 39; CLR 13; MAICYA 1, 2; SAAS 16; SATA 4, 68, 136

Brant, Beth (E.) 1941- .... **NNAL**
See also CA 144; FW

Brant, Sebastian 1457-1521 .... **LC 112**
See also DLB 179; RGWL 2, 3

Brathwaite, Edward Kamau
1930- .... **BLCS; CLC 11; PC 56**
See also BW 2, 3; CA 25-28R; CANR 11, 26, 47, 107; CDWLB 3; CP 1, 2, 3, 4, 5, 6, 7; DAM POET; DLB 125; EWL 3

Brathwaite, Kamau
See Brathwaite, Edward Kamau

Brautigan, Richard (Gary)
1935-1984 .... **CLC 1, 3, 5, 9, 12, 34, 42; TCLC 133**
See also BPFB 1; CA 53-56; 113; CANR 34; CN 1, 2, 3; CP 1, 2, 3, 4; DA3; DAM NOV; DLB 2, 5, 206; DLBY 1980, 1984; FANT; MAL 5; MTCW 1; RGAL 4; SATA 56

Brave Bird, Mary .... **NNAL**
See Crow Dog, Mary (Ellen)

Braverman, Kate 1950- .... **CLC 67**
See also CA 89-92; CANR 141

Brecht, (Eugen) Bertolt (Friedrich)
1898-1956 ...... **DC 3; TCLC 1, 6, 13, 35, 169; WLC**
See also CA 104; 133; CANR 62; CDWLB 2; DA; DA3; DAB; DAC; DAM DRAM, MST; DFS 4, 5, 9; DLB 56, 124; EW 11; EWL 3; IDTP; MTCW 1, 2; MTFW 2005; RGWL 2, 3; TWA

Brecht, Eugen Berthold Friedrich
See Brecht, (Eugen) Bertolt (Friedrich)

Bremer, Fredrika 1801-1865 .... **NCLC 11**
See also DLB 254

Brennan, Christopher John
1870-1932 .... **TCLC 17**
See also CA 117; 188; DLB 230; EWL 3

Brennan, Maeve 1917-1993 ... **CLC 5; TCLC 124**
See also CA 81-84; CANR 72, 100

Brenner, Jozef 1887-1919
See Csath, Geza
See also CA 240

Brent, Linda
See Jacobs, Harriet A(nn)

Brentano, Clemens (Maria)
1778-1842 .... **NCLC 1**
See also DLB 90; RGWL 2, 3

Brent of Bin Bin
See Franklin, (Stella Maria Sarah) Miles (Lampe)

Brenton, Howard 1942- .... **CLC 31**
See also CA 69-72; CANR 33, 67; CBD; CD 5, 6; DLB 13; MTCW 1

Breslin, James 1930-
See Breslin, Jimmy
See also CA 73-76; CANR 31, 75, 139; DAM NOV; MTCW 1, 2; MTFW 2005

Breslin, Jimmy .... **CLC 4, 43**
See Breslin, James
See also AITN 1; DLB 185; MTCW 2

Bresson, Robert 1901(?)-1999 .... **CLC 16**
See also CA 110; 187; CANR 49

Breton, Andre 1896-1966 .. **CLC 2, 9, 15, 54; PC 15**
See also CA 19-20; 25-28R; CANR 40, 60; CAP 2; DLB 65, 258; EW 11; EWL 3; GFL 1789 to the Present; LMFS 2; MTCW 1, 2; MTFW 2005; RGWL 2, 3; TWA; WP

Breytenbach, Breyten 1939(?)- .. **CLC 23, 37, 126**
See also CA 113; 129; CANR 61, 122; CWW 2; DAM POET; DLB 225; EWL 3

Bridgers, Sue Ellen 1942- .... **CLC 26**
See also AAYA 8, 49; BYA 7, 8; CA 65-68; CANR 11, 36; CLR 18; DLB 52; JRDA; MAICYA 1, 2; SAAS 1; SATA 22, 90; SATA-Essay 109; WYA; YAW

Bridges, Robert (Seymour)
1844-1930 .... **PC 28; TCLC 1**
See also BRW 6; CA 104; 152; CDBLB 1890-1914; DAM POET; DLB 19, 98

Bridie, James .... **TCLC 3**
See Mavor, Osborne Henry
See also DLB 10; EWL 3

Brin, David 1950- .... **CLC 34**
See also AAYA 21; CA 102; CANR 24, 70, 125, 127; INT CANR-24; SATA 65; SCFW 2; SFW 4

Brink, Andre (Philippus) 1935- . **CLC 18, 36, 106**
See also AFW; BRWS 6; CA 104; CANR 39, 62, 109, 133; CN 4, 5, 6, 7; DLB 225; EWL 3; INT CA-103; LATS 1:2; MTCW 1, 2; MTFW 2005; WLIT 2

Brinsmead, H. F(ay)
See Brinsmead, H(esba) F(ay)

Brinsmead, H. F.
See Brinsmead, H(esba) F(ay)

Brinsmead, H(esba) F(ay) 1922- ...... **CLC 21**
See also CA 21-24R; CANR 10; CLR 47; CWRI 5; MAICYA 1, 2; SAAS 5; SATA 18, 78

Brittain, Vera (Mary) 1893(?)-1970 . **CLC 23**
See also BRWS 10; CA 13-16; 25-28R; CANR 58; CAP 1; DLB 191; FW; MTCW 1, 2

Broch, Hermann 1886-1951 .... **TCLC 20**
See also CA 117; 211; CDWLB 2; DLB 85, 124; EW 10; EWL 3; RGWL 2, 3

Brock, Rose
See Hansen, Joseph
See also GLL 1

Brod, Max 1884-1968 .... **TCLC 115**
See also CA 5-8R; 25-28R; CANR 7; DLB 81; EWL 3

Brodkey, Harold (Roy) 1930-1996 .. **CLC 56; TCLC 123**
See also CA 111; 151; CANR 71; CN 4, 5, 6; DLB 130

Brodsky, Iosif Alexandrovich 1940-1996
See Brodsky, Joseph
See also AITN 1; CA 41-44R; 151; CANR 37, 106; DA3; DAM POET; MTCW 1, 2; MTFW 2005; RGWL 2, 3

Brodsky, Joseph . **CLC 4, 6, 13, 36, 100; PC 9**
See Brodsky, Iosif Alexandrovich
See also AMWS 8; CWW 2; DLB 285; EWL 3; MTCW 1

Brodsky, Michael (Mark) 1948- .... **CLC 19**
See also CA 102; CANR 18, 41, 58; DLB 244

Brodzki, Bella ed. .... **CLC 65**

Brome, Richard 1590(?)-1652 .... **LC 61**
See also BRWS 10; DLB 58

Bromell, Henry 1947- .... **CLC 5**
See also CA 53-56; CANR 9, 115, 116

Bryant, William Cullen 1794-1878 . **NCLC 6, 46; PC 20**
See also AMWS 1; CDALB 1640-1865; DA; DAB; DAC; DAM MST, POET; DLB 3, 43, 59, 189, 250; EXPP; PAB; RGAL 4; TUS

Bryusov, Valery Yakovlevich 1873-1924 .... **TCLC 10**
See also CA 107; 155; EWL 3; SFW 4

Buchan, John 1875-1940 .... **TCLC 41**
See also CA 108; 145; CMW 4; DAB; DAM POP; DLB 34, 70, 156; HGG; MSW; MTCW 2; RGEL 2; RHW; YABC 2

Buchanan, George 1506-1582 .... **LC 4**
See also DLB 132

Buchanan, Robert 1841-1901 .... **TCLC 107**
See also CA 179; DLB 18, 35

Buchheim, Lothar-Guenther 1918- .... **CLC 6**
See also CA 85-88

Buchner, (Karl) Georg
1813-(1837) .... **NCLC 26, 146**
See also CDWLB 2; DLB 133; EW 6; RGSF 2; RGWL 2, 3; TWA

Buchwald, Art(hur) 1925- .... **CLC 33**
See also AITN 1; CA 5-8R; CANR 21, 67, 107; MTCW 1, 2; SATA 10

Buck, Pearl S(ydenstricker)
1892-1973 .... **CLC 7, 11, 18, 127**
See also AAYA 42; AITN 1; AMWS 2; BPFB 1; CA 1-4R; 41-44R; CANR 1, 34; CDALBS; CN 1; DA; DA3; DAB; DAC; DAM MST, NOV; DLB 9, 102; EWL 3; LAIT 3; MAL 5; MTCW 1, 2; MTFW 2005; RGAL 4; RHW; SATA 1, 25; TUS

Buckler, Ernest 1908-1984 .... **CLC 13**
See also CA 11-12; 114; CAP 1; CCA 1; CN 1, 2, 3; DAC; DAM MST; DLB 68; SATA 47

Buckley, Christopher (Taylor)
1952- .... **CLC 165**
See also CA 139; CANR 119

Buckley, Vincent (Thomas)
1925-1988 .... **CLC 57**
See also CA 101; CP 1, 2, 3, 4; DLB 289

Buckley, William F(rank), Jr. 1925- . **CLC 7, 18, 37**
See also AITN 1; BPFB 1; CA 1-4R; CANR 1, 24, 53, 93, 133; CMW 4; CPW; DA3; DAM POP; DLB 137; DLBY 1980; INT CANR-24; MTCW 1, 2; MTFW 2005; TUS

Buechner, (Carl) Frederick 1926- . **CLC 2, 4, 6, 9**
See also AMWS 12; BPFB 1; CA 13-16R; CANR 11, 39, 64, 114, 138; CN 1, 2, 3, 4, 5, 6, 7; DAM NOV; DLBY 1980; INT CANR-11; MAL 5; MTCW 1, 2; MTFW 2005; TCLE 1:1

Buell, John (Edward) 1927- .... **CLC 10**
See also CA 1-4R; CANR 71; DLB 53

Buero Vallejo, Antonio 1916-2000 ... **CLC 15, 46, 139; DC 18**
See also CA 106; 189; CANR 24, 49, 75; CWW 2; DFS 11; EWL 3; HW 1; MTCW 1, 2

Bufalino, Gesualdo 1920-1996 .... **CLC 74**
See also CA 209; CWW 2; DLB 196

Bugayev, Boris Nikolayevich
1880-1934 .... **PC 11; TCLC 7**
See Bely, Andrey; Belyi, Andrei
See also CA 104; 165; MTCW 2; MTFW 2005

Bukowski, Charles 1920-1994 ... **CLC 2, 5, 9, 41, 82, 108; PC 18; SSC 45**
See also CA 17-20R; 144; CANR 40, 62, 105; CN 4, 5; CP 1, 2, 3, 4; CPW; DA3; DAM NOV, POET; DLB 5, 130, 169; EWL 3; MAL 5; MTCW 1, 2; MTFW 2005

Bulgakov, Mikhail (Afanas'evich)
1891-1940 ..... **SSC 18; TCLC 2, 16, 159**
See also BPFB 1; CA 105; 152; DAM DRAM, NOV; DLB 272; EWL 3; MTCW 2; MTFW 2005; NFS 8; RGSF 2; RGWL 2, 3; SFW 4; TWA

Bulgya, Alexander Alexandrovich
1901-1956 .... **TCLC 53**
See Fadeev, Aleksandr Aleksandrovich; Fadeev, Alexandr Alexandrovich; Fadeyev, Alexander
See also CA 117; 181

Bullins, Ed 1935- ... **BLC 1; CLC 1, 5, 7; DC 6**
See also BW 2, 3; CA 49-52; CAAS 16; CAD; CANR 24, 46, 73, 134; CD 5, 6; DAM DRAM, MULT; DLB 7, 38, 249; EWL 3; MAL 5; MTCW 1, 2; MTFW 2005; RGAL 4

Bulosan, Carlos 1911-1956 .... **AAL**
See also CA 216; DLB 312; RGAL 4

Bulwer-Lytton, Edward (George Earle Lytton) 1803-1873 .... **NCLC 1, 45**
See also DLB 21; RGEL 2; SFW 4; SUFW 1; TEA

Bunin, Ivan Alexeyevich 1870-1953 ... **SSC 5; TCLC 6**
See also CA 104; DLB 317; EWL 3; RGSF 2; RGWL 2, 3; TWA

Bunting, Basil 1900-1985 ...... **CLC 10, 39, 47**
See also BRWS 7; CA 53-56; 115; CANR 7; CP 1, 2, 3, 4; DAM POET; DLB 20; EWL 3; RGEL 2

Bunuel, Luis 1900-1983 ... **CLC 16, 80; HLC 1**
See also CA 101; 110; CANR 32, 77; DAM MULT; HW 1

Bunyan, John 1628-1688 ..... **LC 4, 69; WLC**
See also BRW 2; BYA 5; CDBLB 1660-1789; DA; DAB; DAC; DAM MST; DLB 39; RGEL 2; TEA; WCH; WLIT 3

Buravsky, Alexandr .... **CLC 59**

Burckhardt, Jacob (Christoph)
1818-1897 .... **NCLC 49**
See also EW 6

Burford, Eleanor
See Hibbert, Eleanor Alice Burford

Burgess, Anthony . **CLC 1, 2, 4, 5, 8, 10, 13, 15, 22, 40, 62, 81, 94**
See Wilson, John (Anthony) Burgess
See also AAYA 25; AITN 1; BRWS 1; CDBLB 1960 to Present; CN 1, 2, 3, 4, 5; DAB; DLB 14, 194, 261; DLBY 1998; EWL 3; RGEL 2; RHW; SFW 4; YAW

Burke, Edmund 1729(?)-1797 .... **LC 7, 36; WLC**
See also BRW 3; DA; DA3; DAB; DAC; DAM MST; DLB 104, 252; RGEL 2; TEA

Burke, Kenneth (Duva) 1897-1993 ... **CLC 2, 24**
See also AMW; CA 5-8R; 143; CANR 39, 74, 136; CN 1, 2; CP 1, 2, 3, 4; DLB 45, 63; EWL 3; MAL 5; MTCW 1, 2; MTFW 2005; RGAL 4

Burke, Leda
See Garnett, David

Burke, Ralph
See Silverberg, Robert

Burke, Thomas 1886-1945 .... **TCLC 63**
See also CA 113; 155; CMW 4; DLB 197

Burney, Fanny 1752-1840 .... **NCLC 12, 54, 107**
See also BRWS 3; DLB 39; FL 1:2; NFS 16; RGEL 2; TEA

Burney, Frances
See Burney, Fanny

Burns, Robert 1759-1796 ... **LC 3, 29, 40; PC 6; WLC**
See also AAYA 51; BRW 3; CDBLB 1789-1832; DA; DA3; DAB; DAC; DAM MST, POET; DLB 109; EXPP; PAB; RGEL 2; TEA; WP

Burns, Tex
See L'Amour, Louis (Dearborn)

Burnshaw, Stanley 1906- .... **CLC 3, 13, 44**
See also CA 9-12R; CP 1, 2, 3, 4, 5, 6, 7; DLB 48; DLBY 1997

Burr, Anne 1937- .... **CLC 6**
See also CA 25-28R

Burroughs, Edgar Rice 1875-1950 . **TCLC 2, 32**
See also AAYA 11; BPFB 1; BYA 4, 9; CA 104; 132; CANR 131; DA3; DAM NOV; DLB 8; FANT; MTCW 1, 2; MTFW 2005; RGAL 4; SATA 41; SCFW 1, 2; SFW 4; TCWW 1, 2; TUS; YAW

Burroughs, William S(eward)
1914-1997 .. **CLC 1, 2, 5, 15, 22, 42, 75, 109; TCLC 121; WLC**
See Lee, William; Lee, Willy
See also AAYA 60; AITN 2; AMWS 3; BG 1:2; BPFB 1; CA 9-12R; 160; CANR 20, 52, 104; CN 1, 2, 3, 4, 5, 6; CPW; DA; DA3; DAB; DAC; DAM MST, NOV, POP; DLB 2, 8, 16, 152, 237; DLBY 1981, 1997; EWL 3; HGG; LMFS 2; MAL 5; MTCW 1, 2; MTFW 2005; RGAL 4; SFW 4

Burton, Sir Richard F(rancis)
1821-1890 .... **NCLC 42**
See also DLB 55, 166, 184; SSFS 21

Burton, Robert 1577-1640 .... **LC 74**
See also DLB 151; RGEL 2

Buruma, Ian 1951- .... **CLC 163**
See also CA 128; CANR 65, 141

Busch, Frederick 1941- ... **CLC 7, 10, 18, 47, 166**
See also CA 33-36R; CAAS 1; CANR 45, 73, 92; CN 1, 2, 3, 4, 5, 6, 7; DLB 6, 218

Bush, Barney (Furman) 1946- .... **NNAL**
See also CA 145

Bush, Ronald 1946- .... **CLC 34**
See also CA 136

Bustos, F(rancisco)
See Borges, Jorge Luis

Bustos Domecq, H(onorio)
See Bioy Casares, Adolfo; Borges, Jorge Luis

Butler, Octavia E(stelle) 1947- .. **BLCS; CLC 38, 121**
See also AAYA 18, 48; AFAW 2; AMWS 13; BPFB 1; BW 2, 3; CA 73-76; CANR 12, 24, 38, 73, 145; CLR 65; CN 7; CPW; DA3; DAM MULT, POP; DLB 33; LATS 1:2; MTCW 1, 2; MTFW 2005; NFS 8, 21; SATA 84; SCFW 2; SFW 4; SSFS 6; TCLE 1:1; YAW

Butler, Robert Olen, (Jr.) 1945- ...... **CLC 81, 162**
See also AMWS 12; BPFB 1; CA 112; CANR 66, 138; CN 7; CSW; DAM POP; DLB 173; INT CA-112; MAL 5; MTCW 2; MTFW 2005; SSFS 11

Butler, Samuel 1612-1680 .... **LC 16, 43**
See also DLB 101, 126; RGEL 2

Butler, Samuel 1835-1902 .... **TCLC 1, 33; WLC**
See also BRWS 2; CA 143; CDBLB 1890-1914; DA; DA3; DAB; DAC; DAM MST, NOV; DLB 18, 57, 174; RGEL 2; SFW 4; TEA

Butler, Walter C.
See Faust, Frederick (Schiller)

Butor, Michel (Marie Francois)
1926- .... **CLC 1, 3, 8, 11, 15, 161**
See also CA 9-12R; CANR 33, 66; CWW
2; DLB 83; EW 13; EWL 3; GFL 1789 to
the Present; MTCW 1, 2; MTFW 2005

Butts, Mary 1890(?)-1937 .... **TCLC 77**
See also CA 148; DLB 240

Buxton, Ralph
See Silverstein, Alvin; Silverstein, Virginia
B(arbara Opshelor)

Buzo, Alex
See Buzo, Alexander (John)
See also DLB 289

Buzo, Alexander (John) 1944- .... **CLC 61**
See also CA 97-100; CANR 17, 39, 69; CD
5, 6

Buzzati, Dino 1906-1972 .... **CLC 36**
See also CA 160; 33-36R; DLB 177; RGWL
2, 3; SFW 4

Byars, Betsy (Cromer) 1928- .... **CLC 35**
See also AAYA 19; BYA 3; CA 33-36R,
183; CAAE 183; CANR 18, 36, 57, 102;
CLR 1, 16, 72; DLB 52; INT CANR-18;
JRDA; MAICYA 1, 2; MAICYAS 1;
MTCW 1; SAAS 1; SATA 4, 46, 80, 163;
SATA-Essay 108; WYA; YAW

Byatt, A(ntonia) S(usan Drabble)
1936- .... **CLC 19, 65, 136**
See also BPFB 1; BRWC 2; BRWS 4; CA
13-16R; CANR 13, 33, 50, 75, 96, 133;
CN 1, 2, 3, 4, 5, 6; DA3; DAM NOV,
POP; DLB 14, 194; EWL 3; MTCW 1, 2;
MTFW 2005; RGSF 2; RHW; TEA

Byrd, William II 1674-1744 .... **LC 112**
See also DLB 24, 140; RGAL 4

Byrne, David 1952- .... **CLC 26**
See also CA 127

Byrne, John Keyes 1926-
See Leonard, Hugh
See also CA 102; CANR 78, 140; INT CA-
102

Byron, George Gordon (Noel)
1788-1824 ..... **DC 24; NCLC 2, 12, 109,
149; PC 16; WLC**
See also AAYA 64; BRW 4; BRWC 2; CD-
BLB 1789-1832; DA; DA3; DAB; DAC;
DAM MST, POET; DLB 96, 110; EXPP;
LMFS 1; PAB; PFS 1, 14; RGEL 2; TEA;
WLIT 3; WP

Byron, Robert 1905-1941 .... **TCLC 67**
See also CA 160; DLB 195

C. 3. 3.
See Wilde, Oscar (Fingal O'Flahertie Wills)

Caballero, Fernan 1796-1877 .... **NCLC 10**

Cabell, Branch
See Cabell, James Branch

Cabell, James Branch 1879-1958 .... **TCLC 6**
See also CA 105; 152; DLB 9, 78; FANT;
MAL 5; MTCW 2; RGAL 4; SUFW 1

Cabeza de Vaca, Alvar Nunez
1490-1557(?) .... **LC 61**

Cable, George Washington
1844-1925 .... **SSC 4; TCLC 4**
See also CA 104; 155; DLB 12, 74; DLBD
13; RGAL 4; TUS

Cabral de Melo Neto, Joao
1920-1999 .... **CLC 76**
See Melo Neto, Joao Cabral de
See also CA 151; DAM MULT; DLB 307;
LAW; LAWS 1

Cabrera Infante, G(uillermo)
1929-2005 ..... **CLC 5, 25, 45, 120; HLC
1; SSC 39**
See also CA 85-88; 236; CANR 29, 65, 110;
CDWLB 3; CWW 2; DA3; DAM MULT;
DLB 113; EWL 3; HW 1, 2; LAW; LAWS
1; MTCW 1, 2; MTFW 2005; RGSF 2;
WLIT 1

Cade, Toni
See Bambara, Toni Cade

Cadmus and Harmonia
See Buchan, John

Caedmon fl. 658-680 .... **CMLC 7**
See also DLB 146

Caeiro, Alberto
See Pessoa, Fernando (Antonio Nogueira)

Caesar, Julius .... **CMLC 47**
See Julius Caesar
See also AW 1; RGWL 2, 3

Cage, John (Milton), (Jr.)
1912-1992 .... **CLC 41; PC 58**
See also CA 13-16R; 169; CANR 9, 78;
DLB 193; INT CANR-9; TCLE 1:1

Cahan, Abraham 1860-1951 .... **TCLC 71**
See also CA 108; 154; DLB 9, 25, 28; MAL
5; RGAL 4

Cain, G.
See Cabrera Infante, G(uillermo)

Cain, Guillermo
See Cabrera Infante, G(uillermo)

Cain, James M(allahan) 1892-1977 .. **CLC 3,
11, 28**
See also AITN 1; BPFB 1; CA 17-20R; 73-
76; CANR 8, 34, 61; CMW 4; CN 1, 2;
DLB 226; EWL 3; MAL 5; MSW; MTCW
1; RGAL 4

Caine, Hall 1853-1931 .... **TCLC 97**
See also RHW

Caine, Mark
See Raphael, Frederic (Michael)

Calasso, Roberto 1941- .... **CLC 81**
See also CA 143; CANR 89

Calderon de la Barca, Pedro
1600-1681 .... **DC 3; HLCS 1; LC 23**
See also EW 2; RGWL 2, 3; TWA

Caldwell, Erskine (Preston)
1903-1987 .... **CLC 1, 8, 14, 50, 60; SSC
19; TCLC 117**
See also AITN 1; AMW; BPFB 1; CA 1-4R;
121; CAAS 1; CANR 2, 33; CN 1, 2, 3,
4; DA3; DAM NOV; DLB 9, 86; EWL 3;
MAL 5; MTCW 1, 2; MTFW 2005;
RGAL 4; RGSF 2; TUS

Caldwell, (Janet Miriam) Taylor (Holland)
1900-1985 .... **CLC 2, 28, 39**
See also BPFB 1; CA 5-8R; 116; CANR 5;
DA3; DAM NOV, POP; DLBD 17;
MTCW 2; RHW

Calhoun, John Caldwell
1782-1850 .... **NCLC 15**
See also DLB 3, 248

Calisher, Hortense 1911- ..... **CLC 2, 4, 8, 38,
134; SSC 15**
See also CA 1-4R; CANR 1, 22, 117; CN
1, 2, 3, 4, 5, 6, 7; DA3; DAM NOV; DLB
2, 218; INT CANR-22; MAL 5; MTCW
1, 2; MTFW 2005; RGAL 4; RGSF 2

Callaghan, Morley Edward
1903-1990 ..... **CLC 3, 14, 41, 65; TCLC
145**
See also CA 9-12R; 132; CANR 33, 73;
CN 1, 2, 3, 4; DAC; DAM MST; DLB
68; EWL 3; MTCW 1, 2; MTFW 2005;
RGEL 2; RGSF 2; SSFS 19

Callimachus c. 305B.C.-c.
240B.C. .... **CMLC 18**
See also AW 1; DLB 176; RGWL 2, 3

Calvin, Jean
See Calvin, John
See also GFL Beginnings to 1789

Calvin, John 1509-1564 .... **LC 37**
See Calvin, Jean

Calvino, Italo 1923-1985 .... **CLC 5, 8, 11, 22,
33, 39, 73; SSC 3, 48**
See also AAYA 58; CA 85-88; 116; CANR
23, 61, 132; DAM NOV; DLB 196; EW
13; EWL 3; MTCW 1, 2; MTFW 2005;
RGSF 2; RGWL 2, 3; SFW 4; SSFS 12;
WLIT 7

Camara Laye
See Laye, Camara
See also EWL 3

Camden, William 1551-1623 .... **LC 77**
See also DLB 172

Cameron, Carey 1952- .... **CLC 59**
See also CA 135

Cameron, Peter 1959- .... **CLC 44**
See also AMWS 12; CA 125; CANR 50,
117; DLB 234; GLL 2

Camoens, Luis Vaz de 1524(?)-1580
See Camoes, Luis de
See also EW 2

Camoes, Luis de 1524(?)-1580 . **HLCS 1; LC
62; PC 31**
See Camoens, Luis Vaz de
See also DLB 287; RGWL 2, 3

Campana, Dino 1885-1932 .... **TCLC 20**
See also CA 117; DLB 114; EWL 3

Campanella, Tommaso 1568-1639 .... **LC 32**
See also RGWL 2, 3

Campbell, John W(ood, Jr.)
1910-1971 .... **CLC 32**
See also CA 21-22; 29-32R; CANR 34;
CAP 2; DLB 8; MTCW 1; SCFW 1, 2;
SFW 4

Campbell, Joseph 1904-1987 .... **CLC 69;
TCLC 140**
See also AAYA 3, 66; BEST 89:2; CA 1-4R;
124; CANR 3, 28, 61, 107; DA3; MTCW
1, 2

Campbell, Maria 1940- .... **CLC 85; NNAL**
See also CA 102; CANR 54; CCA 1; DAC

Campbell, (John) Ramsey 1946- ..... **CLC 42;
SSC 19**
See also AAYA 51; CA 57-60, 228; CAAE
228; CANR 7, 102; DLB 261; HGG; INT
CANR-7; SUFW 1, 2

Campbell, (Ignatius) Roy (Dunnachie)
1901-1957 .... **TCLC 5**
See also AFW; CA 104; 155; DLB 20, 225;
EWL 3; MTCW 2; RGEL 2

Campbell, Thomas 1777-1844 .... **NCLC 19**
See also DLB 93, 144; RGEL 2

Campbell, Wilfred .... **TCLC 9**
See Campbell, William

Campbell, William 1858(?)-1918
See Campbell, Wilfred
See also CA 106; DLB 92

Campbell, William Edward March
1893-1954
See March, William
See also CA 108

Campion, Jane 1954- .... **CLC 95**
See also AAYA 33; CA 138; CANR 87

Campion, Thomas 1567-1620 .... **LC 78**
See also CDBLB Before 1660; DAM POET;
DLB 58, 172; RGEL 2

Camus, Albert 1913-1960 ...... **CLC 1, 2, 4, 9,
11, 14, 32, 63, 69, 124; DC 2; SSC 9,
76; WLC**
See also AAYA 36; AFW; BPFB 1; CA 89-
92; CANR 131; DA; DA3; DAB; DAC;
DAM DRAM, MST, NOV; DLB 72, 321;
EW 13; EWL 3; EXPN; EXPS; GFL 1789
to the Present; LATS 1:2; LMFS 2;
MTCW 1, 2; MTFW 2005; NFS 6, 16;
RGSF 2; RGWL 2, 3; SSFS 4; TWA

Canby, Vincent 1924-2000 .... **CLC 13**
See also CA 81-84; 191

Cancale
See Desnos, Robert

Canetti, Elias 1905-1994 .. **CLC 3, 14, 25, 75,
86; TCLC 157**
See also CA 21-24R; 146; CANR 23, 61,
79; CDWLB 2; CWW 2; DA3; DLB 85,
124; EW 12; EWL 3; MTCW 1, 2; MTFW
2005; RGWL 2, 3; TWA

Davies, William Henry 1871-1940 ... **TCLC 5**
See also BRWS 11; CA 104; 179; DLB 19, 174; EWL 3; RGEL 2

Da Vinci, Leonardo 1452-1519 ..... **LC 12, 57, 60**
See also AAYA 40

Davis, Angela (Yvonne) 1944- .... **CLC 77**
See also BW 2, 3; CA 57-60; CANR 10, 81; CSW; DA3; DAM MULT; FW

Davis, B. Lynch
See Bioy Casares, Adolfo; Borges, Jorge Luis

Davis, Frank Marshall 1905-1987 ...... **BLC 1**
See also BW 2, 3; CA 125; 123; CANR 42, 80; DAM MULT; DLB 51

Davis, Gordon
See Hunt, E(verette) Howard, (Jr.)

Davis, H(arold) L(enoir) 1896-1960 . **CLC 49**
See also ANW; CA 178; 89-92; DLB 9, 206; SATA 114; TCWW 1, 2

Davis, Natalie Zemon 1928- .... **CLC 204**
See also CA 53-56; CANR 58, 100

Davis, Rebecca (Blaine) Harding
1831-1910 .... **SSC 38; TCLC 6**
See also CA 104; 179; DLB 74, 239; FW; NFS 14; RGAL 4; TUS

Davis, Richard Harding
1864-1916 .... **TCLC 24**
See also CA 114; 179; DLB 12, 23, 78, 79, 189; DLBD 13; RGAL 4

Davison, Frank Dalby 1893-1970 ..... **CLC 15**
See also CA 217; 116; DLB 260

Davison, Lawrence H.
See Lawrence, D(avid) H(erbert Richards)

Davison, Peter (Hubert) 1928-2004 . **CLC 28**
See also CA 9-12R; 234; CAAS 4; CANR 3, 43, 84; CP 1, 2, 3, 4, 5, 6, 7; DLB 5

Davys, Mary 1674-1732 .... **LC 1, 46**
See also DLB 39

Dawson, (Guy) Fielding (Lewis)
1930-2002 .... **CLC 6**
See also CA 85-88; 202; CANR 108; DLB 130; DLBY 2002

Dawson, Peter
See Faust, Frederick (Schiller)
See also TCWW 1, 2

Day, Clarence (Shepard, Jr.)
1874-1935 .... **TCLC 25**
See also CA 108; 199; DLB 11

Day, John 1574(?)-1640(?) .... **LC 70**
See also DLB 62, 170; RGEL 2

Day, Thomas 1748-1789 .... **LC 1**
See also DLB 39; YABC 1

Day Lewis, C(ecil) 1904-1972 . **CLC 1, 6, 10; PC 11**
See Blake, Nicholas; Lewis, C. Day
See also BRWS 3; CA 13-16; 33-36R; CANR 34; CAP 1; CP 1; CWRI 5; DAM POET; DLB 15, 20; EWL 3; MTCW 1, 2; RGEL 2

Dazai Osamu .... **SSC 41; TCLC 11**
See Tsushima, Shuji
See also CA 164; DLB 182; EWL 3; MJW; RGSF 2; RGWL 2, 3; TWA

de Andrade, Carlos Drummond
See Drummond de Andrade, Carlos

de Andrade, Mario 1892(?)-1945
See Andrade, Mario de
See also CA 178; HW 2

Deane, Norman
See Creasey, John

Deane, Seamus (Francis) 1940- ...... **CLC 122**
See also CA 118; CANR 42

de Beauvoir, Simone (Lucie Ernestine Marie Bertrand)
See Beauvoir, Simone (Lucie Ernestine Marie Bertrand) de

de Beer, P.
See Bosman, Herman Charles

De Botton, Alain 1969- .... **CLC 203**
See also CA 159; CANR 96

de Brissac, Malcolm
See Dickinson, Peter (Malcolm de Brissac)

de Campos, Alvaro
See Pessoa, Fernando (Antonio Nogueira)

de Chardin, Pierre Teilhard
See Teilhard de Chardin, (Marie Joseph) Pierre

de Crenne, Helisenne c. 1510-c.
1560 .... **LC 113**

Dee, John 1527-1608 .... **LC 20**
See also DLB 136, 213

Deer, Sandra 1940- .... **CLC 45**
See also CA 186

De Ferrari, Gabriella 1941- .... **CLC 65**
See also CA 146

de Filippo, Eduardo 1900-1984 ... **TCLC 127**
See also CA 132; 114; EWL 3; MTCW 1; RGWL 2, 3

Defoe, Daniel 1660(?)-1731 .... **LC 1, 42, 108; WLC**
See also AAYA 27; BRW 3; BRWR 1; BYA 4; CDBLB 1660-1789; CLR 61; DA; DA3; DAB; DAC; DAM MST, NOV; DLB 39, 95, 101; JRDA; LAIT 1; LMFS 1; MAICYA 1, 2; NFS 9, 13; RGEL 2; SATA 22; TEA; WCH; WLIT 3

de Gourmont, Remy(-Marie-Charles)
See Gourmont, Remy(-Marie-Charles) de

de Gournay, Marie le Jars
1566-1645 .... **LC 98**
See also FW

de Hartog, Jan 1914-2002 .... **CLC 19**
See also CA 1-4R; 210; CANR 1; DFS 12

de Hostos, E. M.
See Hostos (y Bonilla), Eugenio Maria de

de Hostos, Eugenio M.
See Hostos (y Bonilla), Eugenio Maria de

Deighton, Len .... **CLC 4, 7, 22, 46**
See Deighton, Leonard Cyril
See also AAYA 6; BEST 89:2; BPFB 1; CD-BLB 1960 to Present; CMW 4; CN 1, 2, 3, 4, 5, 6, 7; CPW; DLB 87

Deighton, Leonard Cyril 1929-
See Deighton, Len
See also AAYA 57; CA 9-12R; CANR 19, 33, 68; DA3; DAM NOV, POP; MTCW 1, 2; MTFW 2005

Dekker, Thomas 1572(?)-1632 ..... **DC 12; LC 22**
See also CDBLB Before 1660; DAM DRAM; DLB 62, 172; LMFS 1; RGEL 2

de Laclos, Pierre Ambroise Franois
See Laclos, Pierre-Ambroise Francois

Delacroix, (Ferdinand-Victor-)Eugene
1798-1863 .... **NCLC 133**
See also EW 5

Delafield, E. M. .... **TCLC 61**
See Dashwood, Edmee Elizabeth Monica de la Pasture
See also DLB 34; RHW

de la Mare, Walter (John)
1873-1956 . **SSC 14; TCLC 4, 53; WLC**
See also CA 163; CDBLB 1914-1945; CLR 23; CWRI 5; DA3; DAB; DAC; DAM MST, POET; DLB 19, 153, 162, 255, 284; EWL 3; EXPP; HGG; MAICYA 1, 2; MTCW 2; MTFW 2005; RGEL 2; RGSF 2; SATA 16; SUFW 1; TEA; WCH

de Lamartine, Alphonse (Marie Louis Prat)
See Lamartine, Alphonse (Marie Louis Prat) de

Delaney, Franey
See O'Hara, John (Henry)

Delaney, Shelagh 1939- .... **CLC 29**
See also CA 17-20R; CANR 30, 67; CBD; CD 5, 6; CDBLB 1960 to Present; CWD; DAM DRAM; DFS 7; DLB 13; MTCW 1

Delany, Martin Robison
1812-1885 .... **NCLC 93**
See also DLB 50; RGAL 4

Delany, Mary (Granville Pendarves)
1700-1788 .... **LC 12**

Delany, Samuel R(ay), Jr. 1942- .... **BLC 1; CLC 8, 14, 38, 141**
See also AAYA 24; AFAW 2; BPFB 1; BW 2, 3; CA 81-84; CANR 27, 43, 116; CN 2, 3, 4, 5, 6, 7; DAM MULT; DLB 8, 33; FANT; MAL 5; MTCW 1, 2; RGAL 4; SATA 92; SCFW 1, 2; SFW 4; SUFW 2

De la Ramee, Marie Louise (Ouida)
1839-1908
See Ouida
See also CA 204; SATA 20

de la Roche, Mazo 1879-1961 .... **CLC 14**
See also CA 85-88; CANR 30; DLB 68; RGEL 2; RHW; SATA 64

De La Salle, Innocent
See Hartmann, Sadakichi

de Laureamont, Comte
See Lautreamont

Delbanco, Nicholas (Franklin)
1942- .... **CLC 6, 13, 167**
See also CA 17-20R, 189; CAAE 189; CAAS 2; CANR 29, 55, 116; CN 7; DLB 6, 234

del Castillo, Michel 1933- .... **CLC 38**
See also CA 109; CANR 77

Deledda, Grazia (Cosima)
1875(?)-1936 .... **TCLC 23**
See also CA 123; 205; DLB 264; EWL 3; RGWL 2, 3; WLIT 7

Deleuze, Gilles 1925-1995 .... **TCLC 116**
See also DLB 296

Delgado, Abelardo (Lalo) B(arrientos)
1930-2004 .... **HLC 1**
See also CA 131; 230; CAAS 15; CANR 90; DAM MST, MULT; DLB 82; HW 1, 2

Delibes, Miguel .... **CLC 8, 18**
See Delibes Setien, Miguel
See also DLB 322; EWL 3

Delibes Setien, Miguel 1920-
See Delibes, Miguel
See also CA 45-48; CANR 1, 32; CWW 2; HW 1; MTCW 1

DeLillo, Don 1936- ..... **CLC 8, 10, 13, 27, 39, 54, 76, 143, 210, 213**
See also AMWC 2; AMWS 6; BEST 89:1; BPFB 1; CA 81-84; CANR 21, 76, 92, 133; CN 3, 4, 5, 6, 7; CPW; DA3; DAM NOV, POP; DLB 6, 173; EWL 3; MAL 5; MTCW 1, 2; MTFW 2005; RGAL 4; TUS

de Lisser, H. G.
See De Lisser, H(erbert) G(eorge)
See also DLB 117

De Lisser, H(erbert) G(eorge)
1878-1944 .... **TCLC 12**
See de Lisser, H. G.
See also BW 2; CA 109; 152

Deloire, Pierre
See Peguy, Charles (Pierre)

Deloney, Thomas 1543(?)-1600 .... **LC 41**
See also DLB 167; RGEL 2

Deloria, Ella (Cara) 1889-1971(?) ..... **NNAL**
See also CA 152; DAM MULT; DLB 175

Deloria, Vine (Victor), Jr.
1933-2005 .... **CLC 21, 122; NNAL**
See also CA 53-56; CANR 5, 20, 48, 98; DAM MULT; DLB 175; MTCW 1; SATA 21

del Valle-Inclan, Ramon (Maria)
See Valle-Inclan, Ramon (Maria) del
See also DLB 322

Del Vecchio, John M(ichael) 1947- .. **CLC 29**
See also CA 110; DLBD 9

de Man, Paul (Adolph Michel)
1919-1983 .... **CLC 55**
See also CA 128; 111; CANR 61; DLB 67;
MTCW 1, 2

DeMarinis, Rick 1934- .... **CLC 54**
See also CA 57-60, 184; CAAE 184; CAAS
24; CANR 9, 25, 50; DLB 218; TCWW 2

de Maupassant, (Henri Rene Albert) Guy
See Maupassant, (Henri Rene Albert) Guy
de

Dembry, R. Emmet
See Murfree, Mary Noailles

Demby, William 1922- .... **BLC 1; CLC 53**
See also BW 1, 3; CA 81-84; CANR 81;
DAM MULT; DLB 33

de Menton, Francisco
See Chin, Frank (Chew, Jr.)

Demetrius of Phalerum c.
307B.C.- .... **CMLC 34**

Demijohn, Thom
See Disch, Thomas M(ichael)

De Mille, James 1833-1880 .... **NCLC 123**
See also DLB 99, 251

Deming, Richard 1915-1983
See Queen, Ellery
See also CA 9-12R; CANR 3, 94; SATA 24

Democritus c. 460B.C.-c. 370B.C. . **CMLC 47**

de Montaigne, Michel (Eyquem)
See Montaigne, Michel (Eyquem) de

de Montherlant, Henry (Milon)
See Montherlant, Henry (Milon) de

Demosthenes 384B.C.-322B.C. ...... **CMLC 13**
See also AW 1; DLB 176; RGWL 2, 3

de Musset, (Louis Charles) Alfred
See Musset, (Louis Charles) Alfred de

de Natale, Francine
See Malzberg, Barry N(athaniel)

de Navarre, Marguerite 1492-1549 ... **LC 61;**
SSC 85
See Marguerite d'Angouleme; Marguerite
de Navarre

Denby, Edwin (Orr) 1903-1983 .... **CLC 48**
See also CA 138; 110; CP 1

de Nerval, Gerard
See Nerval, Gerard de

Denham, John 1615-1669 .... **LC 73**
See also DLB 58, 126; RGEL 2

Denis, Julio
See Cortazar, Julio

Denmark, Harrison
See Zelazny, Roger (Joseph)

Dennis, John 1658-1734 .... **LC 11**
See also DLB 101; RGEL 2

Dennis, Nigel (Forbes) 1912-1989 ...... **CLC 8**
See also CA 25-28R; 129; CN 1, 2, 3, 4;
DLB 13, 15, 233; EWL 3; MTCW 1

Dent, Lester 1904-1959 .... **TCLC 72**
See also CA 112; 161; CMW 4; DLB 306;
SFW 4

De Palma, Brian (Russell) 1940- ...... **CLC 20**
See also CA 109

De Quincey, Thomas 1785-1859 ..... **NCLC 4,**
87
See also BRW 4; CDBLB 1789-1832; DLB
110, 144; RGEL 2

Deren, Eleanora 1908(?)-1961
See Deren, Maya
See also CA 192; 111

Deren, Maya .... **CLC 16, 102**
See Deren, Eleanora

Derleth, August (William)
1909-1971 .... **CLC 31**
See also BPFB 1; BYA 9, 10; CA 1-4R; 29-
32R; CANR 4; CMW 4; CN 1; DLB 9;
DLBD 17; HGG; SATA 5; SUFW 1

Der Nister 1884-1950 .... **TCLC 56**
See Nister, Der

de Routisie, Albert
See Aragon, Louis

Derrida, Jacques 1930-2004 .... **CLC 24, 87**
See also CA 124; 127; 232; CANR 76, 98,
133; DLB 242; EWL 3; LMFS 2; MTCW
2; TWA

Derry Down Derry
See Lear, Edward

Dersonnes, Jacques
See Simenon, Georges (Jacques Christian)

Der Stricker c. 1190-c. 1250 .... **CMLC 75**
See also DLB 138

Desai, Anita 1937- .... **CLC 19, 37, 97, 175**
See also BRWS 5; CA 81-84; CANR 33,
53, 95, 133; CN 1, 2, 3, 4, 5, 6, 7; CWRI
5; DA3; DAB; DAM NOV; DLB 271;
DNFS 2; EWL 3; FW; MTCW 1, 2;
MTFW 2005; SATA 63, 126

Desai, Kiran 1971- .... **CLC 119**
See also BYA 16; CA 171; CANR 127

de Saint-Luc, Jean
See Glassco, John

de Saint Roman, Arnaud
See Aragon, Louis

Desbordes-Valmore, Marceline
1786-1859 .... **NCLC 97**
See also DLB 217

Descartes, Rene 1596-1650 .... **LC 20, 35**
See also DLB 268; EW 3; GFL Beginnings
to 1789

Deschamps, Eustache 1340(?)-1404 .. **LC 103**
See also DLB 208

De Sica, Vittorio 1901(?)-1974 .... **CLC 20**
See also CA 117

Desnos, Robert 1900-1945 .... **TCLC 22**
See also CA 121; 151; CANR 107; DLB
258; EWL 3; LMFS 2

Destouches, Louis-Ferdinand
1894-1961 .... **CLC 9, 15**
See Celine, Louis-Ferdinand
See also CA 85-88; CANR 28; MTCW 1

de Tolignac, Gaston
See Griffith, D(avid Lewelyn) W(ark)

Deutsch, Babette 1895-1982 .... **CLC 18**
See also BYA 3; CA 1-4R; 108; CANR 4,
79; CP 1, 2, 3; DLB 45; SATA 1; SATA-
Obit 33

Devenant, William 1606-1649 .... **LC 13**

Devkota, Laxmiprasad 1909-1959 . **TCLC 23**
See also CA 123

De Voto, Bernard (Augustine)
1897-1955 .... **TCLC 29**
See also CA 113; 160; DLB 9, 256; MAL
5; TCWW 1, 2

De Vries, Peter 1910-1993 ..... **CLC 1, 2, 3, 7,**
10, 28, 46
See also CA 17-20R; 142; CANR 41; CN
1, 2, 3, 4, 5; DAM NOV; DLB 6; DLBY
1982; MAL 5; MTCW 1, 2; MTFW 2005

Dewey, John 1859-1952 .... **TCLC 95**
See also CA 114; 170; CANR 144; DLB
246, 270; RGAL 4

Dexter, John
See Bradley, Marion Zimmer
See also GLL 1

Dexter, Martin
See Faust, Frederick (Schiller)

Dexter, Pete 1943- .... **CLC 34, 55**
See also BEST 89:2; CA 127; 131; CANR
129; CPW; DAM POP; INT CA-131;
MAL 5; MTCW 1; MTFW 2005

Diamano, Silmang
See Senghor, Leopold Sedar

Diamond, Neil 1941- .... **CLC 30**
See also CA 108

Diaz del Castillo, Bernal c.
1496-1584 .... **HLCS 1; LC 31**
See also DLB 318; LAW

di Bassetto, Corno
See Shaw, George Bernard

Dick, Philip K(indred) 1928-1982 ... **CLC 10,**
30, 72; SSC 57
See also AAYA 24; BPFB 1; BYA 11; CA
49-52; 106; CANR 2, 16, 132; CN 2, 3;
CPW; DA3; DAM NOV, POP; DLB 8;
MTCW 1, 2; MTFW 2005; NFS 5; SCFW
1, 2; SFW 4

Dickens, Charles (John Huffam)
1812-1870 .... **NCLC 3, 8, 18, 26, 37, 50,**
86, 105, 113, 161; SSC 17, 49, 88; WLC
See also AAYA 23; BRW 5; BRWC 1, 2;
BYA 1, 2, 3, 13, 14; CDBLB 1832-1890;
CLR 95; CMW 4; DA; DA3; DAB; DAC;
DAM MST, NOV; DLB 21, 55, 70, 159,
166; EXPN; GL 2; HGG; JRDA; LAIT 1,
2; LATS 1:1; LMFS 1; MAICYA 1, 2;
NFS 4, 5, 10, 14, 20; RGEL 2; RGSF 2;
SATA 15; SUFW 1; TEA; WCH; WLIT
4; WYA

Dickey, James (Lafayette)
1923-1997 .... **CLC 1, 2, 4, 7, 10, 15, 47,**
109; PC 40; TCLC 151
See also AAYA 50; AITN 1, 2; AMWS 4;
BPFB 1; CA 9-12R; 156; CABS 2; CANR
10, 48, 61, 105; CDALB 1968-1988; CP
1, 2, 3, 4; CPW; CSW; DA3; DAM NOV,
POET, POP; DLB 5, 193; DLBD 7;
DLBY 1982, 1993, 1996, 1997, 1998;
EWL 3; INT CANR-10; MAL 5; MTCW
1, 2; NFS 9; PFS 6, 11; RGAL 4; TUS

Dickey, William 1928-1994 .... **CLC 3, 28**
See also CA 9-12R; 145; CANR 24, 79; CP
1, 2, 3, 4; DLB 5

Dickinson, Charles 1951- .... **CLC 49**
See also CA 128; CANR 141

Dickinson, Emily (Elizabeth)
1830-1886 ... **NCLC 21, 77; PC 1; WLC**
See also AAYA 22; AMW; AMWR 1;
CDALB 1865-1917; DA; DA3; DAB;
DAC; DAM MST, POET; DLB 1, 243;
EXPP; FL 1:3; MAWW; PAB; PFS 1, 2,
3, 4, 5, 6, 8, 10, 11, 13, 16; RGAL 4;
SATA 29; TUS; WP; WYA

Dickinson, Mrs. Herbert Ward
See Phelps, Elizabeth Stuart

Dickinson, Peter (Malcolm de Brissac)
1927- .... **CLC 12, 35**
See also AAYA 9, 49; BYA 5; CA 41-44R;
CANR 31, 58, 88, 134; CLR 29; CMW 4;
DLB 87, 161, 276; JRDA; MAICYA 1, 2;
SATA 5, 62, 95, 150; SFW 4; WYA; YAW

Dickson, Carr
See Carr, John Dickson

Dickson, Carter
See Carr, John Dickson

Diderot, Denis 1713-1784 .... **LC 26**
See also DLB 313; EW 4; GFL Beginnings
to 1789; LMFS 1; RGWL 2, 3

Didion, Joan 1934- . **CLC 1, 3, 8, 14, 32, 129**
See also AITN 1; AMWS 4; CA 5-8R;
CANR 14, 52, 76, 125; CDALB 1968-
1988; CN 2, 3, 4, 5, 6, 7; DA3; DAM
NOV; DLB 2, 173, 185; DLBY 1981,
1986; EWL 3; MAL 5; MAWW; MTCW
1, 2; MTFW 2005; NFS 3; RGAL 4;
TCLE 1:1; TCWW 2; TUS

di Donato, Pietro 1911-1992 .... **TCLC 159**
See also CA 101; 136; DLB 9

Dietrich, Robert
See Hunt, E(verette) Howard, (Jr.)

Difusa, Pati
See Almodovar, Pedro

Dillard, Annie 1945- .... **CLC 9, 60, 115, 216**
See also AAYA 6, 43; AMWS 6; ANW; CA
49-52; CANR 3, 43, 62, 90, 125; DA3;
DAM NOV; DLB 275, 278; DLBY 1980;
LAIT 4, 5; MAL 5; MTCW 1, 2; MTFW
2005; NCFS 1; RGAL 4; SATA 10, 140;
TCLE 1:1; TUS

Dillard, R(ichard) H(enry) W(ilde)
1937- .... **CLC 5**
See also CA 21-24R; CAAS 7; CANR 10;
CP 2, 3, 4, 5, 6, 7; CSW; DLB 5, 244

Dillon, Eilis 1920-1994 .... **CLC 17**
See also CA 9-12R, 182; 147; CAAE 182;
CAAS 3; CANR 4, 38, 78; CLR 26; MAI-
CYA 1, 2; MAICYAS 1; SATA 2, 74;
SATA-Essay 105; SATA-Obit 83; YAW

Dimont, Penelope
See Mortimer, Penelope (Ruth)

Dinesen, Isak ..... **CLC 10, 29, 95; SSC 7, 75**
See Blixen, Karen (Christentze Dinesen)
See also EW 10; EWL 3; EXPS; FW; GL
2; HGG; LAIT 3; MTCW 1; NCFS 2;
NFS 9; RGSF 2; RGWL 2, 3; SSFS 3, 6,
13; WLIT 2

Ding Ling .... **CLC 68**
See Chiang, Pin-chin
See also RGWL 3

Diphusa, Patty
See Almodovar, Pedro

Disch, Thomas M(ichael) 1940- ... **CLC 7, 36**
See Disch, Tom
See also AAYA 17; BPFB 1; CA 21-24R;
CAAS 4; CANR 17, 36, 54, 89; CLR 18;
CP 7; DA3; DLB 8; HGG; MAICYA 1, 2;
MTCW 1, 2; MTFW 2005; SAAS 15;
SATA 92; SCFW 1, 2; SFW 4; SUFW 2

Disch, Tom
See Disch, Thomas M(ichael)
See also DLB 282

d'Isly, Georges
See Simenon, Georges (Jacques Christian)

Disraeli, Benjamin 1804-1881 ... **NCLC 2, 39, 79**
See also BRW 4; DLB 21, 55; RGEL 2

Ditcum, Steve
See Crumb, R(obert)

Dixon, Paige
See Corcoran, Barbara (Asenath)

Dixon, Stephen 1936- .... **CLC 52; SSC 16**
See also AMWS 12; CA 89-92; CANR 17,
40, 54, 91; CN 4, 5, 6, 7; DLB 130; MAL
5

Dixon, Thomas, Jr. 1864-1946 ..... **TCLC 163**
See also RHW

Djebar, Assia 1936- .... **CLC 182**
See also CA 188; EWL 3; RGWL 3; WLIT
2

Doak, Annie
See Dillard, Annie

Dobell, Sydney Thompson
1824-1874 .... **NCLC 43**
See also DLB 32; RGEL 2

Doblin, Alfred .... **TCLC 13**
See Doeblin, Alfred
See also CDWLB 2; EWL 3; RGWL 2, 3

Dobroliubov, Nikolai Aleksandrovich
See Dobrolyubov, Nikolai Alexandrovich
See also DLB 277

Dobrolyubov, Nikolai Alexandrovich
1836-1861 .... **NCLC 5**
See Dobroliubov, Nikolai Aleksandrovich

Dobson, Austin 1840-1921 .... **TCLC 79**
See also DLB 35, 144

Dobyns, Stephen 1941- .... **CLC 37**
See also AMWS 13; CA 45-48; CANR 2,
18, 99; CMW 4; CP 4, 5, 6, 7; PFS 23

Doctorow, E(dgar) L(aurence)
1931- .... **CLC 6, 11, 15, 18, 37, 44, 65, 113, 214**
See also AAYA 22; AITN 2; AMWS 4;
BEST 89:3; BPFB 1; CA 45-48; CANR
2, 33, 51, 76, 97, 133; CDALB 1968-
1988; CN 3, 4, 5, 6, 7; CPW; DA3; DAM
NOV, POP; DLB 2, 28, 173; DLBY 1980;

EWL 3; LAIT 3; MAL 5; MTCW 1, 2;
MTFW 2005; NFS 6; RGAL 4; RHW;
TCLE 1:1; TCWW 1, 2; TUS

Dodgson, Charles L(utwidge) 1832-1898
See Carroll, Lewis
See also CLR 2; DA; DA3; DAB; DAC;
DAM MST, NOV, POET; MAICYA 1, 2;
SATA 100; YABC 2

Dodsley, Robert 1703-1764 .... **LC 97**
See also DLB 95; RGEL 2

Dodson, Owen (Vincent) 1914-1983 .. **BLC 1; CLC 79**
See also BW 1; CA 65-68; 110; CANR 24;
DAM MULT; DLB 76

Doeblin, Alfred 1878-1957 .... **TCLC 13**
See Doblin, Alfred
See also CA 110; 141; DLB 66

Doerr, Harriet 1910-2002 .... **CLC 34**
See also CA 117; 122; 213; CANR 47; INT
CA-122; LATS 1:2

Domecq, H(onorio Bustos)
See Bioy Casares, Adolfo

Domecq, H(onorio) Bustos
See Bioy Casares, Adolfo; Borges, Jorge
Luis

Domini, Rey
See Lorde, Audre (Geraldine)
See also GLL 1

Dominique
See Proust, (Valentin-Louis-George-Eugene)
Marcel

Don, A
See Stephen, Sir Leslie

Donaldson, Stephen R(eeder)
1947- .... **CLC 46, 138**
See also AAYA 36; BPFB 1; CA 89-92;
CANR 13, 55, 99; CPW; DAM POP;
FANT; INT CANR-13; SATA 121; SFW
4; SUFW 1, 2

Donleavy, J(ames) P(atrick) 1926- .... **CLC 1, 4, 6, 10, 45**
See also AITN 2; BPFB 1; CA 9-12R;
CANR 24, 49, 62, 80, 124; CBD; CD 5,
6; CN 1, 2, 3, 4, 5, 6, 7; DLB 6, 173; INT
CANR-24; MAL 5; MTCW 1, 2; MTFW
2005; RGAL 4

Donnadieu, Marguerite
See Duras, Marguerite

Donne, John 1572-1631 ... **LC 10, 24, 91; PC 1, 43; WLC**
See also AAYA 67; BRW 1; BRWC 1;
BRWR 2; CDBLB Before 1660; DA;
DAB; DAC; DAM MST, POET; DLB
121, 151; EXPP; PAB; PFS 2, 11; RGEL
3; TEA; WLIT 3; WP

Donnell, David 1939(?)- .... **CLC 34**
See also CA 197

Donoghue, Denis 1928- .... **CLC 209**
See also CA 17-20R; CANR 16, 102

Donoghue, P. S.
See Hunt, E(verette) Howard, (Jr.)

Donoso (Yanez), Jose 1924-1996 ... **CLC 4, 8, 11, 32, 99; HLC 1; SSC 34; TCLC 133**
See also CA 81-84; 155; CANR 32, 73; CD-
WLB 3; CWW 2; DAM MULT; DLB 113;
EWL 3; HW 1, 2; LAW; LAWS 1; MTCW
1, 2; MTFW 2005; RGSF 2; WLIT 1

Donovan, John 1928-1992 .... **CLC 35**
See also AAYA 20; CA 97-100; 137; CLR
3; MAICYA 1, 2; SATA 72; SATA-Brief
29; YAW

Don Roberto
See Cunninghame Graham, Robert
(Gallnigad) Bontine

Doolittle, Hilda 1886-1961 . **CLC 3, 8, 14, 31, 34, 73; PC 5; WLC**
See H. D.
See also AAYA 66; AMWS 1; CA 97-100;
CANR 35, 131; DA; DAC; DAM MST,

POET; DLB 4, 45; EWL 3; FW; GLL 1;
LMFS 2; MAL 5; MAWW; MTCW 1, 2;
MTFW 2005; PFS 6; RGAL 4

Doppo, Kunikida .... **TCLC 99**
See Kunikida Doppo

Dorfman, Ariel 1942- .... **CLC 48, 77, 189; HLC 1**
See also CA 124; 130; CANR 67, 70, 135;
CWW 2; DAM MULT; DFS 4; EWL 3;
HW 1, 2; INT CA-130; WLIT 1

Dorn, Edward (Merton)
1929-1999 .... **CLC 10, 18**
See also CA 93-96; 187; CANR 42, 79; CP
1, 2, 3, 4, 5, 6, 7; DLB 5; INT CA-93-96;
WP

Dor-Ner, Zvi .... **CLC 70**

Dorris, Michael (Anthony)
1945-1997 .... **CLC 109; NNAL**
See also AAYA 20; BEST 90:1; BYA 12;
CA 102; 157; CANR 19, 46, 75; CLR 58;
DA3; DAM MULT, NOV; DLB 175;
LAIT 5; MTCW 2; MTFW 2005; NFS 3;
RGAL 4; SATA 75; SATA-Obit 94;
TCWW 2; YAW

Dorris, Michael A.
See Dorris, Michael (Anthony)

Dorsan, Luc
See Simenon, Georges (Jacques Christian)

Dorsange, Jean
See Simenon, Georges (Jacques Christian)

Dorset
See Sackville, Thomas

Dos Passos, John (Roderigo)
1896-1970 ... **CLC 1, 4, 8, 11, 15, 25, 34, 82; WLC**
See also AMW; BPFB 1; CA 1-4R; 29-32R;
CANR 3; CDALB 1929-1941; DA; DA3;
DAB; DAC; DAM MST, NOV; DLB 4,
9, 274, 316; DLBD 1, 15; DLBY 1996;
EWL 3; MAL 5; MTCW 1, 2; MTFW
2005; NFS 14; RGAL 4; TUS

Dossage, Jean
See Simenon, Georges (Jacques Christian)

Dostoevsky, Fedor Mikhailovich
1821-1881 .. **NCLC 2, 7, 21, 33, 43, 119, 167; SSC 2, 33, 44; WLC**
See Dostoevsky, Fyodor
See also AAYA 40; DA; DA3; DAB; DAC;
DAM MST, NOV; EW 7; EXPN; NFS 3,
8; RGSF 2; RGWL 2, 3; SSFS 8; TWA

Dostoevsky, Fyodor
See Dostoevsky, Fedor Mikhailovich
See also DLB 238; LATS 1:1; LMFS 1, 2

Doty, M. R.
See Doty, Mark (Alan)

Doty, Mark
See Doty, Mark (Alan)

Doty, Mark (Alan) 1953(?)- .... **CLC 176; PC 53**
See also AMWS 11; CA 161, 183; CAAE
183; CANR 110

Doty, Mark A.
See Doty, Mark (Alan)

Doughty, Charles M(ontagu)
1843-1926 .... **TCLC 27**
See also CA 115; 178; DLB 19, 57, 174

Douglas, Ellen .... **CLC 73**
See Haxton, Josephine Ayres; Williamson,
Ellen Douglas
See also CN 5, 6, 7; CSW; DLB 292

Douglas, Gavin 1475(?)-1522 .... **LC 20**
See also DLB 132; RGEL 2

Douglas, George
See Brown, George Douglas
See also RGEL 2

Douglas, Keith (Castellain)
1920-1944 .... **TCLC 40**
See also BRW 7; CA 160; DLB 27; EWL
3; PAB; RGEL 2

Douglas, Leonard
See Bradbury, Ray (Douglas)
Douglas, Michael
See Crichton, (John) Michael
Douglas, (George) Norman
1868-1952 .... **TCLC 68**
See also BRW 6; CA 119; 157; DLB 34, 195; RGEL 2
Douglas, William
See Brown, George Douglas
Douglass, Frederick 1817(?)-1895 ..... **BLC 1; NCLC 7, 55, 141; WLC**
See also AAYA 48; AFAW 1, 2; AMWC 1; AMWS 3; CDALB 1640-1865; DA; DA3; DAC; DAM MST, MULT; DLB 1, 43, 50, 79, 243; FW; LAIT 2; NCFS 2; RGAL 4; SATA 29
Dourado, (Waldomiro Freitas) Autran
1926- .... **CLC 23, 60**
See also CA 25-28R, 179; CANR 34, 81; DLB 145, 307; HW 2
Dourado, Waldomiro Freitas Autran
See Dourado, (Waldomiro Freitas) Autran
Dove, Rita (Frances) 1952- . **BLCS; CLC 50, 81; PC 6**
See also AAYA 46; AMWS 4; BW 2; CA 109; CAAS 19; CANR 27, 42, 68, 76, 97, 132; CDALBS; CP 7; CSW; CWP; DA3; DAM MULT, POET; DLB 120; EWL 3; EXPP; MAL 5; MTCW 2; MTFW 2005; PFS 1, 15; RGAL 4
Doveglion
See Villa, Jose Garcia
Dowell, Coleman 1925-1985 .... **CLC 60**
See also CA 25-28R; 117; CANR 10; DLB 130; GLL 2
Dowson, Ernest (Christopher)
1867-1900 .... **TCLC 4**
See also CA 105; 150; DLB 19, 135; RGEL 2
Doyle, A. Conan
See Doyle, Sir Arthur Conan
Doyle, Sir Arthur Conan
1859-1930 . **SSC 12, 83; TCLC 7; WLC**
See Conan Doyle, Arthur
See also AAYA 14; BRWS 2; CA 104; 122; CANR 131; CDBLB 1890-1914; CMW 4; DA; DA3; DAB; DAC; DAM MST, NOV; DLB 18, 70, 156, 178; EXPS; HGG; LAIT 2; MSW; MTCW 1, 2; MTFW 2005; RGEL 2; RGSF 2; RHW; SATA 24; SCFW 1, 2; SFW 4; SSFS 2; TEA; WCH; WLIT 4; WYA; YAW
Doyle, Conan
See Doyle, Sir Arthur Conan
Doyle, John
See Graves, Robert (von Ranke)
Doyle, Roddy 1958- .... **CLC 81, 178**
See also AAYA 14; BRWS 5; CA 143; CANR 73, 128; CN 6, 7; DA3; DLB 194; MTCW 2; MTFW 2005
Doyle, Sir A. Conan
See Doyle, Sir Arthur Conan
Dr. A
See Asimov, Isaac; Silverstein, Alvin; Silverstein, Virginia B(arbara Opshelor)
Drabble, Margaret 1939- ...... **CLC 2, 3, 5, 8, 10, 22, 53, 129**
See also BRWS 4; CA 13-16R; CANR 18, 35, 63, 112, 131; CDBLB 1960 to Present; CN 1, 2, 3, 4, 5, 6, 7; CPW; DA3; DAB; DAC; DAM MST, NOV, POP; DLB 14, 155, 231; EWL 3; FW; MTCW 1, 2; MTFW 2005; RGEL 2; SATA 48; TEA
Drakulic, Slavenka 1949- .... **CLC 173**
See also CA 144; CANR 92
Drakulic-Ilic, Slavenka
See Drakulic, Slavenka

Drapier, M. B.
See Swift, Jonathan
Drayham, James
See Mencken, H(enry) L(ouis)
Drayton, Michael 1563-1631 .... **LC 8**
See also DAM POET; DLB 121; RGEL 2
Dreadstone, Carl
See Campbell, (John) Ramsey
Dreiser, Theodore (Herman Albert)
1871-1945 .... **SSC 30; TCLC 10, 18, 35, 83; WLC**
See also AMW; AMWC 2; AMWR 2; BYA 15, 16; CA 106; 132; CDALB 1865-1917; DA; DA3; DAC; DAM MST, NOV; DLB 9, 12, 102, 137; DLBD 1; EWL 3; LAIT 2; LMFS 2; MAL 5; MTCW 1, 2; MTFW 2005; NFS 8, 17; RGAL 4; TUS
Drexler, Rosalyn 1926- .... **CLC 2, 6**
See also CA 81-84; CAD; CANR 68, 124; CD 5, 6; CWD; MAL 5
Dreyer, Carl Theodor 1889-1968 ...... **CLC 16**
See also CA 116
Drieu la Rochelle, Pierre(-Eugene)
1893-1945 .... **TCLC 21**
See also CA 117; DLB 72; EWL 3; GFL 1789 to the Present
Drinkwater, John 1882-1937 .... **TCLC 57**
See also CA 109; 149; DLB 10, 19, 149; RGEL 2
Drop Shot
See Cable, George Washington
Droste-Hulshoff, Annette Freiin von
1797-1848 .... **NCLC 3, 133**
See also CDWLB 2; DLB 133; RGSF 2; RGWL 2, 3
Drummond, Walter
See Silverberg, Robert
Drummond, William Henry
1854-1907 .... **TCLC 25**
See also CA 160; DLB 92
Drummond de Andrade, Carlos
1902-1987 .... **CLC 18; TCLC 139**
See Andrade, Carlos Drummond de
See also CA 132; 123; DLB 307; LAW
Drummond of Hawthornden, William
1585-1649 .... **LC 83**
See also DLB 121, 213; RGEL 2
Drury, Allen (Stuart) 1918-1998 .... **CLC 37**
See also CA 57-60; 170; CANR 18, 52; CN 1, 2, 3, 4, 5, 6; INT CANR-18
Druse, Eleanor
See King, Stephen
Dryden, John 1631-1700 ..... **DC 3; LC 3, 21, 115; PC 25; WLC**
See also BRW 2; CDBLB 1660-1789; DA; DAB; DAC; DAM DRAM, MST, POET; DLB 80, 101, 131; EXPP; IDTP; LMFS 1; RGEL 2; TEA; WLIT 3
du Bellay, Joachim 1524-1560 .... **LC 92**
See also GFL Beginnings to 1789; RGWL 2, 3
Duberman, Martin (Bauml) 1930- ..... **CLC 8**
See also CA 1-4R; CAD; CANR 2, 63, 137; CD 5, 6
Dubie, Norman (Evans) 1945- .... **CLC 36**
See also CA 69-72; CANR 12, 115; CP 3, 4, 5, 6, 7; DLB 120; PFS 12
Du Bois, W(illiam) E(dward) B(urghardt)
1868-1963 ..... **BLC 1; CLC 1, 2, 13, 64, 96; HR 1:2; TCLC 169; WLC**
See also AAYA 40; AFAW 1, 2; AMWC 1; AMWS 2; BW 1, 3; CA 85-88; CANR 34, 82, 132; CDALB 1865-1917; DA; DA3; DAC; DAM MST, MULT, NOV; DLB 47, 50, 91, 246, 284; EWL 3; EXPP; LAIT 2; LMFS 2; MAL 5; MTCW 1, 2; MTFW 2005; NCFS 1; PFS 13; RGAL 4; SATA 42

Dubus, Andre 1936-1999 ..... **CLC 13, 36, 97; SSC 15**
See also AMWS 7; CA 21-24R; 177; CANR 17; CN 5, 6; CSW; DLB 130; INT CANR-17; RGAL 4; SSFS 10; TCLE 1:1
Duca Minimo
See D'Annunzio, Gabriele
Ducharme, Rejean 1941- .... **CLC 74**
See also CA 165; DLB 60
du Chatelet, Emilie 1706-1749 .... **LC 96**
See Chatelet, Gabrielle-Emilie Du
Duchen, Claire .... **CLC 65**
Duclos, Charles Pinot- 1704-1772 .... **LC 1**
See also GFL Beginnings to 1789
Dudek, Louis 1918-2001 .... **CLC 11, 19**
See also CA 45-48; 215; CAAS 14; CANR 1; CP 1, 2, 3, 4, 5, 6, 7; DLB 88
Duerrenmatt, Friedrich 1921-1990 ... **CLC 1, 4, 8, 11, 15, 43, 102**
See Durrenmatt, Friedrich
See also CA 17-20R; CANR 33; CMW 4; DAM DRAM; DLB 69, 124; MTCW 1, 2
Duffy, Bruce 1953(?)- .... **CLC 50**
See also CA 172
Duffy, Maureen (Patricia) 1933- ...... **CLC 37**
See also CA 25-28R; CANR 33, 68; CBD; CN 1, 2, 3, 4, 5, 6, 7; CP 7; CWD; CWP; DFS 15; DLB 14, 310; FW; MTCW 1
Du Fu
See Tu Fu
See also RGWL 2, 3
Dugan, Alan 1923-2003 .... **CLC 2, 6**
See also CA 81-84; 220; CANR 119; CP 1, 2, 3, 4, 5, 6, 7; DLB 5; MAL 5; PFS 10
du Gard, Roger Martin
See Martin du Gard, Roger
Duhamel, Georges 1884-1966 .... **CLC 8**
See also CA 81-84; 25-28R; CANR 35; DLB 65; EWL 3; GFL 1789 to the Present; MTCW 1
Dujardin, Edouard (Emile Louis)
1861-1949 .... **TCLC 13**
See also CA 109; DLB 123
Duke, Raoul
See Thompson, Hunter S(tockton)
Dulles, John Foster 1888-1959 .... **TCLC 72**
See also CA 115; 149
Dumas, Alexandre (pere)
1802-1870 .... **NCLC 11, 71; WLC**
See also AAYA 22; BYA 3; DA; DA3; DAB; DAC; DAM MST, NOV; DLB 119, 192; EW 6; GFL 1789 to the Present; LAIT 1, 2; NFS 14, 19; RGWL 2, 3; SATA 18; TWA; WCH
Dumas, Alexandre (fils) 1824-1895 ...... **DC 1; NCLC 9**
See also DLB 192; GFL 1789 to the Present; RGWL 2, 3
Dumas, Claudine
See Malzberg, Barry N(athaniel)
Dumas, Henry L. 1934-1968 .... **CLC 6, 62**
See also BW 1; CA 85-88; DLB 41; RGAL 4
du Maurier, Daphne 1907-1989 .. **CLC 6, 11, 59; SSC 18**
See also AAYA 37; BPFB 1; BRWS 3; CA 5-8R; 128; CANR 6, 55; CMW 4; CN 1, 2, 3, 4; CPW; DA3; DAB; DAC; DAM MST, POP; DLB 191; GL 2; HGG; LAIT 3; MSW; MTCW 1, 2; NFS 12; RGEL 2; RGSF 2; RHW; SATA 27; SATA-Obit 60; SSFS 14, 16; TEA
Du Maurier, George 1834-1896 ..... **NCLC 86**
See also DLB 153, 178; RGEL 2
Dunbar, Paul Laurence 1872-1906 ... **BLC 1; PC 5; SSC 8; TCLC 2, 12; WLC**
See also AFAW 1, 2; AMWS 2; BW 1, 3; CA 104; 124; CANR 79; CDALB 1865-1917; DA; DA3; DAC; DAM MST, MULT, POET; DLB 50, 54, 78; EXPP; MAL 5; RGAL 4; SATA 34

Gent, Peter 1942- .... **CLC 29**
See also AITN 1; CA 89-92; DLBY 1982

Gentile, Giovanni 1875-1944 .... **TCLC 96**
See also CA 119

Gentlewoman in New England, A
See Bradstreet, Anne

Gentlewoman in Those Parts, A
See Bradstreet, Anne

Geoffrey of Monmouth c.
1100-1155 .... **CMLC 44**
See also DLB 146; TEA

George, Jean
See George, Jean Craighead

George, Jean Craighead 1919- .... **CLC 35**
See also AAYA 8; BYA 2, 4; CA 5-8R;
CANR 25; CLR 1; 80; DLB 52; JRDA;
MAICYA 1, 2; SATA 2, 68, 124; WYA;
YAW

George, Stefan (Anton) 1868-1933 . **TCLC 2,
14**
See also CA 104; 193; EW 8; EWL 3

Georges, Georges Martin
See Simenon, Georges (Jacques Christian)

Gerald of Wales c. 1146-c. 1223 ... **CMLC 60**

Gerhardi, William Alexander
See Gerhardie, William Alexander

Gerhardie, William Alexander
1895-1977 .... **CLC 5**
See also CA 25-28R; 73-76; CANR 18; CN
1, 2; DLB 36; RGEL 2

Gerson, Jean 1363-1429 .... **LC 77**
See also DLB 208

Gersonides 1288-1344 .... **CMLC 49**
See also DLB 115

Gerstler, Amy 1956- .... **CLC 70**
See also CA 146; CANR 99

Gertler, T. .... **CLC 34**
See also CA 116; 121

Gertsen, Aleksandr Ivanovich
See Herzen, Aleksandr Ivanovich

Ghalib .... **NCLC 39, 78**
See Ghalib, Asadullah Khan

Ghalib, Asadullah Khan 1797-1869
See Ghalib
See also DAM POET; RGWL 2, 3

Ghelderode, Michel de 1898-1962 ..... **CLC 6,
11; DC 15**
See also CA 85-88; CANR 40, 77; DAM
DRAM; DLB 321; EW 11; EWL 3; TWA

Ghiselin, Brewster 1903-2001 .... **CLC 23**
See also CA 13-16R; CAAS 10; CANR 13;
CP 1, 2, 3, 4, 5, 6, 7

Ghose, Aurabinda 1872-1950 .... **TCLC 63**
See Ghose, Aurobindo
See also CA 163

Ghose, Aurobindo
See Ghose, Aurabinda
See also EWL 3

Ghose, Zulfikar 1935- .... **CLC 42, 200**
See also CA 65-68; CANR 67; CN 1, 2, 3,
4, 5, 6, 7; CP 1, 2, 3, 4, 5, 6, 7; EWL 3

Ghosh, Amitav 1956- .... **CLC 44, 153**
See also CA 147; CANR 80; CN 6, 7;
WWE 1

Giacosa, Giuseppe 1847-1906 .... **TCLC 7**
See also CA 104

Gibb, Lee
See Waterhouse, Keith (Spencer)

Gibbon, Edward 1737-1794 .... **LC 97**
See also BRW 3; DLB 104; RGEL 2

Gibbon, Lewis Grassic .... **TCLC 4**
See Mitchell, James Leslie
See also RGEL 2

Gibbons, Kaye 1960- .... **CLC 50, 88, 145**
See also AAYA 34; AMWS 10; CA 151;
CANR 75, 127; CN 7; CSW; DA3; DAM
POP; DLB 292; MTCW 2; MTFW 2005;
NFS 3; RGAL 4; SATA 117

Gibran, Kahlil 1883-1931 . **PC 9; TCLC 1, 9**
See also CA 104; 150; DA3; DAM POET,
POP; EWL 3; MTCW 2; WLIT 6

Gibran, Khalil
See Gibran, Kahlil

Gibson, Mel 1956- .... **CLC 215**

Gibson, William 1914- .... **CLC 23**
See also CA 9-12R; CAD; CANR 9, 42, 75,
125; CD 5, 6; DA; DAB; DAC; DAM
DRAM, MST; DFS 2; DLB 7; LAIT 2;
MAL 5; MTCW 2; MTFW 2005; SATA
66; YAW

Gibson, William (Ford) 1948- ... **CLC 39, 63,
186, 192; SSC 52**
See also AAYA 12, 59; BPFB 2; CA 126;
133; CANR 52, 90, 106; CN 6, 7; CPW;
DA3; DAM POP; DLB 251; MTCW 2;
MTFW 2005; SCFW 2; SFW 4

Gide, Andre (Paul Guillaume)
1869-1951 ..... **SSC 13; TCLC 5, 12, 36;
WLC**
See also CA 104; 124; DA; DA3; DAB;
DAC; DAM MST, NOV; DLB 65, 321;
EW 8; EWL 3; GFL 1789 to the Present;
MTCW 1, 2; MTFW 2005; NFS 21;
RGSF 2; RGWL 2, 3; TWA

Gifford, Barry (Colby) 1946- .... **CLC 34**
See also CA 65-68; CANR 9, 30, 40, 90

Gilbert, Frank
See De Voto, Bernard (Augustine)

Gilbert, W(illiam) S(chwenck)
1836-1911 .... **TCLC 3**
See also CA 104; 173; DAM DRAM, POET;
RGEL 2; SATA 36

Gilbreth, Frank B(unker), Jr.
1911-2001 .... **CLC 17**
See also CA 9-12R; SATA 2

Gilchrist, Ellen (Louise) 1935- .. **CLC 34, 48,
143; SSC 14, 63**
See also BPFB 2; CA 113; 116; CANR 41,
61, 104; CN 4, 5, 6, 7; CPW; CSW; DAM
POP; DLB 130; EWL 3; EXPS; MTCW
1, 2; MTFW 2005; RGAL 4; RGSF 2;
SSFS 9

Giles, Molly 1942- .... **CLC 39**
See also CA 126; CANR 98

Gill, Eric .... **TCLC 85**
See Gill, (Arthur) Eric (Rowton Peter
Joseph)

Gill, (Arthur) Eric (Rowton Peter Joseph)
1882-1940
See Gill, Eric
See also CA 120; DLB 98

Gill, Patrick
See Creasey, John

Gillette, Douglas .... **CLC 70**

Gilliam, Terry (Vance) 1940- .... **CLC 21, 141**
See Monty Python
See also AAYA 19, 59; CA 108; 113; CANR
35; INT CA-113

Gillian, Jerry
See Gilliam, Terry (Vance)

Gilliatt, Penelope (Ann Douglass)
1932-1993 .... **CLC 2, 10, 13, 53**
See also AITN 2; CA 13-16R; 141; CANR
49; CN 1, 2, 3, 4, 5; DLB 14

Gilligan, Carol 1936- .... **CLC 208**
See also CA 142; CANR 121; FW

Gilman, Charlotte (Anna) Perkins (Stetson)
1860-1935 ...... **SSC 13, 62; TCLC 9, 37,
117**
See also AMWS 11; BYA 11; CA 106; 150;
DLB 221; EXPS; FL 1:5; FW; HGG;
LAIT 2; MAWW; MTCW 2; MTFW
2005; RGAL 4; RGSF 2; SFW 4; SSFS 1,
18

Gilmour, David 1946- .... **CLC 35**

Gilpin, William 1724-1804 .... **NCLC 30**

Gilray, J. D.
See Mencken, H(enry) L(ouis)

Gilroy, Frank D(aniel) 1925- .... **CLC 2**
See also CA 81-84; CAD; CANR 32, 64,
86; CD 5, 6; DFS 17; DLB 7

Gilstrap, John 1957(?)- .... **CLC 99**
See also AAYA 67; CA 160; CANR 101

Ginsberg, Allen 1926-1997 .... **CLC 1, 2, 3, 4,
6, 13, 36, 69, 109; PC 4, 47; TCLC
120; WLC**
See also AAYA 33; AITN 1; AMWC 1;
AMWS 2; BG 1:2; CA 1-4R; 157; CANR
2, 41, 63, 95; CDALB 1941-1968; CP 1,
2, 3, 4, 5, 6; DA; DA3; DAB; DAC; DAM
MST, POET; DLB 5, 16, 169, 237; EWL
3; GLL 1; LMFS 2; MAL 5; MTCW 1, 2;
MTFW 2005; PAB; PFS 5; RGAL 4;
TUS; WP

Ginzburg, Eugenia .... **CLC 59**
See Ginzburg, Evgeniia

Ginzburg, Evgeniia 1904-1977
See Ginzburg, Eugenia
See also DLB 302

Ginzburg, Natalia 1916-1991 .... **CLC 5, 11,
54, 70; SSC 65; TCLC 156**
See also CA 85-88; 135; CANR 33; DFS
14; DLB 177; EW 13; EWL 3; MTCW 1,
2; MTFW 2005; RGWL 2, 3

Giono, Jean 1895-1970 .... **CLC 4, 11; TCLC
124**
See also CA 45-48; 29-32R; CANR 2, 35;
DLB 72, 321; EWL 3; GFL 1789 to the
Present; MTCW 1; RGWL 2, 3

Giovanni, Nikki 1943- ...... **BLC 2; CLC 2, 4,
19, 64, 117; PC 19; WLCS**
See also AAYA 22; AITN 1; BW 2, 3; CA
29-32R; CAAS 6; CANR 18, 41, 60, 91,
130; CDALBS; CLR 6, 73; CP 2, 3, 4, 5,
6, 7; CSW; CWP; CWRI 5; DA; DA3;
DAB; DAC; DAM MST, MULT, POET;
DLB 5, 41; EWL 3; EXPP; INT CANR-
18; MAICYA 1, 2; MAL 5; MTCW 1, 2;
MTFW 2005; PFS 17; RGAL 4; SATA
24, 107; TUS; YAW

Giovene, Andrea 1904-1998 .... **CLC 7**
See also CA 85-88

Gippius, Zinaida (Nikolaevna) 1869-1945
See Hippius, Zinaida (Nikolaevna)
See also CA 106; 212

Giraudoux, Jean(-Hippolyte)
1882-1944 .... **TCLC 2, 7**
See also CA 104; 196; DAM DRAM; DLB
65, 321; EW 9; EWL 3; GFL 1789 to the
Present; RGWL 2, 3; TWA

Gironella, Jose Maria (Pous)
1917-2003 .... **CLC 11**
See also CA 101; 212; EWL 3; RGWL 2, 3

Gissing, George (Robert)
1857-1903 .... **SSC 37; TCLC 3, 24, 47**
See also BRW 5; CA 105; 167; DLB 18,
135, 184; RGEL 2; TEA

Gitlin, Todd 1943- .... **CLC 201**
See also CA 29-32R; CANR 25, 50, 88

Giurlani, Aldo
See Palazzeschi, Aldo

Gladkov, Fedor Vasil'evich
See Gladkov, Fyodor (Vasilyevich)
See also DLB 272

Gladkov, Fyodor (Vasilyevich)
1883-1958 .... **TCLC 27**
See Gladkov, Fedor Vasil'evich
See also CA 170; EWL 3

Glancy, Diane 1941- .... **CLC 210; NNAL**
See also CA 136, 225; CAAE 225; CAAS
24; CANR 87; DLB 175

Glanville, Brian (Lester) 1931- .... **CLC 6**
See also CA 5-8R; CAAS 9; CANR 3, 70;
CN 1, 2, 3, 4, 5, 6, 7; DLB 15, 139; SATA
42

Glasgow, Ellen (Anderson Gholson)
1873-1945 .... **SSC 34; TCLC 2, 7**
See also AMW; CA 104; 164; DLB 9, 12;
MAL 5; MAWW; MTCW 2; MTFW 2005;
RGAL 4; RHW; SSFS 9; TUS

Glaspell, Susan 1882(?)-1948 ..... **DC 10; SSC
41; TCLC 55, 175**
See also AMWS 3; CA 110; 154; DFS 8,
18; DLB 7, 9, 78, 228; MAWW; RGAL
4; SSFS 3; TCWW 2; TUS; YABC 2

Glassco, John 1909-1981 .... **CLC 9**
See also CA 13-16R; 102; CANR 15; CN
1, 2; CP 1, 2, 3; DLB 68

Glasscock, Amnesia
See Steinbeck, John (Ernst)

Glasser, Ronald J. 1940(?)- .... **CLC 37**
See also CA 209

Glassman, Joyce
See Johnson, Joyce

Gleick, James (W.) 1954- .... **CLC 147**
See also CA 131; 137; CANR 97; INT CA-
137

Glendinning, Victoria 1937- .... **CLC 50**
See also CA 120; 127; CANR 59, 89; DLB
155

Glissant, Edouard (Mathieu)
1928- .... **CLC 10, 68**
See also CA 153; CANR 111; CWW 2;
DAM MULT; EWL 3; RGWL 3

Gloag, Julian 1930- .... **CLC 40**
See also AITN 1; CA 65-68; CANR 10, 70;
CN 1, 2, 3, 4, 5, 6

Glowacki, Aleksander
See Prus, Boleslaw

Gluck, Louise (Elisabeth) 1943- .. **CLC 7, 22,
44, 81, 160; PC 16**
See also AMWS 5; CA 33-36R; CANR 40,
69, 108, 133; CP 1, 2, 3, 4, 5, 6, 7; CWP;
DA3; DAM POET; DLB 5; MAL 5;
MTCW 2; MTFW 2005; PFS 5, 15;
RGAL 4; TCLE 1:1

Glyn, Elinor 1864-1943 .... **TCLC 72**
See also DLB 153; RHW

Gobineau, Joseph-Arthur
1816-1882 .... **NCLC 17**
See also DLB 123; GFL 1789 to the Present

Godard, Jean-Luc 1930- .... **CLC 20**
See also CA 93-96

Godden, (Margaret) Rumer
1907-1998 .... **CLC 53**
See also AAYA 6; BPFB 2; BYA 2, 5; CA
5-8R; 172; CANR 4, 27, 36, 55, 80; CLR
20; CN 1, 2, 3, 4, 5, 6; CWRI 5; DLB
161; MAICYA 1, 2; RHW; SAAS 12;
SATA 3, 36; SATA-Obit 109; TEA

Godoy Alcayaga, Lucila 1899-1957 .. **HLC 2;
PC 32; TCLC 2**
See Mistral, Gabriela
See also BW 2; CA 104; 131; CANR 81;
DAM MULT; DNFS; HW 1, 2; MTCW 1,
2; MTFW 2005

Godwin, Gail 1937- ...... **CLC 5, 8, 22, 31, 69,
125**
See also BPFB 2; CA 29-32R; CANR 15,
43, 69, 132; CN 3, 4, 5, 6, 7; CPW; CSW;
DA3; DAM POP; DLB 6, 234; INT
CANR-15; MAL 5; MTCW 1, 2; MTFW
2005

Godwin, Gail Kathleen
See Godwin, Gail

Godwin, William 1756-1836 .. **NCLC 14, 130**
See also CDBLB 1789-1832; CMW 4; DLB
39, 104, 142, 158, 163, 262; GL 2; HGG;
RGEL 2

Goebbels, Josef
See Goebbels, (Paul) Joseph

Goebbels, (Paul) Joseph
1897-1945 .... **TCLC 68**
See also CA 115; 148

Goebbels, Joseph Paul
See Goebbels, (Paul) Joseph

Goethe, Johann Wolfgang von
1749-1832 . **DC 20; NCLC 4, 22, 34, 90,
154; PC 5; SSC 38; WLC**
See also CDWLB 2; DA; DA3; DAB;
DAC; DAM DRAM, MST, POET; DLB
94; EW 5; GL 2; LATS 1; LMFS 1:1;
RGWL 2, 3; TWA

Gogarty, Oliver St. John
1878-1957 .... **TCLC 15**
See also CA 109; 150; DLB 15, 19; RGEL
2

Gogol, Nikolai (Vasilyevich)
1809-1852 .... **DC 1; NCLC 5, 15, 31,
162; SSC 4, 29, 52; WLC**
See also DA; DAB; DAC; DAM DRAM,
MST; DFS 12; DLB 198; EW 6; EXPS;
RGSF 2; RGWL 2, 3; SSFS 7; TWA

Goines, Donald 1937(?)-1974 ...... **BLC 2; CLC
80**
See also AITN 1; BW 1, 3; CA 124; 114;
CANR 82; CMW 4; DA3; DAM MULT,
POP; DLB 33

Gold, Herbert 1924- ... **CLC 4, 7, 14, 42, 152**
See also CA 9-12R; CANR 17, 45, 125; CN
1, 2, 3, 4, 5, 6, 7; DLB 2; DLBY 1981;
MAL 5

Goldbarth, Albert 1948- .... **CLC 5, 38**
See also AMWS 12; CA 53-56; CANR 6,
40; CP 3, 4, 5, 6, 7; DLB 120

Goldberg, Anatol 1910-1982 .... **CLC 34**
See also CA 131; 117

Goldemberg, Isaac 1945- .... **CLC 52**
See also CA 69-72; CAAS 12; CANR 11,
32; EWL 3; HW 1; WLIT 1

Golding, Arthur 1536-1606 .... **LC 101**
See also DLB 136

Golding, William (Gerald)
1911-1993 ..... **CLC 1, 2, 3, 8, 10, 17, 27,
58, 81; WLC**
See also AAYA 5, 44; BPFB 2; BRWR 1;
BRWS 1; BYA 2; CA 5-8R; 141; CANR
13, 33, 54; CD 5; CDBLB 1945-1960;
CLR 94; CN 1, 2, 3, 4; DA; DA3; DAB;
DAC; DAM MST, NOV; DLB 15, 100,
255; EWL 3; EXPN; HGG; LAIT 4;
MTCW 1, 2; MTFW 2005; NFS 2; RGEL
2; RHW; SFW 4; TEA; WLIT 4; YAW

Goldman, Emma 1869-1940 .... **TCLC 13**
See also CA 110; 150; DLB 221; FW;
RGAL 4; TUS

Goldman, Francisco 1954- .... **CLC 76**
See also CA 162

Goldman, William (W.) 1931- ...... **CLC 1, 48**
See also BPFB 2; CA 9-12R; CANR 29,
69, 106; CN 1, 2, 3, 4, 5, 6, 7; DLB 44;
FANT; IDFW 3, 4

Goldmann, Lucien 1913-1970 .... **CLC 24**
See also CA 25-28; CAP 2

Goldoni, Carlo 1707-1793 .... **LC 4**
See also DAM DRAM; EW 4; RGWL 2, 3;
WLIT 7

Goldsberry, Steven 1949- .... **CLC 34**
See also CA 131

Goldsmith, Oliver 1730-1774 .... **DC 8; LC 2,
48, 122; WLC**
See also BRW 3; CDBLB 1660-1789; DA;
DAB; DAC; DAM DRAM, MST, NOV,
POET; DFS 1; DLB 39, 89, 104, 109, 142;
IDTP; RGEL 2; SATA 26; TEA; WLIT 3

Goldsmith, Peter
See Priestley, J(ohn) B(oynton)

Gombrowicz, Witold 1904-1969 .... **CLC 4, 7,
11, 49**
See also CA 19-20; 25-28R; CANR 105;
CAP 2; CDWLB 4; DAM DRAM; DLB
215; EW 12; EWL 3; RGWL 2, 3; TWA

Gomez de Avellaneda, Gertrudis
1814-1873 .... **NCLC 111**
See also LAW

Gomez de la Serna, Ramon
1888-1963 .... **CLC 9**
See also CA 153; 116; CANR 79; EWL 3;
HW 1, 2

Goncharov, Ivan Alexandrovich
1812-1891 .... **NCLC 1, 63**
See also DLB 238; EW 6; RGWL 2, 3

Goncourt, Edmond (Louis Antoine Huot) de
1822-1896 .... **NCLC 7**
See also DLB 123; EW 7; GFL 1789 to the
Present; RGWL 2, 3

Goncourt, Jules (Alfred Huot) de
1830-1870 .... **NCLC 7**
See also DLB 123; EW 7; GFL 1789 to the
Present; RGWL 2, 3

Gongora (y Argote), Luis de
1561-1627 .... **LC 72**
See also RGWL 2, 3

Gontier, Fernande 19(?)- .... **CLC 50**

Gonzalez Martinez, Enrique
See Gonzalez Martinez, Enrique
See also DLB 290

Gonzalez Martinez, Enrique
1871-1952 .... **TCLC 72**
See Gonzalez Martinez, Enrique
See also CA 166; CANR 81; EWL 3; HW
1, 2

Goodison, Lorna 1947- .... **PC 36**
See also CA 142; CANR 88; CP 7; CWP;
DLB 157; EWL 3

Goodman, Paul 1911-1972 ..... **CLC 1, 2, 4, 7**
See also CA 19-20; 37-40R; CAD; CANR
34; CAP 2; CN 1; DLB 130, 246; MAL
5; MTCW 1; RGAL 4

GoodWeather, Harley
See King, Thomas

Googe, Barnabe 1540-1594 .... **LC 94**
See also DLB 132; RGEL 2

Gordimer, Nadine 1923- ...... **CLC 3, 5, 7, 10,
18, 33, 51, 70, 123, 160, 161; SSC 17,
80; WLCS**
See also AAYA 39; AFW; BRWS 2; CA
5-8R; CANR 3, 28, 56, 88, 131; CN 1, 2,
3, 4, 5, 6, 7; DA; DA3; DAB; DAC; DAM
MST, NOV; DLB 225; EWL 3; EXPS;
INT CANR-28; LATS 1:2; MTCW 1, 2;
MTFW 2005; NFS 4; RGEL 2; RGSF 2;
SSFS 2, 14, 19; TWA; WLIT 2; YAW

Gordon, Adam Lindsay
1833-1870 .... **NCLC 21**
See also DLB 230

Gordon, Caroline 1895-1981 . **CLC 6, 13, 29,
83; SSC 15**
See also AMW; CA 11-12; 103; CANR 36;
CAP 1; CN 1, 2; DLB 4, 9, 102; DLBD
17; DLBY 1981; EWL 3; MAL 5; MTCW
1, 2; MTFW 2005; RGAL 4; RGSF 2

Gordon, Charles William 1860-1937
See Connor, Ralph
See also CA 109

Gordon, Mary (Catherine) 1949- .... **CLC 13,
22, 128, 216; SSC 59**
See also AMWS 4; BPFB 2; CA 102;
CANR 44, 92; CN 4, 5, 6, 7; DLB 6;
DLBY 1981; FW; INT CA-102; MAL 5;
MTCW 1

Gordon, N. J.
See Bosman, Herman Charles

Gordon, Sol 1923- .... **CLC 26**
See also CA 53-56; CANR 4; SATA 11

Gordone, Charles 1925-1995 .. **CLC 1, 4; DC
8**
See also BW 1, 3; CA 93-96; 180; 150;
CAAE 180; CAD; CANR 55; DAM
DRAM; DLB 7; INT CA-93-96; MTCW
1

Green, Paul (Eliot) 1894-1981 .... **CLC 25**
    See also AITN 1; CA 5-8R; 103; CAD;
    CANR 3; DAM DRAM; DLB 7, 9, 249;
    DLBY 1981; MAL 5; RGAL 4
Greenaway, Peter 1942- .... **CLC 159**
    See also CA 127
Greenberg, Ivan 1908-1973
    See Rahv, Philip
    See also CA 85-88
Greenberg, Joanne (Goldenberg)
    1932- .... **CLC 7, 30**
    See also AAYA 12, 67; CA 5-8R; CANR
    14, 32, 69; CN 6, 7; SATA 25; YAW
Greenberg, Richard 1959(?)- .... **CLC 57**
    See also CA 138; CAD; CD 5, 6
Greenblatt, Stephen J(ay) 1943- ...... **CLC 70**
    See also CA 49-52; CANR 115
Greene, Bette 1934- .... **CLC 30**
    See also AAYA 7; BYA 3; CA 53-56; CANR
    4, 146; CLR 2; CWRI 5; JRDA; LAIT 4;
    MAICYA 1, 2; NFS 10; SAAS 16; SATA
    8, 102, 161; WYA; YAW
Greene, Gael .... **CLC 8**
    See also CA 13-16R; CANR 10
Greene, Graham (Henry)
    1904-1991 .... **CLC 1, 3, 6, 9, 14, 18, 27,
    37, 70, 72, 125; SSC 29; WLC**
    See also AAYA 61; AITN 2; BPFB 2;
    BRWR 2; BRWS 1; BYA 3; CA 13-16R;
    133; CANR 35, 61, 131; CBD; CDBLB
    1945-1960; CMW 4; CN 1, 2, 3, 4; DA;
    DA3; DAB; DAC; DAM MST, NOV;
    DLB 13, 15, 77, 100, 162, 201, 204;
    DLBY 1991; EWL 3; MSW; MTCW 1, 2;
    MTFW 2005; NFS 16; RGEL 2; SATA
    20; SSFS 14; TEA; WLIT 4
Greene, Robert 1558-1592 .... **LC 41**
    See also BRWS 8; DLB 62, 167; IDTP;
    RGEL 2; TEA
Greer, Germaine 1939- .... **CLC 131**
    See also AITN 1; CA 81-84; CANR 33, 70,
    115, 133; FW; MTCW 1, 2; MTFW 2005
Greer, Richard
    See Silverberg, Robert
Gregor, Arthur 1923- .... **CLC 9**
    See also CA 25-28R; CAAS 10; CANR 11;
    CP 1, 2, 3, 4, 5, 6, 7; SATA 36
Gregor, Lee
    See Pohl, Frederik
Gregory, Lady Isabella Augusta (Persse)
    1852-1932 .... **TCLC 1, 176**
    See also BRW 6; CA 104; 184; DLB 10;
    IDTP; RGEL 2
Gregory, J. Dennis
    See Williams, John A(lfred)
Grekova, I. .... **CLC 59**
    See Ventsel, Elena Sergeevna
    See also CWW 2
Grendon, Stephen
    See Derleth, August (William)
Grenville, Kate 1950- .... **CLC 61**
    See also CA 118; CANR 53, 93; CN 7
Grenville, Pelham
    See Wodehouse, P(elham) G(renville)
Greve, Felix Paul (Berthold Friedrich)
    1879-1948
    See Grove, Frederick Philip
    See also CA 104; 141, 175; CANR 79;
    DAC; DAM MST
Greville, Fulke 1554-1628 .... **LC 79**
    See also BRWS 11; DLB 62, 172; RGEL 2
Grey, Lady Jane 1537-1554 .... **LC 93**
    See also DLB 132
Grey, Zane 1872-1939 .... **TCLC 6**
    See also BPFB 2; CA 104; 132; DA3; DAM
    POP; DLB 9, 212; MTCW 1, 2; MTFW
    2005; RGAL 4; TCWW 1, 2; TUS

Griboedov, Aleksandr Sergeevich
    1795(?)-1829 .... **NCLC 129**
    See also DLB 205; RGWL 2, 3
Grieg, (Johan) Nordahl (Brun)
    1902-1943 .... **TCLC 10**
    See also CA 107; 189; EWL 3
Grieve, C(hristopher) M(urray)
    1892-1978 .... **CLC 11, 19**
    See MacDiarmid, Hugh; Pteleon
    See also CA 5-8R; 85-88; CANR 33, 107;
    DAM POET; MTCW 1; RGEL 2
Griffin, Gerald 1803-1840 .... **NCLC 7**
    See also DLB 159; RGEL 2
Griffin, John Howard 1920-1980 ..... **CLC 68**
    See also AITN 1; CA 1-4R; 101; CANR 2
Griffin, Peter 1942- .... **CLC 39**
    See also CA 136
Griffith, D(avid Lewelyn) W(ark)
    1875(?)-1948 .... **TCLC 68**
    See also CA 119; 150; CANR 80
Griffith, Lawrence
    See Griffith, D(avid Lewelyn) W(ark)
Griffiths, Trevor 1935- .... **CLC 13, 52**
    See also CA 97-100; CANR 45; CBD; CD
    5, 6; DLB 13, 245
Griggs, Sutton (Elbert)
    1872-1930 .... **TCLC 77**
    See also CA 123; 186; DLB 50
Grigson, Geoffrey (Edward Harvey)
    1905-1985 .... **CLC 7, 39**
    See also CA 25-28R; 118; CANR 20, 33;
    CP 1, 2, 3, 4; DLB 27; MTCW 1, 2
Grile, Dod
    See Bierce, Ambrose (Gwinett)
Grillparzer, Franz 1791-1872 .... **DC 14;
    NCLC 1, 102; SSC 37**
    See also CDWLB 2; DLB 133; EW 5;
    RGWL 2, 3; TWA
Grimble, Reverend Charles James
    See Eliot, T(homas) S(tearns)
Grimke, Angelina (Emily) Weld
    1880-1958 .... **HR 1:2**
    See Weld, Angelina (Emily) Grimke
    See also BW 1; CA 124; DAM POET; DLB
    50, 54
Grimke, Charlotte L(ottie) Forten
    1837(?)-1914
    See Forten, Charlotte L.
    See also BW 1; CA 117; 124; DAM MULT,
    POET
Grimm, Jacob Ludwig Karl
    1785-1863 .... **NCLC 3, 77; SSC 36, 88**
    See also DLB 90; MAICYA 1, 2; RGSF 2;
    RGWL 2, 3; SATA 22; WCH
Grimm, Wilhelm Karl 1786-1859 .. **NCLC 3,
    77; SSC 36, 88**
    See also CDWLB 2; DLB 90; MAICYA 1,
    2; RGSF 2; RGWL 2, 3; SATA 22; WCH
**Grimmelshausen, Hans Jakob Christoffel
    von**
    See Grimmelshausen, Johann Jakob Christ-
    offel von
    See also RGWL 2, 3
**Grimmelshausen, Johann Jakob Christoffel
    von** 1621-1676 .... **LC 6**
    See Grimmelshausen, Hans Jakob Christof-
    fel von
    See also CDWLB 2; DLB 168
Grindel, Eugene 1895-1952
    See Eluard, Paul
    See also CA 104; 193; LMFS 2
Grisham, John 1955- .... **CLC 84**
    See also AAYA 14, 47; BPFB 2; CA 138;
    CANR 47, 69, 114, 133; CMW 4; CN 6,
    7; CPW; CSW; DA3; DAM POP; MSW;
    MTCW 2; MTFW 2005
Grosseteste, Robert 1175(?)-1253 . **CMLC 62**
    See also DLB 115

Grossman, David 1954- .... **CLC 67**
    See also CA 138; CANR 114; CWW 2;
    DLB 299; EWL 3; WLIT 6
Grossman, Vasilii Semenovich
    See Grossman, Vasily (Semenovich)
    See also DLB 272
Grossman, Vasily (Semenovich)
    1905-1964 .... **CLC 41**
    See Grossman, Vasilii Semenovich
    See also CA 124; 130; MTCW 1
Grove, Frederick Philip .... **TCLC 4**
    See Greve, Felix Paul (Berthold Friedrich)
    See also DLB 92; RGEL 2; TCWW 1, 2
Grubb
    See Crumb, R(obert)
Grumbach, Doris (Isaac) 1918- . **CLC 13, 22,
    64**
    See also CA 5-8R; CAAS 2; CANR 9, 42,
    70, 127; CN 6, 7; INT CANR-9; MTCW
    2; MTFW 2005
Grundtvig, Nikolai Frederik Severin
    1783-1872 .... **NCLC 1, 158**
    See also DLB 300
Grunge
    See Crumb, R(obert)
Grunwald, Lisa 1959- .... **CLC 44**
    See also CA 120
Gryphius, Andreas 1616-1664 .... **LC 89**
    See also CDWLB 2; DLB 164; RGWL 2, 3
Guare, John 1938- .... **CLC 8, 14, 29, 67; DC
    20**
    See also CA 73-76; CAD; CANR 21, 69,
    118; CD 5, 6; DAM DRAM; DFS 8, 13;
    DLB 7, 249; EWL 3; MAL 5; MTCW 1,
    2; RGAL 4
Guarini, Battista 1537-1612 .... **LC 102**
Gubar, Susan (David) 1944- .... **CLC 145**
    See also CA 108; CANR 45, 70, 139; FW;
    MTCW 1; RGAL 4
Gudjonsson, Halldor Kiljan 1902-1998
    See Halldor Laxness
    See also CA 103; 164
Guenter, Erich
    See Eich, Gunter
Guest, Barbara 1920- .... **CLC 34; PC 55**
    See also BG 1:2; CA 25-28R; CANR 11,
    44, 84; CP 1, 2, 3, 4, 5, 6, 7; CWP; DLB
    5, 193
Guest, Edgar A(lbert) 1881-1959 ... **TCLC 95**
    See also CA 112; 168
Guest, Judith (Ann) 1936- .... **CLC 8, 30**
    See also AAYA 7, 66; CA 77-80; CANR
    15, 75, 138; DA3; DAM NOV, POP;
    EXPN; INT CANR-15; LAIT 5; MTCW
    1, 2; MTFW 2005; NFS 1
Guevara, Che .... **CLC 87; HLC 1**
    See Guevara (Serna), Ernesto
Guevara (Serna), Ernesto
    1928-1967 .... **CLC 87; HLC 1**
    See Guevara, Che
    See also CA 127; 111; CANR 56; DAM
    MULT; HW 1
Guicciardini, Francesco 1483-1540 ..... **LC 49**
Guild, Nicholas M. 1944- .... **CLC 33**
    See also CA 93-96
Guillemin, Jacques
    See Sartre, Jean-Paul
Guillen, Jorge 1893-1984 . **CLC 11; HLCS 1;
    PC 35**
    See also CA 89-92; 112; DAM MULT,
    POET; DLB 108; EWL 3; HW 1; RGWL
    2, 3
Guillen, Nicolas (Cristobal)
    1902-1989 .... **BLC 2; CLC 48, 79; HLC
    1; PC 23**
    See also BW 2; CA 116; 125; 129; CANR
    84; DAM MST, MULT, POET; DLB 283;
    EWL 3; HW 1; LAW; RGWL 2, 3; WP

Guillen y Alvarez, Jorge
See Guillen, Jorge

Guillevic, (Eugene) 1907-1997 .... **CLC 33**
See also CA 93-96; CWW 2

Guillois
See Desnos, Robert

Guillois, Valentin
See Desnos, Robert

Guimaraes Rosa, Joao 1908-1967 .... **HLCS 2**
See Rosa, Joao Guimaraes
See also CA 175; LAW; RGSF 2; RGWL 2, 3

Guiney, Louise Imogen
1861-1920 .... **TCLC 41**
See also CA 160; DLB 54; RGAL 4

Guinizelli, Guido c. 1230-1276 ...... **CMLC 49**
See Guinizzelli, Guido

Guinizzelli, Guido
See Guinizelli, Guido
See also WLIT 7

Guiraldes, Ricardo (Guillermo)
1886-1927 .... **TCLC 39**
See also CA 131; EWL 3; HW 1; LAW; MTCW 1

Gumilev, Nikolai (Stepanovich)
1886-1921 .... **TCLC 60**
See Gumilyov, Nikolay Stepanovich
See also CA 165; DLB 295

Gumilyov, Nikolay Stepanovich
See Gumilev, Nikolai (Stepanovich)
See also EWL 3

Gump, P. Q.
See Card, Orson Scott

Gunesekera, Romesh 1954- .... **CLC 91**
See also BRWS 10; CA 159; CANR 140; CN 6, 7; DLB 267

Gunn, Bill .... **CLC 5**
See Gunn, William Harrison
See also DLB 38

Gunn, Thom(son William)
1929-2004 . **CLC 3, 6, 18, 32, 81; PC 26**
See also BRWS 4; CA 17-20R; 227; CANR 9, 33, 116; CDBLB 1960 to Present; CP 1, 2, 3, 4, 5, 6, 7; DAM POET; DLB 27; INT CANR-33; MTCW 1; PFS 9; RGEL 2

Gunn, William Harrison 1934(?)-1989
See Gunn, Bill
See also AITN 1; BW 1, 3; CA 13-16R; 128; CANR 12, 25, 76

Gunn Allen, Paula
See Allen, Paula Gunn

Gunnars, Kristjana 1948- .... **CLC 69**
See also CA 113; CCA 1; CP 7; CWP; DLB 60

Gunter, Erich
See Eich, Gunter

Gurdjieff, G(eorgei) I(vanovich)
1877(?)-1949 .... **TCLC 71**
See also CA 157

Gurganus, Allan 1947- .... **CLC 70**
See also BEST 90:1; CA 135; CANR 114; CN 6, 7; CPW; CSW; DAM POP; GLL 1

Gurney, A. R.
See Gurney, A(lbert) R(amsdell), Jr.
See also DLB 266

Gurney, A(lbert) R(amsdell), Jr.
1930- .... **CLC 32, 50, 54**
See Gurney, A. R.
See also AMWS 5; CA 77-80; CAD; CANR 32, 64, 121; CD 5, 6; DAM DRAM; EWL 3

Gurney, Ivor (Bertie) 1890-1937 ... **TCLC 33**
See also BRW 6; CA 167; DLBY 2002; PAB; RGEL 2

Gurney, Peter
See Gurney, A(lbert) R(amsdell), Jr.

Guro, Elena (Genrikhovna)
1877-1913 .... **TCLC 56**
See also DLB 295

Gustafson, James M(oody) 1925- ... **CLC 100**
See also CA 25-28R; CANR 37

Gustafson, Ralph (Barker)
1909-1995 .... **CLC 36**
See also CA 21-24R; CANR 8, 45, 84; CP 1, 2, 3, 4; DLB 88; RGEL 2

Gut, Gom
See Simenon, Georges (Jacques Christian)

Guterson, David 1956- .... **CLC 91**
See also CA 132; CANR 73, 126; CN 7; DLB 292; MTCW 2; MTFW 2005; NFS 13

Guthrie, A(lfred) B(ertram), Jr.
1901-1991 .... **CLC 23**
See also CA 57-60; 134; CANR 24; CN 1, 2, 3; DLB 6, 212; MAL 5; SATA 62; SATA-Obit 67; TCWW 1, 2

Guthrie, Isobel
See Grieve, C(hristopher) M(urray)

Guthrie, Woodrow Wilson 1912-1967
See Guthrie, Woody
See also CA 113; 93-96

Guthrie, Woody .... **CLC 35**
See Guthrie, Woodrow Wilson
See also DLB 303; LAIT 3

Gutierrez Najera, Manuel
1859-1895 .... **HLCS 2; NCLC 133**
See also DLB 290; LAW

Guy, Rosa (Cuthbert) 1925- .... **CLC 26**
See also AAYA 4, 37; BW 2; CA 17-20R; CANR 14, 34, 83; CLR 13; DLB 33; DNFS 1; JRDA; MAICYA 1, 2; SATA 14, 62, 122; YAW

Gwendolyn
See Bennett, (Enoch) Arnold

H. D. .... **CLC 3, 8, 14, 31, 34, 73; PC 5**
See Doolittle, Hilda
See also FL 1:5

H. de V.
See Buchan, John

Haavikko, Paavo Juhani 1931- .. **CLC 18, 34**
See also CA 106; CWW 2; EWL 3

Habbema, Koos
See Heijermans, Herman

Habermas, Juergen 1929- .... **CLC 104**
See also CA 109; CANR 85; DLB 242

Habermas, Jurgen
See Habermas, Juergen

Hacker, Marilyn 1942- ...... **CLC 5, 9, 23, 72, 91; PC 47**
See also CA 77-80; CANR 68, 129; CP 3, 4, 5, 6, 7; CWP; DAM POET; DLB 120, 282; FW; GLL 2; MAL 5; PFS 19

Hadewijch of Antwerp fl. 1250- ... **CMLC 61**
See also RGWL 3

Hadrian 76-138 .... **CMLC 52**

Haeckel, Ernst Heinrich (Philipp August)
1834-1919 .... **TCLC 83**
See also CA 157

Hafiz c. 1326-1389(?) .... **CMLC 34**
See also RGWL 2, 3; WLIT 6

Hagedorn, Jessica T(arahata)
1949- .... **CLC 185**
See also CA 139; CANR 69; CWP; DLB 312; RGAL 4

Haggard, H(enry) Rider
1856-1925 .... **TCLC 11**
See also BRWS 3; BYA 4, 5; CA 108; 148; CANR 112; DLB 70, 156, 174, 178; FANT; LMFS 1; MTCW 2; RGEL 2; RHW; SATA 16; SCFW 1, 2; SFW 4; SUFW 1; WLIT 4

Hagiosy, L.
See Larbaud, Valery (Nicolas)

Hagiwara, Sakutaro 1886-1942 .... **PC 18; TCLC 60**
See Hagiwara Sakutaro
See also CA 154; RGWL 3

Hagiwara Sakutaro
See Hagiwara, Sakutaro
See also EWL 3

Haig, Fenil
See Ford, Ford Madox

Haig-Brown, Roderick (Langmere)
1908-1976 .... **CLC 21**
See also CA 5-8R; 69-72; CANR 4, 38, 83; CLR 31; CWRI 5; DLB 88; MAICYA 1, 2; SATA 12; TCWW 2

Haight, Rip
See Carpenter, John (Howard)

Hailey, Arthur 1920-2004 .... **CLC 5**
See also AITN 2; BEST 90:3; BPFB 2; CA 1-4R; 233; CANR 2, 36, 75; CCA 1; CN 1, 2, 3, 4, 5, 6, 7; CPW; DAM NOV, POP; DLB 88; DLBY 1982; MTCW 1, 2; MTFW 2005

Hailey, Elizabeth Forsythe 1938- ..... **CLC 40**
See also CA 93-96, 188; CAAE 188; CAAS 1; CANR 15, 48; INT CANR-15

Haines, John (Meade) 1924- .... **CLC 58**
See also AMWS 12; CA 17-20R; CANR 13, 34; CP 1, 2, 3, 4; CSW; DLB 5, 212; TCLE 1:1

Hakluyt, Richard 1552-1616 .... **LC 31**
See also DLB 136; RGEL 2

Haldeman, Joe (William) 1943- .... **CLC 61**
See Graham, Robert
See also AAYA 38; CA 53-56, 179; CAAE 179; CAAS 25; CANR 6, 70, 72, 130; DLB 8; INT CANR-6; SCFW 2; SFW 4

Hale, Janet Campbell 1947- .... **NNAL**
See also CA 49-52; CANR 45, 75; DAM MULT; DLB 175; MTCW 2; MTFW 2005

Hale, Sarah Josepha (Buell)
1788-1879 .... **NCLC 75**
See also DLB 1, 42, 73, 243

Halevy, Elie 1870-1937 .... **TCLC 104**

Haley, Alex(ander Murray Palmer)
1921-1992 .... **BLC 2; CLC 8, 12, 76; TCLC 147**
See also AAYA 26; BPFB 2; BW 2, 3; CA 77-80; 136; CANR 61; CDALBS; CPW; CSW; DA; DA3; DAB; DAC; DAM MST, MULT, POP; DLB 38; LAIT 5; MTCW 1, 2; NFS 9

Haliburton, Thomas Chandler
1796-1865 .... **NCLC 15, 149**
See also DLB 11, 99; RGEL 2; RGSF 2

Hall, Donald (Andrew, Jr.) 1928- ...... **CLC 1, 13, 37, 59, 151; PC 70**
See also AAYA 63; CA 5-8R; CAAS 7; CANR 2, 44, 64, 106, 133; CP 1, 2, 3, 4, 5, 6, 7; DAM POET; DLB 5; MAL 5; MTCW 2; MTFW 2005; RGAL 4; SATA 23, 97

Hall, Frederic Sauser
See Sauser-Hall, Frederic

Hall, James
See Kuttner, Henry

Hall, James Norman 1887-1951 ..... **TCLC 23**
See also CA 123; 173; LAIT 1; RHW 1; SATA 21

Hall, Joseph 1574-1656 .... **LC 91**
See also DLB 121, 151; RGEL 2

Hall, (Marguerite) Radclyffe
1880-1943 .... **TCLC 12**
See also BRWS 6; CA 110; 150; CANR 83; DLB 191; MTCW 2; MTFW 2005; RGEL 2; RHW

Hall, Rodney 1935- .... **CLC 51**
See also CA 109; CANR 69; CN 6, 7; CP 1, 2, 3, 4, 5, 6, 7; DLB 289

Heyerdahl, Thor 1914-2002 .... **CLC 26**
See also CA 5-8R; 207; CANR 5, 22, 66, 73; LAIT 4; MTCW 1, 2; MTFW 2005; SATA 2, 52

Heym, Georg (Theodor Franz Arthur)
1887-1912 .... **TCLC 9**
See also CA 106; 181

Heym, Stefan 1913-2001 .... **CLC 41**
See also CA 9-12R; 203; CANR 4; CWW 2; DLB 69; EWL 3

Heyse, Paul (Johann Ludwig von)
1830-1914 .... **TCLC 8**
See also CA 104; 209; DLB 129

Heyward, (Edwin) DuBose
1885-1940 .... **HR 1:2; TCLC 59**
See also CA 108; 157; DLB 7, 9, 45, 249; MAL 5; SATA 21

Heywood, John 1497(?)-1580(?) .... **LC 65**
See also DLB 136; RGEL 2

Heywood, Thomas 1573(?)-1641 .... **LC 111**
See also DAM DRAM; DLB 62; LMFS 1; RGEL 2; TEA

Hibbert, Eleanor Alice Burford
1906-1993 .... **CLC 7**
See Holt, Victoria
See also BEST 90:4; CA 17-20R; 140; CANR 9, 28, 59; CMW 4; CPW; DAM POP; MTCW 2; MTFW 2005; RHW; SATA 2; SATA-Obit 74

Hichens, Robert (Smythe)
1864-1950 .... **TCLC 64**
See also CA 162; DLB 153; HGG; RHW; SUFW

Higgins, Aidan 1927- .... **SSC 68**
See also CA 9-12R; CANR 70, 115; CN 1, 2, 3, 4, 5, 6, 7; DLB 14

Higgins, George V(incent)
1939-1999 .... **CLC 4, 7, 10, 18**
See also BPFB 2; CA 77-80; 186; CAAS 5; CANR 17, 51, 89, 96; CMW 4; CN 2, 3, 4, 5, 6; DLB 2; DLBY 1981, 1998; INT CANR-17; MSW; MTCW 1

Higginson, Thomas Wentworth
1823-1911 .... **TCLC 36**
See also CA 162; DLB 1, 64, 243

Higgonet, Margaret ed. .... **CLC 65**

Highet, Helen
See MacInnes, Helen (Clark)

Highsmith, (Mary) Patricia
1921-1995 .... **CLC 2, 4, 14, 42, 102**
See Morgan, Claire
See also AAYA 48; BRWS 5; CA 1-4R; 147; CANR 1, 20, 48, 62, 108; CMW 4; CN 1, 2, 3, 4, 5; CPW; DA3; DAM NOV, POP; DLB 306; MSW; MTCW 1, 2; MTFW 2005

Highwater, Jamake (Mamake)
1942(?)-2001 .... **CLC 12**
See also AAYA 7; BPFB 2; BYA 4; CA 65-68; 199; CAAS 7; CANR 10, 34, 84; CLR 17; CWRI 5; DLB 52; DLBY 1985; JRDA; MAICYA 1, 2; SATA 32, 69; SATA-Brief 30

Highway, Tomson 1951- ...... **CLC 92; NNAL**
See also CA 151; CANR 75; CCA 1; CD 5, 6; CN 7; DAC; DAM MULT; DFS 2; MTCW 2

Hijuelos, Oscar 1951- .... **CLC 65; HLC 1**
See also AAYA 25; AMWS 8; BEST 90:1; CA 123; CANR 50, 75, 125; CPW; DA3; DAM MULT, POP; DLB 145; HW 1, 2; LLW; MAL 5; MTCW 2; MTFW 2005; NFS 17; RGAL 4; WLIT 1

Hikmet, Nazim 1902-1963 .... **CLC 40**
See Nizami of Ganja
See also CA 141; 93-96; EWL 3; WLIT 6

Hildegard von Bingen 1098-1179 . **CMLC 20**
See also DLB 148

Hildesheimer, Wolfgang 1916-1991 .. **CLC 49**
See also CA 101; 135; DLB 69, 124; EWL 3

Hill, Geoffrey (William) 1932- ...... **CLC 5, 8, 18, 45**
See also BRWS 5; CA 81-84; CANR 21, 89; CDBLB 1960 to Present; CP 1, 2, 3, 4, 5, 6, 7; DAM POET; DLB 40; EWL 3; MTCW 1; RGEL 2

Hill, George Roy 1921-2002 .... **CLC 26**
See also CA 110; 122; 213

Hill, John
See Koontz, Dean R.

Hill, Susan (Elizabeth) 1942- ...... **CLC 4, 113**
See also CA 33-36R; CANR 29, 69, 129; CN 2, 3, 4, 5, 6, 7; DAB; DAM MST, NOV; DLB 14, 139; HGG; MTCW 1; RHW

Hillard, Asa G. III .... **CLC 70**

Hillerman, Tony 1925- .... **CLC 62, 170**
See also AAYA 40; BEST 89:1; BPFB 2; CA 29-32R; CANR 21, 42, 65, 97, 134; CMW 4; CPW; DA3; DAM POP; DLB 206, 306; MAL 5; MSW; MTCW 2; MTFW 2005; RGAL 4; SATA 6; TCWW 2; YAW

Hillesum, Etty 1914-1943 .... **TCLC 49**
See also CA 137

Hilliard, Noel (Harvey) 1929-1996 ... **CLC 15**
See also CA 9-12R; CANR 7, 69; CN 1, 2, 3, 4, 5, 6

Hillis, Rick 1956- .... **CLC 66**
See also CA 134

Hilton, James 1900-1954 .... **TCLC 21**
See also CA 108; 169; DLB 34, 77; FANT; SATA 34

Hilton, Walter (?)-1396 .... **CMLC 58**
See also DLB 146; RGEL 2

Himes, Chester (Bomar) 1909-1984 .. **BLC 2; CLC 2, 4, 7, 18, 58, 108; TCLC 139**
See also AFAW 2; BPFB 2; BW 2; CA 25-28R; 114; CANR 22, 89; CMW 4; CN 1, 2, 3; DAM MULT; DLB 2, 76, 143, 226; EWL 3; MAL 5; MSW; MTCW 1, 2; MTFW 2005; RGAL 4

Himmelfarb, Gertrude 1922- .... **CLC 202**
See also CA 49-52; CANR 28, 66, 102

Hinde, Thomas .... **CLC 6, 11**
See Chitty, Thomas Willes
See also CN 1, 2, 3, 4, 5, 6; EWL 3

Hine, (William) Daryl 1936- .... **CLC 15**
See also CA 1-4R; CAAS 15; CANR 1, 20; CP 1, 2, 3, 4, 5, 6, 7; DLB 60

Hinkson, Katharine Tynan
See Tynan, Katharine

Hinojosa(-Smith), Rolando (R.)
1929- .... **HLC 1**
See Hinojosa-Smith, Rolando
See also CA 131; CAAS 16; CANR 62; DAM MULT; DLB 82; HW 1, 2; LLW; MTCW 2; MTFW 2005; RGAL 4

Hinton, S(usan) E(loise) 1950- .. **CLC 30, 111**
See also AAYA 2, 33; BPFB 2; BYA 2, 3; CA 81-84; CANR 32, 62, 92, 133; CDALBS; CLR 3, 23; CPW; DA; DA3; DAB; DAC; DAM MST, NOV; JRDA; LAIT 5; MAICYA 1, 2; MTCW 1, 2; MTFW 2005 !**; NFS 5, 9, 15, 16; SATA 19, 58, 115, 160; WYA; YAW

Hippius, Zinaida (Nikolaevna) .... **TCLC 9**
See Gippius, Zinaida (Nikolaevna)
See also DLB 295; EWL 3

Hiraoka, Kimitake 1925-1970
See Mishima, Yukio
See also CA 97-100; 29-32R; DA3; DAM DRAM; GLL 1; MTCW 1, 2

Hirsch, E(ric) D(onald), Jr. 1928- .... **CLC 79**
See also CA 25-28R; CANR 27, 51; DLB 67; INT CANR-27; MTCW 1

Hirsch, Edward 1950- .... **CLC 31, 50**
See also CA 104; CANR 20, 42, 102; CP 7; DLB 120; PFS 22

Hitchcock, Alfred (Joseph)
1899-1980 .... **CLC 16**
See also AAYA 22; CA 159; 97-100; SATA 27; SATA-Obit 24

Hitchens, Christopher (Eric)
1949- .... **CLC 157**
See also CA 152; CANR 89

Hitler, Adolf 1889-1945 .... **TCLC 53**
See also CA 117; 147

Hoagland, Edward (Morley) 1932- .. **CLC 28**
See also ANW; CA 1-4R; CANR 2, 31, 57, 107; CN 1, 2, 3, 4, 5, 6, 7; DLB 6; SATA 51; TCWW 2

Hoban, Russell (Conwell) 1925- ... **CLC 7, 25**
See also BPFB 2; CA 5-8R; CANR 23, 37, 66, 114, 138; CLR 3, 69; CN 4, 5, 6, 7; CWRI 5; DAM NOV; DLB 52; FANT; MAICYA 1, 2; MTCW 1, 2; MTFW 2005; SATA 1, 40, 78, 136; SFW 4; SUFW 2; TCLE 1:1

Hobbes, Thomas 1588-1679 .... **LC 36**
See also DLB 151, 252, 281; RGEL 2

Hobbs, Perry
See Blackmur, R(ichard) P(almer)

Hobson, Laura Z(ametkin)
1900-1986 .... **CLC 7, 25**
See also BPFB 2; CA 17-20R; 118; CANR 55; CN 1, 2, 3, 4; DLB 28; SATA 52

Hoccleve, Thomas c. 1368-c. 1437 ...... **LC 75**
See also DLB 146; RGEL 2

Hoch, Edward D(entinger) 1930-
See Queen, Ellery
See also CA 29-32R; CANR 11, 27, 51, 97; CMW 4; DLB 306; SFW 4

Hochhuth, Rolf 1931- .... **CLC 4, 11, 18**
See also CA 5-8R; CANR 33, 75, 136; CWW 2; DAM DRAM; DLB 124; EWL 3; MTCW 1, 2; MTFW 2005

Hochman, Sandra 1936- .... **CLC 3, 8**
See also CA 5-8R; CP 1, 2, 3, 4; DLB 5

Hochwaelder, Fritz 1911-1986 .... **CLC 36**
See Hochwalder, Fritz
See also CA 29-32R; 120; CANR 42; DAM DRAM; MTCW 1; RGWL 3

Hochwalder, Fritz
See Hochwaelder, Fritz
See also EWL 3; RGWL 2

Hocking, Mary (Eunice) 1921- .... **CLC 13**
See also CA 101; CANR 18, 40

Hodgins, Jack 1938- .... **CLC 23**
See also CA 93-96; CN 4, 5, 6, 7; DLB 60

Hodgson, William Hope
1877(?)-1918 .... **TCLC 13**
See also CA 111; 164; CMW 4; DLB 70, 153, 156, 178; HGG; MTCW 2; SFW 4; SUFW 1

Hoeg, Peter 1957- .... **CLC 95, 156**
See also CA 151; CANR 75; CMW 4; DA3; DLB 214; EWL 3; MTCW 2; MTFW 2005; NFS 17; RGWL 3; SSFS 18

Hoffman, Alice 1952- .... **CLC 51**
See also AAYA 37; AMWS 10; CA 77-80; CANR 34, 66, 100, 138; CN 4, 5, 6, 7; CPW; DAM NOV; DLB 292; MAL 5; MTCW 1, 2; MTFW 2005; TCLE 1:1

Hoffman, Daniel (Gerard) 1923- . **CLC 6, 13, 23**
See also CA 1-4R; CANR 4, 142; CP 1, 2, 3, 4, 5, 6, 7; DLB 5; TCLE 1:1

Hoffman, Eva 1945- .... **CLC 182**
See also CA 132; CANR 146

Hoffman, Stanley 1944- .... **CLC 5**
See also CA 77-80

Hoffman, William 1925- .... **CLC 141**
See also CA 21-24R; CANR 9, 103; CSW; DLB 234; TCLE 1:1

Hoffman, William M.
See Hoffman, William M(oses)
See also CAD; CD 5, 6
Hoffman, William M(oses) 1939- ..... **CLC 40**
See Hoffman, William M.
See also CA 57-60; CANR 11, 71
Hoffmann, E(rnst) T(heodor) A(madeus)
1776-1822 .... **NCLC 2; SSC 13**
See also CDWLB 2; DLB 90; EW 5; GL 2;
RGSF 2; RGWL 2, 3; SATA 27; SUFW
1; WCH
Hofmann, Gert 1931-1993 .... **CLC 54**
See also CA 128; CANR 145; EWL 3
Hofmannsthal, Hugo von 1874-1929 ... **DC 4;
TCLC 11**
See also CA 106; 153; CDWLB 2; DAM
DRAM; DFS 17; DLB 81, 118; EW 9;
EWL 3; RGWL 2, 3
Hogan, Linda 1947- ..... **CLC 73; NNAL; PC
35**
See also AMWS 4; ANW; BYA 12; CA 120,
226; CAAE 226; CANR 45, 73, 129;
CWP; DAM MULT; DLB 175; SATA
132; TCWW 2
Hogarth, Charles
See Creasey, John
Hogarth, Emmett
See Polonsky, Abraham (Lincoln)
Hogarth, William 1697-1764 .... **LC 112**
See also AAYA 56
Hogg, James 1770-1835 .... **NCLC 4, 109**
See also BRWS 10; DLB 93, 116, 159; GL
2; HGG; RGEL 2; SUFW 1
Holbach, Paul-Henri Thiry
1723-1789 .... **LC 14**
See also DLB 313
Holberg, Ludvig 1684-1754 .... **LC 6**
See also DLB 300; RGWL 2, 3
Holcroft, Thomas 1745-1809 .... **NCLC 85**
See also DLB 39, 89, 158; RGEL 2
Holden, Ursula 1921- .... **CLC 18**
See also CA 101; CAAS 8; CANR 22
Holderlin, (Johann Christian) Friedrich
1770-1843 .... **NCLC 16; PC 4**
See also CDWLB 2; DLB 90; EW 5; RGWL
2, 3
Holdstock, Robert
See Holdstock, Robert P.
Holdstock, Robert P. 1948- .... **CLC 39**
See also CA 131; CANR 81; DLB 261;
FANT; HGG; SFW 4; SUFW 2
Holinshed, Raphael fl. 1580- .... **LC 69**
See also DLB 167; RGEL 2
Holland, Isabelle (Christian)
1920-2002 .... **CLC 21**
See also AAYA 11, 64; CA 21-24R; 205;
CAAE 181; CANR 10, 25, 47; CLR 57;
CWRI 5; JRDA; LAIT 4; MAICYA 1, 2;
SATA 8, 70; SATA-Essay 103; SATA-Obit
132; WYA
Holland, Marcus
See Caldwell, (Janet Miriam) Taylor
(Holland)
Hollander, John 1929- .... **CLC 2, 5, 8, 14**
See also CA 1-4R; CANR 1, 52, 136; CP 1,
2, 3, 4, 5, 6, 7; DLB 5; MAL 5; SATA 13
Hollander, Paul
See Silverberg, Robert
Holleran, Andrew .... **CLC 38**
See Garber, Eric
See also CA 144; GLL 1
Holley, Marietta 1836(?)-1926 .... **TCLC 99**
See also CA 118; DLB 11; FL 1:3
Hollinghurst, Alan 1954- .... **CLC 55, 91**
See also BRWS 10; CA 114; CN 5, 6, 7;
DLB 207; GLL 1
Hollis, Jim
See Summers, Hollis (Spurgeon, Jr.)

Holly, Buddy 1936-1959 .... **TCLC 65**
See also CA 213
Holmes, Gordon
See Shiel, M(atthew) P(hipps)
Holmes, John
See Souster, (Holmes) Raymond
Holmes, John Clellon 1926-1988 ...... **CLC 56**
See also BG 1:2; CA 9-12R; 125; CANR 4;
CN 1, 2, 3, 4; DLB 16, 237
Holmes, Oliver Wendell, Jr.
1841-1935 .... **TCLC 77**
See also CA 114; 186
Holmes, Oliver Wendell
1809-1894 .... **NCLC 14, 81**
See also AMWS 1; CDALB 1640-1865;
DLB 1, 189, 235; EXPP; RGAL 4; SATA
34
Holmes, Raymond
See Souster, (Holmes) Raymond
Holt, Victoria
See Hibbert, Eleanor Alice Burford
See also BPFB 2
Holub, Miroslav 1923-1998 .... **CLC 4**
See also CA 21-24R; 169; CANR 10; CD-
WLB 4; CWW 2; DLB 232; EWL 3;
RGWL 3
Holz, Detlev
See Benjamin, Walter
Homer c. 8th cent. B.C.- .... **CMLC 1, 16, 61;
PC 23; WLCS**
See also AW 1; CDWLB 1; DA; DA3;
DAB; DAC; DAM MST, POET; DLB
176; EFS 1; LAIT 1; LMFS 1; RGWL 2,
3; TWA; WP
Hongo, Garrett Kaoru 1951- .... **PC 23**
See also CA 133; CAAS 22; CP 7; DLB
120, 312; EWL 3; EXPP; RGAL 4
Honig, Edwin 1919- .... **CLC 33**
See also CA 5-8R; CAAS 8; CANR 4, 45,
144; CP 1, 2, 3, 4, 5, 6, 7; DLB 5
Hood, Hugh (John Blagdon) 1928- . **CLC 15,
28; SSC 42**
See also CA 49-52; CAAS 17; CANR 1,
33, 87; CN 1, 2, 3, 4, 5, 6, 7; DLB 53;
RGSF 2
Hood, Thomas 1799-1845 .... **NCLC 16**
See also BRW 4; DLB 96; RGEL 2
Hooker, (Peter) Jeremy 1941- .... **CLC 43**
See also CA 77-80; CANR 22; CP 2, 3, 4,
5, 6, 7; DLB 40
Hooker, Richard 1554-1600 .... **LC 95**
See also BRW 1; DLB 132; RGEL 2
hooks, bell
See Watkins, Gloria Jean
Hope, A(lec) D(erwent) 1907-2000 .... **CLC 3,
51; PC 56**
See also BRWS 7; CA 21-24R; 188; CANR
33, 74; CP 1, 2, 3, 4; DLB 289; EWL 3;
MTCW 1, 2; MTFW 2005; PFS 8; RGEL
2
Hope, Anthony 1863-1933 .... **TCLC 83**
See also CA 157; DLB 153, 156; RGEL 2;
RHW
Hope, Brian
See Creasey, John
Hope, Christopher (David Tully)
1944- .... **CLC 52**
See also AFW; CA 106; CANR 47, 101;
CN 4, 5, 6, 7; DLB 225; SATA 62
Hopkins, Gerard Manley
1844-1889 .... **NCLC 17; PC 15; WLC**
See also BRW 5; BRWR 2; CDBLB 1890-
1914; DA; DA3; DAB; DAC; DAM MST,
POET; DLB 35, 57; EXPP; PAB; RGEL
2; TEA; WP
Hopkins, John (Richard) 1931-1998 .. **CLC 4**
See also CA 85-88; 169; CBD; CD 5, 6

Hopkins, Pauline Elizabeth
1859-1930 .... **BLC 2; TCLC 28**
See also AFAW 2; BW 2, 3; CA 141; CANR
82; DAM MULT; DLB 50
Hopkinson, Francis 1737-1791 .... **LC 25**
See also DLB 31; RGAL 4
Hopley-Woolrich, Cornell George 1903-1968
See Woolrich, Cornell
See also CA 13-14; CANR 58; CAP 1;
CMW 4; DLB 226; MTCW 2
Horace 65B.C.-8B.C. .... **CMLC 39; PC 46**
See also AW 2; CDWLB 1; DLB 211;
RGWL 2, 3
Horatio
See Proust, (Valentin-Louis-George-Eugene)
Marcel
**Horgan, Paul (George Vincent
O'Shaughnessy)** 1903-1995 .. **CLC 9, 53**
See also BPFB 2; CA 13-16R; 147; CANR
9, 35; CN 1, 2, 3, 4, 5; DAM NOV; DLB
102, 212; DLBY 1985; INT CANR-9;
MTCW 1, 2; MTFW 2005; SATA 13;
SATA-Obit 84; TCWW 1, 2
Horkheimer, Max 1895-1973 .... **TCLC 132**
See also CA 216; 41-44R; DLB 296
Horn, Peter
See Kuttner, Henry
Horne, Frank (Smith) 1899-1974 ...... **HR 1:2**
See also BW 1; CA 125; 53-56; DLB 51;
WP
Horne, Richard Henry Hengist
1802(?)-1884 .... **NCLC 127**
See also DLB 32; SATA 29
Hornem, Horace Esq.
See Byron, George Gordon (Noel)
**Horney, Karen (Clementine Theodore
Danielsen)** 1885-1952 .... **TCLC 71**
See also CA 114; 165; DLB 246; FW
Hornung, E(rnest) W(illiam)
1866-1921 .... **TCLC 59**
See also CA 108; 160; CMW 4; DLB 70
Horovitz, Israel (Arthur) 1939- .... **CLC 56**
See also CA 33-36R; CAD; CANR 46, 59;
CD 5, 6; DAM DRAM; DLB 7; MAL 5
Horton, George Moses
1797(?)-1883(?) .... **NCLC 87**
See also DLB 50
Horvath, odon von 1901-1938
See von Horvath, Odon
See also EWL 3
Horvath, Oedoen von -1938
See von Horvath, Odon
Horwitz, Julius 1920-1986 .... **CLC 14**
See also CA 9-12R; 119; CANR 12
Hospital, Janette Turner 1942- .... **CLC 42,
145**
See also CA 108; CANR 48; CN 5, 6, 7;
DLBY 2002; RGSF 2
Hostos, E. M. de
See Hostos (y Bonilla), Eugenio Maria de
Hostos, Eugenio M. de
See Hostos (y Bonilla), Eugenio Maria de
Hostos, Eugenio Maria
See Hostos (y Bonilla), Eugenio Maria de
Hostos (y Bonilla), Eugenio Maria de
1839-1903 .... **TCLC 24**
See also CA 123; 131; HW 1
Houdini
See Lovecraft, H(oward) P(hillips)
Houellebecq, Michel 1958- .... **CLC 179**
See also CA 185; CANR 140; MTFW 2005
Hougan, Carolyn 1943- .... **CLC 34**
See also CA 139
Household, Geoffrey (Edward West)
1900-1988 .... **CLC 11**
See also CA 77-80; 126; CANR 58; CMW
4; CN 1, 2, 3, 4; DLB 87; SATA 14;
SATA-Obit 59

Jabran, Kahlil
　See Gibran, Kahlil
Jabran, Khalil
　See Gibran, Kahlil
Jackson, Daniel
　See Wingrove, David (John)
Jackson, Helen Hunt 1830-1885 .... **NCLC 90**
　See also DLB 42, 47, 186, 189; RGAL 4
Jackson, Jesse 1908-1983 .... **CLC 12**
　See also BW 1; CA 25-28R; 109; CANR
　27; CLR 28; CWRI 5; MAICYA 1, 2;
　SATA 2, 29; SATA-Obit 48
Jackson, Laura (Riding) 1901-1991 .... **PC 44**
　See Riding, Laura
　See also CA 65-68; 135; CANR 28, 89;
　DLB 48
Jackson, Sam
　See Trumbo, Dalton
Jackson, Sara
　See Wingrove, David (John)
Jackson, Shirley 1919-1965 . **CLC 11, 60, 87;**
　　SSC 9, 39; WLC
　See also AAYA 9; AMWS 9; BPFB 2; CA
　1-4R; 25-28R; CANR 4, 52; CDALB
　1941-1968; DA; DA3; DAC; DAM MST;
　DLB 6, 234; EXPS; HGG; LAIT 4; MAL
　5; MTCW 2; MTFW 2005; RGAL 4;
　RGSF 2; SATA 2; SSFS 1; SUFW 1, 2
Jacob, (Cyprien-)Max 1876-1944 .... **TCLC 6**
　See also CA 104; 193; DLB 258; EWL 3;
　GFL 1789 to the Present; GLL 2; RGWL
　2, 3
Jacobs, Harriet A(nn)
　　1813(?)-1897 .... **NCLC 67, 162**
　See also AFAW 1, 2; DLB 239; FL 1:3; FW;
　LAIT 2; RGAL 4
Jacobs, Jim 1942- .... **CLC 12**
　See also CA 97-100; INT CA-97-100
Jacobs, W(illiam) W(ymark)
　　1863-1943 .... **SSC 73; TCLC 22**
　See also CA 121; 167; DLB 135; EXPS;
　HGG; RGEL 2; RGSF 2; SSFS 2; SUFW
　1
Jacobsen, Jens Peter 1847-1885 .... **NCLC 34**
Jacobsen, Josephine (Winder)
　　1908-2003 .... **CLC 48, 102; PC 62**
　See also CA 33-36R; 218; CAAS 18; CANR
　23, 48; CCA 1; CP 2, 3, 4, 5, 6, 7; DLB
　244; PFS 23; TCLE 1:1
Jacobson, Dan 1929- .... **CLC 4, 14**
　See also AFW; CA 1-4R; CANR 2, 25, 66;
　CN 1, 2, 3, 4, 5, 6, 7; DLB 14, 207, 225,
　319; EWL 3; MTCW 1; RGSF 2
Jacqueline
　See Carpentier (y Valmont), Alejo
Jacques de Vitry c. 1160-1240 ...... **CMLC 63**
　See also DLB 208
Jagger, Michael Philip
　See Jagger, Mick
Jagger, Mick 1943- .... **CLC 17**
　See also CA 239
Jahiz, al- c. 780-c. 869 .... **CMLC 25**
　See also DLB 311
Jakes, John (William) 1932- .... **CLC 29**
　See also AAYA 32; BEST 89:4; BPFB 2;
　CA 57-60, 214; CAAE 214; CANR 10,
　43, 66, 111, 142; CPW; CSW; DA3; DAM
　NOV, POP; DLB 278; DLBY 1983;
　FANT; INT CANR-10; MTCW 1, 2;
　MTFW 2005; RHW; SATA 62; SFW 4;
　TCWW 1, 2
James I 1394-1437 .... **LC 20**
　See also RGEL 2
James, Andrew
　See Kirkup, James
James, C(yril) L(ionel) R(obert)
　　1901-1989 .... **BLCS; CLC 33**
　See also BW 2; CA 117; 125; 128; CANR
　62; CN 1, 2, 3, 4; DLB 125; MTCW 1

James, Daniel (Lewis) 1911-1988
　See Santiago, Danny
　See also CA 174; 125
James, Dynely
　See Mayne, William (James Carter)
James, Henry Sr. 1811-1882 .... **NCLC 53**
James, Henry 1843-1916 .... **SSC 8, 32, 47;**
　　TCLC 2, 11, 24, 40, 47, 64, 171; WLC
　See also AMW; AMWC 1; AMWR 1; BPFB
　2; BRW 6; CA 104; 132; CDALB 1865-
　1917; DA; DA3; DAB; DAC; DAM MST,
　NOV; DLB 12, 71, 74, 189; DLBD 13;
　EWL 3; EXPS; GL 2; HGG; LAIT 2;
　MAL 5; MTCW 1, 2; MTFW 2005; NFS
　12, 16, 19; RGAL 4; RGEL 2; RGSF 2;
　SSFS 9; SUFW 1; TUS
James, M. R.
　See James, Montague (Rhodes)
　See also DLB 156, 201
James, Montague (Rhodes)
　　1862-1936 .... **SSC 16; TCLC 6**
　See James, M. R.
　See also CA 104; 203; HGG; RGEL 2;
　RGSF 2; SUFW 1
James, P. D. .... **CLC 18, 46, 122**
　See White, Phyllis Dorothy James
　See also BEST 90:2; BPFB 2; BRWS 4;
　CDBLB 1960 to Present; CN 4, 5, 6; DLB
　87, 276; DLBD 17; MSW
James, Philip
　See Moorcock, Michael (John)
James, Samuel
　See Stephens, James
James, Seumas
　See Stephens, James
James, Stephen
　See Stephens, James
James, William 1842-1910 .... **TCLC 15, 32**
　See also AMW; CA 109; 193; DLB 270,
　284; MAL 5; NCFS 5; RGAL 4
Jameson, Anna 1794-1860 .... **NCLC 43**
　See also DLB 99, 166
Jameson, Fredric (R.) 1934- .... **CLC 142**
　See also CA 196; DLB 67; LMFS 2
James VI of Scotland 1566-1625 .... **LC 109**
　See also DLB 151, 172
Jami, Nur al-Din 'Abd al-Rahman
　　1414-1492 .... **LC 9**
Jammes, Francis 1868-1938 .... **TCLC 75**
　See also CA 198; EWL 3; GFL 1789 to the
　Present
Jandl, Ernst 1925-2000 .... **CLC 34**
　See also CA 200; EWL 3
Janowitz, Tama 1957- .... **CLC 43, 145**
　See also CA 106; CANR 52, 89, 129; CN
　5, 6, 7; CPW; DAM POP; DLB 292;
　MTFW 2005
Japrisot, Sebastien 1931- .... **CLC 90**
　See Rossi, Jean-Baptiste
　See also CMW 4; NFS 18
Jarrell, Randall 1914-1965 .... **CLC 1, 2, 6, 9,**
　　13, 49; PC 41
　See also AMW; BYA 5; CA 5-8R; 25-28R;
　CABS 2; CANR 6, 34; CDALB 1941-
　1968; CLR 6; CWRI 5; DAM POET;
　DLB 48, 52; EWL 3; EXPP; MAICYA 1,
　2; MAL 5; MTCW 1, 2; PAB; PFS 2;
　RGAL 4; SATA 7
Jarry, Alfred 1873-1907 .... **SSC 20; TCLC 2,**
　　14, 147
　See also CA 104; 153; DA3; DAM DRAM;
　DFS 8; DLB 192, 258; EW 9; EWL 3;
　GFL 1789 to the Present; RGWL 2, 3;
　TWA
Jarvis, E. K.
　See Ellison, Harlan (Jay)
Jawien, Andrzej
　See John Paul II, Pope

Jaynes, Roderick
　See Coen, Ethan
Jeake, Samuel, Jr.
　See Aiken, Conrad (Potter)
Jean Paul 1763-1825 .... **NCLC 7**
Jefferies, (John) Richard
　　1848-1887 .... **NCLC 47**
　See also DLB 98, 141; RGEL 2; SATA 16;
　SFW 4
Jeffers, (John) Robinson 1887-1962 .. **CLC 2,**
　　3, 11, 15, 54; PC 17; WLC
　See also AMWS 2; CA 85-88; CANR 35;
　CDALB 1917-1929; DA; DAC; DAM
　MST, POET; DLB 45, 212; EWL 3; MAL
　5; MTCW 1, 2; MTFW 2005; PAB; PFS
　3, 4; RGAL 4
Jefferson, Janet
　See Mencken, H(enry) L(ouis)
Jefferson, Thomas 1743-1826 . **NCLC 11, 103**
　See also AAYA 54; ANW; CDALB 1640-
　1865; DA3; DLB 31, 183; LAIT 1; RGAL
　4
Jeffrey, Francis 1773-1850 .... **NCLC 33**
　See Francis, Lord Jeffrey
Jelakowitch, Ivan
　See Heijermans, Herman
Jelinek, Elfriede 1946- .... **CLC 169**
　See also AAYA 68; CA 154; DLB 85; FW
Jellicoe, (Patricia) Ann 1927- .... **CLC 27**
　See also CA 85-88; CBD; CD 5, 6; CWD;
　CWRI 5; DLB 13, 233; FW
Jelloun, Tahar ben 1944- .... **CLC 180**
　See Ben Jelloun, Tahar
　See also CA 162; CANR 100
Jemyma
　See Holley, Marietta
Jen, Gish .... **AAL; CLC 70, 198**
　See Jen, Lillian
　See also AMWC 2; CN 7; DLB 312
Jen, Lillian 1955-
　See Jen, Gish
　See also CA 135; CANR 89, 130
Jenkins, (John) Robin 1912- .... **CLC 52**
　See also CA 1-4R; CANR 1, 135; CN 1, 2,
　3, 4, 5, 6, 7; DLB 14, 271
Jennings, Elizabeth (Joan)
　　1926-2001 .... **CLC 5, 14, 131**
　See also BRWS 5; CA 61-64; 200; CAAS
　5; CANR 8, 39, 66, 127; CP 1, 2, 3, 4, 5,
　6, 7; CWP; DLB 27; EWL 3; MTCW 1;
　SATA 66
Jennings, Waylon 1937-2002 .... **CLC 21**
Jensen, Johannes V(ilhelm)
　　1873-1950 .... **TCLC 41**
　See also CA 170; DLB 214; EWL 3; RGWL
　3
Jensen, Laura (Linnea) 1948- .... **CLC 37**
　See also CA 103
Jerome, Saint 345-420 .... **CMLC 30**
　See also RGWL 3
Jerome, Jerome K(lapka)
　　1859-1927 .... **TCLC 23**
　See also CA 119; 177; DLB 10, 34, 135;
　RGEL 2
Jerrold, Douglas William
　　1803-1857 .... **NCLC 2**
　See also DLB 158, 159; RGEL 2
Jewett, (Theodora) Sarah Orne
　　1849-1909 .... **SSC 6, 44; TCLC 1, 22**
　See also AMW; AMWC 2; AMWR 2; CA
　108; 127; CANR 71; DLB 12, 74, 221;
　EXPS; FL 1:3; FW; MAL 5; MAWW;
　NFS 15; RGAL 4; RGSF 2; SATA 15;
　SSFS 4
Jewsbury, Geraldine (Endsor)
　　1812-1880 .... **NCLC 22**
　See also DLB 21

Jhabvala, Ruth Prawer 1927- . **CLC 4, 8, 29, 94, 138**
See also BRWS 5; CA 1-4R; CANR 2, 29, 51, 74, 91, 128; CN 1, 2, 3, 4, 5, 6, 7; DAB; DAM NOV; DLB 139, 194; EWL 3; IDFW 3, 4; INT CANR-29; MTCW 1, 2; MTFW 2005; RGSF 2; RGWL 2; RHW; TEA

Jibran, Kahlil
See Gibran, Kahlil

Jibran, Khalil
See Gibran, Kahlil

Jiles, Paulette 1943- .... **CLC 13, 58**
See also CA 101; CANR 70, 124; CWP

Jimenez (Mantecon), Juan Ramon
1881-1958 .... **HLC 1; PC 7; TCLC 4**
See also CA 104; 131; CANR 74; DAM MULT, POET; DLB 134; EW 9; EWL 3; HW 1; MTCW 1, 2; MTFW 2005; RGWL 2, 3

Jimenez, Ramon
See Jimenez (Mantecon), Juan Ramon

Jimenez Mantecon, Juan
See Jimenez (Mantecon), Juan Ramon

Jin, Ha .... **CLC 109**
See Jin, Xuefei
See also CA 152; DLB 244, 292; SSFS 17

Jin, Xuefei 1956-
See Jin, Ha
See also CANR 91, 130; MTFW 2005; SSFS 17

Jodelle, Etienne 1532-1573 .... **LC 119**
See also GFL Beginnings to 1789

Joel, Billy .... **CLC 26**
See Joel, William Martin

Joel, William Martin 1949-
See Joel, Billy
See also CA 108

John, Saint 10(?)-100 .... **CMLC 27, 63**

John of Salisbury c. 1115-1180 ..... **CMLC 63**

John of the Cross, St. 1542-1591 .... **LC 18**
See also RGWL 2, 3

John Paul II, Pope 1920-2005 .... **CLC 128**
See also CA 106; 133; 238

Johnson, B(ryan) S(tanley William)
1933-1973 .... **CLC 6, 9**
See also CA 9-12R; 53-56; CANR 9; CN 1; CP 1, 2; DLB 14, 40; EWL 3; RGEL 2

Johnson, Benjamin F., of Boone
See Riley, James Whitcomb

Johnson, Charles (Richard) 1948- .... **BLC 2; CLC 7, 51, 65, 163**
See also AFAW 2; AMWS 6; BW 2, 3; CA 116; CAAS 18; CANR 42, 66, 82, 129; CN 5, 6, 7; DAM MULT; DLB 33, 278; MAL 5; MTCW 2; MTFW 2005; RGAL 4; SSFS 16

Johnson, Charles S(purgeon)
1893-1956 .... **HR 1:3**
See also BW 1, 3; CA 125; CANR 82; DLB 51, 91

Johnson, Denis 1949- . **CLC 52, 160; SSC 56**
See also CA 117; 121; CANR 71, 99; CN 4, 5, 6, 7; DLB 120

Johnson, Diane 1934- .... **CLC 5, 13, 48**
See also BPFB 2; CA 41-44R; CANR 17, 40, 62, 95; CN 4, 5, 6, 7; DLBY 1980; INT CANR-17; MTCW 1

Johnson, E(mily) Pauline 1861-1913 . **NNAL**
See also CA 150; CCA 1; DAC; DAM MULT; DLB 92, 175; TCWW 2

Johnson, Eyvind (Olof Verner)
1900-1976 .... **CLC 14**
See also CA 73-76; 69-72; CANR 34, 101; DLB 259; EW 12; EWL 3

Johnson, Fenton 1888-1958 .... **BLC 2**
See also BW 1; CA 118; 124; DAM MULT; DLB 45, 50

Johnson, Georgia Douglas (Camp)
1880-1966 .... **HR 1:3**
See also BW 1; CA 125; DLB 51, 249; WP

Johnson, Helene 1907-1995 .... **HR 1:3**
See also CA 181; DLB 51; WP

Johnson, J. R.
See James, C(yril) L(ionel) R(obert)

Johnson, James Weldon 1871-1938 .. **BLC 2; HR 1:3; PC 24; TCLC 3, 19, 175**
See also AFAW 1, 2; BW 1, 3; CA 104; 125; CANR 82; CDALB 1917-1929; CLR 32; DA3; DAM MULT, POET; DLB 51; EWL 3; EXPP; LMFS 2; MAL 5; MTCW 1, 2; MTFW 2005; NFS 22; PFS 1; RGAL 4; SATA 31; TUS

Johnson, Joyce 1935- .... **CLC 58**
See also BG 1:3; CA 125; 129; CANR 102

Johnson, Judith (Emlyn) 1936- .... **CLC 7, 15**
See Sherwin, Judith Johnson
See also CA 25-28R; 153; CANR 34; CP 7

Johnson, Lionel (Pigot)
1867-1902 .... **TCLC 19**
See also CA 117; 209; DLB 19; RGEL 2

Johnson, Marguerite Annie
See Angelou, Maya

Johnson, Mel
See Malzberg, Barry N(athaniel)

Johnson, Pamela Hansford
1912-1981 .... **CLC 1, 7, 27**
See also CA 1-4R; 104; CANR 2, 28; CN 1, 2, 3; DLB 15; MTCW 1, 2; MTFW 2005; RGEL 2

Johnson, Paul (Bede) 1928- .... **CLC 147**
See also BEST 89:4; CA 17-20R; CANR 34, 62, 100

Johnson, Robert .... **CLC 70**

Johnson, Robert 1911(?)-1938 .... **TCLC 69**
See also BW 3; CA 174

Johnson, Samuel 1709-1784 .... **LC 15, 52; WLC**
See also BRW 3; BRWR 1; CDBLB 1660-1789; DA; DAB; DAC; DAM MST; DLB 39, 95, 104, 142, 213; LMFS 1; RGEL 2; TEA

Johnson, Uwe 1934-1984 .. **CLC 5, 10, 15, 40**
See also CA 1-4R; 112; CANR 1, 39; CD-WLB 2; DLB 75; EWL 3; MTCW 1; RGWL 2, 3

Johnston, Basil H. 1929- .... **NNAL**
See also CA 69-72; CANR 11, 28, 66; DAC; DAM MULT; DLB 60

Johnston, George (Benson) 1913- .... **CLC 51**
See also CA 1-4R; CANR 5, 20; CP 1, 2, 3, 4, 5, 6, 7; DLB 88

Johnston, Jennifer (Prudence)
1930- .... **CLC 7, 150**
See also CA 85-88; CANR 92; CN 4, 5, 6, 7; DLB 14

Joinville, Jean de 1224(?)-1317 ..... **CMLC 38**

Jolley, (Monica) Elizabeth 1923- ..... **CLC 46; SSC 19**
See also CA 127; CAAS 13; CANR 59; CN 4, 5, 6, 7; EWL 3; RGSF 2

Jones, Arthur Llewellyn 1863-1947
See Machen, Arthur
See also CA 104; 179; HGG

Jones, D(ouglas) G(ordon) 1929- ..... **CLC 10**
See also CA 29-32R; CANR 13, 90; CP 1, 2, 3, 4, 5, 6, 7; DLB 53

Jones, David (Michael) 1895-1974 .... **CLC 2, 4, 7, 13, 42**
See also BRW 6; BRWS 7; CA 9-12R; 53-56; CANR 28; CDBLB 1945-1960; CP 1, 2; DLB 20, 100; EWL 3; MTCW 1; PAB; RGEL 2

Jones, David Robert 1947-
See Bowie, David
See also CA 103; CANR 104

Jones, Diana Wynne 1934- .... **CLC 26**
See also AAYA 12; BYA 6, 7, 9, 11, 13, 16; CA 49-52; CANR 4, 26, 56, 120; CLR 23; DLB 161; FANT; JRDA; MAICYA 1, 2; MTFW 2005; SAAS 7; SATA 9, 70, 108, 160; SFW 4; SUFW 2; YAW

Jones, Edward P. 1950- .... **CLC 76**
See also BW 2, 3; CA 142; CANR 79, 134; CSW; MTFW 2005

Jones, Gayl 1949- ...... **BLC 2; CLC 6, 9, 131**
See also AFAW 1, 2; BW 2, 3; CA 77-80; CANR 27, 66, 122; CN 4, 5, 6, 7; CSW; DA3; DAM MULT; DLB 33, 278; MAL 5; MTCW 1, 2; MTFW 2005; RGAL 4

Jones, James 1921-1977 ...... **CLC 1, 3, 10, 39**
See also AITN 1, 2; AMWS 11; BPFB 2; CA 1-4R; 69-72; CANR 6; CN 1, 2; DLB 2, 143; DLBD 17; DLBY 1998; EWL 3; MAL 5; MTCW 1; RGAL 4

Jones, John J.
See Lovecraft, H(oward) P(hillips)

Jones, LeRoi .... **CLC 1, 2, 3, 5, 10, 14**
See Baraka, Amiri
See also CN 1, 2; CP 1, 2, 3; MTCW 2

Jones, Louis B. 1953- .... **CLC 65**
See also CA 141; CANR 73

Jones, Madison (Percy, Jr.) 1925- ...... **CLC 4**
See also CA 13-16R; CAAS 11; CANR 7, 54, 83; CN 1, 2, 3, 4, 5, 6, 7; CSW; DLB 152

Jones, Mervyn 1922- .... **CLC 10, 52**
See also CA 45-48; CAAS 5; CANR 1, 91; CN 1, 2, 3, 4, 5, 6, 7; MTCW 1

Jones, Mick 1956(?)- .... **CLC 30**

Jones, Nettie (Pearl) 1941- .... **CLC 34**
See also BW 2; CA 137; CAAS 20; CANR 88

Jones, Peter 1802-1856 .... **NNAL**

Jones, Preston 1936-1979 .... **CLC 10**
See also CA 73-76; 89-92; DLB 7

Jones, Robert F(rancis) 1934-2003 .... **CLC 7**
See also CA 49-52; CANR 2, 61, 118

Jones, Rod 1953- .... **CLC 50**
See also CA 128

Jones, Terence Graham Parry
1942- .... **CLC 21**
See Jones, Terry; Monty Python
See also CA 112; 116; CANR 35, 93; INT CA-116; SATA 127

Jones, Terry
See Jones, Terence Graham Parry
See also SATA 67; SATA-Brief 51

Jones, Thom (Douglas) 1945(?)- ..... **CLC 81; SSC 56**
See also CA 157; CANR 88; DLB 244

Jong, Erica 1942- .... **CLC 4, 6, 8, 18, 83**
See also AITN 1; AMWS 5; BEST 90:2; BPFB 2; CA 73-76; CANR 26, 52, 75, 132; CN 3, 4, 5, 6, 7; CP 2, 3, 4, 5, 6, 7; CPW; DA3; DAM NOV, POP; DLB 2, 5, 28, 152; FW; INT CANR-26; MAL 5; MTCW 1, 2; MTFW 2005

Jonson, Ben(jamin) 1572(?)-1637 . **DC 4; LC 6, 33, 110; PC 17; WLC**
See also BRW 1; BRWC 1; BRWR 1; CD-BLB Before 1660; DA; DAB; DAC; DAM DRAM, MST, POET; DFS 4, 10; DLB 62, 121; LMFS 1; PFS 23; RGEL 2; TEA; WLIT 3

Jordan, June (Meyer)
1936-2002 .. **BLCS; CLC 5, 11, 23, 114; PC 38**
See also AAYA 2, 66; AFAW 1, 2; BW 2, 3; CA 33-36R; 206; CANR 25, 70, 114; CLR 10; CP 3, 4, 5, 6, 7; CWP; DAM MULT, POET; DLB 38; GLL 2; LAIT 5; MAICYA 1, 2; MTCW 1; SATA 4, 136; YAW

Jordan, Neil (Patrick) 1950- .... **CLC 110**
   See also CA 124; 130; CANR 54; CN 4, 5,
   6, 7; GLL 2; INT CA-130
Jordan, Pat(rick M.) 1941- .... **CLC 37**
   See also CA 33-36R; CANR 121
Jorgensen, Ivar
   See Ellison, Harlan (Jay)
Jorgenson, Ivar
   See Silverberg, Robert
Joseph, George Ghevarughese .... **CLC 70**
Josephson, Mary
   See O'Doherty, Brian
Josephus, Flavius c. 37-100 .... **CMLC 13**
   See also AW 2; DLB 176
Josiah Allen's Wife
   See Holley, Marietta
Josipovici, Gabriel (David) 1940- ...... **CLC 6,**
   43, 153
   See also CA 37-40R, 224; CAAE 224;
   CAAS 8; CANR 47, 84; CN 3, 4, 5, 6, 7;
   DLB 14, 319
Joubert, Joseph 1754-1824 .... **NCLC 9**
Jouve, Pierre Jean 1887-1976 .... **CLC 47**
   See also CA 65-68; DLB 258; EWL 3
Jovine, Francesco 1902-1950 .... **TCLC 79**
   See also DLB 264; EWL 3
Joyce, James (Augustine Aloysius)
   1882-1941 .... **DC 16; PC 22; SSC 3, 26,**
   44, 64; TCLC 3, 8, 16, 35, 52, 159;
   WLC
   See also AAYA 42; BRW 7; BRWC 1;
   BRWR 1; BYA 11, 13; CA 104; 126; CD-
   BLB 1914-1945; DA; DA3; DAB; DAC;
   DAM MST, NOV, POET; DLB 10, 19,
   36, 162, 247; EWL 3; EXPN; EXPS;
   LAIT 3; LMFS 1, 2; MTCW 1, 2; MTFW
   2005; NFS 7; RGSF 2; SSFS 1, 19; TEA;
   WLIT 4
Jozsef, Attila 1905-1937 .... **TCLC 22**
   See also CA 116; 230; CDWLB 4; DLB
   215; EWL 3
Juana Ines de la Cruz, Sor
   1651(?)-1695 ...... **HLCS 1; LC 5; PC 24**
   See also DLB 305; FW; LAW; RGWL 2, 3;
   WLIT 1
Juana Inez de La Cruz, Sor
   See Juana Ines de la Cruz, Sor
Judd, Cyril
   See Kornbluth, C(yril) M.; Pohl, Frederik
Juenger, Ernst 1895-1998 .... **CLC 125**
   See Junger, Ernst
   See also CA 101; 167; CANR 21, 47, 106;
   DLB 56
Julian of Norwich 1342(?)-1416(?) . **LC 6, 52**
   See also DLB 146; LMFS 1
Julius Caesar 100B.C.-44B.C.
   See Caesar, Julius
   See also CDWLB 1; DLB 211
Junger, Ernst
   See Juenger, Ernst
   See also CDWLB 2; EWL 3; RGWL 2, 3
Junger, Sebastian 1962- .... **CLC 109**
   See also AAYA 28; CA 165; CANR 130;
   MTFW 2005
Juniper, Alex
   See Hospital, Janette Turner
Junius
   See Luxemburg, Rosa
Junzaburo, Nishiwaki
   See Nishiwaki, Junzaburo
   See also EWL 3
Just, Ward (Swift) 1935- .... **CLC 4, 27**
   See also CA 25-28R; CANR 32, 87; CN 6,
   7; INT CANR-32

Justice, Donald (Rodney)
   1925-2004 .... **CLC 6, 19, 102; PC 64**
   See also AMWS 7; CA 5-8R; 230; CANR
   26, 54, 74, 121, 122; CP 1, 2, 3, 4, 5, 6,
   7; CSW; DAM POET; DLBY 1983; EWL
   3; INT CANR-26; MAL 5; MTCW 2; PFS
   14; TCLE 1:1
Juvenal c. 60-c. 130 .... **CMLC 8**
   See also AW 2; CDWLB 1; DLB 211;
   RGWL 2, 3
Juvenis
   See Bourne, Randolph S(illiman)
K., Alice
   See Knapp, Caroline
Kabakov, Sasha .... **CLC 59**
Kabir 1398(?)-1448(?) .... **LC 109; PC 56**
   See also RGWL 2, 3
Kacew, Romain 1914-1980
   See Gary, Romain
   See also CA 108; 102
Kadare, Ismail 1936- .... **CLC 52, 190**
   See also CA 161; EWL 3; RGWL 3
Kadohata, Cynthia (Lynn)
   1956(?)- .... **CLC 59, 122**
   See also CA 140; CANR 124; SATA 155
Kafka, Franz 1883-1924 .. **SSC 5, 29, 35, 60;**
   TCLC 2, 6, 13, 29, 47, 53, 112; WLC
   See also AAYA 31; BPFB 2; CA 105; 126;
   CDWLB 2; DA; DA3; DAB; DAC; DAM
   MST, NOV; DLB 81; EW 9; EWL 3;
   EXPS; LATS 1:1; LMFS 1; MTCW 1, 2;
   MTFW 2005; NFS 7; RGSF 2; RGWL 1,
   3; SFW 4; SSFS 3, 7, 12; TWA
Kahanovitsch, Pinkhes
   See Der Nister
Kahn, Roger 1927- .... **CLC 30**
   See also CA 25-28R; CANR 44, 69; DLB
   171; SATA 37
Kain, Saul
   See Sassoon, Siegfried (Lorraine)
Kaiser, Georg 1878-1945 .... **TCLC 9**
   See also CA 106; 190; CDWLB 2; DLB
   124; EWL 3; LMFS 2; RGWL 2, 3
Kaledin, Sergei .... **CLC 59**
Kaletski, Alexander 1946- .... **CLC 39**
   See also CA 118; 143
Kalidasa fl. c. 400-455 .... **CMLC 9; PC 22**
   See also RGWL 2, 3
Kallman, Chester (Simon)
   1921-1975 .... **CLC 2**
   See also CA 45-48; 53-56; CANR 3; CP 1,
   2
Kaminsky, Melvin 1926-
   See Brooks, Mel
   See also CA 65-68; CANR 16; DFS 21
Kaminsky, Stuart M(elvin) 1934- ..... **CLC 59**
   See also CA 73-76; CANR 29, 53, 89;
   CMW 4
Kamo no Chomei 1153(?)-1216 .... **CMLC 66**
   See also DLB 203
Kamo no Nagaakira
   See Kamo no Chomei
Kandinsky, Wassily 1866-1944 .... **TCLC 92**
   See also AAYA 64; CA 118; 155
Kane, Francis
   See Robbins, Harold
Kane, Henry 1918-
   See Queen, Ellery
   See also CA 156; CMW 4
Kane, Paul
   See Simon, Paul (Frederick)
Kanin, Garson 1912-1999 .... **CLC 22**
   See also AITN 1; CA 5-8R; 177; CAD;
   CANR 7, 78; DLB 7; IDFW 3, 4
Kaniuk, Yoram 1930- .... **CLC 19**
   See also CA 134; DLB 299
Kant, Immanuel 1724-1804 ..... **NCLC 27, 67**
   See also DLB 94

Kantor, MacKinlay 1904-1977 .... **CLC 7**
   See also CA 61-64; 73-76; CANR 60, 63;
   CN 1, 2; DLB 9, 102; MAL 5; MTCW 2;
   RHW; TCWW 1, 2
Kanze Motokiyo
   See Zeami
Kaplan, David Michael 1946- .... **CLC 50**
   See also CA 187
Kaplan, James 1951- .... **CLC 59**
   See also CA 135; CANR 121
Karadzic, Vuk Stefanovic
   1787-1864 .... **NCLC 115**
   See also CDWLB 4; DLB 147
Karageorge, Michael
   See Anderson, Poul (William)
Karamzin, Nikolai Mikhailovich
   1766-1826 .... **NCLC 3**
   See also DLB 150; RGSF 2
Karapanou, Margarita 1946- .... **CLC 13**
   See also CA 101
Karinthy, Frigyes 1887-1938 .... **TCLC 47**
   See also CA 170; DLB 215; EWL 3
Karl, Frederick R(obert)
   1927-2004 .... **CLC 34**
   See also CA 5-8R; 226; CANR 3, 44, 143
Karr, Mary 1955- .... **CLC 188**
   See also AMWS 11; CA 151; CANR 100;
   MTFW 2005; NCFS 5
Kastel, Warren
   See Silverberg, Robert
Kataev, Evgeny Petrovich 1903-1942
   See Petrov, Evgeny
   See also CA 120
Kataphusin
   See Ruskin, John
Katz, Steve 1935- .... **CLC 47**
   See also CA 25-28R; CAAS 14, 64; CANR
   12; CN 4, 5, 6, 7; DLBY 1983
Kauffman, Janet 1945- .... **CLC 42**
   See also CA 117; CANR 43, 84; DLB 218;
   DLBY 1986
Kaufman, Bob (Garnell) 1925-1986 . **CLC 49**
   See also BG 1:3; BW 1; CA 41-44R; 118;
   CANR 22; CP 1; DLB 16, 41
Kaufman, George S. 1889-1961 ...... **CLC 38;**
   DC 17
   See also CA 108; 93-96; DAM DRAM;
   DFS 1, 10; DLB 7; INT CA-108; MTCW
   2; MTFW 2005; RGAL 4; TUS
Kaufman, Moises 1964- .... **DC 26**
   See also CA 211; DFS 22; MTFW 2005
Kaufman, Sue .... **CLC 3, 8**
   See Barondess, Sue K(aufman)
Kavafis, Konstantinos Petrou 1863-1933
   See Cavafy, C(onstantine) P(eter)
   See also CA 104
Kavan, Anna 1901-1968 .... **CLC 5, 13, 82**
   See also BRWS 7; CA 5-8R; CANR 6, 57;
   DLB 255; MTCW 1; RGEL 2; SFW 4
Kavanagh, Dan
   See Barnes, Julian (Patrick)
Kavanagh, Julie 1952- .... **CLC 119**
   See also CA 163
Kavanagh, Patrick (Joseph)
   1904-1967 .... **CLC 22; PC 33**
   See also BRWS 7; CA 123; 25-28R; DLB
   15, 20; EWL 3; MTCW 1; RGEL 2
Kawabata, Yasunari 1899-1972 ..... **CLC 2, 5,**
   9, 18, 107; SSC 17
   See Kawabata Yasunari
   See also CA 93-96; 33-36R; CANR 88;
   DAM MULT; MJW; MTCW 2; MTFW
   2005; RGSF 2; RGWL 2, 3
Kawabata Yasunari
   See Kawabata, Yasunari
   See also DLB 180; EWL 3

Khayyam, Omar 1048-1131 ... **CMLC 11; PC 8**
See Omar Khayyam
See also DA3; DAM POET; WLIT 6

Kherdian, David 1931- .... **CLC 6, 9**
See also AAYA 42; CA 21-24R, 192; CAAE 192; CAAS 2; CANR 39, 78; CLR 24; JRDA; LAIT 3; MAICYA 1, 2; SATA 16, 74; SATA-Essay 125

Khlebnikov, Velimir .... **TCLC 20**
See Khlebnikov, Viktor Vladimirovich
See also DLB 295; EW 10; EWL 3; RGWL 2, 3

Khlebnikov, Viktor Vladimirovich 1885-1922
See Khlebnikov, Velimir
See also CA 117; 217

Khodasevich, Vladislav (Felitsianovich)
1886-1939 .... **TCLC 15**
See also CA 115; DLB 317; EWL 3

Kielland, Alexander Lange
1849-1906 .... **TCLC 5**
See also CA 104

Kiely, Benedict 1919- ... **CLC 23, 43; SSC 58**
See also CA 1-4R; CANR 2, 84; CN 1, 2, 3, 4, 5, 6, 7; DLB 15, 319; TCLE 1:1

Kienzle, William X(avier)
1928-2001 .... **CLC 25**
See also CA 93-96; 203; CAAS 1; CANR 9, 31, 59, 111; CMW 4; DA3; DAM POP; INT CANR-31; MSW; MTCW 1, 2; MTFW 2005

Kierkegaard, Soren 1813-1855 ..... **NCLC 34, 78, 125**
See also DLB 300; EW 6; LMFS 2; RGWL 3; TWA

Kieslowski, Krzysztof 1941-1996 .... **CLC 120**
See also CA 147; 151

Killens, John Oliver 1916-1987 .... **CLC 10**
See also BW 2; CA 77-80; 123; CAAS 2; CANR 26; CN 1, 2, 3, 4; DLB 33; EWL 3

Killigrew, Anne 1660-1685 .... **LC 4, 73**
See also DLB 131

Killigrew, Thomas 1612-1683 .... **LC 57**
See also DLB 58; RGEL 2

Kim
See Simenon, Georges (Jacques Christian)

Kincaid, Jamaica 1949- ...... **BLC 2; CLC 43, 68, 137; SSC 72**
See also AAYA 13, 56; AFAW 2; AMWS 7; BRWS 7; BW 2, 3; CA 125; CANR 47, 59, 95, 133; CDALBS; CDWLB 3; CLR 63; CN 4, 5, 6, 7; DA3; DAM MULT, NOV; DLB 157, 227; DNFS 1; EWL 3; EXPS; FW; LATS 1:2; LMFS 2; MAL 5; MTCW 2; MTFW 2005; NCFS 1; NFS 3; SSFS 5, 7; TUS; WWE 1; YAW

King, Francis (Henry) 1923- .... **CLC 8, 53, 145**
See also CA 1-4R; CANR 1, 33, 86; CN 1, 2, 3, 4, 5, 6, 7; DAM NOV; DLB 15, 139; MTCW 1

King, Kennedy
See Brown, George Douglas

King, Martin Luther, Jr. 1929-1968 . **BLC 2; CLC 83; WLCS**
See also BW 2, 3; CA 25-28; CANR 27, 44; CAP 2; DA; DA3; DAB; DAC; DAM MST, MULT; LAIT 5; LATS 1:2; MTCW 1, 2; MTFW 2005; SATA 14

King, Stephen 1947- .... **CLC 12, 26, 37, 61, 113; SSC 17, 55**
See also AAYA 1, 17; AMWS 5; BEST 90:1; BPFB 2; CA 61-64; CANR 1, 30, 52, 76, 119, 134; CN 7; CPW; DA3; DAM NOV, POP; DLB 143; DLBY 1980; HGG; JRDA; LAIT 5; MTCW 1, 2; MTFW 2005; RGAL 4; SATA 9, 55, 161; SUFW 1, 2; WYAS 1; YAW

King, Stephen Edwin
See King, Stephen

King, Steve
See King, Stephen

King, Thomas 1943- .... **CLC 89, 171; NNAL**
See also CA 144; CANR 95; CCA 1; CN 6, 7; DAC; DAM MULT; DLB 175; SATA 96

Kingman, Lee .... **CLC 17**
See Natti, (Mary) Lee
See also CWRI 5; SAAS 3; SATA 1, 67

Kingsley, Charles 1819-1875 .... **NCLC 35**
See also CLR 77; DLB 21, 32, 163, 178, 190; FANT; MAICYA 2; MAICYAS 1; RGEL 2; WCH; YABC 2

Kingsley, Henry 1830-1876 .... **NCLC 107**
See also DLB 21, 230; RGEL 2

Kingsley, Sidney 1906-1995 .... **CLC 44**
See also CA 85-88; 147; CAD; DFS 14, 19; DLB 7; MAL 5; RGAL 4

Kingsolver, Barbara 1955- .... **CLC 55, 81, 130, 216**
See also AAYA 15; AMWS 7; CA 129; 134; CANR 60, 96, 133; CDALBS; CN 7; CPW; CSW; DA3; DAM POP; DLB 206; INT CA-134; LAIT 5; MTCW 2; MTFW 2005; NFS 5, 10, 12; RGAL 4; TCLE 1:1

Kingston, Maxine (Ting Ting) Hong
1940- .... **AAL; CLC 12, 19, 58, 121; WLCS**
See also AAYA 8, 55; AMWS 5; BPFB 2; CA 69-72; CANR 13, 38, 74, 87, 128; CDALBS; CN 6, 7; DA3; DAM MULT, NOV; DLB 173, 212, 312; DLBY 1980; EWL 3; FL 1:6; FW; INT CANR-13; LAIT 5; MAL 5; MAWW; MTCW 1, 2; MTFW 2005; NFS 6; RGAL 4; SATA 53; SSFS 3; TCWW 2

Kinnell, Galway 1927- ..... **CLC 1, 2, 3, 5, 13, 29, 129; PC 26**
See also AMWS 3; CA 9-12R; CANR 10, 34, 66, 116, 138; CP 1, 2, 3, 4, 5, 6, 7; DLB 5; DLBY 1987; EWL 3; INT CANR-34; MAL 5; MTCW 1, 2; MTFW 2005; PAB; PFS 9; RGAL 4; TCLE 1:1; WP

Kinsella, Thomas 1928- .... **CLC 4, 19, 138; PC 69**
See also BRWS 5; CA 17-20R; CANR 15, 122; CP 1, 2, 3, 4, 5, 6, 7; DLB 27; EWL 3; MTCW 1, 2; MTFW 2005; RGEL 2; TEA

Kinsella, W(illiam) P(atrick) 1935- . **CLC 27, 43, 166**
See also AAYA 7, 60; BPFB 2; CA 97-100; 222; CAAE 222; CAAS 7; CANR 21, 35, 66, 75, 129; CN 4, 5, 6, 7; CPW; DAC; DAM NOV, POP; FANT; INT CANR-21; LAIT 5; MTCW 1, 2; MTFW 2005; NFS 15; RGSF 2

Kinsey, Alfred C(harles)
1894-1956 .... **TCLC 91**
See also CA 115; 170; MTCW 2

Kipling, (Joseph) Rudyard 1865-1936 . **PC 3; SSC 5, 54; TCLC 8, 17, 167; WLC**
See also AAYA 32; BRW 6; BRWC 1, 2; BYA 4; CA 105; 120; CANR 33; CDBLB 1890-1914; CLR 39, 65; CWRI 5; DA; DA3; DAB; DAC; DAM MST, POET; DLB 19, 34, 141, 156; EWL 3; EXPS; FANT; LAIT 3; LMFS 1; MAICYA 1, 2; MTCW 1, 2; MTFW 2005; NFS 21; PFS 22; RGEL 2; RGSF 2; SATA 100; SFW 4; SSFS 8, 21; SUFW 1; TEA; WCH; WLIT 4; YABC 2

Kircher, Athanasius 1602-1680 .... **LC 121**
See also DLB 164

Kirk, Russell (Amos) 1918-1994 .. **TCLC 119**
See also AITN 1; CA 1-4R; 145; CAAS 9; CANR 1, 20, 60; HGG; INT CANR-20; MTCW 1, 2

Kirkham, Dinah
See Card, Orson Scott

Kirkland, Caroline M. 1801-1864 . **NCLC 85**
See also DLB 3, 73, 74, 250, 254; DLBD 13

Kirkup, James 1918- .... **CLC 1**
See also CA 1-4R; CAAS 4; CANR 2; CP 1, 2, 3, 4, 5, 6, 7; DLB 27; SATA 12

Kirkwood, James 1930(?)-1989 .... **CLC 9**
See also AITN 2; CA 1-4R; 128; CANR 6, 40; GLL 2

Kirsch, Sarah 1935- .... **CLC 176**
See also CA 178; CWW 2; DLB 75; EWL 3

Kirshner, Sidney
See Kingsley, Sidney

Kis, Danilo 1935-1989 .... **CLC 57**
See also CA 109; 118; 129; CANR 61; CD-WLB 4; DLB 181; EWL 3; MTCW 1; RGSF 2; RGWL 2, 3

Kissinger, Henry A(lfred) 1923- ..... **CLC 137**
See also CA 1-4R; CANR 2, 33, 66, 109; MTCW 1

Kivi, Aleksis 1834-1872 .... **NCLC 30**

Kizer, Carolyn (Ashley) 1925- ... **CLC 15, 39, 80; PC 66**
See also CA 65-68; CAAS 5; CANR 24, 70, 134; CP 1, 2, 3, 4, 5, 6, 7; CWP; DAM POET; DLB 5, 169; EWL 3; MAL 5; MTCW 2; MTFW 2005; PFS 18; TCLE 1:1

Klabund 1890-1928 .... **TCLC 44**
See also CA 162; DLB 66

Klappert, Peter 1942- .... **CLC 57**
See also CA 33-36R; CSW; DLB 5

Klein, A(braham) M(oses)
1909-1972 .... **CLC 19**
See also CA 101; 37-40R; CP 1; DAB; DAC; DAM MST; DLB 68; EWL 3; RGEL 2

Klein, Joe
See Klein, Joseph

Klein, Joseph 1946- .... **CLC 154**
See also CA 85-88; CANR 55

Klein, Norma 1938-1989 .... **CLC 30**
See also AAYA 2, 35; BPFB 2; BYA 6, 7, 8; CA 41-44R; 128; CANR 15, 37; CLR 2, 19; INT CANR-15; JRDA; MAICYA 1, 2; SAAS 1; SATA 7, 57; WYA; YAW

Klein, T(heodore) E(ibon) D(onald)
1947- .... **CLC 34**
See also CA 119; CANR 44, 75; HGG

Kleist, Heinrich von 1777-1811 ...... **NCLC 2, 37; SSC 22**
See also CDWLB 2; DAM DRAM; DLB 90; EW 5; RGSF 2; RGWL 2, 3

Klima, Ivan 1931- .... **CLC 56, 172**
See also CA 25-28R; CANR 17, 50, 91; CDWLB 4; CWW 2; DAM NOV; DLB 232; EWL 3; RGWL 3

Klimentev, Andrei Platonovich
See Klimentov, Andrei Platonovich

Klimentov, Andrei Platonovich
1899-1951 .... **SSC 42; TCLC 14**
See Platonov, Andrei Platonovich; Platonov, Andrey Platonovich
See also CA 108; 232

Klinger, Friedrich Maximilian von
1752-1831 .... **NCLC 1**
See also DLB 94

Klingsor the Magician
See Hartmann, Sadakichi

Klopstock, Friedrich Gottlieb
1724-1803 .... **NCLC 11**
See also DLB 97; EW 4; RGWL 2, 3

Kluge, Alexander 1932- .... **SSC 61**
See also CA 81-84; DLB 75

Knapp, Caroline 1959-2002 .... **CLC 99**
See also CA 154; 207

Limonov, Edward 1944- .... **CLC 67**
See Limonov, Eduard
See also CA 137

Lin, Frank
See Atherton, Gertrude (Franklin Horn)

Lin, Yutang 1895-1976 .... **TCLC 149**
See also CA 45-48; 65-68; CANR 2; RGAL
4

Lincoln, Abraham 1809-1865 .... **NCLC 18**
See also LAIT 2

Lind, Jakov .... **CLC 1, 2, 4, 27, 82**
See Landwirth, Heinz
See also CAAS 4; DLB 299; EWL 3

Lindbergh, Anne (Spencer) Morrow
1906-2001 .... **CLC 82**
See also BPFB 2; CA 17-20R; 193; CANR
16, 73; DAM NOV; MTCW 1, 2; MTFW
2005; SATA 33; SATA-Obit 125; TUS

Lindsay, David 1878(?)-1945 .... **TCLC 15**
See also CA 113; 187; DLB 255; FANT;
SFW 4; SUFW 1

Lindsay, (Nicholas) Vachel
1879-1931 .... **PC 23; TCLC 17; WLC**
See also AMWS 1; CA 114; 135; CANR
79; CDALB 1865-1917; DA; DA3; DAC;
DAM MST, POET; DLB 54; EWL 3;
EXPP; MAL 5; RGAL 4; SATA 40; WP

Linke-Poot
See Doeblin, Alfred

Linney, Romulus 1930- .... **CLC 51**
See also CA 1-4R; CAD; CANR 40, 44,
79; CD 5, 6; CSW; RGAL 4

Linton, Eliza Lynn 1822-1898 .... **NCLC 41**
See also DLB 18

Li Po 701-763 .... **CMLC 2; PC 29**
See also PFS 20; WP

Lipsius, Justus 1547-1606 .... **LC 16**

Lipsyte, Robert (Michael) 1938- ...... **CLC 21**
See also AAYA 7, 45; CA 17-20R; CANR
8, 57; CLR 23, 76; DA; DAC; DAM
MST, NOV; JRDA; LAIT 5; MAICYA 1,
2; SATA 5, 68, 113, 161; WYA; YAW

Lish, Gordon (Jay) 1934- ... **CLC 45; SSC 18**
See also CA 113; 117; CANR 79; DLB 130;
INT CA-117

Lispector, Clarice 1925(?)-1977 .... **CLC 43;**
HLCS 2; SSC 34
See also CA 139; 116; CANR 71; CDWLB
3; DLB 113, 307; DNFS 1; EWL 3; FW;
HW 2; LAW; RGSF 2; RGWL 2, 3; WLIT
1

Littell, Robert 1935(?)- .... **CLC 42**
See also CA 109; 112; CANR 64, 115;
CMW 4

Little, Malcolm 1925-1965
See Malcolm X
See also BW 1, 3; CA 125; 111; CANR 82;
DA; DA3; DAB; DAC; DAM MST,
MULT; MTCW 1, 2; MTFW 2005

Littlewit, Humphrey Gent.
See Lovecraft, H(oward) P(hillips)

Litwos
See Sienkiewicz, Henryk (Adam Alexander
Pius)

Liu, E. 1857-1909 .... **TCLC 15**
See also CA 115; 190

Lively, Penelope 1933- .... **CLC 32, 50**
See also BPFB 2; CA 41-44R; CANR 29,
67, 79, 131; CLR 7; CN 5, 6, 7; CWRI 5;
DAM NOV; DLB 14, 161, 207; FANT;
JRDA; MAICYA 1, 2; MTCW 1, 2;
MTFW 2005; SATA 7, 60, 101, 164; TEA

Lively, Penelope Margaret
See Lively, Penelope

Livesay, Dorothy (Kathleen)
1909-1996 .... **CLC 4, 15, 79**
See also AITN 2; CA 25-28R; CAAS 8;
CANR 36, 67; CP 1, 2, 3, 4; DAC; DAM
MST, POET; DLB 68; FW; MTCW 1;
RGEL 2; TWA

Livy c. 59B.C.-c. 12 .... **CMLC 11**
See also AW 2; CDWLB 1; DLB 211;
RGWL 2, 3

Lizardi, Jose Joaquin Fernandez de
1776-1827 .... **NCLC 30**
See also LAW

Llewellyn, Richard
See Llewellyn Lloyd, Richard Dafydd Viv-
ian
See also DLB 15

Llewellyn Lloyd, Richard Dafydd Vivian
1906-1983 .... **CLC 7, 80**
See Llewellyn, Richard
See also CA 53-56; 111; CANR 7, 71;
SATA 11; SATA-Obit 37

Llosa, (Jorge) Mario (Pedro) Vargas
See Vargas Llosa, (Jorge) Mario (Pedro)
See also RGWL 3

Llosa, Mario Vargas
See Vargas Llosa, (Jorge) Mario (Pedro)

Lloyd, Manda
See Mander, (Mary) Jane

Lloyd Webber, Andrew 1948-
See Webber, Andrew Lloyd
See also AAYA 1, 38; CA 116; 149; DAM
DRAM; SATA 56

Llull, Ramon c. 1235-c. 1316 .... **CMLC 12**

Lobb, Ebenezer
See Upward, Allen

Locke, Alain (Le Roy)
1886-1954 .... **BLCS; HR 1:3; TCLC 43**
See also AMWS 14; BW 1, 3; CA 106; 124;
CANR 79; DLB 51; LMFS 2; MAL 5;
RGAL 4

Locke, John 1632-1704 .... **LC 7, 35**
See also DLB 31, 101, 213, 252; RGEL 2;
WLIT 3

Locke-Elliott, Sumner
See Elliott, Sumner Locke

Lockhart, John Gibson 1794-1854 .. **NCLC 6**
See also DLB 110, 116, 144

Lockridge, Ross (Franklin), Jr.
1914-1948 .... **TCLC 111**
See also CA 108; 145; CANR 79; DLB 143;
DLBY 1980; MAL 5; RGAL 4; RHW

Lockwood, Robert
See Johnson, Robert

Lodge, David (John) 1935- .... **CLC 36, 141**
See also BEST 90:1; BRWS 4; CA 17-20R;
CANR 19, 53, 92, 139; CN 1, 2, 3, 4, 5,
6, 7; CPW; DAM POP; DLB 14, 194;
EWL 3; INT CANR-19; MTCW 1, 2;
MTFW 2005

Lodge, Thomas 1558-1625 .... **LC 41**
See also DLB 172; RGEL 2

Loewinsohn, Ron(ald William)
1937- .... **CLC 52**
See also CA 25-28R; CANR 71; CP 1, 2, 3,
4

Logan, Jake
See Smith, Martin Cruz

Logan, John (Burton) 1923-1987 .... **CLC 5**
See also CA 77-80; 124; CANR 45; CP 1,
2, 3, 4; DLB 5

Lo Kuan-chung 1330(?)-1400(?) .... **LC 12**

Lombard, Nap
See Johnson, Pamela Hansford

Lombard, Peter 1100(?)-1160(?) ... **CMLC 72**

London, Jack 1876-1916 .. **SSC 4, 49; TCLC**
9, 15, 39; WLC
See London, John Griffith
See also AAYA 13; AITN 2; AMW; BPFB
2; BYA 4, 13; CDALB 1865-1917; DLB
8, 12, 78, 212; EWL 3; EXPS; LAIT 3;
MAL 5; NFS 8; RGAL 4; RGSF 2; SATA
18; SFW 4; SSFS 7; TCWW 1, 2; TUS;
WYA; YAW

London, John Griffith 1876-1916
See London, Jack
See also CA 110; 119; CANR 73; DA; DA3;
DAB; DAC; DAM MST, NOV; JRDA;
MAICYA 1, 2; MTCW 1, 2; MTFW 2005;
NFS 19

Long, Emmett
See Leonard, Elmore (John, Jr.)

Longbaugh, Harry
See Goldman, William (W.)

Longfellow, Henry Wadsworth
1807-1882 .... **NCLC 2, 45, 101, 103; PC**
30; WLCS
See also AMW; AMWR 2; CDALB 1640-
1865; CLR 99; DA; DA3; DAB; DAC;
DAM MST, POET; DLB 1, 59, 235;
EXPP; PAB; PFS 2, 7, 17; RGAL 4;
SATA 19; TUS; WP

Longinus c. 1st cent. - .... **CMLC 27**
See also AW 2; DLB 176

Longley, Michael 1939- .... **CLC 29**
See also BRWS 8; CA 102; CP 1, 2, 3, 4, 5,
6, 7; DLB 40

Longstreet, Augustus Baldwin
1790-1870 .... **NCLC 159**
See also DLB 3, 11, 74, 248; RGAL 4

Longus fl. c. 2nd cent. - .... **CMLC 7**

Longway, A. Hugh
See Lang, Andrew

Lonnbohm, Armas Eino Leopold 1878-1926
See Leino, Eino
See also CA 123

Lonnrot, Elias 1802-1884 .... **NCLC 53**
See also EFS 1

Lonsdale, Roger ed. .... **CLC 65**

Lopate, Phillip 1943- .... **CLC 29**
See also CA 97-100; CANR 88; DLBY
1980; INT CA-97-100

Lopez, Barry (Holstun) 1945- .... **CLC 70**
See also AAYA 9, 63; ANW; CA 65-68;
CANR 7, 23, 47, 68, 92; DLB 256, 275;
INT CANR-7, -23; MTCW 1; RGAL 4;
SATA 67

Lopez de Mendoza, Inigo
See Santillana, Inigo Lopez de Mendoza,
Marques de

Lopez Portillo (y Pacheco), Jose
1920-2004 .... **CLC 46**
See also CA 129; 224; HW 1

Lopez y Fuentes, Gregorio
1897(?)-1966 .... **CLC 32**
See also CA 131; EWL 3; HW 1

Lorca, Federico Garcia
See Garcia Lorca, Federico
See also DFS 4; EW 11; PFS 20; RGWL 2,
3; WP

Lord, Audre
See Lorde, Audre (Geraldine)
See also EWL 3

Lord, Bette Bao 1938- .... **AAL; CLC 23**
See also BEST 90:3; BPFB 2; CA 107;
CANR 41, 79; INT CA-107; SATA 58

Lord Auch
See Bataille, Georges

Lord Brooke
See Greville, Fulke

Lord Byron
See Byron, George Gordon (Noel)

MacDiarmid, Hugh .... **CLC 2, 4, 11, 19, 63; PC 9**
See Grieve, C(hristopher) M(urray)
See also CDBLB 1945-1960; CP 1, 2; DLB 20; EWL 3; RGEL 2

MacDonald, Anson
See Heinlein, Robert A(nson)

Macdonald, Cynthia 1928- .... **CLC 13, 19**
See also CA 49-52; CANR 4, 44, 146; DLB 105

MacDonald, George 1824-1905 .... **TCLC 9, 113**
See also AAYA 57; BYA 5; CA 106; 137; CANR 80; CLR 67; DLB 18, 163, 178; FANT; MAICYA 1, 2; RGEL 2; SATA 33, 100; SFW 4; SUFW; WCH

Macdonald, John
See Millar, Kenneth

MacDonald, John D(ann)
1916-1986 .... **CLC 3, 27, 44**
See also BPFB 2; CA 1-4R; 121; CANR 1, 19, 60; CMW 4; CPW; DAM NOV, POP; DLB 8, 306; DLBY 1986; MSW; MTCW 1, 2; MTFW 2005; SFW 4

Macdonald, John Ross
See Millar, Kenneth

Macdonald, Ross ..... **CLC 1, 2, 3, 14, 34, 41**
See Millar, Kenneth
See also AMWS 4; BPFB 2; CN 1, 2, 3; DLBD 6; MSW; RGAL 4

MacDougal, John
See Blish, James (Benjamin)

MacDougal, John
See Blish, James (Benjamin)

MacDowell, John
See Parks, Tim(othy Harold)

MacEwen, Gwendolyn (Margaret)
1941-1987 .... **CLC 13, 55**
See also CA 9-12R; 124; CANR 7, 22; CP 1, 2, 3, 4; DLB 53, 251; SATA 50; SATA-Obit 55

Macha, Karel Hynek 1810-1846 .... **NCLC 46**

Machado (y Ruiz), Antonio
1875-1939 .... **TCLC 3**
See also CA 104; 174; DLB 108; EW 9; EWL 3; HW 2; PFS 23; RGWL 2, 3

Machado de Assis, Joaquim Maria
1839-1908 .... **BLC 2; HLCS 2; SSC 24; TCLC 10**
See also CA 107; 153; CANR 91; DLB 307; LAW; RGSF 2; RGWL 2, 3; TWA; WLIT 1

Machaut, Guillaume de c.
1300-1377 .... **CMLC 64**
See also DLB 208

Machen, Arthur .... **SSC 20; TCLC 4**
See Jones, Arthur Llewellyn
See also CA 179; DLB 156, 178; RGEL 2; SUFW 1

Machiavelli, Niccolo 1469-1527 ... **DC 16; LC 8, 36; WLCS**
See also AAYA 58; DA; DAB; DAC; DAM MST; EW 2; LAIT 1; LMFS 1; NFS 9; RGWL 2, 3; TWA; WLIT 7

MacInnes, Colin 1914-1976 .... **CLC 4, 23**
See also CA 69-72; 65-68; CANR 21; CN 1, 2; DLB 14; MTCW 1, 2; RGEL 2; RHW

MacInnes, Helen (Clark)
1907-1985 .... **CLC 27, 39**
See also BPFB 2; CA 1-4R; 117; CANR 1, 28, 58; CMW 4; CN 1, 2; CPW; DAM POP; DLB 87; MSW; MTCW 1, 2; MTFW 2005; SATA 22; SATA-Obit 44

Mackay, Mary 1855-1924
See Corelli, Marie
See also CA 118; 177; FANT; RHW

Mackay, Shena 1944- .... **CLC 195**
See also CA 104; CANR 88, 139; DLB 231, 319; MTFW 2005

Mackenzie, Compton (Edward Montague)
1883-1972 .... **CLC 18; TCLC 116**
See also CA 21-22; 37-40R; CAP 2; CN 1; DLB 34, 100; RGEL 2

Mackenzie, Henry 1745-1831 .... **NCLC 41**
See also DLB 39; RGEL 2

Mackey, Nathaniel (Ernest) 1947- .... **PC 49**
See also CA 153; CANR 114; CP 7; DLB 169

MacKinnon, Catharine A. 1946- .... **CLC 181**
See also CA 128; 132; CANR 73, 140; FW; MTCW 2; MTFW 2005

Mackintosh, Elizabeth 1896(?)-1952
See Tey, Josephine
See also CA 110; CMW 4

MacLaren, James
See Grieve, C(hristopher) M(urray)

MacLaverty, Bernard 1942- .... **CLC 31**
See also CA 116; 118; CANR 43, 88; CN 5, 6, 7; DLB 267; INT CA-118; RGSF 2

MacLean, Alistair (Stuart)
1922(?)-1987 .... **CLC 3, 13, 50, 63**
See also CA 57-60; 121; CANR 28, 61; CMW 4; CP 2, 3, 4, 5, 6, 7; CPW; DAM POP; DLB 276; MTCW 1; SATA 23; SATA-Obit 50; TCWW 2

Maclean, Norman (Fitzroy)
1902-1990 .... **CLC 78; SSC 13**
See also AMWS 14; CA 102; 132; CANR 49; CPW; DAM POP; DLB 206; TCWW 2

MacLeish, Archibald 1892-1982 ... **CLC 3, 8, 14, 68; PC 47**
See also AMW; CA 9-12R; 106; CAD; CANR 33, 63; CDALBS; CP 1, 2; DAM POET; DFS 15; DLB 4, 7, 45; DLBY 1982; EWL 3; EXPP; MAL 5; MTCW 1, 2; MTFW 2005; PAB; PFS 5; RGAL 4; TUS

MacLennan, (John) Hugh
1907-1990 .... **CLC 2, 14, 92**
See also CA 5-8R; 142; CANR 33; CN 1, 2, 3, 4; DAC; DAM MST; DLB 68; EWL 3; MTCW 1, 2; MTFW 2005; RGEL 2; TWA

MacLeod, Alistair 1936- .. **CLC 56, 165; SSC 90**
See also CA 123; CCA 1; DAC; DAM MST; DLB 60; MTCW 2; MTFW 2005; RGSF 2; TCLE 1:2

Macleod, Fiona
See Sharp, William
See also RGEL 2; SUFW

MacNeice, (Frederick) Louis
1907-1963 .... **CLC 1, 4, 10, 53; PC 61**
See also BRW 7; CA 85-88; CANR 61; DAB; DAM POET; DLB 10, 20; EWL 3; MTCW 1, 2; MTFW 2005; RGEL 2

MacNeill, Dand
See Fraser, George MacDonald

Macpherson, James 1736-1796 .... **LC 29**
See Ossian
See also BRWS 8; DLB 109; RGEL 2

Macpherson, (Jean) Jay 1931- .... **CLC 14**
See also CA 5-8R; CANR 90; CP 1, 2, 3, 4, 5, 6, 7; CWP; DLB 53

Macrobius fl. 430- .... **CMLC 48**

MacShane, Frank 1927-1999 .... **CLC 39**
See also CA 9-12R; 186; CANR 3, 33; DLB 111

Macumber, Mari
See Sandoz, Mari(e Susette)

Madach, Imre 1823-1864 .... **NCLC 19**

Madden, (Jerry) David 1933- .... **CLC 5, 15**
See also CA 1-4R; CAAS 3; CANR 4, 45; CN 3, 4, 5, 6, 7; CSW; DLB 6; MTCW 1

Maddern, Al(an)
See Ellison, Harlan (Jay)

Madhubuti, Haki R. 1942- ... **BLC 2; CLC 6, 73; PC 5**
See Lee, Don L.
See also BW 2, 3; CA 73-76; CANR 24, 51, 73, 139; CP 5, 6, 7; CSW; DAM MULT, POET; DLB 5, 41; DLBD 8; EWL 3; MAL 5; MTCW 2; MTFW 2005; RGAL 4

Madison, James 1751-1836 .... **NCLC 126**
See also DLB 37

Maepenn, Hugh
See Kuttner, Henry

Maepenn, K. H.
See Kuttner, Henry

Maeterlinck, Maurice 1862-1949 ..... **TCLC 3**
See also CA 104; 136; CANR 80; DAM DRAM; DLB 192; EW 8; EWL 3; GFL 1789 to the Present; LMFS 2; RGWL 2, 3; SATA 66; TWA

Maginn, William 1794-1842 .... **NCLC 8**
See also DLB 110, 159

Mahapatra, Jayanta 1928- .... **CLC 33**
See also CA 73-76; CAAS 9; CANR 15, 33, 66, 87; CP 4, 5, 6, 7; DAM MULT

Mahfouz, Naguib (Abdel Aziz Al-Sabilgi)
1911(?)- .... **CLC 153; SSC 66**
See Mahfuz, Najib (Abdel Aziz al-Sabilgi)
See also AAYA 49; BEST 89:2; CA 128; CANR 55, 101; DA3; DAM NOV; MTCW 1, 2; MTFW 2005; RGWL 2, 3; SSFS 9

Mahfuz, Najib (Abdel Aziz al-Sabilgi)
.... **CLC 52, 55**
See Mahfouz, Naguib (Abdel Aziz Al-Sabilgi)
See also AFW; CWW 2; DLBY 1988; EWL 3; RGSF 2; WLIT 6

Mahon, Derek 1941- .... **CLC 27; PC 60**
See also BRWS 6; CA 113; 128; CANR 88; CP 1, 2, 3, 4, 5, 6, 7; DLB 40; EWL 3

Maiakovskii, Vladimir
See Mayakovski, Vladimir (Vladimirovich)
See also IDTP; RGWL 2, 3

Mailer, Norman (Kingsley) 1923- . **CLC 1, 2, 3, 4, 5, 8, 11, 14, 28, 39, 74, 111**
See also AAYA 31; AITN 2; AMW; AMWC 2; AMWR 2; BPFB 2; CA 9-12R; CABS 1; CANR 28, 74, 77, 130; CDALB 1968-1988; CN 1, 2, 3, 4, 5, 6, 7; CPW; DA; DA3; DAB; DAC; DAM MST, NOV, POP; DLB 2, 16, 28, 185, 278; DLBD 3; DLBY 1980, 1983; EWL 3; MAL 5; MTCW 1, 2; MTFW 2005; NFS 10; RGAL 4; TUS

Maillet, Antonine 1929- .... **CLC 54, 118**
See also CA 115; 120; CANR 46, 74, 77, 134; CCA 1; CWW 2; DAC; DLB 60; INT CA-120; MTCW 2; MTFW 2005

Maimonides, Moses 1135-1204 ..... **CMLC 76**
See also DLB 115

Mais, Roger 1905-1955 .... **TCLC 8**
See also BW 1, 3; CA 105; 124; CANR 82; CDWLB 3; DLB 125; EWL 3; MTCW 1; RGEL 2

Maistre, Joseph 1753-1821 .... **NCLC 37**
See also GFL 1789 to the Present

Maitland, Frederic William
1850-1906 .... **TCLC 65**

Maitland, Sara (Louise) 1950- .... **CLC 49**
See also BRWS 11; CA 69-72; CANR 13, 59; DLB 271; FW

Major, Clarence 1936- ... **BLC 2; CLC 3, 19, 48**
See also AFAW 2; BW 2, 3; CA 21-24R; CAAS 6; CANR 13, 25, 53, 82; CN 3, 4, 5, 6, 7; CP 2, 3, 4, 5, 6, 7; CSW; DAM MULT; DLB 33; EWL 3; MAL 5; MSW

Major, Kevin (Gerald) 1949- .... **CLC 26**
See also AAYA 16; CA 97-100; CANR 21, 38, 112; CLR 11; DAC; DLB 60; INT CANR-21; JRDA; MAICYA 1, 2; MAICYAS 1; SATA 32, 82, 134; WYA; YAW

Maki, James
See Ozu, Yasujiro

Makine, Andrei 1957- .... **CLC 198**
See also CA 176; CANR 103; MTFW 2005

Malabaila, Damiano
See Levi, Primo

Malamud, Bernard 1914-1986 .. **CLC 1, 2, 3, 5, 8, 9, 11, 18, 27, 44, 78, 85; SSC 15; TCLC 129; WLC**
See also AAYA 16; AMWS 1; BPFB 2; BYA 15; CA 5-8R; 118; CABS 1; CANR 28, 62, 114; CDALB 1941-1968; CN 1, 2, 3, 4; CPW; DA; DA3; DAB; DAC; DAM MST, NOV, POP; DLB 2, 28, 152; DLBY 1980, 1986; EWL 3; EXPS; LAIT 4; LATS 1:1; MAL 5; MTCW 1, 2; MTFW 2005; NFS 4, 9; RGAL 4; RGSF 2; SSFS 8, 13, 16; TUS

Malan, Herman
See Bosman, Herman Charles; Bosman, Herman Charles

Malaparte, Curzio 1898-1957 .... **TCLC 52**
See also DLB 264

Malcolm, Dan
See Silverberg, Robert

Malcolm, Janet 1934- .... **CLC 201**
See also CA 123; CANR 89; NCFS 1

Malcolm X .... **BLC 2; CLC 82, 117; WLCS**
See Little, Malcolm
See also LAIT 5; NCFS 3

Malherbe, Francois de 1555-1628 .... **LC 5**
See also GFL Beginnings to 1789

Mallarme, Stephane 1842-1898 ...... **NCLC 4, 41; PC 4**
See also DAM POET; DLB 217; EW 7; GFL 1789 to the Present; LMFS 2; RGWL 2, 3; TWA

Mallet-Joris, Francoise 1930- .... **CLC 11**
See also CA 65-68; CANR 17; CWW 2; DLB 83; EWL 3; GFL 1789 to the Present

Malley, Ern
See McAuley, James Phillip

Mallon, Thomas 1951- .... **CLC 172**
See also CA 110; CANR 29, 57, 92

Mallowan, Agatha Christie
See Christie, Agatha (Mary Clarissa)

Maloff, Saul 1922- .... **CLC 5**
See also CA 33-36R

Malone, Louis
See MacNeice, (Frederick) Louis

Malone, Michael (Christopher)
1942- .... **CLC 43**
See also CA 77-80; CANR 14, 32, 57, 114

Malory, Sir Thomas 1410(?)-1471(?) . **LC 11, 88; WLCS**
See also BRW 1; BRWR 2; CDBLB Before 1660; DA; DAB; DAC; DAM MST; DLB 146; EFS 2; RGEL 2; SATA 59; SATA-Brief 33; TEA; WLIT 3

Malouf, (George Joseph) David
1934- .... **CLC 28, 86**
See also CA 124; CANR 50, 76; CN 3, 4, 5, 6, 7; CP 1, 3, 4, 5, 6, 7; DLB 289; EWL 3; MTCW 2; MTFW 2005

Malraux, (Georges-)Andre
1901-1976 ...... **CLC 1, 4, 9, 13, 15, 57**
See also BPFB 2; CA 21-22; 69-72; CANR 34, 58; CAP 2; DA3; DAM NOV; DLB 72; EW 12; EWL 3; GFL 1789 to the Present; MTCW 1, 2; MTFW 2005; RGWL 2, 3; TWA

Malthus, Thomas Robert
1766-1834 .... **NCLC 145**
See also DLB 107, 158; RGEL 2

Malzberg, Barry N(athaniel) 1939- ... **CLC 7**
See also CA 61-64; CAAS 4; CANR 16; CMW 4; DLB 8; SFW 4

Mamet, David (Alan) 1947- .. **CLC 9, 15, 34, 46, 91, 166; DC 4, 24**
See also AAYA 3, 60; AMWS 14; CA 81-84; CABS 3; CAD; CANR 15, 41, 67, 72, 129; CD 5, 6; DA3; DAM DRAM; DFS 2, 3, 6, 12, 15; DLB 7; EWL 3; IDFW 4; MAL 5; MTCW 1, 2; MTFW 2005; RGAL 4

Mamoulian, Rouben (Zachary)
1897-1987 .... **CLC 16**
See also CA 25-28R; 124; CANR 85

Mandelshtam, Osip
See Mandelstam, Osip (Emilievich)
See also EW 10; EWL 3; RGWL 2, 3

Mandelstam, Osip (Emilievich)
1891(?)-1943(?) .... **PC 14; TCLC 2, 6**
See Mandelshtam, Osip
See also CA 104; 150; MTCW 2; TWA

Mander, (Mary) Jane 1877-1949 ... **TCLC 31**
See also CA 162; RGEL 2

Mandeville, Bernard 1670-1733 .... **LC 82**
See also DLB 101

Mandeville, Sir John fl. 1350- ...... **CMLC 19**
See also DLB 146

Mandiargues, Andre Pieyre de ...... **CLC 41**
See Pieyre de Mandiargues, Andre
See also DLB 83

Mandrake, Ethel Belle
See Thurman, Wallace (Henry)

Mangan, James Clarence
1803-1849 .... **NCLC 27**
See also RGEL 2

Maniere, J.-E.
See Giraudoux, Jean(-Hippolyte)

Mankiewicz, Herman (Jacob)
1897-1953 .... **TCLC 85**
See also CA 120; 169; DLB 26; IDFW 3, 4

Manley, (Mary) Delariviere
1672(?)-1724 .... **LC 1, 42**
See also DLB 39, 80; RGEL 2

Mann, Abel
See Creasey, John

Mann, Emily 1952- .... **DC 7**
See also CA 130; CAD; CANR 55; CD 5, 6; CWD; DLB 266

Mann, (Luiz) Heinrich 1871-1950 ... **TCLC 9**
See also CA 106; 164, 181; DLB 66, 118; EW 8; EWL 3; RGWL 2, 3

Mann, (Paul) Thomas 1875-1955 . **SSC 5, 80, 82; TCLC 2, 8, 14, 21, 35, 44, 60, 168; WLC**
See also BPFB 2; CA 104; 128; CANR 133; CDWLB 2; DA; DA3; DAB; DAC; DAM MST, NOV; DLB 66; EW 9; EWL 3; GLL 1; LATS 1:1; LMFS 1; MTCW 1, 2; MTFW 2005; NFS 17; RGSF 2; RGWL 2, 3; SSFS 4, 9; TWA

Mannheim, Karl 1893-1947 .... **TCLC 65**
See also CA 204

Manning, David
See Faust, Frederick (Schiller)

Manning, Frederic 1882-1935 .... **TCLC 25**
See also CA 124; 216; DLB 260

Manning, Olivia 1915-1980 .... **CLC 5, 19**
See also CA 5-8R; 101; CANR 29; CN 1, 2; EWL 3; FW; MTCW 1; RGEL 2

Mano, D. Keith 1942- .... **CLC 2, 10**
See also CA 25-28R; CAAS 6; CANR 26, 57; DLB 6

Mansfield, Katherine .... **SSC 9, 23, 38, 81; TCLC 2, 8, 39, 164; WLC**
See Beauchamp, Kathleen Mansfield
See also BPFB 2; BRW 7; DAB; DLB 162; EWL 3; EXPS; FW; GLL 1; RGEL 2; RGSF 2; SSFS 2, 8, 10, 11; WWE 1

Manso, Peter 1940- .... **CLC 39**
See also CA 29-32R; CANR 44

Mantecon, Juan Jimenez
See Jimenez (Mantecon), Juan Ramon

Mantel, Hilary (Mary) 1952- .... **CLC 144**
See also CA 125; CANR 54, 101; CN 5, 6, 7; DLB 271; RHW

Manton, Peter
See Creasey, John

Man Without a Spleen, A
See Chekhov, Anton (Pavlovich)

Manzano, Juan Franciso
1797(?)-1854 .... **NCLC 155**

Manzoni, Alessandro 1785-1873 ... **NCLC 29, 98**
See also EW 5; RGWL 2, 3; TWA; WLIT 7

Map, Walter 1140-1209 .... **CMLC 32**

Mapu, Abraham (ben Jekutiel)
1808-1867 .... **NCLC 18**

Mara, Sally
See Queneau, Raymond

Maracle, Lee 1950- .... **NNAL**
See also CA 149

Marat, Jean Paul 1743-1793 .... **LC 10**

Marcel, Gabriel Honore 1889-1973 . **CLC 15**
See also CA 102; 45-48; EWL 3; MTCW 1, 2

March, William .... **TCLC 96**
See Campbell, William Edward March
See also CA 216; DLB 9, 86, 316; MAL 5

Marchbanks, Samuel
See Davies, (William) Robertson
See also CCA 1

Marchi, Giacomo
See Bassani, Giorgio

Marcus Aurelius
See Aurelius, Marcus
See also AW 2

Marguerite
See de Navarre, Marguerite

Marguerite d'Angouleme
See de Navarre, Marguerite
See also GFL Beginnings to 1789

Marguerite de Navarre
See de Navarre, Marguerite
See also RGWL 2, 3

Margulies, Donald 1954- .... **CLC 76**
See also AAYA 57; CA 200; CD 6; DFS 13; DLB 228

Marie de France c. 12th cent. - ..... **CMLC 8; PC 22**
See also DLB 208; FW; RGWL 2, 3

Marie de l'Incarnation 1599-1672 ...... **LC 10**

Marier, Captain Victor
See Griffith, D(avid Lewelyn) W(ark)

Mariner, Scott
See Pohl, Frederik

Marinetti, Filippo Tommaso
1876-1944 .... **TCLC 10**
See also CA 107; DLB 114, 264; EW 9; EWL 3; WLIT 7

Marivaux, Pierre Carlet de Chamblain de
1688-1763 .... **DC 7; LC 4, 123**
See also DLB 314; GFL Beginnings to 1789; RGWL 2, 3; TWA

Markandaya, Kamala .... **CLC 8, 38**
See Taylor, Kamala (Purnaiya)
See also BYA 13; CN 1, 2, 3, 4, 5, 6, 7; EWL 3

Markfield, Wallace (Arthur)
1926-2002 .... **CLC 8**
See also CA 69-72; 208; CAAS 3; CN 1, 2, 3, 4, 5, 6, 7; DLB 2, 28; DLBY 2002

Markham, Edwin 1852-1940 .... **TCLC 47**
See also CA 160; DLB 54, 186; MAL 5; RGAL 4

Markham, Robert
See Amis, Kingsley (William)

Markoosie .... **NNAL**
See Patsauq, Markoosie
See also CLR 23; DAM MULT

Marks, J.
See Highwater, Jamake (Mamake)

Marks, J
See Highwater, Jamake (Mamake)

Marks-Highwater, J
See Highwater, Jamake (Mamake)

Marks-Highwater, J.
See Highwater, Jamake (Mamake)

Markson, David M(errill) 1927- .... **CLC 67**
See also CA 49-52; CANR 1, 91; CN 5, 6

Marlatt, Daphne (Buckle) 1942- .... **CLC 168**
See also CA 25-28R; CANR 17, 39; CN 6,
7; CP 4, 5, 6, 7; CWP; DLB 60; FW

Marley, Bob .... **CLC 17**
See Marley, Robert Nesta

Marley, Robert Nesta 1945-1981
See Marley, Bob
See also CA 107; 103

Marlowe, Christopher 1564-1593 . **DC 1; LC
22, 47, 117; PC 57; WLC**
See also BRW 1; BRWR 1; CDBLB Before
1660; DA; DA3; DAB; DAC; DAM
DRAM, MST; DFS 1, 5, 13, 21; DLB 62;
EXPP; LMFS 1; PFS 22; RGEL 2; TEA;
WLIT 3

Marlowe, Stephen 1928- .... **CLC 70**
See Queen, Ellery
See also CA 13-16R; CANR 6, 55; CMW
4; SFW 4

Marmion, Shakerley 1603-1639 .... **LC 89**
See also DLB 58; RGEL 2

Marmontel, Jean-Francois 1723-1799 .. **LC 2**
See also DLB 314

Maron, Monika 1941- .... **CLC 165**
See also CA 201

Marquand, John P(hillips)
1893-1960 .... **CLC 2, 10**
See also AMW; BPFB 2; CA 85-88; CANR
73; CMW 4; DLB 9, 102; EWL 3; MAL
5; MTCW 2; RGAL 4

Marques, Rene 1919-1979 .. **CLC 96; HLC 2**
See also CA 97-100; 85-88; CANR 78;
DAM MULT; DLB 305; EWL 3; HW 1,
2; LAW; RGSF 2

Marquez, Gabriel (Jose) Garcia
See Garcia Marquez, Gabriel (Jose)

Marquis, Don(ald Robert Perry)
1878-1937 .... **TCLC 7**
See also CA 104; 166; DLB 11, 25; MAL
5; RGAL 4

Marquis de Sade
See Sade, Donatien Alphonse Francois

Marric, J. J.
See Creasey, John
See also MSW

Marryat, Frederick 1792-1848 .... **NCLC 3**
See also DLB 21, 163; RGEL 2; WCH

Marsden, James
See Creasey, John

Marsh, Edward 1872-1953 .... **TCLC 99**

Marsh, (Edith) Ngaio 1895-1982 .. **CLC 7, 53**
See also CA 9-12R; CANR 6, 58; CMW 4;
CN 1, 2, 3; CPW; DAM POP; DLB 77;
MSW; MTCW 1, 2; RGEL 2; TEA

Marshall, Allen
See Westlake, Donald E(dwin)

Marshall, Garry 1934- .... **CLC 17**
See also AAYA 3; CA 111; SATA 60

Marshall, Paule 1929- .. **BLC 3; CLC 27, 72;
SSC 3**
See also AFAW 1, 2; AMWS 11; BPFB 2;
BW 2, 3; CA 77-80; CANR 25, 73, 129;
CN 1, 2, 3, 4, 5, 6, 7; DA3; DAM MULT;
DLB 33, 157, 227; EWL 3; LATS 1:2;
MAL 5; MTCW 1, 2; MTFW 2005;
RGAL 4; SSFS 15

Marshallik
See Zangwill, Israel

Marsten, Richard
See Hunter, Evan

Marston, John 1576-1634 .... **LC 33**
See also BRW 2; DAM DRAM; DLB 58,
172; RGEL 2

Martel, Yann 1963- .... **CLC 192**
See also AAYA 67; CA 146; CANR 114;
MTFW 2005

Martens, Adolphe-Adhemar
See Ghelderode, Michel de

Martha, Henry
See Harris, Mark

Marti, Jose
See Marti (y Perez), Jose (Julian)
See also DLB 290

Marti (y Perez), Jose (Julian)
1853-1895 .... **HLC 2; NCLC 63**
See Marti, Jose
See also DAM MULT; HW 2; LAW; RGWL
2, 3; WLIT 1

Martial c. 40-c. 104 .... **CMLC 35; PC 10**
See also AW 2; CDWLB 1; DLB 211;
RGWL 2, 3

Martin, Ken
See Hubbard, L(afayette) Ron(ald)

Martin, Richard
See Creasey, John

Martin, Steve 1945- .... **CLC 30, 217**
See also AAYA 53; CA 97-100; CANR 30,
100, 140; DFS 19; MTCW 1; MTFW
2005

Martin, Valerie 1948- .... **CLC 89**
See also BEST 90:2; CA 85-88; CANR 49,
89

Martin, Violet Florence 1862-1915 .. **SSC 56;
TCLC 51**

Martin, Webber
See Silverberg, Robert

Martindale, Patrick Victor
See White, Patrick (Victor Martindale)

Martin du Gard, Roger
1881-1958 .... **TCLC 24**
See also CA 118; CANR 94; DLB 65; EWL
3; GFL 1789 to the Present; RGWL 2, 3

Martineau, Harriet 1802-1876 ...... **NCLC 26,
137**
See also DLB 21, 55, 159, 163, 166, 190;
FW; RGEL 2; YABC 2

Martines, Julia
See O'Faolain, Julia

Martinez, Enrique Gonzalez
See Gonzalez Martinez, Enrique

Martinez, Jacinto Benavente y
See Benavente (y Martinez), Jacinto

Martinez de la Rosa, Francisco de Paula
1787-1862 .... **NCLC 102**
See also TWA

Martinez Ruiz, Jose 1873-1967
See Azorin; Ruiz, Jose Martinez
See also CA 93-96; HW 1

Martinez Sierra, Gregorio
1881-1947 .... **TCLC 6**
See also CA 115; EWL 3

Martinez Sierra, Maria (de la O'LeJarraga)
1874-1974 .... **TCLC 6**
See also CA 115; EWL 3

Martinsen, Martin
See Follett, Ken(neth Martin)

Martinson, Harry (Edmund)
1904-1978 .... **CLC 14**
See also CA 77-80; CANR 34, 130; DLB
259; EWL 3

Martyn, Edward 1859-1923 .... **TCLC 131**
See also CA 179; DLB 10; RGEL 2

Marut, Ret
See Traven, B.

Marut, Robert
See Traven, B.

Marvell, Andrew 1621-1678 .... **LC 4, 43; PC
10; WLC**
See also BRW 2; BRWR 2; CDBLB 1660-
1789; DA; DAB; DAC; DAM MST,
POET; DLB 131; EXPP; PFS 5; RGEL 2;
TEA; WP

Marx, Karl (Heinrich)
1818-1883 .... **NCLC 17, 114**
See also DLB 129; LATS 1:1; TWA

Masaoka, Shiki -1902 .... **TCLC 18**
See Masaoka, Tsunenori
See also RGWL 3

Masaoka, Tsunenori 1867-1902
See Masaoka, Shiki
See also CA 117; 191; TWA

Masefield, John (Edward)
1878-1967 .... **CLC 11, 47**
See also CA 19-20; 25-28R; CANR 33;
CAP 2; CDBLB 1890-1914; DAM POET;
DLB 10, 19, 153, 160; EWL 3; EXPP;
FANT; MTCW 1, 2; PFS 5; RGEL 2;
SATA 19

Maso, Carole (?)- .... **CLC 44**
See also CA 170; CN 7; GLL 2; RGAL 4

Mason, Bobbie Ann 1940- ... **CLC 28, 43, 82,
154; SSC 4**
See also AAYA 5, 42; AMWS 8; BPFB 2;
CA 53-56; CANR 11, 31, 58, 83, 125;
CDALBS; CN 5, 6, 7; CSW; DA3; DLB
173; DLBY 1987; EWL 3; EXPS; INT
CANR-31; MAL 5; MTCW 1, 2; MTFW
2005; NFS 4; RGAL 4; RGSF 2; SSFS 3,
8, 20; TCLE 1:2; YAW

Mason, Ernst
See Pohl, Frederik

Mason, Hunni B.
See Sternheim, (William Adolf) Carl

Mason, Lee W.
See Malzberg, Barry N(athaniel)

Mason, Nick 1945- .... **CLC 35**

Mason, Tally
See Derleth, August (William)

Mass, Anna .... **CLC 59**

Mass, William
See Gibson, William

Massinger, Philip 1583-1640 .... **LC 70**
See also BRWS 11; DLB 58; RGEL 2

Master Lao
See Lao Tzu

Masters, Edgar Lee 1868-1950 ...... **PC 1, 36;
TCLC 2, 25; WLCS**
See also AMWS 1; CA 104; 133; CDALB
1865-1917; DA; DAC; DAM MST,
POET; DLB 54; EWL 3; EXPP; MAL 5;
MTCW 1, 2; MTFW 2005; RGAL 4;
TUS; WP

Masters, Hilary 1928- .... **CLC 48**
See also CA 25-28R; 217; CAAE 217;
CANR 13, 47, 97; CN 6, 7; DLB 244

Mastrosimone, William 1947- .... **CLC 36**
See also CA 186; CAD; CD 5, 6

Mathe, Albert
See Camus, Albert

Mather, Cotton 1663-1728 .... **LC 38**
See also AMWS 2; CDALB 1640-1865;
DLB 24, 30, 140; RGAL 4; TUS

Mather, Increase 1639-1723 .... **LC 38**
See also DLB 24

Matheson, Richard (Burton) 1926- .. **CLC 37**
See also AAYA 31; CA 97-100; CANR 88,
99; DLB 8, 44; HGG; INT CA-97-100;
SCFW 1, 2; SFW 4; SUFW 2

Mathews, Harry (Burchell) 1930- ..... **CLC 6,
52**
See also CA 21-24R; CAAS 6; CANR 18,
40, 98; CN 5, 6, 7

Mathews, John Joseph 1894-1979 .. **CLC 84;**
NNAL
See also CA 19-20; 142; CANR 45; CAP 2;
DAM MULT; DLB 175; TCWW 1, 2
Mathias, Roland (Glyn) 1915- .... **CLC 45**
See also CA 97-100; CANR 19, 41; CP 1,
2, 3, 4, 5, 6, 7; DLB 27
Matsuo Basho 1644(?)-1694 ...... **LC 62; PC 3**
See Basho, Matsuo
See also DAM POET; PFS 2, 7, 18
Mattheson, Rodney
See Creasey, John
Matthews, (James) Brander
1852-1929 .... **TCLC 95**
See also CA 181; DLB 71, 78; DLBD 13
Matthews, Greg 1949- .... **CLC 45**
See also CA 135
Matthews, William (Procter III)
1942-1997 .... **CLC 40**
See also AMWS 9; CA 29-32R; 162; CAAS
18; CANR 12, 57; CP 2, 3, 4; DLB 5
Matthias, John (Edward) 1941- ...... **CLC 9**
See also CA 33-36R; CANR 56; CP 4, 5, 6,
7
Matthiessen, F(rancis) O(tto)
1902-1950 .... **TCLC 100**
See also CA 185; DLB 63; MAL 5
Matthiessen, Peter 1927- ... **CLC 5, 7, 11, 32,**
64
See also AAYA 6, 40; AMWS 5; ANW;
BEST 90:4; BPFB 2; CA 9-12R; CANR
21, 50, 73, 100, 138; CN 1, 2, 3, 4, 5, 6,
7; DA3; DAM NOV; DLB 6, 173, 275;
MAL 5; MTCW 1, 2; MTFW 2005; SATA
27
Maturin, Charles Robert
1780(?)-1824 .... **NCLC 6**
See also BRWS 8; DLB 178; GL 3; HGG;
LMFS 1; RGEL 2; SUFW
Matute (Ausejo), Ana Maria 1925- .. **CLC 11**
See also CA 89-92; CANR 129; CWW 2;
DLB 322; EWL 3; MTCW 1; RGSF 2
Maugham, W. S.
See Maugham, W(illiam) Somerset
Maugham, W(illiam) Somerset
1874-1965 .. **CLC 1, 11, 15, 67, 93; SSC**
8; WLC
See also AAYA 55; BPFB 2; BRW 6; CA
5-8R; 25-28R; CANR 40, 127; CDBLB
1914-1945; CMW 4; DA; DA3; DAB;
DAC; DAM DRAM, MST, NOV; DFS
22; DLB 10, 36, 77, 100, 162, 195; EWL
3; LAIT 3; MTCW 1, 2; MTFW 2005;
RGEL 2; RGSF 2; SATA 54; SSFS 17
Maugham, William Somerset
See Maugham, W(illiam) Somerset
Maupassant, (Henri Rene Albert) Guy de
1850-1893 . **NCLC 1, 42, 83; SSC 1, 64;**
WLC
See also BYA 14; DA; DA3; DAB; DAC;
DAM MST; DLB 123; EW 7; EXPS; GFL
1789 to the Present; LAIT 2; LMFS 1;
RGSF 2; RGWL 2, 3; SSFS 4, 21; SUFW
TWA
Maupin, Armistead (Jones, Jr.)
1944- .... **CLC 95**
See also CA 125; 130; CANR 58, 101;
CPW; DA3; DAM POP; DLB 278; GLL
1; INT CA-130; MTCW 2; MTFW 2005
Maurhut, Richard
See Traven, B.
Mauriac, Claude 1914-1996 .... **CLC 9**
See also CA 89-92; 152; CWW 2; DLB 83;
EWL 3; GFL 1789 to the Present
Mauriac, Francois (Charles)
1885-1970 .... **CLC 4, 9, 56; SSC 24**
See also CA 25-28; CAP 2; DLB 65; EW
10; EWL 3; GFL 1789 to the Present;
MTCW 1, 2; MTFW 2005; RGWL 2, 3;
TWA

Mavor, Osborne Henry 1888-1951
See Bridie, James
See also CA 104
Maxwell, William (Keepers, Jr.)
1908-2000 .... **CLC 19**
See also AMWS 8; CA 93-96; 189; CANR
54, 95; CN 1, 2, 3, 4, 5, 6, 7; DLB 218,
278; DLBY 1980; INT CA-93-96; SATA-
Obit 128
May, Elaine 1932- .... **CLC 16**
See also CA 124; 142; CAD; CWD; DLB
44
Mayakovski, Vladimir (Vladimirovich)
1893-1930 .... **TCLC 4, 18**
See Maiakovskii, Vladimir; Mayakovsky,
Vladimir
See also CA 104; 158; EWL 3; MTCW 2;
MTFW 2005; SFW 4; TWA
Mayakovsky, Vladimir
See Mayakovski, Vladimir (Vladimirovich)
See also EW 11; WP
Mayhew, Henry 1812-1887 .... **NCLC 31**
See also DLB 18, 55, 190
Mayle, Peter 1939(?)- .... **CLC 89**
See also CA 139; CANR 64, 109
Maynard, Joyce 1953- .... **CLC 23**
See also CA 111; 129; CANR 64
Mayne, William (James Carter)
1928- .... **CLC 12**
See also AAYA 20; CA 9-12R; CANR 37,
80, 100; CLR 25; FANT; JRDA; MAI-
CYA 1, 2; MAICYAS 1; SAAS 11; SATA
6, 68, 122; SUFW 2; YAW
Mayo, Jim
See L'Amour, Louis (Dearborn)
Maysles, Albert 1926- .... **CLC 16**
See also CA 29-32R
Maysles, David 1932-1987 .... **CLC 16**
See also CA 191
Mazer, Norma Fox 1931- .... **CLC 26**
See also AAYA 5, 36; BYA 1, 8; CA 69-72;
CANR 12, 32, 66, 129; CLR 23; JRDA;
MAICYA 1, 2; SAAS 1; SATA 24, 67,
105; WYA; YAW
Mazzini, Guiseppe 1805-1872 .... **NCLC 34**
McAlmon, Robert (Menzies)
1895-1956 .... **TCLC 97**
See also CA 107; 168; DLB 4, 45; DLBD
15; GLL 1
McAuley, James Phillip 1917-1976 .. **CLC 45**
See also CA 97-100; CP 1, 2; DLB 260;
RGEL 2
McBain, Ed
See Hunter, Evan
See also MSW
McBrien, William (Augustine)
1930- .... **CLC 44**
See also CA 107; CANR 90
McCabe, Patrick 1955- .... **CLC 133**
See also BRWS 9; CA 130; CANR 50, 90;
CN 6, 7; DLB 194
McCaffrey, Anne 1926- .... **CLC 17**
See also AAYA 6, 34; AITN 2; BEST 89:2;
BPFB 2; BYA 5; CA 25-28R, 227; CAAE
227; CANR 15, 35, 55, 96; CLR 49;
CPW; DA3; DAM NOV, POP; DLB 8;
JRDA; MAICYA 1, 2; MTCW 1, 2;
MTFW 2005; SAAS 11; SATA 8, 70, 116,
152; SATA-Essay 152; SFW 4; SUFW 2;
WYA; YAW
McCaffrey, Anne Inez
See McCaffrey, Anne
McCall, Nathan 1955(?)- .... **CLC 86**
See also AAYA 59; BW 3; CA 146; CANR
88
McCann, Arthur
See Campbell, John W(ood, Jr.)
McCann, Edson
See Pohl, Frederik

McCarthy, Charles, Jr. 1933-
See McCarthy, Cormac
See also CANR 42, 69, 101; CPW; CSW;
DA3; DAM POP; MTCW 2; MTFW 2005
McCarthy, Cormac ...... **CLC 4, 57, 101, 204**
See McCarthy, Charles, Jr.
See also AAYA 41; AMWS 8; BPFB 2; CA
13-16R; CANR 10; CN 6, 7; DLB 6, 143,
256; EWL 3; LATS 1:2; MAL 5; TCLE
1:2; TCWW 2
McCarthy, Mary (Therese)
1912-1989 .. **CLC 1, 3, 5, 14, 24, 39, 59;**
SSC 24
See also AMW; BPFB 2; CA 5-8R; 129;
CANR 16, 50, 64; CN 1, 2, 3, 4; DA3;
DLB 2; DLBY 1981; EWL 3; FW; INT
CANR-16; MAL 5; MAWW; MTCW 1,
2; MTFW 2005; RGAL 4; TUS
McCartney, (James) Paul 1942- . **CLC 12, 35**
See also CA 146; CANR 111
McCauley, Stephen (D.) 1955- .... **CLC 50**
See also CA 141
McClaren, Peter .... **CLC 70**
McClure, Michael (Thomas) 1932- ... **CLC 6,**
10
See also BG 1:3; CA 21-24R; CAD; CANR
17, 46, 77, 131; CD 5, 6; CP 1, 2, 3, 4, 5,
6, 7; DLB 16; WP
McCorkle, Jill (Collins) 1958- .... **CLC 51**
See also CA 121; CANR 113; CSW; DLB
234; DLBY 1987
McCourt, Frank 1930- .... **CLC 109**
See also AAYA 61; AMWS 12; CA 157;
CANR 97, 138; MTFW 2005; NCFS 1
McCourt, James 1941- .... **CLC 5**
See also CA 57-60; CANR 98
McCourt, Malachy 1931- .... **CLC 119**
See also SATA 126
McCoy, Horace (Stanley)
1897-1955 .... **TCLC 28**
See also AMWS 13; CA 108; 155; CMW 4;
DLB 9
McCrae, John 1872-1918 .... **TCLC 12**
See also CA 109; DLB 92; PFS 5
McCreigh, James
See Pohl, Frederik
McCullers, (Lula) Carson (Smith)
1917-1967 .... **CLC 1, 4, 10, 12, 48, 100;**
SSC 9, 24; TCLC 155; WLC
See also AAYA 21; AMW; AMWC 2; BPFB
2; CA 5-8R; 25-28R; CABS 1, 3; CANR
18, 132; CDALB 1941-1968; DA; DA3;
DAB; DAC; DAM MST, NOV; DFS 5,
18; DLB 2, 7, 173, 228; EWL 3; EXPS;
FW; GLL 1; LAIT 3, 4; MAL 5; MAWW;
MTCW 1, 2; MTFW 2005; NFS 6, 13;
RGAL 4; RGSF 2; SATA 27; SSFS 5;
TUS; YAW
McCulloch, John Tyler
See Burroughs, Edgar Rice
McCullough, Colleen 1937- ...... **CLC 27, 107**
See also AAYA 36; BPFB 2; CA 81-84;
CANR 17, 46, 67, 98, 139; CPW; DA3;
DAM NOV, POP; MTCW 1, 2; MTFW
2005; RHW
McCunn, Ruthanne Lum 1946- .... **AAL**
See also CA 119; CANR 43, 96; DLB 312;
LAIT 2; SATA 63
McDermott, Alice 1953- .... **CLC 90**
See also CA 109; CANR 40, 90, 126; CN
7; DLB 292; MTFW 2005
McElroy, Joseph (Prince) 1930- ... **CLC 5, 47**
See also CA 17-20R; CN 3, 4, 5, 6, 7
McEwan, Ian (Russell) 1948- .... **CLC 13, 66,**
169
See also BEST 90:4; BRWS 4; CA 61-64;
CANR 14, 41, 69, 87, 132; CN 3, 4, 5, 6,
7; DAM NOV; DLB 14, 194, 319; HGG;
MTCW 1, 2; MTFW 2005; RGSF 2;
SUFW 2; TEA

McFadden, David 1940- .... **CLC 48**
    See also CA 104; CP 1, 2, 3, 4, 5, 6, 7; DLB
    60; INT CA-104
McFarland, Dennis 1950- .... **CLC 65**
    See also CA 165; CANR 110
McGahern, John 1934- ... **CLC 5, 9, 48, 156;**
    SSC 17
    See also CA 17-20R; CANR 29, 68, 113;
    CN 1, 2, 3, 4, 5, 6, 7; DLB 14, 231, 319;
    MTCW 1
McGinley, Patrick (Anthony) 1937- . **CLC 41**
    See also CA 120; 127; CANR 56; INT CA-
    127
McGinley, Phyllis 1905-1978 .... **CLC 14**
    See also CA 9-12R; 77-80; CANR 19; CP
    1, 2; CWRI 5; DLB 11, 48; MAL 5; PFS
    9, 13; SATA 2, 44; SATA-Obit 24
McGinniss, Joe 1942- .... **CLC 32**
    See also AITN 2; BEST 89:2; CA 25-28R;
    CANR 26, 70; CPW; DLB 185; INT
    CANR-26
McGivern, Maureen Daly
    See Daly, Maureen
McGrath, Patrick 1950- .... **CLC 55**
    See also CA 136; CANR 65; CN 5, 6, 7;
    DLB 231; HGG; SUFW 2
McGrath, Thomas (Matthew)
    1916-1990 .... **CLC 28, 59**
    See also AMWS 10; CA 9-12R; 132; CANR
    6, 33, 95; CP 1, 2, 3, 4; DAM POET;
    MAL 5; MTCW 1; SATA 41; SATA-Obit
    66
McGuane, Thomas (Francis III)
    1939- .... **CLC 3, 7, 18, 45, 127**
    See also AITN 2; BPFB 2; CA 49-52;
    CANR 5, 24, 49, 94; CN 2, 3, 4, 5, 6, 7;
    DLB 2, 212; DLBY 1980; EWL 3; INT
    CANR-24; MAL 5; MTCW 1; MTFW
    2005; TCWW 1, 2
McGuckian, Medbh 1950- .... **CLC 48, 174;**
    PC 27
    See also BRWS 5; CA 143; CP 4, 5, 6, 7;
    CWP; DAM POET; DLB 40
McHale, Tom 1942(?)-1982 .... **CLC 3, 5**
    See also AITN 1; CA 77-80; 106; CN 1, 2,
    3
McHugh, Heather 1948- .... **PC 61**
    See also CA 69-72; CANR 11, 28, 55, 92;
    CP 4, 5, 6, 7; CWP
McIlvanney, William 1936- .... **CLC 42**
    See also CA 25-28R; CANR 61; CMW 4;
    DLB 14, 207
McIlwraith, Maureen Mollie Hunter
    See Hunter, Mollie
    See also SATA 2
McInerney, Jay 1955- .... **CLC 34, 112**
    See also AAYA 18; BPFB 2; CA 116; 123;
    CANR 45, 68, 116; CN 5, 6, 7; CPW;
    DA3; DAM POP; DLB 292; INT CA-123;
    MAL 5; MTCW 2; MTFW 2005
McIntyre, Vonda N(eel) 1948- .... **CLC 18**
    See also CA 81-84; CANR 17, 34, 69;
    MTCW 1; SFW 4; YAW
McKay, Claude .... **BLC 3; HR 1:3; PC 2;**
    TCLC 7, 41; WLC
    See McKay, Festus Claudius
    See also AFAW 1, 2; AMWS 10; DAB;
    DLB 4, 45, 51, 117; EWL 3; EXPP; GLL
    2; LAIT 3; LMFS 2; MAL 5; PAB; PFS
    4; RGAL 4; WP
McKay, Festus Claudius 1889-1948
    See McKay, Claude
    See also BW 1, 3; CA 104; 124; CANR 73;
    DA; DAC; DAM MST, MULT, NOV,
    POET; MTCW 1, 2; MTFW 2005; TUS
McKuen, Rod 1933- .... **CLC 1, 3**
    See also AITN 1; CA 41-44R; CANR 40;
    CP 1
McLoughlin, R. B.
    See Mencken, H(enry) L(ouis)

McLuhan, (Herbert) Marshall
    1911-1980 .... **CLC 37, 83**
    See also CA 9-12R; 102; CANR 12, 34, 61;
    DLB 88; INT CANR-12; MTCW 1, 2;
    MTFW 2005
McManus, Declan Patrick Aloysius
    See Costello, Elvis
McMillan, Terry (L.) 1951- . **BLCS; CLC 50,**
    61, 112
    See also AAYA 21; AMWS 13; BPFB 2;
    BW 2, 3; CA 140; CANR 60, 104, 131;
    CN 7; CPW; DA3; DAM MULT, NOV,
    POP; MAL 5; MTCW 2; MTFW 2005;
    RGAL 4; YAW
McMurtry, Larry 1936- .... **CLC 2, 3, 7, 11,**
    27, 44, 127
    See also AAYA 15; AITN 2; AMWS 5;
    BEST 89:2; BPFB 2; CA 5-8R; CANR
    19, 43, 64, 103; CDALB 1968-1988; CN
    2, 3, 4, 5, 6, 7; CPW; CSW; DA3; DAM
    NOV, POP; DLB 2, 143, 256; DLBY
    1980, 1987; EWL 3; MAL 5; MTCW 1,
    2; MTFW 2005; RGAL 4; TCWW 1, 2
McNally, T. M. 1961- .... **CLC 82**
McNally, Terrence 1939- ... **CLC 4, 7, 41, 91;**
    DC 27
    See also AAYA 62; AMWS 13; CA 45-48;
    CAD; CANR 2, 56, 116; CD 5, 6; DA3;
    DAM DRAM; DFS 16, 19; DLB 7, 249;
    EWL 3; GLL 1; MTCW 2; MTFW 2005
McNamer, Deirdre 1950- .... **CLC 70**
McNeal, Tom .... **CLC 119**
McNeile, Herman Cyril 1888-1937
    See Sapper
    See also CA 184; CMW 4; DLB 77
McNickle, (William) D'Arcy
    1904-1977 .... **CLC 89; NNAL**
    See also CA 9-12R; 85-88; CANR 5, 45;
    DAM MULT; DLB 175, 212; RGAL 4;
    SATA-Obit 22; TCWW 1, 2
McPhee, John (Angus) 1931- .... **CLC 36**
    See also AAYA 61; AMWS 3; ANW; BEST
    90:1; CA 65-68; CANR 20, 46, 64, 69,
    121; CPW; DLB 185, 275; MTCW 1, 2;
    MTFW 2005; TUS
McPherson, James Alan 1943- . **BLCS; CLC**
    19, 77
    See also BW 1, 3; CA 25-28R; CAAS 17;
    CANR 24, 74, 140; CN 3, 4, 5, 6; CSW;
    DLB 38, 244; EWL 3; MTCW 1, 2;
    MTFW 2005; RGAL 4; RGSF 2
McPherson, William (Alexander)
    1933- .... **CLC 34**
    See also CA 69-72; CANR 28; INT
    CANR-28
McTaggart, J. McT. Ellis
    See McTaggart, John McTaggart Ellis
McTaggart, John McTaggart Ellis
    1866-1925 .... **TCLC 105**
    See also CA 120; DLB 262
Mead, George Herbert 1863-1931 . **TCLC 89**
    See also CA 212; DLB 270
Mead, Margaret 1901-1978 .... **CLC 37**
    See also AITN 1; CA 1-4R; 81-84; CANR
    4; DA3; FW; MTCW 1, 2; SATA-Obit 20
Meaker, Marijane (Agnes) 1927-
    See Kerr, M. E.
    See also CA 107; CANR 37, 63, 145; INT
    CA-107; JRDA; MAICYA 1, 2; MAIC-
    YAS 1; MTCW 1; SATA 20, 61, 99, 160;
    SATA-Essay 111; YAW
Medoff, Mark (Howard) 1940- .... **CLC 6, 23**
    See also AITN 1; CA 53-56; CAD; CANR
    5; CD 5, 6; DAM DRAM; DFS 4; DLB
    7; INT CANR-5
Medvedev, P. N.
    See Bakhtin, Mikhail Mikhailovich
Meged, Aharon
    See Megged, Aharon

Meged, Aron
    See Megged, Aharon
Megged, Aharon 1920- .... **CLC 9**
    See also CA 49-52; CAAS 13; CANR 1,
    140; EWL 3
Mehta, Deepa 1950- .... **CLC 208**
Mehta, Gita 1943- .... **CLC 179**
    See also CA 225; CN 7; DNFS 2
Mehta, Ved (Parkash) 1934- .... **CLC 37**
    See also CA 1-4R, 212; CAAE 212; CANR
    2, 23, 69; MTCW 1; MTFW 2005
Melanchthon, Philipp 1497-1560 .... **LC 90**
    See also DLB 179
Melanter
    See Blackmore, R(ichard) D(oddridge)
Meleager c. 140B.C.-c. 70B.C. ...... **CMLC 53**
Melies, Georges 1861-1938 .... **TCLC 81**
Melikow, Loris
    See Hofmannsthal, Hugo von
Melmoth, Sebastian
    See Wilde, Oscar (Fingal O'Flahertie Wills)
Melo Neto, Joao Cabral de
    See Cabral de Melo Neto, Joao
    See also CWW 2; EWL 3
Meltzer, Milton 1915- .... **CLC 26**
    See also AAYA 8, 45; BYA 2, 6; CA 13-
    16R; CANR 38, 92, 107; CLR 13; DLB
    61; JRDA; MAICYA 1, 2; SAAS 1; SATA
    1, 50, 80, 128; SATA-Essay 124; WYA;
    YAW
Melville, Herman 1819-1891 ..... **NCLC 3, 12,**
    29, 45, 49, 91, 93, 123, 157; SSC 1, 17,
    46; WLC
    See also AAYA 25; AMW; AMWR 1;
    CDALB 1640-1865; DA; DA3; DAB;
    DAC; DAM MST, NOV; DLB 3, 74, 250,
    254; EXPN; EXPS; GL 3; LAIT 1, 2; NFS
    7, 9; RGAL 4; RGSF 2; SATA 59; SSFS
    3; TUS
Members, Mark
    See Powell, Anthony (Dymoke)
Membreno, Alejandro .... **CLC 59**
Menand, Louis 1952- .... **CLC 208**
    See also CA 200
Menander c. 342B.C.-c. 293B.C. .... **CMLC 9,**
    51; DC 3
    See also AW 1; CDWLB 1; DAM DRAM;
    DLB 176; LMFS 1; RGWL 2, 3
Menchu, Rigoberta 1959- .. **CLC 160; HLCS**
    2
    See also CA 175; CANR 135; DNFS 1;
    WLIT 1
Mencken, H(enry) L(ouis)
    1880-1956 .... **TCLC 13**
    See also AMW; CA 105; 125; CDALB
    1917-1929; DLB 11, 29, 63, 137, 222;
    EWL 3; MAL 5; MTCW 1, 2; MTFW
    2005; NCFS 4; RGAL 4; TUS
Mendelsohn, Jane 1965- .... **CLC 99**
    See also CA 154; CANR 94
Mendoza, Inigo Lopez de
    See Santillana, Inigo Lopez de Mendoza,
    Marques de
Menton, Francisco de
    See Chin, Frank (Chew, Jr.)
Mercer, David 1928-1980 .... **CLC 5**
    See also CA 9-12R; 102; CANR 23; CBD;
    DAM DRAM; DLB 13, 310; MTCW 1;
    RGEL 2
Merchant, Paul
    See Ellison, Harlan (Jay)
Meredith, George 1828-1909 .. **PC 60; TCLC**
    17, 43
    See also CA 117; 153; CANR 80; CDBLB
    1832-1890; DAM POET; DLB 18, 35, 57,
    159; RGEL 2; TEA

Meredith, William (Morris) 1919- .... **CLC 4, 13, 22, 55; PC 28**
See also CA 9-12R; CAAS 14; CANR 6, 40, 129; CP 1, 2, 3, 4, 5, 6, 7; DAM POET; DLB 5; MAL 5

Merezhkovsky, Dmitrii Sergeevich
See Merezhkovsky, Dmitry Sergeyevich
See also DLB 295

Merezhkovsky, Dmitry Sergeevich
See Merezhkovsky, Dmitry Sergeyevich
See also EWL 3

Merezhkovsky, Dmitry Sergeyevich
1865-1941 .... **TCLC 29**
See Merezhkovsky, Dmitrii Sergeevich; Merezhkovsky, Dmitry Sergeyevich
See also CA 169

Merimee, Prosper 1803-1870 ... **NCLC 6, 65; SSC 7, 77**
See also DLB 119, 192; EW 6; EXPS; GFL 1789 to the Present; RGSF 2; RGWL 2, 3; SSFS 8; SUFW

Merkin, Daphne 1954- .... **CLC 44**
See also CA 123

Merleau-Ponty, Maurice
1908-1961 .... **TCLC 156**
See also CA 114; 89-92; DLB 296; GFL 1789 to the Present

Merlin, Arthur
See Blish, James (Benjamin)

Mernissi, Fatima 1940- .... **CLC 171**
See also CA 152; FW

Merrill, James (Ingram) 1926-1995 .. **CLC 2, 3, 6, 8, 13, 18, 34, 91; PC 28; TCLC 173**
See also AMWS 3; CA 13-16R; 147; CANR 10, 49, 63, 108; CP 1, 2, 3, 4; DA3; DAM POET; DLB 5, 165; DLBY 1985; EWL 3; INT CANR-10; MAL 5; MTCW 1, 2; MTFW 2005; PAB; PFS 23; RGAL 4

Merriman, Alex
See Silverberg, Robert

Merriman, Brian 1747-1805 .... **NCLC 70**

Merritt, E. B.
See Waddington, Miriam

Merton, Thomas (James)
1915-1968 . **CLC 1, 3, 11, 34, 83; PC 10**
See also AAYA 61; AMWS 8; CA 5-8R; 25-28R; CANR 22, 53, 111, 131; DA3; DLB 48; DLBY 1981; MAL 5; MTCW 1, 2; MTFW 2005

Merwin, W(illiam) S(tanley) 1927- ... **CLC 1, 2, 3, 5, 8, 13, 18, 45, 88; PC 45**
See also AMWS 3; CA 13-16R; CANR 15, 51, 112, 140; CP 1, 2, 3, 4, 5, 6, 7; DA3; DAM POET; DLB 5, 169; EWL 3; INT CANR-15; MAL 5; MTCW 1, 2; MTFW 2005; PAB; PFS 5, 15; RGAL 4

Metastasio, Pietro 1698-1782 .... **LC 115**
See also RGWL 2, 3

Metcalf, John 1938- .... **CLC 37; SSC 43**
See also CA 113; CN 4, 5, 6, 7; DLB 60; RGSF 2; TWA

Metcalf, Suzanne
See Baum, L(yman) Frank

Mew, Charlotte (Mary) 1870-1928 .. **TCLC 8**
See also CA 105; 189; DLB 19, 135; RGEL 2

Mewshaw, Michael 1943- .... **CLC 9**
See also CA 53-56; CANR 7, 47; DLBY 1980

Meyer, Conrad Ferdinand
1825-1898 .... **NCLC 81; SSC 30**
See also DLB 129; EW; RGWL 2, 3

Meyer, Gustav 1868-1932
See Meyrink, Gustav
See also CA 117; 190

Meyer, June
See Jordan, June (Meyer)

Meyer, Lynn
See Slavitt, David R(ytman)

Meyers, Jeffrey 1939- .... **CLC 39**
See also CA 73-76; 186; CAAE 186; CANR 54, 102; DLB 111

Meynell, Alice (Christina Gertrude Thompson) 1847-1922 .... **TCLC 6**
See also CA 104; 177; DLB 19, 98; RGEL 2

Meyrink, Gustav .... **TCLC 21**
See Meyer, Gustav
See also DLB 81; EWL 3

Michaels, Leonard 1933-2003 ..... **CLC 6, 25; SSC 16**
See also CA 61-64; 216; CANR 21, 62, 119; CN 3, 45, 6, 7; DLB 130; MTCW 1; TCLE 1:2

Michaux, Henri 1899-1984 .... **CLC 8, 19**
See also CA 85-88; 114; DLB 258; EWL 3; GFL 1789 to the Present; RGWL 2, 3

Micheaux, Oscar (Devereaux)
1884-1951 .... **TCLC 76**
See also BW 3; CA 174; DLB 50; TCWW 2

Michelangelo 1475-1564 .... **LC 12**
See also AAYA 43

Michelet, Jules 1798-1874 .... **NCLC 31**
See also EW 5; GFL 1789 to the Present

Michels, Robert 1876-1936 .... **TCLC 88**
See also CA 212

Michener, James A(lbert)
1907(?)-1997 .. **CLC 1, 5, 11, 29, 60, 109**
See also AAYA 27; AITN 1; BEST 90:1; BPFB 2; CA 5-8R; 161; CANR 21, 45, 68; CN 1, 2, 3, 4, 5, 6; CPW; DA3; DAM NOV, POP; DLB 6; MAL 5; MTCW 1, 2; MTFW 2005; RHW; TCWW 1, 2

Mickiewicz, Adam 1798-1855 . **NCLC 3, 101; PC 38**
See also EW 5; RGWL 2, 3

Middleton, (John) Christopher
1926- .... **CLC 13**
See also CA 13-16R; CANR 29, 54, 117; CP 1, 2, 3, 4, 5, 6, 7; DLB 40

Middleton, Richard (Barham)
1882-1911 .... **TCLC 56**
See also CA 187; DLB 156; HGG

Middleton, Stanley 1919- .... **CLC 7, 38**
See also CA 25-28R; CAAS 23; CANR 21, 46, 81; CN 1, 2, 3, 4, 5, 6, 7; DLB 14

Middleton, Thomas 1580-1627 ...... **DC 5; LC 33, 123**
See also BRW 2; DAM DRAM, MST; DFS 18, 22; DLB 58; RGEL 2

Migueis, Jose Rodrigues 1901-1980 . **CLC 10**
See also DLB 287

Mikszath, Kalman 1847-1910 .... **TCLC 31**
See also CA 170

Miles, Jack .... **CLC 100**
See also CA 200

Miles, John Russiano
See Miles, Jack

Miles, Josephine (Louise)
1911-1985 .... **CLC 1, 2, 14, 34, 39**
See also CA 1-4R; 116; CANR 2, 55; CP 1, 2, 3, 4; DAM POET; DLB 48; MAL 5; TCLE 1:2

Militant
See Sandburg, Carl (August)

Mill, Harriet (Hardy) Taylor
1807-1858 .... **NCLC 102**
See also FW

Mill, John Stuart 1806-1873 .... **NCLC 11, 58**
See also CDBLB 1832-1890; DLB 55, 190, 262; FW 1; RGEL 2; TEA

Millar, Kenneth 1915-1983 .... **CLC 14**
See Macdonald, Ross
See also CA 9-12R; 110; CANR 16, 63, 107; CMW 4; CPW; DA3; DAM POP; DLB 2, 226; DLBD 6; DLBY 1983; MTCW 1, 2; MTFW 2005

Millay, E. Vincent
See Millay, Edna St. Vincent

Millay, Edna St. Vincent 1892-1950 ..... **PC 6, 61; TCLC 4, 49, 169; WLCS**
See Boyd, Nancy
See also AMW; CA 104; 130; CDALB 1917-1929; DA; DA3; DAB; DAC; DAM MST, POET; DLB 45, 249; EWL 3; EXPP; FL 1:6; MAL 5; MAWW; MTCW 1, 2; MTFW 2005; PAB; PFS 3, 17; RGAL 4; TUS; WP

Miller, Arthur 1915-2005 ..... **CLC 1, 2, 6, 10, 15, 26, 47, 78, 179; DC 1; WLC**
See also AAYA 15; AITN 1; AMW; AMWC 1; CA 1-4R; 236; CABS 3; CAD; CANR 2, 30, 54, 76, 132; CD 5, 6; CDALB 1941-1968; DA; DA3; DAB; DAC; DAM DRAM, MST; DFS 1, 3, 8; DLB 7, 266; EWL 3; LAIT 1, 4; LATS 1:2; MAL 5; MTCW 1, 2; MTFW 2005; RGAL 4; TUS; WYAS 1

Miller, Henry (Valentine)
1891-1980 .... **CLC 1, 2, 4, 9, 14, 43, 84; WLC**
See also AMW; BPFB 2; CA 9-12R; 97-100; CANR 33, 64; CDALB 1929-1941; CN 1, 2; DA; DA3; DAB; DAC; DAM MST, NOV; DLB 4, 9; DLBY 1980; EWL 3; MAL 5; MTCW 1, 2; MTFW 2005; RGAL 4; TUS

Miller, Hugh 1802-1856 .... **NCLC 143**
See also DLB 190

Miller, Jason 1939(?)-2001 .... **CLC 2**
See also AITN 1; CA 73-76; 197; CAD; CANR 130; DFS 12; DLB 7

Miller, Sue 1943- .... **CLC 44**
See also AMWS 12; BEST 90:3; CA 139; CANR 59, 91, 128; DA3; DAM POP; DLB 143

Miller, Walter M(ichael, Jr.)
1923-1996 .... **CLC 4, 30**
See also BPFB 2; CA 85-88; CANR 108; DLB 8; SCFW 1, 2; SFW 4

Millett, Kate 1934- .... **CLC 67**
See also AITN 1; CA 73-76; CANR 32, 53, 76, 110; DA3; DLB 246; FW; GLL 1; MTCW 1, 2; MTFW 2005

Millhauser, Steven (Lewis) 1943- .... **CLC 21, 54, 109; SSC 57**
See also CA 110; 111; CANR 63, 114, 133; CN 6, 7; DA3; DLB 2; FANT; INT CA-111; MAL 5; MTCW 2; MTFW 2005

Millin, Sarah Gertrude 1889-1968 ... **CLC 49**
See also CA 102; 93-96; DLB 225; EWL 3

Milne, A(lan) A(lexander)
1882-1956 .... **TCLC 6, 88**
See also BRWS 5; CA 104; 133; CLR 1, 26; CMW 4; CWRI 5; DA3; DAB; DAC; DAM MST; DLB 10, 77, 100, 160; FANT; MAICYA 1, 2; MTCW 1, 2; MTFW 2005; RGEL 2; SATA 100; WCH; YABC 1

Milner, Ron(ald) 1938-2004 ..... **BLC 3; CLC 56**
See also AITN 1; BW 1; CA 73-76; 230; CAD; CANR 24, 81; CD 5, 6; DAM MULT; DLB 38; MAL 5; MTCW 1

Milnes, Richard Monckton
1809-1885 .... **NCLC 61**
See also DLB 32, 184

Milosz, Czeslaw 1911-2004 .... **CLC 5, 11, 22, 31, 56, 82; PC 8; WLCS**
See also AAYA 62; CA 81-84; 230; CANR 23, 51, 91, 126; CDWLB 4; CWW 2;

Mott, Michael (Charles Alston)
1930- .... **CLC 15, 34**
See also CA 5-8R; CAAS 7; CANR 7, 29

Mountain Wolf Woman 1884-1960 . **CLC 92;
NNAL**
See also CA 144; CANR 90

Moure, Erin 1955- .... **CLC 88**
See also CA 113; CP 7; CWP; DLB 60

Mourning Dove 1885(?)-1936 .... **NNAL**
See also CA 144; CANR 90; DAM MULT;
DLB 175, 221

Mowat, Farley (McGill) 1921- .... **CLC 26**
See also AAYA 1, 50; BYA 2; CA 1-4R;
CANR 4, 24, 42, 68, 108; CLR 20; CPW;
DAC; DAM MST; DLB 68; INT CANR-
24; JRDA; MAICYA 1, 2; MTCW 1, 2;
MTFW 2005; SATA 3, 55; YAW

Mowatt, Anna Cora 1819-1870 ..... **NCLC 74**
See also RGAL 4

Moyers, Bill 1934- .... **CLC 74**
See also AITN 2; CA 61-64; CANR 31, 52

Mphahlele, Es'kia
See Mphahlele, Ezekiel
See also AFW; CDWLB 3; CN 4, 5, 6; DLB
125, 225; RGSF 2; SSFS 11

Mphahlele, Ezekiel 1919- ... **BLC 3; CLC 25,
133**
See Mphahlele, Es'kia
See also BW 2, 3; CA 81-84; CANR 26,
76; CN 1, 2, 3; DA3; DAM MULT; EWL
3; MTCW 2; MTFW 2005; SATA 119

Mqhayi, S(amuel) E(dward) K(rune Loliwe)
1875-1945 .... **BLC 3; TCLC 25**
See also CA 153; CANR 87; DAM MULT

Mrozek, Slawomir 1930- .... **CLC 3, 13**
See also CA 13-16R; CAAS 10; CANR 29;
CDWLB 4; CWW 2; DLB 232; EWL 3;
MTCW 1

Mrs. Belloc-Lowndes
See Lowndes, Marie Adelaide (Belloc)

Mrs. Fairstar
See Horne, Richard Henry Hengist

M'Taggart, John M'Taggart Ellis
See McTaggart, John McTaggart Ellis

Mtwa, Percy (?)- .... **CLC 47**
See also CD 6

Mueller, Lisel 1924- .... **CLC 13, 51; PC 33**
See also CA 93-96; CP 7; DLB 105; PFS 9,
13

Muggeridge, Malcolm (Thomas)
1903-1990 .... **TCLC 120**
See also AITN 1; CA 101; CANR 33, 63;
MTCW 1, 2

Muhammad 570-632 .... **WLCS**
See also DA; DAB; DAC; DAM MST;
DLB 311

Muir, Edwin 1887-1959 . **PC 49; TCLC 2, 87**
See Moore, Edward
See also BRWS 6; CA 104; 193; DLB 20,
100, 191; EWL 3; RGEL 2

Muir, John 1838-1914 .... **TCLC 28**
See also AMWS 9; ANW; CA 165; DLB
186, 275

Mujica Lainez, Manuel 1910-1984 ... **CLC 31**
See Lainez, Manuel Mujica
See also CA 81-84; 112; CANR 32; EWL
3; HW 1

Mukherjee, Bharati 1940- ..... **AAL; CLC 53,
115; SSC 38**
See also AAYA 46; BEST 89:2; CA 107,
232; CAAE 232; CANR 45, 72, 128; CN
5, 6, 7; DAM NOV; DLB 60, 218; DNFS
1, 2; EWL 3; FW; MAL 5; MTCW 1, 2;
MTFW 2005; RGAL 4; RGSF 2; SSFS 7;
TUS; WWE 1

Muldoon, Paul 1951- .... **CLC 32, 72, 166**
See also BRWS 4; CA 113; 129; CANR 52,
91; CP 2, 3, 4, 5, 6, 7; DAM POET; DLB
40; INT CA-129; PFS 7, 22; TCLE 1:2

Mulisch, Harry (Kurt Victor)
1927- .... **CLC 42**
See also CA 9-12R; CANR 6, 26, 56, 110;
CWW 2; DLB 299; EWL 3

Mull, Martin 1943- .... **CLC 17**
See also CA 105

Muller, Wilhelm .... **NCLC 73**

Mulock, Dinah Maria
See Craik, Dinah Maria (Mulock)
See also RGEL 2

Multatuli 1820-1887 .... **NCLC 165**
See also RGWL 2, 3

Munday, Anthony 1560-1633 .... **LC 87**
See also DLB 62, 172; RGEL 2

Munford, Robert 1737(?)-1783 .... **LC 5**
See also DLB 31

Mungo, Raymond 1946- .... **CLC 72**
See also CA 49-52; CANR 2

Munro, Alice (Anne) 1931- .... **CLC 6, 10, 19,
50, 95; SSC 3; WLCS**
See also AITN 2; BPFB 2; CA 33-36R;
CANR 33, 53, 75, 114; CCA 1; CN 1, 2,
3, 4, 5, 6, 7; DA3; DAC; DAM MST,
NOV; DLB 53; EWL 3; MTCW 1, 2;
MTFW 2005; RGEL 2; RGSF 2; SATA
29; SSFS 5, 13, 19; TCLE 1:2; WWE 1

Munro, H(ector) H(ugh) 1870-1916 .... **WLC**
See Saki
See also AAYA 56; CA 104; 130; CANR
104; CDBLB 1890-1914; DA; DA3;
DAB; DAC; DAM MST, NOV; DLB 34,
162; EXPS; MTCW 1, 2; MTFW 2005;
RGEL 2; SSFS 15

Murakami, Haruki 1949- .... **CLC 150**
See Murakami Haruki
See also CA 165; CANR 102, 146; MJW;
RGWL 3; SFW 4

Murakami Haruki
See Murakami, Haruki
See also CWW 2; DLB 182; EWL 3

Murasaki, Lady
See Murasaki Shikibu

Murasaki Shikibu 978(?)-1026(?) .. **CMLC 1,
79**
See also EFS 2; LATS 1:1; RGWL 2, 3

Murdoch, (Jean) Iris 1919-1999 ... **CLC 1, 2,
3, 4, 6, 8, 11, 15, 22, 31, 51; TCLC 171**
See also BRWS 1; CA 13-16R; 179; CANR
8, 43, 68, 103, 142; CBD; CDBLB 1960
to Present; CN 1, 2, 3, 4, 5, 6; CWD;
DA3; DAB; DAC; DAM MST, NOV;
DLB 14, 194, 233; EWL 3; INT CANR-8;
MTCW 1, 2; MTFW 2005; NFS 18;
RGEL 2; TCLE 1:2; TEA; WLIT 4

Murfree, Mary Noailles 1850-1922 .. **SSC 22;
TCLC 135**
See also CA 122; 176; DLB 12, 74; RGAL
4

Murnau, Friedrich Wilhelm
See Plumpe, Friedrich Wilhelm

Murphy, Richard 1927- .... **CLC 41**
See also BRWS 5; CA 29-32R; CP 1, 2, 3,
4, 5, 6, 7; DLB 40; EWL 3

Murphy, Sylvia 1937- .... **CLC 34**
See also CA 121

Murphy, Thomas (Bernard) 1935- ... **CLC 51**
See Murphy, Tom
See also CA 101

Murphy, Tom
See Murphy, Thomas (Bernard)
See also DLB 310

Murray, Albert L. 1916- .... **CLC 73**
See also BW 2; CA 49-52; CANR 26, 52,
78; CN 7; CSW; DLB 38; MTFW 2005

Murray, James Augustus Henry
1837-1915 .... **TCLC 117**

Murray, Judith Sargent
1751-1820 .... **NCLC 63**
See also DLB 37, 200

Murray, Les(lie Allan) 1938- .... **CLC 40**
See also BRWS 7; CA 21-24R; CANR 11,
27, 56, 103; CP 1, 2, 3, 4, 5, 6, 7; DAM
POET; DLB 289; DLBY 2001; EWL 3;
RGEL 2

Murry, J. Middleton
See Murry, John Middleton

Murry, John Middleton
1889-1957 .... **TCLC 16**
See also CA 118; 217; DLB 149

Musgrave, Susan 1951- .... **CLC 13, 54**
See also CA 69-72; CANR 45, 84; CCA 1;
CP 2, 3, 4, 5, 6, 7; CWP

Musil, Robert (Edler von)
1880-1942 .... **SSC 18; TCLC 12, 68**
See also CA 109; CANR 55, 84; CDWLB
2; DLB 81, 124; EW 9; EWL 3; MTCW
2; RGSF 2; RGWL 2, 3

Muske, Carol .... **CLC 90**
See Muske-Dukes, Carol (Anne)

Muske-Dukes, Carol (Anne) 1945-
See Muske, Carol
See also CA 65-68, 203; CAAE 203; CANR
32, 70; CWP

Musset, (Louis Charles) Alfred de
1810-1857 .... **DC 27; NCLC 7, 150**
See also DLB 192, 217; EW 6; GFL 1789
to the Present; RGWL 2, 3; TWA

Mussolini, Benito (Amilcare Andrea)
1883-1945 .... **TCLC 96**
See also CA 116

Mutanabbi, Al-
See al-Mutanabbi, Ahmad ibn al-Husayn
Abu al-Tayyib al-Jufi al-Kindi
See also WLIT 6

My Brother's Brother
See Chekhov, Anton (Pavlovich)

Myers, L(eopold) H(amilton)
1881-1944 .... **TCLC 59**
See also CA 157; DLB 15; EWL 3; RGEL
2

Myers, Walter Dean 1937- .. **BLC 3; CLC 35**
See also AAYA 4, 23; BW 2; BYA 6, 8, 11;
CA 33-36R; CANR 20, 42, 67, 108; CLR
4, 16, 35; DAM MULT, NOV; DLB 33;
INT CANR-20; JRDA; LAIT 5; MAICYA
1, 2; MAICYAS 1; MTCW 2; MTFW
2005; SAAS 2; SATA 41, 71, 109, 157;
SATA-Brief 27; WYA; YAW

Myers, Walter M.
See Myers, Walter Dean

Myles, Symon
See Follett, Ken(neth Martin)

Nabokov, Vladimir (Vladimirovich)
1899-1977 .... **CLC 1, 2, 3, 6, 8, 11, 15,
23, 44, 46, 64; SSC 11, 86; TCLC 108;
WLC**
See also AAYA 45; AMW; AMWC 1;
AMWR 1; BPFB 2; CA 5-8R; 69-72;
CANR 20, 102; CDALB 1941-1968; CN
1, 2; CP 2; DA; DA3; DAB; DAC; DAM
MST, NOV; DLB 2, 244, 278, 317; DLBD
3; DLBY 1980, 1991; EWL 3; EXPS;
LATS 1:2; MAL 5; MTCW 1, 2; MTFW
2005; NCFS 4; NFS 9; RGAL 4; RGSF
2; SSFS 6, 15; TUS

Naevius c. 265B.C.-201B.C. .... **CMLC 37**
See also DLB 211

Nagai, Kafu .... **TCLC 51**
See Nagai, Sokichi
See also DLB 180

Nagai, Sokichi 1879-1959
See Nagai, Kafu
See also CA 117

Nagy, Laszlo 1925-1978 .... **CLC 7**
See also CA 129; 112

Naidu, Sarojini 1879-1949 .... **TCLC 80**
See also EWL 3; RGEL 2

Nishiwaki, Junzaburo 1894-1982 .... **PC 15**
See Junzaburo, Nishiwaki
See also CA 194; 107; MJW; RGWL 3

Nissenson, Hugh 1933- .... **CLC 4, 9**
See also CA 17-20R; CANR 27, 108; CN
5, 6; DLB 28

Nister, Der
See Der Nister
See also EWL 3

Niven, Larry .... **CLC 8**
See Niven, Laurence Van Cott
See also AAYA 27; BPFB 2; BYA 10; DLB
8; SCFW 1, 2

Niven, Laurence Van Cott 1938-
See Niven, Larry
See also CA 21-24R, 207; CAAE 207;
CAAS 12; CANR 14, 44, 66, 113; CPW;
DAM POP; MTCW 1, 2; SATA 95; SFW
4

Nixon, Agnes Eckhardt 1927- .... **CLC 21**
See also CA 110

Nizan, Paul 1905-1940 .... **TCLC 40**
See also CA 161; DLB 72; EWL 3; GFL
1789 to the Present

Nkosi, Lewis 1936- .... **BLC 3; CLC 45**
See also BW 1, 3; CA 65-68; CANR 27,
81; CBD; CD 5, 6; DAM MULT; DLB
157, 225; WWE 1

Nodier, (Jean) Charles (Emmanuel)
1780-1844 .... **NCLC 19**
See also DLB 119; GFL 1789 to the Present

Noguchi, Yone 1875-1947 .... **TCLC 80**

Nolan, Christopher 1965- .... **CLC 58**
See also CA 111; CANR 88

Noon, Jeff 1957- .... **CLC 91**
See also CA 148; CANR 83; DLB 267;
SFW 4

Norden, Charles
See Durrell, Lawrence (George)

Nordhoff, Charles Bernard
1887-1947 .... **TCLC 23**
See also CA 108; 211; DLB 9; LAIT 1;
RHW 1; SATA 23

Norfolk, Lawrence 1963- .... **CLC 76**
See also CA 144; CANR 85; CN 6, 7; DLB
267

Norman, Marsha (Williams) 1947- . **CLC 28,
186; DC 8**
See also CA 105; CABS 3; CAD; CANR
41, 131; CD 5, 6; CSW; CWD; DAM
DRAM; DFS 2; DLB 266; DLBY 1984;
FW; MAL 5

Normyx
See Douglas, (George) Norman

Norris, (Benjamin) Frank(lin, Jr.)
1870-1902 .... **SSC 28; TCLC 24, 155**
See also AAYA 57; AMW; AMWC 2; BPFB
2; CA 110; 160; CDALB 1865-1917; DLB
12, 71, 186; LMFS 2; NFS 12; RGAL 4;
TCWW 1, 2; TUS

Norris, Leslie 1921- .... **CLC 14**
See also CA 11-12; CANR 14, 117; CAP 1;
CP 1, 2, 3, 4, 5, 6, 7; DLB 27, 256

North, Andrew
See Norton, Andre

North, Anthony
See Koontz, Dean R.

North, Captain George
See Stevenson, Robert Louis (Balfour)

North, Captain George
See Stevenson, Robert Louis (Balfour)

North, Milou
See Erdrich, (Karen) Louise

Northrup, B. A.
See Hubbard, L(afayette) Ron(ald)

North Staffs
See Hulme, T(homas) E(rnest)

Northup, Solomon 1808-1863 ...... **NCLC 105**

Norton, Alice Mary
See Norton, Andre
See also MAICYA 1; SATA 1, 43

Norton, Andre 1912-2005 .... **CLC 12**
See Norton, Alice Mary
See also AAYA 14; BPFB 2; BYA 4, 10,
12; CA 1-4R; 237; CANR 68; CLR 50;
DLB 8, 52; JRDA; MAICYA 2; MTCW
1; SATA 91; SUFW 1, 2; YAW

Norton, Caroline 1808-1877 .... **NCLC 47**
See also DLB 21, 159, 199

Norway, Nevil Shute 1899-1960
See Shute, Nevil
See also CA 102; 93-96; CANR 85; MTCW
2

Norwid, Cyprian Kamil
1821-1883 .... **NCLC 17**
See also RGWL 3

Nosille, Nabrah
See Ellison, Harlan (Jay)

Nossack, Hans Erich 1901-1978 .... **CLC 6**
See also CA 93-96; 85-88; DLB 69; EWL 3

Nostradamus 1503-1566 .... **LC 27**

Nosu, Chuji
See Ozu, Yasujiro

Notenburg, Eleanora (Genrikhovna) von
See Guro, Elena (Genrikhovna)

Nova, Craig 1945- .... **CLC 7, 31**
See also CA 45-48; CANR 2, 53, 127

Novak, Joseph
See Kosinski, Jerzy (Nikodem)

Novalis 1772-1801 .... **NCLC 13**
See also CDWLB 2; DLB 90; EW 5; RGWL
2, 3

Novick, Peter 1934- .... **CLC 164**
See also CA 188

Novis, Emile
See Weil, Simone (Adolphine)

Nowlan, Alden (Albert) 1933-1983 ... **CLC 15**
See also CA 9-12R; CANR 5; CP 1, 2, 3;
DAC; DAM MST; DLB 53; PFS 12

Noyes, Alfred 1880-1958 ...... **PC 27; TCLC 7**
See also CA 104; 188; DLB 20; EXPP;
FANT; PFS 4; RGEL 2

Nugent, Richard Bruce
1906(?)-1987 .... **HR 1:3**
See also BW 1; CA 125; DLB 51; GLL 2

Nunn, Kem .... **CLC 34**
See also CA 159

Nussbaum, Martha Craven 1947- .. **CLC 203**
See also CA 134; CANR 102

Nwapa, Flora (Nwanzuruaha)
1931-1993 .... **BLCS; CLC 133**
See also BW 2; CA 143; CANR 83; CD-
WLB 3; CWRI 5; DLB 125; EWL 3;
WLIT 4

Nye, Robert 1939- .... **CLC 13, 42**
See also BRWS 10; CA 33-36R; CANR 29,
67, 107; CN 1, 2, 3, 4, 5, 6, 7; CP 1, 2, 3,
4, 5, 6, 7; CWRI 5; DAM NOV; DLB 14,
271; FANT; HGG; MTCW 1; RHW;
SATA 6

Nyro, Laura 1947-1997 .... **CLC 17**
See also CA 194

Oates, Joyce Carol 1938- .. **CLC 1, 2, 3, 6, 9,
11, 15, 19, 33, 52, 108, 134; SSC 6, 70;
WLC**
See also AAYA 15, 52; AITN 1; AMWS 2;
BEST 89:2; BPFB 2; BYA 11; CA 5-8R;
CANR 25, 45, 74, 113, 129; CDALB
1968-1988; CN 1, 2, 3, 4, 5, 6, 7; CP 7;
CPW; CWP; DA; DA3; DAB; DAC;
DAM MST, NOV, POP; DLB 2, 5, 130;
DLBY 1981; EWL 3; EXPS; FL 1:6; FW;
GL 3; HGG; INT CANR-25; LAIT 4;
MAL 5; MAWW; MTCW 1, 2; MTFW
2005; NFS 8; RGAL 4; RGSF 2; SATA
159; SSFS 1, 8, 17; SUFW 2; TUS

O'Brian, E. G.
See Clarke, Arthur C(harles)

O'Brian, Patrick 1914-2000 .... **CLC 152**
See also AAYA 55; CA 144; 187; CANR
74; CPW; MTCW 2; MTFW 2005; RHW

O'Brien, Darcy 1939-1998 .... **CLC 11**
See also CA 21-24R; 167; CANR 8, 59

O'Brien, Edna 1932- ..... **CLC 3, 5, 8, 13, 36,
65, 116; SSC 10, 77**
See also BRWS 5; CA 1-4R; CANR 6, 41,
65, 102; CDBLB 1960 to Present; CN 1,
2, 3, 4, 5, 6, 7; DA3; DAM NOV; DLB
14, 231, 319; EWL 3; FW; MTCW 1, 2;
MTFW 2005; RGSF 2; WLIT 4

O'Brien, Fitz-James 1828-1862 ..... **NCLC 21**
See also DLB 74; RGAL 4; SUFW

O'Brien, Flann .... **CLC 1, 4, 5, 7, 10, 47**
See O Nuallain, Brian
See also BRWS 2; DLB 231; EWL 3;
RGEL 2

O'Brien, Richard 1942- .... **CLC 17**
See also CA 124

O'Brien, (William) Tim(othy) 1946- . **CLC 7,
19, 40, 103, 211; SSC 74**
See also AAYA 16; AMWS 5; CA 85-88;
CANR 40, 58, 133; CDALBS; CN 5, 6,
7; CPW; DA3; DAM POP; DLB 152;
DLBD 9; DLBY 1980; LATS 1:2; MAL
5; MTCW 2; MTFW 2005; RGAL 4;
SSFS 5, 15; TCLE 1:2

Obstfelder, Sigbjoern 1866-1900 .... **TCLC 23**
See also CA 123

O'Casey, Sean 1880-1964 .... **CLC 1, 5, 9, 11,
15, 88; DC 12; WLCS**
See also BRW 7; CA 89-92; CANR 62;
CBD; CDBLB 1914-1945; DA3; DAB;
DAC; DAM DRAM, MST; DFS 19; DLB
10; EWL 3; MTCW 1, 2; MTFW 2005;
RGEL 2; TEA; WLIT 4

O'Cathasaigh, Sean
See O'Casey, Sean

Occom, Samson 1723-1792 .... **LC 60; NNAL**
See also DLB 175

Ochs, Phil(ip David) 1940-1976 .... **CLC 17**
See also CA 185; 65-68

O'Connor, Edwin (Greene)
1918-1968 .... **CLC 14**
See also CA 93-96; 25-28R; MAL 5

O'Connor, (Mary) Flannery
1925-1964 .... **CLC 1, 2, 3, 6, 10, 13, 15,
21, 66, 104; SSC 1, 23, 61, 82; TCLC
132; WLC**
See also AAYA 7; AMW; AMWR 2; BPFB
3; BYA 16; CA 1-4R; CANR 3, 41;
CDALB 1941-1968; DA; DA3; DAB;
DAC; DAM MST, NOV; DLB 2, 152;
DLBD 12; DLBY 1980; EWL 3; EXPS;
LAIT 5; MAL 5; MAWW; MTCW 1, 2;
MTFW 2005; NFS 3, 21; RGAL 4; RGSF
2; SSFS 2, 7, 10, 19; TUS

O'Connor, Frank .... **CLC 23; SSC 5**
See O'Donovan, Michael Francis
See also DLB 162; EWL 3; RGSF 2; SSFS
5

O'Dell, Scott 1898-1989 .... **CLC 30**
See also AAYA 3, 44; BPFB 3; BYA 1, 2,
3, 5; CA 61-64; 129; CANR 12, 30, 112;
CLR 1, 16; DLB 52; JRDA; MAICYA 1,
2; SATA 12, 60, 134; WYA; YAW

Odets, Clifford 1906-1963 ..... **CLC 2, 28, 98;
DC 6**
See also AMWS 2; CA 85-88; CAD; CANR
62; DAM DRAM; DFS 3, 17, 20; DLB 7,
26; EWL 3; MAL 5; MTCW 1, 2; MTFW
2005; RGAL 4; TUS

O'Doherty, Brian 1928- .... **CLC 76**
See also CA 105; CANR 108

O'Donnell, K. M.
See Malzberg, Barry N(athaniel)

Osborne, Lawrence 1958- .... **CLC 50**
See also CA 189

Osbourne, Lloyd 1868-1947 .... **TCLC 93**

Osgood, Frances Sargent
1811-1850 .... **NCLC 141**
See also DLB 250

Oshima, Nagisa 1932- .... **CLC 20**
See also CA 116; 121; CANR 78

Oskison, John Milton
1874-1947 .... **NNAL; TCLC 35**
See also CA 144; CANR 84; DAM MULT;
DLB 175

Ossian c. 3rd cent. - .... **CMLC 28**
See Macpherson, James

Ossoli, Sarah Margaret (Fuller)
1810-1850 .... **NCLC 5, 50**
See Fuller, Margaret; Fuller, Sarah Margaret
See also CDALB 1640-1865; FW; LMFS 1;
SATA 25

Ostriker, Alicia (Suskin) 1937- .... **CLC 132**
See also CA 25-28R; CAAS 24; CANR 10,
30, 62, 99; CWP; DLB 120; EXPP; PFS
19

Ostrovsky, Aleksandr Nikolaevich
See Ostrovsky, Alexander
See also DLB 277

Ostrovsky, Alexander 1823-1886 .. **NCLC 30,
57**
See Ostrovsky, Aleksandr Nikolaevich

Otero, Blas de 1916-1979 .... **CLC 11**
See also CA 89-92; DLB 134; EWL 3

O'Trigger, Sir Lucius
See Horne, Richard Henry Hengist

Otto, Rudolf 1869-1937 .... **TCLC 85**

Otto, Whitney 1955- .... **CLC 70**
See also CA 140; CANR 120

Otway, Thomas 1652-1685 ... **DC 24; LC 106**
See also DAM DRAM; DLB 80; RGEL 2

Ouida .... **TCLC 43**
See De la Ramee, Marie Louise (Ouida)
See also DLB 18, 156; RGEL 2

Ouologuem, Yambo 1940- .... **CLC 146**
See also CA 111; 176

Ousmane, Sembene 1923- ... **BLC 3; CLC 66**
See Sembene, Ousmane
See also BW 1, 3; CA 117; 125; CANR 81;
CWW 2; MTCW 1

Ovid 43B.C.-17 .... **CMLC 7; PC 2**
See also AW 2; CDWLB 1; DA3; DAM
POET; DLB 211; PFS 22; RGWL 2, 3;
WP

Owen, Hugh
See Faust, Frederick (Schiller)

Owen, Wilfred (Edward Salter)
1893-1918 ... **PC 19; TCLC 5, 27; WLC**
See also BRW 6; CA 104; 141; CDBLB
1914-1945; DA; DAB; DAC; DAM MST,
POET; DLB 20; EWL 3; EXPP; MTCW
2; MTFW 2005; PFS 10; RGEL 2; WLIT
4

Owens, Louis (Dean) 1948-2002 .... **NNAL**
See also CA 137, 179; 207; CAAE 179;
CAAS 24; CANR 71

Owens, Rochelle 1936- .... **CLC 8**
See also CA 17-20R; CAAS 2; CAD;
CANR 39; CD 5, 6; CP 1, 2, 3, 4, 5, 6, 7;
CWD; CWP

Oz, Amos 1939- ...... **CLC 5, 8, 11, 27, 33, 54;
SSC 66**
See also CA 53-56; CANR 27, 47, 65, 113,
138; CWW 2; DAM NOV; EWL 3;
MTCW 1, 2; MTFW 2005; RGSF 2;
RGWL 3; WLIT 6

Ozick, Cynthia 1928- .... **CLC 3, 7, 28, 62,
155; SSC 15, 60**
See also AMWS 5; BEST 90:1; CA 17-20R;
CANR 23, 58, 116; CN 3, 4, 5, 6, 7;
CPW; DA3; DAM NOV, POP; DLB 28,

152, 299; DLBY 1982; EWL 3; EXPS;
INT CANR-23; MAL 5; MTCW 1, 2;
MTFW 2005; RGAL 4; RGSF 2; SSFS 3,
12

Ozu, Yasujiro 1903-1963 .... **CLC 16**
See also CA 112

Pabst, G. W. 1885-1967 .... **TCLC 127**

Pacheco, C.
See Pessoa, Fernando (Antonio Nogueira)

Pacheco, Jose Emilio 1939- .... **HLC 2**
See also CA 111; 131; CANR 65; CWW 2;
DAM MULT; DLB 290; EWL 3; HW 1,
2; RGSF 2

Pa Chin .... **CLC 18**
See Li Fei-kan
See also EWL 3

Pack, Robert 1929- .... **CLC 13**
See also CA 1-4R; CANR 3, 44, 82; CP 1,
2, 3, 4, 5, 6, 7; DLB 5; SATA 118

Padgett, Lewis
See Kuttner, Henry

Padilla (Lorenzo), Heberto
1932-2000 .... **CLC 38**
See also AITN 1; CA 123; 131; 189; CWW
2; EWL 3; HW 1

Page, James Patrick 1944-
See Page, Jimmy
See also CA 204

Page, Jimmy 1944- .... **CLC 12**
See Page, James Patrick

Page, Louise 1955- .... **CLC 40**
See also CA 140; CANR 76; CBD; CD 5,
6; CWD; DLB 233

Page, P(atricia) K(athleen) 1916- ...... **CLC 7,
18; PC 12**
See Cape, Judith
See also CA 53-56; CANR 4, 22, 65; CP 1,
2, 3, 4, 5, 6, 7; DAC; DAM MST; DLB
68; MTCW 1; RGEL 2

Page, Stanton
See Fuller, Henry Blake

Page, Stanton
See Fuller, Henry Blake

Page, Thomas Nelson 1853-1922 .... **SSC 23**
See also CA 118; 177; DLB 12, 78; DLBD
13; RGAL 4

Pagels, Elaine Hiesey 1943- .... **CLC 104**
See also CA 45-48; CANR 2, 24, 51; FW;
NCFS 4

Paget, Violet 1856-1935
See Lee, Vernon
See also CA 104; 166; GLL 1; HGG

Paget-Lowe, Henry
See Lovecraft, H(oward) P(hillips)

Paglia, Camille (Anna) 1947- .... **CLC 68**
See also CA 140; CANR 72, 139; CPW;
FW; GLL 2; MTCW 2; MTFW 2005

Paige, Richard
See Koontz, Dean R.

Paine, Thomas 1737-1809 .... **NCLC 62**
See also AMWS 1; CDALB 1640-1865;
DLB 31, 43, 73, 158; LAIT 1; RGAL 4;
RGEL 2; TUS

Pakenham, Antonia
See Fraser, Antonia (Pakenham)

Palamas, Costis
See Palamas, Kostes

Palamas, Kostes 1859-1943 .... **TCLC 5**
See Palamas, Kostis
See also CA 105; 190; RGWL 2, 3

Palamas, Kostis
See Palamas, Kostes
See also EWL 3

Palazzeschi, Aldo 1885-1974 .... **CLC 11**
See also CA 89-92; 53-56; DLB 114, 264;
EWL 3

Pales Matos, Luis 1898-1959 .... **HLCS 2**
See Pales Matos, Luis
See also DLB 290; HW 1; LAW

Paley, Grace 1922- .. **CLC 4, 6, 37, 140; SSC
8**
See also AMWS 6; CA 25-28R; CANR 13,
46, 74, 118; CN 2, 3, 4, 5, 6, 7; CPW;
DA3; DAM POP; DLB 28, 218; EWL 3;
EXPS; FW; INT CANR-13; MAL 5;
MAWW; MTCW 1, 2; MTFW 2005;
RGAL 4; RGSF 2; SSFS 3, 20

Palin, Michael (Edward) 1943- .... **CLC 21**
See Monty Python
See also CA 107; CANR 35, 109; SATA 67

Palliser, Charles 1947- .... **CLC 65**
See also CA 136; CANR 76; CN 5, 6, 7

Palma, Ricardo 1833-1919 .... **TCLC 29**
See also CA 168; LAW

Pamuk, Orhan 1952- .... **CLC 185**
See also CA 142; CANR 75, 127; CWW 2;
WLIT 6

Pancake, Breece Dexter 1952-1979
See Pancake, Breece D'J
See also CA 123; 109

Pancake, Breece D'J .... **CLC 29; SSC 61**
See Pancake, Breece Dexter
See also DLB 130

Panchenko, Nikolai .... **CLC 59**

Pankhurst, Emmeline (Goulden)
1858-1928 .... **TCLC 100**
See also CA 116; FW

Panko, Rudy
See Gogol, Nikolai (Vasilyevich)

Papadiamantis, Alexandros
1851-1911 .... **TCLC 29**
See also CA 168; EWL 3

Papadiamantopoulos, Johannes 1856-1910
See Moreas, Jean
See also CA 117

Papini, Giovanni 1881-1956 .... **TCLC 22**
See also CA 121; 180; DLB 264

Paracelsus 1493-1541 .... **LC 14**
See also DLB 179

Parasol, Peter
See Stevens, Wallace

Pardo Bazan, Emilia 1851-1921 .... **SSC 30**
See also EWL 3; FW; RGSF 2; RGWL 2, 3

Pareto, Vilfredo 1848-1923 .... **TCLC 69**
See also CA 175

Paretsky, Sara 1947- .... **CLC 135**
See also AAYA 30; BEST 90:3; CA 125;
129; CANR 59, 95; CMW 4; CPW; DA3;
DAM POP; DLB 306; INT CA-129;
MSW; RGAL 4

Parfenie, Maria
See Codrescu, Andrei

Parini, Jay (Lee) 1948- .... **CLC 54, 133**
See also CA 97-100, 229; CAAE 229;
CAAS 16; CANR 32, 87

Park, Jordan
See Kornbluth, C(yril) M.; Pohl, Frederik

Park, Robert E(zra) 1864-1944 ..... **TCLC 73**
See also CA 122; 165

Parker, Bert
See Ellison, Harlan (Jay)

Parker, Dorothy (Rothschild)
1893-1967 . **CLC 15, 68; PC 28; SSC 2;
TCLC 143**
See also AMWS 9; CA 19-20; 25-28R; CAP
2; DA3; DAM POET; DLB 11, 45, 86;
EXPP; FW; MAL 5; MAWW; MTCW 1,
2; MTFW 2005; PFS 18; RGAL 4; RGSF
2; TUS

Parker, Robert B(rown) 1932- .... **CLC 27**
See also AAYA 28; BEST 89:4; BPFB 3;
CA 49-52; CANR 1, 26, 52, 89, 128;
CMW 4; CPW; DAM NOV, POP; DLB
306; INT CANR-26; MSW; MTCW 1;
MTFW 2005

Parkin, Frank 1940- .... **CLC 43**
See also CA 147

PEPECE
See Prado (Calvo), Pedro

Pepys, Samuel 1633-1703 ... **LC 11, 58; WLC**
See also BRW 2; CDBLB 1660-1789; DA; DA3; DAB; DAC; DAM MST; DLB 101, 213; NCFS 4; RGEL 2; TEA; WLIT 3

Percy, Thomas 1729-1811 .... **NCLC 95**
See also DLB 104

Percy, Walker 1916-1990 .... **CLC 2, 3, 6, 8, 14, 18, 47, 65**
See also AMWS 3; BPFB 3; CA 1-4R; 131; CANR 1, 23, 64; CN 1, 2, 3, 4; CPW; CSW; DA3; DAM NOV, POP; DLB 2; DLBY 1980, 1990; EWL 3; MAL 5; MTCW 1, 2; MTFW 2005; RGAL 4; TUS

Percy, William Alexander 1885-1942 .... **TCLC 84**
See also CA 163; MTCW 2

Perec, Georges 1936-1982 .... **CLC 56, 116**
See also CA 141; DLB 83, 299; EWL 3; GFL 1789 to the Present; RGWL 3

Pereda (y Sanchez de Porrua), Jose Maria de 1833-1906 .... **TCLC 16**
See also CA 117

Pereda y Porrua, Jose Maria de
See Pereda (y Sanchez de Porrua), Jose Maria de

Peregoy, George Weems
See Mencken, H(enry) L(ouis)

Perelman, S(idney) J(oseph) 1904-1979 .. **CLC 3, 5, 9, 15, 23, 44, 49; SSC 32**
See also AITN 1, 2; BPFB 3; CA 73-76; 89-92; CANR 18; DAM DRAM; DLB 11, 44; MTCW 1, 2; MTFW 2005; RGAL 4

Peret, Benjamin 1899-1959 .... **PC 33; TCLC 20**
See also CA 117; 186; GFL 1789 to the Present

Peretz, Isaac Leib
See Peretz, Isaac Loeb
See also CA 201

Peretz, Isaac Loeb 1851(?)-1915 ...... **SSC 26; TCLC 16**
See Peretz, Isaac Leib
See also CA 109

Peretz, Yitzkhok Leibush
See Peretz, Isaac Loeb

Perez Galdos, Benito 1843-1920 ..... **HLCS 2; TCLC 27**
See Galdos, Benito Perez
See also CA 125; 153; EWL 3; HW 1; RGWL 2, 3

Peri Rossi, Cristina 1941- .. **CLC 156; HLCS 2**
See also CA 131; CANR 59, 81; CWW 2; DLB 145, 290; EWL 3; HW 1, 2

Perlata
See Peret, Benjamin

Perloff, Marjorie G(abrielle) 1931- .... **CLC 137**
See also CA 57-60; CANR 7, 22, 49, 104

Perrault, Charles 1628-1703 .... **LC 2, 56**
See also BYA 4; CLR 79; DLB 268; GFL Beginnings to 1789; MAICYA 1, 2; RGWL 2, 3; SATA 25; WCH

Perry, Anne 1938- .... **CLC 126**
See also CA 101; CANR 22, 50, 84; CMW 4; CN 6, 7; CPW; DLB 276

Perry, Brighton
See Sherwood, Robert E(mmet)

Perse, St.-John
See Leger, (Marie-Rene Auguste) Alexis Saint-Leger

Perse, Saint-John
See Leger, (Marie-Rene Auguste) Alexis Saint-Leger
See also DLB 258; RGWL 3

Persius 34-62 .... **CMLC 74**
See also AW 2; DLB 211; RGWL 2, 3

Perutz, Leo(pold) 1882-1957 .... **TCLC 60**
See also CA 147; DLB 81

Peseenz, Tulio F.
See Lopez y Fuentes, Gregorio

Pesetsky, Bette 1932- .... **CLC 28**
See also CA 133; DLB 130

Peshkov, Alexei Maximovich 1868-1936
See Gorky, Maxim
See also CA 105; 141; CANR 83; DA; DAC; DAM DRAM, MST, NOV; MTCW 2; MTFW 2005

Pessoa, Fernando (Antonio Nogueira) 1888-1935 ..... **HLC 2; PC 20; TCLC 27**
See also CA 125; 183; DAM MULT; DLB 287; EW 10; EWL 3; RGWL 2, 3; WP

Peterkin, Julia Mood 1880-1961 ...... **CLC 31**
See also CA 102; DLB 9

Peters, Joan K(aren) 1945- .... **CLC 39**
See also CA 158; CANR 109

Peters, Robert L(ouis) 1924- .... **CLC 7**
See also CA 13-16R; CAAS 8; CP 1, 7; DLB 105

Petofi, Sandor 1823-1849 .... **NCLC 21**
See also RGWL 2, 3

Petrakis, Harry Mark 1923- .... **CLC 3**
See also CA 9-12R; CANR 4, 30, 85; CN 1, 2, 3, 4, 5, 6, 7

Petrarch 1304-1374 .... **CMLC 20; PC 8**
See also DA3; DAM POET; EW 2; LMFS 1; RGWL 2, 3; WLIT 7

Petronius c. 20-66 .... **CMLC 34**
See also AW 2; CDWLB 1; DLB 211; RGWL 2, 3

Petrov, Evgeny .... **TCLC 21**
See Kataev, Evgeny Petrovich

Petry, Ann (Lane) 1908-1997 .. **CLC 1, 7, 18; TCLC 112**
See also AFAW 1, 2; BPFB 3; BW 1, 3; BYA 2; CA 5-8R; 157; CAAS 6; CANR 4, 46; CLR 12; CN 1, 2, 3, 4, 5, 6; DLB 76; EWL 3; JRDA; LAIT 1; MAICYA 1, 2; MAICYAS 1; MTCW 1; RGAL 4; SATA 5; SATA-Obit 94; TUS

Petursson, Halligrimur 1614-1674 .... **LC 8**

Peychinovich
See Vazov, Ivan (Minchov)

Phaedrus c. 15B.C.-c. 50 .... **CMLC 25**
See also DLB 211

Phelps (Ward), Elizabeth Stuart
See Phelps, Elizabeth Stuart
See also FW

Phelps, Elizabeth Stuart 1844-1911 .... **TCLC 113**
See Phelps (Ward), Elizabeth Stuart
See also DLB 74

Philips, Katherine 1632-1664 . **LC 30; PC 40**
See also DLB 131; RGEL 2

Philipson, Morris H. 1926- .... **CLC 53**
See also CA 1-4R; CANR 4

Phillips, Caryl 1958- .... **BLCS; CLC 96**
See also BRWS 5; BW 2; CA 141; CANR 63, 104, 140; CBD; CD 5, 6; CN 5, 6, 7; DA3; DAM MULT; DLB 157; EWL 3; MTCW 2; MTFW 2005; WLIT 4; WWE 1

Phillips, David Graham 1867-1911 .... **TCLC 44**
See also CA 108; 176; DLB 9, 12, 303; RGAL 4

Phillips, Jack
See Sandburg, Carl (August)

Phillips, Jayne Anne 1952- .... **CLC 15, 33, 139; SSC 16**
See also AAYA 57; BPFB 3; CA 101; CANR 24, 50, 96; CN 5, 6, 7; CSW; DLBY 1980; INT CANR-24; MTCW 1, 2; MTFW 2005; RGAL 4; RGSF 2; SSFS 4

Phillips, Richard
See Dick, Philip K(indred)

Phillips, Robert (Schaeffer) 1938- .... **CLC 28**
See also CA 17-20R; CAAS 13; CANR 8; DLB 105

Phillips, Ward
See Lovecraft, H(oward) P(hillips)

Philostratus, Flavius c. 179-c. 244 .... **CMLC 62**

Piccolo, Lucio 1901-1969 .... **CLC 13**
See also CA 97-100; DLB 114; EWL 3

Pickthall, Marjorie L(owry) C(hristie) 1883-1922 .... **TCLC 21**
See also CA 107; DLB 92

Pico della Mirandola, Giovanni 1463-1494 .... **LC 15**
See also LMFS 1

Piercy, Marge 1936- .... **CLC 3, 6, 14, 18, 27, 62, 128; PC 29**
See also BPFB 3; CA 21-24R; 187; CAAE 187; CAAS 1; CANR 13, 43, 66, 111; CN 3, 4, 5, 6, 7; CP 1, 2, 3, 4, 5, 6, 7; CWP; DLB 120, 227; EXPP; FW; MAL 5; MTCW 1, 2; MTFW 2005; PFS 9, 22; SFW 4

Piers, Robert
See Anthony, Piers

Pieyre de Mandiargues, Andre 1909-1991
See Mandiargues, Andre Pieyre de
See also CA 103; 136; CANR 22, 82; EWL 3; GFL 1789 to the Present

Pilnyak, Boris 1894-1938 . **SSC 48; TCLC 23**
See Vogau, Boris Andreyevich
See also EWL 3

Pinchback, Eugene
See Toomer, Jean

Pincherle, Alberto 1907-1990 ...... **CLC 11, 18**
See Moravia, Alberto
See also CA 25-28R; 132; CANR 33, 63, 142; DAM NOV; MTCW 1; MTFW 2005

Pinckney, Darryl 1953- .... **CLC 76**
See also BW 2, 3; CA 143; CANR 79

Pindar 518(?)B.C.-438(?)B.C. .... **CMLC 12; PC 19**
See also AW 1; CDWLB 1; DLB 176; RGWL 2

Pineda, Cecile 1942- .... **CLC 39**
See also CA 118; DLB 209

Pinero, Arthur Wing 1855-1934 .... **TCLC 32**
See also CA 110; 153; DAM DRAM; DLB 10; RGEL 2

Pinero, Miguel (Antonio Gomez) 1946-1988 .... **CLC 4, 55**
See also CA 61-64; 125; CAD; CANR 29, 90; DLB 266; HW 1; LLW

Pinget, Robert 1919-1997 .... **CLC 7, 13, 37**
See also CA 85-88; 160; CWW 2; DLB 83; EWL 3; GFL 1789 to the Present

Pink Floyd
See Barrett, (Roger) Syd; Gilmour, David; Mason, Nick; Waters, Roger; Wright, Rick

Pinkney, Edward 1802-1828 .... **NCLC 31**
See also DLB 248

Pinkwater, D. Manus
See Pinkwater, Daniel Manus

Pinkwater, Daniel
See Pinkwater, Daniel Manus

Pinkwater, Daniel M.
See Pinkwater, Daniel Manus

Pinkwater, Daniel Manus 1941- .... **CLC 35**
See also AAYA 1, 46; BYA 9; CA 29-32R; CANR 12, 38, 89, 143; CLR 4; CSW; FANT; JRDA; MAICYA 1, 2; SAAS 3; SATA 8, 46, 76, 114, 158; SFW 4; YAW

Pinkwater, Manus
See Pinkwater, Daniel Manus

DLBY 1980; EWL 3; EXPS; LAIT 3;
MAL 5; MAWW; MTCW 1, 2; MTFW
2005; NFS 14; RGAL 4; RGSF 2; SATA
39; SATA-Obit 23; SSFS 1, 8, 11, 16;
TCWW 2; TUS

Porter, Peter (Neville Frederick)
1929- .... **CLC 5, 13, 33**
See also CA 85-88; CP 1, 2, 3, 4, 5, 6, 7;
DLB 40, 289; WWE 1

Porter, William Sydney 1862-1910
See Henry, O.
See also CA 104; 131; CDALB 1865-1917;
DA; DA3; DAB; DAC; DAM MST; DLB
12, 78, 79; MAL 5; MTCW 1, 2; MTFW
2005; TUS; YABC 2

Portillo (y Pacheco), Jose Lopez
See Lopez Portillo (y Pacheco), Jose

Portillo Trambley, Estela 1927-1998 .. **HLC 2**
See Trambley, Estela Portillo
See also CANR 32; DAM MULT; DLB
209; HW 1

Posey, Alexander (Lawrence)
1873-1908 .... **NNAL**
See also CA 144; CANR 80; DAM MULT;
DLB 175

Posse, Abel .... **CLC 70**

Post, Melville Davisson
1869-1930 .... **TCLC 39**
See also CA 110; 202; CMW 4

Potok, Chaim 1929-2002 ... **CLC 2, 7, 14, 26,**
112
See also AAYA 15, 50; AITN 1, 2; BPFB 3;
BYA 1; CA 17-20R; 208; CANR 19, 35,
64, 98; CLR 92; CN 4, 5, 6; DA3; DAM
NOV; DLB 28, 152; EXPN; INT CANR-
19; LAIT 4; MTCW 1, 2; MTFW 2005;
NFS 4; SATA 33, 106; SATA-Obit 134;
TUS; YAW

Potok, Herbert Harold -2002
See Potok, Chaim

Potok, Herman Harold
See Potok, Chaim

Potter, Dennis (Christopher George)
1935-1994 .... **CLC 58, 86, 123**
See also BRWS 10; CA 107; 145; CANR
33, 61; CBD; DLB 233; MTCW 1

Pound, Ezra (Weston Loomis)
1885-1972 .. **CLC 1, 2, 3, 4, 5, 7, 10, 13,**
18, 34, 48, 50, 112; PC 4; WLC
See also AAYA 47; AMW; AMWR 1; CA
5-8R; 37-40R; CANR 40; CDALB 1917-
1929; CP 1; DA; DA3; DAB; DAC; DAM
MST, POET; DLB 4, 45, 63; DLBD 15;
EFS 2; EWL 3; EXPP; LMFS 2; MAL 5;
MTCW 1, 2; MTFW 2005; PAB; PFS 2,
8, 16; RGAL 4; TUS; WP

Povod, Reinaldo 1959-1994 .... **CLC 44**
See also CA 136; 146; CANR 83

Powell, Adam Clayton, Jr.
1908-1972 .... **BLC 3; CLC 89**
See also BW 1, 3; CA 102; 33-36R; CANR
86; DAM MULT

Powell, Anthony (Dymoke)
1905-2000 .... **CLC 1, 3, 7, 9, 10, 31**
See also BRW 7; CA 1-4R; 189; CANR 1,
32, 62, 107; CDBLB 1945-1960; CN 1, 2,
3, 4, 5, 6; DLB 15; EWL 3; MTCW 1, 2;
MTFW 2005; RGEL 2; TEA

Powell, Dawn 1896(?)-1965 .... **CLC 66**
See also CA 5-8R; CANR 121; DLBY 1997

Powell, Padgett 1952- .... **CLC 34**
See also CA 126; CANR 63, 101; CSW;
DLB 234; DLBY 01

Powell, (Oval) Talmage 1920-2000
See Queen, Ellery
See also CA 5-8R; CANR 2, 80

Power, Susan 1961- .... **CLC 91**
See also BYA 14; CA 160; CANR 135; NFS
11

Powers, J(ames) F(arl) 1917-1999 ..... **CLC 1,**
4, 8, 57; SSC 4
See also CA 1-4R; 181; CANR 2, 61; CN
1, 2, 3, 4, 5, 6; DLB 130; MTCW 1;
RGAL 4; RGSF 2

Powers, John J(ames) 1945-
See Powers, John R.
See also CA 69-72

Powers, John R. .... **CLC 66**
See Powers, John J(ames)

Powers, Richard (S.) 1957- .... **CLC 93**
See also AMWS 9; BPFB 3; CA 148;
CANR 80; CN 6, 7; MTFW 2005; TCLE
1:2

Pownall, David 1938- .... **CLC 10**
See also CA 89-92, 180; CAAS 18; CANR
49, 101; CBD; CD 5, 6; CN 4, 5, 6, 7;
DLB 14

Powys, John Cowper 1872-1963 ... **CLC 7, 9,**
15, 46, 125
See also CA 85-88; CANR 106; DLB 15,
255; EWL 3; FANT; MTCW 1, 2; MTFW
2005; RGEL 2; SUFW

Powys, T(heodore) F(rancis)
1875-1953 .... **TCLC 9**
See also BRWS 8; CA 106; 189; DLB 36,
162; EWL 3; FANT; RGEL 2; SUFW

Pozzo, Modesta
See Fonte, Moderata

Prado (Calvo), Pedro 1886-1952 ... **TCLC 75**
See also CA 131; DLB 283; HW 1; LAW

Prager, Emily 1952- .... **CLC 56**
See also CA 204

Pratchett, Terry 1948- .... **CLC 197**
See also AAYA 19, 54; BPFB 3; CA 143;
CANR 87, 126; CLR 64; CN 6, 7; CPW;
CWRI 5; FANT; MTFW 2005; SATA 82,
139; SFW 4; SUFW 2

Pratolini, Vasco 1913-1991 .... **TCLC 124**
See also CA 211; DLB 177; EWL 3; RGWL
2, 3

Pratt, E(dwin) J(ohn) 1883(?)-1964 . **CLC 19**
See also CA 141; 93-96; CANR 77; DAC;
DAM POET; DLB 92; EWL 3; RGEL 2;
TWA

Premchand .... **TCLC 21**
See Srivastava, Dhanpat Rai
See also EWL 3

Prescott, William Hickling
1796-1859 .... **NCLC 163**
See also DLB 1, 30, 59, 235

Preseren, France 1800-1849 .... **NCLC 127**
See also CDWLB 4; DLB 147

Preussler, Otfried 1923- .... **CLC 17**
See also CA 77-80; SATA 24

Prevert, Jacques (Henri Marie)
1900-1977 .... **CLC 15**
See also CA 77-80; 69-72; CANR 29, 61;
DLB 258; EWL 3; GFL 1789 to the
Present; IDFW 3, 4; MTCW 1; RGWL 2,
3; SATA-Obit 30

Prevost, (Antoine Francois)
1697-1763 .... **LC 1**
See also DLB 314; EW 4; GFL Beginnings
to 1789; RGWL 2, 3

Price, (Edward) Reynolds 1933- ... **CLC 3, 6,**
13, 43, 50, 63, 212; SSC 22
See also AMWS 6; CA 1-4R; CANR 1, 37,
57, 87, 128; CN 1, 2, 3, 4, 5, 6, 7; CSW;
DAM NOV; DLB 2, 218, 278; EWL 3;
INT CANR-37; MAL 5; MTCW 2; MTFW
2005; NFS 18

Price, Richard 1949- .... **CLC 6, 12**
See also CA 49-52; CANR 3; CN 7; DLBY
1981

Prichard, Katharine Susannah
1883-1969 .... **CLC 46**
See also CA 11-12; CANR 33; CAP 1; DLB
260; MTCW 1; RGEL 2; RGSF 2; SATA
66

Priestley, J(ohn) B(oynton)
1894-1984 .... **CLC 2, 5, 9, 34**
See also BRW 7; CA 9-12R; 113; CANR
33; CDBLB 1914-1945; CN 1, 2, 3; DA3;
DAM DRAM, NOV; DLB 10, 34, 77,
100, 139; DLBY 1984; EWL 3; MTCW
1, 2; MTFW 2005; RGEL 2; SFW 4

Prince 1958- .... **CLC 35**
See also CA 213

Prince, F(rank) T(empleton)
1912-2003 .... **CLC 22**
See also CA 101; 219; CANR 43, 79; CP 1,
2, 3, 4, 5, 6, 7; DLB 20

Prince Kropotkin
See Kropotkin, Peter (Aleksieevich)

Prior, Matthew 1664-1721 .... **LC 4**
See also DLB 95; RGEL 2

Prishvin, Mikhail 1873-1954 .... **TCLC 75**
See Prishvin, Mikhail Mikhailovich

Prishvin, Mikhail Mikhailovich
See Prishvin, Mikhail
See also DLB 272; EWL 3

Pritchard, William H(arrison)
1932- .... **CLC 34**
See also CA 65-68; CANR 23, 95; DLB
111

Pritchett, V(ictor) S(awdon)
1900-1997 ... **CLC 5, 13, 15, 41; SSC 14**
See also BPFB 3; BRWS 3; CA 61-64; 157;
CANR 31, 63; CN 1, 2, 3, 4, 5, 6; DA3;
DAM NOV; DLB 15, 139; EWL 3;
MTCW 1, 2; MTFW 2005; RGEL 2;
RGSF 2; TEA

Private 19022
See Manning, Frederic

Probst, Mark 1925- .... **CLC 59**
See also CA 130

Procaccino, Michael
See Cristofer, Michael

Proclus c. 412-485 .... **CMLC 81**

Prokosch, Frederic 1908-1989 ...... **CLC 4, 48**
See also CA 73-76; 128; CANR 82; CN 1,
2, 3, 4; CP 1, 2, 3, 4; DLB 48; MTCW 2

Propertius, Sextus c. 50B.C.-c.
16B.C. .... **CMLC 32**
See also AW 2; CDWLB 1; DLB 211;
RGWL 2, 3

Prophet, The
See Dreiser, Theodore (Herman Albert)

Prose, Francine 1947- .... **CLC 45**
See also CA 109; 112; CANR 46, 95, 132;
DLB 234; MTFW 2005; SATA 101, 149

Proudhon
See Cunha, Euclides (Rodrigues Pimenta)
da

Proulx, Annie
See Proulx, E. Annie

Proulx, E. Annie 1935- .... **CLC 81, 158**
See also AMWS 7; BPFB 3; CA 145;
CANR 65, 110; CN 6, 7; CPW 1; DA3;
DAM POP; MAL 5; MTCW 2; MTFW
2005; SSFS 18

Proulx, Edna Annie
See Proulx, E. Annie

Proust, (Valentin-Louis-George-Eugene)
Marcel 1871-1922 ..... **SSC 75; TCLC 7,**
13, 33; WLC
See also AAYA 58; BPFB 3; CA 104; 120;
CANR 110; DA; DA3; DAB; DAC; DAM
MST, NOV; DLB 65; EW 8; EWL 3; GFL
1789 to the Present; MTCW 1, 2; MTFW
2005; RGWL 2, 3; TWA

Prowler, Harley
See Masters, Edgar Lee

Prudentius, Aurelius Clemens 348-c. 405 .... **CMLC 78**
See also EW 1; RGWL 2, 3

Prus, Boleslaw 1845-1912 .... **TCLC 48**
See also RGWL 2, 3

Pryor, Richard (Franklin Lenox Thomas) 1940-2005 .... **CLC 26**
See also CA 122; 152

Przybyszewski, Stanislaw 1868-1927 .... **TCLC 36**
See also CA 160; DLB 66; EWL 3

Pteleon
See Grieve, C(hristopher) M(urray)
See also DAM POET

Puckett, Lute
See Masters, Edgar Lee

Puig, Manuel 1932-1990 .... **CLC 3, 5, 10, 28, 65, 133; HLC 2**
See also BPFB 3; CA 45-48; CANR 2, 32, 63; CDWLB 3; DA3; DAM MULT; DLB 113; DNFS 1; EWL 3; GLL 1; HW 1, 2; LAW; MTCW 1, 2; MTFW 2005; RGWL 2, 3; TWA; WLIT 1

Pulitzer, Joseph 1847-1911 .... **TCLC 76**
See also CA 114; DLB 23

Purchas, Samuel 1577(?)-1626 .... **LC 70**
See also DLB 151

Purdy, A(lfred) W(ellington) 1918-2000 .... **CLC 3, 6, 14, 50**
See also CA 81-84; 189; CAAS 17; CANR 42, 66; CP 1, 2, 3, 4, 5, 6, 7; DAC; DAM MST, POET; DLB 88; PFS 5; RGEL 2

Purdy, James (Amos) 1923- .... **CLC 2, 4, 10, 28, 52**
See also AMWS 7; CA 33-36R; CAAS 1; CANR 19, 51, 132; CN 1, 2, 3, 4, 5, 6, 7; DLB 2, 218; EWL 3; INT CANR-19; MAL 5; MTCW 1; RGAL 4

Pure, Simon
See Swinnerton, Frank Arthur

Pushkin, Aleksandr Sergeevich
See Pushkin, Alexander (Sergeyevich)
See also DLB 205

Pushkin, Alexander (Sergeyevich) 1799-1837 .... **NCLC 3, 27, 83; PC 10; SSC 27, 55; WLC**
See Pushkin, Aleksandr Sergeevich
See also DA; DA3; DAB; DAC; DAM DRAM, MST, POET; EW 5; EXPS; RGSF 2; RGWL 2, 3; SATA 61; SSFS 9; TWA

P'u Sung-ling 1640-1715 .... **LC 49; SSC 31**

Putnam, Arthur Lee
See Alger, Horatio, Jr.

Puttenham, George 1529(?)-1590 ...... **LC 116**
See also DLB 281

Puzo, Mario 1920-1999 .... **CLC 1, 2, 6, 36, 107**
See also BPFB 3; CA 65-68; 185; CANR 4, 42, 65, 99, 131; CN 1, 2, 3, 4, 5, 6; CPW; DA3; DAM NOV, POP; DLB 6; MTCW 1, 2; MTFW 2005; NFS 16; RGAL 4

Pygge, Edward
See Barnes, Julian (Patrick)

Pyle, Ernest Taylor 1900-1945
See Pyle, Ernie
See also CA 115; 160

Pyle, Ernie .... **TCLC 75**
See Pyle, Ernest Taylor
See also DLB 29; MTCW 2

Pyle, Howard 1853-1911 .... **TCLC 81**
See also AAYA 57; BYA 2, 4; CA 109; 137; CLR 22; DLB 42, 188; DLBD 13; LAIT 1; MAICYA 1, 2; SATA 16, 100; WCH; YAW

Pym, Barbara (Mary Crampton) 1913-1980 .... **CLC 13, 19, 37, 111**
See also BPFB 3; BRWS 2; CA 13-14; 97-100; CANR 13, 34; CAP 1; DLB 14, 207; DLBY 1987; EWL 3; MTCW 1, 2; MTFW 2005; RGEL 2; TEA

Pynchon, Thomas (Ruggles, Jr.) 1937- ...... **CLC 2, 3, 6, 9, 11, 18, 33, 62, 72, 123, 192, 213; SSC 14, 84; WLC**
See also AMWS 2; BEST 90:2; BPFB 3; CA 17-20R; CANR 22, 46, 73, 142; CN 1, 2, 3, 4, 5, 6, 7; CPW 1; DA; DA3; DAB; DAC; DAM MST, NOV, POP; DLB 2, 173; EWL 3; MAL 5; MTCW 1, 2; MTFW 2005; RGAL 4; SFW 4; TCLE 1:2; TUS

Pythagoras c. 582B.C.-c. 507B.C. . **CMLC 22**
See also DLB 176

Q
See Quiller-Couch, Sir Arthur (Thomas)

Qian, Chongzhu
See Ch'ien, Chung-shu

Qian, Sima 145B.C.-c. 89B.C. .... **CMLC 72**

Qian Zhongshu
See Ch'ien, Chung-shu
See also CWW 2

Qroll
See Dagerman, Stig (Halvard)

Quarles, Francis 1592-1644 .... **LC 117**
See also DLB 126; RGEL 2

Quarrington, Paul (Lewis) 1953- ..... **CLC 65**
See also CA 129; CANR 62, 95

Quasimodo, Salvatore 1901-1968 .... **CLC 10; PC 47**
See also CA 13-16; 25-28R; CAP 1; DLB 114; EW 12; EWL 3; MTCW 1; RGWL 2, 3

Quatermass, Martin
See Carpenter, John (Howard)

Quay, Stephen 1947- .... **CLC 95**
See also CA 189

Quay, Timothy 1947- .... **CLC 95**
See also CA 189

Queen, Ellery .... **CLC 3, 11**
See Dannay, Frederic; Davidson, Avram (James); Deming, Richard; Fairman, Paul W.; Flora, Fletcher; Hoch, Edward D(entinger); Kane, Henry; Lee, Manfred B(ennington); Marlowe, Stephen; Powell, (Oval) Talmage; Sheldon, Walter J(ames); Sturgeon, Theodore (Hamilton); Tracy, Don(ald Fiske); Vance, John Holbrook
See also BPFB 3; CMW 4; MSW; RGAL 4

Queen, Ellery, Jr.
See Dannay, Frederic; Lee, Manfred B(ennington)

Queneau, Raymond 1903-1976 ..... **CLC 2, 5, 10, 42**
See also CA 77-80; 69-72; CANR 32; DLB 72, 258; EW 12; EWL 3; GFL 1789 to the Present; MTCW 1, 2; RGWL 2, 3

Quevedo, Francisco de 1580-1645 .... **LC 23**

Quiller-Couch, Sir Arthur (Thomas) 1863-1944 .... **TCLC 53**
See also CA 118; 166; DLB 135, 153, 190; HGG; RGEL 2; SUFW 1

Quin, Ann (Marie) 1936-1973 .... **CLC 6**
See also CA 9-12R; 45-48; CN 1; DLB 14, 231

Quincey, Thomas de
See De Quincey, Thomas

Quindlen, Anna 1953- .... **CLC 191**
See also AAYA 35; CA 138; CANR 73, 126; DA3; DLB 292; MTCW 2; MTFW 2005

Quinn, Martin
See Smith, Martin Cruz

Quinn, Peter 1947- .... **CLC 91**
See also CA 197

Quinn, Simon
See Smith, Martin Cruz

Quintana, Leroy V. 1944- ...... **HLC 2; PC 36**
See also CA 131; CANR 65, 139; DAM MULT; DLB 82; HW 1, 2

Quintilian c. 40-c. 100 .... **CMLC 77**
See also AW 2; DLB 211; RGWL 2, 3

Quintillian 0035-0100 .... **CMLC 77**

Quiroga, Horacio (Sylvestre) 1878-1937 ... **HLC 2; SSC 89; TCLC 20**
See also CA 117; 131; DAM MULT; EWL 3; HW 1; LAW; MTCW 1; RGSF 2; WLIT 1

Quoirez, Francoise 1935-2004 .... **CLC 9**
See Sagan, Francoise
See also CA 49-52; 231; CANR 6, 39, 73; MTCW 1, 2; MTFW 2005; TWA

Raabe, Wilhelm (Karl) 1831-1910 . **TCLC 45**
See also CA 167; DLB 129

Rabe, David (William) 1940- .. **CLC 4, 8, 33, 200; DC 16**
See also CA 85-88; CABS 3; CAD; CANR 59, 129; CD 5, 6; DAM DRAM; DFS 3, 8, 13; DLB 7, 228; EWL 3; MAL 5

Rabelais, Francois 1494-1553 .... **LC 5, 60; WLC**
See also DA; DAB; DAC; DAM MST; EW 2; GFL Beginnings to 1789; LMFS 1; RGWL 2, 3; TWA

Rabinovitch, Sholem 1859-1916
See Aleichem, Sholom
See also CA 104

Rabinyan, Dorit 1972- .... **CLC 119**
See also CA 170

Rachilde
See Vallette, Marguerite Eymery; Vallette, Marguerite Eymery
See also EWL 3

Racine, Jean 1639-1699 .... **LC 28, 113**
See also DA3; DAB; DAM MST; DLB 268; EW 3; GFL Beginnings to 1789; LMFS 1; RGWL 2, 3; TWA

Radcliffe, Ann (Ward) 1764-1823 ... **NCLC 6, 55, 106**
See also DLB 39, 178; GL 3; HGG; LMFS 1; RGEL 2; SUFW; WLIT 3

Radclyffe-Hall, Marguerite
See Hall, (Marguerite) Radclyffe

Radiguet, Raymond 1903-1923 ...... **TCLC 29**
See also CA 162; DLB 65; EWL 3; GFL 1789 to the Present; RGWL 2, 3

Radnoti, Miklos 1909-1944 .... **TCLC 16**
See also CA 118; 212; CDWLB 4; DLB 215; EWL 3; RGWL 2, 3

Rado, James 1939- .... **CLC 17**
See also CA 105

Radvanyi, Netty 1900-1983
See Seghers, Anna
See also CA 85-88; 110; CANR 82

Rae, Ben
See Griffiths, Trevor

Raeburn, John (Hay) 1941- .... **CLC 34**
See also CA 57-60

Ragni, Gerome 1942-1991 .... **CLC 17**
See also CA 105; 134

Rahv, Philip .... **CLC 24**
See Greenberg, Ivan
See also DLB 137; MAL 5

Raimund, Ferdinand Jakob 1790-1836 .... **NCLC 69**
See also DLB 90

Raine, Craig (Anthony) 1944- .. **CLC 32, 103**
See also CA 108; CANR 29, 51, 103; CP 3, 4, 5, 6, 7; DLB 40; PFS 7

Raine, Kathleen (Jessie) 1908-2003 .. **CLC 7, 45**
See also CA 85-88; 218; CANR 46, 109; CP 1, 2, 3, 4, 5, 6, 7; DLB 20; EWL 3; MTCW 1; RGEL 2

Rainis, Janis 1865-1929 .... **TCLC 29**
See also CA 170; CDWLB 4; DLB 220; EWL 3

Rakosi, Carl .... **CLC 47**
See Rawley, Callman
See also CA 228; CAAS 5; CP 1, 2, 3, 4, 5, 6, 7; DLB 193

Ralegh, Sir Walter
  See Raleigh, Sir Walter
  See also BRW 1; RGEL 2; WP
Raleigh, Richard
  See Lovecraft, H(oward) P(hillips)
Raleigh, Sir Walter 1554(?)-1618 .... **LC 31, 39; PC 31**
  See Ralegh, Sir Walter
  See also CDBLB Before 1660; DLB 172; EXPP; PFS 14; TEA
Rallentando, H. P.
  See Sayers, Dorothy L(eigh)
Ramal, Walter
  See de la Mare, Walter (John)
Ramana Maharshi 1879-1950 .... **TCLC 84**
Ramoacn y Cajal, Santiago 1852-1934 .... **TCLC 93**
Ramon, Juan
  See Jimenez (Mantecon), Juan Ramon
Ramos, Graciliano 1892-1953 .... **TCLC 32**
  See also CA 167; DLB 307; EWL 3; HW 2; LAW; WLIT 1
Rampersad, Arnold 1941- .... **CLC 44**
  See also BW 2, 3; CA 127; 133; CANR 81; DLB 111; INT CA-133
Rampling, Anne
  See Rice, Anne
  See also GLL 2
Ramsay, Allan 1686(?)-1758 .... **LC 29**
  See also DLB 95; RGEL 2
Ramsay, Jay
  See Campbell, (John) Ramsey
Ramuz, Charles-Ferdinand 1878-1947 .... **TCLC 33**
  See also CA 165; EWL 3
Rand, Ayn 1905-1982 ...... **CLC 3, 30, 44, 79; WLC**
  See also AAYA 10; AMWS 4; BPFB 3; BYA 12; CA 13-16R; 105; CANR 27, 73; CDALBS; CN 1, 2, 3; CPW; DA; DA3; DAC; DAM MST, NOV, POP; DLB 227, 279; MTCW 1, 2; MTFW 2005; NFS 10, 16; RGAL 4; SFW 4; TUS; YAW
Randall, Dudley (Felker) 1914-2000 . **BLC 3; CLC 1, 135**
  See also BW 1, 3; CA 25-28R; 189; CANR 23, 82; CP 1, 2, 3, 4; DAM MULT; DLB 41; PFS 5
Randall, Robert
  See Silverberg, Robert
Ranger, Ken
  See Creasey, John
Rank, Otto 1884-1939 .... **TCLC 115**
Ransom, John Crowe 1888-1974 .. **CLC 2, 4, 5, 11, 24; PC 61**
  See also AMW; CA 5-8R; 49-52; CANR 6, 34; CDALBS; CP 1, 2; DA3; DAM POET; DLB 45, 63; EWL 3; EXPP; MAL 5; MTCW 1, 2; MTFW 2005; RGAL 4; TUS
Rao, Raja 1909- .... **CLC 25, 56**
  See also CA 73-76; CANR 51; CN 1, 2, 3, 4, 5, 6; DAM NOV; EWL 3; MTCW 1, 2; MTFW 2005; RGEL 2; RGSF 2
Raphael, Frederic (Michael) 1931- ... **CLC 2, 14**
  See also CA 1-4R; CANR 1, 86; CN 1, 2, 3, 4, 5, 6, 7; DLB 14, 319; TCLE 1:2
Ratcliffe, James P.
  See Mencken, H(enry) L(ouis)
Rathbone, Julian 1935- .... **CLC 41**
  See also CA 101; CANR 34, 73
Rattigan, Terence (Mervyn) 1911-1977 .... **CLC 7; DC 18**
  See also BRWS 7; CA 85-88; 73-76; CBD; CDBLB 1945-1960; DAM DRAM; DFS 8; DLB 13; IDFW 3, 4; MTCW 1, 2; MTFW 2005; RGEL 2
Ratushinskaya, Irina 1954- .... **CLC 54**
  See also CA 129; CANR 68; CWW 2

Raven, Simon (Arthur Noel) 1927-2001 .... **CLC 14**
  See also CA 81-84; 197; CANR 86; CN 1, 2, 3, 4, 5, 6; DLB 271
Ravenna, Michael
  See Welty, Eudora (Alice)
Rawley, Callman 1903-2004
  See Rakosi, Carl
  See also CA 21-24R; 228; CANR 12, 32, 91
Rawlings, Marjorie Kinnan 1896-1953 .... **TCLC 4**
  See also AAYA 20; AMWS 10; ANW; BPFB 3; BYA 3; CA 104; 137; CANR 74; CLR 63; DLB 9, 22, 102; DLBD 17; JRDA; MAICYA 1, 2; MAL 5; MTCW 2; MTFW 2005; RGAL 4; SATA 100; WCH; YABC 1; YAW
Ray, Satyajit 1921-1992 .... **CLC 16, 76**
  See also CA 114; 137; DAM MULT
Read, Herbert Edward 1893-1968 ..... **CLC 4**
  See also BRW 6; CA 85-88; 25-28R; DLB 20, 149; EWL 3; PAB; RGEL 2
Read, Piers Paul 1941- .... **CLC 4, 10, 25**
  See also CA 21-24R; CANR 38, 86; CN 2, 3, 4, 5, 6, 7; DLB 14; SATA 21
Reade, Charles 1814-1884 .... **NCLC 2, 74**
  See also DLB 21; RGEL 2
Reade, Hamish
  See Gray, Simon (James Holliday)
Reading, Peter 1946- .... **CLC 47**
  See also BRWS 8; CA 103; CANR 46, 96; CP 7; DLB 40
Reaney, James 1926- .... **CLC 13**
  See also CA 41-44R; CAAS 15; CANR 42; CD 5, 6; CP 1, 2, 3, 4, 5, 6, 7; DAC; DAM MST; DLB 68; RGEL 2; SATA 43
Rebreanu, Liviu 1885-1944 .... **TCLC 28**
  See also CA 165; DLB 220; EWL 3
Rechy, John (Francisco) 1934- ...... **CLC 1, 7, 14, 18, 107; HLC 2**
  See also CA 5-8R, 195; CAAE 195; CAAS 4; CANR 6, 32, 64; CN 1, 2, 3, 4, 5, 6, 7; DAM MULT; DLB 122, 278; DLBY 1982; HW 1, 2; INT CANR-6; LLW; MAL 5; RGAL 4
Redcam, Tom 1870-1933 .... **TCLC 25**
Reddin, Keith 1956- .... **CLC 67**
  See also CAD; CD 6
Redgrove, Peter (William) 1932-2003 .... **CLC 6, 41**
  See also BRWS 6; CA 1-4R; 217; CANR 3, 39, 77; CP 1, 2, 3, 4, 5, 6, 7; DLB 40; TCLE 1:2
Redmon, Anne .... **CLC 22**
  See Nightingale, Anne Redmon
  See also DLBY 1986
Reed, Eliot
  See Ambler, Eric
Reed, Ishmael (Scott) 1938- . **BLC 3; CLC 2, 3, 5, 6, 13, 32, 60, 174; PC 68**
  See also AFAW 1, 2; AMWS 10; BPFB 3; BW 2, 3; CA 21-24R; CANR 25, 48, 74, 128; CN 1, 2, 3, 4, 5, 6, 7; CP 1, 2, 3, 4, 5, 6, 7; CSW; DA3; DAM MULT; DLB 2, 5, 33, 169, 227; DLBD 8; EWL 3; LMFS 2; MAL 5; MSW; MTCW 1, 2; MTFW 2005; PFS 6; RGAL 4; TCWW 2
Reed, John (Silas) 1887-1920 .... **TCLC 9**
  See also CA 106; 195; MAL 5; TUS
Reed, Lou .... **CLC 21**
  See Firbank, Louis
Reese, Lizette Woodworth 1856-1935 . **PC 29**
  See also CA 180; DLB 54
Reeve, Clara 1729-1807 .... **NCLC 19**
  See also DLB 39; RGEL 2
Reich, Wilhelm 1897-1957 .... **TCLC 57**
  See also CA 199

Reid, Christopher (John) 1949- .... **CLC 33**
  See also CA 140; CANR 89; CP 4, 5, 6, 7; DLB 40; EWL 3
Reid, Desmond
  See Moorcock, Michael (John)
Reid Banks, Lynne 1929-
  See Banks, Lynne Reid
  See also AAYA 49; CA 1-4R; CANR 6, 22, 38, 87; CLR 24; CN 1, 2, 3, 7; JRDA; MAICYA 1, 2; SATA 22, 75, 111, 165; YAW
Reilly, William K.
  See Creasey, John
Reiner, Max
  See Caldwell, (Janet Miriam) Taylor (Holland)
Reis, Ricardo
  See Pessoa, Fernando (Antonio Nogueira)
Reizenstein, Elmer Leopold
  See Rice, Elmer (Leopold)
  See also EWL 3
Remarque, Erich Maria 1898-1970 . **CLC 21**
  See also AAYA 27; BPFB 3; CA 77-80; 29-32R; CDWLB 2; DA; DA3; DAB; DAC; DAM MST, NOV; DLB 56; EWL 3; EXPN; LAIT 3; MTCW 1, 2; MTFW 2005; NFS 4; RGWL 2, 3
Remington, Frederic S(ackrider) 1861-1909 .... **TCLC 89**
  See also CA 108; 169; DLB 12, 186, 188; SATA 41; TCWW 2
Remizov, A.
  See Remizov, Aleksei (Mikhailovich)
Remizov, A. M.
  See Remizov, Aleksei (Mikhailovich)
Remizov, Aleksei (Mikhailovich) 1877-1957 .... **TCLC 27**
  See Remizov, Alexey Mikhaylovich
  See also CA 125; 133; DLB 295
Remizov, Alexey Mikhaylovich
  See Remizov, Aleksei (Mikhailovich)
  See also EWL 3
Renan, Joseph Ernest 1823-1892 . **NCLC 26, 145**
  See also GFL 1789 to the Present
Renard, Jules(-Pierre) 1864-1910 .. **TCLC 17**
  See also CA 117; 202; GFL 1789 to the Present
Renault, Mary .... **CLC 3, 11, 17**
  See Challans, Mary
  See also BPFB 3; BYA 2; CN 1, 2, 3; DLBY 1983; EWL 3; GLL 1; LAIT 1; RGEL 2; RHW
Rendell, Ruth (Barbara) 1930- .. **CLC 28, 48**
  See Vine, Barbara
  See also BPFB 3; BRWS 9; CA 109; CANR 32, 52, 74, 127; CN 5, 6, 7; CPW; DAM POP; DLB 87, 276; INT CANR-32; MSW; MTCW 1, 2; MTFW 2005
Renoir, Jean 1894-1979 .... **CLC 20**
  See also CA 129; 85-88
Resnais, Alain 1922- .... **CLC 16**
Revard, Carter (Curtis) 1931- .... **NNAL**
  See also CA 144; CANR 81; PFS 5
Reverdy, Pierre 1889-1960 .... **CLC 53**
  See also CA 97-100; 89-92; DLB 258; EWL 3; GFL 1789 to the Present
Rexroth, Kenneth 1905-1982 .... **CLC 1, 2, 6, 11, 22, 49, 112; PC 20**
  See also BG 1:3; CA 5-8R; 107; CANR 14, 34, 63; CDALB 1941-1968; CP 1, 2, 3; DAM POET; DLB 16, 48, 165, 212; DLBY 1982; EWL 3; INT CANR-14; MAL 5; MTCW 1, 2; MTFW 2005; RGAL 4
Reyes, Alfonso 1889-1959 .... **HLCS 2; TCLC 33**
  See also CA 131; EWL 3; HW 1; LAW

Robbins, Tom .... **CLC 9, 32, 64**
See Robbins, Thomas Eugene
See also AAYA 32; AMWS 10; BEST 90:3;
BPFB 3; CN 3, 4, 5, 6, 7; DLBY 1980
Robbins, Trina 1938- .... **CLC 21**
See also AAYA 61; CA 128
Roberts, Charles G(eorge) D(ouglas)
1860-1943 .... **TCLC 8**
See also CA 105; 188; CLR 33; CWRI 5;
DLB 92; RGEL 2; RGSF 2; SATA 88;
SATA-Brief 29
Roberts, Elizabeth Madox
1886-1941 .... **TCLC 68**
See also CA 111; 166; CLR 100; CWRI 5;
DLB 9, 54, 102; RGAL 4; RHW; SATA
33; SATA-Brief 27; TCWW 2; WCH
Roberts, Kate 1891-1985 .... **CLC 15**
See also CA 107; 116; DLB 319
Roberts, Keith (John Kingston)
1935-2000 .... **CLC 14**
See also BRWS 10; CA 25-28R; CANR 46;
DLB 261; SFW 4
Roberts, Kenneth (Lewis)
1885-1957 .... **TCLC 23**
See also CA 109; 199; DLB 9; MAL 5;
RGAL 4; RHW
Roberts, Michele (Brigitte) 1949- .... **CLC 48,
178**
See also CA 115; CANR 58, 120; CN 6, 7;
DLB 231; FW
Robertson, Ellis
See Ellison, Harlan (Jay); Silverberg, Rob-
ert
Robertson, Thomas William
1829-1871 .... **NCLC 35**
See Robertson, Tom
See also DAM DRAM
Robertson, Tom
See Robertson, Thomas William
See also RGEL 2
Robeson, Kenneth
See Dent, Lester
Robinson, Edwin Arlington
1869-1935 .... **PC 1, 35; TCLC 5, 101**
See also AMW; CA 104; 133; CDALB
1865-1917; DA; DAC; DAM MST,
POET; DLB 54; EWL 3; EXPP; MAL 5;
MTCW 1, 2; MTFW 2005; PAB; PFS 4;
RGAL 4; WP
Robinson, Henry Crabb
1775-1867 .... **NCLC 15**
See also DLB 107
Robinson, Jill 1936- .... **CLC 10**
See also CA 102; CANR 120; INT CA-102
Robinson, Kim Stanley 1952- .... **CLC 34**
See also AAYA 26; CA 126; CANR 113,
139; CN 6, 7; MTFW 2005; SATA 109;
SCFW 2; SFW 4
Robinson, Lloyd
See Silverberg, Robert
Robinson, Marilynne 1944- ...... **CLC 25, 180**
See also CA 116; CANR 80, 140; CN 4, 5,
6, 7; DLB 206; MTFW 2005
Robinson, Mary 1758-1800 .... **NCLC 142**
See also DLB 158; FW
Robinson, Smokey .... **CLC 21**
See Robinson, William, Jr.
Robinson, William, Jr. 1940-
See Robinson, Smokey
See also CA 116
Robison, Mary 1949- .... **CLC 42, 98**
See also CA 113; 116; CANR 87; CN 4, 5,
6, 7; DLB 130; INT CA-116; RGSF 2
Roches, Catherine des 1542-1587 ...... **LC 117**
Rochester
See Wilmot, John
See also RGEL 2
Rod, Edouard 1857-1910 .... **TCLC 52**

Roddenberry, Eugene Wesley 1921-1991
See Roddenberry, Gene
See also CA 110; 135; CANR 37; SATA 45;
SATA-Obit 69
Roddenberry, Gene .... **CLC 17**
See Roddenberry, Eugene Wesley
See also AAYA 5; SATA-Obit 69
Rodgers, Mary 1931- .... **CLC 12**
See also BYA 5; CA 49-52; CANR 8, 55,
90; CLR 20; CWRI 5; INT CANR-8;
JRDA; MAICYA 1, 2; SATA 8, 130
Rodgers, W(illiam) R(obert)
1909-1969 .... **CLC 7**
See also CA 85-88; DLB 20; RGEL 2
Rodman, Eric
See Silverberg, Robert
Rodman, Howard 1920(?)-1985 .... **CLC 65**
See also CA 118
Rodman, Maia
See Wojciechowska, Maia (Teresa)
Rodo, Jose Enrique 1871(?)-1917 .... **HLCS 2**
See also CA 178; EWL 3; HW 2; LAW
Rodolph, Utto
See Ouologuem, Yambo
Rodriguez, Claudio 1934-1999 .... **CLC 10**
See also CA 188; DLB 134
Rodriguez, Richard 1944- .... **CLC 155; HLC
2**
See also AMWS 14; CA 110; CANR 66,
116; DAM MULT; DLB 82, 256; HW 1,
2; LAIT 5; LLW; MTFW 2005; NCFS 3;
WLIT 1
Roelvaag, O(le) E(dvart) 1876-1931
See Rolvaag, O(le) E(dvart)
See also CA 117; 171
Roethke, Theodore (Huebner)
1908-1963 .... **CLC 1, 3, 8, 11, 19, 46,
101; PC 15**
See also AMW; CA 81-84; CABS 2;
CDALB 1941-1968; DA3; DAM POET;
DLB 5, 206; EWL 3; EXPP; MAL 5;
MTCW 1, 2; PAB; PFS 3; RGAL 4; WP
Rogers, Carl R(ansom)
1902-1987 .... **TCLC 125**
See also CA 1-4R; 121; CANR 1, 18;
MTCW 1
Rogers, Samuel 1763-1855 .... **NCLC 69**
See also DLB 93; RGEL 2
Rogers, Thomas Hunton 1927- .... **CLC 57**
See also CA 89-92; INT CA-89-92
Rogers, Will(iam Penn Adair)
1879-1935 .... **NNAL; TCLC 8, 71**
See also CA 105; 144; DA3; DAM MULT;
DLB 11; MTCW 2
Rogin, Gilbert 1929- .... **CLC 18**
See also CA 65-68; CANR 15
Rohan, Koda
See Koda Shigeyuki
Rohlfs, Anna Katharine Green
See Green, Anna Katharine
Rohmer, Eric .... **CLC 16**
See Scherer, Jean-Marie Maurice
Rohmer, Sax .... **TCLC 28**
See Ward, Arthur Henry Sarsfield
See also DLB 70; MSW; SUFW
Roiphe, Anne (Richardson) 1935- .. **CLC 3, 9**
See also CA 89-92; CANR 45, 73, 138;
DLBY 1980; INT CA-89-92
Rojas, Fernando de 1475-1541 ... **HLCS 1, 2;
LC 23**
See also DLB 286; RGWL 2, 3
Rojas, Gonzalo 1917- .... **HLCS 2**
See also CA 178; HW 2; LAWS 1
Roland (de la Platiere), Marie-Jeanne
1754-1793 .... **LC 98**
See also DLB 314

**Rolfe, Frederick (William Serafino Austin
Lewis Mary)** 1860-1913 .... **TCLC 12**
See Al Siddik
See also CA 107; 210; DLB 34, 156; RGEL
2
Rolland, Romain 1866-1944 .... **TCLC 23**
See also CA 118; 197; DLB 65, 284; EWL
3; GFL 1789 to the Present; RGWL 2, 3
Rolle, Richard c. 1300-c. 1349 ...... **CMLC 21**
See also DLB 146; LMFS 1; RGEL 2
Rolvaag, O(le) E(dvart) .... **TCLC 17**
See Roelvaag, O(le) E(dvart)
See also DLB 9, 212; MAL 5; NFS 5;
RGAL 4
Romain Arnaud, Saint
See Aragon, Louis
Romains, Jules 1885-1972 .... **CLC 7**
See also CA 85-88; CANR 34; DLB 65,
321; EWL 3; GFL 1789 to the Present;
MTCW 1
Romero, Jose Ruben 1890-1952 .... **TCLC 14**
See also CA 114; 131; EWL 3; HW 1; LAW
Ronsard, Pierre de 1524-1585 . **LC 6, 54; PC
11**
See also EW 2; GFL Beginnings to 1789;
RGWL 2, 3; TWA
Rooke, Leon 1934- .... **CLC 25, 34**
See also CA 25-28R; CANR 23, 53; CCA
1; CPW; DAM POP
Roosevelt, Franklin Delano
1882-1945 .... **TCLC 93**
See also CA 116; 173; LAIT 3
Roosevelt, Theodore 1858-1919 ..... **TCLC 69**
See also CA 115; 170; DLB 47, 186, 275
Roper, William 1498-1578 .... **LC 10**
Roquelaure, A. N.
See Rice, Anne
Rosa, Joao Guimaraes 1908-1967 ... **CLC 23;
HLCS 1**
See Guimaraes Rosa, Joao
See also CA 89-92; DLB 113, 307; EWL 3;
WLIT 1
Rose, Wendy 1948- . **CLC 85; NNAL; PC 13**
See also CA 53-56; CANR 5, 51; CWP;
DAM MULT; DLB 175; PFS 13; RGAL
4; SATA 12
Rosen, R. D.
See Rosen, Richard (Dean)
Rosen, Richard (Dean) 1949- .... **CLC 39**
See also CA 77-80; CANR 62, 120; CMW
4; INT CANR-30
Rosenberg, Isaac 1890-1918 .... **TCLC 12**
See also BRW 6; CA 107; 188; DLB 20,
216; EWL 3; PAB; RGEL 2
Rosenblatt, Joe .... **CLC 15**
See Rosenblatt, Joseph
See also CP 3, 4, 5, 6, 7
Rosenblatt, Joseph 1933-
See Rosenblatt, Joe
See also CA 89-92; CP 1, 2; INT CA-89-92
Rosenfeld, Samuel
See Tzara, Tristan
Rosenstock, Sami
See Tzara, Tristan
Rosenstock, Samuel
See Tzara, Tristan
Rosenthal, M(acha) L(ouis)
1917-1996 .... **CLC 28**
See also CA 1-4R; 152; CAAS 6; CANR 4,
51; CP 1, 2, 3, 4; DLB 5; SATA 59
Ross, Barnaby
See Dannay, Frederic
Ross, Bernard L.
See Follett, Ken(neth Martin)
Ross, J. H.
See Lawrence, T(homas) E(dward)
Ross, John Hume
See Lawrence, T(homas) E(dward)

Ross, Martin 1862-1915
See Martin, Violet Florence
See also DLB 135; GLL 2; RGEL 2; RGSF 2

Ross, (James) Sinclair 1908-1996 ... **CLC 13; SSC 24**
See also CA 73-76; CANR 81; CN 1, 2, 3, 4, 5, 6; DAC; DAM MST; DLB 88; RGEL 2; RGSF 2; TCWW 1, 2

Rossetti, Christina 1830-1894 ... **NCLC 2, 50, 66; PC 7; WLC**
See also AAYA 51; BRW 5; BYA 4; DA; DA3; DAB; DAC; DAM MST, POET; DLB 35, 163, 240; EXPP; FL 1:3; LATS 1:1; MAICYA 1, 2; PFS 10, 14; RGEL 2; SATA 20; TEA; WCH

Rossetti, Christina Georgina
See Rossetti, Christina

Rossetti, Dante Gabriel 1828-1882 . **NCLC 4, 77; PC 44; WLC**
See also AAYA 51; BRW 5; CDBLB 1832-1890; DA; DAB; DAC; DAM MST, POET; DLB 35; EXPP; RGEL 2; TEA

Rossi, Cristina Peri
See Peri Rossi, Cristina

Rossi, Jean-Baptiste 1931-2003
See Japrisot, Sebastien
See also CA 201; 215

Rossner, Judith (Perelman) 1935- . **CLC 6, 9, 29**
See also AITN 2; BEST 90:3; BPFB 3; CA 17-20R; CANR 18, 51, 73; CN 4, 5, 6, 7; DLB 6; INT CANR-18; MAL 5; MTCW 1, 2; MTFW 2005

Rostand, Edmond (Eugene Alexis) 1868-1918 .... **DC 10; TCLC 6, 37**
See also CA 104; 126; DA; DA3; DAB; DAC; DAM DRAM, MST; DFS 1; DLB 192; LAIT 1; MTCW 1; RGWL 2, 3; TWA

Roth, Henry 1906-1995 ..... **CLC 2, 6, 11, 104**
See also AMWS 9; CA 11-12; 149; CANR 38, 63; CAP 1; CN 1, 2, 3, 4, 5, 6; DA3; DLB 28; EWL 3; MAL 5; MTCW 1, 2; MTFW 2005; RGAL 4

Roth, (Moses) Joseph 1894-1939 ... **TCLC 33**
See also CA 160; DLB 85; EWL 3; RGWL 2, 3

Roth, Philip (Milton) 1933- ... **CLC 1, 2, 3, 4, 6, 9, 15, 22, 31, 47, 66, 86, 119, 201; SSC 26; WLC**
See also AAYA 67; AMWR 2; AMWS 3; BEST 90:3; BPFB 3; CA 1-4R; CANR 1, 22, 36, 55, 89, 132; CDALB 1968-1988; CN 3, 4, 5, 6, 7; CPW 1; DA; DA3; DAB; DAC; DAM MST, NOV, POP; DLB 2, 28, 173; DLBY 1982; EWL 3; MAL 5; MTCW 1, 2; MTFW 2005; RGAL 4; RGSF 2; SSFS 12, 18; TUS

Rothenberg, Jerome 1931- .... **CLC 6, 57**
See also CA 45-48; CANR 1, 106; CP 1, 2, 3, 4, 5, 6, 7; DLB 5, 193

Rotter, Pat ed. .... **CLC 65**

Roumain, Jacques (Jean Baptiste) 1907-1944 .... **BLC 3; TCLC 19**
See also BW 1; CA 117; 125; DAM MULT; EWL 3

Rourke, Constance Mayfield 1885-1941 .... **TCLC 12**
See also CA 107; 200; MAL 5; YABC 1

Rousseau, Jean-Baptiste 1671-1741 ...... **LC 9**

Rousseau, Jean-Jacques 1712-1778 .... **LC 14, 36, 122; WLC**
See also DA; DA3; DAB; DAC; DAM MST; DLB 314; EW 4; GFL Beginnings to 1789; LMFS 1; RGWL 2, 3; TWA

Roussel, Raymond 1877-1933 .... **TCLC 20**
See also CA 117; 201; EWL 3; GFL 1789 to the Present

Rovit, Earl (Herbert) 1927- .... **CLC 7**
See also CA 5-8R; CANR 12

Rowe, Elizabeth Singer 1674-1737 ..... **LC 44**
See also DLB 39, 95

Rowe, Nicholas 1674-1718 .... **LC 8**
See also DLB 84; RGEL 2

Rowlandson, Mary 1637(?)-1678 .... **LC 66**
See also DLB 24, 200; RGAL 4

Rowley, Ames Dorrance
See Lovecraft, H(oward) P(hillips)

Rowley, William 1585(?)-1626 ... **LC 100, 123**
See also DFS 22; DLB 58; RGEL 2

Rowling, J. K. 1966- .... **CLC 137, 217**
See also AAYA 34; BYA 11, 13, 14; CA 173; CANR 128; CLR 66, 80; MAICYA 2; MTFW 2005; SATA 109; SUFW 2

Rowling, Joanne Kathleen
See Rowling, J.K.

Rowson, Susanna Haswell 1762(?)-1824 .... **NCLC 5, 69**
See also AMWS 15; DLB 37, 200; RGAL 4

Roy, Arundhati 1960(?)- .... **CLC 109, 210**
See also CA 163; CANR 90, 126; CN 7; DLBY 1997; EWL 3; LATS 1:2; MTFW 2005; NFS 22; WWE 1

Roy, Gabrielle 1909-1983 .... **CLC 10, 14**
See also CA 53-56; 110; CANR 5, 61; CCA 1; DAB; DAC; DAM MST; DLB 68; EWL 3; MTCW 1; RGWL 2, 3; SATA 104; TCLE 1:2

Royko, Mike 1932-1997 .... **CLC 109**
See also CA 89-92; 157; CANR 26, 111; CPW

Rozanov, Vasilii Vasil'evich
See Rozanov, Vassili
See also DLB 295

Rozanov, Vasily Vasilyevich
See Rozanov, Vassili
See also EWL 3

Rozanov, Vassili 1856-1919 .... **TCLC 104**
See also Rozanov, Vasilii Vasil'evich; Rozanov, Vasily Vasilyevich

Rozewicz, Tadeusz 1921- ...... **CLC 9, 23, 139**
See also CA 108; CANR 36, 66; CWW 2; DA3; DAM POET; DLB 232; EWL 3; MTCW 1, 2; MTFW 2005; RGWL 3

Ruark, Gibbons 1941- .... **CLC 3**
See also CA 33-36R; CAAS 23; CANR 14, 31, 57; DLB 120

Rubens, Bernice (Ruth) 1923-2004 . **CLC 19, 31**
See also CA 25-28R; 232; CANR 33, 65, 128; CN 1, 2, 3, 4, 5, 6, 7; DLB 14, 207; MTCW 1

Rubin, Harold
See Robbins, Harold

Rudkin, (James) David 1936- .... **CLC 14**
See also CA 89-92; CBD; CD 5, 6; DLB 13

Rudnik, Raphael 1933- .... **CLC 7**
See also CA 29-32R

Ruffian, M.
See Hasek, Jaroslav (Matej Frantisek)

Ruiz, Jose Martinez .... **CLC 11**
See Martinez Ruiz, Jose

Ruiz, Juan c. 1283-c. 1350 .... **CMLC 66**

Rukeyser, Muriel 1913-1980 . **CLC 6, 10, 15, 27; PC 12**
See also AMWS 6; CA 5-8R; 93-96; CANR 26, 60; CP 1, 2, 3; DA3; DAM POET; DLB 48; EWL 3; FW; GLL 2; MAL 5; MTCW 1, 2; PFS 10; RGAL 4; SATA-Obit 22

Rule, Jane (Vance) 1931- .... **CLC 27**
See also CA 25-28R; CAAS 18; CANR 12, 87; CN 4, 5, 6, 7; DLB 60; FW

Rulfo, Juan 1918-1986 .. **CLC 8, 80; HLC 2; SSC 25**
See also CA 85-88; 118; CANR 26; CDWLB 3; DAM MULT; DLB 113; EWL 3; HW 1, 2; LAW; MTCW 1, 2; RGSF 2; RGWL 2, 3; WLIT 1

Rumi, Jalal al-Din 1207-1273 ...... **CMLC 20; PC 45**
See also AAYA 64; RGWL 2, 3; WLIT 6; WP

Runeberg, Johan 1804-1877 .... **NCLC 41**

Runyon, (Alfred) Damon 1884(?)-1946 .... **TCLC 10**
See also CA 107; 165; DLB 11, 86, 171; MAL 5; MTCW 2; RGAL 4

Rush, Norman 1933- .... **CLC 44**
See also CA 121; 126; CANR 130; INT CA-126

Rushdie, (Ahmed) Salman 1947- .... **CLC 23, 31, 55, 100, 191; SSC 83; WLCS**
See also AAYA 65; BEST 89:3; BPFB 3; BRWS 4; CA 108; 111; CANR 33, 56, 108, 133; CN 4, 5, 6, 7; CPW 1; DA3; DAB; DAC; DAM MST, NOV, POP; DLB 194; EWL 3; FANT; INT CA-111; LATS 1:2; LMFS 2; MTCW 1, 2; MTFW 2005; NFS 22; RGEL 2; RGSF 2; TEA; WLIT 4

Rushforth, Peter (Scott) 1945- .... **CLC 19**
See also CA 101

Ruskin, John 1819-1900 .... **TCLC 63**
See also BRW 5; BYA 5; CA 114; 129; CDBLB 1832-1890; DLB 55, 163, 190; RGEL 2; SATA 24; TEA; WCH

Russ, Joanna 1937- .... **CLC 15**
See also BPFB 3; CA 25-28; CANR 11, 31, 65; CN 4, 5, 6, 7; DLB 8; FW; GLL 1; MTCW 1; SCFW 1, 2; SFW 4

Russ, Richard Patrick
See O'Brian, Patrick

Russell, George William 1867-1935
See A.E.; Baker, Jean H.
See also BRWS 8; CA 104; 153; CDBLB 1890-1914; DAM POET; EWL 3; RGEL 2

Russell, Jeffrey Burton 1934- .... **CLC 70**
See also CA 25-28R; CANR 11, 28, 52

Russell, (Henry) Ken(neth Alfred) 1927- .... **CLC 16**
See also CA 105

Russell, William Martin 1947-
See Russell, Willy
See also CA 164; CANR 107

Russell, Willy .... **CLC 60**
See Russell, William Martin
See also CBD; CD 5, 6; DLB 233

Russo, Richard 1949- .... **CLC 181**
See also AMWS 12; CA 127; 133; CANR 87, 114

Rutherford, Mark .... **TCLC 25**
See White, William Hale
See also DLB 18; RGEL 2

Ruyslinck, Ward .... **CLC 14**
See Belser, Reimond Karel Maria de

Ryan, Cornelius (John) 1920-1974 ..... **CLC 7**
See also CA 69-72; 53-56; CANR 38

Ryan, Michael 1946- .... **CLC 65**
See also CA 49-52; CANR 109; DLBY 1982

Ryan, Tim
See Dent, Lester

Rybakov, Anatoli (Naumovich) 1911-1998 .... **CLC 23, 53**
See Rybakov, Anatolii (Naumovich)
See also CA 126; 135; 172; SATA 79; SATA-Obit 108

Rybakov, Anatolii (Naumovich)
See Rybakov, Anatoli (Naumovich)
See also DLB 302

Ryder, Jonathan
See Ludlum, Robert

Ryga, George 1932-1987 .... **CLC 14**
See also CA 101; 124; CANR 43, 90; CCA 1; DAC; DAM MST; DLB 60

S. H.
See Hartmann, Sadakichi

S. S.
See Sassoon, Siegfried (Lorraine)

Sa'adawi, al- Nawal
See El Saadawi, Nawal
See also AFW; EWL 3

Saadawi, Nawal El
See El Saadawi, Nawal
See also WLIT 2

Saba, Umberto 1883-1957 .... **TCLC 33**
See also CA 144; CANR 79; DLB 114; EWL 3; RGWL 2, 3

Sabatini, Rafael 1875-1950 .... **TCLC 47**
See also BPFB 3; CA 162; RHW

Sabato, Ernesto (R.) 1911- .... **CLC 10, 23; HLC 2**
See also CA 97-100; CANR 32, 65; CD-WLB 3; CWW 2; DAM MULT; DLB 145; EWL 3; HW 1, 2; LAW; MTCW 1, 2; MTFW 2005

Sa-Carneiro, Mario de 1890-1916 . **TCLC 83**
See also DLB 287; EWL 3

Sacastru, Martin
See Bioy Casares, Adolfo
See also CWW 2

Sacher-Masoch, Leopold von 1836(?)-1895 .... **NCLC 31**

Sachs, Hans 1494-1576 .... **LC 95**
See also CDWLB 2; DLB 179; RGWL 2, 3

Sachs, Marilyn 1927- .... **CLC 35**
See also AAYA 2; BYA 6; CA 17-20R; CANR 13, 47; CLR 2; JRDA; MAICYA 1, 2; SAAS 2; SATA 3, 68, 164; SATA-Essay 110; WYA; YAW

Sachs, Marilyn Stickle
See Sachs, Marilyn

Sachs, Nelly 1891-1970 .... **CLC 14, 98**
See also CA 17-18; 25-28R; CANR 87; CAP 2; EWL 3; MTCW 1, 2; MTFW 2005; PFS 20; RGWL 2, 3

Sackler, Howard (Oliver) 1929-1982 .... **CLC 14**
See also CA 61-64; 108; CAD; CANR 30; DFS 15; DLB 7

Sacks, Oliver (Wolf) 1933- .... **CLC 67, 202**
See also CA 53-56; CANR 28, 50, 76; CPW; DA3; INT CANR-28; MTCW 1, 2; MTFW 2005

Sackville, Thomas 1536-1608 .... **LC 98**
See also DAM DRAM; DLB 62, 132; RGEL 2

Sadakichi
See Hartmann, Sadakichi

Sa'dawi, Nawal al-
See El Saadawi, Nawal
See also CWW 2

Sade, Donatien Alphonse Francois 1740-1814 .... **NCLC 3, 47**
See also DLB 314; EW 4; GFL Beginnings to 1789; RGWL 2, 3

Sade, Marquis de
See Sade, Donatien Alphonse Francois

Sadoff, Ira 1945- .... **CLC 9**
See also CA 53-56; CANR 5, 21, 109; DLB 120

Saetone
See Camus, Albert

Safire, William 1929- .... **CLC 10**
See also CA 17-20R; CANR 31, 54, 91

Sagan, Carl (Edward) 1934-1996 .... **CLC 30, 112**
See also AAYA 2, 62; CA 25-28R; 155; CANR 11, 36, 74; CPW; DA3; MTCW 1, 2; MTFW 2005; SATA 58; SATA-Obit 94

Sagan, Françoise .... **CLC 3, 6, 9, 17, 36**
See Quoirez, Francoise
See also CWW 2; DLB 83; EWL 3; GFL 1789 to the Present; MTCW 2

Sahgal, Nayantara (Pandit) 1927- .... **CLC 41**
See also CA 9-12R; CANR 11, 88; CN 1, 2, 3, 4, 5, 6, 7

Said, Edward W. 1935-2003 .... **CLC 123**
See also CA 21-24R; 220; CANR 45, 74, 107, 131; DLB 67; MTCW 2; MTFW 2005

Saint, H(arry) F. 1941- .... **CLC 50**
See also CA 127

St. Aubin de Teran, Lisa 1953-
See Teran, Lisa St. Aubin de
See also CA 118; 126; CN 6, 7; INT CA-126

Saint Birgitta of Sweden c. 1303-1373 .... **CMLC 24**

Saint Gregory of Nazianzus 329-389 .... **CMLC 82**

Sainte-Beuve, Charles Augustin 1804-1869 .... **NCLC 5**
See also DLB 217; EW 6; GFL 1789 to the Present

Saint-Exupery, Antoine (Jean Baptiste Marie Roger) de 1900-1944 .... **TCLC 2, 56, 169; WLC**
See also AAYA 63; BPFB 3; BYA 3; CA 108; 132; CLR 10; DA3; DAM NOV; DLB 72; EW 12; EWL 3; GFL 1789 to the Present; LAIT 3; MAICYA 1, 2; MTCW 1, 2; MTFW 2005; RGWL 2, 3; SATA 20; TWA

St. John, David
See Hunt, E(verette) Howard, (Jr.)

St. John, J. Hector
See Crevecoeur, Michel Guillaume Jean de

Saint-John Perse
See Leger, (Marie-Rene Auguste) Alexis Saint-Leger
See also EW 10; EWL 3; GFL 1789 to the Present; RGWL 2

Saintsbury, George (Edward Bateman) 1845-1933 .... **TCLC 31**
See also CA 160; DLB 57, 149

Sait Faik .... **TCLC 23**
See Abasiyanik, Sait Faik

Saki .... **SSC 12; TCLC 3**
See Munro, H(ector) H(ugh)
See also BRWS 6; BYA 11; LAIT 2; RGEL 2; SSFS 1; SUFW

Sala, George Augustus 1828-1895 . **NCLC 46**

Saladin 1138-1193 .... **CMLC 38**

Salama, Hannu 1936- .... **CLC 18**
See also EWL 3

Salamanca, J(ack) R(ichard) 1922- .. **CLC 4, 15**
See also CA 25-28R, 193; CAAE 193

Salas, Floyd Francis 1931- .... **HLC 2**
See also CA 119; CAAS 27; CANR 44, 75, 93; DAM MULT; DLB 82; HW 1, 2; MTCW 2; MTFW 2005

Sale, J. Kirkpatrick
See Sale, Kirkpatrick

Sale, Kirkpatrick 1937- .... **CLC 68**
See also CA 13-16R; CANR 10

Salinas, Luis Omar 1937- ... **CLC 90; HLC 2**
See also AMWS 13; CA 131; CANR 81; DAM MULT; DLB 82; HW 1, 2

Salinas (y Serrano), Pedro 1891(?)-1951 .... **TCLC 17**
See also CA 117; DLB 134; EWL 3

Salinger, J(erome) D(avid) 1919- .. **CLC 1, 3, 8, 12, 55, 56, 138; SSC 2, 28, 65; WLC**
See also AAYA 2, 36; AMW; AMWC 1; BPFB 3; CA 5-8R; CANR 39, 129; CDALB 1941-1968; CLR 18; CN 1, 2, 3, 4, 5, 6, 7; CPW 1; DA; DA3; DAB; DAC; DAM MST, NOV, POP; DLB 2, 102, 173; EWL 3; EXPN; LAIT 4; MAICYA 1, 2; MAL 5; MTCW 1, 2; MTFW 2005; NFS 1; RGAL 4; RGSF 2; SATA 67; SSFS 17; TUS; WYA; YAW

Salisbury, John
See Caute, (John) David

Sallust c. 86B.C.-35B.C. .... **CMLC 68**
See also AW 2; CDWLB 1; DLB 211; RGWL 2, 3

Salter, James 1925- .. **CLC 7, 52, 59; SSC 58**
See also AMWS 9; CA 73-76; CANR 107; DLB 130

Saltus, Edgar (Everton) 1855-1921 . **TCLC 8**
See also CA 105; DLB 202; RGAL 4

Saltykov, Mikhail Evgrafovich 1826-1889 .... **NCLC 16**
See also DLB 238:

Saltykov-Shchedrin, N.
See Saltykov, Mikhail Evgrafovich

Samarakis, Andonis
See Samarakis, Antonis
See also EWL 3

Samarakis, Antonis 1919-2003 .... **CLC 5**
See Samarakis, Andonis
See also CA 25-28R; 224; CAAS 16; CANR 36

Sanchez, Florencio 1875-1910 .... **TCLC 37**
See also CA 153; DLB 305; EWL 3; HW 1; LAW

Sanchez, Luis Rafael 1936- .... **CLC 23**
See also CA 128; DLB 305; EWL 3; HW 1; WLIT 1

Sanchez, Sonia 1934- .... **BLC 3; CLC 5, 116, 215; PC 9**
See also BW 2, 3; CA 33-36R; CANR 24, 49, 74, 115; CLR 18; CP 2, 3, 4, 5, 6, 7; CSW; CWP; DA3; DAM MULT; DLB 41; DLBD 8; EWL 3; MAICYA 1, 2; MAL 5; MTCW 1, 2; MTFW 2005; SATA 22, 136; WP

Sancho, Ignatius 1729-1780 .... **LC 84**

Sand, George 1804-1876 ..... **NCLC 2, 42, 57; WLC**
See also DA; DA3; DAB; DAC; DAM MST, NOV; DLB 119, 192; EW 6; FL 1:3; FW; GFL 1789 to the Present; RGWL 2, 3; TWA

Sandburg, Carl (August) 1878-1967 . **CLC 1, 4, 10, 15, 35; PC 2, 41; WLC**
See also AAYA 24; AMW; BYA 1, 3; CA 5-8R; 25-28R; CANR 35; CDALB 1865-1917; CLR 67; DA; DA3; DAB; DAC; DAM MST, POET; DLB 17, 54, 284; EWL 3; EXPP; LAIT 2; MAICYA 1, 2; MAL 5; MTCW 1, 2; MTFW 2005; PAB; PFS 3, 6, 12; RGAL 4; SATA 8; TUS; WCH; WP; WYA

Sandburg, Charles
See Sandburg, Carl (August)

Sandburg, Charles A.
See Sandburg, Carl (August)

Sanders, (James) Ed(ward) 1939- .... **CLC 53**
See Sanders, Edward
See also BG 1:3; CA 13-16R; CAAS 21; CANR 13, 44, 78; CP 1, 2, 3, 4, 5, 6, 7; DAM POET; DLB 16, 244

Sanders, Edward
See Sanders, (James) Ed(ward)
See also DLB 244

Sanders, Lawrence 1920-1998 .... **CLC 41**
See also BEST 89:4; BPFB 3; CA 81-84; 165; CANR 33, 62; CMW 4; CPW; DA3; DAM POP; MTCW 1

Senghor, Leopold Sedar 1906-2001 ... **BLC 3; CLC 54, 130; PC 25**
See also AFW; BW 2; CA 116; 125; 203; CANR 47, 74, 134; CWW 2; DAM MULT, POET; DNFS 2; EWL 3; GFL 1789 to the Present; MTCW 1, 2; MTFW 2005; TWA

Senior, Olive (Marjorie) 1941- .... **SSC 78**
See also BW 3; CA 154; CANR 86, 126; CN 6; CP 7; CWP; DLB 157; EWL 3; RGSF 2

Senna, Danzy 1970- .... **CLC 119**
See also CA 169; CANR 130

Serling, (Edward) Rod(man)
1924-1975 .... **CLC 30**
See also AAYA 14; AITN 1; CA 162; 57-60; DLB 26; SFW 4

Serna, Ramon Gomez de la
See Gomez de la Serna, Ramon

Serpieres
See Guillevic, (Eugene)

Service, Robert
See Service, Robert W(illiam)
See also BYA 4; DAB; DLB 92

Service, Robert W(illiam)
1874(?)-1958 ... **PC 70; TCLC 15; WLC**
See also Service, Robert
See also CA 115; 140; CANR 84; DA; DAC; DAM MST, POET; PFS 10; RGEL 2; SATA 20

Seth, Vikram 1952- .... **CLC 43, 90**
See also BRWS 1; CA 121; 127; CANR 50, 74, 131; CN 6, 7; CP 7; DA3; DAM MULT; DLB 120, 271, 282; EWL 3; INT CA-127; MTCW 2; MTFW 2005; WWE 1

Seton, Cynthia Propper 1926-1982 .. **CLC 27**
See also CA 5-8R; 108; CANR 7

Seton, Ernest (Evan) Thompson
1860-1946 .... **TCLC 31**
See also ANW; BYA 3; CA 109; 204; CLR 59; DLB 92; DLBD 13; JRDA; SATA 18

Seton-Thompson, Ernest
See Seton, Ernest (Evan) Thompson

Settle, Mary Lee 1918-2005 .... **CLC 19, 61**
See also BPFB 3; CA 89-92; CAAS 1; CANR 44, 87, 126; CN 6, 7; CSW; DLB 6; INT CA-89-92

Seuphor, Michel
See Arp, Jean

Sevigne, Marie (de Rabutin-Chantal)
1626-1696 .... **LC 11**
See Sevigne, Marie de Rabutin Chantal
See also GFL Beginnings to 1789; TWA

Sevigne, Marie de Rabutin Chantal
See Sevigne, Marie (de Rabutin-Chantal)
See also DLB 268

Sewall, Samuel 1652-1730 .... **LC 38**
See also DLB 24; RGAL 4

Sexton, Anne (Harvey) 1928-1974 ..... **CLC 2, 4, 6, 8, 10, 15, 53, 123; PC 2; WLC**
See also AMWS 2; CA 1-4R; 53-56; CABS 2; CANR 3, 36; CDALB 1941-1968; CP 1, 2; DA; DA3; DAB; DAC; DAM MST, POET; DLB 5, 169; EWL 3; EXPP; FL 1:6; FW; MAL 5; MAWW; MTCW 1, 2; MTFW 2005; PAB; PFS 4, 14; RGAL 4; SATA 10; TUS

Shaara, Jeff 1952- .... **CLC 119**
See also CA 163; CANR 109; CN 7; MTFW 2005

Shaara, Michael (Joseph, Jr.)
1929-1988 .... **CLC 15**
See also AITN 1; BPFB 3; CA 102; 125; CANR 52, 85; DAM POP; DLBY 1983; MTFW 2005

Shackleton, C. C.
See Aldiss, Brian W(ilson)

Shacochis, Bob .... **CLC 39**
See Shacochis, Robert G.

Shacochis, Robert G. 1951-
See Shacochis, Bob
See also CA 119; 124; CANR 100; INT CA-124

Shadwell, Thomas 1641(?)-1692 .... **LC 114**
See also DLB 80; IDTP; RGEL 2

Shaffer, Anthony (Joshua)
1926-2001 .... **CLC 19**
See also CA 110; 116; 200; CBD; CD 5, 6; DAM DRAM; DFS 13; DLB 13

Shaffer, Peter (Levin) 1926- .. **CLC 5, 14, 18, 37, 60; DC 7**
See also BRWS 1; CA 25-28R; CANR 25, 47, 74, 118; CBD; CD 5, 6; CDBLB 1960 to Present; DA3; DAB; DAM DRAM, MST; DFS 5, 13; DLB 13, 233; EWL 3; MTCW 1, 2; MTFW 2005; RGEL 2; TEA

Shakespeare, William 1564-1616 .... **WLC**
See also AAYA 35; BRW 1; CDBLB Before 1660; DA; DA3; DAB; DAC; DAM DRAM, MST, POET; DFS 20, 21; DLB 62, 172, 263; EXPP; LAIT 1; LATS 1:1; LMFS 1; PAB; PFS 1, 2, 3, 4, 5, 8, 9; RGEL 2; TEA; WLIT 3; WP; WS; WYA

Shakey, Bernard
See Young, Neil

Shalamov, Varlam (Tikhonovich)
1907-1982 .... **CLC 18**
See also CA 129; 105; DLB 302; RGSF 2

Shamloo, Ahmad
See Shamlu, Ahmad

Shamlou, Ahmad
See Shamlu, Ahmad

Shamlu, Ahmad 1925-2000 .... **CLC 10**
See also CA 216; CWW 2

Shammas, Anton 1951- .... **CLC 55**
See also CA 199

Shandling, Arline
See Berriault, Gina

Shange, Ntozake 1948- ... **BLC 3; CLC 8, 25, 38, 74, 126; DC 3**
See also AAYA 9, 66; AFAW 1, 2; BW 2; CA 85-88; CABS 3; CAD; CANR 27, 48, 74, 131; CD 5, 6; CP 7; CWD; CWP; DA3; DAM DRAM, MULT; DFS 2, 11; DLB 38, 249; FW; LAIT 4, 5; MAL 5; MTCW 1, 2; MTFW 2005; NFS 11; RGAL 4; SATA 157; YAW

Shanley, John Patrick 1950- .... **CLC 75**
See also AMWS 14; CA 128; 133; CAD; CANR 83; CD 5, 6

Shapcott, Thomas W(illiam) 1935- .. **CLC 38**
See also CA 69-72; CANR 49, 83, 103; CP 1, 2, 3, 4, 5, 6, 7; DLB 289

Shapiro, Jane 1942- .... **CLC 76**
See also CA 196

Shapiro, Karl (Jay) 1913-2000 ...... **CLC 4, 8, 15, 53; PC 25**
See also AMWS 2; CA 1-4R; 188; CAAS 6; CANR 1, 36, 66; CP 1, 2, 3, 4, 5, 6; DLB 48; EWL 3; EXPP; MAL 5; MTCW 1, 2; MTFW 2005; PFS 3; RGAL 4

Sharp, William 1855-1905 .... **TCLC 39**
See Macleod, Fiona
See also CA 160; DLB 156; RGEL 2

Sharpe, Thomas Ridley 1928-
See Sharpe, Tom
See also CA 114; 122; CANR 85; INT CA-122

Sharpe, Tom .... **CLC 36**
See Sharpe, Thomas Ridley
See also CN 4, 5, 6, 7; DLB 14, 231

Shatrov, Mikhail .... **CLC 59**

Shaw, Bernard
See Shaw, George Bernard
See also DLB 10, 57, 190

Shaw, G. Bernard
See Shaw, George Bernard

Shaw, George Bernard 1856-1950 ..... **DC 23; TCLC 3, 9, 21, 45; WLC**
See Shaw, Bernard
See also AAYA 61; BRW 6; BRWC 1; BRWR 2; CA 104; 128; CDBLB 1914-1945; DA; DA3; DAB; DAC; DAM DRAM, MST; DFS 1, 3, 6, 11, 19, 22; EWL 3; LAIT 3; LATS 1:1; MTCW 1, 2; MTFW 2005; RGEL 2; TEA; WLIT 4

Shaw, Henry Wheeler 1818-1885 .. **NCLC 15**
See also DLB 11; RGAL 4

Shaw, Irwin 1913-1984 .... **CLC 7, 23, 34**
See also AITN 1; BPFB 3; CA 13-16R; 112; CANR 21; CDALB 1941-1968; CN 1, 2, 3; CPW; DAM DRAM, POP; DLB 6, 102; DLBY 1984; MAL 5; MTCW 1, 21; MTFW 2005

Shaw, Robert (Archibald)
1927-1978 .... **CLC 5**
See also AITN 1; CA 1-4R; 81-84; CANR 4; CN 1, 2; DLB 13, 14

Shaw, T. E.
See Lawrence, T(homas) E(dward)

Shawn, Wallace 1943- .... **CLC 41**
See also CA 112; CAD; CD 5, 6; DLB 266

Shchedrin, N.
See Saltykov, Mikhail Evgrafovich

Shea, Lisa 1953- .... **CLC 86**
See also CA 147

Sheed, Wilfrid (John Joseph) 1930- . **CLC 2, 4, 10, 53**
See also CA 65-68; CANR 30, 66; CN 1, 2, 3, 4, 5, 6, 7; DLB 6; MAL 5; MTCW 1, 2; MTFW 2005

Sheehy, Gail 1937- .... **CLC 171**
See also CA 49-52; CANR 1, 33, 55, 92; CPW; MTCW 1

Sheldon, Alice Hastings Bradley
1915(?)-1987
See Tiptree, James, Jr.
See also CA 108; 122; CANR 34; INT CA-108; MTCW 1

Sheldon, John
See Bloch, Robert (Albert)

Sheldon, Walter J(ames) 1917-1996
See Queen, Ellery
See also AITN 1; CA 25-28R; CANR 10

Shelley, Mary Wollstonecraft (Godwin)
1797-1851 ...... **NCLC 14, 59, 103; WLC**
See also AAYA 20; BPFB 3; BRW 3; BRWC 2; BRWS 3; BYA 5; CDBLB 1789-1832; DA; DA3; DAB; DAC; DAM MST, NOV; DLB 110, 116, 159, 178; EXPN; FL 1:3; GL 3; HGG; LAIT 1; LMFS 1, 2; NFS 1; RGEL 2; SATA 29; SCFW 1, 2; SFW 4; TEA; WLIT 3

Shelley, Percy Bysshe 1792-1822 .. **NCLC 18, 93, 143; PC 14, 67; WLC**
See also AAYA 61; BRW 4; BRWR 1; CDBLB 1789-1832; DA; DA3; DAB; DAC; DAM MST, POET; DLB 96, 110, 158; EXPP; LMFS 1; PAB; PFS 2; RGEL 2; TEA; WLIT 3; WP

Shepard, James R. .... **CLC 36**
See also CA 137; CANR 59, 104; SATA 90, 164

Shepard, Jim
See Shepard, James R.

Shepard, Lucius 1947- .... **CLC 34**
See also CA 128; 141; CANR 81, 124; HGG; SCFW 2; SFW 4; SUFW 2

Shepard, Sam 1943- .... **CLC 4, 6, 17, 34, 41, 44, 169; DC 5**
See also AAYA 1, 58; AMWS 3; CA 69-72; CABS 3; CAD; CANR 22, 120, 140; CD 5, 6; DA3; DAM DRAM; DFS 3, 6, 7, 14; DLB 7, 212; EWL 3; IDFW 3, 4; MAL 5; MTCW 1, 2; MTFW 2005; RGAL 4

Shepherd, Michael
See Ludlum, Robert
Sherburne, Zoa (Lillian Morin)
1912-1995 .... CLC 30
See also AAYA 13; CA 1-4R; 176; CANR
3, 37; MAICYA 1, 2; SAAS 18; SATA 3;
YAW
Sheridan, Frances 1724-1766 .... LC 7
See also DLB 39, 84
Sheridan, Richard Brinsley
1751-1816 .... DC 1; NCLC 5, 91; WLC
See also BRW 3; CDBLB 1660-1789; DA;
DAB; DAC; DAM DRAM, MST; DFS
15; DLB 89; WLIT 3
Sherman, Jonathan Marc 1968- .... CLC 55
See also CA 230
Sherman, Martin 1941(?)- .... CLC 19
See also CA 116; 123; CAD; CANR 86;
CD 5, 6; DFS 20; DLB 228; GLL 1; IDTP
Sherwin, Judith Johnson
See Johnson, Judith (Emlyn)
See also CANR 85; CP 2, 3, 4; CWP
Sherwood, Frances 1940- .... CLC 81
See also CA 146, 220; CAAE 220
Sherwood, Robert E(mmet)
1896-1955 .... TCLC 3
See also CA 104; 153; CANR 86; DAM
DRAM; DFS 11, 15, 17; DLB 7, 26, 249;
IDFW 3, 4; MAL 5; RGAL 4
Shestov, Lev 1866-1938 .... TCLC 56
Shevchenko, Taras 1814-1861 .... NCLC 54
Shiel, M(atthew) P(hipps)
1865-1947 .... TCLC 8
See Holmes, Gordon
See also CA 106; 160; DLB 153; HGG;
MTCW 2; MTFW 2005; SCFW 1, 2;
SFW 4; SUFW
Shields, Carol (Ann) 1935-2003 ...... CLC 91,
113, 193
See also AMWS 7; CA 81-84; 218; CANR
51, 74, 98, 133; CCA 1; CN 6, 7; CPW;
DA3; DAC; MTCW 2; MTFW 2005
Shields, David (Jonathan) 1956- ...... CLC 97
See also CA 124; CANR 48, 99, 112
Shiga, Naoya 1883-1971 .... CLC 33; SSC 23;
TCLC 172
See Shiga Naoya
See also CA 101; 33-36R; MJW; RGWL 3
Shiga Naoya
See Shiga, Naoya
See also DLB 180; EWL 3; RGWL 3
Shilts, Randy 1951-1994 .... CLC 85
See also AAYA 19; CA 115; 127; 144;
CANR 45; DA3; GLL 1; INT CA-127;
MTCW 2; MTFW 2005
Shimazaki, Haruki 1872-1943
See Shimazaki Toson
See also CA 105; 134; CANR 84; RGWL 3
Shimazaki Toson .... TCLC 5
See Shimazaki, Haruki
See also DLB 180; EWL 3
Shirley, James 1596-1666 .... DC 25; LC 96
See also DLB 58; RGEL 2
Sholokhov, Mikhail (Aleksandrovich)
1905-1984 .... CLC 7, 15
See also CA 101; 112; DLB 272; EWL 3;
MTCW 1, 2; MTFW 2005; RGWL 2, 3;
SATA-Obit 36
Shone, Patric
See Hanley, James
Showalter, Elaine 1941- .... CLC 169
See also CA 57-60; CANR 58, 106; DLB
67; FW; GLL 2
Shreve, Susan
See Shreve, Susan Richards
Shreve, Susan Richards 1939- .... CLC 23
See also CA 49-52; CAAS 5; CANR 5, 38,
69, 100; MAICYA 1, 2; SATA 46, 95, 152;
SATA-Brief 41

Shue, Larry 1946-1985 .... CLC 52
See also CA 145; 117; DAM DRAM; DFS
7
Shu-Jen, Chou 1881-1936
See Lu Hsun
See also CA 104
Shulman, Alix Kates 1932- .... CLC 2, 10
See also CA 29-32R; CANR 43; FW; SATA
7
Shuster, Joe 1914-1992 .... CLC 21
See also AAYA 50
Shute, Nevil .... CLC 30
See Norway, Nevil Shute
See also BPFB 3; DLB 255; NFS 9; RHW;
SFW 4
Shuttle, Penelope (Diane) 1947- .... CLC 7
See also CA 93-96; CANR 39, 84, 92, 108;
CP 3, 4, 5, 6, 7; CWP; DLB 14, 40
Shvarts, Elena 1948- .... PC 50
See also CA 147
Sidhwa, Bapsi
See Sidhwa, Bapsy (N.)
See also CN 6, 7
Sidhwa, Bapsy (N.) 1938- .... CLC 168
See Sidhwa, Bapsi
See also CA 108; CANR 25, 57; FW
Sidney, Mary 1561-1621 .... LC 19, 39
See Sidney Herbert, Mary
Sidney, Sir Philip 1554-1586 . LC 19, 39; PC
32
See also BRW 1; BRWR 2; CDBLB Before
1660; DA; DA3; DAB; DAC; DAM MST,
POET; DLB 167; EXPP; PAB; RGEL 2;
TEA; WP
Sidney Herbert, Mary
See Sidney, Mary
See also DLB 167
Siegel, Jerome 1914-1996 .... CLC 21
See Siegel, Jerry
See also CA 116; 169; 151
Siegel, Jerry
See Siegel, Jerome
See also AAYA 50
Sienkiewicz, Henryk (Adam Alexander Pius)
1846-1916 .... TCLC 3
See also CA 104; 134; CANR 84; EWL 3;
RGSF 2; RGWL 2, 3
Sierra, Gregorio Martinez
See Martinez Sierra, Gregorio
Sierra, Maria (de la O'LeJarraga) Martinez
See Martinez Sierra, Maria (de la
O'LeJarraga)
Sigal, Clancy 1926- .... CLC 7
See also CA 1-4R; CANR 85; CN 1, 2, 3,
4, 5, 6, 7
Siger of Brabant 1240(?)-1284(?) . CMLC 69
See also DLB 115
Sigourney, Lydia H.
See Sigourney, Lydia Howard (Huntley)
See also DLB 73, 183
Sigourney, Lydia Howard (Huntley)
1791-1865 .... NCLC 21, 87
See Sigourney, Lydia H.; Sigourney, Lydia
Huntley
See also DLB 1
Sigourney, Lydia Huntley
See Sigourney, Lydia Howard (Huntley)
See also DLB 42, 239, 243
Siguenza y Gongora, Carlos de
1645-1700 .... HLCS 2; LC 8
See also LAW
Sigurjonsson, Johann
See Sigurjonsson, Johann
Sigurjonsson, Johann 1880-1919 ... TCLC 27
See also CA 170; DLB 293; EWL 3
Sikelianos, Angelos 1884-1951 .... PC 29;
TCLC 39
See also EWL 3; RGWL 2, 3

Silkin, Jon 1930-1997 .... CLC 2, 6, 43
See also CA 5-8R; CAAS 5; CANR 89; CP
1, 2, 3, 4, 5, 6; DLB 27
Silko, Leslie (Marmon) 1948- .... CLC 23, 74,
114, 211; NNAL; SSC 37, 66; WLCS
See also AAYA 14; AMWS 4; ANW; BYA
12; CA 115; 122; CANR 45, 65, 118; CN
4, 5, 6, 7; CP 4, 5, 6, 7; CPW 1; CWP;
DA; DA3; DAC; DAM MST, MULT,
POP; DLB 143, 175, 256, 275; EWL 3;
EXPP; EXPS; LAIT 4; MAL 5; MTCW
2; MTFW 2005; NFS 4; PFS 9, 16; RGAL
4; RGSF 2; SSFS 4, 8, 10, 11; TCWW 1,
2
Sillanpaa, Frans Eemil 1888-1964 ... CLC 19
See also CA 129; 93-96; EWL 3; MTCW 1
Sillitoe, Alan 1928- .. CLC 1, 3, 6, 10, 19, 57,
148
See also AITN 1; BRWS 5; CA 9-12R, 191;
CAAE 191; CAAS 2; CANR 8, 26, 55,
139; CDBLB 1960 to Present; CN 1, 2, 3,
4, 5, 6; CP 1, 2, 3, 4; DLB 14, 139; EWL
3; MTCW 1, 2; MTFW 2005; RGEL 2;
RGSF 2; SATA 61
Silone, Ignazio 1900-1978 .... CLC 4
See also CA 25-28; 81-84; CANR 34; CAP
2; DLB 264; EW 12; EWL 3; MTCW 1;
RGSF 2; RGWL 2, 3
Silone, Ignazione
See Silone, Ignazio
Silver, Joan Micklin 1935- .... CLC 20
See also CA 114; 121; INT CA-121
Silver, Nicholas
See Faust, Frederick (Schiller)
Silverberg, Robert 1935- .... CLC 7, 140
See also AAYA 24; BPFB 3; BYA 7, 9; CA
1-4R, 186; CAAE 186; CAAS 3; CANR
1, 20, 36, 85, 140; CLR 59; CN 6, 7;
CPW; DAM POP; DLB 8; INT CANR-
20; MAICYA 1, 2; MTCW 1, 2; MTFW
2005; SATA 13, 91; SATA-Essay 104;
SCFW 1, 2; SFW 4; SUFW 2
Silverstein, Alvin 1933- .... CLC 17
See also CA 49-52; CANR 2; CLR 25;
JRDA; MAICYA 1, 2; SATA 8, 69, 124
Silverstein, Shel(don Allan)
1932-1999 .... PC 49
See also AAYA 40; BW 3; CA 107; 179;
CANR 47, 74, 81; CLR 5, 96; CWRI 5;
JRDA; MAICYA 1, 2; MTCW 2; MTFW
2005; SATA 33, 92; SATA-Brief 27;
SATA-Obit 116
Silverstein, Virginia B(arbara Opshelor)
1937- .... CLC 17
See also CA 49-52; CANR 2; CLR 25;
JRDA; MAICYA 1, 2; SATA 8, 69, 124
Sim, Georges
See Simenon, Georges (Jacques Christian)
Simak, Clifford D(onald) 1904-1988 . CLC 1,
55
See also CA 1-4R; 125; CANR 1, 35; DLB
8; MTCW 1; SATA-Obit 56; SCFW 1, 2;
SFW 4
Simenon, Georges (Jacques Christian)
1903-1989 .... CLC 1, 2, 3, 8, 18, 47
See also BPFB 3; CA 85-88; 129; CANR
35; CMW 4; DA3; DAM POP; DLB 72;
DLBY 1989; EW 12; EWL 3; GFL 1789
to the Present; MSW; MTCW 1, 2; MTFW
2005; RGWL 2, 3
Simic, Charles 1938- .... CLC 6, 9, 22, 49, 68,
130; PC 69
See also AMWS 8; CA 29-32R; CAAS 4;
CANR 12, 33, 52, 61, 96, 140; CP 2, 3, 4,
5, 6, 7; DA3; DAM POET; DLB 105;
MAL 5; MTCW 2; MTFW 2005; PFS 7;
RGAL 4; WP
Simmel, Georg 1858-1918 .... TCLC 64
See also CA 157; DLB 296

Simmons, Charles (Paul) 1924- .... **CLC 57**
See also CA 89-92; INT CA-89-92
Simmons, Dan 1948- .... **CLC 44**
See also AAYA 16, 54; CA 138; CANR 53,
81, 126; CPW; DAM POP; HGG; SUFW
2
Simmons, James (Stewart Alexander)
1933- .... **CLC 43**
See also CA 105; CAAS 21; CP 1, 2, 3, 4,
5, 6, 7; DLB 40
Simms, William Gilmore
1806-1870 .... **NCLC 3**
See also DLB 3, 30, 59, 73, 248, 254;
RGAL 4
Simon, Carly 1945- .... **CLC 26**
See also CA 105
Simon, Claude 1913-2005 ... **CLC 4, 9, 15, 39**
See also CA 89-92; 241; CANR 33, 117;
CWW 2; DAM NOV; DLB 83; EW 13;
EWL 3; GFL 1789 to the Present; MTCW
1
Simon, Claude Eugene Henri
See Simon, Claude
Simon, Claude Henri Eugene
See Simon, Claude
Simon, Myles
See Follett, Ken(neth Martin)
Simon, (Marvin) Neil 1927- ... **CLC 6, 11, 31,**
39, 70; DC 14
See also AAYA 32; AITN 1; AMWS 4; CA
21-24R; CAD; CANR 26, 54, 87, 126;
CD 5, 6; DA3; DAM DRAM; DFS 2, 6,
12, 18; DLB 7, 266; LAIT 4; MAL 5;
MTCW 1, 2; MTFW 2005; RGAL 4; TUS
Simon, Paul (Frederick) 1941(?)- ..... **CLC 17**
See also CA 116; 153
Simonon, Paul 1956(?)- .... **CLC 30**
Simonson, Rick ed. .... **CLC 70**
Simpson, Harriette
See Arnow, Harriette (Louisa) Simpson
Simpson, Louis (Aston Marantz)
1923- .... **CLC 4, 7, 9, 32, 149**
See also AMWS 9; CA 1-4R; CAAS 4;
CANR 1, 61, 140; CP 1, 2, 3, 4, 5, 6, 7;
DAM POET; DLB 5; MAL 5; MTCW 1,
2; MTFW 2005; PFS 7, 11, 14; RGAL 4
Simpson, Mona (Elizabeth) 1957- ... **CLC 44,**
146
See also CA 122; 135; CANR 68, 103; CN
6, 7; EWL 3
Simpson, N(orman) F(rederick)
1919- .... **CLC 29**
See also CA 13-16R; CBD; DLB 13; RGEL
2
Sinclair, Andrew (Annandale) 1935- . **CLC 2,**
14
See also CA 9-12R; CAAS 5; CANR 14,
38, 91; CN 1, 2, 3, 4, 5, 6, 7; DLB 14;
FANT; MTCW 1
Sinclair, Emil
See Hesse, Hermann
Sinclair, Iain 1943- .... **CLC 76**
See also CA 132; CANR 81; CP 7; HGG
Sinclair, Iain MacGregor
See Sinclair, Iain
Sinclair, Irene
See Griffith, D(avid Lewelyn) W(ark)
Sinclair, Mary Amelia St. Clair 1865(?)-1946
See Sinclair, May
See also CA 104; HGG; RHW
Sinclair, May .... **TCLC 3, 11**
See Sinclair, Mary Amelia St. Clair
See also CA 166; DLB 36, 135; EWL 3;
RGEL 2; SUFW
Sinclair, Roy
See Griffith, D(avid Lewelyn) W(ark)

Sinclair, Upton (Beall) 1878-1968 ..... **CLC 1,**
11, 15, 63; TCLC 160; WLC
See also AAYA 63; AMWS 5; BPFB 3;
BYA 2; CA 5-8R; 25-28R; CANR 7;
CDALB 1929-1941; DA; DA3; DAB;
DAC; DAM MST, NOV; DLB 9; EWL 3;
INT CANR-7; LAIT 3; MAL 5; MTCW
1, 2; MTFW 2005; NFS 6; RGAL 4;
SATA 9; TUS; YAW
Singe, (Edmund) J(ohn) M(illington)
1871-1909 .... **WLC**
Singer, Isaac
See Singer, Isaac Bashevis
Singer, Isaac Bashevis 1904-1991 .. **CLC 1, 3,**
6, 9, 11, 15, 23, 38, 69, 111; SSC 3, 53,
80; WLC
See also AAYA 32; AITN 1, 2; AMW;
AMWR 2; BPFB 3; BYA 1, 4; CA 1-4R;
134; CANR 1, 39, 106; CDALB 1941-
1968; CLR 1; CN 1, 2, 3, 4; CWRI 5;
DA; DA3; DAB; DAC; DAM MST, NOV;
DLB 6, 28, 52, 278; DLBY 1991; EWL
3; EXPS; HGG; JRDA; LAIT 3; MAI-
CYA 1, 2; MAL 5; MTCW 1, 2; MTFW
2005; RGAL 4; RGSF 2; SATA 3, 27;
SATA-Obit 68; SSFS 2, 12, 16; TUS;
TWA
Singer, Israel Joshua 1893-1944 .... **TCLC 33**
See also CA 169; EWL 3
Singh, Khushwant 1915- .... **CLC 11**
See also CA 9-12R; CAAS 9; CANR 6, 84;
CN 1, 2, 3, 4, 5, 6, 7; EWL 3; RGEL 2
Singleton, Ann
See Benedict, Ruth (Fulton)
Singleton, John 1968(?)- .... **CLC 156**
See also AAYA 50; BW 2, 3; CA 138;
CANR 67, 82; DAM MULT
Siniavskii, Andrei
See Sinyavsky, Andrei (Donatevich)
See also CWW 2
Sinjohn, John
See Galsworthy, John
Sinyavsky, Andrei (Donatevich)
1925-1997 .... **CLC 8**
See Siniavskii, Andrei; Sinyavsky, Andrey
Donatovich; Tertz, Abram
See also CA 85-88; 159
Sinyavsky, Andrey Donatovich
See Sinyavsky, Andrei (Donatevich)
See also EWL 3
Sirin, V.
See Nabokov, Vladimir (Vladimirovich)
Sissman, L(ouis) E(dward)
1928-1976 .... **CLC 9, 18**
See also CA 21-24R; 65-68; CANR 13; CP
2; DLB 5
Sisson, C(harles) H(ubert)
1914-2003 .... **CLC 8**
See also BRWS 11; CA 1-4R; 220; CAAS
3; CANR 3, 48, 84; CP 1, 2, 3, 4, 5, 6, 7;
DLB 27
Sitting Bull 1831(?)-1890 .... **NNAL**
See also DA3; DAM MULT
Sitwell, Dame Edith 1887-1964 ..... **CLC 2, 9,**
67; PC 3
See also BRW 7; CA 9-12R; CANR 35;
CDBLB 1945-1960; DAM POET; DLB
20; EWL 3; MTCW 1, 2; MTFW 2005;
RGEL 2; TEA
Siwaarmill, H. P.
See Sharp, William
Sjoewall, Maj 1935- .... **CLC 7**
See Sjowall, Maj
See also CA 65-68; CANR 73
Sjowall, Maj
See Sjoewall, Maj
See also BPFB 3; CMW 4; MSW
Skelton, John 1460(?)-1529 ..... **LC 71; PC 25**
See also BRW 1; DLB 136; RGEL 2

Skelton, Robin 1925-1997 .... **CLC 13**
See Zuk, Georges
See also AITN 2; CA 5-8R; 160; CAAS 5;
CANR 28, 89; CCA 1; CP 1, 2, 3, 4; DLB
27, 53
Skolimowski, Jerzy 1938- .... **CLC 20**
See also CA 128
Skram, Amalie (Bertha)
1847-1905 .... **TCLC 25**
See also CA 165
Skvorecky, Josef (Vaclav) 1924- ...... **CLC 15,**
39, 69, 152
See also CA 61-64; CAAS 1; CANR 10,
34, 63, 108; CDWLB 4; CWW 2; DA3;
DAC; DAM NOV; DLB 232; EWL 3;
MTCW 1, 2; MTFW 2005
Slade, Bernard 1930- .... **CLC 11, 46**
See Newbound, Bernard Slade
See also CAAS 9; CCA 1; CD 6; DLB 53
Slaughter, Carolyn 1946- .... **CLC 56**
See also CA 85-88; CANR 85; CN 5, 6, 7
Slaughter, Frank G(ill) 1908-2001 ... **CLC 29**
See also AITN 2; CA 5-8R; 197; CANR 5,
85; INT CANR-5; RHW
Slavitt, David R(ytman) 1935- ..... **CLC 5, 14**
See also CA 21-24R; CAAS 3; CANR 41,
83; CN 1, 2; CP 1, 2, 3, 4, 5, 6, 7; DLB
5, 6
Slesinger, Tess 1905-1945 .... **TCLC 10**
See also CA 107; 199; DLB 102
Slessor, Kenneth 1901-1971 .... **CLC 14**
See also CA 102; 89-92; DLB 260; RGEL
2
Slowacki, Juliusz 1809-1849 .... **NCLC 15**
See also RGWL 3
Smart, Christopher 1722-1771 . **LC 3; PC 13**
See also DAM POET; DLB 109; RGEL 2
Smart, Elizabeth 1913-1986 .... **CLC 54**
See also CA 81-84; 118; CN 4; DLB 88
Smiley, Jane (Graves) 1949- ...... **CLC 53, 76,**
144
See also AAYA 66; AMWS 6; BPFB 3; CA
104; CANR 30, 50, 74, 96; CN 6, 7; CPW
1; DA3; DAM POP; DLB 227, 234; EWL
3; INT CANR-30; MAL 5; MTFW 2005;
SSFS 19
Smith, A(rthur) J(ames) M(arshall)
1902-1980 .... **CLC 15**
See also CA 1-4R; 102; CANR 4; CP 1, 2,
3; DAC; DLB 88; RGEL 2
Smith, Adam 1723(?)-1790 .... **LC 36**
See also DLB 104, 252; RGEL 2
Smith, Alexander 1829-1867 .... **NCLC 59**
See also DLB 32, 55
Smith, Anna Deavere 1950- .... **CLC 86**
See also CA 133; CANR 103; CD 5, 6; DFS
2, 22
Smith, Betty (Wehner) 1904-1972 .... **CLC 19**
See also BPFB 3; BYA 3; CA 5-8R; 33-
36R; DLBY 1982; LAIT 3; RGAL 4;
SATA 6
Smith, Charlotte (Turner)
1749-1806 .... **NCLC 23, 115**
See also DLB 39, 109; RGEL 2; TEA
Smith, Clark Ashton 1893-1961 .... **CLC 43**
See also CA 143; CANR 81; FANT; HGG;
MTCW 2; SCFW 1, 2; SFW 4; SUFW
Smith, Dave .... **CLC 22, 42**
See Smith, David (Jeddie)
See also CAAS 7; CP 3, 4, 5, 6, 7; DLB 5
Smith, David (Jeddie) 1942-
See Smith, Dave
See also CA 49-52; CANR 1, 59, 120;
CSW; DAM POET
Smith, Florence Margaret 1902-1971
See Smith, Stevie
See also CA 17-18; 29-32R; CANR 35;
CAP 2; DAM POET; MTCW 1, 2; TEA

Smith, Iain Crichton 1928-1998 .... **CLC 64**
See also BRWS 9; CA 21-24R; 171; CN 1,
2, 3, 4, 5, 6; CP 1, 2, 3, 4; DLB 40, 139,
319; RGSF 2

Smith, John 1580(?)-1631 .... **LC 9**
See also DLB 24, 30; TUS

Smith, Johnston
See Crane, Stephen (Townley)

Smith, Joseph, Jr. 1805-1844 .... **NCLC 53**

Smith, Lee 1944- .... **CLC 25, 73**
See also CA 114; 119; CANR 46, 118; CN
7; CSW; DLB 143; DLBY 1983; EWL 3;
INT CA-119; RGAL 4

Smith, Martin
See Smith, Martin Cruz

Smith, Martin Cruz 1942- .. **CLC 25; NNAL**
See also BEST 89:4; BPFB 3; CA 85-88;
CANR 6, 23, 43, 65, 119; CMW 4; CPW;
DAM MULT, POP; HGG; INT CANR-
23; MTCW 2; MTFW 2005; RGAL 4

Smith, Patti 1946- .... **CLC 12**
See also CA 93-96; CANR 63

Smith, Pauline (Urmson)
1882-1959 .... **TCLC 25**
See also DLB 225; EWL 3

Smith, Rosamond
See Oates, Joyce Carol

Smith, Sheila Kaye
See Kaye-Smith, Sheila

Smith, Stevie .... **CLC 3, 8, 25, 44; PC 12**
See Smith, Florence Margaret
See also BRWS 2; CP 1; DLB 20; EWL 3;
PAB; PFS 3; RGEL 2

Smith, Wilbur (Addison) 1933- .... **CLC 33**
See also CA 13-16R; CANR 7, 46, 66, 134;
CPW; MTCW 1, 2; MTFW 2005

Smith, William Jay 1918- .... **CLC 6**
See also AMWS 13; CA 5-8R; CANR 44,
106; CP 1, 2, 3, 4, 5, 6, 7; CSW; CWRI
5; DLB 5; MAICYA 1, 2; SAAS 22;
SATA 2, 68, 154; SATA-Essay 154; TCLE
1:2

Smith, Woodrow Wilson
See Kuttner, Henry

Smith, Zadie 1976- .... **CLC 158**
See also AAYA 50; CA 193; MTFW 2005

Smolenskin, Peretz 1842-1885 .... **NCLC 30**

Smollett, Tobias (George) 1721-1771 ... **LC 2,
46**
See also BRW 3; CDBLB 1660-1789; DLB
39, 104; RGEL 2; TEA

Snodgrass, W(illiam) D(e Witt)
1926- .... **CLC 2, 6, 10, 18, 68**
See also AMWS 6; CA 1-4R; CANR 6, 36,
65, 85; CP 1, 2, 3, 4, 5, 6, 7; DAM POET;
DLB 5; MAL 5; MTCW 1, 2; MTFW
2005; RGAL 4; TCLE 1:2

Snorri Sturluson 1179-1241 .... **CMLC 56**
See also RGWL 2, 3

Snow, C(harles) P(ercy) 1905-1980 ... **CLC 1,
4, 6, 9, 13, 19**
See also BRW 7; CA 5-8R; 101; CANR 28;
CDBLB 1945-1960; CN 1, 2; DAM NOV;
DLB 15, 77; DLBD 17; EWL 3; MTCW
1, 2; MTFW 2005; RGEL 2; TEA

Snow, Frances Compton
See Adams, Henry (Brooks)

Snyder, Gary (Sherman) 1930- . **CLC 1, 2, 5,
9, 32, 120; PC 21**
See also AMWS 8; ANW; BG 1:3; CA 17-
20R; CANR 30, 60, 125; CP 1, 2, 3, 4, 5,
6, 7; DA3; DAM POET; DLB 5, 16, 165,
212, 237, 275; EWL 3; MAL 5; MTCW
2; MTFW 2005; PFS 9, 19; RGAL 4; WP

Snyder, Zilpha Keatley 1927- .... **CLC 17**
See also AAYA 15; BYA 1; CA 9-12R;
CANR 38; CLR 31; JRDA; MAICYA 1,
2; SAAS 2; SATA 1, 28, 75, 110, 163;
SATA-Essay 112, 163; YAW

Soares, Bernardo
See Pessoa, Fernando (Antonio Nogueira)

Sobh, A.
See Shamlu, Ahmad

Sobh, Alef
See Shamlu, Ahmad

Sobol, Joshua 1939- .... **CLC 60**
See Sobol, Yehoshua
See also CA 200

Sobol, Yehoshua 1939-
See Sobol, Joshua
See also CWW 2

Socrates 470B.C.-399B.C. .... **CMLC 27**

Soderberg, Hjalmar 1869-1941 .... **TCLC 39**
See also DLB 259; EWL 3; RGSF 2

Soderbergh, Steven 1963- .... **CLC 154**
See also AAYA 43

Sodergran, Edith (Irene) 1892-1923
See Soedergran, Edith (Irene)
See also CA 202; DLB 259; EW 11; EWL
3; RGWL 2, 3

Soedergran, Edith (Irene)
1892-1923 .... **TCLC 31**
See Sodergran, Edith (Irene)

Softly, Edgar
See Lovecraft, H(oward) P(hillips)

Softly, Edward
See Lovecraft, H(oward) P(hillips)

Sokolov, Alexander V(sevolodovich) 1943-
See Sokolov, Sasha
See also CA 73-76

Sokolov, Raymond 1941- .... **CLC 7**
See also CA 85-88

Sokolov, Sasha .... **CLC 59**
See Sokolov, Alexander V(sevolodovich)
See also CWW 2; DLB 285; EWL 3; RGWL
2, 3

Solo, Jay
See Ellison, Harlan (Jay)

Sologub, Fyodor .... **TCLC 9**
See Teternikov, Fyodor Kuzmich
See also EWL 3

Solomons, Ikey Esquir
See Thackeray, William Makepeace

Solomos, Dionysios 1798-1857 .... **NCLC 15**

Solwoska, Mara
See French, Marilyn

Solzhenitsyn, Aleksandr I(sayevich)
1918- .. **CLC 1, 2, 4, 7, 9, 10, 18, 26, 34,
78, 134; SSC 32; WLC**
See Solzhenitsyn, Aleksandr Isaevich
See also AAYA 49; AITN 1; BPFB 3; CA
69-72; CANR 40, 65, 116; DA; DA3;
DAB; DAC; DAM MST, NOV; DLB 302;
EW 13; EXPS; LAIT 4; MTCW 1, 2;
MTFW 2005; NFS 6; RGSF 2; RGWL 2,
3; SSFS 9; TWA

Solzhenitsyn, Aleksandr Isaevich
See Solzhenitsyn, Aleksandr I(sayevich)
See also CWW 2; EWL 3

Somers, Jane
See Lessing, Doris (May)

Somerville, Edith Oenone
1858-1949 .... **SSC 56; TCLC 51**
See also CA 196; DLB 135; RGEL 2; RGSF
2

Somerville & Ross
See Martin, Violet Florence; Somerville,
Edith Oenone

Sommer, Scott 1951- .... **CLC 25**
See also CA 106

Sommers, Christina Hoff 1950- ...... **CLC 197**
See also CA 153; CANR 95

Sondheim, Stephen (Joshua) 1930- . **CLC 30,
39, 147; DC 22**
See also AAYA 11, 66; CA 103; CANR 47,
67, 125; DAM DRAM; LAIT 4

Sone, Monica 1919- .... **AAL**
See also DLB 312

Song, Cathy 1955- .... **AAL; PC 21**
See also CA 154; CANR 118; CWP; DLB
169, 312; EXPP; FW; PFS 5

Sontag, Susan 1933-2004 ... **CLC 1, 2, 10, 13,
31, 105, 195**
See also AMWS 3; CA 17-20R; 234; CANR
25, 51, 74, 97; CN 1, 2, 3, 4, 5, 6, 7;
CPW; DA3; DAM POP; DLB 2, 67; EWL
3; MAL 5; MAWW; MTCW 1, 2; MTFW
2005; RGAL 4; RHW; SSFS 10

Sophocles 496(?)B.C.-406(?)B.C. .... **CMLC 2,
47, 51; DC 1; WLCS**
See also AW 1; CDWLB 1; DA; DA3;
DAB; DAC; DAM DRAM, MST; DFS 1,
4, 8; DLB 176; LAIT 1; LATS 1:1; LMFS
1; RGWL 2, 3; TWA

Sordello 1189-1269 .... **CMLC 15**

Sorel, Georges 1847-1922 .... **TCLC 91**
See also CA 118; 188

Sorel, Julia
See Drexler, Rosalyn

Sorokin, Vladimir .... **CLC 59**
See Sorokin, Vladimir Georgievich

Sorokin, Vladimir Georgievich
See Sorokin, Vladimir
See also DLB 285

Sorrentino, Gilbert 1929- .. **CLC 3, 7, 14, 22,
40**
See also CA 77-80; CANR 14, 33, 115; CN
3, 4, 5, 6, 7; CP 1, 2, 3, 4, 5, 6, 7; DLB 5,
173; DLBY 1980; INT CANR-14

Soseki
See Natsume, Soseki
See also MJW

Soto, Gary 1952- ... **CLC 32, 80; HLC 2; PC
28**
See also AAYA 10, 37; BYA 11; CA 119;
125; CANR 50, 74, 107; CLR 38; CP 4,
5, 6, 7; DAM MULT; DLB 82; EWL 3;
EXPP; HW 1, 2; INT CA-125; JRDA;
LLW; MAICYA 2; MAICYAS 1; MAL 5;
MTCW 2; MTFW 2005; PFS 7; RGAL 4;
SATA 80, 120; WYA; YAW

Soupault, Philippe 1897-1990 .... **CLC 68**
See also CA 116; 147; 131; EWL 3; GFL
1789 to the Present; LMFS 2

Souster, (Holmes) Raymond 1921- .... **CLC 5,
14**
See also CA 13-16R; CAAS 14; CANR 13,
29, 53; CP 1, 2, 3, 4, 5, 6, 7; DA3; DAC;
DAM POET; DLB 88; RGEL 2; SATA 63

Southern, Terry 1924(?)-1995 .... **CLC 7**
See also AMWS 11; BPFB 3; CA 1-4R;
150; CANR 1, 55, 107; CN 1, 2, 3, 4, 5,
6; DLB 2; IDFW 3, 4

Southerne, Thomas 1660-1746 .... **LC 99**
See also DLB 80; RGEL 2

Southey, Robert 1774-1843 .... **NCLC 8, 97**
See also BRW 4; DLB 93, 107, 142; RGEL
2; SATA 54

Southwell, Robert 1561(?)-1595 .... **LC 108**
See also DLB 167; RGEL 2; TEA

Southworth, Emma Dorothy Eliza Nevitte
1819-1899 .... **NCLC 26**
See also DLB 239

Souza, Ernest
See Scott, Evelyn

Soyinka, Wole 1934- .. **BLC 3; CLC 3, 5, 14,
36, 44, 179; DC 2; WLC**
See also AFW; BW 2, 3; CA 13-16R;
CANR 27, 39, 82, 136; CD 5, 6; CDWLB
3; CN 6, 7; CP 1, 2, 3, 4, 5, 6 ,7; DA;
DA3; DAB; DAC; DAM DRAM, MST,
MULT; DFS 10; DLB 125; EWL 3;
MTCW 1, 2; MTFW 2005; RGEL 2;
TWA; WLIT 2; WWE 1

Spackman, W(illiam) M(ode)
1905-1990 .... **CLC 46**
See also CA 81-84; 132

Stephen, Adeline Virginia
See Woolf, (Adeline) Virginia
Stephen, Sir Leslie 1832-1904 .... **TCLC 23**
See also BRW 5; CA 123; DLB 57, 144, 190
Stephen, Sir Leslie
See Stephen, Sir Leslie
Stephen, Virginia
See Woolf, (Adeline) Virginia
Stephens, James 1882(?)-1950 .... **SSC 50; TCLC 4**
See also CA 104; 192; DLB 19, 153, 162; EWL 3; FANT; RGEL 2; SUFW
Stephens, Reed
See Donaldson, Stephen R(eeder)
Stephenson, Neal 1959- .... **CLC 220**
See also AAYA 38; CA 122; CANR 88, 138; CN 7; MTCW 2005; SFW 4
Steptoe, Lydia
See Barnes, Djuna
See also GLL 1
Sterchi, Beat 1949- .... **CLC 65**
See also CA 203
Sterling, Brett
See Bradbury, Ray (Douglas); Hamilton, Edmond
Sterling, Bruce 1954- .... **CLC 72**
See also CA 119; CANR 44, 135; CN 7; MTFW 2005; SCFW 2; SFW 4
Sterling, George 1869-1926 .... **TCLC 20**
See also CA 117; 165; DLB 54
Stern, Gerald 1925- .... **CLC 40, 100**
See also AMWS 9; CA 81-84; CANR 28, 94; CP 3, 4, 5, 6, 7; DLB 105; RGAL 4
Stern, Richard (Gustave) 1928- ... **CLC 4, 39**
See also CA 1-4R; CANR 1, 25, 52, 120; CN 1, 2, 3, 4, 5, 6, 7; DLB 218; DLBY 1987; INT CANR-25
Sternberg, Josef von 1894-1969 .... **CLC 20**
See also CA 81-84
Sterne, Laurence 1713-1768 .... **LC 2, 48; WLC**
See also BRW 3; BRWC 1; CDBLB 1660-1789; DA; DAB; DAC; DAM MST, NOV; DLB 39; RGEL 2; TEA
Sternheim, (William Adolf) Carl
1878-1942 .... **TCLC 8**
See also CA 105; 193; DLB 56, 118; EWL 3; IDTP; RGWL 2, 3
Stevens, Margaret Dean
See Aldrich, Bess Streeter
Stevens, Mark 1951- .... **CLC 34**
See also CA 122
Stevens, Wallace 1879-1955 . **PC 6; TCLC 3, 12, 45; WLC**
See also AMW; AMWR 1; CA 104; 124; CDALB 1929-1941; DA; DA3; DAB; DAC; DAM MST, POET; DLB 54; EWL 3; EXPP; MAL 5; MTCW 1, 2; PAB; PFS 13, 16; RGAL 4; TUS; WP
Stevenson, Anne (Katharine) 1933- .. **CLC 7, 33**
See also BRWS 6; CA 17-20R; CAAS 9; CANR 9, 33, 123; CP 3, 4, 5, 6, 7; CWP; DLB 40; MTCW 1; RHW
Stevenson, Robert Louis (Balfour)
1850-1894 ...... **NCLC 5, 14, 63; SSC 11, 51; WLC**
See also AAYA 24; BPFB 3; BRW 5; BRWC 1; BRWR 1; BYA 1, 2, 4, 13; CD-BLB 1890-1914; CLR 10, 11; DA; DA3; DAB; DAC; DAM MST, NOV; DLB 18, 57, 141, 156, 174; DLBD 13; GL 3; HGG; JRDA; LAIT 1, 3; MAICYA 1, 2; NFS 11, 20; RGEL 2; RGSF 2; SATA 100; SUFW; TEA; WCH; WLIT 4; WYA; YABC 2; YAW

Stewart, J(ohn) I(nnes) M(ackintosh)
1906-1994 .... **CLC 7, 14, 32**
See Innes, Michael
See also CA 85-88; 147; CAAS 3; CANR 47; CMW 4; CN 1, 2, 3, 4, 5; MTCW 1, 2
Stewart, Mary (Florence Elinor)
1916- .... **CLC 7, 35, 117**
See also AAYA 29; BPFB 3; CA 1-4R; CANR 1, 59, 130; CMW 4; CPW; DAB; FANT; RHW; SATA 12; YAW
Stewart, Mary Rainbow
See Stewart, Mary (Florence Elinor)
Stifle, June
See Campbell, Maria
Stifter, Adalbert 1805-1868 .. **NCLC 41; SSC 28**
See also CDWLB 2; DLB 133; RGSF 2; RGWL 2, 3
Still, James 1906-2001 .... **CLC 49**
See also CA 65-68; 195; CAAS 17; CANR 10, 26; CSW; DLB 9; DLBY 01; SATA 29; SATA-Obit 127
Sting 1951-
See Sumner, Gordon Matthew
See also CA 167
Stirling, Arthur
See Sinclair, Upton (Beall)
Stitt, Milan 1941- .... **CLC 29**
See also CA 69-72
Stockton, Francis Richard 1834-1902
See Stockton, Frank R.
See also AAYA 68; CA 108; 137; MAICYA 1, 2; SATA 44; SFW 4
Stockton, Frank R. .... **TCLC 47**
See Stockton, Francis Richard
See also BYA 4, 13; DLB 42, 74; DLBD 13; EXPS; SATA-Brief 32; SSFS 3; SUFW; WCH
Stoddard, Charles
See Kuttner, Henry
Stoker, Abraham 1847-1912
See Stoker, Bram
See also CA 105; 150; DA; DA3; DAC; DAM MST, NOV; HGG; MTFW 2005; SATA 29
Stoker, Bram . **SSC 62; TCLC 8, 144; WLC**
See Stoker, Abraham
See also AAYA 23; BPFB 3; BRWS 3; BYA 5; CDBLB 1890-1914; DAB; DLB 304; GL 3; LATS 1:1; NFS 18; RGEL 2; SUFW; TEA; WLIT 4
Stolz, Mary (Slattery) 1920- .... **CLC 12**
See also AAYA 8; AITN 1; CA 5-8R; CANR 13, 41, 112; JRDA; MAICYA 1, 2; SAAS 3; SATA 10, 71, 133; YAW
Stone, Irving 1903-1989 .... **CLC 7**
See also AITN 1; BPFB 3; CA 1-4R; 129; CAAS 3; CANR 1, 23; CN 1, 2, 3, 4; CPW; DA3; DAM POP; INT CANR-23; MTCW 1, 2; MTFW 2005; RHW; SATA 3; SATA-Obit 64
Stone, Oliver (William) 1946- .... **CLC 73**
See also AAYA 15, 64; CA 110; CANR 55, 125
Stone, Robert (Anthony) 1937- ... **CLC 5, 23, 42, 175**
See also AMWS 5; BPFB 3; CA 85-88; CANR 23, 66, 95; CN 4, 5, 6, 7; DLB 152; EWL 3; INT CANR-23; MAL 5; MTCW 1; MTFW 2005
Stone, Ruth 1915- .... **PC 53**
See also CA 45-48; CANR 2, 91; CP 7; CSW; DLB 105; PFS 19
Stone, Zachary
See Follett, Ken(neth Martin)

Stoppard, Tom 1937- ... **CLC 1, 3, 4, 5, 8, 15, 29, 34, 63, 91; DC 6; WLC**
See also AAYA 63; BRWC 1; BRWR 2; BRWS 1; CA 81-84; CANR 39, 67, 125; CBD; CD 5, 6; CDBLB 1960 to Present; DA; DA3; DAB; DAC; DAM DRAM, MST; DFS 2, 5, 8, 11, 13, 16; DLB 13, 233; DLBY 1985; EWL 3; LATS 1:2; MTCW 1, 2; MTFW 2005; RGEL 2; TEA; WLIT 4
Storey, David (Malcolm) 1933- . **CLC 2, 4, 5, 8**
See also BRWS 1; CA 81-84; CANR 36; CBD; CD 5, 6; CN 1, 2, 3, 4, 5, 6; DAM DRAM; DLB 13, 14, 207, 245; EWL 3; MTCW 1; RGEL 2
Storm, Hyemeyohsts 1935- ... **CLC 3; NNAL**
See also CA 81-84; CANR 45; DAM MULT
Storm, (Hans) Theodor (Woldsen)
1817-1888 .... **NCLC 1; SSC 27**
See also CDWLB 2; DLB 129; EW; RGSF 2; RGWL 2, 3
Storni, Alfonsina 1892-1938 . **HLC 2; PC 33; TCLC 5**
See also CA 104; 131; DAM MULT; DLB 283; HW 1; LAW
Stoughton, William 1631-1701 .... **LC 38**
See also DLB 24
Stout, Rex (Todhunter) 1886-1975 ..... **CLC 3**
See also AITN 2; BPFB 3; CA 61-64; CANR 71; CMW 4; CN 2; DLB 306; MSW; RGAL 4
Stow, (Julian) Randolph 1935- ... **CLC 23, 48**
See also CA 13-16R; CANR 33; CN 1, 2, 3, 4, 5, 6, 7; CP 1, 2, 3, 4; DLB 260; MTCW 1; RGEL 2
Stowe, Harriet (Elizabeth) Beecher
1811-1896 .... **NCLC 3, 50, 133; WLC**
See also AAYA 53; AMWS 1; CDALB 1865-1917; DA; DA3; DAB; DAC; DAM MST, NOV; DLB 1, 12, 42, 74, 189, 239, 243; EXPN; FL 1:3; JRDA; LAIT 2; MAICYA 1, 2; NFS 6; RGAL 4; TUS; YABC 1
Strabo c. 64B.C.-c. 25 .... **CMLC 37**
See also DLB 176
Strachey, (Giles) Lytton
1880-1932 .... **TCLC 12**
See also BRWS 2; CA 110; 178; DLB 149; DLBD 10; EWL 3; MTCW 2; NCFS 4
Stramm, August 1874-1915 .... **PC 50**
See also CA 195; EWL 3
Strand, Mark 1934- .. **CLC 6, 18, 41, 71; PC 63**
See also AMWS 4; CA 21-24R; CANR 40, 65, 100; CP 1, 2, 3, 4, 5, 6, 7; DAM POET; DLB 5; EWL 3; MAL 5; PAB; PFS 9, 18; RGAL 4; SATA 41; TCLE 1:2
Stratton-Porter, Gene(va Grace) 1863-1924
See Porter, Gene(va Grace) Stratton
See also ANW; CA 137; CLR 87; DLB 221; DLBD 14; MAICYA 1, 2; SATA 15
Straub, Peter (Francis) 1943- ... **CLC 28, 107**
See also BEST 89:1; BPFB 3; CA 85-88; CANR 28, 65, 109; CPW; DAM POP; DLBY 1984; HGG; MTCW 1, 2; MTFW 2005; SUFW 2
Strauss, Botho 1944- .... **CLC 22**
See also CA 157; CWW 2; DLB 124
Strauss, Leo 1899-1973 .... **TCLC 141**
See also CA 101; 45-48; CANR 122
Streatfeild, (Mary) Noel
1897(?)-1986 .... **CLC 21**
See also CA 81-84; 120; CANR 31; CLR 17, 83; CWRI 5; DLB 160; MAICYA 1, 2; SATA 20; SATA-Obit 48
Stribling, T(homas) S(igismund)
1881-1965 .... **CLC 23**
See also CA 189; 107; CMW 4; DLB 9; RGAL 4

Synge, (Edmund) J(ohn) M(illington)
1871-1909 .... **DC 2; TCLC 6, 37**
See also BRW 6; BRWR 1; CA 104; 141;
CDBLB 1890-1914; DAM DRAM; DFS
18; DLB 10, 19; EWL 3; RGEL 2; TEA;
WLIT 4

Syruc, J.
See Milosz, Czeslaw

Szirtes, George 1948- .... **CLC 46; PC 51**
See also CA 109; CANR 27, 61, 117; CP 4,
5, 6, 7

Szymborska, Wislawa 1923- ... **CLC 99, 190;**
PC 44
See also CA 154; CANR 91, 133; CDWLB
4; CWP; CWW 2; DA3; DLB 232; DLBY
1996; EWL 3; MTCW 2; MTFW 2005;
PFS 15; RGWL 3

T. O., Nik
See Annensky, Innokenty (Fyodorovich)

Tabori, George 1914- .... **CLC 19**
See also CA 49-52; CANR 4, 69; CBD; CD
5, 6; DLB 245

Tacitus c. 55-c. 117 .... **CMLC 56**
See also AW 2; CDWLB 1; DLB 211;
RGWL 2, 3

Tagore, Rabindranath 1861-1941 .... **PC 8;**
SSC 48; TCLC 3, 53
See also CA 104; 120; DA3; DAM DRAM,
POET; EWL 3; MTCW 1, 2; MTFW
2005; PFS 18; RGEL 2; RGSF 2; RGWL
2, 3; TWA

Taine, Hippolyte Adolphe
1828-1893 .... **NCLC 15**
See also EW 7; GFL 1789 to the Present

Talayesva, Don C. 1890-(?) .... **NNAL**

Talese, Gay 1932- .... **CLC 37**
See also AITN 1; CA 1-4R; CANR 9, 58,
137; DLB 185; INT CANR-9; MTCW 1,
2; MTFW 2005

Tallent, Elizabeth (Ann) 1954- .... **CLC 45**
See also CA 117; CANR 72; DLB 130

Tallmountain, Mary 1918-1997 .... **NNAL**
See also CA 146; 161; DLB 193

Tally, Ted 1952- .... **CLC 42**
See also CA 120; 124; CAD; CANR 125;
CD 5, 6; INT CA-124

Talvik, Heiti 1904-1947 .... **TCLC 87**
See also EWL 3

Tamayo y Baus, Manuel
1829-1898 .... **NCLC 1**

Tammsaare, A(nton) H(ansen)
1878-1940 .... **TCLC 27**
See also CA 164; CDWLB 4; DLB 220;
EWL 3

Tam'si, Tchicaya U
See Tchicaya, Gerald Felix

Tan, Amy (Ruth) 1952- . **AAL; CLC 59, 120,**
151
See also AAYA 9, 48; AMWS 10; BEST
89:3; BPFB 3; CA 136; CANR 54, 105,
132; CDALBS; CN 6, 7; CPW 1; DA3;
DAM MULT, NOV, POP; DLB 173, 312;
EXPN; FL 1:6; FW; LAIT 3, 5; MAL 5;
MTCW 2; MTFW 2005; NFS 1, 13, 16;
RGAL 4; SATA 75; SSFS 9; YAW

Tandem, Felix
See Spitteler, Carl (Friedrich Georg)

Tanizaki, Jun'ichiro 1886-1965 ... **CLC 8, 14,**
28; SSC 21
See Tanizaki Jun'ichiro
See also CA 93-96; 25-28R; MJW; MTCW
2; MTFW 2005; RGSF 2; RGWL 2

Tanizaki Jun'ichiro
See Tanizaki, Jun'ichiro
See also DLB 180; EWL 3

Tannen, Deborah F(rances) 1945- .. **CLC 206**
See also CA 118; CANR 95

Tanner, William
See Amis, Kingsley (William)

Tao Lao
See Storni, Alfonsina

Tapahonso, Luci 1953- .... **NNAL; PC 65**
See also CA 145; CANR 72, 127; DLB 175

Tarantino, Quentin (Jerome)
1963- .... **CLC 125**
See also AAYA 58; CA 171; CANR 125

Tarassoff, Lev
See Troyat, Henri

Tarbell, Ida M(inerva) 1857-1944 . **TCLC 40**
See also CA 122; 181; DLB 47

Tarkington, (Newton) Booth
1869-1946 .... **TCLC 9**
See also BPFB 3; BYA 3; CA 110; 143;
CWRI 5; DLB 9, 102; MAL 5; MTCW 2;
RGAL 4; SATA 17

Tarkovskii, Andrei Arsen'evich
See Tarkovsky, Andrei (Arsenyevich)

Tarkovsky, Andrei (Arsenyevich)
1932-1986 .... **CLC 75**
See also CA 127

Tartt, Donna 1964(?)- .... **CLC 76**
See also AAYA 56; CA 142; CANR 135;
MTFW 2005

Tasso, Torquato 1544-1595 .... **LC 5, 94**
See also EFS 2; EW 2; RGWL 2, 3; WLIT
7

Tate, (John Orley) Allen 1899-1979 .. **CLC 2,**
4, 6, 9, 11, 14, 24; PC 50
See also AMW; CA 5-8R; 85-88; CANR
32, 108; CN 1, 2; CP 1, 2; DLB 4, 45, 63;
DLBD 17; EWL 3; MAL 5; MTCW 1, 2;
MTFW 2005; RGAL 4; RHW

Tate, Ellalice
See Hibbert, Eleanor Alice Burford

Tate, James (Vincent) 1943- ..... **CLC 2, 6, 25**
See also CA 21-24R; CANR 29, 57, 114;
CP 1, 2, 3, 4, 5, 6, 7; DLB 5, 169; EWL
3; PFS 10, 15; RGAL 4; WP

Tate, Nahum 1652(?)-1715 .... **LC 109**
See also DLB 80; RGEL 2

Tauler, Johannes c. 1300-1361 ...... **CMLC 37**
See also DLB 179; LMFS 1

Tavel, Ronald 1940- .... **CLC 6**
See also CA 21-24R; CAD; CANR 33; CD
5, 6

Taviani, Paolo 1931- .... **CLC 70**
See also CA 153

Taylor, Bayard 1825-1878 .... **NCLC 89**
See also DLB 3, 189, 250, 254; RGAL 4

Taylor, C(ecil) P(hilip) 1929-1981 .... **CLC 27**
See also CA 25-28R; 105; CANR 47; CBD

Taylor, Edward 1642(?)-1729 . **LC 11; PC 63**
See also AMW; DA; DAB; DAC; DAM
MST, POET; DLB 24; EXPP; RGAL 4;
TUS

Taylor, Eleanor Ross 1920- .... **CLC 5**
See also CA 81-84; CANR 70

Taylor, Elizabeth 1912-1975 ..... **CLC 2, 4, 29**
See also CA 13-16R; CANR 9, 70; CN 1,
2; DLB 139; MTCW 1; RGEL 2; SATA
13

Taylor, Frederick Winslow
1856-1915 .... **TCLC 76**
See also CA 188

Taylor, Henry (Splawn) 1942- .... **CLC 44**
See also CA 33-36R; CAAS 7; CANR 31;
CP 7; DLB 5; PFS 10

Taylor, Kamala (Purnaiya) 1924-2004
See Markandaya, Kamala
See also CA 77-80; 227; MTFW 2005; NFS
13

Taylor, Mildred D(elois) 1943- .... **CLC 21**
See also AAYA 10, 47; BW 1; BYA 3, 8;
CA 85-88; CANR 25, 115, 136; CLR 9,
59, 90; CSW; DLB 52; JRDA; LAIT 3;
MAICYA 1, 2; MTFW 2005; SAAS 5;
SATA 135; WYA; YAW

Taylor, Peter (Hillsman) 1917-1994 .. **CLC 1,**
4, 18, 37, 44, 50, 71; SSC 10, 84
See also AMWS 5; BPFB 3; CA 13-16R;
147; CANR 9, 50; CN 1, 2, 3, 4, 5; CSW;
DLB 218, 278; DLBY 1981, 1994; EWL
3; EXPS; INT CANR-9; MAL 5; MTCW
1, 2; MTFW 2005; RGSF 2; SSFS 9; TUS

Taylor, Robert Lewis 1912-1998 .... **CLC 14**
See also CA 1-4R; 170; CANR 3, 64; CN
1, 2; SATA 10; TCWW 1, 2

Tchekhov, Anton
See Chekhov, Anton (Pavlovich)

Tchicaya, Gerald Felix 1931-1988 .. **CLC 101**
See Tchicaya U Tam'si
See also CA 129; 125; CANR 81

Tchicaya U Tam'si
See Tchicaya, Gerald Felix
See also EWL 3

Teasdale, Sara 1884-1933 .... **PC 31; TCLC 4**
See also CA 104; 163; DLB 45; GLL 1;
PFS 14; RGAL 4; SATA 32; TUS

Tecumseh 1768-1813 .... **NNAL**
See also DAM MULT

Tegner, Esaias 1782-1846 .... **NCLC 2**

Teilhard de Chardin, (Marie Joseph) Pierre
1881-1955 .... **TCLC 9**
See also CA 105; 210; GFL 1789 to the
Present

Temple, Ann
See Mortimer, Penelope (Ruth)

Tennant, Emma (Christina) 1937- .. **CLC 13,**
52
See also BRWS 9; CA 65-68; CAAS 9;
CANR 10, 38, 59, 88; CN 3, 4, 5, 6, 7;
DLB 14; EWL 3; SFW 4

Tenneshaw, S. M.
See Silverberg, Robert

Tenney, Tabitha Gilman
1762-1837 .... **NCLC 122**
See also DLB 37, 200

Tennyson, Alfred 1809-1892 ... **NCLC 30, 65,**
115; PC 6; WLC
See also AAYA 50; BRW 4; CDBLB 1832-
1890; DA; DA3; DAB; DAC; DAM MST,
POET; DLB 32; EXPP; PAB; PFS 1, 2, 4,
11, 15, 19; RGEL 2; TEA; WLIT 4; WP

Teran, Lisa St. Aubin de .... **CLC 36**
See St. Aubin de Teran, Lisa

Terence c. 184B.C.-c. 159B.C. ...... **CMLC 14;**
DC 7
See also AW 1; CDWLB 1; DLB 211;
RGWL 2, 3; TWA

Teresa de Jesus, St. 1515-1582 .... **LC 18**

Teresa of Avila, St.
See Teresa de Jesus, St.

Terkel, Louis 1912-
See Terkel, Studs
See also CA 57-60; CANR 18, 45, 67, 132;
DA3; MTCW 1, 2; MTFW 2005

Terkel, Studs .... **CLC 38**
See Terkel, Louis
See also AAYA 32; AITN 1; MTCW 2; TUS

Terry, C. V.
See Slaughter, Frank G(ill)

Terry, Megan 1932- .... **CLC 19; DC 13**
See also CA 77-80; CABS 3; CAD; CANR
43; CD 5, 6; CWD; DFS 18; DLB 7, 249;
GLL 2

Tertullian c. 155-c. 245 .... **CMLC 29**

Tertz, Abram
See Sinyavsky, Andrei (Donatevich)
See also RGSF 2

Tesich, Steve 1943(?)-1996 .... **CLC 40, 69**
See also CA 105; 152; CAD; DLBY 1983

Tesla, Nikola 1856-1943 .... **TCLC 88**

Teternikov, Fyodor Kuzmich 1863-1927
See Sologub, Fyodor
See also CA 104

Tolkien, J(ohn) R(onald) R(euel)
1892-1973 .... **CLC 1, 2, 3, 8, 12, 38;
TCLC 137; WLC**
See also AAYA 10; AITN 1; BPFB 3;
BRWC 2; BRWS 2; CA 17-18; 45-48;
CANR 36, 134; CAP 2; CDBLB 1914-
1945; CLR 56; CN 1; CPW 1; CWRI 5;
DA; DA3; DAB; DAC; DAM MST, NOV,
POP; DLB 15, 160, 255; EFS 2; EWL 3;
FANT; JRDA; LAIT 1; LATS 1:2; LMFS
2; MAICYA 1, 2; MTCW 1, 2; MTFW
2005; NFS 8; RGEL 2; SATA 2, 32, 100;
SATA-Obit 24; SFW 4; SUFW; TEA;
WCH; WYA; YAW
Toller, Ernst 1893-1939 .... **TCLC 10**
See also CA 107; 186; DLB 124; EWL 3;
RGWL 2, 3
Tolson, M. B.
See Tolson, Melvin B(eaunorus)
Tolson, Melvin B(eaunorus)
1898(?)-1966 .... **BLC 3; CLC 36, 105**
See also AFAW 1, 2; BW 1, 3; CA 124; 89-
92; CANR 80; DAM MULT, POET; DLB
48, 76; MAL 5; RGAL 4
Tolstoi, Aleksei Nikolaevich
See Tolstoy, Alexey Nikolaevich
Tolstoi, Lev
See Tolstoy, Leo (Nikolaevich)
See also RGSF 2; RGWL 2, 3
Tolstoy, Aleksei Nikolaevich
See Tolstoy, Alexey Nikolaevich
See also DLB 272
Tolstoy, Alexey Nikolaevich
1882-1945 .... **TCLC 18**
See Tolstoy, Aleksei Nikolaevich
See also CA 107; 158; EWL 3; SFW 4
Tolstoy, Leo (Nikolaevich)
1828-1910 . **SSC 9, 30, 45, 54; TCLC 4,
11, 17, 28, 44, 79, 173; WLC**
See Tolstoy, Lev
See also AAYA 56; CA 104; 123; DA; DA3;
DAB; DAC; DAM MST, NOV; DLB 238;
EFS 2; EW 7; EXPS; IDTP; LAIT 2;
LATS 1:1; LMFS 1; NFS 10; SATA 26;
SSFS 5; TWA
Tolstoy, Count Leo
See Tolstoy, Leo (Nikolaevich)
Tomalin, Claire 1933- .... **CLC 166**
See also CA 89-92; CANR 52, 88; DLB
155
Tomasi di Lampedusa, Giuseppe 1896-1957
See Lampedusa, Giuseppe (Tomasi) di
See also CA 111; DLB 177; EWL 3; WLIT
7
Tomlin, Lily .... **CLC 17**
See Tomlin, Mary Jean
Tomlin, Mary Jean 1939(?)-
See Tomlin, Lily
See also CA 117
Tomline, F. Latour
See Gilbert, W(illiam) S(chwenck)
Tomlinson, (Alfred) Charles 1927- .... **CLC 2,
4, 6, 13, 45; PC 17**
See also CA 5-8R; CANR 33; CP 1, 2, 3, 4,
5, 6, 7; DAM POET; DLB 40; TCLE 1:2
Tomlinson, H(enry) M(ajor)
1873-1958 .... **TCLC 71**
See also CA 118; 161; DLB 36, 100, 195
Tonna, Charlotte Elizabeth
1790-1846 .... **NCLC 135**
See also DLB 163
Tonson, Jacob fl. 1655(?)-1736 .... **LC 86**
See also DLB 170
Toole, John Kennedy 1937-1969 ..... **CLC 19,
64**
See also BPFB 3; CA 104; DLBY 1981;
MTCW 2; MTFW 2005
Toomer, Eugene
See Toomer, Jean

Toomer, Eugene Pinchback
See Toomer, Jean
Toomer, Jean 1894-1967 .. **BLC 3; CLC 1, 4,
13, 22; HR 1:3; PC 7; SSC 1, 45;
TCLC 172; WLCS**
See also AFAW 1, 2; AMWS 3, 9; BW 1;
CA 85-88; CDALB 1917-1929; DA3;
DAM MULT; DLB 45, 51; EWL 3; EXPP;
EXPS; LMFS 2; MAL 5; MTCW 1, 2;
MTFW 2005; NFS 11; RGAL 4; RGSF 2;
SSFS 5
Toomer, Nathan Jean
See Toomer, Jean
Toomer, Nathan Pinchback
See Toomer, Jean
Torley, Luke
See Blish, James (Benjamin)
Tornimparte, Alessandra
See Ginzburg, Natalia
Torre, Raoul della
See Mencken, H(enry) L(ouis)
Torrence, Ridgely 1874-1950 .... **TCLC 97**
See also DLB 54, 249; MAL 5
Torrey, E(dwin) Fuller 1937- .... **CLC 34**
See also CA 119; CANR 71
Torsvan, Ben Traven
See Traven, B.
Torsvan, Benno Traven
See Traven, B.
Torsvan, Berick Traven
See Traven, B.
Torsvan, Berwick Traven
See Traven, B.
Torsvan, Bruno Traven
See Traven, B.
Torsvan, Traven
See Traven, B.
Tourneur, Cyril 1575(?)-1626 .... **LC 66**
See also BRW 2; DAM DRAM; DLB 58;
RGEL 2
Tournier, Michel (Edouard) 1924- .... **CLC 6,
23, 36, 95; SSC 88**
See also CA 49-52; CANR 3, 36, 74; CWW
2; DLB 83; EWL 3; GFL 1789 to the
Present; MTCW 1, 2; SATA 23
Tournimparte, Alessandra
See Ginzburg, Natalia
Towers, Ivar
See Kornbluth, C(yril) M.
Towne, Robert (Burton) 1936(?)- ..... **CLC 87**
See also CA 108; DLB 44; IDFW 3, 4
Townsend, Sue .... **CLC 61**
See Townsend, Susan Lilian
See also AAYA 28; CA 119; 127; CANR
65, 107; CBD; CD 5, 6; CPW; CWD;
DAB; DAC; DAM MST; DLB 271; INT
CA-127; SATA 55, 93; SATA-Brief 48;
YAW
Townsend, Susan Lilian 1946-
See Townsend, Sue
Townshend, Pete
See Townshend, Peter (Dennis Blandford)
Townshend, Peter (Dennis Blandford)
1945- .... **CLC 17, 42**
See also CA 107
Tozzi, Federigo 1883-1920 .... **TCLC 31**
See also CA 160; CANR 110; DLB 264;
EWL 3; WLIT 7
Tracy, Don(ald Fiske) 1905-1970(?)
See Queen, Ellery
See also CA 1-4R; 176; CANR 2
Trafford, F. G.
See Riddell, Charlotte
Traherne, Thomas 1637(?)-1674 .. **LC 99; PC
70**
See also BRW 2; BRWS 11; DLB 131;
PAB; RGEL 2
Traill, Catharine Parr 1802-1899 .. **NCLC 31**
See also DLB 99

Trakl, Georg 1887-1914 .... **PC 20; TCLC 5**
See also CA 104; 165; EW 10; EWL 3;
LMFS 2; MTCW 2; RGWL 2, 3
Trambley, Estela Portillo .... **TCLC 163**
See Portillo Trambley, Estela
See also CA 77-80; RGAL 4
Tranquilli, Secondino
See Silone, Ignazio
Transtroemer, Tomas Gosta
See Transtromer, Tomas (Goesta)
Transtromer, Tomas (Gosta)
See Transtromer, Tomas (Goesta)
See also CWW 2
Transtromer, Tomas (Goesta)
1931- .... **CLC 52, 65**
See Transtromer, Tomas (Gosta)
See also CA 117; 129; CAAS 17; CANR
115; DAM POET; DLB 257; EWL 3; PFS
21
Transtromer, Tomas Gosta
See Transtromer, Tomas (Goesta)
Traven, B. 1882(?)-1969 .... **CLC 8, 11**
See also CA 19-20; 25-28R; CAP 2; DLB
9, 56; EWL 3; MTCW 1; RGAL 4
Trediakovsky, Vasilii Kirillovich
1703-1769 .... **LC 68**
See also DLB 150
Treitel, Jonathan 1959- .... **CLC 70**
See also CA 210; DLB 267
Trelawny, Edward John
1792-1881 .... **NCLC 85**
See also DLB 110, 116, 144
Tremain, Rose 1943- .... **CLC 42**
See also CA 97-100; CANR 44, 95; CN 4,
5, 6, 7; DLB 14, 271; RGSF 2; RHW
Tremblay, Michel 1942- .... **CLC 29, 102**
See also CA 116; 128; CCA 1; CWW 2;
DAC; DAM MST; DLB 60; EWL 3; GLL
1; MTCW 1, 2; MTFW 2005
Trevanian .... **CLC 29**
See Whitaker, Rod(ney)
Trevor, Glen
See Hilton, James
Trevor, William .. **CLC 7, 9, 14, 25, 71, 116;
SSC 21, 58**
See Cox, William Trevor
See also BRWS 4; CBD; CD 5, 6; CN 1, 2,
3, 4, 5, 6, 7; DLB 14, 139; EWL 3; LATS
1:2; RGEL 2; RGSF 2; SSFS 10; TCLE
1:2
Trifonov, Iurii (Valentinovich)
See Trifonov, Yuri (Valentinovich)
See also DLB 302; RGWL 2, 3
Trifonov, Yuri (Valentinovich)
1925-1981 .... **CLC 45**
See Trifonov, Iurii (Valentinovich); Tri-
fonov, Yury Valentinovich
See also CA 126; 103; MTCW 1
Trifonov, Yury Valentinovich
See Trifonov, Yuri (Valentinovich)
See also EWL 3
Trilling, Diana (Rubin) 1905-1996 . **CLC 129**
See also CA 5-8R; 154; CANR 10, 46; INT
CANR-10; MTCW 1, 2
Trilling, Lionel 1905-1975 ..... **CLC 9, 11, 24;
SSC 75**
See also AMWS 3; CA 9-12R; 61-64;
CANR 10, 105; CN 1, 2; DLB 28, 63;
EWL 3; INT CANR-10; MAL 5; MTCW
1, 2; RGAL 4; TUS
Trimball, W. H.
See Mencken, H(enry) L(ouis)
Tristan
See Gomez de la Serna, Ramon
Tristram
See Housman, A(lfred) E(dward)

Usk, Thomas (?)-1388 .... **CMLC 76**
See also DLB 146

Ustinov, Peter (Alexander)
1921-2004 .... **CLC 1**
See also AITN 1; CA 13-16R; 225; CANR
25, 51; CBD; CD 5, 6; DLB 13; MTCW
2

U Tam'si, Gerald Felix Tchicaya
See Tchicaya, Gerald Felix

U Tam'si, Tchicaya
See Tchicaya, Gerald Felix

Vachss, Andrew (Henry) 1942- .... **CLC 106**
See also CA 118, 214; CAAE 214; CANR
44, 95; CMW 4.

Vachss, Andrew H.
See Vachss, Andrew (Henry)

Vaculik, Ludvik 1926- .... **CLC 7**
See also CA 53-56; CANR 72; CWW 2;
DLB 232; EWL 3

Vaihinger, Hans 1852-1933 .... **TCLC 71**
See also CA 116; 166

Valdez, Luis (Miguel) 1940- ..... **CLC 84; DC
10; HLC 2**
See also CA 101; CAD; CANR 32, 81; CD
5, 6; DAM MULT; DFS 5; DLB 122;
EWL 3; HW 1; LAIT 4; LLW

Valenzuela, Luisa 1938- .... **CLC 31, 104;
HLCS 2; SSC 14, 82**
See also CA 101; CANR 32, 65, 123; CD-
WLB 3; CWW 2; DAM MULT; DLB 113;
EWL 3; FW; HW 1, 2; LAW; RGSF 2;
RGWL 3

Valera y Alcala-Galiano, Juan
1824-1905 .... **TCLC 10**
See also CA 106

Valerius Maximus fl. 20- .... **CMLC 64**
See also DLB 211

Valery, (Ambroise) Paul (Toussaint Jules)
1871-1945 .... **PC 9; TCLC 4, 15**
See also CA 104; 122; DA3; DAM POET;
DLB 258; EW 8; EWL 3; GFL 1789 to
the Present; MTCW 1, 2; MTFW 2005;
RGWL 2, 3; TWA

Valle-Inclan, Ramon (Maria) del
1866-1936 .... **HLC 2; TCLC 5**
See del Valle-Inclan, Ramon (Maria)
See also CA 106; 153; CANR 80; DAM
MULT; DLB 134; EW 8; EWL 3; HW 2;
RGSF 2; RGWL 2, 3

Vallejo, Antonio Buero
See Buero Vallejo, Antonio

Vallejo, Cesar (Abraham)
1892-1938 .... **HLC 2; TCLC 3, 56**
See also CA 105; 153; DAM MULT; DLB
290; EWL 3; HW 1; LAW; RGWL 2, 3

Valles, Jules 1832-1885 .... **NCLC 71**
See also DLB 123; GFL 1789 to the Present

Vallette, Marguerite Eymery
1860-1953 .... **TCLC 67**
See Rachilde
See also CA 182; DLB 123, 192

Valle Y Pena, Ramon del
See Valle-Inclan, Ramon (Maria) del

Van Ash, Cay 1918-1994 .... **CLC 34**
See also CA 220

Vanbrugh, Sir John 1664-1726 .... **LC 21**
See also BRW 2; DAM DRAM; DLB 80;
IDTP; RGEL 2

Van Campen, Karl
See Campbell, John W(ood, Jr.)

Vance, Gerald
See Silverberg, Robert

Vance, Jack .... **CLC 35**
See Vance, John Holbrook
See also DLB 8; FANT; SCFW 1, 2; SFW
4; SUFW 1, 2

Vance, John Holbrook 1916-
See Queen, Ellery; Vance, Jack
See also CA 29-32R; CANR 17, 65; CMW
4; MTCW 1

**Van Den Bogarde, Derek Jules Gaspard
Ulric Niven** 1921-1999 .... **CLC 14**
See Bogarde, Dirk
See also CA 77-80; 179

Vandenburgh, Jane .... **CLC 59**
See also CA 168

Vanderhaeghe, Guy 1951- .... **CLC 41**
See also BPFB 3; CA 113; CANR 72, 145;
CN 7

van der Post, Laurens (Jan)
1906-1996 .... **CLC 5**
See also AFW; CA 5-8R; 155; CANR 35;
CN 1, 2, 3, 4, 5, 6; DLB 204; RGEL 2

van de Wetering, Janwillem 1931- ... **CLC 47**
See also CA 49-52; CANR 4, 62, 90; CMW
4

Van Dine, S. S. .... **TCLC 23**
See Wright, Willard Huntington
See also DLB 306; MSW

Van Doren, Carl (Clinton)
1885-1950 .... **TCLC 18**
See also CA 111; 168

Van Doren, Mark 1894-1972 .... **CLC 6, 10**
See also CA 1-4R; 37-40R; CANR 3; CN
1; CP 1; DLB 45, 284; MAL 5; MTCW
1, 2; RGAL 4

Van Druten, John (William)
1901-1957 .... **TCLC 2**
See also CA 104; 161; DLB 10; MAL 5;
RGAL 4

Van Duyn, Mona (Jane) 1921-2004 .. **CLC 3,
7, 63, 116**
See also CA 9-12R; 234; CANR 7, 38, 60,
116; CP 1, 2, 3, 4, 5, 6, 7; CWP; DAM
POET; DLB 5; MAL 5; MTFW 2005;
PFS 20

Van Dyne, Edith
See Baum, L(yman) Frank

van Itallie, Jean-Claude 1936- .... **CLC 3**
See also CA 45-48; CAAS 2; CAD; CANR
1, 48; CD 5, 6; DLB 7

Van Loot, Cornelius Obenchain
See Roberts, Kenneth (Lewis)

van Ostaijen, Paul 1896-1928 .... **TCLC 33**
See also CA 163

Van Peebles, Melvin 1932- .... **CLC 2, 20**
See also BW 2, 3; CA 85-88; CANR 27,
67, 82; DAM MULT

van Schendel, Arthur(-Francois-Emile)
1874-1946 .... **TCLC 56**
See also EWL 3

Vansittart, Peter 1920- .... **CLC 42**
See also CA 1-4R; CANR 3, 49, 90; CN 4,
5, 6, 7; RHW

Van Vechten, Carl 1880-1964 ... **CLC 33; HR
1:3**
See also AMWS 2; CA 183; 89-92; DLB 4,
9, 51; RGAL 4

van Vogt, A(lfred) E(lton) 1912-2000 . **CLC 1**
See also BPFB 3; BYA 13, 14; CA 21-24R;
190; CANR 28; DLB 8, 251; SATA 14;
SATA-Obit 124; SCFW 1, 2; SFW 4

Vara, Madeleine
See Jackson, Laura (Riding)

Varda, Agnes 1928- .... **CLC 16**
See also CA 116; 122

Vargas Llosa, (Jorge) Mario (Pedro)
1936- .... **CLC 3, 6, 9, 10, 15, 31, 42, 85,
181; HLC 2**
See Llosa, (Jorge) Mario (Pedro) Vargas
See also BPFB 3; CA 73-76; CANR 18, 32,
42, 67, 116, 140; CDWLB 3; CWW 2;
DA; DA3; DAB; DAC; DAM MST,
MULT, NOV; DLB 145; DNFS 2; EWL

3; HW 1, 2; LAIT 5; LATS 1:2; LAW;
LAWS 1; MTCW 1, 2; MTFW 2005;
RGWL 2; SSFS 14; TWA; WLIT 1

Varnhagen von Ense, Rahel
1771-1833 .... **NCLC 130**
See also DLB 90

Vasari, Giorgio 1511-1574 .... **LC 114**

Vasiliu, George
See Bacovia, George

Vasiliu, Gheorghe
See Bacovia, George
See also CA 123; 189

Vassa, Gustavus
See Equiano, Olaudah

Vassilikos, Vassilis 1933- .... **CLC 4, 8**
See also CA 81-84; CANR 75; EWL 3

Vaughan, Henry 1621-1695 .... **LC 27**
See also BRW 2; DLB 131; PAB; RGEL 2

Vaughn, Stephanie .... **CLC 62**

Vazov, Ivan (Minchov) 1850-1921 . **TCLC 25**
See also CA 121; 167; CDWLB 4; DLB
147

Veblen, Thorstein B(unde)
1857-1929 .... **TCLC 31**
See also AMWS 1; CA 115; 165; DLB 246;
MAL 5

Vega, Lope de 1562-1635 ... **HLCS 2; LC 23,
119**
See also EW 2; RGWL 2, 3

Vendler, Helen (Hennessy) 1933- ... **CLC 138**
See also CA 41-44R; CANR 25, 72, 136;
MTCW 1, 2; MTFW 2005

Venison, Alfred
See Pound, Ezra (Weston Loomis)

Ventsel, Elena Sergeevna 1907-2002
See Grekova, I.
See also CA 154

Verdi, Marie de
See Mencken, H(enry) L(ouis)

Verdu, Matilde
See Cela, Camilo Jose

Verga, Giovanni (Carmelo)
1840-1922 .... **SSC 21, 87; TCLC 3**
See also CA 104; 123; CANR 101; EW 7;
EWL 3; RGSF 2; RGWL 2, 3; WLIT 7

Vergil 70B.C.-19B.C. ... **CMLC 9, 40; PC 12;
WLCS**
See Virgil
See also AW 2; DA; DA3; DAB; DAC;
DAM MST, POET; EFS 1; LMFS 1

Vergil, Polydore c. 1470-1555 .... **LC 108**
See also DLB 132

Verhaeren, Emile (Adolphe Gustave)
1855-1916 .... **TCLC 12**
See also CA 109; EWL 3; GFL 1789 to the
Present

Verlaine, Paul (Marie) 1844-1896 .. **NCLC 2,
51; PC 2, 32**
See also DAM POET; DLB 217; EW 7;
GFL 1789 to the Present; LMFS 2; RGWL
2, 3; TWA

Verne, Jules (Gabriel) 1828-1905 ... **TCLC 6,
52**
See also AAYA 16; BYA 4; CA 110; 131;
CLR 88; DA3; DLB 123; GFL 1789 to
the Present; JRDA; LAIT 2; LMFS 2;
MAICYA 1, 2; MTFW 2005; RGWL 2, 3;
SATA 21; SCFW 1, 2; SFW 4; TWA;
WCH

Verus, Marcus Annius
See Aurelius, Marcus

Very, Jones 1813-1880 .... **NCLC 9**
See also DLB 1, 243; RGAL 4

Vesaas, Tarjei 1897-1970 .... **CLC 48**
See also CA 190; 29-32R; DLB 297; EW
11; EWL 3; RGWL 3

Vialis, Gaston
See Simenon, Georges (Jacques Christian)

Vian, Boris 1920-1959(?) .... **TCLC 9**
  See also CA 106; 164; CANR 111; DLB
    72, 321; GFL 1789 to the Present;
    MTCW 2; RGWL 2, 3
Viaud, (Louis Marie) Julien 1850-1923
  See Loti, Pierre
  See also CA 107
Vicar, Henry
  See Felsen, Henry Gregor
Vicente, Gil 1465-c. 1536 .... **LC 99**
  See also DLB 318; IDTP; RGWL 2, 3
Vicker, Angus
  See Felsen, Henry Gregor
Vidal, (Eugene Luther) Gore 1925- .. **CLC 2,
  4, 6, 8, 10, 22, 33, 72, 142**
  See Box, Edgar
  See also AAYA 64; AITN 1; AMWS 4;
    BEST 90:2; BPFB 3; CA 5-8R; CAD;
    CANR 13, 45, 65, 100, 132; CD 5, 6;
    CDALBS; CN 1, 2, 3, 4, 5, 6, 7; CPW;
    DA3; DAM NOV, POP; DFS 2; DLB 6,
    152; EWL 3; INT CANR-13; MAL 5;
    MTCW 1, 2; MTFW 2005; RGAL 4;
    RHW; TUS
Viereck, Peter (Robert Edwin)
  1916- .... **CLC 4; PC 27**
  See also CA 1-4R; CANR 1, 47; CP 1, 2, 3,
    4, 5, 6, 7; DLB 5; MAL 5; PFS 9, 14
Vigny, Alfred (Victor) de
  1797-1863 .... **NCLC 7, 102; PC 26**
  See also DAM POET; DLB 119, 192, 217;
    EW 5; GFL 1789 to the Present; RGWL
    2, 3
Vilakazi, Benedict Wallet
  1906-1947 .... **TCLC 37**
  See also CA 168
Villa, Jose Garcia 1908-1997 ... **AAL; PC 22,
  TCLC 176**
  See also CA 25-28R; CANR 12, 118; CP 1,
    2, 3, 4; DLB 312; EWL 3; EXPP
Villard, Oswald Garrison
  1872-1949 .... **TCLC 160**
  See also CA 113; 162; DLB 25, 91
Villarreal, Jose Antonio 1924- .... **HLC 2**
  See also CA 133; CANR 93; DAM MULT;
    DLB 82; HW 1; LAIT 4; RGAL 4
Villaurrutia, Xavier 1903-1950 ...... **TCLC 80**
  See also CA 192; EWL 3; HW 1; LAW
Villaverde, Cirilo 1812-1894 .... **NCLC 121**
  See also LAW
Villehardouin, Geoffroi de
  1150(?)-1218(?) .... **CMLC 38**
Villiers, George 1628-1687 .... **LC 107**
  See also DLB 80; RGEL 2
**Villiers de l'Isle Adam, Jean Marie Mathias
  Philippe Auguste** 1838-1889 ... **NCLC 3;
  SSC 14**
  See also DLB 123, 192; GFL 1789 to the
    Present; RGSF 2
Villon, Francois 1431-1463(?) . **LC 62; PC 13**
  See also DLB 208; EW 2; RGWL 2, 3;
    TWA
Vine, Barbara .... **CLC 50**
  See Rendell, Ruth (Barbara)
  See also BEST 90:4
Vinge, Joan (Carol) D(ennison)
  1948- .... **CLC 30; SSC 24**
  See also AAYA 32; BPFB 3; CA 93-96;
    CANR 72; SATA 36, 113; SFW 4; YAW
Viola, Herman J(oseph) 1938- .... **CLC 70**
  See also CA 61-64; CANR 8, 23, 48, 91;
    SATA 126
Violis, G.
  See Simenon, Georges (Jacques Christian)
Viramontes, Helena Maria 1954- .... **HLCS 2**
  See also CA 159; DLB 122; HW 2; LLW

Virgil
  See Vergil
  See also CDWLB 1; DLB 211; LAIT 1;
    RGWL 2, 3; WP
Visconti, Luchino 1906-1976 .... **CLC 16**
  See also CA 81-84; 65-68; CANR 39
Vitry, Jacques de
  See Jacques de Vitry
Vittorini, Elio 1908-1966 .... **CLC 6, 9, 14**
  See also CA 133; 25-28R; DLB 264; EW
    12; EWL 3; RGWL 2, 3
Vivekananda, Swami 1863-1902 .... **TCLC 88**
Vizenor, Gerald Robert 1934- .... **CLC 103;
  NNAL**
  See also CA 13-16R, 205; CAAE 205;
    CAAS 22; CANR 5, 21, 44, 67; DAM
    MULT; DLB 175, 227; MTCW 2; MTFW
    2005; TCWW 2
Vizinczey, Stephen 1933- .... **CLC 40**
  See also CA 128; CCA 1; INT CA-128
Vliet, R(ussell) G(ordon)
  1929-1984 .... **CLC 22**
  See also CA 37-40R; 112; CANR 18; CP 2,
    3
Vogau, Boris Andreyevich 1894-1938
  See Pilnyak, Boris
  See also CA 123; 218
Vogel, Paula A(nne) 1951- ... **CLC 76; DC 19**
  See also CA 108; CAD; CANR 119, 140;
    CD 5, 6; CWD; DFS 14; MTFW 2005;
    RGAL 4
Voigt, Cynthia 1942- .... **CLC 30**
  See also AAYA 3, 30; BYA 1, 3, 6, 7, 8;
    CA 106; CANR 18, 37, 40, 94, 145; CLR
    13, 48; INT CANR-18; JRDA; LAIT 5;
    MAICYA 1, 2; MAICYAS 1; MTFW
    2005; SATA 48, 79, 116, 160; SATA-Brief
    33; WYA; YAW
Voigt, Ellen Bryant 1943- .... **CLC 54**
  See also CA 69-72; CANR 11, 29, 55, 115;
    CP 7; CSW; CWP; DLB 120; PFS 23
Voinovich, Vladimir (Nikolaevich)
  1932- .... **CLC 10, 49, 147**
  See also CA 81-84; CAAS 12; CANR 33,
    67; CWW 2; DLB 302; MTCW 1
Vollmann, William T. 1959- .... **CLC 89**
  See also CA 134; CANR 67, 116; CN 7;
    CPW; DA3; DAM NOV, POP; MTCW 2;
    MTFW 2005
Voloshinov, V. N.
  See Bakhtin, Mikhail Mikhailovich
Voltaire 1694-1778 . **LC 14, 79, 110; SSC 12;
  WLC**
  See also BYA 13; DA; DA3; DAB; DAC;
    DAM DRAM, MST; DLB 314; EW 4;
    GFL Beginnings to 1789; LATS 1:1;
    LMFS 1; NFS 7; RGWL 2, 3; TWA
von Aschendrof, Baron Ignatz
  See Ford, Ford Madox
von Chamisso, Adelbert
  See Chamisso, Adelbert von
von Daeniken, Erich 1935- .... **CLC 30**
  See also AITN 1; CA 37-40R; CANR 17,
    44
von Daniken, Erich
  See von Daeniken, Erich
von Hartmann, Eduard
  1842-1906 .... **TCLC 96**
von Hayek, Friedrich August
  See Hayek, F(riedrich) A(ugust von)
von Heidenstam, (Carl Gustaf) Verner
  See Heidenstam, (Carl Gustaf) Verner von
von Heyse, Paul (Johann Ludwig)
  See Heyse, Paul (Johann Ludwig von)
von Hofmannsthal, Hugo
  See Hofmannsthal, Hugo von
von Horvath, Odon
  See von Horvath, Odon

von Horvath, Odon
  See von Horvath, Odon
von Horvath, Odon 1901-1938 .... **TCLC 45**
  See von Horvath, Oedoen
  See also CA 118; 194; DLB 85, 124; RGWL
    2, 3
von Horvath, Oedoen
  See von Horvath, Odon
  See also CA 184
von Kleist, Heinrich
  See Kleist, Heinrich von
**von Liliencron, (Friedrich Adolf Axel)
  Detlev**
  See Liliencron, (Friedrich Adolf Axel) De-
    tlev von
Vonnegut, Kurt, Jr. 1922- . **CLC 1, 2, 3, 4, 5,
  8, 12, 22, 40, 60, 111, 212; SSC 8;
  WLC**
  See also AAYA 6, 44; AITN 1; AMWS 2;
    BEST 90:4; BPFB 3; BYA 3, 14; CA
    1-4R; CANR 1, 25, 49, 75, 92; CDALB
    1968-1988; CN 1, 2, 3, 4, 5, 6, 7; CPW 1;
    DA; DA3; DAB; DAC; DAM MST, NOV,
    POP; DLB 2, 8, 152; DLBD 3; DLBY
    1980; EWL 3; EXPN; EXPS; LAIT 4;
    LMFS 2; MAL 5; MTCW 1, 2; MTFW
    2005; NFS 3; RGAL 4; SCFW; SFW 4;
    SSFS 5; TUS; YAW
Von Rachen, Kurt
  See Hubbard, L(afayette) Ron(ald)
von Rezzori (d'Arezzo), Gregor
  See Rezzori (d'Arezzo), Gregor von
von Sternberg, Josef
  See Sternberg, Josef von
Vorster, Gordon 1924- .... **CLC 34**
  See also CA 133
Vosce, Trudie
  See Ozick, Cynthia
Voznesensky, Andrei (Andreievich)
  1933- .... **CLC 1, 15, 57**
  See Voznesensky, Andrey
  See also CA 89-92; CANR 37; CWW 2;
    DAM POET; MTCW 1
Voznesensky, Andrey
  See Voznesensky, Andrei (Andreievich)
  See also EWL 3
Wace, Robert c. 1100-c. 1175 .... **CMLC 55**
  See also DLB 146
Waddington, Miriam 1917-2004 .... **CLC 28**
  See also CA 21-24R; 225; CANR 12, 30;
    CCA 1; CP 1, 2, 3, 4, 5, 6, 7; DLB 68
Wagman, Fredrica 1937- .... **CLC 7**
  See also CA 97-100; INT CA-97-100
Wagner, Linda W.
  See Wagner-Martin, Linda (C.)
Wagner, Linda Welshimer
  See Wagner-Martin, Linda (C.)
Wagner, Richard 1813-1883 ..... **NCLC 9, 119**
  See also DLB 129; EW 6
Wagner-Martin, Linda (C.) 1936- .... **CLC 50**
  See also CA 159; CANR 135
Wagoner, David (Russell) 1926- .... **CLC 3, 5,
  15; PC 33**
  See also AMWS 9; CA 1-4R; CAAS 3;
    CANR 2, 71; CN 1, 2, 3, 4, 5, 6, 7; CP 1,
    2, 3, 4, 5, 6, 7; DLB 5, 256; SATA 14;
    TCWW 1, 2
Wah, Fred(erick James) 1939- .... **CLC 44**
  See also CA 107; 141; CP 1, 7; DLB 60
Wahloo, Per 1926-1975 .... **CLC 7**
  See also BPFB 3; CA 61-64; CANR 73;
    CMW 4; MSW
Wahloo, Peter
  See Wahloo, Per

Wain, John (Barrington) 1925-1994 . **CLC 2, 11, 15, 46**
See also CA 5-8R; 145; CAAS 4; CANR 23, 54; CDBLB 1960 to Present; CN 1, 2, 3, 4, 5; CP 1, 2, 3, 4; DLB 15, 27, 139, 155; EWL 3; MTCW 1, 2; MTFW 2005

Wajda, Andrzej 1926- .... **CLC 16, 219**
See also CA 102

Wakefield, Dan 1932- .... **CLC 7**
See also CA 21-24R; 211; CAAE 211; CAAS 7; CN 4, 5, 6, 7

Wakefield, Herbert Russell
1888-1965 .... **TCLC 120**
See also CA 5-8R; CANR 77; HGG; SUFW

Wakoski, Diane 1937- ...... **CLC 2, 4, 7, 9, 11, 40; PC 15**
See also CA 13-16R, 216; CAAE 216; CAAS 1; CANR 9, 60, 106; CP 1, 2, 3, 4, 5, 6, 7; CWP; DAM POET; DLB 5; INT CANR-9; MAL 5; MTCW 2; MTFW 2005

Wakoski-Sherbell, Diane
See Wakoski, Diane

Walcott, Derek (Alton) 1930- ... **BLC 3; CLC 2, 4, 9, 14, 25, 42, 67, 76, 160; DC 7; PC 46**
See also BW 2; CA 89-92; CANR 26, 47, 75, 80, 130; CBD; CD 5, 6; CDWLB 3; CP 1, 2, 3, 4, 5, 6, 7; DA3; DAB; DAC; DAM MST, MULT, POET; DLB 117; DLBY 1981; DNFS 1; EFS 1; EWL 3; LMFS 2; MTCW 1, 2; MTFW 2005; PFS 6; RGEL 2; TWA; WWE 1

Waldman, Anne (Lesley) 1945- .... **CLC 7**
See also BG 1:3; CA 37-40R; CAAS 17; CANR 34, 69, 116; CP 1, 2, 3, 4, 5, 6, 7; CWP; DLB 16

Waldo, E. Hunter
See Sturgeon, Theodore (Hamilton)

Waldo, Edward Hamilton
See Sturgeon, Theodore (Hamilton)

Walker, Alice (Malsenior) 1944- .... **BLC 3; CLC 5, 6, 9, 19, 27, 46, 58, 103, 167; PC 30; SSC 5; WLCS**
See also AAYA 3, 33; AFAW 1, 2; AMWS 3; BEST 89:4; BPFB 3; BW 2, 3; CA 37-40R; CANR 9, 27, 49, 66, 82, 131; CDALB 1968-1988; CN 4, 5, 6, 7; CPW; CSW; DA; DA3; DAB; DAC; DAM MST, MULT, NOV, POET, POP; DLB 6, 33, 143; EWL 3; EXPN; EXPS; FL 1:6; FW; INT CANR-27; LAIT 3; MAL 5; MAWW; MTCW 1, 2; MTFW 2005; NFS 5; RGAL 4; RGSF 2; SATA 31; SSFS 2, 11; TUS; YAW

Walker, David Harry 1911-1992 ...... **CLC 14**
See also CA 1-4R; 137; CANR 1; CN 1, 2; CWRI 5; SATA 8; SATA-Obit 71

Walker, Edward Joseph 1934-2004
See Walker, Ted
See also CA 21-24R; 226; CANR 12, 28, 53

Walker, George F(rederick) 1947- .. **CLC 44, 61**
See also CA 103; CANR 21, 43, 59; CD 5, 6; DAB; DAC; DAM MST; DLB 60

Walker, Joseph A. 1935-2003 .... **CLC 19**
See also BW 1, 3; CA 89-92; CAD; CANR 26, 143; CD 5, 6; DAM DRAM, MST; DFS 12; DLB 38

Walker, Margaret (Abigail)
1915-1998 .... **BLC; CLC 1, 6; PC 20; TCLC 129**
See also AFAW 1, 2; BW 2, 3; CA 73-76; 172; CANR 26, 54, 76, 136; CN 1, 2, 3, 4, 5, 6; CP 1, 2, 3, 4; CSW; DAM MULT; DLB 76, 152; EXPP; FW; MAL 5; MTCW 1, 2; MTFW 2005; RGAL 4; RHW

Walker, Ted .... **CLC 13**
See Walker, Edward Joseph
See also CP 1, 2, 3, 4, 5, 6, 7; DLB 40

Wallace, David Foster 1962- ... **CLC 50, 114; SSC 68**
See also AAYA 50; AMWS 10; CA 132; CANR 59, 133; CN 7; DA3; MTCW 2; MTFW 2005

Wallace, Dexter
See Masters, Edgar Lee

Wallace, (Richard Horatio) Edgar
1875-1932 .... **TCLC 57**
See also CA 115; 218; CMW 4; DLB 70; MSW; RGEL 2

Wallace, Irving 1916-1990 .... **CLC 7, 13**
See also AITN 1; BPFB 3; CA 1-4R; 132; CAAS 1; CANR 1, 27; CPW; DAM NOV, POP; INT CANR-27; MTCW 1, 2

Wallant, Edward Lewis 1926-1962 ... **CLC 5, 10**
See also CA 1-4R; CANR 22; DLB 2, 28, 143, 299; EWL 3; MAL 5; MTCW 1, 2; RGAL 4

Wallas, Graham 1858-1932 .... **TCLC 91**

Waller, Edmund 1606-1687 .... **LC 86**
See also BRW 2; DAM POET; DLB 126; PAB; RGEL 2

Walley, Byron
See Card, Orson Scott

Walpole, Horace 1717-1797 .... **LC 2, 49**
See also BRW 3; DLB 39, 104, 213; GL 3; HGG; LMFS 1; RGEL 2; SUFW 1; TEA

Walpole, Hugh (Seymour)
1884-1941 .... **TCLC 5**
See also CA 104; 165; DLB 34; HGG; MTCW 2; RGEL 2; RHW

Walrond, Eric (Derwent) 1898-1966 . **HR 1:3**
See also BW 1; CA 125; DLB 51

Walser, Martin 1927- .... **CLC 27, 183**
See also CA 57-60; CANR 8, 46, 145; CWW 2; DLB 75, 124; EWL 3

Walser, Robert 1878-1956 ..... **SSC 20; TCLC 18**
See also CA 118; 165; CANR 100; DLB 66; EWL 3

Walsh, Gillian Paton
See Paton Walsh, Gillian

Walsh, Jill Paton .... **CLC 35**
See Paton Walsh, Gillian
See also CLR 2, 65; WYA

Walter, Villiam Christian
See Andersen, Hans Christian

Walters, Anna L(ee) 1946- .... **NNAL**
See also CA 73-76

Walther von der Vogelweide c.
1170-1228 .... **CMLC 56**

Walton, Izaak 1593-1683 .... **LC 72**
See also BRW 2; CDBLB Before 1660; DLB 151, 213; RGEL 2

Wambaugh, Joseph (Aloysius), Jr.
1937- .... **CLC 3, 18**
See also AITN 1; BEST 89:3; BPFB 3; CA 33-36R; CANR 42, 65, 115; CMW 4; CPW 1; DA3; DAM NOV, POP; DLB 6; DLBY 1983; MSW; MTCW 1, 2

Wang Wei 699(?)-761(?) .... **PC 18**
See also TWA

Warburton, William 1698-1779 .... **LC 97**
See also DLB 104

Ward, Arthur Henry Sarsfield 1883-1959
See Rohmer, Sax
See also CA 108; 173; CMW 4; HGG

Ward, E. D.
See Lucas, E(dward) V(errall)

Ward, Mrs. Humphry 1851-1920
See Ward, Mary Augusta
See also RGEL 2

Ward, Mary Augusta 1851-1920 ... **TCLC 55**
See Ward, Mrs. Humphry
See also DLB 18

Ward, Nathaniel 1578(?)-1652 .... **LC 114**
See also DLB 24

Ward, Peter
See Faust, Frederick (Schiller)

Warhol, Andy 1928(?)-1987 .... **CLC 20**
See also AAYA 12; BEST 89:4; CA 89-92; 121; CANR 34

Warner, Francis (Robert le Plastrier)
1937- .... **CLC 14**
See also CA 53-56; CANR 11; CP 1, 2, 3, 4

Warner, Marina 1946- .... **CLC 59**
See also CA 65-68; CANR 21, 55, 118; CN 5, 6, 7; DLB 194; MTFW 2005

Warner, Rex (Ernest) 1905-1986 ...... **CLC 45**
See also CA 89-92; 119; CN 1, 2, 3, 4; CP 1, 2, 3, 4; DLB 15; RGEL 2; RHW

Warner, Susan (Bogert)
1819-1885 .... **NCLC 31, 146**
See also DLB 3, 42, 239, 250, 254

Warner, Sylvia (Constance) Ashton
See Ashton-Warner, Sylvia (Constance)

Warner, Sylvia Townsend
1893-1978 .. **CLC 7, 19; SSC 23; TCLC 131**
See also BRWS 7; CA 61-64; 77-80; CANR 16, 60, 104; CN 1, 2; DLB 34, 139; EWL 3; FANT; FW; MTCW 1, 2; RGEL 2; RGSF 2; RHW

Warren, Mercy Otis 1728-1814 ..... **NCLC 13**
See also DLB 31, 200; RGAL 4; TUS

Warren, Robert Penn 1905-1989 .. **CLC 1, 4, 6, 8, 10, 13, 18, 39, 53, 59; PC 37; SSC 4, 58; WLC**
See also AITN 1; AMW; AMWC 2; BPFB 3; BYA 1; CA 13-16R; 129; CANR 10, 47; CDALB 1968-1988; CN 1, 2, 3, 4; CP 1, 2, 3, 4; DA; DA3; DAB; DAC; DAM MST, NOV, POET; DLB 2, 48, 152, 320; DLBY 1980, 1989; EWL 3; INT CANR-10; MAL 5; MTCW 1, 2; MTFW 2005; NFS 13; RGAL 4; RGSF 2; RHW; SATA 46; SATA-Obit 63; SSFS 8; TUS

Warrigal, Jack
See Furphy, Joseph

Warshofsky, Isaac
See Singer, Isaac Bashevis

Warton, Joseph 1722-1800 .... **NCLC 118**
See also DLB 104, 109; RGEL 2

Warton, Thomas 1728-1790 .... **LC 15, 82**
See also DAM POET; DLB 104, 109; RGEL 2

Waruk, Kona
See Harris, (Theodore) Wilson

Warung, Price .... **TCLC 45**
See Astley, William
See also DLB 230; RGEL 2

Warwick, Jarvis
See Garner, Hugh
See also CCA 1

Washington, Alex
See Harris, Mark

Washington, Booker T(aliaferro)
1856-1915 .... **BLC 3; TCLC 10**
See also BW 1; CA 114; 125; DA3; DAM MULT; LAIT 2; RGAL 4; SATA 28

Washington, George 1732-1799 .... **LC 25**
See also DLB 31

Wassermann, (Karl) Jakob
1873-1934 .... **TCLC 6**
See also CA 104; 163; DLB 66; EWL 3

Wessel, Johan Herman 1742-1785 .... **LC 7**
See also DLB 300
West, Anthony (Panther)
1914-1987 .... **CLC 50**
See also CA 45-48; 124; CANR 3, 19; CN
1, 2, 3, 4; DLB 15
West, C. P.
See Wodehouse, P(elham) G(renville)
West, Cornel (Ronald) 1953- .... **BLCS; CLC
134**
See also CA 144; CANR 91; DLB 246
West, Delno C(loyde), Jr. 1936- .... **CLC 70**
See also CA 57-60
West, Dorothy 1907-1998 ...... **HR 1:3; TCLC
108**
See also BW 2; CA 143; 169; DLB 76
West, (Mary) Jessamyn 1902-1984 ... **CLC 7,
17**
See also CA 9-12R; 112; CANR 27; CN 1,
2, 3; DLB 6; DLBY 1984; MTCW 1, 2;
RGAL 4; RHW; SATA-Obit 37; TCWW
2; TUS; YAW
West, Morris L(anglo) 1916-1999 ..... **CLC 6,
33**
See also BPFB 3; CA 5-8R; 187; CANR
24, 49, 64; CN 1, 2, 3, 4, 5, 6; CPW; DLB
289; MTCW 1, 2; MTFW 2005
West, Nathanael 1903-1940 .. **SSC 16; TCLC
1, 14, 44**
See also AMW; AMWR 2; BPFB 3; CA
104; 125; CDALB 1929-1941; DA3; DLB
4, 9, 28; EWL 3; MAL 5; MTCW 1, 2;
MTFW 2005; NFS 16; RGAL 4; TUS
West, Owen
See Koontz, Dean R.
West, Paul 1930- .... **CLC 7, 14, 96**
See also CA 13-16R; CAAS 7; CANR 22,
53, 76, 89, 136; CN 1, 2, 3, 4, 5, 6, 7;
DLB 14; INT CANR-22; MTCW 2;
MTFW 2005
West, Rebecca 1892-1983 ... **CLC 7, 9, 31, 50**
See also BPFB 3; BRWS 3; CA 5-8R; 109;
CANR 19; CN 1, 2, 3; DLB 36; DLBY
1983; EWL 3; FW; MTCW 1, 2; MTFW
2005; NCFS 4; RGEL 2; TEA
Westall, Robert (Atkinson)
1929-1993 .... **CLC 17**
See also AAYA 12; BYA 2, 6, 7, 8, 9, 15;
CA 69-72; 141; CANR 18, 68; CLR 13;
FANT; JRDA; MAICYA 1, 2; MAICYAS
1; SAAS 2; SATA 23, 69; SATA-Obit 75;
WYA; YAW
Westermarck, Edward 1862-1939 . **TCLC 87**
Westlake, Donald E(dwin) 1933- . **CLC 7, 33**
See also BPFB 3; CA 17-20R; CAAS 13;
CANR 16, 44, 65, 94, 137; CMW 4;
CPW; DAM POP; INT CANR-16; MSW;
MTCW 2; MTFW 2005
Westmacott, Mary
See Christie, Agatha (Mary Clarissa)
Weston, Allen
See Norton, Andre
Wetcheek, J. L.
See Feuchtwanger, Lion
Wetering, Janwillem van de
See van de Wetering, Janwillem
Wetherald, Agnes Ethelwyn
1857-1940 .... **TCLC 81**
See also CA 202; DLB 99
Wetherell, Elizabeth
See Warner, Susan (Bogert)
Whale, James 1889-1957 .... **TCLC 63**
Whalen, Philip (Glenn) 1923-2002 .... **CLC 6,
29**
See also BG 1:3; CA 9-12R; 209; CANR 5,
39; CP 1, 2, 3, 4, 5, 6, 7; DLB 16; WP

Wharton, Edith (Newbold Jones)
1862-1937 ... **SSC 6, 84; TCLC 3, 9, 27,
53, 129, 149; WLC**
See also AAYA 25; AMW; AMWC 2;
AMWR 1; BPFB 3; CA 104; 132; CDALB
1865-1917; DA; DA3; DAB; DAC; DAM
MST, NOV; DLB 4, 9, 12, 78, 189; DLBD
13; EWL 3; EXPS; FL 1:6; GL 3; HGG;
LAIT 2, 3; LATS 1:1; MAL 5; MAWW;
MTCW 1, 2; MTFW 2005; NFS 5, 11,
15, 20; RGAL 4; RGSF 2; RHW; SSFS 6,
7; SUFW; TUS
Wharton, James
See Mencken, H(enry) L(ouis)
Wharton, William (a pseudonym)
1925- .... **CLC 18, 37**
See also CA 93-96; CN 4, 5, 6, 7; DLBY
1980; INT CA-93-96
Wheatley (Peters), Phillis
1753(?)-1784 ... **BLC 3; LC 3, 50; PC 3;
WLC**
See also AFAW 1, 2; CDALB 1640-1865;
DA; DA3; DAC; DAM MST, MULT,
POET; DLB 31, 50; EXPP; FL 1:1; PFS
13; RGAL 4
Wheelock, John Hall 1886-1978 .... **CLC 14**
See also CA 13-16R; 77-80; CANR 14; CP
1, 2; DLB 45; MAL 5
Whim-Wham
See Curnow, (Thomas) Allen (Monro)
White, Babington
See Braddon, Mary Elizabeth
White, E(lwyn) B(rooks)
1899-1985 .... **CLC 10, 34, 39**
See also AAYA 62; AITN 2; AMWS 1; CA
13-16R; 116; CANR 16, 37; CDALBS;
CLR 1, 21; CPW; DA3; DAM POP; DLB
11, 22; EWL 3; FANT; MAICYA 1, 2;
MAL 5; MTCW 1, 2; MTFW 2005; NCFS
5; RGAL 4; SATA 2, 29, 100; SATA-Obit
44; TUS
White, Edmund (Valentine III)
1940- .... **CLC 27, 110**
See also AAYA 7; CA 45-48; CANR 3, 19,
36, 62, 107, 133; CN 5, 6, 7; DA3; DAM
POP; DLB 227; MTCW 1, 2; MTFW
2005
White, Hayden V. 1928- .... **CLC 148**
See also CA 128; CANR 135; DLB 246
White, Patrick (Victor Martindale)
1912-1990 ...... **CLC 3, 4, 5, 7, 9, 18, 65,
69; SSC 39; TCLC 176**
See also BRWS 1; CA 81-84; 132; CANR
43; CN 1, 2, 3, 4; DLB 260; EWL 3;
MTCW 1; RGEL 2; RGSF 2; RHW;
TWA; WWE 1
White, Phyllis Dorothy James 1920-
See James, P. D.
See also CA 21-24R; CANR 17, 43, 65,
112; CMW 4; CN 7; CPW; DA3; DAM
POP; MTCW 1, 2; MTFW 2005; TEA
White, T(erence) H(anbury)
1906-1964 .... **CLC 30**
See also AAYA 22; BPFB 3; BYA 4, 5; CA
73-76; CANR 37; DLB 160; FANT;
JRDA; LAIT 1; MAICYA 1, 2; RGEL 2;
SATA 12; SUFW 1; YAW
White, Terence de Vere 1912-1994 ... **CLC 49**
See also CA 49-52; 145; CANR 3
White, Walter
See White, Walter F(rancis)
White, Walter F(rancis) 1893-1955 ... **BLC 3;
HR 1:3; TCLC 15**
See also BW 1; CA 115; 124; DAM MULT;
DLB 51
White, William Hale 1831-1913
See Rutherford, Mark
See also CA 121; 189

Whitehead, Alfred North
1861-1947 .... **TCLC 97**
See also CA 117; 165; DLB 100, 262
Whitehead, E(dward) A(nthony)
1933- .... **CLC 5**
See Whitehead, Ted
See also CA 65-68; CANR 58, 118; CBD;
CD 5; DLB 310
Whitehead, Ted
See Whitehead, E(dward) A(nthony)
See also CD 6
Whiteman, Roberta J. Hill 1947- ...... **NNAL**
See also CA 146
Whitemore, Hugh (John) 1936- .... **CLC 37**
See also CA 132; CANR 77; CBD; CD 5,
6; INT CA-132
Whitman, Sarah Helen (Power)
1803-1878 .... **NCLC 19**
See also DLB 1, 243
Whitman, Walt(er) 1819-1892 .. **NCLC 4, 31,
81; PC 3; WLC**
See also AAYA 42; AMW; AMWR 1;
CDALB 1640-1865; DA; DA3; DAB;
DAC; DAM MST, POET; DLB 3, 64,
224, 250; EXPP; LAIT 2; LMFS 1; PAB;
PFS 2, 3, 13, 22; RGAL 4; SATA 20;
TUS; WP; WYAS 1
Whitney, Phyllis A(yame) 1903- .... **CLC 42**
See also AAYA 36; AITN 2; BEST 90:3;
CA 1-4R; CANR 3, 25, 38, 60; CLR 59;
CMW 4; CPW; DA3; DAM POP; JRDA;
MAICYA 1, 2; MTCW 2; RHW; SATA 1,
30; YAW
Whittemore, (Edward) Reed, Jr.
1919- .... **CLC 4**
See also CA 9-12R; 219; CAAE 219; CAAS
8; CANR 4, 119; CP 1, 2, 3, 4, 5, 6, 7;
DLB 5; MAL 5
Whittier, John Greenleaf
1807-1892 .... **NCLC 8, 59**
See also AMWS 1; DLB 1, 243; RGAL 4
Whittlebot, Hernia
See Coward, Noel (Peirce)
Wicker, Thomas Grey 1926-
See Wicker, Tom
See also CA 65-68; CANR 21, 46, 141
Wicker, Tom .... **CLC 7**
See Wicker, Thomas Grey
Wideman, John Edgar 1941- ... **BLC 3; CLC
5, 34, 36, 67, 122; SSC 62**
See also AFAW 1, 2; AMWS 10; BPFB 4;
BW 2, 3; CA 85-88; CANR 14, 42, 67,
109, 140; CN 4, 5, 6, 7; DAM MULT;
DLB 33, 143; MAL 5; MTCW 2; MTFW
2005; RGAL 4; RGSF 2; SSFS 6, 12;
TCLE 1:2
Wiebe, Rudy (Henry) 1934- .. **CLC 6, 11, 14,
138**
See also CA 37-40R; CANR 42, 67, 123;
CN 1, 2, 3, 4, 5, 6, 7; DAC; DAM MST;
DLB 60; RHW; SATA 156
Wieland, Christoph Martin
1733-1813 .... **NCLC 17**
See also DLB 97; EW 4; LMFS 1; RGWL
2, 3
Wiene, Robert 1881-1938 .... **TCLC 56**
Wieners, John 1934- .... **CLC 7**
See also BG 1:3; CA 13-16R; CP 1, 2, 3, 4,
5, 6, 7; DLB 16; WP
Wiesel, Elie(zer) 1928- .... **CLC 3, 5, 11, 37,
165; WLCS**
See also AAYA 7, 54; AITN 1; CA 5-8R;
CAAS 4; CANR 8, 40, 65, 125; CDALBS;
CWW 2; DA; DA3; DAB; DAC; DAM
MST, NOV; DLB 83, 299; DLBY 1987;
EWL 3; INT CANR-8; LAIT 4; MTCW
1, 2; MTFW 2005; NCFS 4; NFS 4;
RGWL 3; SATA 56; YAW

Wilson, John (Anthony) Burgess 1917-1993
See Burgess, Anthony
See also CA 1-4R; 143; CANR 2, 46; DA3;
DAC; DAM NOV; MTCW 1, 2; MTFW
2005; NFS 15; TEA

Wilson, Lanford 1937- .. **CLC 7, 14, 36, 197;**
DC 19
See also CA 17-20R; CABS 3; CAD; CANR
45, 96; CD 5, 6; DAM DRAM; DFS 4, 9,
12, 16, 20; DLB 7; EWL 3; MAL 5; TUS

Wilson, Robert M. 1941- .... **CLC 7, 9**
See also CA 49-52; CAD; CANR 2, 41; CD
5, 6; MTCW 1

Wilson, Robert McLiam 1964- .... **CLC 59**
See also CA 132; DLB 267

Wilson, Sloan 1920-2003 .... **CLC 32**
See also CA 1-4R; 216; CANR 1, 44; CN
1, 2, 3, 4, 5, 6

Wilson, Snoo 1948- .... **CLC 33**
See also CA 69-72; CBD; CD 5, 6

Wilson, William S(mith) 1932- .... **CLC 49**
See also CA 81-84

Wilson, (Thomas) Woodrow
1856-1924 .... **TCLC 79**
See also CA 166; DLB 47

Wilson and Warnke eds. .... **CLC 65**

Winchilsea, Anne (Kingsmill) Finch
1661-1720
See Finch, Anne
See also RGEL 2

Windham, Basil
See Wodehouse, P(elham) G(renville)

Wingrove, David (John) 1954- .... **CLC 68**
See also CA 133; SFW 4

Winnemucca, Sarah 1844-1891 .... **NCLC 79;**
NNAL
See also DAM MULT; DLB 175; RGAL 4

Winstanley, Gerrard 1609-1676 .... **LC 52**

Wintergreen, Jane
See Duncan, Sara Jeannette

Winters, Arthur Yvor
See Winters, Yvor

Winters, Janet Lewis .... **CLC 41**
See Lewis, Janet
See also DLBY 1987

Winters, Yvor 1900-1968 .... **CLC 4, 8, 32**
See also AMWS 2; CA 11-12; 25-28R; CAP
1; DLB 48; EWL 3; MAL 5; MTCW 1;
RGAL 4

Winterson, Jeanette 1959- .... **CLC 64, 158**
See also BRWS 4; CA 136; CANR 58, 116;
CN 5, 6, 7; CPW; DA3; DAM POP; DLB
207, 261; FANT; FW; GLL 1; MTCW 2;
MTFW 2005; RHW

Winthrop, John 1588-1649 .... **LC 31, 107**
See also DLB 24, 30

Wirth, Louis 1897-1952 .... **TCLC 92**
See also CA 210

Wiseman, Frederick 1930- .... **CLC 20**
See also CA 159

Wister, Owen 1860-1938 .... **TCLC 21**
See also BPFB 3; CA 108; 162; DLB 9, 78,
186; RGAL 4; SATA 62; TCWW 1, 2

Wither, George 1588-1667 .... **LC 96**
See also DLB 121; RGEL 2

Witkacy
See Witkiewicz, Stanislaw Ignacy

Witkiewicz, Stanislaw Ignacy
1885-1939 .... **TCLC 8**
See also CA 105; 162; CDWLB 4; DLB
215; EW 10; EWL 3; RGWL 2, 3; SFW 4

Wittgenstein, Ludwig (Josef Johann)
1889-1951 .... **TCLC 59**
See also CA 113; 164; DLB 262; MTCW 2

Wittig, Monique 1935-2003 .... **CLC 22**
See also CA 116; 135; 212; CANR 143;
CWW 2; DLB 83; EWL 3; FW; GLL 1

Wittlin, Jozef 1896-1976 .... **CLC 25**
See also CA 49-52; 65-68; CANR 3; EWL
3

Wodehouse, P(elham) G(renville)
1881-1975 . **CLC 1, 2, 5, 10, 22; SSC 2;**
TCLC 108
See also AAYA 65; AITN 2; BRWS 3; CA
45-48; 57-60; CANR 3, 33; CDBLB
1914-1945; CN 1, 2; CPW 1; DA3; DAB;
DAC; DAM NOV; DLB 34, 162; EWL 3;
MTCW 1, 2; MTFW 2005; RGEL 2;
RGSF 2; SATA 22; SSFS 10

Woiwode, L.
See Woiwode, Larry (Alfred)

Woiwode, Larry (Alfred) 1941- ... **CLC 6, 10**
See also CA 73-76; CANR 16, 94; CN 3, 4,
5, 6, 7; DLB 6; INT CANR-16

Wojciechowska, Maia (Teresa)
1927-2002 .... **CLC 26**
See also AAYA 8, 46; BYA 3; CA 9-12R,
183; 209; CAAE 183; CANR 4, 41; CLR
1; JRDA; MAICYA 1, 2; SAAS 1; SATA
1, 28, 83; SATA-Essay 104; SATA-Obit
134; YAW

Wojtyla, Karol (Jozef)
See John Paul II, Pope

Wojtyla, Karol (Josef)
See John Paul II, Pope

Wolf, Christa 1929- .... **CLC 14, 29, 58, 150**
See also CA 85-88; CANR 45, 123; CD-
WLB 2; CWW 2; DLB 75; EWL 3; FW;
MTCW 1; RGWL 2, 3; SSFS 14

Wolf, Naomi 1962- .... **CLC 157**
See also CA 141; CANR 110; FW; MTFW
2005

Wolfe, Gene 1931- .... **CLC 25**
See also AAYA 35; CA 57-60; CAAS 9;
CANR 6, 32, 60; CPW; DAM POP; DLB
8; FANT; MTCW 2; MTFW 2005; SATA
118, 165; SCFW 2; SFW 4; SUFW 2

Wolfe, Gene Rodman
See Wolfe, Gene

Wolfe, George C. 1954- .... **BLCS; CLC 49**
See also CA 149; CAD; CD 5, 6

Wolfe, Thomas (Clayton)
1900-1938 ...... **SSC 33; TCLC 4, 13, 29,**
61; WLC
See also AMW; BPFB 3; CA 104; 132;
CANR 102; CDALB 1929-1941; DA;
DA3; DAB; DAC; DAM MST, NOV;
DLB 9, 102, 229; DLBD 2, 16; DLBY
1985, 1997; EWL 3; MAL 5; MTCW 1,
2; NFS 18; RGAL 4; SSFS 18; TUS

Wolfe, Thomas Kennerly, Jr.
1931- .... **CLC 147**
See Wolfe, Tom
See also CA 13-16R; CANR 9, 33, 70, 104;
DA3; DAM POP; DLB 185; EWL 3; INT
CANR-9; MTCW 1, 2; MTFW 2005; TUS

Wolfe, Tom .... **CLC 1, 2, 9, 15, 35, 51**
See Wolfe, Thomas Kennerly, Jr.
See also AAYA 8, 67; AITN 2; AMWS 3;
BEST 89:1; BPFB 3; CN 5, 6, 7; CPW;
CSW; DLB 152; LAIT 5; RGAL 4

Wolff, Geoffrey (Ansell) 1937- .... **CLC 41**
See also CA 29-32R; CANR 29, 43, 78

Wolff, Sonia
See Levitin, Sonia (Wolff)

Wolff, Tobias (Jonathan Ansell)
1945- .... **CLC 39, 64, 172; SSC 63**
See also AAYA 16; AMWS 7; BEST 90:2;
BYA 12; CA 114; 117; CAAS 22; CANR
54, 76, 96; CN 5, 6, 7; CSW; DA3; DLB
130; EWL 3; INT CA-117; MTCW 2;
MTFW 2005; RGAL 4; RGSF 2; SSFS 4,
11

Wolfram von Eschenbach c. 1170-c.
1220 .... **CMLC 5**
See Eschenbach, Wolfram von
See also CDWLB 2; DLB 138; EW 1;
RGWL 2

Wolitzer, Hilma 1930- .... **CLC 17**
See also CA 65-68; CANR 18, 40; INT
CANR-18; SATA 31; YAW

Wollstonecraft, Mary 1759-1797 .... **LC 5, 50,**
90
See also BRWS 3; CDBLB 1789-1832;
DLB 39, 104, 158, 252; FL 1:1; FW;
LAIT 1; RGEL 2; TEA; WLIT 3

Wonder, Stevie .... **CLC 12**
See Morris, Steveland Judkins

Wong, Jade Snow 1922- .... **CLC 17**
See also CA 109; CANR 91; SATA 112

Woodberry, George Edward
1855-1930 .... **TCLC 73**
See also CA 165; DLB 71, 103

Woodcott, Keith
See Brunner, John (Kilian Houston)

Woodruff, Robert W.
See Mencken, H(enry) L(ouis)

Woolf, (Adeline) Virginia 1882-1941 .. **SSC 7,**
79; TCLC 1, 5, 20, 43, 56, 101, 123,
128; WLC
See also AAYA 44; BPFB 3; BRW 7;
BRWC 2; BRWR 1; CA 104; 130; CANR
64, 132; CDBLB 1914-1945; DA; DA3;
DAB; DAC; DAM MST, NOV; DLB 36,
100, 162; DLBD 10; EWL 3; EXPS; FL
1:6; FW; LAIT 3; LATS 1:1; LMFS 2;
MTCW 1, 2; MTFW 2005; NCFS 2; NFS
8, 12; RGEL 2; RGSF 2; SSFS 4, 12;
TEA; WLIT 4

Woollcott, Alexander (Humphreys)
1887-1943 .... **TCLC 5**
See also CA 105; 161; DLB 29

Woolrich, Cornell .... **CLC 77**
See Hopley-Woolrich, Cornell George
See also MSW

Woolson, Constance Fenimore
1840-1894 .... **NCLC 82; SSC 90**
See also DLB 12, 74, 189, 221; RGAL 4

Wordsworth, Dorothy 1771-1855 . **NCLC 25,**
138
See also DLB 107

Wordsworth, William 1770-1850 .. **NCLC 12,**
38, 111; PC 4, 67; WLC
See also BRW 4; BRWC 1; CDBLB 1789-
1832; DA; DA3; DAB; DAC; DAM MST,
POET; DLB 93, 107; EXPP; LATS 1:1;
LMFS 1; PAB; PFS 2; RGEL 2; TEA;
WLIT 3; WP

Wotton, Sir Henry 1568-1639 .... **LC 68**
See also DLB 121; RGEL 2

Wouk, Herman 1915- .... **CLC 1, 9, 38**
See also BPFB 2, 3; CA 5-8R; CANR 6,
33, 67, 146; CDALBS; CN 1, 2, 3, 4, 5,
6; CPW; DA3; DAM NOV, POP; DLBY
1982; INT CANR-6; LAIT 4; MAL 5;
MTCW 1, 2; MTFW 2005; NFS 7; TUS

Wright, Charles (Penzel, Jr.) 1935- .. **CLC 6,**
13, 28, 119, 146
See also AMWS 5; CA 29-32R; CAAS 7;
CANR 23, 36, 62, 88, 135; CP 3, 4, 5, 6,
7; DLB 165; DLBY 1982; EWL 3;
MTCW 1, 2; MTFW 2005; PFS 10

Wright, Charles Stevenson 1932- ..... **BLC 3;**
CLC 49
See also BW 1; CA 9-12R; CANR 26; CN
1, 2, 3, 4, 5, 6, 7; DAM MULT, POET;
DLB 33

Wright, Frances 1795-1852 .... **NCLC 74**
See also DLB 73

Wright, Frank Lloyd 1867-1959 .... **TCLC 95**
See also AAYA 33; CA 174

Wright, Jack R.
See Harris, Mark

Wright, James (Arlington)
1927-1980 .... **CLC 3, 5, 10, 28; PC 36**
See also AITN 2; AMWS 3; CA 49-52; 97-100; CANR 4, 34, 64; CDALBS; CP 1, 2; DAM POET; DLB 5, 169; EWL 3; EXPP; MAL 5; MTCW 1, 2; MTFW 2005; PFS 7, 8; RGAL 4; TUS; WP

Wright, Judith (Arundell)
1915-2000 .... **CLC 11, 53; PC 14**
See also CA 13-16R; 188; CANR 31, 76, 93; CP 1, 2, 3, 4, 5, 6, 7; CWP; DLB 260; EWL 3; MTCW 1, 2; MTFW 2005; PFS 8; RGEL 2; SATA 14; SATA-Obit 121

Wright, L(aurali) R. 1939- .... **CLC 44**
See also CA 138; CMW 4

Wright, Richard (Nathaniel)
1908-1960 ... **BLC 3; CLC 1, 3, 4, 9, 14, 21, 48, 74; SSC 2; TCLC 136; WLC**
See also AAYA 5, 42; AFAW 1, 2; AMW; BPFB 3; BW 1; BYA 2; CA 108; CANR 64; CDALB 1929-1941; DA; DA3; DAB; DAC; DAM MST, MULT, NOV; DLB 76, 102; DLBD 2; EWL 3; EXPN; LAIT 3, 4; MAL 5; MTCW 1, 2; MTFW 2005; NCFS 1; NFS 1, 7; RGAL 4; RGSF 2; SSFS 3, 9, 15, 20; TUS; YAW

Wright, Richard B(ruce) 1937- .... **CLC 6**
See also CA 85-88; CANR 120; DLB 53

Wright, Rick 1945- .... **CLC 35**

Wright, Rowland
See Wells, Carolyn

Wright, Stephen 1946- .... **CLC 33**
See also CA 237

Wright, Willard Huntington 1888-1939
See Van Dine, S. S.
See also CA 115; 189; CMW 4; DLBD 16

Wright, William 1930- .... **CLC 44**
See also CA 53-56; CANR 7, 23

Wroth, Lady Mary 1587-1653(?) .... **LC 30; PC 38**
See also DLB 121

Wu Ch'eng-en 1500(?)-1582(?) .... **LC 7**

Wu Ching-tzu 1701-1754 .... **LC 2**

Wulfstan c. 10th cent. -1023 .... **CMLC 59**

Wurlitzer, Rudolph 1938(?)- ... **CLC 2, 4, 15**
See also CA 85-88; CN 4, 5, 6, 7; DLB 173

Wyatt, Sir Thomas c. 1503-1542 . **LC 70; PC 27**
See also BRW 1; DLB 132; EXPP; RGEL 2; TEA

Wycherley, William 1640-1716 .... **LC 8, 21, 102**
See also BRW 2; CDBLB 1660-1789; DAM DRAM; DLB 80; RGEL 2

Wyclif, John c. 1330-1384 .... **CMLC 70**
See also DLB 146

Wylie, Elinor (Morton Hoyt)
1885-1928 .... **PC 23; TCLC 8**
See also AMWS 1; CA 105; 162; DLB 9, 45; EXPP; MAL 5; RGAL 4

Wylie, Philip (Gordon) 1902-1971 ... **CLC 43**
See also CA 21-22; 33-36R; CAP 2; CN 1; DLB 9; SFW 4

Wyndham, John .... **CLC 19**
See Harris, John (Wyndham Parkes Lucas) Beynon
See also DLB 255; SCFW 1, 2

Wyss, Johann David Von
1743-1818 .... **NCLC 10**
See also CLR 92; JRDA; MAICYA 1, 2; SATA 29; SATA-Brief 27

Xenophon c. 430B.C.-c. 354B.C. ... **CMLC 17**
See also AW 1; DLB 176; RGWL 2, 3

Xingjian, Gao 1940-
See Gao Xingjian
See also CA 193; DFS 21; RGWL 3

Yakamochi 718-785 .... **CMLC 45; PC 48**

Yakumo Koizumi
See Hearn, (Patricio) Lafcadio (Tessima Carlos)

Yamada, Mitsuye (May) 1923- .... **PC 44**
See also CA 77-80

Yamamoto, Hisaye 1921- .... **AAL; SSC 34**
See also CA 214; DAM MULT; DLB 312; LAIT 4; SSFS 14

Yamauchi, Wakako 1924- .... **AAL**
See also CA 214; DLB 312

Yanez, Jose Donoso
See Donoso (Yanez), Jose

Yanovsky, Basile S.
See Yanovsky, V(assily) S(emenovich)

Yanovsky, V(assily) S(emenovich)
1906-1989 .... **CLC 2, 18**
See also CA 97-100; 129

Yates, Richard 1926-1992 .... **CLC 7, 8, 23**
See also AMWS 11; CA 5-8R; 139; CANR 10, 43; CN 1, 2, 3, 4, 5; DLB 2, 234; DLBY 1981, 1992; INT CANR-10

Yau, John 1950- .... **PC 61**
See also CA 154; CANR 89; CP 4, 5, 6, 7; DLB 234, 312

Yeats, W. B.
See Yeats, William Butler

Yeats, William Butler 1865-1939 . **PC 20, 51; TCLC 1, 11, 18, 31, 93, 116; WLC**
See also AAYA 48; BRW 6; BRWR 1; CA 104; 127; CANR 45; CDBLB 1890-1914; DA; DA3; DAB; DAC; DAM DRAM, MST, POET; DLB 10, 19, 98, 156; EWL 3; EXPP; MTCW 1, 2; MTFW 2005; NCFS 3; PAB; PFS 1, 2, 5, 7, 13, 15; RGEL 2; TEA; WLIT 4; WP

Yehoshua, A(braham) B. 1936- .. **CLC 13, 31**
See also CA 33-36R; CANR 43, 90, 145; CWW 2; EWL 3; RGSF 2; RGWL 3; WLIT 6

Yellow Bird
See Ridge, John Rollin

Yep, Laurence Michael 1948- .... **CLC 35**
See also AAYA 5, 31; BYA 7; CA 49-52; CANR 1, 46, 92; CLR 3, 17, 54; DLB 52, 312; FANT; JRDA; MAICYA 1, 2; MAICYAS 1; SATA 7, 69, 123; WYA; YAW

Yerby, Frank G(arvin) 1916-1991 ..... **BLC 3; CLC 1, 7, 22**
See also BPFB 3; BW 1, 3; CA 9-12R; 136; CANR 16, 52; CN 1, 2, 3, 4, 5; DAM MULT; DLB 76; INT CANR-16; MTCW 1; RGAL 4; RHW

Yesenin, Sergei Alexandrovich
See Esenin, Sergei (Alexandrovich)

Yesenin, Sergey
See Esenin, Sergei (Alexandrovich)
See also EWL 3

Yevtushenko, Yevgeny (Alexandrovich)
1933- ...... **CLC 1, 3, 13, 26, 51, 126; PC 40**
See Evtushenko, Evgenii Aleksandrovich
See also CA 81-84; CANR 33, 54; DAM POET; EWL 3; MTCW 1

Yezierska, Anzia 1885(?)-1970 .... **CLC 46**
See also CA 126; 89-92; DLB 28, 221; FW; MTCW 1; RGAL 4; SSFS 15

Yglesias, Helen 1915- .... **CLC 7, 22**
See also CA 37-40R; CAAS 20; CANR 15, 65, 95; CN 4, 5, 6, 7; INT CANR-15; MTCW 1

Yokomitsu, Riichi 1898-1947 .... **TCLC 47**
See also CA 170; EWL 3

Yonge, Charlotte (Mary)
1823-1901 .... **TCLC 48**
See also CA 109; 163; DLB 18, 163; RGEL 2; SATA 17; WCH

York, Jeremy
See Creasey, John

York, Simon
See Heinlein, Robert A(nson)

Yorke, Henry Vincent 1905-1974 ..... **CLC 13**
See Green, Henry
See also CA 85-88; 49-52

Yosano Akiko 1878-1942 .... **PC 11; TCLC 59**
See also CA 161; EWL 3; RGWL 3

Yoshimoto, Banana .... **CLC 84**
See Yoshimoto, Mahoko
See also AAYA 50; NFS 7

Yoshimoto, Mahoko 1964-
See Yoshimoto, Banana
See also CA 144; CANR 98; SSFS 16

Young, Al(bert James) 1939- ... **BLC 3; CLC 19**
See also BW 2, 3; CA 29-32R; CANR 26, 65, 109; CN 2, 3, 4, 5, 6, 7; CP 1, 2, 3, 4, 5, 6, 7; DAM MULT

Young, Andrew (John) 1885-1971 ...... **CLC 5**
See also CA 5-8R; CANR 7, 29; CP 1; RGEL 2

Young, Collier
See Bloch, Robert (Albert)

Young, Edward 1683-1765 .... **LC 3, 40**
See also DLB 95; RGEL 2

Young, Marguerite (Vivian)
1909-1995 .... **CLC 82**
See also CA 13-16; 150; CAP 1; CN 1, 2, 3, 4, 5, 6

Young, Neil 1945- .... **CLC 17**
See also CA 110; CCA 1

Young Bear, Ray A. 1950- ... **CLC 94; NNAL**
See also CA 146; DAM MULT; DLB 175; MAL 5

Yourcenar, Marguerite 1903-1987 ... **CLC 19, 38, 50, 87**
See also BPFB 3; CA 69-72; CANR 23, 60, 93; DAM NOV; DLB 72; DLBY 1988; EW 12; EWL 3; GFL 1789 to the Present; GLL 1; MTCW 1, 2; MTFW 2005; RGWL 2, 3

Yuan, Chu 340(?)B.C.-278(?)B.C. . **CMLC 36**

Yurick, Sol 1925- .... **CLC 6**
See also CA 13-16R; CANR 25; CN 1, 2, 3, 4, 5, 6, 7; MAL 5

Zabolotsky, Nikolai Alekseevich
1903-1958 .... **TCLC 52**
See Zabolotsky, Nikolay Alekseevich
See also CA 116; 164

Zabolotsky, Nikolay Alekseevich
See Zabolotsky, Nikolai Alekseevich
See also EWL 3

Zagajewski, Adam 1945- .... **PC 27**
See also CA 186; DLB 232; EWL 3

Zalygin, Sergei -2000 .... **CLC 59**

Zalygin, Sergei (Pavlovich)
1913-2000 .... **CLC 59**
See also DLB 302

Zamiatin, Evgenii
See Zamyatin, Evgeny Ivanovich
See also RGSF 2; RGWL 2, 3

Zamiatin, Evgenii Ivanovich
See Zamyatin, Evgeny Ivanovich
See also DLB 272

Zamiatin, Yevgenii
See Zamyatin, Evgeny Ivanovich

Zamora, Bernice (B. Ortiz) 1938- .. **CLC 89; HLC 2**
See also CA 151; CANR 80; DAM MULT; DLB 82; HW 1, 2

Zamyatin, Evgeny Ivanovich
1884-1937 .... **SSC 89; TCLC 8, 37**
See Zamiatin, Evgenii; Zamiatin, Evgenii Ivanovich; Zamiatin, Yevgeny Ivanovich
See also CA 105; 166; SFW 4

Zamyatin, Yevgeny Ivanovich
See Zamyatin, Evgeny Ivanovich
See also EW 10; EWL 3

Zangwill, Israel 1864-1926 ... **SSC 44; TCLC 16**
　　See also CA 109; 167; CMW 4; DLB 10, 135, 197; RGEL 2

Zanzotto, Andrea 1921- .... **PC 65**
　　See also CA 208; CWW 2; DLB 128; EWL 3

Zappa, Francis Vincent, Jr. 1940-1993
　　See Zappa, Frank
　　See also CA 108; 143; CANR 57

Zappa, Frank .... **CLC 17**
　　See Zappa, Francis Vincent, Jr.

Zaturenska, Marya 1902-1982 ..... **CLC 6, 11**
　　See also CA 13-16R; 105; CANR 22; CP 1, 2, 3

Zayas y Sotomayor, Maria de 1590-c. 1661 .... **LC 102**
　　See also RGSF 2

Zeami 1363-1443 .... **DC 7; LC 86**
　　See also DLB 203; RGWL 2, 3

Zelazny, Roger (Joseph) 1937-1995 . **CLC 21**
　　See also AAYA 7, 68; BPFB 3; CA 21-24R; 148; CANR 26, 60; CN 6; DLB 8; FANT; MTCW 1, 2; MTFW 2005; SATA 57; SATA-Brief 39; SCFW 1, 2; SFW 4; SUFW 1, 2

Zhang Ailing
　　See Chang, Eileen
　　See also CWW 2; RGSF 2

Zhdanov, Andrei Alexandrovich 1896-1948 .... **TCLC 18**
　　See also CA 117; 167

Zhukovsky, Vasilii Andreevich
　　See Zhukovsky, Vasily (Andreevich)
　　See also DLB 205

Zhukovsky, Vasily (Andreevich) 1783-1852 .... **NCLC 35**
　　See Zhukovsky, Vasilii Andreevich

Ziegenhagen, Eric .... **CLC 55**

Zimmer, Jill Schary
　　See Robinson, Jill

Zimmerman, Robert
　　See Dylan, Bob

Zindel, Paul 1936-2003 ...... **CLC 6, 26; DC 5**
　　See also AAYA 2, 37; BYA 2, 3, 8, 11, 14; CA 73-76; 213; CAD; CANR 31, 65, 108; CD 5, 6; CDALBS; CLR 3, 45, 85; DA; DA3; DAB; DAC; DAM DRAM, MST, NOV; DFS 12; DLB 7, 52; JRDA; LAIT 5; MAICYA 1, 2; MTCW 1, 2; MTFW 2005; NFS 14; SATA 16, 58, 102; SATA-Obit 142; WYA; YAW

Zinn, Howard 1922- .... **CLC 199**
　　See also CA 1-4R; CANR 2, 33, 90

Zinov'Ev, A. A.
　　See Zinoviev, Alexander (Aleksandrovich)

Zinov'ev, Aleksandr (Aleksandrovich)
　　See Zinoviev, Alexander (Aleksandrovich)
　　See also DLB 302

Zinoviev, Alexander (Aleksandrovich) 1922- .... **CLC 19**
　　See Zinov'ev, Aleksandr (Aleksandrovich)
　　See also CA 116; 133; CAAS 10

Zizek, Slavoj 1949- .... **CLC 188**
　　See also CA 201; MTFW 2005

Zoilus
　　See Lovecraft, H(oward) P(hillips)

Zola, Emile (Edouard Charles Antoine) 1840-1902 ...... **TCLC 1, 6, 21, 41; WLC**
　　See also CA 104; 138; DA; DA3; DAB; DAC; DAM MST, NOV; DLB 123; EW 7; GFL 1789 to the Present; IDTP; LMFS 1, 2; RGWL 2; TWA

Zoline, Pamela 1941- .... **CLC 62**
　　See also CA 161; SFW 4

Zoroaster 628(?)B.C.-551(?)B.C. ... **CMLC 40**

Zorrilla y Moral, Jose 1817-1893 .... **NCLC 6**

Zoshchenko, Mikhail (Mikhailovich) 1895-1958 .... **SSC 15; TCLC 15**
　　See also CA 115; 160; EWL 3; RGSF 2; RGWL 3

Zuckmayer, Carl 1896-1977 .... **CLC 18**
　　See also CA 69-72; DLB 56, 124; EWL 3; RGWL 2, 3

Zuk, Georges
　　See Skelton, Robin
　　See also CCA 1

Zukofsky, Louis 1904-1978 ... **CLC 1, 2, 4, 7, 11, 18; PC 11**
　　See also AMWS 3; CA 9-12R; 77-80; CANR 39; CP 1, 2; DAM POET; DLB 5, 165; EWL 3; MAL 5; MTCW 1; RGAL 4

Zweig, Paul 1935-1984 .... **CLC 34, 42**
　　See also CA 85-88; 113

Zweig, Stefan 1881-1942 .... **TCLC 17**
　　See also CA 112; 170; DLB 81, 118; EWL 3

Zwingli, Huldreich 1484-1531 .... **LC 37**
　　See also DLB 179

Literary Criticism Series
Cumulative Topic Index

This index lists all topic entries in Thompson Gale's *Children's Literature Review* (CLR), *Classical and Medieval Literature Criticism* (CMLC), *Contemporary Literary Criticism* (CLC), *Drama Criticism* (DC), *Literature Criticism from 1400 to 1800* (LC), *Nineteenth-Century Literature Criticism* (NCLC), *Short Story Criticism* (SSC), and *Twentieth-Century Literary Criticism* (TCLC). The index also lists topic entries in the Gale Critical Companion Collection, which includes the following publications: *The Beat Generation* (BG), *Feminism in Literature* (FL), *Gothic Literature* (GL), and *Harlem Renaissance* (HR).

Topic Index

Topic Index

Topic Index

NCLC Cumulative Nationality Index

Nationality Index

ISBN 0-7876-8652-2

90000

9 780787 686529